Collins

— POCKET —

English
Dictionary
& Thesaurus

HarperCollins Publishers
Westerhill Road
Bishopbriggs
Glasgow
G64 2QT

Sixth Edition 2012

Reprint 10 9 8 7 6 5 4 3 2 1

© HarperCollins Publishers 2009, 2012

ISBN 978-0-00-745701-4

Collins® is a registered trademark of
HarperCollins Publishers Limited

www.collinslanguage.com

A catalogue record for this book is
available from the British Library

Typeset by MacMillan Publishing Solutions
and Davidson Publishing Solutions,
Glasgow

Printed and bound in Italy by LEGO
SpA, Lavis (Trento)

Acknowledgements
We would like to thank those authors and
publishers who kindly gave permission for
copyright material to be used in the Collins
Corpus. We would also like to thank Times
Newspapers Ltd for providing valuable
data.

Editorial staff
Duncan Black
Gerry Breslin
Freddy Chick
Robert Groves
Helen Hucker
Persephone Lock
Cormac McKeown

Supplement
Martin and Simon Toseland

For the publisher
Lucy Cooper
Kerry Ferguson
Elaine Higgleton

Contents

Features of this

Headwords in colour

a

adage *n* wise saying, proverb.
adagio *n, pl* **-gios** *adv Music* (piece to be played) slowly and gracefully.
adamant ❶ *adj* unshakable in determination or purpose.
Adam's apple *n* projecting lump of thyroid cartilage at the front of the throat.

Short, clear definitions

adapt ❶ *v* alter for new use or new conditions. **adaptable** *adj* **adaptability** *n* **adaptation** *n* **1** thing produced by adapting something. **2** adapting. **adaptor, adapter** *n* device for connecting several electrical appliances to a single socket.

❶ Symbol directs you to the thesaurus entry

add ❶ *v* **1** combine (numbers or quantities). **2** join (to something). **3** say or write further. **addition** *n* thing added.
addendum ❶ *n, pl* **-da 1** an addition. **2** appendix to a book etc.
adder *n* small poisonous snake.
addict ❶ *n* **1** person who is unable to stop taking drugs. **2** *informal* person devoted to something. **addicted** *adj* **addiction** *n* **addictive** *adj* causing addiction.

Usage labels

address ❶ *n* **1** place where a person lives. **2** direction on a letter. **3** location. **4** *formal* public speech. ▷ *v* **5** mark the destination, as on an envelope. **6** speak to.

Key synonyms highlighted

adamant *adj* = **determined**, firm, fixed, obdurate, resolute, stubborn, unbending, uncompromising
adapt *v* = **adjust**, acclimatize, accommodate, alter, change, conform, convert, modify, remodel, tailor
add *v* **1** = **count up**, add up, compute, reckon, total, tot up **2** = **include**, adjoin, affix, append, attach, augment, supplement
addendum *n* **1** = **addition**, appendage, attachment, extension, extra **2** = **appendix**, postscript, supplement

Generous choice of synonyms

addict *n* **1** = **junkie**, fiend (*inf*), freak (*inf*) (*inf*) **2** *Inf* = **fan**, adherent, buff (*inf*), devotee, enthusiast, follower, nut (*sl*)
address *n* **1, 3** = **location**, abode, dwelling, home, house, residence, situation,

Dictionary & Thesaurus

7 give attention to (a problem, task, etc.). **addressee** *n* person addressed.

● **SPELLING TIP**
● If you spell **address** wrongly, you
● probably miss out one *d*. Remember to
● double the *d* and the *s*.

— Spelling tips

adenoids [**ad**-in-oidz] *pl n* mass of tissue at the back of the throat. **adenoidal** *adj* having a nasal voice caused by swollen adenoids.

adept ❶ *adj, n* very skilful (person).

adequate ❶ *adj* **1** sufficient, enough. **2** not outstanding. **adequately** *adv* **adequacy** *n*.

adhere ❶ *v* **1** stick (to). **2** be devoted (to). **adherence** *n* **adherent** *n* devotee, follower. **adhesion** *n* **1** sticking (to). **2** joining together of parts of the body that are normally separate, as after surgery.

ad hoc *adj, adv Latin* for a particular purpose only.

— Pronunciation help

adieu ❶ [a-**dew**] *interj* farewell, goodbye.

adjacent ❶ *adj* **1** near or next (to). **2** having a common boundary. **3** *Geom* (of a side in a right-angled triangle) lying between a specified angle and the right angle.

adjective *n* word that adds information about a noun or pronoun. **adjectival** *adj*.

whereabouts **4** = **speech**, discourse, dissertation, lecture, oration, sermon, talk ▷ *v* **6** = **speak to**, approach, greet, hail, talk to **7** = **concentrate on**, apply (oneself) to, attend to, devote (oneself) to, engage in, focus on, take care of

— Numbers link thesaurus and dictionary meanings

adept *adj* = **skilful**, able, accomplished, adroit, expert, practised, proficient, skilled, versed *n* = **expert**, dab hand (*Brit inf*), fundi (*S Afr*), genius, hotshot (*inf*), master

— Labels give context of use

adequate *adj* **1** = **enough**, satisfactory, sufficient **2** = **fair**, competent, satisfactory, tolerable, up to scratch (*inf*)

adhere *v* **1** = **stick**, attach, cleave, cling, fasten, fix, glue, hold fast, paste

adieu *interj* = **goodbye**, farewell

adjacent *adj* **1** = **next**, adjoining, beside, bordering, close, near, neighbouring, next

v

Abbreviations

abbrev	abbreviation	lb(s)	pound(s)
adj	adjective	*lit*	Literary
adv	adverb	*masc*	masculine
Afr	African	*Maths*	Mathematics
Anat	Anatomy	*Med*	Medicine
arch	Archaic	*Mil*	Military
Aust	Australian	*Myth*	Mythology
Bot	Botany	*n*	noun
Brit	Britain, British	*N*	North(ern)
Canad	Canadian	*Naut*	Nautical
cap.	capital	*NZ*	New Zealand
Chem	Chemistry	*obs*	Obsolete
comb.	combining	*offens*	Offensive
conj	conjuction	oft.	often
dial	Dialect	orig.	originally
E	East(ern)	*Pathol*	Pathology
Eng	England, English	pert.	pertaining
e.g.	for example	*Photog*	Photography
esp.	especially	*pl*	plural
etc.	et cetera	*Poet*	Poetic
fem	feminine	*prep*	preposition
fig	Figurative	*pron*	pronoun
foll.	followed	*S*	South(ern)
Fr	French	*Scot*	Scottish
Geog	Geography	*sing.*	singular
Hist	History	*sl*	slang
inf	Informal	*US*	United States
interj	interjection	usu.	usually
kg	kilogram(s)	*v*	verb
km	kilometre(s)	*Vulg*	Vulgar
Lat	Latin	*W*	West(ern)

a *adj* indefinite article, used before a noun being mentioned for the first time.

AA 1 Alcoholics Anonymous. **2** Automobile Association.

aardvark *n* S African anteater with long ears and snout.

aback *adv* **taken aback** startled or disconcerted.

abandon ① *v* **1** desert or leave (one's wife, children, etc.). **2** give up (hope etc.) altogether. ▷ *n* **3** lack of inhibition. **abandoned** *adj* **1** deserted. **2** uninhibited. **abandonment** *n*.

abase *v* humiliate or degrade (oneself). **abasement** *n*.

abashed ① *adj* embarrassed and ashamed.

abate ① *v* make or become less strong. **abatement** *n*.

abattoir [**ab**-a-twahr] *n* slaughterhouse.

abbey ① *n* dwelling place of, or a church belonging to, a community of monks or nuns.

abbreviate ① *v* shorten (a word) by leaving out some letters. **abbreviation** *n* shortened form of a word or words.

abdicate ① *v* give up (the throne or a responsibility). **abdication** *n*.

abdomen *n* part of the body containing the stomach and intestines. **abdominal** *adj*.

abduct ① *v* carry off, kidnap. **abduction** *n* **abductor** *n*.

aberration ① *n* **1** sudden change from what is normal, accurate, or correct. **2** brief lapse in control of one's thoughts or feelings. **aberrant** *adj*.

abet ① *v* **abetting**, **abetted** help or encourage in wrongdoing. **abettor** *n*.

abeyance ① *n* **in abeyance** not in use.

abhor ① *v* **-horring**, **-horred** detest utterly. **abhorrent** *adj* hateful, loathsome. **abhorrence** *n*.

abide ① *v* **1** endure, put up with. **2** *obs* stay or dwell, e.g. *abide with me*. **abide by** *v* obey (the law, rules, etc.). **abiding** *adj* lasting.

ability ① *n*, *pl* **-ties 1** competence, power. **2** talent.

———— THESAURUS ————

abandon *v* **1** = **leave**, desert, forsake, strand **2** = **give up**, relinquish, surrender, yield ▷ *n* **3** = **wildness**, recklessness

abashed *adj* = **embarrassed**, ashamed, chagrined, disconcerted, dismayed, humiliated, mortified, shamefaced, taken aback

abate *v* = **decrease**, decline, diminish, dwindle, fade, lessen, let up, moderate, outspan (*S Afr*), relax, slacken, subside, weaken

abbey *n* = **monastery**, convent, friary, nunnery, priory

abbreviate *v* = **shorten**, abridge, compress, condense, contract, cut, reduce, summarize

abdicate *v* = **give up**, abandon, quit, relinquish, renounce, resign, step down (*inf*)

abduct *v* = **kidnap**, carry off, seize, snatch (*sl*)

aberration *n* **1** = **oddity**, abnormality, anomaly, defect, irregularity, peculiarity, quirk **2** = **lapse**

abet *v* = **help**, aid, assist, connive at, support

abeyance *n* **in abeyance** = **shelved**, hanging fire, on ice (*inf*), pending, suspended

abhor *v* = **hate**, abominate, detest, loathe, shrink from, shudder at

abide *v* **1** = **tolerate**, accept, bear, endure, put up with, stand, suffer

ability *n* **1** = **skill**, aptitude, capability, competence, expertise, proficiency **2** = **talent**

a

abject ❶ *adj* **1** utterly miserable. **2** lacking all self-respect.

ablaze ❶ *adj* burning fiercely.

able ❶ *adj* capable, competent. **ably** *adv* **able-bodied** *adj* strong and healthy.

abnormal ❶ *adj* not normal or usual. **abnormally** *adv* **abnormality** *n*.

aboard *adv, prep* on, in, onto, or into (a ship, train, or plane).

abolish ❶ *v* do away with. **abolition** *n*.

abort ❶ *v* **1** have an abortion or perform an abortion on. **2** have a miscarriage. **3** end a plan or process before completion. **abortion** *n* **1** operation to end a pregnancy. **2** *informal* something grotesque. **abortionist** *n* person who performs abortions, esp. illegally. **abortive** *adj* unsuccessful.

abound ❶ *v* be plentiful. **abounding** *adj*.

about ❶ *prep* **1** concerning, on the subject of. **2** in or near (a place). ▷ *adv* **3** nearly, approximately. **4** nearby. **about to** shortly going to. **about-turn** *n* complete change of attitude or opinion.

above ❶ *adv, prep* **1** over or higher (than). **2** greater (than). **3** superior (to). **above board** in the open, without dishonesty.

abrasion ❶ *n* scraped area on the skin. **abrasive** *adj* harsh and unpleasant in manner.

abreast ❶ *adv, adj* side by side. **abreast of** up to date with.

abridge ❶ *v* shorten by using fewer words. **abridgment, abridgement** *n*.

abroad ❶ *adv* **1** to or in a foreign country. **2** at large.

abrupt ❶ *adj* **1** sudden, unexpected. **2** blunt and rude. **abruptly** *adv* **abruptness** *n*.

abs *pl n informal* abdominal muscles.

abscess *n* inflamed swelling containing pus.

abscond ❶ *v* leave secretly.

absent ❶ *adj* **1** not present. **2** lacking. **3** inattentive. ▷ *v* **4** stay away. **absently** *adv* **absence** *n* **1** being away. **2** lack.

——————————————— THESAURUS ———————

abject *adj* **1** = **miserable**, deplorable, forlorn, hopeless, pitiable, wretched **2** = **servile**, cringing, degraded, fawning, grovelling, submissive

ablaze *adj* = **on fire**, aflame, alight, blazing, burning, fiery, flaming, ignited, lighted

able *adj* = **capable**, accomplished, competent, efficient, proficient, qualified, skilful

abnormal *adj* = **unusual**, atypical, exceptional, extraordinary, irregular, munted (*NZ sl*), odd, peculiar, strange, uncommon

abolish *v* = **do away with**, annul, cancel, destroy, eliminate, end, eradicate, put an end to, quash, rescind, revoke, stamp out

abort *v* **1** = **terminate** (*a pregnancy*) **2** = **miscarry 3** = **stop**, arrest, axe (*inf*), call off, check, end, fail, halt, terminate

abound *v* = **be plentiful**, flourish, proliferate, swarm, swell, teem, thrive

about *prep* **1** = **regarding**, as regards, concerning, dealing with, on, referring to, relating to **2** = **near**, adjacent to, beside, circa (*used with dates*), close to, nearby ▷ *adv* **3** = **nearly**, almost, approaching, approximately, around, close to, more or less, roughly

above *prep* **1** = **over**, higher than, on top of, upon **2** = **greater than**, beyond, exceeding

abrasion *n* = **graze**, chafe, scrape, scratch, scuff, surface injury

abreast *adv, adj* = **alongside**, beside, side by side

abridge *v* = **shorten**, abbreviate, condense, cut, decrease, reduce, summarize

abroad *adv* **1** = **overseas**, in foreign lands, out of the country

abrupt *adj* **1** = **sudden**, precipitate, quick, surprising, unexpected **2** = **curt**, brusque, gruff, impatient, rude, short, terse

abscond *v* = **flee**, clear out, disappear, escape, make off, run off, steal away

absent *adj* **1** = **missing**, away, elsewhere,

absentee n person who should be present but is not. **absenteeism** n persistent absence from work or school. **absent-minded** adj inattentive or forgetful.

absolute ⊙ adj 1 complete, perfect. 2 not limited, unconditional. 3 pure, e.g. absolute alcohol. **absolutely** adv 1 completely. ▷ interj 2 certainly, yes. **absolutism** n government by a ruler with unrestricted power.

absolve ⊙ v declare to be free from blame or sin. **absolution** n.

absorb ⊙ v 1 soak up (a liquid). 2 take in. 3 engage the interest of (someone). **absorption** n **absorbent** adj able to absorb liquid. **absorbency** n.

abstain ⊙ v 1 choose not to do something. 2 choose not to vote. **abstainer** n **abstention** n abstaining, esp. from voting. **abstinence** n abstaining, esp. from drinking alcohol. **abstinent** adj.

abstemious ⊙ adj taking very little alcohol or food.

abstract ⊙ adj 1 existing as a quality or idea rather than a material object. 2 theoretical. 3 (of art) using patterns of shapes and colours rather than realistic likenesses. ▷ n 4 summary. 5 abstract work of art. 6 abstract word or idea. ▷ v 7 summarize. 8 remove. **abstracted** adj lost in thought. **abstraction** n.

abstruse ⊙ adj not easy to understand.

absurd ⊙ adj incongruous or ridiculous. **absurdity** n.

abundant ⊙ adj plentiful. **abundantly** adv **abundance** n.

abuse ⊙ v 1 use wrongly. 2 ill-treat violently. 3 speak harshly and rudely to. ▷ n 4 prolonged ill-treatment. 5 harsh and vulgar comments. 6 wrong use. **abuser** n **abusive** adj **abusively** adv **abusiveness** n.

——————————— THESAURUS ———————————

gone, nonexistent, out 2 = **lacking**, unavailable 3 = **absent-minded**, blank, distracted, inattentive, oblivious, preoccupied, vacant, vague ▷ v 4 **absent oneself** = **stay away**, keep away, play truant, withdraw

absolute adj 1 = **total**, complete, outright, perfect, pure, sheer, thorough, utter 2 = **supreme**, full, sovereign, unbounded, unconditional, unlimited, unrestricted

absolve v = **forgive**, deliver, exculpate, excuse, let off, pardon, release, set free

absorb v 1 = **soak up**, suck up 2 = **take in**, consume, digest, imbibe, incorporate, receive 3 = **preoccupy**, captivate, engage, engross, fascinate, rivet

abstain v 1 = **refrain**, avoid, decline, deny yourself, desist, fast, forbear, forgo, give up, keep from

abstemious adj = **self-denying**, ascetic, austere, frugal, moderate, sober, temperate

abstract adj 1 = **indefinite**, general 2 = **theoretical**, hypothetical, notional ▷ n 4 = **summary**, abridgment, digest,

epitome, outline, précis, résumé, synopsis ▷ v 7 = **summarize**, abbreviate, abridge, condense, digest, epitomize, outline, précis, shorten 8 = **remove**, detach, extract, isolate, separate, take away, take out, withdraw

abstruse adj = **obscure**, arcane, complex, deep, enigmatic, esoteric, recondite, unfathomable, vague

absurd adj = **ridiculous**, crazy (inf), farcical, foolish, idiotic, illogical, inane, incongruous, irrational, ludicrous, nonsensical, preposterous, senseless, silly, stupid, unreasonable

abundant adj = **plentiful**, ample, bountiful, copious, exuberant, filled, full, luxuriant, profuse, rich, teeming

abuse v 1 = **misuse** 2 = **ill-treat**, damage, exploit, harm, hurt, injure, maltreat, take advantage of 3 = **insult**, castigate, curse, defame, disparage, malign, rouse on (Aust), scold, vilify ▷ n 4 = **ill-treatment**, damage, exploitation, harm, hurt, injury, maltreatment, manhandling 5 = **insults**, blame, castigation, censure, defamation,

abut v **abutting**, **abutted** be next to or touching.

abysmal ❶ adj informal extremely bad, awful. **abysmally** adv.

abyss ❶ n very deep hole or chasm.

AC alternating current.

acacia [a-**kay**-sha] n tree or shrub with yellow or white flowers.

academy n, pl **-mies 1** society to advance arts or sciences. **2** institution for training in a particular skill. **3** Scot secondary school. **academic** adj **1** of an academy or university. **2** of theoretical interest only. ▷ n **3** lecturer or researcher at a university. **academically** adv **academician** n member of an academy.

accede ❶ v **1** consent or agree (to). **2** take up (an office or position).

accelerate ❶ v (cause to) move faster. **acceleration** n **accelerator** n pedal in a motor vehicle to increase speed.

accent ❶ n **1** distinctive style of pronunciation of a local, national, or social group. **2** mark over a letter to show how it is pronounced. **3** stress on a syllable or musical note. ▷ v **4** place emphasis on.

accentuate ❶ v stress, emphasize. **accentuation** n.

accept ❶ v **1** receive willingly. **2** agree to. **3** consider to be true. **acceptance** n **acceptable** adj **1** tolerable. **2** satisfactory. **acceptably** adv **acceptability** n.

access ❶ n **1** means of or right to approach or enter. ▷ v **2** obtain (data) from a computer. **accessible** adj easy to reach. **accessibility** n.

accession n taking up of an office or position.

accessory ❶ n, pl **-ries 1** supplementary part or object. **2** person involved in a crime although not present when it is committed.

accident ❶ n **1** mishap, usu. one causing injury or death. **2** event happening by chance. **accidental** adj happening by chance or unintentionally. **accidentally** adv.

acclaim ❶ v **1** applaud, praise. ▷ n

————————————————————— THESAURUS —————————

derision, disparagement, invective, reproach, scolding, vilification **6** = **misuse**, misapplication

abysmal adj Inf = **terrible**, appalling, awful, bad, dire, dreadful

abyss n = **pit**, chasm, crevasse, fissure, gorge, gulf, void

accede v **1** = **agree**, accept, acquiesce, admit, assent, comply, concede, concur, consent, endorse, grant **2** = **inherit**, assume, attain, come to, enter upon, succeed, succeed to (as heir)

accelerate v = **speed up**, advance, expedite, further, hasten, hurry, quicken

accent n **1** = **pronunciation**, articulation, brogue, enunciation, inflection, intonation, modulation, tone **3** = **emphasis**, beat, cadence, force, pitch, rhythm, stress, timbre ▷ v **4** = **emphasize**, accentuate, stress, underline, underscore

accentuate v = **emphasize**, accent, draw attention to, foreground, highlight, stress,

underline, underscore

accept v **1** = **receive**, acquire, gain, get, obtain, secure, take **2** = **agree to**, approve, concur with, consent to, cooperate with **3** = **believe**, admit, recognize

access n **1** = **entrance**, admission, admittance, approach, entry, passage, path, road

accessory n **1** = **addition**, accompaniment, adjunct, adornment, appendage, attachment, decoration, extra, supplement, trimming **2** = **accomplice**, abettor, assistant, associate (in crime), colleague, confederate, helper, partner

accident n **1** = **misfortune**, calamity, collision, crash, disaster, misadventure, mishap **2** = **chance**, fate, fluke, fortuity, fortune, hazard, luck

acclaim v **1** = **praise**, applaud, approve, celebrate, cheer, clap, commend, exalt,

2 enthusiastic approval. **acclamation** n.

acclimatize ❶ v adapt to a new climate or environment. **acclimatization** n.

accolade ❶ n 1 award, honour, or praise. 2 award of knighthood.

accommodate ❶ v 1 provide with lodgings. 2 have room for. 3 oblige, do a favour for. 4 adapt or adjust (to something). **accommodation** n house or room for living in. **accommodating** adj obliging.

● **SPELLING TIP**
● The Bank of English shows that people
● usually remember that **accommoda-**
● **tion** and **accommodate** have two cs,
● but they often forget that these words
● have two ms as well.

accompany ❶ v -nying, -nied 1 go along with. 2 occur with. 3 provide a musical accompaniment for. **accompaniment** n 1 something that accompanies. 2 Music supporting part that goes with a solo. **accompanist** n.

accomplice ❶ n person who helps another to commit a crime.

accomplish ❶ v 1 manage to do. 2 finish. **accomplishment** n 1 completion. 2 personal ability or skill. **accomplished** adj expert, proficient.

accord ❶ n 1 agreement, harmony. ▷ v 2 fit in with.

accordion n portable musical instrument played by moving the two sides apart and together, and pressing a keyboard or buttons to produce the notes. **accordionist** n.

accost ❶ v approach and speak to.

account ❶ n 1 report, description. 2 business arrangement making credit available. 3 record of money received and paid out with the resulting balance. 4 importance, value. ▷ v 5 judge to be. **on account of** because of. **accountable** adj responsible to someone or for something. **accountability** n.

accoutrements pl n clothing and equipment for a particular activity.

accredited ❶ adj authorized, officially recognized.

──────── THESAURUS ────────

hail, honour, salute ▷ n 2 = **praise**, acclamation, applause, approval, celebration, commendation, honour, kudos

acclimatize v = **adapt**, accommodate, accustom, adjust, get used to, habituate, inure, naturalize

accolade n 1 = **praise**, acclaim, applause, approval, commendation, compliment, ovation, recognition, tribute

accommodate v 1 = **house**, cater for, entertain, lodge, put up, shelter 3 = **help**, aid, assist, oblige, serve 4 = **adapt**, adjust, comply, conform, fit, harmonize, modify, reconcile, settle

accompany v 1 = **go with**, attend, chaperon, conduct, convoy, escort, hold (someone's) hand 2 = **occur with**, belong to, come with, follow, go together with, supplement

accomplice n = **helper**, abettor, accessory, ally, assistant, associate, collaborator, colleague, henchman, partner

accomplish v 1 = **do**, achieve, attain, bring about, carry out, effect, execute, fulfil, manage, perform, produce 2 = **finish**, complete

accord n 1 = **agreement**, conformity, correspondence, harmony, rapport, sympathy, unison v 2 = **agree**, conform, correspond, fit, harmonize, match, suit, tally

accost v = **approach**, buttonhole, confront, greet, hail

account n 1 = **description**, explanation, narrative, report, statement, story, tale, version 3 = **statement**, balance, bill, books, charge, invoice, reckoning, register, score, tally 4 = **importance**, consequence, honour, note, significance, standing, value, worth ▷ v 5 = **consider**, count, estimate, judge, rate, reckon, regard, think, value

accredited adj = **authorized**, appointed, certified, empowered, endorsed, guaranteed, licensed, official, recognized

accrue ❶ v -cruing, -crued increase gradually. **accrual** n.

accumulate ❶ v gather together in increasing quantity. **accumulation** n **accumulator** n rechargeable electric battery.

accurate ❶ adj exact, correct. **accurately** adv **accuracy** n.

accursed ❶ adj 1 under a curse. 2 detestable.

accuse ❶ v charge with wrongdoing. **accused** n **accuser** n **accusation** n **accusatory** adj.

accustom ❶ v make used to. **accustomed** adj 1 usual. 2 used (to). 3 in the habit (of).

ace ❶ n 1 playing card with one symbol on it. 2 informal expert. 3 Tennis unreturnable serve. ▷ adj 4 informal excellent.

acetylene [ass-**set**-ill-een] n colourless flammable gas used in welding metals.

ache ❶ n 1 dull continuous pain. ▷ v 2 be in or cause continuous dull pain.

achieve ❶ v gain by hard work or ability. **achievement** n something accomplished.

acid ❶ n 1 Chem one of a class of compounds, corrosive and sour when dissolved in water, that combine with a base to form a salt. 2 slang LSD. ▷ adj 3 containing acid. 4 sour-tasting. 5 sharp or sour in manner. **acidic** adj **acidity** n **acid rain** rain containing acid from atmospheric pollution. **acid test** conclusive test of value.

acknowledge ❶ v 1 admit, recognize. 2 indicate recognition of (a person). 3 say one has received. **acknowledgment**, **acknowledgement** n.

acme [**ak**-mee] n highest point of achievement or excellence.

acne [**ak**-nee] n pimply skin disease.

acorn n nut of the oak tree.

acoustic adj 1 of sound and hearing. 2 (of a musical instrument) not electronically amplified. **acoustics** n 1 science of sounds. ▷ pl 2 features of a room or building determining how sound is heard within it.

acquaint ❶ v make familiar, inform. **acquainted** adj **acquaintance** n 1 person

———————— THESAURUS ————————

accrue v = **increase**, accumulate, amass, arise, be added, build up, collect, enlarge, flow, follow, grow

accumulate v = **collect**, accrue, amass, build up, gather, hoard, increase, pile up, store

accurate adj = **exact**, authentic, careful, close, correct, faithful, precise, scrupulous, spot-on (Brit inf), strict, true, unerring

accursed adj 1 = **cursed**, bewitched, condemned, damned, doomed, hopeless, ill-fated, ill-omened, jinxed, unfortunate, unlucky, wretched 2 = **hateful**, abominable, despicable, detestable, execrable, hellish, horrible

accuse v = **charge**, blame, censure, denounce, impeach, impute, incriminate, indict

accustom v = **adapt**, acclimatize, acquaint, discipline, exercise, familiarize, train

ace n 1 = **one**, single point 2 Inf = **expert**, champion, dab hand (Brit inf), fundi (S Afr), master, star, virtuoso, wizard (inf) ▷ adj 4 Inf = **excellent**, awesome (sl), brilliant, fine, great, outstanding, superb

ache n 1 = **pain**, hurt, pang, pounding, soreness, suffering, throbbing ▷ v 2 = **hurt**, pain, pound, smart, suffer, throb, twinge

achieve v = **attain**, accomplish, acquire, bring about, carry out, complete, do, execute, fulfil, gain, get, obtain, perform

acid adj 4 = **sour**, acerbic, acrid, pungent, tart, vinegary 5 = **sharp**, biting, bitter, caustic, cutting, harsh, trenchant, vitriolic

acknowledge v 1 = **accept**, admit, allow, concede, confess, declare, grant, own, profess, recognize, yield 2 = **greet**, address, hail, notice, recognize, salute 3 = **reply to**, answer, notice, react to, recognize, respond to, return

acquaint v = **tell**, disclose, divulge, enlighten, familiarize, inform, let (someone) know, notify, reveal

known. **2** personal knowledge.

acquiesce ⊙ [ak-wee-**ess**] *v* agree to what someone wants. **acquiescence** *n* **acquiescent** *adj*.

acquire ⊙ *v* gain, get. **acquisition** *n* **1** thing acquired. **2** act of getting.

acquit *v* **-quitting, -quitted**
1 pronounce (someone) innocent.
2 behave in a particular way. **acquittal** *n*.

acre *n* measure of land, 4840 square yards.
acreage [**ake**-er-rij] *n* land area in acres.

acrid ⊙ [**ak**-rid] *adj* pungent, bitter.
acridity *n*.

acrobat *n* person skilled in gymnastic feats requiring agility and balance. **acrobatic** *adj* **acrobatics** *pl n* acrobatic feats.

acronym *n* word formed from the initial letters of other words, such as NASA.

across *adv, prep* **1** from side to side (of). **2** on or to the other side (of). **across the board** applying equally to all.

acrylic *n, adj* (synthetic fibre, paint, etc.) made from acrylic acid.

act ⊙ *n* **1** thing done. **2** law or decree.
3 section of a play or opera. **4** one of several short performances in a show.
5 pretended attitude. ▷ *v* **6** do something.

7 behave in a particular way. **8** perform in a play, film, etc. **act of God** unpredictable natural event. **acting** *n* **1** art of an actor. ▷ *adj* **2** temporarily performing the duties of. **action** *n* process of doing something. **active** *adj* moving, working. **actor**, **actress** *n* person who acts in a play, film, etc.

ACT Australian Capital Territory.

actual ⊙ *adj* existing in reality. **actually** *adv* really, indeed. **actuality** *n*.

actuary *n, pl* **-aries** statistician who calculates insurance risks. **actuarial** *adj*.

actuate *v* start up (a device).

acumen ⊙ [**ak**-yew-men] *n* ability to make good judgments.

acupuncture *n* medical treatment involving the insertion of needles at various points on the body. **acupuncturist** *n*.

acute ⊙ *adj* **1** severe. **2** keen, shrewd.
3 sharp, sensitive. **4** (of an angle) less than 90° ▷ *n* **5** accent (´) over a letter to indicate the quality or length of its sound, as in café **acutely** *adv*.

ad *n informal* advertisement.

AD anno Domini.

———————————————— THESAURUS ————————————————

acquiesce *v* = **agree**, accede, accept, allow, approve, assent, comply, concur, conform, consent, give in, go along with, submit, yield

acquire *v* = **get**, amass, attain, buy, collect, earn, gain, gather, obtain, receive, secure, win

acquit *v* **1** = **clear**, discharge, free, liberate, release, vindicate **2** = **behave**, bear, comport, conduct, perform

acrid *adj* = **pungent**, bitter, caustic, harsh, sharp, vitriolic

act *n* **1** = **deed**, accomplishment, achievement, action, exploit, feat, performance, undertaking **2** = **law**, bill, decree, edict, enactment, measure, ordinance, resolution, statute
4 = **performance**, routine, show, sketch,

turn **5** = **pretence**, affectation, attitude, front, performance, pose, posture, show ▷ *v* **6** = **do**, carry out, enact, execute, function, operate, perform, take effect, work **8** = **perform**, act out, impersonate, mimic, play, play *or* take the part of, portray, represent

actual *adj* = **definite**, concrete, factual, physical, positive, real, substantial, tangible

acumen *n* = **judgment**, astuteness, cleverness, ingenuity, insight, intelligence, perspicacity, shrewdness

acute *adj* **1** = **sharp**, excruciating, fierce, intense, piercing, powerful, severe, shooting, violent **2** = **perceptive**, astute, clever, insightful, keen, observant, sensitive, sharp, smart

a

adage n wise saying, proverb.

adagio n, pl **-gios** adv Music (piece to be played) slowly and gracefully.

adamant ❶ adj unshakable in determination or purpose.

Adam's apple n projecting lump of thyroid cartilage at the front of the throat.

adapt ❶ v alter for new use or new conditions. **adaptable** adj **adaptability** n **adaptation** n 1 thing produced by adapting something. 2 adapting. **adaptor**, **adapter** n device for connecting several electrical appliances to a single socket.

add ❶ v 1 combine (numbers or quantities). 2 join (to something). 3 say or write further. **addition** n thing added.

addendum ❶ n, pl **-da** 1 an addition. 2 appendix to a book etc.

adder n small poisonous snake.

addict ❶ n 1 person who is unable to stop taking drugs. 2 informal person devoted to something. **addicted** adj **addiction** n **addictive** adj causing addiction.

address ❶ n 1 place where a person lives. 2 direction on a letter. 3 location. 4 formal public speech. ▷ v 5 mark the destination, as on an envelope. 6 speak to.

7 give attention to (a problem, task, etc.). **addressee** n person addressed.

● **SPELLING TIP**
● If you spell **address** wrongly, you
● probably miss out one d. Remember to
● double the d and the s.

adenoids [ad-in-oidz] pl n mass of tissue at the back of the throat. **adenoidal** adj having a nasal voice caused by swollen adenoids.

adept ❶ adj, n very skilful (person).

adequate ❶ adj 1 sufficient, enough. 2 not outstanding. **adequately** adv **adequacy** n.

adhere ❶ v 1 stick (to). 2 be devoted (to). **adherence** n **adherent** n devotee, follower. **adhesion** n 1 sticking (to). 2 joining together of parts of the body that are normally separate, as after surgery.

ad hoc adj, adv Latin for a particular purpose only.

adieu ❶ [a-dew] interj farewell, goodbye.

adjacent ❶ adj 1 near or next (to). 2 having a common boundary. 3 Geom (of a side in a right-angled triangle) lying between a specified angle and the right angle.

adjective n word that adds information about a noun or pronoun. **adjectival** adj.

———————————————————————— THESAURUS ——————

adamant adj = **determined**, firm, fixed, obdurate, resolute, stubborn, unbending, uncompromising

adapt v = **adjust**, acclimatize, accommodate, alter, change, conform, convert, modify, remodel, tailor

add v 1 = **count up**, add up, compute, reckon, total, tot up 2 = **include**, adjoin, affix, append, attach, augment, supplement

addendum n 1 = **addition**, appendage, attachment, extension, extra
2 = **appendix**, postscript, supplement

addict n 1 = **junkie**, fiend (inf), freak (inf) (inf) 2 Inf = **fan**, adherent, buff (inf), devotee, enthusiast, follower, nut (sl)

address n 1,3 = **location**, abode, dwelling, home, house, residence, situation,

whereabouts 4 = **speech**, discourse, dissertation, lecture, oration, sermon, talk ▷ v 6 = **speak to**, approach, greet, hail, talk to 7 = **concentrate on**, apply (oneself) to, attend to, devote (oneself) to, engage in, focus on, take care of

adept adj = **skilful**, able, accomplished, adroit, expert, practised, proficient, skilled, versed n = **expert**, dab hand (Brit inf), fundi (S Afr), genius, hotshot (inf), master

adequate adj 1 = **enough**, satisfactory, sufficient 2 = **fair**, competent, satisfactory, tolerable, up to scratch (inf)

adhere v 1 = **stick**, attach, cleave, cling, fasten, fix, glue, hold fast, paste

adieu interj = **goodbye**, farewell

adjacent adj 1 = **next**, adjoining, beside, bordering, close, near, neighbouring, next

adjoin ❶ v be next to. **adjoining** adj.
adjourn ❶ v **1** close (a court) at the end
of a session. **2** postpone temporarily.
3 informal go elsewhere.
adjournment n.
adjudge v declare (to be).
adjudicate ❶ v **1** give a formal decision
on (a dispute). **2** judge (a competition).
adjudication n **adjudicator** n.
adjunct n subordinate or additional person
or thing.
adjure v **1** command (to do). **2** appeal
earnestly.
adjust ❶ v **1** adapt to new conditions.
2 alter slightly so as to be suitable.
adjustable adj **adjuster** n **adjustment** n.
adjutant [aj-oo-tant] n army officer in
charge of routine administration.
ad-lib ❶ v **-libbing**, **-libbed 1** improvise
a speech etc. without preparation. ▷ n
2 improvised remark.
administer ❶ v **1** manage (business
affairs). **2** organize and put into practice.
3 give (medicine or treatment).
administrate v manage (an
organization). **administration** n
administrative adj **administrator** n.

admiral n highest naval rank. **Admiralty** n
former government department in charge
of the Royal Navy.
admire ❶ v regard with esteem and
approval. **admirable** adj **admirably** adv
admiration n **admirer** n **admiring** adj.
admit ❶ v **-mitting**, **-mitted 1** confess,
acknowledge. **2** concede the truth of.
3 allow in. **admission** n permission to
enter. **admittance** n permission to enter.
admittedly adv it must be agreed.
admonish ❶ v reprove sternly.
admonition n.
ad nauseam [ad naw-zee-am] adv Latin
to a boring or sickening extent.
ado n fuss, trouble.
adolescence ❶ n period between puberty
and adulthood. **adolescent** n, adj (person)
between puberty and adulthood.
adopt ❶ v **1** take (someone else's child) as
one's own. **2** take up (a plan or principle).
adoption n **adoptive** adj related by
adoption.
adore ❶ v **1** love intensely. **2** worship.
adorable adj **adoration** n **adoring** adj.
adorn ❶ v decorate, embellish.
adornment n.

───── THESAURUS ─────

door, touching
adjoin v = **connect**, border, join, link,
touch
adjourn v **2** = **postpone**, defer, delay,
discontinue, interrupt, put off, suspend
adjudicate v **1** = **judge**, adjudge, arbitrate,
decide, determine, mediate, referee, settle,
umpire
adjust v **1** = **adapt**, accustom **2** = **alter**,
make conform, modify
ad-lib v **1** = **improvise**, busk, extemporize,
make up, speak off the cuff, wing it (inf)
administer v **1,2** = **manage**, conduct,
control, direct, govern, handle, oversee,
run, supervise **3** = **give**, apply, dispense,
impose, mete out, perform, provide
admire v = **respect**, appreciate, approve,
esteem, look up to, praise, prize, think
highly of, value

admit v **1** = **confess**, acknowledge, declare,
disclose, divulge, own, reveal **2** = **allow**,
agree, grant, let, permit, recognize **3** = **let
in**, accept, allow, give access, initiate,
introduce, receive, take in
admonish v = **reprimand**, berate, chide,
rebuke, rouse on (Aust), scold, slap on the
wrist, tell off (inf)
adolescence n = **youth**, boyhood,
childishness, girlhood, immaturity,
minority, teens, youthfulness
adopt v **1** = **foster**, take in **2** = **choose**,
assume, espouse, follow, maintain, take
up
adore v **1** = **love**, admire, cherish, dote
on, esteem, honour **2** = **worship**, exalt,
glorify, idolize, revere
adorn v = **decorate**, array, embellish,
festoon

adrenal [ad-**reen**-al] *adj* near the kidneys. **adrenal glands** glands covering the top of the kidneys.

adrift ● *adj, adv* 1 drifting. 2 without a clear purpose.

adroit ● *adj* quick and skilful. **adroitly** *adv*.

adulation ● *n* uncritical admiration.

adult ● *adj* 1 fully grown, mature. ▷ *n* 2 adult person or animal. **adulthood** *n*.

adulterate *v* spoil something by adding inferior material. **adulteration** *n*.

adultery *n, pl* **-teries** sexual unfaithfulness of a husband or wife. **adulterer**, **adulteress** *n* **adulterous** *adj*.

advance ● *v* 1 go or bring forward. 2 further (a cause). 3 propose (an idea). 4 lend (a sum of money). ▷ *n* 5 forward movement. 6 improvement. 7 loan. ▷ *pl* 8 approaches to a person with the hope of starting a romantic or sexual relationship. ▷ *adj* 9 done or happening before an event. **in advance** ahead. **advanced** *adj* 1 at a late stage in development. 2 not elementary. **advancement** *n* promotion.

advantage ● *n* 1 more favourable position or state. 2 benefit or profit. 3 *Tennis* point scored after deuce. **take advantage of 1** use (a person) unfairly. 2 use (an opportunity). **advantageous** *adj*.

advent *n* 1 arrival. 2 (A-) season of four weeks before Christmas.

adventure ● *n* exciting and risky undertaking or exploit. **adventurer**, **adventuress** *n* 1 person who unscrupulously seeks money or power. 2 person who seeks adventures. **adventurous** *adj*.

adverb *n* word that adds information about a verb, adjective, or other adverb. **adverbial** *adj*.

adverse ● *adj* 1 unfavourable. 2 antagonistic or hostile. **adversely** *adv* **adversity** *n* very difficult or hard circumstances.

advert ● *n informal* advertisement.

advertise ● *v* 1 present or praise (goods or services) to the public in order to encourage sales. 2 make (a vacancy, event,

━━━━━━━━━━━━━━━ THESAURUS ━━━━━━━━━━━━━━━

adrift *adj* 1 = **drifting**, afloat, unanchored, unmoored 2 = **aimless**, directionless, goalless, purposeless

adroit *adj* = **skilful**, adept, clever, deft, dexterous, expert, masterful, neat, proficient, skilled

adulation *n* = **worship**, fawning, fulsome praise, servile flattery, sycophancy

adult *adj* 1 = **fully grown**, full grown, fully developed, grown-up, mature, of age, ripe ▷ *n* 2 = **grown-up**, grown or grown-up person (man *or* woman), person of mature age

advance *v* 1 = **progress**, accelerate, bring forward, come forward, go on, hasten, make inroads, proceed, speed 2 = **benefit**, further, improve, prosper 3 = **suggest**, offer, present, proffer, put forward, submit 4 = **lend**, pay beforehand, supply on credit ▷ *n* 5 = **progress**, advancement, development, forward movement, headway, inroads, onward movement

6 = **improvement**, breakthrough, gain, growth, progress, promotion, step 7 = **loan**, credit, deposit, down payment, prepayment, retainer ▷ *pl* 8 = **overtures**, approach, approaches, moves, proposals, proposition ▷ *adj* 9 = **prior**, beforehand, early, forward, in front **in advance** = **beforehand**, ahead, earlier, previously

advantage *n* 1 = **superiority**, ascendancy, dominance, lead, precedence, sway 2 = **benefit**, good, help, profit

adventure *n* = **escapade**, enterprise, experience, exploit, incident, occurrence, undertaking, venture

adverse *adj* 1 = **unfavourable**, contrary, detrimental, inopportune, negative 2 = **hostile**, antagonistic, opposing

advert *n Inf* = **advertisement**, ad (*inf*), announcement, blurb, commercial, notice, plug (*inf*), poster

advertise *v* 1 = **publicize**, plug (*inf*), promote, tout 2 = **announce**, make known

etc.) known publicly. **advertisement** n public announcement to sell goods or publicize an event. **advertiser** n **advertising** adj, n.

● SPELLING TIP
● Some verbs can be spelt ending in either
● -ise or -ize, but **advertise** and **advise**
● always have an s.

advice ❶ n recommendation as to what to do. **advise** v 1 offer advice to. 2 notify (someone). **adviser**, **advisor** n **advisable** adj prudent, sensible. **advisability** n **advisory** adj giving advice. **advised** adj considered, thought-out, e.g. ill-advised. **advisedly** adv deliberately.

● SPELLING TIP
● The Bank of English shows that people
● sometimes write **advise** with an s
● where they ought to write **advice** with
● a c. The verb is **advise** and the noun is
● **advice**.

advocate ❶ v 1 propose or recommend. ▷ n 2 person who publicly supports a cause. 3 Scot barrister. **advocacy** n.

aeon [ee-on] n immeasurably long period of time.

aerate v put gas into (a liquid), as when making a fizzy drink. **aeration** n.

aerial adj 1 in, from, or operating in the air. 2 relating to aircraft. ▷ n 3 metal pole, wire, etc., for receiving or transmitting radio or TV signals.

aerobatics pl n stunt flying. **aerobatic** adj.

aerobics n exercises designed to increase the amount of oxygen in the blood. **aerobic** adj.

aerodrome n small airport.

aerodynamics n study of how air flows around moving solid objects. **aerodynamic** adj.

aeronautics n study or practice of aircraft flight. **aeronautical** adj.

aeroplane n powered flying vehicle with fixed wings.

aerosol n pressurized can from which a substance can be dispensed as a fine spray.

aerospace n earth's atmosphere and space beyond.

aesthetic [iss-**thet**-ik] adj relating to the appreciation of art and beauty. **aesthetics** n study of art, beauty, and good taste. **aesthetically** adv **aesthete** [**eess**-theet] n person who has or affects an extravagant love of art. **aestheticism** n.

afar adv from or at a great distance.

affable ❶ adj friendly and easy to talk to. **affability** n.

affair ❶ n 1 event or happening. 2 sexual relationship outside marriage. 3 thing to be done or attended to. ▷ pl 4 personal or business interests. 5 matters of public interest.

affect¹ ❶ v 1 act on, influence. 2 move (someone) emotionally.

affect² ❶ v 1 put on a show of. 2 wear or use by preference. **affectation** n attitude or manner put on to impress. **affected** adj 1 displaying affectation. 2 pretended.

THESAURUS

advice n = **guidance**, counsel, help, opinion, recommendation, suggestion

advocate v 1 = **recommend**, advise, argue for, campaign for, champion, commend, encourage, promote, propose, support, uphold ▷ n 2 = **supporter**, campaigner, champion, counsellor, defender, promoter, proponent, spokesman, upholder 3 Scot = **lawyer**, attorney, barrister, counsel, solicitor

affable adj = **friendly**, amiable, amicable, approachable, congenial, cordial, courteous, genial, pleasant, sociable, urbane

affair n 1 = **event**, activity, business, episode, happening, incident, matter, occurrence 2 = **relationship**, amour, intrigue, liaison, romance

affect¹ v 1 = **influence**, act on, alter, bear upon, change, concern, impinge upon, relate to 2 = **move**, disturb, overcome, perturb, stir, touch, upset

affect² v 1 = **put on**, adopt, aspire to, assume, contrive, feign, imitate, pretend, simulate

affection n fondness or love.

affidavit [af-fid-**dave**-it] n written statement made on oath.

affiliate ❶ v (of a group) link up with a larger group. **affiliation** n.

affinity ❶ n, pl -**ties 1** close connection or liking. **2** close resemblance. **3** chemical attraction.

affirm ❶ v **1** declare to be true. **2** uphold or confirm (an idea or belief). **affirmation** n **affirmative** n, adj (word or phrase) indicating agreement.

affix v **1** attach or fasten. ▷ n **2** word or syllable added to a word to change its meaning.

afflict ❶ v give pain or grief to. **affliction** n.

affluent ❶ adj having plenty of money. **affluence** n wealth.

afford ❶ v **1** have enough money to buy. **2** be able to spare (the time etc.). **3** give or supply. **affordable** adj.

affront ❶ v, n insult.

afield adv **far afield** far away.

aflame ❶ adj burning.

afloat adv, adj **1** floating. **2** at sea.

afoot ❶ adv, adj happening, in operation.

aforesaid, aforementioned adj referred to previously.

afraid ❶ adj **1** frightened. **2** regretful.

afresh ❶ adv again, anew.

African adj **1** of Africa. ▷ n **2** person from Africa.

aft adv at or towards the rear of a ship or aircraft.

after ❶ prep **1** following in time or place. **2** in pursuit of. **3** in imitation of. ▷ conj **4** at a later time than. ▷ adv **5** at a later time. **afters** pl n informal dessert.

afterbirth n material expelled from the womb after childbirth.

aftermath ❶ n results of an event considered together.

afternoon n time between noon and evening.

aftershave n lotion applied to the face after shaving.

afterwards, afterward adv later.

again ❶ adv **1** once more. **2** in addition.

—————————————————— THESAURUS ——————————————————

affiliate v = **join**, ally, amalgamate, associate, band together, combine, incorporate, link, unite

affinity n **1** = **attraction**, fondness, inclination, leaning, liking, partiality, rapport, sympathy **2** = **similarity**, analogy, closeness, connection, correspondence, kinship, likeness, relationship, resemblance

affirm v **1** = **declare**, assert, maintain, state, swear **2** = **confirm**, certify, pronounce, testify

afflict v = **torment**, distress, grieve, harass, hurt, oppress, pain, plague, trouble

affluent adj = **wealthy**, loaded (sl), moneyed, opulent, prosperous, rich, well-heeled (inf), well-off, well-to-do

afford v **2** = **spare**, bear, manage, stand, sustain **3** = **give**, offer, produce, provide, render, supply, yield

affront v = **offend**, anger, annoy, displease,

insult, outrage, provoke, slight ▷ n = **insult**, offence, outrage, provocation, slap in the face (inf), slight, slur

aflame adj = **burning**, ablaze, alight, blazing, fiery, flaming, lit, on fire

afoot adj = **going on**, abroad, brewing, current, happening, in preparation, in progress, on the go (inf), up (inf)

afraid adj **1** = **scared**, apprehensive, cowardly, faint-hearted, fearful, frightened, nervous **2** = **sorry**, regretful, unhappy

afresh adv = **again**, anew, newly, once again, once more, over again

after adv **5** = **following**, afterwards, behind, below, later, subsequently, succeeding, thereafter

aftermath n = **effects**, aftereffects, consequences, end result, outcome, results, sequel, upshot, wake

again adv **1** = **once more**, afresh, anew, another time **2** = **also**, besides,

against ❶ *prep* **1** in opposition or contrast to. **2** in contact with. **3** as a protection from.

agape *adj* **1** (of the mouth) wide open. **2** (of a person) very surprised.

agate [**ag**-git] *n* semiprecious form of quartz with striped colouring.

age ❶ *n* **1** length of time a person or thing has existed. **2** time of life. **3** latter part of human life. **4** period of history. **5** long time. ▷ *v* **ageing** *or* **aging, aged 6** make or grow old. **aged** *adj* **1** [**ay**-jid] old. **2** [rhymes with **raged**] being at the age of. **ageing, aging** *n, adj* **ageless** *adj* **1** apparently never growing old. **2** seeming to have existed for ever. **age-old** *adj* very old.

agenda ❶ *n* list of things to be dealt with, esp. at a meeting.

agent ❶ *n* **1** person acting on behalf of another. **2** person or thing producing an effect. **agency** *n* organization providing a service.

aggrandize *v* make greater in size, power, or rank. **aggrandizement** *n*.

aggravate ❶ *v* **1** make worse.

2 *informal* annoy. **aggravating** *adj* **aggravation** *n*.

- SPELLING TIP
- The biggest problem with spelling
- **aggravate** is not how many *g*s there are
- at the beginning, but that there is an *a*
- (not an *e*) in the middle.

aggregate ❶ *n* **1** total. **2** rock consisting of a mixture of minerals. **3** sand or gravel used to make concrete. ▷ *adj* **4** gathered into a mass. **5** total or final. ▷ *v* **6** combine into a whole. **aggregation** *n*

aggression ❶ *n* **1** hostile behaviour. **2** unprovoked attack. **aggressive** *adj* **1** showing aggression. **2** forceful. **aggressively** *adv* **aggressiveness** *n* **aggressor** *n*.

- SPELLING TIP
- The Bank of English shows that
- **aggressive** is quite a common word
- and that *agressive* is a common way of
- misspelling it.

aggrieved ❶ *adj* upset and angry.

aghast ❶ *adj* overcome with amazement or horror.

—— THESAURUS ——

furthermore, in addition, moreover

against *prep* **1 = opposed to**, anti (*inf*), averse to, hostile to, in defiance of, in opposition to, resisting, versus **2 = beside**, abutting, facing, in contact with, on, opposite to, touching, upon **3 = in preparation for**, in anticipation of, in expectation of, in provision for

age 1 = lifetime, generation ▷ *n* **3 = old age**, advancing years, decline (*of life*), majority, maturity, senescence, senility, seniority **4 = time**, date, day(s), duration, epoch, era, period, span

agenda *n* **= list**, calendar, diary, plan, programme, schedule, timetable

agent *n* **1 = representative**, envoy, go-between, negotiator, rep (*inf*), surrogate **2 = force**, agency, cause, instrument, means, power, vehicle

aggravate *v* **1 = make worse**, exacerbate,

exaggerate, increase, inflame, intensify, magnify, worsen **2** *Inf* **= annoy**, bother, get on one's nerves (*inf*), irritate, nettle, provoke

aggregate *n* **1 = total**, accumulation, amount, body, bulk, collection, combination, mass, pile, sum, whole ▷ *adj* **4 = accumulated**, collected, combined, composite, mixed **5 = total**, cumulative ▷ *v* **6 = combine**, accumulate, amass, assemble, collect, heap, mix, pile

aggression *n* **1 = hostility**, antagonism, belligerence, destructiveness, pugnacity **2 = attack**, assault, injury, invasion, offensive, onslaught, raid

aggrieved *adj* **= hurt**, afflicted, distressed, disturbed, harmed, injured, unhappy, wronged

aghast *adj* **= horrified**, amazed, appalled, astonished, astounded, awestruck,

agile ❶ *adj* **1** nimble, quick-moving.
2 mentally quick. **agilely** *adv* **agility** *n*.
agitate ❶ *v* **1** disturb or excite. **2** stir or
shake (a liquid). **3** stir up public opinion
for or against something. **agitation** *n*
agitator *n*.
aglow *adj* glowing.
AGM annual general meeting.
agnostic *n* **1** person who believes that it is
impossible to know whether God exists.
▷ *adj* **2** of agnostics. **agnosticism** *n*.
ago *adv* in the past.
agog ❶ *adj* eager or curious.
agony ❶ *n, pl* **-nies** extreme physical or
mental pain. **agonize** *v* **1** worry greatly.
2 (cause to) suffer agony. **agonizing** *adj*
agony aunt journalist who gives advice
in an agony column. **agony column**
newspaper or magazine feature offering
advice on personal problems.
agoraphobia *n* fear of open spaces.
agoraphobic *n, adj*.
agree ❶ *v* **agreeing, agreed 1** be of the
same opinion. **2** consent. **3** reach a joint
decision. **4** be consistent. **5** (foll. by *with*)
be suitable to (one's health or digestion).

agreeable *adj* **1** pleasant and enjoyable.
2 prepared to consent. **agreeably** *adv*
agreement *n* **1** agreeing. **2** contract.
agriculture ❶ *n* raising of crops and
livestock. **agricultural** *adj* **agriculturalist**
n.
aground ❶ *adv* onto the bottom of shallow
water.
ahead ❶ *adv* **1** in front. **2** forwards.
ahoy *interj* shout used at sea to attract
attention.
aid ❶ *v, n* (give) assistance or support.
aide ❶ *n* assistant.
AIDS acquired immunodeficiency
syndrome, a viral disease that destroys the
body's ability to fight infection.
ail *v* **1** trouble, afflict. **2** be ill. **ailing** *adj*
sickly. **ailment** *n* illness.
aim ❶ *v* **1** point (a weapon or missile) or
direct (a blow or remark) at a target.
2 propose or intend. ▷ *n* **3** aiming.
4 intention, purpose. **aimless** *adj* having
no purpose. **aimlessly** *adv*.
ain't *not standard* **1** am not. **2** is not. **3** are
not. **4** has not. **5** have not.
air ❶ *n* **1** mixture of gases forming the

━━━━━━━━━━━━━━━━━━━━━━━ THESAURUS ━━━

confounded, shocked, startled, stunned
agile *adj* **1** = **nimble**, active, brisk, lithe,
quick, sprightly, spry, supple, swift
2 = **acute**, alert, bright (*inf*), clever, lively,
quick-witted, sharp
agitate *v* **1** = **upset**, disconcert, distract,
excite, fluster, perturb, trouble, unnerve,
worry **2** = **stir**, beat, convulse, disturb,
rouse, shake, toss
agog *adj* = **eager**, avid, curious, enthralled,
enthusiastic, excited, expectant,
impatient, in suspense
agony *n* = **suffering**, anguish, distress,
misery, pain, throes, torment, torture
agree *v* **1** = **concur**, assent, be of the
same opinion, comply, consent, see eye
to eye **4** = **match**, coincide, conform,
correspond, tally
agriculture *n* = **farming**, cultivation,
culture, husbandry, tillage

aground *adv* = **beached**, ashore,
foundered, grounded, high and dry, on the
rocks, stranded, stuck
ahead *adv* **1** = **in front**, at an advantage, at
the head, before, in advance, in the lead,
leading, to the fore
aid *v* = **help**, assist, encourage, favour,
promote, serve, subsidize, support,
sustain ▷ *n* = **help**, assistance, benefit,
encouragement, favour, promotion, relief,
service, support
aide *n* = **assistant**, attendant, helper,
right-hand man, second, supporter
aim *v* **2** = **intend**, attempt, endeavour,
mean, plan, point, propose, seek, set one's
sights on, strive, try ▷ *n* **4** = **intention**,
ambition, aspiration, desire, goal,
objective, plan, purpose, target
air *n* **1, 2** = **atmosphere**, heavens, sky
3 = **wind**, breeze, draught, zephyr

# # #

a

earth's atmosphere. **2** space above the ground, sky. **3** breeze. **4** quality or manner. **5** tune. ▷ *pl* **6** affected manners. ▷ *v* **7** make known publicly. **8** expose to air to dry or ventilate. **on the air** in the act of broadcasting on radio or television. **airless** *adj* stuffy. **airborne** *adj* **1** carried by air. **2** (of aircraft) flying. **airbrush** *n* atomizer spraying paint by compressed air. **airfield** *n* place where aircraft can land and take off. **air force** branch of the armed forces responsible for air warfare. **air gun** gun fired by compressed air. **airlift** *n* **1** transport of troops or cargo by aircraft when other routes are blocked. ▷ *v* **2** transport by airlift. **airlock** *n* air bubble blocking the flow of liquid in a pipe. **airmail** *n* **1** system of sending mail by aircraft. **2** mail sent in this way. **airman** *n* member of the air force. **airplay** *n* broadcast performances of a record on radio. **airport** *n* airfield for civilian aircraft, with facilities for aircraft maintenance and passengers. **air raid** attack by aircraft. **airship** *n* lighter-than-air self-propelled aircraft. **airspace** *n* atmosphere above a country, regarded as its territory. **airstrip** *n* cleared area where aircraft can take off and land. **airtight** *adj* sealed so that air cannot enter.

aisle ❶ [rhymes with **mile**] *n* passageway separating seating areas in a church, theatre, etc., or row of shelves in a supermarket.

ajar *adj, adv* (of a door) partly open.

AK Alaska.
akimbo *adv* **with arms akimbo** with hands on hips and elbows outwards.
akin *adj* **akin to** similar, related.
AL Alabama.
alabaster *n* soft white translucent stone.
à la carte *adj, adv* (of a menu) having dishes individually priced.
alacrity ❶ *n* speed, eagerness.
alarm ❶ *n* **1** sudden fear caused by awareness of danger. **2** warning sound. **3** device that gives this. **4** alarm clock. ▷ *v* **5** fill with fear. **alarming** *adj* **alarmist** *n* person who alarms others needlessly. **alarm clock** clock which sounds at a set time to wake someone up.
alas *adv* unfortunately, regrettably.
albatross *n* large sea bird with very long wings.
albino *n, pl* **-nos** person or animal with white skin and hair and pink eyes.
album *n* **1** book with blank pages for keeping photographs or stamps in. **2** long-playing record.
alchemy *n* medieval form of chemistry concerned with trying to turn base metals into gold and to find the elixir of life. **alchemist** *n*.
alcohol *n* **1** colourless flammable liquid present in intoxicating drinks. **2** intoxicating drinks generally. **alcoholic** *adj* **1** of alcohol. ▷ *n* **2** person addicted to alcohol. **alcoholism** *n* addiction to alcohol.
alcove ❶ *n* recess in the wall of a room.

— **THESAURUS** —

4 = **manner**, appearance, atmosphere, aura, demeanour, impression, look, mood **5** = **tune**, aria, lay, melody, song ▷ *pl* **6** = **affectation**, arrogance, hauteur, haughtiness, pomposity, pretensions, superciliousness, swank (*inf*) ▷ *v* **7** = **publicize**, circulate, display, exhibit, express, give vent to, make known, make public, reveal, voice **8** = **ventilate**, aerate, expose, freshen
aisle *n* = **passageway**, alley, corridor, gangway, lane, passage, path

alacrity *n* = **eagerness**, alertness, enthusiasm, promptness, quickness, readiness, speed, willingness, zeal
alarm *n* **1** = **fear**, anxiety, apprehension, consternation, fright, nervousness, panic, scare, trepidation **2, 3** = **danger signal**, alarm bell, alert, bell, distress signal, hooter, siren, warning ▷ *v* **5** = **frighten**, daunt, dismay, distress, give (someone) a turn (*inf*), panic, scare, startle, unnerve
alcove *n* = **recess**, bay, compartment,

alder n tree related to the birch.
alderman n formerly, senior member of a local council.
ale n kind of beer.
alert ❶ adj **1** watchful, attentive. ▷ n **2** warning of danger. ▷ v **3** warn of danger. **4** make (someone) aware of (a fact). **on the alert** watchful. **alertness** n.
alfresco adv, adj in the open air.
algae [al-jee] pl n plants which live in or near water and have no true stems, leaves, or roots.
algebra n branch of mathematics using symbols to represent numbers. **algebraic** adj.
Algonquin, Algonkin n a member of a North American Indian people formerly living along the Lawrence and Ottawa Rivers in Canada.
alias ❶ adv **1** also known as. ▷ n **2** false name.
alibi ❶ n **1** plea of being somewhere else when a crime was committed. **2** informal excuse.

alien ❶ adj **1** foreign. **2** repugnant (to). **3** from another world. ▷ n **4** foreigner. **5** being from another world. **alienate** v cause to become hostile. **alienation** n.
alight¹ ❶ v **1** step out of (a vehicle). **2** land.
alight² ❶ adj **1** on fire. **2** lit up.
align ❶ [a-line] v **1** bring (a person or group) into agreement with the policy of another. **2** place in a line. **alignment** n.
alike ❶ adj **1** like, similar. ▷ adv **2** in the same way.
alimony n allowance paid under a court order to a separated or divorced spouse.
alive ❶ adj **1** living, in existence. **2** lively. **alive to** aware of. **alive with** swarming with.
alkali [alk-a-lie] n substance which combines with acid and neutralizes it to form a salt. **alkaline** adj **alkalinity** n **alkaloid** n any of a group of organic compounds containing nitrogen.
all ❶ adj **1** whole quantity or number (of). ▷ adv **2** wholly, entirely. **3** (in the score of games) each. **give one's all** make

——————————————————————— THESAURUS ————————

corner, cubbyhole, cubicle, niche, nook
alert adj **1** = **watchful**, attentive, awake, circumspect, heedful, observant, on guard, on one's toes, on the lookout, vigilant, wide-awake n **2** = **warning**, alarm, signal, siren v **3** = **warn**, alarm, forewarn, signal **4** = **inform**, notify
alias adv **1** = **also known as**, also called, otherwise, otherwise known as ▷ n **2** = **pseudonym**, assumed name, nom de guerre, nom de plume, pen name, stage name
alibi n **2** Inf = **excuse**, defence, explanation, justification, plea, pretext, reason
alien adj **1** = **strange**, exotic, foreign, unfamiliar n **4** = **foreigner**, newcomer, outsider, stranger
alight¹ v **1** = **get off**, descend, disembark, dismount, get down **2** = **land**, come down, come to rest, descend, light, perch, settle, touch down

alight² adj **1** = **on fire**, ablaze, aflame, blazing, burning, fiery, flaming, lighted, lit **2** = **lit up**, bright, brilliant, illuminated, shining
align v **1** = **ally**, affiliate, agree, associate, cooperate, join, side, sympathize **2** = **line up**, even up, order, range, regulate, straighten
alike adj **1** = **similar**, akin, analogous, corresponding, identical, of a piece, parallel, resembling, the same ▷ adv **2** = **similarly**, analogously, correspondingly, equally, evenly, identically, uniformly
alive adj **1** = **living**, animate, breathing, existing, extant, in existence, in the land of the living (inf), subsisting **2** = **lively**, active, alert, animated, energetic, full of life, vital, vivacious
all adj **1** = **entire**, complete, each, each and every, every, every bit of, every one of, every single, full, the whole of, total ▷ adv

the greatest possible effort. **all in** *adj*
1 exhausted. **2** (of wrestling) with no
style forbidden. ▷ *adv* **3** with all expenses
included. **all right** *adj* **1** adequate,
satisfactory. **2** unharmed. ▷ *interj*
3 expression of approval or agreement.
all-rounder *n* person with ability in many
fields.

allay *v* reduce (fear or anger).

allege ❶ *v* state without proof. **allegedly**
adv **allegation** *n* unproved accusation.

allegiance ❶ *n* loyalty to a person,
country, or cause.

allegory ❶ *n, pl* **-ries** story with an
underlying meaning as well as the literal
one. **allegorical** *adj*.

allegro *n, pl* **-gros** *adv Music* (piece to be
played) in a brisk lively manner.

allergy ❶ *n, pl* **-gies** extreme sensitivity to a
substance, which causes the body to react
to it. **allergic** *adj* having or caused by an
allergy. **allergen** *n* substance capable of
causing an allergic reaction.

alleviate ❶ *v* lessen (pain or suffering).
alleviation *n*.

alley ❶ *n* **1** narrow street or path. **2** long
narrow enclosure in which tenpin bowling

or skittles is played.

alliance ❶ *n* **1** state of being allied.
2 formal relationship between countries or
groups for a shared purpose.

alligator *n* reptile of the crocodile family,
found in the southern US and China.

alliteration *n* use of the same sound at
the start of words occurring together.
alliterative *adj*.

allocate ❶ *v* assign to someone or for a
particular purpose. **allocation** *n*.

allot ❶ *v* **-lotting, -lotted** assign as a share
or for a particular purpose. **allotment**
n **1** distribution. **2** portion allotted.
3 small piece of public land rented to grow
vegetables on.

allow ❶ *v* **1** permit. **2** set aside.
3 acknowledge (a point or claim). **allow
for** *v* take into account. **allowable** *adj*
allowance *n* **1** amount of money given at
regular intervals. **2** amount permitted.
make allowances for 1 treat or judge
(someone) less severely because he or she
has special problems. **2** take into account.

alloy ❶ *n* **1** mixture of two or more metals.
▷ *v* **2** mix (metals).

allude ❶ *v* (foll. by *to*) refer indirectly to.

———————————— THESAURUS ————————————

2 = completely, altogether, entirely, fully,
totally, utterly, wholly

allege *v* = **claim**, affirm, assert, charge,
declare, maintain, state

allegiance *n* = **loyalty**, constancy,
devotion, faithfulness, fidelity, obedience

allegory *n* = **symbol**, fable, myth, parable,
story, symbolism, tale

allergy *n* = **sensitivity**, antipathy,
hypersensitivity, susceptibility

alleviate *v* = **ease**, allay, lessen, lighten,
moderate, reduce, relieve, soothe

alley *n* **1** = **passage**, alleyway, backstreet,
lane, passageway, pathway, walk

alliance *n* **1** = **connection**, affiliation,
agreement, association, combination,
marriage, partnership **2** = **union**,
coalition, confederation, federation,
league, pact, treaty

allocate *v* = **assign**, allot, allow, apportion,
budget, designate, earmark, mete, set
aside, share out

allot *v* = **assign**, allocate, apportion,
budget, designate, earmark, mete, set
aside, share out

allow *v* **1** = **permit**, approve, authorize,
enable, endure, let, sanction, stand,
suffer, tolerate **2** = **set aside**, allocate,
allot, assign, give, grant, provide, spare
3 = **acknowledge**, admit, concede,
confess, grant, own

alloy *n* **1** = **mixture**, admixture, amalgam,
blend, combination, composite,
compound, hybrid ▷ *v* **2** = **mix**,
amalgamate, blend, combine, compound,
fuse

allude *v* (foll. by *to*) = **refer**, hint, imply,
intimate, mention, suggest, touch upon

allusion n indirect reference. **allusive** adj.
allure ❶ n 1 attractiveness. ▷ v 2 entice or attract. **alluring** adj.
ally ❶ n, pl **-lies** 1 country, person, or group with an agreement to support another. ▷ v **-lying, -lied** 2 **ally oneself with** join as an ally. **allied** adj.
almanac n yearly calendar with detailed information on anniversaries, phases of the moon, etc.
almighty ❶ adj 1 having absolute power. 2 informal very great. ▷ n 3 **the Almighty** God.
almond n edible oval-shaped nut which grows on a small tree.
almost ❶ adv very nearly.
alms [ahmz] pl n old-fashioned gifts to the poor.
aloft adv 1 in the air. 2 in a ship's rigging.
alone ❶ adj, adv without anyone or anything else.
along prep 1 over part or all the length of. ▷ adv 2 forward. 3 in company with others. **alongside** prep, adv beside (something).
aloof ❶ adj distant or haughty in manner.

aloofly adv **aloofness** n.
aloud ❶ adv in an audible voice.
alphabet n set of letters used in writing a language. **alphabetical** adj in the conventional order of the letters of an alphabet. **alphabetically** adv **alphabetize** v put in alphabetical order.
already ❶ adv 1 before the present time. 2 sooner than expected.
Alsatian n large wolflike dog.
also ❶ adv in addition, too. **also-ran** n loser in a race, competition, or election.
alt. combining form informal alternative, e.g. alt. rock.
altar n 1 table used for Communion in Christian churches. 2 raised structure on which sacrifices are offered and religious rites are performed. **altarpiece** n work of art above and behind the altar in some Christian churches.
alter ❶ v make or become different. **alteration** n.
altercation n heated argument.
alternate ❶ v 1 (cause to) occur by turns. ▷ adj 2 occurring by turns. 3 every second (one) of a series. **alternately**

────────────────────────────────────── THESAURUS ──────

allure n 1 = **attractiveness**, appeal, attraction, charm, enchantment, enticement, glamour, lure, persuasion, seductiveness, temptation ▷ v 2 = **attract**, captivate, charm, enchant, entice, lure, persuade, seduce, tempt, win over
ally n 1 = **partner**, accomplice, associate, cobber (Aust or old-fashioned NZ inf), collaborator, colleague, friend, helper ▷ v 2 **ally oneself with** = **unite with**, associate with, collaborate with, combine with, join forces with, join with
almighty adj 1 = **all-powerful**, absolute, invincible, omnipotent, supreme, unlimited 2 Inf = **great**, enormous, excessive, intense, loud, severe, terrible
almost adv = **nearly**, about, approximately, close to, just about, not quite, on the brink of, practically, virtually

alone adj = **by oneself**, apart, detached, isolated, lonely, lonesome (chiefly US & Canad), only, on one's tod (sl), separate, single, solitary, unaccompanied
aloof adj = **distant**, detached, haughty, remote, standoffish, supercilious, unapproachable, unfriendly
aloud adv = **out loud**, audibly, clearly, distinctly, intelligibly, plainly
already adv = **before now**, at present, before, by now, by then, even now, heretofore, just now, previously
also adv = **too**, additionally, and, as well, besides, further, furthermore, in addition, into the bargain, moreover, to boot
alter v = **change**, adapt, adjust, amend, convert, modify, reform, revise, transform, turn, vary
alternate v 1 = **change**, act reciprocally, fluctuate, interchange, oscillate, rotate,

a

adv **alternative** *n* one of two choices.
alternator *n* electric generator
for producing alternating current.
alternating current electric current that
reverses direction at frequent regular
intervals.
although ❶ *conj* despite the fact that.
altitude *n* height above sea level.
alto *n, pl* **-tos** *Music* **1** short for CONTRALTO.
2 (singer with) the highest adult male
voice. **3** instrument with the second-
highest pitch in its group.
altogether ❶ *adv* **1** entirely. **2** on the
whole. **3** in total.
altruism *n* unselfish concern for the
welfare of others. **altruistic** *adj*.
aluminium *n Chem* light silvery-white
metal that does not rust.
always ❶ *adv* **1** at all times. **2** for ever.
am *v* see BE.
a.m. ante meridiem: before noon.
amalgamate ❶ *v* combine or unite.
amalgamation *n*.
amass ❶ *v* collect or accumulate.
amateur ❶ *n* **1** person who engages in
a sport or activity as a pastime rather

than as a profession. **2** person unskilled
in something. ▷ *adj* **3** not professional.
amateurish *adj* lacking skill.
amaut, amowt *n Canad* a hood on an
Eskimo woman's parka for carrying a child.
amaze ❶ *v* surprise greatly, astound.
amazing *adj* **amazement** *n*.
ambassador ❶ *n* senior diplomat who
represents his or her country in another
country. **ambassadorial** *adj*.
amber *n* **1** clear yellowish fossil resin. ▷ *adj*
2 brownish-yellow.
ambidextrous *adj* able to use both hands
with equal ease.
ambience *n* atmosphere of a place.
ambiguous ❶ *adj* having more than one
possible meaning. **ambiguity** *n*.
ambition ❶ *n* **1** desire for success.
2 something so desired, goal. **ambitious**
adj.
ambivalence *n* state of feeling two
conflicting emotions at the same time.
ambivalent *adj*.
amble ❶ *v* **1** walk at a leisurely pace. ▷ *n*
2 leisurely walk or pace.
ambulance *n* motor vehicle designed to

—— THESAURUS ——

substitute, take turns ▷ *adj* **3** = **every
other**, alternating, every second
although *conj* = **though**, albeit, despite
the fact that, even if, even though,
notwithstanding, while
altogether *adv* **1** = **completely**,
absolutely, fully, perfectly, quite,
thoroughly, totally, utterly, wholly **2** = **on
the whole**, all in all, all things considered,
as a whole, collectively, generally, in
general **3** = **in total**, all told, everything
included, in all, in sum, taken together
always *adv* **1** = **continually**, consistently,
constantly, every time, invariably,
perpetually, repeatedly, twenty-four-seven
(*inf*), without exception **2** = **forever**,
eternally, evermore
amalgamate *v* = **combine**, ally, blend,
fuse, incorporate, integrate, merge,
mingle, unite

amass *v* = **collect**, accumulate, assemble,
compile, gather, hoard, pile up
amateur *n* **1** = **nonprofessional**, dabbler,
dilettante, layman
amaze *v* = **astonish**, alarm, astound,
bewilder, dumbfound, shock, stagger,
startle, stun, surprise
ambassador *n* = **representative**, agent,
consul, deputy, diplomat, envoy, legate,
minister
ambiguous *adj* = **unclear**, dubious,
enigmatic, equivocal, inconclusive,
indefinite, indeterminate, obscure, vague
ambition *n* **1** = **enterprise**, aspiration,
desire, drive, eagerness, longing, striving,
yearning, zeal **2** = **goal**, aim, aspiration,
desire, dream, hope, intent, objective,
purpose, wish
amble *v* **1** = **stroll**, dawdle, meander, mosey
(*inf*), ramble, saunter, walk, wander

carry sick or injured people.

ambush ❶ n **1** act of waiting in a concealed position to make a surprise attack. **2** attack from a concealed position. ▷ v **3** attack from a concealed position.

ameliorate [am-**meal**-yor-rate] v make (something) better. **amelioration** n.

amen interj so be it: used at the end of a prayer.

amenable ❶ adj likely or willing to cooperate.

amend ❶ v make small changes to correct or improve (something). **amendment** n.

amenity ❶ n, pl -**ties** useful or enjoyable feature.

amiable ❶ adj friendly, pleasant-natured. **amiably** adv.

amicable ❶ adj friendly. **amicably** adv.

amid, amidst ❶ prep in the middle of, among. **amidships** adv at or towards the middle of a ship.

amiss ❶ adv **1** wrongly, badly. ▷ adj **2** wrong, faulty. **take something amiss** be offended by something.

ammonia n **1** strong-smelling alkaline gas containing hydrogen and nitrogen. **2** solution of this in water.

ammunition ❶ n **1** bullets, bombs, and shells that can be fired from or as a weapon. **2** facts that can be used in an argument.

amnesia n loss of memory. **amnesiac** adj, n.

amnesty ❶ n, pl -**ties** general pardon for offences against a government.

amoeba [am-**mee**-ba] n, pl -**bae**, -**bas** microscopic single-celled animal able to change its shape.

amok ❶ adv **run amok** run about in a violent frenzy.

among, amongst ❶ prep **1** in the midst of. **2** in the group or number of. **3** to each of, e.g. divide it among yourselves.

amoral [aim-**mor**-ral] adj without moral standards.

amorous ❶ adj feeling, showing, or relating to sexual love or desire.

amorphous adj without distinct shape.

——————————————— THESAURUS ———

ambush n **1** = **trap**, lying in wait, waylaying ▷ v **3** = **trap**, attack, bushwhack (US), ensnare, surprise, waylay

amenable adj = **receptive**, able to be influenced, acquiescent, agreeable, compliant, open, persuadable, responsive, susceptible

amend v = **change**, alter, correct, fix, improve, mend, modify, reform, remedy, repair, revise

amenity n = **facility**, advantage, comfort, convenience, service

amiable adj = **pleasant**, affable, agreeable, charming, congenial, engaging, friendly, genial, likable or likeable, lovable

amicable adj = **friendly**, amiable, civil, cordial, courteous, harmonious, neighbourly, peaceful, sociable

amid, amidst prep = **in the middle of**, among, amongst, in the midst of, in the thick of, surrounded by

amiss adv **1** = **wrongly**, erroneously,

improperly, inappropriately, incorrectly, mistakenly, unsuitably ▷ adj **2** = **wrong**, awry, faulty, incorrect, mistaken, untoward

ammunition n **1** = **munitions**, armaments, explosives, powder, rounds, shells, shot

amnesty n = **general pardon**, absolution, dispensation, forgiveness, immunity, remission (of penalty), reprieve

amok adv **run amok** = **madly**, berserk, destructively, ferociously, in a frenzy, murderously, savagely, uncontrollably, violently, wildly

among, amongst prep **1** = **in the midst of**, amid, amidst, in the middle of, in the thick of, surrounded by, together with, with **2** = **in the group of**, in the class of, in the company of, in the number of, out of **3** = **to each of**, between

amorous adj = **loving**, erotic, impassioned, in love, lustful, passionate, tender

amount ❶ n 1 extent or quantity. ▷ v 2 (foll. by to) be equal or add up to.

amp n 1 ampere. 2 informal amplifier.

ampere [am-pair] n basic unit of electric current.

ampersand n the character (&), meaning and.

amphetamine [am-fet-am-mean] n drug used as a stimulant.

amphibian n 1 animal that lives on land but breeds in water. 2 vehicle that can travel on both land and water. **amphibious** adj living or operating both on land and in water.

amphitheatre n open oval or circular building with tiers of seats rising round an arena.

ample ❶ adj 1 more than sufficient. 2 large. **amply** adv.

amplify ❶ v -fying, -fied 1 increase the strength of (a current or sound signal). 2 explain in more detail. 3 increase the size or effect of. **amplification** n **amplifier** n device used to amplify a current or sound signal.

amplitude n greatness of extent.

amputate ❶ v cut off (a limb or part of a limb) for medical reasons. **amputation** n.

amulet n something carried or worn as a protection against evil.

amuse ❶ v 1 cause to laugh or smile. 2 entertain or divert. **amusing** adj

amusement n 1 state of being amused. 2 something that amuses.

an adj form of a used before vowels, and sometimes before h.

anachronism [an-nak-kron-iz-zum] n person or thing placed in the wrong historical period or seeming to belong to another time. **anachronistic** adj.

anaconda n large S American snake which kills by constriction.

anaemia [an-neem-ee-a] n deficiency in the number of red blood cells. **anaemic** adj 1 having anaemia. 2 pale and sickly. 3 lacking vitality.

anaesthetic ❶ [an-niss-thet-ik] n, adj (substance) causing loss of bodily feeling. **anaesthesia** [an-niss-theez-ee-a] n loss of bodily feeling. **anaesthetist** [an-neess-thet-ist] n doctor trained to administer anaesthetics. **anaesthetize** v.

anagram n word or phrase made by rearranging the letters of another word or phrase.

anal [ain-al] adj of the anus.

analgesic [an-nal-jeez-ik] n, adj (drug) relieving pain. **analgesia** n absence of pain.

analogy ❶ n, pl -gies 1 similarity in some respects. 2 comparison made to show such a similarity. **analogical** adj.

analysis ❶ n, pl -ses 1 separation of a whole into its parts for study and

amount n 1 = **quantity**, expanse, extent, magnitude, mass, measure, number, supply, volume ▷ v 2 (foll. by to) = **add up to**, become, come to, develop into, equal, mean, total

ample adj 1 = **plenty**, abundant, bountiful, copious, expansive, extensive, full, generous, lavish, plentiful, profuse

amplify v 2 = **go into detail**, develop, elaborate, enlarge, expand, explain, flesh out 3 = **expand**, enlarge, extend, heighten, increase, intensify, magnify, strengthen, widen

amputate v = **cut off**, curtail, lop, remove, separate, sever, truncate

amuse v = **entertain**, charm, cheer, delight, interest, please

anaesthetic n = **painkiller**, analgesic, anodyne, narcotic, opiate, sedative, soporific ▷ adj = **pain-killing**, analgesic, anodyne, deadening, dulling, numbing, sedative, soporific

analogy n 1 = **similarity**, correlation, correspondence, likeness, parallel, relation, resemblance 2 = **comparison**

analysis n 1 = **examination**, breakdown, dissection, inquiry,

interpretation. **2** psychoanalysis. **analyse**
v **1** make an analysis of (something).
2 psychoanalyse. **analyst** *n* person skilled
in analysis. **analytical**, **analytic** *adj*
analytically *adv*.
anarchy ❶ [an-ark-ee] *n* **1** lawlessness and
disorder. **2** lack of government in a state.
anarchic *adj*.
anathema [an-**nath**-im-a] *n* detested
person or thing.
anatomy ❶ *n*, *pl* -**mies** **1** science of the
structure of the body. **2** physical structure.
3 person's body. **4** detailed analysis.
anatomical *adj* **anatomically** *adv*
anatomist *n* expert in anatomy.
ancestor ❶ *n* **1** person from whom one is
descended. **2** forerunner. **ancestral** *adj*
ancestry *n* lineage or descent.
anchor *n* **1** heavy hooked device attached
to a boat by a cable and dropped overboard
to fasten the ship to the sea bottom.
▷ *v* **2** fasten with or as if with an anchor.
anchorage *n* place where boats can be
anchored. **anchorman**, **anchorwoman**
n **1** broadcaster in a central studio who
links up and presents items from outside
camera units and other studios. **2** last
person to compete in a relay team.
anchovy [an-chov-ee] *n*, *pl* -**vies** small
strong-tasting fish.

ancient ❶ *adj* **1** dating from very long ago.
2 very old.
ancillary ❶ *adj* **1** supporting the main
work of an organization. **2** used as an
extra or supplement.
and ❶ *conj* **1** in addition to. **2** as a
consequence. **3** then, afterwards.
andante [an-**dan**-tay] *n*, *adv Music* (piece
to be played) moderately slowly.
androgynous *adj* having both male and
female characteristics.
android *n* robot resembling a human.
anecdote ❶ *n* short amusing account of an
incident. **anecdotal** *adj*.
anemone [an-**nem**-on-ee] *n* plant with
white, purple, or red flowers.
anew *adv* **1** once more. **2** in a different way.
angel ❶ *n* **1** spiritual being believed to be an
attendant or messenger of God. **2** person
who is kind, pure, or beautiful. **angelic** *adj*
angelically *adv*.
anger ❶ *n* **1** fierce displeasure or extreme
annoyance. ▷ *v* **2** make (someone) angry.
angina [an-**jine**-a] *n* heart disorder causing
sudden severe chest pains (also **angina
pectoris**).
angle¹ ❶ *n* **1** space between or shape
formed by two lines or surfaces that meet.
2 divergence between these, measured
in degrees. **3** corner. **4** point of view. ▷ *v*

————————————— THESAURUS —————————

investigation, scrutiny, sifting, test
anarchy *n* = **lawlessness**, chaos,
confusion, disorder, disorganization,
revolution, riot
anatomy *n* **2** = **structure**, build,
composition, frame, framework, make-up
4 = **examination**, analysis, dissection,
division, inquiry, investigation, study
ancestor *n* = **forefather**, forebear,
forerunner, precursor, predecessor
ancient *adj* = **old**, aged, antique, archaic,
old-fashioned, primeval, primordial,
timeworn
ancillary *adj* **1** = **supporting**, auxiliary,
secondary, subordinate, subsidiary
2 = **supplementary**, additional, extra

and *conj* **1** = **also**, along with, as well as,
furthermore, in addition to, including,
moreover, plus, together with
anecdote *n* = **story**, reminiscence, short
story, sketch, tale, urban legend, urban
myth, yarn
angel *n* **1** = **divine messenger**, archangel,
cherub, seraph **2** = **dear**, beauty, darling,
gem, jewel, paragon, saint, treasure
anger *n* **1** = **rage**, annoyance, displeasure,
exasperation, fury, ire, outrage,
resentment, temper, wrath ▷ *v* **2** = **enrage**,
annoy, displease, exasperate, gall, incense,
infuriate, madden, outrage, rile, vex
angle¹ *n* **1** = **intersection**, bend, crook,
elbow, nook **2** = **corner**, edge, point

5 bend or place (something) at an angle.

angle² ● v **1** fish with a hook and line.
2 (foll. by *for*) try to get by hinting. **angler**
n **angling** *n*.

Anglican *n, adj* (member) of the Church of
England.

Anglo- *combining form* **1** English, e.g.
Anglo-Scottish. **2** British, e.g. *Anglo-
American*.

angora *n* **1** variety of goat, cat, or rabbit
with long silky hair. **2** hair of the angora
goat or rabbit. **3** cloth made from this hair.

anguish ● *n* great mental pain. **anguished**
adj.

angular *adj* **1** (of a person) lean and bony.
2 having angles. **3** measured by an angle.
angularity *n*.

animal ● *n* **1** living creature with
specialized sense organs and capable of
voluntary motion, esp. one other than
a human being. **2** quadruped. **3** of
animals. **4** sensual, physical. ▷ *adj* **3** of

animate ● v **1** give life to. **2** make
lively. **3** make a cartoon film of. ▷ *adj*
4 having life. **animated** *adj* **animation**
n **1** technique of making cartoon films.
2 liveliness and enthusiasm. **animator** *n*.

animosity ● *n, pl* **-ties** hostility, hatred.

animus *n* hatred, animosity.

aniseed *n* liquorice-flavoured seeds of the
anise plant.

ankle *n* joint between the foot and leg.
anklet *n* ornamental chain worn round
the ankle.

annals ● *pl n* yearly records of events.

annex ● v **1** seize (territory). **2** take
(something) without permission. **3** join
or add (something) to something larger.
annexation *n*.

annexe *n* **1** extension to a building.
2 nearby building used as an extension.

annihilate ● v destroy utterly.
annihilation *n*.

anniversary *n, pl* **-ries 1** date on which
something occurred in a previous year.
2 celebration of this.

anno Domini *adv Latin* (indicating years
numbered from the supposed year of the
birth of Christ) in the year of our Lord.

annotate v add notes to (a written work).
annotation *n*.

announce ● v **1** make known publicly.
2 proclaim. **announcement** *n* **announcer**
n person who introduces radio or television
programmes.

annoy ● v irritate or displease.
annoyance *n*.

annual ● *adj* **1** happening once a year.

———— THESAURUS ————

4 = **point of view**, approach, aspect,
outlook, perspective, position, side, slant,
standpoint, viewpoint

angle² v **1** = **fish**, cast

anguish *n* = **suffering**, agony, distress,
grief, heartache, misery, pain, sorrow,
torment, woe

animal *n* **2** = **creature**, beast, brute ▷ *adj*
4 = **physical**, bestial, bodily, brutish,
carnal, gross, sensual

animate v **2** = **enliven**, energize, excite,
fire, inspire, invigorate, kindle, move,
stimulate *adj* **4** = **living**, alive, alive and
kicking, breathing, live, moving

animosity *n* = **hostility**, acrimony,
antipathy, bitterness, enmity, hatred, ill will,
malevolence, malice, rancour, resentment

annals *pl n* = **records**, accounts, archives,
chronicles, history

annex v **1** = **seize**, acquire, appropriate,
conquer, occupy, take over **3** = **join**, add,
adjoin, attach, connect, fasten

annihilate v = **destroy**, abolish, eradicate,
exterminate, extinguish, obliterate, wipe
out

announce v = **make known**, advertise,
broadcast, declare, disclose, proclaim,
report, reveal, tell

annoy v = **irritate**, anger, bother, displease,
disturb, exasperate, get on one's nerves
(*inf*), hassle (*inf*), madden, molest, pester,
plague, trouble, vex

annual *adj* **1** = **yearly**, once a year
2 = **yearlong**

a

2 lasting for a year. ▷ *n* 3 plant that completes its life cycle in a year. 4 book published once every year. **annually** *adv*.

annul ❶ *v* **-nulling, -nulled** declare (something, esp. a marriage) invalid. **annulment** *n*.

anodyne *n* 1 something that relieves pain or distress. ▷ *adj* 2 relieving pain or distress.

anoint ❶ *v* smear with oil as a sign of consecration.

anomaly ❶ [an-**nom**-a-lee] *n, pl* **-lies** something that deviates from the normal, irregularity. **anomalous** *adj*.

anon. anonymous.

anonymous ❶ *adj* 1 by someone whose name is unknown or withheld. 2 having no known name. **anonymously** *adv* **anonymity** *n*.

anorak *n* waterproof hooded jacket.

anorexia *n* psychological disorder characterized by fear of becoming fat and refusal to eat (also **anorexia nervosa**). **anorexic** *adj, n*.

another *adj, pron* 1 one more. 2 a different (one).

answer ❶ *n* 1 reply to a question, request, letter, etc. 2 solution to a problem. 3 reaction or response. ▷ *v* 4 give an answer (to). 5 be responsible to (a person). 6 respond or react. **answerable** *adj* (foll. by *for* or *to*) responsible for or accountable to. **answering machine** device for answering a telephone automatically and recording messages.

ant *n* small insect living in highly organized colonies. **anteater** *n* mammal which feeds on ants by means of a long snout.

antagonist ❶ *n* opponent or adversary. **antagonism** *n* open opposition or hostility. **antagonistic** *adj* **antagonize** *v* arouse hostility in, annoy.

Antarctic *n* 1 **the Antarctic** area around the South Pole. ▷ *adj* 2 of this region.

● **SPELLING TIP**
● Almost one in every hundred references
● to the **Antarctic** in the Bank of English
● is written without its first *c* as *Antartic*.
● Note there is a *c* after the *r*.

ante- *prefix* before in time or position, e.g. *antedate; antechamber.*

antecedent *n* 1 event or circumstance happening or existing before another. ▷ *adj* 2 preceding, prior.

antelope *n* deerlike mammal with long legs and horns.

antenatal *adj* during pregnancy, before birth.

antenna *n* 1 *pl* **-nae** insect's feeler. 2 *pl* **-nas** aerial.

anterior *adj* 1 to the front. 2 earlier.

anthem ❶ *n* 1 song of loyalty, esp. to a country. 2 piece of music for a choir, usu. set to words from the Bible.

anther *n* part of a flower's stamen containing pollen.

anthology ❶ *n, pl* **-gies** collection of poems or other literary pieces by various authors.

———————————————————— THESAURUS ————————————————————

annul *v* = **invalidate**, abolish, cancel, declare *or* render null and void, negate, nullify, repeal, retract

anoint *v* = **consecrate**, bless, hallow, sanctify

anomaly *n* = **irregularity**, abnormality, eccentricity, exception, incongruity, inconsistency, oddity, peculiarity

anonymous *adj* 1 = **uncredited**, unacknowledged, unknown, unsigned 2 = **unnamed**, incognito, nameless, unidentified

answer *n* 1 = **reply**, comeback, defence,

rejoinder, response, retort, return, riposte 2 = **solution**, explanation 3 = **reaction**, response ▷ *v* 4 = **reply**, respond, retort, return 6 = **react**, respond

antagonist *n* = **opponent**, adversary, competitor, contender, enemy, foe, rival

anthem *n* 1 = **song of praise**, paean 2 = **hymn**, canticle, carol, chant, chorale, psalm

anthology *n* = **collection**, compendium, compilation, miscellany, selection, treasury

a

anthracite n hard coal burning slowly with little smoke or flame but intense heat.

anthrax n dangerous disease of cattle and sheep, communicable to humans.

anthropoid adj **1** like a human. ▷ n **2** ape, such as a chimpanzee, that resembles a human.

anthropology n study of human origins, institutions, and beliefs. **anthropological** adj **anthropologist** n.

anti- prefix **1** against, opposed to, e.g. anti-war. **2** opposite to, e.g. anticlimax. **3** counteracting, e.g. antifreeze.

antibiotic n **1** chemical substance capable of destroying bacteria. ▷ adj **2** of antibiotics.

antibody n, pl **-bodies** protein produced in the blood, which destroys bacteria.

anticipate ❶ v **1** foresee and act in advance of. **2** look forward to. **anticipation** n.

anticlimax ❶ n disappointing conclusion to a series of events.

anticlockwise adv, adj in the opposite direction to the rotation of the hands of a clock.

antics ❶ pl n absurd acts or postures.

anticyclone n area of moving air of high pressure in which the winds rotate outwards.

antidote ❶ n substance that counteracts a poison.

antifreeze n liquid added to water to lower its freezing point, used in car radiators.

antihistamine n drug used to treat allergies.

antimony n Chem brittle silvery-white metallic element.

antipathy ❶ [an-**tip**-a-thee] n dislike, hostility. **antipathetic** adj.

antiperspirant n substance used to reduce or prevent sweating.

antipodes [an-**tip**-pod-deez] pl n any two places diametrically opposite one another on the earth's surface. **the Antipodes** Australia and New Zealand. **antipodean** adj.

antique ❶ n **1** object of an earlier period, valued for its beauty, workmanship, or age. ▷ adj **2** made in an earlier period. **3** old-fashioned.

antiseptic ❶ adj **1** preventing infection by killing germs. ▷ n **2** antiseptic substance.

antisocial ❶ adj **1** avoiding the company of other people. **2** (of behaviour) harmful to society.

antithesis ❶ [an-**tith**-iss-iss] n, pl **-ses** [-seez] **1** exact opposite. **2** placing together of contrasting ideas or words to produce an effect of balance. **antithetical** adj.

antitrust adj Aust, S Afr & US (of laws) opposing business monopolies.

antler n branched horn of male deer.

antonym n word that means the opposite

—————— THESAURUS ——————

anticipate v **1** = **expect**, await, foresee, foretell, predict, prepare for **2** = **look forward to**, hope for

anticlimax n = **disappointment**, bathos, comedown (inf), letdown

antics pl n = **clowning**, escapades, horseplay, mischief, playfulness, pranks, tomfoolery, tricks

antidote n = **cure**, countermeasure, remedy

antipathy n = **hostility**, aversion, bad blood, dislike, enmity, hatred, ill will

antique n **1** = **period piece**, bygone, heirloom, relic ▷ adj **2** = **vintage**,

antiquarian, classic, olden **3** = **old-fashioned**, archaic, obsolete, outdated

antiseptic adj **1** = **hygienic**, clean, germ-free, pure, sanitary, sterile, uncontaminated ▷ n **2** = **disinfectant**, germicide, purifier

antisocial adj **1** = **unsociable**, alienated, misanthropic, reserved, retiring, uncommunicative, unfriendly, withdrawn **2** = **disruptive**, antagonistic, belligerent, disorderly, hostile, menacing, rebellious, uncooperative

antithesis n **1** = **opposite**, contrary, contrast, converse, inverse, reverse

of another word.

anus [**ain**-uss] n opening at the end of the alimentary canal, through which faeces are discharged.

anvil n heavy iron block on which metals are hammered into particular shapes.

anxious ❶ adj **1** worried and tense. **2** intensely desiring. **anxiety** n **anxiously** adv.

any adj, pron **1** one or some, no matter which. ▷ adv **2** at all, e.g. it isn't any worse. **anybody** pron anyone. **anyhow** adv anyway. **anyone** pron **1** any person. **2** person of any importance. **anything** pron **anyway** adv **1** at any rate, nevertheless. **2** in any manner. **anywhere** adv in, at, or to any place.

aorta [eh-**or**-ta] n main artery of the body, carrying oxygen-rich blood from the heart.

apace adv lit swiftly.

apart ❶ adv **1** to or in pieces. **2** to or at a distance. **3** individual, distinct.

apartheid n former official government policy of racial segregation in S Africa.

apartment ❶ n **1** room in a building. **2** flat.

apathy ❶ n lack of interest or enthusiasm. **apathetic** adj.

ape n **1** tailless monkey such as the chimpanzee or gorilla. **2** stupid, clumsy, or

ugly man. ▷ v **3** imitate.

aperitif [ap-per-rit-**teef**] n alcoholic drink taken before a meal.

aperture n opening or hole.

apex ❶ n highest point.

aphid [**eh**-fid], **aphis** [**eh**-fiss] n small insect which sucks the sap from plants.

aphorism n short clever saying expressing a general truth.

aphrodisiac [af-roh-**diz**-zee-ak] n **1** substance that arouses sexual desire. ▷ adj **2** arousing sexual desire.

apiece ❶ adv each.

aplomb ❶ n calm self-possession.

apocalypse n **1** end of the world. **2** event of great destruction. **the Apocalypse** book of Revelation, the last book of the New Testament. **apocalyptic** adj.

apocryphal ❶ adj (of a story) of questionable authenticity.

apology ❶ n, pl -**gies 1** expression of regret for wrongdoing. **2** (foll. by for) poor example (of). **3 apologetic** adj showing or expressing regret. **apologetically** adv **apologist** n person who formally defends a cause. **apologize** v make an apology.

● **SPELLING TIP**
● Remember that the correct way to spell
● **apology** is with one p and one l.

apoplexy n Med stroke. **apoplectic** adj **1** of

─────────────────────────── THESAURUS ───────────────

anxious adj **1** = **uneasy**, apprehensive, concerned, fearful, in suspense, nervous, on tenterhooks, tense, troubled, worried **2** = **eager**, desirous, impatient, intent, itching, keen, yearning

apart adv **1** = **to pieces**, asunder, in bits, in pieces, to bits **2** = **separate**, alone, aside, away, by oneself, isolated, to one side

apartment n **1** = **room**, accommodation, living quarters, quarters, rooms, suite **2** = **flat**, penthouse, duplex (US & Canad)

apathy n = **lack of interest**, coolness, indifference, inertia, nonchalance, passivity, torpor, unconcern

apex n = **highest point**, crest, crown,

culmination, peak, pinnacle, point, summit, top

apiece adv = **each**, for each, from each, individually, respectively, separately

aplomb n = **self-possession**, calmness, composure, confidence, level-headedness, poise, sang-froid, self-assurance, self-confidence

apocryphal adj = **dubious**, doubtful, legendary, mythical, questionable, unauthenticated, unsubstantiated

apology n **1** = **defence**, acknowledgment, confession, excuse, explanation, justification, plea **2** (foll. by for) = **mockery**, caricature, excuse, imitation, travesty

apoplexy. **2** *informal* furious.

Apostle *n* **1** one of the twelve disciples chosen by Christ to preach his gospel. **2** (**a-**) ardent supporter of a cause or movement. **apostolic** *adj*.

apostrophe [ap-**poss**-trof-fee] *n* **1** punctuation mark (') showing the omission of a letter or letters in a word, e.g. *don't*, or forming the possessive, e.g. *Jill's car*. **2** digression from a speech to address an imaginary or absent person or thing.

appal ❶ *v* -**palling**, -**palled** dismay, terrify. **appalling** *adj* dreadful, terrible.

- **SPELLING TIP**
- The verb **appal** has two *p*s, but only
- one *l*. If you extend it with an ending
- beginning with a vowel, you must add
- another *l*, as in **appalling**.

apparatus ❶ *n* equipment for a particular purpose.

apparel *n* old-fashioned clothing.

apparent ❶ *adj* **1** readily seen, obvious. **2** seeming as opposed to real. **apparently** *adv*.

- **SPELLING TIP**
- It's quite common to spell **apparently**
- with three *a*s, but there should only be
- two – and then an *e*.

apparition ❶ *n* ghost or ghostlike figure.

appeal ❶ *v* **1** make an earnest request. **2** attract, please, or interest. **3** request a review of a lower court's decision by a higher court. ▷ *n* **4** earnest request for money or help. **5** power to attract, please, or interest people. **6** request for a review of a lower court's decision by a higher court. **appealing** *adj*.

appear ❶ *v* **1** become visible or present. **2** seem. **3** be seen in public. **appearance** *n* **1** an appearing. **2** outward aspect.

appease ❶ *v* **1** pacify (a person) by yielding to his or her demands. **2** satisfy or relieve (a feeling). **appeasement** *n*.

append *v* join on, add. **appendage** *n* thing joined on or added.

appendicitis *n* inflammation of the appendix.

appendix ❶ *n*, *pl* -**dices**, -**dixes** **1** separate additional material at the end of a book. **2** *Anat* short closed tube attached to the large intestine.

- **USAGE NOTE**
- Extra sections at the end of a book are
- *appendices*. The plural *appendixes* is used
- in medicine.

appertain *v* (foll. by *to*) **1** belong to. **2** be connected with.

appetite ❶ *n* **1** desire for food or drink.

—— THESAURUS ——

Apostle *n* **1** = **evangelist**, herald, messenger, missionary, preacher **2** (not cap.) = **supporter**, advocate, champion, pioneer, propagandist, proponent

appal *v* = **horrify**, alarm, daunt, dishearten, dismay, frighten, outrage, shock, unnerve

apparatus *n* = **equipment**, appliance, contraption (*inf*), device, gear, machinery, mechanism, tackle, tools

apparent *adj* **1** = **obvious**, discernible, distinct, evident, manifest, marked, unmistakable, visible **2** = **seeming**, ostensible, outward, superficial

apparition *n* = **ghost**, chimera, phantom, spectre, spirit, wraith

appeal *v* **1** = **plead**, ask, beg, call upon, entreat, pray, request **2** = **attract**, allure,

charm, entice, fascinate, interest, please, tempt ▷ *n* **4** = **plea**, application, entreaty, petition, prayer, request, supplication **5** = **attraction**, allure, beauty, charm, fascination

appear *v* **1** = **come into view**, be present, come out, come to light, crop up (*inf*), emerge, occur, show up (*inf*), surface, turn up **2** = **look (like** *or* **as if)**, occur, seem, strike one as

appease *v* **1** = **pacify**, calm, conciliate, mollify, placate, quiet, satisfy, soothe **2** = **ease**, allay, alleviate, calm, relieve, soothe

appendix *n* **1** = **supplement**, addendum, addition, adjunct, appendage, postscript

appetite *n* **1** = **desire**, craving, demand,

2 liking or willingness. **appetizer** n thing eaten or drunk to stimulate the appetite. **appetizing** adj stimulating the appetite.

applaud ❶ v **1** show approval of by clapping one's hands. **2** approve strongly. **applause** n approval shown by clapping one's hands.

apple n round firm fleshy fruit that grows on trees. **in apple-pie order** informal very tidy.

appliance ❶ n device with a specific function.

apply ❶ v -plying, -plied **1** make a formal request. **2** put to practical use. **3** put onto a surface. **4** be relevant or appropriate. **apply oneself** concentrate one's efforts. **applicant** n **application** n formal request. **applied** adj (of a skill, science, etc.) put to practical use.

appoint ❶ v **1** assign to a job or position. **2** fix or decide, e.g. appoint a time. **3** equip or furnish. **appointment** n **1** arrangement to meet a person. **2** act of placing someone in a job. **3** the job itself. ▷ pl

4 fixtures or fittings.

apportion ❶ v divide out in shares.

apposite ❶ adj suitable, apt. **apposition** n grammatical construction in which two nouns or phrases referring to the same thing are placed one after another without a conjunction, e.g. my son the doctor.

appraise ❶ v estimate the value or quality of. **appraisal** n.

appreciate ❶ v **1** value highly. **2** be aware of and understand. **3** be grateful for. **4** rise in value. **appreciable** adj enough to be noticed. **appreciably** adv **appreciation** n **appreciative** adj feeling or showing appreciation.

apprehend ❶ v **1** arrest and take into custody. **2** grasp (something) mentally. **apprehension** n **1** dread, anxiety. **2** arrest. **3** understanding. **apprehensive** adj fearful or anxious.

apprentice ❶ n **1** someone working for a skilled person for a fixed period in order to learn his or her trade. ▷ v **2** take or place (someone) as an apprentice.

——————————— THESAURUS ———————————

hunger, relish, stomach, taste **2** = **liking**, longing, passion, yearning

applaud v **1** = **clap**, cheer **2** = **approve**, acclaim, commend, compliment, encourage, extol, praise

appliance n = **device**, apparatus, gadget, implement, instrument, machine, mechanism, tool

apply v **1** = **request**, appeal, claim, inquire, petition, put in, requisition **2** = **use**, bring to bear, carry out, employ, exercise, exert, implement, practise, utilize **3** = **put on**, cover with, lay on, paint, place, smear, spread on **4** = **be relevant**, be applicable, be appropriate, bear upon, be fitting, fit, pertain, refer, relate

appoint v **1** = **assign**, choose, commission, delegate, elect, name, nominate, select **2** = **decide**, allot, arrange, assign, choose, designate, establish, fix, set **3** = **equip**, fit out, furnish, provide, supply

apportion v = **divide**, allocate, allot,

assign, dispense, distribute, dole out, give out, ration out, share

apposite adj = **appropriate**, applicable, apt, fitting, pertinent, relevant, suitable, to the point

appraise v = **assess**, estimate, evaluate, gauge, judge, rate, review, value

appreciate v **1** = **value**, admire, enjoy, like, prize, rate highly, respect, treasure **2** = **be aware of**, perceive, realize, recognize, sympathize with, take account of, understand **3** = **be grateful for**, be appreciative, be indebted, be obliged, be thankful for, give thanks for **4** = **increase**, enhance, gain, grow, improve, rise

apprehend v **1** = **arrest**, capture, catch, nick (sl, chiefly Brit), seize, take prisoner **2** = **understand**, comprehend, conceive, get the picture, grasp, perceive, realize, recognize

apprentice n **1** = **trainee**, beginner, learner, novice, probationer, pupil, student

a

apprenticeship n.

apprise v make aware (of).

approach ❶ v **1** come near or nearer (to). **2** make a proposal or suggestion to. **3** begin to deal with (a matter). ▷ n **4** approaching or means of approaching. **5** approximation. **approachable** adj.

approbation n approval.

appropriate ❶ adj **1** suitable, fitting. ▷ v **2** take for oneself. **3** put aside for a particular purpose. **appropriately** adv **appropriateness** n **appropriation** n.

approve ❶ v **1** consider good or right. **2** authorize, agree to. **approval** n **1** consent. **2** favourable opinion. **on approval** (of goods) with an option to be returned without payment if unsatisfactory.

approx. approximate(ly).

approximate ❶ adj **1** almost but not quite exact. ▷ v (foll. by to) **2** come close to. **3** be almost the same as. **approximately** adv **approximation** n.

Apr. April.

après-ski [ap-ray-**skee**] n social activities after a day's skiing.

apricot n **1** yellowish-orange juicy fruit like a small peach. ▷ adj **2** yellowish-orange.

April n fourth month of the year. **April fool** victim of a practical joke played on April 1 (**April Fools' Day**).

apron ❶ n **1** garment worn over the front of the body to protect the clothes. **2** area at an airport or hangar for manoeuvring and loading aircraft. **3** part of a stage in front of the curtain.

apropos [ap-prop-**poh**] adj, adv appropriate(ly). **apropos of** with regard to.

apt ❶ adj **1** having a specified tendency. **2** suitable. **3** quick to learn. **aptly** adv **aptness** n **aptitude** n natural ability.

aqualung n mouthpiece attached to air cylinders, worn for underwater swimming.

aquamarine n **1** greenish-blue gemstone. ▷ adj **2** greenish-blue.

aquarium n, pl **aquariums**, **aquaria 1** tank in which fish and other underwater creatures are kept. **2** building containing such tanks.

aquatic adj **1** living in or near water. **2** done in or on water. **aquatics** pl n water sports.

aqueduct n structure carrying water across a valley or river.

aquiline adj **1** (of a nose) curved like an eagle's beak. **2** of or like an eagle.

THESAURUS

approach v **1** = **move towards**, come close, come near, draw near, near, reach **2** = **make a proposal to**, appeal to, apply to, make overtures to, sound out **3** = **set about**, begin work on, commence, embark on, enter upon, make a start, undertake ▷ n **4** = **coming**, advance, arrival, drawing near, nearing **5** = **likeness**, approximation, semblance

appropriate adj **1** = **suitable**, apt, befitting, fitting, pertinent, relevant, to the point, well-suited ▷ v **2** = **seize**, commandeer, confiscate, embezzle, filch, impound, misappropriate, pilfer, pocket, steal, take possession of, usurp **3** = **allocate**, allot, apportion, assign, devote, earmark, set aside

approve v **1** = **favour**, admire, commend, have a good opinion of, like, praise, regard highly, respect **2** = **agree to**, allow, assent to, authorize, consent to, endorse, pass, permit, recommend, sanction

approximate adj **1** = **close**, estimated, inexact, loose, near, rough ▷ v (foll. by to) **2** = **come close**, approach, border on, come near, reach, touch, verge on **3** = **resemble**

apron n **1** = **pinny** (inf), pinafore

apt adj **1** = **inclined**, disposed, given, liable, likely, of a mind, prone, ready **2** = **appropriate**, fitting, pertinent, relevant, suitable, to the point **3** = **gifted**, clever, quick, sharp, smart, talented

arable ❶ *adj* suitable for growing crops on.

arbiter ❶ *n* 1 person empowered to judge in a dispute. 2 person with influential opinions about something.

arboreal *adj* of or living in trees.

arc ❶ *n* 1 part of a circle or other curve. 2 luminous discharge of electricity across a small gap between two electrodes. ▷ *v* 3 form an arc.

arcade ❶ *n* 1 covered passageway lined with shops. 2 set of arches and their supporting columns.

arcane ❶ *adj* mysterious and secret.

arch¹ ❶ *n* 1 curved structure supporting a bridge or roof. 2 something curved. 3 curved lower part of the foot. ▷ *v* 4 (cause to) form an arch. **archway** *n* passageway under an arch.

arch² ❶ *adj* 1 superior, knowing. 2 coyly playful.

arch- *combining form* chief, principal, e.g. *archenemy*.

archaeology *n* study of ancient cultures from their physical remains. **archaeological** *adj* **archaeologist** *n*.

archaic ❶ [ark-**kay**-ik] *adj* 1 ancient. 2 out-of-date. **archaism** [**ark**-kay-iz-zum] *n* archaic word or phrase.

archbishop *n* chief bishop.

archetype ❶ [**ark**-ee-type] *n* 1 perfect specimen. 2 original model. **archetypal** *adj*.

archipelago [ark-ee-**pel**-a-go] *n*, *pl* **-gos** 1 group of islands. 2 sea full of small islands.

architect ❶ *n* person qualified to design and supervise the construction of buildings. **architecture** *n* 1 style in which a building is designed and built. 2 designing and construction of buildings. **architectural** *adj*.

Arctic ❶ *n* 1 **the Arctic** area around the North Pole. ▷ *adj* 2 of this region. 3 (**a-**) *informal* very cold.

ardent ❶ *adj* 1 passionate. 2 eager, zealous. **ardently** *adv* **ardour** *n* 1 passion. 2 enthusiasm, zeal.

arduous ❶ *adj* hard to accomplish, strenuous.

are *v* see BE.

area ❶ *n* 1 part or region. 2 size of a

—————————————————————— THESAURUS ——————————————

arable *adj* = **productive**, farmable, fertile, fruitful

arbiter *n* 1 = **judge**, adjudicator, arbitrator, referee, umpire 2 = **authority**, controller, dictator, expert, governor, lord, mana (*NZ*), master, pundit, ruler

arc *n* 1 = **curve**, arch, bend, bow, crescent, half-moon

arcade *n* = **gallery**, cloister, colonnade, portico

arcane *adj* = **mysterious**, esoteric, hidden, occult, recondite, secret

arch¹ *n* 1 = **archway**, curve, dome, span, vault 2 = **curve**, arc, bend, bow, hump, semicircle ▷ *v* 4 = **curve**, arc, bend, bow, bridge, span

arch² *adj* 2 = **playful**, frolicsome, mischievous, pert, roguish, saucy, sly, waggish

archaic *adj* 1 = **old**, ancient, antique,

bygone, olden (*arch*), primitive 2 = **old-fashioned**, antiquated, behind the times, obsolete, outmoded, out of date, passé

archetype *n* 1 = **standard**, model, paradigm, pattern, prime example 2 = **original**, prototype

architect *n* = **designer**, master builder, planner

Arctic *adj* 2 = **polar**, far-northern, hyperborean 3 (not cap.) *Inf* = **freezing**, chilly, cold, frigid, frozen, glacial, icy

ardent *adj* 1 = **passionate**, amorous, hot-blooded, impassioned, intense, lusty 2 = **enthusiastic**, avid, eager, keen, zealous

arduous *adj* = **difficult**, exhausting, fatiguing, gruelling, laborious, onerous, punishing, rigorous, strenuous, taxing, tiring

area *n* 1 = **region**, district, locality,

two-dimensional surface. **3** subject field. **4** small sunken yard giving access to a basement.

arena ❶ *n* **1** seated enclosure for sports events. **2** area of a Roman amphitheatre where gladiators fought. **3** sphere of intense activity.

argon *n Chem* inert gas found in the air.

argue ❶ *v* **-guing, -gued 1** try to prove by giving reasons. **2** debate. **3** quarrel, dispute. **arguable** *adj* **arguably** *adv* **argument** *n* **1** quarrel. **2** discussion. **3** point presented for or against something. **argumentative** *adj* given to arguing.

● **SPELLING TIP**
● There's an *e* at the end of **argue**, but you
● should leave it out when you write **argu-
● ment**. A lot of people get that wrong.

aria [**ah**-ree-a] *n* elaborate song for solo voice, esp. one from an opera.

arid ❶ *adj* **1** parched, dry. **2** uninteresting. **aridity** *n*.

arise ❶ *v* **arising, arose, arisen 1** come about. **2** come into notice. **3** get up.

aristocracy ❶ *n, pl* **-cies** highest social class. **aristocrat** *n* member of the aristocracy. **aristocratic** *adj*.

arithmetic *n* **1** calculation by or

of numbers. ▷ *adj* **2** of arithmetic. **arithmetical** *adj* **arithmetician** *n*.

ark *n* **1** *Old Testament* boat built by Noah, which survived the Flood. **2 (A-)** *Judaism* chest containing the writings of Jewish Law.

arm¹ ❶ *n* **1** upper limb from the shoulder to the wrist. **2** sleeve of a garment. **3** side of a chair. **armful** *n* as much as can be held in the arms. **armchair** *n* upholstered chair with side supports for the arms. **armhole** *n* opening in a garment through which the arm passes. **armpit** *n* hollow under the arm at the shoulder.

arm² ❶ *v* **1** supply with weapons. **2** prepare (a bomb etc.) for use. **arms** *pl n* **1** weapons. **2** military exploits. **3** heraldic emblem.

armada ❶ *n* large number of warships.

armadillo *n, pl* **-los** small S American mammal covered in strong bony plates.

armistice ❶ [**arm**-miss-stiss] *n* agreed suspension of fighting.

armour ❶ *n* **1** metal clothing formerly worn to protect the body in battle. **2** metal plating of tanks, warships, etc. **armourer** *n* maker, repairer, or keeper of arms or armour. **armoury** *n* place where weapons are stored.

army ❶ *n, pl* **armies 1** military land forces

——— THESAURUS ———

neighbourhood, part, portion, section, sector, zone **3** = **field**, department, domain, province, realm, sphere, territory

arena *n* **1** = **ring**, bowl, enclosure, field, ground, stadium **2** = **amphitheatre** **3** = **sphere**, area, domain, field, province, realm, sector, territory

argue *v* **1** = **maintain**, assert, claim, dispute, remonstrate **2** = **debate**, discuss, reason **3** = **quarrel**, bicker, disagree, dispute, fall out (*inf*), fight, squabble

arid *adj* **1** = **dry**, barren, desert, parched, sterile, torrid, waterless **2** = **boring**, dreary, dry, dull, tedious, tiresome, uninspired, uninteresting

arise *v* **1** = **happen**, begin, emerge, ensue, follow, occur, result, start, stem **3** = **get**

up, get to one's feet, go up, rise, stand up, wake up

aristocracy *n* = **upper class**, elite, gentry, nobility, patricians, peerage, ruling class

arm¹ *n* **1** = **upper limb**, appendage, limb

arm² *v* **1** = **equip**, accoutre, array, deck out, furnish, issue with, provide, supply **2** = **prime**

armada *n* = **fleet**, flotilla, navy, squadron

armistice *n* = **truce**, ceasefire, peace, suspension of hostilities

armour *n* **1, 2** = **protection**, armour plate, covering, sheathing, shield

army *n* **1** = **soldiers**, armed force, legions, military, military force, soldiery, troops **2** = **vast number**, array, horde, host, multitude, pack, swarm, throng

of a nation. **2** great number.

aroma ❶ *n* pleasant smell. **aromatic** *adj*
aromatherapy *n* massage with fragrant
oils to relieve tension.

around ❶ *prep, adv* **1** on all sides (of).
2 from place to place (in). **3** somewhere in
or near. **4** approximately.

arouse ❶ *v* **1** stimulate, make active.
2 awaken.

arraign [ar-**rain**] *v* **1** bring (a prisoner)
before a court to answer a charge.
2 accuse. **arraignment** *n*.

arrange ❶ *v* **1** plan. **2** agree. **3** put in
order. **4** adapt (music) for performance in a
certain way. **arrangement** *n*.

array ❶ *n* **1** impressive display or collection.
2 orderly arrangement, esp. of troops.
3 *poetic* rich clothing. ▷ *v* **4** arrange in
order. **5** dress in rich clothing.

arrears *pl n* money owed. **in arrears** late in
paying a debt.

arrest ❶ *v* **1** take (a person) into custody.
2 stop the movement or development of.
3 catch and hold (the attention). ▷ *n* **4** act
of taking a person into custody. **5** slowing
or stopping. **arresting** *adj* attracting
attention, striking.

arrive ❶ *v* **1** reach a place or destination.
2 happen, come. **3** *informal* be born.
4 *informal* attain success. **arrival** *n*
1 arriving. **2** person or thing that has just
arrived.

arrow ❶ *n* **1** pointed shaft shot from a bow.
2 arrow-shaped sign or symbol used to
show direction. **arrowhead** *n* pointed tip
of an arrow.

arsenal ❶ *n* place where arms and
ammunition are made or stored.

arsenic *n* **1** toxic grey element. **2** highly
poisonous compound of this.

arson *n* crime of intentionally setting
property on fire. **arsonist** *n*.

---

aroma *n* = **scent**, bouquet, fragrance,
odour, perfume, redolence, savour, smell

around *prep* **1** = **surrounding**, about,
encircling, enclosing, encompassing,
on all sides of, on every side of
4 = **approximately**, about, circa
(*used with dates*), roughly ▷ *adv*
1 = **everywhere**, about, all over,
here and there, in all directions, on all
sides, throughout **3** = **near**, at hand,
close, close at hand, nearby, nigh (*arch*
or *dial*)

arouse *v* **1** = **stimulate**, excite, incite,
instigate, provoke, spur, stir up, summon
up, whip up **2** = **awaken**, rouse, waken,
wake up

arrange *v* **1** = **plan**, construct, contrive,
devise, fix up, organize, prepare **2** = **agree**,
adjust, come to terms, compromise,
determine, settle **3** = **put in order**, classify,
group, line up, order, organize, position,
sort **4** = **adapt**, instrument, orchestrate,
score

array *n* **1, 2** = **arrangement**, collection,
display, exhibition, formation, line-up,

parade, show, supply **3** *Poet* = **clothing**,
apparel, attire, clothes, dress, finery,
garments, regalia ▷ *v* **4** = **arrange**, display,
exhibit, group, parade, range, show
5 = **dress**, adorn, attire, clothe, deck,
decorate, festoon

arrest *v* **1** = **capture**, apprehend, catch,
detain, nick (*sl, chiefly Brit*), seize, take
prisoner **2** = **stop**, block, delay, end,
inhibit, interrupt, obstruct, slow, suppress
3 = **grip**, absorb, engage, engross,
fascinate, hold, intrigue, occupy ▷ *n*
4 = **capture**, bust (*inf*), cop (*sl*), detention,
seizure **5** = **stopping**, blockage, delay,
end, hindrance, interruption, obstruction,
suppression

arrive *v* **1** = **come**, appear, enter, get
to, reach, show up (*inf*), turn up **4** *Inf*
= **succeed**, become famous, make good,
make it (*inf*), make the grade (*inf*)

arrow *n* **1** = **dart**, bolt, flight, quarrel, shaft
(*arch*) **2** = **pointer**, indicator

arsenal *n* = **armoury**, ammunition dump,
arms depot, ordnance depot, stockpile,
store, storehouse, supply

art ❶ n 1 creation of works of beauty, esp. paintings or sculpture. 2 works of art collectively. 3 skill. ▷ pl 4 nonscientific branches of knowledge. **artist** n 1 person who produces works of art, esp. paintings or sculpture. 2 person skilled at something. 3 artiste. **artiste** n professional entertainer such as a singer or dancer. **artistic** adj **artistically** adv **artistry** n artistic skill. **arty** adj **artier**, **artiest** informal having an affected interest in art.

artefact n something made by human beings.

artery n, pl **-teries** 1 one of the tubes carrying blood from the heart. 2 major road or means of communication. **arterial** adj 1 of an artery. 2 (of a route) major.

arthritis n painful inflammation of a joint or joints. **arthritic** adj, n.

artichoke n flower head of a thistle-like plant, cooked as a vegetable.

article ❶ n 1 written piece in a magazine or newspaper. 2 item or object. 3 clause in a document. 4 Grammar any of the words the, a, or an.

articulate ❶ adj 1 able to express oneself clearly and coherently. 2 (of speech) clear, distinct. 3 Zool having joints. ▷ v 4 speak or say clearly and coherently. **articulately**

adv **articulated** adj jointed. **articulated lorry** large lorry in two separate sections joined by a pivoted bar. **articulation** n.

artifice ❶ n 1 clever trick. 2 cleverness, skill. **artificial** adj man-made, not occurring naturally.

artillery ❶ n 1 large-calibre guns. 2 branch of the army who use these.

artisan ❶ n skilled worker, craftsman.

as ❶ conj 1 while, when. 2 in the way that. 3 that which, e.g. do as you are told. 4 since, seeing that. 5 for instance. ▷ adv, conj 6 used to indicate amount or extent in comparisons, e.g. he is as tall as you. ▷ prep 7 in the role of, being, e.g. as a mother, I am concerned.

asbestos n fibrous mineral which does not burn. **asbestosis** n lung disease caused by inhalation of asbestos fibre.

ASBO Brit anti-social behaviour order: a civil order made against a persistently antisocial person.

ascend ❶ v go or move up. **ascent** n 1 ascending. 2 upward slope. **ascendant** adj 1 dominant or influential. ▷ n 2 **in the ascendant** increasing in power or influence. **ascendancy** n condition of being dominant.

ascertain ❶ v find out definitely. **ascertainable** adj **ascertainment** n.

THESAURUS

art n 3 = **skill**, craft, expertise, ingenuity, mastery, virtuosity

article n 1 = **piece**, composition, discourse, essay, feature, item, paper, story, treatise 2 = **thing**, commodity, item, object, piece, substance, unit 3 = **clause**, item, paragraph, part, passage, point, portion, section

articulate adj 1, 2 = **expressive**, clear, coherent, eloquent, fluent, lucid, well-spoken ▷ v 4 = **express**, enunciate, pronounce, say, speak, state, talk, utter, voice

artifice n 1 = **trick**, contrivance, device, machination, manoeuvre, stratagem, subterfuge, tactic 2 = **cleverness**,

ingenuity, inventiveness, skill

artillery n 1 = **big guns**, battery, cannon, cannonry, gunnery, ordnance

artisan n = **craftsman**, journeyman, mechanic, skilled workman, technician

as conj 1 = **when**, at the time that, during the time that, just as, while 2 = **in the way that**, in the manner that, like 3 = **what**, that which 4 = **since**, because, considering that, seeing that 5 = **for instance**, like, such as ▷ prep 7 = **being**, in the character of, in the role of, under the name of

ascend v = **move up**, climb, go up, mount, scale

ascertain v = **find out**, confirm,

ascetic ❶ [ass-**set**-tik] *n, adj* (person) abstaining from worldly pleasures and comforts. **asceticism** *n*.

ascribe ❶ *v* attribute, as to a particular origin. **ascription** *n*.

asexual [eh-**sex**-yew-al] *adj* without sex. **asexually** *adv*.

ash¹ *n* **1** powdery substance left when something is burnt. ▷ *pl* **2** remains after burning, esp. of a human body after cremation. **ashen** *adj* pale with shock. **ashtray** *n* receptacle for tobacco ash and cigarette butts.

ash² *n* tree with grey bark.

ashamed ❶ *adj* feeling shame.

ashore ❶ *adv* towards or on land.

aside ❶ *adv* **1** to one side. **2** out of other people's hearing, e.g. *he took me aside to tell me his plans.* ▷ *n* **3** remark not meant to be heard by everyone present.

asinine ❶ *adj* stupid, idiotic.

ask ❶ *v* **1** say or write (something) in a form that requires an answer. **2** make a request or demand. **3** invite.

askance [ass-**kanss**] *adv* **look askance at 1** look at with an oblique glance. **2** regard with suspicion.

askew ❶ *adv, adj* to one side, crooked.

asleep ❶ *adj* **1** sleeping. **2** (of limbs) numb.

asp *n* small poisonous snake.

asparagus *n* plant whose shoots are cooked as a vegetable.

aspect ❶ *n* **1** feature or element. **2** position facing a particular direction. **3** appearance or look.

aspen *n* kind of poplar tree.

aspersion *n* **cast aspersions on** make derogatory remarks about.

asphalt *n* **1** black hard tarlike substance used for road surfaces etc.

aspic *n* savoury jelly used to coat meat, eggs, fish, etc.

aspidistra *n* plant with long tapered leaves.

aspire ❶ *v* (foll. by *to*) yearn (for), hope (to do or be). **aspiration** *n* strong desire or aim.

aspirin *n* **1** drug used to relieve pain and fever. **2** tablet of this.

ass ❶ *n* **1** donkey. **2** stupid person.

——————————————————————— THESAURUS ————

determine, discover, establish, learn

ascetic *n* = **monk**, abstainer, hermit, nun, recluse ▷ *adj* = **self-denying**, abstinent, austere, celibate, frugal, puritanical, self-disciplined

ascribe *v* = **attribute**, assign, charge, credit, impute, put down, refer, set down

ashamed *adj* = **embarrassed**, distressed, guilty, humiliated, mortified, remorseful, shamefaced, sheepish, sorry

ashore *adv* = **on land**, aground, landwards, on dry land, on the beach, on the shore, shorewards, to the shore

aside *adv* **1** = **to one side**, apart, beside, on one side, out of the way, privately, separately, to the side ▷ *n* **3** = **interpolation**, parenthesis

asinine *adj* = **stupid**, fatuous, foolish, idiotic, imbecilic, moronic, senseless

ask *v* **1** = **inquire**, interrogate, query, question, quiz **2** = **request**, appeal, beg, demand, plead, seek **3** = **invite**, bid, summon

askew *adv* = **crookedly**, aslant, awry, obliquely, off-centre, to one side ▷ *adj* = **crooked**, awry, cockeyed (*inf*), lopsided, oblique, off-centre, skewwhiff (*Brit inf*)

asleep *adj* **1** = **sleeping**, dormant, dozing, fast asleep, napping, slumbering, snoozing (*inf*), sound asleep

aspect *n* **1** = **feature**, angle, facet, side **2** = **position**, outlook, point of view, prospect, scene, situation, view **3** = **appearance**, air, attitude, bearing, condition, demeanour, expression, look, manner

aspire *v* (foll. by *to*) = **aim**, desire, dream, hope, long, seek, set one's heart on, wish

ass *n* **1** = **donkey**, moke (*sl*) **2** = **fool**, blockhead, halfwit, idiot, jackass,

assail ❶ v attack violently. **assailant** n.

assassin ❶ n person who murders a prominent person. **assassinate** v murder (a prominent person). **assassination** n.

assault ❶ n 1 violent attack. ▷ v 2 attack violently. **assault course** series of obstacles used in military training.

assemble ❶ v 1 collect or congregate. 2 put together the parts of (a machine). **assemblage** n 1 collection or group. 2 assembling. **assembly** n 1 pl -blies assembled group. 2 assembling. **assembly line** sequence of machines and workers in a factory assembling a product.

assent ❶ n 1 agreement or consent. ▷ v 2 agree or consent.

assert ❶ v 1 declare forcefully. 2 insist upon (one's rights etc.). **assert oneself** put oneself forward forcefully. **assertion** n **assertive** adj **assertively** adv.

assess ❶ v 1 judge the worth or importance of. 2 estimate the value of (income or property) for taxation purposes. **assessment** n **assessor** n.

asset ❶ n 1 valuable or useful person or thing. ▷ pl 2 property that a person or firm can sell, esp. to pay debts.

assiduous ❶ adj hard-working. **assiduously** adv **assiduity** n.

assign ❶ v 1 appoint (someone) to a job or task. 2 allot (a task). 3 attribute. **assignation** n 1 assigning. 2 secret arrangement to meet. **assignment** n 1 task assigned. 2 assigning.

assimilate ❶ v 1 learn and understand (information). 2 absorb or be absorbed or incorporated. **assimilation** n.

assist ❶ v give help or support. **assistance** n **assistant** n 1 helper. ▷ adj 2 junior or deputy.

—————————— THESAURUS ——————————

numbskull or numskull, oaf, twit (inf, chiefly Brit)

assail v = **attack**, assault, fall upon, lay into (inf), set upon

assassin n = **murderer**, executioner, hatchet man (sl), hit man (sl), killer, liquidator, slayer

assault n 1 = **attack**, charge, invasion, offensive, onslaught v 2 = **attack**, beset, fall upon, lay into (inf), set about, set upon, strike at

assemble v 1 = **gather**, amass, bring together, call together, collect, come together, congregate, meet, muster, rally 2 = **put together**, build up, connect, construct, fabricate, fit together, join, piece together, set up

assent n 1 = **agreement**, acceptance, approval, compliance, concurrence, consent, permission, sanction ▷ v 2 = **agree**, allow, approve, consent, grant, permit

assert v 1 = **state**, affirm, declare, maintain, profess, pronounce, swear 2 = **insist upon**, claim, defend, press, put forward, stand up for, stress,

uphold **assert oneself** = **be forceful**, exert one's influence, make one's presence felt, put oneself forward, put one's foot down (inf)

assess v 1 = **judge**, appraise, estimate, evaluate, rate, size up (inf), value, weigh 2 = **evaluate**, fix, impose, levy, rate, tax, value

asset n 1 = **benefit**, advantage, aid, blessing, boon, feather in one's cap, help, resource, service pl 2 = **property**, capital, estate, funds, goods, money, possessions, resources, wealth

assiduous adj = **diligent**, hard-working, indefatigable, industrious, persevering, persistent, unflagging

assign v 1 = **select**, appoint, choose, delegate, designate, name, nominate 2 = **give**, allocate, allot, apportion, consign, distribute, give out, grant 3 = **attribute**, accredit, ascribe, put down

assimilate v 1 = **learn**, absorb, digest, take in 2 = **adjust**, adapt, blend in, digest, incorporate, mingle, take in

assist v = **help**, abet, aid, cooperate, lend a helping hand, serve, support

associate ❶ v 1 connect in the mind. 2 mix socially. ▷ n 3 partner in business. 4 friend or companion. ▷ adj 5 having partial rights or subordinate status, e.g. *associate member*. **association** n 1 society or club. 2 associating.

assonance n rhyming of vowel sounds but not consonants, as in *time* and *light*.

assorted ❶ adj consisting of various types mixed together. **assortment** n assorted mixture.

assume ❶ v 1 take to be true without proof. 2 take upon oneself, e.g. *he assumed command*. 3 pretend, e.g. *I assumed indifference*. **assumption** n 1 thing assumed. 2 assuming.

assure ❶ v 1 promise or guarantee. 2 convince. 3 make (something) certain. 4 insure against loss of life. **assured** adj 1 confident. 2 certain to happen. **assuredly** adv definitely. **assurance** n assuring or being assured.

aster n plant with daisy-like flowers.

asterisk n 1 star-shaped symbol (*) used in printing or writing to indicate a footnote etc. ▷ v 2 mark with an asterisk.

astern adv 1 at or towards the stern of a ship. 2 backwards.

asteroid n any of the small planets that orbit the sun between Mars and Jupiter.

asthma [**ass**-ma] n illness causing difficulty in breathing. **asthmatic** adj, n.

astigmatism [eh-**stig**-mat-tiz-zum] n inability of a lens, esp. of the eye, to focus properly. **astigmatic** adj.

astir adj 1 out of bed. 2 in motion.

astonish ❶ v surprise greatly. **astonishment** n.

astound v overwhelm with amazement. **astounding** adj.

astral adj 1 of stars. 2 of the spirit world.

astray ❶ adv off the right path.

astride adv, prep with a leg on either side (of).

astringent adj 1 causing contraction of body tissue. 2 checking the flow of blood from a cut. 3 severe or harsh. ▷ n 4 astringent substance. **astringency** n.

astrology n study of the alleged influence of the stars, planets, and moon on human affairs. **astrologer** n **astrological** adj.

astronaut n person trained for travelling in space.

astronomy n scientific study of heavenly bodies. **astronomer** n **astronomical** adj 1 very large. 2 of astronomy. **astronomically** adv.

astute ❶ adj perceptive or shrewd.

——————————————————— THESAURUS ———————————————————

associate v 1 = **connect**, ally, combine, identify, join, link, lump together 2 = **mix**, accompany, consort, hobnob, mingle, socialize ▷ n 3 = **partner**, collaborator, colleague, confederate, co-worker 4 = **friend**, ally, cobber (*Aust or old-fashioned NZ inf*), companion, comrade, mate (*inf*)

assorted adj = **various**, different, diverse, miscellaneous, mixed, motley, sundry, varied

assume v 1 = **take for granted**, believe, expect, fancy, imagine, infer, presume, suppose, surmise, think 2 = **take on**, accept, enter upon, put on, shoulder, take, take over 3 = **put on**, adopt, affect, feign, imitate, impersonate, mimic,

pretend to, simulate

assure v 1 = **promise**, certify, confirm, declare confidently, give one's word to, guarantee, pledge, swear, vow 2 = **convince**, comfort, embolden, encourage, hearten, persuade, reassure 3 = **make certain**, clinch, complete, confirm, ensure, guarantee, make sure, seal, secure

astonish v = **amaze**, astound, bewilder, confound, daze, dumbfound, stagger, stun, surprise

astray adv = **off the right track**, adrift, amiss, lost, off, off course, off the mark

astute adj = **intelligent**, canny, clever, crafty, cunning, perceptive, sagacious, sharp, shrewd, subtle

astutely adv **astuteness** n.

asunder adv into parts or pieces.

asylum ❶ n 1 refuge or sanctuary. 2 old name for a mental hospital.

asymmetry n lack of symmetry. **asymmetrical, asymmetric** adj.

at prep indicating position in space or time, movement towards an object, etc. e.g. at midnight; throwing stones at windows.

atheism ❶ [**aith**-ee-iz-zum] n belief that there is no God. **atheist** n **atheistic** adj.

atigi n a type of parka worn by the Inuit in Canada.

atlas n book of maps.

atmosphere ❶ n 1 mass of gases surrounding a heavenly body, esp. the earth. 2 prevailing tone or mood (of a place etc.). 3 unit of pressure. **atmospheric** adj **atmospherics** pl n radio interference due to electrical disturbance in the atmosphere.

atoll n ring-shaped coral reef enclosing a lagoon.

atom ❶ n 1 smallest unit of matter which can take part in a chemical reaction. 2 very small amount. **atom bomb** same as ATOMIC BOMB.

atonal [eh-**tone**-al] adj (of music) not written in an established key.

atone ❶ v make amends (for sin or wrongdoing). **atonement** n.

atop prep on top of.

atrocious ❶ adj 1 extremely cruel or wicked. 2 horrifying or shocking. 3 informal very bad. **atrociously** adv **atrocity** n 1 wickedness. 2 pl **-ties** act of cruelty.

atrophy [**at**-trof-fee] n, pl **-phies** 1 wasting away of an organ or part. ▷ v **-phying, -phied** 2 (cause to) waste away.

attach ❶ v 1 join, fasten, or connect. 2 attribute or ascribe. **attached** adj (foll. by to) fond of. **attachment** n.

attaché [at-**tash**-shay] n specialist attached to a diplomatic mission. **attaché case** flat rectangular briefcase for papers.

attack ❶ v 1 launch a physical assault (against). 2 criticize. 3 set about (a job or problem) with vigour. 4 affect adversely. ▷ n 5 act of attacking. 6 sudden bout of illness. **attacker** n.

attain ❶ v 1 achieve or accomplish (a task or aim). 2 reach. **attainable** adj **attainment** n accomplishment.

—————— THESAURUS ——————

asylum n 1 = **refuge**, harbour, haven, preserve, retreat, safety, sanctuary, shelter 2 Old-fashioned = **mental hospital**, hospital, institution, madhouse (inf), psychiatric hospital

atheism n = **nonbelief**, disbelief, godlessness, heathenism, infidelity, irreligion, paganism, scepticism, unbelief

atmosphere n 1 = **air**, aerosphere, heavens, sky 2 = **feeling**, ambience, character, climate, environment, mood, spirit, surroundings, tone

atom n 2 = **particle**, bit, dot, speck, spot, trace

atone v = **make amends**, compensate, do penance, make redress, make reparation, make up for, pay for, recompense, redress

atrocious adj 1 = **cruel**, barbaric, brutal, fiendish, infernal, monstrous, savage,

vicious, wicked 2 = **shocking**, appalling, detestable, grievous, horrible, horrifying, terrible

attach v 1 = **connect**, add, couple, fasten, fix, join, link, secure, stick, tie 2 = **put**, ascribe, assign, associate, attribute, connect

attack v 1 = **assault**, invade, lay into (inf), raid, set upon, storm, strike (at) 2 = **criticize**, abuse, blame, censure, have a go (at) (inf), put down, vilify ▷ n 5 **a** = **assault**, campaign, charge, foray, incursion, invasion, offensive, onslaught, raid, strike **b** = **criticism**, abuse, blame, censure, denigration, stick (sl), vilification 6 = **bout**, convulsion, fit, paroxysm, seizure, spasm, stroke

attain v 1 = **achieve**, accomplish, acquire, complete, fulfil, gain, get, obtain

a

attempt ❶ v 1 try, make an effort. ▷ n 2 effort or endeavour.

attend ❶ v 1 be present at. 2 go regularly to a school, college, etc. 3 look after. 4 pay attention. 5 apply oneself (to). **attendance** n 1 attending. 2 number attending. **attendant** n 1 person who assists, guides, or provides a service. ▷ adj 2 accompanying. **attention** n 1 concentrated direction of the mind. 2 consideration. 3 care. 4 alert position in military drill. **attentive** adj 1 giving attention. 2 considerately helpful. **attentively** adv **attentiveness** n.

attest v affirm the truth of, be proof of.

attic ❶ n space or room within the roof of a house.

attire ❶ n fine or formal clothes.

attitude ❶ n 1 way of thinking and behaving. 2 posture of the body.

attorney n 1 person legally appointed to act for another. 2 US lawyer.

attract ❶ v 1 arouse the interest or admiration of. 2 draw (something) closer to it by exerting a force on it. **attraction** n 1 power to attract. 2 something that attracts. **attractive** adj **attractively** adv **attractiveness** n.

attribute ❶ v 1 (usu. foll. by to) regard as belonging to or produced by. ▷ n 2 quality or feature representative of a person or thing. **attributable** adj **attribution** n **attributive** adj Grammar (of an adjective) preceding the noun modified.

attrition n constant wearing down to weaken or destroy.

attune ❶ v adjust or accustom (a person or thing).

atypical [eh-**tip**-ik-al] adj not typical.

aubergine [**oh**-bur-zheen] n dark purple tropical fruit, cooked and eaten as a vegetable.

auburn adj (of hair) reddish-brown.

auction n 1 public sale in which articles are sold to the highest bidder. ▷ v 2 sell by auction. **auctioneer** n person who conducts an auction.

audacious ❶ adj 1 recklessly bold or daring. 2 impudent. **audaciously** adv **audacity** n.

audible ❶ adj loud enough to be heard. **audibly** adv **audibility** n.

THESAURUS

---

attempt v 1 = **try**, endeavour, seek, strive, undertake, venture ▷ n 2 = **try**, bid, crack (inf), effort, go (inf), shot (inf), stab (inf), trial

attend v 1 = **be present**, appear, frequent, go to, haunt, put in an appearance, show oneself, turn up, visit 3 = **look after**, care for, mind, minister to, nurse, take care of, tend 4 = **pay attention**, hear, heed, listen, mark, note, observe, pay heed 5 **attend to** = **apply oneself to**, concentrate on, devote oneself to, get to work on, look after, occupy oneself with, see to, take care of

attic n = **loft**, garret

attire n = **clothes**, apparel, costume, dress, garb, garments, outfit, robes, wear

attitude n 1 = **disposition**, approach, frame of mind, mood, opinion, outlook, perspective, point of view, position, stance 2 = **position**, pose, posture, stance

attract v 1 = **appeal to**, charm, enchant 2 = **draw**, allure, entice, lure, pull (inf), tempt

attribute v 1 (usu. foll. by to) = **ascribe**, charge, credit, put down to, set down to ▷ n 2 = **quality**, aspect, character, characteristic, facet, feature, peculiarity, property, trait

attune v = **accustom**, adapt, adjust, familiarize, harmonize, regulate

audacious adj 1 = **daring**, bold, brave, courageous, fearless, intrepid, rash, reckless 2 = **cheeky**, brazen, defiant, impertinent, impudent, insolent, presumptuous, shameless

audible adj = **clear**, detectable, discernible, distinct, hearable, perceptible

audience ❶ n 1 group of spectators or listeners. 2 formal interview.

audio adj 1 of sound or hearing. 2 of or for the transmission or reproduction of sound.

audit n 1 official examination of business accounts. ▷ v **auditing, audited** 2 examine (business accounts) officially. **auditor** n.

audition n 1 test of a performer's ability for a particular role or job. ▷ v 2 test or be tested in an audition.

Aug. August.

augment v increase or enlarge. **augmentation** n.

augur v be a sign of (future events). **augury** n 1 foretelling of the future. 2 pl **-ries** omen.

August n eighth month of the year.

auk n northern sea bird with short wings and black-and-white plumage.

aunt n 1 father's or mother's sister. 2 uncle's wife. **auntie, aunty** n, pl **aunties** informal aunt. **Aunt Sally** 1 figure used in fairgrounds as a target. 2 target of abuse or criticism.

au pair n young foreign woman who does housework in return for board and lodging.

aura ❶ n distinctive air or quality of a person or thing.

aural adj of or using the ears or hearing.

auricle n 1 upper chamber of the heart. 2 outer part of the ear. **auricular** adj.

aurora n, pl **-ras, -rae** bands of light sometimes seen in the sky in polar regions. **aurora australis** aurora seen near the South Pole. **aurora borealis** aurora seen near the North Pole.

auspices [aw-spiss-siz] pl n **under the auspices of** with the support and approval of.

austere ❶ adj 1 stern or severe. 2 ascetic or self-disciplined. 3 severely simple or plain. **austerely** adv **austerity** n.

authentic ❶ adj known to be real, genuine. **authentically** adv **authenticity** n **authenticate** v establish as genuine. **authentication** n.

author ❶ n 1 writer of a book etc. 2 originator or creator. **authorship** n.

authority ❶ n, pl **-ties** 1 power to command or control others. 2 (often pl) person or group having this power. 3 expert in a particular field. **authoritarian** n, adj (person) insisting on strict obedience to authority. **authoritative** adj 1 recognized as being reliable. 2 possessing authority. **authoritatively** adv **authorize** v 1 give authority to. 2 give permission for. **authorization** n.

autism n Psychiatry disorder, usu. of children, characterized by lack of response to people and limited ability to communicate. **autistic** adj.

auto- combining form self-, e.g. autobiography.

——————————— THESAURUS ———————————

audience n 1 = **spectators**, assembly, crowd, gallery, gathering, listeners, onlookers, turnout, viewers 2 = **interview**, consultation, hearing, meeting, reception

aura n = **air**, ambience, atmosphere, feeling, mood, quality, tone

austere adj 1 = **stern**, forbidding, formal, serious, severe, solemn, strict 2 = **ascetic**, abstemious, puritanical, self-disciplined, sober, solemn, strait-laced, strict 3 = **plain**, bleak, harsh, simple, spare, Spartan, stark

authentic adj = **genuine**, actual, authoritative, bona fide, legitimate, pure, real, true-to-life, valid

author n 1 = **writer**, composer, creator 2 = **creator**, architect, designer, father, founder, inventor, originator, producer

authority n 1 = **power**, command, control, direction, influence, mana (NZ), supremacy, sway, weight 2 (often pl) = **powers that be**, administration, government, management, officialdom, police, the Establishment 3 = **expert**, connoisseur, guru, judge, master,

autobiography *n, pl* **-phies** account of a person's life written by that person. **autobiographical** *adj*.

autocrat ❶ *n* 1 ruler with absolute authority. 2 dictatorial person. **autocratic** *adj* **autocratically** *adv* **autocracy** *n* government by an autocrat.

Autocue *n* ® electronic television prompting device displaying a speaker's script, unseen by the audience.

autogiro, autogyro *n, pl* **-ros** self-propelled aircraft resembling a helicopter but with an unpowered rotor.

autograph *n* 1 handwritten signature of a (famous) person. ▷ *v* 2 write one's signature on or in.

automatic ❶ *adj* 1 (of a device) operating mechanically by itself. 2 (of a process) performed by automatic equipment. 3 done without conscious thought. 4 (of a firearm) self-loading. ▷ *n* 5 self-loading firearm. 6 vehicle with automatic transmission. **automatically** *adv*.

automobile *n* US motor car.

autonomy ❶ *n* self-government. **autonomous** *adj*.

autopsy *n, pl* **-sies** examination of a corpse to determine the cause of death.

autumn *n* season between summer and winter. **autumnal** *adj*.

auxiliary ❶ *adj* 1 secondary or supplementary. 2 supporting. ▷ *n, pl* **-ries** 3 person or thing that supplements or supports. **auxiliary verb** verb used to form the tense, voice, or mood of another, such as *will* in *I will go*.

avail ❶ *v* 1 be of use or advantage (to). ▷ *n* 2 use or advantage, esp. in *to no avail*. **avail oneself of** make use of. **available** obtainable or accessible.

avalanche ❶ *n* 1 mass of snow or ice falling down a mountain. 2 sudden overwhelming quantity of anything.

avant-garde ❶ [av-ong-**gard**] *n* 1 group of innovators, esp. in the arts. ▷ *adj* 2 innovative and progressive.

avarice ❶ [**av**-a-riss] *n* greed for wealth. **avaricious** *adj*.

avenge ❶ *v* take revenge in retaliation for (harm done) or on behalf of (a person harmed). **avenger** *n*.

avenue ❶ *n* 1 wide street. 2 road between two rows of trees. 3 way of approach.

aver [av-**vur**] *v* **averring, averred** state to be true.

——————————————————————————————— THESAURUS ———————

professional, specialist

autocrat *n* 1 = **dictator**, absolutist, despot, tyrant

automatic *adj* 1, 2 = **mechanical**, automated, mechanized, push-button, self-propelling 3 = **involuntary**, instinctive, mechanical, natural, reflex, spontaneous, unconscious, unwilling

autonomy *n* = **independence**, freedom, home rule, self-determination, self-government, self-rule, sovereignty

auxiliary *adj* 1 = **supplementary**, back-up, emergency, fall-back, reserve, secondary, subsidiary, substitute 2 = **supporting**, accessory, aiding, ancillary, assisting, helping *n* 3 = **helper**, assistant, associate, backup, companion, reserve, subordinate, supporter

avail *v* 1 = **benefit**, aid, assist, be of advantage, be useful, help, profit ▷ *n* 2 = **benefit**, advantage, aid, good, help, profit, use

avalanche *n* 1 = **snow-slide**, landslide, landslip 2 = **flood**, barrage, deluge, inundation, torrent

avant-garde *adj* 2 = **progressive**, experimental, ground-breaking, innovative, pioneering, unconventional

avarice *n* = **greed**, covetousness, meanness, miserliness, niggardliness, parsimony, stinginess

avenge *v* = **get revenge for**, get even for (*inf*), get one's own back, hit back, punish, repay, retaliate

avenue *n* 1 = **street**, boulevard, course, drive, passage, path, road, route, way

a

average ❶ n 1 typical or normal amount or quality. 2 result obtained by adding quantities together and dividing the total by the number of quantities. ▷ adj 3 usual or typical. 4 calculated as an average. ▷ v 5 calculate the average of. 6 amount to as an average.

averse ❶ adj (usu. foll. by to) disinclined or unwilling. **aversion** n 1 strong dislike. 2 person or thing disliked.

avert ❶ v 1 turn away. 2 ward off.

aviary n, pl **aviaries** large cage or enclosure for birds.

aviation n art of flying aircraft. **aviator** n.

avid ❶ adj 1 keen or enthusiastic. 2 greedy (for). **avidly** adv **avidity** n.

avocado n, pl **-dos** pear-shaped tropical fruit with a leathery green skin and yellowish-green flesh.

avoid ❶ v 1 prevent from happening.

2 refrain from. 3 keep away from. **avoidable** adj **avoidance** n.

avow v 1 state or affirm. 2 admit openly. **avowal** n **avowed** adj.

await ❶ v 1 wait for. 2 be in store for.

awake ❶ v awaking, awoke, awoken 1 emerge or rouse from sleep. 2 (cause to) become alert. ▷ adj 3 not sleeping. 4 alert.

award ❶ v 1 give (something, such as a prize) formally. ▷ n 2 something awarded, such as a prize.

aware ❶ adj having knowledge, informed. **awareness** n.

awash adv washed over by water.

away ❶ adv 1 from a place, e.g. go away. 2 to another place, e.g. put that gun away. 3 out of existence, e.g. laughing away. 4 continuously, e.g. laughing away. ▷ adj 5 not present. 6 distant, e.g. two miles away. 7 Sport played on an opponent's ground.

──────── THESAURUS ────────

average n 1 = **usual**, norm, normal, par, standard 2 = **mean**, medium, midpoint ▷ adj 3 = **usual**, commonplace, fair, general, normal, ordinary, regular, standard, typical 4 = **mean**, intermediate, median, medium, middle ▷ v 6 = **make on average**, balance out to, be on average, do on average, even out to

averse adj (usu. foll. by to) = **opposed**, disinclined, hostile, ill-disposed, loath, reluctant, unwilling

avert v 1 = **turn away**, turn aside 2 = **ward off**, avoid, fend off, forestall, frustrate, preclude, prevent, stave off

avid adj 1 = **enthusiastic**, ardent, devoted, eager, fanatical, intense, keen, passionate, zealous 2 = **insatiable**, grasping, greedy, hungry, rapacious, ravenous, thirsty, voracious

avoid v 1 = **prevent**, avert 2 = **refrain from**, dodge, duck (out of) (inf), eschew, fight shy of, shirk 3 = **keep away from**, bypass, dodge, elude, escape, evade, shun, steer clear of

await v 1 = **wait for**, abide, anticipate, expect, look for, look forward to, stay for

2 = **be in store for**, attend, be in readiness for, be prepared for, be ready for, wait for

awake v 1 = **wake up**, awaken, rouse, wake 2 = **alert**, arouse, kindle, provoke, revive, stimulate, stir up ▷ adj 3 = **not sleeping**, aroused, awakened, aware, conscious, wakeful, wide-awake 4 = **alert**, alive, attentive, aware, heedful, observant, on the lookout, vigilant, watchful

award v 1 = **give**, bestow, confer, endow, grant, hand out, present ▷ n 2 = **prize**, decoration, gift, grant, trophy

aware adj = **knowing**, acquainted with, conscious of, conversant with, enlightened, familiar with, informed, in the loop, in the picture, knowledgeable, mindful of

away adv 1 = **from here**, abroad, apart, at a distance, elsewhere, far, from home, hence, off, remote 2 = **aside**, out of the way, to one side 4 = **continuously**, incessantly, interminably, relentlessly, repeatedly, uninterruptedly, unremittingly ▷ adj 5 = **not present**, abroad, absent, elsewhere, gone, not at home, not here, out

awe ❶ n 1 wonder and respect mixed with dread. ▷ v 2 fill with awe. **awesome** adj 1 inspiring awe. 2 slang excellent or outstanding. **awestruck** adj filled with awe.

awful ❶ adj 1 very bad or unpleasant. 2 informal very great. 3 obs inspiring awe. **awfully** adv 1 in an unpleasant way. 2 informal very.

awhile adv for a brief time.

awkward ❶ adj 1 clumsy or ungainly. 2 embarrassed. 3 difficult to use or handle. 4 inconvenient. **awkwardly** adv **awkwardness** n.

awl n pointed tool for piercing wood, leather, etc.

awning n canvas roof supported by a frame to give protection against the weather.

AWOL adj Mil absent without leave.

awry [a-**rye**] adv, adj 1 with a twist to one side, askew. 2 amiss.

axe ❶ n 1 tool with a sharp blade for felling trees or chopping wood. 2 informal dismissal from employment etc. ▷ v 3 informal dismiss (employees), restrict (expenditure), or terminate (a project).

axiom ❶ n 1 generally accepted principle. 2 self-evident statement. **axiomatic** adj 1 self-evident.

axis ❶ n, pl **axes** 1 (imaginary) line round which a body can rotate or about which an object or geometrical figure is symmetrical. 2 one of two fixed lines on a graph, against which quantities or positions are measured. **axial** adj.

axle ❶ n shaft on which a wheel or pair of wheels turns.

aye, ay interj 1 yes. ▷ n 2 affirmative vote or voter.

azalea [az-**zale**-ya] n garden shrub grown for its showy flowers.

azure adj, n (of) the colour of a clear blue sky.

———————————————— THESAURUS ————————

awe n 1 = **wonder**, admiration, amazement, astonishment, dread, fear, horror, respect, reverence, terror ▷ v 2 = **impress**, amaze, astonish, frighten, horrify, intimidate, stun, terrify

awful adj 1 = **terrible**, abysmal, appalling, deplorable, dreadful, frightful, ghastly, horrendous 3 Obs = **awe-inspiring**, awesome, fearsome, majestic, solemn

awkward adj 1 = **clumsy**, gauche, gawky, inelegant, lumbering, uncoordinated, ungainly 2 = **embarrassed**, ill at ease, uncomfortable 3 = **difficult**, cumbersome, troublesome, unmanageable, unwieldy 4 = **inconvenient**

axe n 1 = **hatchet**, adze, chopper 2 Inf = **the sack**, dismissal, termination, the boot (sl), the chop (sl) (inf) ▷ v 3 Inf = **cut back**, cancel, dismiss, dispense with, eliminate, fire (inf), get rid of, remove, sack (inf)

axiom n 1 = **principle**, adage, aphorism, dictum, maxim, precept 2 = **truism**

axis n 1 = **pivot**, axle, centre line, shaft, spindle

axle n = **shaft**, axis, pin, pivot, rod, spindle

Bb

BA Bachelor of Arts.

baas n S Afr boss.

babble ❶ v 1 talk excitedly or foolishly. 2 (of streams) make a low murmuring sound. ▷ n 3 muddled or foolish speech.

babe n baby.

babiche n Canad thongs or lacings of rawhide.

baboon n large monkey with a pointed face and a long tail.

baby ❶ n, pl **-bies** 1 very young child or animal. 2 slang sweetheart. ▷ adj 3 comparatively small of its type. **babyish** adj **baby-sit** v take care of a child while the parents are out. **baby-sitter** n.

bach n NZ small holiday cottage.

bachelor n 1 unmarried man. 2 person who holds the lowest university or college degree.

- **SPELLING TIP**
- We find *batchelor* spelt with a *t* 14 times in
- the Bank of English. The correct spelling
- has no *t*: **bachelor**.

bacillus [bass-**ill**-luss] n, pl -**li** [-lie] rod-shaped bacterium, esp. one causing disease.

back ❶ n 1 rear part of the human body, from the neck to the pelvis. 2 part or side of an object opposite the front. 3 part of anything less often seen or used. 4 Ball games defensive player or position. ▷ v 5 (cause to) move backwards. 6 provide money for (a person or enterprise). 7 bet on the success of. 8 (foll. by onto) have the back facing towards. ▷ adj 9 situated behind. 10 owing from an earlier date. ▷ adv 11 at, to, or towards the rear. 12 to or towards the original starting point or condition. **backer** n person who gives financial support. **backfire** v fail to have the desired effect. **background** n space behind chief figures of a picture, etc. **backing** n 1 support. 2 musical accompaniment for a pop singer. **backlash** n sudden and adverse reaction. **backward** adj 1 directed towards the rear. 2 retarded in physical, material, or intellectual development. **backwardness** n **backwards** adv 1 towards the rear. 2 with the back foremost. 3 in the reverse of the usual direction. **back up** v support. **backup** n 1 support or reinforcement. 2 reserve or substitute.

bacon n salted or smoked pig meat.

bacteria ❶ pl n, sing -**rium** large group of microorganisms, many of which cause disease. **bacterial** adj **bacteriology** n study of bacteria.

bad ❶ adj **worse**, **worst** 1 of poor quality. 2 lacking skill or talent. 3 harmful. 4 immoral or evil. 5 naughty or mischievous. 6 rotten or decayed. 7 unpleasant. **badly** adv **badness** n.

— THESAURUS —

babble v 1 = **gabble**, burble, chatter, gibber, jabber, prattle, waffle (inf, chiefly Brit) 2 = **gurgle** ▷ n 3 = **gabble**, burble, drivel, gibberish, waffle (inf, chiefly Brit)

baby n 1 = **infant**, babe, babe in arms, bairn (Scot), child, newborn child ▷ adj 3 = **small**, little, mini, miniature, minute, teeny-weeny, tiny, wee

back n 1 = **rear**, end, hindquarters 3 = **end**, far end, hind part, rear, reverse, stern, tail end ▷ v 6 = **support**, advocate, assist, champion, endorse, promote, sponsor ▷ adj 9 = **rear**, end, hind, hindmost, posterior, tail 10 = **previous**, delayed, earlier, elapsed, former, overdue, past

bacteria pl n = **microorganisms**, bacilli, bugs (sl), germs, microbes, pathogens, viruses

bad adj 1 = **inferior**, defective, faulty, imperfect, inadequate, poor, substandard, unsatisfactory 3 = **harmful**, damaging, dangerous, deleterious, detrimental,

badge ❶ n emblem worn to show membership, rank, etc.

badger ❶ n **1** nocturnal burrowing mammal with a black and white head. ▷ v **2** pester or harass.

badminton n game played with rackets and a shuttlecock, which is hit back and forth over a high net.

baffle ❶ v **1** perplex or puzzle. ▷ n **2** device to limit or regulate the flow of fluid, light, or sound. **bafflement** n.

bag ❶ n **1** flexible container with an opening at one end. **2** handbag or piece of luggage. **3** offens ugly or bad-tempered woman. ▷ v **bagging, bagged 4** put into a bag. **5** succeed in capturing, killing or scoring. **baggy** adj (of clothes) hanging loosely.

bagatelle n **1** something of little value. **2** board game in which balls are struck into holes.

baggage ❶ n suitcases packed for a journey.

bagpipes pl n musical wind instrument with reed pipes and an inflatable bag.

bail¹ ❶ n **1** Law money deposited with a court as security for a person's reappearance in court. ▷ v **2** pay bail for (a person).

bail², bale ❶ v (foll. by out) **1** remove (water) from (a boat). **2** informal help

(a person or organization) out of a predicament. **3** make an emergency parachute jump from an aircraft.

bail³ n Cricket either of two wooden bars across the tops of the stumps.

bailiff n **1** sheriff's officer who serves writs and summonses. **2** landlord's agent.

bait ❶ n **1** piece of food on a hook or in a trap to attract fish or animals. ▷ v **2** put a piece of food on or in (a hook or trap). **3** persecute or tease.

baize n woollen fabric used to cover billiard and card tables.

bake v **1** cook by dry heat as in an oven. **2** make or become hardened by heat. **baker** n person whose business is to make or sell bread, cakes, etc. **baker's dozen** thirteen. **bakery** n, pl **-eries** place where bread, cakes, etc. are baked or sold. **baking powder** powdered mixture containing sodium bicarbonate, used as a raising agent in baking.

bakeapple n cloudberry.

bakkie n S Afr small truck.

balaclava, balaclava helmet n close-fitting woollen hood that covers the ears and neck.

balalaika n guitar-like musical instrument with a triangular body.

—————————————————— THESAURUS ——————————————————

hurtful, ruinous, unhealthy **4 = wicked**, corrupt, criminal, evil, immoral, mean, sinful, wrong **5 = naughty**, disobedient, mischievous, unruly **6 = rotten**, decayed, mouldy, off, putrid, rancid, sour, spoiled **7 = unfavourable**, adverse, distressing, gloomy, grim, troubled, unfortunate, unpleasant

badge n **= mark**, brand, device, emblem, identification, insignia, sign, stamp, token

badger v **2 = pester**, bully, goad, harass, hound, importune, nag, plague, torment

baffle v **= puzzle**, bewilder, confound, confuse, flummox, mystify, nonplus, perplex, stump

bag n **1 = container**, receptacle, sac, sack

▷ v **5 = catch**, acquire, capture, kill, land, shoot, trap

baggage n **= luggage**, accoutrements, bags, belongings, equipment, gear, paraphernalia, suitcases, things

bail¹ n **1** Law **= security**, bond, guarantee, pledge, surety, warranty

bail², bale v (foll. by out) **2** Inf **= help**, aid, relieve, rescue, save (someone's) bacon (inf, chiefly Brit) ▷ v **3 = escape**, quit, retreat, withdraw

bait n **1 = lure**, allurement, attraction, decoy, enticement, incentive, inducement, snare, temptation ▷ v **3 = tease**, annoy, bother, harass, hassle (inf), hound, irritate, persecute, torment, wind up (Brit sl)

b

balance ❶ n 1 state in which a weight or amount is evenly distributed. 2 amount that remains, e.g. *the balance of what you owe*. 3 weighing device. 4 difference between the credits and debits of an account. ▷ v 5 weigh in a balance. 6 make or remain steady. 7 consider or compare. 8 compare or equalize the money going into or coming out of an account.

balcony ❶ n, pl **-nies** 1 platform on the outside of a building with a rail along the outer edge. 2 upper tier of seats in a theatre or cinema.

bald ❶ adj 1 having little or no hair on the scalp. 2 plain or blunt. 3 (of a tyre) having a worn tread. **balding** adj becoming bald. **baldness** n.

bale n 1 large bundle of hay or goods tightly bound together. ▷ v 2 make or put into bales.

baleful adj vindictive or menacing.

balk, baulk ❶ v 1 be reluctant to (do something). 2 thwart or hinder.

ball¹ ❶ n 1 round or nearly round object, esp. one used in games. 2 single delivery of the ball in a game. ▷ pl taboo slang 3 testicles. 4 nonsense. ▷ v 5 form into a ball. **ball bearings** steel balls between moving parts of a machine to reduce friction. **ballpoint**, **ballpoint pen** n pen with a tiny ball

bearing as a writing point.

ball² n formal social function for dancing. **ballroom** n.

ballad n 1 narrative poem or song. 2 slow sentimental song.

ballast ❶ n substance, such as sand, used to stabilize a ship when it is not carrying cargo.

ballet n 1 classical style of expressive dancing based on conventional steps. 2 theatrical performance of this. **ballerina** n female ballet dancer.

ballistics n study of the flight of projectiles, such as bullets. **ballistic missile** missile guided automatically in flight but which falls freely at its target.

balloon ❶ n 1 inflatable rubber bag used as a plaything or decoration. 2 large bag inflated with air or gas, designed to float in the atmosphere with passengers in a basket underneath. ▷ v 3 fly in a balloon. 4 swell or increase rapidly in size. **balloonist** n.

ballot ❶ n 1 method of voting secretly. 2 actual vote or paper indicating a person's choice. ▷ v **-loting**, **-loted** 3 vote or ask for a vote from.

balm ❶ n 1 aromatic substance used for healing and soothing. 2 anything that comforts or soothes.

--- THESAURUS ---

balance n 1 = **equilibrium**, correspondence, equity, equivalence, evenness, parity, symmetry 2 = **remainder**, difference, residue, rest, surplus ▷ v 5 = **weigh** 6 = **stabilize**, level, match, parallel, steady 7 = **compare**, assess, consider, deliberate, estimate, evaluate 8 = **calculate**, compute, settle, square, tally, total

balcony n 1 = **terrace**, veranda 2 = **upper circle**, gallery, gods

bald adj 1 = **hairless**, baldheaded, depilated 2 = **plain**, blunt, direct, forthright, straightforward, unadorned, unvarnished

balk, baulk v 1 = **recoil**, evade, flinch, hesitate, jib, refuse, resist, shirk, shrink

from 2 = **foil**, check, counteract, defeat, frustrate, hinder, obstruct, prevent, thwart

ball¹ n 1 = **sphere**, drop, globe, globule, orb, pellet, spheroid

ballast n = **counterbalance**, balance, counterweight, equilibrium, sandbag, stability, stabilizer, weight

balloon v 4 = **swell**, billow, blow up, dilate, distend, expand, grow rapidly, inflate, puff out

ballot n 1 = **vote**, election, poll, polling, voting

balm n 1 = **ointment**, balsam, cream, embrocation, emollient, lotion, salve, unguent 2 = **comfort**, anodyne, consolation, curative, palliative, restorative, solace

balmy ❶ *adj* **balmier, balmiest** (of weather) mild and pleasant.

balsa [**bawl**-sa] *n* very light wood from a tropical American tree.

balsam *n* soothing ointment.

bamboo *n* tall treelike tropical grass with hollow stems.

bamboozle ❶ *v informal* **1** cheat or mislead. **2** confuse, puzzle.

ban ❶ *v* **banning, banned 1** prohibit or forbid officially. ▷ *n* **2** official prohibition.

banal ❶ [ban-**nahl**] *adj* ordinary and unoriginal. **banality** *n*.

banana *n* yellow crescent-shaped fruit.

band¹ ❶ *n* **1** group of musicians playing together. **2** group of people having a common purpose. **bandstand** *n* roofed outdoor platform for a band. **band together** *v* unite.

band² ❶ *n* **1** strip of some material, used to hold objects. **2** *Physics* range of frequencies or wavelengths between two limits.

bandanna, bandana *n* large brightly coloured handkerchief or neckerchief.

B & B bed and breakfast.

bandit ❶ *n* robber, esp. a member of an armed gang. **banditry** *n*.

bandwagon *n* **jump, climb on the bandwagon** join a party or movement that seems assured of success.

bandy *adj* **-dier, -diest 1** (also **bandy-legged**) having legs curved outwards at the knees. ▷ *v* **-dying, -died 2** exchange (words) in a heated manner. **3** use (a name, term, etc.) frequently.

bane ❶ *n* person or thing that causes misery or distress. **baneful** *adj*.

bang ❶ *n* **1** short loud explosive noise. **2** hard blow or loud knock. ▷ *v* **3** hit or knock, esp. with a loud noise. **4** close (a door) noisily. ▷ *adv* **5** precisely. **6** with a sudden impact.

banger *n* **1** *informal* old decrepit car. **2** *slang* sausage. **3** firework that explodes loudly.

bangle *n* bracelet worn round the arm or the ankle.

banish ❶ *v* **1** send (someone) into exile. **2** drive away. **banishment** *n*.

banisters ❶ *pl n* railing supported by posts on a staircase.

banjo *n, pl* **-jos, -joes** guitar-like musical instrument with a circular body.

bank¹ ❶ *n* **1** institution offering services such as the safekeeping and lending of

———————————— THESAURUS ————————

balmy *adj* = **mild**, clement, pleasant, summery, temperate

bamboozle *v Inf* **1** = **cheat**, con (*inf*), deceive, dupe, fool, hoodwink, swindle, trick ▷ *v* **2** = **puzzle**, baffle, befuddle, confound, confuse, mystify, perplex, stump

ban *v* **1** = **prohibit**, banish, bar, block, boycott, disallow, disqualify, exclude, forbid, outlaw *n* **2** = **prohibition**, boycott, disqualification, embargo, restriction, taboo

banal *adj* = **unoriginal**, hackneyed, humdrum, mundane, pedestrian, stale, stereotyped, trite, unimaginative

band¹ *n* **1** = **ensemble**, combo, group, orchestra **2** = **gang**, body, company, group, party, posse (*inf*)

band² *n* **1** = **strip**, belt, bond, chain, cord, ribbon, strap

bandit *n* = **robber**, brigand, desperado,

highwayman, marauder, outlaw, thief

bane *n* = **plague**, bête noire, curse, nuisance, pest, ruin, scourge, torment

bang *n* **1** = **explosion**, clang, clap, clash, pop, slam, thud, thump **2** = **blow**, bump, cuff, knock, punch, smack, stroke, whack ▷ *v* **3** = **hit**, belt (*inf*), clatter, knock, slam, strike, thump ▷ *adv* **5** = **straight**, precisely, slap, smack **6** = **hard**, abruptly, headlong, noisily, suddenly

banish *v* **1** = **expel**, deport, eject, evict, exile, outlaw **2** = **get rid of**, ban, cast out, discard, dismiss, oust, remove

banisters *pl n* = **railing**, balusters, balustrade, handrail, rail

bank¹ *n* **1** = **storehouse**, depository, repository **2** = **store**, accumulation, fund, hoard, reserve, reservoir, savings, stock, stockpile ▷ *v* **3** = **save**, deposit, keep

money. **2** any supply, store, or reserve. ▷ v **3** deposit (cash or cheques) in a bank. **4** transact business with a bank. **banking** n **bank holiday** public holiday when banks are closed by law. **banknote** n piece of paper money. **bank on** v rely on.

bank² ❶ n **1** raised mass, esp. of earth. **2** slope, as of a hill. **3** sloping ground at the side of a river. ▷ v **4** form into a bank. **5** cover (a fire) with ashes and fuel so that it will burn slowly. **6** cause (an aircraft) or (of an aircraft) to tip to one side on turning.

bankrupt ❶ n **1** person declared by a court to be unable to pay his or her debts. ▷ adj **2** financially ruined. ▷ v **3** make bankrupt. **bankruptcy** n.

banner ❶ n **1** long strip of cloth displaying a slogan, advertisement, etc. **2** placard carried in a demonstration or procession.

banns pl n public declaration, esp. in a church, of an intended marriage.

banquet ❶ n elaborate formal dinner.

banshee n (in Irish folklore) female spirit whose wailing warns of a coming death.

bantam n small breed of chicken. **bantamweight** n boxer weighing up to 118lb (professional) or 54kg (amateur).

banter ❶ v **1** tease jokingly. ▷ n **2** teasing or joking conversation.

bar ❶ n **1** rigid length of metal, wood, etc. **2** solid, usu. rectangular block, of any material. **3** anything that obstructs or prevents. **4** counter or room where drinks are served. **5** heating element in an electric fire. **6** place in court where the accused stands during trial. **7** Music group of beats repeated throughout a piece of music. ▷ v **barring**, **barred** **8** secure with a bar. **9** obstruct. **10** ban or forbid. ▷ prep **11** (also **barring**) except for. **the Bar** n barristers collectively. **barman**, **barmaid**, **bartender** n.

barachois [bar-ah-**shwah**] n (in the Atlantic Provinces of Canada) a shallow lagoon formed by a sand bar.

barb ❶ n **1** cutting remark. **2** point facing in the opposite direction to the main point of a fish-hook etc. **barbed wire** strong wire with protruding sharp points.

barbecue n **1** grill on which food is cooked over hot charcoal, usu. outdoors. ▷ v **2** cook (food) on a barbecue.

barber n person who cuts men's hair and shaves beards.

barbiturate n drug used as a sedative.

THESAURUS

bank² n **1** = **mound**, banking, embankment, heap, mass, pile, ridge **3** = **side**, brink, edge, margin, shore ▷ v **4** = **pile**, amass, heap, mass, mound, stack **6** = **tilt**, camber, cant, heel, incline, pitch, slant, slope, tip

bankrupt adj **2** = **insolvent**, broke (inf), destitute, impoverished, in queer street, in the red, munted (NZ sl), ruined, wiped out (inf)

banner n **1** = **flag**, colours, ensign, pennant, standard, streamer **2** = **placard**

banquet n = **feast**, dinner, meal, repast, revel, treat

banter v **1** = **joke**, jest, kid (inf), rib (inf), taunt, tease ▷ n **2** = **joking**, badinage, jesting, kidding (inf), repartee, teasing, wordplay

bar n **1** = **rod**, paling, palisade, pole, rail, shaft, stake, stick **3** = **obstacle**, barricade, barrier, block, deterrent, hindrance, impediment, obstruction, stop **4** = **public house**, boozer (Brit, Aust & NZ inf), beer parlour (Canad), beverage room (Canad), canteen, counter, inn, pub (inf, chiefly Brit), saloon, tavern, watering hole (facetious sl) ▷ v **8** = **fasten**, barricade, bolt, latch, lock, secure **9** = **obstruct**, hinder, prevent, restrain **10** = **exclude**, ban, black, blackball, forbid, keep out, prohibit **the Bar** = **barristers**, body of lawyers, counsel, court, judgment, tribunal

barb n **1** = **dig**, affront, cut, gibe, insult, sarcasm, scoff, sneer **2** = **point**, bristle, prickle, prong, quill, spike, spur, thorn

b

bard n lit same as POET.

bare ❶ adj 1 unclothed, naked.
2 without the natural or usual covering.
3 unembellished, simple. 4 just sufficient.
▷ v 5 uncover. **barely** adv only just.
bareness n.

bargain ❶ n 1 agreement establishing what
each party will give, receive, or perform
in a transaction. 2 something bought
or offered at a low price. ▷ v 3 negotiate
the terms of an agreement. **bargain for** v
anticipate or take into account.

barge ❶ n 1 flat-bottomed boat used to
transport freight. ▷ v 2 informal push
violently. **barge in, into** v interrupt rudely.

barista n person who makes and sells
coffee in a coffee bar.

baritone n (singer with) the second lowest
adult male voice.

barium n Chem soft white metallic element.

bark¹ ❶ n 1 loud harsh cry of a dog. ▷ v 2 (of
a dog) make its typical cry. 3 shout in an
angry tone.

bark² ❶ n tough outer layer of a tree.

barley n tall grasslike plant cultivated for
grain.

barmy ❶ adj **-mier, -miest** slang insane.

barn n large building on a farm used for
storing grain.

barnacle n shellfish that lives attached to
rocks, ship bottoms, etc.

barometer n instrument for measuring
atmospheric pressure. **barometric** adj.

baron n 1 member of the lowest rank
of nobility. 2 powerful businessman.
baroness n **baronial** adj.

baronet n commoner who holds the
lowest hereditary British title.

baroque [bar-**rock**] n 1 highly ornate style
of art, architecture, or music from the
late 16th to the early 18th century. ▷ adj
2 ornate in style.

barque [**bark**] n sailing ship, esp. one with
three masts.

barracks ❶ pl n building used to
accommodate military personnel.

barracouta n large Pacific fish with a
protruding lower jaw and strong teeth.

barrage ❶ [bar-**rahzh**] n 1 continuous
delivery of questions, complaints, etc.
2 continuous artillery fire. 3 artificial
barrier across a river to control the
water level.

barrel n 1 cylindrical container with
rounded sides and flat ends. 2 tube in a
firearm through which the bullet is fired.
barrel organ musical instrument played
by turning a handle.

barren ❶ adj 1 (of a woman or female
animal) incapable of producing offspring.
2 (of land) unable to support the growth of
crops, fruit, etc. **barrenness** n.

———————————————————— THESAURUS ————

bare adj 1 = **naked**, nude, stripped, unclad,
unclothed, uncovered, undressed, without
a stitch on (inf) 3 = **plain**, austere, basic,
sheer, simple, spare, spartan, stark,
unadorned, unembellished

bargain n 1 = **agreement**, arrangement,
contract, pact, pledge, promise 2 = **good
buy**, (cheap) purchase, discount,
giveaway, good deal, reduction, snip
(inf), steal (inf) ▷ v 3 = **negotiate**, agree,
contract, covenant, cut a deal, promise,
stipulate, transact

barge n 1 = **canal boat**, flatboat, lighter,
narrow boat

bark¹ n 1 = **yap**, bay, howl, woof, yelp ▷ v

2 = **yap**, bay, howl, woof, yelp

bark² n = **covering**, casing, cortex (Anat,
bot), crust, husk, rind, skin

barmy adj Sl = **insane**, crazy, daft (inf),
foolish, idiotic, nuts (sl), out of one's mind,
stupid

barracks pl n = **camp**, billet, encampment,
garrison, quarters

barrage n 1 = **torrent**, burst, deluge,
hail, mass, onslaught, plethora, stream
2 = **bombardment**, battery, cannonade,
fusillade, gunfire, salvo, shelling, volley

barren adj 1 = **infertile**, childless, sterile
2 = **unproductive**, arid, desert, desolate,
dry, empty, unfruitful, waste

barricade ❶ *n* **1** barrier, esp. one erected hastily for defence. ▷ *v* **2** erect a barricade across (an entrance).

barrier ❶ *n* anything that prevents access, progress, or union.

barrister *n* lawyer qualified to plead in a higher court.

barrow *n* **1** wheelbarrow. **2** movable stall used by street traders.

barter ❶ *v* **1** trade (goods) in exchange for other goods. ▷ *n* **2** trade by the exchange of goods.

base¹ ❶ *n* **1** bottom or supporting part of anything. **2** fundamental part. **3** centre of operations, organization, or supply. **4** starting point. ▷ *v* **5** (foll. by *on* or *upon*) use as a basis (for). **6** (foll. by *at* or *in*) station or place. **baseless** *adj* **basement** *n* partly or wholly underground storey of a building.

base² ❶ *adj* **1** dishonourable or immoral. **2** of inferior quality or value. **basely** *adv* **baseness** *n*.

baseball *n* **1** team game in which runs are scored by hitting a ball with a bat then running round four bases. **2** ball used for this.

bash ❶ *informal* ▷ *v* **1** hit violently or

forcefully. ▷ *n* **2** heavy blow.

bashful ❶ *adj* shy or modest.

basic ❶ *adj* **1** of or forming a base or basis. **2** elementary or simple. **basics** *pl n* fundamental principles, facts, etc. **basically** *adv*.

basil *n* aromatic herb used in cooking.

basin *n* **1** round open container. **2** sink for washing the hands and face. **3** sheltered area of water where boats may be moored. **4** catchment area of a particular river.

basis ❶ *n*, *pl* **-ses** fundamental principles etc. from which something is started or developed.

bask ❶ *v* lie in or be exposed to something, esp. pleasant warmth.

basket *n* container made of interwoven strips of wood or cane.

bass¹ ❶ [base] *n* **1** (singer with) the lowest adult male voice. ▷ *adj* **2** of the lowest range of musical notes.

bass² *n* edible sea fish.

bassoon *n* low-pitched woodwind instrument.

bastard ❶ *n* **1** *offens* obnoxious or despicable person. **2** person born of

barricade *n* **1** = **barrier**, blockade, bulwark, fence, obstruction, palisade, rampart, stockade ▷ *v* **2** = **bar**, block, blockade, defend, fortify, obstruct, protect, shut in

barrier *n* **a** = **barricade**, bar, blockade, boundary, fence, obstacle, obstruction, wall **b** = **hindrance**, difficulty, drawback, handicap, hurdle, obstacle, restriction, stumbling block

barter *v* **1** = **trade**, bargain, drive a hard bargain, exchange, haggle, sell, swap, traffic

base¹ *n* **1** = **bottom**, bed, foot, foundation, pedestal, rest, stand, support **2** = **basis**, core, essence, heart, key, origin, root, source **3** = **centre**, camp, headquarters, home, post, settlement, starting point, station ▷ *v* **5** (foll. by *on*) (*upon*) = **found**, build, construct, depend, derive, establish, ground, hinge **6** (foll. by *at* or *in*) = **place**, locate, post, station

base² *adj* **1** = **dishonourable**, contemptible, despicable, disreputable, evil, immoral, scungy (*Aust & NZ inf*), shameful, sordid, wicked

bash *inf v* **1** = **hit**, belt (*inf*), smash, sock (*sl*), strike, wallop (*inf*)

bashful *adj* = **shy**, blushing, coy, diffident, reserved, reticent, retiring, timid

basic *adj* **1** = **essential**, fundamental, key, necessary, primary, vital **2** = **elementary**, simple

basis *n* = **foundation**, base, bottom, footing, ground, groundwork, support

bask *v* = **lie in**, laze, loll, lounge, outspan (*S Afr*), relax, sunbathe

bass¹ *adj* **2** = **deep**, deep-toned, low, low-pitched, resonant, sonorous

bastard *n* **1** *Offens* = **rogue**, blackguard, miscreant, reprobate, scoundrel, villain,

parents not married to each other.
bastardize v debase or corrupt.

baste v moisten (meat) during cooking with hot fat.

bastion ❶ n 1 projecting part of a fortification. 2 thing or person regarded as defending a principle.

bat¹ ❶ n 1 any of various types of club used to hit the ball in certain sports. ▷ v **batting, batted** 2 strike with or as if with a bat. **batsman** n Cricket person who bats or specializes in batting.

bat² n nocturnal mouselike flying animal.

batch ❶ n group of people or things dealt with at the same time.

bated adj **with bated breath** in suspense or fear.

bath ❶ n 1 large container in which to wash the body. 2 act of washing in such a container. ▷ pl 3 public swimming pool. ▷ v 4 wash in a bath. **bathroom** n room with a bath, sink, and usu. a toilet.

bathe ❶ v 1 swim in open water for pleasure. 2 apply liquid to (the skin or a wound) in order to cleanse or soothe. 3 (foll. by in) fill (with), e.g. bathed in sunlight. **bather** n.

baton ❶ n 1 thin stick used by the conductor of an orchestra. 2 short bar

transferred in a relay race. 3 police officer's truncheon.

battalion n army unit consisting of three or more companies.

batten n strip of wood fixed to something, esp. to hold it in place. **batten down** v secure with battens.

batter¹ ❶ v 1 hit repeatedly. 2 damage or injure, as by blows, heavy wear, etc. e. g. battered by gales. **battering ram** large beam used to break down fortifications.

batter² n mixture of flour, eggs, and milk, used in cooking.

battery ❶ n, pl **-teries** 1 device that produces electricity in a torch, radio, etc. 2 group of heavy guns operating as a single unit. ▷ adj 3 kept in series of cages for intensive rearing.

battle ❶ n 1 fight between large armed forces. 2 conflict or struggle. ▷ v 3 struggle.

battlement n wall with gaps along the top for firing through.

battleship ❶ n large heavily armoured warship.

batty ❶ adj **-tier, -tiest** slang eccentric or crazy.

bauble ❶ n trinket of little value.

——————— THESAURUS ———————

wretch 2 = **illegitimate child**, love child, natural child

bastion n 1 = **stronghold**, bulwark, citadel, defence, fortress 2 = **tower of strength**, mainstay, prop, rock, support

bat¹ v 2 = **hit**, bang, smack, strike, swat, thump, wallop (inf), whack

batch n = **group**, amount, assemblage, bunch, collection, crowd, lot, pack, quantity, set

bath n 2 = **wash**, cleansing, douche, scrubbing, shower, soak, tub ▷ v 4 = **wash**, bathe, clean, douse, scrub down, shower, soak

bathe v 1 = **swim** 2 = **wash**, cleanse, rinse 3 (foll. by in) = **cover**, flood, immerse, steep, suffuse

baton n 1 = **stick**, wand 3 = **truncheon**,

club, rod

batter¹ v 1 = **beat**, buffet, clobber (sl), pelt, pound, pummel, thrash, wallop (inf).

battery n 2 = **artillery**, cannon, cannonry, gun emplacements, guns

battle n 1 = **fight**, action, attack, combat, encounter, engagement, hostilities, skirmish 2 = **conflict**, campaign, contest, crusade, dispute, struggle ▷ v 3 = **struggle**, argue, clamour, dispute, fight, lock horns, strive, war

battleship n = **warship**, gunboat, man-of-war

batty adj Sl = **crazy**, daft (inf), dotty (sl, chiefly Brit), eccentric, mad, munted (NZ sl), odd, peculiar, potty (Brit inf), touched

bauble n = **trinket**, bagatelle, gewgaw, gimcrack, knick-knack, plaything, toy, trifle

b

bawdy ① *adj* **bawdier, bawdiest** (of writing etc.) containing humorous references to sex. **bawdiness** *n*.

bawl ① *v* shout or weep noisily.

bay¹ ① *n* stretch of coastline that curves inwards.

bay² ① *n* **1** recess in a wall. **2** area set aside for a particular purpose, e.g. *loading bay*. **3** compartment in an aircraft, e.g. *bomb bay*. **bay window** window projecting from a wall.

bay³ ① *n* **1** deep howl of a hound or wolf. ▷ *v* **2** howl in deep prolonged tones. **at bay 1** forced to turn and face attackers. **2** at a safe distance.

bayonet *n* **1** sharp blade that can be fixed to the end of a rifle. ▷ *v* **-neting, -neted 2** stab with a bayonet.

bazaar ① *n* **1** sale in aid of charity. **2** market area, esp. in Eastern countries.

bazooka *n* portable rocket launcher that fires an armour-piercing projectile.

BBC British Broadcasting Corporation.

BC 1 before Christ. **2** British Columbia.

be ① *v, present sing 1st person* **am**. *2nd person* **are**. *3rd person* **is**. *present pl* **are**. *past sing 1st person* **was**. *2nd person* **were**. *3rd person* **was**. *past pl* **were**. *present participle* **being**. *past participle* **been 1** exist or live. **2** used as a linking between the subject of a sentence and its complement, e.g. *John is a musician*. **3** forms the progressive present tense,

e.g. *the man is running*. **4** forms the passive voice of all transitive verbs, e.g. *a good film is being shown on television tonight*.

beach ① *n* **1** area of sand or pebbles on a shore. ▷ *v* **2** run or haul (a boat) onto a beach.

beacon ① *n* fire or light on a hill or tower, used as a warning.

bead ① *n* **1** small piece of plastic, wood, etc., pierced for threading on a string to form a necklace etc. **2** small drop of moisture. **beaded** *adj* **beading** *n* strip of moulding used for edging furniture. **beady** *adj* small, round, and glittering, e.g. *beady eyes*.

beagle *n* small hound with short legs and drooping ears.

beak ① *n* **1** projecting horny jaws of a bird. **2** *slang* nose. **beaky** *adj* **beakier, beakiest**.

beaker *n* **1** large drinking cup. **2** lipped glass container used in laboratories.

beam ① *n* **1** broad smile. **2** ray of light. **3** narrow flow of electromagnetic radiation or particles. **4** long thick piece of wood, metal, etc., used in building. ▷ *v* **5** smile broadly. **6** divert or aim (a radio signal, light, etc.) in a certain direction.

bean *n* seed or pod of various plants, eaten as a vegetable or used to make coffee etc.

beanie *n Brit, Aust & NZ* close-fitting woolen hat.

bear¹ ① *v* **bearing, bore, borne 1** support or hold up. **2** bring, e.g. *to bear gifts*. **3** *passive*

bawdy *adj* = **rude**, coarse, dirty, indecent, lascivious, lecherous, lewd, ribald, salacious, scungy (*Aust & NZ inf*), smutty

bawl *v* **a** = **shout**, bellow, call, clamour, howl, roar, yell **b** = **cry**, blubber, sob, wail, weep

bay¹ *n* = **inlet**, bight, cove, gulf, natural harbour, sound

bay² *n* **1** = **recess**, alcove, compartment, niche, nook, opening

bay³ *n* **1** = **howl**, bark, clamour, cry, yelp ▷ *v* **2** = **howl**, bark, clamour, cry, yelp

bazaar *n* **1** = **fair**, bring-and-buy, fete, sale of work **2** = **market**, exchange, marketplace

be *v* **1** = **exist**, be alive, breathe, inhabit, live

beach *n* **1** = **shore**, coast, sands, seashore, seaside, water's edge

beacon *n* = **signal**, beam, bonfire, flare, sign

bead *n* **2** = **drop**, bubble, droplet, globule

beak *n* **1** = **bill**, mandible, neb (*arch or dial*), nib **2** *Sl* = **nose**, proboscis, snout

beam *n* **1** = **smile**, grin **2** = **ray**, gleam, glimmer, glint, glow, shaft, streak, stream **4** = **rafter**, girder, joist, plank, spar, support, timber ▷ *v* **5** = **smile**, grin **6** = **send out**, broadcast, emit, transmit

bear¹ *v* **1** = **support**, have, hold, maintain, possess, shoulder, sustain, uphold

b

born give birth to. **4** produce as by natural growth. **5** tolerate or endure. **6** hold in the mind. **7** show or be marked with. **8** move in a specified direction. **bearable** adj **bear out** v show to be truthful.

bear² n large heavy mammal with a shaggy coat. **bearskin** n tall fur helmet worn by some British soldiers.

beard n hair growing on the lower parts of a man's face.

bearing ❶ n **1** relevance (to). **2** person's general social conduct. **3** part of a machine that supports another part, esp. one that reduces friction. ▷ pl **4** sense of one's own relative position.

beast ❶ n **1** large wild animal. **2** brutal or uncivilized person. **beastly** adj unpleasant or disagreeable.

beat ❶ v **beating, beat, beaten** or **beat** **1** hit hard and repeatedly. **2** move (wings) up and down. **3** throb rhythmically. **4** stir or mix vigorously. **5** overcome or defeat. ▷ n **6** regular throb. **7** assigned route, as of a policeman. **8** basic rhythmic unit in a piece of music. **beat up** v injure (someone)

by repeated blows or kicks.

beau ❶ [boh] n, pl **beaux, beaus** **1** boyfriend or admirer. **2** man greatly concerned with his appearance.

beauty ❶ n, pl **-ties 1** combination of all the qualities of a person or thing that delight the senses and mind. **2** very attractive woman. **3** informal something outstanding of its kind. **beautiful** adj very attractive to look at.

beaver n amphibious rodent with a big flat tail. **beaver away** v work industriously.

becalmed ❶ adj (of a sailing ship) motionless through lack of wind.

because ❶ conj on account of the fact that. **because of** on account of.

beck n **at someone's beck and call** having to be constantly available to do as someone asks.

beckon ❶ v summon with a gesture.

become ❶ v **-coming, -came, -come** **1** come to be. **2** (foll. by of) happen to. **3** suit. **becoming** adj **1** attractive or pleasing. **2** appropriate or proper.

────────────────────────────── THESAURUS ──────────

2 = carry, bring, convey, hump (Brit sl), move, take, transport **3, 4 = produce**, beget, breed, bring forth, engender, generate, give birth to, yield **5 = tolerate**, abide, allow, brook, endure, permit, put up with (inf), stomach, suffer

bearing n **1 = relevance**, application, connection, import, pertinence, reference, relation, significance **2 = manner**, air, aspect, attitude, behaviour, demeanour, deportment, posture ▷ pl **4 = position**, aim, course, direction, location, orientation, situation, track, way, whereabouts

beast n **1 = animal**, brute, creature **2 = brute**, barbarian, fiend, monster, ogre, sadist, savage, swine

beat v **1 = hit**, bang, batter, buffet, knock, pound, strike, thrash **2 = flap**, flutter **3 = throb**, palpitate, pound, pulsate, quake, thump, vibrate **5 = defeat**, conquer, outdo, overcome, overwhelm, surpass,

vanquish ▷ n **6 = throb**, palpitation, pulsation, pulse **7 = route**, circuit, course, path, rounds, way **8 = rhythm**, accent, cadence, metre, stress, time

beau n **1 = boyfriend**, admirer, fiancé, lover, suitor, sweetheart **2 = dandy**, coxcomb, fop, gallant, ladies' man

beauty n **1 = attractiveness**, charm, comeliness, elegance, exquisiteness, glamour, grace, handsomeness, loveliness **2 = belle**, good-looker, lovely (sl), stunner (inf)

becalmed adj **= still**, motionless, settled, stranded, stuck

because conj **= since**, as, by reason of, in that, on account of, owing to, thanks to

beckon v **= gesture**, bid, gesticulate, motion, nod, signal, summon, wave at

become v **1 = come to be**, alter to, be transformed into, change into, develop into, grow into, mature into, ripen into **3 = suit**, embellish, enhance, fit, flatter, set off

bed ❶ *n* **1** piece of furniture on which to sleep. **2** garden plot. **3** bottom of a river, lake, or sea. **4** layer of rock. **bed down** *v* go to or put into a place to sleep or rest. **bedpan** *n* shallow bowl used as a toilet by bedridden people. **bedridden** *adj* confined to bed because of illness or old age. **bedrock** *n* **1** solid rock beneath the surface soil. **2** basic facts or principles. **bedroom** *n* **bedsit**, **bedsitter** *n* furnished sitting room with a bed.

bedevil ❶ *v* **-illing**, **-illed** harass, confuse, or torment.

bedlam ❶ *n* noisy confused situation.

bedraggled ❶ *adj* untidy, wet, or dirty.

bee *n* insect that makes wax and honey. **beehive** *n* structure in which bees live. **beeswax** *n* wax secreted by bees, used in polishes etc.

beech *n* European tree with a smooth greyish bark.

beef *n* flesh of a cow, bull, or ox. **beefy** *adj* **1** like beef. **2** *informal* strong and muscular. **beefburger** *n* flat grilled or fried cake of minced beef.

beer *n* alcoholic drink brewed from malt and hops.

beer parlour ❶ *n Canad* tavern.

beet *n* plant with an edible root and leaves. **beetroot** *n* type of beet plant with a dark red root.

beetle *n* insect with a hard wing cover on its back.

befall ❶ *v old-fashioned* happen to (someone).

befit *v* be appropriate or suitable for. **befitting** *adj*.

before ❶ *conj, prep, adv* indicating something earlier in time, in front of, or preferred to, e.g. *before the war*; *brought before a judge*; *death before dishonour*. **beforehand** *adv* in advance.

befriend ❶ *v* become friends with.

beg ❶ *v* **begging**, **begged** **1** solicit (for money or food), esp. in the street. **2** ask formally or humbly.

begin ❶ *v* **-ginning**, **-gan**, **-gun** **1** start. **2** bring or come into being. **beginner** *n* person who has just started learning to do something. **beginning** *n*.

begonia *n* tropical plant with waxy flowers.

begrudge ❶ *v* **1** envy (someone) the possession of something. **2** give or allow unwillingly.

———— THESAURUS ————

bed *n* **1** = **bedstead**, berth, bunk, cot, couch, divan **2** = **plot**, area, border, garden, patch, row, strip **3** = **bottom**, base

bedevil *v* = **torment**, afflict, confound, confuse, distress, harass, plague, trouble, vex, worry

bedlam *n* = **pandemonium**, chaos, commotion, confusion, furore, tumult, turmoil, uproar

bedraggled *adj* = **messy**, dirty, dishevelled, disordered, muddied, unkempt, untidy

beer parlour *n* (*Canad*) = **tavern**, inn, bar, pub (*informal, chiefly Brit*), public house, beverage room (*Canad*), hostelry, alehouse (*archaic*)

befall *v Old-fashioned* = **happen**, chance, come to pass, fall, occur, take place, transpire (*inf*)

before *prep* **a** = **earlier than**, in advance of, prior to **b** = **ahead of**, in advance of, in front of **c** = **previously**, ahead, earlier, formerly, in advance, sooner **d** = **in front**, ahead

befriend *v* = **help**, aid, assist, back, encourage, side with, stand by, support, welcome

beg *v* **1** = **scrounge**, bludge (*Aust & NZ*), cadge, seek charity, solicit charity, sponge on, touch (someone) for (*sl*) **2** = **implore**, beseech, entreat, petition, plead, request, solicit

begin *v* **1** = **start**, commence, embark on, initiate, instigate, institute, prepare, set about **2** = **happen**, appear, arise, come into being, emerge, originate, start

begrudge *v* **1** = **resent**, be jealous, envy, grudge

b

beguile ❶ [big-**gile**] v **1** cheat or mislead. **2** charm or amuse. **beguiling** adj.

behalf n **on behalf of** in the interest of or for the benefit of.

behave ❶ v **1** act or function in a particular way. **2** conduct (oneself) properly. **behaviour** n manner of behaving.

behead v remove the head from.

behest n order or earnest request.

behind ❶ prep, adv **1** indicating position to the rear, lateness, responsibility, etc. e.g. *behind the wall; behind schedule; the reasons behind her departure.* ▷ n **2** informal buttocks.

behold v -**holding**, -**held** old-fashioned look (at). **beholder** n.

beholden ❶ adj indebted or obliged.

beige adj pale brown.

being ❶ n **1** state or fact of existing. **2** something that exists or is thought to exist. **3** human being. ▷ v **4** present participle of BE.

belated ❶ adj late or too late. **belatedly** adv.

belch ❶ v **1** expel wind from the stomach noisily through the mouth. **2** expel or be

expelled forcefully, e.g. *smoke belched from the factory.* ▷ n **3** act of belching.

beleaguered ❶ adj **1** struggling against difficulties or criticism. **2** besieged by an enemy.

belfry n, pl -**fries** part of a tower where bells are hung.

belie v show to be untrue.

belief n **1** faith or confidence. **2** opinion. **3** principle accepted as true, often without proof. **believe** v **1** accept as true or real. **2** think, assume, or suppose. **3** accept (someone's) statement or opinion as true, e.g. *I don't believe you!* **believe in** be convinced of the truth or existence of. **believable** adj.

belittle ❶ v treat as having little value or importance.

bell n **1** hollow, usu. metal, cup-shaped instrument that emits a ringing sound when struck. **2** device that rings or buzzes as a signal.

belle n beautiful woman, esp. the most attractive woman at a function.

bellicose adj warlike and aggressive.

———————————————————————— THESAURUS ————

beguile v **1** = **fool**, cheat, deceive, delude, dupe, hoodwink, mislead, take for a ride (inf), trick **2** = **charm**, amuse, distract, divert, engross, entertain, occupy

behave v **1** = **act**, function, operate, perform, run, work **2** = **conduct oneself properly**, act correctly, keep one's nose clean, mind one's manners (inf)

behind prep **a** = **after**, at the back of, at the heels of, at the rear of, following, later than **b** = **causing**, at the bottom of, initiating, instigating, responsible for **c** = **after**, afterwards, following, in the wake (of), next, subsequently **d** = **overdue**, behindhand, in arrears, in debt

behold v Old-fashioned = **look at**, observe, perceive, regard, survey, view, watch, witness

beholden adj = **indebted**, bound, grateful, obliged, owing, under obligation

being n **1** = **existence**, life, reality

2 = **nature**, entity, essence, soul, spirit, substance **3** = **human being**, creature, individual

belated adj = **late**, behindhand, behind time, delayed, late in the day, overdue, tardy

belch v **1** = **burp** (inf), hiccup **2** = **emit**, discharge, disgorge, erupt, give off, spew forth, vent

beleaguered adj **1** = **harassed**, badgered, hassled (inf), persecuted, pestered, plagued, put upon, vexed **2** = **besieged**, assailed, beset, blockaded, hemmed in, surrounded

belief n **1** = **faith**, assurance, confidence, conviction, trust **2** = **opinion**, feeling, impression, judgment, notion **3** = **faith**, credo, creed, doctrine, dogma, ideology, principles, tenet

belittle v = **disparage**, decry, denigrate, deprecate, deride, scoff at, scorn, sneer at

belligerent ❶ *adj* 1 hostile and aggressive. 2 engaged in war. ▷ *n* 3 person or country engaged in war. **belligerence** *n*.

bellow ❶ *v* 1 make a low deep cry like that of a bull. 2 shout in anger. ▷ *n* 3 loud deep roar.

bellows *pl n* instrument for pumping a stream of air into something.

belly ❶ *n, pl* -**lies** 1 part of the body of a vertebrate which contains the intestines. 2 stomach. 3 front, lower, or inner part of something. ▷ *v* -**lying**, -**lied** 4 (cause to) swell out.

belong ❶ *v* 1 (foll. by *to*) be the property of. 2 (foll. by *to*) be a part or member of. **belongings** *pl n* personal possessions.

beloved ❶ *adj* 1 dearly loved. ▷ *n* 2 person dearly loved.

below ❶ *prep, adv* at or to a position lower than, under.

belt ❶ *n* 1 band of cloth, leather, etc., worn usu. around the waist. 2 long narrow area, e.g. *a belt of trees*. 3 circular strip of rubber that drives moving parts in a machine. ▷ *v* 4 fasten with a belt. 5 *slang* hit very hard. 6 *slang* move very fast.

bemoan ❶ *v* express sorrow or dissatisfaction about.

bench ❶ *n* 1 long seat. 2 long narrow work table. **the bench** *n* judge or magistrate sitting in court, or judges and magistrates collectively. **benchmark** *n* criterion by which to measure something.

bend ❶ *v* **bending**, **bent** 1 (cause to) form a curve. 2 (often foll. by *down*) etc. incline the body. ▷ *n* 3 curved part. ▷ *pl* 4 *informal* decompression sickness. **bendy** *adj*.

beneath ❶ *adv, prep* 1 below. 2 not worthy of.

benefit ❶ *n* 1 something that improves or promotes. 2 advantage or sake, e.g. *I'm doing this for your benefit*. 3 payment made by a government to a poor, ill, or unemployed person. ▷ *v* -**fiting**, -**fited** 4 do or receive good. **beneficial** *adj*.

THESAURUS

---

belligerent *adj* 1 = **aggressive**, bellicose, combative, hostile, pugnacious, unfriendly, warlike, warring *n* 3 = **fighter**, combatant, warring nation

bellow *v* 2 = **shout**, bawl, cry, howl, roar, scream, shriek, yell ▷ *n* 3 = **shout**, bawl, cry, howl, roar, scream, shriek, yell

belly *n* 1, 2 = **stomach**, abdomen, corporation (*inf*), gut, insides (*inf*), paunch, potbelly, tummy ▷ *v* 4 = **swell out**, billow, bulge, fill, spread, swell

belong *v* 1 (foll. by *to*) = **be the property of**, be at the disposal of, be held by, be owned by 2 (foll. by *to*) = **be a member of**, be affiliated to, be allied to, be associated with, be included in

beloved *adj* 1 = **dear**, admired, adored, darling, loved, pet, precious, prized, treasured, valued, worshipped

below *prep* = **lower than**, inferior, lesser, less than, subject, subordinate ▷ *adv* = **lower**, beneath, down, under, underneath

belt *n* 1 = **waistband**, band, cummerbund, girdle, girth, sash 2 = **zone**, area, district, layer, region, stretch, strip, tract

bemoan *v* = **lament**, bewail, deplore, grieve for, mourn, regret, rue, weep for

bench *n* 1 = **seat**, form, pew, settle, stall 2 = **worktable**, board, counter, table, trestle table, workbench **the bench** = **court**, courtroom, judges, judiciary, magistrates, tribunal

bend *v* 1 = **curve**, arc, arch, bow, turn, twist, veer 2 = **lean**, bow ▷ *n* 3 = **curve**, angle, arc, arch, bow, corner, loop, turn, twist

beneath *adv* 1 = **underneath**, below, in a lower place ▷ *prep* 1 = **under**, below, lower than, underneath 2 = **unworthy of**, below, inferior to, less than, unbefitting

benefit *n* 1 = **help**, advantage, aid, asset, assistance, favour, good, profit ▷ *v* 4 = **help**, aid, assist, avail, enhance, further, improve, profit

b

benign ❶ [bin-**nine**] *adj* 1 showing kindliness. 2 (of a tumour) not threatening to life.

bent ❶ *v* 1 past of BEND. ▷ *adj* 2 curved. 3 *slang* dishonest or corrupt. ▷ *n* 4 personal inclination or aptitude. **bent on** determined to pursue (a course of action).

bento, bento box *n* thin lightweight box divided into compartments, which contain small separate dishes comprising a Japanese meal.

benzene *n* flammable poisonous liquid used as a solvent, insecticide, etc.

bequeath ❶ *v* dispose of (property) as in a will. **bequest** *n* legal gift of money or property by someone who has died.

berate ❶ *v* scold harshly.

beret [**ber**-ray] *n* round flat close-fitting brimless cap.

berg *n* S *Afr* mountain.

berm *n* NZ narrow grass strip between the road and the footpath in a residential area.

berry *n*, *pl* -**ries** small soft stoneless fruit.

berserk ❶ *adj* **go berserk** become violent or destructive.

berth ❶ *n* 1 bunk in a ship or train. 2 place assigned to a ship at a mooring. ▷ *v* 3 dock (a ship).

beryl *n* hard transparent mineral.

beseech ❶ *v*-**seeching, -sought** or -**seeched** ask earnestly; beg.

beset ❶ *v* trouble or harass constantly.

beside ❶ *prep* 1 at, by, or to the side of. 2 as compared with. **beside oneself** overwhelmed or overwrought. **besides** *adv*, *prep* in addition.

besiege ❶ *v* 1 surround with military forces. 2 overwhelm, as with requests.

besotted ❶ *adj* infatuated.

bespoke *adj* (esp. of a suit) made to the customer's specifications.

best ❶ *adj* 1 most excellent of a particular group etc. ▷ *adv* 2 in a manner surpassing all others. ▷ *n* 3 most outstanding or excellent person, thing, or group in a category. **best man** groom's attendant at a wedding. **bestseller** *n* book or other product that has sold in great numbers.

bestial ❶ *adj* 1 brutal or savage. 2 of or like a beast. **bestiality** *n*.

bestir *v* cause (oneself) to become active.

——————————————————————————— THESAURUS ——————

benign *adj* 1 = **kindly**, amiable, friendly, genial, kind, obliging, sympathetic 2 = **harmless**, curable, remediable

bent *adj* 2 = **curved**, angled, arched, bowed, crooked, hunched, stooped, twisted *n* 4 = **inclination**, ability, aptitude, leaning, penchant, preference, propensity, tendency

bequeath *v* = **leave**, endow, entrust, give, grant, will

berate *v* = **scold**, castigate, censure, chide, criticize, harangue, rebuke, reprimand, reprove, rouse on (*Aust*), tell off (*inf*), upbraid

berserk *adj* **go berserk** = **go crazy**, go mad, go wild, raging, rampage, run amok

berth *n* 1 = **bunk**, bed, billet, hammock 2 = **anchorage**, dock, harbour, haven, pier, port, quay, wharf ▷ *v* 3 = **anchor**, dock, drop anchor, land, moor, tie up

beseech *v* = **beg**, ask, call upon, entreat, implore, plead, pray, solicit

beset *v* = **plague**, bedevil, harass, pester, trouble

beside *prep* 1 = **next to**, abreast of, adjacent to, alongside, at the side of, close to, near, nearby, neighbouring

besiege *v* 1 = **surround**, blockade, encircle, hem in, lay siege to, shut in 2 = **harass**, badger, harry, hassle (*inf*), hound, nag, pester, plague

besotted *adj* = **infatuated**, doting, hypnotized, smitten, spellbound

best *adj* 1 = **finest**, foremost, leading, most excellent, outstanding, pre-eminent, principal, supreme, unsurpassed ▷ *adv* 2 = **most highly**, extremely, greatly, most deeply, most fully ▷ *n* 3 = **finest**, cream, elite, flower, pick, prime, top

bestial *adj* 1 = **brutal**, barbaric, beastly, brutish, inhuman, savage

b

bestow ● v present (a gift) or confer (an honour).

bet ● n 1 the act of staking a sum of money or other stake on the outcome of an event. **2** stake risked. ▷ v **betting**, **bet** or **betted 3** make or place (a bet). **4** informal predict.

betray ● v 1 hand over or expose (one's nation, friend, etc.) treacherously to an enemy. **2** disclose (a secret or confidence) treacherously. **3** reveal unintentionally. **betrayal** n **betrayer** n.

better ● adj 1 more excellent than others. **2** improved or fully recovered in health. ▷ adv **3** in a more excellent manner. **4** in or to a greater degree. ▷ pl n **5** one's superiors. ▷ v **6** improve upon.

between ● prep, adv indicating position in the middle, alternatives, etc.

bevel n 1 slanting edge. ▷ v **-elling**, **-elled 2** cut a bevel on (a piece of timber etc.).

beverage ● n drink.

beverage room ● n Canad tavern.

bevy ● n, pl **bevies** flock or group.

bewail ● v express great sorrow over.

beware ● v be on one's guard (against).

bewilder ● v confuse utterly. **bewildering** adj **bewilderment** n.

bewitch ● v 1 attract and fascinate. **2** cast a spell over. **bewitching** adj.

beyond ● prep 1 at or to a point on the other side of. **2** outside the limits or scope of. ▷ adv **3** at or to the far side of something.

bias ● n 1 mental tendency, esp. prejudice. **2** diagonal cut across the weave of a fabric. **3** Bowls bulge or weight on one side of a bowl that causes it to roll in a curve. ▷ v **-asing**, **-ased** or **-assing**, **-assed 4** cause to have a bias. **biased**, **biassed** adj.

———— THESAURUS ————

bestow v = **present**, award, commit, give, grant, hand out, impart, lavish

bet n 1 = **gamble**, long shot, risk, speculation, venture, wager **2** = **stake** ▷ v **3** = **gamble**, chance, hazard, risk, speculate, stake, venture, wager

betray v 1 = **be disloyal**, be treacherous, be unfaithful, break one's promise, double-cross (inf), inform on or against, sell out (inf), stab in the back **2, 3** = **give away**, disclose, divulge, let slip, reveal

better adj 1 = **superior**, excelling, finer, greater, higher-quality, more desirable, preferable, surpassing **2** = **well**, cured, fully recovered, on the mend (inf), recovering, stronger ▷ adv **3** = **in a more excellent manner**, in a superior way, more advantageously, more attractively, more competently, more effectively **4** = **to a greater degree**, more completely, more thoroughly ▷ v **6** = **improve**, enhance, further, raise

between prep = **amidst**, among, betwixt, in the middle of, mid

beverage n = **drink**, liquid, liquor, refreshment

beverage room n (Canad) = **tavern**, inn, bar, pub (informal, chiefly Brit), public house, beer parlour (Canad), hostelry, alehouse (archaic)

bevy n = **group**, band, bunch (inf), collection, company, crowd, gathering, pack, troupe

bewail v = **lament**, bemoan, cry over, deplore, grieve for, moan, mourn, regret

beware v = **be careful**, be cautious, be wary, guard against, heed, look out, mind, take heed, watch out

bewilder v = **confound**, baffle, bemuse, confuse, flummox, mystify, nonplus, perplex, puzzle

bewitch v = **enchant**, beguile, captivate, charm, enrapture, entrance, fascinate, hypnotize

beyond prep 1 = **past**, above, apart from, at a distance, away from, over **2** = **exceeding**, out of reach of, superior to, surpassing

bias n 1 = **prejudice**, favouritism, inclination, leaning, partiality, tendency ▷ v **4** = **prejudice**, distort, influence, mana (NZ), predispose, slant, sway, twist, warp, weight

bib n 1 piece of cloth or plastic worn to protect a young child's clothes when eating. 2 upper front part of dungarees etc.

Bible n 1 sacred writings of the Christian religion. 2 (b-) book regarded as authoritative. **biblical** adj.

bibliography n, pl **-phies** 1 list of books on a subject. 2 list of sources used in a book etc.

bicentenary n, pl **-naries** 200th anniversary.

biceps n muscle with two origins, esp. the muscle that flexes the forearm.

bicker ❶ v argue over petty matters.

bicycle n vehicle with two wheels, one behind the other, pedalled by the rider.

bid ❶ v **bidding, bade, bidden** 1 say (a greeting). 2 command. 3 past **bid** offer (an amount) in an attempt to buy something. ▷ n 4 offer of a specified amount. 5 attempt. **bidder** n **biddable** adj obedient. **bidding** n command.

bide v **bide one's time** wait patiently for an opportunity.

bier n stand on which a corpse or coffin rests before burial.

big ❶ adj **bigger, biggest** 1 of considerable size, height, number, or capacity. 2 important through having power, wealth, etc. 3 elder. 4 generous. ▷ adv

5 on a grand scale. **bighead** n informal conceited person. **big-headed** adj **big shot, bigwig** n informal important person.

bigamy n crime of marrying a person while still legally married to someone else. **bigamist** n **bigamous** adj.

bigot ❶ n person who is intolerant, esp. regarding religion or race. **bigoted** adj **bigotry** n.

bike n informal bicycle or motorcycle.

bikini n woman's brief two-piece swimming costume.

bilberry n bluish-black edible berry.

bile n bitter yellow fluid secreted by the liver.

bilge n 1 informal nonsense. 2 ship's bottom.

bilingual adj involving or using two languages.

bill¹ ❶ n 1 statement of money owed for goods or services supplied. 2 draft of a proposed new law. 3 poster. 4 US & Canad banknote. 5 list of events, such as a theatre programme. ▷ v 6 send or present a bill to. 7 advertise by posters.

bill² ❶ n bird's beak.

billet ❶ v **-leting, -leted** 1 assign a lodging to (a soldier). ▷ n 2 accommodation for a soldier in civil lodgings.

billiards n game played on a table with balls and a cue.

━━━━━━━━━━━━━━━━━━━━━━━━━━━ THESAURUS ━━━━━━

bicker v = **quarrel**, argue, disagree, dispute, fight, row (inf), squabble, wrangle

bid v 1 = **say**, call, greet, tell, wish 2 = **tell**, ask, command, direct, instruct, order, require 3 = **offer**, proffer, propose, submit, tender ▷ n 4 = **offer**, advance, amount, price, proposal, sum, tender 5 = **attempt**, crack (inf), effort, go (inf), stab (inf), try

big adj 1 = **large**, enormous, extensive, great, huge, immense, massive, substantial, vast 2 = **important**, eminent, influential, leading, main, powerful, prominent, significant, skookum (Canad) 3 = **grown-up**, adult, elder, grown, mature 4 = **generous**, altruistic, benevolent, gracious, magnanimous, noble, unselfish

bigot n = **fanatic**, racist, sectarian, zealot

bill¹ n 1 = **charges**, account, invoice, reckoning, score, statement, tally 2 = **proposal**, measure, piece of legislation, projected law 3 = **advertisement**, bulletin, circular, handbill, hand-out, leaflet, notice, placard, poster 5 = **list**, agenda, card, catalogue, inventory, listing, programme, roster, schedule ▷ v 6 = **charge**, debit, invoice 7 = **advertise**, announce, give advance notice of, post

bill² n = **beak**, mandible, neb (arch or dial), nib

billet v 1 = **quarter**, accommodate, berth, station ▷ n 2 = **quarters**, accommodation, barracks, lodging

b

billion *n* **1** one thousand million. **2** formerly, one million million. **billionth** *adj*.

billow ❶ *n* **1** large sea wave. ▷ *v* **2** rise up or swell out.

biltong *n S Afr* strips of dried meat.

bin *n* container for rubbish or for storing grain, coal, etc.

binary *adj* **1** composed of two parts. **2** *Maths, computers* of or in a counting system with only two digits, 0 and 1.

bind ❶ *v* **binding, bound 1** make secure with or as if with a rope. **2** place (someone) under obligation. **3** enclose and fasten (the pages of a book) between covers. ▷ *n* **4** *informal* annoying situation. **binder** *n* firm cover for holding loose sheets of paper together. **binding** *n* **1** anything that binds or fastens. **2** book cover.

binge ❶ *n informal* bout of excessive indulgence, esp. in drink.

bingo *n* gambling game in which numbers are called out and covered by the players on their individual cards.

binoculars *pl n* optical instrument consisting of two small telescopes joined together.

bio- *combining form* life or living organisms, e.g. *biology*.

biodegradable *adj* capable of being decomposed by natural means.

biography ❶ *n, pl* **-phies** account of a person's life by another person. **biographical** *adj* **biographer** *n*.

biology *n* study of living organisms. **biologist** *n*.

bionic *adj* having a part of the body that is operated electronically.

biopsy *n, pl* **-sies** examination of tissue from a living body.

bioterrorism *n* use of viruses, bacteria, etc., by terrorists. **bioterrorist** *n*.

biped [**bye**-ped] *n* animal with two feet.

birch *n* **1** tree with thin peeling bark. **2** birch rod or twigs used, esp. formerly, for flogging offenders.

bird *n* **1** creature with feathers and wings, most types of which can fly. **2** *slang* young woman.

birdie *n Golf* score of one stroke under par for a hole.

Biro *n* ® ballpoint pen.

birth ❶ *n* **1** process of bearing young; childbirth. **2** act of being born. **3** ancestry. **give birth to** bear (offspring). **birth control** any method of contraception. **birthday** *n* anniversary of the day of one's birth. **birthmark** *n* blemish on the skin formed before birth. **birthright** *n* privileges or possessions that someone is entitled to as soon as he or she is born.

biscuit *n* small flat dry sweet or plain cake.

bisect ❶ *v* divide into two equal parts.

bisexual *adj* sexually attracted to both men and women.

bishop *n* **1** clergyman who governs a diocese. **2** chessman which is moved diagonally. **bishopric** *n* diocese or office of a bishop.

bison *n, pl* **-son** large hairy animal of the cattle family.

bistro *n, pl* **-tros** small restaurant.

— THESAURUS —

billow *n* **1** = **wave**, breaker, crest, roller, surge, swell, tide ▷ *v* **2** = **surge**, balloon, belly, puff up, rise up, roll, swell

bind *v* **1** = **tie**, fasten, hitch, lash, secure, stick, strap, wrap **2** = **oblige**, compel, constrain, engage, force, necessitate, require ▷ *n* **4** *Inf* = **nuisance**, bore, difficulty, dilemma, drag (*inf*), pain in the neck (*inf*), quandary, spot (*inf*)

binge *n Inf* = **bout**, bender (*inf*), feast, fling,

orgy, spree

biography *n* = **life story**, account, curriculum vitae, CV, life, memoir, profile, record

birth *n* **1** = **childbirth**, delivery, parturition **2** = **nativity 3** = **ancestry**, background, blood, breeding, lineage, parentage, pedigree, stock

bisect *v* = **cut in two**, cross, cut across, divide in two, halve, intersect, separate, split

b

bit¹ ❶ n 1 small piece, portion, or quantity.
2 short time or distance. **a bit** rather,
somewhat. **bit by bit** gradually.

bit² ❶ n 1 metal mouthpiece on a bridle.
2 cutting or drilling part of a tool.

bit³ v past tense of BITE.

bit⁴ n Maths, computers 1 single digit of
binary notation, either 0 or 1. 2 smallest
unit of information.

bitch n 1 female dog, fox, or wolf. 2 offens
spiteful woman. ▷ v 3 informal complain or
grumble. **bitchy** adj **bitchiness** n.

bite ❶ v biting, bit, bitten 1 grip, tear, or
puncture the skin, as with the teeth or
jaws. 2 take firm hold of or act effectively
upon. ▷ n 3 act of biting. 4 wound or sting
inflicted by biting. 5 snack. **biting** adj
1 piercing or keen. 2 sarcastic.

bitter ❶ adj 1 having a sharp unpleasant
taste. 2 showing or caused by hostility
or resentment. 3 extremely cold. ▷ n
4 beer with a slightly bitter taste. ▷ pl
5 bitter-tasting alcoholic drink. **bitterly**
adv **bitterness** n.

bittern n wading marsh bird with a
booming call.

bitumen n black sticky substance obtained
from tar or petrol.

bivouac n 1 temporary camp in the open
air. ▷ v -**acking**, -**acked** 2 camp in a
bivouac.

bizarre ❶ adj odd or unusual.

blab ❶ v blabbing, blabbed reveal (secrets)
indiscreetly.

black ❶ adj 1 of the darkest colour, like
coal. 2 (B-) dark-skinned. 3 without
hope. 4 angry or resentful, e.g. black
looks. 5 unpleasant in a macabre manner,
e.g. black comedy. ▷ n 6 darkest colour.
7 (B-) member of a dark-skinned race.
8 complete darkness. ▷ v 9 make black.
10 (of trade unionists) boycott (goods or
people). **blackness** n **blacken** v 1 make or
become black. 2 defame or slander. **black
magic** magic used for evil purposes. **black
market** illegal trade in goods or currencies.
black sheep person who is regarded as a
disgrace by his or her family. **black spot**
place on a road where accidents frequently
occur.

blackguard ❶ [blag-gard] n unprincipled
person.

blackmail ❶ n 1 act of attempting
to extort money by threats.
▷ v 2 (attempt to) obtain money by
blackmail.

━━━━━━━━━━━━━━━━━━━━ THESAURUS ━━━━━━━━

bit¹ n 1 = **piece**, crumb, fragment, grain,
morsel, part, scrap, speck

bit² n 1 = **curb**, brake, check, restraint,
snaffle

bite v 1 = **cut**, chew, gnaw, nip, pierce,
pinch, snap, tear, wound ▷ n 4 = **wound**,
nip, pinch, prick, smarting, sting, tooth
marks 5 = **snack**, food, light meal, morsel,
mouthful, piece, refreshment, taste,
tucker (Aust & NZ inf)

bitter adj 1 = **sour**, acid, acrid, astringent,
harsh, sharp, tart, unsweetened, vinegary
2 = **resentful**, acrimonious, begrudging,
hostile, fierce, sore, sour, sullen 3 = **freezing**,
biting, fierce, intense, severe, stinging

bizarre adj = **strange**, eccentric,
extraordinary, fantastic, freakish,
ludicrous, munted (NZ sl), outlandish,

peculiar, unusual, weird, zany

blab v = **tell**, blurt out, disclose, divulge, give
away, let slip, let the cat out of the bag,
reveal, spill the beans (inf)

black adj 1 = **dark**, dusky, ebony, jet,
pitch-black, raven, sable, swarthy
3 = **gloomy**, depressing, dismal,
foreboding, hopeless, ominous, sad,
sombre 4 = **angry**, furious, hostile,
menacing, resentful, sullen, threatening
▷ v 10 = **boycott**, ban, bar, blacklist

blackguard n = **scoundrel**, bastard
(offens), bounder (old-fashioned Brit sl),
rascal, rogue, swine, villain

blackmail n 1 = **threat**, extortion, hush
money (sl), intimidation, ransom ▷ v
2 = **threaten**, coerce, compel, demand,
extort, hold to ransom, intimidate, squeeze

blackout ❶ n **1** extinguishing of all light as a precaution against an air attack. **2** momentary loss of consciousness or memory. **black out** v **1** extinguish (lights). **2** lose consciousness or memory temporarily.

blacksmith n person who works iron with a furnace, anvil, etc.

bladder n **1** sac in the body where urine is held. **2** hollow bag which may be filled with air or liquid.

blade n **1** cutting edge of a weapon or tool. **2** thin flattish part of a propeller, oar, etc. **3** leaf of grass.

blame ❶ v **1** consider (someone) responsible for. ▷ n **2** responsibility for something that is wrong. **blameless** adj **blameworthy** adj deserving blame.

blanch v **1** become white or pale. **2** prepare (vegetables etc.) by plunging them in boiling water.

blancmange [blam-**monzh**] n jelly-like dessert made with milk.

bland ❶ adj dull and uninteresting. **blandly** adv.

blank ❶ adj **1** not written on. **2** showing no interest or expression. ▷ n **3** empty space. **4** cartridge containing no bullet. **blankly** adv **blank verse** unrhymed verse.

blanket ❶ n **1** large thick cloth used as covering for a bed. **2** concealing cover, as of snow. ▷ v **3** cover as with a blanket.

blare ❶ v **1** sound loudly and harshly. ▷ n **2** loud harsh noise.

blarney ❶ n flattering talk.

blasé [**blah**-zay] adj indifferent or bored through familiarity.

blaspheme ❶ v speak disrespectfully of (God or sacred things). **blasphemy** n **blasphemous** adj.

blast ❶ n **1** explosion. **2** sudden strong gust of air or wind. **3** sudden loud sound, as of a trumpet. ▷ v **4** blow up (a rock etc.) with explosives. **blastoff** n launching of a rocket.

blatant ❶ adj glaringly obvious. **blatantly** adv.

blaze¹ ❶ n **1** strong fire or flame. **2** very bright light. ▷ v **3** burn or shine brightly.

—————————————————— THESAURUS ——————————————————

blackout n **2** = **unconsciousness**, coma, faint, loss of consciousness, oblivion, swoon

blame v **1** = **hold responsible**, accuse, censure, chide, condemn, criticize, find fault with, reproach ▷ n **2** = **responsibility**, accountability, accusation, culpability, fault, guilt, liability, onus

bland adj = **dull**, boring, flat, humdrum, insipid, tasteless, unexciting, uninspiring, vapid

blank adj **1** = **unmarked**, bare, clean, clear, empty, void, white **2** = **expressionless**, deadpan, empty, impassive, poker-faced (inf), vacant, vague ▷ n **3** = **empty space**, emptiness, gap, nothingness, space, vacancy, vacuum, void

blanket n **1** = **cover**, coverlet, rug **2** = **covering**, carpet, cloak, coat, layer, mantle, sheet ▷ v **3** = **cover**, cloak, coat, conceal, hide, mask, obscure, suppress

blare v **1** = **sound out**, blast, clamour, clang, resound, roar, scream, trumpet

blarney n = **flattery**, blandishments, cajolery, coaxing, soft soap (inf), spiel, sweet talk (inf), wheedling

blasé adj = **indifferent**, apathetic, lukewarm, nonchalant, offhand, unconcerned

blaspheme v = **profane**, desecrate

blast n **1** = **explosion**, bang, burst, crash, detonation, discharge, eruption, outburst, salvo, volley **2** = **gust**, gale, squall, storm, strong breeze, tempest **3** = **blare**, blow, clang, honk, peal, scream, toot, wail ▷ v **4** = **blow up**, break up, burst, demolish, destroy, explode, put paid to, ruin, shatter

blatant adj = **obvious**, brazen, conspicuous, flagrant, glaring, obtrusive, ostentatious, overt

blaze¹ n **1** = **fire**, bonfire, conflagration, flames **2** = **glare**, beam, brilliance, flare,

blaze² n mark made on a tree to indicate a route.

blazer n lightweight jacket, often in the colours of a school etc.

bleach ❶ v 1 make or become white or colourless. ▷ n 2 bleaching agent.

bleak ❶ adj 1 exposed and barren. 2 offering little hope.

bleary ❶ adj **-rier, -riest** with eyes dimmed, as by tears or tiredness. **blearily** adv.

bleat v 1 (of a sheep, goat, or calf) utter its plaintive cry. ▷ n 2 cry of sheep, goats, and calves.

bleed ❶ v bleeding, bled 1 lose or emit blood. 2 draw blood from (a person or animal). 3 informal obtain money by extortion.

bleep n 1 short high-pitched sound made by an electrical device. ▷ v 2 make a bleeping sound. **bleeper** n small portable radio receiver that makes a bleeping signal.

blemish ❶ n 1 defect or stain. ▷ v 2 spoil or tarnish.

blend ❶ v 1 mix or mingle (components or ingredients). 2 look good together. ▷ n 3 mixture. **blender** n electrical appliance for puréeing vegetables etc.

bless ❶ v 1 make holy by means of a religious rite. 2 call upon God to protect. 3 endow with health, talent, etc. **blessed** adj holy. **blessing** n 1 invoking of divine aid. 2 approval. 3 happy event.

blether Scot ▷ v talk, esp. foolishly or at length.

blight ❶ n 1 person or thing that spoils or prevents growth. 2 withering plant disease. ▷ v 3 frustrate or disappoint.

blighter n informal irritating person.

blind ❶ adj 1 unable to see. 2 unable or unwilling to understand. 3 not determined by reason, e.g. blind hatred. ▷ v 4 deprive of sight. 5 deprive of good sense, reason, or judgment. ▷ n 6 covering for a window. 7 something that serves to conceal the truth. **blindly** adv **blindness** n.

————————————————— THESAURUS —————————————————

flash, gleam, glitter, glow, light, radiance ▷ v 3 = **burn**, beam, fire, flame, flare, flash, glare, gleam, glow, shine

bleach v 1 = **whiten**, blanch, fade, grow pale, lighten, wash out

bleak adj 1 = **exposed**, bare, barren, desolate, unsheltered, weather-beaten, windswept 2 = **dismal**, cheerless, depressing, discouraging, dreary, gloomy, grim, hopeless, joyless, sombre

bleary adj = **dim**, blurred, blurry, foggy, fuzzy, hazy, indistinct, misty, murky

bleed v 1 = **lose blood**, flow, gush, ooze, run, shed blood, spurt 2 = **draw** or **take blood**, extract, leech 3 Inf = **extort**, drain, exhaust, fleece, milk, squeeze

blemish n 1 = **mark**, blot, defect, disfigurement, fault, flaw, imperfection, smudge, stain, taint v 2 = **mark**, damage, disfigure, impair, injure, mar, spoil, stain, sully, taint, tarnish

blend v 1 = **mix**, amalgamate, combine, compound, merge, mingle, unite 2 = **go**

well, complement, fit, go with, harmonize, suit ▷ n 3 = **mixture**, alloy, amalgamation, combination, compound, concoction, mix, synthesis, union

bless v 1 = **sanctify**, anoint, consecrate, dedicate, exalt, hallow, ordain 3 = **endow**, bestow, favour, give, grace, grant, provide

blight n 1 = **curse**, affliction, bane, contamination, corruption, evil, plague, pollution, scourge, woe 2 = **disease**, canker, decay, fungus, infestation, mildew, pest, pestilence, rot ▷ v 3 = **frustrate**, crush, dash, disappoint, mar, ruin, spoil, undo, wreck

blind adj 1 = **sightless**, eyeless, unseeing, unsighted, visionless 2 = **unaware of**, careless, heedless, ignorant, inattentive, inconsiderate, indifferent, insensitive, oblivious, unconscious of 3 = **unreasoning**, indiscriminate, prejudiced ▷ n 7 = **cover**, camouflage, cloak, facade, feint, front, mask, masquerade, screen, smoke screen

blink ❶ v **1** close and immediately reopen (the eyes). **2** shine intermittently. ▷ n **3** act of blinking. **on the blink** slang not working properly.

blip n spot of light on a radar screen indicating the position of an object.

bliss ❶ n perfect happiness. **blissful** adj **blissfully** adv.

blister ❶ n **1** small bubble on the skin. **2** swelling, as on a painted surface. ▷ v **3** (cause to) have blisters. **blistering** adj **1** (of weather) very hot. **2** (of criticism) extremely harsh.

blithe ❶ adj casual and indifferent. **blithely** adv.

blitz ❶ n **1** violent and sustained attack by aircraft. **2** intensive attack or concerted effort. ▷ v **3** attack suddenly and intensively.

blizzard ❶ n blinding storm of wind and snow.

blob ❶ n **1** soft mass or drop. **2** indistinct or shapeless form.

block ❶ n **1** large solid piece of wood, stone, etc. **2** large building of offices, flats, etc. **3** group of buildings enclosed by intersecting streets. **4** obstruction or hindrance. **5** slang person's head. ▷ v **6** obstruct or impede

by introducing an obstacle. **blockage** n **blockhead** n stupid person.

blockade ❶ n **1** sealing off of a place to prevent the passage of goods. ▷ v **2** impose a blockade on.

blog n **1** journal published on the internet. ▷ v **blogging**, **blogged 2** write a journal on the internet. **blogger** n.

bloke ❶ n informal man.

blood ❶ n **1** red fluid that flows around the body. **2** race or kinship. **in cold blood** done deliberately. **bloodless** adj **blood bath** massacre. **bloodhound** n large dog formerly used for tracking. **bloodshed** n slaughter or killing. **bloodshot** adj (of an eye) inflamed. **blood sport** sport involving the killing of animals. **bloodstream** n flow of blood round the body. **bloodsucker** n **1** animal that sucks blood. **2** informal person who extorts money from other people. **bloodthirsty** adj taking pleasure in violence.

bloom ❶ n **1** blossom on a flowering plant. **2** youthful or healthy glow. ▷ v **3** bear flowers. **4** be in a healthy, glowing condition.

bloomer n informal stupid mistake.

bloomers pl n woman's baggy knickers.

THESAURUS

blink v **1** = **wink**, bat, flutter **2** = **flicker**, flash, gleam, glimmer, shine, twinkle, wink **on the blink** Sl = **not working (properly)**, faulty, malfunctioning, out of action, out of order, playing up

bliss n = **joy**, beatitude, blessedness, blissfulness, ecstasy, euphoria, felicity, gladness, happiness, heaven, nirvana, paradise, rapture

blister n **1** = **sore**, abscess, boil, carbuncle, cyst, pimple, pustule, swelling

blithe adj = **heedless**, careless, casual, indifferent, nonchalant, thoughtless, unconcerned, untroubled

blitz n **1** = **attack**, assault, blitzkrieg, bombardment, offensive, onslaught, raid, strike

blizzard n = **snowstorm**, blast, gale, squall, storm, tempest

blob n **1** = **drop**, ball, bead, bubble, dab, droplet, globule, lump, mass

block n **1** = **piece**, bar, brick, chunk, hunk, ingot, lump, mass **4** = **obstruction**, bar, barrier, hindrance, impediment, jam, obstacle ▷ v **6** = **obstruct**, bung up (inf), choke, clog, close, impede, plug, stem the flow, stop up

blockade n **1** = **stoppage**, barricade, barrier, block, hindrance, impediment, obstacle, obstruction, restriction, siege

bloke n Inf = **man**, chap, character (inf), fellow, guy (inf), individual, person

blood n **1** = **lifeblood**, gore, vital fluid **2** = **family**, ancestry, birth, descent, extraction, kinship, lineage, relations

bloom n **1** = **flower**, blossom, blossoming, bud, efflorescence, opening **2** = **glow**, freshness, lustre, radiance ▷ v **3** = **blossom**,

blossom ❶ *n* **1** flowers of a plant. ▷ *v* **2** (of plants) flower. **3** come to a promising stage.

blot ❶ *n* **1** spot or stain. **2** something that spoils. ▷ *v* **blotting**, **blotted 3** cause a blemish in or on. **4** soak up (ink) by using blotting paper. **blotter** *n* **blot out** *v* darken or hide completely. **blotting paper** soft absorbent paper for soaking up ink.

blotch *n* discoloured area or stain. **blotchy** *adj*.

blouse *n* woman's shirtlike garment.

blow¹ ❶ *v* **blowing**, **blew**, **blown 1** (of air, the wind, etc.) move. **2** move or be carried as if by the wind. **3** expel (air etc.) through the mouth or nose. **4** cause (a musical instrument) to sound by forcing air into it. **5** burn out (a fuse etc.). **6** *slang* spend (money) freely. **blower** *n* **blowy** *adj* windy. **blow-dry** *v* style (the hair) with a hand-held dryer. **blowout** *n* **1** sudden loss of air in a tyre. **2** escape of oil or gas from a well. **blow up** *v* **1** explode. **2** fill with air. **3** *informal* lose one's temper. **4** *informal* enlarge (a photograph).

blow² ❶ *n* **1** hard hit. **2** sudden setback. **3** attacking action.

blowie *n* *Aust informal* bluebottle.

blubber *n* **1** fat of whales, seals, etc. ▷ *v* **2** sob without restraint.

bludge *v* **1** *Aust & NZ informal* evade work. **2** scrounge. **bludger** *n* person who scrounges.

bludgeon ❶ *n* **1** short thick club. ▷ *v* **2** hit with a bludgeon. **3** force or bully.

blue ❶ *n* **1** colour of a clear unclouded sky. ▷ *pl* **2** feeling of depression. **3** type of folk music of Black American origin. ▷ *adj* **bluer**, **bluest 4** of the colour blue. **5** depressed. **6** pornographic. **out of the blue** unexpectedly. **bluish** *adj* **bluebell** *n* flower with blue bell-shaped flowers. **bluebottle** *n* large fly with a dark-blue body. **blue-collar** *adj* denoting manual industrial workers. **blue heeler** *Aust & NZ informal* dog that controls cattle by biting their heels. **blueprint** *n* **1** photographic print of a plan. **2** description of how a plan is expected to work. **bluetongue** *n* Australian lizard with a blue tongue.

bluff¹ ❶ *v* **1** pretend to be confident in order to influence (someone). ▷ *n* **2** act of bluffing.

————————————— THESAURUS —————————————

blow, bud, burgeon, open, sprout **4** = **flourish**, develop, fare well, grow, prosper, succeed, thrive, wax

blossom *n* **1** = **flower**, bloom, bud, floret, flowers ▷ *v* **2** = **flower**, bloom, burgeon **3** = **grow**, bloom, develop, flourish, mature, progress, prosper, thrive

blot *n* **1** = **spot**, blotch, mark, patch, smear, smudge, speck, splodge **2** = **stain**, blemish, defect, fault, flaw, scar, spot, taint ▷ *v* **3** = **stain**, disgrace, mark, smirch, smudge, spoil, spot, sully, tarnish **4** = **soak up**, absorb, dry, take up

blow¹ *v* **2** = **carry**, drive, fling, flutter, move, sweep, waft **3** = **exhale**, breathe, pant, puff **4** = **play**, blare, mouth, pipe, sound, toot, trumpet, vibrate

blow² *n* **1** = **knock**, bang, clout (*inf*), punch, smack, sock (*sl*), stroke, thump, wallop (*inf*), whack **2** = **setback**, bombshell,

calamity, catastrophe, disappointment, disaster, misfortune, reverse, shock

bludgeon *n* **1** = **club**, cosh (*Brit*), cudgel, truncheon ▷ *v* **2** = **club**, beat up, cosh (*Brit*), cudgel, knock down, strike **3** = **bully**, bulldoze (*inf*), coerce, force, railroad (*inf*), steamroller

blue *n* **1** = **azure**, cobalt, cyan, navy, sapphire, ultramarine ▷ *pl* **2** = **depression**, doldrums, dumps (*inf*), gloom, low spirits, melancholy, unhappiness ▷ *adj* **4** = **azure**, cerulean, cobalt, cyan, navy, sapphire, sky-coloured, ultramarine **5** = **depressed**, dejected, despondent, downcast, low, melancholy, sad, unhappy **6** = **smutty**, indecent, lewd, obscene, risqué, X-rated (*inf*)

bluff¹ *v* **1** = **deceive**, con, delude, fake, feign, mislead, pretend, pull the wool over someone's eyes ▷ *n* **2** = **deception**, bluster,

bluff² ⓘ n 1 steep cliff or bank. ▷ adj 2 good-naturedly frank and hearty.

blunder ⓘ n 1 clumsy mistake. ▷ v 2 make a blunder. 3 act clumsily.

blunt ⓘ adj 1 not having a sharp edge or point. 2 (of people, speech, etc.) straightforward or uncomplicated. ▷ v 3 make less sharp. **bluntly** adv.

blur ⓘ v blurring, blurred 1 make or become vague or less distinct. ▷ n 2 something vague, hazy, or indistinct. **blurry** adj.

blurb n promotional description, as on the jacket of a book.

blurt ⓘ v (foll. by out) utter suddenly and involuntarily.

blush ⓘ v 1 become red in the face, esp. from embarrassment or shame. ▷ n 2 reddening of the face.

bluster ⓘ v 1 speak loudly or in a bullying way. ▷ n 2 empty threats or protests. **blustery** adj (of weather) rough and windy.

BO informal body odour.

boa n 1 large nonvenomous snake. 2 long scarf of fur or feathers. **boa constrictor**

large snake that kills its prey by crushing.

boab [boh-ab] n Aust informal short for BAOBAB.

boar n 1 uncastrated male pig. 2 wild pig.

board ⓘ n 1 long flat piece of sawn timber. 2 smaller flat piece of rigid material for a specific purpose, e.g. ironing board; chess board. 3 group of people who administer a company, trust, etc. 4 meals provided for money. ▷ v 5 go aboard (a train, aeroplane, etc.). 6 cover with boards. 7 receive meals and lodgings in return for money. **on board** on or in a ship, aeroplane, etc. **boarder** n pupil who lives at school during the school term. **boarding house** private house that provides meals and accommodation for paying guests. **boardroom** n room where the board of a company meets.

boast ⓘ v 1 speak too proudly about one's talents etc. 2 possess (something to be proud of). ▷ n 3 bragging statement. **boastful** adj.

boat n small vehicle for travelling across water. **boater** n flat straw hat.

bravado, deceit, fraud, humbug, pretence, sham, subterfuge

bluff² n 1 = **precipice**, bank, cliff, crag, escarpment, headland, peak, promontory, ridge ▷ adj 2 = **hearty**, blunt, blustering, genial, good-natured, open, outspoken, plain-spoken

blunder n 1 = **mistake**, bloomer (Brit inf), clanger (inf), error, fault, faux pas, gaffe, howler (inf), inaccuracy, indiscretion, oversight, slip, slip-up (inf) ▷ v 2 = **make a mistake**, botch, bungle, err, put one's foot in it (inf), slip up (inf) 3 = **stumble**, bumble, flounder

blunt adj 1 = **dull**, dulled, edgeless, pointless, rounded, unsharpened 2 = **forthright**, bluff, brusque, frank, outspoken, plain-spoken, rude, straightforward, tactless ▷ v 3 = **dull**, dampen, deaden, numb, soften, take the edge off, water down, weaken

blur v 1 = **make indistinct**, cloud, darken,

make hazy, make vague, mask, obscure ▷ n 2 = **indistinctness**, confusion, fog, haze, obscurity

blurt v (foll. by out) = **exclaim**, disclose, let the cat out of the bag, reveal, spill the beans (inf), tell all, utter suddenly

blush v 1 = **turn red**, colour, flush, go red (as a beetroot), redden, turn scarlet ▷ n 2 = **reddening**, colour, flush, glow, pink tinge, rosiness, rosy tint, ruddiness

bluster v 1 = **roar**, bully, domineer, hector, rant, storm ▷ n 2 = **hot air**, bluff, bombast, bravado (inf)

board n 1 = **plank**, panel, piece of timber, slat, timber 3 = **directors**, advisers, committee, conclave, council, panel, trustees 4 = **meals**, daily meals, provisions, victuals ▷ v 5 = **get on**, embark, enter, mount 7 = **lodge**, put up, quarter, room

boast v 1 = **brag**, blow one's own trumpet, crow, skite (Aust & NZ), strut, swagger, talk big (sl), vaunt 2 = **possess**, be proud of,

bob¹ ❶ v **bobbing, bobbed 1** move up and down repeatedly. ▷ n **2** short abrupt movement.

bob² n **1** hairstyle in which the hair is cut short evenly all round the head. **2** weight on a pendulum or plumb line. ▷ v **bobbing, bobbed 3** cut (the hair) in a bob.

bobbin n reel on which thread is wound.

bobble n small ball of material, usu. for decoration.

bobby n, pl **-bies** informal policeman.

bobotie n S Afr dish of curried mince.

bobsleigh n **1** sledge for racing down an icy track. ▷ v **2** ride on a bobsleigh.

bode ❶ v be an omen of (good or ill).

bodice n upper part of a dress.

bodkin n blunt large-eyed needle.

body ❶ n, pl **bodies 1** entire physical structure of an animal or human. **2** trunk or torso. **3** corpse. **4** group regarded as a single entity. **5** main part of anything. **6** woman's one-piece undergarment. **bodily** adj **1** relating to the body. ▷ adv **2** by taking hold of the body. **body-board** n Aust, NZ, S Afr & US small polystyrene surfboard. **bodyguard** n person or group of people employed to protect someone. **bodywork** n outer shell of a motor vehicle.

boffin ❶ n Brit informal scientist or expert.

bog ❶ n **1** wet spongy ground. **2** slang toilet. **boggy** adj **bog down** v **bogging, bogged** impede physically or mentally.

bogan n Aust dated & NZ slang youth who dresses and behaves rebelliously.

bogey, bogy ❶ n **1** something that worries or annoys. **2** Golf score of one stroke over par on a hole.

boggle v be surprised, confused, or alarmed.

bogus ❶ adj not genuine.

bohemian ❶ n, adj (person) leading an unconventional life.

boil¹ ❶ v **1** (cause to) change from a liquid to a vapour so quickly that bubbles are formed. **2** cook by the process of boiling. ▷ n **3** state or action of boiling. **boiler** n piece of equipment which provides hot water.

boil² ❶ n red pus-filled swelling on the skin.

boisterous ❶ adj noisy and lively.

bold ❶ adj **1** confident and fearless. **2** immodest or impudent. **boldly** adv **boldness** n.

— THESAURUS —

congratulate oneself on, exhibit, flatter oneself, pride oneself on, show off ▷ n **3** = **brag**, avowal

bob¹ v **1** = **duck**, bounce, hop, nod, oscillate, waggle, wobble

bode v = **portend**, augur, be an omen of, forebode, foretell, predict, signify, threaten

body n **1** = **physique**, build, figure, form, frame, shape **2** = **torso**, trunk **3** = **corpse**, cadaver, carcass, dead body, remains, stiff (sl) **4** = **organization**, association, band, bloc, collection, company, confederation, congress, corporation, society **5** = **main part**, bulk, essence, mass, material, matter, substance

boffin n Brit inf = **expert**, brainbox, egghead, fundi (S Afr), genius, intellectual, inventor, mastermind

bog n **1** = **marsh**, fen, mire, morass, quagmire, slough, swamp, wetlands, muskeg (Canad)

bogey n **1** = **bugbear**, bête noire, bugaboo, nightmare

bogus adj = **fake**, artificial, counterfeit, false, forged, fraudulent, imitation, phoney or phony (inf), sham

bohemian n = **nonconformist**, beatnik, dropout, hippy, iconoclast ▷ adj = **unconventional**, alternative, artistic, arty (inf), left bank, nonconformist, offbeat, unorthodox

boil¹ v **1** = **bubble 3** = **froth**, bubble, effervesce, fizz, foam, seethe

boil² n = **pustule**, blister, carbuncle, gathering, swelling, tumour, ulcer

boisterous adj = **unruly**, disorderly, loud, noisy, riotous, rollicking, rowdy, unrestrained, vociferous, wild

bold adj **1** = **fearless**, adventurous, audacious, brave, courageous, daring, enterprising, heroic, intrepid, valiant

bole *n* trunk of a tree.

bolero *n*, *pl* **-ros 1** (music for) traditional Spanish dance. **2** short open jacket.

bollard *n* short thick post used to prevent the passage of motor vehicles.

bolshie, bolshy *adj informal* difficult or rebellious.

bolster ⊙ *v* **1** support or strengthen. ▷ *n* **2** long narrow pillow.

bolt ⊙ *n* **1** sliding metal bar for fastening a door etc. **2** metal pin which screws into a nut. **3** flash (of lightning). ▷ *v* **4** run away suddenly. **5** fasten with a bolt. **6** eat hurriedly. **bolt upright** stiff and rigid. **bolt hole** place of escape.

bomb ⊙ *n* **1** container fitted with explosive material. **2** *slang* large amount of money. ▷ *v* **3** attack with bombs. **4** move very quickly. **bomber** *n* **1** aircraft that drops bombs. **2** person who throws or puts a bomb in a particular place. **bombshell** *n* shocking or unwelcome surprise.

bona fide ⊙ [**bone**-a **fide**-ee] *adj* genuine.

bonanza *n* sudden good luck or wealth.

bond ⊙ *n* **1** something that binds, fastens or holds together. **2** something that unites people. **3** written or spoken agreement. **4** *Finance* certificate of debt issued to raise funds. **5** *S Afr* conditional pledging of property, esp. a house, as security for the repayment of a loan. ▷ *pl* **6** something that restrains or imprisons. ▷ *v* **7** bind.

bondage ⊙ *n* slavery.

bone *n* **1** any of the hard parts in the body that form the skeleton. ▷ *v* **2** remove the bones from (meat for cooking etc.). **bony** *adj* **1** having many bones. **2** thin or emaciated. **bone-dry** *adj* completely dry. **bone-idle** *adj* extremely lazy.

bonfire *n* large outdoor fire.

bongo *n*, *pl* **-gos**, **-goes** small drum played with the fingers.

bonito [ba-**nee**-toh] *n*, *pl* **-os 1** small tunny-like marine food fish. **2** related fish, whose flesh is dried and flaked and used in Japanese cookery.

bonk *v informal* **1** have sex with. **2** hit.

bonnet *n* **1** metal cover over a vehicle's engine. **2** hat which ties under the chin.

bonny *adj* **-nier**, **-niest** *Scot* beautiful.

bonsai *n*, *pl* **-sai** ornamental miniature tree or shrub.

bonus ⊙ *n* something given, paid, or received above what is due or expected.

boo *interj* **1** shout of disapproval. ▷ *v* **booing**, **booed 2** shout 'boo' to show disapproval.

boob *slang* ▷ *n* **1** foolish mistake. **2** female breast.

boobook [**boo**-book] *n* small spotted Australian brown owl.

THESAURUS

2 = **impudent**, barefaced, brazen, cheeky, confident, forward, feisty (*US & Canad*), insolent, rude, shameless

bolster *v* **1** = **support**, augment, boost, help, reinforce, shore up, strengthen

bolt *n* **1** = **bar**, catch, fastener, latch, lock, sliding bar **2** = **pin**, peg, rivet, rod ▷ *v* **4** = **run away**, abscond, dash, escape, flee, fly, make a break (for it), run for it **5** = **lock**, bar, fasten, latch, secure **6** = **gobble**, cram, devour, gorge, gulp, guzzle, stuff, swallow whole, wolf

bomb *n* **1** = **explosive**, device, grenade, mine, missile, projectile, rocket, shell, torpedo ▷ *v* **3** = **blow up**, attack, blow sky-high, bombard, destroy, shell, strafe, torpedo

bona fide *adj* = **genuine**, actual, authentic, honest, kosher (*inf*), legitimate, real, true

bond *n* **1** = **fastening**, chain, cord, fetter, ligature, manacle, shackle, tie **2** = **tie**, affiliation, affinity, attachment, connection, link, relation, union **3** = **agreement**, contract, covenant, guarantee, obligation, pledge, promise, word ▷ *v* **7** = **hold together**, bind, connect, fasten, fix together, glue, paste

bondage *n* = **slavery**, captivity, confinement, enslavement, imprisonment, subjugation

bonus *n* = **extra**, dividend, gift, icing on the cake, plus, premium, prize, reward

boogie v informal dance to fast pop music.

book ❶ n **1** number of pages bound together between covers. **2** long written work. **3** number of tickets, stamps, etc. fastened together. ▷ pl **4** record of transactions of a business or society. ▷ v **5** reserve (a place, passage, etc.) in advance. **6** record the name of (a person) who has committed an offence. **booklet** n thin book with paper covers.

bookmark v Computers store (a website) so that one can return to it easily.

boom¹ ❶ v **1** make a loud deep echoing sound. **2** prosper vigorously and rapidly. ▷ n **3** loud deep echoing sound. **4** period of high economic growth. **boomer** n Aust large male kangaroo.

boom² n **1** pole to which the foot of a sail is attached. **2** pole carrying an overhead microphone. **3** barrier across a waterway.

boomerang n **1** curved wooden missile which can be made to return to the thrower. ▷ v **2** (of a plan) recoil unexpectedly.

boon ❶ n something helpful or beneficial.

boongary [**boong**-gar-ree], pl **-garies** tree kangaroo of NE Queensland, Australia.

boor n rude or insensitive person. **boorish** adj.

boost ❶ n **1** encouragement or help. **2** increase. ▷ v **3** improve. **4** increase. **booster** n small additional injection of a vaccine.

boot ❶ n **1** outer covering for the foot that extends above the ankle. **2** space in a car for luggage. **3** informal kick. **4** slang dismissal from employment. ▷ v **5** informal kick. **6** start up (a computer). **bootee** n baby's soft shoe. **boot camp** centre for young offenders, with strict discipline and hard physical exercise.

booth n **1** small partly enclosed cubicle. **2** stall at a fair or market.

bootleg adj **1** produced, distributed, or sold illicitly. ▷ v **-legging, -legged** **2** make, carry, or sell (illicit goods). **bootlegger** n.

booty ❶ n, pl **-ties** valuable articles obtained as plunder.

booze v, n informal (consume) alcoholic drink. **boozy** adj **boozer** n informal **1** person who is fond of drinking. **2** pub. **booze-up** n informal drinking spree.

border ❶ n **1** dividing line between political or geographical regions. **2** band around or along the edge of something. ▷ v **3** provide

— THESAURUS —

book n **1** = **notebook**, album, diary, e-book or ebook, exercise book, iPad®, jotter, Kindle®, pad **2** = **work**, publication, title, tome, tract, volume ▷ v **5** = **reserve**, arrange for, charter, engage, make reservations, organize, programme, schedule **6** = **note**, enter, list, log, mark down, put down, record, register, write down

boom¹ v **1** = **bang**, blast, crash, explode, resound, reverberate, roar, roll, rumble, thunder **2** = **flourish**, develop, expand, grow, increase, intensify, prosper, strengthen, swell, thrive ▷ n **3** = **bang**, blast, burst, clap, crash, explosion, roar, rumble, thunder **4** = **expansion**, boost, development, growth, improvement, increase, jump, upsurge, upswing, upturn

boon n = **benefit**, advantage, blessing,

favour, gift, godsend, manna from heaven, windfall

boost n **1** = **help**, encouragement, gee-up, praise, promotion **2** = **rise**, addition, expansion, improvement, increase, increment, jump ▷ v **3** = **promote**, advertise, encourage, foster, further, gee up, hype, improve, plug (inf), praise **4** = **increase**, add to, amplify, develop, enlarge, expand, heighten, raise

boot v Inf **5** = **kick**, drive, drop-kick, knock, punt, put the boot in(to) (sl), shove

booty n = **plunder**, gains, haul, loot, prey, spoils, swag (sl), takings, winnings

border n **1** = **frontier**, borderline, boundary, line, march **2** = **edge**, bounds, brink, limits, margin, rim, verge ▷ v **3** = **edge**, bind, decorate, fringe, hem, rim, trim with a border. **4** be nearly the same as, e.g. *resentment that borders on hatred.*

bore¹ ❶ v **1** make (a hole) with a drill etc. ▷ n **2** hole or tunnel drilled in search of oil, minerals, etc. **3** (diameter of) the hollow of a gun barrel.

bore² ❶ v **1** make weary by being dull or repetitious. ▷ n **2** dull or repetitious person or thing. **bored** *adj* **boredom** n.

boree [**baw-ree**] n *Aust* same as MYALL.

boron n *Chem* element used in hardening steel.

boronia n Australian aromatic flowering shrub.

borough n town or district with its own council.

borrow ❶ v **1** obtain (something) temporarily. **2** adopt (ideas etc.) from another source. **borrower** n.

borstal n (formerly) prison for young criminals.

borzoi n tall dog with a long silky coat.

bosom ❶ n **1** chest of a person, esp. the female breasts. ▷ adj **2** very dear, e.g. *a bosom friend.*

boss ❶ n **1** person in charge of or employing others. ▷ v **2** **boss around**, **about** be domineering towards. **bossy** *adj* **bossier**, **bossiest**.

botany n study of plants. **botanical**, **botanic** *adj* **botanist** n.

botch ❶ v **1** spoil through clumsiness. ▷ n **2** (also **botch-up**) badly done piece of work or repair.

both *adj*, *pron* two considered together.

bother ❶ v **1** take the time or trouble. **2** give annoyance or trouble to. **3** pester. ▷ n **4** trouble, fuss, or difficulty. **bothersome** *adj*.

bottle n **1** container for holding liquids. **2** *slang* courage. ▷ v **3** put in a bottle. **bottleneck** n narrow stretch of road where traffic is held up. **bottle tree** Australian tree with a bottle-shaped swollen trunk. **bottle up** v restrain (powerful emotion).

bottom ❶ n **1** lowest, deepest, or farthest removed part of a thing. **2** buttocks. ▷ adj **3** lowest or last. **bottomless** *adj*.

bough n large branch of a tree.

boulder n large rounded rock.

boulevard n wide, usu. tree-lined, street.

bounce ❶ v **1** (of a ball etc.) rebound from an impact. **2** *slang* (of a cheque) be returned uncashed owing to a lack of funds in the account. ▷ n **3** act of rebounding.

— THESAURUS —

bore¹ v **1** = **drill**, burrow, gouge out, mine, penetrate, perforate, pierce, sink, tunnel

bore² v **1** = **tire**, be tedious, fatigue, jade, pall on, send to sleep, wear out, weary ▷ n **2** = **nuisance**, anorak (*inf*), pain (*inf*), yawn (*inf*)

borrow v **1** = **take on loan**, bludge (*Aust & NZ*), cadge, scrounge (*inf*), touch (someone) for (*sl*), use temporarily **2** = **steal**, adopt, copy, obtain, plagiarize, take, usurp

bosom n **1** = **breast**, bust, chest ▷ adj **2** = **intimate**, boon, cherished, close, confidential, dear, very dear

boss n **1** = **head**, chief, director, employer, gaffer (*inf, chiefly Brit*), leader, manager, master, supervisor

botch v **1** = **spoil**, blunder, bungle, cock up (*Brit sl*), make a pig's ear of (*inf*), mar, mess

up, screw up (*inf*) ▷ n **2** = **mess**, blunder, bungle, cock-up (*Brit sl*), failure, hash, pig's ear (*inf*)

bother v **3** = **trouble**, disturb, harass, hassle (*inf*), inconvenience, pester, plague, worry ▷ n **4** = **trouble**, difficulty, fuss, hassle (*inf*), inconvenience, irritation, nuisance, problem, worry

bottom n **1** = **lowest part**, base, bed, depths, floor, foot, foundation, lower side, sole, underneath, underside **2** = **buttocks**, backside, behind (*inf*), posterior, rear, rump, seat ▷ adj **3** = **lowest**, last

bounce v **1** = **rebound**, bob, bound, jump, leap, recoil, ricochet, spring ▷ n **4** = **springiness**, elasticity, give, recoil, resilience, spring **5** *Inf* = **life**, dynamism, energy, go (*inf*), liveliness, vigour, vivacity, zip (*inf*)

b

4 springiness. **5** *informal* vitality or vigour. **bouncer** n person employed at a disco etc. to remove unwanted people. **bouncing** adj vigorous and robust.

bound¹ ⓞ v **1** past of BIND. ▷ adj **2** destined or certain. **3** compelled or obliged.

bound² ⓞ v **1** move forwards by jumps. ▷ n **2** jump upwards or forwards.

bound³ ⓞ v **1** form a boundary of. ▷ pl n **2** limit. **boundary** n dividing line that indicates the farthest limit.

bound⁴ adj going or intending to go towards, e.g. *homeward bound*.

bounty ⓞ n, pl **-ties 1** generosity. **2** generous gift or reward. **bountiful**, **bounteous** adj.

bouquet ⓞ n **1** bunch of flowers. **2** aroma of wine.

bourbon [**bur**-bn] n whiskey made from maize.

bourgeois ⓞ [**boor**-zhwah] adj, n offens middle-class (person).

bout ⓞ n **1** period of activity or illness. **2** boxing or wrestling match.

boutique n small clothes shop.

bow¹ ⓞ [rhymes with **now**] v **1** lower (one's head) or bend (one's knee or body) as a sign of respect or shame. **2** comply or accept. ▷ n **3** movement made when bowing.

bow² [rhymes with **go**] n **1** knot with two loops and loose ends. **2** weapon for shooting arrows. **3** long stick stretched with horsehair for playing stringed instruments. **bow-legged** adj having legs that curve outwards at the knees.

bow³ ⓞ [rhymes with **now**] n front end of a ship.

bowel n **1** intestine, esp. the large intestine. ▷ pl **2** innermost part.

bower n shady leafy shelter. **bowerbird** n songbird of Australia and New Guinea, the males of which build bower-like display grounds to attract females.

bowl¹ ⓞ n **1** round container with an open top. **2** hollow part of an object.

bowl² ⓞ n **1** large heavy ball. ▷ pl **2** game played on smooth grass with wooden bowls. ▷ v **3** *Cricket* send (a ball) towards the batsman. **bowler** n **bowling** n game in which bowls are rolled at a group of pins.

bowler n stiff felt hat with a rounded crown.

THESAURUS

bound¹ adj **1** = **tied**, cased, fastened, fixed, pinioned, secured, tied up **2** = **certain**, destined, doomed, fated, sure **3** = **obliged**, beholden, committed, compelled, constrained, duty-bound, forced, pledged, required

bound² v **1** = **leap**, bob, bounce, gambol, hurdle, jump, skip, spring, vault ▷ n **2** = **leap**, bob, bounce, gambol, hurdle, jump, skip, spring, vault

bound³ v **1** = **limit**, confine, demarcate, encircle, enclose, hem in, restrain, restrict, surround ▷ pl n **2** = **boundary**, border, confine, edge, extremity, limit, rim, verge

bounty n **1** = **generosity**, benevolence, charity, kindness, largesse or largess, liberality, philanthropy **2** = **reward**, bonus, gift, present

bouquet n **1** = **bunch of flowers**, buttonhole, corsage, garland, nosegay, posy, spray, wreath **2** = **aroma**, fragrance, perfume, redolence, savour, scent

bourgeois adj Offens = **middle-class**, conventional, hidebound, materialistic, traditional

bout n **1** = **period**, fit, spell, stint, term, turn **2** = **fight**, boxing match, competition, contest, encounter, engagement, match, set-to, struggle

bow¹ v **1** = **bend**, bob, droop, genuflect, nod, stoop **2** = **give in**, acquiesce, comply, concede, defer, kowtow, relent, submit, succumb, surrender, yield ▷ n **3** = **bending**, bob, genuflexion, kowtow, nod, obeisance

bow³ n = **prow**, beak, fore, head, stem

bowl¹ n **1** = **basin**, dish, vessel

bowl² v **3** *Cricket* = **throw**, fling, hurl, pitch

box¹ ❶ n 1 container with a firm flat base and sides. 2 separate compartment in a theatre, stable, etc. ▷ v 3 put into a box. **the box** *informal* television. **box jellyfish** highly venomous jellyfish of Australian tropical waters with a cuboidal body. **box office** place where theatre or cinema tickets are sold.

box² ❶ v fight (an opponent) in a boxing match. **boxer** n 1 person who participates in the sport of boxing. 2 medium-sized dog with smooth hair and a short nose. **boxer shorts**, **boxers** pl n men's underpants shaped like shorts but with a front opening. **boxing** n sport of fighting with the fists.

box³ n 1 evergreen tree with shiny leaves. 2 eucalyptus with similar timber and foliage, and with rough bark.

boy ❶ n male child. **boyish** adj **boyhood** n **boyfriend** n male friend with whom a person is romantically or sexually involved.

boycott ❶ v 1 refuse to deal with (an organization or country). ▷ n 2 instance of boycotting.

● SPELLING TIP
● The word **boycott** has two ts, whether
● or not it has an ending such as in
● **boycotting**.

bra n woman's undergarment for supporting the breasts.

braaivlies, **braai** SAfr ▷ n 1 grill on which food is cooked over hot charcoal, usu. outdoors. ▷ v 2 cook (food) in this way.

brace ❶ n 1 object fastened to something to straighten or support it. 2 pair, esp. of game birds. ▷ pl 3 straps worn over the shoulders to hold up trousers. ▷ v 4 steady or prepare (oneself) for something unpleasant. 5 strengthen or fit with a brace. **bracing** adj refreshing and invigorating.

bracken n large fern.

bracket n 1 pair of characters used to enclose a section of writing. 2 group falling within certain defined limits. 3 support fixed to a wall. ▷ v **-eting**, **-eted** 4 put in brackets. 5 class together.

brackish adj (of water) slightly salty.

brag ❶ v **bragging**, **bragged** speak arrogantly and boastfully. **braggart** n.

braid ❶ v 1 interweave (hair, thread, etc.). ▷ n 2 length of hair etc. that has been braided. 3 narrow ornamental tape of woven silk etc.

Braille n system of writing for the blind, consisting of raised dots interpreted by touch.

brain ❶ n 1 soft mass of nervous tissue in the head. 2 intellectual ability. ▷ v 3 hit (someone) hard on the head. **brainless** adj stupid. **brainy** adj informal clever. **brainchild** n idea produced by creative thought. **brainwash** v cause (a person) to alter his or her beliefs, esp. by methods based on isolation, sleeplessness, etc. **brainwave** n sudden idea.

braise v cook slowly in a covered pan with a little liquid.

brake ❶ n 1 device for slowing or stopping a vehicle. ▷ v 2 slow down or stop by using a brake.

——— THESAURUS ———

box¹ n 1 = **container**, carton, case, casket, chest, pack, package, receptacle, trunk ▷ v 3 = **pack**, package, wrap

box² v = **fight**, exchange blows, spar

boy n = **lad**, fellow, junior, schoolboy, stripling, youngster, youth

boycott v 1 = **embargo**, ban, bar, black, exclude, outlaw, prohibit, refuse, reject

brace n 1 = **support**, bolster, bracket, buttress, prop, reinforcement, stay, strut, truss ▷ v 5 = **support**, bolster, buttress, fortify, reinforce, steady, strengthen

brag v = **boast**, blow one's own trumpet, bluster, crow, skite (Aust & NZ), swagger, talk big (sl), vaunt

braid v 1 = **interweave**, entwine, interlace, intertwine, lace, plait, twine, weave

brain n 2 = **intelligence**, intellect, sense, understanding

brake¹ n 1 = **control**, check, constraint, curb, rein, restraint ▷ v 2 = **slow**, check,

bramble n prickly shrub that produces blackberries.

bran n husks of cereal grain.

branch ❶ n 1 secondary stem of a tree. 2 offshoot or subsidiary part of something larger or more complex. ▷ v 3 (of stems, roots, etc.) divide, then develop in different directions. **branch out** v expand one's interests.

brand ❶ n 1 particular product. 2 particular kind or variety. 3 identifying mark burnt onto the skin of an animal. ▷ v 4 mark with a brand. 5 denounce as being. **brand-new** adj absolutely new.

brandish ❶ v wave (a weapon etc.) in a threatening way.

brandy n, pl -dies alcoholic spirit distilled from wine.

brash ❶ adj offensively loud, showy, or self-confident. **brashness** n.

brass n 1 alloy of copper and zinc. 2 family of wind instruments made of brass. **brassy** adj 1 brazen or flashy. 2 like brass, esp. in colour.

brassiere n bra.

brat n unruly child.

bravado ❶ n showy display of self-confidence.

brave ❶ adj 1 having or showing courage, resolution, and daring. ▷ n 2 Native American warrior. ▷ v 3 confront with resolution or courage. **bravery** n.

bravo interj well done!

brawl ❶ n 1 noisy fight. ▷ v 2 fight noisily.

brawn ❶ n 1 physical strength. 2 pressed meat from the head of a pig or calf. **brawny** adj.

bray v 1 (of a donkey) utter its loud harsh sound. ▷ n 2 donkey's loud harsh sound.

brazen ❶ adj 1 shameless and bold.

brazier [bray-zee-er] n portable container for burning charcoal or coal.

breach ❶ n 1 breaking of a promise, obligation, etc. 2 gap or break. ▷ v 3 break (a promise, law, etc.). 4 make a gap in.

bread ❶ n 1 food made by baking a mixture of flour and water or milk. 2 slang money. **breadwinner** n person whose earnings support a family.

————————————————————————————————— THESAURUS ————

decelerate, halt, moderate, reduce speed, slacken, stop

branch ❶ n 1 = **bough**, arm, limb, offshoot, shoot, spray, sprig 2 = **division**, chapter, department, office, part, section, subdivision, subsection, wing

brand n 1 = **label**, emblem, hallmark, logo, mark, marker, sign, stamp, symbol, trademark 2 = **kind**, cast, class, grade, make, quality, sort, species, type, variety ▷ v 4 = **mark**, burn, burn in, label, scar, stamp 5 = **stigmatize**, censure, denounce, discredit, disgrace, expose, mark

brandish v = **wave**, display, exhibit, flaunt, flourish, parade, raise, shake, swing, wield

brash adj = **bold**, brazen, cocky, impertinent, impudent, insolent, pushy (inf), rude

bravado n = **swagger**, bluster, boastfulness, boasting, bombast, swashbuckling, vaunting

brave adj 1 = **courageous**, bold, daring, fearless, heroic, intrepid, plucky, resolute, valiant ▷ v 3 = **confront**, defy, endure, face, stand up to, suffer, tackle, withstand

brawl n 1 = **fight**, affray, altercation, clash, dispute, fracas, fray, mêlée, punch-up (inf), rumpus, scuffle, skirmish ▷ v 2 = **fight**, scrap (inf), scuffle, tussle, wrestle

brawn n 1 = **muscle**, beef (inf), might, muscles, power, strength, vigour

brazen adj = **bold**, audacious, barefaced, brash, defiant, impudent, insolent, shameless, unabashed, unashamed

breach n 1 = **nonobservance**, contravention, infraction, infringement, noncompliance, transgression, trespass, violation 2 = **crack**, cleft, fissure, gap, opening, rift, rupture, split

bread n 2 Sl = **money**, cash, dough (sl), lolly (Aust & NZ sl)

breadth ❶ n extent of something from side to side.

break ❶ v **breaking**, **broke**, **broken**
1 separate or become separated into two or more pieces. 2 damage or become damaged so as to be inoperative. 3 fail to observe (an agreement etc.). 4 disclose or be disclosed, e.g. *he broke the news.* 5 bring or come to an end, e.g. *the good weather broke at last.* 6 weaken or be weakened, as in spirit. 7 cut through or penetrate. 8 improve on or surpass, e.g. *break a record.* 9 (of the male voice) become permanently deeper at puberty. ▷ n 10 act or result of breaking. 11 gap or interruption in continuity. 12 *informal* fortunate opportunity. **break even** make neither a profit nor a loss. **breakable** adj **breakage** n **breaker** n large wave. **break down** v 1 cease to function. 2 yield to strong emotion. **breakdown** n 1 act or instance of breaking down. 2 nervous breakdown. **break-in** n illegal entering of a building, esp. by thieves. **breakneck** adj fast and dangerous. **break off** v 1 sever or detach. 2 end (a relationship etc.). **break out** v begin or arise suddenly. **breakthrough** n important development or discovery. **break up** v 1 (cause to) separate. 2 come to an end. 3 (of a school) close for the holidays. **breakwater** n wall that extends into the sea to protect a harbour or beach from the force of waves.

bream n freshwater silvery fish.

breast ❶ n 1 either of the two soft fleshy milk-secreting glands on a woman's chest. 2 chest. **breastbone** n long flat bone in the front of the body, to which most of the ribs are attached. **breaststroke** n swimming stroke in which the arms are extended in front of the head and swept back on either side.

breath ❶ n 1 taking in and letting out of air during breathing. 2 air taken in and let out during breathing. **breathless** adj **breathtaking** adj causing awe or excitement. **breathe** v 1 take in oxygen and give out carbon dioxide. 2 whisper. **breather** n informal short rest. **breathing** n.

Breathalyser n ® device for estimating the amount of alcohol in the breath. **breathalyse** v.

breech n 1 buttocks. 2 part of a firearm behind the barrel.

breed ❶ v **breeding**, **bred** 1 produce new or improved strains of (domestic animals or plants). 2 bear (offspring). 3 produce or be produced, e.g. *breed trouble.* ▷ n 4 group of animals etc. within a species that have

---

breadth n = **width**, broadness, latitude, span, spread, wideness

break v 1 = **separate**, burst, crack, destroy, disintegrate, fracture, fragment, shatter, smash, snap, split, tear 3 = **disobey**, breach, contravene, disregard, infringe, renege on, transgress, violate 4 = **reveal**, announce, disclose, divulge, impart, inform, let out, make public, proclaim, tell 5 = **stop**, abandon, cut, discontinue, give up, interrupt, pause, rest, suspend 6 = **weaken**, demoralize, dispirit, subdue, tame, undermine 8 = **beat**, better, exceed, excel, go beyond, outdo, outstrip, surpass, top ▷ n 10 = **division**, crack, fissure, fracture, gap, hole, opening, split, tear

11 = **rest**, breather (*inf*), hiatus, interlude, intermission, interruption, interval, let-up (*inf*), lull, pause, respite 12 *Inf* = **stroke of luck**, advantage, chance, fortune, opening, opportunity

breast n 1 = **bosom**, bust, chest, front, teat, udder

breath n 1 = **respiration**, breathing, exhalation, gasp, gulp, inhalation, pant, wheeze

breed v 1 = **cultivate**, develop
2 = **reproduce**, bear, bring forth, hatch, multiply, procreate, produce, propagate
3 = **produce**, arouse, bring about, cause, create, generate, give rise to, stir up ▷ n
4 = **variety**, pedigree, race, species, stock,

certain clearly defined characteristics.
5 kind or sort. **breeder** n **breeding** n result
of good upbringing or training.
breeze ❶ n **1** gentle wind. ▷ v **2** move
quickly or casually. **breezy** adj **1** windy.
2 casual or carefree.
brethren pl n old-fashioned (used in religious
contexts) brothers.
brevity ❶ n shortness.
brew ❶ v **1** make (beer etc.) by steeping,
boiling, and fermentation. **2** prepare (a
drink) by infusing. **3** be about to happen
or forming. ▷ n **4** beverage produced by
brewing. **brewer** n **brewery** n, pl **-eries**
place where beer etc. is brewed.
briar, brier n **1** European shrub with a
hard woody root. **2** tobacco pipe made
from this root.
bribe ❶ v **1** offer or give something to
someone to gain favour, influence, etc. ▷ n
2 something given or offered as a bribe.
bribery n.
bric-a-brac ❶ n miscellaneous small
ornamental objects.
brick n **1** (rectangular block of) baked clay
used in building. ▷ v **2** (foll. by up or over)

build, enclose, or fill with bricks. **bricklayer**
n person who builds with bricks.
bride n woman who has just been
or is about to be married. **bridal** adj
bridegroom n man who has just been or
is about to be married. **bridesmaid** n girl
who attends a bride at her wedding.
bridge¹ ❶ n **1** structure for crossing a
river etc. **2** platform from which a ship
is steered or controlled. **3** upper part of
the nose. **4** piece of wood supporting the
strings of a violin etc. ▷ v **5** build a bridge
over (something). **bridgehead** n fortified
position at the end of a bridge nearest
the enemy.
bridge² n card game based on whist, played
between two pairs.
bridle ❶ n **1** headgear for controlling a
horse. ▷ v **2** show anger or indignation.
bridle path path suitable for riding horses.
brief ❶ adj **1** short in duration. ▷ n
2 condensed statement or written
synopsis. **3** (also **briefing**) set of
instructions. ▷ pl **4** men's or women's
underpants. ▷ v **5** give information and
instructions to (a person). **briefly** adv

— THESAURUS —

strain, type **5** = **kind**, brand, sort, stamp,
type, variety
breeze n **1** = **light wind**, air, breath of wind,
current of air, draught, gust, waft, zephyr
▷ v **2** = **move briskly**, flit, glide, hurry,
pass, sail, sweep
brevity n = **shortness**, briefness,
conciseness, crispness, curtness, economy,
impermanence, pithiness, succinctness,
terseness, transience, transitoriness
brew v **1, 2** = **make** (beer), boil, ferment,
infuse (tea), soak, steep, stew **3** = **develop**,
foment, form, gather, start, stir up ▷ n
4 = **drink**, beverage, blend, concoction,
infusion, liquor, mixture, preparation
bribe v **1** = **buy off**, corrupt, grease the
palm or hand of (sl), pay off (inf), reward,
suborn ▷ n **2** = **inducement**, allurement,
backhander (sl), enticement, kickback
(US), pay-off (inf), sweetener (sl)

bric-a-brac n = **knick-knacks**, baubles,
curios, ornaments, trinkets
bridge¹ n **1** = **arch**, flyover, overpass,
span, viaduct ▷ v **5** = **connect**, join, link,
span
bridle n **1** = **curb**, check, control, rein,
restraint ▷ v **2** = **get angry**, be indignant,
bristle, draw (oneself) up, get one's back
up, raise one's hackles, rear up
brief adj **1** = **short**, ephemeral, fleeting,
momentary, quick, short-lived, swift,
transitory ▷ n **2** = **summary**, abridgment,
abstract, digest, epitome, outline, précis,
sketch, synopsis **3** = **instructions**,
conference, directions, guidance,
information, preparation, priming,
rundown ▷ v **5** = **inform**, advise, explain,
fill in (inf), instruct, keep posted,
prepare, prime, put (someone) in the
picture (inf)

briefcase n small flat case for carrying papers, books, etc.

brier, briar n wild rose with long thorny stems.

brigade ❶ n 1 army unit smaller than a division. 2 group of people organized for a certain task. **brigadier** n high-ranking army officer.

brigand ❶ n bandit.

bright ❶ adj 1 emitting or reflecting much light. 2 (of colours) intense. 3 clever. **brightly** adv **brightness** n **brighten** v.

brilliant ❶ adj 1 shining with light. 2 splendid. 3 extremely clever. **brilliance**, **brilliancy** n.

brim ❶ n 1 upper rim of a cup etc. 2 projecting edge of a hat. ▷ v **brimming**, **brimmed** 3 be full to the brim.

brine n salt water. **briny** adj very salty.

bring ❶ v **bringing**, **brought** 1 carry, convey, or take to a designated place or person. 2 cause to happen. 3 Law put

forward (charges) officially. **bring about** v cause to happen. **bring off** v succeed in achieving. **bring out** v 1 publish or have (a book) published. 2 reveal or cause to be seen. **bring up** v 1 rear (a child). 2 mention. 3 vomit (food).

brinjal n S Afr dark purple tropical fruit, cooked and eaten as a vegetable.

brink ❶ n edge of a steep place.

brisk ❶ adj lively and quick. **briskly** adv.

brisket n beef from the breast of a cow.

bristle ❶ n 1 short stiff hair. ▷ v 2 (cause to) stand up like bristles. 3 show anger. **bristly** adj.

brittle ❶ adj hard but easily broken. **brittleness** n.

broach ❶ v 1 introduce (a topic) for discussion. 2 open (a bottle or barrel).

broad ❶ adj 1 having great breadth or width. 2 not detailed. 3 extensive, e.g. broad support. 4 strongly marked, e.g. a broad Bristol accent. **broadly** adv **broaden**

———— THESAURUS ————

brigade n 2 = **group**, band, company, corps, force, outfit, squad, team, troop, unit

brigand n = **bandit**, desperado, freebooter, gangster, highwayman, marauder, outlaw, plunderer, robber

bright adj 1, 2 = **shining**, brilliant, dazzling, gleaming, glowing, luminous, lustrous, radiant, shimmering, vivid 3 = **intelligent**, astute, aware, clever, inventive, quick-witted, sharp, smart, wide-awake

brilliant adj 1 = **shining**, bright, dazzling, glittering, intense, luminous, radiant, sparkling, vivid 2 = **splendid**, celebrated, famous, glorious, illustrious, magnificent, notable, outstanding, superb 3 = **intelligent**, clever, expert, gifted, intellectual, inventive, masterly, penetrating, profound, talented

brim n 1 = **rim**, border, brink, edge, lip, margin, skirt, verge ▷ v 3 = **be full**, fill, fill up, hold no more, overflow, run over, spill, well over

bring v 1 = **take**, bear, carry, conduct,

convey, deliver, escort, fetch, guide, lead, transfer, transport 2 = **cause**, contribute to, create, effect, inflict, occasion, produce, result in, wreak

brink n = **edge**, border, boundary, brim, fringe, frontier, limit, lip, margin, rim, skirt, threshold, verge

brisk adj = **lively**, active, bustling, busy, energetic, quick, sprightly, spry, vigorous

bristle n 1 = **hair**, barb, prickle, spine, stubble, thorn, whisker ▷ v 2 = **stand up**, rise, stand on end 3 = **be angry**, bridle, flare up, rage, see red, seethe

brittle adj = **fragile**, breakable, crisp, crumbling, crumbly, delicate, frail, frangible, friable

broach v 1 = **bring up**, introduce, mention, open up, propose, raise the subject, speak of, suggest, talk of, touch on 2 = **open**, crack, draw off, pierce, puncture, start, tap, uncork

broad adj 1 = **wide**, ample, expansive, extensive, generous, large, roomy, spacious, vast, voluminous, widespread

v **broadband** n telecommunication transmission technique using a wide range of frequencies. **broad bean** thick flat edible bean. **broadcast** n programme or announcement on radio or television. **broad-minded** adj tolerant. **broadside** n 1 strong verbal or written attack. 2 Naval firing of all the guns on one side of a ship at once.

brocade n rich fabric woven with a raised design.

broccoli n type of cabbage with greenish flower heads.

● SPELLING TIP
● You might expect a word that sounds
● like **broccoli** to have two ls at the end,
● but it has only one because it comes
● from Italian and ends with an i.

brochure ❶ n booklet that contains information about a product or service.

broekies [**brook**-eez] pl n S Afr informal underpants.

brogue¹ n sturdy walking shoe.

brogue² n strong accent, esp. Irish.

broil v Aust, NZ, US & Canad same as GRILL.

broke ❶ v 1 past tense of BREAK. ▷ adj 2 informal having no money.

broker ❶ n agent who buys or sells goods, securities, etc.

brolga n large grey Australian crane with a trumpeting call (also **native companion**).

bromide n chemical compound used in medicine and photography.

bromine n Chem dark red liquid element that gives off a pungent vapour.

bronco n, pl -cos (in the US) wild or partially tamed pony.

brontosaurus n very large plant-eating four-footed dinosaur.

bronze ❶ n 1 alloy of copper and tin. 2 statue, medal, etc. made of bronze. ▷ adj 3 made of, or coloured like, bronze. ▷ v 4 (esp. of the skin) make or become brown.

brooch n ornament with a pin, worn fastened to clothes.

brood ❶ n 1 number of birds produced at one hatching. 2 all the children of a family. ▷ v 3 think long and unhappily. **broody** adj 1 moody and sullen. 2 informal (of a woman) wishing to have a baby.

brook¹ ❶ n small stream.

brook² ❶ v bear or tolerate.

broom n 1 long-handled sweeping brush. 2 yellow-flowered shrub. **broomstick** n handle of a broom.

broth n soup, usu. containing vegetables.

brothel n house where men pay to have sex with prostitutes.

brother ❶ n 1 boy or man with the same parents as another person. 2 member of a male religious order. **brotherly** adj **brotherhood** n 1 fellowship. 2 association, such as a trade union. **brother-in-law** n, pl **brothers-in-law**

— THESAURUS —

3 = **general**, all-embracing, comprehensive, encyclopedic, inclusive, overarching, sweeping, wide, wide-ranging

brochure n = **booklet**, advertisement, circular, folder, handbill, hand-out, leaflet, mailshot, pamphlet

broke adj 2 Inf = **penniless**, bankrupt, bust (inf), down and out, impoverished, insolvent, in the red, munted (NZ sl), ruined, short, skint (Brit sl)

broker n = **dealer**, agent, factor, go-between, intermediary, middleman, negotiator

bronze adj 3 = **reddish-brown**, brownish, chestnut, copper, rust, tan

brood n 1 = **offspring**, clutch, family, issue, litter, progeny ▷ v 3 = **think upon**, agonize, dwell upon, mope, mull over, muse, obsess, ponder, ruminate

brook¹ n = **stream**, beck, burn, rill, rivulet, watercourse

brook² v = **tolerate**, abide, accept, allow, bear, countenance, endure, hack (sl), put up with (inf), stand, stomach, suffer, support, swallow, thole (dial), withstand

brother n 1 = **sibling**, blood brother, kin, kinsman, relation, relative 2 = **monk**, cleric, friar

1 brother of one's husband or wife.
2 husband of one's sister.

brow n 1 part of the face from the eyes to the hairline. 2 eyebrow. 3 top of a hill.

brown ❶ n 1 colour of earth or wood. ▷ adj 2 of the colour brown. ▷ v 3 make or become brown. **browned-off** adj informal bored and depressed.

browse ❷ v 1 look through (a book or articles for sale) in a casual manner. 2 nibble on young shoots or leaves. ▷ n 3 instance of browsing. **browser** n Computers software package that enables a user to read hypertext, esp. on the Internet.

bruise ❶ n 1 discoloured area on the skin caused by an injury. ▷ v 2 cause a bruise on. **bruiser** n strong tough person.

brumby n Aust 1 wild horse. 2 unruly person.

brunch n informal breakfast and lunch combined.

brunette n girl or woman with dark brown hair.

brunt ❶ n main force or shock of a blow, attack, etc.

brush¹ ❶ n 1 device made of bristles,

wires, etc. used for cleaning, painting, etc. 2 brief unpleasant encounter. 3 fox's tail. ▷ v 4 clean, scrub, or paint with a brush. 5 touch lightly and briefly. **brush off** v slang dismiss or ignore (someone). **brush up** v refresh one's knowledge of (a subject).

brush² ❶ n thick growth of shrubs.

brush turkey n bird of New Guinea and Australia resembling the domestic fowl, with black plumage.

brusque ❶ adj blunt or curt in manner or speech. **brusquely** adv **brusqueness** n.

Brussels sprout n vegetable like a tiny cabbage.

brute ❶ n 1 brutal person. 2 animal other than man. ▷ adj 3 wholly instinctive or physical, like an animal. 4 without reason. **brutish** adj of or like an animal. **brutal** adj 1 cruel and vicious. 2 extremely honest in speech or manner. **brutally** adv **brutality** n **brutalize** v.

BSc Bachelor of Science.

BST British Summer Time.

bubble ❶ n 1 ball of air in a liquid or solid. ▷ v 2 form bubbles. 3 move or flow with a gurgling sound. **bubbly** adj 1 excited and lively. 2 full of bubbles.

THESAURUS

---

brown adj 2 = **brunette**, auburn, bay, bronze, chestnut, chocolate, coffee, dun, hazel, sunburnt, tan, tanned, tawny, umber ▷ v 3 = **fry**, cook, grill, sauté, seal, sear

browse v 1 = **skim**, dip into, examine cursorily, flip through, glance at, leaf through, look round, look through, peruse, scan, survey 2 = **graze**, eat, feed, nibble

bruise n 1 = **discoloration**, black mark, blemish, contusion, injury, mark, swelling ▷ v 2 = **discolour**, damage, injure, mar, mark, pound

brunt n = **full force**, burden, force, impact, pressure, shock, strain, stress, thrust, violence

brush¹ n 1 = **broom**, besom, sweeper 2 = **encounter**, clash, conflict, confrontation, skirmish, tussle ▷ v

4 = **clean**, buff, paint, polish, sweep, wash
5 = **touch**, flick, glance, graze, kiss, scrape, stroke, sweep

brush² n = **shrubs**, brushwood, bushes, copse, scrub, thicket, undergrowth

brusque adj = **curt**, abrupt, discourteous, gruff, impolite, sharp, short, surly, terse

brute n 1 = **savage**, barbarian, beast, devil, fiend, monster, sadist, swine
2 = **animal**, beast, creature, wild animal ▷ adj 3 = **physical**, bodily, carnal, fleshly
4 = **mindless**, instinctive, senseless, unthinking

bubble n 1 = **air ball**, bead, blister, blob, drop, droplet, globule ▷ v 2 = **foam**, boil, effervesce, fizz, froth, percolate, seethe, sparkle 3 = **gurgle**, babble, burble, murmur, ripple, trickle

bubonic plague [bew-**bonn**-ik] *n* acute infectious disease characterized by swellings.

buccaneer ❶ *n* pirate.

buck¹ *n* **1** male of the goat, hare, kangaroo, rabbit, and reindeer. ▷ *v* **2** (of a horse etc.) jump with legs stiff and back arched. **3** *informal* resist or oppose obstinately, e.g. *to buck a trend*. **buckshot** *n* large lead pellets used for shooting game. **buck up** *v* make or become more cheerful.

buck² *n US, Canad & Aust slang* dollar.

bucket *n* **1** open-topped round container with a handle. ▷ *v* **-eting, -eted** rain heavily. **bucketful** *n*.

buckle ❶ *n* **1** clasp for fastening a belt or strap. ▷ *v* **2** fasten or be fastened with a buckle. **3** (cause to) bend out of shape through pressure or heat. **buckle down** *v* *informal* apply oneself with determination.

bud ❶ *n* **1** swelling on a tree or plant that develops into a leaf or flower. ▷ *v* **budding, budded 2** produce buds. **budding** *adj* beginning to develop or grow.

budge ❶ *v* move slightly.

budgerigar *n* small cage bird bred in many different-coloured varieties.

budget ❶ *n* **1** financial plan for a period of time. **2** money allocated for a specific purpose. ▷ *v* **-eting, -eted 3** plan the expenditure of (money or time). ▷ *adj* **4** cheap. **budgetary** *adj*.

- **SPELLING TIP**
- A lot of verbs ending in *et* have two *t*s
- when you add an ending like *-ing*, but
- **budget** is not one of them: **budgeting**
- and **budgeted** have a single *t*.

buff¹ ❶ *adj* **1** dull yellowish-brown. ▷ *v* **2** clean or polish with soft material.

buff² ❶ *n informal* expert on or devotee of a given subject.

buffalo *n* **1** type of cattle. **2** *US* bison.

buffer ❶ *n* something that lessens shock or protects from damaging impact, circumstances, etc.

buffet¹ ❶ [**boof**-ay] *n* counter where drinks and snacks are served.

buffet² ❶ [**buff**-it] *v* **-feting, -feted** knock against or about.

buffoon ❶ *n* clown or fool. **buffoonery** *n*.

bug ❶ *n* **1** small insect. **2** *informal* minor illness. **3** small mistake in a computer program. **4** concealed microphone. ▷ *v* **bugging, bugged 5** *informal* irritate

————————————— THESAURUS —————————————

buccaneer *n* = **pirate**, corsair, freebooter, privateer, sea-rover

buckle *n* **1** = **fastener**, catch, clasp, clip, hasp ▷ *v* **2** = **fasten**, clasp, close, hook, secure **3** = **distort**, bend, bulge, cave in, collapse, contort, crumple, fold, twist, warp

bud *n* **1** = **shoot**, embryo, germ, sprout ▷ *v* **2** = **develop**, burgeon, burst forth, grow, shoot, sprout

budge *v* = **move**, dislodge, push, shift, stir

budget *n* **2** = **allowance**, allocation, cost, finances, funds, means, resources ▷ *v* **3** = **plan**, allocate, apportion, cost, estimate, ration

buff¹ *adj* **1** = **yellowish-brown**, sandy, straw, tan, yellowish ▷ *v* **2** = **polish**, brush, burnish, rub, shine, smooth

buff² *n Inf* = **expert**, addict, admirer, aficionado, connoisseur, devotee, enthusiast, fan, fundi (*S Afr*)

buffer¹ *n* = **safeguard**, bulwark, bumper, cushion, fender, intermediary, screen, shield, shock absorber

buffet¹ *n* = **snack bar**, brasserie, café, cafeteria, refreshment counter, sideboard

buffet² *v* = **batter**, beat, bump, knock, pound, pummel, strike, thump, wallop (*inf*)

buffoon *n* = **clown**, comedian, comic, fool, harlequin, jester, joker, wag

bug *n* **2** *Inf* = **illness**, disease, infection, virus **3** = **fault**, defect, error, flaw, glitch, gremlin ▷ *v* **5** = **annoy**, bother, disturb, get on one's nerves (*inf*), hassle (*inf*), irritate, pester, vex **6** = **tap**, eavesdrop, listen in, spy

(someone). **6** conceal a microphone in (a room or phone).

bugbear ❶ n thing that causes obsessive anxiety.

bugger n **1** taboo slang unpleasant or difficult person or thing. ▷ v **2** slang tire. **3** practise buggery with. **buggery** n anal intercourse.

bugle n instrument like a small trumpet. **bugler** n.

build ❶ v **building**, **built** **1** make, construct, or form by joining parts or materials. ▷ n **2** shape of the body. **builder** n **building** n structure with walls and a roof. **building society** organization where money can be borrowed or invested. **build-up** n gradual increase.

bulb n **1** same as LIGHT BULB. **2** onion-shaped root which grows into a flower or plant. **bulbous** adj round and fat.

bulge ❶ n **1** swelling on a normally flat surface. **2** sudden increase in number. ▷ v **3** swell outwards.

bulk ❶ n **1** size or volume, esp. when great. **2** main part. **in bulk** in large quantities. **bulky** adj.

bull n male of some animals, such as cattle, elephants, and whales. **bullock** n castrated bull. **bulldog** n thickset dog with a broad head and a muscular body.

bulldozer n powerful tractor for moving earth. **bulldoze** v **1** demolish or flatten with a bulldozer. **2** informal achieve (something) or persuade (someone) by intimidation, e.g. the new law was bulldozed through parliament. **bullfight** n public show in which a matador kills a bull. **bullfinch** n common European songbird. **bullfrog** n large American frog with a deep croak. **bull's-eye** n central disc of a target. **bull terrier** terrier with a short smooth coat.

bullet ❶ n small piece of metal fired from a gun.

bulletin ❶ n short official report or announcement.

bullion n gold or silver in the form of bars.

bully ❶ n, pl **-lies** **1** person who hurts, persecutes, or intimidates a weaker person. ▷ v **-lying**, **-lied** **2** hurt, intimidate, or persecute (a weaker person).

bulrush n tall stiff reed.

bulwark ❶ n **1** wall used as a fortification. **2** person or thing acting as a defence.

bum n slang buttocks or anus. **bumbag** n small bag attached to a belt and worn round the waist.

bumble v speak, do, or move in a clumsy way. **bumbling** adj, n.

bumblebee n large hairy bee.

bugbear n = **pet hate**, bane, bête noire, bogey, dread, horror, nightmare

build v **1** = **construct**, assemble, erect, fabricate, form, make, put up, raise ▷ n **2** = **physique**, body, figure, form, frame, shape, structure

bulge n **1** = **swelling**, bump, hump, lump, projection, protrusion, protuberance **2** = **increase**, boost, intensification, rise, surge ▷ v **3** = **swell out**, dilate, distend, expand, project, protrude, puff out, stick out

bulk n **1** = **size**, dimensions, immensity, largeness, magnitude, substance, volume, weight **2** = **main part**, better part, body, lion's share, majority, mass, most, nearly all, preponderance

bullet n = **projectile**, ball, missile, pellet, shot, slug

bulletin n = **announcement**, account, communication, communiqué, dispatch, message, news flash, notification, report, statement

bully n **1** = **persecutor**, browbeater, bully boy, coercer, intimidator, oppressor, ruffian, tormentor, tough ▷ v **2** = **persecute**, browbeat, coerce, domineer, hector, intimidate, oppress, push around (sl), terrorize, tyrannize

bulwark n **1** = **fortification**, bastion, buttress, defence, embankment, partition, rampart **2** = **defence**, buffer, guard, mainstay, safeguard, security, support

bumf, bumph n informal official documents or forms.

bump ❶ v 1 knock or strike with a jolt. 2 travel in jerks and jolts. ▷ n 3 dull thud from an impact or collision. 4 raised uneven part. **bumpy** adj **bump off** v informal murder.

bumper n bar on the front and back of a vehicle to protect against damage.

bumpkin ❶ n awkward simple country person.

bumptious ❶ adj offensively self-assertive.

bun n 1 small sweet bread roll or cake. 2 hair gathered into a bun shape at the back of the head.

bunch ❶ n 1 number of things growing, fastened, or grouped together. ▷ v 2 group or be grouped together in a bunch.

bundle ❶ n 1 number of things gathered loosely together. ▷ v 2 cause to go roughly or unceremoniously.

bung n 1 stopper for a cask etc. ▷ v 2 (foll. by up) informal close with a bung. 3 slang throw (something) somewhere in a careless manner.

bungalow n one-storey house.

bungle ❶ v spoil through incompetence. **bungler** n **bungling** adj, n.

bunion n inflamed swelling on the big toe.

bunk n narrow shelflike bed. **bunk bed** one of a pair of beds constructed one above the other.

bunker n 1 sand-filled hollow forming an obstacle on a golf course. 2 underground shelter. 3 large storage container for coal etc.

bunny n, pl -nies child's word for a rabbit.

bunting n decorative flags.

bunya n tall dome-shaped Australian coniferous tree (also **bunya-bunya**).

bunyip n Aust legendary monster said to live in swamps and lakes.

buoy ❶ n 1 floating marker anchored in the sea. ▷ v 2 prevent from sinking. 3 encourage or hearten. **buoyant** adj 1 able to float. 2 cheerful or resilient. **buoyancy** n.

burden ❶ n 1 heavy load. 2 something difficult to cope with. ▷ v 3 put a burden on. 4 oppress. **burdensome** adj.

bureau ❶ n, pl -reaus, -reaux 1 office that provides a service. 2 writing desk with shelves and drawers. **bureaucracy** n administrative system based on complex rules and procedures.

burgeon v develop or grow rapidly.

———————————— THESAURUS ————————————

bump v 1 = **knock**, bang, collide (with), crash, hit, slam, smash into, strike 2 = **jerk**, bounce, jolt, rattle, shake ▷ n 3 = **knock**, bang, blow, collision, crash, impact, jolt, thud, thump 4 = **lump**, bulge, contusion, hump, nodule, protuberance, swelling

bumpkin n = **yokel**, country bumpkin, hick (inf, chiefly US & Canad), hillbilly, peasant, rustic

bumptious adj = **cocky**, arrogant, brash, conceited, forward, full of oneself, overconfident, pushy (inf), self-assertive

bunch n 1 = **number**, assortment, batch, bundle, clump, cluster, collection, heap, lot, mass, pile ▷ v 2 = **group**, assemble, bundle, cluster, collect, huddle, mass, pack

bundle n 1 = **bunch**, assortment, batch, collection, group, heap, mass, pile, stack

▷ v 2 = **push**, hurry, hustle, rush, shove, thrust

bungle v = **mess up**, blow (sl), blunder, botch, foul up, make a mess of, muff, ruin, spoil

buoy n 1 = **marker**, beacon, float, guide, signal ▷ v 3 = **encourage**, boost, cheer, cheer up, hearten, lift, raise, support, sustain

burden n 1 = **load**, encumbrance, weight 2 = **trouble**, affliction, millstone, onus, responsibility, strain, weight, worry ▷ v 3 = **weigh down**, bother, encumber, handicap, load, oppress, saddle with, tax, worry

bureau n 1 = **office**, agency, branch, department, division, service 2 = **desk**, writing desk

b

burglar ⊕ n person who enters a building to commit a crime, esp. theft. **burglary** n **burgle** v.

burgundy adj dark-purplish red.

burlesque ⊕ n artistic work which satirizes a subject by caricature.

burly ⊕ adj -lier, -liest (of a person) broad and strong.

burn ⊕ v **burning**, **burnt** or **burned** 1 be or set on fire. 2 destroy or be destroyed by fire. 3 damage, injure, or mark by heat. 4 feel strong emotion. 5 to record data on (a compact disc). ▷ n 6 injury or mark caused by fire or exposure to heat. **burner** n part of a stove or lamp that produces the flame. **burning** adj 1 intense. 2 urgent or crucial.

burnish ⊕ v make smooth and shiny by rubbing.

burp v, n informal belch.

burrawang n Australian plant with fernlike leaves and an edible nut.

burrow ⊕ n 1 hole dug in the ground by a rabbit etc. ▷ v 2 dig holes in the ground.

bursar n treasurer of a school, college, or university. **bursary** n scholarship.

burst ⊕ v **bursting**, **burst** 1 (cause to) break open or apart noisily and suddenly. 2 come or go suddenly and forcibly. 3 be full to the point of breaking open. ▷ n 4 instance of breaking open suddenly. 5 sudden outbreak or occurrence.

bury ⊕ v **burying**, **buried** 1 place in a grave. 2 place in the earth and cover with soil. 3 conceal or hide.

bus n 1 large motor vehicle for carrying passengers. ▷ v **bussing**, **bussed** 2 travel or transport by bus.

bush ⊕ n 1 dense woody plant, smaller than a tree. 2 wild uncultivated part of a country. **bushy** adj (of hair) thick and shaggy. **bushbaby** n small African tree-living mammal with large eyes.

bushel n obsolete unit of measure equal to 8 gallons.

business ⊕ n 1 purchase and sale of goods and services. 2 commercial establishment. 3 trade or profession. 4 proper concern or responsibility. 5 affair, e.g. *it's a dreadful business.* **businesslike** adj

— THESAURUS —

burglar n = **housebreaker**, cat burglar, filcher, pilferer, robber, sneak thief, thief

burlesque n = **parody**, caricature, mockery, satire, send-up (Brit inf), spoof (inf), takeoff (inf), travesty

burly adj = **brawny**, beefy (inf), bulky, hefty, stocky, stout, sturdy, thickset, well-built

burn v 1 = **be on fire**, be ablaze, blaze, flame, flare, glow, go up in flames, smoke 3 = **set on fire**, char, ignite, incinerate, kindle, light, parch, scorch, sear, singe, toast 4 = **be passionate**, be angry, be aroused, be inflamed, fume, seethe, simmer, smoulder

burnish v = **polish**, brighten, buff, furbish, glaze, rub up, shine, smooth

burrow n 1 = **hole**, den, lair, retreat, shelter, tunnel ▷ v 2 = **dig**, delve, excavate, hollow out, scoop out, tunnel

burst v 1 = **explode**, blow up, break, crack, puncture, rupture, shatter, split, tear apart 2 = **rush**, barge, break, break out, erupt, gush forth, run, spout ▷ n 4 = **explosion**, bang, blast, blowout, break, crack, discharge, rupture, split 5 = **rush**, gush, gust, outbreak, outburst, outpouring, spate, spurt, surge, torrent

bury v 1 = **inter**, consign to the grave, entomb, inhume, lay to rest 2 = **embed**, engulf, submerge 3 = **hide**, conceal, cover, enshroud, secrete, stow away

bush n 1 = **shrub**, hedge, plant, shrubbery, thicket 2 = **the wild**, backwoods, brush, scrub, scrubland, woodland

business n 1 = **trade**, bargaining, commerce, dealings, industry, manufacturing, selling, transaction 2 = **establishment**, company, concern, corporation, enterprise, firm, organization, venture 3 = **profession**, career, employment, function, job, line,

efficient and methodical. **businessman**, **businesswoman** n.

busker n street entertainer. **busk** v act as a busker.

bust¹ ❶ n 1 woman's bosom. 2 sculpture of the head and shoulders.

bust² ❶ informal ▷ v **busting**, **bust** or **busted** 1 burst or break. 2 (of the police) raid (a place) or arrest (someone). ▷ adj 3 broken. **go bust** become bankrupt.

bustard n bird with long strong legs, a heavy body, a long neck, and speckled plumage.

bustle ❶ v 1 hurry with a show of activity or energy. ▷ n 2 energetic and noisy activity. **bustling** adj.

busy ❶ adj **busier**, **busiest** 1 actively employed. 2 crowded or full of activity. ▷ v **busying**, **busied** 3 keep (someone, esp. oneself) busy. **busily** adv **busybody** n meddlesome or nosy person.

but ❶ conj 1 contrary to expectation. 2 in contrast. 3 other than. 4 without it happening. ▷ prep 5 except. ▷ adv 6 only. **but for** were it not for.

butane n gas used for fuel.

butch adj slang markedly or aggressively masculine.

butcher ❶ n 1 person who slaughters animals or sells their meat. 2 brutal murderer. ▷ v 3 kill and prepare (animals) for meat. 4 kill (people) brutally or indiscriminately. **butcherbird** n Australian magpie that impales its prey on thorns. **butchery** n.

butler n chief male servant.

butt¹ ❶ n 1 thicker end of something. 2 unused end of a cigar or cigarette. 3 Chiefly US & Canad slang buttocks.

butt² ❶ n 1 person or thing that is the target of ridicule. 2 mound of earth behind a target. ▷ pl 3 target range.

butt³ ❶ v 1 strike with the head or horns. ▷ n 2 blow with the head or horns. **butt in** v interrupt a conversation.

butter n 1 edible fatty solid made by churning cream. ▷ v 2 put butter on. **buttery** adj **butter up** v flatter.

buttercup n small yellow flower.

butterfly n 1 insect with brightly coloured

——————————————— THESAURUS ———————

occupation, trade, vocation, work, yakka (Aust & NZ inf) 4 = **concern**, affair, assignment, duty, pigeon (inf), problem, responsibility, task

bust¹ n 1 = **bosom**, breast, chest, front, torso

bust² Inf v 1 = **break**, burst, fracture, rupture 2 = **arrest**, catch, fossick (Aust & NZ), raid, search **go bust** = **go bankrupt**, become insolvent, be ruined, fail

bustle v 1 = **hurry**, fuss, hasten, rush, scamper, scurry, scuttle ▷ n 2 = **activity**, ado, commotion, excitement, flurry, fuss, hurly-burly, stir, to-do

busy adj 1 = **occupied**, active, employed, engaged, hard at work, industrious, on duty, rushed off one's feet, working 2 = **lively**, energetic, exacting, full, hectic, hustling ▷ v 3 = **occupy**, absorb, employ, engage, engross, immerse, interest

but conj 1 = **however**, further, moreover, nevertheless, on the contrary, on the other hand, still, yet ▷ prep 5 = **except**, bar, barring, excepting, excluding, notwithstanding, save, with the exception of ▷ adv 6 = **only**, just, merely, simply, singly, solely

butcher n 2 = **murderer**, destroyer, killer, slaughterer, slayer ▷ v 3 = **slaughter**, carve, clean, cut, cut up, dress, joint, prepare 4 = **kill**, assassinate, cut down, destroy, exterminate, liquidate, massacre, put to the sword, slaughter, slay

butt¹ n 1 = **end**, haft, handle, hilt, shaft, shank, stock 2 = **stub**, fag end (inf), leftover, tip

butt² n 1 = **target**, Aunt Sally, dupe, laughing stock, victim

butt³ v 1 = **knock**, bump, poke, prod, push, ram, shove, thrust ▷ n 2 = **knock**, bump, poke, prod, push, ram, shove, thrust

wings. **2** swimming stroke in which both arms move together in a forward circular action.

butterscotch n kind of hard brittle toffee.

buttock n either of the two fleshy masses that form the human rump.

button n **1** small disc or knob sewn to clothing, which can be passed through a slit in another piece of fabric to fasten them. **2** knob that operates a piece of equipment when pressed. ▷ v **3** fasten with buttons. **buttonhole** n **1** slit in a garment through which a button is passed. **2** flower worn on a lapel. ▷ v **3** detain (someone) in conversation.

buttress ❶ n **1** structure to support a wall. ▷ v **2** support with, or as if with, a buttress.

buxom ❶ adj (of a woman) healthily plump and full-bosomed.

buy ❶ v **buying**, **bought 1** acquire by paying money for. **2** slang accept as true. ▷ n **3** thing acquired through payment. **buyer** n **1** customer. **2** person employed to buy merchandise.

buzz n **1** rapidly vibrating humming sound. **2** informal sense of excitement. ▷ v **3** make a humming sound. **4** be filled with an air of excitement. **buzzer** n **buzz word** jargon word which becomes fashionably popular.

buzzard n bird of prey of the hawk family.

by ❶ prep **1** indicating the doer of an action, nearness, movement past, time before or during which, etc. e.g. *bitten by a dog*; *down by the river*; *driving by the school*; *in bed by midnight*. ▷ adv **2** near. **3** past. **by and by** eventually. **by and large** in general.

bye, bye-bye interj informal goodbye.

by-election n election held during parliament to fill a vacant seat.

bygone ❶ adj past or former.

bylaw, bye-law n rule made by a local authority.

bypass ❶ n **1** main road built to avoid a city. **2** operation to divert blood flow away from a damaged part of the heart. ▷ v **3** go round or avoid.

byre n shelter for cows.

byte n Computers group of bits processed as one unit of data.

byway n minor road.

byword ❶ n person or thing regarded as a perfect example of something.

THESAURUS

buttress n **1** = **support**, brace, mainstay, prop, reinforcement, stanchion, strut ▷ v **2** = **support**, back up, bolster, prop up, reinforce, shore up, strengthen, sustain, uphold

buxom adj = **plump**, ample, bosomy, busty, curvaceous, healthy, voluptuous, well-rounded

buy v **1** = **purchase**, acquire, get, invest in, obtain, pay for, procure, shop for ▷ n **3** = **purchase**, acquisition, bargain, deal

by prep **1 a** = **via**, by way of, over

b = **through**, through the agency of

c = **near**, along, beside, close to, next to, past ▷ adv **2** = **near**, at hand, close, handy, in reach

bygone adj = **past**, antiquated, extinct, forgotten, former, lost, of old, olden

bypass v **3** = **go round**, avoid, circumvent, depart from, detour round, deviate from, get round, give a wide berth to, pass round

byword n = **saying**, adage, maxim, motto, precept, proverb, slogan

C 1 *Chem* carbon. 2 Celsius. 3 centigrade. 4 century. 5 the Roman numeral for 100.

c. circa.

CA California.

cab ❶ *n* 1 taxi. 2 enclosed driver's compartment on a train, lorry, etc. **cabbie**, **cabby** *n, pl* **-bies** *informal* taxi driver.

cabal [kab-**bal**] *n* 1 small group of political plotters. 2 secret plot.

cabaret [kab-a-ray] *n* dancing and singing show in a nightclub.

cabbage *n* vegetable with a large head of green leaves.

cabin ❶ *n* 1 compartment in a ship or aircraft. 2 small hut.

cabinet ❶ *n* 1 piece of furniture with drawers or shelves. 2 (**C-**) committee of senior government ministers. **cabinet-maker** *n* person who makes fine furniture.

cable *n* 1 strong thick rope. 2 bundle of wires that carries electricity or electronic signals. 3 telegram sent abroad. ▷ *v* 4 send (someone) a message by cable. **cable car** vehicle pulled up a steep slope by a moving cable. **cable television** television service conveyed by cable to subscribers.

cache [kash] *n* hidden store of weapons or treasure.

cackle *v* 1 laugh shrilly. 2 (of a hen) squawk with shrill broken notes. ▷ *n* 3 cackling noise.

cacophony [kak-**koff**-on-ee] *n* harsh discordant sound. **cacophonous** *adj*.

cactus *n, pl* **-tuses, -ti** fleshy desert plant with spines but no leaves.

cad ❶ *n* old-fashioned dishonourable man. **caddish** *adj*.

cadaver [kad-**dav**-ver] *n* corpse. **cadaverous** *adj* pale, thin, and haggard.

caddie, caddy *n, pl* **-dies** 1 person who carries a golfer's clubs. ▷ *v* **-dying**, **-died** 2 act as a caddie.

caddy *n, pl* **-dies** small container for tea.

cadence [**kade**-enss] *n* 1 rise and fall in the pitch of the voice. 2 close of a musical phrase.

cadenza *n* complex solo passage in a piece of music.

cadet *n* young person training for the armed forces or police.

cadge *v informal* get (something) by taking advantage of someone's generosity.

cadmium *n Chem* bluish-white metallic element used in alloys.

caecum [**seek**-um] *n, pl* **-ca** [-ka] pouch at the beginning of the large intestine.

Caesarean section [see-**zair**-ee-an] *n* surgical incision into the womb to deliver a baby.

caesium *n Chem* silvery-white metallic element used in photocells.

café ❶ *n* 1 small or inexpensive restaurant serving light refreshments. 2 *SAfr* corner shop or grocer. **cafeteria** *n* self-service restaurant.

THESAURUS

cab *n* 1 = **taxi**, hackney carriage, minicab, taxicab

cabal *n* 1 = **clique**, caucus, conclave, faction, league, party, set 2 = **plot**, conspiracy, intrigue, machination, scheme

cabin *n* 1 = **room**, berth, compartment, quarters 2 = **hut**, chalet, cottage, lodge, shack, shanty, shed

cabinet *n* 1 = **cupboard**, case, chiffonier,

closet, commode, dresser, escritoire, locker 2 (usu. cap.) = **council**, administration, assembly, counsellors, ministry

cad *n Old-fashioned* = **scoundrel**, bounder (*old-fashioned Brit sl*), heel (*sl*), rat (*inf*), rotter (*sl, chiefly Brit*)

café *n* = **snack bar**, brasserie, cafeteria, coffee bar, coffee shop, lunchroom, restaurant, tearoom

caffeine n stimulant found in tea and coffee.

caftan n same as KAFTAN.

cage ⊕ n 1 enclosure of bars or wires, for keeping animals or birds. 2 enclosed platform of a lift in a mine.

cagoule n lightweight hooded waterproof jacket.

cairn n mound of stones erected as a memorial or marker.

cajole ⊕ v persuade by flattery.

cake ⊕ n 1 sweet food baked from a mixture of flour, eggs, etc. 2 flat compact mass of something, such as soap. ▷ v 3 form into a hardened mass or crust.

calamine n pink powder consisting chiefly of zinc oxide, used in skin lotions and ointments.

calamity ⊕ n, pl **-ties** disaster. **calamitous** adj

calcium n Chem silvery-white metallic element found in bones, teeth, limestone, and chalk.

calculate ⊕ v 1 solve or find out by a mathematical procedure or by reasoning. 2 aim to have a particular effect. **calculable** adj **calculating** adj selfishly scheming. **calculation** n **calculator** n small electronic device for making calculations.

calendar n 1 chart showing a year divided up into months, weeks, and days. 2 system for determining the beginning, length, and division of years. 3 schedule of events or appointments.

calf¹ n, pl **calves** 1 young cow, bull, elephant, whale, or seal. 2 leather made from calf skin. **calve** v give birth to a calf. **calf love** adolescent infatuation.

calf² n, pl **calves** back of the leg between the ankle and knee.

calibre ⊕ n 1 person's ability or worth. 2 diameter of the bore of a gun or of a shell or bullet. **calibrate** v mark the scale or check the accuracy of (a measuring instrument). **calibration** n.

calico n, pl **-coes** white cotton fabric.

call ⊕ v 1 name. 2 shout to attract attention. 3 telephone. 4 summon. 5 (often foll. by on) visit. 6 arrange (a meeting, strike, etc.). ▷ n 7 cry, shout. 8 animal's or bird's cry. 9 telephone communication. 10 short visit. 11 summons, invitation. 12 need, demand. **caller** n **calling** n vocation, profession. **call box** kiosk for a public telephone. **call for** v require. **call off** v cancel. **call up** v 1 summon to serve in the armed forces. 2 cause one to remember.

calligraphy n (art of) beautiful handwriting.

callous ⊕ adj showing no concern for other

cage n 1 = **enclosure**, pen, pound

cajole v = **persuade**, coax, flatter, seduce, sweet-talk (inf), wheedle

cake n 2 = **block**, bar, cube, loaf, lump, mass, slab ▷ v 3 = **encrust**, bake, coagulate, congeal, solidify

calamity n = **disaster**, cataclysm, catastrophe, misadventure, misfortune, mishap, ruin, tragedy, tribulation

calculate v 1 = **work out**, compute, count, determine, enumerate, estimate, figure, reckon 2 = **plan**, aim, design, intend

calibre n 1 = **worth**, ability, capacity, distinction, merit, quality, stature, talent 2 = **diameter**, bore, gauge, measure

call v 1 = **name**, christen, describe as, designate, dub, entitle, label, style, term 2 = **cry**, arouse, hail, rouse, shout, yell 3 = **phone**, ring up (inf, chiefly Brit), telephone 4 = **summon**, assemble, convene, gather, muster, rally 5 (often foll. by on) = **visit**, drop in on, look in on, look up, see ▷ n 7 = **cry**, hail, scream, shout, signal, whoop, yell 11 = **summons**, appeal, command, demand, invitation, notice, order, plea, request 12 = **need**, cause, excuse, grounds, justification, occasion, reason

callous adj = **heartless**, cold, hard-bitten, hardened, hardhearted, insensitive,

people's feelings; insensitive.
callow ❶ *adj* young and inexperienced.
callus *n, pl* **-luses** area of thick hardened skin.

c

calm ❶ *adj* **1** not agitated or excited. **2** not ruffled by the wind. **3** windless. ▷ *n* **4** peaceful state. ▷ *v* **5** (often foll. by *down*) make or become calm. **calmly** *adv* **calmness** *n*.
calorie *n* unit of measurement for the energy value of food. **2** unit of heat. **calorific** *adj* of calories or heat.
calypso *n, pl* **-sos** West Indian song with improvised topical lyrics.
cam *n* device that converts a circular motion to a to-and-fro motion. **camshaft** *n* part of an engine consisting of a rod to which cams are fixed.
camaraderie *n* comradeship.
camber *n* slight upward curve to the centre of a surface.
cambric *n* fine white linen fabric.
camcorder *n* combined portable video camera and recorder.
camel *n* humped mammal that can survive long periods without food or water in desert regions.
camellia [kam-**meal**-ya] *n* evergreen ornamental shrub with white, pink, or red flowers.
cameo *n, pl* **cameos** brooch or ring with a profile head carved in relief. **2** small part in a film or play performed by a well-known actor or actress.

camera *n* apparatus used for taking photographs or pictures for television or cinema. **in camera** in private session.
camisole *n* woman's bodice-like garment.
camouflage ❶ [**kam**-moo-flahzh] *n* **1** use of natural surroundings or artificial aids to conceal or disguise something. ▷ *v* **2** conceal by camouflage.
camp¹ ❶ *n* **1** (place for) temporary lodgings consisting of tents, huts, or cabins. **2** group supporting a particular doctrine. ▷ *v* **3** stay in a camp. **camper** *n*.
camp² ❶ *adj informal* **1** effeminate or homosexual. **2** consciously artificial or affected.
campaign ❶ *n* **1** series of coordinated activities designed to achieve a goal. ▷ *v* **2** take part in a campaign.
camphor *n* aromatic crystalline substance used medicinally and in mothballs.
campus *n, pl* **-puses** grounds of a university or college.
can¹ *v, past* **could 1** be able to. **2** be allowed to.
can² *n* **1** metal container for food or liquids. ▷ *v* **canning**, **canned 2** put (something) into a can. **canned** *adj* **1** preserved in a can. **2** (of music) prerecorded. **cannery** *n, pl* factory where food is canned.
Canada Day *n* July 1, the anniversary of the day when Canada became the first British colony to receive dominion status.
Canada goose *n* large greyish-brown N American goose with a black neck and

—————————————————————— THESAURUS ————

uncaring, unfeeling, unsympathetic
callow *adj* = **inexperienced**, green, guileless, immature, naive, raw, unsophisticated
calm *adj* **1** = **cool**, collected, composed, dispassionate, relaxed, sedate, self-possessed, unemotional **2, 3** = **still**, balmy, mild, quiet, serene, smooth, tranquil, windless ▷ *n* **4** = **peacefulness**, hush, peace, quiet, repose, serenity, stillness ▷ *v* **5** (often foll. by *down*) = **quieten**, hush, mollify, outspan (*SAfr*), placate, relax, soothe

camouflage *n* **1** = **disguise**, blind, cloak, concealment, cover, mask, masquerade, screen, subterfuge ▷ *v* **2** = **disguise**, cloak, conceal, cover, hide, mask, obfuscate, obscure, screen, veil
camp¹ *n* **1** = **camp site**, bivouac, camping ground, encampment, tents
camp² *adj Inf* **1** = **effeminate 2** = **affected**, artificial, mannered, ostentatious, posturing
campaign *n* **1** = **operation**, crusade, drive, movement, push

head and a white throat patch.

Canada jay *n* a large common jay of North America with a grey body, and a white-and-black crestless head.

canal ❶ *n* **1** artificial waterway. **2** passage in the body.

canary *n, pl* **-ries** small yellow songbird often kept as a pet.

canasta *n* card game like rummy, played with two packs.

cancan *n* lively high-kicking dance performed by a female group.

cancel ❶ *v* **-celling, -celled 1** stop (something that has been arranged) from taking place. **2** mark (a cheque or stamp) with an official stamp to prevent further use. **cancellation** *n* **cancel out** *v* counterbalance, neutralize.

cancer ❶ *n* **1** serious disease resulting from a malignant growth or tumour. **2** malignant growth or tumour. **cancerous** *adj*.

candid ❶ *adj* honest and straightforward.

candidate ❶ *n* **1** person seeking a job or position. **2** person taking an examination. **candidacy, candidature** *n*.

candle *n* stick of wax enclosing a wick, which is burned to produce light. **candlestick** *n* holder for a candle.

candy *n, pl* **-dies** *US* a sweet or sweets. **candied** *adj* coated with sugar. **candyfloss** *n* light fluffy mass of spun sugar on a stick. **candy-striped** *adj* having coloured stripes on a white background.

cane *n* **1** stem of the bamboo or similar plant. **2** flexible rod used to beat someone. **3** slender walking stick. ▷ *v* **4** beat with a cane. **cane toad** large toad used to control insects and other pests of sugar-cane plantations.

canine *adj* **1** of or like a dog. ▷ *n* **2** sharp pointed tooth between the incisors and the molars.

canister *n* metal container.

canker ❶ *n* **1** ulceration, ulcerous disease. **2** something evil that spreads and corrupts.

cannabis *n* **1** Asian plant with tough fibres. **2** drug obtained from the dried leaves and flowers of this plant, which can be smoked or chewed.

cannelloni *pl n* tubular pieces of pasta filled with meat etc.

cannibal *n* **1** person who eats human flesh. **2** animal that eats others of its own kind. **cannibalism** *n* **cannibalize** *v* use parts from (one machine) to repair another.

cannon ❶ *n* **1** large gun on wheels. **2** billiard stroke in which the cue ball hits two balls successively. **cannonade** *n* continuous heavy gunfire. **cannonball** *n* heavy metal ball fired from a cannon.

cannot can not.

canny ❶ *adj* **-nier, -niest** shrewd, cautious. **cannily** *adv*.

canoe *n* light narrow open boat propelled by a paddle or paddles. **canoeing** *n* sport of rowing in a canoe. **canoeist** *n*.

canon ❶ *n* **1** Church decree regulating morals or religious practices. **2** general

---

canal *n* **1** = **waterway**, channel, conduit, duct, passage, watercourse

cancel *v* **1** = **call off**, abolish, abort, annul, delete, do away with, eliminate, erase, expunge, obliterate, repeal, revoke

cancer *n* **1** = **sickness**, pestilence **2** = **growth**, malignancy, tumour

candid *adj* = **honest**, blunt, forthright, frank, open, outspoken, plain, straightforward, truthful

candidate *n* **1** = **contender**, applicant, claimant, competitor, contestant, entrant, nominee, runner

canker *n* **1** = **disease**, cancer, infection, rot, sore, ulcer **2** = **corruption**, blight, rot, scourge

cannon *n* **1** = **gun**, big gun, field gun, mortar

canny *adj* = **shrewd**, astute, careful, cautious, clever, judicious, prudent, wise

canon *n* **2** = **rule**, criterion, dictate, formula, precept, principle, regulation,

rule or standard. **3** list of the works of an author that are accepted as authentic. **4** piece of music in which the same melody is taken up in different parts. **canonical** *adj* **canonize** *v* declare (a person) officially to be a saint. **canonization** *n*.

canopy ⊙ *n*, *pl* **-pies 1** covering above a bed, door, etc. **2** any large or wide covering.

cant ⊙ *n* **1** insincere talk. **2** specialized vocabulary of a particular group. ▷ *v* **3** use cant.

cantankerous ⊙ *adj* quarrelsome, bad-tempered.

cantata *n* musical work consisting of arias, duets, and choruses.

canteen *n* **1** restaurant attached to a workplace or school. **2** box containing a set of cutlery.

canter ⊙ *n* **1** horse's gait between a trot and a gallop. ▷ *v* **2** move at a canter.

cantilever *n* beam or girder fixed at one end only.

Canuck *n*, *adj informal* Canadian.

canvas *n* **1** heavy coarse cloth used for sails and tents, and for oil painting. **2** an oil painting on canvas.

canvass ⊙ *v* **1** try to get votes or support (from). **2** find out the opinions of (people) by conducting a survey. ▷ *n* **3** canvassing.

canyon *n* deep narrow valley.

cap ⊙ *n* **1** soft close-fitting covering for the head. **2** small lid. **3** small explosive device used in a toy gun. ▷ *v* **capping**, **capped 4** cover or top with something. **5** select (a player) for a national team. **6** impose an upper limit on (a tax). **7** outdo, excel.

capable ⊙ *adj* **1** (foll. by *of*) having the ability (for). **2** competent and efficient. **capably** *adv* **capability** *n*, *pl* **-ties.**

capacity ⊙ *n*, *pl* **-ties 1** ability to contain, absorb, or hold. **2** maximum amount that can be contained or produced. **3** physical or mental ability. **4** position, function. **capacious** *adj* roomy. **capacitor** *n* device for storing electrical charge.

cape¹ *n* short cloak.

cape² ⊙ *n* large piece of land that juts out into the sea.

caper ⊙ *n* **1** high-spirited prank. ▷ *v* **2** skip about.

capillary *n*, *pl* **-laries** very fine blood vessel.

capital ⊙ *n* **1** chief city of a country. **2** accumulated wealth. **3** wealth used

——————————————————— THESAURUS ————————

standard, statute, yardstick **3** = **list**, catalogue, roll

canopy *n* **1** = **awning**, covering, shade, sunshade

cant *n* **1** = **hypocrisy**, humbug, insincerity, lip service, pretence, pretentiousness, sanctimoniousness **2** = **jargon**, argot, lingo, patter, slang, vernacular

cantankerous *adj* = **bad-tempered**, choleric, contrary, disagreeable, grumpy, irascible, irritable, testy, waspish

canter *n* **1** = **jog**, amble, dogtrot, lope ▷ *v* **2** = **jog**, amble, lope

canvass *v* **1** = **campaign**, electioneer, solicit, solicit votes **2** = **poll**, examine, inspect, investigate, scrutinize, study ▷ *n* **3** = **poll**, examination, investigation, scrutiny, survey, tally

cap *v* **7** = **beat**, better, crown, eclipse,

exceed, outdo, outstrip, surpass, top, transcend

capable *adj* **1** = **able**, accomplished, gifted, qualified, talented **2** = **competent**, efficient, proficient

capacity *n* **1** = **size**, amplitude, compass, dimensions, extent, magnitude, range, room, scope, space, volume **3** = **ability**, aptitude, aptness, capability, competence, facility, genius, gift **4** = **function**, office, position, post, province, role, sphere

cape² *n* = **headland**, head, peninsula, point, promontory

caper *n* **1** = **escapade**, antic, high jinks, jape, lark (*inf*), mischief, practical joke, prank, stunt ▷ *v* **2** = **dance**, bound, cavort, frolic, gambol, jump, skip, spring, trip

capital *n* **2** = **money**, assets, cash, finances, funds, investment(s), lolly (*Aust*

to produce more wealth. **4** large letter, as used at the beginning of a name or sentence. ▷ *adj* **5** involving or punishable by death. **6** *old-fashioned* excellent.
capitalize *v* **1** write or print (words) in capitals. **2** convert into or provide with capital. **capitalize on** take advantage of (a situation). **capital gain** profit from the sale of an asset. **capitalism** *n* economic system based on the private ownership of industry.
capitulate ❶ *v* surrender on agreed terms.
capon *n* castrated cock fowl fattened for eating.
cappuccino [kap-poo-**cheen**-oh] *n*, *pl* **-nos** coffee with steamed milk, sprinkled with powdered chocolate.
caprice ❶ [kap-**reess**] *n* sudden change of attitude. **capricious** *adj* tending to have sudden changes of attitude.
capsize ❶ *v* overturn accidentally.
capstan *n* rotating cylinder round which a ship's rope is wound.
capsule ❶ *n* **1** soluble gelatine case containing a dose of medicine. **2** plant's seed case. **3** detachable crew compartment of a spacecraft.
captain ❶ *n* **1** commander of a ship or civil aircraft. **2** middle-ranking naval officer. **3** junior officer in the army. **4** leader of a team or group. ▷ *v* **5** be captain of. **captaincy** *n*.

caption *n* **1** title or explanation accompanying an illustration. ▷ *v* **2** provide with a caption.
captive ❶ *n* **1** person kept in confinement. ▷ *adj* **2** kept in confinement. **3** (of an audience) unable to leave. **captivity** *n*.
capture ❶ *v* **1** take by force. **2** succeed in representing (something elusive) artistically. ▷ *n* **3** capturing.
car ❶ *n* **1** motor vehicle designed to carry a small number of people. **2** passenger compartment of a cable car, lift, etc. **3** *US* railway carriage. **car park** area or building reserved for parking cars.
carafe [kar-**raff**] *n* glass bottle for serving water or wine.
caramel *n* **1** chewy sweet made from sugar and milk. **2** burnt sugar, used for colouring and flavouring food. **caramelize** *v* turn into caramel.
carat *n* **1** unit of weight of precious stones. **2** measure of the purity of gold in an alloy.
caravan *n* **1** large enclosed vehicle for living in, designed to be towed by a car or horse. **2** group travelling together in Eastern countries.
caraway *n* plant whose seeds are used as a spice.
carb *n* *informal* short for CARBOHYDRATE.
carbohydrate *n* any of a large group of energy-producing compounds in food, such as sugars and starches.

THESAURUS

& NZ sl), means, principal, resources, wealth, wherewithal ▷ *adj* **6** Old-fashioned = **first-rate**, excellent, fine, splendid, sterling, superb
capitulate *v* = **give in**, cave in (*inf*), come to terms, give up, relent, submit, succumb, surrender, yield
caprice *n* = **whim**, fad, fancy, fickleness, impulse, inconstancy, notion, whimsy
capsize *v* = **overturn**, invert, keel over, tip over, turn over, turn turtle, upset
capsule *n* **1** = **pill**, lozenge, tablet **2** = **pod**, case, receptacle, seed case, sheath, shell, vessel

captain *n* = **leader**, boss, chief, commander, head, master, skipper
captive *n* **1** = **prisoner**, convict, detainee, hostage, internee, prisoner of war, slave ▷ *adj* **2** = **confined**, caged, enslaved, ensnared, imprisoned, incarcerated, locked up, penned, restricted, subjugated
capture *v* **1** = **catch**, apprehend, arrest, bag, collar (*inf*), secure, seize, take, take prisoner ▷ *n* **3** = **catching**, apprehension, arrest, imprisonment, seizure, taking, taking captive, trapping
car *n* **1** = **vehicle**, auto (*US*), automobile, jalopy (*inf*), machine, motor, motorcar,

carbon n nonmetallic element occurring as charcoal, graphite, and diamond, found in all organic matter. **carbonate** n salt or ester of carbonic acid. **carbonated** adj (of a drink) containing carbon dioxide. **carbonize** v 1 turn into carbon as a result of heating. 2 coat with carbon. **carbon copy** 1 copy made with carbon paper. 2 very similar person or thing. **carbon dioxide** colourless gas exhaled by people and animals. **carbon footprint** measure of the carbon dioxide produced by an individual or organization. **carbon paper** paper coated on one side with a dark waxy pigment, used to make a copy of something as it is typed or written.

carbuncle n inflamed boil.

carburettor n device which mixes petrol and air in an internal-combustion engine.

carcass, carcase ❶ n dead body of an animal.

card n 1 piece of thick stiff paper or cardboard used for identification, reference, or sending greetings or messages. 2 one of a set of cards with a printed pattern, used for playing games. 3 small rectangle of stiff plastic with identifying numbers for use as a credit card, cheque card, or charge card. 4 old-fashioned witty or eccentric person. ▷ pl 5 any card game, or card games in general. **cardboard** n thin stiff board made from

paper pulp. **cardsharp** n professional card player who cheats.

cardiac adj of the heart. **cardiograph** n electrocardiograph. **cardiology** n study of the heart and its diseases. **cardiologist** n **cardiovascular** adj of the heart and the blood vessels.

cardigan n knitted jacket.

cardinal ❶ n 1 any of the high-ranking clergymen of the RC Church who elect the Pope and act as his counsellors. ▷ adj 2 fundamentally important. **cardinal number** number denoting quantity but not order in a group, for example four as distinct from fourth. **cardinal points** the four main points of the compass.

care ❶ v 1 be concerned. 2 like (to do something). 3 (foll. by for) like, be fond of. 4 (foll. by for) look after. ▷ n 5 careful attention, caution. 6 protection, charge. 7 trouble, worry. **carefree** adj **careful** adj **carefully** adv **carefulness** n **careless** adj **carelessly** adv **carelessness** n.

career ❶ n 1 series of jobs in a profession or occupation that a person has through their life. 2 part of a person's life spent in a particular occupation. ▷ v 3 rush in an uncontrolled way.

caress ❶ n 1 gentle affectionate touch or embrace. ▷ v 2 touch gently and affectionately.

caret [**kar**-rett] n symbol (^) indicating a

——————————————— THESAURUS ———————————————

wheels (inf) 3 US = **(railway) carriage**, buffet car, cable car, coach, dining car, sleeping car, van

carcass n = **body**, cadaver (Med), corpse, dead body, framework, hulk, remains, shell, skeleton

cardinal adj 2 = **principal**, capital, central, chief, essential, first, fundamental, key, leading, main, paramount, primary

care v 1 = **be concerned**, be bothered, be interested, mind 4 (foll. by for) = **look after**, attend, foster, mind, minister to, nurse, protect, provide for, tend, watch over ▷ n 5 = **caution**, attention, carefulness, consideration, forethought,

heed, management, pains, prudence, vigilance, watchfulness 6 = **protection**, charge, control, custody, guardianship, keeping, management, supervision 7 = **worry**, anxiety, concern, disquiet, perplexity, pressure, responsibility, stress, trouble

career n 1 = **occupation**, calling, employment, life's work, livelihood, pursuit, vocation ▷ v 3 = **rush**, barrel (along) (inf, chiefly US & Canad), bolt, dash, hurtle, race, speed, tear

caress n 1 = **stroke**, cuddle, embrace, fondling, hug, kiss, pat ▷ v 2 = **stroke**, cuddle, embrace, fondle, hug, kiss, neck

place in written or printed matter where something is to be inserted.

cargo ❶ *n, pl* **-goes** goods carried by a ship, aircraft, etc. **cargo pants**, **trousers** *pl n* loose trousers with a large pocket on each leg.

caribou *n, pl* **-bou** or **-bous** large N American reindeer.

caricature ❶ *n* **1** drawing or description of a person that exaggerates features for comic effect. ▷ *v* **2** make a caricature of.

cark *v Aust & NZ slang* die.

carnage ❶ *n* extensive slaughter of people.

carnal ❶ *adj* of a sexual or sensual nature. **carnal knowledge** sexual intercourse.

carnation *n* cultivated plant with fragrant white, pink, or red flowers.

carnival ❶ *n* festive period with processions, music, and dancing in the street.

carol ❶ *n* joyful Christmas hymn.

carouse *v* have a merry drinking party. **carousal** *n* merry drinking party.

carousel [kar-roo-**sell**] *n* **1** revolving conveyor belt for luggage or photographic slides. **2** US merry-go-round.

carp¹ *n* large freshwater fish.

carp² ❶ *v* complain, find fault.

carpenter ❶ *n* person who makes or repairs wooden structures. **carpentry** *n*.

carpet *n* **1** heavy fabric for covering floors. ▷ *v* **carpeting**, **carpeted 2** cover with a carpet. **on the carpet** *informal* being reprimanded. **carpet snake** or **python** large nonvenomous Australian snake with a carpet-like pattern on its back.

carriage ❶ *n* **1** one of the sections of a train for passengers. **2** way a person holds his or her head and body. **3** four-wheeled horse-drawn vehicle. **4** moving part of a machine that supports and shifts another part. **5** charge made for conveying goods. **carriageway** *n* part of a road along which traffic passes in one direction.

carrion *n* dead and rotting flesh.

carrot *n* **1** long tapering orange root vegetable. **2** something offered as an incentive.

carry ❶ *v* **-rying**, **-ried 1** take from one place to another. **2** have with one habitually, in one's pocket etc. **3** transmit (a disease). **4** have as a factor or result. **5** hold (one's head or body) in a specified manner. **6** secure the adoption of (a bill or motion). **7** (of sound) travel a certain distance. **carry on** *v* **1** continue. **2** *informal* cause a fuss. **carry out** *v* follow, accomplish.

cart *n* **1** open two-wheeled horse-drawn vehicle for carrying goods or passengers. ▷ *v* **2** carry, usu. with some effort.

(*inf*), nuzzle, pet, touch

cargo *n* = **load**, baggage, consignment, contents, freight, goods, merchandise, shipment

caricature *n* **1** = **parody**, burlesque, cartoon, distortion, farce, lampoon, satire, send-up (*Brit inf*), takeoff (*inf*), travesty ▷ *v* **2** = **parody**, burlesque, distort, lampoon, mimic, mock, ridicule, satirize, send up (*Brit inf*), take off (*inf*)

carnage *n* = **slaughter**, blood bath, bloodshed, butchery, havoc, holocaust, massacre, mass murder, murder, shambles

carnal *adj* = **sexual**, erotic, fleshly, lascivious, lewd, libidinous, lustful, sensual

carnival *n* = **festival**, celebration, fair, fete, fiesta, gala, holiday, jamboree, jubilee, merrymaking, revelry

carol *n* = **song**, chorus, ditty, hymn, lay

carp² *v* = **find fault**, cavil, complain, criticize, pick holes, quibble, reproach

carpenter *n* = **joiner**, cabinet-maker, woodworker

carriage *n* **1** = **vehicle**, cab, coach, conveyance **2** = **bearing**, air, behaviour, comportment, conduct, demeanour, deportment, gait, manner, posture

carry *v* **1** = **transport**, bear, bring, conduct, convey, fetch, haul, lug, move, relay, take,

carthorse *n* large heavily built horse.

cartwheel *n* sideways somersault supported by the hands with legs outstretched.

carte blanche *n French* complete authority.

cartel *n* association of competing firms formed to fix prices.

cartilage *n* strong flexible tissue forming part of the skeleton. **cartilaginous** *adj*

cartography *n* map making. **cartographic** *adj*.

carton ❶ *n* container made of cardboard or waxed paper.

cartoon ❶ *n* **1** humorous or satirical drawing. **2** sequence of these telling a story. **3** film made by photographing a series of drawings which give the illusion of movement when projected. **cartoonist** *n*.

cartridge ❶ *n* **1** casing containing an explosive charge and bullet for a gun. **2** part of the pick-up of a record player that converts the movements of the stylus into electrical signals. **3** sealed container of film, tape, etc. **cartridge paper** strong thick drawing paper.

carve ❶ *v* **1** cut to form an object. **2** form (an object or design) by cutting. **3** slice (cooked meat). **carving** *n*.

cascade ❶ *n* **1** waterfall. **2** something flowing or falling like a waterfall. ▷ *v* **3** flow or fall in a cascade.

case¹ ❶ *n* **1** instance, example. **2** matter for discussion. **3** condition, state of affairs. **4** set of arguments supporting an action or cause. **5** person or problem dealt with by a doctor, social worker, or solicitor. **6** action, lawsuit. **7** *Grammar* form of a noun, pronoun, or adjective showing its relation to other words in the sentence. **in case** so as to allow for the possibility that.

case² ❶ *n* **1** container, protective covering. ▷ *v* **2** *slang* inspect (a building) with the intention of burgling it. **case-hardened** *adj* having been made callous by experience.

cash ❶ *n* **1** banknotes and coins. ▷ *v* **2** obtain cash for. **cash in on** *v informal* gain profit or advantage from. **cash register** till that displays and adds the prices of the goods sold.

cashier¹ ❶ *n* person responsible for handling cash in a bank, shop, etc.

cashier² ❶ *v* dismiss with dishonour from the armed forces.

cashmere *n* fine soft wool obtained from goats.

━━━━━━━━━━━━━━━━━━━━━━━━━━ THESAURUS ━━━━━━

transfer **6** = **win**, accomplish, capture, effect, gain, secure

carton *n* = **box**, case, container, pack, package, packet

cartoon *n* **1** = **drawing**, caricature, lampoon, parody, satire, sketch **2** = **comic strip 3** = **animation**, animated cartoon, animated film

cartridge *n* **1** = **shell**, charge, round **3** = **container**, capsule, case, cassette, cylinder, magazine

carve *v* **1, 2** = **cut**, chip, chisel, engrave, etch, hew, mould, sculpt, whittle **3** = **slice**

cascade *n* **1** = **waterfall**, avalanche, cataract, deluge, downpour, falls, flood, fountain, outpouring, shower, torrent ▷ *v* **3** = **flow**, descend, fall, flood, gush, overflow, pitch, plunge, pour, spill, surge, teem, tumble

case¹ *n* **1** = **instance**, example, illustration, occasion, occurrence, specimen **3** = **situation**, circumstance(s), condition, context, contingency, event, position, state **6** = **lawsuit**, action, dispute, proceedings, suit, trial

case² *n* **1** = **container**, box, canister, capsule, carton, casing, chest, covering, crate, envelope, holder, jacket, receptacle, sheath, shell, wrapper

cash *n* **1** = **money**, brass (*N Eng dial*), coinage, currency, dough (*sl*), funds, lolly (*Aust & NZ sl*), notes, ready money, silver

cashier¹ *n* = **teller**, bank clerk, banker, bursar, clerk, purser, treasurer

cashier² *v* = **dismiss**, discard, discharge, drum out, expel, give the boot to (*sl*)

casino n, pl **-nos** public building or room where gambling games are played.

cask n barrel used to hold alcoholic drink.

casket ❶ n 1 small box for valuables. 2 US coffin.

casserole n 1 covered dish in which food is cooked slowly, usu. in an oven. 2 dish cooked in this way. ▷ v 3 cook in a casserole.

cassette n plastic case containing a reel of film or magnetic tape.

cassock n long tunic, usu. black, worn by priests.

cast ❶ n 1 actors in a play or film collectively. 2 object shaped by a mould while molten. 3 mould used to shape such an object. 4 rigid plaster-of-Paris casing for immobilizing broken bones while they heal. 5 sort, kind. 6 slight squint in the eye. ▷ v **casting**, **cast** 7 select (an actor) to play a part in a play or film. 8 give (a vote). 9 let fall, shed. 10 shape (molten material) in a mould. 11 throw with force. 12 direct (a glance). **castaway** n shipwrecked person. **casting vote** deciding vote used by the chairman of a meeting when the votes on each side are equal. **cast-iron** adj 1 made of a hard but brittle type of iron. 2 definite, unchallengeable. **cast-off** adj, n discarded (person or thing).

castanets pl n musical instrument, used by Spanish dancers, consisting of curved pieces of hollow wood clicked together in the hand.

caste ❶ n 1 any of the hereditary classes into which Hindu society is divided. 2 social rank.

caster sugar n finely ground white sugar.

castigate ❶ v reprimand severely.

castle ❶ n 1 large fortified building, often built as a ruler's residence. 2 rook in chess.

castor n small swivelling wheel fixed to the bottom of a piece of furniture for easy moving.

castor oil n oil obtained from an Indian plant, used as a lubricant and purgative.

castrate ❶ v 1 remove the testicles of. 2 deprive of vigour or masculinity. **castration** n.

casual ❶ adj 1 careless, nonchalant. 2 (of work or workers) occasional. 3 for informal wear. 4 happening by chance. **casually** adv **casualty** n person killed or injured in an accident or war.

cat ❶ n 1 small domesticated furry mammal. 2 related wild mammal, such as the lion or tiger. **catty** adj informal spiteful. **catkin** n drooping flower spike of certain trees. **catcall** n derisive whistle or cry. **catfish** n fish with whisker-like barbels round the mouth. **catgut** n strong cord used to string musical instruments and sports rackets. **catnap** n, v doze. **Catseyes** pl n ® glass reflectors set in the road to

casket n 1 = **box**, case, chest, coffer, jewel box

cast n 1 = **actors**, characters, company, dramatis personae, players, troupe 5 = **type**, complexion, manner, stamp, style ▷ v 7, 8 = **choose**, allot, appoint, assign, name, pick, select 9 = **give out**, deposit, diffuse, distribute, emit, radiate, scatter, shed, spread 10 = **form**, found, model, mould, set, shape 11 = **throw**, fling, hurl, launch, pitch, sling, thrust, toss

caste n 2 = **class**, estate, grade, order, rank, social order, status, stratum

castigate v = **reprimand**, berate, censure, chastise, criticize, lambast(e), rebuke, rouse on (Aust), scold

castle n 1 = **fortress**, chateau, citadel, keep, palace, stronghold, tower

castrate v 1 = **neuter**, emasculate, geld

casual adj 1 = **careless**, blasé, cursory, lackadaisical, nonchalant, offhand, relaxed, unconcerned 2 = **occasional**, irregular 3 = **informal**, non-dressy, sporty 4 = **chance**, accidental, incidental, random, unexpected

cat n 1 = **feline**, kitty (inf), moggy (sl), puss (inf), pussy (inf), tabby

indicate traffic lanes. **cat's paw** person used by another to do unpleasant things for him or her. **catwalk** n narrow pathway or platform.

cataclysm [kat-a-kliz-zum] n 1 violent upheaval. 2 disaster, such as an earthquake. **cataclysmic** adj.

catalogue ❶ n 1 book containing details of items for sale. 2 systematic list of items. ▷ v 3 make a systematic list of.

catalyst n substance that speeds up a chemical reaction without itself changing. **catalyse** v speed up (a chemical reaction) by a catalyst. **catalytic** adj.

catamaran n boat with twin parallel hulls.

catapult ❶ n 1 Y-shaped device with a loop of elastic, used by children for firing stones. ▷ v 2 shoot forwards or upwards violently.

cataract n 1 eye disease in which the lens becomes opaque. 2 opaque area of an eye. 3 large waterfall.

catarrh [kat-**tar**] n excessive mucus in the nose and throat, during or following a cold. **catarrhal** adj.

catastrophe ❶ [kat-**ass**-trof-fee] n great and sudden disaster. **catastrophic** adj.

catch ❶ v catching, caught 1 seize, capture. 2 surprise in an act, e.g. *two boys were caught stealing.* 3 hit unexpectedly. 4 be in time for (a bus, train, etc.). 5 see or hear. 6 be infected with (an illness). 7 entangle. 8 understand, make out.

9 start burning. ▷ n 10 device for fastening a door, window, etc. 11 total number of fish caught. 12 *informal* concealed or unforeseen drawback. 13 *informal* person considered worth having as a husband or wife. **catch it** *informal* be punished. **catching** adj infectious. **catchy** adj (of a tune) pleasant and easily remembered. **catchment area** area served by a particular school or hospital. **catch on** v *informal* 1 become popular. 2 understand. **catch out** v *informal* trap (someone) in an error or lie. **catch phrase** well-known phrase associated with a particular entertainer. **catch 22** inescapable dilemma. **catchword** n well-known and frequently used phrase.

catechism [**kat**-ti-kiz-zum] n instruction on the doctrine of a Christian Church in a series of questions and answers. **catechize** v 1 instruct by using a catechism. 2 question (someone) thoroughly.

category ❶ n, pl -ries class, group. **categorical** adj absolutely clear and certain. **categorically** adv **categorize** v put in a category. **categorization** n.

cater ❶ v provide what is needed or wanted, esp. food or services. **caterer** n.

caterpillar n 1 wormlike larva of a moth or butterfly. 2 ® endless track, driven by cogged wheels, used to propel a heavy vehicle.

THESAURUS

catalogue n 1 = **directory**, gazetteer 2 = **list**, index, inventory, record, register, roll ▷ v 3 = **list**, alphabetize, classify, inventory, tabulate

catapult n 1 = **sling**, slingshot (US) ▷ v 2 = **shoot**, heave, hurl, pitch, plunge, propel

catastrophe n = **disaster**, adversity, calamity, cataclysm, fiasco, misfortune, tragedy, trouble

catch v 1 = **seize**, apprehend, arrest, capture, clutch, ensnare, entrap, get, grab, grasp, grip, lay hold of, snare, snatch, take, trap 2 = **discover**, catch in the act, detect,

expose, find out, surprise, take unawares, unmask 6 = **contract**, develop, get, go down with, incur, succumb to, suffer from 8 = **make out**, comprehend, discern, get, grasp, hear, perceive, recognize, sense, take in ▷ n 10 = **fastener**, bolt, clasp, clip, latch 12 *Inf* = **drawback**, disadvantage, fly in the ointment, hitch, snag, stumbling block, trap, trick

category n = **class**, classification, department, division, grade, grouping, heading, section, sort, type

cater v = **provide**, furnish, outfit, purvey, supply

catharsis [kath-**thar**-siss] n, pl -**ses** relief of strong suppressed emotions. **cathartic** adj.

cathedral n principal church of a diocese.

Catherine wheel n rotating firework.

catholic adj **1** (of tastes or interests) covering a wide range. ▷ n, adj **2** (**C-**) (member) of the Roman Catholic Church. **Catholicism** n.

cattle pl n domesticated cows and bulls.

cauldron n large pot used for boiling.

cauliflower n vegetable with a large head of white flower buds surrounded by green leaves.

cause ❶ n **1** something that produces a particular effect. **2** (foll. by for) reason, motive. **3** aim or principle supported by a person or group. ▷ v **4** be the cause of.

causeway n raised path or road across water or marshland.

caustic ❶ adj **1** capable of burning by chemical action. **2** bitter and sarcastic.

cauterize v burn (a wound) with heat or a caustic agent to prevent infection.

caution ❶ n **1** care, esp. in the face of danger. **2** warning. ▷ v **3** warn, advise. **cautionary** adj warning. **cautious** adj showing or having caution.

cavalcade ❶ n procession of people on horseback or in cars.

cavalier ❶ adj showing haughty disregard.

cavalry ❶ n, pl -**ries** part of the army orig. on horseback, but now often using fast armoured vehicles.

cave ❶ n hollow in the side of a hill or cliff. **caving** n sport of exploring caves. **cave in** v **1** collapse inwards. **2** informal yield under pressure. **caveman** n prehistoric cave dweller.

caviar, caviare n salted sturgeon roe, regarded as a delicacy.

cavil v -**illing, -illed 1** make petty objections. ▷ n **2** petty objection.

cavort v skip about.

CBE Commander of the Order of the British Empire.

cc cubic centimetre.

CD compact disc.

cease ❶ v bring or come to an end. **ceaseless** adj **ceasefire** n temporary truce.

cedar n **1** evergreen coniferous tree. **2** its wood.

cede ❶ v surrender (territory or legal rights).

cedilla n character (¸) placed under a c

——————— THESAURUS ———————

cattle pl n = **cows**, beasts, bovines, livestock, stock

cause n **1** = **origin**, agent, beginning, creator, genesis, mainspring, maker, producer, root, source, spring **2** (foll. by for) = **reason**, basis, grounds, incentive, inducement, justification, motivation, motive, purpose **3** = **aim**, belief, conviction, enterprise, ideal, movement, principle ▷ v **4** = **produce**, bring about, create, generate, give rise to, incite, induce, lead to, result in

caustic adj **1** = **burning**, acrid, astringent, biting, corroding, corrosive, mordant, vitriolic **2** = **sarcastic**, acrimonious, cutting, pungent, scathing, stinging, trenchant, virulent, vitriolic

caution n **1** = **care**, alertness, carefulness, circumspection, deliberation, discretion, forethought, heed, prudence, vigilance, watchfulness **2** = **warning**, admonition, advice, counsel, injunction ▷ v **3** = **warn**, admonish, advise, tip off, urge

cavalcade n = **parade**, array, march-past, procession, spectacle, train

cavalier adj = **haughty**, arrogant, disdainful, lofty, lordly, offhand, scornful, supercilious

cavalry n = **horsemen**, horse, mounted troops

cave n = **hollow**, cavern, cavity, den, grotto

cease v = **stop**, break off, conclude, discontinue, end, finish, halt, leave off, refrain, terminate

cede v = **surrender**, concede, hand over, make over, relinquish, renounce, resign, transfer, yield

in some languages, to show that it is
pronounced *s*, not *k*.

ceilidh [**kay**-lee] *n* informal social gathering
for singing and dancing, esp. in Scotland.

ceiling *n* **1** inner upper surface of a room.
2 upper limit set on something.

celebrate ❶ *v* **1** hold festivities to mark (a
happy event, anniversary, etc.). **2** perform
(a religious ceremony). **celebrated** *adj*
well known. **celebration** *n* **celebrant** *n*
person who performs a religious ceremony.
celebrity *n, pl* **-rities 1** famous person.
2 state of being famous.

celery *n* vegetable with long green crisp
edible stalks.

celestial ❶ *adj* **1** heavenly, divine. **2** of
the sky.

cell ❶ *n* **1** smallest unit of an organism
that is able to function independently.
2 small room for a prisoner, monk, or nun.
3 small compartment of a honeycomb
etc. **4** small group operating as the core
of a larger organization. **cellular** *adj*
1 of or consisting of cells. **cell phone**,
cellular phone telephone operating by
radio communication via a network of
transmitters each serving a small area.

cellar *n* **1** underground room for storage.
2 stock of wine.

cello [**chell**-oh] *n, pl* **-los** large low-pitched
instrument of the violin family. **cellist** *n*.

Cellophane *n* ® thin transparent cellulose
sheeting used as wrapping.

cellulose *n* main constituent of plant cell
walls, used in making paper, plastics, etc.

Celsius *adj* of the temperature scale in
which water freezes at 0° and boils at 100°.

cement ❶ *n* **1** fine grey powder mixed
with water and sand to make mortar or
concrete. **2** something that unites, binds,
or joins. **3** material used to fill teeth. ▷ *v*
4 join, bind, or cover with cement. **5** make
(a relationship) stronger.

cemetery ❶ *n, pl* **-teries** place where dead
people are buried.

cenotaph *n* monument honouring soldiers
who died in a war.

censor ❶ *n* **1** person authorized to examine
films, books, etc., to ban or cut anything
considered obscene or objectionable. ▷ *v*
2 ban or cut parts of (a film, book, etc.).
censorship *n* **censorious** *adj* harshly
critical.

censure ❶ *n* **1** severe disapproval. ▷ *v*
2 criticize severely.

census *n, pl* **-suses** official count of a
population.

cent *n* hundredth part of a monetary unit
such as the dollar or euro.

centaur *n* mythical creature with the head,
arms, and torso of a man, and the lower
body and legs of a horse.

centenary [sen-**teen**-a-ree] *n, pl* **-naries**
100th anniversary or its celebration.
centenarian *n* person at least 100 years
old. **centennial** *n US* centenary.

——————————————— THESAURUS ———————————————

celebrate *v* **1** = **rejoice**, commemorate,
drink to, keep, kill the fatted calf, observe,
put the flags out, toast **2** = **perform**, bless,
honour, solemnize

celestial *adj* **1** = **heavenly**, angelic,
astral, divine, ethereal, spiritual, sublime,
supernatural

cell *n* **2** = **room**, chamber, compartment,
cubicle, dungeon, stall **3** = **compartment**,
cavity **4** = **unit**, caucus, core, coterie,
group, nucleus

cement 1 *n* = **mortar**, plaster ▷ *n* **2** = **glue**,
adhesive, gum, paste, sealant ▷ *v* **4** = **stick**

together, attach, bind, bond, combine,
glue, join, plaster, seal, unite, weld

cemetery *n* = **graveyard**, burial ground,
churchyard, God's acre, necropolis

censor *v* **2** = **cut**, blue-pencil, bowdlerize,
expurgate

censure *n* **1** = **disapproval**, blame,
condemnation, criticism, obloquy, rebuke,
reprimand, reproach, reproof, stick (*sl*) ▷ *v*
2 = **criticize**, blame, castigate, condemn,
denounce, rap over the knuckles, rebuke,
reprimand, reproach, rouse on (*Aust*),
scold, slap on the wrist

centigrade *adj* same as CELSIUS.
centimetre *n* one hundredth of a metre.
centipede *n* small wormlike creature with many legs.
centre **❶** *n* **1** middle point or part. **2** place for a specified activity. **3** political party or group favouring moderation. **4** *Sport* player who plays in the middle of the field. ▷ *v* **5** put in the centre of something. **central** *adj* **centrist** *n* person favouring political moderation. **centre on** *v* have as a centre or main theme.
centurion *n* (in ancient Rome) officer commanding 100 men.
century *n, pl* **-ries** **1** period of 100 years. **2** cricket score of 100 runs.
CEO chief executive officer.
cereal *n* **1** grass plant with edible grain, such as oat or wheat. **2** this grain. **3** breakfast food made from this grain, eaten mixed with milk.
cerebral [**ser**-rib-ral] *adj* **1** of the brain. **2** intellectual.
ceremony **❶** *n, pl* **-nies** **1** formal act or ritual. **2** formally polite behaviour. **ceremonial** *adj, n* **ceremonious** *adj* excessively polite or formal.
certain **❶** *adj* **1** positive and confident. **2** definite. **3** some but not much. **certainly** *adv* **certainty** *n* **1** state of being sure. ▷ *pl* **-ties** **2** something that is inevitable.

certify **❶** *v* **-fying**, **-fied** **1** confirm, attest to. **2** guarantee. **3** declare legally insane. **certifiable** *adj* considered legally insane. **certification** *n*.
cervix *n, pl* **cervixes**, **cervices** **1** narrow entrance of the womb. **2** neck. **cervical** *adj*.
cessation *n* ceasing.
CGI computer-generated image(s).
chafe **❶** *v* **1** make sore or worn by rubbing. **2** be annoyed or impatient.
chaff¹ **❶** *n* **1** grain husks. **2** something of little worth.
chaff² **❶** *v* tease good-naturedly.
chaffinch *n* small European songbird.
chagrin [**shag**-grin] *n* annoyance and disappointment.
chain **❶** *n* **1** flexible length of connected metal links. **2** series of connected facts or events. **3** group of shops, hotels, etc. owned by one firm. ▷ *v* **4** restrict or fasten with or as if with a chain. **chain reaction** series of events, each of which causes the next. **chain-smoke** *v* smoke (cigarettes) continuously.
chair *n* **1** seat with a back, for one person. **2** official position of authority. **3** person holding this. **4** professorship. ▷ *v* **5** preside over (a meeting). **chairlift** series of chairs suspended from a moving cable for carrying people up a slope. **chairman**, **chairwoman** *n* person in charge of a

centre *n* **1** = **middle**, core, heart, hub, kernel, midpoint, nucleus, pivot ▷ *v* **5** = **focus**, cluster, concentrate, converge, revolve
ceremony *n* **1** = **ritual**, commemoration, function, observance, parade, rite, service, show, solemnities **2** = **formality**, ceremonial, decorum, etiquette, niceties, pomp, propriety, protocol
certain *adj* **1** = **sure**, assured, confident, convinced, positive, satisfied **2** = **definite**, conclusive, decided, established, fixed, incontrovertible, inevitable, irrefutable, known, settled, sure, true, undeniable, unequivocal

certify *v* **1** = **confirm**, attest, authenticate, declare, testify, validate, verify **2** = **guarantee**, assure
chafe *v* **1** = **rub**, abrade, rasp, scrape, scratch **2** = **be annoyed**, be impatient, fret, fume, rage, worry
chaff¹ *n* **1** = **husks** **2** = **rubbish**, dregs, refuse, remains, trash, waste
chaff² *v* = **tease**, mock, rib (*inf*), ridicule, scoff, taunt
chain *n* **1** = **link**, bond, coupling, fetter, manacle, shackle **2** = **series**, progression, sequence, set, string, succession, train ▷ *v* **4** = **bind**, confine, enslave, fetter, handcuff, manacle, restrain, shackle, tether

company's board of directors or a meeting (also **chairperson**).

chalet *n* 1 kind of Swiss wooden house with a steeply sloping roof. 2 similar house, used as a holiday home.

chalice *n* large goblet.

chalk *n* 1 soft white rock consisting of calcium carbonate. 2 piece of chalk, often coloured, used for drawing and writing on blackboards. ▷ *v* 3 draw or mark with chalk. **chalky** *adj*.

challenge ❶ *n* 1 demanding or stimulating situation. 2 call to take part in a contest or fight. 3 questioning of a statement of fact. 4 demand by a sentry for identification or a password. ▷ *v* 5 issue a challenge to. **challenged** *adj* disabled as specified, e.g. *physically challenged*; *mentally challenged*. **challenger** *n*.

chamber ❶ *n* 1 hall used for formal meetings. 2 legislative or judicial assembly. 3 *old-fashioned* bedroom. 4 compartment, cavity. ▷ *pl* 5 set of rooms used as offices by a barrister. **chambermaid** *n* woman employed to clean bedrooms in a hotel. **chamber music** classical music to be performed by a small group of musicians. **chamber pot** bowl for urine, formerly used in bedrooms.

chameleon [kam-**meal**-yon] *n* small lizard that changes colour to blend in with its surroundings.

chamois [**sham**-wah] *n*, *pl* **-ois** 1 small mountain antelope. 2 [**sham**-ee] soft suede leather. 3 piece of this, used for cleaning or polishing.

champ *v* chew noisily. **champ at the bit** *informal* be impatient to do something.

champagne *n* sparkling white French wine.

champion ❶ *n* 1 overall winner of a competition. 2 (foll. by *of*) someone who defends a person or cause. ▷ *v* 3 support. ▷ *adj* 4 *dialect* excellent. **championship** *n*.

chance ❶ *n* 1 likelihood, probability. 2 opportunity to do something. 3 risk, gamble. 4 unpredictable element that causes things to happen one way rather than another. ▷ *v* 5 risk, hazard. **chancy** *adj* uncertain, risky.

chancel *n* part of a church containing the altar and choir.

chancellor *n* 1 head of government in some European countries. 2 honorary head of a university. **chancellorship** *n*.

chandelier [shan-dill-**eer**] *n* ornamental light with branches and holders for several candles or bulbs.

change ❶ *n* 1 becoming different. 2 variety or novelty. 3 different set, esp. of clothes.

——————— THESAURUS ———————

challenge *n* 1 = **trial**, test 2 = **confrontation**, provocation, ultimatum 3 = **question** ▷ *v* 5 = **test**, confront, defy, dispute, object to, question, tackle, throw down the gauntlet

chamber *n* 1 = **hall**, room 2 = **council**, assembly, legislative body, legislature 3 *Old-fashioned* = **bedroom**, apartment, room 4 = **compartment**, cubicle, enclosure

champion *n* 1 = **winner**, conqueror, hero, title holder, victor 2 (foll. by *of*) = **defender**, backer, guardian, patron, protector, upholder ▷ *v* 3 = **support**, advocate, back, commend, defend,

encourage, espouse, fight for, promote, uphold

chance *n* 1 = **probability**, likelihood, odds, possibility, prospect 2 = **opportunity**, occasion, opening, time 3 = **risk**, gamble, hazard, jeopardy, speculation, uncertainty 4 = **luck**, accident, coincidence, destiny, fate, fortune, providence ▷ *v* 5 = **risk**, endanger, gamble, hazard, jeopardize, stake, try, venture, wager

change *n* 1 = **alteration**, difference, innovation, metamorphosis, modification, mutation, revolution, transformation, transition 2 = **variety**, break (*inf*), departure, diversion, novelty, variation ▷ *v* 6 = **alter**, convert, modify, mutate, reform,

4 balance received when the amount paid is more than the cost of a purchase. 5 coins of low value. ▷ v 6 make or become different. 7 give and receive (something) in return. 8 exchange (money) for its equivalent in a smaller denomination or different currency. 9 put on other clothes. 10 leave one vehicle and board another. **changeable** adj changing often. **changeling** n child believed to have been exchanged by fairies for another.

channel **❶** n 1 band of broadcasting frequencies. 2 means of access or communication. 3 broad strait connecting two areas of sea. 4 bed or course of a river, stream, or canal. 5 groove. ▷ v -**nelling**, -**nelled** 6 direct or convey through a channel.

chant **❶** v 1 utter or sing (a slogan or psalm). ▷ n 2 rhythmic or repetitious slogan. 3 psalm that has a short simple melody with several words sung on one note.

chaos **❶** n complete disorder or confusion. **chaotic** adj

chap **❶** n informal man or boy.

chapati, chapatti n (in Indian cookery) flat thin unleavened bread.

chapel n 1 place of worship with its own altar, within a church. 2 similar place of worship in a large house or institution. 3 Nonconformist place of worship.

chaplain n clergyman attached to a chapel, military body, or institution. **chaplaincy** n, pl -**cies**

chapter **❶** n 1 division of a book. 2 period in a life or history. 3 branch of a society or club.

char v **charring**, **charred** blacken by partial burning.

character **❶** n 1 combination of qualities distinguishing a person, group, or place. 2 reputation, esp. good reputation. 3 person represented in a play, film, or story. 4 unusual or amusing person. 5 letter, numeral, or symbol used in writing or printing. **characteristic** . n 1 distinguishing feature or quality. ▷ adj 2 typical. **characteristically** adv **characterize** v 1 be a characteristic of. 2 (foll. by as) describe. **characterization** n.

charade **❶** [shar-**rahd**] n 1 absurd pretence. ▷ pl 2 game in which one team acts out a word or phrase, which the other team has to guess.

charcoal n black substance formed by partially burning wood.

charge **❶** v 1 ask as a price. 2 enter a debit against a person's account for (a purchase). 3 accuse formally. 4 make a

---

reorganize, restyle, shift, transform, vary 7 = **exchange**, barter, convert, interchange, replace, substitute, swap, trade

channel n 2 = **route**, approach, artery, avenue, canal, conduit, course, duct, means, medium, passage, path, way 3 = **strait** 5 = **groove**, furrow, gutter ▷ v 6 = **direct**, conduct, convey, guide, transmit

chant v 1 = **sing**, carol, chorus, descant, intone, recite, warble ▷ n 3 = **song**, carol, chorus, melody, psalm

chaos n = **disorder**, anarchy, bedlam, confusion, disorganization, lawlessness, mayhem, pandemonium, tumult

chap n Inf = **fellow**, bloke (Brit inf),

character, guy (inf), individual, man, person

chapter n 1 = **section**, clause, division, episode, part, topic 2 = **period**, part, phase, stage

character n 1 = **nature**, attributes, calibre, complexion, disposition, personality, quality, temperament, type 2 = **reputation**, honour, integrity, rectitude, strength, uprightness 3 = **role**, part, persona, portrayal 4 = **eccentric**, card (inf), oddball (inf), original 5 = **symbol**, device, figure, hieroglyph, letter, mark, rune, sign

charade n 1 = **pretence**, fake, farce, pantomime, parody, travesty

charge v 3 = **accuse**, arraign, blame,

rush at or sudden attack upon. **5** fill (a glass). **6** fill (a battery) with electricity. **7** command, assign. ▷ *n* **8** price charged. **9** formal accusation. **10** attack. **11** command, exhortation. **12** custody, guardianship. **13** person or thing entrusted to someone's care. **14** amount of electricity stored in a battery. **in charge of** in control of. **chargeable** *adj* **charger** *n* **1** device for charging an accumulator. **2** (in the Middle Ages) warhorse.

chargé d'affaires [shar-zhay daf-**fair**] *n*, *pl* **chargés d'affaires** head of a diplomatic mission in the absence of an ambassador or in a small mission.

chariot *n* two-wheeled horse-drawn vehicle used in ancient times in wars and races. **charioteer** *n* chariot driver.

charisma ❶ [kar-**rizz**-ma] *n* person's power to attract or influence people. **charismatic** [kar-rizz-**mat**-ik] *adj*.

charity ❶ *n*, *pl* -**ties** **1** organization that gives help, such as money or food, to those in need. **2** giving of help to those in need. **3** help given to those in need. **4** kindly attitude towards people. **charitable** *adj* **charitably** *adv*.

charlatan ❶ [**shar**-lat-tan] *n* person who claims expertise that he or she does not have.

charm ❶ *n* **1** attractive quality. **2** trinket worn on a bracelet. **3** magic spell. ▷ *v* **4** attract, delight. **5** influence by personal charm. **6** protect or influence as if by magic. **charmer** *n* **charming** *adj* attractive.

chart ❶ *n* **1** graph, table, or diagram showing information. **2** map of the sea or stars. ▷ *v* **3** plot the course of. **4** make a chart of. **the charts** *informal* weekly lists of the bestselling pop records.

charter ❶ *n* **1** document granting or demanding certain rights. **2** fundamental principles of an organization. **3** hire of transport for private use. ▷ *v* **4** hire by charter. **5** grant a charter to. **chartered** *adj* officially qualified to practise a profession.

charwoman *n* woman whose job is to clean other people's homes.

——————— THESAURUS ———————

impeach, incriminate, indict **4** = **attack**, assail, assault, rush, stampede, storm **5** = **fill**, load **7** = **command**, bid, commit, demand, entrust, instruct, order, require ▷ *n* **8** = **price**, amount, cost, expenditure, expense, outlay, payment, rate, toll **9** = **accusation**, allegation, imputation, indictment **10** = **attack**, assault, onset, onslaught, rush, sortie, stampede **11** = **instruction**, command, demand, direction, injunction, mandate, order, precept **12** = **care**, custody, duty, office, responsibility, safekeeping, trust **13** = **ward**

charisma *n* = **charm**, allure, attraction, lure, magnetism, personality

charity *n* **2** = **help**, assistance, benefaction, philanthropy, relief **3** = **donations**, contributions, endowment, fund, gift, hand-out, largesse *or* largess **4** = **kindness**, altruism, benevolence, compassion, fellow feeling, generosity, goodwill, humanity, indulgence

charlatan *n* = **fraud**, cheat, con man (*inf*), fake, impostor, phoney *or* phony (*inf*), pretender, quack, sham, swindler

charm *n* **1** = **attraction**, allure, appeal, fascination, magnetism **2** = **trinket** **3** = **spell**, enchantment, magic, sorcery ▷ *v* **4** = **attract**, allure, beguile, bewitch, captivate, delight, enchant, enrapture, entrance, fascinate, mesmerize **5** = **win over**

chart *n* **1** = **table**, blueprint, diagram, graph, plan **2** = **map** ▷ *v* **3** = **plot**, map out **4** = **outline**, delineate, draft, shape, sketch

charter *n* **1** = **document**, contract, deed, licence, permit ▷ *v* **4** = **hire**, commission, employ, lease, rent **5** = **authorize**, sanction

chary [**chair**-ee] *adj* -**rier**, -**riest** wary, careful. **charily** *adv*.

chase ❶ *v* 1 run after quickly in order to catch or drive away. 2 *informal* rush, run. 3 *informal* try energetically to obtain. ▷ *n* 4 chasing, pursuit. **chaser** *n* milder drink drunk after another stronger one.

chasm ❶ [**kaz**-zum] *n* deep crack in the earth.

chassis [**shass**-ee] *n*, *pl* -**sis** frame, wheels, and mechanical parts of a vehicle.

chaste ❶ *adj* 1 abstaining from sex outside marriage or altogether. 2 (of style) simple. **chastely** *adv* **chastity** *n*.

chasten ❶ [**chase**-en] *v* subdue by criticism.

chat ❶ *n* 1 informal conversation. ▷ *v* **chatting**, **chatted** 2 have an informal conversation. **chatty** *adj* **chatroom** *n* site on the Internet where users have group discussions by email.

chateau [**shat**-toe] *n*, *pl* -**teaux**, -**teaus** French castle.

chauffeur *n* person employed to drive a car for someone. **chauffeuse** *n fem*.

chauvinism [**show**-vin-iz-zum] *n* irrational belief that one's own country, race, group, or sex is superior. **chauvinist**

n, *adj* **chauvinistic** *adj*.

chav *n Brit informal* young working-class person considered to have vulgar tastes.

cheap ❶ *adj* 1 costing relatively little. 2 of poor quality. 3 not valued highly. 4 mean, despicable. **cheaply** *adv* **cheapen** *v* 1 lower the reputation of. 2 reduce the price of. **cheapskate** *n informal* miserly person.

cheat ❶ *v* 1 act dishonestly to gain profit or advantage. ▷ *n* 2 person who cheats. 3 fraud, deception.

check ❶ *v* 1 examine, investigate. 2 slow the growth or progress of. 3 correspond, agree. ▷ *n* 4 test to ensure accuracy or progress. 5 break in progress. 6 *US* cheque. 7 pattern of squares or crossed lines. 8 *Chess* position of a king under attack. **check in** *v* register one's arrival. **checkmate** *n* 1 *Chess* winning position in which an opponent's king is under attack and unable to escape. 2 utter defeat. ▷ *v* 3 *Chess* place the king of (one's opponent) in checkmate. 4 thwart, defeat. **check out** *v* 1 pay the bill and leave a hotel. 2 examine, investigate. **checkout** *n* counter in a supermarket, where customers pay. **checkup** *n* thorough

---

chase *v* 1 = **pursue**, course, drive, drive away, expel, follow, hound, hunt, put to flight, run after, track ▷ *n* 4 = **pursuit**, hunt, hunting, race

chasm *n* = **gulf**, abyss, crater, crevasse, fissure, gap, gorge, ravine

chaste *adj* = **pure**, immaculate, innocent, modest, unaffected, undefiled, virtuous 2 = **simple**

chasten *v* = **subdue**, chastise, correct, discipline, humble, humiliate, put in one's place, tame

chat *n* 1 = **talk**, chatter, chinwag (*Brit inf*), conversation, gossip, heart-to-heart, natter, tête-à-tête ▷ *v* 2 = **talk**, chatter, gossip, jaw (*sl*), natter

cheap *adj* 1 = **inexpensive**, bargain, cut-price, economical, keen, low-cost, low-

priced, reasonable, reduced 2 = **inferior**, common, poor, second-rate, shoddy, tatty, tawdry, two a penny, worthless 4 = **despicable**, contemptible, mean

cheat *v* 1 = **deceive**, beguile, con (*inf*), defraud, double-cross (*inf*), dupe, fleece, fool, mislead, rip off (*sl*), swindle, trick ▷ *n* 2 = **deceiver**, charlatan, con man (*inf*), double-crosser (*inf*), shark, sharper, swindler, trickster 3 = **deception**, deceit, fraud, rip-off (*sl*), scam (*sl*), swindle, trickery

check *v* 1 = **examine**, inquire into, inspect, investigate, look at, make sure, monitor, research, scrutinize, study, test, vet 2 = **stop**, delay, halt, hinder, impede, inhibit, limit, obstruct, restrain, retard *n* 4 = **examination**, inspection,

medical examination.

Cheddar n firm orange or yellowy-white cheese.

cheek ● n 1 either side of the face below the eye. 2 informal impudence, boldness. ▷ v 3 informal speak impudently to. **cheeky** adj impudent, disrespectful. **cheekily** adv **cheekiness** n.

cheep n 1 young bird's high-pitched cry. ▷ v 2 utter a cheep.

cheer ● v 1 applaud or encourage with shouts. 2 make or become happy. ▷ n 3 shout of applause or encouragement. **cheerful** adj **cheerfully** adv **cheerfulness** n **cheerless** adj dreary, gloomy. **cheery** adj **cheerily** adv.

cheerio interj informal goodbye.

cheese n 1 food made from coagulated milk curd. 2 block of this. **cheesy** adj **cheeseburger** n hamburger topped with melted cheese. **cheesecake** n 1 dessert with a biscuit-crumb base covered with a sweet cream-cheese mixture. 2 slang photographs of naked or near-naked women. **cheesecloth** n light cotton cloth. **cheesed off** bored, annoyed. **cheeseparing** adj mean, miserly.

cheetah n large fast-running spotted African wild cat.

chef n cook in a restaurant.

chemistry n science of the composition, properties, and reactions of substances. **chemical** n substance used in or resulting from a reaction involving changes to atoms or molecules. **chemist** n 1 shop selling medicines and cosmetics. 2 qualified dispenser of prescribed

medicines. 3 specialist in chemistry.

chemotherapy n treatment of disease, often cancer, using chemicals.

chenille [shen-**neel**] n (fabric of) thick tufty yarn.

cheque n written order to one's bank to pay money from one's account. **cheque card** plastic card issued by a bank guaranteeing payment of a customer's cheques.

chequer n 1 piece used in Chinese chequers. ▷ pl 2 game of draughts. **chequered** adj 1 marked by varied fortunes. 2 having a pattern of squares.

cherish ● v 1 cling to (an idea or feeling). 2 care for.

cherry n, pl -ries 1 small red or black fruit with a stone. 2 tree on which it grows. ▷ adj 3 deep red.

cherub n, pl -ubs, -ubim 1 angel, often represented as a winged child. 2 sweet child. **cherubic** [cher-**rew**-bik] adj.

chess n game for two players with 16 pieces each, played on a chequered board of 64 squares. **chessman** n piece used in chess.

chest ● n 1 front of the body, from neck to waist. 2 large strong box. **chest of drawers** piece of furniture consisting of drawers in a frame.

chestnut n 1 reddish-brown edible nut. 2 tree on which it grows. 3 reddish-brown horse. 4 informal old joke. ▷ adj 5 (of hair or a horse) reddish-brown.

chevron [**shev**-ron] n V-shaped pattern, esp. on the sleeve of a military uniform to indicate rank.

━━━━━━━━━━━━━━━━━━━━ THESAURUS ━━━━━━━━

investigation, once-over (inf), research, scrutiny, test

cheek n 2 Inf = **impudence**, audacity, chutzpah (US & Canad inf), disrespect, effrontery, impertinence, insolence, lip (sl), nerve, temerity

cheer v 1 = **applaud**, acclaim, clap, hail 2 = **cheer up**, brighten, buoy up, comfort, encourage, gladden, hearten, uplift n

3 = **applause**, acclamation, ovation, plaudits

cherish v 1 = **cling to**, cleave to, encourage, entertain, foster, harbour, hold dear, nurture, prize, sustain, treasure 2 = **care for**, comfort, hold dear, love, nurse, shelter, support

chest n 2 = **box**, case, casket, coffer, crate, strongbox, trunk

chew ❶ v grind (food) between the teeth. **chewy** adj requiring a lot of chewing. **chewing gum** flavoured gum to be chewed but not swallowed.

chianti [kee-**ant**-ee] n dry red Italian wine.

chic ❶ [**sheek**] adj **1** stylish, elegant. ▷ n **2** stylishness, elegance.

chicane [shik-**kane**] n obstacle in a motor-racing circuit.

chick n baby bird. **chickpea** n edible yellow pealike seed. **chickweed** n weed with small white flowers.

chicken n **1** domestic fowl. **2** its flesh, used as food. **3** slang coward. ▷ adj **4** slang cowardly. **chicken feed** slang trifling amount of money. **chicken out** v informal fail to do something through cowardice. **chickenpox** n infectious disease with an itchy rash.

chicory n, pl **-ries 1** plant whose leaves are used in salads. **2** root of this plant, used as a coffee substitute.

chide ❶ v **chiding**, **chided** or **chid**, **chid** or **chidden** rebuke, scold.

chief ❶ n **1** head of a group of people. ▷ adj **2** most important. **chiefly** adv **1** especially. **2** mainly. **chieftain** n leader of a tribe.

chiffon [**shif**-fon] n fine see-through fabric.

chilblain n inflammation of the fingers or toes, caused by exposure to cold.

child ❶ n, pl **children 1** young human being,

boy or girl. **2** son or daughter. **childhood** n **childish** adj **1** immature, silly. **2** of or like a child. **childless** adj **childlike** adj innocent, trustful. **childbirth** n giving birth to a child. **child's play** very easy task.

chill ❶ n **1** a feverish cold. **2** moderate coldness. ▷ v **3** make (something) cool or cold. **4** cause (someone) to feel cold or frightened. ▷ adj **5** unpleasantly cold. **chilly** adj **1** moderately cold. **2** unfriendly. **chilly-bin** n NZ informal insulated container for carrying food and drink. **chilliness** n **chill out** informal ▷ vb to relax, esp. after energetic dancing at a rave.

chilli, chili n **1** small red or green hot-tasting capsicum pod, used in cooking. **2** (also **chilli con carne**) hot-tasting Mexican dish of meat, onions, beans, and chilli powder.

chime ❶ n **1** musical ringing sound of a bell or clock. ▷ v **2** make a musical ringing sound. **3** indicate (the time) by chiming. **4** (foll. by with) be consistent with.

chimney n hollow vertical structure for carrying away smoke from a fire.

chimpanzee n intelligent black African ape.

chin n part of the face below the mouth. **chinwag** n informal chat.

china ❶ n **1** fine earthenware or porcelain. **2** dishes or ornaments made of this.

— THESAURUS —

chew v = **bite**, champ, chomp, crunch, gnaw, grind, masticate, munch

chic adj **1** = **stylish**, elegant, fashionable, smart, trendy (Brit inf)

chide v = **scold**, admonish, berate, censure, criticize, lecture, rebuke, reprimand, reproach, reprove, rouse on (Aust), tell off (inf), tick off (inf)

chief n **1** = **head**, boss (inf), captain, commander, director, governor, leader, manager, master, principal, ruler adj **2** = **primary**, foremost, highest, key, leading, main, predominant, pre-eminent, premier, prime, principal, supreme, uppermost

child n **1** = **youngster**, babe, baby, bairn (Scot), infant, juvenile, kid (inf), offspring, toddler, tot

chill n **2** = **cold**, bite, coldness, coolness, crispness, frigidity, nip, rawness, sharpness ▷ v **3** = **cool**, freeze, refrigerate **4** = **dishearten**, dampen, deject, depress, discourage, dismay ▷ adj **5** = **cold**, biting, bleak, chilly, freezing, frigid, raw, sharp, wintry

chime n **1** = **ring**, clang, jingle, peal, sound, tinkle, toll ▷ v **2** = **ring**, clang, jingle, peal, sound, tinkle, toll

china n **1** = **pottery**, ceramics, porcelain **2** = **crockery**, service, tableware, ware

chinchilla n 1 S American rodent bred for its soft grey fur. 2 its fur.

chink ❶ n small narrow opening, e.g. *a chink of light*.

chintz n printed cotton fabric with a glazed finish.

chip ❶ n 1 strip of potato, fried in deep fat. 2 tiny wafer of semiconductor material forming an integrated circuit. 3 counter used to represent money in gambling games. 4 small piece removed by chopping, breaking, etc. ▷ v **chipping**, **chipped** 5 break small pieces from. **have a chip on one's shoulder** *informal* bear a grudge. **chip in** v *informal* 1 contribute (money). 2 interrupt with a remark. **chippie** n *Brit, Aust & NZ informal* carpenter.

chipmunk n small squirrel-like N American rodent with a striped back.

chiropodist [kir-**rop**-pod-ist] n person who treats minor foot complaints. **chiropody** n.

chirp ❶ v 1 (of a bird or insect) make a short high-pitched sound. ▷ n 2 chirping sound. **chirpy** adj *informal* lively and cheerful.

chisel n 1 metal tool with a sharp end for shaping wood or stone. ▷ v **-elling**, **-elled** 2 carve or form with a chisel.

chit n short official note, such as a receipt.

chitchat n chat, gossip.

chivalry ❶ n 1 courteous behaviour, esp. by men towards women. 2 medieval system and principles of knighthood. **chivalrous** adj.

chlorine n strong-smelling greenish-yellow gaseous element, used to disinfect water. **chlorinate** v disinfect (water) with chlorine. **chlorination** n **chloride** n compound of chlorine and another substance.

chloroform n strong-smelling liquid formerly used as an anaesthetic.

chlorophyll n green colouring matter of plants, which enables them to convert sunlight into energy.

chock n block or wedge used to prevent a heavy object from moving. **chock-full**, **chock-a-block** adj completely full.

chocolate n 1 sweet food made from cacao seeds. 2 sweet or drink made from this. ▷ adj 3 dark brown.

choice ❶ n 1 choosing. 2 opportunity or power of choosing. 3 person or thing chosen or that may be chosen. 4 alternative action or possibility. ▷ adj 5 of high quality.

choir n 1 organized group of singers, esp. in church. 2 part of a church occupied by the choir.

choke ❶ v 1 hinder or stop the breathing of (a person) by strangling or smothering. 2 have trouble in breathing. 3 block, clog up. ▷ n 4 device controlling the amount of air that is mixed with the fuel in a petrol engine. **choker** n tight-fitting necklace. **choke back** v suppress (tears or anger).

cholera [**kol**-ler-a] n serious infectious disease causing severe vomiting and diarrhoea.

choleric [**kol**-ler-ik] adj bad-tempered.

cholesterol [kol-**lest**-er-oll] n fatty substance found in animal tissue, an

──────────── THESAURUS ────────────

chink n 1 = **opening**, aperture, cleft, crack, cranny, crevice, fissure, gap

chip n 4 = **scratch**, fragment, nick, notch, shard, shaving, sliver, wafer ▷ v 5 = **nick**, chisel, damage, gash, whittle

chirp v 1 = **tweet**, cheep, peep, pipe, twitter, warble

chivalry n 1 = **courtesy**, gallantry, gentlemanliness, politeness
2 = **knighthood**, courage, knight-errantry

choice n 2 = **option**, alternative, pick, preference, say 3 = **selection**, range, variety ▷ adj 5 = **best**, elite, excellent, exclusive, prime, rare, select

choke v 1 = **strangle**, asphyxiate, gag, overpower, smother, stifle, suffocate, suppress, throttle 3 = **block**, bar, bung, clog, congest, constrict, obstruct, stop

excess of which can cause heart disease.

chook *n Aust & NZ* hen or chicken.

choose ⓘ *v* **choosing, chose, chosen**
1 select from a number of alternatives.
2 decide (to do something) because one
wants to. **choosy** *adj informal* fussy, hard
to please.

chop ⓘ *v* **chopping, chopped 1** cut with
a blow from an axe or knife. **2** cut into
pieces. **3** *Boxing, karate* hit (an opponent)
with a short sharp blow. ▷ *n* **4** cutting or
sharp blow. **5** slice of lamb or pork, usu.
with a rib. **chopper** *n* **1** *informal* helicopter.
2 small axe. **3** butcher's cleaver. **4** cycle
with very high handlebars. **choppy** *adj*
-pier, -piest (of the sea) fairly rough.

chopsticks *pl n* pair of thin sticks used to
eat Chinese food.

choral *adj* of a choir.

chorale [kor-**rahl**] *n* slow stately hymn tune.

chord *n* simultaneous sounding of three or
more musical notes.

chore ⓘ *n* routine task.

choreography *n* composition of
steps and movements for dancing.
choreographer *n*

chorister *n* singer in a choir.

chortle ⓘ *v* **1** chuckle in amusement. ▷ *n*
2 amused chuckle.

chorus ⓘ *n, pl* **-ruses 1** large choir. **2** part
of a song repeated after each verse.
3 something expressed by many people
at once. **4** group of singers or dancers
who perform together in a show. ▷ *v*

chorusing, chorused 5 sing or say
together. **in chorus** in unison.

chow *n* thick-coated dog with a curled tail,
orig. from China.

Christian *n* **1** person who believes in
and follows Christ. ▷ *adj* **2** of Christ or
Christianity. **3** kind, good. **Christianity** *n*
religion based on the life and teachings of
Christ. **Christian name** person's first name.

Christmas ⓘ *n* **1** annual festival on
December 25 commemorating the birth
of Christ **2** period around this time.
Christmassy *adj*.

chromosome *n* microscopic gene-
carrying body in the nucleus of a cell.

chronic *adj* **1** (of an illness) lasting a long
time. **2** habitual, e.g. *chronic drinking*.
3 *informal* of poor quality. **chronically** *adv*.

chronicle ⓘ *n* **1** record of events in order
of occurrence. ▷ *v* **2** record in or as if in a
chronicle. **chronicler** *n*.

chrysalis [**kriss**-a-liss] *n* insect in the stage
between larva and adult, when it is in a
cocoon.

chrysanthemum *n* garden flower with a
large head made up of thin petals.

chub *n* freshwater fish of the carp family.

chubby ⓘ *adj* **-bier, -biest** plump and
round. **chubbiness** *n*.

chuck ⓘ *v* **1** *informal* throw. **2** *informal*
give up, reject. **3** touch (someone)
affectionately under the chin.

chuckle ⓘ *v* **1** laugh softly. ▷ *n* **2** soft laugh.

chuffed *adj informal* very pleased.

THESAURUS

choose *v* = **pick**, adopt, designate, elect,
opt for, prefer, select, settle upon

chop *v* **1** = **cut**, cleave, fell, hack, hew, lop,
sever

chore *n* = **task**, duty, errand, job

chortle *v* **1** = **chuckle**, cackle, crow, guffaw
▷ *n* **2** = **chuckle**, cackle, crow, guffaw

chorus *n* **1** = **choir**, choristers, ensemble,
singers, vocalists **2** = **refrain**, burden,
response, strain **3** = **unison**, accord,
concert, harmony

Christmas *n* = **festive season**, Noel, Xmas

(*inf*), Yule (*arch*)

chronicle *n* **1** = **record**, account, annals,
diary, history, journal, narrative, register,
story ▷ *v* **2** = **record**, enter, narrate, put on
record, recount, register, relate, report, set
down, tell

chubby *adj* = **plump**, buxom, flabby, podgy,
portly, roly-poly, rotund, round, stout, tubby

chuck *v* **1** *Inf* = **throw**, cast, fling, heave,
hurl, pitch, sling, toss

chuckle *v* **1** = **laugh**, chortle, crow, exult,
giggle, snigger, titter

chum ❶ *informal* ▷ *n* **1** close friend. ▷ *v* **chumming**, **chummed 2 chum up with** form a close friendship with. **chummy** *adj*.

chunk ❶ *n* **1** thick solid piece. **2** considerable amount. **chunky** *adj* **1** (of a person) broad and heavy. **2** (of an object) large and thick.

church *n* **1** building for public Christian worship. **2** particular Christian denomination. **3** clergy. **churchgoer** *n* person who attends church regularly. **churchyard** *n* grounds round a church, used as a graveyard.

churlish ❶ *adj* surly and rude.

churn ❶ *n* **1** machine in which cream is shaken to make butter. **2** large container for milk. ▷ *v* **3** stir (cream) vigorously to make butter. **4** move about violently. **churn out** *v informal* produce (things) rapidly in large numbers.

chute [**shoot**] *n* steep slope down which things may be slid.

chutney *n* pickle made from fruit, vinegar, spices, and sugar.

CIA (in the US) Central Intelligence Agency.

CID Criminal Investigation Department.

cider *n* alcoholic drink made from fermented apple juice.

cigar *n* roll of cured tobacco leaves for smoking.

cigarette *n* thin roll of shredded tobacco in thin paper, for smoking.

cilantro *n* the US and Canadian word for CORIANDER.

cinch [**sinch**] *n informal* easy task.

cinder *n* piece of material that will not burn, left after burning coal.

cinema ❶ *n* **1** place for showing films. **2** films collectively. **cinematic** *adj* **cinematography** *n* technique of making films. **cinematographer** *n*.

cinnamon *n* spice obtained from the bark of an Asian tree.

- SPELLING TIP
- **Cinnamon** is a tricky word to spell. The
- Bank of English shows at least 3 differ-
- ent ways of getting it wrong. The correct
- spelling has two *n*s in the middle and
- only one *m*.

cipher ❶ [**sife**-er] *n* **1** system of secret writing. **2** unimportant person.

circa [**sir**-ka] *prep Latin* approximately, about.

circle ❶ *n* **1** perfectly round geometric figure, line, or shape. **2** group of people sharing an interest or activity. **3** *Theatre* section of seats above the main level of the auditorium. ▷ *v* **4** move in a circle (round). **5** enclose in a circle. **circular** *adj* round. **circulate** *v* move round.

circuit ❶ *n* **1** complete route or course, esp. a circular one. **2** complete path through which an electric current can flow. **3** periodical journey round a district, as made by judges. **4** motor-racing track. **circuitous** [sir-**kew**-it-uss] *adj* indirect and lengthy. **circuitry** [**sir**-kit-tree] *n* electrical circuit(s).

circumcise *v* remove the foreskin of. **circumcision** *n*.

———————————— THESAURUS ————————————

chum *Inf n* **1** = **friend**, cobber (*Aust or old-fashioned NZ inf*), companion, comrade, crony, mate (*inf*), pal (*inf*)

chunk *n* **1** = **piece**, block, dollop (*inf*), hunk, lump, mass, nugget, portion, slab

churlish *adj* = **rude**, brusque, harsh, ill-tempered, impolite, sullen, surly, uncivil

churn *v* **4** = **stir up**, agitate, beat, convulse, swirl, toss

cinema *n* **1** = **pictures**, flicks (*sl*), movies **2** = **films**, big screen (*inf*), flicks (*sl*), motion

pictures, movies, pictures

cipher *n* **1** = **code**, cryptograph **2** = **nobody**, nonentity

circle *n* **1** = **ring**, disc, globe, orb, sphere **2** = **group**, clique, club, company, coterie, set, society ▷ *v* **4** = **go round**, circumnavigate, circumscribe, wheel **5** = **enclose**, circumscribe, encircle, envelop, ring, surround

circuit *n* **1** = **course**, journey, lap, orbit, revolution, route, tour **4** = **track**

circumference ❶ n 1 boundary of a specified area or shape, esp. of a circle. 2 distance round this.

circumflex n mark (ˆ) over a vowel to show that it is pronounced in a particular way.

circumnavigate v sail right round. **circumnavigation** n.

circumscribe v 1 limit, restrict. 2 draw a line round.

circumspect adj cautious and careful not to take risks. **circumspection** n.

circumstance ❶ n (usu. pl) occurrence or condition that accompanies or influences a person or event. **circumstantial** adj 1 (of evidence) strongly suggesting something but not proving it. 2 very detailed.

circumvent v avoid or get round (a rule etc.). **circumvention** n.

circus n, pl -cuses (performance given by) a travelling company of acrobats, clowns, performing animals, etc.

cirrhosis [sir-**roh**-siss] n serious liver disease, often caused by drinking too much alcohol.

cirrus n, pl -ri high wispy cloud.

cistern ❶ n water tank, esp. one that holds water for flushing a toilet.

citadel ❶ n fortress in a city.

cite ❶ v 1 quote, refer to. 2 bring forward as proof. **citation** n.

citizen ❶ n 1 native or naturalized member of a state or nation. 2 inhabitant of a city or town. **citizenship** n.

citrus fruit n juicy sharp-tasting fruit such as an orange or lemon.

city ❶ n, pl -ties large or important town.

civic ❶ adj of a city or citizens. **civics** n study of the rights and responsibilities of citizenship.

civil ❶ adj 1 relating to the citizens of a state as opposed to the armed forces or the Church. 2 polite, courteous. **civilly** adv **civility** n polite or courteous behaviour. **civilian** n, adj (person) not belonging to the armed forces. **civil service** service responsible for the administration of the government. **civil servant** member of the civil service. **civil war** war between people of the same country.

civilize ❶ v 1 refine or educate (a person). 2 make (a place) more pleasant or more acceptable. **civilization** n 1 high level of human cultural and social development. 2 particular society which has reached this level.

claim ❶ v 1 assert as a fact. 2 demand as a right. 3 need, require. ▷ n 4 assertion that something is true. 5 assertion of a right. 6 something claimed as a right. **claimant** n.

clairvoyance n power of perceiving things

THESAURUS

circumference n 1 = **boundary**, border, edge, extremity, limits, outline, perimeter, periphery, rim

circumstance n (usu. pl) = **situation**, condition, contingency, event, happening, incident, occurrence, position, state, state of affairs, status

cistern n = **tank**, basin, reservoir, sink, vat

citadel n = **fortress**, bastion, fortification, keep, stronghold, tower

cite v 1 = **quote**, adduce, advance, allude to, enumerate, extract, mention, name, specify

citizen n = **inhabitant**, denizen, dweller, resident, subject, townsman

city n = **town**, conurbation, metropolis, municipality

civic adj = **public**, communal, local, municipal

civil adj 1 = **civic**, domestic, municipal, political 2 = **polite**, affable, courteous, obliging, refined, urbane, well-mannered

civilize v 1 = **cultivate**, educate, enlighten, refine, sophisticate, tame

claim v 1 = **assert**, allege, challenge, insist, maintain, profess, uphold 2 = **demand**, ask, call for, insist, need, require ▷ n 4 = **assertion**, affirmation, allegation, pretension 6 = **demand**, application, call, petition, request, requirement

beyond the natural range of the senses. **clairvoyant** *n, adj*.

clam ❶ *n* **1** edible shellfish with a hinged shell. ▷ *v* **clamming, clammed 2 clam up** *informal* stop talking, esp. through nervousness.

clamber ❶ *v* climb awkwardly.

clammy ❶ *adj* **-mier, -miest** unpleasantly moist and sticky.

clamour ❶ *n* **1** loud protest. **2** loud persistent noise or outcry. ▷ *v* **3** make a loud noise or outcry. **clamorous** *adj* **clamour for** *v* demand noisily.

clamp ❶ *n* **1** tool with movable jaws for holding things together tightly. ▷ *v* **2** fasten with a clamp. **clamp down on** *v* **1** become stricter about. **2** suppress.

clan ❶ *n* **1** group of families with a common ancestor, esp. among Scottish Highlanders. **2** close group. **clannish** *adj* (of a group) tending to exclude outsiders.

clandestine ❶ *adj* secret and concealed.

clang *v* **1** make a loud ringing metallic sound. ▷ *n* **2** ringing metallic sound. **clanger** *n informal* obvious mistake.

clap ❶ *v* **clapping, clapped 1** applaud by hitting the palms of one's hands sharply together. **2** put quickly or forcibly. **3** strike (someone) lightly with an open hand, for

example in greeting. ▷ *n* **4** act or sound of clapping. **5** sudden loud noise, e.g. *a clap of thunder*. **clapped out** *slang* worn out, dilapidated.

claret [**klar**-rit] *n* dry red wine from Bordeaux.

clarify ❶ *v* **-fying, -fied** make (a matter) clear and unambiguous. **clarification** *n*.

clarinet *n* keyed woodwind instrument with a single reed. **clarinettist** *n*.

clash ❶ *v* **1** come into conflict. **2** (of events) happen at the same time. **3** (of colours) look unattractive together. **4** (of objects) make a loud harsh sound by being hit together. ▷ *n* **5** fight, argument. **6** fact of two events happening at the same time.

clasp ❶ *n* **1** device for fastening things. **2** firm grasp or embrace. ▷ *v* **3** grasp or embrace firmly. **4** fasten with a clasp.

class ❶ *n* **1** group of people sharing a similar social position. **2** system of dividing society into such groups. **3** group of people or things sharing a common characteristic. **4** group of pupils or students taught together. **5** standard of quality. **6** *informal* elegance or excellence, e.g. *a touch of class*. ▷ *v* **7** place in a class.

classic ❶ *adj* **1** being a typical example of something. **2** of lasting interest because

━━━━━━━━━━━━━━━━━━━━━━━━━━━━━━━━━━ THESAURUS ━━━

clamber *v* = **climb**, claw, scale, scrabble, scramble, shin

clammy *adj* = **moist**, close, damp, dank, sticky, sweaty

clamour *n* **2** = **noise**, commotion, din, hubbub, outcry, racket, shouting, uproar

clamp *n* **1** = **vice**, bracket, fastener, grip, press ▷ *v* **2** = **fasten**, brace, fix, make fast, secure

clan *n* **1** = **family**, tribe **2** = **group**, brotherhood, faction, fraternity, society

clandestine *adj* = **secret**, cloak-and-dagger, concealed, covert, furtive, private, stealthy, surreptitious, underground

clap *v* **1** = **applaud**, acclaim, cheer

clarify *v* = **explain**, clear up, elucidate, illuminate, interpret, make plain, simplify,

throw *or* shed light on

clash *v* **1** = **conflict**, cross swords, feud, grapple, lock horns, quarrel, war, wrangle **4** = **crash**, bang, clang, clank, clatter, jangle, jar, rattle ▷ *n* **5** = **conflict**, brush, collision, confrontation, difference of opinion, disagreement, fight, showdown (*inf*)

clasp *n* **1** = **fastening**, brooch, buckle, catch, clip, fastener, grip, hook, pin **2** = **grasp**, embrace, grip, hold, hug ▷ *v* **3** = **grasp**, clutch, embrace, grip, hold, hug, press, seize, squeeze **4** = **fasten**, connect

class *n* **3** = **group**, category, division, genre, kind, set, sort, type ▷ *v* **7** = **classify**, brand, categorize, designate, grade, group, label, rank, rate

classic *adj* **1** = **typical**, archetypal,

of excellence. **3** attractive because of simplicity of form. ▷ *n* **4** author, artist, or work of art of recognized excellence. ▷ *pl* **5** study of ancient Greek and Roman literature and culture. **classical** *adj* **1** of or in a restrained conservative style. **2** denoting serious art music. **3** of or influenced by ancient Greek and Roman culture. **classically** *adv* **classicism** *n* artistic style showing emotional restraint and regularity of form. **classicist** *n*.

clatter *v, n* (make) a rattling noise.

clause ❶ *n* **1** section of a legal document. **2** part of a sentence, containing a verb.

claustrophobia *n* abnormal fear of confined spaces. **claustrophobic** *adj*

clavicle *n* same as COLLARBONE.

claw ❶ *n* **1** sharp hooked nail of a bird or beast. **2** similar part, such as a crab's pincer. ▷ *v* **3** tear with claws or nails.

clay *n* fine-grained earth, soft when moist and hardening when baked, used to make bricks and pottery. **clayey** *adj* **clay pigeon** baked clay disc hurled into the air as a target for shooting.

clean ❶ *adj* **1** free from dirt or impurities. **2** not yet used. **3** morally acceptable, inoffensive. **4** (of a reputation or record) free from dishonesty or corruption. **5** complete, e.g. *a clean break.* **6** smooth and regular. ▷ *v* **7** make (something) free from dirt. ▷ *adv* **8** *not standard* completely, e.g. *I clean forgot.* **come clean** *informal* reveal or admit something. **cleaner** *n* **cleanly** *adv* **cleanliness** *n*.

clear ❶ *adj* **1** free from doubt or confusion. **2** easy to see or hear. **3** able to be seen through. **4** free from darkness or obscurity. **5** free of obstruction. **6** (of weather) free from clouds. **7** (of skin) without blemish. **8** (of money) without deduction. ▷ *adv* **9** in a clear or distinct manner. **10** out of the way. ▷ *v* **11** make or become clear. **12** pass by or over (something) without contact. **13** prove (someone) innocent of a crime or mistake. **14** make as profit. **clearly** *adv* **clearance** *n* **1** clearing. **2** official permission. **clearing** *n* treeless area in a wood. **clear off** *v informal* go away. **clear out** *v* **1** remove and sort the contents of. **2** *informal* go away. **clearway** *n* stretch of road on which motorists may stop in an emergency.

cleave¹ *v* **cleaving, cleft, cleaved** *or* **clove, cleft, cleaved** *or* **cloven** split apart. **cleavage** *n* **1** space between a woman's breasts, as revealed by a low-cut dress. **2** division, split. **cleaver** *n* butcher's heavy knife with a square blade.

cleave² *v* cling or stick.

characteristic, definitive, exemplary, ideal, model, quintessential, standard **2 = best**, consummate, finest, first-rate, masterly, world-class *n* **4 = standard**, exemplar, masterpiece, model, paradigm, prototype

clause *n* **1 = section**, article, chapter, condition, paragraph, part, passage

claw *n* **1 = nail**, talon **2 = pincer** ▷ *v* **3 = scratch**, dig, lacerate, maul, rip, scrape, tear

clean *adj* **1 = pure**, antiseptic, decontaminated, flawless, hygienic, immaculate, impeccable, purified, spotless, sterile, sterilized, unblemished, uncontaminated, unpolluted **3 = moral**, chaste, decent, good, honourable, innocent, pure, respectable, upright, virtuous **5 = complete**, conclusive, decisive, entire, final, perfect, thorough, total, unimpaired, whole ▷ *v* **7 = cleanse**, disinfect, launder, purge, purify, rinse, sanitize, scour, scrub, wash

clear *adj* **1 = certain**, convinced, decided, definite, positive, resolved, satisfied, sure **2 = obvious**, apparent, blatant, comprehensible, conspicuous, distinct, evident, manifest, palpable, plain, pronounced, recognizable, unmistakable **3 = transparent**, crystalline, glassy, limpid, pellucid, see-through, translucent **5 = unobstructed**, empty, free, open, smooth, unhindered, unimpeded

clef *n Music* symbol at the beginning of a stave to show the pitch.

cleft *n* 1 narrow opening or crack. ▷ *v* 2 a past of CLEAVE¹. **in a cleft stick** in a very difficult position.

clematis *n* climbing plant with large colourful flowers.

clement *adj* (of weather) mild. **clemency** *n* kind or lenient treatment.

clench *v* 1 close or squeeze (one's teeth or fist) tightly. 2 grasp firmly.

clergy ❶ *n* priests and ministers as a group. **clergyman** *n*.

clerical *adj* 1 of clerks or office work. 2 of the clergy.

clerk *n* employee in an office, bank, or court who keeps records, files, and accounts.

clever ❶ *adj* 1 intelligent, quick at learning. 2 showing skill. **cleverly** *adv* **cleverness** *n*.

clianthus [klee-**anth**-us] *n* Australian or NZ plant with slender scarlet flowers.

cliché ❶ [**klee**-shay] *n* expression or idea that is no longer effective because of overuse. **clichéd** *adj*.

click *n* 1 short sharp sound. ▷ *v* 2 make this sound. 3 *informal* (of two people) get on well together. 4 *informal* become suddenly clear. 5 *slang* be a success. 6 (also **click on**) *Computers* to select a particular function by pressing a button on a mouse.

client ❶ *n* 1 person who uses the services of a professional person or company. 2 *Computers* a program or work station that requests data from a server. **clientele** [klee-on-**tell**] *n* clients collectively.

cliff ❶ *n* steep rock face, esp. along the sea shore. **cliffhanger** *n* film, game, etc., that is tense and exciting because its outcome is uncertain.

climate ❶ *n* typical weather conditions of an area. **climatic** *adj*.

climax ❶ *n* 1 most intense point of an experience, series of events, or story. 2 same as ORGASM. **climactic** *adj*.

climb ❶ *v* 1 go up, ascend. 2 rise to a higher point or intensity. ▷ *n* 3 climbing. 4 place to be climbed. **climber** *n* **climb down** *v* retreat from an opinion or position.

clinch ❶ *v* settle (an argument or agreement) decisively. **clincher** *n informal* something decisive.

cling ❶ *v* clinging, clung hold tightly or stick closely. **clingfilm** *n* thin polythene material for wrapping food.

clinic *n* 1 building where outpatients receive medical treatment or advice. 2 private or specialized hospital. **clinical** *adj* 1 of a clinic. 2 logical and unemotional. **clinically** *adv*.

clink *v, n* (make) a light sharp metallic sound.

———————————————————————— THESAURUS ————

6 = **bright**, cloudless, fair, fine, light, luminous, shining, sunny, unclouded
7 = **unblemished**, clean, immaculate
▷ *v* 11 = **unblock**, disentangle, extricate, free, open, rid 12 = **pass over**, jump, leap, miss, vault 13 = **absolve**, acquit, excuse, exonerate, justify, vindicate 14 = **gain**, acquire, earn, make, reap, secure

clergy *n* = **priesthood**, churchmen, clergymen, clerics, holy orders, ministry, the cloth

clever *adj* 1 = **intelligent**, bright, ingenious, knowledgeable, quick-witted, resourceful, shrewd, smart 2 = **talented**, gifted

cliché *n* = **platitude**, banality,

commonplace, hackneyed phrase, stereotype, truism

client *n* = **customer**, applicant, buyer, consumer, patient, patron, shopper

cliff *n* = **rock face**, bluff, crag, escarpment, overhang, precipice, scar, scarp

climate *n* = **weather**, temperature

climax *n* 1 = **culmination**, height, highlight, high point, peak, summit, top, zenith

climb *v* 1 = **ascend**, clamber, mount, rise, scale, shin up, soar, top

clinch *v* = **settle**, conclude, confirm, decide, determine, seal, secure, set the seal on, sew up (*inf*)

cling *v* = **stick**, adhere, clasp, clutch,

clip¹ ⊕ v **clipping**, **clipped** 1 cut with shears or scissors. 2 *informal* hit sharply. ▷ n 3 short extract of a film. 4 *informal* sharp blow. **clippers** pl n tool for clipping. **clipping** n something cut out, esp. an article from a newspaper.

clip² ⊕ n 1 device for attaching or holding things together. ▷ v **clipping**, **clipped** 2 attach or hold together with a clip.

clipper n fast commercial sailing ship.

clique ⊕ [kleek] n small exclusive group.

clitoris [klit-or-iss] n small sexually sensitive organ at the front of the vulva. **clitoral** adj.

cloak ⊕ n 1 loose sleeveless outer garment. ▷ v 2 cover or conceal. **cloakroom** n room where coats may be left temporarily.

clobber v *informal* 1 hit. 2 defeat utterly.

clock n 1 instrument for showing the time. 2 device with a dial for recording or measuring. **clockwise** adv, adj in the direction in which the hands of a clock rotate. **clock in** or **on**, **out** or **off** v register arrival at or departure from work on an automatic time recorder. **clock up** v reach (a total). **clockwork** n mechanism similar to the kind in a clock, used in wind-up toys.

clod n 1 lump of earth. 2 stupid person.

clog ⊕ v **clogging**, **clogged** 1 obstruct. ▷ n 2 wooden or wooden-soled shoe.

cloister n covered pillared arcade, usu. in a monastery. **cloistered** adj sheltered.

clone n 1 animal or plant produced artificially from the cells of another animal or plant, and identical to the original. 2 *informal* person who closely resembles another. ▷ v 3 produce as a clone.

close¹ ⊕ v [rhymes with **nose**] 1 shut. 2 prevent access to. 3 end, terminate. 4 bring or come nearer together. ▷ n 5 end, conclusion. 6 [rhymes with **dose**] street closed at one end. 7 [rhymes with **dose**] courtyard, quadrangle. **closed shop** place of work in which all workers must belong to a particular trade union.

close² ⊕ adj [rhymes with **dose**] 1 near. 2 intimate. 3 careful, thorough. 4 compact, dense. 5 oppressive, stifling. 6 secretive. ▷ adv 7 closely, tightly. **closely** adv **closeness** n **close season** period when it is illegal to kill certain game or fish. **close shave** *informal* narrow escape. **close-up** n photograph or film taken at close range.

closet n 1 US cupboard. 2 small private

---

embrace, grasp, grip, hug
clip¹ v 1 = **trim**, crop, curtail, cut, pare, prune, shear, shorten, snip 2 *Inf* = **smack**, clout (*inf*), cuff, knock, punch, strike, thump, wallop (*inf*), whack ▷ n 4 *Inf* = **smack**, clout (*inf*), cuff, knock, punch, strike, thump, wallop (*inf*), whack
clip² v 2 = **attach**, fasten, fix, hold, pin, staple
clique n = **group**, cabal, circle, coterie, faction, gang, set
cloak n 1 = **cape**, coat, mantle, wrap ▷ v 2 = **cover**, camouflage, conceal, disguise, hide, mask, obscure, screen, veil
clog v 1 = **obstruct**, block, congest, hinder, impede, jam
close¹ v 1 = **shut**, bar, block, lock, plug, seal, secure, stop up 2 = **end**, cease, complete,

conclude, finish, shut down, terminate, wind up 4 = **connect**, come together, couple, fuse, join, unite n 5 = **end**, completion, conclusion, culmination, denouement, ending, finale, finish
close² adj 1 = **near**, adjacent, adjoining, at hand, cheek by jowl, handy, impending, nearby, neighbouring, nigh 2 = **intimate**, attached, confidential, dear, devoted, familiar, inseparable, loving 3 = **careful**, detailed, intense, minute, painstaking, rigorous, thorough 4 = **compact**, congested, crowded, dense, impenetrable, jam-packed, packed, tight 5 = **stifling**, airless, heavy, humid, muggy, oppressive, stuffy, suffocating, sweltering 6 = **secretive**, private, reticent, secret, taciturn, uncommunicative

room. ▷ *adj* **3** private, secret. ▷ *v* **closeting**, **closeted 4** shut (oneself) away in private.

clot *n* **1** soft thick lump formed from liquid. **2** *informal* stupid person. ▷ *v* **clotting**, **clotted 3** form soft thick lumps.

cloth ❶ *n* (piece of) woven fabric.

cloud ❶ *n* **1** mass of condensed water vapour floating in the sky. **2** floating mass of smoke, dust, etc. **3** *Computers* internet server used to store data and services. ▷ *v* **4** (foll. by *over*) become cloudy. **5** confuse. **6** make gloomy or depressed. **cloudy** *adj* **1** having a lot of clouds. **2** (of liquid) not clear. **cloudburst** *n* heavy fall of rain. **cloud computing** model of computer use in which internet services are provided to users on a temporary basis.

clout ❶ *informal* ▷ *n* **1** hard blow. **2** power, influence. ▷ *v* **3** hit hard.

clove¹ *n* dried flower bud of a tropical tree, used as a spice.

clove² *n* segment of a bulb of garlic.

clover *n* plant with three-lobed leaves.

clown ❶ *n* **1** comic entertainer in a circus. **2** amusing person. **3** stupid person. ▷ *v* **4** behave foolishly. **5** perform as a clown.

club ❶ *n* **1** association of people with common interests. **2** building used by such a group. **3** thick stick used as a weapon. **4** stick with a curved end used to hit the ball in golf. **5** playing card with black three-leaved symbols. ▷ *v* **clubbing, clubbed 6** hit with a club. **club together** *v* combine resources for a common purpose.

cluck *n* **1** low clicking noise made by a hen. ▷ *v* **2** make this noise.

clue ❶ *n* something that helps to solve a mystery or puzzle. **not have a clue** be completely baffled. **clueless** *adj* stupid.

clump ❶ *n* **1** small group of things or people. **2** dull heavy tread. ▷ *v* **3** walk heavily. **4** form into clumps.

clumsy ❶ *adj* **-sier, -siest 1** lacking skill or physical coordination. **2** badly made or done. **clumsily** *adv* **clumsiness** *n*.

cluster ❶ *n* **1** small close group. ▷ *v* **2** gather in clusters.

clutch ❶ *v* **1** grasp tightly. **2** (foll. by *at*) try to get hold of. ▷ *n* **3** device enabling two revolving shafts to be connected and disconnected, esp. in a motor vehicle. **4** tight grasp.

clutter ❶ *v* **1** scatter objects about (a place)

——————————————— THESAURUS ———————————————

cloth *n* **1** = **fabric**, material, textiles

cloud *n* **1, 2** = **mist**, gloom, haze, murk, vapour ▷ *v* **4** (foll. by *over*) = **obscure**, becloud, darken, dim, eclipse, obfuscate, overshadow, shade, shadow, veil **5** = **confuse**, disorient, distort, impair, muddle, muddy the waters

clout *Inf n* **2** = **influence**, authority, mana (*NZ*), power, prestige, pull, weight ▷ *v* **3** = **hit**, clobber (*sl*), punch, sock (*sl*), strike, thump, wallop (*inf*)

clown *n* **1** = **comedian**, buffoon, comic, fool, harlequin, jester **2** = **joker**, prankster ▷ *v* **4** = **play the fool**, act the fool, jest, mess about

club *n* **1** = **association**, fraternity, group, guild, lodge, set, society, union **3** = **stick**, bat, bludgeon, cosh (*Brit*), cudgel, truncheon ▷ *v* **6** = **beat**, bash, batter,

bludgeon, cosh (*Brit*), hammer, pummel, strike

clue *n* = **indication**, evidence, hint, lead, pointer, sign, suggestion, suspicion, trace

clump *n* **1** = **cluster**, bunch, bundle, group, mass ▷ *v* **3** = **stomp**, lumber, plod, thud, thump, tramp

clumsy *adj* **1** = **awkward**, bumbling, gauche, gawky, ham-fisted (*inf*), lumbering, maladroit, ponderous, uncoordinated, ungainly, unwieldy

cluster *n* **1** = **gathering**, assemblage, batch, bunch, clump, collection, group, knot ▷ *v* **2** = **gather**, assemble, bunch, collect, flock, group

clutch *v* **1** = **seize**, catch, clasp, cling to, embrace, grab, grasp, grip, snatch

clutter *v* **1** = **litter**, scatter, strew ▷ *n*

untidily. ▷ *n* **2** untidy mess.

cm centimetre.

Co. **1** Company. **2** County.

co- *prefix* together, joint, or jointly, e.g. *coproduction*.

c/o **1** care of. **2** *Book-keeping* carried over.

coach **❶** *n* **1** long-distance bus. **2** railway carriage. **3** large four-wheeled horse-drawn carriage. **4** trainer, instructor. ▷ *v* **5** train, teach.

coagulate [koh-**ag**-yew-late] *v* change from a liquid to a semisolid mass. **coagulation** *n*.

coal *n* black rock consisting mainly of carbon, used as fuel. **coalfield** *n* area with coal under the ground.

coalesce **❶** [koh-a-**less**] *v* come together, merge. **coalescence** *n*.

coalition **❶** [koh-a-**lish**-un] *n* temporary alliance, esp. between political parties.

coarse **❶** *adj* **1** rough in texture. **2** unrefined, indecent. **coarsely** *adv* **coarseness** *n* **coarsen** *v*.

coast **❶** *n* **1** place where the land meets the sea. ▷ *v* **2** move by momentum, without the use of power. **coastal** *adj* **coaster** *n* small mat placed under a glass. **coastguard** *n* **1** organization that aids ships and swimmers in trouble and prevents smuggling. **2** member of this. **coastline** *n*.

coat **❶** *n* **1** outer garment with long sleeves. **2** animal's fur or hair. **3** covering layer,

e.g. *a coat of paint.* ▷ *v* **4** cover with a layer. **coating** *n* covering layer. **coat of arms** heraldic emblem of a family or institution.

coax **❶** *v* **1** persuade gently. **2** obtain by persistent coaxing.

cob *n* **1** stalk of an ear of maize. **2** thickset type of horse. **3** round loaf of bread. **4** male swan.

cobalt *n Chem* brittle silvery-white metallic element.

cobber *n Aust or NZ informal* friend.

cobble *n* cobblestone. **cobbler** *n* shoe mender. **cobblestone** *n* rounded stone used for paving. **cobble together** *v* put together clumsily.

cobia [**koh**-bee-a] *n* large dark-striped game fish of tropical and subtropical seas.

cobra *n* venomous hooded snake of Asia and Africa.

cobweb *n* spider's web.

cocaine *n* addictive drug used as a narcotic and as an anaesthetic.

cochineal *n* red dye obtained from a Mexican insect, used for food colouring.

cock *n* **1** male bird, esp. of domestic fowl. **2** stopcock. ▷ *v* **3** draw back (the hammer of a gun) to firing position. **4** lift and turn (part of the body). **cockerel** *n* young domestic cock. **cock-a-hoop** *adj* in high spirits. **cock-and-bull story** improbable story.

cockatiel, cockateel *n* crested Australian parrot with a greyish-brown

——— THESAURUS ———

2 = **untidiness**, confusion, disarray, disorder, hotchpotch, jumble, litter, mess, muddle

coach *n* **1** = **bus**, car, charabanc, vehicle **3** = **carriage 4** = **instructor**, handler, teacher, trainer, tutor ▷ *v* **5** = **instruct**, drill, exercise, prepare, train, tutor

coalesce *v* = **blend**, amalgamate, combine, fuse, incorporate, integrate, merge, mix, unite

coalition *n* = **alliance**, amalgamation, association, bloc, combination, confederation, conjunction, fusion,

merger, union

coarse *adj* **1** = **rough 2** = **vulgar**, earthy, improper, indecent, indelicate, ribald, rude, smutty

coast *n* **1** = **shore**, beach, border, coastline, seaboard, seaside ▷ *v* **2** = **cruise**, drift, freewheel, glide, sail, taxi

coat *n* **2** = **fur**, fleece, hair, hide, pelt, skin, wool **3** = **layer**, coating, covering, overlay ▷ *v* **4** = **cover**, apply, plaster, smear, spread

coax *v* **1** = **persuade**, allure, cajole, entice, prevail upon, sweet-talk (*inf*), talk into, wheedle

and yellow plumage.

cockatoo n crested parrot of Australia or the East Indies.

cockie, cocky n, pl **-kies** Aust & NZ informal farmer.

cockle n edible shellfish.

cockpit n 1 pilot's compartment in an aircraft. 2 driver's compartment in a racing car.

cockroach n beetle-like insect which is a household pest.

cocktail n 1 mixed alcoholic drink. 2 appetizer of seafood or mixed fruits.

cocky ❶ adj **cockier**, **cockiest** conceited and overconfident. **cockily** adv **cockiness** n.

cocoa n 1 powder made from the seed of the cacao tree. 2 drink made from this powder.

coconut n 1 large hard fruit of a type of palm tree. 2 edible flesh of this fruit.

cocoon n 1 silky protective covering of a silkworm. 2 protective covering. ▷ v 3 wrap up tightly for protection.

cod n 1 large food fish of the North Atlantic. 2 any other fish of the same family.

COD cash on delivery.

coda n final part of a musical composition.

code ❶ n 1 system of letters, symbols, or prearranged signals by which messages can be communicated secretly or briefly. 2 set of principles or rules. ▷ v 3 put into code. **codify** v **-fying**, **-fied** organize (rules or procedures) systematically. **codification** n.

codeine [kode-een] n drug used as a painkiller.

coerce [koh-**urss**] v compel, force. **coercion** n **coercive** adj.

coexist v exist together, esp. peacefully despite differences. **coexistence** n.

C of E Church of England.

coffee n 1 drink made from the roasted and ground seeds of a tropical shrub. 2 beanlike seeds of this shrub. ▷ adj 3 medium-brown.

coffer n 1 chest for valuables. ▷ pl 2 store of money.

coffin n box in which a corpse is buried or cremated.

cog n 1 one of the teeth on the rim of a gearwheel. 2 unimportant person in a big organization.

cogent ❶ [**koh**-jent] adj forcefully convincing. **cogency** n.

cogitate ❶ [**koj**-it-tate] v think deeply about. **cogitation** n.

cognac [**kon**-yak] n French brandy.

cognizance n knowledge, understanding. **cognizant** adj.

cohabit v live together as husband and wife without being married. **cohabitation** n.

cohere v 1 hold or stick together. 2 be logically connected or consistent. **coherence** n **coherent** adj 1 logical and consistent. 2 capable of intelligible speech. **coherently** adv **cohesion** n sticking together. **cohesive** adj.

cohort n 1 band of associates. 2 tenth part of an ancient Roman legion.

coiffure n hairstyle. **coiffeur**, **coiffeuse** n hairdresser.

coil ❶ v 1 wind in loops. 2 move in a winding course. ▷ n 3 something coiled. 4 single loop of this. 5 coil-shaped contraceptive device inserted in the womb.

coin ❶ n 1 piece of metal money. 2 metal

————————————————————————————————— THESAURUS ——————

cocky adj = **overconfident**, arrogant, brash, cocksure, conceited, egotistical, full of oneself, swaggering, vain

code n 1 = **cipher**, cryptograph 2 = **principles**, canon, convention, custom, ethics, etiquette, manners, maxim, regulations, rules, system

cogent adj = **convincing**, compelling,

effective, forceful, influential, potent, powerful, strong, weighty

cogitate v = **think**, consider, contemplate, deliberate, meditate, mull over, muse, ponder, reflect, ruminate

coil v 1 = **wind**, curl, loop, snake, spiral, twine, twist, wreathe, writhe

coin n 1,2 = **money**, cash, change, copper,

currency collectively. ▷ *v* **3** invent (a word or phrase). **coinage** *n* **1** coins collectively. **2** word or phrase coined. **3** coining.

coincide ⓘ *v* **1** happen at the same time. **2** agree or correspond exactly. **coincidence** *n* **1** occurrence of simultaneous or apparently connected events. **2** coinciding. **coincident** *adj* in agreement. **coincidental** *adj* resulting from coincidence. **coincidentally** *adv*.

coke¹ *n* solid fuel left after gas has been distilled from coal.

coke² *n slang* cocaine.

cola *n* dark brown fizzy soft drink.

colander *n* perforated bowl for straining or rinsing foods.

cold ⓘ *adj* **1** lacking heat. **2** lacking affection or enthusiasm. **3** (of a colour) giving an impression of coldness. **4** *slang* unconscious, e.g. *out cold*. ▷ *n* **5** lack of heat. **6** mild illness causing a runny nose, sneezing, and coughing. **coldly** *adv* **coldness** *n* **cold-blooded** *adj* **1** cruel, unfeeling. **2** having a body temperature that varies according to the surrounding temperature. **cold feet** *slang* nervousness, fear. **cold-shoulder** *v* treat with indifference. **cold war** political hostility between countries without actual warfare.

coleslaw *n* salad dish of shredded raw cabbage in a dressing.

colic *n* severe pains in the stomach and bowels. **colicky** *adj*.

collaborate ⓘ *v* **1** work with another on a project. **2** cooperate with an enemy invader. **collaboration** *n* **collaborative** *adj* **collaborator** *n*.

collage [kol-**lahzh**] *n* **1** art form in which various materials or objects are glued onto a surface. **2** picture made in this way.

collapse ⓘ *v* **1** fall down suddenly. **2** fail completely. **3** fold compactly. ▷ *n* **4** collapsing. **5** sudden failure or breakdown. **collapsible** *adj*.

collar ⓘ *n* **1** part of a garment round the neck. **2** band put round an animal's neck. **3** cut of meat from an animal's neck. ▷ *v* **4** *informal* seize, arrest. **5** catch in order to speak to. **collarbone** *n* bone joining the shoulder blade to the breastbone.

collate *v* gather together, examine, and put in order. **collation** *n* **1** collating. **2** light meal.

collateral *n* security pledged for the repayment of a loan.

colleague ⓘ *n* fellow worker, esp. in a profession.

collect ⓘ *v* **1** gather together. **2** accumulate (stamps etc.) as a hobby.

silver, specie ▷ *v* **3** = **invent**, create, fabricate, make up, originate

coincide *v* **1** = **occur simultaneously**, be concurrent, coexist, synchronize **2** = **agree**, accord, concur, correspond, harmonize, match, square, tally

cold *adj* **1** = **chilly**, arctic, bleak, cool, freezing, frigid, frosty, frozen, icy, wintry **2** = **unfriendly**, aloof, distant, frigid, indifferent, reserved, standoffish ▷ *n* **5** = **coldness**, chill, frigidity, frostiness, iciness

collaborate *v* **1** = **work together**, cooperate, join forces, participate, play ball (*inf*), team up **2** = **conspire**, collude,

cooperate, fraternize

collapse *v* **1** = **fall down**, cave in, crumple, fall, fall apart at the seams, give way, subside **2** = **fail**, come to nothing, fold, founder, go belly-up (*inf*) ▷ *n* **4** = **falling down**, cave-in, disintegration, falling apart, ruin, subsidence **5** = **failure**, downfall, flop, slump

collar *v* **4** *Inf* = **seize**, apprehend, arrest, capture, catch, grab, nab (*inf*), nail (*inf*)

colleague *n* = **fellow worker**, ally, assistant, associate, collaborator, comrade, helper, partner, team-mate, workmate

collect *v* **1** = **assemble**, cluster, congregate, convene, converge, flock together, rally

3 fetch. **4** receive payments of (taxes etc.). **5** regain control of (oneself). **collected** *adj* calm and controlled. **collection** *n* **1** things collected. **2** collecting. **3** sum of money collected. **collective** *adj* of or done by a group. **collector** *n*.

college *n* **1** place of higher education. **2** group of people of the same profession or with special duties. **collegiate** *adj*.

collide ❶ *v* **1** crash together violently. **2** have an argument. **collision** *n*.

collie *n* silky-haired sheepdog.

colliery *n, pl* **-lieries** coal mine. **collier** *n* **1** coal miner. **2** coal ship.

colloquial ❶ *adj* suitable for informal speech or writing. **colloquialism** *n* colloquial word or phrase.

collusion *n* secret or illegal cooperation. **collude** *v* act in collusion.

cologne *n* mild perfume.

colon¹ *n* punctuation mark (:).

colon² *n* part of the large intestine connected to the rectum.

colonel *n* senior commissioned army or air-force officer.

colonnade *n* row of columns.

colony ❶ *n, pl* **-nies 1** group of people who settle in a new country but remain under the rule of their homeland. **2** territory occupied by a colony. **3** group of people or animals of the same kind living together. **colonial** *adj, n* (inhabitant) of a colony.

colonialism *n* policy of acquiring and maintaining colonies. **colonist** *n* settler in a colony. **colonize** *v* make into a colony. **colonization** *n*.

colossal ❶ *adj* very large.

colour ❶ *n* **1** appearance of things as a result of reflecting light. **2** substance that gives colour. **3** complexion. ▷ *pl* **4** flag of a country or regiment. **5** *Sport* badge or symbol denoting membership of a team. ▷ *v* **6** apply colour to. **7** influence (someone's judgment). **8** blush. **colourful** *adj* **1** with bright or varied colours. **2** vivid, distinctive. **colourfully** *adv* **colourless** *adj* **colour-blind** *adj* unable to distinguish between certain colours.

colt *n* young male horse.

columbine *n* garden flower with five petals.

column ❶ *n* **1** pillar. **2** vertical division of a newspaper page. **3** regular feature in a newspaper. **4** vertical arrangement of numbers. **5** narrow formation of troops. **columnist** *n* journalist who writes a regular feature in a newspaper.

coma ❶ *n* state of deep unconsciousness. **comatose** *adj* **1** in a coma. **2** sound asleep.

comb ❶ *n* **1** toothed implement for arranging the hair. **2** cock's crest. **3** honeycomb. ▷ *v* **4** use a comb on. **5** search with great care.

THESAURUS

2 = gather, accumulate, amass, assemble, heap, hoard, save, stockpile

collide *v* **1 = crash**, clash, come into collision, meet head-on **2 = conflict**, clash

colloquial *adj* **= informal**, conversational, demotic, everyday, familiar, idiomatic, vernacular

colony *n* **1 = settlement**, community, dependency, dominion, outpost, possession, province, satellite state **2 = territory**

colossal *adj* **= huge**, enormous, gigantic, immense, mammoth, massive, monumental, prodigious, vast

colour *n* **1 = hue**, shade, tint **2 = pigment**, colorant, dye, paint, tint ▷ *v* **6 = paint**, dye, stain, tinge, tint **8 = blush**, flush, redden

column *n* **1 = pillar**, obelisk, post, shaft, support, upright **5 = line**, file, procession, rank, row

coma *n* **= unconsciousness**, oblivion, stupor, trance

comb *v* **4 = untangle**, arrange, dress, groom **5 = search**, forage, fossick, hunt (*Aust & NZ*), rake, ransack, rummage, scour, sift

combat ⊕ n, v **-bating, -bated** fight, struggle. **combatant** n **combative** adj.

combine ⊕ v 1 join together. ▷ n 2 association of people or firms for a common purpose. **combination** n 1 combining. 2 people or things combined. 3 set of numbers that opens a special lock. ▷ pl 4 old-fashioned undergarment with long sleeves and long legs. **combine harvester** machine that reaps and threshes grain in one process.

combustion n process of burning. **combustible** adj burning easily.

come ⊕ v **coming, came, come** 1 move towards a place, arrive. 2 occur. 3 reach a specified point or condition. 4 be produced. 5 (foll. by *from*) be born in. 6 become, e.g. *a dream come true*. **come across** v 1 meet or find by accident. 2 (often foll. by *as*) give an impression of (being). **comeback** n informal 1 return to a former position. 2 retort. **comedown** n 1 decline in status. 2 disappointment. **comeuppance** n informal deserved punishment.

comedy ⊕ n, pl **-dies** humorous play, film, or programme. **comedian, comedienne** n 1 entertainer who tells jokes. 2 person who performs in comedy.

comely adj **-lier, -liest** old-fashioned nice-looking.

comet n heavenly body with a long luminous tail.

comfort ⊕ n 1 physical ease or wellbeing. 2 consolation. 3 means of consolation. ▷ v 4 soothe, console. **comfortable** adj 1 giving comfort. 2 free from pain. 3 informal well-off financially. **comfortably** adv **comforter** n.

comic ⊕ adj 1 humorous, funny. 2 of comedy. ▷ n 3 comedian. 4 magazine containing strip cartoons. **comical** adj amusing. **comically** adv.

comma n punctuation mark (,).

command ⊕ v 1 order. 2 have authority over. 3 deserve and get. 4 look down over. ▷ n 5 authoritative instruction that something must be done. 6 authority to command. 7 knowledge. 8 military or naval unit with a specific function. **commandant** n officer commanding a military group. **commandeer** v seize for military use. **commander** n 1 military officer in command of a group or operation. 2 middle-ranking naval officer. **commandment** n command from God, esp. one of the Ten Commandments in the Old Testament.

commando n, pl **-dos, -does** (member

combat n = **fight**, action, battle, conflict, contest, encounter, engagement, skirmish, struggle, war, warfare ▷ v = **fight**, defy, do battle with, oppose, resist, withstand

combine v 1 = **join together**, amalgamate, blend, connect, integrate, link, merge, mix, pool, unite

come v 1 = **arrive**, advance, appear, approach, draw near, materialize, move towards, near, reach, show up (*inf*), turn up (*inf*) 2 = **happen**, fall, occur, take place 4 = **result**, arise, be produced, emanate, emerge, flow, issue, originate

comedy n = **light entertainment**, farce

comfort n 1 = **luxury**, cosiness, ease,

opulence, snugness, wellbeing 2 = **relief**, compensation, consolation, help, succour, support ▷ v 4 = **console**, commiserate with, hearten, reassure, soothe

comic adj 1 = **funny**, amusing, comical, droll, farcical, humorous, jocular, witty ▷ n 3 = **comedian**, buffoon, clown, funny man, humorist, jester, wag, wit

command v 1 = **order**, bid, charge, compel, demand, direct, require 2 = **have authority over**, control, dominate, govern, handle, head, lead, manage, rule, supervise n 5 = **order**, commandment, decree, demand, directive, instruction, requirement, ultimatum 6 = **authority**,

of) a military unit trained for swift raids in
enemy territory.

commemorate ❶ v honour the memory
of. **commemoration** n **commemorative**
adj.

commence ❶ v begin. **commencement** n.

commend ❶ v 1 praise. 2 recommend.
commendable adj **commendably** adv
commendation n.

commensurate adj corresponding in
degree, size, or value.

comment ❶ n 1 remark. 2 talk, gossip.
3 explanatory note. ▷ v 4 make a
comment. **commentary** n, pl -**taries**
1 spoken accompaniment to a broadcast
or film. 2 series of explanatory notes
on a subject. **commentate** v provide a
commentary. **commentator** n.

commerce ❶ n buying and selling, trade.
commercial adj 1 of commerce. 2 (of
television or radio) paid for by advertisers.
3 having profit as the main aim. ▷ n
4 television or radio advertisement.
commercialization n.

commiserate ❶ v (foll. by with) express
sympathy (for). **commiseration** n.

● SPELLING TIP
● The most popular way to misspell
● **commiserate** and **commiseration** is
● to double the s as well as the m. There
● should indeed be two ms, but only one s.

commission ❶ n 1 piece of work that
an artist is asked to do. 2 duty, task.
3 percentage paid to a salesperson for each
sale made. 4 group of people appointed
to perform certain duties. 5 committing
of a crime. 6 Mil rank or authority
officially given to an officer. ▷ v 7 place
an order for. 8 Mil give a commission to.
9 grant authority to. **out of commission**
not in working order. **commissioner**
n 1 appointed official in a government
department. 2 member of a commission.

commissionaire n uniformed doorman
at a hotel, theatre, etc.

commit ❶ v -mitting, -mitted 1 perform
(a crime or error). 2 pledge (oneself) to
a course of action. 3 send (someone)
to prison or hospital. **committal** n
sending someone to prison or hospital.
commitment n 1 dedication to a cause.
2 responsibility that restricts freedom of
action.

● SPELLING TIP
● The correct spelling of **commitment**
● has three ms altogether, but only two
● ts (which are not next to each other).
● Although the Bank of English has 176
● examples of committment, with three ms
● and three ts, this spelling is wrong.

committee n group of people appointed
to perform a specified service or function.

————————————————————————— THESAURUS ———————————

charge, control, government, mana (NZ),
management, mastery, power, rule,
supervision

commemorate v = **remember**, celebrate,
honour, immortalize, pay tribute to,
recognize, salute

commence v = **begin**, embark on, enter
upon, initiate, open, originate, start

commend v 1 = **praise**, acclaim, applaud,
approve, compliment, extol, speak highly
of 2 = **recommend**

comment n 1 = **remark**, observation,
statement 3 = **note**, annotation,
commentary, explanation, exposition,
illustration ▷ v 4 = **remark**, mention, note,

observe, point out, say, utter

commerce n = **trade**, business, dealing,
exchange, traffic

commiserate v (foll. by with)
= **sympathize**, console, feel for, pity

commission n 2 = **duty**, errand, mandate,
mission, task 3 = **fee**, cut, percentage,
rake-off (sl), royalties 4 = **committee**,
board, commissioners, delegation,
deputation, representatives ▷ v
7 = **appoint**, contract, engage, nominate,
order, select 9 = **authorize**, delegate,
depute, empower

commit v 1 = **do**, carry out, enact, execute,
perform, perpetrate 3 = **put in custody**,

commode n 1 seat with a hinged flap concealing a chamber pot. 2 chest of drawers.

commodity n, pl **-ities** article of trade.

commodore n senior commissioned officer in the navy.

common ❶ adj 1 occurring often. 2 belonging to two or more people. 3 public, general. 4 lacking in taste or manners. ▷ n 5 area of grassy land belonging to a community. **commonly** adv **commoner** n person who does not belong to the nobility. **common-law** adj (of a relationship) regarded as a marriage through being long-standing. **commonplace** adj 1 ordinary, everyday. ▷ n 2 trite remark. **common sense** good practical understanding.

commotion ❶ n noisy disturbance.

commune¹ ❶ n group of people who live together and share everything. **communal** adj shared. **communally** adv.

commune² ❶ v (foll. by with) feel very close (to), e.g. *communing with nature*. **communion** n 1 sharing of thoughts or feelings. 2 (**C-**) Christian ritual of sharing consecrated bread and wine. 3 religious group with shared beliefs and practices.

communicate ❶ v make known or share (information, thoughts, or feelings). **communicable** adj (of a disease) able to be passed on. **communicant** n person who receives Communion. **communicating** adj (of a door) joining two rooms. **communication** n 1 communicating. 2 thing communicated. ▷ pl 3 means of travelling or sending messages. **communicative** adj talking freely.

communiqué [kom-**mune**-ik-kay] n official announcement.

communism ❶ n 1 belief that all property and means of production should be shared by the community. 2 (**C-**) system of state control of the economy and society in some countries. **communist** n, adj.

community ❶ n, pl **-ties** 1 all the people living in one district. 2 group with shared origins or interests. 3 the public, society.

commute v 1 travel daily to and from work. 2 reduce (a sentence) to a less severe one. **commuter** n person who commutes to and from work.

compact¹ ❶ adj 1 closely packed. 2 neatly arranged. 3 concise, brief. ▷ n 4 small flat case containing a mirror and face powder. ▷ v 5 pack closely together. **compact disc**

——————————— THESAURUS ———————————

confine, consign, imprison

common adj 1 = **average**, commonplace, conventional, customary, everyday, familiar, frequent, habitual, ordinary, regular, routine, standard, stock, usual 2 = **collective**, communal, public 3 = **popular**, accepted, general, prevailing, prevalent, universal, widespread 4 = **vulgar**, coarse, inferior, plebeian

commotion n = **disturbance**, disorder, excitement, furore, fuss, hue and cry, rumpus, tumult, turmoil, upheaval, uproar

commune¹ n = **community**, collective, cooperative, kibbutz

commune² v (foll. by with) = **contemplate**, meditate on, muse on, ponder, reflect on

communicate v 1 = **make known**, convey, declare, disclose, impart, inform, pass on, proclaim, transmit

communism n (also cap.) = **socialism**, Bolshevism, collectivism, Marxism, state socialism

community n 1 = **populace**, commonwealth, residents, society, state 2 = **public**, general public, people 3 = **group**, brotherhood, company, society

compact¹ adj 1 = **closely packed**, compressed, condensed, dense,

small digital audio disc on which the sound is read by an optical laser system.

compact² ❶ n contract, agreement.

companion ❶ n person who associates with or accompanies someone. **companionable** adj friendly. **companionship** n.

company ❶ n, pl **-nies** 1 business organization. 2 group of actors. 3 small unit of troops. 4 crew of a ship. 5 fact of being with someone. 6 gathering of people. 7 guest or guests. 8 person's associates.

compare ❶ v 1 examine (things) and point out the resemblances or differences. 2 (foll. by to) declare to be (like). 3 (foll. by with) be worthy of comparison. **comparable** adj **comparability** n **comparative** adj 1 relative. 2 involving comparison. 3 Grammar denoting the form of an adjective or adverb indicating more. ▷ n 4 Grammar comparative form of

a word. **comparatively** adv **comparison** n 1 comparing. 2 similarity or equivalence.

compartment ❶ n 1 section of a railway carriage. 2 separate section.

compass ❶ n 1 instrument for showing direction, with a needle that points north. 2 limits, range. ▷ pl 3 hinged instrument for drawing circles.

compassion ❶ n pity, sympathy. **compassionate** adj.

compatible ❶ adj able to exist, work, or be used together. **compatibility** n.

compatriot n fellow countryman or countrywoman.

compel ❶ v **-pelling, -pelled** force (to be or do).

compendium n, pl **-diums, -dia** selection of board games in one box. **compendious** adj brief but comprehensive.

compensate ❶ v 1 make amends to (someone), esp. for injury or loss. 2 (foll. by for) cancel out (a bad effect).

————————————————————————————— THESAURUS —————————————————————————————

pressed together, solid, thick 3 = **brief**, compendious, concise, succinct, terse, to the point ▷ v 5 = **pack closely**, compress, condense, cram, stuff, tamp

compact² n = **agreement**, arrangement, bargain, bond, contract, covenant, deal, pact, treaty, understanding

companion n = **friend**, accomplice, ally, associate, cobber (Aust or old-fashioned NZ inf), colleague, comrade, consort, mate (inf), partner

company n 1 = **business**, association, concern, corporation, establishment, firm, house, partnership, syndicate 5 = **companionship**, fellowship, presence, society 6 = **group**, assembly, band, collection, community, crowd, gathering, party, set 7 = **guests**, callers, party, visitors

compare v 1 = **weigh**, balance, contrast, juxtapose, set against 2 (foll. by to) = **liken to**, correlate to, equate to, identify with, mention in the same breath as, parallel, resemble 3 (foll. by with) = **be on a par**

with, approach, bear comparison, be in the same class as, be the equal of, compete with, equal, hold a candle to, match

compartment n 1 = **carriage** 2 = **section**, alcove, bay, berth, booth, cubbyhole, cubicle, locker, niche, pigeonhole

compass n 2 = **range**, area, boundary, circumference, extent, field, limit, reach, realm, scope

compassion n = **sympathy**, condolence, fellow feeling, humanity, kindness, mercy, pity, sorrow, tenderness, understanding

compatible adj = **harmonious**, adaptable, congruous, consistent, in harmony, in keeping, suitable

compel v = **force**, coerce, constrain, dragoon, impel, make, oblige, railroad (inf)

compensate v 1 = **recompense**, atone, make amends, make good, refund, reimburse, remunerate, repay 2 (foll. by for) = **cancel (out)**, balance, counteract, counterbalance, make up for, offset, redress

compensation n payment to make up for loss or injury. **compensatory** adj.

compere n 1 person who presents a stage, radio, or television show. ▷ v 2 be the compere of.

compete ❶ v try to win or achieve (a prize, profit, etc.). **competition** n 1 competing. 2 event in which people compete. 3 people against whom one competes. **competitive** adj **competitor** n.

competent ❶ adj having the skill or knowledge to do something well. **competently** adv **competence** n.

compile ❶ v collect and arrange (information), esp. to make a book. **compilation** n **compiler** n.

complacent ❶ adj self-satisfied. **complacency** n.

complain ❶ v 1 express resentment or displeasure. 2 (foll. by of) say that one is suffering from (an illness). **complaint** n 1 complaining. 2 mild illness.

complainant n Law plaintiff.

complement ❶ n 1 thing that completes something. 2 complete amount or number. 3 Grammar word or words added to a verb to complete the meaning. ▷ v 4 make complete. **complementary** adj.

complete ❶ adj 1 thorough, absolute. 2 finished. 3 having all the necessary parts. ▷ v 4 finish. 5 make whole or perfect. **completely** adv **completeness** n **completion** n finishing.

complex ❶ adj 1 made up of parts. 2 complicated. ▷ n 3 whole made up of parts. 4 group of unconscious feelings that influences behaviour. **complexity** n.

complexion ❶ n 1 skin of the face. 2 character, nature.

complicate ❶ v make or become complex or difficult to deal with. **complication** n

complicity n fact of being an accomplice in a crime.

compliment ❶ n 1 expression of praise.

THESAURUS
---

compete v = **contend**, be in the running, challenge, contest, fight, strive, struggle, vie

competent adj = **able**, adequate, capable, fit, proficient, qualified, suitable

compile v = **put together**, accumulate, amass, collect, cull, garner, gather, marshal, organize

complacent adj = **self-satisfied**, contented, pleased with oneself, resting on one's laurels, satisfied, serene, smug, unconcerned

complain v 1 = **find fault**, bemoan, bewail, carp, deplore, groan, grouse, grumble, lament, moan, whine, whinge (inf)

complement n 1 = **completion**, companion, consummation, counterpart, finishing touch, rounding-off, supplement 2 = **total**, aggregate, capacity, entirety, quota, totality, wholeness ▷ v 4 = **complete**, cap (inf), crown, round off, set off

complete adj 1 = **total**, absolute,

consummate, outright, perfect, thorough, thoroughgoing, utter 2 = **finished**, accomplished, achieved, concluded, ended 3 = **entire**, all, faultless, full, intact, plenary, unbroken, whole ▷ v 4 = **finish**, close, conclude, crown, end, finalize, round off, settle, wrap up (inf)

complex adj 1 = **compound**, composite, heterogeneous, manifold, multifarious, multiple 2 = **complicated**, convoluted, elaborate, intricate, involved, labyrinthine, tangled, tortuous ▷ n 3 = **structure**, aggregate, composite, network, organization, scheme, system 4 = **obsession**, fixation, fixed idea, phobia, preoccupation

complexion n 1 = **skin**, colour, colouring, hue, pigmentation, skin tone 2 = **nature**, appearance, aspect, character, guise, light, look, make-up

complicate v = **make difficult**, confuse, entangle, involve, muddle, ravel

compliment n 1 = **praise**, bouquet, commendation, congratulations, eulogy,

▷ *pl* **2** formal greetings. ▷ *v* **3** praise.
complimentary *adj* **1** expressing praise.
2 free of charge.
comply ❶ *v*-**plying**, -**plied** (foll. by *with*) act
in accordance (with).
component ❶ *n, adj* (being) part of a
whole.
compose ❶ *v* **1** put together. **2** be the
component parts of. **3** create (a piece
of music or writing). **4** calm (oneself).
5 arrange artistically. **composer** *n*
person who writes music. **composition**
n way that something is put together or
arranged.
compos mentis *adj Latin* sane.
compost *n* decayed plants used as a
fertilizer.
compound¹ ❶ *n, adj* **1** (thing, esp.
chemical) made up of two or more
combined parts or elements. ▷ *v*
2 combine or make by combining.
3 intensify, make worse.
compound² *n* fenced enclosure containing

buildings, e.g. *a prison compound*.
comprehend ❶ *v* understand.
comprehensible *adj* **comprehension** *n*
comprehensive *adj* **1** of broad scope, fully
inclusive. ▷ *n* **2** comprehensive school.
comprehensive school secondary school
for children of all abilities.
compress ❶ *v* [kum-**press**] **1** squeeze
together. **2** make shorter. ▷ *n* [**kom**-
press]. **3** pad applied to stop bleeding
or cool inflammation. **compression** *n*
compressor *n* machine that compresses
gas or air.
comprise ❶ *v* be made up of or make up.
compromise ❶ [**kom**-prom-mize] *n*
1 settlement reached by concessions on
each side. ▷ *v* **2** settle a dispute by making
concessions. **3** put in a dishonourable
position.
compulsion ❶ *n* **1** irresistible urge.
2 forcing by threats or violence.
compulsive *adj* **compulsively** *adv*
compulsory *adj* required by rules or laws.

— THESAURUS —

flattery, honour, tribute **2** *pl* = **greetings**,
good wishes, regards, remembrances,
respects, salutation ▷ *v* **3** = **praise**,
commend, congratulate, extol, flatter, pay
tribute to, salute, speak highly of
comply *v* (foll. by *with*) = **obey**, abide by,
acquiesce, adhere to, conform to, follow,
observe, submit, toe the line
component *n* = **part**, constituent,
element, ingredient, item, piece, unit ▷ *adj*
= **constituent**, inherent, intrinsic
compose *v* **1** = **put together**, build,
comprise, constitute, construct, fashion,
form, make, make up **3** = **create**, contrive,
devise, invent, produce, write **4** = **calm**,
collect, control, pacify, placate, quiet,
soothe **5** = **arrange**, adjust
compound¹ *n* **1** = **combination**,
alloy, amalgam, blend, composite,
fusion, medley, mixture, synthesis
▷ *v* **2** = **combine**, amalgamate, blend,
intermingle, mix, synthesize, unite
3 = **intensify**, add to, aggravate, augment,

complicate, exacerbate, heighten,
magnify, worsen
comprehend *v* = **understand**, apprehend,
conceive, fathom, grasp, know, make out,
perceive, see, take in
compress *v* **1** = **squeeze**, concentrate,
condense, contract, crush, press, squash
2 = **shorten**, abbreviate, contract
comprise *v* = **be composed of**, compose,
consist of, constitute, contain, embrace,
encompass, form, include, make up,
take in
compromise *n* **1** = **give-and-take**,
accommodation, adjustment, agreement,
concession, settlement, trade-off ▷ *v*
2 = **meet halfway**, adjust, agree, concede,
give and take, go fifty-fifty (*inf*), settle,
strike a balance **3** = **weaken**, discredit,
dishonour, embarrass, expose, jeopardize,
prejudice
compulsion *n* **1** = **urge**, drive, necessity,
need, obsession, preoccupation **2** = **force**,
coercion, constraint, demand, duress,

compunction n feeling of guilt or shame.

compute ❶ v calculate, esp. using a computer. **computation** n computer n electronic machine that stores and processes data. **computerize** v 1 adapt (a system) to be handled by computer. 2 store or process in a computer.

comrade ❶ n 1 fellow member of a union or socialist political party. 2 companion. **comradeship** n.

con¹ ❶ informal n 1 short for CONFIDENCE TRICK. ▷ v **conning, conned** 2 deceive, swindle.

con² n an argument against **pros and cons** see PRO¹.

concave ❶ adj curving inwards.

conceal ❶ v 1 cover and hide. 2 keep secret. **concealment** n.

concede ❶ v 1 admit to be true. 2 acknowledge defeat in (a contest or argument). 3 grant as a right.

conceit ❶ n 1 too high an opinion of oneself. 2 far-fetched or clever comparison. **conceited** adj.

conceive ❶ v 1 imagine, think. 2 form in the mind. 3 become pregnant. **conceivable** adj imaginable, possible.

concentrate ❶ v 1 fix one's attention or efforts on something. 2 bring or come together in large numbers in one place. 3 make (a liquid) stronger by removing water from it. ▷ n 4 concentrated liquid. **concentration** n 1 concentrating. 2 proportion of a substance in a mixture or solution. **concentration camp** prison camp for civilian prisoners, esp. in Nazi Germany.

concentric adj having the same centre.

concept ❶ n abstract or general idea. **conceptual** adj of or based on concepts. **conceptualize** v form a concept of.

conception ❶ n 1 general idea. 2 becoming pregnant.

concern ❶ n 1 anxiety, worry. 2 something that is of importance to someone. 3 business, firm. ▷ v 4 worry (someone). 5 involve (oneself). 6 be relevant or important to. **concerned** adj 1 interested, involved. 2 anxious, worried. **concerning** prep about, regarding.

obligation, pressure, urgency

compute v = **calculate**, add up, count, enumerate, figure out, reckon, tally, total

comrade n 2 = **companion**, ally, associate, cobber (Aust or old-fashioned NZ inf), colleague, co-worker, fellow, friend, partner

con¹ Inf n 1 = **swindle**, deception, fraud, scam (sl), sting (inf), trick ▷ v 2 = **swindle**, cheat, deceive, defraud, double-cross (inf), dupe, hoodwink, rip off (sl), trick

concave adj = **hollow**, indented

conceal v 1 = **hide**, bury, camouflage, cover, disguise, mask, obscure, screen

concede v 1 = **admit**, accept, acknowledge, allow, confess, grant, own 2 = **give up**, cede, hand over, relinquish, surrender, yield

conceit n 1 = **self-importance**, arrogance, egotism, narcissism, pride, swagger, vanity 2 = **fancy**, fantasy, image, whim, whimsy

conceive v 1 = **imagine**, believe, comprehend, envisage, fancy, suppose, think, understand 2 = **think up**, contrive, create, design, devise, formulate 3 = **become pregnant**, become impregnated

concentrate v 1 = **focus one's attention on**, be engrossed in, put one's mind to, rack one's brains 2 = **gather**, accumulate, centre, cluster, collect, congregate, converge, focus, huddle

concept n = **idea**, abstraction, conception, conceptualization, hypothesis, image, notion, theory, view

conception n 1 = **idea**, concept, design, image, notion, plan 2 = **impregnation**, fertilization, germination, insemination

concern n 1 = **worry**, anxiety, apprehension, burden, care, disquiet, distress 2 = **business**, affair, interest,

concert *n* musical entertainment. **in concert** **1** working together. **2** (of musicians) performing live. **concerted** *adj* done together.

concession ⓘ *n* **1** grant of rights, land, or property. **2** reduction in price for a specified category of people. **3** conceding. **4** thing conceded. **concessionary** *adj*.

concession road *n* Canad (esp. in Ontario) one of a series of roads separating land concessions in a township.

conch *n* **1** shellfish with a large spiral shell. **2** its shell.

conciliate ⓘ *v* try to end a disagreement (with). **conciliation** *n* **conciliatory** *adj*.

concise ⓘ *adj* brief and to the point. **concisely** *adv* **concision, conciseness** *n*.

conclave *n* **1** secret meeting. **2** private meeting of cardinals to elect a new pope.

conclude ⓘ *v* **1** decide by reasoning. **2** end, finish. **3** arrange or settle finally. **conclusion** *n* **1** decision based on reasoning. **2** ending. **3** final arrangement or settlement. **conclusive** *adj* ending doubt, convincing. **conclusively** *adv*.

concoct ⓘ *v* **1** make up (a story or plan). **2** make by combining different ingredients.

concoction *n* **concoctive** *adj*.

concord *n* state of peaceful agreement, harmony. **concordance** *n* **1** similarity or consistency. **2** index of words in a book. **concordant** *adj* agreeing.

concourse *n* **1** large open public place where people can gather. **2** large crowd.

concrete ⓘ *n* **1** mixture of cement, sand, stone, and water, used in building. ▷ *adj* **2** made of concrete. **3** particular, specific. **4** real or solid, not abstract.

concubine [kon-kew-bine] *n* woman living with a man as his wife, but not married to him.

concur ⓘ *v* **-curring, -curred** agree. **concurrence** *n* **concurrent** *adj* happening at the same time or place. **concurrently** *adv* at the same time.

concussion *n* period of unconsciousness caused by a blow to the head.

condemn ⓘ *v* **1** express disapproval of. **2** sentence, e.g. *he was condemned to death*. **3** force into an unpleasant situation. **4** declare unfit for use. **condemnation** *n* **condemnatory** *adj*.

condense ⓘ *v* **1** make shorter. **2** turn from gas into liquid. **condensation** *n*

— THESAURUS —

job, responsibility, task **3** = **business**, company, corporation, enterprise, establishment, firm, organization ▷ *v* **4** = **worry**, bother, disquiet, distress, disturb, make anxious, perturb, trouble **6** = **be relevant to**, affect, apply to, bear on, interest, involve, pertain to, regard, touch

concession *n* **1, 2** = **grant**, adjustment, allowance, boon, compromise, indulgence, permit, privilege **3** = **conceding**, acknowledgment, admission, assent, confession, surrender, yielding

conciliate *v* = **pacify**, appease, clear the air, mediate, mollify, placate, reconcile, soothe, win over

concise *adj* = **brief**, compendious, condensed, laconic, pithy, short, succinct, terse

conclude *v* **1** = **decide**, assume, deduce, gather, infer, judge, surmise, work out **2** = **end**, cease, close, complete, finish, round off, terminate, wind up **3** = **accomplish**, bring about, carry out, effect, pull off

concoct *v* **1** = **make up**, contrive, devise, formulate, hatch, invent, think up **2** = **prepare**, brew

concrete *adj* **3** = **specific**, definite, explicit **4** = **real**, actual, factual, material, sensible, substantial, tangible

concur *v* = **agree**, acquiesce, assent, consent

condemn *v* **1** = **disapprove**, blame, censure, criticize, damn, denounce, reproach, reprove, upbraid **2** = **sentence**, convict, damn, doom, pass sentence on

condense *v* **1** = **abridge**, abbreviate,

condenser n Electricity capacitor.

condescend ❶ v 1 behave patronizingly towards someone. 2 agree to do something, but as if doing someone a favour. **condescension** n.

condiment n seasoning for food, such as salt or pepper.

condition ❶ n 1 particular state of being. 2 necessary requirement for something else to happen. 3 restriction, qualification. 4 state of health, physical fitness. 5 medical problem. ▷ pl 6 circumstances. ▷ v 7 train or influence to behave in a particular way. 8 treat with conditioner. **on condition that** only if. **conditional** adj depending on circumstances. **conditioner** n thick liquid used when washing to make hair or clothes feel softer.

condo n, pl **-dos** informal a condominium building or apartment.

condolence n 1 sympathy. ▷ pl 2 expression of sympathy.

condom n rubber sheath worn on the penis or in the vagina during sexual intercourse to prevent conception or infection.

condone ❶ v overlook or forgive (wrongdoing).

conducive adj (foll. by to) likely to lead (to).

conduct ❶ n 1 management of an activity. 2 behaviour. ▷ v 3 carry out (a task). 4 behave (oneself). 5 direct (musicians) by moving the hands or a baton. 6 lead, guide. 7 transmit (heat or electricity). **conduction** n transmission of heat or electricity. **conductivity** n ability to transmit heat or electricity. **conductive** adj **conductor** n 1 person who conducts musicians. 2 (fem **conductress**) official on a bus who collects fares. 3 something that conducts heat or electricity.

conduit [**kon**-dew-it] n channel or tube for fluid or cables.

cone n 1 object with a circular base, tapering to a point. 2 cone-shaped ice-cream wafer. 3 plastic cone used as a traffic marker on the roads. 4 scaly fruit of a conifer tree.

confederate n 1 member of a confederacy. 2 accomplice. ▷ adj 3 united, allied. ▷ v 4 unite in a confederacy. **confederacy** n, pl **-cies** union of states or people for a common purpose. **confederation** n alliance of political units.

confer ❶ v **-ferring, -ferred** 1 discuss together. 2 grant, give. **conference** n meeting for discussion. **conferment** n.

compress, concentrate, epitomize, shorten, summarize 2 = **concentrate**, boil down, reduce, thicken

condescend v 1 = **patronize**, talk down to 2 = **lower oneself**, bend, deign, humble or demean oneself, see fit, stoop

condition n 1 = **state**, circumstances, lie of the land, position, shape, situation, state of affairs 2, 3 = **requirement**, limitation, prerequisite, proviso, qualification, restriction, rider, stipulation, terms 4 = **health**, fettle, fitness, kilter, order, shape, state of health, trim 5 = **ailment**, complaint, infirmity, malady, problem, weakness ▷ pl 6 = **circumstances**, environment, milieu, situation, surroundings, way of life ▷ v 7 = **accustom**, adapt, equip, prepare,

ready, tone up, train, work out

condone v = **overlook**, excuse, forgive, let pass, look the other way, make allowance for, pardon, turn a blind eye to

conduct n 1 = **management**, administration, control, direction, guidance, handling, organization, running, supervision 2 = **behaviour**, attitude, bearing, demeanour, deportment, manners, ways ▷ v 3 = **carry out**, administer, control, direct, handle, manage, organize, preside over, run, supervise 4 = **behave**, acquit, act, carry, comport, deport 5 = **accompany**, convey, escort, guide, lead, steer, usher

confer v 1 = **discuss**, consult, converse, deliberate, discourse, talk 2 = **grant**, accord, award, bestow, give, hand out, present

confess ❶ v 1 admit (a fault or crime).
2 admit to be true. 3 declare (one's sins)
to God or a priest, in hope of forgiveness.
confession n 1 something confessed.
2 confessing. **confessional** n small stall
in which a priest hears confessions.
confessor n priest who hears confessions.
confetti n small pieces of coloured paper
thrown at weddings.
confide ❶ v 1 tell someone (a secret).
2 entrust. **confidence** n 1 trust. 2 self-
assurance. 3 something confided. **in
confidence** as a secret. **confidence trick**
swindle involving gaining a person's trust
in order to cheat him or her. **confident**
adj sure, esp. of oneself. **confidential**
adj 1 private, secret. 2 entrusted with
someone's secret affairs. **confidentiality** n.
configuration n arrangement of parts.
confine ❶ v 1 keep within bounds.
2 restrict the free movement of. **confines**
pl n boundaries, limits. **confinement** n
1 being confined. 2 period of childbirth.
confirm ❶ v 1 prove to be true. 2 reaffirm,
strengthen. 3 administer the rite
of confirmation to. **confirmation** n
1 confirming. 2 something that confirms.

3 *Christianity* rite that admits a baptized
person to full church membership.
confirmed adj firmly established in a habit
or condition.
confiscate ❶ v seize (property) by
authority. **confiscation** n.
conflict ❶ n 1 disagreement. 2 struggle or
fight. ▷ v 3 be incompatible.
conform ❶ v 1 comply with accepted
standards or customs. 2 (foll. by *to* or *with*)
be like or in accordance with. **conformist**
n, adj (person) complying with accepted
standards or customs. **conformity** n
compliance with accepted standards or
customs.
confound ❶ v 1 astound, bewilder.
2 confuse. **confounded** adj informal
damned.
confront ❶ v come face to face with.
confrontation n serious argument.
confuse ❶ v 1 mix up. 2 perplex,
disconcert. 3 make unclear. **confusion** n.
conga n 1 dance performed by a number of
people in single file. 2 large single-headed
drum played with the hands.
congeal v (of a liquid) become thick and
sticky.

━━━━━━━━━━━━━━━━━━━━━━━━━━━━ THESAURUS ━━━

confess v 1 = **admit**, acknowledge, come
clean (*inf*), concede, confide, disclose,
divulge, own up 2 = **declare**, affirm,
assert, confirm, profess, reveal
confide v 1 = **tell**, admit, confess,
disclose, divulge, impart, reveal, whisper
2 = **entrust**, commend, commit, consign
confine v 1 = **imprison**, cage, enclose,
incarcerate, intern, shut up 2 = **restrict**,
hem in, hold back, keep, limit
confirm v 1 = **prove**, authenticate,
bear out, corroborate, endorse,
ratify, substantiate, validate, verify
2 = **strengthen**, buttress, establish, fix,
fortify, reinforce
confiscate v = **seize**, appropriate,
commandeer, impound, sequester,
sequestrate
conflict n 1 = **opposition**, antagonism,

difference, disagreement, discord,
dissension, friction, hostility, strife
2 = **battle**, clash, combat, contest,
encounter, fight, strife, war ▷ v 3 = **be
incompatible**, be at variance, clash,
collide, differ, disagree, interfere
conform v 1 = **comply**, adapt, adjust, fall
in with, follow, obey, toe the line 2 (foll. by
to or *with*) = **agree**, accord, correspond,
harmonize, match, suit, tally
confound v 1 = **bewilder**, astound, baffle,
dumbfound, flummox, mystify, nonplus,
perplex
confront v = **face**, accost, challenge, defy,
encounter, oppose, stand up to, tackle
confuse v 1 = **mix up**, disarrange,
disorder, jumble, mingle, muddle, ravel
2 = **bewilder**, baffle, bemuse, faze,
flummox, mystify, nonplus, perplex, puzzle

congenial ⊕ *adj* **1** pleasant, agreeable. **2** having similar interests and attitudes. **congeniality** *n*.

congenital ⊕ *adj* (of a condition) existing from birth. **congenitally** *adv*.

conger *n* large sea eel.

conglomerate *n* **1** large corporation made up of many companies. **2** thing made up of several different elements. ▷ *v* **3** form into a mass. ▷ *adj* **4** made up of several different elements. **conglomeration** *n*.

congratulate ⊕ *v* express one's pleasure to (someone) at his or her good fortune or success. **congratulations** *pl n, interj* **congratulatory** *adj*.

congregate ⊕ *v* gather together in a crowd. **congregation** *n* people who attend a church. **congregational** *adj*.

congress ⊕ *n* **1** formal meeting for discussion. **2** (**C-**) federal parliament of the US. **congressional** *adj*.

conifer *n* cone-bearing tree, such as the fir or pine. **coniferous** *adj*.

conjecture ⊕ *n, v* guess. **conjectural** *adj*.

conjoined twins *pl n* the technical name for SIAMESE TWINS.

conjugal ⊕ *adj* of marriage.

conjugate *v* give the inflections of (a verb). **conjugation** *n* complete set of inflections of a verb.

conjunction *n* **1** combination. **2** simultaneous occurrence of events. **3** part of speech joining words, phrases, or clauses.

conjunctivitis *n* inflammation of the membrane covering the eyeball and inner eyelid. **conjunctiva** *n* this membrane.

conjure ⊕ *v* perform tricks that appear to be magic. **conjuror** *n* **conjure up** *v* produce as if by magic.

conker *n informal* nut of the horse chestnut.

connect ⊕ *v* **1** join together. **2** associate in the mind. **connection, connexion** *n* **1** relationship, association. **2** link or bond. **3** opportunity to transfer from one public vehicle to another. **4** influential acquaintance. **connective** *adj*.

connive ⊕ *v* **1** (foll. by *at*) allow (wrongdoing) by ignoring it. **2** conspire. **connivance** *n*.

connoisseur ⊕ [kon-noss-**sir**] *n* person with special knowledge of the arts, food, or drink.

conquer ⊕ *v* **1** defeat. **2** overcome (a difficulty). **3** take (a place) by force.

THESAURUS

congenial *adj* **1** = **pleasant**, affable, agreeable, companionable, favourable, friendly, genial, kindly **2** = **compatible**, kindred, like-minded, sympathetic, well-suited

congenital *adj* = **inborn**, immanent, inbred, inherent, innate, natural

congratulate *v* = **compliment**, pat on the back, wish joy to

congregate *v* = **come together**, assemble, collect, convene, converge, flock, gather, mass, meet

congress *n* **1** = **meeting**, assembly, conclave, conference, convention, council, legislature, parliament

conjecture *n* = **guess**, hypothesis, shot in the dark, speculation, supposition, surmise, theory ▷ *v* = **guess**, hypothesize,

imagine, speculate, suppose, surmise, theorize

conjugal *adj* = **marital**, bridal, connubial, married, matrimonial, nuptial, wedded

conjure *v* = **perform tricks**, juggle

connect *v* **1** = **join**, affix, attach, couple, fasten, link

connive *v* **1** (foll. by *at*) = **turn a blind eye to**, abet, disregard, let pass, look the other way, overlook, wink at **2** = **conspire**, collude, cook up (*inf*), intrigue, plot, scheme

connoisseur *n* = **expert**, aficionado, appreciator, authority, buff (*inf*), devotee, fundi (*S Afr*), judge, mana (*NZ*)

conquer *v* **1** = **defeat**, beat, crush, get the better of, master, overcome, overpower, overthrow, quell, subjugate, vanquish **3** = **seize**, acquire, annex, obtain, occupy,

conqueror n **conquest** n 1 conquering.
2 person or thing conquered.

conscience ⓘ n sense of right or wrong as regards thoughts and actions.

conscious ⓘ adj 1 alert and awake.
2 aware. 3 deliberate, intentional.
consciousness n.

conscript n 1 person enrolled for compulsory military service. ▷ v 2 enrol (someone) for compulsory military service.
conscription n.

consecrate ⓘ v 1 make sacred. 2 dedicate to a specific purpose. **consecration** n.

consecutive ⓘ adj in unbroken succession. **consecutively** adv.

consensus ⓘ n general agreement.

● **SPELLING TIP**
● The Bank of English has 6694 examples
● of the word **consensus** and another 112
● of *concensus* with a *c* in the middle. The
● correct spelling is **consensus** and it has
● only one *c*.

consent ⓘ n 1 agreement, permission. ▷ v
2 (foll. by *to*) permit, agree to.

consequence ⓘ n 1 result, effect.
2 importance. **consequent** adj resulting.

consequently adv as a result, therefore.
consequential adj important.

conserve ⓘ v 1 protect from harm, decay, or loss. 2 preserve (fruit) with sugar. ▷ n 3 jam containing large pieces of fruit. **conservancy** n environmental conservation. **conservation** n
1 protection of natural resources and the environment. 2 conserving.
conservationist n **conservative** adj opposing change.

consider ⓘ v 1 regard as. 2 think about.
3 be considerate of. 4 discuss. 5 look at. **considerable** adj large in amount or degree. **considerably** adv **considerate** adj thoughtful towards others. **considerately** adv **consideration** n 1 careful thought.
2 fact that should be considered.
3 thoughtfulness. 4 payment for a service.
considering prep taking (a specified fact) into account.

consign v 1 put somewhere. 2 send (goods).
consignment n shipment of goods.

consist ⓘ v 1 **consist of** be made up of.
2 **consist in** have as its main or only feature.
consistent adj unchanging, constant.

           THESAURUS

overrun, win

conscience n = **principles**, moral sense, scruples, sense of right and wrong, still small voice

conscious adj 1 = **alert**, awake, responsive
2 = **aware**, alive to, sensible, sentient
3 = **deliberate**, calculated, intentional, knowing, premeditated, self-conscious, studied, wilful

consecrate v 1 = **sanctify**, hallow, ordain, venerate 2 = **dedicate**, devote, set apart

consecutive adj = **successive**, in sequence, in turn, running, sequential, succeeding, uninterrupted

consensus n = **agreement**, assent, common consent, concord, general agreement, harmony, unanimity, unity

consent n 1 = **agreement**, acquiescence,

approval, assent, compliance, go-ahead (inf), O.K. or okay (inf), permission, sanction ▷ v 2 = **agree**, acquiesce, allow, approve, assent, concur, permit

consequence n 1 = **result**, effect, end result, issue, outcome, repercussion, sequel, upshot 2 = **importance**, account, concern, import, moment, significance, value, weight

conserve v 1 = **protect**, hoard, husband, keep, nurse, preserve, save, store up, take care of, use sparingly

consider v 1 = **think**, believe, deem, hold to be, judge, rate, regard as 2 = **think about**, cogitate, contemplate, deliberate, meditate, ponder, reflect, ruminate, turn over in one's mind, weigh 3 = **bear in mind**, keep in view, make allowance for, reckon with, remember, respect, take into account

consist v 1 **consist of** = **be made up of**,

console¹ ❶ v comfort in distress.
consolation n 1 consoling. 2 person or thing that consoles.

console² n 1 panel of controls for electronic equipment. 2 cabinet for a television or audio equipment. 3 ornamental wall bracket. 4 part of an organ containing the pedals, stops, and keys.

consolidate ❶ v 1 make or become stronger or more stable. 2 combine into a whole. **consolidation** n.

consommé [kon-**som**-may] n thin clear meat soup.

consonant n 1 speech sound made by partially or completely blocking the breath stream, such as b or f. 2 letter representing this. ▷ adj 3 (foll. by with) agreeing (with). **consonance** n agreement, harmony.

consort ❶ v 1 (foll. by with) keep company (with). ▷ n 2 husband or wife of a monarch.

conspicuous ❶ adj 1 clearly visible. 2 noteworthy, striking.

conspire ❶ v 1 plan a crime together in secret. 2 act together as if by design. **conspiracy** n 1 conspiring. 2 pl **-cies**

plan made by conspiring. **conspirator** n **conspiratorial** adj.

constable n police officer of the lowest rank. **constabulary** n, pl **-laries** police force of an area.

constant ❶ adj 1 continuous. 2 unchanging. 3 faithful. ▷ n 4 unvarying quantity. 5 something that stays the same. **constantly** adv **constancy** n.

constellation n group of stars.

consternation ❶ n anxiety or dismay.

constipation n difficulty in defecating.

constituent ❶ n 1 member of a constituency. 2 component part. ▷ adj 3 forming part of a whole. **constituency** n, pl **-cies** 1 area represented by a Member of Parliament. 2 voters in such an area.

constitute ❶ v form, make up. **constitution** n 1 principles on which a state is governed. 2 physical condition. 3 structure. **constitutional** adj 1 of a constitution. 2 in accordance with a political constitution. ▷ n 3 walk taken for exercise. **constitutionally** adv.

constrain ❶ v 1 compel, force. 2 limit,

——— THESAURUS ———

amount to, be composed of, comprise, contain, embody, include, incorporate, involve **2 = consist in = lie in**, be expressed by, be found or contained in, inhere in, reside in

console¹ v **= comfort**, calm, cheer, encourage, express sympathy for, soothe

consolidate v **1 = strengthen**, fortify, reinforce, secure, stabilize **2 = combine**, amalgamate, federate, fuse, join, unite

consort v **1** (foll. by with) **= associate**, fraternize, go around with, hang about, around or out with, keep company, mix ▷ n **2 = spouse**, companion, husband, partner, wife

conspicuous adj **1 = obvious**, blatant, clear, evident, noticeable, patent, salient **2 = noteworthy**, illustrious, notable, outstanding, prominent, remarkable, salient, signal, striking

conspire v **1 = plot**, contrive, intrigue,

machinate, manoeuvre, plan, scheme **2 = work together**, combine, concur, contribute, cooperate, tend

constant adj **1 = continuous**, ceaseless, incessant, interminable, nonstop, perpetual, sustained, unrelenting **2 = unchanging**, even, fixed, invariable, permanent, stable, steady, uniform, unvarying **3 = faithful**, devoted, loyal, stalwart, staunch, true, trustworthy, trusty

consternation n **= dismay**, alarm, anxiety, distress, dread, fear, trepidation

constituent n **1 = voter**, elector **2 = component**, element, factor, ingredient, part, unit ▷ adj **3 = component**, basic, elemental, essential, integral

constitute v **= make up**, compose, comprise, establish, form, found, set up

constrain v **1 = force**, bind, coerce,

restrict. **constraint** n.
construct ❶ v build or put together.
construction n 1 constructing.
2 thing constructed. **3** interpretation.
4 *Grammar* way in which words are
arranged in a sentence, clause, or phrase.
constructive adj (of advice, criticism, etc.)
useful and helpful. **constructively** adv.
construe v **-struing, -strued** interpret.
consul n 1 official representing a state in
a foreign country. **2** one of the two chief
magistrates in ancient Rome. **consular**
adj **consulate** n workplace or position of
a consul.
consult ❶ v go to for advice or information.
consultant n 1 specialist doctor
with a senior position in a hospital.
2 specialist who gives professional advice.
consultancy n, pl **-cies** work or position of
a consultant. **consultation** n (meeting for)
consulting. **consultative** adj giving advice.
consume ❶ v 1 eat or drink. **2** use
up. **3** destroy. **4** obsess. **consumer** n
person who buys goods or uses services.
consumption n 1 amount consumed.
2 consuming. **3** *old-fashioned* tuberculosis.

consumptive n, adj *old-fashioned* (person)
having tuberculosis.
consummate ❶ [kon-sum-mate]
v **1** make (a marriage) legal by sexual
intercourse. **2** complete or fulfil. ▷ adj
[kon-**sum**-mit] **3** supremely skilled.
4 complete, extreme. **consummation** n.
cont. continued.
contact ❶ n 1 communicating. **2** touching.
3 useful acquaintance. **4** connection
between two electrical conductors in a
circuit. ▷ v **5** get in touch with. **contact
lens** lens placed on the eyeball to correct
defective vision.
contain ❶ v 1 hold or be capable of holding.
2 consist of. **3** control, restrain. **container**
n **1** object used to hold or store things in.
2 large standard-sized box for transporting
cargo by lorry or ship. **containment** n
prevention of the spread of something
harmful.
contaminate ❶ v 1 make impure,
pollute. **2** make radioactive.
contaminant n contaminating substance.
contamination n.
contemplate ❶ v 1 think deeply.

— THESAURUS —

compel, impel, necessitate, oblige,
pressurize **2** = **restrict**, check, confine,
constrict, curb, restrain, straiten
construct v = **build**, assemble, compose,
create, fashion, form, make, manufacture,
put together
consult v = **ask**, compare notes, confer,
pick (someone's) brains, question, refer to,
take counsel, turn to
consume v 1 = **eat**, devour, eat up, gobble
(up), put away, swallow **2** = **use up**,
absorb, dissipate, exhaust, expend, spend,
squander, waste **3** = **destroy**, annihilate,
demolish, devastate, lay waste, ravage
4 = **obsess**, absorb, dominate, eat up,
engross, monopolize, preoccupy
consummate v 2 = **complete**,
accomplish, conclude, crown, end, finish,
fulfil ▷ adj **3** = **skilled**, accomplished,
matchless, perfect, polished, practised,

superb, supreme **4** = **complete**, absolute,
conspicuous, extreme, supreme, total,
utter
contact n 1 = **communication**,
association, connection **2** = **touch**,
contiguity **3** = **acquaintance**, connection
▷ v **5** = **get** or **be in touch with**, approach,
call, communicate with, reach, speak to,
write to
contain v 1 = **hold**, accommodate,
enclose, have capacity for, incorporate,
seat **2** = **include**, comprehend, comprise,
consist of, embody, embrace, involve
3 = **restrain**, control, curb, hold back, hold
in, keep a tight rein on, repress, stifle
contaminate v 1 = **pollute**, adulterate,
befoul, corrupt, defile, infect, stain, taint,
tarnish
contemplate v 1 = **think about**,
consider, deliberate, meditate, muse over,

2 consider as a possibility. **3** gaze at. **contemplation** n **contemplative** adj

contemporary ❶ adj **1** present-day, modern. **2** living or occurring at the same time. ▷ n, pl **-raries 3** person or thing living or occurring at the same time as another. **contemporaneous** adj happening at the same time.

● SPELLING TIP
● It's easy to miss a syllable out when you
● say **contemporary**. The Bank of English
● shows that syllables get lost from spell-
● ings too - for example, *contempory* is a
● common mistake. But remember that
● the correct spelling ends in *orary*.

contempt ❶ n **1** dislike and disregard. **2** open disrespect for the authority of a court. **contemptible** adj deserving contempt. **contemptuous** adj showing contempt.

contend ❶ v **1** (foll. by *with*) deal with. **2** state, assert. **3** compete. **contender** n.

content¹ ❶ n **1** meaning or substance of a piece of writing. **2** amount of a substance in a mixture. ▷ pl **3** what something contains. **4** list of chapters at the front of a book.

content² ❶ adj **1** satisfied with things as they are. ▷ v **2** make (someone) content. ▷ n **3** happiness and satisfaction. **contented** adj **contentment** n.

contest ❶ n **1** competition or struggle. ▷ v **2** dispute, object to. **3** fight or compete for. **contestant** n.

context ❶ n **1** circumstances of an event or fact. **2** words before and after a word or sentence that help make its meaning clear. **contextual** adj.

continent¹ n one of the earth's large masses of land. **continental** adj.

continent² adj **1** able to control one's bladder and bowels. **2** sexually restrained. **continence** n.

contingent n **1** group of people that represents or is part of a larger group. ▷ adj **2** (foll. by *on*) dependent on (something uncertain). **contingency** n, pl **-cies** something that may happen.

continue ❶ v **-tinuing, -tinued 1** (cause to) remain in a condition or place.

──── THESAURUS ────

ponder, reflect upon, ruminate (upon) **2** = **consider**, envisage, expect, foresee, intend, plan, think of **3** = **look at**, examine, eye up, gaze at, inspect, regard, stare at, study, survey, view

contemporary adj **1** = **modern**, à la mode, current, newfangled, present, present-day, recent, up-to-date **2** = **coexisting**, concurrent, contemporaneous ▷ n **3** = **peer**, fellow

contempt n **1** = **scorn**, derision, disdain, disregard, disrespect, mockery, slight

contend v **1** (foll. by *with*) = **compete**, clash, contest, fight, jostle, strive, struggle, vie **2** = **argue**, affirm, allege, assert, dispute, hold, maintain

content¹ n **1** = **meaning**, essence, gist, significance, substance **2** = **amount**, capacity, load, measure, size, volume ▷ pl **3** = **constituents**, elements,

ingredients, load

content² adj **1** = **satisfied**, agreeable, at ease, comfortable, contented, fulfilled ▷ v **2** = **satisfy**, appease, humour, indulge, mollify, placate, please ▷ n **3** = **satisfaction**, comfort, contentment, ease, gratification, peace of mind, pleasure

contest n **1** = **competition**, game, match, tournament, trial ▷ v **2** = **dispute**, argue, call in or into question, challenge, debate, doubt, object to, oppose, question **3** = **compete**, contend, fight, strive, vie

context n **1** = **circumstances**, ambience, background, conditions, frame of reference, situation

continue v **1** = **remain**, abide, carry on, endure, last, live on, persist, stay, survive **2** = **keep on**, carry on, go on, maintain, persevere, persist in, stick at, sustain **3** = **resume**, carry on, pick up where one

2 carry on (doing something). **3** resume.
continual *adj* **1** constant. **2** recurring
frequently. **continually** *adv* **continuance** *n*
continuing. **continuation** *n* **1** continuing.
2 part added. **continuity** *n, pl* smooth
development or sequence. **continuous** *adj*
continuing uninterrupted.
contort *v* twist out of shape. **contortion** *n*
contortionist *n* performer who contorts
his or her body to entertain.
contour *n* **1** outline. **2** (also **contour line**)
line on a map joining places of the same
height.
contra- *prefix* against or contrasting, e.g.
contraflow.
contraband ❶ *n, adj* smuggled (goods).
contraception *n* prevention of pregnancy
by artificial means. **contraceptive**
n **1** device used or pill taken to prevent
pregnancy. ▷ *adj* **2** preventing pregnancy.
contract ❶ *n* **1** (document setting out) a
formal agreement. ▷ *v* **2** make a formal
agreement (to do something). **3** make or
become smaller or shorter. **4** catch (an
illness). **contraction** *n* **contractor** *n* firm
that supplies materials or labour, esp. for

building. **contractual** *adj*.
contradict ❶ *v* **1** declare the opposite of
(a statement) to be true. **2** be at variance
with. **contradiction** *n* **contradictory** *adj*.
contraflow *n* flow of traffic going
alongside but in an opposite direction to
the usual flow.
contralto *n, pl* **-tos** (singer with) the
lowest female voice.
contraption ❶ *n* strange-looking device.
contrary ❶ *n* **1** complete opposite.
▷ *adj* **2** opposed, completely different.
3 perverse, obstinate. ▷ *adv* **4** in
opposition. **contrarily** *adv* **contrariness** *n*.
contrast ❶ *n* **1** obvious difference.
2 person or thing very different from
another. ▷ *v* **3** compare in order to show
differences. **4** (foll. by *with*) be very
different (from).
contravene *v* break (a rule or law).
contravention *n*.
contribute ❶ *v* **1** give for a common
purpose or fund. **2** (foll. by *to*) be partly
responsible (for). **contribution** *n*
contributor *n* **contributory** *adj*.
contrite ❶ *adj* sorry and apologetic.

——————————————————————— THESAURUS ———

left off, proceed, recommence, return to,
take up
contraband *n* = **smuggling**, black-
marketing, bootlegging, trafficking ▷ *adj*
= **smuggled**, banned, bootleg, forbidden,
hot (*inf*), illegal, illicit, prohibited, unlawful
contract *n* **1** = **agreement**, arrangement,
bargain, commitment, covenant, pact,
settlement ▷ *v* **2** = **agree**, bargain, come
to terms, commit oneself, covenant,
negotiate, pledge **3** = **shorten**, abbreviate,
curtail, diminish, dwindle, lessen, narrow,
reduce, shrink, shrivel **4** = **catch**, acquire,
be afflicted with, develop, get, go down
with, incur
contradict *v* **1** = **deny**, challenge, rebut
2 = **be at variance with**, belie, controvert,
fly in the face of, negate
contraption *n Inf* = **device**, apparatus,
contrivance, gadget, instrument,

mechanism
contrary *n* **1** = **opposite**, antithesis,
converse, reverse ▷ *adj* **2** = **opposed**,
adverse, clashing, contradictory, counter,
discordant, hostile, inconsistent, opposite,
paradoxical **3** = **perverse**, awkward,
cantankerous, difficult, disobliging,
intractable, obstinate, stroppy (*Brit sl*),
unaccommodating
contrast *n* **1** = **difference**, comparison,
disparity, dissimilarity, distinction,
divergence, opposition ▷ *v* **3** = **compare**,
differentiate, distinguish, set in opposition,
set off **4** (foll. by *with*) = **differ**, oppose
contribute *v* **1** = **give**, add, bestow, chip
in (*inf*), donate, provide, subscribe, supply
2 (foll. by *to*) = **be partly responsible for**,
be conducive to, be instrumental in, help,
lead to, tend to
contrite *adj* = **sorry**, chastened,

contritely *adv* **contrition** *n*.
contrive ❶ *v* **1** make happen. **2** devise or construct. **contrivance** *n* **1** device. **2** plan. **3** contriving. **contrived** *adj* planned or artificial.
control ❶ *n* **1** power to direct something. **2** curb or check. ▷ *pl* **3** instruments used to operate a machine. ▷ *v* **-trolling, -trolled 4** have power over. **5** limit, restrain. **6** regulate, operate. **controllable** *adj* **controller** *n*.
controversy ❶ *n, pl* **-sies** fierce argument or debate. **controversial** *adj* causing controversy.
contusion *n formal* bruise.
conundrum *n* riddle.
conurbation *n* large urban area formed by the growth and merging of towns.
convalesce *v* recover after an illness or operation. **convalescence** *n* **convalescent** *n, adj.*
convection *n* transmission of heat in liquids or gases by the circulation of currents. **convector** *n* heater that gives out hot air.

convene ❶ *v* gather or summon for a formal meeting. **convener, convenor** *n* person who calls a meeting.
convenient ❶ *adj* **1** suitable or opportune. **2** easy to use. **3** nearby. **conveniently** *adv* **convenience** *n* **1** quality of being convenient. **2** useful object. **3** *euphemistic* public toilet.
convent *n* **1** building where nuns live. **2** school run by nuns.
convention ❶ *n* **1** widely accepted view of proper behaviour. **2** assembly or meeting. **3** formal agreement. **conventional** *adj* **1** (unthinkingly) following the accepted customs. **2** customary. **3** (of weapons or warfare) not nuclear. **conventionally** *adv* **conventionality** *n*.
converge ❶ *v* meet or join. **convergence** *n*
conversant *adj* **conversant with** having knowledge or experience of.
converse¹ ❶ *v* have a conversation. **conversation** *n* informal talk. **conversational** *adj* **conversationalist** *n* person with a specified ability at conversation.

— THESAURUS —

conscience-stricken, humble, penitent, regretful, remorseful, repentant, sorrowful
contrive *v* **1 = bring about**, arrange, effect, manage, manoeuvre, plan, plot, scheme, succeed **2 = devise**, concoct, construct, create, design, fabricate, improvise, invent, manufacture
control *n* **1 = power**, authority, charge, command, guidance, mana (NZ), management, oversight, supervision, supremacy **2 = restraint**, brake, check, curb, limitation, regulation ▷ *pl* **3 = instruments**, console, control panel, dash, dashboard, dials ▷ *v* **4 = have power over**, administer, command, direct, govern, handle, have charge of, manage, manipulate, supervise **5 = restrain**, check, constrain, contain, curb, hold back, limit, repress, subdue
controversy *n* **= argument**, altercation,

debate, dispute, quarrel, row, squabble, wrangling
convene *v* **= gather**, assemble, bring together, call, come together, congregate, convoke, meet, summon
convenient *adj* **1 = suitable**, appropriate, fit, timely **2 = useful**, handy, helpful, labour-saving, serviceable **3 = nearby**, accessible, at hand, available, close at hand, handy, just round the corner, within reach
convention *n* **1 = custom**, code, etiquette, practice, propriety, protocol, tradition, usage **2 = assembly**, conference, congress, convocation, council, meeting **3 = agreement**, bargain, contract, pact, protocol, treaty
converge *v* **= come together**, coincide, combine, gather, join, meet, merge
converse¹ *v* **= talk**, chat, commune, confer, discourse, exchange views

c

converse² ❶ *adj, n* opposite or contrary. **conversely** *adv*.

convert ❶ *v* 1 change in form, character, or function. 2 cause to change in opinion or belief. ▷ *n* 3 person who has converted to a different belief or religion. **conversion** *n* 1 (thing resulting from) converting. 2 *Rugby* score made after a try by kicking the ball over the crossbar. **convertible** *adj* 1 capable of being converted. ▷ *n* 2 car with a folding or removable roof.

convex ❶ *adj* curving outwards.

convey ❶ *v* 1 communicate (information). 2 carry, transport. **conveyance** *n* 1 *old-fashioned* vehicle. 2 transfer of the legal title to property. **conveyancing** *n* branch of law dealing with the transfer of ownership of property. **conveyor belt** continuous moving belt for transporting things, esp. in a factory.

convict ❶ *v* 1 declare guilty. ▷ *n* 2 person serving a prison sentence. **conviction** *n* 1 firm belief. 2 instance of being convicted.

convince ❶ *v* persuade by argument or evidence. **convincing** *adj*.

convivial *adj* sociable, lively. **conviviality** *n*

convoluted *adj* 1 coiled, twisted. 2 (of an argument or sentence) complex and hard to understand. **convolution** *n*.

convoy *n* group of vehicles or ships travelling together.

convulse *v* 1 (of part of the body) undergo violent spasms. 2 *informal* (be) overcome with laughter. **convulsion** *n* 1 violent muscular spasm. ▷ *pl* 2 uncontrollable laughter. **convulsive** *adj*.

coo *v* **cooing, cooed** (of a dove or pigeon) make a soft murmuring sound.

cook *v* 1 prepare (food) by heating. 2 (of food) be cooked. ▷ *n* 3 person who cooks food. **cook the books** falsify accounts. **cooker** *n* apparatus for cooking heated by gas or electricity. **cookery** *n* art of cooking. **cookie** *n* US biscuit. **cook up** *v informal* devise (a story or scheme).

Cooktown orchid *n* purple Australian orchid.

cool ❶ *adj* 1 moderately cold. 2 calm and unemotional. 3 indifferent or unfriendly. 4 *informal* sophisticated or excellent. 5 *informal* (of a large sum of money) without exaggeration, e.g. *a cool million*. ▷ *v* 6 make or become cool. ▷ *n* 7 coolness. 8 *slang* calmness, composure. **coolly** *adv* **coolant** *n* fluid used to cool machinery while it is working. **cool drink** *n* S *Afr* nonalcoholic drink. **cooler** *n* container for making or keeping things cool.

coop¹ *n* cage or pen for poultry. **coop up** *v* confine in a restricted place.

———————————————————————— THESAURUS ————

converse² *adj* = **opposite**, contrary, counter, reverse, reversed, transposed ▷ *n* = **opposite**, antithesis, contrary, obverse, other side of the coin, reverse

convert *v* 1 = **change**, adapt, alter, customize, modify, remodel, reorganize, restyle, revise, transform, transpose, turn 2 = **reform**, convince, proselytize ▷ *n* 3 = **neophyte**, disciple, proselyte

convex *adj* = **rounded**, bulging, gibbous, protuberant

convey *v* 1 = **communicate**, disclose, impart, make known, relate, reveal, tell 2 = **carry**, bear, bring, conduct, fetch, guide, move, send, transport

convict *v* 1 = **find guilty**, condemn, imprison, pronounce guilty, sentence ▷ *n* 2 = **prisoner**, criminal, culprit, felon, jailbird, lag (*sl*)

convince *v* = **persuade**, assure, bring round, prevail upon, satisfy, sway, win over

cool *adj* 1 = **cold**, chilled, chilly, nippy, refreshing 2 = **calm**, collected, composed, relaxed, sedate, self-controlled, self-possessed, unemotional, unruffled 3 = **unfriendly**, aloof, distant, indifferent, lukewarm, offhand, standoffish, unenthusiastic, unwelcoming ▷ *v* 6 = **chill**, cool off, freeze, lose heat, refrigerate ▷ *n* 8 *Sl* = **calmness**, composure, control, poise, self-control, self-discipline, self-possession, temper

coop² [**koh**-op] *n* (shop run by) a cooperative society.

cooperate ❶ *v* work or act together. **cooperation** *n* **cooperative** *adj* **1** willing to cooperate. **2** (of an enterprise) owned and managed collectively. ▷ *n* **3** cooperative organization.

coordinate ❶ *v* **1** bring together and cause to work together efficiently. ▷ *n* **2** *Maths* any of a set of numbers defining the location of a point. ▷ *pl* **3** clothes designed to be worn together. **coordination** *n* **coordinator** *n*.

coot *n* small black water bird.

cop *slang n* **1** policeman. ▷ *v* **copping, copped 2** take or seize. **cop it** get into trouble or be punished. **cop out** *v* avoid taking responsibility or committing oneself.

cope ❶ *v* (often foll. by *with*) **1** deal successfully (with). **2** tolerate, endure.

coping *n* sloping top row of a wall.

copious ❶ [**kope**-ee-uss] *adj* abundant, plentiful.

copper¹ *n* **1** soft reddish-brown metal. **2** copper or bronze coin. **copper-bottomed** *adj* financially reliable. **copperplate** *n* fine handwriting style.

copper² *n slang* policeman.

coppice, copse *n* small group of trees growing close together.

copulate *v* have sexual intercourse; mate.

copulation *n* **copulatory** *adj*.

copy ❶ *n, pl* **copies 1** thing made to look exactly like another. **2** single specimen of a book etc. **3** material for printing. ▷ *v* **copying, copied 4** make a copy of. **5** act or try to be like. **copyright** *n* **1** exclusive legal right to reproduce and control a book, work of art, etc. ▷ *v* **2** take out a copyright on. ▷ *adj* **3** protected by copyright. **copywriter** *n* person who writes advertising copy.

coquette *n* woman who flirts. **coquettish** *adj*.

coracle *n* small round boat of wicker covered with skins.

coral *n* **1** hard substance formed from the skeletons of very small sea animals. ▷ *adj* **2** orange-pink.

cord ❶ *n* **1** thin rope or thick string. **2** cordlike structure in the body. **3** corduroy. ▷ *pl* **4** corduroy trousers.

cordial ❶ *adj* **1** warm and friendly. ▷ *n* **2** drink with a fruit base. **cordially** *adv* **cordiality** *n*.

cordon ❶ *n* chain of police, soldiers, etc., guarding an area. **cordon off** *v* form a cordon round.

cordon bleu [**bluh**] *adj* (of cookery or cooks) of the highest standard.

corduroy *n* cotton fabric with a velvety ribbed surface.

core ❶ *n* **1** central part of certain fruits,

cooperate *v* = **work together**, collaborate, combine, conspire, coordinate, join forces, pool resources, pull together

coordinate *v* **1** = **bring together**, harmonize, integrate, match, organize, synchronize, systematize

cope *v* (often foll. by *with*) **1** = **manage**, carry on, get by (*inf*), hold one's own, make the grade, struggle through, survive ▷ *v* **2** = **deal with**, contend with, grapple with, handle, struggle with, weather, wrestle with

copious *adj* = **abundant**, ample, bountiful,

extensive, full, lavish, plentiful, profuse

copy *n* **1** = **reproduction**, counterfeit, duplicate, facsimile, forgery, imitation, likeness, model, replica ▷ *v* **4** = **reproduce**, counterfeit, duplicate, replicate, transcribe **5** = **imitate**, act like, ape, behave like, emulate, follow, mimic, mirror, repeat

cord *n* **1** = **rope**, line, string, twine

cordial *adj* **1** = **warm**, affable, agreeable, cheerful, congenial, friendly, genial, hearty, sociable

cordon *n* = **chain**, barrier, line, ring

core *n* **1** = **kernel**, pith **2** = **centre**, crux,

containing the seeds. **2** central or essential part. ▷ *v* **3** remove the core from.

corella *n* white Australian cockatoo.

corgi *n* short-legged sturdy dog.

coriander *n* plant grown for its aromatic seeds and leaves.

cork *n* **1** thick light bark of a Mediterranean oak. **2** piece of this used as a stopper. ▷ *v* **3** seal with a cork. **corkscrew** *n* spiral metal tool for pulling corks from bottles.

corm *n* bulblike underground stem of certain plants.

cormorant *n* large dark-coloured long-necked sea bird.

corn¹ *n* **1** cereal plant such as wheat or oats. **2** grain of such plants. **3** *US* maize. **4** *slang* something unoriginal or oversentimental. **corny** *adj slang* unoriginal or oversentimental. **cornflakes** *pl n* breakfast cereal made from toasted maize. **cornflour** *n* fine maize flour *NZ* fine wheat flour. **cornflower** *n* plant with blue flowers.

corn² *n* painful hard skin on the toe.

cornea [**korn**-ee-a] *n*, *pl* **-neas**, **-neae** transparent membrane covering the eyeball.

corner ❶ *n* **1** area or angle where two converging lines or surfaces meet. **2** place where two streets meet. **3** remote place. **4** *Sport* free kick or shot from the corner of the field. ▷ *v* **5** force into a difficult or inescapable position. **6** (of a vehicle) turn a corner. **7** obtain a monopoly of. **cornerstone** *n* indispensable part or basis.

cornet *n* **1** brass instrument similar to the trumpet. **2** cone-shaped ice-cream wafer.

cornice *n* decorative moulding round the top of a wall or building.

cornucopia [korn-yew-**kope**-ee-a] *n* **1** great abundance. **2** symbol of plenty, consisting of a horn overflowing with fruit and flowers.

corollary *n*, *pl* **-laries** idea, fact, or proposition which is the natural result of something else.

coronary [**kor**-ron-a-ree] *adj* **1** of the arteries surrounding the heart. ▷ *n*, *pl* **-naries 2** coronary thrombosis. **coronary thrombosis** condition in which the flow of blood to the heart is blocked by a blood clot.

coronation *n* ceremony of crowning a monarch.

coroner *n* official responsible for the investigation of violent, sudden, or suspicious deaths.

coronet *n* small crown.

corporal¹ *n* noncommissioned officer in an army.

corporal² *adj* of the body. **corporal punishment** physical punishment, such as caning.

corporation ❶ *n* **1** large business or company. **2** city or town council. **3** *informal* large paunch. **corporate** *adj* **1** of business corporations. **2** shared by a group.

corps ❶ [kore] *n*, *pl* **corps 1** military unit with a specific function. **2** organized body of people.

corpse ❶ *n* dead body.

corpulent *adj* fat or plump. **corpulence** *n*.

corpus *n*, *pl* **corpora** collection of writings, esp. by a single author.

corpuscle *n* red or white blood cell.

corral *US* ▷ *n* **1** enclosure for cattle or

——————— THESAURUS ———————

essence, gist, heart, nub, nucleus

corner *n* **1 = angle**, bend, crook, joint **3 = space**, hideaway, hide-out, nook, retreat ▷ *v* **5 = trap**, run to earth **7 = monopolize**, dominate, engross, hog (*sl*)

corporation *n* **1 = business**, association, corporate body, society **2 = town council**, civic authorities, council, municipal authorities **3** *Inf* **= paunch**, beer belly (*inf*), middle-age spread (*inf*), potbelly, spare tyre (*Brit sl*), spread (*inf*)

corps *n* **1 = team**, band, company, detachment, division, regiment, squadron, troop, unit

corpse *n* **= body**, cadaver, carcass, remains, stiff (*sl*)

horses. ▷ v **-ralling, -ralled 2** put in a corral.

correct ❶ adj **1** free from error, true. **2** in accordance with accepted standards. ▷ v **3** put right. **4** indicate the errors in. **5** rebuke or punish. **correctly** adv **correctness** n **correction** n **1** correcting. **2** alteration correcting something. **corrective** adj intended to put right something wrong.

correlate v place or be placed in a mutual relationship. **correlation** n.

correspond ❶ v **1** be consistent or compatible (with). **2** be the same or similar. **3** communicate by letter. **corresponding** adj **correspondence** n **1** communication by letters. **2** letters so exchanged. **3** relationship or similarity. **correspondent** n **1** person employed by a newspaper etc. to report on a special subject or from a foreign country. **2** letter writer.

corridor ❶ n **1** passage in a building or train. **2** strip of land or airspace providing access through foreign territory.

corroborate ❶ v support (a fact or opinion) by giving proof. **corroboration** n **corroborative** adj.

corroboree n Aust Aboriginal gathering of festive or warlike character.

corrode ❶ v eat or be eaten away by chemical action or rust. **corrosion** n **corrosive** adj.

corrupt ❶ adj **1** open to or involving bribery. **2** morally depraved. **3** (of a text or data) unreliable through errors or alterations. ▷ v **4** make corrupt. **corruption** n **corruptible** adj.

corsage [kor-**sahzh**] n small bouquet worn on the bodice of a dress.

corset ❶ n women's close-fitting undergarment worn to shape the torso.

cortege [kor-**tayzh**] n funeral procession.

cortex n, pl **-tices** Anat outer layer of the brain or other internal organ. **cortical** adj.

cortisone n steroid hormone used to treat various diseases.

cosh n **1** heavy blunt weapon. ▷ v **2** hit with a cosh.

cosine [**koh**-sine] n (in trigonometry) ratio of the length of the adjacent side to that of the hypotenuse in a right-angled triangle.

cosmetic ❶ n **1** preparation used to improve the appearance of a person's skin. ▷ adj **2** improving the appearance only.

cosmic ❶ adj of the whole universe. **cosmic rays** electromagnetic radiation from outer space.

correct adj **1** = **true**, accurate, exact, faultless, flawless, O.K. or okay (inf), precise, right **2** = **proper**, acceptable, appropriate, fitting, kosher (inf), O.K. or okay (inf), seemly, standard ▷ v **3** = **rectify**, adjust, amend, cure, emend, redress, reform, remedy, right **5** = **punish**, admonish, chasten, chastise, chide, discipline, rebuke, reprimand, reprove, rouse (Aust)

correspond v **1** = **be consistent**, accord, agree, conform, fit, harmonize, match, square, tally **3** = **communicate**, exchange letters, keep in touch, write

corridor n **1** = **passage**, aisle, alley, hallway, passageway

corroborate v = **support**, authenticate,

back up, bear out, confirm, endorse, ratify, substantiate, validate

corrode v = **eat away**, consume, corrupt, erode, gnaw, oxidize, rust, wear away

corrupt adj **1** = **dishonest**, bent (sl), bribable, crooked (inf), fraudulent, unprincipled, unscrupulous, venal **2** = **depraved**, debased, degenerate, dissolute, profligate, vicious **3** = **distorted**, altered, doctored, falsified ▷ v **4 a** = **bribe**, buy off, entice, fix (inf), grease (someone's) palm (sl), lure, suborn **b** = **deprave**, debauch, pervert, subvert

corset n **1** = **girdle**, belt, bodice

cosmetic adj **2** = **beautifying**, nonessential, superficial, surface

cosmic adj = **universal**, stellar

cosmopolitan ❶ *adj* **1** composed of people or elements from many countries. **2** having lived and travelled in many countries. ▷ *n* **3** cosmopolitan person. **cosmopolitanism** *n*.

cosmos *n* the universe. **cosmology** *n* study of the origin and nature of the universe. **cosmological** *adj*.

cosset *v* **cosseting**, **cosseted** pamper.

cost ❶ *n* **1** amount of money, time, labour, etc., required for something. ▷ *pl* **2** expenses of a lawsuit. ▷ *v* **costing**, **cost 3** have as its cost. **4** involve the loss or sacrifice of. **5** *past* **costed** estimate the cost of. **costly** *adj* **1** expensive. **2** involving great loss or sacrifice.

costume ❶ *n* **1** style of dress of a particular place or time, or for a particular activity. **2** clothes worn by an actor or performer. **costumier** *n* maker or seller of costumes. **costume jewellery** inexpensive artificial jewellery.

cosy ❶ *adj* **-sier**, **-siest 1** warm and snug. **2** intimate, friendly. ▷ *n* **3** cover for keeping things warm, e.g. a *tea cosy*. **cosily** *adv* **cosiness** *n*.

cot *n* **1** baby's bed with high sides. **2** small portable bed. **cot death** unexplained death of a baby while asleep.

cote *n* shelter for birds or animals.

coterie [**kote**-er-ee] *n* exclusive group, clique.

cottage ❶ *n* small house in the country.

cottage cheese soft mild white cheese. **cottage industry** craft industry in which employees work at home. **cottage pie** dish of minced meat topped with mashed potato.

cotton *n* **1** white downy fibre covering the seeds of a tropical plant. **2** cloth or thread made from this. **cotton on (to)** *v informal* understand. **cotton wool** fluffy cotton used for surgical dressings etc.

couch *n* **1** piece of upholstered furniture for seating more than one person. ▷ *v* **2** express in a particular way. **couch potato** *slang* lazy person whose only hobby is watching television.

cougar *n* puma.

cough ❶ *v* **1** expel air from the lungs abruptly and noisily. ▷ *n* **2** act or sound of coughing. **3** illness which causes coughing.

could *v* past tense of CAN¹.

coulomb [**koo**-lom] *n* SI unit of electric charge.

council ❶ *n* **1** group meeting for discussion or consultation. **2** local governing body of a town or region. ▷ *adj* **3** of or by a council. **councillor** *n* member of a council. **council tax** tax based on the value of property, to fund local services.

counsel ❶ *n* **1** advice or guidance. **2** barrister or barristers. ▷ *v* **-selling**, **-selled 3** give guidance to. **4** urge, recommend. **counsellor** *n*.

— THESAURUS —

cosmopolitan *adj* **2** = **sophisticated**, broad-minded, catholic, open-minded, universal, urbane, well-travelled, worldly-wise *n* **3** = **man** *or* **woman of the world**, jet-setter, sophisticate

cost *n* **1** = **price**, amount, charge, damage (*inf*), expense, outlay, payment, worth ▷ *v* **3** = **sell at**, come to, command a price of, set (someone) back (*inf*) **4** = **lose**, do disservice to, harm, hurt, injure

costume *n* **1** = **outfit**, apparel, attire, clothing, dress, ensemble, garb, livery, uniform

cosy *adj* **1** = **snug**, comfortable, comfy (*inf*), homely, sheltered, tucked up, warm **2** = **intimate**, friendly

cottage *n* = **cabin**, chalet, hut, lodge, shack

cough *v* **1** = **clear one's throat**, bark, hack ▷ *n* **2** = **frog** *or* **tickle in one's throat**, bark, hack

council *n* **1,2** = **governing body**, assembly, board, cabinet, committee, conference, congress, convention, panel, parliament

counsel *n* **1** = **advice**, direction, guidance, information, recommendation, suggestion, warning **2** = **legal adviser**,

count¹ ❶ v **1** say numbers in order. **2** find the total of. **3** be important. **4** regard as. **5** take into account. ▷ v **6** counting. **7** number reached by counting. **8** Law one of a number of charges. **countless** adj too many to count. **count on** v rely or depend on.

count² n European nobleman.

countenance n **1** (expression of) the face. ▷ v **2** allow or tolerate.

counter¹ n **1** long flat surface in a bank or shop, on which business is transacted. **2** small flat disc used in board games.

counter² ❶ v **1** oppose, retaliate against. ▷ adv **2** in the opposite direction. **3** in direct contrast. ▷ n **4** opposing or retaliatory action.

counter- prefix **1** opposite, against, e.g. counterattack. **2** complementary, corresponding, e.g. counterpart.

counteract ❶ v act against or neutralize.

counterattack n, v attack in response to an attack.

counterbalance ❶ n **1** weight or force balancing or neutralizing another. ▷ v **2** act as a counterbalance to.

counterfeit ❶ adj **1** fake, forged. ▷ n **2** fake, forgery. ▷ v **3** fake, forge.

counterfoil n part of a cheque or receipt kept as a record.

countermand ❶ v cancel (a previous order).

counterpane n bed covering.

counterpart ❶ n person or thing complementary to or corresponding to another.

counterpoint n Music technique of combining melodies.

countersign v sign (a document already signed by someone) as confirmation.

countersink v drive (a screw) into a shaped hole so that its head is below the surface.

countertenor n male alto.

country ❶ n, pl -tries **1** nation. **2** nation's territory. **3** nation's people. **4** part of the land away from cities. **countrified** adj rustic in manner or appearance. **country and western**, **country music** popular music based on American White folk

—— THESAURUS ——

advocate, attorney, barrister, lawyer, solicitor ▷ v **3** = **advise**, instruct, warn **4** = **urge**, advocate, exhort, recommend

count¹ v **1** = **enumerate 2** = **add (up)**, calculate, compute, number, reckon, tally, tot up **3** = **matter**, be important, carry weight, rate, signify, tell, weigh **4** = **consider**, deem, judge, look upon, rate, regard, think **5** = **take into account** or **consideration**, include, number among ▷ n **6** = **calculation**, computation, enumeration, numbering, poll **7** = **sum**, reckoning, tally

counter² v **1** = **retaliate**, answer, hit back, meet, oppose, parry, resist, respond, ward off ▷ adv **3** = **opposite to**, against, at variance with, contrariwise, conversely, in defiance of, versus

counteract v = **act against**, foil, frustrate, negate, neutralize, offset, resist, thwart

counterbalance v **2** = **offset**, balance,

compensate, make up for, set off

counterfeit adj **1** = **fake**, bogus, false, forged, imitation, phoney or phony (inf), sham, simulated ▷ n **2** = **fake**, copy, forgery, fraud, imitation, phoney or phony (inf), reproduction, sham ▷ v **3** = **fake**, copy, fabricate, feign, forge, imitate, impersonate, pretend, sham, simulate

countermand v = **cancel**, annul, override, repeal, rescind, retract, reverse, revoke

counterpart n = **opposite number**, complement, equal, fellow, match, mate, supplement, tally, twin

country n **1** = **nation**, commonwealth, kingdom, people, realm, state **2** = **territory**, land, region, terrain **3** = **people**, citizens, community, inhabitants, nation, populace, public, society **4** = **countryside**, backwoods, farmland, green belt, outback (Aust & NZ), provinces, sticks (inf)

music. **countryman**, **countrywoman** n
1 person from one's native land. 2 person
who lives in the country. **countryside** n
land away from cities.

county ❶ n, pl **-ties** division of a country.

coup ❶ [koo] n 1 successful action. 2 coup
d'état.

coupé [koo-pay] n sports car with two
doors and a sloping fixed roof.

couple ❶ n 1 two people who are married
or romantically involved. 2 two partners in
a dance or game. ▷ v 3 connect, associate.
a couple 1 a pair. 2 informal a few. **couplet**
n two consecutive lines of verse, usu.
rhyming and of the same metre. **coupling**
n device for connecting things, such as
railway carriages.

coupon ❶ n 1 piece of paper entitling the
holder to a discount or gift. 2 detachable
order form. 3 football pools entry form.

courage ❶ n ability to face danger or
pain without fear. **courageous** adj
courageously adv.

courgette n type of small vegetable
marrow.

courier ❶ n 1 person employed to look

after holiday-makers. 2 person employed
to deliver urgent messages.

course ❶ n 1 series of lessons or medical
treatment. 2 onward movement in
space or time. 3 route or direction taken.
4 area where golf is played or a race is run.
5 any of the successive parts of a meal.
6 continuous layer of masonry at one level
in a building. 7 mode of conduct or action.
8 natural development of events. ▷ v 9 (of
liquid) run swiftly. 10 hunt with hounds
that follow the quarry by sight and not
scent. **of course** as expected, naturally.

court ❶ n 1 body which decides legal
cases. 2 place where it meets. 3 marked
area for playing a racket game.
4 courtyard. 5 residence, household,
or retinue of a sovereign. ▷ v 6 old-
fashioned try to gain the love of. 7 try to
win the favour of. 8 invite, e.g. to court
disaster. **courtier** n attendant at a royal
court. **courtly** adj ceremoniously polite.
courtship n courting of an intended
spouse or mate. **court martial** n, pl
courts martial court for trying naval
or military offences. **courtyard** n paved

━━━━━━━━━━━━━━━━━━━━━━━ **THESAURUS** ━━━━━━━━━━━━━━━━━━━━━━━

county n = **province**, shire

coup n 1 = **masterstroke**, accomplishment,
action, deed, exploit, feat, manoeuvre,
stunt

couple n 1 = **pair**, two, twosome ▷ v
3 = **link**, connect, hitch, join, marry, pair,
unite, wed, yoke

coupon n 1 = **slip**, card, certificate, ticket,
token, voucher

courage n = **bravery**, daring, fearlessness,
gallantry, heroism, mettle, nerve, pluck,
resolution, valour

courier n 1 = **guide**, representative
2 = **messenger**, bearer, carrier, envoy,
runner

course n 1 = **classes**, curriculum, lectures,
programme, schedule 2 = **progression**,
development, flow, movement, order,
progress, sequence, unfolding 3 = **route**,
direction, line, passage, path, road, track,

trajectory, way 4 = **racecourse**, cinder
track, circuit 7 = **procedure**, behaviour,
conduct, manner, method, mode, plan,
policy, programme 8 = **period**, duration,
lapse, passage, passing, sweep, term,
time ▷ v 9 = **run**, flow, gush, race, speed,
stream, surge 10 = **hunt**, chase, follow,
pursue **of course** = **naturally**, certainly,
definitely, indubitably, needless to say,
obviously, undoubtedly, without a doubt

court n 1 = **law court**, bar, bench, tribunal
4 = **courtyard**, cloister, piazza, plaza,
quad (inf), quadrangle, square, yard 5
a = **palace**, hall, manor, royal household
b = **retinue**, attendants, cortege,
entourage, suite, train ▷ v 6 Old-fashioned
= **woo**, date, go (out) with, run after,
serenade, set one's cap at, take out, walk
out with 7 = **cultivate**, curry favour with,
fawn upon, flatter, pander to, seek, solicit

space enclosed by buildings or walls.

courtesy ❶ *n* 1 politeness, good manners. 2 *pl* **-sies** courteous act. **(by) courtesy of** by permission of. **courteous** *adj* polite.

cousin *n* child of one's uncle or aunt.

cove ❶ *n* small bay or inlet.

coven [**kuv**-ven] *n* meeting of witches.

covenant ❶ [**kuv**-ven-ant] *n* 1 formal agreement to make an annual (charitable) payment. ▷ *v* 2 agree by a covenant.

cover ❶ *v* 1 place something over, to protect or conceal. 2 extend over or lie on the surface of. 3 travel over. 4 keep a gun or missile aimed at. 5 insure against loss or risk. 6 include. 7 report (an event) for a newspaper. 8 be enough to pay for. ▷ *n* 9 anything that covers. 10 outside of a book or magazine. 11 pretext or disguise. 12 insurance. 13 shelter or protection. **coverage** *n* amount or extent covered. **coverlet** *n* bed cover.

covert *adj* 1 concealed, secret. ▷ *n* 2 thicket giving shelter to game birds or animals.

covet ❶ *v* **coveting, coveted** long to possess (what belongs to someone else). **covetous** *adj.*

cow¹ *n* 1 mature female of cattle and of certain other mammals, such as the

elephant or seal. 2 *informal, offens* a disagreeable woman. **cowboy** *n* 1 (in the US) ranch worker who herds and tends cattle, usu. on horseback. 2 *informal* irresponsible or unscrupulous worker.

cow² *v* intimidate, subdue.

coward ❶ *n* person who lacks courage. **cowardly** *adj* **cowardice** *n* lack of courage.

cower ❶ *v* cringe in fear.

cowl *n* 1 loose hood. 2 monk's hooded robe. 3 cover on a chimney to increase ventilation.

cowslip *n* small yellow wild flower.

coxswain [**kok**-sn] *n* person who steers a rowing boat.

coy ❶ *adj* affectedly shy or modest. **coyly** *adv* **coyness** *n.*

coyote [koy-**ote**-ee] *n* prairie wolf of N America.

coypu *n* beaver-like aquatic rodent, bred for its fur.

crab *n* edible shellfish with ten legs, the first pair modified into pincers.

crab apple *n* small sour apple.

crack ❶ *v* 1 break or split partially. 2 break with a sharp noise. 3 (cause to) make a sharp noise. 4 (of the voice) become harsh or change pitch suddenly. 5 break

———— THESAURUS ————

8 = **invite**, attract, bring about, incite, prompt, provoke, seek

courtesy *n* 1 = **politeness**, affability, civility, courteousness, gallantry, good manners, graciousness, urbanity 2 = **favour**, indulgence, kindness

cove *n* = **bay**, anchorage, inlet, sound

covenant *n* 1 = **promise**, agreement, arrangement, commitment, contract, pact, pledge ▷ *v* 2 = **promise**, agree, contract, pledge, stipulate, undertake

cover *v* 1 = **envelop**, cloak, coat, conceal, encase, enshroud, hide, mask, obscure, overlay, put on, shroud, veil, wrap 2 = **submerge**, engulf, flood, overrun, wash over 3 = **travel over**, cross, pass through *or* over, traverse 7 = **report**, describe, investigate, narrate, relate, tell

of, write up ▷ *n* 9 = **covering**, canopy, case, coating, envelope, jacket, lid, top, wrapper 11 = **disguise**, camouflage, concealment, facade, front, mask, pretext, screen, smoke screen, veil 12 = **insurance**, compensation, indemnity, protection, reimbursement 13 = **protection**, defence, guard, shelter, shield

covet *v* = **long for**, aspire to, crave, desire, envy, lust after, set one's heart on, yearn for

coward *n* = **wimp** (*inf*), chicken (*sl*), scaredy-cat (*inf*), yellow-belly (*sl*)

cower *v* = **cringe**, draw back, flinch, grovel, quail, shrink, tremble

coy *adj* = **shy**, bashful, demure, modest, reserved, retiring, shrinking, timid

crack *v* 1 = **break**, burst, cleave, fracture, snap, splinter, split 2, 3 = **snap**, burst,

down or yield under strain. **6** hit suddenly.
7 solve (a code or problem). **8** tell (a joke).
▷ *n* **9** sudden sharp noise. **10** narrow
gap. **11** sharp blow. **12** *informal* gibe, joke.
13 *slang* highly addictive form of cocaine.
▷ *adj* **14** *informal* first-rate, excellent,
e.g. *a crack shot*. **cracking** *adj* very
good. **crackdown** *n* severe disciplinary
measures. **crack down on** *v* take severe
measures against.

cradle ❶ *n* **1** baby's bed on rockers. **2** place
where something originates. **3** supporting
structure. ▷ *v* **4** hold gently as if in a cradle.

craft ❶ *n* **1** occupation requiring skill with
the hands. **2** skill or ability. **3** *pl* **craft**
boat, ship, aircraft, or spaceship. **crafty**
adj skilled in deception. **craftsman**,
craftswoman *n* skilled worker.
craftsmanship *n*.

crag ❶ *n* steep rugged rock. **craggy** *adj*

cram ❶ *v* **cramming, crammed 1** force
into too small a space. **2** fill too full.
3 study hard just before an examination.

cramp¹ ❶ *n* **1** painful muscular contraction.
2 clamp for holding masonry or timber
together.

cramp² ❷ *v* confine, restrict.

cranberry *n* sour edible red berry.

crane *n* **1** machine for lifting and moving
heavy weights. **2** large wading bird with
a long neck and legs. ▷ *v* **3** stretch (one's
neck) to see something.

cranium *n*, *pl* **-niums, -nia** skull. **cranial**
adj.

crank *n* **1** arm projecting at right angles
from a shaft, for transmitting or
converting motion. **2** *informal* eccentric
person. ▷ *v* **3** start (an engine) with a
crank. **cranky** *adj informal* **1** eccentric.
2 bad-tempered. **crankshaft** *n* shaft driven
by a crank.

cranny ❶ *n*, *pl* **-nies** narrow opening.

crash ❶ *n* **1** collision involving a vehicle or
vehicles. **2** sudden loud smashing noise.
3 financial collapse. ▷ *v* **4** (cause to) collide
violently with a vehicle, a stationary
object, or the ground. **5** (cause to) make
a loud smashing noise. **6** (cause to) fall
with a crash. **7** collapse or fail financially.
crash course short, very intensive course
in a particular subject. **crash helmet**
protective helmet worn by a motorcyclist.

━━━━━━━━━━━━━━━━━━━━━━━━━━━━━━━━━━━ THESAURUS ━━━

crash, detonate, explode, pop **5** = **give
in**, break down, collapse, give way, go
to pieces, lose control, succumb, yield
6 = **hit**, clip (*inf*), clout (*inf*), cuff, slap,
smack, whack **7** = **solve**, decipher,
fathom, get the answer to, work out ▷ *n*
9 = **snap**, burst, clap, crash, explosion,
pop, report **10** = **break**, chink, cleft,
cranny, crevice, fissure, fracture, gap, rift
11 = **blow**, clip (*inf*), clout (*inf*), cuff, slap,
smack, whack **12** *Inf* = **joke**, dig, funny
remark, gag (*inf*), jibe, quip, wisecrack,
witticism ▷ *adj* **14** *Inf* = **first-class**, ace,
choice, elite, excellent, first-rate, hand-
picked, superior, world-class
cradle *n* **1** = **crib**, bassinet, cot, Moses
basket **2** = **birthplace**, beginning, fount,
fountainhead, origin, source, spring,
wellspring ▷ *v* **4** = **hold**, lull, nestle, nurse,
rock, support

craft *n* **1** = **occupation**, business,
employment, handicraft, pursuit, trade,
vocation, work, yakka (*Aust & NZ inf*)
2 = **skill**, ability, aptitude, art, artistry,
expertise, ingenuity, know-how (*inf*),
technique, workmanship **3** = **vessel**,
aircraft, boat, plane, ship, spacecraft
crag *n* = **rock**, bluff, peak, pinnacle, tor
cram *v* **1** = **stuff**, compress, force, jam, pack
in, press, shove, squeeze **3** = **study**, bone
up (*inf*), mug up (*sl*), revise, swot
cramp¹ *n* **1** = **spasm**, ache, contraction,
convulsion, pain, pang, stitch, twinge
cramp² *v* = **restrict**, constrain, hamper,
handicap, hinder, impede, inhibit, obstruct
cranny *n* = **crevice**, chink, cleft, crack,
fissure, gap, hole, opening
crash *n* **1** = **collision**, accident, bump,
pile-up (*inf*), prang (*inf*), smash, wreck
2 = **smash**, bang, boom, clang, clash,

crash-land v (of an aircraft) land in an emergency, causing damage. **crash-landing** n.

crass ❶ adj stupid and insensitive.

crate ❶ n large wooden container for packing goods.

crater ❶ n very large hole in the ground or in the surface of the moon.

cravat n man's scarf worn like a tie.

crave ❶ v 1 desire intensely. 2 beg or plead for. **craving** n.

craven adj cowardly.

crawl ❶ v 1 move on one's hands and knees. 2 move very slowly. 3 (foll. by to) flatter in order to gain some advantage. 4 feel as if covered with crawling creatures. ▷ n 5 crawling motion or pace. 6 overarm swimming stroke.

crayfish n 1 edible freshwater shellfish like a lobster. 2 any similar shellfish, e.g. the spiny lobster.

crayon v, n (draw or colour with) a stick or pencil of coloured wax or clay.

craze ❶ n short-lived fashion or enthusiasm. **crazed** adj 1 wild and uncontrolled. 2 (of porcelain) having fine cracks. **crazy** adj 1 ridiculous. 2 (foll. by about) very fond (of). 3 insane. **craziness** n

creak ❶ v, n (make) a harsh squeaking sound. **creaky** adj.

cream ❶ n 1 fatty part of milk. 2 food or cosmetic resembling cream in consistency. 3 best part (of something). ▷ adj 4 yellowish-white. ▷ v 5 beat to a creamy consistency. **creamy** adj **cream cheese** rich soft white cheese. **cream off** v take the best part from.

crease ❶ n 1 line made by folding or pressing. 2 Cricket line marking the bowler's and batsman's positions. ▷ v 3 crush or line.

create ❶ v 1 make, cause to exist. 2 appoint to a new rank or position. 3 slang make an angry fuss. **creation** n **creative** adj 1 imaginative or inventive. **creativity** n **creator** n.

creature ❶ n animal, person, or other being.

THESAURUS

---

clatter, din, racket, thunder 3 = **collapse**, debacle, depression, downfall, failure, ruin ▷ v 4 = **collide**, bump (into), crash-land (an aircraft), drive into, have an accident, hit, plough into, wreck 6 = **hurtle**, fall headlong, give way, lurch, overbalance, plunge, topple 7 = **collapse**, be ruined, fail, fold, fold up, go belly up (inf), go bust (inf), go to the wall, go under

crass adj = **insensitive**, boorish, gross, indelicate, oafish, stupid, unrefined, witless

crate n = **container**, box, case, packing case, tea chest

crater n = **hollow**, depression, dip

crave v 1 = **long for**, desire, hanker after, hope for, lust after, want, yearn for 2 = **beg**, ask, beseech, entreat, implore, petition, plead for, pray for, seek, solicit, supplicate

crawl v 1, 2 = **creep**, advance slowly, inch, slither, worm one's way, wriggle, writhe

3 (foll. by to) = **grovel**, creep, fawn, humble oneself, toady 4 = **be full of**, be alive, be overrun (sl), swarm, teem

craze n = **fad**, enthusiasm, fashion, infatuation, mania, rage, trend, vogue

creak v, n = **squeak**, grate, grind, groan, scrape, scratch, screech

cream n 2 = **lotion**, cosmetic, emulsion, essence, liniment, oil, ointment, paste, salve, unguent 3 = **best**, elite, flower, pick, prime ▷ adj 4 = **off-white**, yellowish-white

crease n = **line**, corrugation, fold, groove, ridge, wrinkle ▷ v 3 = **wrinkle**, corrugate, crumple, double up, fold, rumple, screw up

create v 1 = **make**, bring about, cause, compose, devise, formulate, invent, lead to, occasion, originate, produce, spawn 2 = **appoint**, constitute, establish, install, invest, make, set up

creature n = **living thing**, animal, beast, being, brute, human being, individual,

crèche *n* place where small children are looked after while their parents are working, shopping, etc.

credentials ❶ *pl n* document giving evidence of a person's identity or qualifications.

credible ❶ *adj* 1 believable. 2 trustworthy. **credibly** *adv* **credibility** *n*.

credit ❶ *n* 1 system of allowing customers to receive goods and pay later. 2 reputation for trustworthiness in paying debts. 3 money at one's disposal in a bank account. 4 side of an account book on which such sums are entered. 5 (source or cause of) praise or approval. 6 influence or reputation based on the good opinion of others. 7 belief or trust. ▷ *pl* 8 list of people responsible for the production of a film, programme, or record. ▷ *v* **crediting**, **credited** 9 enter as a credit in an account. 10 (foll. by *with*) attribute (to). 11 believe. **creditable** *adj* praiseworthy. **creditably** *adv* **creditor** *n* person to whom money is owed. **credit card** card allowing a person to buy on credit

credulous *adj* too willing to believe. **credulity** *n*.

creed ❶ *n* statement or system of (Christian) beliefs or principles.

creek ❶ *n* 1 narrow inlet or bay. 2 *Aust, NZ, US & Canad* small stream.

creep ❶ *v* **creeping**, **crept** 1 move quietly and cautiously. 2 crawl with the body near to the ground. 3 (of a plant) grow along the ground or over rocks. ▷ *n* 4 *slang* obnoxious or servile person. **give one the creeps** *informal* make one feel fear or disgust. **creeper** *n* creeping plant. **creepy** *adj informal* causing a feeling of fear or disgust.

creole *n* language developed from a mixture of languages.

creosote *n* 1 dark oily liquid made from coal tar and used for preserving wood. ▷ *v* 2 treat with creosote.

crepe [**krayp**] *n* 1 fabric or rubber with a crinkled texture. 2 very thin pancake.

crescendo [krish-**end**-oh] *n, pl* **-dos** gradual increase in loudness, esp. in music.

crescent ❶ *n* 1 (curved shape of) the moon as seen in its first or last quarter. 2 crescent-shaped street.

cress *n* plant with strong-tasting leaves, used in salads.

━━━━━━━━━━━━━━━━━━━━ THESAURUS ━━━━━━━━

man, mortal, person, soul, woman

credentials *pl n* = **certification**, authorization, document, licence, papers, passport, reference(s), testimonial

credible *adj* 1 = **believable**, conceivable, imaginable, likely, plausible, possible, probable, reasonable, thinkable 2 = **reliable**, dependable, honest, sincere, trustworthy, trusty

credit *n* 1 = **deferred payment**, hire-purchase, (the) H.P., the slate (*inf*), tick (*inf*) 5 = **praise**, acclaim, acknowledgment, approval, commendation, honour, kudos, recognition, tribute 6 = **prestige**, esteem, good name, influence, mana (*NZ*), position, regard, reputation, repute, standing, status 7 = **belief**, confidence, credence, faith, reliance, trust ▷ *v* 10 (foll.

by *with*) = **attribute to**, ascribe to, assign to, impute to 11 = **believe**, accept, have faith in, rely on, trust

creed *n* = **belief**, articles of faith, catechism, credo, doctrine, dogma, principles

creek *n* 1 = **inlet**, bay, bight, cove, firth or frith (*Scot*) 2 *Aust & NZ, US, & Canadian* = **stream**, bayou, brook, rivulet, runnel, tributary, watercourse

creep *v* 1 = **sneak**, approach unnoticed, skulk, slink, steal, tiptoe 2 = **crawl**, glide, slither, squirm, wriggle, writhe ▷ *n* 4 *Sl* = **bootlicker** (*inf*), crawler (*sl*), sneak, sycophant, toady ▷ *pl* **give one the creeps** *Inf* = **disgust**, frighten, make one's hair stand on end, make one squirm, repel, repulse, scare

crescent *n* 1 = **meniscus**, new moon, sickle

crest ❶ n 1 top of a mountain, hill, or wave. 2 tuft or growth on a bird's or animal's head. 3 heraldic design used on a coat of arms and elsewhere. **crested** adj **crestfallen** adj disheartened.

cretin n 1 informal stupid person. 2 obs person afflicted with physical and mental retardation caused by a thyroid deficiency. **cretinous** adj.

crevasse n deep open crack in a glacier.

crevice ❶ n narrow crack or gap in rock.

crew ❶ n 1 people who work on a ship or aircraft. 2 group of people working together. 3 informal any group of people. ▷ v 4 serve as a crew member (on). **crew cut** man's closely cropped haircut.

crib ❶ n 1 piece of writing stolen from elsewhere. 2 translation or list of answers used by students, often illicitly. 3 baby's cradle. 4 rack for fodder. 5 short for CRIBBAGE. ▷ v **cribbing, cribbed** 6 copy (someone's work) dishonestly.

cribbage n card game for two to four players.

crick n 1 muscle spasm or cramp in the back or neck. ▷ v 2 cause a crick in.

cricket¹ n outdoor game played with bats, a ball, and wickets by two teams of eleven. **cricketer** n.

cricket² n chirping insect like a grasshopper.

crime ❶ n 1 unlawful act. 2 unlawful acts collectively. **criminal** n 1 person guilty of a crime. ▷ adj 2 of crime. 3 informal deplorable. **criminality** n **criminology** n study of crime.

crimson adj deep purplish-red.

cringe ❶ v 1 flinch in fear. 2 behave in a submissive or timid way.

crinkle v, n wrinkle, crease, or fold.

crinoline n hooped petticoat.

cripple ❶ n 1 person who is lame or disabled. ▷ v 2 make lame or disabled. 3 damage (something).

crisis ❶ n, pl **-ses** 1 crucial stage, turning point. 2 time of extreme trouble.

crisp ❶ adj 1 fresh and firm. 2 dry and brittle. 3 clean and neat. 4 (of weather) cold but invigorating. 5 lively or brisk. ▷ n 6 very thin slice of potato fried till crunchy. **crispy** adj hard and crunchy. **crispbread** n thin dry biscuit.

crisscross v 1 move in or mark with a crosswise pattern. ▷ adj 2 (of lines)

THESAURUS

crest n 1 = **top**, apex, crown, highest point, peak, pinnacle, ridge, summit 2 = **tuft**, comb, crown, mane, plume 3 = **emblem**, badge, bearings, device, insignia, symbol

crevice n = **gap**, chink, cleft, crack, cranny, fissure, hole, opening, slit

crew¹ n 1 = **(ship's) company**, hands, (ship's) complement 2 = **team**, corps, gang, posse, squad 3 Inf = **crowd**, band, bunch (inf), gang, horde, mob, pack, set

crib n 2 = **translation**, key 3 = **cradle**, bassinet, bed, cot 4 = **manger**, rack, stall ▷ v 6 = **copy**, cheat, pirate, plagiarize, purloin, steal

crime n 1 = **offence**, felony, misdeed, misdemeanour, transgression, trespass, unlawful act, violation 2 = **lawbreaking**, corruption, illegality, misconduct, vice, wrongdoing

cringe v 1 = **shrink**, cower, draw back, flinch, recoil, shy, wince 2 = **grovel**, bootlick (inf), crawl, creep, fawn, kowtow, pander to, toady

cripple v 2 = **disable**, hamstring, incapacitate, lame, maim, paralyse, weaken 3 = **damage**, destroy, impair, put out of action, put paid to, ruin, spoil

crisis n 1 = **critical point**, climax, crunch (inf), crux, culmination, height, moment of truth, turning point 2 = **emergency**, deep water, dire straits, meltdown (inf), panic stations (inf), plight, predicament, trouble

crisp adj 1 = **firm**, crispy, crunchy, fresh 2 = **brittle**, crumbly 3 = **clean**, neat, smart, spruce, tidy, trim, well-groomed, well-pressed 4 = **bracing**, brisk, fresh, invigorating, refreshing

crossing in different directions.

criterion ❶ *n, pl* **-ria** standard of judgment.

critic ❶ *n* **1** professional judge of any of the arts. **2** person who finds fault. **critical** *adj* **1** very important or dangerous. **2** very seriously ill or injured. **3** fault-finding. **4** able to examine and judge carefully. **criticism** *n* **1** fault-finding. **2** analysis of a work of art.

croak ❶ *v* **1** (of a frog or crow) give a low hoarse cry. **2** utter or speak with a croak. ▷ *n* **3** low hoarse sound.

crochet [**kroh**-shay] *v* **-cheting**, **-cheted** **1** make by looping and intertwining yarn with a hooked needle. ▷ *n* **2** work made in this way.

crock *n* earthenware pot or jar. **crockery** *n* dishes.

crocodile *n* **1** large amphibious tropical reptile. **2** a line of people, esp. schoolchildren, walking two by two. **crocodile tears** insincere show of grief.

crocus *n, pl* **-cuses** small plant with yellow, white, or purple flowers in spring.

croft *n* small farm worked by one family in Scotland. **crofter** *n*.

croissant [**krwah**-son] *n* rich flaky crescent-shaped roll.

crone *n* witchlike old woman.

crony *n, pl* **-nies** close friend.

crook ❶ *n* **1** *informal* criminal. **2** bent or curved part. **3** hooked pole. ▷ *adj* **4** *Aust &* *NZ slang* unwell, injured **go crook** *Aust &* *NZ slang* become angry. **crooked** *adj* **1** bent or twisted. **2** set at an angle. **3** *informal* dishonest.

croon ❶ *v* sing, hum, or speak in a soft low tone. **crooner** *n* male singer of sentimental ballads.

crop ❶ *n* **1** cultivated plant. **2** season's total yield of produce. **3** group of things appearing at one time. **4** (handle of) a whip. **5** pouch in a bird's gullet. **6** very short haircut. ▷ *v* **cropping**, **cropped** **7** cut very short. **8** produce or harvest as a crop. **9** (of animals) feed on (grass). **cropper** *n* **come a cropper** *informal* have a disastrous failure or heavy fall. **crop-top** *n* short T-shirt or vest that reveals the wearer's midriff. **crop up** *v informal* happen unexpectedly.

croquet [**kroh**-kay] *n* game played on a lawn in which balls are hit through hoops.

croquette [kroh-**kett**] *n* fried cake of potato, meat, or fish.

cross ❶ *v* **1** move or go across (something). **2** meet and pass. **3** mark with a cross. **4** (with *out*) delete with a cross or lines. **5** place (one's arms or legs) crosswise. **6** make the sign of the cross on (oneself). **7** challenge or oppose. **8** cross-fertilize. ▷ *n* **9** structure, symbol, or mark of two intersecting lines. **10** such a structure of wood as a means of execution.

———————————————————————— THESAURUS ————————

criterion *n* = **standard**, bench mark, gauge, measure, principle, rule, test, touchstone, yardstick

critic *n* **1** = **judge**, analyst, authority, commentator, connoisseur, expert, mana (*NZ*), pundit, reviewer **2** = **fault-finder**, attacker, detractor, knocker (*inf*)

croak *v* **1,2** = **squawk**, caw, grunt, utter or speak huskily, wheeze

crook *n* **1** *Inf* = **criminal**, cheat, racketeer, robber, rogue, shark, swindler, thief, villain

croon *v* = **sing**, hum, purr, warble

crop *n* **2** = **produce**, fruits, gathering, harvest, reaping, vintage, yield ▷ *v* **7** = **cut**, clip, lop, pare, prune, shear, snip, trim **9** = **graze**, browse, nibble

cross *v* **1** = **go across**, bridge, cut across, extend over, move across, pass over, span, traverse **2** = **intersect**, crisscross, intertwine **4** (with *out*) = **strike off** *or* **out**, blue-pencil, cancel, delete, eliminate, score off *or* out **7** = **oppose**, block, impede, interfere, obstruct, resist **8** = **interbreed**, blend, crossbreed, cross-fertilize, cross-pollinate, hybridize, intercross, mix, mongrelize ▷ *n* **11** = **crucifix**, rood **12** = **mixture**,

11 representation of the Cross as an emblem of Christianity. 12 mixture of two things. ▷ *adj* 13 angry, annoyed. 14 lying or placed across. **crossing** *n* 1 place where a street may be crossed safely. 2 place where one thing crosses another. 3 journey across water. **crossbar** *n* horizontal bar across goalposts or on a bicycle. **crossbow** *n* weapon consisting of a bow fixed across a wooden stock. **crossbred** *adj* bred from two different types of animal or plant. **crossbreed** *n* crossbred animal or plant. **crosscheck** *v* check using a different method. **cross-country** *adj, adv* by way of open country or fields. **cross-examine** *v Law* question (a witness for the opposing side) to check his or her testimony. **cross-examination** *n* **cross-eyed** *adj* with eyes looking towards each other. **cross-fertilize** *v* fertilize (an animal or plant) from one of a different kind. **crossfire** *n* gunfire crossing another line of fire. **cross-ply** *adj* (of a tyre) having the fabric cords in the outer casing running diagonally. **cross-purposes** *pl n* **at cross-purposes** misunderstanding each other. **cross-reference** *n* reference within a text to another part. **crossroads** *n* place where roads intersect. **cross section** 1 (diagram of) a surface made by cutting across something. 2 representative sample. **crosswise** *adj, adv* 1 across. 2 in the shape

of a cross. **crossword puzzle**, **crossword** *n* puzzle in which words suggested by clues are written into a grid of squares.

crosswalk *n Canad* place marked where pedestrians may cross a road.

crotch *n* part of the body between the tops of the legs.

crotchet *n* musical note half the length of a minim.

crotchety *adj informal* bad-tempered.

crouch ➊ *v* 1 bend low with the legs and body close. ▷ *n* 2 this position.

croupier [**kroop**-ee-ay] *n* person who collects bets and pays out winnings at a gambling table in a casino.

crouton *n* small piece of fried or toasted bread served in soup.

crow¹ *n* large black bird with a harsh call. **as the crow flies** in a straight line. **crow's feet** wrinkles at the corners of the eyes. **crow's nest** lookout platform at the top of a ship's mast **stone the crows!** *Brit & Aust slang* expression of surprise, dismay, etc.

crow² ➊ *v* 1 (of a cock) make a shrill squawking sound. 2 boast or gloat.

crowbar *n* iron bar used as a lever.

crowd ➊ *n* 1 large group of people or things. 2 particular group of people. ▷ *v* 3 gather together in large numbers. 4 press together in a confined space. 5 fill or occupy fully.

crown ➊ *n* 1 monarch's headdress of

---

amalgam, blend, combination ▷ *adj* 13 = **angry**, annoyed, grumpy, ill-tempered, in a bad mood, irascible, put out, short 14 = **transverse**, crosswise, diagonal, intersecting, oblique

crouch *v* 1 = **bend down**, bow, duck, hunch, kneel, squat, stoop

crow² *v* 2 = **gloat**, blow one's own trumpet, boast, brag, exult, skite (*Aust & NZ*), strut, swagger, triumph

crowd *n* 1 = **multitude**, army, horde, host, mass, mob, pack, swarm, throng 2 = **group**, bunch (*inf*), circle, clique, lot,

set ▷ *v* 3 = **flock**, congregate, gather, mass, stream, surge, swarm, throng 4 = **squeeze**, bundle, congest, cram, pack, pile

crown *n* 1 = **coronet**, circlet, diadem, tiara 2 = **laurel wreath**, garland, honour, laurels, prize, trophy, wreath 3 = **high point**, apex, crest, pinnacle, summit, tip, top ▷ *v* 5 = **honour**, adorn, dignify, festoon 7 = **cap**, be the climax or culmination of, complete, finish, perfect, put the finishing touch to, round off, top 10 *Inf* = **strike**, belt (*inf*), biff (*sl*), box, cuff, hit over the head, punch

gold and jewels. **2** wreath for the head, given as an honour. **3** top of the head or of a hill. **4** artificial cover for a broken or decayed tooth. ▷ v **5** put a crown on the head of (someone) to proclaim him or her monarch. **6** put on or form the top of. **7** put the finishing touch to (a series of events). **8** *informal* hit on the head. **the Crown** power of the monarchy. **crown-of-thorns** n starfish with a spiny outer covering that feeds on living coral.

crucial ❶ adj very important. **crucially** adv.

crucible n pot in which metals are melted.

crude ❶ adj **1** rough and simple. **2** tasteless, vulgar. **3** in a natural or unrefined state. **crudely** adv **crudity** n.

cruel ❶ adj **1** delighting in others' pain. **2** causing pain or suffering. **cruelly** adv **cruelty** n.

cruet n small container for salt, pepper, etc., at table.

cruise ❶ n **1** sail for pleasure. ▷ v **2** sail from place to place for pleasure. **3** (of a vehicle) travel at a moderate and economical speed. **cruiser** n **1** fast warship.

2 motorboat with a cabin.

crumb ❶ n **1** small fragment of bread or other dry food. **2** small amount.

crumble ❶ v **1** break into fragments. **2** fall apart or decay. ▷ n **3** pudding of stewed fruit with a crumbly topping. **crumbly** adj.

crumpet n **1** round soft yeast cake, eaten buttered. **2** *slang* sexually attractive women collectively.

crumple ❶ v **1** crush, crease. **2** collapse, esp. from shock.

crunch ❶ v **1** bite or chew with a noisy crushing sound. **2** make a crisp or brittle sound. ▷ n **3** crunching sound. **4** *informal* critical moment. **crunchy** adj.

crusade ❶ n **1** medieval Christian war to recover the Holy Land from the Muslims. **2** vigorous campaign in favour of a cause. ▷ v **3** take part in a crusade. **crusader** n.

crush ❶ v **1** compress so as to injure, break, or crumple. **2** break into small pieces. **3** defeat or humiliate utterly. ▷ n **4** dense crowd. **5** *informal* infatuation. **6** drink made by crushing fruit.

crust ❶ n **1** hard outer part of something,

— THESAURUS —

crucial adj = **vital**, central, critical, decisive, essential, high-priority, important, momentous, pivotal, pressing, urgent

crude adj **1** = **primitive**, clumsy, makeshift, rough, rough-and-ready, rudimentary, unpolished **2** = **vulgar**, coarse, dirty, gross, indecent, obscene, scungy (*Aust & NZ inf*), smutty, tasteless, uncouth **3** = **unrefined**, natural, raw, unprocessed

cruel adj **1** = **brutal**, barbarous, callous, hard-hearted, heartless, inhumane, malevolent, sadistic, spiteful, unkind, vicious

cruise n **1** = **sail**, boat trip, sea trip, voyage ▷ v **2** = **sail**, coast, voyage **3** = **travel along**, coast, drift, keep a steady pace

crumb n = **bit**, fragment, grain, morsel, scrap, shred, soupçon

crumble v **1** = **crush**, fragment, granulate, grind, pound, powder, pulverize **2** = **disintegrate**, collapse,

decay, degenerate, deteriorate, fall apart, go to pieces, go to wrack and ruin, tumble down

crumple v **1** = **crush**, crease, rumple, screw up, wrinkle **2** = **collapse**, break down, cave in, fall, give way, go to pieces

crunch v **1** = **chomp**, champ, chew noisily, grind, munch ▷ n **4** *Inf* = **critical point**, crisis, crux, emergency, moment of truth, test

crusade n **2** = **campaign**, cause, drive, movement, push

crush v **1** = **squash**, break, compress, press, pulverize, squeeze **3 a** = **overcome**, conquer, overpower, overwhelm, put down, quell, stamp out, subdue **b** = **humiliate**, abash, mortify, put down (*sl*), quash, shame ▷ n **4** = **crowd**, huddle, jam

crust n **1** = **layer**, coating, covering, shell, skin, surface

esp. bread. ▷ v **2** cover with or form a crust.
crusty adj **1** having a crust. **2** irritable.

crustacean n hard-shelled, usu. aquatic
animal with several pairs of legs, such as
the crab or lobster.

crutch n **1** long sticklike support with a
rest for the armpit, used by a lame person.
2 person or thing that gives support.
3 crotch.

crux n, pl **cruxes** crucial or decisive point.

cry ❶ v **crying**, **cried 1** shed tears. **2** call or
utter loudly. ▷ n, pl **cries 3** fit of weeping.
4 loud utterance. **5** urgent appeal, e.g. a
cry for help. **crybaby** n person, esp. a child,
who cries too readily. **cry off** v informal
withdraw from an arrangement. **cry out
for** v need urgently.

crypt n vault under a church, esp. one used
as a burial place.

crystal n **1** (single grain of) a symmetrically
shaped solid formed naturally by some
substances. **2** very clear and brilliant glass,
usu. with the surface cut in many planes.
3 tumblers, vases, etc., made of crystal.
▷ adj **4** bright and clear. **crystalline** adj
1 of or like crystal or crystals. **2** clear.
crystallize v **1** make or become definite.
2 form into crystals. **crystallization** n.

cu. cubic.

cub ❶ n **1** young wild animal such as a bear
or fox. ▷ v **cubbing**, **cubbed 2** give birth
to cubs.

cubbyhole n small enclosed space or
room.

cube n **1** object with six equal square sides.
2 number resulting from multiplying a
number by itself twice. ▷ v **3** cut into
cubes. **4** find the cube of (a number). **cubic**

adj **1** having three dimensions. **2** cube-
shaped. **cubism** n style of art in which
objects are represented by geometrical
shapes. **cubist** adj, n **cube root** number
whose cube is a given number.

cubicle n enclosed part of a large room,
screened for privacy.

cuckoo n **1** migratory bird with a
characteristic two-note call, which lays
its eggs in the nests of other birds. ▷ adj
2 informal insane or foolish.

cucumber n long green-skinned fleshy
fruit used in salads.

cud n partially digested food which a
ruminant brings back into its mouth to
chew again. **chew the cud** think deeply.

cuddle ❶ v, n hug. **cuddly** adj.

cudgel ❶ n short thick stick used as a
weapon.

cue¹ ❶ n **1** signal to an actor or musician
to begin speaking or playing. **2** signal or
reminder. ▷ v **cueing**, **cued 3** give a cue to.

cue² n **1** long tapering stick used in billiards,
snooker, or pool. ▷ v **cueing**, **cued 2** hit (a
ball) with a cue.

cuff¹ n end of a sleeve. **off the cuff** informal
without preparation. **cuff link** one of a pair
of decorative fastenings for shirt cuffs.

cuff² v **1** hit with an open hand. ▷ n **2** blow
with an open hand.

cuisine [quiz-**zeen**] n style of cooking.

cul-de-sac ❶ n road with one end blocked
off.

culinary adj of kitchens or cookery.

cull v **1** choose, gather. **2** remove or kill
(inferior or surplus animals) from a herd.
▷ n **3** culling.

culminate ❶ v reach the highest point or

—————————— THESAURUS ——————————

cry v **1** = **weep**, blubber, shed tears, snivel,
sob **2** = **shout**, bawl, bellow, call out,
exclaim, howl, roar, scream, shriek, yell
▷ n **3** = **weeping**, blubbering, snivelling,
sob, sobbing, weep **4** = **shout**, bellow, call,
exclamation, howl, roar, scream, screech,
shriek, yell **5** = **appeal**, plea

cub n **1** = **young**, offspring, whelp

cuddle v = **hug**, bill and coo, cosset,
embrace, fondle, pet, snuggle

cudgel n = **club**, baton, bludgeon, cosh
(Brit), stick, truncheon

cue¹ n **1** = **prompt**, catchword **2** = **signal**,
hint, reminder, sign, suggestion

cul-de-sac n = **dead end**, blind alley

culminate v = **end up**, climax, close, come

climax. **culmination** n.

culottes pl n women's knee-length trousers cut to look like a skirt.

culpable ❶ adj deserving blame. **culpability** n.

culprit ❶ n person guilty of an offence or misdeed.

cult ❶ n 1 specific system of worship. 2 devotion to a person, idea, or activity. 3 popular fashion.

cultivate ❶ v 1 prepare (land) to grow crops. 2 grow (plants). 3 develop or improve (something). 4 try to develop a friendship with (someone). **cultivated** adj well-educated. **cultivation** n.

culture ❶ n 1 ideas, customs, and art of a particular society. 2 particular society. 3 developed understanding of the arts. 4 cultivation of plants or rearing of animals. 5 growth of bacteria for study. **cultural** adj **cultured** adj showing good taste or manners.

culvert ❶ n drain under a road or railway.

cumbersome ❶ adj awkward because of size or shape.

cummerbund n wide sash worn round the waist.

cumulative adj increasing steadily.

cumulus [**kew**-myew-luss] n, pl **-li** thick white or dark grey cloud.

cunjevoi n 1 Aust plant of tropical Asia and Australia with small flowers, cultivated for its edible rhizome. 2 sea squirt.

cunning ❶ adj 1 clever at deceiving. 2 ingenious. ▷ n 3 cleverness at deceiving. 4 ingenuity.

cup ❶ n 1 small bowl-shaped drinking container with a handle. 2 contents of a cup. 3 (competition with) a cup-shaped trophy given as a prize. 4 hollow rounded shape. ▷ v **cupping, cupped** 5 form (one's hands) into the shape of a cup. 6 hold in cupped hands. **cupful** n.

cur n lit 1 mongrel dog. 2 contemptible person.

curate n clergyman who assists a parish priest. **curacy** [**kew**-rah-see] n, pl **-cies** work or position of a curate.

curator n person in charge of a museum or art gallery.

curb ❶ n 1 something that restrains. ▷ v 2 control, restrain.

curd n coagulated milk, used to make cheese. **curdle** v turn into curd, coagulate.

cure ❶ v 1 get rid of (an illness or problem). 2 make (someone) well again. 3 preserve

——————————————————————— THESAURUS ———————————————————————

to a climax, come to a head, conclude, finish, wind up

culpable adj = **blameworthy**, at fault, found wanting, guilty, in the wrong, to blame, wrong

culprit n = **offender**, criminal, evildoer, felon, guilty party, miscreant, transgressor, wrongdoer

cult n 2 = **devotion**, idolization, worship

cultivate v 1 = **farm**, plant, plough, tend, till, work 3 = **develop**, foster, improve, promote, refine 4 = **court**, dance attendance upon, run after, seek out

culture n 1 = **civilization**, customs, lifestyle, mores, society, way of life 3 = **refinement**, education, enlightenment, good taste, sophistication, urbanity 4 = **farming**, cultivation, husbandry

culvert n = **drain**, channel, conduit, gutter, watercourse

cumbersome adj = **awkward**, bulky, burdensome, heavy, unmanageable, unwieldy, weighty

cunning adj 1 = **crafty**, artful, devious, Machiavellian, sharp, shifty, sly, wily 2 = **skilful**, imaginative, ingenious n 3 = **craftiness**, artfulness, deviousness, guile, slyness, trickery 4 = **skill**, artifice, cleverness, ingenuity, subtlety

cup n 1 = **mug**, beaker, bowl, chalice, goblet, teacup 3 = **trophy**

curb n 1 = **restraint**, brake, check, control, deterrent, limitation ▷ v 2 = **restrain**, check, control, hinder, impede, inhibit, restrict, retard, suppress

cure v 1, 2 = **make better**, correct, ease,

by salting, smoking, or drying. ▷ *n*
4 (treatment causing) curing of an illness or person. **5** remedy or solution. **curable** *adj*.
curfew *n* **1** law ordering people to stay inside their homes after a specific time at night. **2** time set as a deadline by such a law.
curio *n, pl* **-rios** rare or unusual object valued as a collector's item.
curious ❶ *adj* **1** eager to learn or know. **2** eager to find out private details. **3** unusual or peculiar. **curiously** *adv* **curiosity** *n* **1** eagerness to know or find out. **2** *pl* **-ties** rare or unusual object.
curl *n* **1** curved piece of hair. **2** curved spiral shape. ▷ *v* **3** make (hair) into curls or (of hair) grow in curls. **4** make into a curved spiral shape. **curly** *adj* **curling** *n* game like bowls, played with heavy stones on ice.
curlew *n* long-billed wading bird.
curmudgeon *n* bad-tempered person.
currajong *n* same as KURRAJONG.
currant *n* **1** small dried grape. **2** small round berry, such as a redcurrant.
current ❶ *adj* **1** of the immediate present. **2** most recent, up-to-date. **3** commonly accepted. ▷ *n* **4** flow of water or air in one direction. **5** flow of electricity. **6** general trend. **currently** *adv* **currency** *n, pl* **-cies**

1 money in use in a particular country.
2 general acceptance or use.
curriculum *n, pl* **-la**, **-lums** all the courses of study offered by a school or college. **curriculum vitae** [**vee**-tie] outline of someone's educational and professional history, prepared for job applications.

● **SPELLING TIP**
● You possibly read the word **curriculum**
● more often than you have to write it. It's
● easy not to notice that the only letter
● that is doubled is the r in the middle.

curry *n, pl* **-ries 1** Indian dish of meat or vegetables in a hot spicy sauce. ▷ *v* **-rying**, **-ried 2** prepare (food) with mixture of hot spices. **curry powder** mixture of spices for making curry.
curse ❶ *v* **1** swear (at). **2** ask a supernatural power to cause harm to. ▷ *n* **3** swearword. **4** (result of) a call to a supernatural power to cause harm to someone. **5** something causing trouble or harm. **cursed** *adj*.
cursor *n* movable point of light that shows a specific position on a visual display unit.
cursory *adj* quick and superficial. **cursorily** *adv*.
curt ❶ *adj* brief and rather rude.
curtail ❶ *v* **1** cut short. **2** restrict. **curtailment** *n*.

heal, mend, relieve, remedy, restore
3 = **preserve**, dry, pickle, salt, smoke ▷ *n*
4 = **remedy**, antidote, medicine, nostrum, panacea, treatment
curious *adj* **1** = **inquiring**, inquisitive, interested, questioning, searching **2** = **inquisitive**, meddling, nosy (*inf*), prying **3** = **unusual**, bizarre, extraordinary, munted (*NZ sl*), mysterious, novel, odd, peculiar, rare, strange, unexpected
curl *n* **2** = **twist**, coil, kink, ringlet, spiral, whorl ▷ *v* **4** = **twirl**, bend, coil, curve, loop, spiral, turn, twist, wind
current *adj* **1** = **present**, contemporary, present-day **2** = **up-to-date**, fashionable, in fashion, in vogue, trendy (*Brit inf*) **3** = **prevalent**, accepted, common,

customary, in circulation, popular, topical, widespread ▷ *n* **4** = **flow**, course, draught, jet, progression, river, stream, tide, undertow **6** = **mood**, atmosphere, feeling, tendency, trend, undercurrent
curse *v* **1** = **swear**, blaspheme, cuss (*inf*), take the Lord's name in vain **2** = **damn**, anathematize, excommunicate ▷ *n* **3** = **oath**, blasphemy, expletive, obscenity, swearing, swearword **4** = **denunciation**, anathema, ban, excommunication, hoodoo (*inf*), jinx **5** = **affliction**, bane, hardship, plague, scourge, torment, trouble
curt *adj* = **short**, abrupt, blunt, brief, brusque, gruff, monosyllabic, succinct, terse
curtail *v* **1** = **cut short**, cut back, decrease,

curtain ❶ *n* **1** piece of cloth hung at a
window or opening as a screen. **2** hanging
cloth separating the audience and the
stage in a theatre. **3** fall or closing of the
curtain at the end, or the rise or opening
of the curtain at the start of a theatrical
performance. **4** something forming
a barrier or screen. ▷ *v* **5** provide with
curtains. **6** (foll. by *off*) separate by a
curtain.

curtsy, curtsey *n*, *pl* **-sies, -seys**
1 woman's gesture of respect made by
bending the knees and bowing the head.
▷ *v* **-sying, -sied** *or* **-seying, -seyed**
2 make a curtsy.

curve ❶ *n* **1** continuously bending line with
no straight parts. ▷ *v* **2** form or move in a
curve. **curvy** *adj* **curvaceous** *adj informal*
(of a woman) having a shapely body.
curvature *n* curved shape. **curvilinear** *adj*
consisting of or bounded by a curve.

cushion ❶ *n* **1** bag filled with soft material,
to make a seat more comfortable.
2 something that provides comfort or
absorbs shock. ▷ *v* **3** lessen the effects of.
4 protect from injury or shock.

cushy ❶ *adj* **cushier, cushiest** *informal*
easy.

custard *n* sweet yellow sauce made from

milk, eggs, and cornflour.

custody ❶ *n* **1** keeping safe.
2 imprisonment prior to being tried.
custodial *adj* **custodian** *n* person in
charge of a public building.

custom ❶ *n* **1** long-established activity
or action. **2** usual habit. **3** regular use of
a shop or business. ▷ *pl* **4** duty charged
on imports or exports. **5** government
department which collects these. **6** area
at a port, airport, or border where
baggage and freight are examined for
dutiable goods. **customary** *adj* **1** usual.
2 established by custom. **customarily** *adv*
customer *n* person who buys goods or
services. **custom-built, custom-made** *adj*
made to the specifications of an individual
customer.

cut ❶ *v* **cutting, cut 1** open up, penetrate,
wound, or divide with a sharp instrument.
2 divide. **3** trim or shape by cutting.
4 abridge, shorten. **5** reduce, restrict.
6 *informal* hurt the feelings of. **7** pretend
not to recognize. ▷ *n* **8** stroke or incision
made by cutting. **9** piece cut off.
10 reduction. **11** deletion in a text, film,
or play. **12** *informal* share, esp. of profits.
13 style in which hair or a garment is cut.
cut in *v* **1** interrupt. **2** obstruct another

━━━━━━━━━━━━━━━━━━━━━━━━━━━ THESAURUS ━━━━

diminish, dock, lessen, reduce, shorten,
truncate
curtain *n* **1** = **hanging**, drape (*chiefly US*)
curve *n* **1** = **bend**, arc, curvature, loop,
trajectory, turn ▷ *v* **2** = **bend**, arc, arch,
coil, hook, spiral, swerve, turn, twist, wind
cushion *n* **1** = **pillow**, beanbag, bolster,
hassock, headrest, pad ▷ *v* **3** = **soften**,
dampen, deaden, muffle, stifle, suppress
cushy *adj Inf* = **easy**, comfortable, soft,
undemanding
custody *n* **1** = **safekeeping**, care,
charge, keeping, protection, supervision
2 = **imprisonment**, confinement,
detention, incarceration
custom *n* **1** = **tradition**, convention, policy,
practice, ritual, rule, usage **2** = **habit**,

practice, procedure, routine, way, wont
3 = **customers**, patronage, trade ▷ *pl*
4 = **duty**, import charges, tariff, tax, toll
cut *v* **1** = **penetrate**, chop, pierce, score,
sever, slash, slice, slit, wound **2** = **divide**,
bisect, dissect, slice, split **3** = **shape**, carve,
chisel, clip, fashion, form, hew, lop, mow,
pare, prune, sculpt, shave, snip, trim,
whittle **4** = **abridge**, abbreviate, condense,
curtail, delete, shorten **5** = **reduce**,
contract, cut back, decrease, diminish,
lower, slash, slim (down) **6** *Inf* = **hurt**,
insult, put down, snub, sting, wound
7 = **ignore**, avoid, cold-shoulder, slight,
spurn, turn one's back on *n* **8** = **incision**,
gash, laceration, nick, slash, slit, stroke,
wound **10** = **reduction**, cutback, decrease,

vehicle in overtaking it.

cute ❶ *adj* 1 appealing or attractive.
2 *informal* clever or shrewd. **cutely** *adv*
cuteness *n*.

cuticle *n* skin at the base of a fingernail or
toenail.

cutlass *n* curved one-edged sword formerly
used by sailors.

cutlery *n* knives, forks, and spoons. **cutler**
n maker of cutlery.

cutlet *n* 1 small piece of meat like a chop.
2 flat croquette of chopped meat or fish.

cuttlefish *n* squidlike sea mollusc.

CV curriculum vitae.

cyanide *n* extremely poisonous chemical
compound.

cyber- *combining form* computers, e.g.
cyberspace.

cybernetics *n* branch of science in which
electronic and mechanical systems are
studied and compared to biological
systems.

cyclamen [**sik**-la-men] *n* plant with red,
pink, or white flowers.

cycle ❶ *v* 1 ride a bicycle. ▷ *n* 2 bicycle.
3 *US* motorcycle. 4 complete series of
recurring events. 5 time taken for one
such series. **cyclical**, **cyclic** *adj* occurring in
cycles. **cyclist** *n* person who rides a bicycle.

cyclone *n* violent wind moving clockwise
round a central area.

cygnet *n* young swan.

cylinder *n* 1 solid or hollow body with
straight sides and circular ends. 2 chamber
within which the piston moves in an
internal-combustion engine. **cylindrical** *adj*.

cymbal *n* percussion instrument consisting
of a brass plate which is struck against
another or hit with a stick.

cynic ❶ [**sin**-ik] *n* person who believes that
people always act selfishly. **cynical** *adj*
cynically *adv* **cynicism** *n*.

cypress *n* evergreen tree with dark green
leaves.

cyst [**sist**] *n* (abnormal) sac in the body
containing fluid or soft matter. **cystic** *adj*
cystitis [siss-**tite**-iss] *n* inflammation of
the bladder.

THESAURUS

---

fall, lowering, saving 12 *Inf* = **share**,
percentage, piece, portion, section, slice
13 = **style**, fashion, look, shape

cute *adj* 1 = **appealing**, attractive,
charming, delightful, engaging, lekker

(*S Afr sl*), lovable

cycle *n* 4, 5 = **era**, circle, period, phase,
revolution, rotation

cynic *n* = **sceptic**, doubter, misanthrope,
misanthropist, pessimist, scoffer

dab ❶ v **dabbing, dabbed 1** pat lightly.
2 apply with short tapping strokes.
▷ n **3** small amount of something soft
or moist. **4** light stroke or tap. **dab
hand** *informal* person who is particularly
good at something.

dabble ❶ v **1** be involved in something
superficially. **2** splash about. **dabbler** n.

dachshund n dog with a long body and
short legs.

dad n *informal* father.

daffodil n yellow trumpet-shaped flower
that blooms in spring.

daft ❶ adj *informal* foolish or crazy.

dagga n S Afr *informal* cannabis.

dagger ❶ n short knifelike weapon with a
pointed blade.

dahlia [**day**-lya] n brightly coloured garden
flower.

daily ❶ adj **1** occurring every day or every
weekday. ▷ adv **2** every day. ▷ n, pl **-lies**
3 daily newspaper. **4** Brit *informal* person
who cleans other people's houses.

dainty ❶ adj **-tier, -tiest** delicate or
elegant. **daintily** adv.

dairy n, pl **dairies 1** place for the processing
or sale of milk and its products. **2** NZ small
shop selling groceries and milk often
outside normal trading hours. ▷ adj **3** of
milk or its products.

dais [**day**-iss] n raised platform in a hall,
used by a speaker.

daisy n, pl **-sies** small wild flower with a
yellow centre and white petals.

dale n (esp. in N England) valley.

dally v **-lying, -lied 1** waste time. **2** (foll.
by *with*) deal frivolously (with). **dalliance**
n flirtation.

Dalmatian n large dog with a white coat
and black spots.

dam ❶ n **1** barrier built across a river to
create a lake. **2** lake created by this. ▷ v
damming, dammed 3 build a dam across
(a river).

damage ❶ v **1** harm, spoil. ▷ n **2** harm to a
person or thing. **3** *informal* cost, e.g. *what's
the damage?* ▷ pl **4** money awarded as
compensation for injury or loss.

damask n fabric with a pattern woven into
it, used for tablecloths etc.

dame ❶ n **1** *slang* woman. **2** (**D-**) title of a
woman who has been awarded the OBE or
another order of chivalry.

damn ❶ interj **1** *slang* exclamation of
annoyance. ▷ adv, adj **2** (also **damned**)

━━━━━━━━━━━━━━━━━━━━━━━━━━━━━━━━ THESAURUS ━━━━━

dab v **1** = **pat**, tap, touch **2** = **daub**, stipple
▷ n **3** = **spot**, bit, drop, pat, smudge, speck
4 = **pat**, flick, stroke, tap, touch

dabble v **1** = **play at**, dip into, potter, tinker,
trifle (with) **2** = **splash**, dip

daft adj *Inf* = **foolish**, absurd, asinine,
crackpot (*inf*), crazy, idiotic, insane, silly,
stupid, witless

dagger n = **knife**, bayonet, dirk, stiletto

daily adj **1** = **everyday**, diurnal, quotidian
▷ adv **2** = **every day**, day by day, once a day

dainty adj = **delicate**, charming, elegant,
exquisite, fine, graceful, neat, petite, pretty

dam n **1** = **barrier**, barrage, embankment,

obstruction, wall ▷ v **3** = **block up**,
barricade, hold back, obstruct, restrict

damage v **1** = **harm**, hurt, impair, injure,
ruin, spoil, weaken, wreck n **2** = **harm**,
destruction, detriment, devastation, hurt,
injury, loss, suffering **3** *Inf* = **cost**, bill, charge,
expense ▷ pl **4** = **compensation**, fine,
reimbursement, reparation, satisfaction

dame n **2** (with cap.) = **noblewoman**,
baroness, dowager, *grande dame*, lady,
peeress

damn v **3** = **criticize**, blast, censure,
condemn, denounce, put down
4 = **sentence**, condemn, doom

slang extreme(ly). ▷ *v* **3** condemn as bad or worthless. **4** (of God) condemn to hell. **damnable** *adj* annoying. **damnably** *adv* **damnation** *interj*, *n* **damning** *adj* proving or suggesting guilt, e.g. *a damning report*.

damp ⓘ *adj* **1** slightly wet. ▷ *n* **2** slight wetness, moisture. ▷ *v* (also **dampen**) **3** make damp. **4** (foll. by *down*) reduce the intensity of (feelings or actions). **damper** *n* **1** movable plate to regulate the draught in a fire. **2** pad in a piano that deadens the vibration of each string. **put a damper on** have a depressing or inhibiting effect on.

damson *n* small blue-black plumlike fruit.

dance ⓘ *v* **1** move the feet and body rhythmically in time to music. **2** perform (a particular dance). **3** skip or leap. **4** move rhythmically. ▷ *n* **5** series of steps and movements in time to music. **6** social meeting arranged for dancing. **dancer** *n*.

dandelion *n* yellow-flowered wild plant.

dandruff *n* loose scales of dry dead skin shed from the scalp.

dandy *n*, *pl* **-dies 1** man who is overconcerned with the elegance of his appearance. ▷ *adj* **-dier, -diest 2** *informal* very good. **dandified** *adj*.

danger ⓘ *n* **1** possibility of being injured or killed. **2** person or thing that may cause injury or harm. **3** likelihood that something unpleasant will happen. **dangerous** *adj* **dangerously** *adv*.

dangle ⓘ *v* **1** hang loosely. **2** display as an enticement.

dank *adj* unpleasantly damp and chilly.

dapper ⓘ *adj* (of a man) neat in appearance and slight in build.

dappled *adj* marked with spots of a different colour. **dapple-grey** *n* horse with a grey coat and darker coloured spots.

dare ⓘ *v* **1** be courageous enough to try (to do something). **2** challenge to do something risky. ▷ *n* **3** challenge to do something risky. **daring** *adj* **1** willing to take risks. ▷ *n* **2** courage to do dangerous things. **daredevil** *adj*, *n* recklessly bold (person).

dark ⓘ *adj* **1** having little or no light. **2** (of a colour) reflecting little light. **3** (of hair or skin) brown or black. **4** gloomy, sad. **5** sinister, evil. **6** secret, e.g. *keep it dark*. ▷ *n* **7** absence of light. **8** night. **darkly** *adv* **darkness** *n* **dark** *v* **dark horse** person about whom little is known. **darkroom** *n* darkened room for processing photographic film.

darling ⓘ *n* **1** much-loved person. **2** favourite. ▷ *adj* **3** much-loved.

damp *adj* **1** = **moist**, clammy, dank, dewy, drizzly, humid, soggy, sopping, wet ▷ *n* **2** = **moisture**, dampness, dankness, drizzle ▷ *v* **3** = **moisten**, dampen, wet **4** (foll. by *down*) = **curb**, allay, check, diminish, dull, inhibit, lessen, moderate, pour cold water on, reduce, restrain, stifle

dance *v* **1** = **prance**, jig, trip, whirl **3** = **skip**, hop ▷ *n* **6** = **ball**, disco, discotheque, hop (*inf*), knees-up (*Brit inf*), social

danger *n* **1, 2** = **peril**, hazard, jeopardy, menace, pitfall, risk, threat

dangle *v* **1** = **hang**, flap, hang down, sway, swing, trail

dapper *adj* = **neat**, natty (*inf*), smart, soigné, spruce, spry, trim, well-groomed, well turned out

dare *v* **1** = **risk**, hazard, make bold, presume, venture **2** = **challenge**, defy, goad, provoke, taunt, throw down the gauntlet ▷ *n* **3** = **challenge**, provocation, taunt

dark *adj* **1** = **dim**, dingy, murky, shadowy, shady, sunless, unlit **3** = **brunette**, black, dark-skinned, dusky, ebony, sable, swarthy **4** = **gloomy**, bleak, dismal, grim, morose, mournful, sad, sombre **5** = **evil**, foul, infernal, sinister, vile, wicked **6** = **secret**, concealed, hidden, mysterious ▷ *n* **7** = **darkness**, dimness, dusk, gloom, murk, obscurity, semi-darkness **8** = **night**, evening, nightfall, night-time, twilight

darling *n* **1** = **beloved**, dear, dearest, love, sweetheart, trueliove ▷ *adj* **3** = **beloved**, adored, cherished, dear, precious, treasured

darn ❶ v 1 mend (a garment) with a series of interwoven stitches. ▷ n 2 patch of darned work.

dart ❶ n 1 small narrow pointed missile that is thrown or shot, esp. in the game of darts. 2 sudden quick movement. 3 tapered tuck made in dressmaking. ▷ pl 4 game in which darts are thrown at a circular numbered board. ▷ v 5 move or direct quickly and suddenly.

dash ❶ v 1 move quickly. 2 hurl or crash. 3 frustrate (someone's hopes). ▷ n 4 sudden quick movement. 5 small amount. 6 mixture of style and courage. 7 punctuation mark (–) indicating a change of subject. 8 longer symbol used in Morse code. **dashing** adj stylish and attractive. **dashboard** n instrument panel in a vehicle.

dastardly adj wicked and cowardly.

dasyure [dass-ee-your] n small marsupial of Australia, New Guinea, and adjacent islands.

data ❶ n 1 information consisting of observations, measurements, or facts. 2 numbers, digits, etc., stored by a computer. **data base** store of information

that can be easily handled by a computer. **data processing** series of operations performed on data, esp. by a computer, to extract or interpret information.

date¹ ❶ n 1 specified day of the month. 2 particular day or year when an event happened. 3 informal appointment, esp. with a person of the opposite sex. 4 informal person with whom one has a date. ▷ v 5 mark with the date. 6 assign a date of occurrence to. 7 become old-fashioned. 8 (foll. by from) originate from. **dated** adj old-fashioned.

date² n dark-brown sweet-tasting fruit of the date palm.

daub ❶ v smear or spread quickly or clumsily.

daughter n 1 female child. 2 woman who comes from a certain place or is connected with a certain thing. **daughter-in-law** n, pl **daughters-in-law** son's wife.

dawdle ❶ v walk slowly, lag behind. **dawdler** n.

dawn ❶ n 1 daybreak. 2 beginning (of something). ▷ v 3 begin to grow light. 4 begin to develop or appear. 5 (foll. by on) become apparent (to).

darn v 1 = **mend**, cobble up, patch, repair, sew up, stitch ▷ n 2 = **mend**, invisible repair, patch, reinforcement

dart v 5 = **dash**, fly, race, run, rush, shoot, spring, sprint, tear

dash v 1 = **rush**, bolt, fly, hurry, race, run, speed, sprint, tear 2 = **throw**, cast, fling, hurl, slam, sling 3 = **frustrate**, blight, foil, ruin, spoil, thwart, undo ▷ n 4 = **rush**, dart, race, run, sortie, sprint, spurt 5 = **little**, bit, drop, hint, pinch, soupçon, sprinkling, tinge, touch 6 = **style**, brio, élan, flair, flourish, panache, spirit, verve

data n 1 = **information**, details, facts, figures, statistics

date¹ n 3 Inf = **appointment**, assignation, engagement, meeting, rendezvous, tryst 4 Inf = **partner**, escort, friend ▷ v 6 = **put a date on**, assign a date to, fix the period

of 7 = **become old-fashioned**, be dated, show one's age 8 (foll. by from) = **come from**, bear a date of, belong to, exist from, originate in

daub v = **smear**, coat, cover, paint, plaster, slap on (inf)

dawdle v = **waste time**, dally, delay, drag one's feet or heels, hang about, idle, loaf, loiter, trail

dawn n 1 = **daybreak**, cockcrow, crack of dawn, daylight, morning, sunrise, sunup 2 = **beginning**, advent, birth, emergence, genesis, origin, rise, start ▷ v 3 = **grow light**, break, brighten, lighten 4 = **begin**, appear, develop, emerge, originate, rise, unfold 5 (foll. by on) = **hit**, become apparent, come into one's head, come to mind, occur, register (inf), strike

day ❶ *n* **1** period of 24 hours. **2** period of light between sunrise and sunset. **3** part of a day occupied with regular activity, esp. work. **4** period or point in time. **5** time of success. **daybreak** *n* time in the morning when light first appears. **daydream** *n* **1** pleasant fantasy indulged in while awake. ▷ *v* **2** indulge in idle fantasy. **daydreamer** *n* **daylight** *n* light from the sun. **day release** system in which workers go to college one day a week. **day-to-day** *adj* routine.

daze ❶ *v* **1** stun, by a blow or shock. ▷ *n* **2** state of confusion or shock.

dazzle ❶ *v* **1** impress greatly. **2** blind temporarily by sudden excessive light. ▷ *n* **3** bright light that dazzles. **dazzling** *adj*.

DC 1 direct current. **2** District of Columbia.

DE Delaware.

de- *prefix* indicating: **1** removal, e.g. *dethrone*. **2** reversal, e.g. *declassify*. **3** departure, e.g. *decamp*.

deacon *n Christianity* **1** ordained minister ranking immediately below a priest. **2** (in some Protestant churches) lay official who assists the minister.

dead ❶ *adj* **1** no longer alive. **2** no longer in use. **3** numb, e.g. *my leg has gone dead*. **4** complete, absolute, e.g. *dead silence*. **5** *informal* very tired. **6** (of a place) lacking activity. ▷ *n* **7** period during which

coldness or darkness is most intense, e.g. *in the dead of night*. ▷ *adv* **8** extremely. **9** suddenly, e.g. *I stopped dead*. **dead set** firmly decided. **deadbeat** *n informal* lazy useless person. **dead beat** *informal* exhausted. **dead end 1** road with one end blocked off. **2** situation in which further progress is impossible. **dead heat** tie for first place between two participants in a contest. **deadline** *n* time limit. **deadlock** *n* point in a dispute at which no agreement can be reached. **deadlocked** *adj* **deadly** *adj* likely to cause death. **deadpan** *adj, adv* showing no emotion or expression. **dead reckoning** method of establishing one's position using the distance and direction travelled. **dead weight** heavy weight.

deaf ❶ *adj* unable to hear. **deaf to** refusing to listen to or take notice of. **deafen** *v* make deaf, esp. temporarily. **deafness** *n*.

deal¹ ❶ *n* **1** agreement or transaction. **2** kind of treatment, e.g. *a fair deal*. **3** large amount. ▷ *v* **dealing, dealt [delt] 4** inflict (a blow) on. **5** *Cards* give out (cards) to the players. **dealer** *n* **dealings** *pl n* transactions or business relations. **deal out** *v* distribute. **deal with** *v* **1** take action on. **2** be concerned with.

deal² *n* plank of fir or pine wood.

dean *n* **1** chief administrative official of a college or university faculty. **2** chief

day *n* **1** = **twenty-four hours 2** = **daylight**, daytime **4** = **point in time**, date, time **5** = **time**, age, epoch, era, heyday, period, zenith

daze *v* **1** = **stun**, benumb, numb, paralyse, shock, stupefy ▷ *n* **2** = **shock**, bewilderment, confusion, distraction, stupor, trance, trancelike state

dazzle *v* **1** = **impress**, amaze, astonish, bowl over (*inf*), overpower, overwhelm, take one's breath away **2** = **blind**, bedazzle, blur, confuse, daze ▷ *n* **3** = **splendour**, brilliance, glitter, magnificence, razzmatazz (*sl*), sparkle

dead *adj* **1** = **deceased**, defunct, departed, extinct, late, passed away, perished

2 = **not working**, inactive, inoperative, stagnant, unemployed, useless **3** = **numb**, inert, paralysed **4** = **total**, absolute, complete, outright, thorough, unqualified, utter **5** *Inf* = **exhausted**, dead beat (*inf*), spent, tired, worn out **6** = **boring**, dull, flat, uninteresting ▷ *n* **7** = **middle**, depth, midst ▷ *adv* **8** = **exactly**, absolutely, completely, directly, entirely, totally

deaf *adj* = **hard of hearing**, stone deaf, without hearing **deaf to** = **oblivious**, indifferent, unconcerned, unhearing, unmoved

deal¹ *n* **1** = **agreement**, arrangement, bargain, contract, pact, transaction,

administrator of a cathedral. **deanery** n,
pl **-eries 1** office or residence of a dean.
2 parishes of a dean.

dear ❶ n **1** someone regarded with
affection. ▷ adj **2** much-loved. **3** costly.
dearly adv.

dearth ❶ [dirth] n inadequate amount,
scarcity.

death ❶ n **1** permanent end of life in a
person or animal. **2** instance of this.
3 ending, destruction. **deathly** adj, adv like
death, e.g. a deathly silence; deathly pale.
death duty former name for INHERITANCE
TAX. **deathtrap** n place or vehicle
considered very unsafe.

debacle ❶ [day-bah-kl] n disastrous failure.

debase ❶ v lower in value, quality, or
character. **debasement** n.

debate ❶ n **1** discussion. ▷ v **2** discuss
formally. **3** consider (a course of action).
debatable adj not absolutely certain.

debilitate v weaken, make feeble.
debilitation n **debility** n weakness, infirmity.

debit n **1** the money, or a record of the
money, withdrawn from a person's bank
account. ▷ v **debiting, debited 2** charge

(an account) with a debt.

debonair ❶ adj (of a man) charming and
refined.

debrief ❶ v receive a report from (a soldier,
diplomat, etc.) after an event. **debriefing** n.

debris ❶ [deb-ree] n fragments of
something destroyed.

debt ❶ n something owed, esp. money. **in
debt** owing money. **debtor** n.

debunk ❶ v informal expose the falseness of.

debut ❶ [day-byoo] n first public
appearance of a performer. **debutante**
[day-byoo-tont] n young upper-class
woman being formally presented to
society.

Dec. December.

decade n period of ten years.

decaffeinated [dee-kaf-fin-ate-id] adj (of
coffee, tea, or cola) with caffeine removed.

decant v **1** pour (a liquid) from one container
to another. **2** rehouse (people) while their
homes are being renovated. **decanter** n
stoppered bottle for wine or spirits.

decapitate ❶ v behead. **decapitation** n.

decathlon n athletic contest with ten
events.

━━━━━━━━━━━━━━━━━━━━━━ THESAURUS ━━━━━━

understanding **3** = **amount**, degree,
extent, portion, quantity, share

dear n **1** = **beloved**, angel, darling, loved
one, precious, treasure ▷ adj **2** = **beloved**,
cherished, close, favourite, intimate,
precious, prized, treasured **3** = **expensive**,
at a premium, costly, high-priced,
overpriced, pricey (inf)

dearth n = **scarcity**, deficiency, inadequacy,
insufficiency, lack, paucity, poverty,
shortage, want

death n **1, 2** = **dying**, demise, departure,
end, exit, passing **3** = **destruction**,
downfall, extinction, finish, ruin, undoing

debacle n = **disaster**, catastrophe,
collapse, defeat, fiasco, reversal, rout

debase v = **degrade**, cheapen, devalue,
lower, reduce

debate n **1** = **discussion**, argument,
contention, controversy, dispute ▷ v

2 = **discuss**, argue, dispute, question
3 = **consider**, deliberate, ponder, reflect,
ruminate, weigh

debonair adj = **elegant**, charming,
courteous, dashing, refined, smooth,
suave, urbane, well-bred

debrief v = **interrogate**, cross-examine,
examine, probe, question, quiz

debris n = **remains**, bits, detritus,
fragments, rubble, ruins, waste, wreckage

debt n = **debit**, commitment, liability,
obligation ▷ n **in debt** = **owing**, in arrears,
in the red (inf), liable

debunk v Inf = **expose**, cut down to size,
deflate, disparage, mock, ridicule,
show up

debut n = **introduction**, beginning, bow,
coming out, entrance, first appearance,
initiation, presentation

decapitate v = **behead**, execute, guillotine

decay ❶ v **1** become weaker or more corrupt. **2** rot. ▷ n **3** process of decaying. **4** state brought about by this process.

decease ❶ n formal death. **deceased** adj formal dead. **the deceased** dead person.

deceive ❶ v **1** mislead by lying. **2** be unfaithful to (one's sexual partner). **deceit** n behaviour intended to deceive. **deceitful** adj.

decelerate v slow down. **deceleration** n.

December n twelfth month of the year.

decent ❶ adj **1** (of a person) polite and morally acceptable. **2** fitting or proper. **3** conforming to conventions of sexual behaviour. **4** informal kind. **decently** adv **decency** n.

deception ❶ n **1** deceiving. **2** something that deceives, trick. **deceptive** adj likely or designed to deceive. **deceptively** adv.

decibel n unit for measuring the intensity of sound.

decide ❶ v **1** (cause to) reach a decision. **2** settle (a contest or question). **decided** adj **1** unmistakable. **2** determined. **decidedly** adv **decision** n judgment, conclusion, or resolution.

deciduous adj (of a tree) shedding its leaves annually.

decimal n **1** fraction written in the form of a dot followed by one or more numbers. ▷ adj **2** relating to or using powers of ten. **3** expressed as a decimal. **decimalize** v change (a system or number) to the decimal system. **decimalization** n **decimal point** dot between the unit and the fraction of a number in the decimal system. **decimal system** number system with a base of ten, in which numbers are expressed by combinations of the digits 0 to 9.

decimate ❶ v destroy or kill a large proportion of. **decimation** n.

decipher ❶ v work out the meaning of (something illegible or in code).

deck n **1** area of a ship that forms a floor. **2** similar area in a bus. **3** platform that supports the turntable and pick-up of a record player. **deck chair** folding chair made of canvas over a wooden frame. **decking** n wooden platform in a garden. **deck out** v decorate.

declaim ❶ v **1** speak loudly and dramatically. **2** protest loudly. **declamatory** adj.

decay v **1** = **decline**, crumble, deteriorate, disintegrate, dwindle, shrivel, wane, waste away, wither **2** = **rot**, corrode, decompose, perish, putrefy ▷ n **3** = **decline**, collapse, degeneration, deterioration, fading, failing, wasting, withering **4** = **rot**, caries, decomposition, gangrene, putrefaction

decease n Formal = **death**, demise, departure, dying, release

deceive v **1** = **take in** (inf), cheat, con (inf), dupe, fool, hoodwink, mislead, swindle, trick

decent adj **1** = **proper**, appropriate, becoming, befitting, fitting, seemly, suitable **3** = **respectable**, chaste, decorous, modest, proper, pure **4** Inf = **kind**, accommodating, courteous, friendly, generous, gracious, helpful, obliging, thoughtful

deception n **1** = **trickery**, cunning, deceit, fraud, guile, legerdemain, treachery **2** = **trick**, bluff, decoy, hoax, illusion, lie, ruse, subterfuge

decide v **1** = **reach** or **come to a decision**, choose, conclude, determine, make up one's mind, resolve **2** = **adjudge**, adjudicate

decimate v = **devastate**, ravage, wreak havoc on

decipher v = **figure out** (inf), crack, decode, deduce, interpret, make out, read, solve

declaim v **1** = **orate**, harangue, hold forth, lecture, proclaim, rant, recite, speak **2** = **protest against**, attack, decry, denounce, inveigh, rail

declare ❶ v 1 state firmly and forcefully.
2 announce officially. 3 acknowledge for
tax purposes. **declaration** n.
decline ❶ v 1 become smaller, weaker, or
less important. 2 refuse politely to accept
or do. 3 *Grammar* list the inflections of (a
noun, pronoun, or adjective). ▷ n 4 gradual
weakening or loss.
decode ❶ v convert from code into ordinary
language. **decoder** n.
decompose ❶ v be broken down
through chemical or bacterial action.
decomposition n.
decongestant n medicine that relieves
nasal congestion.
decontaminate v make safe by
removing poisons, radioactivity, etc.
decontamination n.
decor ❶ [**day**-core] n style in which a room
or house is decorated.
decorate, ❶ v 1 make more attractive by

adding something ornamental. 2 paint or
wallpaper. 3 award a (military) medal to.
decoration n **decorative** adj **decorator** n.
decorum ❶ [dik-**core**-um] n polite and
socially correct behaviour.
decoy ❶ n 1 person or thing used to lure
someone into danger. 2 dummy bird or
animal, used to lure game within shooting
range. ▷ v 3 lure away by means of a trick.
decrease ❶ v 1 make or become less. ▷ n
2 lessening, reduction. 3 amount by which
something has decreased.
decree ❶ n 1 law made by someone in
authority. 2 court judgment. ▷ v 3 order
by decree.
decrepit ❶ adj weakened or worn out by
age or long use. **decrepitude** n.
decry ❶ v -**crying**, -**cried** express
disapproval of.
dedicate ❶ v 1 commit (oneself or one's
time) wholly to a special purpose or

——————————————— THESAURUS ———————————————

declare v 1 = **state**, affirm, announce,
assert, claim, maintain, proclaim, profess,
pronounce, swear, utter
decline v 1 a = **lessen**, decrease,
diminish, dwindle, ebb, fade, fall off,
shrink, wane, weaken b = **deteriorate**,
decay, degenerate, sink, worsen
2 = **refuse**, abstain, avoid, reject, say 'no',
turn down ▷ n 4 = **deterioration**, decay,
degeneration, downturn, drop, dwindling,
failing, falling off, lessening, recession,
slump, weakening, worsening
decode v = **decipher**, crack, decrypt,
interpret, solve, unscramble, work out
decompose v = **rot**, break up, crumble,
decay, fall apart, fester, putrefy
decor n = **decoration**, colour scheme,
furnishing style, ornamentation
decorate v 1 = **adorn**, beautify, embellish,
festoon, grace, ornament, trim 2 = **do
up** (*inf*), colour, furbish, paint, paper,
renovate, wallpaper 3 = **pin a medal on**,
cite, confer an honour on *or* upon
decorum n = **propriety**, decency, dignity,
etiquette, good manners, politeness,

protocol, respectability
decoy n 1 = **lure**, bait, enticement,
inducement, pretence, trap ▷ v 3 = **lure**,
deceive, ensnare, entice, entrap, seduce,
tempt
decrease v 1 = **lessen**, cut down, decline,
diminish, drop, dwindle, lower, reduce,
shrink, subside ▷ n 2 = **lessening**,
contraction, cutback, decline, dwindling,
falling off, loss, reduction, subsidence
decree n 1 = **law**, act, command, edict,
order, proclamation, ruling, statute ▷ v
3 = **order**, command, demand, ordain,
prescribe, proclaim, pronounce, rule
decrepit adj a = **weak**, aged, doddering,
feeble, frail, infirm b = **worn-out**,
battered, beat-up (*inf*), broken-down,
dilapidated, ramshackle, rickety, run-
down, tumbledown, weather-beaten
decry v = **condemn**, belittle, criticize,
denigrate, denounce, discredit, disparage,
put down, run down
dedicate v 1 = **devote**, commit, give
over to, pledge, surrender 2 = **inscribe**,
address

cause. **2** inscribe or address (a book etc.) to someone as a tribute. **dedicated** *adj* devoted to a particular purpose or cause. **dedication** *n*.

deduce ● *v* reach (a conclusion) by reasoning from evidence. **deducible** *adj*.

deduct ● *v* subtract.

deed ● *n* **1** something that is done. **2** legal document.

deem *v* consider, judge.

deep ● *adj* **1** extending or situated far down, inwards, backwards, or sideways. **2** of a specified dimension downwards, inwards, or backwards. **3** difficult to understand. **4** of great intensity. **5** (foll. by *in*) absorbed in (an activity). **6** (of a colour) strong or dark. **7** low in pitch. **the deep** *poetic* the sea. **deeply** *adv* profoundly or intensely (also **deep down**). **deepen** *v* **deep-freeze** *n* same as FREEZER.

deer *n*, *pl* **deer** large wild animal, the male of which has antlers.

deface ● *v* deliberately spoil the appearance of.

defame ● *v* attack the good name or reputation of. **defamation** *n* **defamatory**

[dif-**fam**-a-tree] *adj*.

default ● *n* **1** failure to do something. **2** *Computers* instruction to a computer to select a particular option unless the user specifies otherwise. ▷ *v* **3** fail to fulfil an obligation. **in default of** in the absence of.

defeat ● *v* **1** win a victory over. **2** thwart, frustrate. ▷ *n* **3** defeating. **defeatism** *n* ready acceptance or expectation of defeat. **defeatist** *adj*, *n*.

defecate *v* discharge waste from the body through the anus.

defect ● *n* **1** imperfection, blemish. ▷ *v* **2** desert one's cause or country to join the opposing forces. **defective** *adj* imperfect, faulty. **defection** *n* **defector** *n*.

defend ● *v* **1** protect from harm or danger. **2** support in the face of criticism. **3** represent (a defendant) in court. **defendant** *n* person accused of a crime. **defender** *n* **defensible** *adj* capable of being defended because believed to be right. **defensive** *adj* **1** intended for defence. **2** overanxious to protect oneself against (threatened) criticism. **defensively** *adv*.

deduce *v* = **conclude**, draw, gather, glean, infer, reason, take to mean, understand

deduct *v* = **subtract**, decrease by, knock off (*inf*), reduce by, remove, take away, take off

deed *n* **1** = **action**, achievement, act, exploit, fact, feat, performance **2** = **document**, contract, title

deep *adj* **1** = **wide**, bottomless, broad, far, profound, unfathomable, yawning **3** = **mysterious**, abstract, abstruse, arcane, esoteric, hidden, obscure, recondite, secret **4** = **intense**, extreme, grave, great, profound, serious (*inf*), unqualified **5** (foll. by *in*) = **absorbed**, engrossed, immersed, lost, preoccupied, rapt **6** = **dark**, intense, rich, strong, vivid **7** = **low**, bass, booming, low-pitched, resonant, sonorous *n* **the deep** *Poet* = **ocean**, briny (*inf*), high seas, main, sea

deface *v* = **vandalize**, damage, deform,

disfigure, mar, mutilate, spoil, tarnish

defame *v* = **slander**, bad-mouth (*sl, chiefly US & Canad*), cast aspersions on, denigrate, discredit, disparage, knock (*inf*), libel, malign, smear

default *n* **1** = **failure**, deficiency, dereliction, evasion, lapse, neglect, nonpayment, omission ▷ *v* **3** = **fail**, dodge, evade, neglect

defeat *v* **1** = **beat**, conquer, crush, master, overwhelm, rout, trounce, vanquish, wipe the floor with (*inf*) **2** = **frustrate**, baffle, balk, confound, foil, get the better of, ruin, thwart ▷ *n* **3** = **conquest**, beating, overthrow, pasting (*sl*), rout

defect *n* **1** = **imperfection**, blemish, blotch, error, failing, fault, flaw, spot, taint ▷ *v* **2** = **desert**, abandon, change sides, go over, rebel, revolt, walk out on (*inf*)

defend *v* **1** = **protect**, cover, guard, keep safe, preserve, safeguard, screen, shelter,

defer¹ ❶ v **-ferring, -ferred** delay
(something) until a future time.
deferment, deferral n.

defer² ❶ v **-ferring, -ferred** (foll. by to)
comply with the wishes (of). **deference** n
polite and respectful behaviour.
deferential adj.

deficient ❶ adj **1** lacking some essential
thing or quality. **2** inadequate in quality
or quantity. **deficiency** n **1** state of being
deficient. **2** lack, shortage. **deficit** n amount
by which a sum of money is too small.

defile v treat (something sacred or
important) without respect. **defilement** n.

define ❶ v **1** state precisely the meaning
of. **2** show clearly the outline of. **definable**
adj **definite** adj **1** firm, clear, and precise.
2 having precise limits. **3** known for
certain. **definitely** adv **definition** n
1 statement of the meaning of a word
or phrase. **2** quality of being clear and
distinct. **definitive** adj **1** providing an
unquestionable conclusion. **2** being the
best example of something.

deflate ❶ v **1** (cause to) collapse through
the release of air. **2** take away the self-
esteem or conceit from. **3** Economics cause

deflation of (an economy). **deflation** n
1 Economics reduction in economic activity
resulting in lower output and investment.
2 feeling of sadness following excitement.
deflationary adj.

deflect ❶ v (cause to) turn aside from a
course. **deflection** n.

deform ❶ v put out of shape or spoil the
appearance of. **deformation** n **deformity** n.

defraud ❶ v cheat out of money, property, etc.

defrost v **1** make or become free of ice.
2 thaw (frozen food) by removing it from
a freezer.

deft ❶ adj quick and skilful in movement.

defunct ❶ adj no longer existing or
operative.

defuse v **1** remove the fuse of (an explosive
device). **2** remove the tension from (a
situation).

defy ❶ v **-fying, -fied 1** resist openly and
boldly. **2** make impossible, e.g. the condition
of the refugees defied description. **defiance** n
open resistance or disobedience. **defiant** adj.

degenerate ❶ adj **1** having deteriorated
to a lower mental, moral, or physical level.
▷ n **2** degenerate person. ▷ v **3** become

——————————————— THESAURUS ———————————————

shield **2 = support**, champion, endorse,
justify, speak up for, stand up for, stick up
for (inf), uphold, vindicate

defer¹ v = **postpone**, delay, hold over,
procrastinate, put off, put on ice (inf),
shelve, suspend

defer² v (foll. by to) = **comply**, accede, bow,
capitulate, give in, give way to, submit, yield

deficient adj **1 = lacking**, inadequate,
insufficient, meagre, scant, scarce, short,
skimpy, wanting **2 = unsatisfactory**,
defective, faulty, flawed, impaired,
imperfect, incomplete, inferior, weak

define v **1 = describe**, characterize, designate,
explain, expound, interpret, specify, spell
out **2 = mark out**, bound, circumscribe,
delineate, demarcate, limit, outline

deflate v **1 = collapse**, empty, exhaust,
flatten, puncture, shrink **2 = humiliate**,
chasten, disconcert, dispirit, humble,

mortify, put down (sl), squash **3** Economics
= **reduce**, depress, devalue, diminish

deflect v = **turn aside**, bend, deviate,
diverge, glance off, ricochet, swerve, veer

deform v = **distort**, buckle, contort, deface,
disfigure, gnarl, maim, mangle, mar,
misshape, mutilate, ruin, spoil, twist, warp

defraud v = **cheat**, con (inf), diddle (inf),
embezzle, fleece, pilfer, rip off (sl), swindle,
trick

deft adj = **skilful**, adept, adroit, agile,
dexterous, expert, neat, nimble, proficient

defunct adj = **dead**, bygone, deceased,
departed, expired, extinct, gone,
inoperative, invalid, nonexistent, obsolete,
out of commission

defy v **1 = resist**, brave, confront, disregard,
flout, scorn, slight, spurn

degenerate adj **1 = depraved**, corrupt,
debauched, decadent, dissolute, immoral,

degenerate. **degeneracy** n degenerate behaviour. **degeneration** n.

degrade ● v 1 reduce to dishonour or disgrace. 2 reduce in status or quality. 3 *Chem* decompose into smaller molecules. **degradation** n.

degree ● n 1 stage in a scale of relative amount or intensity. 2 academic award given by a university or college on successful completion of a course. 3 unit of measurement for temperature, angles, or latitude and longitude.

dehydrate v remove water from (food) to preserve it. **be dehydrated** become weak through losing too much water from the body. **dehydration** n.

deify [**day**-if-fie] v **-fying, -fied** treat or worship as a god. **deification** n.

deign [**dane**] v agree (to do something), but as if doing someone a favour.

dejected ● adj unhappy. **dejection** n

delay ● v 1 put off to a later time. 2 slow up or cause to be late. ▷ n 3 act of delaying. 4 interval of time between events.

delectable adj delightful, very attractive. **delectation** n formal great pleasure.

delegate ● n 1 person chosen to represent others, esp. at a meeting. ▷ v 2 entrust (duties or powers) to someone. 3 appoint as a delegate. **delegation** n 1 group chosen to represent others. 2 delegating.

delete ● v remove (something written or printed). **deletion** n.

deliberate ● adj 1 planned in advance, intentional. 2 careful and unhurried. ▷ v 3 think something over. **deliberately** adv **deliberation** n **deliberative** adj.

delicate ● adj 1 fine or subtle in quality or workmanship. 2 having a fragile beauty. 3 (of a taste etc.) pleasantly subtle. 4 easily damaged. 5 requiring tact. **delicately** adv **delicacy** n 1 being delicate. 2 pl **-cies** something particularly good to eat.

delicatessen n shop selling imported or unusual foods, often already cooked or prepared.

low, perverted ▷ v 3 = **worsen**, decay, decline, decrease, deteriorate, fall off, lapse, sink, slip

degrade v 1 = **demean**, debase, discredit, disgrace, dishonour, humble, humiliate, shame 2 = **demote**, downgrade, lower

degree n 1 = **stage**, grade, notch, point, rung, step, unit

dejected adj = **downhearted**, crestfallen, depressed, despondent, disconsolate, disheartened, downcast, glum, miserable, sad

delay v 1 = **put off**, defer, hold over, postpone, procrastinate, shelve, suspend 2 = **hold up**, bog down, detain, hinder, hold back, impede, obstruct, set back, slow down ▷ n 3 = **putting off**, deferment, postponement, procrastination, suspension 4 = **hold-up**, hindrance, impediment, interruption, interval, setback, stoppage, wait

delegate n 1 = **representative**, agent, ambassador, commissioner, deputy,

envoy, legate ▷ v 2 = **entrust**, assign, consign, devolve, give, hand over, pass on, transfer 3 = **appoint**, accredit, authorize, commission, depute, designate, empower, mandate

delete v = **remove**, cancel, cross out, efface, erase, expunge, obliterate, rub out, strike out

deliberate adj 1 = **intentional**, calculated, conscious, planned, prearranged, premeditated, purposeful, wilful 2 = **unhurried**, careful, cautious, circumspect, measured, methodical, ponderous, slow, thoughtful ▷ v 3 = **consider**, cogitate, consult, debate, discuss, meditate, ponder, reflect, think, weigh

delicate adj 1 = **fine**, deft, elegant, exquisite, graceful, precise, skilled, subtle 3 = **subtle**, choice, dainty, delicious, fine, savoury, tender 4 = **fragile**, flimsy, frail, slender, slight, tender, weak 5 = **considerate**, diplomatic, discreet, sensitive, tactful

delicious ❶ *adj* very appealing to taste or smell. **deliciously** *adv*.

delight ❶ *n* 1 (source of) great pleasure. ▷*v* 2 please greatly. 3 (foll. by *in*) take great pleasure (in). **delightful** *adj* **delightfully** *adv*.

delinquent ❶ *n* 1 someone, esp. a young person, who repeatedly breaks the law. ▷*adj* 2 repeatedly breaking the law. **delinquency** *n*.

delirium ❶ *n* 1 state of excitement and mental confusion, often with hallucinations. 2 great excitement. **delirious** *adj* **deliriously** *adv*.

deliver ❶ *v* 1 carry (goods etc.) to a destination. 2 hand over. 3 aid in the birth of. 4 present (a lecture or speech). 5 release or rescue. 6 strike (a blow). **deliverance** *n* rescue from captivity or evil. **delivery** *n*, *pl* **-eries** 1 delivering. 2 something that is delivered. 3 act of giving birth to a baby. 4 style in public speaking.

dell *n* small wooded hollow.

delta *n* 1 fourth letter in the Greek alphabet. 2 flat area at the mouth of some rivers where the main stream splits up into several branches.

delude ❶ *v* deceive.

deluge ❶ [**del**-lyooj] *n* 1 great flood. 2 torrential rain. 3 overwhelming number. ▷*v* 4 flood. 5 overwhelm.

de luxe ❶ *adj* rich or sumptuous, superior in quality.

delve ❶ *v* research deeply (for information).

demagogue ❶ *n* political agitator who appeals to the prejudice and passions of the mob. **demagogic** *adj* **demagogy** *n*.

demand ❶ *v* 1 request forcefully. 2 require as just, urgent, etc. 3 claim as a right. ▷*n* 4 forceful request. 5 *Economics* willingness and ability to purchase goods and services. 6 something that requires special effort or sacrifice. **demanding** *adj* requiring a lot of time or effort.

——————————— THESAURUS ———————————

delicious *adj* = **delectable**, appetizing, choice, dainty, lekker (*S Afr sl*), mouthwatering, savoury, scrumptious (*inf*), tasty, toothsome

delight *n* 1 = **pleasure**, ecstasy, enjoyment, gladness, glee, happiness, joy, rapture ▷*v* 2 = **please**, amuse, charm, cheer, enchant, gratify, thrill 3 (foll. by *in*) = **take pleasure in**, appreciate, enjoy, feast on, like, love, relish, revel in, savour

delinquent *n* 1 = **criminal**, culprit, lawbreaker, miscreant, offender, villain, wrongdoer

delirium *n* 1 = **madness**, derangement, hallucination, insanity, raving 2 = **frenzy**, ecstasy, fever, hysteria, passion

deliver *v* 1 = **carry**, bear, bring, cart, convey, distribute, transport 2 = **hand over**, commit, give up, grant, make over, relinquish, surrender, transfer, turn over, yield 4 = **give**, announce, declare, present, read, utter 5 = **release**, emancipate, free, liberate, loose, ransom, rescue, save 6 = **strike**, administer, aim, deal, direct, give,

inflict, launch

delude *v* = **deceive**, beguile, dupe, fool, hoodwink, kid (*inf*), mislead, take in (*inf*), trick

deluge *n* 1 = **flood**, cataclysm, downpour, inundation, overflowing, spate, torrent 3 = **rush**, avalanche, barrage, flood, spate, torrent ▷*v* 4 = **flood**, douse, drench, drown, inundate, soak, submerge, swamp 5 = **overwhelm**, engulf, inundate, overload, overrun, swamp

de luxe *adj* = **luxurious**, costly, exclusive, expensive, grand, opulent, select, special, splendid, superior

delve *v* = **research**, burrow, explore, ferret out, forage, investigate, look into, probe, rummage, search

demagogue *n* = **agitator**, firebrand, rabble-rouser

demand *v* 1 = **request**, ask, challenge, inquire, interrogate, question 2 = **require**, call for, cry out for, entail, involve, necessitate, need, want 3 = **claim**, exact, expect, insist on, order ▷*n* 4 = **request**, inquiry, order, question, requisition

demean ❶ v **demean oneself** do something unworthy of one's status or character.

demeanour ❶ n way a person behaves.

demented ❶ adj mad. **dementia** [dim-**men**-sha] n state of serious mental deterioration.

demerit n fault, disadvantage.

demi- combining form half.

demijohn n large bottle with a short neck, often encased in wicker.

demilitarize v remove the military forces from. **demilitarization** n.

demise ❶ n 1 eventual failure (of something successful). 2 formal death.

demobilize v release from the armed forces. **demobilization** n.

democracy ❶ n, pl -cies 1 government by the people or their elected representatives. 2 state governed in this way. **democrat** n 1 advocate of democracy. 2 (D-) member or supporter of the Democratic Party in the US. **democratic** adj 1 of democracy. 2 upholding democracy. 3 (D-) of the Democratic Party, the more liberal of the two main political parties in the US. **democratically** adv.

demolish ❶ v 1 knock down or destroy (a building). 2 disprove (an argument). **demolition** n.

demon ❶ n 1 evil spirit. 2 person who does something with great energy or skill. **demonic** adj evil. **demoniac, demoniacal** adj 1 appearing to be possessed by a devil. 2 frenzied. **demonology** n study of demons.

demonstrate ❶ v 1 show or prove by reasoning or evidence. 2 display and explain the workings of. 3 reveal the existence of. 4 show support or opposition by public parades or rallies. **demonstrable** adj able to be proved. **demonstrably** adv. **demonstration** n 1 organized expression of public opinion. 2 explanation or display of how something works. 3 proof. **demonstrative** adj tending to show one's feelings unreservedly. **demonstrator** n 1 person who demonstrates how a device or machine works. 2 person who takes part in a public demonstration.

demoralize ❶ v undermine the morale of. **demoralization** n.

demote ❶ v reduce in status or rank. **demotion** n.

demur ❶ v -murring, -murred 1 show reluctance. ▷ n 2 **without demur** without objecting.

d

THESAURUS

5 Economics = **need**, call, claim, market, requirement, want

demean v = **lower**, abase, debase, degrade, descend, humble, stoop

demeanour n = **behaviour**, air, bearing, carriage, comportment, conduct, deportment, manner

demented adj = **mad**, crazed, crazy, deranged, frenzied, insane, maniacal, unbalanced, unhinged

demise n 1 = **failure**, collapse, downfall, end, fall, ruin 2 Formal = **death**, decease, departure

democracy n 1 = **self-government** 2 = **republic**, commonwealth

demolish v 1 = **knock down**, bulldoze, destroy, dismantle, flatten, level, raze, tear down

demon n 1 = **evil spirit**, devil, fiend, ghoul, goblin, malignant spirit 2 = **wizard**, ace (inf), fiend, master

demonstrate v 1 = **prove**, display, exhibit, indicate, manifest, show, testify to 2 = **show how**, describe, explain, illustrate, make clear, teach 4 = **march**, parade, picket, protest, rally

demoralize v = **dishearten**, deject, depress, discourage, dispirit, undermine, unnerve, weaken

demote v = **downgrade**, degrade, kick downstairs (sl), lower in rank, relegate

demur v 1 = **object**, balk, dispute, hesitate, protest, refuse, take exception, waver ▷ n 2 **without demur** = **without objection**, without a qualm, without compunction,

demure ❶ *adj* quiet, reserved, and rather shy. **demurely** *adv*.

den ❶ *n* **1** home of a wild animal. **2** small secluded room in a home. **3** place where people indulge in criminal or immoral activities.

denigrate ❶ *v* criticize unfairly. **denigration** *n*.

denim *n* **1** hard-wearing cotton fabric, usu. blue. ▷ *pl* **2** jeans made of denim.

denizen *n* inhabitant.

denote ❶ *v* **1** be a sign of. **2** have as a literal meaning.

denouement [day-**noo**-mon] *n* final outcome or solution in a play or book.

denounce ❶ *v* **1** speak vehemently against. **2** give information against. **denunciation** *n* open condemnation.

dense ❶ *adj* **1** closely packed. **2** difficult to see through. **3** stupid. **densely** *adv* **density** *n, pl* **-ties 1** degree to which something is filled or occupied. **2** measure of the compactness of a substance, expressed as its mass per unit volume.

dent ❶ *n* **1** hollow in the surface of something, made by hitting it. ▷ *v* **2** make

impress or be impressed with a dent.

dental *adj* of teeth or dentistry. **dental floss** waxed thread used to remove food particles from between the teeth. **dentifrice** [**den**-tif-riss] *n* paste or powder for cleaning the teeth. **dentine** [**den**-teen] *n* hard dense tissue forming the bulk of a tooth. **dentist** *n* person qualified to practise dentistry. **denture** *n* false tooth.

denude *v* remove the covering or protection from.

deny ❶ *v* **-nying, -nied 1** declare to be untrue. **2** refuse to give or allow. **3** refuse to acknowledge. **denial** *n* **1** statement that something is not true. **2** rejection of a request.

depart ❶ *v* **1** leave. **2** differ, deviate. **departed** *adj euphemistic* dead. **departure** *n*.

department ❶ *n* **1** specialized division of a large organization. **2** major subdivision of the administration of a government. **departmental** *adj* **department store** large shop selling many kinds of goods.

depend ❶ *v* (foll. by *on*) **1** put trust (in). **2** be influenced or determined (by). **3** rely (on) for income or support.

———————— THESAURUS ————————

without hesitation, without misgivings, without protest

demure *adj* = **shy**, diffident, modest, reserved, reticent, retiring, sedate, unassuming

den *n* **1** = **lair**, cave, cavern, haunt, hide-out, hole, shelter **2** = **study**, cubbyhole, hideaway, retreat, sanctuary, sanctum

denigrate *v* = **disparage**, bad-mouth (*sl, chiefly US & Canad*), belittle, knock (*inf*), malign, rubbish (*inf*), run down, slander, vilify

denote *v* **1** = **indicate**, betoken, designate, express, imply, mark, mean, show, signify

denounce *v* **1** = **condemn**, attack, censure, revile, stigmatize, vilify **2** = **accuse**, denunciate

dense *adj* **1** = **thick**, close-knit, compact, condensed, heavy, impenetrable, solid **2** = **opaque 3** = **stupid**, dozy (*Brit inf*), dull,

dumb (*inf*), obtuse, slow-witted, stolid, thick

dent *n* **1** = **hollow**, chip, crater, depression, dimple, dip, impression, indentation, pit ▷ *v* **2** = **make a dent in**, gouge, hollow, press in, push in

deny *v* **1** = **contradict**, disagree with, disprove, rebuff, rebut, refute **2** = **refuse**, begrudge, disallow, forbid, reject, turn down, withhold **3** = **renounce**, disclaim, disown, recant, repudiate, retract

depart *v* **1** = **leave**, absent (oneself), disappear, exit, go, go away, quit, retire, retreat, withdraw **2** = **change**, deviate, differ, digress, diverge, stray, swerve, turn aside, vary, veer

department *n* **1** = **section**, branch, bureau, division, office, station, subdivision, unit

depend *v* (foll. by *on*) **1** = **trust in**, bank on, count on, lean on, reckon on, rely upon,

dependable *adj* **dependably** *adv*
dependability *n* **dependant** *n* person
who depends on another for financial
support. **dependence** *n* state of being
dependent. **dependency** *n, pl* **-cies**
1 country controlled by another country.
2 overreliance on another person or on
a drug. **dependent** *adj* depending on
someone or something.

● **SPELLING TIP**
● The words **dependant** and **dependent**
● are easy to confuse. The first, ending in
● *-ant*, is a noun meaning a person who is
● dependent (adjective ending in *-ent*) on
● someone else.

depict ❶ *v* 1 produce a picture of.
2 describe in words. **depiction** *n*.
deplete ❶ *v* 1 use up. 2 reduce in number.
depletion *n*.
deplore ❶ *v* condemn strongly. **deplorable**
adj very bad or unpleasant.
deploy ❶ *v* organize (troops or resources)
into a position ready for immediate action.
deployment *n*.
depopulate *v* reduce the population of.
depopulation *n*.

deport ❶ *v* remove forcibly from a country.
deportation *n* **deportee** *n*.
deportment *n* way in which a person
moves or stands.
depose ❶ *v* 1 remove from an office or
position of power. 2 *Law* testify on oath.
deposit ❶ *v* 1 put down. 2 entrust
for safekeeping, esp. to a bank. 3 lay
down naturally. ▷ *n* 4 sum of money
paid into a bank account. 5 money
given in part payment for goods or
services. 6 accumulation of sediments,
minerals, etc. **depositary** *n* person to
whom something is entrusted for safety.
depositor *n* **depository** *n* store for
furniture etc.
depot ❶ [**dep-**oh] *n* 1 building where
goods or vehicles are kept when not in use.
2 *Chiefly US* bus or railway station.
deprecate *v* express disapproval of.
deprecation *n* **deprecatory** *adj*.
depreciate ❶ *v* 1 decline in value or price.
2 criticize. **depreciation** *n*.
depress ❶ *v* 1 make sad. 2 lower (prices
or wages). 3 push down. **depressing** *adj*
depression *n* 1 mental state in which

turn to 2 = **be determined by**, be based
on, be contingent on, be subject to, be
subordinate to, hang on, hinge on, rest on,
revolve around
depict *v* 1 = **draw**, delineate, illustrate,
outline, paint, picture, portray, sketch
2 = **describe**, characterize, narrate,
outline, represent
deplete *v* 1 = **use up**, consume, drain,
empty, exhaust, expend, impoverish
2 = **reduce**, lessen
deplore *v* = **disapprove of**, abhor, censure,
condemn, denounce, object to, take a dim
view of
deploy *v* = **position**, arrange, set out,
station, use, utilize
deport *v* = **expel**, banish, exile, expatriate,
extradite, oust **deport oneself** = **behave**,
acquit oneself, act, bear oneself, carry
oneself, comport oneself, conduct oneself,

hold oneself
depose *v* 1 = **remove from office**,
demote, dethrone, dismiss, displace, oust
2 *Law* = **testify**, avouch, declare, make a
deposition
deposit *v* 1 = **put**, drop, lay, locate, place
2 = **store**, bank, consign, entrust, lodge
▷ *n* 5 = **down payment**, instalment, part
payment, pledge, retainer, security, stake
6 = **sediment**, accumulation, dregs, lees,
precipitate, silt
depot *n* 1 = **storehouse**, depository,
repository, warehouse 2 *Chiefly US* = **bus
station**, garage, terminus
depreciate *v* 1 = **decrease**, deflate,
devalue, lessen, lose value, lower, reduce
2 = **disparage**, belittle, denigrate, deride,
detract, run down, scorn, sneer at
depress *v* 1 = **sadden**, deject, discourage,
dishearten, dispirit, make despondent,

a person has feelings of gloom and inadequacy. **2** economic condition in which there is high unemployment and low output and investment. **3** area of low air pressure. **4** sunken place. **depressive** *adj* **1** tending to cause depression. ▷ *n* **2** person who suffers from depression.

deprive ❶ *v* (foll. by *of*) prevent from (having or enjoying). **deprivation** *n* **deprived** *adj* lacking adequate living conditions, education, etc.

depth ❶ *n* **1** distance downwards, backwards, or inwards. **2** intensity of emotion. **3** profundity of character or thought. **depth charge** bomb used to attack submarines by exploding at a preset depth of water.

deregulate *v* remove regulations or controls from. **deregulation** *n*.

derelict ❶ *adj* **1** unused and falling into ruins. ▷ *n* **2** social outcast, vagrant. **dereliction** *n* state of being abandoned.

deride ❶ *v* treat with contempt or ridicule. **derision** *n* **derisive** *adj* mocking, scornful. **derisory** *adj* too small or inadequate to be considered seriously.

derive ❶ *v* (foll. by *from*) take or develop

(from). **derivation** *n* **derivative** *adj* word, idea, etc., derived from another.

dermatitis *n* inflammation of the skin.

derogatory ❶ [dir-**rog**-a-tree] *adj* intentionally offensive.

derv *n* diesel oil, when used for road transport.

descant *n* tune played or sung above a basic melody.

descend ❶ *v* **1** move down (a slope etc.). **2** move to a lower level, pitch, etc. **3** (foll. by *to*) stoop to (unworthy behaviour). **4** (foll. by *on*) visit unexpectedly. **be descended from** be connected by a blood relationship to. **descendant** *n* person or animal descended from an individual, race, or species. **descendent** *adj* descending. **descent** *n* **1** descending. **2** downward slope. **3** derivation from an ancestor.

describe ❶ *v* **1** give an account of (something or someone) in words. **2** trace the outline of (a circle etc.). **description** *n* **1** statement that describes something or someone. **2** sort, e.g. *flowers of every description*. **descriptive** *adj* **descriptively** *adv*.

desecrate *v* damage or insult (something sacred). **desecration** *n*.

————————————— THESAURUS —————————————

oppress, weigh down **2** = **lower**, cheapen, depreciate, devalue, diminish, downgrade, lessen, reduce **3** = **press down**, flatten, level, lower, push down

deprive *v* (foll. by *of*) = **withhold**, bereave, despoil, dispossess, rob, strip

depth *n* **1** = **deepness**, drop, extent, measure **3** = **profoundness**, astuteness, discernment, insight, penetration, profundity, sagacity, wisdom

derelict *adj* **1** = **abandoned**, deserted, dilapidated, discarded, forsaken, munted (*NZ sl*), neglected, ruined ▷ *n* **2** = **tramp**, bag lady, down-and-out, outcast, vagrant

deride *v* = **mock**, disdain, disparage, insult, jeer, ridicule, scoff, scorn, sneer, taunt

derive *v* (foll. by *from*) = **come from**, arise from, emanate from, flow from, issue

from, originate from, proceed from, spring from, stem from

derogatory *adj* = **disparaging**, belittling, defamatory, offensive, slighting, uncomplimentary, unfavourable, unflattering

descend *v* **1** = **move down**, drop, fall, go down, plummet, plunge, sink, subside, tumble **2** = **slope**, dip, incline, slant **3** (foll. by *to*) = **lower oneself**, degenerate, deteriorate, stoop **4** (foll. by *on*) = **attack**, arrive, invade, raid, swoop **be descended from** = **originate from**, be handed down from, be passed down from, derive from, issue from, proceed from, spring from

describe *v* **1** = **relate**, depict, explain, express, narrate, portray, recount, report, tell **2** = **trace**, delineate, draw, mark out, outline

desert¹ ❶ n region with little or no vegetation because of low rainfall.

desert² ❶ v 1 abandon (a person or place) without intending to return. 2 *Mil* leave (a post or duty) with no intention of returning. **deserter** n **desertion** n.

deserve ❶ v be entitled to or worthy of. **deserved** adj rightfully earned. **deservedly** adv **deserving** adj worthy of help, praise, or reward.

design ❶ v 1 work out the structure or form of (something), by making a sketch or plans. 2 plan and make artistically. 3 intend for a specific purpose. ▷ n 4 sketch, plan, or preliminary drawing. 5 arrangement or features of an artistic or decorative work. 6 finished artistic or decorative creation. 7 art of designing. 8 intention, e.g. *by design*. **designer** n 1 person who draws up original sketches or plans from which things are made. ▷ adj 2 designed by a well-known designer. **designing** adj cunning and scheming.

designate ❶ [dez-zig-nate] v 1 give a name to. 2 select (someone) for an office or duty. ▷ adj 3 appointed but not yet in office. **designation** n name.

desire ❶ v 1 want very much. ▷ n 2 wish, longing. 3 sexual appetite. 4 person or thing desired. **desirable** adj 1 worth having. 2 arousing sexual desire. **desirability** n **desirous of** having a desire for.

desist ❶ v (foll. by *from*) stop (doing something).

desk n 1 piece of furniture with a writing surface and drawers. 2 service counter in a public building. 3 section of a newspaper covering a specific subject, e.g. *the sports desk*. **desktop** adj (of a computer) small enough to use at a desk.

desolate ❶ adj 1 uninhabited and bleak. 2 very sad. ▷ v 3 deprive of inhabitants. 4 make (someone) very sad. **desolation** n.

despair ❶ n 1 total loss of hope. ▷ v 2 lose hope.

desperate ❶ adj 1 in despair and reckless. 2 (of an action) undertaken as a last resort. 3 having a strong need or desire.

— THESAURUS —

desert¹ n = **wilderness**, solitude, waste, wasteland, wilds

desert² v 1 = **abandon**, abscond, forsake, jilt, leave, leave stranded, maroon, quit, strand, walk out on (*inf*)

deserve v = **merit**, be entitled to, be worthy of, earn, justify, rate, warrant

design v 1 = **plan**, draft, draw, outline, sketch, trace 2 = **create**, conceive, fabricate, fashion, invent, originate, think up 3 = **intend**, aim, mean, plan, propose, purpose ▷ n 4 = **plan**, blueprint, draft, drawing, model, outline, scheme, sketch 5 = **arrangement**, construction, form, organization, pattern, shape, style 8 = **intention**, aim, end, goal, object, objective, purpose, target

designate v 1 = **name**, call, dub, entitle, label, style, term 2 = **appoint**, assign, choose, delegate, depute, nominate, select

desire v 1 = **want**, crave, hanker after, hope for, long for, set one's heart on, thirst for, wish for, yearn for ▷ n 2 = **wish**, aspiration, craving, hankering, hope, longing, thirst, want 3 = **lust**, appetite, libido, passion

desist v (foll. by *from*) = **stop**, break off, cease, discontinue, end, forbear, leave off, pause, refrain from

desolate adj 1 = **uninhabited**, bare, barren, bleak, dreary, godforsaken, solitary, wild 2 = **miserable**, dejected, despondent, disconsolate, downcast, forlorn, gloomy, wretched ▷ v 3 = **lay waste**, depopulate, despoil, destroy, devastate, lay low, pillage, plunder, ravage, ruin 4 = **deject**, depress, discourage, dishearten, dismay, distress, grieve

despair n 1 = **despondency**, anguish, dejection, depression, desperation, gloom, hopelessness, misery, wretchedness ▷ v 2 = **lose hope**, give up, lose heart

desperate adj 1 = **reckless**, audacious,

desperately adv **desperation** n.

● SPELLING TIP
● It's often difficult to decide whether
● to write an a or an e when it doesn't
● seem to affect a word's pronunciation.
● An example in the Bank of English is
● *desparate*, which should, of course, be
● spelt **desperate**.

despise ❶ v regard with contempt.
despicable adj deserving contempt.

despite ❶ prep in spite of.

despoil v formal plunder.

despondent ❶ adj unhappy.
despondency n.

despot ❶ n person in power who acts
unfairly or cruelly. **despotic** adj **despotism**
n unfair or cruel government or behaviour.

dessert n sweet course served at the end of
a meal. **dessertspoon** n spoon between a
tablespoon and a teaspoon in size.

destination ❶ n place to which someone
or something is going.

destitute ❶ adj having no money or
possessions. **destitution** n.

destroy ❶ v 1 ruin, demolish. 2 put an end

to. 3 kill (an animal). **destroyer** n 1 small
heavily armed warship. 2 person or thing
that destroys. **destruction** n ruin.

desultory [**dez**-zl-tree] adj 1 jumping
from one thing to another, disconnected.
2 random.

detach ❶ v disengage and separate.
detachable adj **detached** adj 1 (of a
house) not joined to another house.
2 showing no emotional involvement.
detachment n 1 lack of emotional
involvement. 2 small group of soldiers.

detail ❶ n 1 individual piece of
information. 2 unimportant item.
3 small individual features of something,
considered collectively. 4 Chiefly
mil (personnel assigned) a specific duty.
▷ v 5 list fully.

detain ❶ v 1 delay (someone). 2 hold
(someone) in custody. **detainee** n.

detect ❶ v 1 notice. 2 discover, find.
detectable adj **detection** n **detective**
n policeman or private agent who
investigates crime. **detector** n instrument
used to find something.

————————————————————————— THESAURUS ——

daring, frantic, furious, risky 2 = **grave**,
drastic, extreme, urgent
despise v = **look down on**, abhor, detest,
loathe, revile, scorn
despite prep = **in spite of**, against,
even with, in the face of, in the teeth of,
notwithstanding, regardless of,
undeterred by
despondent adj = **dejected**, depressed,
disconsolate, disheartened, dispirited,
downhearted, glum, in despair, sad,
sorrowful
despot n = **tyrant**, autocrat, dictator,
oppressor
destination n = **journey's end**, haven,
resting-place, station, stop, terminus
destitute adj = **penniless**, down and
out, impoverished, indigent, insolvent,
moneyless, penurious, poor, poverty-
stricken
destroy v 1, 2 = **ruin**, annihilate, crush,

demolish, devastate, eradicate, shatter,
wipe out, wreck
detach v = **separate**, cut off, disconnect,
disengage, divide, remove, sever, tear off,
unfasten
detail n 2 = **fine point**, nicety, particular,
triviality 3 = **point**, aspect, component,
element, fact, factor, feature, particular,
respect 4 Chiefly mil = **party**, assignment,
body, detachment, duty, fatigue, force,
squad ▷ v 5 = **list**, catalogue, enumerate,
itemize, recite, recount, rehearse, relate,
tabulate
detain v 1 = **delay**, check, hinder, hold up,
impede, keep back, retard, slow up (or
down) 2 = **hold**, arrest, confine, intern,
restrain
detect v 1 = **notice**, ascertain, identify,
note, observe, perceive, recognize, spot
2 = **discover**, find, track down, uncover,
unmask

deter ❶ v **-terring, -terred** discourage (someone) from doing something by instilling fear or doubt. **deterrent** n **1** something that deters. **2** weapon, esp. nuclear, intended to deter attack. ▷ adj **3** tending to deter.

detergent ❶ n chemical substance for washing clothes or dishes.

deteriorate ❶ v become worse. **deterioration** n.

determine ❶ v **1** settle (an argument or a question) conclusively. **2** find out the facts about. **3** make a firm decision (to do something). **determinant** n factor that determines. **determinate** adj definitely limited or fixed. **determination** n **1** being determined or resolute. **determined** adj firmly decided, unable to be dissuaded. **determinedly** adv **determiner** n Grammar word that determines the object to which a noun phrase refers, e.g. all. **determinism** n theory that human choice is not free, but decided by past events.

detest ❶ v dislike intensely. **detestable** adj **detestation** n.

dethrone v remove from a throne or position of power.

detonate ❶ v explode. **detonation** n **detonator** n small amount of explosive, or a device, used to set off an explosion.

detour ❶ n route that is not the most direct one.

detract ❶ v (foll. by from) make (something) seem less good. **detractor** n.

detriment ❶ n disadvantage or damage. **detrimental** adj **detrimentally** adv.

deuce [**dyewss**] n **1** Tennis score of forty all. **2** playing card with two symbols or dice with two spots.

devalue v **-valuing, -valued 1** reduce the exchange value of (a currency). **2** reduce the value of (something or someone). **devaluation** n.

devastate ❶ v destroy. **devastated** adj shocked and extremely upset. **devastation** n.

develop ❶ v **1** grow or bring to a later, more elaborate, or more advanced stage. **2** come or bring into existence. **3** build houses or factories on (an area of land). **4** produce (photographs) by making negatives or prints from a film. **developer** n **1** person who develops property. **2** chemical used to develop photographs or films. **development** n **developing country** poor or nonindustrial country that is trying to develop its resources by industrialization.

deviate ❶ v **1** differ from others in belief or thought. **2** depart from one's previous

deter v = **discourage**, dissuade, frighten, inhibit from, intimidate, prevent, put off, stop, talk out of

detergent n = **cleaner**, cleanser

deteriorate v = **decline**, degenerate, go downhill (inf), lower, slump, worsen

determine v **1** = **settle**, conclude, decide, end, finish, ordain, regulate **2** = **find out**, ascertain, detect, discover, establish, learn, verify, work out **3** = **decide**, choose, elect, make up one's mind, resolve

detest v = **hate**, abhor, abominate, despise, dislike intensely, loathe, recoil from

detonate v = **explode**, blast, blow up, discharge, set off, trigger

detour n = **diversion**, bypass, indirect course, roundabout way

detract v (foll. by from) = **lessen**, devaluate, diminish, lower, reduce, take away from

detriment n = **damage**, disadvantage, disservice, harm, hurt, impairment, injury, loss

devastate v = **destroy**, demolish, lay waste, level, ravage, raze, ruin, sack, wreck

develop v **1** = **advance**, amplify, augment, broaden, elaborate, enlarge, evolve, expand, flourish, grow, mature, progress, prosper, ripen **2** = **form**, breed, establish, generate, invent, originate

deviate v **1, 2** = **differ**, depart, diverge, stray, swerve, veer, wander

behaviour. **deviation** n **deviant** n, adj
(person) deviating from what is considered
acceptable behaviour. **deviance** n.
device ❶ n **1** machine or tool used for a
specific task. **2** scheme or plan.
devil ❶ n **1** evil spirit. **2** evil person.
3 person, e.g. *poor devil*. **4** daring person,
e.g. *be a devil!* **5** *informal* something difficult
or annoying, e.g. *a devil of a long time.*
▷ v **-illing**, **-illed 6** prepare (food) with
a highly flavoured spiced mixture. **the
Devil** Theology chief spirit of evil and enemy
of God. **devilish** adj cruel or unpleasant.
▷ adv **2** (also **devilishly**) *informal*
extremely. **devilment** n mischievous
conduct. **devilry** n mischievousness.
devil-may-care adj carefree and cheerful.
devil's advocate person who takes an
opposing or unpopular point of view for
the sake of argument.
devise ❶ v work out (something) in one's
mind.
devoid ❶ adj (foll. by *of*) completely lacking
(in).
devolve v (foll. by *on* or *to*) pass (power or
duties) or (of power or duties) be passed
to a successor or substitute. **devolution**
n transfer of authority from a central
government to regional governments.

devote ❶ v apply or dedicate to a
particular purpose. **devoted** adj
showing loyalty or devotion. **devotee** n
1 person who is very enthusiastic about
something. **2** zealous follower
of a religion. **devotion** n **1** strong
affection for or loyalty to someone or
something. **2** religious zeal. ▷ pl **3** prayers.
devotional adj.
devour ❶ v **1** eat greedily. **2** (of an
emotion) engulf and destroy. **3** read
eagerly.
devout ❶ adj deeply religious.
dew n drops of water that form on the
ground at night from vapour in the air.
dewy adj.
dexterity ❶ n **1** skill in using one's hands.
2 mental quickness. **dexterous** adj.
diabetes [die-a-**beet**-eez] n disorder
in which an abnormal amount of urine
containing an excess of sugar is excreted.
diabetic n, adj.
diabolic adj of the Devil. **diabolical** adj
informal extremely bad.
diadem n old-fashioned crown.
diagnosis ❶ [die-ag-**no**-siss] n, pl **-ses**
[-seez] discovery and identification of
diseases from the examination of
symptoms. **diagnose** v **diagnostic** adj.

——————————————————————— THESAURUS ———————

device n **1** = **gadget**, apparatus, appliance,
contraption, implement, instrument,
machine, tool **2** = **ploy**, gambit, manoeuvre,
plan, scheme, stratagem, trick, wile
devil n **1** = **brute**, beast, demon, fiend,
monster, ogre, terror **2** = **scamp**, rascal,
rogue, scoundrel **3** = **person**, beggar,
creature, thing, wretch **the Devil** Theology
= **Satan**, Beelzebub, Evil One, Lucifer,
Mephistopheles, Old Nick (*inf*), Prince of
Darkness
devise v = **work out**, conceive, construct,
contrive, design, dream up, formulate,
invent, think up
devoid adj (foll. by *of*) = **lacking**, bereft,
deficient, destitute, empty, free from,
wanting, without

devote v = **dedicate**, allot, apply, assign,
commit, give, pledge, reserve, set apart
devour v **1** = **eat**, consume, gobble,
gulp, guzzle, polish off (*inf*), swallow,
wolf **2** = **destroy**, annihilate, consume,
ravage, waste, wipe out **3** = **enjoy**,
read compulsively or voraciously, take in
devout adj = **religious**, godly, holy,
orthodox, pious, prayerful, pure, reverent,
saintly
dexterity n **1** = **skill**, adroitness, deftness,
expertise, finesse, nimbleness, proficiency,
touch **2** = **cleverness**, ability, aptitude,
ingenuity
diagnosis n = **analysis**, conclusion,
examination, investigation, opinion,
scrutiny

diagonal ❶ adj **1** from corner to corner. **2** slanting. ▷ n **3** diagonal line. **diagonally** adv.

diagram ❶ n sketch showing the form or workings of something. **diagrammatic** adj.

dial n **1** face of a clock or watch. **2** graduated disc on a measuring instrument. **3** control on a radio or television set used to change the station. **4** numbered disc on the front of some telephones. ▷ v **dialling, dialled 5** operate the dial or buttons on a telephone in order to contact (a number).

dialect ❶ n form of a language spoken in a particular area. **dialectal** adj.

dialogue ❶ n **1** conversation between two people, esp. in a book, film, or play. **2** discussion between representatives of two nations or groups. **dialogue box** n small window on a computer screen prompting the user to enter information.

dialysis [die-**al**-iss-iss] n Med filtering of blood through a membrane to remove waste products.

diameter n (length of) a straight line through the centre of a circle or sphere. **diametric, diametrical** adj **1** of a diameter. **2** completely opposed, e.g. the diametric opposite. **diametrically** adv.

diamond n **1** exceptionally hard, usu. colourless, precious stone. **2** Geom figure with four sides of equal length forming two acute and two obtuse angles. **3** playing card marked with red diamond-shaped symbols. **diamond wedding** sixtieth anniversary of a wedding.

diaper US & Canad n towelling cloth to absorb a baby's excrement.

diaphragm [**die**-a-fram] n **1** muscular partition that separates the abdominal cavity and chest cavity. **2** contraceptive device placed over the neck of the womb.

diarrhoea [die-a-**ree**-a] n frequent discharge of abnormally liquid faeces.

● SPELLING TIP
● It's possibly because people don't write
● the word **diarrhoea** very often that
● there's only one example of diarhoea,
● with only one r, in the Bank of English.
● Or is it because it's such a difficult word
● to spell, we always look it up to get it
● right?

diary ❶ n, pl -ries (book for) a record of daily events, appointments, or observations. **diarist** n.

diatribe n bitter critical attack.

dice n, pl **dice 1** small cube each of whose sides has a different number of spots (1 to 6), used in games of chance. ▷ v **2** cut (food) into small cubes. **dice with death** take a risk. **dicey** adj informal dangerous or risky.

dichotomy [die-**kot**-a-mee] n, pl -mies division into two opposed groups or parts.

dicky ❶ adj dickier, dickiest informal shaky or weak, e.g. a dicky heart.

dictate ❶ v **1** say aloud for someone else to write down. **2** (foll. by to) seek to impose one's will on (other people). ▷ n **3** authoritative command. **4** guiding principle. **dictation** n **dictator** n **1** ruler who has complete power. **2** person in power who acts unfairly or cruelly. **dictatorship** n **dictatorial** adj like a dictator.

diagonal adj **1** = **crossways**, cross, crosswise **2** = **slanting**, angled, oblique

diagram n = **plan**, chart, drawing, figure, graph, representation, sketch

dialect n = **language**, brogue, idiom, jargon, patois, provincialism, speech, vernacular

dialogue n **1** = **conversation**, communication, discourse, exchange **2** = **discussion**, conference

diary n = **journal**, appointment book, chronicle, daily record, engagement book, Filofax ®

dicky adj Inf = **weak**, fluttery, shaky, shonky (Aust & NZ inf), unreliable, unsound, unsteady

dictate v **1** = **speak**, read out, say, utter **2** (foll. by to) = **order**, command, decree, demand, direct, impose, lay down the law, pronounce ▷ n **3** = **command**, decree,

diction ❶ *n* manner of pronouncing words and sounds.

dictionary ❶ *n, pl -aries* **1** book consisting of an alphabetical list of words with their meanings. **2** alphabetically ordered reference book of terms relating to a particular subject.

did *v* past tense of DO.

die¹ ❶ *v* **dying, died 1** (of a person, animal, or plant) cease all biological activity permanently. **2** (of something inanimate) cease to exist or function. **be dying for, to do something** *informal* be eager for or to do something. **die-hard** *n* person who resists change.

die² *n* shaped block used to cut or form metal.

diesel *n* **1** diesel engine. **2** vehicle driven by a diesel engine. **3** diesel oil. **diesel engine** internal-combustion engine in which oil is ignited by compression. **diesel oil** fuel obtained from petroleum distillation.

diet ❶ *n* **1** food that a person or animal regularly eats. **2** specific range of foods, to control weight or for health reasons. ▷ *v* **3** follow a special diet so as to lose weight. ▷ *adj* **4** (of food) suitable for a weight-reduction diet. **dietary** *adj* **dietary fibre**

fibrous substances in fruit and vegetables that aid digestion. **dieter** *n* **dietetic** *adj* prepared for special dietary requirements. **dietetics** *n* study of diet and nutrition. **dietician** *n* person who specializes in dietetics.

differ ❶ *v* **1** be unlike. **2** disagree. **difference** *n* **1** state of being unlike. **2** disagreement. **3** remainder left after subtraction. **different** *adj* **1** unlike. **2** unusual. **differently** *adv*.

differential *adj* **1** of or using a difference. **2** *Maths* involving differentials. ▷ *n* **3** factor that differentiates between two comparable things. **4** *Maths* tiny difference between values in a scale. **5** difference between rates of pay for different types of work. **differential calculus** branch of calculus concerned with derivatives and differentials. **differentiate** *v* **1** perceive or show the difference (between). **2** make (one thing) distinct from other such things. **differentiation** *n*.

difficult ❶ *adj* **1** requiring effort or skill to do or understand. **2** not easily pleased. **difficulty** *n*.

diffident ❶ *adj* lacking self-confidence. **diffidence** *n*.

━━━━━━━━━━━━━━━━━━━━━━━━ THESAURUS ━━━━━━━

demand, direction, edict, fiat, injunction, order **4** = **principle**, code, law, rule

diction *n* = **pronunciation**, articulation, delivery, elocution, enunciation, fluency, inflection, intonation, speech

dictionary *n* **1, 2** = **wordbook**, glossary, lexicon, vocabulary

die¹ *v* **1** = **pass away**, breathe one's last, cark (*Aust & NZ sl*), croak (*sl*), expire, give up the ghost, kick the bucket (*sl*), peg out (*inf*), perish, snuff it (*sl*) **2** = **stop**, break down, fade out *or* away, fail, fizzle out, halt, lose power, peter out, run down **be dying for, to do something** *Inf* = **long for**, ache for, be eager for, desire, hunger for, pine for, yearn for

diet *n* **1** = **food**, fare, nourishment, nutriment, provisions, rations, sustenance, tucker (*Aust & NZ inf*), victuals

2 = **regime**, abstinence, fast, regimen ▷ *v*
3 = **slim**, abstain, eat sparingly, fast, lose weight

differ *v* **1** = **be dissimilar**, contradict, contrast, depart from, diverge, run counter to, stand apart, vary **2** = **disagree**, clash, contend, debate, demur, dispute, dissent, oppose, take exception, take issue

difficult *adj* **1 a** = **hard**, arduous, demanding, formidable, laborious, onerous, strenuous, uphill **b** = **problematical**, abstruse, baffling, complex, complicated, intricate, involved, knotty, obscure
2 = **troublesome**, demanding, fastidious, fussy, hard to please, perverse, refractory, unaccommodating

diffident *adj* = **shy**, bashful, doubtful, hesitant, insecure, modest, reserved, self-conscious, timid, unassertive, unassuming

diffuse v **1** spread over a wide area. ▷ adj **2** widely spread. **3** lacking concision. **diffusion** n.

dig ❶ v **digging, dug 1** cut into, break up, and turn over or remove (earth), esp. with a spade. **2** (foll. by out or up) find by effort or searching. **3** (foll. by in or into) thrust or jab. ▷ n **4** digging. **5** archaeological excavation. **6** thrust or poke. **7** spiteful remark. ▷ pl **8** informal lodgings. **digger** n machine used for digging.

digest ❶ v **1** subject to a process of digestion. **2** absorb mentally. ▷ n **3** shortened version of a book, report, or article. **digestible** adj **digestion** n (body's system for) breaking down food into easily absorbed substances. **digestive** adj **digestive biscuit** biscuit made from wholemeal flour.

digit [**dij**-it] n **1** finger or toe. **2** numeral from 0 to 9. **digital** adj displaying information as numbers rather than with hands and a dial, e.g. a digital clock. **digital recording** sound-recording process that converts audio or analogue signals into a series of pulses. **digital television** television in which the picture is transmitted in digital form and then decoded. **digitally** adv.

dignity ❶ n, pl **-ties 1** serious, calm, and controlled behaviour or manner. **2** quality of being worthy of respect. **3** sense of self-importance. **dignify** v add distinction to. **dignitary** n person of high official position.

digress ❶ v depart from the main subject in speech or writing. **digression** n.

dike n same as DYKE.

dilapidated ❶ adj (of a building) having fallen into ruin. **dilapidation** n.

dilate ❶ v make or become wider or larger. **dilation, dilatation** n.

dilemma ❶ n situation offering a choice between two equally undesirable alternatives.

dilettante ❶ [dill-it-**tan**-tee] n, pl **-tantes, -tanti** person whose interest in a subject is superficial rather than serious. **dilettantism** n.

diligent ❶ adj **1** careful and persevering in carrying out duties. **2** carried out with care and perseverance. **diligently** adv **diligence** n.

— THESAURUS —

dig v **1, 2** = **excavate**, burrow, delve, hollow out, mine, quarry, scoop, tunnel **3** (foll. by out or up) = **find**, delve, dig down, discover, expose, fossick (Aust & NZ), go into, investigate, probe, research, search, uncover, unearth, uproot **4** (foll. by in or into) = **poke**, drive, jab, prod, punch, thrust ▷ n **6** = **poke**, jab, prod, punch, thrust **7** = **cutting remark**, barb, crack (sl), gibe, insult, jeer, sneer, taunt, wisecrack (inf)

digest v **1** = **ingest**, absorb, assimilate, dissolve, incorporate **2** = **take in**, absorb, consider, contemplate, grasp, study, understand ▷ n **3** = **summary**, abridgment, abstract, epitome, précis, résumé, synopsis

dignity n **1** = **decorum**, courtliness, grandeur, gravity, loftiness, majesty, nobility, solemnity, stateliness **2** = **honour**, eminence, importance, rank, respectability, standing, status **3** = **self-importance**, pride, self-esteem, self-respect

digress v = **wander**, depart, deviate, diverge, drift, get off the point or subject, go off at a tangent, ramble, stray

dilapidated adj = **ruined**, broken-down, crumbling, decrepit, in ruins, munted (NZ sl), ramshackle, rickety, run-down, tumbledown

dilate v = **enlarge**, broaden, expand, puff out, stretch, swell, widen

dilemma n = **predicament**, difficulty, mess, plight, problem, puzzle, quandary, spot (inf)

dilettante n = **amateur**, aesthete, dabbler, trifler

diligent adj **1** = **hard-working**, assiduous, attentive, careful, conscientious, industrious, painstaking, persistent, studious, tireless

dill *n* sweet-smelling herb.

dilute *v* 1 make (a liquid) less concentrated, esp. by adding water. 2 make (a quality etc.) weaker in force. **dilution** *n*.

dim ❶ *adj* **dimmer**, **dimmest** 1 badly lit. 2 not clearly seen. 3 unintelligent. ▷ *v* **dimming**, **dimmed** 4 make or become dim. **take a dim view of** disapprove of. **dimly** *adv* **dimness** *n* **dimmer** *n* device for dimming an electric light.

dime *n* coin of the US and Canada, worth ten cents.

dimension ❶ *n* 1 measurement of the size of something in a particular direction. 2 aspect, factor.

diminish ❶ *v* make or become smaller, fewer, or less. **diminution** *n* **diminutive** *adj* 1 very small. ▷ *n* 2 word or affix which implies smallness or unimportance.

diminuendo *n Music* gradual decrease in loudness.

dimple *n* 1 small natural dent, esp. in the cheeks or chin. ▷ *v* 2 produce dimples by smiling.

din ❶ *n* 1 loud unpleasant confused noise. ▷ *v* **dinning**, **dinned** 2 (foll. by *into*) instil (something) into someone by constant repetition.

dine ❶ *v* eat dinner. **diner** *n* 1 person eating a meal. 2 *Chiefly US* small cheap restaurant. **dining room** room where meals are eaten.

dinghy [**ding**-ee] *n, pl* **-ghies** small boat, powered by sails, oars, or a motor.

dingo *n, pl* **-goes** Australian wild dog (also **native dog**).

dingy ❶ [**din**-jee] *adj* **-gier**, **-giest** dull and drab. **dinginess** *n*.

dinner ❶ *n* main meal of the day, eaten either in the evening or at midday. **dinner jacket** man's semiformal black evening jacket.

dinosaur *n* extinct gigantic prehistoric reptile.

dint *n* **by dint of** by means of.

diocese [**die**-a-siss] *n* district over which a bishop has control. **diocesan** *adj*.

diode *n* semiconductor device for converting alternating current to direct current.

dip ❶ *v* **dipping**, **dipped** 1 plunge quickly or briefly into a liquid. 2 slope downwards. 3 switch (car headlights) from the main to the lower beam. 4 lower briefly. ▷ *n* 5 dipping. 6 brief swim. 7 liquid chemical in which farm animals are dipped to rid them of insects. 8 depression in a landscape. 9 creamy mixture into which pieces of food are dipped before being eaten. **dip into** *v* read passages at random from (a book or journal).

---

dilute *v* 1 = **water down**, adulterate, cut, make thinner, thin (out), weaken 2 = **reduce**, attenuate, decrease, diffuse, diminish, lessen, mitigate, temper, weaken

dim *adj* 1 = **poorly lit**, cloudy, dark, grey, overcast, shadowy, tenebrous 2 = **unclear**, bleary, blurred, faint, fuzzy, ill-defined, indistinct, obscured, shadowy 3 = **stupid**, dense, dozy (*Brit inf*), dull, dumb (*inf*), obtuse, slow on the uptake (*inf*), thick ▷ *v* 4 = **dull**, blur, cloud, darken, fade, obscure **take a dim view of** = **disapprove of**, be displeased with, be sceptical of, look askance at, reject, suspect, take exception to, view with disfavour

dimension *n* 1 = **measurement**, amplitude, bulk, capacity, extent, proportions, size, volume

diminish *v* = **decrease**, curtail, cut, decline, die out, dwindle, lessen, lower, recede, reduce, shrink, subside, wane

din *n* 1 = **noise**, clamour, clatter, commotion, crash, pandemonium, racket, row, uproar ▷ *v* 2 (foll. by *into*) = **instil**, drum into, go on at, hammer into, inculcate, instruct, teach

dine *v* = **eat**, banquet, feast, lunch, sup

dingy *adj* = **dull**, dark, dim, drab, dreary, gloomy, murky, obscure, sombre

dinner *n* = **meal**, banquet, feast, main meal, repast, spread (*inf*)

dip *v* 1 = **plunge**, bathe, douse, duck, dunk, immerse 2 = **slope**, decline, descend, drop (down), fall, lower, sink, subside ▷ *n* 5 = **plunge**, douche, drenching, ducking,

diphtheria [dif-**theer**-ya] n contagious disease producing fever and difficulty in breathing and swallowing.

diphthong n union of two vowel sounds in a single compound sound.

diploma n qualification awarded by a college on successful completion of a course.

diplomacy ❶ n **1** conduct of the relations between nations by peaceful means. **2** tact or skill in dealing with people. **diplomat** n official engaged in diplomacy. **diplomatic** adj **1** of diplomacy. **2** tactful in dealing with people. **diplomatically** adv.

dipper n **1** ladle used for dipping. **2** (also **ousel**, **ouzel**) songbird that lives by a river.

diprotodont [die-**pro**-toe-dont] n marsupial with fewer than three upper incisor teeth on each side of the jaw.

dipsomania n compulsive craving for alcohol. **dipsomaniac** n, adj.

dire ❶ adj disastrous, urgent, or terrible.

direct ❶ adj **1** (of a route) shortest, straight. **2** without anyone or anything intervening. **3** likely to have an immediate effect. **4** honest, frank. ▷ adv **5** in a direct manner. ▷ v **6** lead and organize. **7** tell (someone) to

do something. **8** tell (someone) the way to a place. **9** address (a letter, package, remark, etc.). **10** provide guidance to (actors, cameramen, etc.) in (a play or film). **directly** adv **1** in a direct manner. **2** at once. ▷ conj **3** as soon as. **directness** n **direct current** electric current that flows in one direction only. **director** n person or thing that directs or controls. **directory** n book listing names, addresses, and telephone numbers.

direction ❶ n **1** course or line along which a person or thing moves, points, or lies. **2** management or guidance. ▷ pl **3** instructions for doing something or for reaching a place.

dirge ❶ n slow sad song of mourning.

dirk n dagger, formerly worn by Scottish Highlanders.

dirt ❶ n **1** unclean substance, filth. **2** earth, soil. **3** obscene speech or writing. **4** informal harmful gossip. **dirt track** racetrack made of packed earth or cinders.

dis- prefix indicating: **1** reversal, e.g. disconnect. **2** negation or lack, e.g. dissimilar; disgrace. **3** removal or release, e.g. disembowel.

────── THESAURUS ──────

immersion, soaking **6** = **bathe**, dive, plunge, swim **8** = **hollow**, basin, concavity, depression, hole, incline, slope

diplomacy n **1** = **statesmanship**, international negotiation, statecraft **2** = **tact**, artfulness, craft, delicacy, discretion, finesse, savoir-faire, skill, subtlety

dire adj **a** = **disastrous**, awful, calamitous, catastrophic, horrible, ruinous, terrible, woeful **b** = **desperate**, critical, crucial, drastic, extreme, now or never, pressing, urgent

direct adj **1** = **straight**, nonstop, not crooked, shortest, through, unbroken, uninterrupted **2** = **first-hand**, face-to-face, head-on, immediate, personal **4** = **straightforward**, blunt, candid, downright, explicit, frank, honest, open, plain, plain-spoken, point-blank, straight,

unambiguous, unequivocal, upfront (inf) ▷ v **6** = **control**, conduct, guide, handle, lead, manage, oversee, run, supervise **7** = **order**, bid, charge, command, demand, dictate, instruct **8** = **guide**, indicate, lead, point in the direction of, point the way, show **9** = **address**, label, mail, route, send

direction n **1** = **way**, aim, bearing, course, line, path, road, route, track **2** = **management**, administration, charge, command, control, guidance, leadership, order, supervision ▷ pl **3** = **instructions**, briefing, guidance, guidelines, plan, recommendation, regulations

dirge n = **lament**, dead march, elegy, funeral song, requiem, threnody

dirt n **1** = **filth**, dust, grime, impurity, muck, mud **2** = **soil**, clay, earth, loam **3** = **obscenity**, indecency, pornography, sleaze, smut

disable ❶ v make ineffective, unfit, or incapable. **disabled** adj lacking a physical power, such as the ability to walk. **disablement** n **disability** n, pl **-ties** 1 condition of being disabled. 2 something that disables someone.

disabuse v (foll. by of) rid (someone) of a mistaken idea.

disadvantage ❶ n unfavourable or harmful circumstance. **disadvantageous** adj **disadvantaged** adj socially or economically deprived.

disaffected adj having lost loyalty to or affection for someone or something. **disaffection** n.

disagree ❶ v -greeing, -greed 1 argue or have different opinions. 2 be different, conflict. 3 (foll. by with) cause physical discomfort (to), e.g. curry disagrees with me. **disagreement** n **disagreeable** adj 1 unpleasant. 2 (of a person) unfriendly or unhelpful.

disallow ❶ v reject as untrue or invalid; cancel.

disappear ❶ v 1 cease to be visible. 2 cease to exist. **disappearance** n.

disappoint ❶ v fail to meet the

expectations or hopes of. **disappointment** n 1 feeling of being disappointed. 2 person or thing that disappoints.

disarm ❶ v 1 deprive of weapons. 2 win the confidence or affection of. 3 (of a country) decrease the size of one's armed forces. **disarmament** n **disarming** adj removing hostility or suspicion.

disarray ❶ n 1 confusion and lack of discipline. 2 extreme untidiness.

disaster ❶ n 1 occurrence that causes great distress or destruction. 2 project etc. that fails. **disastrous** adj.

disband v (cause to) cease to function as a group.

disbelieve v 1 reject as false. 2 (foll. by in) have no faith (in). **disbelief** n.

disburse v pay out. **disbursement** n

disc n 1 flat circular object. 2 gramophone record. 3 Anat circular flat structure in the body, esp. between the vertebrae. 4 Computers same as DISK. **disc jockey** person who introduces and plays pop records on a radio programme or at a disco.

discard ❶ v get rid of (something or someone) as useless or undesirable.

——————————————— THESAURUS ———————

disable v = **handicap**, cripple, damage, enfeeble, immobilize, impair, incapacitate, paralyse, render or declare incapable

disadvantage n = **drawback**, damage, detriment, disservice, downside, handicap, harm, hurt, inconvenience, injury, loss, nuisance, snag, trouble

disagree v 1 = **differ (in opinion)**, argue, clash, cross swords, dispute, dissent, object, quarrel, take issue with 2 = **conflict**, be dissimilar, contradict, counter, differ, diverge, run counter to, vary 3 (foll. by with) = **make ill**, bother, discomfort, distress, hurt, nauseate, sicken, trouble, upset

disallow v = **reject**, disavow, dismiss, disown, rebuff, refuse, repudiate

disappear v 1 = **vanish**, evanesce, fade away, pass, recede 2 = **cease**, die out,

dissolve, evaporate, leave no trace, melt away, pass away, perish

disappoint v = **let down**, disenchant, disgruntle, dishearten, disillusion, dismay, dissatisfy, fail

disarm v 1 = **render defenceless**, disable 2 = **win over**, persuade, set at ease 3 = **demilitarize**, deactivate, demobilize, disband (US & Canad)

disarray n 1 = **confusion**, disorder, disorganization, disunity, indiscipline, unruliness 2 = **untidiness**, chaos, clutter, hotchpotch, jumble, mess, muddle, shambles

disaster n 1 = **catastrophe**, adversity, calamity, cataclysm, misfortune, ruin, tragedy, trouble

discard v = **get rid of**, abandon, cast aside, dispense with, dispose of, drop, dump

discern v see or be aware of (something) clearly. **discernible** adj **discerning** adj having good judgment. **discernment** n.

discharge ❶ v 1 release, allow to go. 2 dismiss (someone) from duty or employment. 3 fire (a gun). 4 pour forth, send out. 5 meet the demands of (a duty or responsibility). 6 relieve oneself of (a debt). ▷ n 7 substance that comes out from a place. 8 discharging.

disciple ❶ [diss-**sipe**-pl] n follower of the doctrines of a teacher, esp. Jesus Christ.

discipline ❶ n 1 practice of imposing strict rules of behaviour. 2 area of academic study. ▷ v 3 attempt to improve the behaviour of (oneself or another) by training or rules. 4 punish. **disciplined** adj able to behave and work in a controlled way. **disciplinarian** n person who practises strict discipline. **disciplinary** adj.

disclaim v deny (responsibility for or

knowledge of something). **disclaimer** n statement denying responsibility.

disclose ❶ v 1 make known. 2 allow to be seen. **disclosure** n.

disco n, pl **-cos** 1 nightclub where people dance to amplified pop records. 2 occasion at which people dance to amplified pop records. 3 mobile equipment for providing music for a disco.

discolour ❶ v change in colour, fade. **discoloration** n.

discomfit v make uneasy or confused. **discomfiture** n.

discomfort ❶ n inconvenience, distress, or mild pain.

disconcert ❶ v embarrass or upset.

disconnect ❶ v 1 undo or break the connection between (two things). 2 stop the supply of electricity or gas of. **disconnected** adj (of speech or ideas) not logically connected. **disconnection** n.

disconsolate ❶ adj sad beyond comfort. **disconsolately** adv.

—————— THESAURUS ——————

(inf), jettison, reject, throw away or out

discharge v 1 = **release**, allow to go, clear, free, liberate, pardon, set free 2 = **dismiss**, cashier, discard, expel, fire (inf), oust, remove, sack (inf) 3 = **fire**, detonate, explode, let loose (inf), let off, set off, shoot 4 = **pour forth**, dispense, emit, exude, give off, leak, ooze, release 5 = **carry out**, accomplish, do, execute, fulfil, observe, perform 6 = **pay**, clear, honour, meet, relieve, satisfy, settle, square up ▷ n 7 = **emission**, excretion, ooze, pus, secretion, seepage, suppuration 8 a = **release**, acquittal, clearance, liberation, pardon b = **dismissal**, demobilization, ejection c = **firing**, blast, burst, detonation, explosion, report, salvo, shot, volley

disciple n = **follower**, adherent, apostle, devotee, pupil, student, supporter

discipline n 1 = **training**, conduct, control, orderliness, practice, regimen, regulation, restraint, self-control, strictness 2 = **field of study**, area, branch of knowledge,

course, curriculum, speciality, subject ▷ v 3 = **train**, bring up, drill, educate, exercise, prepare 4 = **punish**, bring to book, castigate, chasten, chastise, correct, penalize, reprimand, reprove

disclose v 1 = **make known**, broadcast, communicate, confess, divulge, let slip, publish, relate, reveal 2 = **show**, bring to light, expose, lay bare, reveal, uncover, unveil

discolour v = **stain**, fade, mark, soil, streak, tarnish, tinge

discomfort n a = **uneasiness**, annoyance, distress, hardship, irritation, nuisance, trouble b = **pain**, ache, hurt, irritation, malaise, soreness

disconcert v = **disturb**, faze, fluster, perturb, rattle (inf), take aback, unsettle, upset, worry

disconnect v 1 = **cut off**, detach, disengage, divide, part, separate, sever, take apart, uncouple

disconsolate adj = **inconsolable**, crushed, dejected, desolate, forlorn, grief-stricken,

discontent ❶ *n* lack of contentment.
discontented *adj*.

discontinue ❶ *v* come or bring to
an end.

discord ❶ *n* 1 lack of agreement or
harmony between people. 2 harsh
confused sounds. **discordant** *adj*
discordance *n*.

discount ❶ *v* 1 take no account of
(something) because it is considered to
be unreliable, prejudiced, or irrelevant.
2 deduct (an amount) from the price of
something. ▷ *n* 3 deduction from the full
price of something.

discourse ❶ *n* 1 conversation. 2 formal
treatment of a subject in speech or writing.
▷ *v* 3 (foll. by *on*) speak or write (about)
at length.

discourteous ❶ *adj* showing bad
manners. **discourtesy** *n*.

discover ❶ *v* 1 be the first to find or to find

out about. 2 learn about for the first time.
3 find after study or search. **discoverer**
n **discovery** *n, pl* **-eries** 1 discovering.
2 person, place, or thing that has been
discovered.

discredit ❶ *v* 1 damage the reputation
of. 2 cause (an idea) to be disbelieved or
distrusted. ▷ *n* 3 damage to someone's
reputation. **discreditable** *adj* bringing
shame.

discreet ❶ *adj* 1 careful to avoid
embarrassment, esp. by keeping
confidences secret. 2 unobtrusive.

discrepancy ❶ *n, pl* **-cies** conflict or
variation between facts, figures, or
claims.

discrete *adj* separate, distinct.

discretion ❶ *n* 1 quality of behaving in a
discreet way. 2 freedom or authority to
make judgments and decide what to do.
discretionary *adj*.

——————————————————————— THESAURUS ———————————————————————

heartbroken, miserable, wretched
discontent *n* = **dissatisfaction**,
displeasure, envy, regret, restlessness,
uneasiness, unhappiness

discontinue *v* = **stop**, abandon, break off,
cease, drop, end, give up, quit, suspend,
terminate

discord *n* 1 = **disagreement**, conflict,
dissension, disunity, division, friction,
incompatibility, strife 2 = **disharmony**,
cacophony, din, dissonance, harshness,
jarring, racket, tumult

discount *v* 1 = **leave out**, brush off (*sl*),
disbelieve, disregard, ignore, overlook,
pass over 2 = **deduct**, lower, mark down,
reduce, take off ▷ *n* 3 = **deduction**,
concession, cut, rebate, reduction

discourse *n* 1 = **conversation**, chat,
communication, dialogue, discussion,
seminar, speech, talk 2 = **speech**,
dissertation, essay, homily, lecture,
oration, sermon, treatise ▷ *v* 3 (foll. by *on*)
= **hold forth**, expatiate, speak, talk

discourteous *adj* = **rude**, bad-
mannered, boorish, disrespectful,

ill-mannered, impolite, insolent, offhand,
ungentlemanly, ungracious

discover *v* 1 = **find**, come across, come
upon, dig up, locate, turn up, uncover,
unearth 2, 3 = **find out**, ascertain, detect,
learn, notice, perceive, realize, recognize,
uncover

discredit *v* 1 = **disgrace**, bring into
disrepute, defame, dishonour, disparage,
slander, smear, vilify 2 = **doubt**, challenge,
deny, disbelieve, discount, dispute, distrust,
mistrust, question ▷ *n* 3 = **disgrace**,
dishonour, disrepute, ignominy, ill-repute,
scandal, shame, stigma

discreet *adj* 1 = **tactful**, careful, cautious,
circumspect, considerate, diplomatic,
guarded, judicious, prudent, wary

discrepancy *n* = **disagreement**, conflict,
contradiction, difference, disparity,
divergence, incongruity, inconsistency,
variation

discretion *n* 1 = **tact**, carefulness, caution,
consideration, diplomacy, judiciousness,
prudence, wariness 2 = **choice**, inclination,
pleasure, preference, volition, will

discriminate ❶ v **1** (foll. by *against* or *in favour of*) single out (a particular person or group) for worse or better treatment than others. **2** (foll. by *between*) recognize or understand the difference (between). **discriminating** *adj* showing good taste and judgment. **discrimination** *n*. **discriminatory** *adj* based on prejudice.

discursive *adj* passing from one topic to another.

discus *n* heavy disc-shaped object thrown in sports competitions.

discuss ❶ v **1** consider (something) by talking it over. **2** treat (a subject) in speech or writing. **discussion** *n*.

disdain ❶ *n* **1** feeling of superiority and dislike. ▷ v **2** refuse with disdain. **disdainful** *adj* **disdainfully** *adv*.

disease ❶ *n* illness, sickness. **diseased** *adj*.

disembark ❶ v get off a ship, aircraft, or bus. **disembarkation** *n*.

disembodied *adj* **1** lacking a body. **2** seeming not to be attached to or coming

from anyone, e.g. *a disembodied voice*.

disembowel v **-elling**, **-elled** remove the entrails of.

disenchanted ❶ *adj* disappointed and disillusioned. **disenchantment** *n*.

disengage ❶ v release from a connection. **disengagement** *n*.

disfavour ❶ *n* disapproval or dislike.

disfigure ❶ v spoil the appearance of. **disfigurement** *n*.

disgrace ❶ *n* **1** condition of shame, loss of reputation, or dishonour. **2** shameful person or thing. ▷ v **3** bring shame upon (oneself or others). **disgraceful** *adj*. **disgracefully** *adv*.

disgruntled ❶ *adj* sulky or discontented. **disgruntlement** *n*.

disguise ❶ v **1** change the appearance or manner in order to conceal the identity of (someone or something). **2** misrepresent (something) in order to obscure its actual nature or meaning. ▷ *n* **3** mask, costume, or manner that

---

discriminate v **1** (foll. by *against* or *in favour of*) = **show prejudice**, favour, show bias, single out, treat as inferior, treat as superior, treat differently, victimize **2** (foll. by *between*) = **differentiate**, distinguish, draw a distinction, segregate, separate, tell the difference

discuss v **1** = **talk about**, argue, confer, consider, converse, debate, deliberate, examine

disdain *n* **1** = **contempt**, arrogance, derision, haughtiness, scorn, superciliousness ▷ v **2** = **scorn**, deride, disregard, look down on, reject, slight, sneer at, spurn

disease *n* = **illness**, affliction, ailment, complaint, condition, disorder, infection, infirmity, malady, sickness

disembark v = **land**, alight, arrive, get off, go ashore, step out of

disenchanted *adj* = **disillusioned**, cynical, disappointed, indifferent, jaundiced, let down, sick of, soured

disengage v = **release**, disentangle,

extricate, free, loosen, set free, unloose, untie

disfavour *n* = **disapproval**, disapprobation, dislike, displeasure

disfigure v = **damage**, blemish, deface, deform, distort, mar, mutilate, scar

disgrace *n* **1** = **shame**, degradation, dishonour, disrepute, ignominy, infamy, odium, opprobrium **2** = **stain**, blemish, blot, reproach, scandal, slur, stigma ▷ v **3** = **bring shame upon**, degrade, discredit, dishonour, humiliate, shame, sully, taint

disgruntled *adj* = **discontented**, annoyed, displeased, dissatisfied, grumpy, irritated, peeved, put out, vexed

disguise v **1** = **hide**, camouflage, cloak, conceal, cover, mask, screen, shroud, veil **2** = **misrepresent**, fake, falsify ▷ *n* **3** = **costume**, camouflage, cover, mask, screen, veil **4** = **facade**, deception, dissimulation, front, pretence, semblance, trickery, veneer

disguises. **4** state of being disguised.

disgust ❶ *n* **1** great loathing or distaste. ▷ *v* **2** sicken, fill with loathing.

dish ❶ *n* **1** shallow container used for holding or serving food. **2** particular kind of food. **3** *informal* attractive person. **dishcloth** *n* cloth for washing dishes. **dish out** *v informal* distribute. **dish up** *v informal* serve (food).

dishearten ❶ *v* weaken or destroy the hope, courage, or enthusiasm of.

dishevelled ❶ *adj* (of a person's hair, clothes, or general appearance) disordered and untidy.

dishonest ❶ *adj* not honest or fair. **dishonesty** *n*.

dishonour ❶ *v* **1** treat with disrespect. ▷ *n* **2** lack of respect. **3** state of shame or disgrace. **4** something that causes a loss of honour. **dishonourable** *adj* **dishonourably** *adv*.

disillusion *v* **1** destroy the illusions or false ideas of. ▷ *n* **2** (also **disillusionment**) state of being disillusioned.

disinformation *n* false information intended to mislead.

disingenuous *adj* not sincere.

disinherit ❶ *v Law* deprive (an heir) of inheritance. **disinheritance** *n*.

disintegrate ❶ *v* break up. **disintegration** *n*.

disinterested ❶ *adj* free from bias or involvement. **disinterest** *n*.

● **USAGE NOTE**
● People sometimes use *disinterested*
● where they mean *uninterested*. If you
● want to say that someone shows a lack
● of interest, use *uninterested*. *Disinterested*
● would be used in a sentence such as
● *We asked him to decide because he was a*
● *disinterested observer.*

disk *n Computers* storage device, consisting of a stack of plates coated with a magnetic layer, which rotates rapidly as a single unit.

dislike ❶ *v* **1** consider unpleasant or disagreeable. ▷ *n* **2** feeling of not liking something or someone.

dislocate *v* **1** displace (a bone or joint) from its normal position. **2** disrupt or shift out of place. **dislocation** *n*.

dislodge ❶ *v* remove (something) from a previously fixed position.

━━━━━━━━━━━━━━━━━━━━━━━━━━━━━━━━━━━━ THESAURUS ━━━━━━

disgust *n* **1** = **loathing**, abhorrence, aversion, dislike, distaste, hatred, nausea, repugnance, repulsion, revulsion ▷ *v* **2** = **sicken**, displease, nauseate, offend, put off, repel, revolt

dish *n* **1** = **bowl**, plate, platter, salver **2** = **food**, fare, recipe

dishearten *v* = **discourage**, cast down, deject, depress, deter, dismay, dispirit, put a damper on

dishevelled *adj* = **untidy**, bedraggled, disordered, messy, ruffled, rumpled, tousled, uncombed, unkempt

dishonest *adj* = **deceitful**, bent (*sl*), cheating, corrupt, crooked (*inf*), disreputable, double-dealing, false, lying, treacherous

dishonour *v* **1** = **disgrace**, debase, debauch, defame, degrade, discredit, shame, sully ▷ *n* **3** = **disgrace**, discredit, disrepute, ignominy, infamy, obloquy,

reproach, scandal, shame **4** = **insult**, abuse, affront, discourtesy, indignity, offence, outrage, sacrilege, slight

disinherit *v Law* = **cut off**, disown, dispossess, oust, repudiate

disintegrate *v* = **break up**, break apart, crumble, fall apart, go to pieces, separate, shatter, splinter

disinterested *adj* = **impartial**, detached, dispassionate, even-handed, impersonal, neutral, objective, unbiased, unprejudiced

dislike *v* **1** = **be averse to**, despise, detest, disapprove, hate, loathe, not be able to bear *or* abide *or* stand, object to, take a dim view of ▷ *n* **2** = **aversion**, animosity, antipathy, disapproval, disinclination, displeasure, distaste, enmity, hostility, repugnance

dislodge *v* = **displace**, disturb, extricate, force out, knock loose, oust, remove, uproot

disloyal ❶ *adj* not loyal, deserting one's allegiance. **disloyalty** *n*.

dismal ❶ *adj* 1 gloomy and depressing. 2 *informal* of poor quality. **dismally** *adv*.

dismantle ❶ *v* take apart piece by piece.

dismay ❶ *v* 1 fill with alarm or depression. ▷ *n* 2 alarm mixed with sadness.

dismember ❶ *v* 1 remove the limbs of. 2 cut to pieces. **dismemberment** *n*.

dismiss ❶ *v* 1 remove (an employee) from a job. 2 allow (someone) to leave. 3 put out of one's mind. 4 (of a judge) state that (a case) will not be brought to trial. **dismissal** *n* **dismissive** *adj* scornful, contemptuous.

dismount *v* get off a horse or bicycle.

disobey ❶ *v* neglect or refuse to obey. **disobedient** *adj* **disobedience** *n*.

disorder ❶ *n* 1 state of untidiness and disorganization. 2 public violence or rioting. 3 an illness. **disordered** *adj* untidy.

disorderly *adj* 1 untidy and disorganized. 2 uncontrolled, unruly.

disorientate, disorient *v* cause (someone) to lose his or her bearings. **disorientation** *n*.

disown ❶ *v* deny any connection with (someone).

disparage ❶ *v* speak contemptuously of. **disparagement** *n*.

dispassionate ❶ *adj* not influenced by emotion. **dispassionately** *adv*.

dispatch ❶ *v* 1 send off to a destination or to perform a task. 2 carry out (a duty or a task) with speed. 3 *old-fashioned* kill. ▷ *n* 4 official communication or report, sent in haste. 5 report sent to a newspaper by a correspondent. **dispatch rider** motorcyclist who carries dispatches.

dispel ❶ *v* -**pelling**, -**pelled** destroy or remove.

———————————————— THESAURUS ————————————————

disloyal *adj* = **treacherous**, faithless, false, subversive, traitorous, two-faced, unfaithful, untrustworthy

dismal *adj* 1 = **gloomy**, bleak, cheerless, dark, depressing, discouraging, dreary, forlorn, sombre, wretched

dismantle *v* = **take apart**, demolish, disassemble, strip, take to pieces

dismay *v* 1 = **alarm**, appal, daunt, discourage, dishearten, dispirit, distress, frighten, horrify, paralyse, put off, scare, terrify, unnerve ▷ *n* 2 = **alarm**, anxiety, apprehension, consternation, discouragement, dread, fear, horror, trepidation

dismember *v* 1 = **amputate** 2 = **cut into pieces**, dissect, sever

dismiss *v* 1 = **sack** (*inf*), axe (*inf*), cashier, discharge, fire (*inf*), give notice to, give (someone) their marching orders, lay off, remove 2 = **let go**, disperse, dissolve, free, release, send away 3 = **put out of one's mind**, banish, discard, dispel, disregard, lay aside, reject, set aside

disobey *v* = **refuse to obey**, contravene, defy, disregard, flout, ignore, infringe,

rebel, violate

disorder *n* 1 = **untidiness**, chaos, clutter, confusion, disarray, jumble, mess, muddle, shambles 2 = **disturbance**, commotion, riot, turmoil, unrest, unruliness, uproar 3 = **illness**, affliction, ailment, complaint, disease, malady, sickness

disown *v* = **deny**, cast off, disavow, disclaim, reject, renounce, repudiate

disparage *v* = **run down**, belittle, denigrate, deprecate, deride, malign, put down, ridicule, slander, vilify

dispassionate *adj* = **unemotional**, calm, collected, composed, cool, detached, disinterested, impersonal, imperturbable, serene, unruffled

dispatch *v* 1 = **send**, consign, dismiss, hasten 2 = **carry out**, discharge, dispose of, finish, perform, settle 3 *Old-fashioned* = **murder**, assassinate, execute, kill, slaughter, slay ▷ *n* 5 = **message**, account, bulletin, communication, communiqué, news, report, story

dispel *v* = **drive away**, banish, chase away, dismiss, disperse, eliminate, expel

dispense ⓿ v 1 distribute in portions.
2 prepare and distribute (medicine).
3 administer (the law etc.). **dispensable**
adj not essential. **dispensation** n
1 dispensing. 2 exemption from an
obligation. **dispenser** n **dispensary** n, pl
-saries place where medicine is dispensed.
dispense with v do away with, manage
without.

disperse ⓿ v 1 scatter over a wide area.
2 (cause to) leave a gathering. **dispersal**,
dispersion n.

displace ⓿ v 1 move from the usual
location. 2 remove from office.
displacement n **displaced person** person
forced from his or her home or country,
esp. by war.

display ⓿ v 1 make visible or noticeable.
▷ n 2 displaying. 3 something displayed.
4 exhibition.

displease ⓿ v annoy or upset. **displeasure** n.

dispose ⓿ v place in a certain order.
disposed adj 1 willing or eager. 2 having

an attitude as specified, e.g. he felt
well disposed towards her. **disposable**
adj 1 designed to be thrown away after
use. 2 available for use, e.g. disposable
income. **disposal** n getting rid of
something. **at one's disposal** available
for use. **disposition** n 1 person's usual
temperament. 2 desire or tendency to do
something. 3 arrangement. **dispose of** v
1 throw away, get rid of. 2 deal with
(a problem etc.). 3 kill.

disprove ⓿ v show (an assertion or claim)
to be incorrect.

dispute ⓿ n 1 disagreement, argument. ▷ v
2 argue about (something). 3 doubt the
validity of. 4 fight over possession of.

disqualify ⓿ v stop (someone) officially
from taking part in something for
wrongdoing. **disqualification** n.

disquiet ⓿ n 1 feeling of anxiety. ▷ v 2 make
(someone) anxious. **disquietude** n.

disregard ⓿ v 1 give little or no attention
to. ▷ n 2 lack of attention or respect.

——————————————— THESAURUS ———————————————

dispense v 1 = **distribute**, allocate,
allot, apportion, assign, deal out, dole
out, share 2 = **prepare**, measure, mix,
supply 3 = **administer**, apply, carry out,
discharge, enforce, execute, implement,
operate ▷ v **dispense with** = **do without**,
abolish, abstain from, brush aside, cancel,
dispose of, do away with, forgo, get rid of,
give up

disperse v 1 = **scatter**, broadcast, diffuse,
disseminate, distribute, spread, strew
2 = **break up**, disband, dissolve, scatter,
separate

displace v 1 = **move**, disturb, misplace,
shift, transpose 2 = **replace**, oust, succeed,
supersede, supplant, take the place of

display v 1 = **show**, demonstrate,
disclose, exhibit, expose, flaunt, flourish,
manifest, present, reveal, show
off, vaunt ▷ n 2, 3 = **exhibition**, array,
demonstration, presentation, show
4 = **show**, pageant, parade, spectacle

displease v = **annoy**, anger, irk, irritate,

offend, pique, put out, upset, vex

dispose v = **arrange**, array, distribute,
group, marshal, order, place, put

disprove v = **prove false**, contradict,
discredit, expose, give the lie to, invalidate,
negate, rebut, refute

dispute n 1 = **disagreement**, altercation,
argument, conflict, contention,
controversy, debate, dissension, feud,
quarrel ▷ v 2 = **argue**, clash, cross swords,
debate, quarrel, squabble 3 = **doubt**,
challenge, contest, contradict, deny,
impugn, question, rebut

disqualify v = **ban**, debar, declare
ineligible, preclude, prohibit, rule out

disquiet n 1 = **uneasiness**, alarm, anxiety,
concern, disturbance, foreboding,
nervousness, trepidation, worry ▷ v
2 = **make uneasy**, bother, concern, disturb,
perturb, trouble, unsettle, upset, worry

disregard v 1 = **ignore**, brush aside or
away, discount, make light of, neglect,
overlook, pass over, pay no heed to,

disrepair ❶ *n* condition of being worn out or in poor working order.

disrepute ❶ *n* loss or lack of good reputation. **disreputable** *adj* having or causing a bad reputation.

disrespect ❶ *n* lack of respect. **disrespectful** *adj*.

disrupt ❶ *v* interrupt the progress of. **disruption** *n* **disruptive** *adj*.

dissatisfied ❶ *adj* not pleased or contented. **dissatisfaction** *n*.

dissect ❶ *v* **1** cut open (a corpse) to examine it. **2** examine critically and minutely. **dissection** *n*.

dissemble *v* conceal one's real motives or emotions by pretence.

disseminate ❶ *v* spread (information). **dissemination** *n*.

dissent ❶ *v* **1** disagree. **2** *Christianity* reject the doctrines of an established church. ▷ *n*

3 disagreement. **4** *Christianity* separation from an established church. **dissension** *n* **dissenter** *n*.

dissertation ❶ *n* **1** written thesis, usu. required for a higher university degree. **2** long formal speech.

disservice ❶ *n* harmful action.

dissident ❶ *n* **1** person who disagrees with and criticizes the government. ▷ *adj* **2** disagreeing with the government. **dissidence** *n*.

dissimilar ❶ *adj* not alike, different. **dissimilarity** *n*.

dissipate ❶ *v* **1** waste or squander. **2** scatter, disappear. **dissipated** *adj* showing signs of overindulgence in alcohol and other physical pleasures. **dissipation** *n*.

dissociate ❶ *v* regard or treat as separate. **dissociate oneself from** deny or break an association with. **dissociation** *n*.

———— THESAURUS ————

turn a blind eye to ▷ *n* **2** = **inattention**, contempt, disdain, disrespect, indifference, neglect, negligence, oversight

disrepair *n* = **dilapidation**, collapse, decay, deterioration, ruination

disrepute *n* = **discredit**, disgrace, dishonour, ignominy, ill repute, infamy, obloquy, shame, unpopularity

disrespect *n* = **contempt**, cheek, impertinence, impoliteness, impudence, insolence, irreverence, lack of respect, rudeness, sauce

disrupt *v* = **disturb**, break up or into, confuse, disorder, disorganize, interfere with, interrupt, intrude, spoil, unsettle, upset

dissatisfied *adj* = **discontented**, disappointed, disgruntled, displeased, fed up, frustrated, unhappy, unsatisfied

dissect *v* **1** = **cut up** or **apart**, anatomize, dismember, lay open **2** = **analyse**, break down, explore, inspect, investigate, research, scrutinize, study

disseminate *v* = **spread**, broadcast, circulate, disperse, distribute, publicize, scatter

dissent *v* **1** = **disagree**, differ, object, protest, refuse, withhold assent or approval ▷ *n* **3** = **disagreement**, discord, dissension, objection, opposition, refusal, resistance

dissertation *n* **1** = **thesis**, critique, discourse, disquisition, essay, exposition, treatise

disservice *n* = **bad turn**, harm, injury, injustice, unkindness, wrong

dissident *n* **1** = **protester**, agitator, dissenter, rebel ▷ *adj* **2** = **dissenting**, disagreeing, discordant, heterodox, nonconformist

dissimilar *adj* = **different**, disparate, divergent, diverse, heterogeneous, unlike, unrelated, various

dissipate *v* **1** = **squander**, consume, deplete, expend, fritter away, run through, spend, waste **2** = **disperse**, disappear, dispel, dissolve, drive away, evaporate, scatter, vanish

dissociate *v* = **separate**, detach, disconnect, distance, divorce, isolate, segregate, set apart ▷ *v* **dissociate oneself from** = **break away from**, break off from, part company from, quit

dissolute ⊙ *adj* leading an immoral life.
dissolution ⊙ *n* **1** official breaking up of an organization or institution, such as Parliament. **2** official ending of a formal agreement, such as a marriage.
dissolve ⊙ *v* **1** (cause to) become liquid. **2** break up or end officially. **3** break down emotionally, e.g. *she dissolved into tears*.
dissuade ⊙ *v* deter (someone) by persuasion from doing something. **dissuasion** *n*.
distance ⊙ *n* **1** space between two points. **2** state of being apart. **3** remoteness in manner. **the distance** most distant part of the visible scene. **distance oneself from** separate oneself mentally from. **distant** *adj* **1** far apart. **2** separated by a specified distance. **3** remote in manner. **distantly** *adv*.
distaste ⊙ *n* dislike, disgust. **distasteful** *adj* unpleasant, offensive.
distemper[1] *n* highly contagious viral disease of dogs.
distemper[2] *n* paint mixed with water, glue, etc., used for painting walls.
distend *v* (of part of the body) swell. **distension** *n*.
distil ⊙ *v* **-tilling, -tilled 1** subject to or obtain by distillation. **2** give off (a substance) in drops. **3** extract the essence of. **distillation** *n* **1** process of evaporating a liquid and condensing its vapour. **2** (also **distillate**) concentrated essence. **distiller** *n* person or company that makes strong alcoholic drink, esp. whisky. **distillery** *n*, *pl* **-leries** place where a strong alcoholic drink, esp. whisky, is made.
distinct ⊙ *adj* **1** not the same. **2** easily sensed or understood. **3** clear and definite. **distinctly** *adv* **distinction** *n* **1** act of distinguishing. **2** distinguishing feature. **3** state of being different. **4** special honour, recognition, or fame. **distinctive** *adj* easily recognizable. **distinctively** *adv* **distinctiveness** *n*.
distinguish ⊙ *v* **1** (usu. foll. by *between*) make, show, or recognize a difference (between). **2** be a distinctive feature of. **3** make out by hearing, seeing, etc. **distinguishable** *adj* **distinguished** *adj* **1** dignified in appearance. **2** highly respected.
distort ⊙ *v* **1** misrepresent (the truth or facts). **2** twist out of shape. **distortion** *n*.

————————————————— THESAURUS —————————————————

dissolute *adj* = **immoral**, debauched, degenerate, depraved, dissipated, profligate, rakish, wanton, wild
dissolution *n* **1** = **breaking up**, disintegration, division, parting, separation **2** = **adjournment**, discontinuation, end, finish, suspension, termination
dissolve *v* **1** = **melt**, deliquesce, fuse, liquefy, soften, thaw **2** = **end**, break up, discontinue, suspend, terminate, wind up
dissuade *v* = **deter**, advise against, discourage, put off, remonstrate, talk out of, warn
distance *n* **1** = **space**, extent, gap, interval, length, range, span, stretch **3** = **reserve**, aloofness, coldness, coolness, remoteness, restraint, stiffness ▷ *v* **distance oneself from** = **separate oneself from**, be distanced from, dissociate oneself from

distaste *n* = **dislike**, aversion, disgust, horror, loathing, odium, repugnance, revulsion
distil *v* **1, 3** = **extract**, condense, purify, refine
distinct *adj* **1** = **different**, detached, discrete, individual, separate, unconnected **3** = **definite**, clear, decided, evident, marked, noticeable, obvious, palpable, unmistakable, well-defined
distinguish *v* **1** (usu. foll. by *between*) = **differentiate**, ascertain, decide, determine, discriminate, judge, tell apart, tell the difference **2** = **characterize**, categorize, classify, mark, separate, set apart, single out **3** = **make out**, discern, know, perceive, pick out, recognize, see, tell
distort *v* **1** = **misrepresent**, bias, colour, falsify, pervert, slant, twist **2** = **deform**,

distract ❶ v 1 draw the attention of (a person) away from something. 2 entertain. **distracted** adj unable to concentrate, preoccupied. **distraction** n.

distraught ❶ [diss-**trawt**] adj extremely anxious or agitated.

distress ❶ n 1 extreme unhappiness. 2 great physical pain. 3 poverty. ▷ v 4 upset badly. **distressed** adj 1 extremely upset. 2 in financial difficulties. **distressing** adj **distressingly** adv.

distribute ❶ v 1 hand out or deliver. 2 share out. **distribution** n 1 distributing. 2 arrangement or spread. **distributor** n 1 wholesaler who distributes goods to retailers in a specific area. 2 device in a petrol engine that sends the electric current to the spark plugs. **distributive** adj.

district ❶ n area of land regarded as an administrative or geographical unit.

distrust ❶ v 1 regard as untrustworthy or dishonest. ▷ n 2 feeling of suspicion or doubt. **distrustful** adj.

disturb ❶ v 1 intrude on. 2 worry, make anxious. 3 change the position or shape of. **disturbance** n **disturbing** adj **disturbingly** adv **disturbed** adj Psychiatry emotionally upset or maladjusted.

disuse ❶ n state of being no longer used. **disused** adj.

ditch ❶ n 1 narrow channel dug in the earth for drainage or irrigation. ▷ v 2 slang abandon.

dither ❶ v 1 be uncertain or indecisive. ▷ n 2 state of indecision or agitation. **ditherer** n **dithery** adj

ditto n, pl **-tos** 1 the same. ▷ adv 2 in the same way.

ditty n, pl **-ties** short simple poem or song.

divan n 1 low backless bed. 2 backless sofa or couch.

dive ❶ v **diving**, **dived** 1 plunge headfirst into water. 2 (of a submarine or diver) submerge under water. 3 fly in a steep

bend, buckle, contort, disfigure, misshape, twist, warp

distract v 1 = **divert**, draw away, sidetrack, turn aside 2 = **amuse**, beguile, engross, entertain, occupy

distraught adj = **frantic**, agitated, beside oneself, desperate, distracted, distressed, out of one's mind, overwrought, worked-up

distress n 1 = **worry**, grief, heartache, misery, pain, sorrow, suffering, torment, wretchedness 2 = **pain**, suffering, torment 3 = **need**, adversity, difficulties, hardship, misfortune, poverty, privation, trouble ▷ v 4 = **upset**, disturb, grieve, harass, sadden, torment, trouble, worry

distribute v 1 = **hand out**, circulate, convey, deliver, pass round 2 = **share**, allocate, allot, apportion, deal, dispense, dole out

district n = **area**, locale, locality, neighbourhood, parish, quarter, region, sector, vicinity

distrust v 1 = **suspect**, be suspicious of, be wary of, disbelieve, doubt, mistrust, question, smell a rat (inf) ▷ n 2 = **suspicion**, disbelief, doubt, misgiving, mistrust, question, scepticism, wariness

disturb v 1 = **interrupt**, bother, butt in on, disrupt, interfere with, intrude on, pester 2 = **upset**, alarm, distress, fluster, harass, perturb, trouble, unnerve, unsettle, worry 3 = **muddle**, disarrange, disorder

disuse n = **neglect**, abandonment, decay, idleness

ditch n 1 = **channel**, drain, dyke, furrow, gully, moat, trench, watercourse ▷ v 2 Sl = **get rid of**, abandon, discard, dispose of, drop, dump (inf), jettison, scrap, throw out or overboard

dither v 1 = **vacillate**, faff about (Brit inf), hesitate, hum and haw, shillyshally (inf), teeter, waver ▷ n 2 = **flutter**, flap (inf), fluster, tizzy (inf)

dive v 1-3 = **plunge**, descend, dip, drop, duck, nose-dive, plummet, swoop

nose-down descending path. **4** move quickly in a specified direction. **5** (foll. by *in* or *into*) start doing (something) enthusiastically. ▷ *n* **6** diving. **7** steep nose-down descent. **8** *slang* disreputable bar or club. **diver** *n* **1** person who works or explores underwater. **2** person who dives for sport.

diverge 1 *v* **1** separate and go in different directions. **2** deviate (from a prescribed course). **divergence** *n* **divergent** *adj*.

diverse 1 *adj* **1** having variety, assorted. **2** different in kind. **diversity** *n*, *pl* **-ties** **1** quality of being different or varied. **2** range of difference. **diversify** *v* **-fying**, **-fied**. **diversification** *n*.

divert 1 *v* **1** change the direction of. **2** entertain, distract the attention of. **diversion** *n* **1** official detour used by traffic when a main route is closed. **2** something that distracts someone's attention. **3** diverting. **4** amusing pastime. **diversionary** *adj*.

divide 1 *v* **1** separate into parts. **2** share or be shared out in parts. **3** (cause to) disagree. **4** keep apart, be a boundary between. **5** calculate how many times (one number) can be contained in

(another). ▷ *n* **6** division, split. **dividend** *n* **1** sum of money representing part of the profit made, paid by a company to its shareholders. **2** extra benefit. **divider** *n* **1** screen used to divide a room into separate areas. ▷ *pl* **2** compasses with two pointed arms, used for measuring or dividing lines.

divine 1 *adj* **1** of God or a god. **2** godlike. **3** *informal* splendid. ▷ *v* **4** discover (something) by intuition or guessing. **divinely** *adv* **divination** *n* art of discovering future events, as though by supernatural powers. **divinity** *n* **1** study of religion. **2** *pl* **-ties** god. **3** state of being divine. **divining rod** forked twig said to move when held over ground in which water or metal is to be found.

division 1 *n* **1** dividing, sharing out. **2** one of the parts into which something is divided. **3** mathematical operation of dividing. **4** difference of opinion. **divisional** *adj* of a division in an organization. **divisible** *adj* **divisibility** *n* **divisive** *adj* tending to cause disagreement. **divisor** *n* number to be divided into another number.

divorce 1 *n* **1** legal ending of a marriage. **2** any separation, esp. a permanent one.

——————————————— THESAURUS ———————

▷ *n* **6** = **plunge**, jump, leap **7** = **nose dive**, descent, drop, plummet, plunge, swoop

diverge *v* **1** = **separate**, branch, divide, fork, part, split, spread **2** = **deviate**, depart, digress, meander, stray, turn aside, wander

diverse *adj* **1** = **various**, assorted, manifold, miscellaneous, of every description, several, sundry, varied **2** = **different**, discrete, disparate, dissimilar, distinct, divergent, separate, unlike, varying

divert *v* **1** = **redirect**, avert, deflect, switch, turn aside **2 a** = **entertain**, amuse, beguile, delight, gratify, regale **b** = **distract**, draw *or* lead away from, lead astray, sidetrack

divide *v* **1** = **separate**, bisect, cut (up), part, partition, segregate, split **2** = **share**, allocate, allot, deal out, dispense,

distribute **3** = **cause to disagree**, break up, come between, estrange, split

divine *adj* **1, 2** = **heavenly**, angelic, celestial, godlike, holy, spiritual, superhuman, supernatural **3** *Inf* = **wonderful**, beautiful, excellent, glorious, marvellous, perfect, splendid, superlative ▷ *v* **4** = **infer**, apprehend, deduce, discern, guess, perceive, suppose, surmise

division *n* **1** = **separation**, cutting up, dividing, partition, splitting up **2** = **share**, allotment, apportionment **4** = **disagreement**, difference of opinion, discord, rupture, split, variance

divorce *n* **1** = **separation**, annulment, dissolution, split-up ▷ *v* **3** = **separate**, disconnect, dissociate, dissolve (*marriage*), divide, part, sever, split up

▷ v **3** legally end one's marriage (to).
4 separate, consider separately. **divorcée**,
(*masc*) **divorcé** *n* person who is divorced.
divulge ❶ *v* make known, disclose.
divulgence *n*.
DIY *Brit, Aust & NZ* do-it-yourself.
dizzy ❶ *adj* **-zier, -ziest 1** having or causing
a whirling sensation. **2** mentally confused.
▷ v **-zying, -zied 3** make dizzy. **dizzily** *adv*
dizziness *n*.
DJ 1 disc jockey. **2** dinner jacket.
DNA *n* deoxyribonucleic acid, the main
constituent of the chromosomes of all
living things.
do ❶ *v* **does, doing, did, done 1** perform
or complete (a deed or action). **2** be
adequate, e.g. *that one will do*. **3** provide,
serve. **4** make (hair) neat or attractive.
5 suit or improve, e.g. *that style does nothing
for you*. **6** find the answer to (a problem or
puzzle). **7** cause, produce, e.g. *it does no
harm to think ahead*. **8** give, grant, e.g. *do
me a favour*. **9** work at, as a course of study
or a job. **10** *informal* cheat or rob. **11** used
to form questions, e.g. *how do you know?*
12 used to intensify positive statements
and commands, e.g. *I do like port; do go
on*. **13** used to form negative statements
and commands, e.g. *I do not know her well;
do not get up*. **14** used to replace an earlier

verb, e.g. *he gets paid more than I do*. ▷ *n, pl*
dos, do's 15 *informal* party, celebration. **do
away with** *v* get rid of. **do-it-yourself** *n*
constructing and repairing things oneself.
do up *v* **1** fasten. **2** decorate and repair.
do with *v* find useful or benefit from, e.g. *I
could do with a rest*. **do without** *v* manage
without.
Doberman pinscher, Doberman *n*
large dog with a black-and-tan coat.
dob in *v* **dobbing, dobbed** *Aust & NZ
informal* **1** inform against. **2** contribute
to a fund.
docile ❶ *adj* (of a person or animal) easily
controlled. **docilely** *adv* **docility** *n*.
dock¹ ❶ *n* **1** enclosed area of water where
ships are loaded, unloaded, or repaired.
▷ *v* **2** bring or be brought into dock. **3** link
(two spacecraft) or (of two spacecraft)
be linked together in space. **docker** *n*
person employed to load and unload ships.
dockyard *n* place where ships are built or
repaired.
dock² ❶ *v* **1** deduct money from (a person's
wages). **2** remove part of (an animal's tail)
by cutting through the bone.
dock³ *n* enclosed space in a court of law
where the accused person sits or stands.
dock⁴ *n* weed with broad leaves.
docket *n* label on a package or other

divulge *v* = **make known**, confess,
declare, disclose, let slip, proclaim,
reveal, tell
dizzy *adj* **1** = **giddy**, faint, light-headed,
off balance, reeling, shaky, swimming,
wobbly, woozy (*inf*) **2** = **confused**, at sea,
befuddled, bemused, bewildered, dazed,
dazzled, muddled
do *v* **1** = **perform**, accomplish, achieve,
carry out, complete, execute **2** = **be
adequate**, be sufficient, cut the mustard,
pass muster, satisfy, suffice **4** = **get
ready**, arrange, fix, look after, prepare,
see to **6** = **solve**, decipher, decode,
figure out, puzzle out, resolve, work
out **7** = **cause**, bring about, create,

effect, produce ▷ *n* **15** *Inf* = **event**, affair,
function, gathering, occasion, party **do
without** = **manage without**, abstain
from, dispense with, forgo, get along
without, give up, kick (*inf*)
docile *adj* = **submissive**, amenable,
biddable, compliant, manageable,
obedient, pliant
dock¹ *n* **1** = **wharf**, harbour, pier, quay,
waterfront ▷ *v* **2** = **moor**, anchor, berth,
drop anchor, land, put in, tie up **3** *Of
spacecraft* = **link up**, couple, hook up, join,
rendezvous, unite
dock² *v* **1** = **deduct**, decrease, diminish,
lessen, reduce, subtract, withhold **2** = **cut
off**, clip, crop, curtail, cut short, shorten

delivery, stating contents, delivery instructions, etc.

doctor ❶ n 1 person licensed to practise medicine. 2 person who has been awarded a doctorate. ▷ v 3 alter in order to deceive. 4 poison or drug (food or drink). 5 informal castrate (an animal). **doctoral** adj **doctorate** n highest academic degree in any field of knowledge.

doctrine ❶ n 1 body of teachings of a religious, political, or philosophical group. 2 principle or body of principles that is taught or advocated. **doctrinal** adj of doctrines. **doctrinaire** adj stubbornly insistent on the application of a theory without regard to practicality.

document ❶ n 1 piece of paper providing an official record of something. ▷ v 2 record or report (something) in detail. 3 support (a claim) with evidence. **documentation** n.

documentary n, pl -ries 1 film or television programme presenting the facts about a particular subject. ▷ adj 2 (of evidence) based on documents.

dodder v move unsteadily. **doddery** adj.

dodge ❶ v 1 avoid (a blow, being seen, etc.) by moving suddenly. 2 evade by cleverness or trickery. ▷ n 3 cunning or deceitful trick. **dodger** n **dodgy** adj **dodgier**, **dodgiest** informal 1 dangerous, risky. 2 untrustworthy.

Dodgem n ® small electric car driven and bumped against similar cars in a rink at a funfair.

dodo n, pl **dodos**, **dodoes** large flightless extinct bird.

doe n female deer, hare, or rabbit.

does v third person singular of the present tense of DO.

doff v take off or lift (one's hat) in polite greeting.

dog ❶ n 1 domesticated four-legged mammal of many different breeds. 2 related wild mammal, such as the dingo or coyote. 4 male animal of the dog family. 4 informal person, e.g. you lucky dog!. ▷ v **dogging**, **dogged** 5 follow (someone) closely. 6 trouble, plague. **go to the dogs** informal go to ruin physically or morally. **let sleeping dogs lie** leave things undisturbed. **doggy**, **doggie** n, pl -**gies** child's word for a dog. **dogcart** n light horse-drawn two-wheeled cart. **dog collar** 1 collar for a dog. 2 informal white collar fastened at the back, worn by members of the clergy. **dog-eared** adj 1 (of a book) having pages folded down at the corner. 2 shabby, worn. **dogfight** n close-quarters combat between fighter aircraft. **dogfish** n small shark. **doghouse** n US kennel. **in the doghouse** informal in disgrace. **dogleg** n sharp bend. **dog-tired** adj informal exhausted.

doggerel n poorly written poetry, usu. comic.

———————————————————————— THESAURUS ————————

doctor n 1 = **G.P.**, general practitioner, medic (inf), medical practitioner, physician ▷ v 3 = **change**, alter, disguise, falsify, misrepresent, pervert, tamper with 4 = **add to**, adulterate, cut, dilute, mix with, spike, water down

doctrine n = **teaching**, article of faith, belief, conviction, creed, dogma, opinion, precept, principle, tenet

document n 1 = **paper**, certificate, record, report ▷ v 3 = **support**, authenticate, certify, corroborate, detail, substantiate,

validate, verify

dodge v 1 = **duck**, dart, sidestep, swerve, turn aside 2 = **evade**, avoid, elude, get out of, shirk ▷ n 3 = **trick**, device, ploy, ruse, scheme, stratagem, subterfuge, wheeze (Brit sl)

dog n 1 = **hound**, canine, cur, man's best friend, pooch (sl) ▷ v 5, 6 = **trouble**, follow, haunt, hound, plague, pursue, track, trail **go to the dogs** Inf = **go to ruin**, degenerate, deteriorate, go doswn the drain, go to pot

dogma ⚊ n doctrine or system of doctrines proclaimed by authority as true. **dogmatic** adj habitually stating one's opinions forcefully or arrogantly. **dogmatism** n

doily n, pl -**lies** decorative lacy paper mat, laid on a plate.

doldrums ⚊ pl n 1 depressed state of mind. 2 state of inactivity.

dole ⚊ n 1 informal money received from the state while unemployed. ▷ v 2 (foll. by out) distribute in small quantities.

doleful adj dreary, unhappy. **dolefully** adv **dolefulness** n.

doll n 1 small model of a human being, used as a toy. 2 slang pretty girl or young woman.

dollar n standard monetary unit of the US, Canada, and various other countries.

dollop ⚊ n informal lump (of food).

dolly n, pl -**lies** 1 child's word for a doll. 2 wheeled support on which a camera may be moved.

dolphin n sea mammal of the whale family, with a beaklike snout.

domain n 1 field of knowledge or activity. 2 land under one ruler or government. 3 Computers group of computers with the same name on the Internet. 4 NZ public park.

dome n 1 rounded roof built on a circular base. 2 something shaped like this. **domed** adj.

domestic ⚊ adj 1 of one's own country or a specific country. 2 of the home or family. 3 enjoying running a home. 4 (of an animal) kept as a pet or to produce food. ▷ n 5 person whose job is to do housework in someone else's house. **domestically** adv **domesticity** n **domesticate** v 1 bring or keep (a wild animal or plant) under control or cultivation. 2 accustom (someone) to home life. **domestication** n **domestic science** study of household skills.

domicile [**dom**-miss-ile] n place where one lives.

dominate ⚊ v 1 control or govern. 2 tower above (surroundings). 3 be very significant in. **domination** n.

dominion ⚊ n 1 control or authority. 2 land governed by one ruler or government. 3 (formerly) self-governing division of the British Empire.

don[1] ⚊ v **donning, donned** put on (clothing).

don[2] n 1 Brit member of the teaching staff at a university or college. 2 Spanish gentleman or nobleman. **donnish** adj serious and academic.

donate ⚊ v give, esp. to a charity or organization. **donation** n 1 donating. 2 thing donated. **donor** n 1 Med person who gives blood or organs for use in the treatment of another person. 2 person who makes a donation.

———————— THESAURUS ————————

dogma n = **doctrine**, belief, credo, creed, opinion, teachings

doldrums n 1 = **depression**, dumps (inf), gloom, malaise 2 = **inactivity**, listlessness

dole n 1 Inf = **benefit**, allowance, gift, grant, hand-out, pogey (Canad) ▷ v 2 (foll. by out) = **give out**, allocate, allot, apportion, assign, dispense, distribute, hand out

dollop n Inf = **lump**, helping, portion, scoop, serving

domestic adj 1 = **native**, indigenous, internal 2 = **home**, family, household, private 3 = **home-loving**, domesticated, homely, housewifely, stay-at-home 4 = **domesticated**, house-trained, pet, tame, trained ▷ n 5 = **servant**, char (inf), charwoman, daily, help, maid

dominate v 1 = **control**, direct, govern, have the whip hand over, monopolize, rule, tyrannize 2 = **tower above**, loom over, overlook, stand head and shoulders above, stand over, survey

dominion n 1 = **control**, authority, command, jurisdiction, mana (NZ), power, rule, sovereignty, supremacy 2 = **kingdom**, country, domain, empire, realm, territory

don[1] v = **put on**, clothe oneself in, dress in, get into, pull on, slip on or into

donate v = **give**, contribute, make a gift of, present, subscribe

done v past participle of DO.

donkey n long-eared member of the horse family. **donkey jacket** man's long thick jacket with a waterproof panel across the shoulders. **donkey's years** informal a long time. **donkey-work** n tedious hard work.

doodle v 1 scribble or draw aimlessly. ▷ n 2 shape or picture drawn aimlessly.

doom ❶ n 1 death or a terrible fate. ▷ v 2 destine or condemn to death or a terrible fate. **doomsday** n 1 Christianity day on which the Last Judgment will occur. 2 any dreaded day.

door ❶ n 1 hinged or sliding panel for closing the entrance to a building, room, etc. 2 entrance. **doormat** n 1 mat for wiping dirt from shoes before going indoors. 2 informal person who offers little resistance to ill-treatment. **doorway** n opening into a building or room.

dope ❶ n 1 slang illegal drug, usu. cannabis. 2 medicine, drug. 3 informal stupid person. ▷ v 4 give a drug to, esp. in order to improve performance in a race. **dopey**, **dopy** adj 1 half-asleep, drowsy. 2 slang silly.

dormant ❶ adj temporarily quiet, inactive, or not being used. **dormancy** n.

dormitory n, pl -ries large room, esp. at a school, containing several beds.

dormouse n, pl -mice small mouselike rodent with a furry tail.

dorp n S Afr small town.

dorsal adj of or on the back.

dory n, pl -ries 1 (also **John Dory**) spiny-finned edible sea fish. 2 same as WALLEYE.

dose ❶ n 1 specific quantity of a medicine taken at one time. 2 informal something unpleasant to experience. ▷ v 3 give a dose to. **dosage** n size of a dose.

dossier [**doss**-ee-ay] n collection of documents about a subject or person.

dot ❶ n 1 small round mark. 2 shorter symbol used in Morse code. ▷ v **dotting**, **dotted** 3 mark with a dot. 4 scatter, spread around. **on the dot** at exactly the arranged time. **dotty** adj slang rather eccentric. **dotcom**, **dot.com** n company that does most of its business on the Internet.

dote ❶ v **dote on** love to an excessive degree. **dotage** n weakness as a result of old age.

double ❶ adj 1 as much again in number, amount, size, etc. 2 composed of two equal or similar parts. 3 designed for two users, e.g. double room. 4 folded in two. ▷ adv 5 twice over. ▷ n 6 twice the number, amount, size, etc. 7 person who looks almost exactly like another. ▷ pl 8 game between two pairs of players. ▷ v 9 make or become twice as much or as many. 10 bend or fold (material etc.). 11 play two parts. 12 turn sharply. **at,**

──────────────────────── THESAURUS ────────────────────────

doom n 1 = **destruction**, catastrophe, downfall, fate, fortune, ruin ▷ v 2 = **condemn**, consign, damn, destine, sentence

door n 2 = **opening**, doorway, entrance, entry, exit

dope n 1 Sl = **drug**, narcotic, opiate 3 Inf = **idiot**, dimwit (inf), dunce, fool, nitwit (inf), numbskull or numbskull, simpleton, twit (inf, chiefly Brit) ▷ v 4 = **drug**, anaesthetize, knock out, narcotize, sedate, stupefy

dormant adj = **inactive**, asleep, hibernating, inert, inoperative, latent,

sleeping, slumbering, suspended

dose n 1 = **quantity**, dosage, draught, measure, portion, potion, prescription

dot n 1 = **spot**, fleck, jot, mark, point, speck, speckle ▷ v 3 = **spot**, dab, dabble, fleck, speckle, sprinkle, stipple, stud **on the dot** = **on time**, exactly, on the button (inf), precisely, promptly, punctually, to the minute

dote v **dote on** = **adore**, admire, hold dear, idolize, lavish affection on, prize, treasure

double adj 1 = **twice**, duplicate, twofold 2 = **dual**, coupled, in pairs, paired, twin ▷ n 7 = **twin**, clone, dead ringer (sl),

on the double quickly or immediately.
doubly adv **double agent** spy employed by two enemy countries at the same time.
double bass stringed instrument, largest and lowest member of the violin family.
double chin fold of fat under the chin.
double cream thick cream with a high fat content. **double-cross** v 1 cheat or betray. ▷ n 2 double-crossing. **double-dealing** n treacherous or deceitful behaviour.
double-decker n 1 bus with two passenger decks one on top of the other.
double Dutch informal incomprehensible talk, gibberish. **double glazing** two panes of glass in a window, fitted to reduce heat loss. **double talk** deceptive or ambiguous talk. **double whammy** informal devastating setback made up of two elements.
doubt ❶ n 1 uncertainty about the truth, facts, or existence of something. 2 unresolved difficulty or point. ▷ v 3 question the truth of. 4 distrust or be suspicious of (someone). **doubtful** adj 1 unlikely. 2 feeling doubt. **doubtfully** adv **doubtless** adv probably or certainly.
dough n 1 thick mixture of flour and water or milk, used for making bread etc. 2 slang money. **doughnut** n small cake of sweetened dough fried in deep fat.
doughty [**dowt**-ee] adj -**tier**, -**tiest** old-fashioned brave and determined.
dour ❶ [**doo**-er] adj sullen and unfriendly.

douse [rhymes with **mouse**] v 1 drench with water or other liquid. 2 put out (a light).
dove n 1 bird with a heavy body, small head, and short legs. 2 Politics person opposed to war. **dovecote**, **dovecot** n structure for housing pigeons. **dovetail** n 1 joint containing wedge-shaped tenons. ▷ v 2 fit together neatly.
dowager n widow possessing property or a title obtained from her husband.
dowdy ❶ adj -**dier**, -**diest** dull and old-fashioned. **dowdily** adv **dowdiness** n.
dowel n wooden or metal peg that fits into two corresponding holes to join two adjacent parts.
down¹ ❶ prep, adv 1 indicating movement to or position in a lower place. ▷ adv 2 indicating completion of an action, lessening of intensity, etc. e.g. calm down. ▷ adj 3 depressed, unhappy. ▷ v 4 informal drink quickly. **have a down on** informal feel hostile towards. **down under** informal (in or to) Australia or New Zealand. **downward** adj, adv (descending) from a higher to a lower level, condition, or position. **downwards** adv from a higher to a lower level, condition, or position. **down-and-out** n 1 person who is homeless and destitute. ▷ adj 2 without any means of support. **down-to-earth** adj sensible or practical.
down² n soft fine feathers. **downy** adj.

doppelgänger, duplicate, lookalike, replica, spitting image (inf) ▷ v 9 = **multiply**, duplicate, enlarge, grow, increase, magnify **at** or **on the double** = **quickly**, at full speed, briskly, immediately, posthaste, without delay
doubt n 1 = **uncertainty**, apprehension, distrust, hesitancy, hesitation, indecision, irresolution, lack of conviction, misgiving, mistrust, qualm, scepticism, suspense, suspicion ▷ v 3 = **be uncertain**, be dubious, demur 4 = **suspect**, discredit, distrust, fear, lack confidence in, mistrust,

query, question
dour adj = **gloomy**, dismal, dreary, forbidding, grim, morose, sour, sullen, unfriendly
dowdy adj = **frumpy**, dingy, drab, frowzy, old-fashioned, shabby, unfashionable
down¹ adj 3 = **depressed**, dejected, disheartened, downcast, low, miserable, sad, unhappy ▷ v 4 Inf = **swallow**, drain, drink (down), gulp, put away, toss off **have a down on** Inf = **be antagonistic** or **hostile to**, bear a grudge towards, be prejudiced against, be set against, have it in for (sl)

download v **1** transfer (data) from the memory of one computer to that of another. ▷ n **2** file transferred in such a way.

downs pl n low grassy hills, esp. in S England.

downtown US, Canad & NZ n **1** the central or lower part of a city, especially the main commercial area. ▷ adv **2** towards, to, or into this area.

dowry n, pl **-ries** property brought by a woman to her husband at marriage.

doyen [**doy**-en] n senior member of a group, profession, or society. **doyenne** [doy-**en**] n fem.

doze ❶ v **1** sleep lightly or briefly. ▷ n **2** short sleep. **dozy** adj **dozier, doziest 1** feeling sleepy. **2** informal stupid. **doze off** v fall into a light sleep.

dozen adj, n twelve.

drab ❶ adj **drabber, drabbest** dull and dreary. **drabness** n.

draconian adj severe, harsh.

draft ❶ n **1** plan, sketch, or drawing of something. **2** preliminary outline of a book, speech, etc. **3** written order for payment of money by a bank. **4** US & Aust selection for compulsory military service. ▷ v **5** draw up an outline or plan of. **6** send (people) from one place to another to do a specific job.

7 US & Aust select for compulsory military service.

drag ❶ v **dragging, dragged 1** pull with force, esp. along the ground. **2** trail on the ground. **3** persuade or force (oneself or someone else) to go somewhere. **4** (foll. by on or out) last or be prolonged tediously. **5** search (a river) with a dragnet or hook. **6** Computers move (an image) on the screen by use of the mouse. ▷ n **7** person or thing that slows up progress. **8** informal tedious thing or person. **9** slang women's clothes worn by a man. **dragnet** n net used to scour the bottom of a pond or river to search for something. **drag race** race in which specially built cars or motorcycles are timed over a measured course.

dragon n **1** mythical fire-breathing monster like a huge lizard. **2** informal fierce woman. **dragonfly** n brightly coloured insect with a long slender body and two pairs of wings.

dragoon ❶ n **1** heavily armed cavalryman. ▷ v **2** coerce, force.

drain ❶ n **1** pipe or channel that carries off water or sewage. **2** cause of a continuous reduction in energy or resources. ▷ v **3** draw off or remove liquid from. **4** flow away or filter off. **5** drink the entire contents of (a glass or cup).

——————————————— THESAURUS ————

doze v **1** = **nap**, kip (Brit sl), nod off (inf), sleep, slumber, snooze (inf) ▷ n **2** = **nap**, catnap, forty winks (inf), kip (Brit sl), shuteye (sl), siesta, snooze (inf)

drab adj = **dull**, dingy, dismal, dreary, flat, gloomy, shabby, sombre

draft n **1** = **outline**, abstract, plan, rough, sketch, version **3** = **order**, bill (of exchange), cheque, postal order ▷ v **5** = **outline**, compose, design, draw, draw up, formulate, plan, sketch

drag v **1** = **pull**, draw, haul, lug, tow, trail, tug **4** (foll. by on or out) = **last**, draw out, extend, keep going, lengthen, persist, prolong, protract, spin out, stretch out ▷ n

8 Inf = **nuisance**, annoyance, bore, bother, pain (inf), pest

dragoon v **2** = **force**, browbeat, bully, coerce, compel, constrain, drive, impel, intimidate, railroad (inf)

drain n **1** = **pipe**, channel, conduit, culvert, ditch, duct, sewer, sink, trench **2** = **reduction**, depletion, drag, exhaustion, sap, strain, withdrawal ▷ v **3** = **remove**, bleed, draw off, dry, empty, pump off or out, tap, withdraw **4** = **flow out**, effuse, exude, leak, ooze, seep, trickle, well out **5** = **drink up**, finish, gulp down, quaff, swallow **6** = **exhaust**, consume, deplete, dissipate, empty, sap, strain, use up

6 make constant demands on (energy or resources), exhaust. **drainage** n **1** system of drains. **2** process or method of draining.

drake n male duck.

dram n **1** small amount of a strong alcoholic drink, esp. whisky. **2** one sixteenth of an ounce.

drama ❶ n **1** serious play for theatre, television, or radio. **2** writing, producing, or acting in plays. **3** situation that is exciting or highly emotional. **dramatic** adj **1** of or like drama. **2** behaving flamboyantly. **dramatically** adv **dramatist** n person who writes plays. **dramatize** v **1** rewrite (a book) in the form of a play. **2** express (something) in a dramatic or exaggerated way. **dramatization** n.

drape ❶ v **1** cover with material, usu. in folds. **2** place casually. ▷ n **3** Aust, US & Canad curtain. **draper** n Brit, Aust & NZ person who sells fabrics and sewing materials. **drapery** n, pl **-peries 1** fabric or clothing arranged and draped. **2** fabrics and cloth collectively.

drastic ❶ adj strong and severe.

draught ❶ n **1** current of cold air, esp. in an enclosed space. **2** portion of liquid to be drunk, esp. medicine. **3** gulp or swallow. **4** one of the flat discs used in the game of draughts. ▷ pl **5** game for two players using a chessboard and twelve draughts each. ▷ adj **6** (of an animal) used for pulling heavy loads. **draughty** adj exposed to draughts of air. **draughtsman** n person

employed to prepare detailed scale drawings of machinery, buildings, etc. **draughtsmanship** n **draught beer** beer stored in a cask.

draw ❶ v drawing, drew, drawn **1** sketch (a figure, picture, etc.) with a pencil or pen. **2** pull (a person or thing) closer to or further away from a place. **3** move in a specified direction, e.g. the car drew near. **4** take from a source, e.g. draw money from bank accounts. **5** attract, interest. **6** formulate or decide, e.g. to draw conclusions. **7** (of two teams or contestants) finish a game with an equal number of points. ▷ n **8** raffle or lottery. **9** contest or game ending in a tie. **10** event, act, etc., that attracts a large audience. **drawing** n **1** picture or plan made by means of lines on a surface. **2** art of making drawings. **drawing pin** short tack with a broad smooth head. **drawing room** old-fashioned room where visitors are received and entertained. **drawback** n disadvantage. **drawbridge** n bridge that may be raised to prevent access or to enable vessels to pass. **draw out** v **1** encourage (someone) to talk freely. **2** make longer. **drawstring** n cord run through a hem around an opening, so that when it is pulled tighter, the opening closes. **draw up** v **1** prepare and write out (a contract). **2** (of a vehicle) come to a stop.

drawl v **1** speak slowly, with long vowel sounds. ▷ n **2** drawling manner of speech.

drama n **1** = **play**, dramatization, show, stage show **2** = **theatre**, acting, dramaturgy, stagecraft **3** = **excitement**, crisis, histrionics, scene, spectacle, turmoil

drape v **1** = **cover**, cloak, fold, swathe, wrap

drastic adj = **extreme**, desperate, dire, forceful, harsh, radical, severe, strong

draught n **1** = **breeze**, current, flow, movement, puff **2** = **drink**, cup, dose,

potion, quantity

draw v **1** = **sketch**, depict, design, map out, mark out, outline, paint, portray, trace **2** = **pull**, drag, haul, tow, tug **4** = **take out**, extract, pull out **5** = **attract**, allure, elicit, entice, evoke, induce, influence, invite, persuade **6** = **deduce**, derive, infer, make, take ▷ n **9** = **tie**, dead heat, deadlock, impasse, stalemate **10** = **attraction**, enticement, lure, pull (inf)

d

drawn ❶ v **1** past participle of DRAW. ▷ *adj* **2** haggard, tired, or tense in appearance.

dread ❶ v **1** anticipate with apprehension or fear. ▷ n **2** great fear. **dreadful** *adj* **1** very disagreeable or shocking. **2** extreme. **dreadfully** *adv*.

dream ❶ n **1** imagined series of events experienced in the mind while asleep. **2** cherished hope. **3** *informal* wonderful person or thing. ▷ v **dreaming**, **dreamed** or **dreamt 4** see imaginary pictures in the mind while asleep. **5** (often foll. by *of* or *about*) have an image (of) or fantasy (about). **6** (foll. by *of*) consider the possibility (of). ▷ *adj* **7** ideal, e.g. *a dream house*. **dreamer** n **dreamy** *adj* **1** vague or impractical. **2** *informal* wonderful. **dreamily** *adv*.

dreary ❶ *adj* **drearier, dreariest**, dull, boring. **drearily** *adv* **dreariness** n.

dredge v clear or search (a river bed or harbour) by removing silt or mud. **dredger** n boat fitted with machinery for dredging. **dredge up** v *informal* remember (something) obscure or half-forgotten.

dregs ❶ pl n **1** solid particles that settle at the bottom of some liquids. **2** most despised elements.

drench ❶ v make completely wet.

dress ❶ n **1** one-piece garment for a woman or girl, consisting of a skirt and bodice and sometimes sleeves. **2** complete style of clothing. ▷ v **3** put clothes on. **4** put on formal clothes. **5** apply a protective covering to (a wound). **6** arrange or prepare. **dressing** n **1** sauce for salad. **2** covering for a wound. **dressing-down** n *informal* severe scolding. **dressing gown** coat-shaped garment worn over pyjamas or nightdress. **dressing room** room used for changing clothes, esp. backstage in a theatre. **dressy** *adj* (of clothes) elegant. **dress circle** first gallery in a theatre. **dressmaker** n person who makes women's clothes. **dressmaking** n **dress rehearsal** last rehearsal of a play or show, using costumes, lighting, etc.

dressage [dress-ahzh] n training of a horse to perform manoeuvres in response to the rider's body signals.

dresser n piece of furniture with shelves and with cupboards, for storing or displaying dishes.

drey n squirrel's nest.

dribble ❶ v **1** (allow to) flow in drops. **2** allow saliva to trickle from the mouth. **3** *Sport* propel (a ball) by repeatedly tapping it with the foot, hand, or a stick.

———————————————————————— THESAURUS ————

drawn *adj* **2** = **tense**, haggard, pinched, stressed, tired, worn

dread v **1** = **fear**, cringe at, have cold feet (*inf*), quail, shrink from, shudder, tremble ▷ n **2** = **fear**, alarm, apprehension, dismay, fright, horror, terror, trepidation

dream n **1** = **vision**, delusion, hallucination, illusion, imagination, trance **2** = **ambition**, aim, aspiration, desire, goal, hope, wish **3** *Inf* = **delight**, beauty, gem, joy, marvel, pleasure, treasure ▷ v **5** (often foll. by *of* or *about*) = **daydream**, build castles in the air or in Spain, conjure up, envisage, fantasize, stargaze, visualize

dreary *adj* = **dull**, boring, drab, humdrum, monotonous, tedious, tiresome,

uneventful, wearisome

dregs pl n **1** = **sediment**, deposit, dross, grounds, lees, resi, residuum, scum, waste **2** = **scum**, good-for-nothings, rabble, ragtag and bobtail, riffraff

drench v = **soak**, drown, flood, inundate, saturate, souse, steep, swamp, wet

dress n **1** = **frock**, gown, outfit, robe **2** = **clothing**, apparel, attire, clothes, costume, garb, garments, togs ▷ v **3** = **put on**, attire, change, clothe, don, garb, robe, slip on or into **5** = **bandage**, bind up, plaster, treat **6** = **arrange**, adjust, align, get ready, prepare, straighten

dribble v **1** = **run**, drip, drop, fall in drops, leak, ooze, seep, trickle **2** = **drool**, drivel, slaver, slobber

▷ *n* **4** small quantity of liquid falling in drops.

drift ❶ *v* **1** be carried along by currents of air or water. **2** move aimlessly from one place or activity to another. ▷ *n* **3** something piled up by the wind or current, such as a snowdrift. **4** general movement or development. **5** point, meaning, e.g. *catch my drift?* **drifter** *n* person who moves aimlessly from place to place or job to job. **driftwood** *n* wood floating on or washed ashore by the sea.

drill¹ ❶ *n* **1** tool or machine for boring holes. **2** strict and often repetitious training. **3** *informal* correct procedure. ▷ *v* **4** bore a hole in (something) with or as if with a drill. **5** teach by rigorous exercises or training.

drill² *n* **1** machine for sowing seed in rows. **2** small furrow for seed. ▷ *v* **3** sow (seed) in drills or furrows.

drink ❶ *v* **drinking, drank, drunk** **1** swallow (a liquid). **2** consume alcohol, esp. to excess. ▷ *n* **3** (portion of) a liquid suitable for drinking. **4** alcohol, or its habitual or excessive consumption. **drinkable** *adj* **drinker** *n* **drink in** *v* pay close attention to. **drink to** *v* drink a toast to.

drip ❶ *v* **dripping, dripped** **1** (let) fall in drops. ▷ *n* **2** falling of drops of liquid. **3** sound made by falling drops. **4** *informal* weak dull person. **5** *Med* device by which a solution is passed in small drops through a tube into a vein. **drip-dry** *adj* denoting clothing that will dry free of creases if hung up when wet.

drive ❶ *v* **driving, drove, driven** **1** guide the movement of (a vehicle). **2** transport in a vehicle. **3** goad into a specified state. **4** push or propel. **5** *Sport* hit (a ball) very hard and straight. ▷ *n* **6** journey by car, van, etc. **7** (also **driveway**) path for vehicles connecting a building to a public road. **8** united effort towards a common goal. **9** energy and ambition. **10** *Psychol* motive or interest, e.g. *sex drive*. **11** means by which power is transmitted in a mechanism. **driver** *n* **drive at** *v* *informal* intend or mean, e.g. *what was he driving at?* **drive-in** *adj, n* (denoting) a cinema, restaurant, etc., used by people in their cars.

drivel ❶ *n* **1** foolish talk. ▷ *v* **-elling, -elled** **2** speak foolishly.

drift *v* **1** = **float**, be carried along, coast, go (aimlessly), meander, stray, waft, wander ▷ *n* **3** = **pile**, accumulation, bank, heap, mass, mound **5** = **meaning**, direction, gist, import, intention, purport, significance, tendency, thrust

drill¹ *n* **1** = **boring tool**, bit, borer, gimlet **2** = **training**, discipline, exercise, instruction, practice, preparation, repetition ▷ *v* **4** = **bore**, penetrate, perforate, pierce, puncture, sink in **5** = **train**, coach, discipline, exercise, instruct, practise, rehearse, teach

drink *v* **1** = **swallow**, gulp, guzzle, imbibe, quaff, sip, suck, sup **2** = **booze** (*inf*), hit the bottle (*inf*), tipple, tope ▷ *n* **3** = **beverage**, cup, draught, glass, liquid, potion, refreshment **4** = **alcohol**, booze (*inf*), hooch *or* hootch (*inf, chiefly US & Canad*), liquor, spirits, the bottle (*inf*)

drip *v* **1** = **drop**, dribble, exude, plop, splash, sprinkle, trickle ▷ *n* **2** = **drop**, dribble, leak, trickle **4** *Inf* = **weakling**, mummy's boy (*inf*), namby-pamby, softie (*inf*), weed (*inf*), wet (*Brit inf*)

drive *v* **1** = **operate**, direct, guide, handle, manage, motor, ride, steer, travel **3** = **goad**, coerce, constrain, force, press, prod, prompt, spur **4** = **push**, hurl, impel, propel, ram, send, thrust ▷ *n* **6** = **run**, excursion, jaunt, journey, outing, ride, spin (*inf*), trip **8** = **campaign**, action, appeal, crusade, effort, push (*inf*) **9** = **initiative**, ambition, energy, enterprise, get-up-and-go (*inf*), motivation, vigour, zip (*inf*)

drivel *n* **1** = **nonsense**, garbage (*inf*), gibberish, hogwash, hot air (*inf*), kak (*S Afr sl*), poppycock (*inf*), rubbish, trash, twaddle, waffle (*inf, chiefly Brit*)

drizzle ❶ n **1** very light rain. ▷ v **2** rain lightly. **drizzly** adj.

droll ❶ adj quaintly amusing.

dromedary [**drom**-mid-er-ee] n, pl -**daries** camel with a single hump.

drone¹ n male bee.

drone² ❶ v, n (make) a monotonous low dull sound. **drone on** v talk for a long time in a monotonous tone.

drongo n, pl -**gos** tropical songbird with a glossy black plumage, a forked tail, and a stout bill.

drool ❶ v **1** (foll. by over) show excessive enthusiasm (for). **2** allow saliva to flow from the mouth.

droop ❶ v hang downwards loosely. **droopy** adj.

drop ❶ v **dropping**, **dropped 1** (allow to) fall vertically. **2** decrease in amount, strength, or value. **3** mention (a hint or name) casually. **4** discontinue. ▷ n **5** small quantity of liquid forming a round shape. **6** any small quantity of liquid. **7** decrease in amount, strength, or value. **8** vertical distance that something may fall. ▷ pl **9** liquid medication

applied in small drops. **droplet** n **droppings** pl n faeces of certain animals, such as rabbits or birds. **drop in**, **by** v pay someone a casual visit. **drop off** v **1** informal fall asleep. **2** grow smaller or less. **dropout** n **1** person who rejects conventional society. **2** person who does not complete a course of study. **drop out (of)** v abandon or withdraw from (a school, job, etc.).

dropsy n illness in which watery fluid collects in the body.

dross n **1** scum formed on the surfaces of molten metals. **2** anything worthless.

drought ❶ n prolonged shortage of rainfall.

drove ❶ n very large group, esp. of people. **drover** n person who drives sheep or cattle.

drown ❶ v **1** die or kill by immersion in liquid. **2** forget (one's sorrows) temporarily by drinking alcohol. **3** drench thoroughly. **4** make (a sound) inaudible by being louder.

drudge ❶ n person who works hard at uninteresting tasks. **drudgery** n.

drug ❶ n **1** substance used in the treatment or prevention of disease. **2** chemical

──────────── THESAURUS ────────────

▷ v **2** = **babble**, blether, gab (inf), prate, ramble, waffle (inf, chiefly Brit)

drizzle n **1** = **fine rain**, Scotch mist ▷ v **2** = **rain**, shower, spot or spit with rain, spray, sprinkle

droll adj = **amusing**, comical, entertaining, funny, humorous, jocular, waggish, whimsical

drone² v = **hum**, buzz, purr, thrum, vibrate, whirr ▷ n = **hum**, buzz, murmuring, purr, thrum, vibration, whirring

drool v **1** (foll. by over) = **gloat over**, dote on, gush, make much of, rave about (inf) **2** = **dribble**, drivel, salivate, slaver, slobber, water at the mouth

droop v = **sag**, bend, dangle, drop, fall down, hang (down), sink

drop v **1** = **fall**, descend, plummet, plunge, sink, tumble **2** = **diminish**, decline, fall, plummet **4** = **discontinue**, axe (inf), give up, kick (inf), quit, relinquish ▷ n

5 = **droplet**, bead, bubble, drip, globule, pearl, tear **6** = **dash**, mouthful, shot (inf), sip, spot, tot, trace, trickle **7** = **decrease**, cut, decline, deterioration, downturn, fall-off, lowering, reduction, slump **8** = **fall**, descent, plunge

drought n = **dry spell**, aridity, dehydration, dryness

drove n = **herd**, collection, company, crowd, flock, horde, mob, multitude, swarm, throng

drown v **3** = **drench**, deluge, engulf, flood, go under, immerse, inundate, sink, submerge, swamp **4** = **overpower**, deaden, muffle, obliterate, overcome, overwhelm, stifle, swallow up, wipe out

drudge n = **menial**, dogsbody (inf), factotum, servant, skivvy (chiefly Brit), slave, toiler, worker

drug n = **medication**, medicament, medicine, physic, poison, remedy **2** = **dope** (sl), narcotic, opiate, stimulant ▷ v

substance, esp. a narcotic, taken for the effects it produces. ▷ v **drugging**, **drugged** **3** give a drug to (a person or animal) to cause sleepiness or unconsciousness. **4** mix a drug with (food or drink). **drugstore** n US pharmacy where a wide range of goods are available.

drum ❶ n **1** percussion instrument sounded by striking a membrane stretched across the opening of a hollow cylinder. **2** cylindrical object or container. ▷ v **drumming**, **drummed** **3** play (music) on a drum. **4** tap rhythmically or regularly. **drummer** n **drum into** v instil into (someone) by constant repetition. **drumstick** n **1** stick used for playing a drum. **2** lower joint of the leg of a cooked chicken etc. **drum up** v obtain (support or business) by making requests or canvassing.

drunk ❶ v **1** past participle of DRINK. ▷ adj **2** intoxicated with alcohol to the extent of losing control over normal functions. **3** overwhelmed by a strong influence or emotion. ▷ n **4** person who is drunk or who frequently gets drunk. **drunkard** n person who frequently gets drunk. **drunken** adj **1** drunk or frequently drunk. **2** caused by or relating to alcoholic intoxication. **drunkenness** n.

dry ❶ adj **drier**, **driest** or **dryer**, **dryest** **1** lacking moisture. **2** having little or no rainfall. **3** informal thirsty. **4** (of wine) not sweet. **5** uninteresting. **6** (of humour) subtle and sarcastic. **7** prohibiting the sale of alcohol, e.g. a dry town. ▷ v **drying**, **dried** **8** make or become dry. **9** preserve (food) by removing the moisture. **drily**, **dryly** adv **dryness** n **dryer** n apparatus for removing moisture. **dry-clean** v clean (clothes etc.) with chemicals rather than water. **dry-cleaner** n **dry-cleaning** n **dry out** v **1** make or become dry. **2** (cause to) undergo treatment for alcoholism. **dry rot** crumbling and drying of timber, caused by certain fungi. **dry run** informal rehearsal.

dual ❶ adj having two parts, functions, or aspects. **duality** n **dual carriageway** Brit, Aust & NZ road on which traffic travelling in opposite directions is separated by a central strip of grass or concrete.

dub¹ v **dubbing**, **dubbed** give (a person or place) a name or nickname.

dub² v **dubbing**, **dubbed** **1** provide (a film) with a new soundtrack, esp. in a different language. **2** provide (a film or tape) with a soundtrack. ▷ n **3** style of reggae record production involving exaggeration of instrumental parts, echo, etc.

dubious ❶ [dew-bee-uss] adj feeling or causing doubt. **dubiety** [dew-**by**-it-ee] n.

duchess n **1** woman who holds the rank of duke. **2** wife or widow of a duke.

duck¹ n **1** water bird with short legs, webbed feet, and a broad blunt bill. **2** its

d

3 = **dose**, administer a drug, anaesthetize, deaden, dope (sl), knock out, medicate, numb, poison, stupefy, treat

drum v **4** = **beat**, pulsate, rap, reverberate, tap, tattoo, throb **drum into** v = **drive home**, din into, hammer away, harp on, instil into, reiterate

drunk adj **2** = **intoxicated**, drunken, inebriated, legless (inf), merry (Brit inf), plastered (sl), tipsy, under the influence (inf) ▷ n **4** = **drunkard**, alcoholic, boozer (inf), inebriate, lush (sl), wino (inf)

dry adj **1** = **dehydrated**, arid, barren,

desiccated, dried up, parched, thirsty **5** = **dull**, boring, dreary, monotonous, plain, tedious, tiresome, uninteresting **6** = **sarcastic**, deadpan, droll, low-key, sly ▷ v **8** = **dehydrate**, dehumidify, desiccate, drain, make dry, parch, sear

dual adj = **twofold**, binary, double, duplex, duplicate, matched, paired, twin

dubious adj **a** = **unsure**, doubtful, hesitant, sceptical, uncertain, unconvinced, undecided, wavering **b** = **suspect**, fishy (inf), questionable, suspicious, unreliable, untrustworthy

d

flesh, used as food. **3** female of this bird.
4 *Cricket* score of nothing. **duckling**
n baby duck. **duck-billed platypus** or
duckbill see PLATYPUS.

duck² ❷ v **1** move (the head or body)
quickly downwards, to avoid being seen
or to dodge a blow. **2** plunge suddenly
under water. **3** *informal* dodge (a duty or
responsibility).

duct n **1** tube, pipe, or channel through
which liquid or gas is conveyed. **2** bodily
passage conveying secretions or
excretions.

dud ❶ *informal* ▷ n **1** ineffectual person or
thing. ▷ *adj* **2** bad or useless.

due ❶ *adj* **1** expected or scheduled to
be present or arrive. **2** owed as a debt.
3 fitting, proper. ▷ n **4** something that
is owed or required. ▷ *pl* **5** charges for
membership of a club or organization.
▷ *adv* **6** directly or exactly, e.g. *due south*.
due to attributable to or caused by.

duel ❶ n **1** formal fight with deadly
weapons between two people, to settle a
quarrel. ▷ v **duelling**, **duelled 2** fight in a
duel. **duellist** n.

duet n piece of music for two performers.

duffel, duffle n short for DUFFEL COAT.

duffel bag cylindrical canvas bag
fastened with a drawstring. **duffel coat**
wool coat with toggle fastenings, usu.
with a hood.

duffer n *informal* dull or incompetent
person.

dugite [doo-gyte] n medium-sized
Australian venomous snake.

dugout n **1** (at a sports ground) covered
bench where managers and substitutes
sit. **2** canoe made by hollowing out a
log. **3** *Mil* covered excavation to provide
shelter.

duke n **1** nobleman of the highest rank.
2 prince or ruler of a small principality or
duchy. **dukedom** n.

dulcet [dull-sit] *adj* (of a sound) soothing
or pleasant.

dulcimer n tuned percussion instrument
consisting of a set of strings stretched
over a sounding board and struck with
hammers.

dull ❶ *adj* **1** not interesting. **2** (of an ache)
not acute. **3** (of weather) not bright
or clear. **4** lacking in spirit. **5** not very
intelligent. **6** (of a blade) not sharp. ▷ v
7 make or become dull. **dullness** n **dully**
adv **dullard** n dull or stupid person.

———————————————————————————— THESAURUS ————————

duck² v **1** = **bob**, bend, bow, crouch, dodge,
drop, lower, stoop **2** = **plunge**, dip, dive,
douse, dunk, immerse, souse, submerge,
wet **3** *Inf* = **dodge**, avoid, escape, evade,
shirk, shun, sidestep

dud *Inf* n **1** = **failure**, flop (*inf*), washout (*inf*)
▷ *adj* **2** = **useless**, broken, duff (*Brit inf*),
failed, inoperative, worthless

due *adj* **1** = **expected**, scheduled
2 = **payable**, in arrears, outstanding,
owed, owing, unpaid **3** = **fitting**,
appropriate, deserved, justified, merited,
proper, rightful, suitable, well-earned ▷ n
4 = **right(s)**, comeuppance (*sl*), deserts,
merits, privilege ▷ *pl* **5** = **membership fee**,
charge, charges, contribution, fee, levy
▷ *adv* **6** = **directly**, dead, exactly, straight,
undeviatingly

duel n **1** = **fight**, affair of honour, clash,
competition, contest, encounter,
engagement, head-to-head, single
combat ▷ v **2** = **fight**, clash, compete,
contend, contest, lock horns, rival,
struggle, vie with

dull *adj* **1** = **boring**, dreary, flat,
humdrum, monotonous, plain, run-
of-the-mill, tedious, uninteresting
3 = **cloudy**, dim, dismal, gloomy,
leaden, overcast **4** = **lifeless**, apathetic,
blank, indifferent, listless, passionless,
unresponsive **5** = **stupid**, dense,
dim-witted (*inf*), dozy (*Brit inf*), slow,
thick, unintelligent **6** = **blunt**, blunted,
unsharpened ▷ v **7** = **relieve**, allay,
alleviate, blunt, lessen, moderate,
soften, take the edge off

dumb ❶ adj **1** lacking the power to speak. **2** silent. **3** informal stupid. **dumbly** adv **dumbness** n **dumbbell** n short bar with a heavy ball or disc at each end, used for physical exercise. **dumbfounded** adj speechless with astonishment. **dumb show** meaningful gestures without speech.

dummy ❶ n, pl **-mies 1** figure representing the human form, used for displaying clothes etc. **2** copy of an object, often lacking some essential feature of the original. **3** rubber teat for a baby to suck. **4** slang stupid person. ▷ adj **5** imitation, substitute. **dummy run** rehearsal.

dump ❶ v **1** drop or let fall in a careless manner. **2** informal get rid of (someone or something no longer wanted). ▷ n **3** place where waste materials are left. **4** informal dirty unattractive place. **5** Mil place where weapons or supplies are stored. **down in the dumps** informal depressed and miserable.

dunce ❶ n person who is stupid or slow to learn.

dune n mound or ridge of drifted sand.

dung n faeces from animals such as cattle.

dungarees pl n trousers with a bib attached.

dungeon ❶ n underground prison cell.

dunk v **1** dip (a biscuit or bread) in a drink or soup before eating it. **2** put (something) in liquid.

duo n, pl **duos 1** pair of performers. **2** informal pair of closely connected people.

duodenum [dew-oh-**deen**-um] n, pl **-na**, **-nums** first part of the small intestine, just below the stomach. **duodenal** adj.

dupe v **1** deceive or cheat. ▷ n **2** person who is easily deceived.

duplicate ❶ adj **1** copied exactly from an original. ▷ n **2** exact copy. ▷ v **3** make an exact copy of. **4** do again (something that has already been done). **duplication** n **duplicator** n.

durable ❶ adj long-lasting. **durability** n.

duration ❶ n length of time that something lasts.

duress ❶ n compulsion by use of force or threats.

———————————— THESAURUS ————————————

dumb adj **1, 2 = mute**, mum, silent, soundless, speechless, tongue-tied, voiceless, wordless **3** Inf = **stupid**, asinine, dense, dim-witted (inf), dull, foolish, thick, unintelligent

dummy n **1 = model**, figure, form, manikin, mannequin **2 = copy**, counterfeit, duplicate, imitation, sham, substitute **4** Sl = **fool**, blockhead, dunce, idiot, nitwit (inf), numbskull or numskull, oaf, simpleton ▷ adj **5 = imitation**, artificial, bogus, fake, false, mock, phoney or phony (inf), sham, simulated

dump v **1 = drop**, deposit, fling down, let fall, throw down **2** Inf = **get rid of**, dispose of, ditch (sl), empty out, jettison, scrap, throw away or out, tip, unload ▷ n **3 = rubbish tip**, junkyard, refuse heap, rubbish heap, tip **4** Inf = **pigsty**, hole (inf), hovel, mess, slum

dunce n = **simpleton**, blockhead, duffer (inf), dunderhead, ignoramus, moron, nincompoop, numbskull or numskull, thickhead

dungeon n = **prison**, cage, cell, oubliette, vault

duplicate adj **1 = identical**, corresponding, matched, matching, twin, twofold ▷ n **2 = copy**, carbon copy, clone, double, facsimile, photocopy, replica, reproduction ▷ v **3 = copy**, clone, double, replicate, reproduce **4 = repeat**

durable adj = **long-lasting**, dependable, enduring, hard-wearing, persistent, reliable, resistant, strong, sturdy, tough

duration n = **length**, extent, period, span, spell, stretch, term, time

duress n = **pressure**, coercion, compulsion, constraint, threat

during *prep* throughout or within the limit of (a period of time).

dusk ❶ *n* time just before nightfall, when it is almost dark. **dusky** *adj* 1 dark in colour. 2 shadowy.

dust ❶ *n* 1 small dry particles of earth, sand, or dirt. ▷ *v* 2 remove dust from (furniture) by wiping. 3 sprinkle (something) with a powdery substance. **duster** *n* cloth used for dusting. **dusty** *adj* covered with dust. **dustbin** *n* large container for household rubbish. **dust bowl** dry area in which the surface soil is exposed to wind erosion. **dust jacket** removable paper cover used to protect a book. **dustman** *n* Brit man whose job is to collect household rubbish. **dustpan** *n* short-handled shovel into which dust is swept from floors.

Dutch *adj* of the Netherlands. **go Dutch** *informal* share the expenses on an outing. **Dutch courage** false courage gained from drinking alcohol.

duty ❶ *n, pl* **-ties** 1 work or a task performed as part of one's job. 2 task that a person feels morally bound to do. 3 government tax on imports. **on duty** at work. **dutiful** *adj* doing what is expected. **dutifully** *adv*.

duvet [**doo**-vay] *n* kind of quilt used in bed instead of a top sheet and blankets.

DVT deep-vein thrombosis.

dwarf ❶ *n, pl* **dwarfs**, **dwarves** 1 person who is smaller than average. 2 (in folklore) small ugly manlike creature, often possessing magical powers. ▷ *adj* 3 (of an animal or plant) much smaller than the usual size for the species. ▷ *v* 4 cause (someone or something) to seem small by being much larger.

dwell ❶ *v* **dwelling**, **dwelt** *or* **dwelled** live, reside. **dwelling** *n* place of residence. **dwell on**, **upon** *v* think, speak, or write at length about.

dwindle ❶ *v* grow less in size, strength, or number.

dye ❶ *n* 1 colouring substance. 2 colour produced by dyeing. ▷ *v* **dyeing**, **dyed** 3 colour (hair or fabric) by applying a dye. **dyer** *n* **dyed-in-the-wool** *adj* uncompromising or unchanging in opinion.

dyke *n* wall built to prevent flooding.

dynamic ❶ *adj* full of energy, ambition, and new ideas.

dynamics *n* 1 branch of mechanics concerned with the forces that change or produce the motions of bodies. ▷ *pl* 2 forces that produce change in a system.

dynamite *n* 1 explosive made of nitroglycerine. 2 *informal* dangerous or exciting person or thing. ▷ *v* 3 blow (something) up with dynamite.

dynamo *n, pl* **-mos** device for converting mechanical energy into electrical energy.

——————————————————————— THESAURUS ———————————

dusk *n* = **twilight**, dark, evening, eventide, gloaming (*Scot or poet*), nightfall, sundown, sunset

dust *n* 1 = **grime**, grit, particles, powder ▷ *v* 3 = **sprinkle**, cover, dredge, powder, scatter, sift, spray, spread

duty *n* 1 = **responsibility**, assignment, function, job, obligation, role, task, work, yakka (*Aust & NZ inf*) 2 = **loyalty**, allegiance, deference, obedience, respect, reverence 3 = **tax**, excise, levy, tariff, toll **on duty** = **at work**, busy, engaged, on active service

dwarf *n* 1 = **midget**, Lilliputian, pygmy or pigmy, Tom Thumb ▷ *adj* 3 = **miniature**, baby, bonsai, diminutive, small, tiny, undersized ▷ *v* 4 = **tower above** *or* **over**, diminish, dominate, overshadow

dwell *v* = **live**, abide, inhabit, lodge, reside

dwindle *v* = **lessen**, decline, decrease, die away, diminish, fade, peter out, shrink, subside, taper off, wane

dye *n* 1 = **colouring**, colorant, colour, pigment, stain, tinge, tint ▷ *v* 3 = **colour**, pigment, stain, tinge, tint

dynamic *adj* = **energetic**, forceful,

dynasty ❶ *n, pl* **-ties** sequence of
hereditary rulers. **dynastic** *adj*.

dysentery *n* infection of the intestine
causing severe diarrhoea.

dysfunction *n Med* disturbance or
abnormality in the function of an organ or
part. **dysfunctional** *adj*.

dyslexia *n* disorder causing impaired ability
to read. **dyslexic** *adj*.

dyspepsia *n* indigestion. **dyspeptic** *adj*.

dystrophy [**diss**-trof-fee] *n* see MUSCULAR
DYSTROPHY.

—— THESAURUS ——

go-ahead, go-getting (*inf*), high-
powered, lively, powerful, storming (*inf*),
vital

dynasty *n* = **empire**, government, house,
regime, rule, sovereignty

Ee

E East(ern).

e- *prefix* electronic, e.g. *e-mail*.

each ❶ *adj, pron* every (one) taken separately.

eager ❶ *adj* showing or feeling great desire, keen. **eagerly** *adv* **eagerness** *n*.

eagle *n* **1** large bird of prey with keen eyesight. **2** *Golf* score of two strokes under par for a hole.

ear¹ ❶ *n* **1** organ of hearing, esp. the external part of it. **2** sensitivity to musical or other sounds. **earbash** *v Aust & NZ informal* talk incessantly. **eardrum** *n* thin piece of skin inside the ear which enables one to hear sounds. **earmark** *v* **1** set (something) aside for a specific purpose. **earphone** *n* receiver for a radio etc., held to or put in the ear. **earring** *n* ornament for the lobe of the ear. **earshot** *n* hearing range.

ear² *n* head of corn.

earl *n* British nobleman ranking next below a marquess. **earldom** *n*.

early ❶ *adj, adv* **-lier, -liest 1** before the expected or usual time. **2** in the first part of a period. **3** in a period far back in time.

earn ❶ *v* **1** obtain by work or merit. **2** (of investments etc.) gain (interest). **earnings** *pl n* money earned.

earnest ❶ *adj* serious and sincere. **in earnest** seriously. **earnestly** *adv*.

earth ❶ *n* **1** planet that we live on. **2** land, the ground. **3** soil. **4** fox's hole. **5** wire connecting an electrical apparatus with the earth. ▷ *v* **6** connect (a circuit) to earth. **earthen** *adj* made of baked clay or earth. **earthenware** *n* pottery made of baked clay. **earthly** *adj* conceivable or possible. **earthy** *adj* **1** coarse or crude. **2** of or like earth. **earthquake** *n* violent vibration of the earth's surface. **earthwork** *n* fortification made of earth. **earthworm** *n* worm which burrows in the soil.

ease ❶ *n* **1** freedom from difficulty, discomfort, or worry. **2** rest or leisure. ▷ *v* **3** give bodily or mental ease to. **4** lessen (severity, tension, pain, etc.). **5** move carefully or gradually.

easel *n* frame to support an artist's canvas or a blackboard.

━━━━━━━━━━━━━━━━━━━━━━━ THESAURUS ━━━━━━

each *adj* = **every** ▷ *pron* = **every one**, each and every one, each one, one and all

eager *adj* = **keen**, agog, anxious, athirst, avid, enthusiastic, fervent, hungry, impatient, longing

ear¹ *n* **2** = **sensitivity**, appreciation, discrimination, taste

early *adj* **1** = **premature**, advanced, forward, untimely **3** = **primitive**, primeval, primordial, undeveloped, young ▷ *adv* **1** = **too soon**, ahead of time, beforehand, in advance, in good time, prematurely

earn *v* **1** = **deserve**, acquire, attain, be entitled to, be worthy of, merit, rate, warrant, win **2** = **make**, bring in, collect, gain, get, gross, net, receive

earnest *adj* = **serious**, grave, intent, resolute, resolved, sincere, solemn, thoughtful **in earnest** = **in seriousness**, in sincerity, in truth

earth *n* **1** = **world**, globe, orb, planet, sphere **2, 3** = **soil**, clay, dirt, ground, land, turf

ease *n* **1 a** = **effortlessness**, easiness, facility, readiness, simplicity **b** = **peace of mind**, comfort, content, happiness, peace, quiet, serenity, tranquillity **2** = **leisure**, relaxation, repose, rest, restfulness ▷ *v* **3** = **comfort**, calm, outspan (*S Afr*), relax, soothe **4** = **relieve**, alleviate, lessen, lighten, soothe **5** = **move carefully**, edge, inch, manoeuvre, slide, slip

east n 1 (direction towards) the part of the horizon where the sun rises. 2 region lying in this direction. ▷ adj 3 to or in the east. 4 (of a wind) from the east. ▷ adv 5 in, to, or towards the east. **easterly** adj **eastern** adj **eastward** adj, adv **eastwards** adv.

Easter n Christian spring festival commemorating the Resurrection of Jesus Christ. **Easter egg** chocolate egg given at Easter.

easy ❶ adj **easier**, **easiest** 1 not needing much work or effort. 2 free from pain, care, or anxiety. 3 easy-going. **easily** adv **easiness** n **easy chair** comfortable armchair. **easy-going** adj relaxed in attitude, tolerant.

eat ❶ v **eating**, **ate**, **eaten** 1 take (food) into the mouth and swallow it. 2 have a meal. 3 (foll. by away or up) destroy. **eatable** adj fit or suitable for eating.

eau de Cologne [**oh** de kol-**lone**] n French light perfume.

eaves pl n overhanging edges of a roof.

ebb ❶ v 1 (of tide water) flow back. 2 fall away or decline. ▷ n 3 flowing back of the

tide. **at a low ebb** in a state of weakness.

ebony n, pl **-onies** 1 hard black wood. ▷ adj 2 deep black.

e-book, ebook n a book in electronic form.

ebullient adj full of enthusiasm or excitement. **ebullience** n.

eccentric ❶ adj 1 odd or unconventional. 2 (of circles) not having the same centre. ▷ n 3 eccentric person. **eccentricity** n.

echo ❶ n, pl **-oes** 1 repetition of sounds by reflection of sound waves off a surface. 2 close imitation. ▷ v **-oing**, **-oed** 3 repeat or be repeated as an echo. 4 imitate (what someone else has said).

éclair n finger-shaped pastry filled with cream and covered with chocolate.

eclectic adj selecting from various styles, ideas, or sources. **eclecticism** n.

eclipse ❶ n 1 temporary obscuring of one star or planet by another. ▷ v 2 surpass or outclass. **ecliptic** n apparent path of the sun.

economy ❶ n, pl **-mies** 1 system of interrelationship of money, industry, and employment in a country. 2 careful

easy adj 1 = **not difficult**, a piece of cake (inf), child's play (inf), effortless, no trouble, painless, plain sailing, simple, straightforward, uncomplicated, undemanding 2 = **carefree**, comfortable, cushy (inf), leisurely, peaceful, quiet, relaxed, serene, tranquil, untroubled 3 = **tolerant**, easy-going, indulgent, lenient, mild, permissive, unoppressive

eat v 1 = **consume**, chew, devour, gobble, ingest, munch, scoff (sl), swallow 2 = **have a meal**, dine, feed, take nourishment 3 (foll. by away or up) = **destroy**, corrode, decay, dissolve, erode, rot, waste away, wear away

ebb v 1 = **flow back**, go out, recede, retire, retreat, subside, wane, withdraw 2 = **decline**, decrease, diminish, dwindle, fade away, fall away, flag, lessen, peter out ▷ n 3 = **flowing back**, going out, low tide, low water, retreat, subsidence,

wane, withdrawal

eccentric adj 1 = **odd**, freakish, idiosyncratic, irregular, munted (NZ sl), outlandish, peculiar, quirky, strange, unconventional ▷ n 3 = **crank** (inf), character (inf), nonconformist, oddball (inf), weirdo or weirdie (inf)

echo n 1 = **repetition**, answer, reverberation 2 = **copy**, imitation, mirror image, parallel, reflection, reiteration, reproduction ▷ v 3 = **repeat**, resound, reverberate 4 = **copy**, ape, imitate, mirror, parallel, recall, reflect, resemble

eclipse n 1 = **obscuring**, darkening, dimming, extinction, shading ▷ v 2 = **surpass**, exceed, excel, outdo, outshine, put in the shade (inf), transcend

economy n 2 = **thrift**, frugality, husbandry, parsimony, prudence, restraint

use of money or resources to avoid waste. **economic** *adj* **1** of economics. **2** profitable. **3** *informal* inexpensive or cheap. **economics** *n* **1** social science concerned with the production and consumption of goods and services. ▷ *pl* **2** financial aspects. **economical** *adj* not wasteful, thrifty. **economist** *n* specialist in economics. **economize** *v* reduce expense or waste.

ecstasy ⊙ *n* state of intense delight. **ecstatic** *adj*.

- ● **SPELLING TIP**
- ● People get confused about how many *cs*
- ● there are in **ecstasy**. The Bank of English
- ● has 119 occurrences of *ecstacy*, but 3379 of
- ● the correct spelling **ecstasy**.

eczema [**ek**-sim-a] *n* skin disease causing intense itching.

eddy ⊙ *n, pl* **eddies 1** circular movement of air, water, etc. ▷ *v* **eddying, eddied 2** move with a circular motion.

edge ⊙ *n* **1** border or line where something ends or begins. **2** cutting side of a blade. **3** sharpness of tone. ▷ *v* **4** provide an edge or border for. **5** push (one's way) gradually. **have the edge on** have an advantage over. **on edge** nervous or irritable.

edgeways *adv* with the edge forwards or uppermost. **edging** *n* anything placed along an edge to finish it. **edgy** *adj* nervous or irritable.

edible ⊙ *adj* fit to be eaten.

edict ⊙ [**ee**-dikt] *n* order issued by an authority.

edifice ⊙ [**ed**-if-iss] *n* large building.

edify ⊙ [**ed**-if-fie] *v* **-fying, -fied** improve morally by instruction. **edification** *n*.

edit ⊙ *v* prepare (a book, film, etc.) for publication or broadcast. **edition** *n* number of copies of a new publication printed at one time. **editor** *n* **1** person who edits. **2** person in charge of one section of a newspaper or magazine. **editorial** *n* **1** newspaper article stating the opinion of the editor. ▷ *adj* **2** of editing or editors.

educate ⊙ *v* **1** teach. **2** provide schooling for. **education** *n* **educational** *adj* **educationalist** *n* expert in the theory of education. **educative** *adj* educating.

eel *n* snakelike fish.

eerie ⊙ *adj* **eerier, eeriest** uncannily frightening or disturbing. **eerily** *adv*.

efface ⊙ *v* **1** remove by rubbing. **2** make (oneself) inconspicuous. **effacement** *n*.

—————————— THESAURUS ——————————

ecstasy *n* = **rapture**, bliss, delight, elation, euphoria, fervour, joy, seventh heaven

eddy *n* **1** = **swirl**, counter-current, undertow, vortex, whirlpool ▷ *v* **2** = **swirl**, whirl

edge *n* **1** = **border**, boundary, brink, fringe, limit, outline, perimeter, rim, side, verge ▷ *v* **4** = **border**, fringe, hem **5** = **inch**, creep, ease, sidle, steal **have the edge on** = **have the advantage over**, have ascendancy over, have dominance over, have superiority over, have the upper hand over **on edge** = **nervous**, apprehensive, edgy, ill at ease, impatient, irritable, keyed up, on tenterhooks, tense, wired (*sl*)

edible *adj* = **eatable**, digestible, fit to eat, good, harmless, palatable, wholesome

edict *n* = **decree**, act, command, injunction, law, order, proclamation, ruling

edifice *n* = **building**, construction, erection, house, structure

edify *v* = **instruct**, educate, enlighten, guide, improve, inform, nurture, school, teach

edit *v* = **revise**, adapt, condense, correct, emend, polish, rewrite

educate *v* **1** = **teach**, discipline, enlighten, improve, inform, instruct, school, train, tutor

eerie *adj* = **frightening**, creepy (*inf*), ghostly, mysterious, scary (*inf*), spooky (*inf*), strange, uncanny, unearthly, weird

efface *v* **1** = **obliterate**, blot out, cancel, delete, destroy, eradicate, erase, rub out, wipe out

effect ❶ *n* **1** change or result caused by someone or something. **2** condition of being operative, e.g. *the law comes into effect next month*. **3** overall impression. ▷ *pl* **4** personal belongings. **5** lighting, sounds, etc. to accompany a film or a broadcast. ▷ *v* **6** cause to happen, accomplish. **effective** *adj* **1** producing a desired result. **2** operative. **effectively** *adv* **effectual** *adj* producing the intended result. **effectually** *adv*.

effeminate ❶ *adj* (of a man) displaying characteristics thought to be typical of a woman. **effeminacy** *n*.

efficient ❶ *adj* functioning effectively with little waste of effort. **efficiently** *adv* **efficiency** *n*.

effigy ❶ [ef-fij-ee] *n*, *pl* **-gies** image or likeness of a person.

effluent ❶ *n* liquid discharged as waste.

effort ❶ *n* **1** physical or mental exertion. **2** attempt. **effortless** *adj*.

effrontery ❶ *n* brazen impudence.

e.g. for example.

egalitarian *adj* **1** upholding the equality of all people. ▷ *n* **2** person who holds egalitarian beliefs. **egalitarianism** *n*.

egg¹ *n* **1** oval or round object laid by the females of birds and other creatures, containing a developing embryo. **2** hen's egg used as food. **3** (also **egg cell**) ovum. **egghead** *n informal* intellectual person. **eggplant** *n US, Canad, & Aust* aubergine.

egg² ❶ *v* **egg on** encourage or incite, esp. to do wrong.

ego *n*, *pl* **egos** **1** the conscious mind of an individual. **2** self-esteem. **egoism**, **egotism** *n* **1** excessive concern for one's own interests. **2** excessively high opinion of oneself. **egotist**, **egoist** *n* **egotistic**, **egoistic** *adj* **egocentric** *adj* self-centred.

egregious [ig-**greej**-uss] *adj* outstandingly bad.

eider *n* Arctic duck. **eiderdown** *n* quilt (orig. stuffed with eider feathers).

eight *adj*, *n* **1** one more than seven. ▷ *n* **2** eight-oared boat. **3** its crew. **eighth** *adj*, *n* (of) number eight in a series. **eighteen** *adj*, *n* eight and ten. **eighteenth** *adj*, *n* **eighty** *adj*, *n* eight times ten. **eightieth** *adj*, *n*.

either *adj*, *pron* **1** one or the other (of two). **2** each of two. ▷ *conj* **3** used preceding two or more possibilities joined by *or*. ▷ *adv* **4** likewise, e.g. *I don't eat meat and he doesn't either*.

ejaculate *v* **1** eject (semen). **2** utter abruptly. **ejaculation** *n*.

effect *n* **1** = **result**, conclusion, consequence, end result, event, outcome, upshot **2** = **operation**, action, enforcement, execution, force, implementation **3** = **impression**, essence, impact, sense, significance, tenor ▷ *pl* **4** = **belongings**, gear, goods, paraphernalia, possessions, property, things ▷ *v* **6** = **bring about**, accomplish, achieve, complete, execute, fulfil, perform, produce

effeminate *adj* = **womanly**, camp (*inf*), feminine, sissy, soft, tender, unmanly, weak, womanish

efficient *adj* = **competent**, businesslike, capable, economic, effective, organized, productive, proficient, well-organized, workmanlike

effigy *n* = **likeness**, dummy, figure, guy, icon, idol, image, picture, portrait, representation, statue

effluent *n* = **waste**, effluvium, pollutant, sewage

effort *n* **1** = **exertion**, application, elbow grease (*facetious*), endeavour, energy, pains, struggle, toil, trouble, work, yakka (*Aust & NZ inf*) **2** = **attempt**, endeavour, essay, go (*inf*), shot (*inf*), stab (*inf*), try

effrontery *n* = **insolence**, arrogance, audacity, brazenness, cheek (*inf*), impertinence, impudence, nerve, presumption, temerity

egg² *v* **egg on** = **encourage**, exhort, goad, incite, prod, prompt, push, spur, urge

e

eject ❶ v force out, expel. **ejection** n **ejector** n.

eke out ❶ v 1 make (a supply) last by frugal use. 2 make (a living) with difficulty.

elaborate ❶ adj 1 with a lot of fine detail. ▷ v 2 expand upon. **elaboration** n.

élan [ale-**an**] n style and vigour.

elapse ❶ v (of time) pass by.

elastic ❶ adj 1 capable of resuming normal shape after distortion. 2 adapting easily to change. ▷ n 3 tape or fabric containing interwoven strands of flexible rubber. **elasticity** n.

elbow ❶ n 1 joint between the upper arm and the forearm. ▷ v 2 shove or strike with the elbow. **elbow grease** vigorous physical labour. **elbow room** sufficient room to move freely.

elder¹ ❶ adj 1 older. ▷ n 2 older person. 3 (in certain Protestant Churches) lay officer. **elderly** adj (fairly) old. **eldest** adj oldest.

elder² n small tree with white flowers and black berries.

elect ❶ v 1 choose by voting. 2 decide (to do something). ▷ adj 3 appointed but not yet in office, e.g. president elect. **election** n 1 choosing of representatives by voting. 2 act of choosing. **electioneering** n active participation in an electoral campaign. **elective** adj 1 chosen by election. 2 optional. **elector** n someone who has the right to vote in an election. **electoral** adj **electorate** n people who have the right to vote.

electricity n 1 form of energy associated with stationary or moving electrons or other charged particles. 2 electric current or charge. **electric** adj 1 produced by, transmitting, or powered by electricity. 2 exciting or tense. **electrical** adj using or concerning electricity. **electrician** n person trained to install and repair electrical equipment. **electrics** pl n electric appliances. **electric chair** US chair in which criminals who have been sentenced to death are electrocuted.

electro- combining form operated by or caused by electricity.

electrocute v kill or injure by electricity. **electrocution** n.

electrode n conductor through which an electric current enters or leaves a battery, vacuum tube, etc.

electron n elementary particle in all atoms that have a negative electrical charge. **electron microscope** microscope that uses electrons, rather than light, to produce a magnified image.

electronic adj 1 (of a device) dependent on the action of electrons. 2 (of a process) using electronic devices.

elegant ❶ adj pleasing or graceful in dress, style, or design. **elegance** n.

elegy [**el**-lij-ee] n, pl **-gies** mournful poem, esp. a lament for the dead. **elegiac** adj mournful or plaintive.

━━━━━━━━━━━━━━━━━━━━━━ THESAURUS ━━━━━━━━

eject v = **throw out**, banish, drive out, evict, expel, oust, remove, turn out

eke out v 1 = **be sparing with**, economize on, husband, stretch out

elaborate adj 1 = **detailed**, complex, complicated, intricate, involved ▷ v 2 = **expand (upon)**, add detail, amplify, develop, embellish, enlarge, flesh out

elapse v = **pass**, glide by, go by, lapse, roll by, slip away

elastic adj 1 = **flexible**, plastic, pliable, pliant, resilient, rubbery, springy, stretchy, supple, tensile 2 = **adaptable**,

accommodating, adjustable, compliant, flexible, supple, tolerant, variable, yielding

elbow n 1 = **joint**, angle ▷ v 2 = **push**, jostle, knock, nudge, shove

elder¹ adj 1 = **older**, first-born, senior ▷ n 2 = **older person**, senior

elect v 1 = **choose**, appoint, determine, opt for, pick, prefer, select, settle on, vote

elegant adj = **stylish**, chic, delicate, exquisite, fine, graceful, handsome, polished, refined, tasteful

element ❶ *n* **1** component part.
2 substance which cannot be separated
into other substances by ordinary
chemical techniques. **3** section of people
within a larger group, e.g. *the rowdy
element*. **4** heating wire in an electric
kettle, stove, etc. ▷ *pl* **5** basic principles
of something. **6** weather conditions, esp.
wind, rain, and cold. **in one's element**
in a situation where one is happiest.
elemental *adj* of primitive natural forces
or passions. **elementary** *adj* simple and
straightforward.

elephant *n* huge four-footed thick-skinned
animal with ivory tusks and a long trunk.
elephantine *adj* unwieldy, clumsy.

elevate ❶ *v* **1** raise in rank or status. **2** lift
up. **elevation** *n* **1** raising. **2** height above
sea level. **3** scale drawing of one side of a
building. **elevator** *n Aust, US & Canad* lift
for carrying people.

eleven *adj, n* **1** one more than ten. ▷ *n*
2 *Sport* team of eleven people. **eleventh**
adj, n (of) number eleven in a series.
elevenses *n informal* mid-morning snack.

elf *n, pl* **elves** (in folklore) small mischievous
fairy. **elfin** *adj* small and delicate.

elicit ❶ *v* **1** bring about (a response or

reaction). **2** find out (information) by
careful questioning.

eligible ❶ *adj* **1** meeting the requirements
or qualifications needed. **2** desirable as a
spouse. **eligibility** *n*.

eliminate ❶ *v* get rid of. **elimination** *n*.

elite ❶ [ill-**eet**] *n* most powerful, rich, or
gifted members of a group. **elitism** *n* belief
that society should be governed by a small
group of superior people. **elitist** *n, adj*.

elixir ❶ [ill-**ix**-er] *n* imaginary liquid that
can prolong life or turn base metals
into gold.

elk *n* large deer of N Europe and Asia.

ellipse *n* oval shape. **elliptical** *adj* **1** oval-
shaped. **2** (of speech or writing) obscure or
ambiguous.

elm *n* tree with serrated leaves.

elocution ❶ *n* art of speaking clearly in
public.

elongate ❶ [**eel**-long-gate] *v* make or
become longer. **elongation** *n*.

elope ❶ *v* (of two people) run away secretly
to get married. **elopement** *n*.

eloquence ❶ *n* fluent powerful use of
language. **eloquent** *adj* **eloquently** *adv*.

else *adv* **1** in addition or more, e.g. *what
else can I do?* **2** other or different, e.g. *it*

THESAURUS

---

element *n* **1** = **component**, constituent,
factor, ingredient, part, section,
subdivision, unit ▷ *pl* **5** = **basics**,
essentials, foundations, fundamentals,
nuts and bolts (*inf*), principles, rudiments
6 = **weather conditions**, atmospheric
conditions, powers of nature

elevate *v* **1** = **promote**, advance,
aggrandize, exalt, prefer, upgrade
2 = **raise**, heighten, hoist, lift, lift up, uplift

elicit *v* **1** = **bring about**, bring forth, bring
out, bring to light, call forth, cause, derive,
evolve, give rise to **2** = **obtain**, draw out,
evoke, exact, extort, extract, wrest

eligible *adj* **1** = **qualified**, acceptable,
appropriate, desirable, fit, preferable,
proper, suitable, worthy

eliminate *v* = **get rid of**, cut out, dispose

of, do away with, eradicate, exterminate,
remove, stamp out, take out

elite *n* = **best**, aristocracy, cream, flower,
nobility, pick, upper class

elixir *n* = **panacea**, nostrum

elocution *n* = **diction**, articulation,
declamation, delivery, enunciation,
oratory, pronunciation, speech,
speechmaking

elongate *v* = **make longer**, draw out,
extend, lengthen, prolong, protract,
stretch

elope *v* = **run away**, abscond, bolt,
decamp, disappear, escape, leave, run off,
slip away, steal away

eloquence *n* = **expressiveness**,
expression, fluency, forcefulness, oratory,
persuasiveness, rhetoric, way with words

was unlike anything else that had happened.
elsewhere *adv* in or to another place.

elucidate ❶ *v* make (something difficult) clear. **elucidation** *n*.

elude ❶ *v* 1 escape from by cleverness or quickness. 2 baffle. **elusive** *adj* difficult to catch or remember.

emaciated ❶ [im-**mace**-ee-ate-id] *adj* abnormally thin. **emaciation** *n*.

email *n* 1 short for electronic mail. ▷ *v* 2 to contact (a person) by email. 3 to send (a message, document, etc) by email.

emanate ❶ [**em**-a-nate] *v* issue, proceed from a source. **emanation** *n*.

emancipate ❶ *v* free from social, political, or legal restraints. **emancipation** *n*.

emasculate *v* deprive of power. **emasculation** *n*.

embalm ❶ *v* preserve (a corpse) from decay by the use of chemicals etc.

embankment *n* man-made ridge that carries a road or railway or holds back water.

embargo ❶ *n*, *pl* **-goes** 1 order by a government prohibiting trade with a country. ▷ *v* **-going, -goed** 2 put an embargo on.

embark ❶ *v* 1 board a ship or aircraft.

2 (foll. by *on*) begin (a new project). **embarkation** *n*.

embarrass ❶ *v* cause to feel self-conscious or ashamed. **embarrassed** *adj* **embarrassing** *adj* **embarrassment** *n*.

● **SPELLING TIP**
● There are 32 examples of the misspelling
● *embarras* in the Bank of English and
● another mistake, *embarassment*, occurs
● 64 times. Both these words should have
● two rs and two ss.

embassy *n*, *pl* **-sies** 1 offices or official residence of an ambassador. 2 ambassador and his staff.

embellish ❶ *v* 1 decorate. 2 embroider (a story). **embellishment** *n*.

ember *n* glowing piece of wood or coal in a dying fire.

embezzle ❶ *v* steal money that has been entrusted to one. **embezzlement** *n* **embezzler** *n*.

emblem ❶ *n* object or design that symbolizes a quality, type, or group. **emblematic** *adj*.

embody ❶ *v* **-bodying, -bodied** 1 be an example or expression of. 2 comprise, include. **embodiment** *n*.

--- THESAURUS ---

elucidate *v* = **clarify**, clear up, explain, explicate, expound, illuminate, illustrate, make plain, shed *or* throw light upon, spell out

elude *v* 1 = **escape**, avoid, dodge, duck (*inf*), evade, flee, get away from, outrun 2 = **baffle**, be beyond (someone), confound, escape, foil, frustrate, puzzle, stump, thwart

emaciated *adj* = **skeletal**, cadaverous, gaunt, haggard, lean, pinched, scrawny, thin, undernourished, wasted

emanate *v* = **flow**, arise, come forth, derive, emerge, issue, originate, proceed, spring, stem

emancipate *v* = **free**, deliver, liberate, release, set free, unchain, unfetter

embalm *v* = **preserve**, mummify

embargo *n* 1 = **ban**, bar, boycott, interdiction, prohibition, restraint,

restriction, stoppage ▷ *v* 2 = **ban**, bar, block, boycott, prohibit, restrict, stop

embark *v* 1 = **go aboard**, board ship, take ship 2 (foll. by *on*) = **begin**, commence, enter, launch, plunge into, set about, set out, start, take up

embarrass *v* = **shame**, discomfit, disconcert, distress, fluster, humiliate, mortify, show up (*inf*)

embellish *v* 1 = **decorate**, adorn, beautify, enhance, enrich, festoon, ornament 2 = **elaborate**, embroider

embezzle *v* = **misappropriate**, appropriate, filch, misuse, peculate, pilfer, purloin, rip off (*sl*), steal

emblem *n* = **symbol**, badge, crest, image, insignia, mark, sign, token

embody *v* 1 = **personify**, exemplify, manifest, represent, stand for, symbolize,

embolism n blocking of a blood vessel by a blood clot or air bubble.

embrace ❶ v 1 clasp in the arms, hug. 2 accept (an idea) eagerly. 3 comprise. ▷ n 4 act of embracing.

embrocation n lotion for rubbing into the skin to relieve pain.

embroider v 1 decorate with needlework. 2 make (a story) more interesting with fictitious detail. **embroidery** n.

embroil ❶ v involve (a person) in problems.

embryo ❶ [em-bree-oh] n, pl -bryos 1 unborn creature in the early stages of development. 2 something at an undeveloped stage. **embryonic** adj at an early stage. **embryology** n.

emend ❶ v remove errors from. **emendation** n.

emerald n 1 bright green precious stone. ▷ adj 2 bright green.

emerge ❶ v 1 come into view. 2 (foll. by from) come out of. 3 become known. **emergence** n **emergent** adj.

emergency ❶ n, pl -cies sudden unforeseen occurrence needing immediate action.

emery n hard, greyish-black mineral used for smoothing and polishing.

emigrate ❶ v go and settle in another country. **emigrant** n **emigration** n.

eminent ❶ adj distinguished, well-known. **eminently** adv **eminence** n 1 position of superiority or fame. 2 (E-) title of a cardinal.

emissary n, pl -saries agent sent on a mission by a government.

emit ❶ v **emitting**, **emitted** 1 give out (heat, light, or a smell). 2 utter. **emission** n.

emollient adj 1 softening, soothing. ▷ n 2 substance which softens or soothes the skin.

emoticon [i-mote-i-kon] n Computers symbol depicting a smile or other facial expression, used in email.

emotion ❶ n strong feeling. **emotional** adj readily affected by or appealing to the emotions. **emotionally** adv **emotive** adj tending to arouse emotion.

empathy n ability to understand someone else's feelings as if they were one's own.

emperor n ruler of an empire. **empress** n fem.

emphasis ❶ n, pl -ses 1 special importance or significance. 2 stress on a word or phrase in speech. **emphasize**

typify 2 = **incorporate**, collect, combine, comprise, contain, include

embrace v 1 = **hug**, clasp, cuddle, envelop, hold, seize, squeeze, take or hold in one's arms 2 = **accept**, adopt, espouse, seize, take on board, take up, welcome 3 = **include**, comprehend, comprise, contain, cover, encompass, involve, take in ▷ n 4 = **hug**, clasp, clinch (sl), cuddle, squeeze

embroil v = **involve**, enmesh, ensnare, entangle, implicate, incriminate, mire, mix up

embryo n 2 = **germ**, beginning, nucleus, root, rudiment

emend v = **revise**, amend, correct, edit, improve, rectify

emerge v 1 = **come into view**, appear, arise, come forth, surface 2 (foll. by from) = **issue**, emanate, rise, spring up 3 = **become apparent**, become known, come out, come out in the wash, come to light, crop up, transpire

emergency n = **crisis**, danger, difficulty, extremity, necessity, plight, predicament, quandary, scrape (inf)

emigrate v = **move abroad**, migrate, move

eminent adj = **prominent**, celebrated, distinguished, esteemed, famous, high-ranking, illustrious, noted, renowned, well-known

emit v 1 = **give off**, cast out, discharge, eject, emanate, exude, radiate, send out, transmit

emotion n = **feeling**, ardour, excitement, fervour, passion, sensation, sentiment, vehemence, warmth

emphasis n 1 = **importance**, accent, attention, force, priority, prominence, significance, stress, weight 2 = **stress**, accent

v **emphatic** *adj* showing emphasis. **emphatically** *adv*.

emphysema [em-fiss-**see**-ma] *n* condition in which the air sacs of the lungs are grossly enlarged, causing breathlessness.

empire ❶ *n* **1** group of territories under the rule of one state or person. **2** large organization that is directed by one person or group.

empirical ❶ *adj* relying on experiment or experience, not on theory. **empirically** *adv* **empiricism** *n* doctrine that all knowledge derives from experience.

emplacement *n* prepared position for a gun.

employ ❶ *v* **1** hire (a person). **2** provide work or occupation for. **3** use. ▷ *n* **4 in the employ of** doing regular paid work for. **employee** *n* **employer** *n* **employment** *n* **1** state of being employed. **2** work done by a person to earn money.

empower ❶ *v* enable, authorize.

empty ❶ *adj* **-tier, -tiest 1** containing nothing. **2** unoccupied. **3** without purpose or value. **4** (of words) insincere. ▷ *v* **-tying, -tied 5** make or become

empty. **empties** *pl n* empty boxes, bottles, etc. **emptiness** *n*.

emu *n* large Australian flightless bird with long legs.

emulate ❶ *v* attempt to equal or surpass by imitating. **emulation** *n*.

emulsion *n* **1** light-sensitive coating on photographic film. **2** type of water-based paint. ▷ *v* **3** paint with emulsion paint. **emulsify** *v* (of two liquids) join together or join (two liquids) together. **emulsifier** *n*.

enable *v* provide (a person) with the means, opportunity, or authority (to do something).

enact ❶ *v* **1** establish by law. **2** perform (a story or play) by acting. **enactment** *n*.

enamel *n* **1** glasslike coating applied to metal etc. to preserve the surface. **2** hard white coating on a tooth. ▷ *v* **-elling, -elled 3** cover with enamel.

encapsulate ❶ *v* **1** summarize. **2** enclose as in a capsule.

enchant ❶ *v* delight and fascinate. **enchantment** *n* **enchantress** *n fem*.

encircle *v* form a circle around. **encirclement** *n*.

enclave *n* part of a country entirely

——————— THESAURUS ———————

empire *n* **1** = **kingdom**, commonwealth, domain, realm

empirical *adj* = **first-hand**, experiential, experimental, observed, practical, pragmatic

employ *v* **1** = **hire**, commission, engage, enlist, retain, take on **2** = **keep busy**, engage, fill, make use of, occupy, take up, use up **3** = **use**, apply, bring to bear, exercise, exert, make use of, ply, put to use, utilize

empower *v* = **enable**, allow, authorize, commission, delegate, entitle, license, permit, qualify, sanction, warrant

empty *adj* **1, 2** = **bare**, blank, clear, deserted, desolate, hollow, unfurnished, uninhabited, unoccupied, vacant, void **3** = **purposeless**, banal, fruitless, futile, hollow, inane, meaningless, senseless,

vain, worthless **4** = **insincere**, cheap, hollow, idle ▷ *v* **5** = **evacuate**, clear, drain, exhaust, pour out, unload, vacate, void

emulate *v* = **imitate**, compete with, copy, echo, follow, mimic, rival

enable *v* = **allow**, authorize, empower, entitle, license, permit, qualify, sanction, warrant

enact *v* **1** = **establish**, authorize, command, decree, legislate, ordain, order, proclaim, sanction **2** = **perform**, act out, depict, play, play the part of, portray, represent

encapsulate *v* **1** = **sum up**, abridge, compress, condense, digest, epitomize, précis, summarize

enchant *v* = **fascinate**, beguile, bewitch, captivate, charm, delight, enrapture,

surrounded by foreign territory.

enclose ❶ v 1 surround completely.
2 include along with something else.
enclosure n.

encompass ❶ v 1 surround. 2 include
comprehensively.

encore interj 1 again, once more. ▷ n
2 extra performance due to enthusiastic
demand.

encounter ❶ v 1 meet unexpectedly. 2 be
faced with. ▷ n 3 unexpected meeting.
4 game or battle.

encourage ❶ v 1 inspire with confidence.
2 spur on. **encouragement** n.

encroach ❶ v intrude gradually on a
person's rights or land. **encroachment** n.

encrust v cover with a layer of something.

encumber ❶ v hinder or impede.
encumbrance n something that impedes
or is burdensome.

encyclopedia, encyclopaedia n book
or set of books containing facts about
many subjects, usu. in alphabetical order.
encyclopedic, encyclopaedic adj.

end ❶ n 1 furthest point or part. 2 limit.
3 last part of something. 4 fragment.
5 death or destruction. 6 purpose.
7 Sport either of the two defended areas
of a playing field. ▷ v 8 bring or come to a
finish. **make ends meet** have just enough
money for one's needs. **ending** n **endless**
adj endways.

endanger ❶ v put in danger.

endear v cause to be liked. **endearing**
adj **endearment** n affectionate word or
phrase.

endeavour ❶ v 1 try. ▷ n 2 effort.

endorse ❶ v 1 give approval to. 2 sign the
back of (a cheque). 3 record a conviction
on (a driving licence). **endorsement** n.

enthral, ravish

enclose v 1 = **surround**, bound, encase,
encircle, fence, hem in, shut in, wall in
2 = **send with**, include, insert, put in

encompass v 1 = **surround**, circle,
encircle, enclose, envelop, ring
2 = **include**, admit, comprise, contain,
cover, embrace, hold, incorporate,
take in

encounter v 1 = **meet**, bump into
(inf), chance upon, come upon, run
across 2 = **face**, confront, experience
▷ n 3 = **meeting**, brush, confrontation,
rendezvous 4 = **battle**, clash, conflict,
contest, head-to-head, run-in (inf)

encourage v 1 = **inspire**, buoy up, cheer,
comfort, console, embolden, hearten,
reassure, support 2 = **spur**, advocate,
egg on, foster, incite, promote, prompt,
urge

encroach v = **intrude**, impinge, infringe,
invade, make inroads, overstep, trespass,
usurp

encumber v = **burden**, hamper, handicap,
hinder, impede, inconvenience, obstruct,
saddle, weigh down

end n 1,2 = **extremity**, boundary,
edge, extent, extreme, limit, point,
terminus, tip 3 = **finish**, cessation,
close, closure, conclusion, culmination,
denouement, ending, expiration, expiry,
finale, resolution, stop, termination
4 = **remnant**, butt, fragment, leftover,
oddment, remainder, scrap, stub
5 = **destruction**, death, demise,
doom, extermination, extinction, ruin
6 = **purpose**, aim, goal, intention, object,
objective, point, reason ▷ v 8 = **finish**,
cease, close, conclude, culminate, stop,
terminate, wind up

endanger v = **put at risk**, compromise,
imperil, jeopardize, put in danger, risk,
threaten

endeavour v 1 = **try**, aim, aspire, attempt,
labour, make an effort, strive, struggle,
take pains ▷ n 2 = **effort**, attempt,
enterprise, trial, try, undertaking,
venture

endorse v 1 = **approve**, advocate,
authorize, back, champion, promote,
ratify, recommend, support 2 = **sign**,
countersign

endow ❶ v provide permanent income for. **endowed with** provided with. **endowment** n.

endure ❶ v 1 bear (hardship) patiently. 2 last for a long time. **endurable** adj **endurance** n act or power of enduring.

enema [en-im-a] n medicine injected into the rectum to empty the bowels.

enemy ❶ n, pl -mies hostile person or nation, opponent.

energy ❶ n, pl -gies 1 capacity for intense activity. 2 capacity to do work and overcome resistance. 3 source of power, such as electricity. **energetic** adj **energetically** adv **energize** v give vigour to. **energy drink** soft drink supposed to boost the drinker's energy levels.

enervate v deprive of strength or vitality. **enervation** n.

enfeeble v weaken.

enfold v 1 cover by wrapping something around. 2 embrace.

enforce ❶ v 1 impose obedience (to a law etc.). 2 impose (a condition). **enforceable** adj **enforcement** n.

enfranchise v grant (a person) the right to

vote. **enfranchisement** n.

engage ❶ v 1 take part, participate. 2 involve (a person or his or her attention) intensely. 3 employ (a person). 4 begin a battle with. 5 bring (a mechanism) into operation. **engaged** adj 1 pledged to be married. 2 in use. **engagement** n **engaging** adj charming.

engender ❶ v produce, cause to occur.

engine ❶ n 1 any machine which converts energy into mechanical work. 2 railway locomotive.

engineer ❶ n 1 person trained in any branch of engineering. ▷ v 2 plan in a clever manner. 3 design or construct as an engineer.

engineering n profession of applying scientific principles to the design and construction of engines, cars, buildings, or machines.

engrave ❶ v 1 carve (a design) onto a hard surface. 2 fix deeply in the mind. **engraver** n **engraving** n print made from an engraved plate.

engross ❶ [en-**groce**] v occupy the attention of (a person) completely.

engulf ❶ v cover or surround completely.

——————————————————— THESAURUS ———————————

endow v = **provide**, award, bequeath, bestow, confer, donate, finance, fund, give

endure v 1 = **bear**, cope with, experience, stand, suffer, sustain, undergo, withstand 2 = **last**, continue, live on, persist, remain, stand, stay, survive

enemy n = **foe**, adversary, antagonist, competitor, opponent, rival, the opposition, the other side

energy n 1, 2 = **vigour**, drive, forcefulness, get-up-and-go (inf), liveliness, pep, stamina, verve, vitality

enforce v 1, 2 = **impose**, administer, apply, carry out, execute, implement, insist on, prosecute, put into effect

engage v 1 = **participate**, embark on, enter into, join, set about, take part, undertake 2 = **preoccupy**, absorb, captivate, engross, fix, grip, involve, occupy 3 = **employ**,

appoint, enlist, enrol, hire, retain, take on 4 = **begin battle with**, assail, attack, encounter, fall on, join battle with, meet, take on 5 = **set going**, activate, apply, bring into operation, energize, switch on

engender v = **produce**, breed, cause, create, generate, give rise to, induce, instigate, lead to

engine n 1 = **machine**, mechanism, motor

engineer v 2 = **bring about**, contrive, create, devise, effect, mastermind, plan, plot, scheme

engrave v 1 = **carve**, chisel, cut, etch, inscribe 2 = **fix**, embed, impress, imprint, ingrain, lodge

engross v = **absorb**, engage, immerse, involve, occupy, preoccupy

engulf v = **immerse**, envelop, inundate, overrun, overwhelm, submerge, swallow

enhance ❶ v increase in quality, value, or attractiveness. **enhancement** n.

enigma ❶ n puzzling thing or person. **enigmatic** adj.

enjoy ❶ v 1 take joy in. 2 have the benefit of. 3 experience. **enjoyable** adj **enjoyment** n.

enlarge ❶ v 1 make or grow larger. 2 (foll. by on) speak or write about in greater detail. **enlargement** n.

enlighten ❶ v give information to. **enlightenment** n.

enlist ❶ v 1 enter the armed forces. 2 obtain the support of. **enlistment** n.

enliven ❶ v make lively or cheerful.

enmity ❶ n, pl **-ties** ill will, hatred.

enormous ❶ adj very big, vast. **enormity** n, pl **-ties 1** great wickedness. 2 gross offence. 3 informal great size.

enough ❶ adj 1 as much as or as many as necessary. ▷ n 2 sufficient quantity. ▷ adv 3 sufficiently. 4 fairly or quite, e.g. that's a common enough experience.

enquire ❶ v same as INQUIRE. **enquiry** n.

enrich ❶ v 1 improve in quality. 2 make wealthy or wealthier.

enrol ❶ v -rolling, -rolled (cause to) become a member. **enrolment** n.

en route ❶ adv French on the way.

ensemble ❶ [on-**som**-bl] n 1 all the parts of something taken together. 2 complete outfit of clothes. 3 company of actors or musicians. 4 Music group of musicians playing together.

enshrine v cherish or treasure.

ensign ❶ n 1 naval flag. 2 banner. 3 US naval officer.

enslave v make a slave of (someone).

up, swamp

enhance v = **improve**, add to, boost, heighten, increase, lift, reinforce, strengthen, swell

enigma n = **mystery**, conundrum, problem, puzzle, riddle, teaser

enjoy v 1 = **take pleasure in** or **from**, appreciate, be entertained by, be pleased with, delight in, like, relish 2 = **have**, be blessed or favoured with, experience, have the benefit of, own, possess, reap the benefits of, use

enlarge v 1 = **increase**, add to, amplify, broaden, expand, extend, grow, magnify, swell, widen 2 (foll. by on) = **expand on**, descant on, develop, elaborate on, expatiate on, give further details about

enlighten v = **inform**, advise, cause to understand, counsel, edify, educate, instruct, make aware, teach

enlist v 1 = **join up**, enrol, enter (into), join, muster, register, sign up, volunteer 2 = **obtain**, engage, procure, recruit

enliven v = **cheer up**, animate, excite, inspire, invigorate, pep up, rouse, spark, stimulate, vitalize

enmity n = **hostility**, acrimony, animosity, bad blood, bitterness, hatred, ill will, malice

enormous adj = **huge**, colossal, gigantic, gross, immense, mammoth, massive, mountainous, tremendous, vast

enough adj 1 = **sufficient**, abundant, adequate, ample, plenty ▷ n 2 = **sufficiency**, abundance, adequacy, ample supply, plenty, right amount ▷ adv 3 = **sufficiently**, abundantly, adequately, amply, reasonably, satisfactorily, tolerably

enquire see INQUIRE.

enrich v 1 = **enhance**, augment, develop, improve, refine, supplement 2 = **make rich**, make wealthy

enrol v = **enlist**, accept, admit, join up, recruit, register, sign up or on, take on

en route adv French = **on** or **along the way**, in transit, on the road

ensemble n 1 = **whole**, aggregate, collection, entirety, set, sum, total, totality 2 = **outfit**, costume, get-up (inf), suit 3 = **group**, band, cast, chorus, company, troupe

ensign n 1, 2 = **flag**, banner, colours, jack, pennant, pennon, standard, streamer

enslavement n **enslaver** n.
ensnare v catch in or as if in a snare.
ensue ❶ v come next, result.
ensure ❶ v 1 make certain or sure. 2 make safe or protect.
entail ❶ v bring about or impose inevitably.
entangle ❶ v catch or involve in or as if in a tangle. **entanglement** n.
entente [on-**tont**] n friendly understanding between nations.
enter ❶ v 1 come or go in. 2 join. 3 become involved in, take part in. 4 record (an item) in a journal etc. 5 begin. **entrance** n 1 way into a place. 2 act of entering. 3 right of entering. **entrant** n person who enters a university, contest, etc. **entry** n, pl **-tries** 1 entrance. 2 entering. 3 item entered in a journal etc.
enterprise ❶ n 1 company or firm. 2 bold or difficult undertaking. 3 boldness and energy. **enterprising** adj full of boldness and initiative.

entertain ❶ v 1 amuse. 2 receive as a guest. 3 consider (an idea). **entertainer** n **entertainment** n.
enthral ❶ [en-**thrawl**] v -thralling, -thralled hold the attention of. **enthralling** adj.
enthusiasm ❶ n ardent interest, eagerness. **enthuse** v (cause to) show enthusiasm. **enthusiast** n ardent supporter of something. **enthusiastic** adj **enthusiastically** adv.
entice ❶ v attract by exciting hope or desire, tempt. **enticement** n.
entire ❶ adj including every detail, part, or aspect of something. **entirely** adv **entirety** n.
entitle ❶ v 1 give a right to. 2 give a title to. **entitlement** n.
entity ❶ n, pl **-ties** separate distinct thing.
entomology n study of insects. **entomologist** n.
entourage ❶ [on-toor-ahzh] n group of

ensue v = **follow**, arise, come next, derive, flow, issue, proceed, result, stem
ensure v 1 = **make certain**, certify, confirm, effect, guarantee, make sure, secure, warrant 2 = **protect**, guard, make safe, safeguard, secure
entail v = **involve**, bring about, call for, demand, give rise to, necessitate, occasion, require
entangle v = **tangle**, catch, embroil, enmesh, ensnare, entrap, implicate, snag, snare, trap
enter v 1 = **come** or **go in** or **into**, arrive, make an entrance, pass into, penetrate, pierce 2 = **join**, enlist, enrol 3 = **start**, commence, embark upon, set out on, take up 4 = **record**, inscribe, list, log, note, register, set down, take down
enterprise n 1 = **firm**, business, company, concern, establishment, operation 2 = **undertaking**, adventure, effort, endeavour, operation, plan, programme, project, venture 3 = **initiative**, adventurousness, boldness, daring, drive,

energy, enthusiasm, resourcefulness
entertain v 1 = **amuse**, charm, cheer, delight, please, regale 2 = **show hospitality to**, accommodate, be host to, harbour, have company, lodge, put up, treat 3 = **consider**, conceive, contemplate, imagine, keep in mind, think about
enthral v = **fascinate**, captivate, charm, enchant, enrapture, entrance, grip, mesmerize
enthusiasm n = **keenness**, eagerness, fervour, interest, passion, relish, zeal, zest
entice v = **attract**, allure, cajole, coax, lead on, lure, persuade, seduce, tempt
entire adj = **whole**, complete, full, gross, total
entitle v 1 = **give the right to**, allow, authorize, empower, enable, license, permit 2 = **call**, christen, dub, label, name, term, title
entity n = **thing**, being, creature, individual, object, organism, substance
entourage n = **retinue**, associates, attendants, company, court, escort,

people who assist an important person.

entrails ❶ *pl n* **1** intestines. **2** innermost parts of something.

entrance¹ ❶ *n* see ENTER.

entrance² ❶ *v* **1** delight. **2** put into a trance.

entreat *v* ask earnestly. **entreaty** *n, pl* **-ties** earnest request.

entrench ❶ *v* **1** establish firmly. **2** establish in a fortified position with trenches. **entrenchment** *n*.

entrepreneur ❶ *n* business person who attempts to make a profit by risk and initiative.

entrust ❶ *v* put into the care or protection of.

entwine ❶ *v* twist together or around.

enumerate ❶ *v* name one by one.

enunciate ❶ *v* **1** pronounce clearly. **2** state precisely or formally.

envelop ❶ *v* **enveloping, enveloped** wrap up, enclose.

envelope ❶ *n* folded gummed paper

covering for a letter, etc.

environment ❶ [en-**vire**-on-ment] *n* external conditions and surroundings in which people, animals, or plants live. **environmental** *adj* **environmentalist** *n* person concerned with the protection of the natural environment.

● **SPELLING TIP**
● For every thousand correct appearances
● of the word **environment** in the Bank of
● English, there is one *enviroment*, without
● the middle *n*.

envisage ❶ *v* conceive of as a possibility.

envoy ❶ *n* **1** messenger. **2** diplomat ranking below an ambassador.

envy ❶ *n* **1** feeling of discontent aroused by another's good fortune. ▷ *v* **-vying, -vied 2** grudge (another's good fortune, success, or qualities). **enviable** *adj* arousing envy, fortunate. **envious** *adj* full of envy.

enzyme *n* any of a group of complex proteins that act as catalysts in specific biochemical reactions.

THESAURUS

followers, staff, train

entrails *pl n* = **intestines**, bowels, guts, innards (*inf*), insides (*inf*), offal, viscera

entrance¹ *n* **1** = **way in**, access, door, doorway, entry, gate, opening, passage **2** = **appearance**, arrival, coming in, entry, introduction **3** = **admission**, access, admittance, entrée, entry, permission to enter

entrance² *v* **1** = **enchant**, bewitch, captivate, charm, delight, enrapture, enthral, fascinate **2** = **mesmerize**, hypnotize, put in a trance

entrepreneur *n* = **businessman** *or* **businesswoman**, impresario, industrialist, magnate, tycoon

entrust *v* = **give custody of**, assign, commit, confide, delegate, deliver, hand over, turn over

entwine *v* = **twist**, interlace, interweave, knit, plait, twine, weave, wind

enumerate *v* = **list**, cite, itemize, mention, name, quote, recite, recount, relate, spell

out

enunciate *v* **1** = **pronounce**, articulate, enounce, say, sound, speak, utter, vocalize, voice **2** = **state**, declare, proclaim, promulgate, pronounce, propound, publish

envelop *v* = **enclose**, cloak, cover, encase, encircle, engulf, shroud, surround, wrap

envelope *n* = **wrapping**, case, casing, cover, covering, jacket, wrapper

environment *n* = **surroundings**, atmosphere, background, conditions, habitat, medium, setting, situation

envisage *v* = **imagine**, conceive (of), conceptualize, contemplate, envision, fancy, foresee, picture, see, think up, visualize

envoy *n* **1** = **messenger**, agent, courier, delegate, emissary, intermediary, representative **2** = **diplomat**, ambassador

envy *n* **1** = **covetousness**, enviousness, jealousy, resentfulness, resentment ▷ *v* **2** = **covet**, be envious (of), begrudge, be jealous (of), grudge, resent

epaulette *n* shoulder ornament on a uniform.

ephemeral ❶ *adj* short-lived.

epic *n* **1** long poem, book, or film about heroic events or actions. ▷ *adj* **2** very impressive or ambitious.

epicentre *n* point on the earth's surface immediately above the origin of an earthquake.

epicure *n* person who enjoys good food and drink. **epicurean** *adj* **1** devoted to sensual pleasures, esp. food and drink. ▷ *n* **2** epicure.

epidemic ❶ *n* **1** widespread occurrence of a disease. **2** rapid spread of something.

epidermis *n* outer layer of the skin.

epidural [ep-pid-**dure**-al] *adj, n* (of) spinal anaesthetic injected to relieve pain during childbirth.

epigram ❶ *n* short witty remark or poem. **epigrammatic** *adj*.

epigraph *n* **1** quotation at the start of a book. **2** inscription.

epilepsy *n* disorder of the nervous system causing loss of consciousness and sometimes convulsions. **epileptic** *adj* **1** of or having epilepsy. ▷ *n* **2** person who has epilepsy.

epilogue ❶ *n* short speech or poem at the end of a literary work, esp. a play.

episcopal [ip-**piss**-kop-al] *adj* of or governed by bishops. **episcopalian** *adj* **1** advocating Church government by bishops. ▷ *n* **2** advocate of such Church government.

episode ❶ *n* **1** incident in a series of incidents. **2** section of a serialized book, television programme, etc. **episodic** *adj* occurring at irregular intervals.

epistle ❶ *n* letter, esp. of an apostle. **epistolary** *adj*.

epitaph ❶ *n* **1** commemorative inscription on a tomb. **2** commemorative speech or passage.

epithet ❶ *n* descriptive word or name.

epitome ❶ [ip-**pit**-a-mee] *n* typical example. **epitomize** *v* be the epitome of.

epoch ❶ [**ee**-pok] *n* period of notable events.

equable ❶ [**ek**-wab-bl] *adj* even-tempered. **equably** *adv*.

equal ❶ *adj* **1** identical in size, quantity, degree, etc. **2** having identical rights or status. **3** evenly balanced. **4** (foll. by *to*) having the necessary ability (for). ▷ *n* **5** person or thing equal to another.

──────────── THESAURUS ────────────

ephemeral *adj* = **brief**, fleeting, momentary, passing, short-lived, temporary, transient, transitory

epidemic *n* **1** = **plague**, contagion, outbreak **2** = **spread**, growth, upsurge, wave

epigram *n* = **witticism**, aphorism, bon mot, quip

epilogue *n* = **conclusion**, coda, concluding speech, postscript

episode *n* **1** = **event**, adventure, affair, escapade, experience, happening, incident, matter, occurrence **2** = **part**, chapter, instalment, passage, scene, section

epistle *n* = **letter**, communication, message, missive, note

epitaph *n* **1** = **monument**, inscription

epithet *n* = **name**, appellation, description, designation (*sl*), nickname, sobriquet, tag, title

epitome *n* = **personification**, archetype, embodiment, essence, quintessence, representation, type, typical example

epoch *n* = **era**, age, date, period, time

equable *adj* = **even-tempered**, calm, composed, easy-going, imperturbable, level-headed, placid, serene, unflappable (*inf*)

equal *adj* **1** = **identical**, alike, corresponding, equivalent, regular, symmetrical, the same, uniform **3** = **even**, balanced, evenly matched, fifty-fifty (*inf*), level pegging (*Brit inf*) **4** (foll. by *to*) = **capable of**, competent to, fit for, good enough for, ready for, strong enough for, suitable for, up to ▷ *n* **5** = **match**, counterpart, equivalent, rival, twin ▷ *v*

▷ *v* **equalling**, **equalled** 6 be equal to.
equally *adv* **equality** *n* state of being
equal. **equalize** *v* 1 make or become equal.
2 reach the same score as one's opponent.
equalization *n* **equal opportunity**
nondiscrimination as to sex, race, etc. in
employment.

equate ❶ *v* make or regard as equivalent.
equation *n* 1 mathematical statement
that two expressions are equal. 2 act of
equating.

equator *n* imaginary circle round the
earth, equidistant from the poles.
equatorial *adj*.

equestrian *adj* of horses and riding.

equilateral *adj* having equal sides.

equilibrium ❶ *n*, *pl* **-ria** steadiness or
stability.

equinox *n* time of year when day and night
are of equal length.

equip ❶ *v* **equipping**, **equipped** provide
with supplies, components, etc.
equipment *n* 1 set of tools or devices
used for a particular purpose. 2 act of
equipping.

equivalent ❶ *adj* 1 equal in value.
2 having the same meaning or result.

▷ *n* 3 something that is equivalent.
equivalence *n*.

equivocal ❶ *adj* 1 ambiguous.
2 deliberately misleading. 3 of doubtful
character or sincerity. **equivocate** *v* use
vague or ambiguous language to mislead
people. **equivocation** *n*.

era ❶ *n* period of time considered as
distinctive.

eradicate ❶ *v* destroy completely.
eradication *n*.

erase ❶ *v* 1 rub out. 2 remove sound or
information from (a magnetic tape or disk).
eraser *n* object for erasing something
written. **erasure** *n* 1 erasing. 2 place or
mark where something has been erased.

ere *prep*, *conj poetic* before.

e-reader, **eReader** *n* portable device that
allows users to download and read texts in
electronic form.

erect ❶ *v* 1 build. 2 found or form.
▷ *adj* 3 upright. 4 (of the penis, clitoris,
or nipples) rigid as a result of sexual
excitement. **erectile** *adj* capable of
becoming erect from sexual excitement.
erection *n*.

erode ❶ *v* wear away. **erosion** *n*.

THESAURUS

6 = **match**, amount to, be tantamount
to, correspond to, equate, level, parallel,
tie with

equate *v* = **make** *or* **be equal**, be
commensurate, compare, correspond with
or to, liken, mention in the same breath,
parallel

equilibrium *n* = **stability**, balance,
equipoise, evenness, rest, steadiness,
symmetry

equip *v* = **supply**, arm, array, fit out,
furnish, kit out, provide, stock

equivalent *adj* 1, 2 = **equal**, alike,
commensurate, comparable,
corresponding, interchangeable, of a
piece, same, similar, tantamount ▷ *n*
3 = **equal**, counterpart, match, opposite
number, parallel, twin

equivocal *adj* 1 = **ambiguous**, indefinite,

indeterminate, oblique, obscure,
uncertain, vague 2 = **misleading**,
evasive

era *n* = **age**, date, day *or* days, epoch,
generation, period, time

eradicate *v* = **wipe out**, annihilate,
destroy, eliminate, erase, exterminate,
extinguish, get rid of, obliterate, remove,
root out

erase *v* 1 = **remove**, blot, cancel, delete,
expunge, obliterate 2 = **wipe out**, rub
out

erect *v* 1 = **build**, construct, put up, raise,
set up 2 = **found**, create, establish, form,
initiate, institute, organize, set up ▷ *adj*
3 = **upright**, elevated, perpendicular,
straight, vertical 4 = **stiff**

erode *v* = **wear down** *or* **away**, abrade,
consume, corrode, destroy, deteriorate,

erotic ① *adj* relating to sexual pleasure or desire. **eroticism** *n* **erotica** *n* sexual literature or art.

err ① *v* make a mistake. **erratum** *n*, *pl* **-ta** error in writing or printing. **erroneous** *adj* incorrect, mistaken. **error** *n* mistake, inaccuracy, or misjudgment.

errand ① *n* short trip to do something for someone.

errant *adj* behaving in a manner considered to be unacceptable.

erstwhile ① *adj* former.

erudite ① *adj* having great academic knowledge. **erudition** *n*.

erupt ① *v* **1** eject (steam, water, or volcanic material) violently. **2** burst forth suddenly and violently. **3** (of a blemish) appear on the skin. **eruption** *n*.

escalate ① *v* increase in extent or intensity. **escalation** *n*.

escalator *n* moving staircase.

escape ① *v* **1** get free (of). **2** avoid, e.g. *escape attention*. **3** (of a gas, liquid, etc.) leak gradually. ▷ *n* **4** act of escaping. **5** means of relaxation. **escapee** *n* person who

has escaped. **escapism** *n* taking refuge in fantasy to avoid unpleasant reality. **escapologist** *n* entertainer who specializes in freeing himself from confinement.

escarpment *n* steep face of a ridge or mountain.

eschew [iss-**chew**] *v* abstain from, avoid.

escort ① *n* **1** people or vehicles accompanying another person for protection or as an honour. **2** person who accompanies a person of the opposite sex to a social event. ▷ *v* **3** act as an escort to.

Eskimo *n* **1** a member of a group of peoples inhabiting N Canada, Greenland, Alaska, and E Siberia, having a material culture adapted to an extremely cold climate. **2** their language.

esoteric [ee-so-**ter**-rik] *adj* understood by only a small number of people with special knowledge.

ESP extrasensory perception.

especial ① *adj formal* special. **especially** *adv* particularly.

espionage ① [ess-pyon-ahzh] *n* spying.

esplanade *n* wide open road used as a

——————— THESAURUS ———————

disintegrate, eat away, grind down

erotic *adj* = **sexual**, amatory, carnal, lustful, seductive, sensual, sexy (*inf*), voluptuous

err *v* = **make a mistake**, blunder, go wrong, miscalculate, misjudge, mistake, slip up (*inf*)

errand *n* = **job**, charge, commission, message, mission, task

erstwhile *adj* = **former**, bygone, late, old, once, one-time, past, previous, sometime

erudite *adj* = **learned**, cultivated, cultured, educated, knowledgeable, scholarly, well-educated, well-read

erupt *v* **1, 2** = **explode**, belch forth, blow up, burst out, gush, pour forth, spew forth or out, spout, throw off **3** = **break out**, appear

escalate *v* = **increase**, expand, extend, grow, heighten, intensify, mount, rise

escape *v* **1** = **get away**, abscond, bolt, break free or out, flee, fly, make one's getaway, run away or off, slip away **2** = **avoid**, dodge, duck, elude, evade, pass, shun, slip **3** = **leak**, emanate, exude, flow, gush, issue, pour forth, seep ▷ *n* **4** = **getaway**, break, break-out, flight **5** = **relaxation**, distraction, diversion, pastime, recreation

escort *n* **1** = **guard**, bodyguard, convoy, cortege, entourage, retinue, train **2** = **companion**, attendant, beau, chaperon, guide, partner ▷ *v* **3** = **accompany**, chaperon, conduct, guide, lead, partner, shepherd, usher

especial *adj Formal* = **exceptional**, noteworthy, outstanding, principal, special, uncommon, unusual

espionage *n* = **spying**, counter-intelligence, intelligence, surveillance, undercover work

public promenade.

espouse ❶ v adopt or give support to (a cause etc.). **espousal** n.

espy v **espying**, **espied** catch sight of.

Esq. esquire.

essay ❶ n 1 short literary composition. 2 short piece of writing on a subject done as an exercise by a student. ▷ v 3 attempt. **essayist** n.

essence ❶ n 1 most important feature of a thing which determines its identity. 2 concentrated liquid used to flavour food. **essential** adj 1 vitally important. 2 basic or fundamental. ▷ n 3 something fundamental or indispensable. **essentially** adv.

establish ❶ v 1 set up on a permanent basis. 2 make secure or permanent in a certain place, job, etc. 3 prove. 4 cause to be accepted. **establishment** n 1 act of establishing. 2 commercial or other institution. **the Establishment** group of people having authority within a society.

estate ❶ n 1 landed property. 2 large area of property development, esp. of new houses or factories. 3 property of a deceased

person. **estate agent** agent concerned with the valuation, lease, and sale of property. **estate car** car with a rear door and luggage space behind the rear seats.

esteem ❶ n 1 high regard. ▷ v 2 think highly of. 3 judge or consider.

ester n Chem compound produced by the reaction between an acid and an alcohol.

estimate ❶ v 1 calculate roughly. 2 form an opinion about. ▷ n 3 approximate calculation. 4 statement from a workman etc. of the likely charge for a job. 5 opinion. **estimable** adj worthy of respect. **estimation** n considered opinion.

estranged adj no longer living with one's spouse. **estrangement** n.

estuary ❶ n, pl **-aries** mouth of a river.

etc. et cetera.

et cetera ❶ [et **set**-ra] Latin 1 and the rest, and others. 2 or the like. **etceteras** pl n miscellaneous extra things or people.

etch ❶ v 1 wear away or cut the surface of (metal, glass, etc.) with acid. 2 imprint vividly (on someone's mind). **etching** n.

———— THESAURUS ————

espouse v = **support**, adopt, advocate, back, champion, embrace, promote, stand up for, take up, uphold

essay n 1 = **composition**, article, discourse, dissertation, paper, piece, tract, treatise ▷ v 3 = **attempt**, aim, endeavour, try, undertake

essence n 1 = **fundamental nature**, being, core, heart, nature, quintessence, soul, spirit, substance 2 = **concentrate**, distillate, extract, spirits, tincture

establish v 1 = **create**, constitute, form, found, ground, inaugurate, institute, settle, set up 3 = **prove**, authenticate, certify, confirm, corroborate, demonstrate, substantiate, verify

estate n 1 = **lands**, area, domain, holdings, manor, property, homestead (US & Canad) 3 = **property**, assets, belongings, effects, fortune, goods, possessions, wealth

esteem n 1 = **respect**, admiration, credit,

estimation, good opinion, honour, regard, reverence, veneration ▷ v 2 = **respect**, admire, love, prize, regard highly, revere, think highly of, treasure, value 3 = **consider**, believe, deem, estimate, judge, reckon, regard, think, view

estimate v 1 = **calculate roughly**, assess, evaluate, gauge, guess, judge, number, reckon, value 2 = **form an opinion**, believe, conjecture, consider, judge, rank, rate, reckon, surmise ▷ n 3 = **approximate calculation**, assessment, ballpark figure (inf), guess, guesstimate (inf), judgment, valuation 5 = **opinion**, appraisal, assessment, belief, estimation, judgment

estuary n = **inlet**, creek, firth, fjord, mouth

et cetera Latin 1, 2 = **and so on**, and others, and so forth, and the like, and the rest, et al.

etch v 1 = **cut**, carve, eat into, engrave, impress, imprint, inscribe, stamp

eternal ❶ adj 1 without beginning or end. 2 unchanging. **eternally** adv **eternity** n 1 infinite time. 2 timeless existence after death.

ether n 1 colourless sweet-smelling liquid used as an anaesthetic. 2 region above the clouds. **ethereal** [eth-**eer**-ee-al] adj extremely delicate.

ethnic ❶ adj 1 relating to a people or group that shares a culture, religion, or language. 2 belonging or relating to such a group, esp. one that is a minority group in a particular place. **ethnic cleansing** practice, by the dominant ethnic group in an area, of removing other ethnic groups by expulsion or extermination. **ethnology** n study of human races. **ethnological** adj.

ethos [**eeth**-oss] n distinctive spirit and attitudes of a people, culture, etc.

etiquette ❶ n conventional code of conduct.

étude [**ay**-tewd] n short musical composition for a solo instrument, esp. intended as a technical exercise.

etymology n, pl -**gies** study of the sources and development of words. **etymological** adj.

eucalyptus, eucalypt n tree, mainly grown in Australia, that provides timber, gum, and medicinal oil from the leaves.

Eucharist [**yew**-kar-ist] n 1 Christian sacrament commemorating Christ's Last Supper. 2 consecrated elements of bread and wine used in religious services.

eugenics [yew-**jen**-iks] n study of methods of improving the human race.

eulogy n, pl -**gies** speech or writing in praise of a person. **eulogize** v praise (a person or thing) highly in speech or writing. **eulogistic** adj.

eunuch n castrated man, esp. (formerly) a guard in a harem.

euphemism n inoffensive word or phrase substituted for one considered offensive or upsetting. **euphemistic** adj.

euphoria ❶ n sense of elation. **euphoric** adj.

eureka [yew-**reek**-a] interj exclamation of triumph at finding something.

euthanasia n act of killing someone painlessly, esp. to relieve his or her suffering.

evacuate ❶ v 1 send (someone) away from a place of danger. 2 empty. **evacuation** n **evacuee** n.

evade ❶ v 1 get away from or avoid. 2 elude. **evasion** n **evasive** adj not straightforward. **evasively** adv.

evaluate ❶ v find or judge the value of. **evaluation** n.

evangelical adj 1 of or according to gospel teaching. 2 of certain Protestant sects which maintain the doctrine of salvation by faith. ▷ n 3 member of an evangelical sect.

evaporate ❶ v 1 change from a liquid or solid to a vapour. 2 disappear.

THESAURUS

eternal adj 1 = **everlasting**, endless, immortal, infinite, never-ending, perpetual, timeless, unceasing, unending 2 = **permanent**, deathless, enduring, immutable, imperishable, indestructible, lasting, unchanging

ethnic adj 1 = **cultural**, folk, indigenous, national, native, racial, traditional

etiquette n = **good** or **proper behaviour**, civility, courtesy, decorum, formalities, manners, politeness, propriety, protocol

euphoria n = **elation**, ecstasy, exaltation, exhilaration, intoxication, joy, jubilation, rapture

evacuate v 1 = **clear**, abandon, desert, forsake, leave, move out, pull out, quit, vacate, withdraw

evade v 1 = **avoid**, dodge, duck, elude, escape, get away from, sidestep, steer clear of 2 = **avoid answering**, equivocate, fend off, fudge, hedge, parry

evaluate v = **assess**, appraise, calculate, estimate, gauge, judge, rate, reckon, size up (inf), weigh

evaporate v 1 = **dry up**, dry, vaporize 2 = **disappear**, dematerialize, dissolve,

evaporation n **evaporated milk** thick unsweetened tinned milk.

eve ❶ n 1 evening or day before some special event. 2 period immediately before an event. **evensong** n evening prayer.

even ❶ adj 1 flat or smooth. 2 (foll. by with) on the same level (as). 3 constant. 4 calm. 5 equally balanced. 6 divisible by two. ▷ adv 7 equally. 8 simply. 9 nevertheless. ▷ v 10 make even.

evening ❶ n 1 end of the day or early part of the night. ▷ adj 2 of or in the evening.

event ❶ n 1 anything that takes place. 2 planned and organized occasion. 3 contest in a sporting programme. **eventful** adj full of exciting incidents.

ever ❶ adv 1 at any time. 2 always. **evergreen** n, adj (tree or shrub) having leaves throughout the year. **everlasting** adj **evermore** adv for all time to come.

every ❶ adj 1 each without exception. 2 all possible. **everybody** pron every person. **everyday** adj usual or ordinary. **everyone** pron every person. **everything** pron **everywhere** adv in all places.

evict ❶ v legally expel (someone) from his or her home. **eviction** n.

evidence ❶ n 1 ground for belief. 2 matter produced before a lawcourt to prove or disprove a point. 3 sign, indication. ▷ v 4 demonstrate, prove. **in evidence** conspicuous. **evident** adj easily seen or understood. **evidently** adv **evidential** adj of, serving as, or based on evidence.

evil ❶ n 1 wickedness. 2 wicked deed. ▷ adj 3 harmful. 4 morally bad. 5 very unpleasant. **evilly** adv **evildoer** n wicked person.

evoke ❶ v call or summon up (a memory, feeling, etc.). **evocation** n **evocative** adj.

e

———————— THESAURUS ————————

fade away, melt away, vanish

eve n 1 = **night before**, day before, vigil 2 = **brink**, edge, point, threshold, verge

even adj 1 = **level**, flat, horizontal, parallel, smooth, steady, straight, true, uniform 2 (foll. by with) = **equal**, comparable, fifty-fifty (inf), identical, level, like, matching, neck and neck, on a par, similar, tied 3 = **regular**, constant, smooth, steady, unbroken, uniform, uninterrupted, unvarying, unwavering 4 = **calm**, composed, cool, even-tempered, imperturbable, placid, unruffled, well-balanced

evening n 1 = **dusk**, gloaming (Scot or poet), twilight

event n 1 = **incident**, affair, business, circumstance, episode, experience, happening, occasion, occurrence 3 = **competition**, bout, contest, game, tournament

ever adv 1 = **at any time**, at all, at any period, at any point, by any chance, in any case, on any occasion 2 = **always**, at all times, constantly, continually, evermore,

for ever, perpetually, twenty-four-seven (inf)

every adj 1 = **each**, all, each one

evict v = **expel**, boot out (inf), eject, kick out (inf), oust, remove, throw out, turf out (inf), turn out

evidence n 1, 2 = **proof**, confirmation, corroboration, demonstration, grounds, substantiation, testimony 3 = **sign**, indication ▷ v 4 = **show**, demonstrate, display, exhibit, indicate, prove, reveal, signify, witness

evil n 1 = **wickedness**, badness, depravity, malignity, sin, vice, villainy, wrongdoing 2 = **harm**, affliction, disaster, hurt, ill, injury, mischief, misfortune, suffering, woe ▷ adj 3 = **harmful**, calamitous, catastrophic, destructive, dire, disastrous, pernicious, ruinous 4 = **wicked**, bad, depraved, immoral, malevolent, malicious, sinful, villainous 5 = **offensive**, foul, noxious, pestilential, unpleasant, vile

evoke v = **arouse**, awaken, call, give rise to, induce, recall, rekindle, stir up, summon up

evolve ❶ v 1 develop gradually. 2 (of an animal or plant species) undergo evolution. **evolution** n gradual change in the characteristics of living things over successive generations, esp. to a more complex form. **evolutionary** adj.

ewe n female sheep.

ex- prefix 1 out of, outside, from, e.g. exodus. 2 former, e.g. ex-wife.

exacerbate [ig-**zass**-er-bate] v make (pain, emotion, or a situation) worse. **exacerbation** n.

exact ❶ adj 1 correct and complete in every detail. 2 precise, as opposed to approximate. ▷ v 3 demand (payment or obedience). **exactly** adv precisely, in every respect. **exactness**, **exactitude** n **exacting** adj making rigorous or excessive demands.

exaggerate ❶ v 1 regard or represent as greater than is true. 2 make greater or more noticeable. **exaggeration** n.

  ● **SPELLING TIP**
  ● Some apparently tricky words, like **ex-**
  ● **aggerate** for example, appear wrongly
  ● spelt relatively rarely in the Bank of
  ● English. Similarly, there is only one
  ● occurrence of exagerration, instead of the
  ● correct **exaggeration**.

exalt ❶ v 1 praise highly. 2 raise to a higher rank. **exalted** adj **exaltation** n.

exam n short for EXAMINATION.

examine ❶ v 1 look at closely. 2 test the knowledge of. 3 ask questions of. **examination** n 1 examining. 2 test of a candidate's knowledge or skill. **examinee** n **examiner** n.

example ❶ n 1 specimen typical of its group. 2 person or thing worthy of imitation. 3 punishment regarded as a warning to others.

exasperate ❶ v cause great irritation to. **exasperation** n.

excavate ❶ v 1 unearth buried objects from (a piece of land) methodically to learn about the past. 2 make (a hole) in solid matter by digging. **excavation** n **excavator** n large machine used for digging.

exceed ❶ v 1 be greater than. 2 go beyond (a limit). **exceedingly** adv very.

excel ❶ v -celling, -celled 1 be superior to. 2 be outstandingly good at something. **excellent** adj exceptionally good. **excellence** n.

───────────────── THESAURUS ─────────────────

evolve v 1 = **develop**, expand, grow, increase, mature, progress, unfold, work out

exact adj 1 = **correct**, faultless, right, true, unerring 2 = **accurate**, definite, precise, specific ▷ v 3 = **demand**, claim, command, compel, extort, extract, force

exaggerate v 1 = **overstate**, amplify, embellish, embroider, enlarge, overemphasize, overestimate

exalt v 1 = **praise**, acclaim, extol, glorify, idolize, set on a pedestal, worship 2 = **raise**, advance, elevate, ennoble, honour, promote, upgrade

examine v 1 = **inspect**, analyse, explore, investigate, peruse, scrutinize, study, survey 2 = **test**, question, quiz 3 = **question**, cross-examine, grill (inf), inquire, interrogate

example n 1 = **specimen**, case, illustration, instance, sample 2 = **model**, archetype, ideal, paradigm, paragon, prototype, standard 3 = **warning**, caution, lesson

exasperate v = **irritate**, anger, annoy, enrage, incense, inflame, infuriate, madden, pique

excavate v 1 = **unearth**, dig out, dig up, mine, quarry, uncover 2 = **dig**, burrow, delve, tunnel

exceed v 1 = **surpass**, beat, better, cap (inf), eclipse, outdo, outstrip, overtake, pass, top 2 = **go over the limit of**, go over the top, overstep

excel v 1 = **be superior**, beat, eclipse, outdo, outshine, surpass, transcend 2 = **be good**, be proficient, be skilful, be talented, shine, show talent

except ⊕ *prep* **1** (sometimes foll. by *for*) other than, not including. ▷ *v* **2** not include. **except that** but for the fact that. **excepting** *prep* except. **exception** *n* **1** excepting. **2** thing that is excluded from or does not conform to the general rule. **exceptionable** *adj* causing offence. **exceptional** *adj* **1** not ordinary. **2** much above the average.

excerpt ⊕ *n* passage taken from a book, speech, etc.

excess ⊕ *n* **1** state or act of exceeding the permitted limits. **2** immoderate amount. **3** amount by which a thing exceeds the permitted limits. **excessive** *adj* **excessively** *adv*.

exchange ⊕ *v* **1** give or receive (something) in return for something else. ▷ *n* **2** act of exchanging. **3** thing given or received in place of another. **4** centre in which telephone lines are interconnected. **5** *Finance* place where securities or commodities are traded. **6** transfer of sums of money of equal value between different currencies. **exchangeable** *adj*.

excise¹ *n* tax on goods produced for the home market.

excise² *v* cut out or away. **excision** *n*.

excite ⊕ *v* **1** arouse to strong emotion. **2** arouse or evoke (an emotion). **3** arouse sexually. **excitement** *n* **excitable** *adj* easily excited.

exclaim ⊕ *v* speak suddenly, cry out. **exclamation** *n* **exclamation mark** punctuation mark (!) used after exclamations. **exclamatory** *adj*.

exclude ⊕ *v* **1** keep out, leave out. **2** leave out of consideration. **exclusion** *n* **exclusive** *adj* **1** excluding everything else. **2** not shared. **3** catering for a privileged minority. ▷ *n* **4** story reported in only one newspaper. **exclusively** *adv* **exclusivity**, **exclusiveness** *n*.

excommunicate ⊕ *v* exclude from membership and the sacraments of the Church. **excommunication** *n*.

excrement *n* waste matter discharged from the body.

excruciating ⊕ *adj* **1** agonizing. **2** hard to bear.

excursion ⊕ *n* short journey, esp. for pleasure.

excuse ⊕ *n* **1** explanation offered to justify (a fault etc.). ▷ *v* **2** put forward a reason or

except *prep* **1** (sometimes foll. by *for*) = **apart from**, barring, besides, but, excepting, excluding, omitting, other than, saving, with the exception of ▷ *v* **2** = **exclude**, leave out, omit, pass over

excerpt *n* = **extract**, fragment, part, passage, piece, quotation, section, selection

excess *n* **1** = **overindulgence**, debauchery, dissipation, dissoluteness, extravagance, intemperance, prodigality **2** = **surfeit**, glut, overload, superabundance, superfluity, surplus, too much

exchange *v* **1** = **interchange**, barter, change, convert into, swap, switch, trade ▷ *n* **2** = **interchange**, barter, quid pro quo, reciprocity, substitution, swap, switch, tit for tat, trade

excite *v* **1, 2** = **arouse**, animate, galvanize,

inflame, inspire, provoke, rouse, stir up **3** = **thrill**, electrify, titillate

exclaim *v* = **cry out**, call out, declare, proclaim, shout, utter, yell

exclude *v* **1** = **keep out**, ban, bar, boycott, disallow, forbid, prohibit, refuse, shut out **3** = **leave out**, count out, eliminate, ignore, omit, pass over, reject, rule out, set aside

excommunicate *v* = **expel**, anathematize, ban, banish, cast out, denounce, exclude, repudiate

excruciating *adj* **1** = **agonizing**, harrowing, intense, piercing, severe, violent **2** = **unbearable**, insufferable

excursion *n* = **trip**, day trip, expedition, jaunt, journey, outing, pleasure trip, ramble, tour

excuse *n* **1** = **justification**, apology, defence, explanation, grounds, mitigation,

e

justification for (a fault etc.). **3** forgive (a person) or overlook (a fault etc.). **4** make allowances for. **5** exempt. **6** allow to leave. **excusable** *adj*.

execrable [**eks**-sik-rab-bl] *adj* of very poor quality.

execute ➊ *v* **1** put (a condemned person) to death. **2** carry out or accomplish. **3** produce (a work of art). **4** render (a legal document) effective, as by signing. **execution** *n* **executioner** *n* **executive** *n* person or group in an administrative position.

exemplify ➊ *v* **-fying, -fied 1** show an example of. **2** be an example of. **exemplification** *n*.

exempt ➊ *adj* **1** not subject to an obligation etc. ▷ *v* **2** release from an obligation etc. **exemption** *n*.

exercise ➊ *n* **1** activity to train the body or mind. **2** set of movements or tasks designed to improve or test a person's ability. **3** performance of a function. ▷ *v* **4** make use of, e.g. *to exercise one's rights*. **5** take exercise or perform exercises.

exert ➊ *v* use (influence, authority, etc.) forcefully or effectively. **exert oneself** make a special effort. **exertion** *n*.

exhale *v* breathe out. **exhalation** *n*.

exhaust ➊ *v* **1** tire out. **2** use up. **3** discuss (a subject) thoroughly. ▷ *n* **4** gases ejected from an engine as waste products. **5** pipe through which an engine's exhaust fumes pass. **exhaustible** *adj* **exhaustion** *n* **1** extreme tiredness. **2** exhausting. **exhaustive** *adj* comprehensive. **exhaustively** *adv*.

exhibit ➊ *v* **1** display to the public. **2** show (a quality or feeling). ▷ *n* **3** object exhibited to the public. **4** *Law* document or object produced in court as evidence. **exhibitor** *n* **exhibition** *n* **1** public display of art, skills, etc. **2** exhibiting. **exhibitionism** *n* **1** compulsive desire to draw attention to oneself. **2** compulsive desire to display one's genitals in public. **exhibitionist** *n*.

exhilarate *v* make lively and cheerful. **exhilaration** *n*.

● **SPELLING TIP**
● It may surprise you that it's the vowels,
● not the consonants, that are a problem
● when people try to spell **exhilarate**
● or **exhilaration**. They often make the
● mistake of writing an *e* instead of an *a* in
● the middle.

———————————————————— THESAURUS ————————————————————

plea, reason, vindication ▷ *v* **2** = **justify**, apologize for, defend, explain, mitigate, vindicate **3, 4** = **forgive**, acquit, exculpate, exonerate, make allowances for, overlook, pardon, tolerate, turn a blind eye to **5** = **free**, absolve, discharge, exempt, let off, release, relieve, spare

execute *v* **1** = **put to death**, behead, electrocute, guillotine, hang, kill, shoot **2** = **carry out**, accomplish, administer, discharge, effect, enact, implement, perform, prosecute

exemplify *v* **1, 2** = **show**, demonstrate, display, embody, exhibit, illustrate, represent, serve as an example of

exempt *adj* **1** = **immune**, excepted, excused, free, not liable, released, spared ▷ *v* **2** = **grant immunity**, absolve, discharge, excuse, free, let off, release,

relieve, spare

exercise *n* **1** = **exertion**, activity, effort, labour, toil, training, work, work-out **2** = **task**, drill, lesson, practice, problem **3** = **use**, application, discharge, fulfilment, implementation, practice, utilization ▷ *v* **4** = **put to use**, apply, bring to bear, employ, exert, use, utilize **5** = **train**, practise, work out

exert *v* = **use**, apply, bring to bear, employ, exercise, make use of, utilize, wield **exert oneself** = **make an effort**, apply oneself, do one's best, endeavour, labour, strain, strive, struggle, toil, work

exhaust *v* **1** = **tire out**, debilitate, drain, enervate, enfeeble, fatigue, sap, weaken, wear out **2** = **use up**, consume, deplete, dissipate, expend, run through, spend, squander, waste

exhibit *v* **1** = **display**, parade, put on view,

exhort ❶ *v* urge earnestly. **exhortation** *n*.

exhume ❶ [ig-**zyume**] *v* dig up (something buried, esp. a corpse).

exigency ❶ *n*, *pl* **-cies** urgent demand or need. **exigent** *adj*.

exile ❶ *n* **1** prolonged, usu. enforced, absence from one's country. **2** person banished or living away from his or her country. ▷ *v* **3** expel from one's country.

exist ❶ *v* **1** have being or reality. **2** eke out a living. **3** live. **existence** *n* **existent** *adj*.

● SPELLING TIP
● People often write -*ance* at the end of a
● word when it should be -*ence*. The Bank
● of English shows this is the case for *ex-*
● *istance* which occurs 43 times. However,
● the correct spelling **existence** is over
● 350 times commoner.

exit ❶ *n* **1** way out. **2** going out. **3** actor's going offstage. ▷ *v* **4** go out. **5** go offstage: used as a stage direction.

exodus ❶ [**eks**-so-duss] *n* departure of a large number of people.

exonerate ❶ *v* free from blame or a criminal charge. **exoneration** *n*.

exorbitant ❶ *adj* (of prices, demands, etc.) excessive, immoderate.

exorcize ❶ *v* expel (evil spirits) by prayers and religious rites. **exorcism** *n* **exorcist** *n*.

exotic ❶ *adj* **1** having a strange allure or beauty. **2** originating in a foreign country. ▷ *n* **3** non-native plant. **exotica** *pl n* (collection of) exotic objects.

expand ❶ *v* **1** make or become larger. **2** spread out. **3** (foll. by *on*) enlarge (on). **4** become more relaxed, friendly, and talkative. **expansion** *n* **expanse** *n* uninterrupted wide area. **expansive** *adj* **1** wide or extensive. **2** friendly and talkative.

expatiate [iks-**pay**-shee-ate] *v* (foll. by *on*) speak or write at great length (on).

expatriate ❶ [eks-**pat**-ree-it] *adj* **1** living outside one's native country. ▷ *n* **2** person living outside his or her native country.

— THESAURUS —

show **2** = **show**, demonstrate, express, indicate, manifest, reveal

exhort *v* = **urge**, advise, beseech, call upon, entreat, persuade, press, spur

exhume *v* = **dig up**, disentomb, disinter, unearth

exigency *n* = **need**, constraint, demand, necessity, requirement

exile *n* **1** = **banishment**, deportation, expatriation, expulsion **2** = **expatriate**, deportee, émigré, outcast, refugee ▷ *v* **3** = **banish**, deport, drive out, eject, expatriate, expel

exist *v* **1** = **be**, be present, occur **2** = **survive**, eke out a living, get along *or* by, keep one's head above water, stay alive, subsist **3** = **live**, endure

exit *n* **1** = **way out**, door, gate, outlet **2** = **departure**, exodus, farewell, going, goodbye, leave-taking, retreat, withdrawal ▷ *v* **4** = **depart**, go away, go out, leave, make tracks, retire, retreat, take one's leave, withdraw **4** = **go offstage** (*Theatre*)

exodus *n* = **departure**, evacuation, exit, flight, going out, leaving, migration, retreat, withdrawal

exonerate *v* = **clear**, absolve, acquit, discharge, exculpate, excuse, justify, pardon, vindicate

exorbitant *adj* = **excessive**, extortionate, extravagant, immoderate, inordinate, outrageous, preposterous, unreasonable

exorcize *v* = **drive out**, cast out, deliver (from), expel, purify

exotic *adj* **1** = **unusual**, colourful, fascinating, glamorous, mysterious, strange, striking, unfamiliar **2** = **foreign**, alien, external, imported, naturalized

expand *v* **1** = **increase**, amplify, broaden, develop, enlarge, extend, grow, magnify, swell, widen **2** = **spread (out)**, diffuse, stretch (out), unfold, unfurl, unravel, unroll **3** (foll. by *on*) = **go into detail about**, amplify, develop, elaborate on, embellish, enlarge on, expatiate on, expound on, flesh out

expatriate *adj* **1** = **exiled**, banished, emigrant, émigré ▷ *n* **2** = **exile**, emigrant, émigré, refugee

expect ❶ v 1 regard as probable. 2 look forward to, await. 3 require as an obligation. **expectancy** n 1 something expected on the basis of an average, e.g. *life expectancy*. 2 feeling of anticipation. **expectant** adj 1 expecting or hopeful. 2 pregnant. **expectation** n 1 act or state of expecting. 2 something looked forward to. 3 attitude of anticipation or hope.

expedient ❶ n 1 something that achieves a particular purpose. ▷ adj 2 suitable to the circumstances, appropriate. **expediency** n.

expedite v hasten the progress of. **expedition** n 1 organized journey, esp. for exploration. 2 people and equipment comprising an expedition. 3 pleasure trip or excursion. **expeditionary** adj relating to an expedition, esp. a military one. **expeditious** adj done quickly and efficiently.

expel ❶ v -pelling, -pelled 1 drive out with force. 2 dismiss from a school etc. permanently. **expulsion** n.

expend ❶ v spend, use up. **expendable** adj able to be sacrificed to achieve an objective. **expenditure** n 1 something expended, esp. money. 2 amount expended. **expense** n 1 cost. 2 (cause of) spending. ▷ pl 3 charges, outlay incurred. **expensive** adj high-priced.

experience ❶ n 1 direct personal participation. 2 particular incident, feeling, etc. that a person has undergone. 3 accumulated knowledge. ▷ v 4 participate in. 5 be affected by (an emotion). **experienced** adj skilful from extensive participation.

experiment ❶ n 1 test to provide evidence to prove or disprove a theory. 2 attempt at something new. ▷ v 3 carry out an experiment. **experimental** adj **experimentation** n.

expert ❶ n 1 person with extensive skill or knowledge in a particular field. ▷ adj 2 skilful or knowledgeable. **expertise** [eks-per-**teez**] n special skill or knowledge.

expiate v make amends for.

expire ❶ v 1 finish or run out. 2 breathe out. 3 *lit* die. **expiration** n **expiry** n end, esp. of a contract period.

———————————————————————————— THESAURUS ——————

expect v 1 = **think**, assume, believe, imagine, presume, reckon, suppose, surmise, trust 2 = **look forward to**, anticipate, await, contemplate, envisage, hope for, predict, watch for 3 = **require**, call for, demand, insist on, want

expedient n 1 = **means**, contrivance, device, makeshift, measure, method, resort, scheme, stopgap ▷ adj 2 = **advantageous**, appropriate, beneficial, convenient, effective, helpful, opportune, practical, suitable, useful

expel v 1 = **drive out**, belch, cast out, discharge, eject, remove, spew 2 = **dismiss**, ban, banish, drum out, evict, exclude, exile, throw out, turf out (*inf*)

expend v = **spend**, consume, dissipate, exhaust, go through, pay out, use (up)

experience n 1 = **participation**, contact, exposure, familiarity, involvement

2 = **event**, adventure, affair, encounter, episode, happening, incident, occurrence 3 = **knowledge**, practice, training ▷ v 4 = **undergo**, encounter, endure, face, feel, go through, live through, sample, taste

experiment n 1 = **test**, examination, experimentation, investigation, procedure, proof, research 2 = **trial**, trial run ▷ v 3 = **test**, examine, investigate, put to the test, research, sample, try, verify

expert n 1 = **master**, authority, connoisseur, dab hand (*Brit inf*), fundi (*S Afr*), guru, mana (*NZ*), past master, professional, specialist, virtuoso ▷ adj 2 = **skilful**, adept, adroit, experienced, masterly, practised, professional, proficient, qualified, virtuoso

expire v 1 = **finish**, cease, close, come to an end, conclude, end, lapse, run out, stop, terminate 2 = **breathe out**, emit,

explain ❶ v 1 make clear and intelligible. 2 account for. **explanation** n **explanatory** adj.

expletive n swearword.

explicable adj able to be explained. **explication** n.

explicit ❶ adj 1 precisely and clearly expressed. 2 shown in realistic detail. **explicitly** adv.

explode ❶ v 1 burst with great violence, blow up. 2 react suddenly with emotion. 3 increase rapidly. 4 show (a theory etc.) to be baseless. **explosion** n **explosive** adj 1 tending to explode. ▷ n 2 substance that causes explosions.

exploit ❶ v 1 take advantage of for one's own purposes. 2 make the best use of. ▷ n 3 notable feat or deed. **exploitation** n **exploiter** n.

explore ❶ v 1 investigate. 2 travel into (unfamiliar regions), esp. for scientific purposes. **exploration** n **exploratory** adj **explorer** n.

exponent ❶ n 1 person who advocates an idea, cause, etc. 2 skilful performer, esp. a musician.

export n 1 selling or shipping of goods to a foreign country. 2 product shipped or sold to a foreign country. ▷ v 3 sell or ship (goods) to a foreign country.

expose ❶ v 1 uncover or reveal. 2 make vulnerable, leave unprotected. 3 subject (a photographic film) to light. **expose oneself** display one's sexual organs in public. **exposure** n 1 exposing. 2 lack of shelter from the weather, esp. the cold. 3 appearance before the public, as on television.

exposé [iks-**pose**-ay] n bringing of a crime, scandal, etc. to public notice.

expound ❶ v explain in detail. **exposition** n 1 explanation. 2 large public exhibition.

express ❶ v 1 put into words. 2 show (an emotion). 3 indicate by a symbol or formula. 4 squeeze out (juice etc.). ▷ adj 5 explicitly stated. 6 (of a purpose) particular. 7 of or for rapid transportation of people, mail, etc. ▷ n 8 fast train or bus stopping at only a few stations. ▷ adv 9 by express delivery. **expression** n 1 expressing. 2 word or phrase. 3 showing or communication of emotion.

———————————— THESAURUS ————————————

exhale, expel 3 *Lit* = **die**, cark (*Aust & NZ sl*), depart, kick the bucket (*inf*), pass away *or* on, perish

explain v 1 = **make clear** *or* **plain**, clarify, clear up, define, describe, elucidate, expound, resolve, teach 2 = **account for**, excuse, give a reason for, justify

explicit adj 1 = **clear**, categorical, definite, frank, precise, specific, straightforward, unambiguous

explode v 1 = **blow up**, burst, detonate, discharge, erupt, go off, set off, shatter 4 = **disprove**, debunk, discredit, give the lie to, invalidate, refute, repudiate

exploit v 1 = **take advantage of**, abuse, manipulate, milk, misuse, play on *or* upon 2 = **make the best use of**, capitalize on, cash in on (*inf*), profit by *or* from, use, utilize ▷ n 3 = **feat**, accomplishment, achievement, adventure, attainment,

deed, escapade, stunt

explore v 1 = **investigate**, examine, fossick (*Aust & NZ*), inquire into, inspect, look into, probe, research, search 2 = **travel**, reconnoitre, scout, survey, tour

exponent n 1 = **advocate**, backer, champion, defender, promoter, proponent, supporter, upholder 2 = **performer**, player

expose v 1 = **uncover**, display, exhibit, present, reveal, show, unveil 2 = **make vulnerable**, endanger, imperil, jeopardize, lay open, leave open, subject

expound v = **explain**, describe, elucidate, interpret, set forth, set out, unfold

express v 1 = **state**, articulate, communicate, declare, phrase, put into words, say, utter, voice, word 2 = **show**, convey, exhibit, intimate, make known, reveal 3 = **represent**, indicate, signify,

4 look on the face that indicates mood. **5** *Maths* variable, function, or some combination of these. **expressionless** *adj* **expressive** *adj*.

expropriate *v* deprive an owner of (property). **expropriation** *n*.

expunge *v* delete, erase, blot out.

expurgate *v* remove objectionable parts from (a book etc.).

exquisite ❶ *adj* **1** of extreme beauty or delicacy. **2** intense in feeling. **exquisitely** *adv*.

extend ❶ *v* **1** draw out or be drawn out, stretch. **2** last for a certain time. **3** (foll. by *to*) include. **4** increase in size or scope. **5** offer, e.g. *extend one's sympathy*. **extendable** *adj* **extension** *n* **1** room or rooms added to an existing building. **2** additional telephone connected to the same line as another. **3** extending. **extensive** *adj* having a large extent, widespread. **extensor** *n* muscle that extends a part of the body. **extent** *n* range over which something extends, area.

● **SPELLING TIP**
● Lots of nouns in English end with *-tion*,
● but **extension** is not one of them.

extenuate *v* make (an offence or fault) less blameworthy.

exterior ❶ *n* **1** part or surface on the outside. **2** outward appearance. ▷ *adj* **3** of, on, or coming from the outside.

exterminate ❶ *v* destroy (animals or people) completely. **extermination** *n*.

external ❶ *adj* of, situated on, or coming from the outside. **externally** *adv*.

extinct ❶ *adj* **1** having died out. **2** (of a volcano) no longer liable to erupt. **extinction** *n*.

extinguish ❶ *v* **1** put out (a fire or light). **2** remove or destroy entirely. **extinguisher** *n*.

extol ❶ *v* **-tolling, -tolled** praise highly.

extort ❶ *v* get (something) by force or threats. **extortion** *n* **extortionate** *adj* (of prices) excessive.

extra ❶ *adj* **1** more than is usual, expected or needed. ▷ *n* **2** additional person or thing. **3** something for which an additional charge is made. **4** *Films* actor hired for crowd scenes. ▷ *adv* **5** unusually or exceptionally.

extra- *prefix* outside or beyond an area or scope, e.g. *extrasensory; extraterritorial*.

───────────────── THESAURUS ─────────────────

stand for, symbolize ▷ *adj* **5** = **explicit**, categorical, clear, definite, distinct, plain, unambiguous **6** = **specific**, clear-cut, especial, particular, singular, special **7** = **fast**, direct, high-speed, nonstop, rapid, speedy, swift

exquisite *adj* **1** = **beautiful**, attractive, comely, dainty, delicate, elegant, fine, lovely, pleasing **2** = **intense**, acute, keen, sharp

extend *v* **1** = **make longer**, drag out, draw out, lengthen, prolong, spin out, spread out, stretch **2** = **last**, carry on, continue, go on **4** = **widen**, add to, augment, broaden, enhance, enlarge, expand, increase, supplement **5** = **offer**, confer, impart, present, proffer

exterior *n* **1** = **outside**, coating, covering, facade, face, shell, skin, surface ▷ *adj*

3 = **outside**, external, outer, outermost, outward, surface

exterminate *v* = **destroy**, abolish, annihilate, eliminate, eradicate

external *adj* = **outer**, exterior, outermost, outside, outward, surface

extinct *adj* **1** = **dead**, defunct, gone, lost, vanished

extinguish *v* **1** = **put out**, blow out, douse, quench, smother, snuff out, stifle **2** = **destroy**, annihilate, eliminate, end, eradicate, exterminate, remove, wipe out

extol *v* = **praise**, acclaim, commend, eulogize, exalt, glorify, sing the praises of

extort *v* = **force**, blackmail, bully, coerce, extract, squeeze

extra *adj* **1 a** = **additional**, added, ancillary, auxiliary, further, more, supplementary **b** = **surplus**, excess, leftover, redundant,

extract ❶ v **1** pull out by force. **2** remove. **3** derive. **4** copy out (an article, passage, etc.) from a publication. ▷ n **5** something extracted, such as a passage from a book etc. **6** preparation containing the concentrated essence of a substance, e.g. *beef extract*. **extraction** n **extractor** n.

extramural adj connected with but outside the normal courses of a university or college.

extraneous ❶ [iks-**train**-ee-uss] adj irrelevant.

extraordinary ❶ adj **1** very unusual. **2** (of a meeting) specially arranged to deal with a particular subject. **extraordinarily** adv.

extrapolate v **1** infer (something not known) from the known facts. **2** *Maths* estimate (a value of a function or measurement) beyond the known values by the extension of a curve. **extrapolation** n.

extrasensory adj **extrasensory perception** supposed ability to obtain information other than through the normal senses.

extravagant ❶ adj **1** spending money excessively. **2** going beyond reasonable limits. **extravagance** n **extravaganza** n elaborate and lavish entertainment, display, etc.

● **SPELLING TIP**
● Make sure that **extravagant** ends in
● -*ant*, even though -*ent* sounds like a
● possibility.

extreme ❶ adj **1** of a high or the highest degree or intensity. **2** severe. **3** immoderate. **4** farthest or outermost. ▷ n **5** either of the two limits of a scale or range. **extremely** adv **extremist** n **1** person who favours immoderate methods. ▷ adj **2** holding extreme opinions. **extremity** n, pl -**ties 1** farthest point. **2** extreme condition, as of misfortune. ▷ pl **3** hands and feet. **extreme sport** sport with a high risk of injury or death.

extricate ❶ v free from complication or difficulty.

extrovert ❶ adj **1** lively and outgoing. **2** concerned more with external reality than inner feelings. ▷ n **3** extrovert person.

extrude v squeeze or force out. **extrusion** n.

exuberant ❶ adj **1** high-spirited. **2** growing luxuriantly. **exuberance** n.

THESAURUS
---

spare, superfluous, unused ▷ n **2** = **addition**, accessory, attachment, bonus, extension, supplement ▷ adv **5** = **exceptionally**, especially, extraordinarily, extremely, particularly, remarkably, uncommonly, unusually

extract v **1** = **pull out**, draw, pluck out, pull, remove, take out, uproot, withdraw **3** = **derive**, draw, elicit, glean, obtain ▷ n **5** = **passage**, citation, clipping, cutting, excerpt, quotation, selection **6** = **essence**, concentrate, distillation, juice

extraneous adj = **irrelevant**, beside the point, immaterial, inappropriate, off the subject, unconnected, unrelated

extraordinary adj **1** = **unusual**, amazing, exceptional, fantastic, outstanding, phenomenal, remarkable, strange, uncommon

extravagant adj **1** = **wasteful**, lavish, prodigal, profligate, spendthrift **2** = **excessive**, outrageous, over the top (sl), preposterous, reckless, unreasonable

extreme adj **1** = **maximum**, acute, great, highest, intense, severe, supreme, ultimate, utmost **2** = **severe**, drastic, harsh, radical, rigid, strict, uncompromising **3** = **excessive**, fanatical, immoderate, radical **4** = **farthest**, far-off, most distant, outermost, remotest ▷ n **5** = **limit**, boundary, edge, end, extremity, pole

extricate v = **free**, disengage, disentangle, get out, release, remove, rescue, wriggle out of

extrovert adj **1** = **outgoing**, exuberant, gregarious, sociable

exuberant adj **1** = **high-spirited**,

exude v 1 (of a liquid or smell) seep or flow out slowly and steadily. 2 make apparent by mood or behaviour, e.g. *exude confidence*.

exult ⊙ v be joyful or jubilant. **exultation** n **exultant** adj.

eye ⊙ n 1 organ of sight. 2 external part of an eye. 3 (often pl) ability to see. 4 attention, e.g. *his new shirt caught my eye*. 5 ability to judge or appreciate, e.g. *a good eye for detail*. 6 one end of a sewing needle. 7 small area of calm at the centre of a hurricane. 8 dark spot on a potato from which a stem grows. ▷ v **eyeing** or **eying**, **eyed** 9 look at carefully or warily. **eyelet** n 1 small hole for a lace or cord to be passed through. 2 ring that

strengthens this. **eyeball** n ball-shaped part of the eye. **eyebrow** n line of hair on the bony ridge above the eye. **eyelash** n short hair that grows out from the eyelid. **eyelid** n fold of skin that covers the eye when it is closed. **eyeliner** n cosmetic used to outline the eyes. **eye-opener** n *informal* something startling or revealing. **eye shadow** coloured cosmetic worn on the upper eyelids. **eyesight** n ability to see. **eyesore** n ugly object. **eyetooth** n canine tooth. **eyewitness** n person who was present at an event and can describe what happened.

eyrie n 1 nest of an eagle. 2 high isolated place.

—————————————————————————— THESAURUS ——————

animated, cheerful, ebullient, energetic, enthusiastic, lively, spirited, vivacious 2 = **luxuriant**, abundant, copious, lavish, plentiful, profuse

exult v = **be joyful**, be overjoyed, celebrate, jump for joy, rejoice

eye n 1 = **eyeball**, optic (*inf*) 5 = **appreciation**, discernment, discrimination, judgment, perception, recognition, taste ▷ v 9 = **look at**, check out (*inf*), contemplate, inspect, study, survey, view, watch

Ff

F Fahrenheit.

fable ● *n* **1** story with a moral. **2** false or fictitious account. **3** legend. **fabled** *adj* made famous in legend. **fabulous** *adj* amazing.

fabric ● *n* **1** knitted or woven cloth. **2** framework or structure.

face ● *n* **1** front of the head. **2** facial expression. **3** distorted expression. **4** outward appearance. **5** front or main side. **6** dial of a clock. **7** exposed area of coal or ore in a mine. **8** dignity, self-respect. ▷ *v* **9** look or turn towards. **10** be opposite. **11** be confronted by. **12** provide with a surface. **faceless** *adj* impersonal, anonymous. **face-lift** *n* operation to tighten facial skin, to remove wrinkles.

face-saving *adj* maintaining dignity or self-respect. **face up to** *v* accept (an unpleasant fact or reality). **face value** apparent worth or meaning.

facetious ● [fas-**see**-shuss] *adj* funny or trying to be funny, esp. at inappropriate times.

facia *n*, *pl* **-ciae** same as FASCIA.

facile ● [**fas**-sile] *adj* (of a remark, argument, etc.) superficial and showing lack of real thought.

facsimile ● [fak-**sim**-ill-ee] *n* exact copy.

fact ● *n* **1** event or thing known to have happened or existed. **2** provable truth. **facts of life** details of sex and reproduction. **factual** *adj*.

faction ● *n* **1** (dissenting) minority group within a larger body. **2** dissension. **factious** *adj* of or producing factions.

factor ● *n* **1** element contributing to a result. **2** *Maths* one of the integers multiplied together to give a given number. **3** *Scot* property manager. **factorial** *n* product of all the integers from one to a given number.

THESAURUS
---

fable *n* **1** = **story**, allegory, legend, myth, parable, tale **2, 3** = **fiction**, fabrication, fantasy, invention, tall story (*inf*), urban legend, urban myth, yarn (*inf*)

fabric *n* **1** = **cloth**, material, stuff, textile, web **2** = **framework**, constitution, construction, foundations, make-up, organization, structure

face *n* **1** = **countenance**, features, mug (*sl*), visage **2** = **expression**, appearance, aspect, look **3** = **scowl**, frown, grimace, pout, smirk **4** = **side**, exterior, front, outside, surface **8** = **self-respect**, authority, dignity, honour, image, prestige, reputation, standing, status ▷ *v* **10** = **look onto**, be opposite, front onto, overlook **11** = **confront**, brave, come up against, deal with, encounter, experience, meet, oppose, tackle **12** = **coat**, clad, cover, dress, finish

facetious *adj* = **funny**, amusing, comical, droll, flippant, frivolous, humorous, jocular, playful, tongue in cheek

facile *adj* = **superficial**, cursory, glib, hasty, shallow, slick

facsimile *n* = **copy**, carbon copy, duplicate, fax, photocopy, print, replica, reproduction, transcript

fact *n* **1** = **event**, *fait accompli*, act, deed, happening, incident, occurrence, performance **2** = **truth**, certainty, reality

faction[1] *n* **1** = **group**, bloc, cabal, clique, contingent, coterie, gang, party, set, splinter group **2** = **dissension**, conflict, disagreement, discord, disunity, division, infighting, rebellion

factor *n* **1** = **element**, aspect, cause, component, consideration, influence, item, part

f

factory ❶ *n, pl* **-ries** building where goods are manufactured.

faculty ❶ *n, pl* **-ties** **1** physical or mental ability. **2** department in a university or college.

fad ❶ *n* **1** short-lived fashion. **2** whim.

fade ❶ *v* **1** (cause to) lose brightness, colour, or strength. **2** vanish slowly.

faeces [**fee**-seez] *pl n* **1** waste matter discharged from the anus. **faecal** [**fee**-kl] *adj*.

fag¹ *n* **1** *informal* boring task. **2** young public schoolboy who does menial chores for a senior boy. ▷ *v* **3** do menial chores in a public school.

fag² *n slang* cigarette. **fag end 1** last and worst part. **2** *slang* cigarette stub.

faggot *n* **1** ball of chopped liver, herbs, and bread. **2** bundle of sticks for fuel.

Fahrenheit [**far**-ren-hite] *adj* of a temperature scale with the freezing point of water at 32° and the boiling point at 212°.

fail ❶ *v* **1** be unsuccessful. **2** stop operating. **3** be or judge to be below the required standard in a test. **4** disappoint or be useless to (someone). **5** neglect or be unable to do (something). ▷ *n* **6** instance of not passing an exam or test. **without fail 1** regularly. **2** definitely. **failing** *n* **1** weak point. ▷ *prep* **2** in the absence of. **failure** *n* **1** act or instance of failing. **2** unsuccessful person or thing.

faint ❶ *adj* **1** lacking clarity, brightness, or volume. **2** feeling dizzy or weak. **3** lacking conviction or force. ▷ *v* **4** lose consciousness temporarily. ▷ *n* **5** temporary loss of consciousness.

fair¹ ❶ *adj* **1** unbiased and reasonable. **2** light in colour. **3** beautiful. **4** quite good, e.g. *a fair attempt*. **5** quite large, e.g. *a fair amount of money*. **6** (of weather) fine. ▷ *adv* **7** fairly. **fairly** *adv* **1** moderately. **2** to a great degree or extent. **3** as deserved, reasonably. **fairness** *n* **fairway** *n Golf* smooth area between the tee and the green.

fair² ❶ *n* **1** travelling entertainment with sideshows, rides, and amusements.

——————————————— THESAURUS ———————————————

factory *n* = **works**, mill, plant

faculty *n* **1** = **ability**, aptitude, capacity, facility, power, propensity, skill **2** = **department**, school

fad *n* **1** = **craze**, fashion, mania, rage, trend, vogue **2** = **whim**

fade *v* **1** = **pale**, bleach, discolour, lose colour, wash out **2** = **dwindle**, decline, die away, disappear, dissolve, melt away, vanish, wane

fail *v* **1** = **be unsuccessful**, bite the dust, break down, come to grief, come unstuck, fall, fizzle out (*inf*), flop (*inf*), founder, miscarry, misfire **2** = **give out**, cark (*Aust & NZ sl*), conk out (*inf*), cut out, die, peter out, stop working **4**, **5** = **disappoint**, abandon, desert, forget, forsake, let down, neglect, omit **without fail 1** = **regularly**, like clockwork, religiously **2** = **dependably**, conscientiously, constantly, without exception

faint *adj* **1** = **dim**, distant, faded, indistinct, low, muted, soft, subdued, vague **2** = **dizzy**, exhausted, giddy, light-headed, muzzy, weak, woozy (*inf*) **3** = **slight**, feeble, remote, unenthusiastic, weak ▷ *v* **4** = **pass out**, black out, collapse, flake out (*inf*), keel over (*inf*), lose consciousness, swoon (*lit*) ▷ *n* **5** = **blackout**, collapse, swoon (*lit*), unconsciousness

fair¹ *adj* **1** = **unbiased**, above board, equitable, even-handed, honest, impartial, just, lawful, legitimate, proper, unprejudiced **2** = **light**, blond, blonde, fair-haired, flaxen-haired, towheaded **3** = **beautiful**, bonny, comely, handsome, lovely, pretty **4**, **5** = **respectable**, adequate, average, decent, moderate, O.K. or okay (*inf*), passable, reasonable, satisfactory, tolerable **6** = **fine**, bright, clear, cloudless, dry, sunny, unclouded

fair² *n* **1** = **carnival**, bazaar, festival, fete, gala, show

2 exhibition of commercial or industrial products. **fairground** n open space used for a fair.

fairy ❶ n, pl **fairies** 1 imaginary small creature with magic powers. 2 *offens* male homosexual. **fairy godmother** person who helps in time of trouble. **fairyland** n **fairy lights** small coloured electric bulbs used as decoration. **fairy penguin** small penguin with a bluish head and back, found on the Australian coast. **fairy tale, story** 1 story about fairies or magic. 2 unbelievable story or explanation.

faith ❶ n 1 strong belief, esp. without proof. 2 religion. 3 complete confidence or trust. 4 allegiance to a person or cause. **faithful** adj 1 loyal. 2 consistently reliable. 3 accurate in detail. **faithfully** adv **faithless** adj disloyal or dishonest.

fake ❶ v 1 cause something not genuine to appear real or more valuable by fraud. 2 pretend to have (an illness, emotion, etc.). ▷ n 3 person, thing, or act that is not genuine. ▷ adj 4 not genuine.

falcon n small bird of prey. **falconry** n 1 art of training falcons. 2 sport of hunting with trained falcons.

fall ❶ v **falling, fell, fallen** 1 drop from a higher to a lower place through the force of gravity. 2 collapse to the ground. 3 decrease in number or quality. 4 slope downwards. 5 die in battle. 6 be captured. 7 pass into a specified condition. 8 (of the face) take on a sad expression. 9 occur. 10 yield to temptation. ▷ n 11 falling. 12 thing or amount that falls. 13 decrease in value or number. 14 decline in power or influence. 15 capture or overthrow. 16 US autumn. ▷ pl 17 waterfall. **fall for** v 1 *informal* fall in love with. 2 be deceived by (a lie or trick). **fall guy** 1 *informal* victim of a confidence trick. 2 scapegoat. **fallout** n radioactive particles spread as a result of a nuclear explosion.

fallacy ❶ n, pl **-cies** 1 false belief. 2 unsound reasoning. **fallacious** adj.

fallow ❶ adj (of land) ploughed but left unseeded to regain fertility.

false ❶ adj 1 not true or correct. 2 artificial, fake. 3 deceptive, e.g. *false promises*. **falsely** adv **falseness** n **falsity** n **falsehood** n 1 quality of being untrue. 2 lie.

fairy n 1 = **sprite**, brownie, elf, leprechaun, peri, pixie

faith n 1, 3 = **confidence**, assurance, conviction, credence, credit, dependence, reliance, trust 2 = **religion**, belief, church, communion, creed, denomination, dogma, persuasion 4 = **allegiance**, constancy, faithfulness, fidelity, loyalty

fake v 1 = **counterfeit**, copy, fabricate, forge 2 = **sham**, feign, pretend, put on, simulate ▷ n 3 = **impostor**, charlatan, copy, forgery, fraud, hoax, imitation, reproduction, sham ▷ adj 4 = **artificial**, counterfeit, false, forged, imitation, mock, phoney or phony (*inf*), sham

fall v 1, 2 = **descend**, cascade, collapse, dive, drop, plummet, plunge, sink, subside, tumble 3 = **decrease**, decline, diminish, drop, dwindle, go down, lessen, slump, subside 4 = **slope**, fall

away, incline 5 = **die**, be killed, cark (*Aust & NZ sl*), meet one's end, perish 6 = **be overthrown**, capitulate, pass into enemy hands, succumb, surrender 9 = **occur**, befall, chance, come about, come to pass, happen, take place 10 = **lapse**, err, go astray, offend, sin, transgress, trespass ▷ n 11 = **descent**, dive, drop, nose dive, plummet, plunge, slip, tumble 13 = **decrease**, cut, decline, dip, drop, lessening, lowering, reduction, slump 14, 15 = **collapse**, capitulation, defeat, destruction, downfall, overthrow, ruin

fallacy n 1 = **error**, delusion, falsehood, flaw, misapprehension, misconception, mistake, untruth

fallow adj = **uncultivated**, dormant, idle, inactive, resting, unplanted, unused

false adj 1 = **incorrect**, erroneous, faulty, inaccurate, inexact, invalid, mistaken,

falsetto n, pl **-tos** voice pitched higher than one's natural range.

falter ⊙ v 1 be hesitant, weak, or unsure. 2 lose power momentarily. 3 utter hesitantly. 4 move unsteadily.

fame ⊙ n state of being widely known or recognized. **famed** adj famous.

familiar ⊙ adj 1 well-known. 2 intimate, friendly. 3 too friendly. ▷ n 4 demon supposed to attend a witch. 5 friend. **familiarly** adv **familiarity** n **familiarize** v acquaint fully with a particular subject.

family ⊙ n, pl **-lies** 1 group of parents and their children. 2 one's spouse and children. 3 group descended from a common ancestor. 4 group of related objects or beings. ▷ adj 5 suitable for parents and children together. **familial** adj **family planning** control of the number of children in a family by the use of contraception.

famine ⊙ n severe shortage of food.

fan¹ ⊙ n 1 hand-held or mechanical object used to create a current of air for ventilation or cooling. ▷ v **fanning, fanned** 2 blow or cool with a fan. 3 spread out like a fan. **fanbase** n body of admirers of a particular pop singer, sports team, etc.

fan² ⊙ n informal devotee of a pop star, sport, or hobby.

fanatic ⊙ n person who is excessively enthusiastic about something. **fanatical** adj **fanatically** adv **fanaticism** n.

fancy ⊙ adj **-cier, -ciest** 1 elaborate, not plain. 2 (of prices) higher than usual. ▷ n, pl **-cies** 3 sudden irrational liking or desire. 4 uncontrolled imagination. ▷ v **-cying, -cied** 5 informal be sexually attracted to. 6 informal have a wish for. 7 picture in the imagination. 8 suppose. **fancy oneself** informal have a high opinion of oneself. **fanciful** adj 1 not based on fact. 2 excessively elaborate. **fancy dress** party costume representing a historical figure, animal, etc. **fancy-free** adj not in love.

fanfare n short loud tune played on brass instruments.

───────── THESAURUS ─────────

wrong 2 = **artificial**, bogus, counterfeit, fake, forged, imitation, sham, simulated 3 = **untrue**, deceitful, deceptive, fallacious, fraudulent, hypocritical, lying, misleading, trumped up, unreliable, unsound, untruthful

falter v 1 = **hesitate**, vacillate, waver 3 = **stutter**, stammer 4 = **stumble**, totter

fame n = **prominence**, celebrity, glory, honour, renown, reputation, repute, stardom

familiar adj 1 = **well-known**, recognizable 2 = **friendly**, amicable, close, easy, intimate, relaxed 3 = **disrespectful**, bold, forward, impudent, intrusive, presumptuous

family n 1, 2 = **relations**, folk (inf), household, kin, kith and kin, one's nearest and dearest, one's own flesh and blood, relatives 3 = **clan**, dynasty, house, race, tribe 4 = **group**, class, genre, network, subdivision, system

famine n = **hunger**, dearth, scarcity, starvation

fan¹ n 1 = **blower**, air conditioner, ventilator ▷ v 2 = **blow**, air-condition, cool, refresh, ventilate

fan² n Inf = **supporter**, admirer, aficionado, buff (inf), devotee, enthusiast, follower, lover

fanatic n = **extremist**, activist, bigot, militant, zealot

fancy adj 1 = **elaborate**, baroque, decorative, embellished, extravagant, intricate, ornamental, ornate ▷ n 3 = **whim**, caprice, desire, humour, idea, impulse, inclination, notion, thought, urge 4 = **delusion**, chimera, daydream, dream, fantasy, vision ▷ v Inf = **be attracted to**, be captivated by, like, lust after, take a liking to, take to 6 Inf = **wish for**, crave, desire, hanker after, hope for, long for, thirst for, yearn for 7, 8 = **suppose**, believe, conjecture, imagine, reckon, think, think likely

fang *n* **1** snake's tooth which injects poison. **2** long pointed tooth.

fantasy ❶ *n, pl* **-sies 1** far-fetched notion. **2** imagination unrestricted by reality. **3** daydream. **4** fiction with a large fantasy content. **fantasize** *v* indulge in daydreams.

far ❶ *adv* **farther** or **further**, **farthest** or **furthest 1** at, to, or from a great distance. **2** at or to a remote time. **3** very much. ▷ *adj* **4** remote in space or time. **Far East** East Asia. **far-fetched** *adj* hard to believe.

farce ❶ *n* **1** boisterous comedy. **2** ludicrous situation. **farcical** *adj* ludicrous.

fare ❶ *n* **1** charge for a passenger's journey. **2** passenger. **3** food provided. ▷ *v* **4** get on (as specified), e.g. *we fared badly*.

farm ❶ *n* **1** area of land for growing crops or rearing livestock. **2** area of land or water for growing or rearing a specified animal or plant, e.g. *fish farm*. ▷ *v* **3** cultivate (land). **4** rear (stock). **farmer** *n* **farmhouse** *n* **farm out** *v* send (work) to be done by others. **farmstead** *n* farm and its buildings. **farmyard** *n*.

fart *taboo* ▷ *n* **1** emission of gas from the anus. ▷ *v* **2** emit gas from the anus.

farther, farthest *adv, adj* see FAR.

farthing *n* former British coin equivalent to a quarter of a penny.

fascia [**fay**-shya] *n, pl* **-ciae, -cias 1** outer surface of a dashboard. **2** flat surface above a shop window.

fascinate ❶ *v* **1** attract and interest strongly. **2** make motionless from fear or awe. **fascinating** *adj* **fascination** *n*.

● **SPELLING TIP**
● Remember that there is a silent *c* after
● the *s* in **fascinate**, **fascinated**, and
● **fascinating**.

fascism [**fash**-iz-zum] *n* right-wing totalitarian political system characterized by state control and extreme nationalism. **fascist** *adj, n*.

fashion ❶ *n* **1** style in clothes, hairstyle, etc., popular at a particular time. **2** way something happens or is done. ▷ *v* **3** form or make into a particular shape. **fashionable** *adj* currently popular. **fashionably** *adv*.

fast¹ ❶ *adj* **1** (capable of) acting or moving quickly. **2** done in or lasting a short time. **3** adapted to or allowing rapid movement. **4** (of a clock or watch) showing a time later than the correct time. **5** dissipated. **6** firmly

—————————————— THESAURUS ——————————————

fantasy *n* **1, 3** = **daydream**, dream, flight of fancy, illusion, mirage, pipe dream, reverie, vision **2** = **imagination**, creativity, fancy, invention, originality

far *adv* **1** = **a long way**, afar, a good way, a great distance, deep, miles **3** = **much**, considerably, decidedly, extremely, greatly, incomparably, very much ▷ *adj* **4** = **remote**, distant, faraway, far-flung, far-off, outlying, out-of-the-way

farce *n* **1** = **comedy**, buffoonery, burlesque, satire, slapstick **2** = **mockery**, joke, nonsense, parody, sham, travesty

fare *n* **1** = **charge**, price, ticket money **3** = **food**, provisions, rations, sustenance, victuals ▷ *v* **4** = **get on**, do, get along, make out, manage, prosper

farm *n* **1** = **smallholding**, croft (*Scot*),

farmstead, grange, homestead, plantation, ranch (*chiefly N Amer*) ▷ *v* **3** = **cultivate**, plant, work

fascinate *v* **1** = **entrance**, absorb, beguile, captivate, engross, enthral, hold spellbound, intrigue **2** = **transfix**, rivet

fashion *n* **1** = **style**, craze, custom, fad, look, mode, rage, trend, vogue **2** = **method**, manner, mode, style, way ▷ *v* **3** = **make**, construct, create, forge, form, manufacture, mould, shape

fast¹ *adj* **1-3** = **quick**, brisk, fleet, flying, hasty, nippy (*Brit inf*), rapid, speedy, swift **5** = **dissipated**, dissolute, extravagant, loose, profligate, reckless, self-indulgent, wanton, wild **6** = **fixed**, close, fastened, firm, immovable, secure, sound, steadfast, tight ▷ *adv* **7** = **quickly**, hastily, hurriedly,

fixed, fastened, or shut. ▷ *adv* **7** quickly.
8 soundly, deeply, e.g. *fast asleep*.
9 tightly and firmly. **fast food** food, such
as hamburgers, prepared and served very
quickly.

fast² ❶ *v* **1** go without food, esp. for
religious reasons. ▷ *n* **2** period of fasting.

fasten ❶ *v* **1** make or become firmly fixed or
joined. **2** close by fixing in place or locking.
3 (foll. by *on*) direct (one's attention)
towards. **fastener**, **fastening** *n* device
that fastens.

fastidious *adj* **1** very fussy about details.
2 excessively concerned with cleanliness.

fat ❶ *adj* **fatter, fattest 1** having excess
flesh on the body. **2** (of meat) containing
a lot of fat. **3** thick. **4** profitable. ▷ *n*
5 extra flesh on the body. **6** oily substance
obtained from animals or plants. **fatten** *v*
(cause to) become fat. **fatty** *adj* containing
fat. **fathead** *n informal* stupid person.

fate ❶ *n* **1** power supposed to predetermine
events. **2** inevitable fortune that befalls
a person or thing. **fated** *adj* **1** destined.
2 doomed to death or destruction. **fateful**
adj having important, usu. disastrous,

consequences.

father ❶ *n* **1** male parent. **2** person who
founds a line or family. **3** man who starts,
creates, or invents something. **4** (**F-**)
God. **5** (**F-**) title of some priests. ▷ *v* **6** be
the father of (offspring). **fatherhood** *n*
fatherless *adj* **fatherly** *adj* **father-in-
law** *n, pl* **fathers-in-law** father of one's
husband or wife. **fatherland** *n* one's native
country.

fathom ❶ *n* **1** unit of measurement of
the depth of water, equal to six feet. ▷ *v*
2 understand. **fathomless** *adj* too deep or
difficult to fathom.

fatigue ❶ [fat-**eeg**] *n* **1** extreme physical
or mental tiredness. **2** weakening of
a material due to stress. **3** soldier's
nonmilitary duty. ▷ *v* **4** tire out.

fatuous ❶ *adj* foolish.

faucet [**faw**-set] *n US & Canad* valve with
handle, plug etc. to regulate or stop flow
of fluid.

fault ❶ *n* **1** responsibility for something
wrong. **2** defect or flaw. **3** mistake or error.
4 *Geology* break in layers of rock. **5** *Tennis,
squash, etc.* invalid serve. ▷ *v* **6** criticize or

— THESAURUS —

in haste, like lightning, rapidly, speedily,
swiftly **8** = **soundly**, deeply, firmly, fixedly,
securely, tightly

fast² *v* **1** = **go hungry**, abstain, deny
oneself, go without food ▷ *n* **2** = **fasting**,
abstinence

fasten *v* **1, 2** = **fix**, affix, attach, bind,
connect, join, link, secure, tie

fat *adj* **1** = **overweight**, corpulent, heavy,
obese, plump, podgy, portly, rotund, stout,
tubby **2** = **fatty**, adipose, greasy, oily,
oleaginous ▷ *n* **5** = **fatness**, blubber, bulk,
corpulence, flab, flesh, obesity, paunch

fate *n* **1** = **destiny**, chance, divine will,
fortune, kismet, nemesis, predestination,
providence **2** = **fortune**, cup, horoscope,
lot, portion, stars

father *n* **1** = **daddy** (*inf*), dad (*inf*), old
man (*inf*), pa (*inf*), papa (*old-fashioned
inf*), pater, pop (*inf*) **2** = **forefather**,

ancestor, forebear, predecessor, progenitor
3 = **founder**, architect, author, creator,
inventor, maker, originator, prime mover
5 (with cap.) = **priest**, padre (*inf*), pastor
▷ *v* **6** = **sire**, beget, get, procreate

fathom *v* **2** = **understand**, comprehend,
get to the bottom of, grasp, interpret

fatigue *n* **1** = **tiredness**, heaviness,
languor, lethargy, listlessness ▷ *v* **4** = **tire**,
drain, exhaust, knacker (*sl*), take it out of
(*inf*), weaken, wear out, weary

fatuous *adj* = **foolish**, brainless, idiotic,
inane, ludicrous, mindless, moronic, silly,
stupid, witless

faucet *noun* (*US & Canad*) = **tap**, spout,
spigot, stopcock, valve

fault *n* **1** = **responsibility**, accountability,
culpability, liability **2** = **flaw**, blemish,
defect, deficiency, failing, imperfection,
shortcoming, weakness, weak point

blame. **at fault** guilty of error. **find fault with** seek out minor imperfections in. **to a fault** excessively. **faulty** *adj* **faultless** *adj*.

faun *n* (in Roman legend) creature with a human face and torso and a goat's horns and legs.

fauna *n*, *pl* **-nas**, **-nae** animals of a given place or time.

faux pas [**foe pah**] *n*, *pl* **faux pas** social blunder.

favour ❶ *n* 1 approving attitude. 2 act of goodwill or generosity. 3 partiality. ▷ *v* 4 prefer. 5 regard or treat with especial kindness. 6 support or advocate. **favourable** *adj* **favourite** *n* favoured person or thing.

fawn¹ ❶ *n* 1 young deer. ▷ *adj* 2 light yellowish-brown.

fawn² ❶ *v* 1 (foll. by *on*) seek attention from (someone) by insincere flattery. 2 (of a dog) try to please by a show of extreme affection.

fax *n* 1 electronic system for sending facsimiles of documents by telephone.

2 document sent by this system. ▷ *v* 3 send (a document) by this system.

FBI *US* Federal Bureau of Investigation.

fear ❶ *n* 1 distress or alarm caused by impending danger or pain. 2 something that causes distress. ▷ *v* 3 be afraid of (something or someone). **fear for** feel anxiety about something. **fearful** *adj* 1 feeling fear. 2 causing fear. 3 *informal* very unpleasant. **fearfully** *adv* **fearless** *adj* **fearsome** *adj* terrifying.

feasible ❶ *adj* able to be done, possible. **feasibly** *adv* **feasibility** *n*.

feast ❶ *n* 1 lavish meal. 2 something extremely pleasing. 3 annual religious celebration. ▷ *v* 4 eat a feast. 5 (foll. by *on*) eat a large amount of.

feat ❶ *n* remarkable, skilful, or daring action.

feather *n* 1 one of the barbed shafts forming the plumage of birds. ▷ *v* 2 fit or cover with feathers. 3 turn (an oar) edgeways. **feather in one's cap** achievement one can be pleased with.

— THESAURUS —

3 = **mistake**, blunder, error, indiscretion, lapse, oversight, slip ▷ *v* 6 = **criticize**, blame, censure, find fault with, hold (someone) responsible, impugn **at fault** = **guilty**, answerable, blamable, culpable, in the wrong, responsible, to blame **find fault with** = **criticize**, carp at, complain, pick holes in, pull to pieces, quibble, take to task **to a fault** = **excessively**, immoderately, in the extreme, overmuch, unduly

favour *n* 1 = **approval**, approbation, backing, good opinion, goodwill, patronage, support 2 = **good turn**, benefit, boon, courtesy, indulgence, kindness, service ▷ *v* 4, 5 = **prefer**, incline towards, indulge, reward, side with, smile upon 6 = **support**, advocate, approve, champion, commend, encourage

fawn¹ *adj* 2 = **beige**, buff, greyish-brown, neutral

fawn² *v* 1 (foll. by *on*) = **ingratiate oneself**, crawl, creep, curry favour, dance

attendance, flatter, grovel, kowtow, pander to

fear *n* 1 = **dread**, alarm, apprehensiveness, fright, horror, panic, terror, trepidation 2 = **bugbear**, bête noire, bogey, horror, nightmare, spectre ▷ *v* 3 = **be afraid**, dread, shake in one's shoes, shudder at, take fright, tremble at ▷ *v* **fear for** = **worry about**, be anxious about, feel concern for

feasible *adj* = **possible**, achievable, attainable, likely, practicable, reasonable, viable, workable

feast *n* 1 = **banquet**, dinner, repast, spread (*inf*), treat 2 = **treat**, delight, enjoyment, gratification, pleasure 3 = **festival**, celebration, fete, holiday, holy day, red-letter day, saint's day ▷ *v* 4 = **eat one's fill**, gorge, gormandize, indulge, overindulge, pig out (*sl*)

feat *n* = **accomplishment**, achievement, act, attainment, deed, exploit, performance

feather one's nest make one's life comfortable. **feathered** adj **feathery** adj
featherweight n 1 boxer weighing up to 126lb (professional) or 57kg (amateur). 2 insignificant person or thing.
feature ❶ n 1 part of the face, such as the eyes. 2 prominent or distinctive part. 3 special article in a newspaper or magazine. 4 main film in a cinema programme. ▷ v 5 have as a feature or be a feature in. 6 give prominence to. **featureless** adj.
Feb. February.
February n second month of the year.
feckless ❶ adj ineffectual or irresponsible.
federal adj 1 of a system in which power is divided between one central government and several regional governments. 2 of the central government of a federation. **federalism** n **federalist** n **federate** v unite in a federation. **federation** n 1 union of several states, provinces, etc. 2 association.
fee ❶ n 1 charge paid to be allowed to do something. 2 payment for professional services.
feeble ❶ adj 1 lacking physical or mental power. 2 unconvincing. **feebleness** n **feebly** adv **feeble-minded** adj unable to think or understand effectively.

feed ❶ v **feeding, fed** 1 give food to. 2 give (something) as food. 3 eat. 4 supply or prepare food for. 5 supply (what is needed). ▷ n 6 act of feeding. 7 food, esp. for babies or animals. 8 informal meal.
feedback n 1 information received in response to something done. 2 return of part of the output of an electrical circuit or loudspeaker to its source.
feel ❶ v **feeling, felt** 1 have a physical or emotional sensation of. 2 become aware of or examine by touch. 3 believe. ▷ n 4 act of feeling. 5 impression. 6 way something feels. 7 sense of touch. 8 instinctive aptitude. **feeler** n 1 organ of touch in some animals. 2 remark made to test others' opinion. **feeling** n 1 emotional reaction. 2 intuitive understanding. 3 opinion. 4 sympathy, understanding. 5 ability to experience physical sensations. 6 sensation experienced. ▷ pl 7 emotional sensitivities. **feel like** wish for, want.
feet n plural of FOOT.
feign [fane] v pretend.
feint [faint] n 1 sham attack or blow meant to distract an opponent. ▷ v 2 make a feint.
feisty ❶ adj inf lively, resilient, and self-reliant. 2 US & Canad frisky. 3 US & Canad irritable.

——————————————————————— THESAURUS ———————————

feature n 2 = **aspect**, characteristic, facet, factor, hallmark, peculiarity, property, quality, trait 3 = **article**, column, item, piece, report, story 4 = **highlight**, attraction, main item, speciality ▷ v 6 = **spotlight**, emphasize, foreground, give prominence to, play up, present, star
feckless adj = **irresponsible**, good-for-nothing, hopeless, incompetent, ineffectual, shiftless, worthless
fee n 1, 2 = **charge**, bill, payment, remuneration, toll
feeble adj 1 = **weak**, debilitated, doddering, effete, frail, infirm, puny, sickly, weedy (inf) 2 = **flimsy**, inadequate, insufficient, lame, paltry, pathetic, poor, tame, thin, unconvincing

feed v 1, 2, 4 = **cater for**, nourish, provide for, provision, supply, sustain, victual, wine and dine 3 = **eat**, devour, exist on, live on, partake of ▷ n 7 = **food**, fodder, pasturage, provender 8 Inf = **meal**, feast, nosh (sl), repast, spread (inf)
feel v 1 = **experience**, be aware of, notice, observe, perceive 2 = **touch**, caress, finger, fondle, handle, manipulate, paw, stroke 3 = **believe**, consider, deem, hold, judge, think ▷ n 5 = **impression**, air, ambience, atmosphere, feeling, quality, sense 6 = **texture**, finish, surface, touch
feisty adjective (Informal, chiefly US & Canad) = **fiery**, spirited, bold, plucky, vivacious

felicity n 1 happiness. 2 pl **-ties** appropriate expression or style. **felicitations** pl n congratulations. **felicitous** adj.

feline adj 1 of cats. 2 catlike. ▷ n 3 member of the cat family.

fell¹ ❶ v 1 cut down (a tree). **2** knock down.

fell² n Scot & N English a mountain, hill, or moor.

fellow ❶ n 1 old-fashioned man or boy. **2** comrade or associate. **3** person in the same group or condition. **4** member of a learned society or the governing body of a college. ▷ adj **5** in the same group or condition. **fellowship** n 1 sharing of aims or interests. **2** group with shared aims or interests. **3** feeling of friendliness. **4** paid research post in a college or university.

felon n Criminal law (formerly) person guilty of a felony. **felony** n, pl **-nies** serious crime. **felonious** adj.

felt n matted fabric made by bonding fibres by pressure. **felt-tip pen** pen with a writing point made from pressed fibres.

female adj 1 of the sex which bears offspring. **2** (of plants) producing fruits. ▷ n **3** female person or animal.

feminine ❶ adj 1 having qualities traditionally regarded as suitable for, or typical of, women. **2** of women. **3** belonging to a particular class of grammatical inflection in some languages. **femininity** n **feminism** n advocacy of equal rights for women. **feminist** n, adj.

fen ❶ n low-lying flat marshy land.

fence ❶ n 1 barrier of posts linked by wire or wood, enclosing an area. **2** slang dealer in stolen property. ▷ v **3** enclose with or as if with a fence. **4** fight with swords as a sport. **5** avoid a question. **fencing** n **1** sport of fighting with swords. **2** material for making fences.

fend v **fend for oneself** provide for oneself. **fend off** v defend oneself against (verbal or physical attack).

feng shui [fung **shway**] n Chinese art of deciding the best design of a building, etc., in order to bring good luck.

fennel n fragrant plant whose seeds, leaves, and root are used in cookery.

feral adj wild.

ferment ❶ n 1 commotion, unrest. ▷ v **2** undergo or cause to undergo fermentation. **fermentation** n reaction in which an organic molecule splits into simpler substances, esp. the conversion of sugar to alcohol.

fern n flowerless plant with fine fronds.

ferocious ❶ adj savagely fierce or cruel. **ferocity** n.

ferret n **1** tamed polecat used to catch rabbits or rats. ▷ v **ferreting**, **ferreted 2** hunt with ferrets. **3** search around. **ferret out** v find by searching.

ferric, ferrous adj of or containing iron.

ferry ❶ n, pl **-ries 1** boat for transporting people and vehicles. ▷ v **-rying**, **-ried**

THESAURUS

---

fell¹ v 1 = **cut down**, cut, hew 2 = **knock down**, demolish, level

fellow n 1 Old-fashioned = **man**, bloke (Brit inf), chap (inf), character, guy (inf), individual, person 2, 3 = **associate**, colleague, companion, comrade, partner, peer

feminine adj 1, 2 = **womanly**, delicate, gentle, ladylike, soft, tender

fen n = **marsh**, bog, morass, quagmire, slough, swamp, muskeg (Canad)

fence n 1 = **barrier**, barricade, defence, hedge, palisade, railings, rampart, wall

▷ v 3 = **enclose**, bound, confine, encircle, pen, protect, surround 5 = **evade**, dodge, equivocate, flannel (Brit inf), parry

ferment n 1 = **commotion**, disruption, excitement, frenzy, furore, stir, tumult, turmoil, unrest, uproar

ferocious adj = **fierce**, bloodthirsty, brutal, cruel, predatory, rapacious, ravening, ruthless, savage, vicious, violent, wild

ferry n 1 = **ferry boat**, packet, packet boat ▷ v 2, 3 = **carry**, chauffeur, convey, run, ship, shuttle, transport

2 carry by ferry. 3 convey (goods or people).

fertile ⊕ adj 1 capable of producing young, crops, or vegetation. 2 highly productive, e.g. *a fertile mind*. **fertility** n **fertilize** v 1 provide (an animal or plant) with sperm or pollen to bring about fertilization. 2 supply (soil) with nutrients. **fertilization** n **fertilizer** n substance added to the soil to increase its productivity.

fervent, fervid ⊕ adj intensely passionate and sincere. **fervour** n intensity of feeling.

fester ⊕ v 1 grow worse and increasingly hostile. 2 (of a wound) form pus. 3 rot and decay.

festival ⊕ n 1 organized series of special events or performances. 2 day or period of celebration. **festive** adj of or like a celebration. **festivity** n, pl **-ties** 1 happy celebration. ▷ pl 2 celebrations.

festoon ⊕ v hang decorations in loops.

fete [**fate**] n 1 gala, bazaar, etc., usu. held outdoors. ▷ v 2 honour or entertain regally.

fetid adj stinking.

fetish ⊕ n 1 form of behaviour in which sexual pleasure is derived from looking at or handling an inanimate object. 2 thing with which one is excessively concerned. 3 object believed to have magical powers.

fetishism n **fetishist** n.

fetter n 1 chain or shackle for the foot. ▷ pl 2 restrictions. ▷ v 3 restrict. 4 bind in fetters.

fettle n state of health or spirits.

fetus [**fee**-tuss] n, pl **-tuses** embryo of a mammal in the later stages of development. **fetal** adj.

feud ⊕ n 1 long bitter hostility between two people or groups. ▷ v 2 carry on a feud.

fever ⊕ n 1 (illness causing) high body temperature. 2 nervous excitement. **fevered** adj **feverish** adj 1 suffering from fever. 2 in a state of nervous excitement.

few ⊕ adj not many. **a few** a small number. **quite a few, a good few** several.

● **USAGE NOTE**
● *Few(er)* is used of things that can be
● counted: *Fewer than five visits*. Compare
● *less*, which is used for quantity: *It uses*
● *less sugar*.

fez n, pl **fezzes** brimless tasselled cap, orig. from Turkey.

fiancé [fee-**on**-say] n man engaged to be married. **fiancée** n fem.

fiasco ⊕ n, pl **-cos, -coes** ridiculous or humiliating failure.

fib ⊕ n 1 trivial lie. ▷ v **fibbing, fibbed** 2 tell a lie. **fibber** n.

——————————————————— THESAURUS ———————————————

fertile adj = **productive**, abundant, fecund, fruitful, luxuriant, plentiful, prolific, rich, teeming

fervent, fervid adj = **intense**, ardent, devout, earnest, enthusiastic, heartfelt, impassioned, passionate, vehement

fester v 1 = **intensify**, aggravate, smoulder 2 = **suppurate**, ulcerate 3 = **putrefy**, decay

festival n 1 = **celebration**, carnival, entertainment, fête, gala, jubilee 2 = **holy day**, anniversary, commemoration, feast, fete, fiesta, holiday, red-letter day, saint's day

festoon v = **decorate**, array, deck, drape, garland, hang, swathe, wreathe

fetish n 1, 2 = **fixation**, mania, obsession,

thing (*inf*) 3 = **talisman**, amulet

feud n 1 = **hostility**, argument, conflict, disagreement, enmity, quarrel, rivalry, row, vendetta ▷ v 2 = **quarrel**, bicker, clash, contend, dispute, fall out, row, squabble, war

fever n 1 = **delirium** 2 = **excitement**, agitation, ferment, fervour, frenzy, restlessness

few adj = **not many**, meagre, negligible, rare, scanty, scarcely any, sparse, sporadic

fiasco n = **flop** (*inf*), catastrophe, cock-up (*Brit sl*), debacle, disaster, failure, mess, washout (*inf*)

fib n 1 = **lie**, fiction, story, untruth, white lie

fibre ❶ n 1 thread that can be spun into yarn. 2 threadlike animal or plant tissue. 3 fibrous material in food. 4 strength of character. 5 essential substance or nature. **fibrous** adj **fibreglass** n material made of fine glass fibres, used as insulation. **fibre optics** transmission of information by light along very thin flexible fibres of glass.

fickle ❶ adj changeable, inconstant. **fickleness** n.

fiction ❶ n 1 literary works of the imagination, such as novels. 2 invented story. **fictional** adj **fictionalize** v turn into fiction. **fictitious** adj 1 not genuine. 2 of or in fiction.

fiddle ❶ n 1 violin. 2 informal dishonest action or scheme. ▷ v 3 play the violin. 4 falsify (accounts). 5 move or touch something restlessly. **fiddling** adj trivial. **fiddly** adj awkward to do or use. **fiddlesticks** interj expression of annoyance or disagreement.

fidelity ❶ n 1 faithfulness. 2 accuracy in detail. 3 quality of sound reproduction.

fidget ❶ v 1 move about restlessly. ▷ n 2 person who fidgets. ▷ pl 3 restlessness.

fidgetingly adv **fidgety** adj.

field ❶ n 1 enclosed piece of agricultural land. 2 marked off area for sports. 3 area rich in a specified natural resource. 4 all the competitors in a competition. 5 all the competitors except the favourite. 6 battlefield. 7 sphere of knowledge or activity. 8 place away from the laboratory or classroom where practical work is done. 9 background, as of a flag. 10 area over which electric, gravitational, or magnetic force is exerted. ▷ v 11 Sport catch and return (a ball). 12 send (a player or team) on to the field. 13 play as a fielder. 14 deal with (a question) successfully. **fielder** n Sport player whose task is to field the ball. **field day** day or time of exciting activity. **field glasses** binoculars. **field marshal** army officer of the highest rank. **field sports** hunting, shooting, and fishing. **fieldwork** n investigation made in the field as opposed to the classroom or the laboratory.

fiend ❶ [feend] n 1 evil spirit. 2 cruel or wicked person. 3 informal person devoted to something, e.g. fitness fiend. **fiendish** adj.

——————— THESAURUS ———————

fibre n 1 = **thread**, filament, pile, strand, texture, wisp 4 = **strength of character**, resolution, stamina, strength, toughness 5 = **essence**, nature, quality, spirit, substance

fickle adj = **changeable**, capricious, faithless, inconstant, irresolute, temperamental, unfaithful, variable, volatile

fiction n 1 = **tale**, fantasy, legend, myth, novel, romance, story, yarn (inf) 2 = **lie**, cock and bull story (inf), fabrication, falsehood, invention, tall story, untruth, urban legend, urban myth

fiddle n 1 = **violin** 2 Inf = **fraud**, fix, racket, scam (sl), swindle ▷ v 4 = **cheat**, cook the books (inf), diddle (inf), fix, swindle, wangle (inf) 5 = **fidget**, finger, interfere with, mess about or around, play, tamper with, tinker

fidelity n 1 = **loyalty**, allegiance, constancy, dependability, devotion, faithfulness, staunchness, trustworthiness 2 = **accuracy**, closeness, correspondence, exactness, faithfulness, precision, scrupulousness

fidget v 1 = **move restlessly**, fiddle (inf), fret, squirm, twitch ▷ pl n 3 = **restlessness**, fidgetiness, jitters (inf), nervousness, unease, uneasiness

field n 1 = **meadow**, grassland, green, lea (poet), pasture 4 = **competitors**, applicants, candidates, competition, contestants, entrants, possibilities, runners 7 = **speciality**, area, department, discipline, domain, line, province, territory ▷ v 11 Sport = **retrieve**, catch, pick up, return, stop 14 = **deal with**, deflect, handle, turn aside

fiend n 1 = **demon**, devil, evil spirit 2 = **brute**, barbarian, beast, ghoul, monster, ogre, savage 3 Inf = **enthusiast**, addict, fanatic, freak (inf), maniac

fierce ❶ *adj* 1 wild or aggressive. 2 intense or strong. **fiercely** *adv* **fierceness** *n*.

fiery ❶ *adj* **fierier, fieriest** 1 consisting of or like fire. 2 easily angered. 3 (of food) very spicy.

fiesta *n* religious festival, carnival.

fifteen *adj*, *n* five and ten. **fifteenth** *adj*, *n*.

fig *n* 1 soft pear-shaped fruit. 2 tree bearing it.

fight ❶ *v* **fighting, fought** 1 struggle (against) in battle or physical combat. 2 struggle to overcome someone or obtain something. 3 carry on (a battle or contest). 4 make (one's way) somewhere with difficulty. ▷ *n* 5 aggressive conflict between two (groups of) people. 6 quarrel or contest. 7 resistance. 8 boxing match. **fighter** *n* 1 boxer. 2 determined person. 3 aircraft designed to destroy other aircraft. **fight off** *v* 1 drive away (an attacker). 2 struggle to avoid.

figment *n* **figment of one's imagination** imaginary thing.

figure ❶ *n* 1 numerical symbol. 2 amount expressed in numbers. 3 bodily shape. 4 well-known person. 5 representation in painting or sculpture of a human form. 6 diagram or illustration. 7 set of movements in dancing or skating. 8 *Maths* any combination of lines, planes, points, or curves. ▷ *v* 9 calculate (sums or amounts). 10 *US & Aust* consider, conclude. 11 (usu. foll. by *in*) be included (in). **figure of speech** expression in which words do not have their literal meaning. **figurative** *adj* (of language) abstract, imaginative, or symbolic. **figuratively** *adv* **figurine** *n* statuette. **figurehead** *n* 1 nominal leader. 2 carved bust at the bow of a ship. **figure out** *v* solve or understand.

filament *n* 1 fine wire in a light bulb that gives out light. 2 fine thread.

filch ❶ *v* steal (small amounts).

file¹ ❶ *n* 1 box or folder used to keep documents in order. 2 documents in a file. 3 information about a person or subject. 4 line of people one behind the other. 5 *Computers* organized collection of related material. ▷ *v* 6 place (a document) in a file. 7 place (a legal document) on official record. 8 bring a lawsuit, esp. for divorce. 9 walk or march in a line.

file² ❶ *n* 1 tool with a roughened blade for smoothing or shaping. ▷ *v* 2 shape or

——————————————————— THESAURUS ———————————————————

fierce *adj* 1 = **wild**, brutal, cruel, dangerous, ferocious, fiery, furious, menacing, powerful, raging, savage, stormy, strong, tempestuous, vicious, violent 2 = **intense**, cut-throat, keen, relentless, strong

fiery *adj* 1 = **burning**, ablaze, afire, aflame, blazing, flaming, on fire 2 = **excitable**, fierce, hot-headed, impetuous, irascible, irritable, passionate

fight *v* 1 = **battle**, box, clash, combat, do battle, grapple, spar, struggle, tussle, wrestle 2 = **oppose**, contest, defy, dispute, make a stand against, resist, stand up to, withstand 3 = **engage in**, carry on, conduct, prosecute, wage ▷ *n* 5, 6 = **battle**, clash, conflict, contest, dispute, duel, encounter, struggle, tussle 7 = **resistance**, belligerence, militancy, pluck, spirit

figure *n* 1 = **number**, character, digit, numeral, symbol 2 = **amount**, cost, price, sum, total, value 3 = **shape**, body, build, frame, physique, proportions 4 = **character**, big name, celebrity, dignitary, personality 5, 6 = **diagram**, design, drawing, illustration, representation, sketch ▷ *v* 9 = **calculate**, compute, count, reckon, tally, tot up, work out 11 (usu. foll. by *in*) = **feature**, act, appear, be featured, contribute to, play a part

filch *v* = **steal**, embezzle, misappropriate, pilfer, pinch (*inf*), take, thieve, walk off with

file¹ *n* 1-3 = **folder**, case, data, documents, dossier, information, portfolio 4 = **line**, column, queue, row ▷ *v* 6 = **put in place**, document, enter, pigeonhole 7 = **register**, record 9 = **march**, parade, troop

file² *v* 2 = **smooth**, abrade, polish, rasp, rub, scrape, shape smooth with a file. **filings** *pl n* shavings removed by a file.

filial *adj* of or befitting a son or daughter.

filibuster *n* **1** obstruction of legislation by making long speeches. **2** person who filibusters. ▷ *v* **3** obstruct (legislation) with such delaying tactics.

filigree *n* **1** delicate ornamental work of gold or silver wire. ▷ *adj* **2** made of filigree.

fill ❶ *v* **1** make or become full. **2** occupy completely. **3** plug (a gap). **4** satisfy (a need). **5** hold and perform the duties of (a position). **6** appoint to (a job or position). **one's fill** sufficient for one's needs or wants. **filling** *n* **1** substance that fills a gap or cavity, esp. in a tooth. ▷ *adj* **2** (of food) substantial and satisfying. **filling station** garage selling petrol, oil, etc.

fillet *n* **1** boneless piece of meat or fish. ▷ *v* **filleting, filleted 2** remove the bones from.

fillip *n* something that adds stimulation or enjoyment.

filly *n, pl* **-lies** young female horse.

film ❶ *n* **1** sequence of images projected on a screen, creating the illusion of movement. **2** story told in such a sequence of images. **3** thin strip of light-sensitive cellulose used to make photographic negatives and transparencies. **4** thin sheet or layer. ▷ *v* **5** photograph with a movie or video camera. **6** make a film of (a scene,

story, etc.). **7** cover or become covered with a thin layer. ▷ *adj* **8** connected with films or the cinema. **filmy** *adj* very thin, delicate.

filth ❶ *n* **1** disgusting dirt. **2** offensive material or language. **filthy** *adj* **filthily** *adv* **filthiness** *n*.

fin *n* **1** projection from a fish's body enabling it to balance and swim. **2** vertical tailplane of an aircraft.

final ❶ *adj* **1** at the end. **2** having no possibility of further change, action, or discussion. ▷ *n* **3** deciding contest between winners of previous rounds in a competition. ▷ *pl* **4** last examinations in an educational course. **finally** *adv* **finality** *n* **finalist** *n* competitor in a final. **finalize** *v* put into final form. **finale** [fin-**nah**-lee] *n* concluding part of a dramatic performance or musical work.

finance ❶ *v* **1** provide or obtain funds for. ▷ *n* **2** management of money, loans, or credits. **3** (provision of) funds. ▷ *pl* **4** money resources. **financial** *adj* **financially** *adv* **financier** *n* person involved in large-scale financial business. **financial year** twelve-month period used for financial calculations.

finch *n, pl* **finches** small songbird with a short strong beak.

find ❶ *v* **finding, found 1** discover by chance. **2** discover by search or effort.

— **THESAURUS** —

fill *v* **1** = **stuff**, cram, crowd, glut, pack, stock, supply, swell **2** = **saturate**, charge, imbue, impregnate, pervade, suffuse **3** = **plug**, block, bung, close, cork, seal, stop **5** = **perform**, carry out, discharge, execute, fulfil, hold, occupy **one's fill** = **sufficient**, all one wants, ample, enough, plenty

film *n* **1, 2** = **movie**, flick (*sl*), motion picture **4** = **layer**, coating, covering, dusting, membrane, skin, tissue ▷ *v* **5, 6** = **photograph**, shoot, take, video, videotape

filth *n* **1** = **dirt**, excrement, grime, muck,

refuse, sewage, slime, sludge, squalor **2** = **obscenity**, impurity, indecency, pornography, smut, vulgarity

final *adj* **1** = **last**, closing, concluding, latest, terminal, ultimate **2** = **conclusive**, absolute, decided, definite, definitive, incontrovertible, irrevocable, settled

finance *v* **1** = **fund**, back, bankroll (*US*), guarantee, pay for, subsidize, support, underwrite ▷ *n* **2** = **economics**, accounts, banking, business, commerce, investment, money

find *v* **1** = **discover**, come across, encounter, hit upon, locate, meet, recognize, spot,

3 become aware of. 4 consider to have a particular quality. 5 experience (a particular feeling). 6 *Law* pronounce (the defendant) guilty or not guilty. 7 provide, esp. with difficulty. ▷ *n* 8 person or thing found, esp. when valuable. **finder** *n* **finding** *n* conclusion from an investigation. **find out** *v* 1 gain knowledge of. 2 detect (a crime, deception, etc.).

fine¹ ❶ *adj* 1 very good. 2 (of weather) clear and dry. 3 in good health. 4 satisfactory. 5 of delicate workmanship. 6 thin or slender. 7 subtle or abstruse, e.g. *a fine distinction*. **finely** *adv* **fineness** *n* **finery** *n* showy clothing. **fine art** art produced to appeal to the sense of beauty. **fine-tune** *v* make small adjustments to (something) so that it works really well.

fine² ❶ *n* 1 payment imposed as a penalty. ▷ *v* 2 impose a fine on.

finger ❶ *n* 1 one of the four long jointed parts of the hand. 2 part of a glove that covers a finger. 3 quantity of liquid in a glass as deep as a finger is wide.

▷ *v* 4 touch or handle with the fingers. **fingering** *n* technique of using the fingers in playing a musical instrument. **fingerboard** *n* part of a stringed instrument against which the strings are pressed. **fingerprint** *n* 1 impression of the ridges on the tip of the finger. ▷ *v* 2 take the fingerprints of (someone).

finicky *adj* 1 excessively particular, fussy. 2 overelaborate.

finish ❶ *v* 1 bring to an end, stop. 2 use up. 3 bring to a desired or completed condition. 4 put a surface texture on (wood, cloth, or metal). 5 defeat or destroy. ▷ *n* 6 end, last part. 7 death or defeat. 8 surface texture.

finite ❶ *adj* having limits in space, time, or size.

fiord *n* same as FJORD.

fir *n* pyramid-shaped tree with needle-like leaves and erect cones.

fire ❶ *n* 1 state of combustion producing heat, flames, and smoke. 2 burning coal or wood, or a gas or electric device,

— THESAURUS —

uncover 2, 3 = **realise**, detect, discover, learn, note, notice, observe, perceive ▷ *n* 8 = **discovery**, acquisition, asset, bargain, catch, good buy
fine¹ *adj* 1 = **excellent**, accomplished, exceptional, exquisite, first-rate, magnificent, masterly, outstanding, splendid, superior 2 = **sunny**, balmy, bright, clear, clement, cloudless, dry, fair, pleasant 4 = **satisfactory**, acceptable, all right, convenient, good, O.K. or okay (*inf*), suitable 5 = **delicate**, dainty, elegant, expensive, exquisite, fragile, quality 6 = **slender**, diaphanous, flimsy, gauzy, gossamer, light, sheer, thin 7 = **subtle**, abstruse, acute, hairsplitting, minute, nice, precise, sharp
fine² *n* 1 = **penalty**, damages, forfeit, punishment ▷ *v* 2 = **penalize**, mulct, punish
finger *v* 4 = **touch**, feel, fiddle with (*inf*), handle, manipulate, maul, paw (*inf*), toy with
finish *v* 1 = **stop**, cease, close, complete,

conclude, end, round off, terminate, wind up, wrap up (*inf*) 2 = **consume**, devour, dispose of, eat, empty, exhaust, use up 3 = **perfect**, polish, refine 4 = **coat**, gild, lacquer, polish, stain, texture, veneer, wax 5 = **destroy**, bring down, defeat, dispose of, exterminate, overcome, put an end to, put paid to, rout, ruin ▷ *n* 6 = **end**, cessation, close, completion, conclusion, culmination, denouement, finale, run-in 7 = **defeat**, annihilation, curtains (*inf*), death, end, end of the road, ruin 8 = **surface**, lustre, patina, polish, shine, smoothness, texture
finite *adj* = **limited**, bounded, circumscribed, delimited, demarcated, restricted
fire *n* 1, 3 = **flames**, blaze, combustion, conflagration, inferno 4 = **bombardment**, barrage, cannonade, flak, fusillade, hail, salvo, shelling, sniping, volley 5 = **passion**, ardour, eagerness, enthusiasm,

used to heat a room. **3** uncontrolled destructive burning. **4** shooting of guns. **5** intense passion, ardour. ▷ v **6** operate (a weapon) so that a bullet or missile is released. **7** *informal* dismiss from employment. **8** bake (ceramics etc.) in a kiln. **9** excite. **firearm** n rifle, pistol, or shotgun. **firebrand** n person who causes unrest. **fireguard** n protective grating in front of a fire. **fire brigade** organized body of people whose job is to put out fires. **fire drill** rehearsal of procedures for escape from a fire. **fire engine** vehicle with apparatus for extinguishing fires. **fire escape** metal staircase or ladder down the outside of a building for escape in the event of fire. **firefighter** n member of a fire brigade. **firefly** n, pl **-flies** beetle that glows in the dark. **fireguard** n protective grating in front of a fire. **fireplace** n recess in a room for a fire. **fire power** *Mil* amount a weapon or unit can fire. **fire station** building where firefighters are stationed. **firewall** n *Computers* computer that prevents unauthorized access to a computer network from the Internet. **firework** n **1** device containing chemicals that is ignited to produce spectacular explosions and coloured sparks. ▷ pl **2** show of fireworks. **3** *informal* outburst of temper. **firing squad** group of soldiers ordered to execute an offender by shooting.

firm ❶ *adj* **1** not soft or yielding. **2** securely

in position. **3** definite. **4** having determination or strength. ▷ *adv* **5** in an unyielding manner, e.g. *hold firm.* ▷ v **6** make or become firm. **firmly** *adv* **firmness** n.

First Nations *pl n Canad* Canadian aboriginal communities.

First Peoples *pl n Canad* a collective term for the Native Canadian peoples, the Inuit, and the Métis.

fiscal *adj* of government finances, esp. taxes.

fish n, pl **fish, fishes 1** cold-blooded vertebrate with gills, that lives in water. **2** its flesh as food. ▷ v **3** try to catch fish. **4** fish in (a particular area of water). **5** (foll. by *for*) grope for and find with difficulty. **6** (foll. by *for*) seek indirectly. **fisherman** n person who catches fish for a living or for pleasure. **fishery** n, pl **-eries** area of the sea used for fishing. **fishy** *adj* **1** of or like fish. **2** *informal* suspicious or questionable. **fishmeal** dried ground fish used as animal feed or fertilizer. **fishmonger** n seller of fish. **fishnet** n open mesh fabric resembling netting. **fishwife** n, pl coarse scolding woman.

fissure ❶ [fish-er] n long narrow cleft or crack.

fist n clenched hand. **fisticuffs** *pl n* fighting with the fists.

fit¹ ❶ v **fitting, fitted 1** be appropriate or suitable for. **2** be of the correct size or shape (for). **3** adjust so as to make

excitement, fervour, intensity, sparkle, spirit, verve, vigour ▷ v **6** = **shoot**, detonate, discharge, explode, let off, pull the trigger, set off, shell **7** *Inf* = **dismiss**, cashier, discharge, make redundant, sack (*inf*), show the door **9** = **inspire**, animate, enliven, excite, galvanize, impassion, inflame, rouse, stir

firm *adj* **1** = **hard**, dense, inflexible, rigid, set, solid, solidified, stiff, unyielding **2** = **secure**, embedded, fast, fixed, immovable, rooted, stable, steady, tight, unshakable **3** = **definite**, **3** = **determined**,

adamant, inflexible, resolute, resolved, set on, unbending, unshakable, unyielding

fissure n = **crack**, breach, cleft, crevice, fault, fracture, opening, rift, rupture, split

fit¹ v **1, 2** = **suit**, accord, belong, conform, correspond, match, meet, tally **3** = **adapt**, adjust, alter, arrange, customize, modify, shape, tweak (*inf*) **5** = **equip**, arm, fit out, kit out, prepare, provide ▷ *adj* **7** = **appropriate**, apt, becoming, correct, fitting, proper, right, seemly, suitable **8** = **healthy**, able-bodied, hale, in good shape, robust, strapping, trim, well

appropriate. **4** try (clothes) on and note any adjustments needed. **5** make competent or ready. **6** correspond with the facts or circumstances. ▷ *adj* **7** appropriate. **8** in good health. **9** worthy or deserving. ▷ *n* **10** way in which something fits. **fitness** *n* **fitter** *n* **1** person skilled in the installation and adjustment of machinery. **2** person who fits garments. **fitting** *adj* **1** appropriate, suitable. ▷ *n* **2** accessory or part. **3** trying on of clothes for size. ▷ *pl* **4** furnishings and accessories in a building. **fitment** *n* detachable part of the furnishings of a room. **fit in** *v* **1** give a place or time to. **2** belong or conform. **fit out** *v* provide with the necessary equipment.

fit² ❶ *n* **1** sudden attack or convulsion, such as an epileptic seizure. **2** sudden short burst or spell.

five *adj, n* one more than four. **fiver** *n informal* five-pound note.

fix ❶ *v* **1** make or become firm, stable, or secure. **2** repair. **3** place permanently. **4** settle definitely. **5** direct (the eyes etc.) steadily. **6** *informal* unfairly influence the outcome of. ▷ *n* **7** *informal* difficult situation. **8** ascertaining of the position of a ship by radar etc. **9** *slang* injection of a narcotic drug. **fixed** *adj* **fixedly** *adv* steadily. **fix up** *v* **1** arrange. **2** provide (with).

fizz ❶ *v* **1** make a hissing or bubbling noise. **2** give off small bubbles. ▷ *n* **3** hissing or bubbling noise. **4** releasing of small bubbles of gas by a liquid. **5** effervescent drink. **fizzy** *adj* **fizziness** *n*.

fizzle *v* make a weak hissing or bubbling sound. **fizzle out** *v informal* come to nothing, fail.

fjord [fee-**ord**] *n* long narrow inlet of the sea between cliffs, esp. in Norway.

FL Florida.

flabby ❶ *adj* **-bier, -biest 1** having flabby flesh. **2** loose or limp.

flag¹ ❶ *n* **1** piece of cloth attached to a pole as an emblem or signal. ▷ *v* **flagging, flagged 2** mark with a flag or sticker. **3** (often foll. by *down*) signal (a vehicle) to stop by waving the arm. **flag day** day on which small stickers are sold in the streets for charity. **flagpole, flagstaff** *n* pole for a flag. **flagship** *n* **1** admiral's ship. **2** most important product of an organization.

flag² ❶ *v* **flagging, flagged** lose enthusiasm or vigour.

flag³, flagstone *n* flat paving-stone.

flagon *n* **1** wide bottle for wine or cider. **2** narrow-necked jug for liquid.

flagrant ❶ [**flayg**-rant] *adj* openly outrageous. **flagrancy** *n*.

flail ❶ *v* **1** wave about wildly. **2** beat or thrash. ▷ *n* **3** tool formerly used for threshing grain by hand.

— THESAURUS —

fit² *n* **1 = seizure**, attack, bout, convulsion, paroxysm, spasm **2 = outbreak**, bout, burst, outburst, spell

fix *v* **1 = fasten**, attach, bind, connect, link, secure, stick, tie **2 = repair**, correct, mend, patch up, put to rights, see to **3 = place**, embed, establish, implant, install, locate, plant, position, set **4 = decide**, agree on, arrange, arrive at, determine, establish, set, settle, specify **5 = focus**, direct **6** *Inf* **= rig**, fiddle (*inf*), influence, manipulate ▷ *n* **7** *Inf* **= predicament**, difficulty, dilemma, embarrassment, mess, pickle (*inf*), plight, quandary

fizz *v* **1, 2 = bubble**, effervesce, fizzle, froth, hiss, sparkle, sputter

flabby *adj* **1 = baggy 2 = limp**, drooping, flaccid, floppy, loose, pendulous, sagging

flag¹ *n* **1 = banner**, colours, ensign, pennant, pennon, standard, streamer ▷ *v* **2 = mark**, indicate, label, note **3** (often foll. by *down*) **= hail**, signal, warn, wave

flag² *v* **= weaken**, abate, droop, fade, languish, peter out, sag, wane, weary, wilt

flagrant *adj* **= outrageous**, barefaced, blatant, brazen, glaring, heinous, scandalous, shameless

flail *v* **1 = windmill 2 = thrash**, beat, thresh

flair ❶ *n* **1** natural ability. **2** stylishness.

flak *n* **1** anti-aircraft fire. **2** *informal* severe criticism.

flake ❶ *n* **1** small thin piece, esp. chipped off something. **2** *Aust, NZ & US informal* unreliable person. ▷ *v* **3** peel off in flakes. **flaky** *adj* **flake out** *v informal* collapse or fall asleep from exhaustion.

flambé [**flahm**-bay] *v* **flambéing, flambéed** cook or serve (food) in flaming brandy.

flamboyant ❶ *adj* **1** behaving in a very noticeable, extravagant way. **2** very bright and showy. **flamboyance** *n*.

flame ❶ *n* **1** luminous burning gas coming from burning material. ▷ *v* **2** burn brightly. **3** become bright red. **old flame** *informal* former sweetheart.

flamenco *n, pl* **-cos 1** rhythmical Spanish dance accompanied by a guitar and vocalist. **2** music for this dance.

flamingo *n, pl* **-gos, -goes** large pink wading bird with a long neck and legs.

flammable *adj* easily set on fire.

flan *n* open sweet or savoury tart.

flange *n* projecting rim or collar.

flank ❶ *n* **1** part of the side between the hips and ribs. **2** side of a body of troops. ▷ *v* **3** be at or move along the side of.

flannel *n* **1** small piece of cloth for washing the face. **2** soft woollen fabric for clothing. **3** *informal* evasive talk. ▷ *pl* **4** trousers made of flannel. ▷ *v* **-nelling, -nelled 5** *informal* talk evasively. **flannelette** *n* cotton imitation of flannel.

flap ❶ *v* **flapping, flapped 1** move back and forwards or up and down. ▷ *n* **2** action or sound of flapping. **3** piece of something attached by one edge only. **4** *informal* state of excitement or panic.

flapjack *n* chewy biscuit made with oats.

flare ❶ *v* **1** blaze with a sudden unsteady flame. **2** *informal* (of temper, violence, or trouble) break out suddenly. **3** (of a skirt or trousers) become wider towards the hem. ▷ *n* **4** sudden unsteady flame. **5** signal light. ▷ *pl* **6** flared trousers. **flared** *adj* (of a skirt or trousers) becoming wider towards the hem.

flash ❶ *n* **1** sudden burst of light or flame. **2** sudden occurrence (of intuition or emotion). **3** very short time. **4** brief unscheduled news announcement. **5** *Photog* small bulb that produces an intense flash of light. ▷ *adj* **6** (also **flashy**) vulgarly showy. ▷ *v* **7** (cause to) burst into flame. **8** (cause to) emit light suddenly or intermittently. **9** move very fast. **10** come rapidly (to mind or view). **11** *informal* display ostentatiously. **12** *slang* expose

— THESAURUS —

flair *n* **1** = **ability**, aptitude, faculty, feel, genius, gift, knack, mastery, talent **2** = **style**, chic, dash, discernment, elegance, panache, stylishness, taste

flake *n* **1** = **chip**, layer, peeling, scale, shaving, sliver, wafer ▷ *v* **2** = **chip**, blister, peel off

flamboyant *adj* **1** = **theatrical**, dashing, extravagant, ostentatious, swashbuckling **2** = **showy**, brilliant, colourful, dazzling, elaborate, florid, glamorous, glitzy (*sl*), ornate

flame *n* **1** = **fire**, blaze ▷ *v* **2** = **burn**, blaze, flare, flash, glare, glow, shine

flank *n* **1** = **side**, hip, loin, thigh

flap *v* **1** = **flutter**, beat, flail, shake, thrash, vibrate, wag, wave ▷ *n* **2** = **flutter**, beating, shaking, swinging, swish, waving **4** *Inf* = **panic**, agitation, commotion, fluster, state (*inf*), sweat (*inf*), tizzy (*inf*)

flare *v* **1** = **blaze**, burn up, flicker, glare ▷ *n* **4** = **flame**, blaze, burst, flash, flicker, glare

flash *n* **1** = **gleam**, blaze, burst, dazzle, flare, flicker, shimmer, spark, streak **3** = **moment**, instant, jiffy (*inf*), second, split second, trice, twinkling of an eye ▷ *adj* **6** (also **flashy**) = **showy**, flamboyant, garish, gaudy, glitzy (*sl*), jazzy (*inf*), ostentatious, snazzy (*inf*), tacky (*inf*), tasteless, vulgar (*inf*) ▷ *v* **7** = **blaze**, flare **8** = **gleam**, flicker, glare, shimmer, sparkle, twinkle **9** = **speed**, dart, dash, fly, race,

oneself indecently. **flasher** *n slang* man who exposes himself indecently. **flashback** *n* scene in a book, play, or film, that shows earlier events **flash flood** sudden short-lived flood. **flashlight** *n US* torch. **flash point 1** critical point beyond which a situation will inevitably erupt into violence. **2** lowest temperature at which vapour given off by a liquid can ignite.

flask *n* **1** same as VACUUM FLASK. **2** flat bottle for carrying alcoholic drink in the pocket. **3** narrow-necked bottle.

flat¹ ❶ *adj* **flatter**, **flattest 1** level and horizontal. **2** even and smooth. **3** (of a tyre) deflated. **4** outright. **5** fixed. **6** without variation or emotion. **7** (of a drink) no longer fizzy. **8** (of a battery) with no electrical charge. **9** *Music* below the true pitch. ▷ *adv* **10** in or into a flat position. **11** completely or absolutely. **12** exactly. **13** *Music* too low in pitch. ▷ *n* **14** flat surface. **15** *Music* symbol lowering the pitch of a note by a semitone. **16** punctured car tyre. **17** level ground. **18** mudbank exposed at low tide. **flat out** with maximum speed or effort. **flatly** *adv* **flatness** *n* **flatten** *v* **flatfish** *n* sea fish, such as the sole, which has a flat body. **flat racing** horse racing over level ground with no jumps.

flat² ❶ *n* set of rooms for living in which are part of a larger building. **flatmate** *n* person with whom one shares a flat.

flatter ❶ *v* **1** praise insincerely. **2** show to advantage. **3** make (a person) appear more attractive in a picture than in reality. **flatterer** *n* **flattery** *n*.

flattie *n NZ & S Afr informal* flat tyre.

flatulent *adj* suffering from or caused by too much gas in the intestines. **flatulence** *n*.

flaunt ❶ *v* display (oneself or one's possessions) arrogantly.

● **USAGE NOTE**
● Be careful not to confuse this with *flout* meaning 'disobey'.

flavour ❶ *n* **1** distinctive taste. **2** distinctive characteristic or quality. ▷ *v* **3** give flavour to. **flavouring** *n* substance used to flavour food.

flaw ❶ *n* **1** imperfection or blemish. **2** mistake that makes a plan or argument invalid. **flawed** *adj* **flawless** *adj*.

flax *n* **1** plant grown for its stem fibres and seeds. **2** its fibres, spun into linen thread. **flaxen** *adj* (of hair) pale yellow.

flay *v* **1** strip the skin off. **2** criticize severely.

flea *n* small wingless jumping bloodsucking insect. **flea market** market for cheap goods. **fleapit** *n informal* shabby cinema or theatre.

— THESAURUS —

shoot, streak, whistle, zoom **11** *Inf* = **show**, display, exhibit, expose, flaunt, flourish

flat¹ *adj* **1, 2** = **even**, horizontal, level, levelled, low, smooth **3** = **punctured**, blown out, burst, collapsed, deflated, empty **4** = **absolute**, categorical, downright, explicit, out-and-out, positive, unequivocal, unqualified **6** = **dull**, boring, dead, lacklustre, lifeless, monotonous, tedious, tiresome, uninteresting *adv* **11** = **completely**, absolutely, categorically, exactly, point blank, precisely, utterly **flat out** = **at full speed**, all out, at full tilt, for all one is worth, hell for leather (*inf*)

flat² *n* = **apartment**, rooms, duplex (*US & Canad*)

flatter *v* **1** = **praise**, butter up, compliment, pander to, soft-soap (*inf*), sweet-talk (*inf*), wheedle **2** = **suit**, become, do something for, enhance, set off, show to advantage

flaunt *v* = **show off**, brandish, display, exhibit, flash about, flourish, parade, sport (*inf*)

flavour *n* **1** = **taste**, aroma, flavouring, piquancy, relish, savour, seasoning, smack, tang, zest **2** = **quality**, character, essence, feel, feeling, style, tinge, tone ▷ *v* **3** = **season**, ginger up, imbue, infuse, leaven, spice

flaw *n* **1** = **weakness**, blemish, chink in one's armour, defect, failing, fault, imperfection, weak spot

fleck *n* **1** small mark, streak, or speck. ▷ *v* **2** speckle.

flee ❶ *v* **fleeing, fled** run away (from).

fleece *n* **1** sheep's coat of wool. **2** sheepskin used as a lining for coats etc. **3** warm polyester fabric. **4** jacket or top made of this fabric. ▷ *v* **5** defraud or overcharge. **fleecy** *adj* made of or like fleece.

fleet¹ ❶ *n* **1** number of warships organized as a unit. **2** number of vehicles under the same ownership.

fleet² ❷ *adj* swift in movement. **fleeting** *adj* rapid and soon passing.

flesh ❶ *n* **1** soft part of a human or animal body. **2** *informal* excess fat. **3** meat of animals as opposed to fish or fowl. **4** thick soft part of a fruit or vegetable. **5** human body as opposed to the soul. **in the flesh** in person, actually present. **one's own flesh and blood** one's family. **flesh-coloured** *adj* yellowish-pink. **fleshy** *adj* **1** plump. **2** like flesh. **flesh wound** wound affecting only superficial tissue.

flex *n* **1** flexible insulated electric cable. ▷ *v* **2** bend. **flexible** *adj* **1** easily bent. **2** adaptable. **flexibly** *adv* **flexibility** *n* **flexitime** *n* system permitting variation in starting and finishing times of work.

flick ❶ *v* **1** touch or move with the finger or hand in a quick movement. **2** move with a short sudden movement, often repeatedly. ▷ *n* **3** tap or quick stroke. ▷ *pl* **4** *slang* the cinema. **flick through** *v* look at (a book or magazine) quickly or idly.

flicker ❶ *v* **1** shine unsteadily or intermittently. **2** move quickly to and fro. ▷ *n* **3** unsteady brief light. **4** brief faint indication.

flight¹ ❶ *n* **1** journey by air. **2** act or manner of flying through the air. **3** group of birds or aircraft flying together. **4** aircraft flying on a scheduled journey. **5** set of stairs between two landings. **6** stabilizing feathers or plastic fins on an arrow or dart. **flight deck 1** crew compartment in an airliner. **2** runway deck on an aircraft carrier. **flight recorder** electronic device in an aircraft storing information about its flight.

flight² ❷ *n* act of running away.

flimsy ❶ *adj* **-sier, -siest 1** not strong or substantial. **2** thin. **3** not very convincing. **flimsily** *adv* **flimsiness** *n*.

flinch ❶ *v* draw back or wince, as from pain. **flinch from** *v* shrink from or avoid.

fling ❶ *v* **flinging, flung 1** throw, send, or move forcefully or hurriedly. ▷ *n* **2** spell of

flee *v* = **run away**, bolt, depart, escape, fly, make one's getaway, scarper (*Brit sl*), take flight, take off (*inf*), take to one's heels, turn tail

fleet¹ *n* **1** = **navy**, armada, flotilla, task force

fleet² *adj* = **swift**, fast, flying, mercurial, meteoric, nimble, nimble-footed, quick, rapid, speedy, winged

flesh *n* **1** = **meat**, tissue **2** = **fat**, brawn, weight **5** = **physical nature**, carnality, flesh and blood, human nature **one's own flesh and blood** = **family**, blood, kin, kinsfolk, kith and kin, relations, relatives

flick *v* **1** = **strike**, dab, flip, hit, tap, touch **flick through** *v* = **browse**, flip through, glance at, skim, skip, thumb

flicker *v* **1** = **twinkle**, flare, flash, glimmer, gutter, shimmer, sparkle **2** = **flutter**,

quiver, vibrate, waver ▷ *n* **3** = **glimmer**, flare, flash, gleam, spark **4** = **trace**, breath, glimmer, iota, spark

flight¹ *n* **1** = **journey**, trip, voyage **2** = **aviation**, aeronautics, flying **3** = **flock**, cloud, formation, squadron, swarm, unit

flight² *n* = **escape**, departure, exit, exodus, fleeing, getaway, retreat, running away

flimsy *adj* **1** = **fragile**, delicate, frail, insubstantial, makeshift, rickety, shaky **2** = **thin**, gauzy, gossamer, light, sheer, transparent **3** = **unconvincing**, feeble, implausible, inadequate, pathetic, poor, unsatisfactory, weak

flinch *v* = **recoil**, cower, cringe, draw back, quail, shirk, shrink, shy away, wince

fling *v* **1** = **throw**, cast, catapult, heave, hurl, propel, sling, toss ▷ *n* **2** = **binge** (*inf*), self-indulgent enjoyment. **3** brief romantic or sexual relationship.

flint *n* **1** hard grey stone. **2** piece of this. **3** small piece of an iron alloy, used in cigarette lighters. **flinty** *adj* **1** cruel. **2** of or like flint.

flip ❶ *v* **flipping, flipped 1** throw (something small or light) carelessly. **2** turn (something) over. **3** (also **flip one's lid**) *slang* fly into an emotional state. ▷ *n* **4** snap or tap. ▷ *adj* **5** *informal* flippant. **flipper** *n* **1** limb of a sea animal adapted for swimming. **2** one of a pair of paddle-like rubber devices worn on the feet to help in swimming. **flip-flop** *n* rubber-soled sandal held on by a thong between the big toe and the next toe.

flirt ❶ *v* **1** behave as if sexually attracted to someone. **2** consider lightly, toy (with). ▷ *n* **3** person who flirts. **flirtation** *n* **flirtatious** *adj*.

flit *v* **flitting, flitted 1** move lightly and rapidly. **2** *Scot* move house. **3** *informal* depart hurriedly and secretly. ▷ *n* **4** act of flitting.

float ❶ *v* **1** rest on the surface of a liquid. **2** move lightly and freely. **3** move about aimlessly. **4** launch (a company). **5** offer for sale on the stock market. **6** allow (a currency) to fluctuate against other currencies. ▷ *n* **7** light object used to help

someone or something float. **8** indicator on a fishing line that moves when a fish bites. **9** decorated lorry in a procession. **10** small delivery vehicle. **11** sum of money used for minor expenses or to provide change. **floating** *adj* **1** moving about, changing, e.g. *floating population*. **2** (of a voter) not committed to one party.

flock ❶ *n* **1** number of animals of one kind together. **2** large group of people. **3** *Christianity* congregation. ▷ *v* **4** gather in a crowd.

floe *n* sheet of floating ice.

flog ❶ *v* **flogging, flogged 1** beat with a whip or stick. **2** *slang* sell. **flogging** *n*.

flood ❶ *n* **1** overflow of water onto a normally dry area. **2** large amount of water. **3** rising of the tide. ▷ *v* **4** cover or become covered with water. **5** fill to overflowing. **6** come in large numbers or quantities. **floodgate** *n* gate used to control the flow of water. **floodlight** *n* **1** lamp that casts a broad intense beam of light. ▷ *v* **-lighting, -lit 2** illuminate by floodlight.

floor ❶ *n* **1** lower surface of a room. **2** level of a building. **3** flat bottom surface. **4** (right to speak in) a legislative hall. ▷ *v* **5** knock down. **6** *informal* disconcert or defeat. **floored** *adj* covered with a floor.

━━━━━━━━━━━━━━━━━━━━━━━━━━━━━━ THESAURUS ━━━━━━━━━━━

bash, good time, party, rave-up (*Brit sl*), spree

flip *v* **1,2** = **toss**, flick, spin, throw ▷ *n* **4** = **snap**

flirt *v* **1** = **chat up** (*inf*), lead on, make advances, make eyes at, make sheep's eyes at, philander **2** = **toy with**, consider, dabble in, entertain, expose oneself to, give a thought to, play with, trifle with ▷ *n* **3** = **tease**, coquette, heart-breaker, philanderer

float *v* **1** = **be buoyant**, bob, sail **2** = **glide**, hang, hover, move gently, slide, slip along **3** = **drift 4** = **launch**, get going, promote, set up

flock *n* **1** = **herd**, colony, drove, flight, gaggle, skein **2** = **crowd**, collection, company, gathering, group, herd, host,

mass **3** *Christianity* = **congregation** ▷ *v* **4** = **gather**, collect, congregate, converge, crowd, herd, huddle, mass, throng

flog *v* **1** = **beat**, flagellate, flay, lash, scourge, thrash, trounce, whack, whip

flood *n* **1** = **overflow**, deluge, downpour, inundation **2** = **torrent**, flow, rush, stream **3** = **tide**, spate ▷ *v* **4** = **immerse**, drown, engulf, inundate, overwhelm, pour over, submerge, surge, swamp **5** = **overflow**, fill, saturate

floor *n* **2** = **tier**, level, stage, storey ▷ *v* **5** = **knock down**, deck (*sl*), prostrate **6** *Inf* = **disconcert**, baffle, bewilder, confound, defeat, dumbfound, perplex, puzzle, stump, throw (*inf*)

flooring n material for floors. **floor show** entertainment in a nightclub.

flop ① v **flopping, flopped 1** bend, fall, or collapse loosely or carelessly. **2** informal fail. ▷ n **3** informal failure. **4** flopping movement. **floppy** adj hanging downwards, loose. **floppy disk** Computers flexible magnetic disk that stores information.

flora n plants of a given place or time.

floret n small flower forming part of a composite flower head.

florid ① adj **1** with a red or flushed complexion. **2** ornate.

floss n fine silky fibres.

flotilla n small fleet or fleet of small ships.

flotsam ① n floating wreckage. **flotsam and jetsam 1** odds and ends. **2** homeless or vagrant people.

flounce¹ v **1** go with emphatic movements. ▷ n **2** flouncing movement.

flounce² n ornamental frill on a garment.

flounder¹ ① v **1** move with difficulty, as in mud. **2** behave or speak in a bungling or hesitating manner.

flounder² n edible flatfish.

flour n **1** powder made by grinding grain, esp. wheat. ▷ v **2** sprinkle with flour. **floury** adj.

flourish ① v **1** be active, successful, or widespread. **2** be at the peak of development. **3** wave (something) dramatically. ▷ n **4** dramatic waving motion. **5** ornamental curly line in writing. **flourishing** adj.

flow ① v **1** (of liquid) move in a stream. **2** (of blood or electricity) circulate. **3** proceed smoothly. **4** hang loosely. **5** be abundant. ▷ n **6** act, rate, or manner of flowing. **7** continuous stream or discharge. **flow chart** diagram showing a sequence of operations in a process.

flower ① n **1** part of a plant that produces seeds. **2** plant grown for its colourful flowers. **3** best or finest part. ▷ v **4** produce flowers, bloom. **5** reach full growth or maturity. **in flower** with flowers open. **flowered** adj decorated with a floral design. **flowery** adj **1** decorated with a floral design. **2** (of language or style) elaborate. **flowerbed** n piece of ground for growing flowers.

fl. oz. fluid ounce(s).

flu n short for INFLUENZA.

fluctuate ① v change frequently and erratically. **fluctuation** n.

flue n passage or pipe for smoke or hot air.

fluent ① adj **1** able to speak or write with ease. **2** spoken or written with ease. **fluency** n.

THESAURUS

---

flop v **1** = **fall**, collapse, dangle, droop, drop, sag, slump **2** Inf = **fail**, come unstuck, fall flat, fold (inf), founder, go belly-up (sl), misfire ▷ n **3** Inf = **failure**, debacle, disaster, fiasco, nonstarter, washout (inf)

florid adj **1** = **flushed**, blowsy, rubicund, ruddy **2** = **ornate**, baroque, flamboyant, flowery, high-flown, overelaborate

flotsam n = **debris**, detritus, jetsam, junk, odds and ends, wreckage

flounder¹ v **1** = **struggle**, fumble, grope, stumble, thrash, toss

flourish v **1, 2** = **thrive**, bloom, blossom, boom, flower, grow, increase, prosper, succeed **3** = **wave**, brandish, display, flaunt, shake, wield ▷ n **4** = **wave**

5 = **ornamentation**, curlicue, decoration, embellishment, plume, sweep

flow v **1** = **pour**, cascade, flood, gush, rush, stream, surge, sweep **2** = **run**, circulate, course, move, roll **3** = **issue**, arise, emanate, emerge, proceed, result, spring ▷ n **6** = **course**, current, drift, flood, flux, outpouring, spate, tide **7** = **stream**

flower n **1, 2** = **bloom**, blossom, efflorescence **3** = **elite**, best, cream, pick ▷ v **4** = **bloom**, blossom, flourish, open, unfold **5** = **mature**

fluctuate v = **change**, alternate, oscillate, seesaw, shift, swing, vary, veer, waver

fluent adj **1** = **flowing**, articulate, natural, smooth, voluble, well-versed **2** = **effortless**, easy

fluff ❶ n 1 soft fibres. 2 informal mistake. ▷ v 3 make or become soft and puffy. 4 informal make a mistake. **fluffy** adj.

fluid ❶ n 1 substance able to flow and change its shape; a liquid or a gas. ▷ adj 2 able to flow or change shape easily. **fluidity** n **fluid ounce** one twentieth of a pint.

fluke ❶ n accidental stroke of luck. **fluky** adj.

flummox v puzzle or confuse.

flunky, flunkey n, pl **flunkies, flunkeys** 1 servile person. 2 manservant who wears a livery.

fluoride n compound containing fluorine. **fluoridate** v add fluoride to (water) as protection against tooth decay. **fluoridation** n.

flurry ❶ n, pl **-ries** 1 sudden commotion. 2 gust of rain or wind or fall of snow. ▷ v **-rying, -ried** 3 confuse.

flush¹ ❶ v 1 blush or cause to blush. 2 send water through (a toilet or pipe) so as to clean it. 3 elate. ▷ n 4 blush. 5 rush of water. 6 excitement or elation. **flushed** adj.

flush² ❶ adj 1 level with the surrounding surface. 2 informal having plenty of money.

fluster ❶ v 1 make nervous or upset. ▷ n 2 nervous or upset state.

flute n 1 wind instrument consisting of a tube with sound holes and a mouth hole in the side. 2 tall narrow wineglass. **fluted** adj having decorative grooves.

flutter ❶ v 1 wave rapidly. 2 flap the wings. 3 move quickly and irregularly. 4 (of the heart) beat abnormally quickly. ▷ n 5 flapping movement. 6 nervous agitation. 7 informal small bet. 8 abnormally fast heartbeat.

flux n 1 constant change or instability. 2 flow or discharge. 3 substance mixed with metal to assist in fusion.

fly¹ ❶ v **flying, flew, flown** 1 move through the air on wings or in an aircraft. 2 control the flight of. 3 float, flutter, display, or be displayed in the air. 4 transport or be transported by air. 5 move quickly or suddenly. 6 (of time) pass rapidly. 7 flee. ▷ n, pl **flies** 8 (often pl) fastening at the front of trousers. 9 flap forming the entrance to a tent. ▷ pl 10 space above a stage, used for storage. **flyer, flier** n 1 small advertising leaflet. 2 aviator. **fly-by-night** adj informal unreliable or untrustworthy. **flyleaf** n blank leaf at the beginning or end of a book. **flyover** n road passing over another by a bridge. **fly-past** n ceremonial

---

fluff n 1 = **fuzz**, down, nap, pile ▷ v 4 Inf = **mess up** (inf), bungle, make a mess off, muddle, spoil

fluid n 1 = **liquid**, liquor, solution adj 2 = **liquid**, flowing, liquefied, melted, molten, runny, watery

fluke n = **stroke of luck**, accident, chance, coincidence, lucky break, quirk of fate, serendipity

flurry n 1 = **commotion**, ado, bustle, disturbance, excitement, flutter, fuss, stir 2 = **gust**, squall

flush¹ v 1 = **blush**, colour, glow, go red, redden 2 = **rinse out**, cleanse, flood, hose down, wash out ▷ n 4 = **blush**, colour, glow, redness, rosiness

flush² adj 1 = **level**, even, flat, square,

true 2 Inf = **wealthy**, in the money (inf), moneyed, rich, well-heeled (inf), well-off

fluster v 1 = **upset**, agitate, bother, confuse, disturb, perturb, rattle (inf), ruffle, unnerve ▷ n 2 = **turmoil**, disturbance, dither, flap (inf), flurry, flutter, furore, state (inf)

flutter v 2 = **beat**, flap 3 = **tremble**, quiver, ripple, waver 4 = **palpitate** ▷ n 5 = **vibration**, quiver, shiver, shudder, tremble, tremor, twitching 6 = **agitation**, commotion, confusion, dither, excitement, fluster, state (inf) 8 = **palpitation**

fly¹ v 1 = **take wing**, flit, flutter, hover, sail, soar, wing 2 = **pilot**, control, manoeuvre, operate 3 = **display**, flap, float, flutter, show, wave 5 = **rush**, career, dart, dash,

flight of aircraft. **flywheel** *n* heavy wheel regulating the speed of a machine.

fly² *n, pl* **flies** two-winged insect. **flycatcher** *n* small insect-eating songbird. **fly-fishing** *n* fishing with an artificial fly as a lure. **flypaper** *n* paper with a sticky poisonous coating, used to kill flies. **flyweight** *n* boxer weighing up to 112lb (professional) or 51kg (amateur).

foal *n* 1 young of a horse or related animal. ▷ *v* 2 give birth to a foal.

foam ❶ *n* 1 mass of small bubbles on a liquid. 2 frothy saliva. 3 light spongelike solid used for insulation, packing, etc. ▷ *v* 4 produce foam. **foamy** *adj*.

fob *n* 1 short watch chain. 2 small pocket in a waistcoat.

focus ❶ *n, pl* **-cuses, -ci** [-sye] 1 point at which light or sound waves converge. 2 state of an optical image when it is clearly defined. 3 state of an instrument producing such an image. 4 centre of interest or activity. ▷ *v* **-cusing, -cused** or **-cussing, -cussed** 5 bring or come into focus. 6 concentrate (on). **focal** *adj* of or at a focus. **focus group** group of people gathered by a market-research company to di scuss and assess a product or service.

fodder *n* feed for livestock.

foe ❶ *n* enemy, opponent.

fog ❶ *n* 1 mass of condensed water vapour in the lower air, often greatly reducing

visibility. ▷ *v* **fogging, fogged** 2 cover with steam. **foggy** *adj* **foghorn** *n* large horn sounded to warn ships in fog.

fogey, fogy *n, pl* **-geys, -gies** old-fashioned person.

foible *n* minor weakness or slight peculiarity.

foil¹ ❶ *v* ruin (someone's plan).

foil² ❶ *n* 1 metal in a thin sheet. 2 anything which sets off another thing to advantage.

foil³ *n* light slender flexible sword tipped with a button.

foist ❶ *v* (foll. by *on* or *upon*) force or impose on.

fold¹ ❶ *v* 1 bend so that one part covers another. 2 interlace (the arms). 3 clasp (in the arms). 4 *Cooking* mix gently. 5 *informal* fail or go bankrupt. ▷ *n* 6 folded piece or part. 7 mark, crease, or hollow made by folding. **folder** *n* piece of folded cardboard for holding loose papers.

fold² *n* 1 enclosure for sheep. 2 church or its members.

foliage *n* leaves.

folio *n, pl* **-lios** 1 sheet of paper folded in half to make two leaves of a book. 2 book made up of such sheets. 3 page number.

folk ❶ *n* 1 people in general. 2 race of people. ▷ *pl* 3 relatives. **folksy** *adj* simple and unpretentious. **folk dance** traditional country dance. **folklore** *n* traditional beliefs and stories of a people. **folk song**

hurry, race, shoot, speed, sprint, tear 6 = **pass**, elapse, flit, glide, pass swiftly, roll on, run its course, slip away 7 = **flee**, escape, get away, run for it, skedaddle (*inf*), take to one's heels

foam *n* 1 = **froth**, bubbles, head, lather, spray, spume, suds ▷ *v* 4 = **bubble**, boil, effervesce, fizz, froth, lather

focus *n* 4 = **centre**, focal point, heart, hub, target ▷ *v* 6 = **concentrate**, aim, centre, direct, fix, pinpoint, spotlight, zoom in

foe *n* = **enemy**, adversary, antagonist, opponent, rival

fog *n* 1 = **mist**, gloom, miasma, murk,

peasouper (*inf*), smog

foil¹ *v* = **thwart**, balk, counter, defeat, disappoint, frustrate, nullify, stop

foil² *n* 2 = **contrast**, antithesis, complement

foist *v* (foll. by *on* or *upon*) = **impose**, fob off, palm off, pass off, sneak in, unload

fold¹ *v* 1 = **bend**, crease, double over 5 *Inf* = **go bankrupt**, collapse, crash, fail, go bust (*inf*), go to the wall, go under, shut down ▷ *n* 7 = **crease**, bend, furrow, overlap, pleat, wrinkle

folk *n* 1 = **people** 2 = **race**, clan, tribe ▷ *pl* 3 = **family**, kin, kindred

1 song handed down among the common people. **2** modern song like this.

follicle *n* small cavity in the body, esp. one from which a hair grows.

follow ❶ *v* **1** go or come after. **2** be a logical or natural consequence of. **3** keep to the course or track of. **4** act in accordance with. **5** accept the ideas or beliefs of. **6** understand. **7** have a keen interest in. **8** *Computers* to receive messages posted by (a blogger). **follower** *n* disciple or supporter. **following** *adj* **1** about to be mentioned. **2** next in time. ▷ *n* **3** group of supporters. ▷ *prep* **4** as a result of. **follow up** *v* **1** investigate. **2** do a second, often similar, thing after (a first). **follow-up** *n* something done to reinforce an initial action.

folly ❶ *n*, *pl* **-lies 1** foolishness. **2** foolish action or idea. **3** useless extravagant building.

foment [foam-**ent**] *v* encourage or stir up (trouble).

fond ❶ *adj* **1** tender, loving. **2** unlikely to be realized, e.g. *a fond hope*. **fond of** having a liking for. **fondness** *n*.

fondant *n* (sweet made from) flavoured paste of sugar and water.

fondle ❶ *v* caress.

font *n* bowl in a church for baptismal water.

fontanelle *n* soft membranous gap between the bones of a baby's skull.

food ❶ *n* what one eats, solid nourishment. **foodie** *n informal* gourmet. **foodstuff** *n* substance used as food.

fool¹ ❶ *n* **1** person lacking sense or judgment. **2** person made to appear ridiculous. **3** *Hist* jester, clown. ▷ *v* **4** deceive (someone). **foolish** *adj* unwise, silly, or absurd. **foolishness** *n* **fool around** *v* act or play irresponsibly or aimlessly. **foolproof** *adj* unable to fail.

fool² *n* dessert of puréed fruit mixed with cream.

foot *n*, *pl* **feet 1** part of the leg below the ankle. **2** unit of length of twelve inches (0.3048 metre). **3** lowest part of anything. **4** unit of poetic rhythm. **foot the bill** pay the entire cost. **footage** *n* amount of film used. **foot-and-mouth disease** infectious viral disease of sheep, cattle, etc. **football** *n* game played by two teams kicking a ball in an attempt to score goals. **footbridge** *n* bridge for pedestrians. **footfall** *n* sound of a footstep. **foothills** *pl n* hills at the foot of a mountain. **foothold** *n* **1** secure position from which progress may be made. **2** small place giving a secure grip for the foot. **footlights** *pl n* lights across the

——————————————————— THESAURUS ———

follow *v* **1** = **come after**, come next, succeed, supersede, supplant, take the place of **2** = **result**, arise, develop, ensue, flow, issue, proceed, spring **3** = **pursue**, chase, dog, hound, hunt, shadow, stalk, track, trail **4** = **obey**, be guided by, conform, heed, observe **6** = **understand**, appreciate, catch on (*inf*), comprehend, fathom, grasp, realize, take in **7** = **be interested in**, cultivate, keep abreast of, support

folly *n* **1** = **foolishness**, imprudence, indiscretion, lunacy, madness, nonsense, rashness, stupidity

fond *adj* **1** = **loving**, adoring, affectionate, amorous, caring, devoted, doting, indulgent, tender, warm **2** = **foolish**,

deluded, delusive, empty, naive, overoptimistic, vain **fond of** = **keen on**, addicted to, attached to, enamoured of, having a soft spot for, hooked on, into (*inf*), partial to

fondle *v* = **caress**, cuddle, dandle, pat, pet, stroke

food *n* = **nourishment**, cuisine, diet, fare, grub (*sl*), nutrition, rations, refreshment

fool¹ *n* **1** = **simpleton**, blockhead, dunce, halfwit, idiot, ignoramus, imbecile (*inf*), numbskull *or* numskull, twit (*inf, chiefly Brit*) **2** = **dupe**, fall guy (*inf*), laughing stock, mug (*Brit sl*), stooge (*sl*), sucker (*sl*) **3** *Hist* = **clown**, buffoon, harlequin, jester ▷ *v* **4** = **deceive**, beguile, con (*inf*), delude, dupe, hoodwink, mislead, take in, trick

front of a stage. **footloose** *adj* free from ties. **footman** *n* male servant in uniform. **footnote** *n* note printed at the foot of a page. **footpath** *n* 1 narrow path for walkers only. 2 *Aust* raised space alongside a road, for pedestrians. **footplate** *n* platform in the cab of a locomotive for the driver. **footprint** *n* mark left by a foot. **footstep** *n* 1 step in walking. 2 sound made by walking. **footstool** *n* low stool used to rest the feet on while sitting. **footwear** *n* anything worn to cover the feet. **footwork** *n* skilful use of the feet, as in sport or dancing.

footle *v informal* loiter aimlessly. **footling** *adj* trivial.

for *prep* 1 indicating a person intended to benefit from or receive something, span of time or distance, person or thing represented by someone, etc. e.g. *a gift for you; for five miles; playing for his country.* ▷ *conj* 2 because. **for it** *informal* liable for punishment or blame.

forage ❶ *v* 1 search about (for). ▷ *n* 2 food for cattle or horses.

foray ❶ *n* 1 brief raid or attack. 2 first attempt or new undertaking.

forbear ❶ *v* cease or refrain (from doing something). **forbearance** *n* tolerance, patience.

forbid ❶ *v* prohibit, refuse to allow. **forbidden** *adj* **forbidding** *adj* severe, threatening.

force ❶ *n* 1 strength or power. 2 compulsion. 3 *Physics* influence tending to produce a change in a physical system. 4 mental or moral strength. 5 person or thing with strength or influence. 6 vehemence or intensity. 7 group of people organized for a particular task or duty. ▷ *v* 8 compel, make (someone) do something. 9 acquire or produce through effort, strength, etc. 10 propel or drive. 11 break open. 12 impose or inflict. 13 cause to grow at an increased rate. **in force** 1 having legal validity. 2 in great numbers. **forced** *adj* 1 compulsory. 2 false or unnatural. 3 due to an emergency. **forceful** *adj* 1 emphatic and confident. 2 effective. **forcefully** *adv* **forcible** *adj* 1 involving physical force or violence. 2 strong and emphatic. **forcibly** *adv*.

forceps *pl n* surgical pincers.

ford *n* 1 shallow place where a river may be crossed. ▷ *v* 2 cross (a river) at a ford.

fore *adj* 1 in, at, or towards the front. ▷ *n* 2 front part. **to the fore** in a conspicuous position.

forearm¹ *n* arm from the wrist to the elbow.

forearm² *v* prepare beforehand.

forebear ❶ *n* ancestor.

forecast ❶ *v* -casting, -cast or -casted 1 predict (weather, events, etc.). ▷ *n* 2 prediction.

forage *v* 1 = **search**, cast about, explore, hunt, rummage, scour, seek ▷ *n* 2 = **fodder**, feed, food, provender

foray *n* 1 = **raid**, incursion, inroad, invasion, sally, sortie, swoop

forbear *v* = **refrain**, abstain, cease, desist, hold back, keep from, restrain oneself, stop

forbid *v* = **prohibit**, ban, disallow, exclude, outlaw, preclude, rule out, veto

force *n* 1 = **power**, energy, impulse, might, momentum, pressure, strength, vigour 2 = **compulsion**, arm-twisting (*inf*), coercion, constraint, duress, pressure, violence 6 = **intensity**, emphasis,

fierceness, vehemence, vigour 7 = **army**, host, legion, patrol, regiment, squad, troop, unit ▷ *v* 8 = **compel**, coerce, constrain, dragoon, drive, impel, make, oblige, press, pressurize 10 = **push**, propel, thrust 11 = **break open**, blast, prise, wrench, wrest **in force** 1 = **valid**, binding, current, effective, in operation, operative, working 2 = **in great numbers**, all together, in full strength

forebear *n* = **ancestor**, father, forefather, forerunner, predecessor

forecast *v* 1 = **predict**, anticipate, augur, divine, foresee, foretell, prophesy

forecastle [**foke**-sl] *n* raised front part of a ship.

foreclose *v* take possession of (property bought with borrowed money which has not been repaid). **foreclosure** *n*.

forecourt *n* courtyard or open space in front of a building.

forefather ❶ *n* ancestor.

forefinger *n* finger next to the thumb.

forefront ❶ *n* **1** most active or prominent position. **2** very front.

foregoing ❶ *adj* going before, preceding. **foregone conclusion** inevitable result.

foreground *n* part of a view, esp. in a picture, nearest the observer.

forehand *n Tennis etc.* stroke played with the palm of the hand facing forward.

forehead *n* part of the face above the eyebrows.

foreign ❶ *adj* **1** not of, or in, one's own country. **2** relating to or connected with other countries. **3** unfamiliar, strange. **4** in an abnormal place or position, e.g. *foreign matter.* **foreigner** *n*.

foreman *n* **1** person in charge of a group of workers. **2** leader of a jury.

foremost ❶ *adj, adv* first in time, place, or importance.

forensic *adj* used in or connected with courts of law. **forensic medicine** use of medical knowledge for the purposes of the law.

forerunner ❶ *n* person or thing that goes before, precursor.

foresee ❶ *v* see or know beforehand. **foreseeable** *adj*.

● **SPELLING TIP**
● There are 665 occurrences of the word
● **unforeseen** in the Bank of English. The
● misspelling *unforseen* occurs 50 times.

foreshadow ❶ *v* show or indicate beforehand.

foresight ❶ *n* ability to anticipate and provide for future needs.

foreskin *n* fold of skin covering the tip of the penis.

forest *n* large area with a thick growth of trees. **forestry** *n* **1** science of planting and caring for trees. **2** management of forests. **forester** *n* person skilled in forestry.

forestall *v* prevent or guard against in advance.

foretaste *n* early limited experience of something to come.

foretell ❶ *v* tell or indicate beforehand.

forethought ❶ *n* thoughtful planning for future events.

forever, for ever ❶ *adv* **1** without end. **2** at all times. **3** *informal* for a long time.

———————————————— THESAURUS ————————————————

▷ *n* **2** = **prediction**, conjecture, guess, prognosis, prophecy

forefather *n* = **ancestor**, father, forebear, forerunner, predecessor

forefront *n* **1** = **foreground**, centre, fore, prominence **2** = **lead**, front, spearhead, vanguard

foregoing *adj* = **preceding**, above, antecedent, anterior, former, previous, prior

foreign *adj* **1, 2** = **external**, exotic, imported, remote **3** = **alien**, strange, unfamiliar, unknown

foremost *adj* = **leading**, chief, highest, paramount, pre-eminent, primary, prime, principal, supreme

forerunner *n* = **precursor**, harbinger, herald, prototype

foresee *v* = **predict**, anticipate, envisage, forecast, foretell, prophesy

foreshadow *v* = **indicate**, augur, forebode, portend, prefigure, presage, promise, signal

foresight *n* = **forethought**, anticipation, far-sightedness, precaution, preparedness, prescience, prudence

foretell *v* = **predict**, forecast, forewarn, presage, prognosticate, prophesy

forethought *n* = **anticipation**, far-sightedness, foresight, precaution, providence, provision, prudence

forever, for ever *adv* **1** = **evermore**, always, endlessly, eternally, for all time, for keeps, in perpetuity **2** = **constantly**,

forewarn ❶ v warn beforehand.
foreword n introduction to a book.
forfeit ❶ [**for**-fit] n 1 thing lost or given
  up as a penalty for a fault or mistake. ▷ v
  2 lose as a forfeit. ▷ adj 3 lost as a forfeit.
  forfeiture n.
forge¹ ❶ n 1 place where metal is worked,
  smithy. 2 furnace for melting metal.
  ▷ v 3 make a fraudulent imitation of
  (something). 4 shape (metal) by heating and
  hammering it. 5 create (an alliance etc.).
forge² v advance steadily. **forge ahead**
  increase speed or take the lead.
forget ❶ v -**getting**, -**got**, -**gotten** 1 fail to
  remember. 2 neglect. 3 leave behind by
  mistake. **forgetful** adj tending to forget.
  forget-me-not n plant with clusters of
  small blue flowers.
forgive ❶ v -**giving**, -**gave**, -**given** cease to
  blame or hold resentment against, pardon.
  forgiveness n.
forgo ❶ v do without or give up.
fork ❶ n 1 tool for eating food, with prongs
and a handle. 2 large similarly-shaped
tool for digging or lifting. 3 point where
a road, river, etc. divides into branches.
4 one of the branches. ▷ v 5 pick up, dig,
etc. with a fork. 6 branch. 7 take one or
other branch at a fork in the road. **forked**
adj **fork-lift truck** vehicle with a forklike
device at the front which can be raised
or lowered to move loads. **fork out** v
informal pay.
forlorn ❶ adj lonely and unhappy. **forlorn
hope** hopeless enterprise.
form ❶ n 1 shape or appearance. 2 mode
in which something appears. 3 type or
kind. 4 printed document with spaces for
details. 5 physical or mental condition.
6 previous record of an athlete, racehorse,
etc. 7 class in school. 8 procedure or
etiquette. 9 bench. 10 hare's nest. ▷ v
11 give a (particular) shape to or take a
(particular) shape. 12 come or bring into
existence. 13 make or be made. 14 train.
15 acquire or develop. 16 be an element

—————— THESAURUS ——————

all the time, continually, incessantly,
interminably, perpetually, twenty-four-
seven (inf), unremittingly 3 Inf = **till the
cows come home**, till Doomsday (inf)
forewarn v = **caution**, advise, alert,
apprise, give fair warning, put on guard,
tip off
forfeit n 1 = **penalty**, damages, fine,
forfeiture, loss, mulct ▷ v 2 = **lose**, be
deprived of, be stripped of, give up,
relinquish, renounce, say goodbye to,
surrender
forge¹ v 3 = **fake**, copy, counterfeit, falsify,
feign, imitate 4 = **shape**, fashion, mould,
work 5 = **create**, construct, devise, form,
frame, make
forget v 1 = **omit**, overlook 2 = **neglect**,
lose sight of 3 = **leave behind**
forgive v = **excuse**, absolve, acquit,
condone, exonerate, let bygones be
bygones, let off (inf), pardon
forgo v = **give up**, abandon, do without,
relinquish, renounce, resign, surrender,
waive, yield
fork v 6 = **branch**, bifurcate, diverge, divide,
part, split
forlorn adj = **miserable**, disconsolate,
down in the dumps (inf), helpless,
hopeless, pathetic, pitiful, unhappy,
woebegone, wretched
form n 1 = **shape**, appearance, structure
2 = **formation**, configuration, pattern
3 = **type**, kind, sort, style, variety
4 = **document**, application, paper,
sheet 5 = **condition**, fettle, fitness,
health, shape, trim 7 = **class**, grade, rank
8 = **procedure**, convention, custom,
etiquette, protocol ▷ v 11 = **arrange**,
combine, draw up, organize 12 = **take
shape**, appear, become visible, come
into being, crystallize, grow, materialize,
rise 13 = **make**, build, construct, create,
fashion, forge, mould, produce, shape
15 = **develop**, acquire, contract, cultivate,
pick up 16 = **constitute**, compose,
comprise, make up

f

of. **formation** *n* structure or shape.
formless *adj*.
formal ❶ *adj* 1 of or characterized by
established conventions of ceremony
and behaviour. 2 of or for formal
occasions. 3 stiff in manner. 4 organized.
5 symmetrical. **formally** *adv* **formality**
n, pl **-ties** 1 requirement of custom or
etiquette. 2 necessary procedure without
real importance. **formalize** *v* make official
or formal.
format ❶ *n* 1 style in which something
is arranged. ▷ *v* **-matting, -matted**
2 arrange in a format.
former ❶ *adj* of an earlier time, previous.
the former first mentioned of two.
formerly *adv*.
Formica *n* ® kind of laminated sheet used
to make heat-resistant surfaces.
formidable ❶ *adj* 1 frightening because
difficult to overcome or manage.
2 extremely impressive.
formula ❶ *n, pl* **-las, -lae** 1 group of
numbers, letters, or symbols expressing a
scientific or mathematical rule. 2 method
or rule for doing or producing something.
3 set form of words used in religion, law, etc.

4 specific category of car in motor racing.
formulaic *adj* **formulate** *v* plan or describe
precisely and clearly. **formulation** *n*.
forsake ❶ *v* **-saking, -sook, -saken**
1 withdraw support or friendship from.
2 give up, renounce.
forswear *v* **-swearing, -swore, -sworn**
renounce or reject.
fort ❶ *n* fortified building or place. **hold
the fort** *informal* keep things going during
someone's absence.
forte¹ ❶ [**for**-tay] *n* thing at which a person
excels.
forte² [**for**-tay] *adv Music* loudly.
forth ❶ *adv* forwards, out, or away.
forthright ❶ *adj* direct and outspoken.
fortify ❶ *v* **-fying, -fied** 1 make (a
place) defensible, as by building walls.
2 strengthen. 3 add vitamins etc. to (food).
4 add alcohol to (wine) to make sherry or
port. **fortification** *n*.
fortitude ❶ *n* courage in adversity or
pain.
fortnight *n* two weeks. **fortnightly** *adv, adj*.
fortress ❶ *n* large fort or fortified town.
fortuitous [for-**tyew**-it-uss] *adj* happening
by (lucky) chance.

——————————————————————— THESAURUS ——————————

formal *adj* 1 = **official**, ceremonial,
ritualistic 2 = **stiff**, affected, precise,
unbending
format *n* 1 = **layout**, construction,
form, make-up, plan 2 = **arrangement**,
appearance, look, style, type
former *adj* = **previous**, earlier, erstwhile,
one-time, prior
formidable *adj* 1 = **intimidating**,
daunting, dismaying, fearful, frightful,
terrifying 2 = **impressive**, awesome,
great, mighty, powerful, redoubtable,
terrific, tremendous
formula *n* 2 = **method**, blueprint, precept,
principle, procedure, recipe, rule
forsake *v* 1 = **desert**, abandon, disown,
leave in the lurch, strand 2 = **give up**,
forgo, relinquish, renounce, set aside,
surrender, yield

fort *n* = **fortress**, blockhouse, camp, castle,
citadel, fortification, garrison, stronghold
hold the fort *Inf* = **carry on**, keep things on
an even keel, stand in, take over the reins
forte¹ *n* = **speciality**, gift, long suit (*inf*),
métier, strength, strong point, talent
forth *adv* = **forward**, ahead, away, onward,
out, outward
forthright *adj* = **outspoken**, blunt,
candid, direct, frank, open, plain-spoken,
straightforward, upfront (*inf*)
fortify *v* 1 = **protect**, buttress, reinforce,
shore up 2 = **strengthen**, augment,
support
fortitude *n* = **courage**, backbone,
bravery, fearlessness, grit, perseverance,
resolution, strength, valour
fortress *n* = **castle**, citadel, fastness, fort,
redoubt, stronghold

fortune ❶ n 1 luck, esp. when favourable. 2 power regarded as influencing human destiny. 3 wealth, large sum of money. ▷ pl 4 person's destiny. **fortunate** adj having good luck. **fortune-teller** n person who claims to predict the future of others.

forty adj, n, pl **-ties** four times ten. **fortieth** adj, n.

forum n meeting or medium for open discussion or debate.

forward ❶ adj 1 directed or moving ahead. 2 in, at, or near the front. 3 presumptuous. 4 well developed or advanced. 5 relating to the future. ▷ n 6 attacking player in various team games, such as football or hockey. ▷ adv 7 forwards. ▷ v 8 send (a letter etc.) on to an ultimate destination. 9 advance or promote. **forwards** adv 1 towards or at a place further ahead in space or time. 2 towards the front.

fossick v Aust & NZ search, esp. for gold or precious stones.

fossil n hardened remains of a prehistoric animal or plant preserved in rock. **fossilize** v 1 turn into a fossil. 2 become out-of-date or inflexible.

foster ❶ v 1 promote the growth or development of. 2 bring up (a child not one's own). ▷ adj 3 of or involved in fostering a child, e.g. foster parents.

foul ❶ adj 1 loathsome or offensive. 2 stinking or dirty. 3 (of language) obscene or vulgar. 4 unfair. ▷ n 5 Sport violation of the rules. ▷ v 6 make dirty or polluted. 7 make or become entangled or clogged. 8 Sport commit a foul against (an opponent). **fall foul of** come into conflict with. **foul-mouthed** adj habitually using foul language. **foul play** unfair conduct, esp. involving violence.

found¹ ❶ v 1 establish or bring into being. 2 lay the foundation of. 3 (foll. by on or upon) have a basis (in). **founder** n **founder member** one of the original members of a club or organization, often someone involved in setting it up.

found² v 1 cast (metal or glass) by melting and setting in a mould. 2 make (articles) by this method.

founder ❶ v 1 break down or fail. 2 (of a ship) sink. 3 stumble or fall.

foundling n abandoned baby.

—— THESAURUS ——

fortune n 1 = **luck**, chance 2 = **fate**, destiny, kismet, providence 3 = **wealth**, affluence, opulence, possessions, property, prosperity, riches, treasure ▷ pl 4 = **destiny**, lot

forward adj 1 = **leading**, advance, head 2 = **front**, first, foremost 3 = **presumptuous**, bold, brash, brazen, cheeky, familiar, impertinent, impudent, pushy (inf) 4 = **well-developed**, advanced, precocious, premature ▷ adv 7 = **forth**, ahead, on, onward 9 = **send**, dispatch, post, send on 9 = **promote**, advance, assist, expedite, further, hasten, hurry

foster v 1 = **promote**, cultivate, encourage, feed, nurture, stimulate, support, uphold 2 = **bring up**, mother, nurse, raise, rear, take care of

foul adj 1 = **offensive**, abhorrent, despicable, detestable, disgraceful, scandalous, shameful, wicked 2 = **dirty**, fetid, filthy, malodorous, nauseating, putrid, repulsive, squalid, stinking, unclean 3 = **obscene**, abusive, blue, coarse, indecent, lewd, profane, scurrilous, vulgar 4 = **unfair**, crooked, dishonest, fraudulent, shady (inf), underhand, unscrupulous ▷ v 6 = **dirty**, besmirch, contaminate, defile, pollute, stain, sully, taint

found¹ v 1 = **establish**, constitute, create, inaugurate, institute, organize, originate, set up, start

founder v 1 = **fail**, break down, collapse, come to grief, come unstuck, fall through, miscarry, misfire 2 = **sink**, be lost, go down, go to the bottom, submerge 3 = **stumble**, lurch, sprawl, stagger, trip

fount n 1 *lit* fountain. 2 source.

fountain ● n 1 jet of water. 2 structure from which such a jet spurts. 3 source. **fountainhead** n original source. **fountain pen** pen supplied with ink from a container inside it.

four adj, n 1 one more than three. ▷ n 2 (crew of) four-oared rowing boat. **on all fours** on hands and knees. **four-letter word** short obscene word referring to sex or excrement. **four-poster** n bed with four posts supporting a canopy. **foursome** n group of four people.

fowl n 1 domestic cock or hen. 2 any bird used for food or hunted as game.

fox n 1 reddish-brown bushy-tailed animal of the dog family. 2 its fur. 3 cunning person. ▷ v 4 *informal* perplex or deceive. **foxy** adj of or like a fox, esp. in craftiness. **foxglove** n tall plant with purple or white flowers. **foxtrot** n 1 ballroom dance with slow and quick steps. 2 music for this.

foyer ● [**foy**-ay] n entrance hall in a theatre, cinema, or hotel.

fracas ● [**frak**-ah] n, pl **-cas** noisy quarrel.

fraction ● n 1 numerical quantity that is not a whole number. 2 fragment, piece. 3 *Chem* substance separated by distillation. **fractional** adj.

fracture ● n 1 breaking, esp. of a bone. ▷ v 2 break or cause to break.

fragile ● adj 1 easily broken or damaged. 2 in a weakened physical state. **fragility** n.

fragrant ● adj sweet-smelling. **fragrance** n 1 pleasant smell. 2 perfume, scent.

frail ● adj 1 physically weak. 2 easily damaged. **frailty** n, pl **-ties** physical or moral weakness.

frame ● n 1 structure giving shape or support. 2 enclosing case or border, as round a picture. 3 person's build. 4 individual exposure on a strip of film. 5 individual game of snooker in a match. ▷ v 6 put together, construct. 7 put into words. 8 put into a frame. 9 *slang* incriminate (a person) on a false charge. **frame of mind** mood or attitude. **frame-up** n *slang* false incrimination. **framework** n supporting structure.

franc n monetary unit of France, Switzerland, Belgium, and various African countries.

franchise n 1 right to vote. 2 authorization to sell a company's goods.

frank ● adj 1 honest and straightforward in speech or attitude. ▷ n 2 official mark on a letter permitting delivery. ▷ v 3 put such a mark on (a letter). **frankly** adv.

frankfurter n smoked sausage.

— THESAURUS —

fountain n 1 = **jet**, spout, spray, spring 2 = **fount**, font, well 3 = **source**, cause, derivation, fount, fountainhead, origin, wellspring

foyer n = **entrance hall**, antechamber, anteroom, lobby, reception area, vestibule

fracas n = **brawl**, affray (*Law*), disturbance, mêlée, riot, rumpus, scuffle, skirmish

fraction n 1 = **percentage** 2 = **piece**, part, portion, section, segment, share, slice

fracture n 1 = **break**, crack ▷ v 2 = **break**, crack, rupture, splinter, split

fragile adj 1 = **delicate**, breakable, brittle, dainty, fine, flimsy, frangible 2 = **weak**, frail

fragrant adj = **aromatic**, balmy, odorous, perfumed, redolent, sweet-scented, sweet-smelling

frail adj 1 = **weak**, feeble, fragile, infirm, puny 2 = **delicate**, flimsy, insubstantial, vulnerable

frame n 1 = **casing**, construction, framework, shell, structure 3 = **physique**, anatomy, body, build, carcass ▷ v 6 = **construct**, assemble, build, make, manufacture, put together 7 = **devise**, compose, draft, draw up, formulate, map out, sketch 8 = **mount**, case, enclose, surround **frame of mind** = **mood**, attitude, disposition, humour, outlook, state, temper

frank adj 1 = **honest**, blunt, candid, direct, forthright, open, outspoken, plain-spoken, sincere, straightforward, truthful

frankincense n aromatic gum resin burned as incense.

frantic ⊙ adj 1 distracted with rage, grief, joy, etc. 2 hurried and disorganized. **frantically** adv.

fraternal adj of a brother, brotherly. **fraternity** n 1 group of people with shared interests, aims, etc. 2 brotherhood. 3 US male social club at college. **fraternize** v associate on friendly terms. **fraternization** n **fratricide** n 1 crime of killing one's brother. 2 person who does this.

fraud ⊙ n 1 (criminal) deception, swindle. 2 person who acts in a deceitful way. **fraudulent** adj **fraudulence** n.

fraught [**frawt**] adj tense or anxious. **fraught with** involving, filled with.

fray¹ n noisy quarrel or conflict.

fray² ⊙ v 1 make or become ragged at the edge. 2 become strained.

frazzle n informal exhausted state.

freak ⊙ n 1 abnormal person or thing. 2 person who is excessively enthusiastic about something. ▷ adj 3 abnormal. **freakish** adj **freak out** v informal (cause to) be in a heightened emotional state.

freckle n small brown spot on the skin. **freckled** adj marked with freckles.

free ⊙ adj **freer**, **freest** 1 able to act at will, not compelled or restrained. 2 not subject (to). 3 independent. 4 provided without charge. 5 generous, lavish. 6 not in use. 7 (of a person) not busy. 8 not fixed or joined. ▷ v **freeing**, **freed** 9 release, liberate. 10 remove (obstacles, pain, etc.) from. 11 make available or usable. **a free hand** unrestricted freedom to act. **freely** adv **free fall** part of a parachute descent before the parachute opens. **free-for-all** n informal brawl. **freehand** adj drawn without guiding instruments. **freehold** n tenure of land held for life without restrictions. **freeholder** n **freelance** adj, n (of) a self-employed person doing specific pieces of work for various employers. **freeloader** n slang habitual scrounger. **free-range** adj kept or produced in natural conditions. **freeway** n Chiefly US motorway. **freewheel** v travel downhill on a bicycle without pedalling.

freeze ⊙ v **freezing**, **froze**, **frozen** 1 change from a liquid to a solid by the reduction of temperature, as water to ice. 2 preserve (food etc.) by extreme cold. 3 (cause to) be very cold. 4 become motionless with fear, shock, etc. 5 fix (prices or wages) at a particular level. 6 ban the exchange

frantic adj 1 = **distraught**, at the end of one's tether, berserk, beside oneself, desperate, distracted, fraught (inf), furious, wild 2 = **hectic**, frenetic, frenzied (sl)

fraud n 1 = **deception**, chicanery, deceit, double-dealing, duplicity, sharp practice, swindling, treachery, trickery 2 = **impostor**, charlatan, fake, hoaxer, phoney or phony (inf), pretender, swindler

fray² v 1 = **wear thin**, wear

freak n 1 = **oddity**, aberration, anomaly, malformation, monstrosity, weirdo or weirdie (inf) 2 = **enthusiast**, addict, aficionado, buff (inf), devotee, fan, fanatic, fiend (inf), nut (sl) ▷ adj 3 = **abnormal**, exceptional, unparalleled, unusual

free adj 1 = **allowed**, able, clear, permitted, unimpeded, unrestricted 2, 3 = **at liberty**, at large, footloose, independent, liberated, loose, on the loose, unfettered 4 = **complimentary**, for free (inf), for nothing, free of charge, gratis, gratuitous, on the house, unpaid, without charge 5 = **generous**, lavish, liberal, unsparing, unstinting 6 = **available**, empty, spare, unoccupied, unused, vacant 7 = **idle**, unemployed ▷ v 9 = **release**, deliver, let out, liberate, loose, set free, turn loose, unchain, untie 10 = **clear**, cut loose, disengage, disentangle, extricate, rescue

freeze v 1 = **ice over** or **up**, harden, stiffen 3 = **chill** 5, 6 = **suspend**, fix, hold up, inhibit, stop

or collection of (loans, assets, etc.). ▷ *n*
7 period of very cold weather. **8** freezing of
prices or wages. **freezer** *n* insulated cabinet
for cold-storage of perishable foods. **freeze-
dry** *v* preserve (food) by rapid freezing and
drying in a vacuum. **freezing** *adj informal*
very cold.

freezing point *n* the temperature below
which a liquid turns into a solid.

freight ① [frate] *n* **1** commercial transport
of goods. **2** cargo transported. **3** cost of
this. ▷ *v* **4** send by freight. **freighter** *n* ship
or aircraft for transporting goods.

frenetic [frin-**net**-ik] *adj* uncontrolled,
excited.

frenzy ① *n, pl* **-zies 1** violent mental
derangement. **2** wild excitement.
frenzied *adj*.

frequent ① *adj* **1** happening often.
2 habitual. ▷ *v* **3** visit habitually.
frequently *adv* **frequency** *n, pl* **-cies**
1 rate of occurrence. **2** *Physics* number
of times a wave repeats itself in a given
time.

fresco *n, pl* **-coes**, **-cos** method of
watercolour painting done on wet plaster
on a wall.

fresh ① *adj* **1** newly made, acquired, etc.
2 novel, original. **3** most recent. **4** further,

additional. **5** (of food) not preserved.
6 (of water) not salty. **7** (of weather) brisk
or invigorating. **8** not tired. **9** *informal*
impudent. **freshly** *adv* **freshness** *n*
freshen *v* make or become fresh or fresher.
fresher, **freshman** *n* first-year student.

fret¹ ① *v* **fretting**, **fretted** be worried.
fretful *adj* irritable.

fret² *n* small bar on the fingerboard of a
guitar etc.

Fri. Friday.

friable *adj* easily crumbled.

friar *n* member of a male Roman Catholic
religious order. **friary** *n, pl* **-ries** house of
friars.

fricassee *n* stewed meat served in a thick
white sauce.

friction ① *n* **1** resistance met with by a body
moving over another. **2** rubbing. **3** clash of
wills or personalities. **frictional** *adj*.

Friday *n* sixth day of the week.

fridge *n* apparatus in which food and drinks
are kept cool.

friend ① *n* **1** person whom one knows well
and likes. **2** supporter or ally. **friendly**
adj **1** showing or expressing liking. **2** not
hostile, on the same side. ▷ *n, pl* **-lies**
3 *Sport* match played for its own sake and
not as part of a competition. **-friendly**

— THESAURUS —

freight *n* **1** = **transportation**, carriage,
conveyance, shipment **2** = **cargo**, burden,
consignment, goods, load, merchandise,
payload

frenzy *n* **1** = **fury**, derangement, hysteria,
paroxysm, passion, rage, seizure

frequent *adj* **1** = **persistent**, recurrent,
repeated **2** = **habitual**, common,
customary, everyday, familiar, usual ▷ *v*
3 = **visit**, attend, hang out at (*inf*), haunt,
patronize

fresh *adj* **1** = **new**, different **2** = **novel**,
original **3** = **recent**, modern, up-
to-date **4** = **additional**, added,
auxiliary, extra, further, more, other,
supplementary **5** = **natural**, unprocessed
7 = **invigorating**, bracing, brisk, clean,

cool, crisp, pure, refreshing, unpolluted
8 = **lively**, alert, energetic, keen, refreshed,
sprightly, spry, vigorous **9** *Inf* = **cheeky**,
disrespectful, familiar, forward, impudent,
insolent, presumptuous

fret¹ *v* = **worry**, agonize, brood, lose sleep
over, obsess about, upset *or* distress
oneself

friction *n* **2** = **rubbing**, abrasion,
chafing, grating, rasping, resistance,
scraping **3** = **hostility**, animosity, bad
blood, conflict, disagreement, discord,
dissension, resentment

friend *n* **1** = **companion**, buddy (*inf*), chum
(*inf*), comrade, mate (*inf*), pal, playmate
2 = **supporter**, ally, associate, patron,
well-wisher

combining form good or easy for the person or thing specified, e.g. *user-friendly*.
friendly fire *n Military* firing by one's own side, esp when it harms one's own person nel. **friendliness** *n* **friendless** *adj* **friendship** *n*.

frieze [**freeze**] *n* ornamental band on a wall.

frigate [**frig**-it] *n* medium-sized fast warship.

fright ❶ *n* 1 sudden fear or alarm. 2 sudden alarming shock. **frighten** *v* 1 scare or terrify. 2 force (someone) to do something from fear. **frightening** *adj* **frightful** *adj* 1 horrifying. 2 *informal* very great. **frightfully** *adv*.

frigid ❶ [**frij**-id] *adj* 1 (of a woman) sexually unresponsive. 2 very cold. 3 excessively formal. **frigidity** *n*.

frill *n* 1 gathered strip of fabric attached at one edge. ▷ *pl* 2 superfluous decorations or details. **frilled lizard** large tree-living Australian lizard with an erectile fold of skin round the neck. **frilly** *adj*.

fringe ❶ *n* 1 hair cut short and hanging over the forehead. 2 ornamental edge of hanging threads, tassels, etc. 3 outer edge. 4 less important parts of an activity or group. ▷ *v* 5 decorate with a fringe. ▷ *adj* 6 (of theatre) unofficial or unconventional. **fringed** *adj* **fringe benefit** benefit given in addition to a regular salary.

frisk ❶ *v* 1 move or leap playfully. 2 *informal* search (a person) for concealed weapons etc. **frisky** *adj* lively or high-spirited. **friskily** *adv*.

frisson [**frees**-sonn] *n* shiver of fear or excitement.

fritter *n* piece of food fried in batter.

frivolous ❶ *adj* 1 not serious or sensible. 2 enjoyable but trivial. **frivolity** *n*.

frizz *v* form (hair) into stiff wiry curls. **frizzy** *adj*.

frock *n* dress. **frock coat** man's skirted coat as worn in the 19th century.

frog *n* smooth-skinned tailless amphibian with long back legs used for jumping. **frog in one's throat** phlegm on the vocal cords, hindering speech. **frogman** *n* swimmer with a rubber suit and breathing equipment for working underwater. **frogmarch** *v* force (a resisting person) to move by holding his arms. **frogspawn** *n* jelly-like substance containing frog's eggs.

frolic ❶ *v* **-icking, -icked** 1 run and play in a lively way. ▷ *n* 2 lively and merry behaviour. **frolicsome** *adj* playful.

from *prep* indicating the point of departure, source, distance, cause, change of state, etc.

frond *n* long leaf or leaflike part of a fern, palm, or seaweed.

front ❶ *n* 1 fore part. 2 position directly before or ahead. 3 seaside promenade.

—— THESAURUS ——

fright *n* 1, 2 = **fear**, alarm, consternation, dread, horror, panic, scare, shock, trepidation

frigid *adj* 1 = **unresponsive** 2 = **cold**, arctic, frosty, frozen, glacial, icy, wintry 3 = **formal**, aloof, austere, forbidding, unapproachable, unfeeling

fringe *n* 2 = **border**, edging, hem, trimming 3 = **edge**, borderline, limits, margin, outskirts, perimeter, periphery ▷ *adj* 6 = **unofficial**, unconventional, unorthodox

frisk *v* 1 = **frolic**, caper, cavort, gambol, jump, play, prance, skip, trip 2 *Inf* = **search**, check, inspect, run over, shake down (*US sl*)

frivolous *adj* 1 = **flippant**, childish, foolish, idle, juvenile, puerile, silly, superficial 2 = **trivial**, footling (*inf*), minor, petty, shallow, trifling, unimportant

frolic *v* 1 = **play**, caper, cavort, frisk, gambol, lark, make merry, romp, sport ▷ *n* 2 = **revel**, antic, game, lark, romp, spree

front *n* 1 = **foreground**, frontage 2 = **forefront**, head, lead, vanguard 4 = **front line** 6 = **exterior**, facade, face 7 *Inf* = **cover**, blind, cover-up, disguise, mask, pretext ▷ *adj* 9 = **foremost**, first, head, lead, leading, topmost ▷ *v* 10 = **face onto**, look over *or* onto, overlook

4 battle line or area. **5** *Meteorol* dividing line between two different air masses. **6** outward appearance. **7** *informal* cover for another, usu. criminal, activity. **8** group with a common goal. ▷ *adj* **9** of or at the front. ▷ *v* **10** face (onto). **11** be the presenter of (a television show). **frontal** *adj* **frontage** *n* facade of a building. **front bench** parliamentary leaders of the government or opposition. **front-bencher** *n* **frontrunner** *n informal* person regarded as most likely to win a race, election, etc.

frost ❶ *n* **1** white frozen dew or mist. **2** atmospheric temperature below freezing point. ▷ *v* **3** become covered with frost. **frosted** *adj* (of glass) having a rough surface to make it opaque. **frosting** *n Chiefly US* sugar icing. **frosty** *adj* **1** characterized or covered by frost. **2** unfriendly. **frostily** *adv* **frostiness** *n* **frostbite** *n* destruction of tissue, esp. of the fingers or ears, by cold.

froth ❶ *n* **1** mass of small bubbles. ▷ *v* **2** foam. **frothy** *adj*.

frown ❶ *v* **1** wrinkle one's brows in worry, anger, or thought. **2** look disapprovingly (on). ▷ *n* **3** frowning expression.

frugal ❶ *adj* **1** thrifty, sparing. **2** meagre and inexpensive. **frugality** *n*.

fruit ❶ *n* **1** part of a plant containing seeds, esp. if edible. **2** any plant product useful to man. **3** (often *pl*) result of an action or effort. ▷ *v* **4** bear fruit. **fruiterer**

n person who sells fruit. **fruitful** *adj* useful or productive. **fruitless** *adj* useless or unproductive. **fruity** *adj* **1** of or like fruit. **2** (of a voice) mellow. **3** *informal* mildly bawdy. **fruit fly 1** small fly that feeds on and lays its eggs in plant tissues. **2** similar fly that feeds on plant sap, decaying fruit, etc., and is widely used in genetics experiments. **fruit machine** coin-operated gambling machine.

frump *n* dowdy woman. **frumpy** *adj*.

frustrate ❶ *v* **1** upset or anger. **2** hinder or prevent. **frustrated** *adj* **frustrating** *adj* **frustration** *n*.

fry¹ *v* **frying**, **fried 1** cook or be cooked in fat or oil. ▷ *n*, *pl* **fries 2** (also **fry-up**) dish of fried food. ▷ *pl* **3** potato chips.

fry² *pl n* young fishes. **small fry** young or insignificant people.

ft. 1 foot. **2** feet.

fuchsia [**fyew**-sha] *n* ornamental shrub with hanging flowers.

fuddle *v* cause to be intoxicated or confused.

fuddy-duddy ❶ *adj*, *n*, *pl* **-dies** *informal* old-fashioned (person).

fudge¹ *n* soft caramel-like sweet.

fudge² ❶ *v* avoid making a firm statement or decision.

fuel ❶ *n* **1** substance burned or treated to produce heat or power. **2** something that intensifies (a feeling etc.). ▷ *v* **fuelling**, **fuelled 3** provide with fuel.

— THESAURUS —

frost *n* **1** = **hoarfrost**, rime ▷ *v* **3** = **freeze**

froth *n* **1** = **foam**, bubbles, effervescence, head, lather, scum, spume, suds ▷ *v* **2** = **fizz**, bubble over, come to a head, effervesce, foam, lather

frown *v* **1** = **scowl**, glare, glower, knit one's brows, look daggers, lour *or* lower **2** = **disapprove of**, discourage, dislike, look askance at, take a dim view of

frugal *adj* **1** = **thrifty**, abstemious, careful, economical, niggardly, parsimonious, prudent, sparing

fruit *n* **2** = **produce**, crop, harvest, product, yield **3** (often *pl*) = **result**, advantage, benefit, consequence, effect, end result, outcome, profit, return, reward

frustrate *v* **2** = **thwart**, balk, block, check, counter, defeat, disappoint, foil, forestall, nullify, stymie

fuddy-duddy *n Inf* = **conservative**, (old) fogey, square (*inf*), stick-in-the-mud (*inf*), stuffed shirt (*inf*)

fudge² *v* = **stall**, hedge

fuel *n* **2** = **incitement**, provocation

fugitive ① [**fyew**-jit-iv] *n* 1 person who flees, esp. from arrest or pursuit. ▷ *adj* 2 fleeing. 3 transient.

fugue [**fyewg**] *n* musical composition in which a theme is repeated in different parts.

fulcrum *n, pl* -**crums**, -**cra** pivot about which a lever turns.

fulfil ① *v* -**filling**, -**filled** 1 bring about the achievement of (a desire or promise). 2 carry out (a request or order). 3 do what is required. **fulfilment** *n* **fulfil oneself** *v* achieve one's potential.

full ① *adj* 1 containing as much or as many as possible. 2 abundant in supply. 3 having had enough to eat. 4 plump. 5 complete, whole. 6 (of a garment) of ample cut. 7 (of a sound or flavour) rich and strong. ▷ *adv* 8 completely. 9 directly. 10 very. **fully** *adv* **fullness** *n* **in full** without shortening. **full-blooded** *adj* vigorous or enthusiastic. **full-blown** *adj* fully developed. **full moon** phase of the moon when it is visible as a fully illuminated disc. **full-scale** *adj* 1 (of a plan) of actual size. 2 using all resources. **full stop** punctuation mark (.) at the end of a

sentence and after abbreviations.

fulminate *v* (foll. by *against*) criticize or denounce angrily.

fulsome ① *adj* distastefully excessive or insincere.

fumble ① *v* 1 handle awkwardly. 2 say awkwardly. ▷ *n* 3 act of fumbling.

fume ① *v* 1 be very angry. 2 give out smoke or vapour. ▷ *pl n* 3 pungent smoke or vapour.

fun ① *n* enjoyment or amusement. **make fun of** mock or tease. **funny** *adj* 1 comical, humorous. 2 odd. **funny bone** part of the elbow where the nerve is near the surface. **funnily** *adv*.

function ① *n* 1 purpose something exists for. 2 way something works. 3 large or formal social event. 4 *Maths* quantity whose value depends on the varying value of another. 5 sequence of operations performed by a computer at a key stroke. ▷ *v* 6 operate or work. 7 (foll. by *as*) fill the role of. **functional** *adj* 1 of or as a function. 2 practical rather than decorative. 3 in working order. **functionary** *n, pl* -**aries** official.

THESAURUS

---

fugitive *n* 1 = **runaway**, deserter, escapee, refugee ▷ *adj* 3 = **momentary**, brief, ephemeral, fleeting, passing, short-lived, temporary, transient, transitory

fulfil *v* 1 = **achieve**, accomplish, realise 2 = **carry out**, complete, perform, satisfy 3 = **comply with**, answer, conform to, fill, meet, obey, observe

full *adj* 1 = **filled**, brimming, complete, loaded, saturated, stocked 2 = **extensive**, abundant, adequate, ample, generous, plentiful 3 = **satiated**, replete 4 = **plump**, buxom, curvaceous, rounded, voluptuous 5 = **comprehensive**, exhaustive 6 = **voluminous**, baggy, capacious, large, loose, puffy 7 = **rich**, clear, deep, distinct, loud, resonant, rounded **in full** = **completely**, in its entirety, in total, without exception

fulsome *adj* = **extravagant**, excessive, immoderate, inordinate, insincere, sycophantic, unctuous

fumble *v* 1 = **grope**, feel around, flounder, scrabble

fume *v* 1 (*inf*) = **rage**, rant, see red (*inf*), seethe, smoulder, storm ▷ *pl n* 3 = **smoke**, exhaust, gas, pollution, smog, vapour

fun *n* = **enjoyment**, amusement, entertainment, jollity, merriment, mirth, pleasure, recreation, sport **make fun of** = **mock**, lampoon, laugh at, parody, poke fun at, ridicule, satirize, send up (*Brit inf*)

function *n* 1 = **purpose**, raison d'être, business, duty, job, mission, responsibility, role, task 3 = **reception**, affair, do (*inf*), gathering, social occasion ▷ *v* 6 = **work**, go, operate, perform, run 7 (foll. by *as*) = **act as**, behave as, do duty as

fund ❶ n 1 stock of money for a special purpose. 2 supply or store. ▷ pl 3 money resources. ▷ v 4 provide money to. **funding** n.

fundamental ❶ adj 1 essential or primary. 2 basic. ▷ n 3 basic rule or fact. **fundamentally** adv **fundamentalism** n literal or strict interpretation of a religion. **fundamentalist** n, adj.

fundi n S Afr expert or boffin.

funeral ❶ n ceremony of burying or cremating a dead person.

fungus n, pl **-gi**, **-guses** plant without leaves, flowers, or roots, such as a mushroom or mould. **fungal**, **fungous** adj **fungicide** n substance that destroys fungi.

funk n style of dance music with a strong beat. **funky** adj **funkier**, **funkiest** (of music) having a strong beat.

funnel ❶ n 1 cone-shaped tube for pouring liquids into a narrow opening. 2 chimney of a ship or locomotive. ▷ v **-nelling**, **-nelled** 3 (cause to) move through or as if through a funnel. **funnel-web** n Aust large poisonous black spider that builds funnel-shaped webs.

fur n 1 soft hair of a mammal. 2 animal skin with the fur left on. 3 garment made of this. 4 whitish coating on the tongue or inside a kettle. ▷ v 5 cover or become covered with fur. **furry** adj **furrier** n dealer in furs.

furious ❶ adj 1 very angry. 2 violent or unrestrained.

furl v roll up and fasten (a sail, umbrella, or flag).

furlong n eighth of a mile.

furnace n enclosed chamber containing a very hot fire.

furnish ❶ v 1 provide (a house or room) with furniture. 2 supply, provide. **furnishings** pl n furniture, carpets, and fittings. **furniture** n large movable articles such as chairs and wardrobes.

furore ❶ [fyew-**ror**-ee] n very excited or angry reaction.

furrow ❶ n 1 trench made by a plough. 2 groove, esp. a wrinkle on the forehead. ▷ v 3 make or become wrinkled. 4 make furrows in.

further ❶ adv 1 in addition. 2 to a greater distance or extent. ▷ adj 3 additional. 4 more distant. ▷ v 5 assist the progress of. **further education** education beyond school other than at a university. **furthest** adv 1 to the greatest distance or extent. ▷ adj 2 most distant. **furtherance** n **furthermore** adv besides. **furthermost** adj most distant.

─────────────── THESAURUS ───────────────

fund n 1 = **kitty**, pool 2 = **reserve**, stock, store, supply ▷ v 4 = **finance**, pay for, subsidize, support

fundamental adj 1 = **essential**, cardinal, central, key, primary, principal 2 = **basic**, elementary, rudimentary, underlying ▷ n 3 = **principle**, axiom, cornerstone, law, rudiment, rule

funeral n = **burial**, cremation, interment, obsequies

funnel v 3 = **channel**, conduct, convey, direct, filter, move, pass, pour

furious adj 1 = **angry**, beside oneself, enraged, fuming, incensed, infuriated, livid (inf), raging, up in arms 2 = **violent**, fierce, intense, savage, turbulent, unrestrained, vehement

furnish v 1 = **decorate**, equip, fit out, stock 2 = **supply**, give, grant, hand out, offer, present, provide

furore n = **commotion**, disturbance, hullabaloo, outcry, stir, to-do, uproar

furrow n 1 = **groove**, channel, hollow, line, rut, seam, trench 2 = **wrinkle**, crease ▷ v 3 = **wrinkle**, corrugate, crease, draw together, knit

further adv 1 = **in addition**, additionally, also, besides, furthermore, into the bargain, moreover, to boot ▷ adj 3 = **additional**, extra, fresh, more, new, other, supplementary ▷ v 5 = **promote**, advance, assist, encourage, forward, help, lend support to, work for

furtive ⊕ *adj* sly and secretive. **furtively** *adv*.
fury ⊕ *n, pl* -**ries** 1 wild anger.
2 uncontrolled violence.
fuse[1] *n* cord containing an explosive for detonating a bomb.
fuse[2] *n* 1 safety device for electric circuits, containing a wire that melts and breaks the connection when the circuit is overloaded. ▷ *v* 2 (cause to) fail as a result of a blown fuse. 3 equip (a plug) with a fuse. 4 join or combine. 5 unite by melting. 6 melt with heat.
fuselage [**fyew**-zill-lahzh] *n* body of an aircraft.
fuss ⊕ *n* 1 needless activity or worry.
2 complaint or objection. 3 great display of attention. ▷ *v* 4 make a fuss. **fussy** *adj* 1 inclined to fuss. 2 overparticular.
3 overelaborate. **fussily** *adv* **fussiness** *n*.

fusty ⊕ *adj* -**tier**, -**tiest** 1 stale-smelling.
2 behind the times.
futile ⊕ *adj* unsuccessful or useless.
futility *n*.
futon [**foo**-tonn] *n* Japanese padded quilt, laid on the floor as a bed.
future ⊕ *n* 1 time to come. 2 what will happen. 3 prospects. ▷ *adj* 4 yet to come or be. 5 of or relating to time to come.
6 (of a verb tense) indicating that the action specified has not yet taken place.
futuristic *adj* of a design appearing to belong to some future time.
fuzz[1] *n* mass of fine or curly hairs or fibres.
fuzzy *adj* **fuzzier**, **fuzziest** 1 of, like, or covered with fuzz. 2 blurred or indistinct.
3 (of hair) tightly curled. **fuzzily** *adv*
fuzziness *n*.
fuzz[2] *n slang* police.

furtive *adj* = **sly**, clandestine, conspiratorial, secretive, sneaky, stealthy, surreptitious, underhand, under-the-table
fury *n* 1 = **anger**, frenzy, impetuosity, madness, passion, rage, wrath
2 = **violence**, ferocity, fierceness, force, intensity, savagery, severity, vehemence
fuss *n* 1 = **bother**, ado, commotion, excitement, hue and cry, palaver, stir, to-do 2 = **argument**, complaint, furore, objection, row, squabble, trouble ▷ *v*

4 = **worry**, fidget, flap (*inf*), fret, get worked up, take pains
fusty *adj* 1 = **stale**, airless, damp, mildewed, mouldering, mouldy, musty, stuffy
futile *adj* = **useless**, fruitless, ineffectual, unavailing, unprofitable, unsuccessful, vain, worthless
future *n* 1 = **time to come**, hereafter
3 = **prospect**, expectation, outlook ▷ *adj* 4,
5 = **forthcoming**, approaching, coming, fated, impending, later, subsequent, to come

Gg

g 1 gram(s). **2** (acceleration due to) gravity.
GA Georgia.
gabardine, gaberdine *n* strong twill cloth used esp. for raincoats.
gabble ❶ *v* **1** speak rapidly and indistinctly. ▷ *n* **2** rapid indistinct speech.
gable *n* triangular upper part of a wall between sloping roofs. **gabled** *adj*.
gad *v* **gadding, gadded. gad about, around** go around in search of pleasure.
gadget ❶ *n* small mechanical device or appliance. **gadgetry** *n* gadgets.
gaffe ❶ *n* social blunder.
gaffer ❶ *n* **1** *informal* foreman or boss. **2** old man.
gag¹ ❶ *v* **gagging, gagged 1** choke or

retch. **2** stop up the mouth of (a person) with cloth etc. **3** deprive of free speech. ▷ *n* **4** cloth etc. put into or tied across the mouth.
gag² ❶ *n informal* joke.
gaggle *n* **1** *informal* disorderly crowd. **2** flock of geese.
gain ❶ *v* **1** acquire or obtain. **2** increase or improve. **3** reach. **4** (of a watch or clock) be or become too fast. ▷ *n* **5** profit or advantage. **6** increase or improvement. **gainful** *adj* useful or profitable. **gainfully** *adv* **gain on, upon** *v* get nearer to or catch up with.
gainsay ❶ *v* **-saying, -said** deny or contradict.
gait ❶ *n* manner of walking.
gala ❶ [**gah**-la] *n* **1** festival. **2** competitive sporting event.
galaxy *n, pl* **-axies 1** system of stars. **2** gathering of famous people. **galactic** *adj*.
gale ❶ *n* **1** strong wind. **2** *informal* loud outburst.
gall¹ ❶ [**gawl**] *n* **1** *informal* impudence.

THESAURUS

gabble *v* **1** = **prattle**, babble, blabber, gibber, gush, jabber, spout ▷ *n* **2** = **gibberish**, babble, blabber, chatter, drivel, prattle, twaddle
gadget *n* = **device**, appliance, contraption (*inf*), contrivance, gizmo (*sl, chiefly US*), instrument, invention, thing, tool
gaffe *n* = **blunder**, bloomer (*inf*), clanger (*inf*), faux pas, howler, indiscretion, lapse, mistake, slip, solecism
gaffer *n* **1** *Inf* = **manager**, boss (*inf*), foreman, overseer, superintendent, supervisor **2** = **old man**, granddad, greybeard, old boy (*inf*), old fellow, old-timer (*US*)
gag¹ *v* **1** = **retch**, heave, puke (*sl*), spew, throw up (*inf*), vomit **2** = **suppress**, curb, muffle, muzzle, quiet, silence, stifle, stop up
gag² *n Inf* = **joke**, crack (*sl*), funny (*inf*), hoax, jest, wisecrack (*inf*), witticism

gain *v* **1** = **acquire**, attain, capture, collect, gather, get, land, secure **2** = **improve**, advance, increase, pick up, profit **3** = **reach**, arrive at, attain, come to, get to ▷ *n* **5** = **profit**, advantage, benefit, dividend, return, yield **6** = **increase**, advance, growth, improvement, progress, rise
gainsay *v* = **contradict**, contravene, controvert, deny, disagree with, dispute, rebut, retract
gait *n* = **walk**, bearing, carriage, pace, step, stride, tread
gala *n* **1** = **festival**, carnival, celebration, festivity, fete, jamboree, pageant
gale *n* **1** = **storm**, blast, cyclone, hurricane, squall, tempest, tornado, typhoon **2** *Inf* = **outburst**, burst, eruption, explosion, fit, howl, outbreak, paroxysm, peal, shout, shriek, storm
gall¹ *n* **1** *Inf* = **impudence**, brazenness,

2 bitter feeling. **3** bile. **gall bladder**
sac attached to the liver, storing bile.
gallstone n hard mass formed in the gall
bladder or its ducts.

gall² ❶ **[gawl]** v **1** annoy. **2** make sore
by rubbing. ▷ n **3** sore caused by
rubbing. **galling** adj annoying or bitterly
humiliating.

gallant ❶ adj **1** brave and noble. **2** (of a
man) attentive to women. **gallantry** n
1 showy, attentive treatment of women.
2 bravery.

galleon n large three-masted sailing ship
of the 15th–17th centuries.

gallery n, pl **-ries 1** room or building for
displaying works of art. **2** balcony in a
church, theatre, etc. **3** passage in a mine.
4 long narrow room for a specific purpose,
e.g. shooting gallery.

galley n **1** kitchen of a ship or aircraft.
2 Hist ship propelled by oars, usu. rowed
by slaves. **galley slave 1** slave forced to
row in a galley. **2** informal drudge.

gallivant ❶ v go about in search of
pleasure.

gallon n liquid measure of eight pints,
equal to 4.55 litres.

gallop ❶ n **1** horse's fastest pace.
2 galloping. ▷ v **galloping, galloped 3** go

or ride at a gallop. **4** move or progress
rapidly.

● **SPELLING TIP**
● Although **gallop** has two ls, remember
● that **galloping** and **galloped** have only
● one p.

gallows n wooden structure used for
hanging criminals.

galore ❶ adv in abundance.

galoshes pl n waterproof overshoes.

gambit n **1** opening line or move intended
to secure an advantage. **2** Chess opening
move involving the sacrifice of a pawn.

gamble ❶ v **1** play games of chance to
win money. **2** act on the expectation of
something. ▷ n **3** risky undertaking. **4** bet
or wager. **gambler** n **gambling** n.

gambol ❶ v **-bolling, -bolled 1** jump about
playfully, frolic. ▷ n **2** frolic.

● **SPELLING TIP**
● Although the pronunciation is the same
● as 'gamble', both the verb and the noun
● **gambol** must always contain an o.

game¹ ❶ n **1** amusement or pastime.
2 contest for amusement. **3** single period
of play in a contest. **4** animals or birds
hunted for sport or food. **5** their flesh.
6 scheme or trick. ▷ v **7** gamble. ▷ adj
8 brave. **9** willing. **gamely** adv **gaming**

cheek (inf), chutzpah (US & Canad inf),
effrontery, impertinence, insolence, nerve
(inf) **2** = **bitterness**, acrimony, animosity,
bile, hostility, rancour

gall² v **1** = **annoy**, exasperate, irk, irritate,
provoke, rankle, vex **2** = **scrape**, abrade,
chafe, irritate

gallant adj **1** = **brave**, bold, courageous,
heroic, honourable, intrepid, manly,
noble, valiant **2** = **courteous**, attentive,
chivalrous, gentlemanly, gracious, noble,
polite

gallivant v = **wander**, gad about, ramble,
roam, rove

gallop v **3, 4** = **run**, bolt, career, dash, hurry,
race, rush, speed, sprint

galore adv = **in abundance**, all over the

place, aplenty, everywhere, in great
quantity, in numbers, in profusion, to
spare

gamble v **1** = **bet**, game, have a flutter
(inf), play, punt, wager **2** = **risk**, chance,
hazard, speculate, stick one's neck out
(inf), take a chance ▷ n **3** = **risk**, chance,
leap in the dark, lottery, speculation,
uncertainty, venture **4** = **bet**, flutter (inf),
punt, wager

gambol v **1** = **frolic**, caper, cavort, frisk,
hop, jump, prance, skip ▷ n **2** = **frolic**,
caper, hop, jump, prance, skip

game¹ n **1** = **pastime**, amusement,
distraction, diversion, entertainment, lark,
recreation, sport **2** = **match**, competition,
contest, event, head-to-head,

g

n gambling. **gamekeeper** *n* person employed to breed game and prevent poaching. **gamer** *n* person who plays computer games. **gamesmanship** *n* art of winning by cunning practices without actually cheating.

game² ❶ *adj Brit, Aust & NZ* lame, crippled.

gammon *n* cured or smoked ham.

gamut ❶ *n* whole range or scale (of music, emotions, etc.).

gander *n* **1** male goose. **2** *informal* quick look.

gang ❶ *n* **1** (criminal) group. **2** organized group of workmen. **gangland** *n* criminal underworld. **gang up** *v* form an alliance (against).

gangling ❶ *adj* lanky and awkward.

gangplank *n* portable bridge for boarding or leaving a ship.

gangrene *n* decay of body tissue as a result of disease or injury. **gangrenous** *adj*.

gangster ❶ *n* member of a criminal gang.

gangway *n* **1** passage between rows of seats. **2** gangplank.

gannet *n* **1** large sea bird. **2** *slang* greedy person.

gantry *n, pl* **-tries** structure supporting something such as a crane or rocket.

gaol [**jayl**] *n* same as JAIL.

gap ❶ *n* **1** break or opening. **2** interruption or interval. **3** divergence or difference. **gappy** *adj*.

gape ❶ *v* **1** stare in wonder. **2** open the mouth wide. **3** be or become wide open. **gaping** *adj*.

garage *n* **1** building used to house cars. **2** place for the refuelling, sale, and repair of cars. ▷ *v* **3** put or keep a car in a garage.

garb *n* **1** clothes. ▷ *v* **2** clothe.

garbage ❶ *n* rubbish.

garden *n* **1** piece of land for growing flowers, fruit, or vegetables. ▷ *pl* **2** ornamental park. ▷ *v* **3** cultivate a garden. **gardener** *n* **gardening** *n* **garden centre** place selling plants and gardening equipment.

garfish *n* **1** freshwater fish with a long body and very long toothed jaws. **2** sea fish with similar characteristics.

gargantuan *adj* huge.

gargle *v* **1** wash the throat with (a liquid) by breathing out slowly through the liquid. ▷ *n* **2** liquid used for gargling.

gargoyle *n* waterspout carved in the form of a grotesque face, esp. on a church.

garish ❶ *adj* crudely bright or colourful.

garland ❶ *n* **1** wreath of flowers worn or hung as a decoration. ▷ *v* **2** decorate with garlands.

——————— THESAURUS —————

meeting, tournament **4** = **wild animals**, prey, quarry **6** = **scheme**, design, plan, plot, ploy, stratagem, tactic, trick ▷ *adj* **8** = **brave**, courageous, gallant, gritty, intrepid, persistent, plucky, spirited, feisty (*US & Canad*) **9** = **willing**, desirous, eager, interested, keen, prepared, ready

game² *adj* = **disabled**, bad, crippled, deformed, gammy (*Brit sl*), incapacitated, injured, lame, maimed

gamut *n* = **range**, area, catalogue, compass, field, scale, scope, series, sweep

gang *n* = **group**, band, clique, club, company, coterie, crowd, mob, pack, squad, team

gangling *adj* = **tall**, angular, awkward, lanky, rangy, rawboned, spindly

gangster *n* = **racketeer**, crook (*inf*), hood (*US sl*), hoodlum (*chiefly US*), mobster (*US sl*)

gap *n* **1** = **opening**, break, chink, cleft, crack, hole, space **2** = **interval**, breathing space, hiatus, interlude, intermission, interruption, lacuna, lull, pause, respite **3** = **difference**, disagreement, disparity, divergence, inconsistency

gape *v* **1** = **stare**, gawk, gawp (*Brit sl*), goggle, wonder **3** = **open**, crack, split, yawn

garbage *n* = **waste**, refuse, rubbish, trash (*chiefly US*)

garish *adj* = **gaudy**, brash, brassy, flashy, loud, showy, tacky (*inf*), tasteless, vulgar

garland *n* **1** = **wreath**, bays, chaplet, crown, festoon, honours, laurels

garlic n pungent bulb of a plant of the onion family, used in cooking.

garment n 1 article of clothing. ▷ pl 2 clothes.

garner ❶ v collect or store.

garnet n red semiprecious stone.

garnish ❶ v 1 decorate (food). ▷ n 2 decoration for food.

garret n attic in a house.

garrison ❶ n 1 troops stationed in a town or fort. 2 fortified place. ▷ v 3 station troops in.

garrotte, garotte n 1 Spanish method of execution by strangling. 2 cord or wire used for this. ▷ v 3 kill by this method.

garrulous ❶ adj talkative.

garter n band worn round the leg to hold up a sock or stocking.

gas n, pl **gases** or **gasses** 1 airlike substance that is not liquid or solid. 2 fossil fuel in the form of a gas, used for heating. 3 gaseous anaesthetic. 4 US & Canad petrol. ▷ v **gassing, gassed** 5 poison or render unconscious with gas. 6 informal talk idly or boastfully. **gassy** adj filled with gas. **gaseous** adj of or like gas. **gasbag** n informal person who talks too much. **gas chamber** airtight room which is filled with poison gas to kill people or animals.

gas mask mask with a chemical filter to protect the wearer against poison gas.

gash ❶ v 1 make a long deep cut in. ▷ n 2 long deep cut.

gasket n piece of rubber etc. placed between the faces of a metal joint to act as a seal.

gasp ❶ v 1 draw in breath sharply or with difficulty. 2 utter breathlessly. ▷ n 3 convulsive intake of breath.

gastric adj of the stomach. **gastritis** n inflammation of the stomach lining.

gastroenteritis n inflammation of the stomach and intestines.

gastronomy n art of good eating. **gastronomic** adj.

gate ❶ n 1 movable barrier, usu. hinged, in a wall or fence. 2 opening with a gate. 3 any entrance or way in. 4 (entrance money paid by) those attending a sporting event. **gate-crash** v enter (a party) uninvited. **gatehouse** n building at or above a gateway. **gateway** n 1 entrance with a gate. 2 means of access, e.g. Bombay, gateway to India.

gâteau [**gat**-toe] n, pl **-teaux** [-toes] rich elaborate cake.

gather ❶ v 1 assemble. 2 collect gradually. 3 increase gradually. 4 learn from

━━━━━━ THESAURUS ━━━━━━

▷ v 2 = **adorn**, crown, deck, festoon, wreathe

garner v = **collect**, accumulate, amass, gather, hoard, save, stockpile, store, stow away

garnish v 1 = **decorate**, adorn, embellish, enhance, ornament, set off, trim ▷ n 2 = **decoration**, adornment, embellishment, enhancement, ornamentation, trimming

garrison n 1 = **troops**, armed force, command, detachment, unit 2 = **fort**, base, camp, encampment, fortification, fortress, post, station, stronghold ▷ v 3 = **station**, assign, position, post, put on duty

garrulous adj = **talkative**, chatty, gossiping, loquacious, prattling, verbose, voluble

gash v 1 = **cut**, gouge, lacerate, slash, slit, split, tear, wound ▷ n 2 = **cut**, gouge, incision, laceration, slash, slit, split, tear, wound

gasp v 1 = **gulp**, blow, catch one's breath, choke, pant, puff ▷ n 3 = **gulp**, exclamation, pant, puff, sharp intake of breath

gate n 1-3 = **barrier**, door, entrance, exit, gateway, opening, passage, portal

gather v 1, 2 = **assemble**, accumulate, amass, collect, garner, mass, muster, stockpile 3 = **intensify**, deepen, expand, grow, heighten, increase, rise, swell, thicken 4 = **learn**, assume, conclude, deduce, hear, infer, surmise, understand

information given. **5** pick or harvest.
6 draw (material) into small tucks or folds.
gathering *n* assembly.
gaudy ⊕ *adj* **gaudier**, **gaudiest** vulgarly
bright or colourful.
gauge ⊕ [**gayj**] *v* **1** estimate or judge.
2 measure the amount or condition of.
▷ *n* **3** measuring instrument. **4** scale or
standard of measurement. **5** distance
between the rails of a railway track.

● **SPELLING TIP**
● The vowels in **gauge** are often confused
● so that the misspelling *guage* is common
● in the Bank of English.

gaunt ⊕ *adj* lean and haggard.
gauntlet *n* **1** heavy glove with a long cuff.
2 medieval armoured glove. **throw down
the gauntlet** offer a challenge.
gauze *n* transparent loosely-woven fabric,
often used for surgical dressings. **gauzy**
adj.
gavel [**gav**-el] *n* small hammer banged on
a table by a judge, auctioneer, or chairman
to call for attention.
gay ⊕ *adj* **1** homosexual. **2** carefree and
merry. **3** colourful. ▷ *n* **4** homosexual.
gaze ⊕ *v* **1** look fixedly. ▷ *n* **2** fixed look.
gazebo [gaz-**zee**-boh] *n, pl* **-bos**, **-boes**
summerhouse with a good view.

gazelle *n* small graceful antelope.
gazette ⊕ *n* official publication containing
announcements. **gazetteer** *n* (part of) a
book that lists and describes places.
GB Great Britain.
GBH grievous bodily harm.
GCE General Certificate of Education.
GCSE General Certificate of Secondary
Education.
gear ⊕ *n* **1** set of toothed wheels
connecting with another or with a rack
to change the direction or speed of
transmitted motion. **2** mechanism for
transmitting motion by gears. **3** setting of
a gear to suit engine speed, e.g. *first gear.*
4 clothing or belongings. **5** equipment.
▷ *v* **6** prepare or organize for something.
in, **out of gear** with the gear mechanism
engaged *or* disengaged. **gearbox** *n* case
enclosing a set of gears in a motor vehicle.
gear up *v* prepare for an activity.
geebung [**gee**-bung] *n* **1** Australian tree
or shrub with an edible but tasteless fruit.
2 fruit of this tree.
geese *n* plural of GOOSE.
geezer *n informal* man.
geisha [**gay**-sha] *n, pl* **-sha**, **-shas** (in
Japan) professional female companion
for men.

——————————————————— THESAURUS ———————

5 = **pick**, cull, garner, glean, harvest, pluck,
reap, select **6** = **fold**, pleat, tuck
gaudy *adj* = **garish**, bright, flashy, loud,
showy, tacky (*inf*), tasteless, vulgar
gauge *v* **1** = **judge**, adjudge, appraise,
assess, estimate, evaluate, guess, rate,
reckon, value **2** = **measure**, ascertain,
calculate, check, compute, count,
determine, weigh ▷ *n* **3, 4** = **indicator**,
criterion, guide, guideline, measure,
meter, standard, test, touchstone,
yardstick
gaunt *adj* = **thin**, angular, bony,
haggard, lean, pinched, scrawny, skinny,
spare
gay *adj* **1** = **homosexual**, lesbian, queer
(*inf, derog*) **2** = **cheerful**, blithe, carefree,

jovial, light-hearted, lively, merry,
sparkling **3** = **colourful**, bright, brilliant,
flamboyant, flashy, rich, showy, vivid ▷ *n*
4 = **homosexual**, lesbian
gaze *v* **1** = **stare**, gape, look, regard, view,
watch, wonder ▷ *n* **2** = **stare**, fixed look,
look
gazette *n* = **newspaper**, journal, news-
sheet, paper, periodical
gear *n* **1** = **cog**, cogwheel, gearwheel
2 = **mechanism**, cogs, machinery,
works **4** = **clothing**, clothes, costume,
dress, garments, outfit, togs, wear
5 = **equipment**, accoutrements,
apparatus, instruments, paraphernalia,
supplies, tackle, tools ▷ *v* **6** = **equip**,
adapt, adjust, fit

gel [**jell**] *n* **1** jelly-like substance, esp. one
used to secure a hairstyle. ▷ *v* **gelling**,
gelled 2 form a gel. **3** *informal* take on a
definite form.

gelatine [**jel**-at-teen], **gelatin** *n*
1 substance made by boiling animal bones.
2 edible jelly made of this. **gelatinous**
[jel-**at**-in-uss] *adj* of or like jelly.

geld *v* castrate. **gelding** *n* castrated horse.

gelignite *n* type of dynamite used for
blasting.

gem ❶ *n* **1** precious stone or jewel. **2** highly
valued person or thing. **gemfish** *n*
Australian food fish with a delicate
flavour.

gen *n informal* information. **gen up on**
v **genning**, **genned** *informal* make or
become fully informed about.

gender *n* **1** state of being male or female.
2 *Grammar* classification of nouns in
certain languages as masculine, feminine,
or neuter.

gene [**jean**] *n* part of a cell which
determines inherited characteristics.

genealogy [jean-ee-**al**-a-gee] *n*, *pl* -**gies**
(study of) the history and descent of a
family or families.

general ❶ *adj* **1** common or widespread.
2 of or affecting all or most. **3** not specific.
4 including or dealing with various
or miscellaneous items. **5** highest in
authority or rank, e.g. *general manager*.
▷ *n* **6** very senior army officer. **in
general** mostly or usually. **generally** *adv*
generality *n*, *pl* **-ties 1** general principle.
2 state of being general. **generalize** *v*
1 draw general conclusions. **2** speak in
generalities. **3** make widely known or
used. **generalization** *n* **general election**
election in which representatives are
chosen for every constituency. **general
practitioner** nonspecialist doctor serving
a local area.

generate ❶ *v* produce or bring into being.
generation *n* all the people born about
the same time. **generative** *adj* capable
of producing. **generator** *n* machine
for converting mechanical energy into
electrical energy.

generous ❶ *adj* **1** free in giving. **2** free
from pettiness. **3** plentiful. **generosity** *n*.

genesis ❶ [**jen**-iss-iss] *n*, *pl* -**eses** [-iss-eez]
beginning or origin.

genial ❶ [**jean**-ee-al] *adj* cheerful and
friendly. **genially** *adv* **geniality** *n*.

genie [**jean**-ee] *n* (in fairy tales) servant
who appears by magic and grants wishes.

genital *adj* of the sexual organs or
reproduction. **genitals**, **genitalia**[jen-it-
ail-ya] *pl n* external sexual organs.

genius ❶ [**jean**-yuss] *n* (person with)
exceptional ability in a particular field.

THESAURUS

---

gem *n* **1** = **precious stone**, jewel, stone
2 = **prize**, jewel, masterpiece, pearl,
treasure

general *adj* **1** = **common**, accepted, broad,
extensive, popular, prevalent, public,
universal, widespread **2, 4** = **universal**,
across-the-board, blanket, collective,
comprehensive, indiscriminate,
miscellaneous, overall, overarching,
sweeping, total **3** = **imprecise**,
approximate, ill-defined, indefinite,
inexact, loose, unspecific, vague

generate *v* = **produce**, breed, cause,
create, engender, give rise to, make,
propagate

generous *adj* **1** = **liberal**, beneficent,
bountiful, charitable, hospitable,
kind, lavish, open-handed, unstinting
2 = **unselfish**, big-hearted, good, high-
minded, lofty, magnanimous, noble
3 = **plentiful**, abundant, ample, copious,
full, lavish, liberal, rich, unstinting

genesis *n* = **beginning**, birth, creation,
formation, inception, origin, start

genial *adj* = **cheerful**, affable, agreeable,
amiable, congenial, friendly, good-
natured, jovial, pleasant, warm

genius *n* = **master**, brainbox, expert,
fundi (*S Afr*), hotshot (*inf*), maestro,
mastermind, virtuoso, whiz (*inf*)

genocide [**jen**-no-side] n murder of a race of people.

genre ❶ [**zhohn**-ra] n style of literary, musical, or artistic work.

gent n informal gentleman. **gents** n men's public toilet.

genteel ❶ adj affectedly proper and polite. **genteelly** adv.

gentile adj, n non-Jewish (person).

gentle ❶ adj 1 mild or kindly. 2 not rough or severe. 3 gradual. 4 easily controlled, tame. **gentleness** n **gently** adv **gentleman** n 1 polite well-bred man. 2 man of high social position. 3 polite name for a man. **gentlemanly** adj **gentlewoman** n fem.

gentry ❶ n people just below the nobility in social rank. **gentrification** n taking-over of a traditionally working-class area by middle-class incomers. **gentrify** v.

genuine ❶ adj 1 not fake, authentic. 2 sincere. **genuinely** adv **genuineness** n.

genus [**jean**-uss] n, pl **genera** 1 group into which a family of animals or plants is divided. 2 kind, type.

geography n study of the earth's physical features, climate, population, etc. **geographer** n **geographical**, **geographic** adj.

geology n study of the earth's origin, structure, and composition. **geological** adj **geologist** n.

geometry n branch of mathematics dealing with points, lines, curves, and surfaces. **geometric**, **geometrical** adj.

geranium n cultivated plant with red, pink, or white flowers.

gerbil [**jer**-bill] n burrowing desert rodent of Asia and Africa.

geriatrics n branch of medicine dealing with old age and its diseases. **geriatric** adj, n old (person).

germ ❶ n 1 microbe, esp. one causing disease. 2 beginning from which something may develop. 3 simple structure that can develop into a complete organism. **germicide** n substance that kills germs.

germinate ❶ v (cause to) sprout or begin to grow. **germination** n **germinal** adj of or in the earliest stage of development.

gestation n 1 (period of) carrying of young in the womb between conception and birth. 2 developing of a plan or idea in the mind.

gesticulate ❶ v make expressive movements with the hands and arms. **gesticulation** n.

gesture ❶ n 1 movement to convey meaning. 2 thing said or done to show one's feelings. ▷ v 3 gesticulate.

——————— THESAURUS ———————

genre n = **type**, category, class, group, kind, sort, species, style

genteel adj = **refined**, courteous, cultured, elegant, gentlemanly, ladylike, polite, respectable, urbane, well-mannered

gentle adj 1 = **mild**, compassionate, humane, kindly, meek, placid, sweet-tempered, tender 2 = **moderate**, light, mild, muted, slight, soft, soothing 3 = **gradual**, easy, imperceptible, light, mild, moderate, slight, slow 4 = **tame**, biddable, broken, docile, manageable, placid, tractable

gentry n = **upper class**, aristocracy, elitey, upper crust (inf)

genuine adj 1 = **authentic**, actual, bona fide, legitimate, real, the real McCoy, true, veritable 2 = **sincere**, candid, earnest, frank, heartfelt, honest, unaffected, unfeigned

germ n 1 = **microbe**, bacterium, bug (inf), microorganism, virus 2 = **beginning**, embryo, origin, root, rudiment, seed, source, spark 3 = **embryo**, seed

germinate v = **sprout**, bud, develop, generate, grow, originate, shoot, swell, vegetate

gesticulate v = **signal**, gesture, indicate, make a sign, motion, sign, wave

gesture n 1 = **signal**, action, gesticulation, indication, motion, sign 2 = **signal**, indication, sign ▷ v 3 = **signal**, gesticulate, indicate, motion, sign, wave

get ❶ v **getting**, **got 1** obtain or receive. **2** bring or fetch. **3** contract (an illness). **4** capture or seize. **5** (cause to) become as specified, e.g. *get wet*. **6** understand. **7** (often foll. by *to*) come (to) or arrive (at). **8** go on board (a plane, bus, etc.). **9** persuade. **10** receive a broadcast signal. **11** *informal* annoy. **12** *informal* have the better of. **13** be revenged on. **get across** v (cause to) be understood. **get at** v **1** gain access to. **2** imply or mean. **3** criticize. **getaway** adj, n (used in) escape. **get by** v manage in spite of difficulties. **get off** v (cause to) avoid the consequences of, or punishment for, an action. **get off with** v *informal* start a romantic or sexual relationship with. **get over** v recover from. **get through** v **1** (cause to) succeed. **2** use up (money or supplies). **get through to** v **1** make (a person) understand. **2** contact by telephone. **get-up** n *informal* costume. **get up to** v be involved in.

geyser [**geez**-er] n **1** spring that discharges steam and hot water. **2** domestic gas water heater.

ghastly ❶ adj **-lier**, **-liest 1** *informal* unpleasant. **2** deathly pale. **3** *informal* unwell. **4** *informal* horrible. **ghastliness** n.

gherkin n small pickled cucumber.

ghetto n, pl **-tos**, **-toes** slum area inhabited by a deprived minority. **ghetto-blaster** n

informal large portable cassette recorder or CD player.

ghost ❶ n **1** disembodied spirit of a dead person. **2** faint trace. ▷ v **3** ghostwrite. **ghost gum** *Aust* eucalyptus with white trunk and branches. **ghostly** adj **ghost town** deserted town. **ghostwrite** v write (a book or article) on behalf of another person who is credited as the author. **ghostwriter** n.

ghoul [**gool**] n **1** person with morbid interests. **2** demon that eats corpses. **ghoulish** adj.

giant ❶ n **1** mythical being of superhuman size. **2** very large person or thing. ▷ adj **3** huge.

gibber [**jib**-ber] v speak or utter rapidly and unintelligibly. **gibberish** n rapid unintelligible talk.

gibbon [**gib**-bon] n agile tree-dwelling ape of S Asia.

gibe ❶ [**jibe**] v, n same as JIBE¹.

giblets [**jib**-lets] pl n gizzard, liver, heart, and neck of a fowl.

gidday, g'day interj *Aust & NZ* expression of greeting.

giddy ❶ adj **-dier**, **-diest** having or causing a feeling of dizziness. **giddily** adv **giddiness** n.

gift ❶ n **1** present. **2** natural talent. ▷ v **3** make a present of. **gifted** adj talented.

---

get v **1** = **obtain**, acquire, attain, gain, land, net, pick up, procure, receive, secure, win **2** = **bring**, fetch **3** = **contract**, catch, come down with, fall victim to, take **4** = **capture**, grab, lay hold of, nab (*inf*), seize, take **5** = **become**, come to be, grow, turn **6** = **understand**, catch, comprehend, fathom, follow, perceive, see, take in, work out **9** = **persuade**, convince, induce, influence, prevail upon **11** *Inf* = **annoy**, bug (*inf*), gall, irritate, upset, vex

ghastly adj **1, 4** *Inf* = **horrible**, dreadful, frightful, gruesome, hideous, horrendous, loathsome, shocking, terrible, terrifying

ghost n **1** = **spirit**, apparition, phantom,

soul, spectre, spook (*inf*), wraith **2** = **trace**, glimmer, hint, possibility, semblance, shadow, suggestion

giant n **1, 2** = **ogre**, colossus, monster, titan ▷ adj **3** = **huge**, colossal, enormous, gargantuan, gigantic, immense, mammoth, titanic, vast

gibe v, n see JIBE¹

giddy adj = **dizzy**, dizzying, faint, light-headed, reeling, unsteady, vertiginous

gift n **1** = **donation**, bequest, bonus, contribution, grant, hand-out, legacy, offering, present **2** = **talent**, ability, capability, capacity, flair, genius, knack, power

gig¹ n **1** single performance by pop or jazz musicians. ▷ v **gigging**, **gigged 2** play a gig or gigs.

gig² n informal short for GIGABYTE.

gigabyte n Computers 1024 megabytes.

gigantic ⊙ adj enormous.

giggle ⊙ v **1** laugh nervously or foolishly. ▷ n **2** such a laugh. **giggly** adj.

gild ⊙ v **gilding**, **gilded** or **gilt 1** put a thin layer of gold on. **2** make falsely attractive.

gill [**jill**] n liquid measure of quarter of a pint, equal to 0.142 litres.

gimmick ⊙ n something designed to attract attention or publicity. **gimmickry** n **gimmicky** adj.

gin n alcoholic drink flavoured with juniper berries.

ginger n **1** root of a tropical plant, used as a spice. **2** light orange-brown colour. **gingery** adj **ginger ale**, **beer** fizzy ginger-flavoured soft drink. **gingerbread** n moist cake flavoured with ginger. **ginger group** group within a larger group that agitates for a more active policy.

gingerly ⊙ adv cautiously.

gingham n cotton cloth, usu. checked or striped.

gingivitis [jin-jiv-**vite**-iss] n inflammation of the gums.

ginseng [**jin**-seng] n (root of) a plant believed to have tonic and energy-giving properties.

Gipsy n, pl **-sies** same as GYPSY.

giraffe n African ruminant mammal with a spotted yellow skin and long neck and legs.

gird ⊙ v **girding**, **girded** or **girt 1** put a belt round. **2** secure with or as if with a belt. **3** surround. **gird (up) one's loins** prepare for action.

girdle ⊙ n **1** woman's elastic corset. **2** belt. **3** Anat encircling structure or part. ▷ v **4** surround or encircle.

girl ⊙ n **1** female child. **2** young woman. **3** girlfriend. **4** informal any woman. **girlhood** n **girlish** adj **girlie** adj informal featuring photographs of naked or scantily clad women. **girlfriend** n **1** girl or woman with whom a person is romantically or sexually involved. **2** female friend.

giro [**jire**-oh] n, pl **-ros 1** system of transferring money within a post office or bank directly from one account to another. **2** informal social security payment by giro cheque.

girth ⊙ n **1** measurement round something. **2** band round a horse to hold the saddle in position.

gist ⊙ [**jist**] n substance or main point of a matter.

give ⊙ v **giving**, **gave**, **given 1** present (something) to another person. **2** transfer

─────────── THESAURUS ───────────

gigantic adj = **enormous**, colossal, giant, huge, immense, mammoth, stupendous, titanic, tremendous

giggle v, n = **laugh**, cackle, chortle, chuckle, snigger, titter, twitter

gild v **2** = **embellish**, adorn, beautify, brighten, coat, dress up, embroider, enhance, ornament

gimmick n = **stunt**, contrivance, device, dodge, ploy, scheme

gingerly adv = **cautiously**, carefully, charily, circumspectly, hesitantly, reluctantly, suspiciously, timidly, warily

gird v **3** = **surround**, encircle, enclose, encompass, enfold, hem in, ring

girdle n **2** = **belt**, band, cummerbund, sash, waistband ▷ v **4** = **surround**, bound, encircle, enclose, encompass, gird, ring

girl n **1, 2** = **female child**, damsel (arch), daughter, lass, lassie (inf), maid (arch), maiden (arch), miss

girth n **1** = **circumference**, bulk, measure, size

gist n = **point**, core, essence, force, idea, meaning, sense, significance, substance

give v **1** = **present**, award, contribute, deliver, donate, grant, hand over or out, provide, supply **3, 7** = **announce**, communicate, issue, notify, pronounce,

in exchange or payment. **3** impart.
4 attribute. **5** administer. **6** be a source
of. **7** utter or emit. **8** sacrifice or devote.
9 organize or host. **10** concede. **11** yield or
break under pressure. ▷ *n* **12** resilience or
elasticity. **give away** *v* **1** donate as a gift.
2 reveal. **giveaway** *n* **1** something that
reveals hidden feelings or intentions. ▷ *adj*
2 very cheap or free. **give in** *v* admit defeat.
give off *v* emit. **give out** *v* **1** distribute.
2 emit. **3** come to an end or fail. **give
over** *v* **1** set aside for a specific purpose.
2 *informal* cease. **give up** *v* **1** abandon.
2 acknowledge defeat.

glacé [**glass**-say] *adj* preserved in a thick
sugary syrup.

glacier *n* slow-moving mass of ice formed
by accumulated snow. **glacial** *adj* **1** of
ice or glaciers. **2** very cold. **3** unfriendly.
glaciation *n*.

glad ❶ *adj* **gladder**, **gladdest** **1** pleased
and happy. **2** causing happiness. **glad to**
very willing to (do something). **gladly** *adv*
gladden *v* make glad. **glad rags** *informal*
best clothes.

glade *n* open space in a forest.

gladiator *n* (in ancient Rome) man
trained to fight in arenas to provide
entertainment.

gladiolus *n*, *pl* **-lus**, **-li**, **-luses** garden plant
with sword-shaped leaves.

glamour ❶ *n* alluring charm or
fascination. **glamorous** *adj* alluring,
attractive, etc. **glamorize** *v*.

- ● **SPELLING TIP**
- ● People often forget to drop the *u* in
- ● **glamour** when they add *ous*. That's why
- ● there are 124 occurrences of *glamourous*
- ● in the Bank of English. But the correct
- ● spelling is **glamorous**.

glance ❶ *v* **1** look rapidly or briefly. **2** glint
or gleam. ▷ *n* **3** brief look. **glancing** *adj*
hitting at an oblique angle. **glance off** *v*
strike and be deflected off (an object) at an
oblique angle.

gland *n* organ that produces and
secretes substances in the body.
glandular *adj*.

glare ❶ *v* **1** stare angrily. **2** be unpleasantly
bright. ▷ *n* **3** angry stare. **4** unpleasant
brightness. **glaring** *adj* **1** conspicuous.
2 unpleasantly bright. **glaringly** *adv*.

glass *n* **1** hard brittle, usu. transparent
substance consisting of metal silicates
or similar compounds. **2** tumbler. **3** its
contents. **4** objects made of glass.
5 mirror. **6** barometer. ▷ *pl* **7** spectacles.
glassy *adj* **1** like glass. **2** expressionless.
glassiness *n* **glasshouse** *n* **1** greenhouse.
2 *informal* army prison.

glaucoma *n* eye disease.

glaze ❶ *v* **1** fit or cover with glass. **2** cover
with a protective shiny coating. ▷ *n*
3 transparent coating. **4** substance used
for this. **glazier** *n* person who fits windows
with glass.

transmit, utter **6** = **produce**, cause,
engender, make, occasion **8** = **devote**,
hand over, relinquish **10** = **concede**, allow,
grant **11** = **surrender**, yield
glad *adj* **1** = **happy**, contented, delighted,
gratified, joyful, overjoyed, pleased
2 = **pleasing**, cheerful, cheering,
gratifying, pleasant
glamour *n* = **charm**, allure, appeal,
attraction, beauty, enchantment,
fascination, prestige
glance *v* **1** = **peek**, glimpse, look, peep,
scan, view **2** = **gleam**, flash, glimmer,

glint, glisten, glitter, reflect, shimmer,
shine, twinkle ▷ *n* **3** = **peek**, dekko (*sl*),
glimpse, look, peep, view
glare *v* **1** = **scowl**, frown, glower,
look daggers, lour *or* lower **2** = **dazzle**,
blaze, flame, flare ▷ *n* **3** = **scowl**, black
look, dirty look, frown, glower, lour *or*
lower **4** = **dazzle**, blaze, brilliance,
flame, glow
glaze *v* **2** = **coat**, enamel, gloss, lacquer,
polish, varnish ▷ *n* **3, 4** = **coat**, enamel,
finish, gloss, lacquer, lustre, patina, polish,
shine, varnish

gleam ❶ *n* **1** small beam or glow of light. **2** brief or faint indication. ▷ *v* **3** emit a gleam. **gleaming** *adj*.

glean *v* **1** gather (facts etc.) bit by bit. **2** gather (the useful remnants of a crop) after harvesting.

glee ❶ *n* triumph and delight. **gleeful** *adj*.

glen *n* deep narrow valley.

glib ❶ *adj* **glibber**, **glibbest** fluent but insincere or superficial.

glide ❶ *v* **1** move easily and smoothly. **2** (of an aircraft) move without the use of engines. ▷ *n* **3** smooth easy movement. **glider** *n* **1** aircraft without an engine which floats on air currents. **2** flying phalanger. **gliding** *n* sport of flying gliders.

glimmer ❶ *v* **1** shine faintly, flicker. ▷ *n* **2** faint gleam. **3** faint indication.

glimpse ❶ *n* **1** brief or incomplete view. ▷ *v* **2** catch a glimpse of.

glint ❶ *v* **1** gleam brightly. ▷ *n* **2** bright gleam.

glisten ❶ *v* gleam by reflecting light.

glitter ❶ *v* **1** shine with bright flashes. **2** be showy. ▷ *n* **3** sparkle or brilliance. **4** tiny pieces of shiny decorative material.

gloat ❶ *v* (often foll. by *over*) regard one's own good fortune or the misfortune of others with smug or malicious pleasure.

globe ❶ *n* **1** sphere with a map of the earth on it. **2** spherical object. **3** *S Afr* light bulb. **the globe** the earth. **global** *adj* **1** worldwide. **2** total or comprehensive. **globalization** *n* process by which a company, etc., expands to operate internationally. **globally** *adv* **globetrotter** *n* habitual worldwide traveller. **globetrotting** *n, adj*.

globule ❶ *n* small round drop. **globular** *adj*.

glockenspiel *n* percussion instrument consisting of small metal bars played with hammers.

gloom ❶ *n* **1** melancholy or depression. **2** darkness. **gloomy** *adj* **gloomier**, **gloomiest**. **gloomily** *adv*.

———————————————— THESAURUS ————————

gleam *n* **1** = **glow**, beam, flash, glimmer, ray, sparkle **2** = **trace**, flicker, glimmer, hint, inkling, suggestion ▷ *v* **3** = **shine**, flash, glimmer, glint, glisten, glitter, glow, shimmer, sparkle

glee *n* = **delight**, elation, exhilaration, exuberance, exultation, joy, merriment, triumph

glib *adj* = **smooth**, easy, fluent, insincere, plausible, quick, ready, slick, suave, voluble

glide *v* **1** = **slide**, coast, drift, float, flow, roll, run, sail, skate, slip

glimmer *v* **1** = **flicker**, blink, gleam, glisten, glitter, glow, shimmer, shine, sparkle, twinkle ▷ *n* **2** = **gleam**, blink, flicker, glow, ray, shimmer, sparkle, twinkle **3** = **trace**, flicker, gleam, hint, inkling, suggestion

glimpse *n* **1** = **look**, glance, peek, peep, sight, sighting ▷ *v* **2** = **catch sight of**, espy, sight, spot, spy, view

glint *v* **1** = **gleam**, flash, glimmer, glitter,

shine, sparkle, twinkle ▷ *n* **2** = **gleam**, flash, glimmer, glitter, shine, sparkle, twinkle, twinkling

glisten *v* = **gleam**, flash, glance, glare, glimmer, glint, glitter, shimmer, shine, sparkle, twinkle

glitter *v* **1** = **shine**, flash, glare, gleam, glimmer, glint, glisten, shimmer, sparkle, twinkle ▷ *n* **3** = **shine**, brightness, flash, glare, gleam, radiance, sheen, shimmer, sparkle

gloat *v* (often foll. by *over*) = **relish**, crow, drool, exult, glory, revel in, rub it in (*inf*), triumph

globe *n* **2** = **sphere**, ball, orb **the globe** = **earth**, planet, world

globule *n* = **droplet**, bead, bubble, drop, particle, pearl, pellet

gloom *n* **1** = **depression**, dejection, despondency, low spirits, melancholy, sorrow, unhappiness, woe **2** = **darkness**, blackness, dark, dusk, murk, obscurity, shade, shadow, twilight

glory ❶ n, pl **-ries** 1 praise or honour.
2 splendour. 3 praiseworthy thing. ▷ v **-rying, -ried** 4 (foll. by in) triumph or exalt.
glorify v 1 make (something) seem more worthy than it is. 2 praise. **glorification** n **glorious** adj 1 brilliantly beautiful.
2 delightful. 3 full of or conferring glory.
gloriously adv **glory hole** informal untidy cupboard or storeroom.

gloss¹ ❶ n 1 surface shine or lustre. 2 paint or cosmetic giving a shiny finish. **glossy** adj **-sier, -siest** 1 smooth and shiny. 2 (of a magazine) printed on shiny paper. **glossily** adv **glossiness** n **gloss over** (try to) cover up or pass over (a fault or error).

gloss² ❷ n 1 explanatory comment added to the text of a book. ▷ v 2 add glosses to.

glove n covering for the hand with individual sheaths for each finger and the thumb. **gloved** adj covered by a glove or gloves. **glove compartment** small storage area in the dashboard of a car.

glow ❶ v 1 emit light and heat without flames. 2 shine. 3 have a feeling of wellbeing or satisfaction. 4 (of a colour) look warm. 5 be hot. ▷ n 6 glowing light.
7 warmth of colour. 8 feeling of wellbeing.

glow-worm n insect giving out a green light.

glower ❶ [rhymes with **power**] v, n scowl.

glucose n kind of sugar found in fruit.

glue ❶ n 1 natural or synthetic sticky substance used as an adhesive. ▷ v **gluing** or **glueing, glued** 2 fasten with glue. 3 (foll. by to) pay full attention to, e.g. her eyes were glued to the TV. **gluey** adj **glue-sniffing** n inhaling of glue fumes for intoxicating or hallucinatory effects.

glum ❶ adj **glummer, glummest** sullen or gloomy.

glut ❶ n 1 excessive supply. ▷ v **glutting, glutted** 2 oversupply.

glutton ❶ n 1 greedy person. 2 person with a great capacity for something. **gluttonous** adj **gluttony** n.

glycerine, glycerin n colourless sweet liquid used widely in chemistry and industry.

GMT Greenwich Mean Time.

gnarled ❶ adj rough, twisted, and knobbly.

gnash v grind (the teeth) together in anger or pain.

gnat n small biting two-winged fly.

gnaw ❶ v **gnawing, gnawed, gnawed** or

──────── THESAURUS ────────

glory n 1 = **honour**, dignity, distinction, eminence, fame, praise, prestige, renown 2 = **splendour**, grandeur, greatness, magnificence, majesty, nobility, pageantry, pomp ▷ v 4 (foll. by in) = **triumph**, exalt, pride oneself, relish, revel, take delight

gloss¹ n 1 = **shine**, brightness, gleam, lustre, patina, polish, sheen, veneer

gloss² n 1 = **comment**, annotation, commentary, elucidation, explanation, footnote, interpretation, note, translation ▷ v 2 = **interpret**, annotate, comment, elucidate, explain, translate

glow v 1 = **smoulder**, burn 2 = **shine**, brighten, burn, gleam, glimmer, redden ▷ n 6 = **light**, burning, gleam, glimmer, luminosity, phosphorescence 7 = **radiance**, brightness, brilliance,

effulgence, splendour, vividness

glower v = **scowl**, frown, give a dirty look, glare, look daggers, lour or lower ▷ n = **scowl**, black look, dirty look, frown, glare, lour or lower

glue n 1 = **adhesive**, cement, gum, paste

glum adj = **gloomy**, crestfallen, dejected, doleful, low, morose, pessimistic, sullen

glut n 1 = **surfeit**, excess, oversupply, plethora, saturation, superfluity, surplus ▷ v 2 = **saturate**, choke, clog, deluge, flood, inundate, overload, oversupply

glutton n 1 = **gourmand**, gannet (sl), pig (inf)

gnarled adj = **twisted**, contorted, knotted, knotty, rough, rugged, weather-beaten, wrinkled

gnaw v 1 = **bite**, chew, munch, nibble

gnawn 1 bite or chew steadily. **2** (foll. by *at*) cause constant distress (to).

gnome *n* imaginary creature like a little old man.

gnu [**noo**] *n* oxlike S African antelope.

go ● *v* **going, went, gone 1** move to or from a place. **2** be in regular attendance at. **3** depart. **4** function. **5** be, do, or become as specified. **6** contribute to a result, e.g. *it just goes to show.* **7** be allotted to a specific purpose or recipient. **8** be sold. **9** blend or harmonize. **10** fail or break down. **11** elapse. **12** be got rid of. **13** attend. **14** reach or exceed certain limits, e.g. *she's gone too far this time.* **15** be acceptable. ▷ *n* **16** attempt. **17** verbal attack. **18** turn. **19** *informal* energy or vigour. **make a go of** be successful at. **go back on** *v* break (a promise etc.). **go-between** *n* intermediary. **go for** *v* **1** *informal* choose. **2** attack. **3** apply to equally. **go-getter** *n* energetically ambitious person. **go off** *v* **1** explode. **2** ring or sound. **3** *informal* become stale or rotten. **4** *informal* stop liking. **go out** *v* **1** go to entertainments or social functions. **2** be romantically involved (with). **3** be extinguished. **go over** *v* examine or check. **go-slow** *n* deliberate slowing of work-rate as an industrial protest. **go through** *v* **1** suffer or undergo. **2** examine or search.

goad ● *v* **1** provoke (someone) to take some kind of action, usu. in anger.

▷ *n* **2** spur or provocation. **3** spiked stick for driving cattle.

goal ● *n* **1** *Sport* posts through which the ball or puck has to be propelled to score. **2** score made in this way. **3** aim or purpose. **goalie** *n informal* goalkeeper. **goalkeeper** *n* player whose task is to stop shots entering the goal. **goalpost** *n* one of the two posts supporting the crossbar of a goal. **move the goalposts** change the aims of an activity to ensure the desired result.

goat *n* sure-footed ruminant animal with horns. **get someone's goat** *slang* annoy someone. **goatee** *n* pointed tuftlike beard.

gobble[1] ● *v* eat hastily and greedily.

gobble[2] *n* **1** rapid gurgling cry of the male turkey. ▷ *v* **2** make this noise.

gobbledegook, gobbledygook ● *n* unintelligible (official) language or jargon.

goblet *n* drinking cup without handles.

goblin *n* (in folklore) small malevolent creature.

god *n* **1** spirit or being worshipped as having supernatural power. **2** object of worship, idol. **3** (**G-**) (in monotheistic religions) the Supreme Being, creator and ruler of the universe. **the gods** top balcony in a theatre. **goddess** *n fem* **godlike** *adj* **godly** *adj* devout or pious. **godliness** *n* **god-fearing** *adj* pious and devout. **godforsaken** *adj* desolate or dismal. **godsend** *n* something unexpected but welcome.

─────────────────────── THESAURUS ───────────────

go *v* **1** = **move**, advance, journey, make for, pass, proceed, set off, travel **3** = **leave**, depart, make tracks, move out, slope off, withdraw **4** = **function**, move, operate, perform, run, work **6** = **contribute**, lead to, serve, tend, work towards **9** = **harmonize**, agree, blend, chime, complement, correspond, fit, match, suit **11** = **elapse**, expire, flow, lapse, pass, slip away ▷ *n* **16, 18** = **attempt**, bid, crack (*inf*), effort, shot (*inf*), try, turn **19** *Inf* = **energy**, drive, force, life, spirit, verve, vigour, vitality, vivacity

goad *v* **1** = **provoke**, drive, egg on, exhort, incite, prod, prompt, spur ▷ *n* **2** = **provocation**, impetus, incentive, incitement, irritation, spur, stimulus, urge

goal *n* **3** = **aim**, ambition, end, intention, object, objective, purpose, target

gobble[1] *v* = **devour**, bolt, cram, gorge, gulp, guzzle, stuff, swallow, wolf

gobbledegook, gobbledygook *n* = **nonsense**, babble, cant, gabble, gibberish, hocus-pocus, jargon, mumbo jumbo, twaddle

gogga n S Afr informal any small insect.

goggle v 1 (of the eyes) bulge. 2 stare. **goggles** pl n protective spectacles.

go-kart n small low-powered racing car.

gold n 1 yellow precious metal. 2 coins or articles made of this. 3 colour of gold. ▷ adj 4 made of gold. 5 gold-coloured. **gold-digger** n 1 informal woman who uses her sexual attractions to get money from a man. **goldfinch** n kind of finch, the male of which has yellow-and-black wings. **goldfish** n orange fish kept in ponds or aquariums. **gold leaf** thin gold sheet used for gilding. **gold medal** given to the winner of a competition or race.

golf n 1 outdoor game in which a ball is struck with clubs into a series of holes. ▷ v 2 play golf. **golfer** n.

gondola n 1 long narrow boat used in Venice. 2 suspended cabin of a cable car, airship, etc. **gondolier** n person who propels a gondola.

gong n 1 rimmed metal disc that produces a note when struck. 2 slang medal.

good ❶ adj **better**, **best** 1 giving pleasure. 2 morally excellent. 3 beneficial. 4 kindly. 5 talented. 6 well-behaved. 7 valid. 8 reliable. 9 financially sound. 10 complete or full. ▷ n 11 benefit. 12 positive moral qualities. ▷ pl 13 merchandise. 14 property. **as good as** virtually. **for good** permanently. **goodness** n **goodly** adj considerable. **goody** n 1 informal hero in a book or film. 2 enjoyable thing. **goody-goody** adj, n smugly virtuous (person). **good-for-nothing** adj, n irresponsible or worthless (person). **Good Samaritan** person who helps another in distress. **goodwill** n 1 kindly feeling. 2 value of a business in reputation etc. over and above its tangible assets.

goodbye ❶ interj, n expression used on parting.

gooey adj **gooier**, **gooiest** informal sticky and soft.

goose n, pl **geese** 1 web-footed bird like a large duck. 2 female of this bird. **goose flesh**, **pimples** bumpy condition of the skin and bristling of the hair due to cold or fright. **goose step** march step in which the leg is raised rigidly.

gooseberry n 1 edible yellowy-green berry. 2 informal unwanted third person accompanying a couple.

gore¹ ❶ n blood from a wound.

gore² ❶ v pierce with horns.

g

—————————————————— THESAURUS ——————————————————

good adj 1 = **excellent**, acceptable, admirable, fine, first-class, first-rate, great, pleasing, satisfactory, splendid, superior 2 = **honourable**, admirable, ethical, honest, moral, praiseworthy, righteous, trustworthy, upright, virtuous, worthy 3 = **favourable**, advantageous, beneficial, convenient, fitting, helpful, profitable, suitable, useful, wholesome 4 = **kind**, altruistic, benevolent, charitable, friendly, humane, kind-hearted, kindly, merciful, obliging 5 = **expert**, able, accomplished, adept, adroit, clever, competent, proficient, skilled, talented 6 = **well-behaved**, dutiful, obedient, orderly, polite, well-mannered 7 = **valid**, authentic, bona fide, genuine, legitimate, proper, real, true 10 = **full**, adequate, ample, complete, considerable, extensive, large, substantial, sufficient n 11 = **benefit**, advantage, gain, interest, profit, use, usefulness, welfare, wellbeing 12 = **virtue**, excellence, goodness, merit, morality, rectitude, right, righteousness, worth ▷ pl 13 = **merchandise**, commodities, stock, stuff, wares 14 = **property**, belongings, chattels, effects, gear, paraphernalia, possessions, things, trappings **for good** = **permanently**, finally, for ever, irrevocably, once and for all

goodbye interj = **farewell**, adieu ▷ n = **parting**, adieu, farewell, leave-taking

gore¹ n = **blood**, bloodshed, butchery, carnage, slaughter

gore² v = **pierce**, impale, transfix, wound

gorge ❶ *n* 1 deep narrow valley. ▷ *v* 2 eat greedily. **make one's gorge rise** cause feelings of disgust or nausea.

gorgeous ❶ *adj* 1 strikingly beautiful or attractive. 2 *informal* very pleasant.

gorilla *n* largest of the apes, found in Africa.

gormless *adj informal* stupid.

gorse *n* prickly yellow-flowered shrub.

gosling *n* young goose.

gospel ❶ *n* 1 (**G-**) any of the first four books of the New Testament. 2 unquestionable truth. 3 Black religious music originating in the churches of the Southern US.

gossamer *n* 1 very fine fabric. 2 filmy cobweb.

gossip ❶ *n* 1 idle talk, esp. about other people. 2 person who engages in gossip. ▷ *v* **gossiping**, **gossiped** 3 engage in gossip. **gossipy** *adj*.

gouge ❶ [**gowj**] *v* 1 scoop or force out. 2 cut (a hole or groove) in (something). ▷ *n* 3 hole or groove. 4 chisel with a curved cutting edge.

goulash [**goo**-lash] *n* rich stew seasoned with paprika.

gourd [**goord**] *n* 1 fleshy fruit of a climbing plant. 2 its dried shell, used as a container.

gourmand [**goor**-mand] *n* person who is very keen on food and drink.

gourmet ❶ [**goor**-may] *n* connoisseur of food and drink.

gout [**gowt**] *n* disease causing inflammation of the joints.

govern ❶ *v* 1 rule, direct, or control. 2 exercise restraint over (temper etc.). **governance** *n* governing. **governess** *n* woman teacher in a private household. **government** *n* 1 executive policy-making body of a state. 2 exercise of political authority over a country or state. 3 system by which a country or state is ruled. **governmental** *adj* **governor** *n* 1 official governing a province or state. 2 senior administrator of a society, institution, or prison.

● **SPELLING TIP**
● In the Bank of English, there are hun-
● dreds of examples of *goverment* without
● its middle *n*. Remember it has two *n*s:
● **government**.

gown ❶ *n* 1 woman's long formal dress. 2 surgeon's overall. 3 official robe worn by judges, clergymen, etc.

GP general practitioner.

GPS Global Positioning System: a satellite-based navigation sys tem.

grab ❶ *v* **grabbing**, **grabbed** 1 grasp

━━━ THESAURUS ━━━━━━

gorge *n* 1 = **ravine**, canyon, chasm, cleft, defile, fissure, pass ▷ *v* 2 = **overeat**, cram, devour, feed, glut, gobble, gulp, guzzle, stuff, wolf

gorgeous *adj* 1 = **beautiful**, dazzling, elegant, magnificent, ravishing, splendid, stunning (*inf*) 2 *Inf* = **pleasing**, delightful, enjoyable, exquisite, fine, glorious, good, lovely

gospel *n* 3 = **truth**, certainty, fact, the last word

gossip *n* 1 = **idle talk**, blether, chinwag (*Brit inf*), chitchat, hearsay, scandal, small talk, tittle-tattle 2 = **busybody**, chatterbox (*inf*), chatterer, gossipmonger, scandalmonger, tattler, telltale, tattletale (*chiefly US & Canad*) ▷ *v* 3 = **chat**, blether,

gabble, jaw (*sl*), prate, prattle, tattle

gouge *v* 1, 2 = **scoop**, chisel, claw, cut, dig (out), hollow (out) ▷ *n* 3 = **gash**, cut, furrow, groove, hollow, scoop, scratch, trench

gourmet *n* = **connoisseur**, bon vivant, epicure, foodie (*inf*), gastronome

govern *v* 1 = **rule**, administer, command, control, direct, guide, handle, lead, manage, order 2 = **restrain**, check, control, curb, discipline, hold in check, master, regulate, subdue, tame

gown *n* 1 = **dress**, frock 3 = **robe**, costume, garb, garment, habit

grab *v* 1 = **snatch**, capture, catch, catch or take hold of, clutch, grasp, grip, pluck, seize, snap up

suddenly, snatch. ▷ *n* **2** sudden snatch.
3 mechanical device for gripping.

grace ❶ *n* **1** beauty and elegance. **2** polite,
kind behaviour. **3** goodwill or favour.
4 courtesy or decency. **5** delay granted.
6 short prayer of thanks for a meal. **7** (**G-**)
title of a duke, duchess, or archbishop ▷ *v*
8 honour. **9** add grace to. **graceful** *adj*
gracefully *adv* **graceless** *adj* **gracious** *adj*
1 kind and courteous. **2** condescendingly
polite. **3** elegant. **graciously**.

grade ❶ *n* **1** place on a scale of quality,
rank, or size. **2** mark or rating. **3** *US*
& Aust class in school. ▷ *v* **4** arrange in
grades. **5** assign a grade to. **make the**
grade succeed. **gradation** *n* **1** (stage in) a
series of degrees or steps. **2** arrangement
in stages.

gradient ❶ *n* (degree of) slope.

gradual ❶ *adj* occurring, developing, or
moving in small stages. **gradually** *adv*.

graduate ❶ *v* **1** receive a degree or
diploma. **2** group by type or quality.
3 mark (a container etc.) with units of
measurement. ▷ *n* **4** holder of a degree.
graduation *n*.

graffiti [graf-**fee**-tee] *pl n* words or
drawings scribbled or sprayed on walls
etc.

graft¹ ❶ *n* **1** surgical transplant of skin or
tissue. **2** shoot of a plant set in the stalk
of another. ▷ *v* **3** transplant (living tissue)
surgically. **4** insert (a plant shoot) in
another stalk.

graft² *informal* ▷ *n* **1** hard work. **2** obtaining
of money by misusing one's position. ▷ *v*
3 work hard.

grain ❶ *n* **1** seedlike fruit of a cereal
plant. **2** cereal plants in general. **3** small
hard particle. **4** very small amount.
5 arrangement of fibres, as in wood.
6 texture or pattern resulting from this.
go against the grain be contrary to one's
natural inclination. **grainy** *adj*.

gram, gramme *n* metric unit of mass
equal to one thousandth of a kilogram.

grammar *n* **1** branch of linguistics dealing
with the form, function, and order of
words. **2** use of words. **3** book on the rules
of grammar. **grammatical** *adj* according
to the rules of grammar. **grammar**
school esp. formerly, a secondary school

———————— THESAURUS ————————

grace *n* **1** = **elegance**, attractiveness, beauty,
charm, comeliness, ease, gracefulness,
poise, polish, refinement, tastefulness **2**,
4 = **manners**, consideration, decency,
decorum, etiquette, propriety, tact
3 = **goodwill**, benefaction, benevolence,
favour, generosity, goodness, kindliness,
kindness **5** = **indulgence**, mercy, pardon,
reprieve **6** = **prayer**, benediction, blessing,
thanks, thanksgiving ▷ *v* **8** = **honour**,
dignify, favour **9** = **enhance**, adorn,
decorate, embellish, enrich, ornament,
set off

grade *n* **1-3** = **level**, category (*US & Aust*)
class, degree, echelon, group, rank, stage
▷ *v* **4**, **5** = **classify**, arrange, class, group,
order, range, rank, rate, sort

gradient *n* = **slope**, bank, declivity, grade,
hill, incline, rise

gradual *adj* = **steady**, gentle, graduated,
piecemeal, progressive, regular, slow,
unhurried

graduate *v* **2** = **classify**, arrange, grade,
group, order, rank, sort **3** = **mark off**,
calibrate, grade, measure out, proportion,
regulate

graft¹ *n* **2** = **shoot**, bud, implant, scion,
splice, sprout ▷ *v* **3**, **4** = **transplant**, affix,
implant, ingraft, insert, join, splice

grain *n* **1** = **seed**, grist, kernel **2** = **cereals**,
corn **4** = **bit**, fragment, granule, modicum,
morsel, particle, piece, scrap, speck, trace
5, **6** = **texture**, fibre, nap, pattern, surface,
weave

g

providing an education with a strong
academic bias.

gramophone n old-fashioned type of
record player.

gran n informal grandmother.

granary n, pl **-ries** storehouse for grain.

grand ❶ adj **1** large or impressive,
imposing. **2** dignified or haughty.
3 informal excellent. **4** (of a total)
final. ▷ n **5** slang thousand pounds or
dollars. **6** grand piano. **grandchild** n
child of one's child. **granddaughter** n
female grandchild. **grandfather** n male
grandparent. **grandfather clock** tall
standing clock with a pendulum and
wooden case. **grandmother** n female
grandparent. **grandparent** n parent
of one's parent. **grand piano** large
harp-shaped piano with the strings set
horizontally. **grand slam** winning of all
the games or major tournaments in a
sport in one season. **grandson** n male
grandchild. **grandstand** n terraced block
of seats giving the best view at a sports
ground.

granite [gran-nit] n very hard igneous rock
often used in building.

grant ❶ v **1** consent to fulfil (a request).
2 give formally. **3** admit. ▷ n **4** sum of
money provided by a government for a
specific purpose, such as education. **take**

for granted 1 accept as true without
proof. **2** take advantage of without due
appreciation.

granule ❶ n small grain. **granular** adj of or
like grains. **granulated** adj (of sugar) in the
form of coarse grains.

grape n small juicy green or purple berry,
eaten raw or used to produce wine,
raisins, currants, or sultanas. **grapevine** n
1 grape-bearing vine. **2** informal unofficial
way of spreading news.

grapefruit n large round yellow citrus
fruit.

graph n drawing showing the relation of
different numbers or quantities plotted
against a set of axes.

graphic ❶ adj **1** vividly descriptive. **2** of or
using drawing, painting, etc. **graphics** pl
n diagrams, graphs, etc., esp. as used on a
television programme or computer screen.
graphically adv.

graphite n soft black form of carbon, used
in pencil leads.

grapple ❶ v **1** try to cope with (something
difficult). **2** come to grips with (a person).
grappling iron grapnel.

grasp ❶ v **1** grip something firmly.
2 understand. **3** try to seize. ▷ n **4** grip
or clasp. **5** understanding. **6** total rule
or possession. **grasping** adj greedy or
avaricious.

— THESAURUS —

grand adj **1** = **impressive**, grandiose,
great, imposing, large, magnificent, regal,
splendid, stately, sublime **3** Inf = **excellent**,
fine, first-class, great (inf), outstanding,
smashing (inf), splendid, wonderful

grant v **1** = **consent to**, accede to, agree
to, allow, permit **2** = **give**, allocate,
allot, assign, award, donate, hand out,
present **3** = **admit**, acknowledge, concede
▷ n **4** = **award**, allowance, donation,
endowment, gift, hand-out, present,
subsidy

granule n = **grain**, atom, crumb, fragment,
molecule, particle, scrap, speck

graphic adj **1** = **vivid**, clear, detailed,

explicit, expressive, lively, lucid, striking
2 = **pictorial**, diagrammatic, visual

grapple v **1** = **deal with**, address oneself
to, confront, get to grips with, tackle, take
on, wrestle **2** = **grip**, clutch, grab, grasp,
seize, struggle, wrestle

grasp v **1, 3** = **grip**, catch, clasp, clinch,
clutch, grab, grapple, hold, lay or take hold
of, seize, snatch **2** = **understand**, catch
on, catch or get the drift of, comprehend,
get, realize, see, take in ▷ n **4** = **grip**, clasp,
clutches, embrace, hold, possession,
tenure **5** = **understanding**, awareness,
comprehension, grip, knowledge, mastery
6 = **control**, power, reach, scope

grass n 1 common type of plant with jointed stems and long narrow leaves, including cereals and bamboo. 2 lawn. 3 pasture land. 4 *slang* marijuana. 5 *slang* person who informs, esp. on criminals. ▷ v 6 cover with grass. 7 (often foll. by *on*) *slang* inform on. **grassy** *adj* **-sier, -siest**. **grasshopper** n jumping insect with long hind legs. **grass roots** 1 ordinary members of a group, as distinct from its leaders. 2 essentials. **grassroots** *adj* **grass tree** Australian plant with stiff grasslike leaves and small white flowers. **grass widow** wife whose husband is absent for a time.

grate¹ ❶ v 1 rub into small bits on a rough surface. 2 scrape with a harsh rasping noise. 3 annoy. **grater** n **grating** *adj* 1 harsh or rasping. 2 annoying.

grate² n framework of metal bars for holding fuel in a fireplace. **grating** n framework of metal bars covering an opening.

grateful ❶ *adj* feeling or showing gratitude. **gratefully** *adv*.

gratify ❶ v **-fying, -fied** 1 satisfy or please. 2 indulge (a desire or whim). **gratification** n.

gratis *adv*, *adj* free, for nothing.

gratitude n feeling of being thankful for a favour or gift.

gratuitous ❶ *adj* 1 unjustified, e.g. *gratuitous violence*. 2 given free.

grave¹ ❶ n hole for burying a corpse. **gravestone** n stone marking a grave. **graveyard** n cemetery.

grave² ❶ *adj* 1 causing concern. 2 serious and solemn. **gravely** *adv*.

grave³ [rhymes with **halve**] n accent (`) over a vowel to indicate a special pronunciation.

gravel n mixture of small stones and coarse sand. **gravelly** *adj* 1 covered with gravel. 2 rough-sounding.

graven *adj* carved or engraved.

gravitate v 1 be influenced or drawn towards. 2 *Physics* move by gravity. **gravitation** n **gravitational** *adj*.

gravity ❶ n, pl **-ties** 1 force of attraction of one object for another, esp. of objects to the earth. 2 seriousness or importance. 3 solemnity.

gravy n, pl **-vies** 1 juices from meat in cooking. 2 sauce made from these.

graze¹ ❶ v feed on grass.

graze² ❶ v 1 scratch or scrape the skin. 2 touch lightly in passing. ▷ n 3 slight scratch or scrape.

grease n 1 soft melted animal fat. 2 any thick oily substance. ▷ v 3 apply grease to.

g

grate¹ v 1 = **scrape**, creak, grind, rasp, rub, scratch 3 = **annoy**, exasperate, get on one's nerves (*inf*), irritate, jar, rankle, set one's teeth on edge

grateful *adj* = **thankful**, appreciative, beholden, indebted, obliged

gratify v = **please**, delight, give pleasure, gladden, humour, requite, satisfy

gratitude n = **thankfulness**, appreciation, gratefulness, indebtedness, obligation, recognition, thanks

gratuitous *adj* 1 = **unjustified**, baseless, causeless, groundless, needless, superfluous, uncalled-for, unmerited, unnecessary, unwarranted, wanton 2 = **voluntary**, complimentary, free, gratis, spontaneous, unasked-for,

unpaid, unrewarded

grave¹ n = **tomb**, burying place, crypt, mausoleum, pit, sepulchre, vault

grave² *adj* 1 = **critical**, acute, pressing, serious, severe, threatening 2 = **serious**, dignified, dour, earnest, sober, solemn, sombre, unsmiling

gravity n 2 = **importance**, acuteness, momentousness, perilousness, seriousness, severity, significance, urgency, weightiness 3 = **solemnity**, dignity, earnestness, seriousness, sobriety

graze¹ v = **feed**, browse, crop, pasture

graze² v 1 = **scratch**, abrade, chafe, scrape, skin 2 = **touch**, brush, glance off, rub, scrape, shave, skim ▷ n 3 = **scratch**, abrasion, scrape

g

greasy *adj* greasier, greasiest covered with or containing grease. greasiness *n* greasepaint *n* theatrical make-up.
great ❶ *adj* 1 large in size or number. 2 important. 3 pre-eminent. 4 *informal* excellent. great- *prefix* one generation older or younger than, e.g. *great-grandfather*. greatly *adv* greatness *n* greatcoat *n* heavy overcoat.
greed ❶ *n* excessive desire for food, wealth, etc. greedy *adj* greedily *adv* greediness *n*.
green ❶ *adj* 1 of a colour between blue and yellow. 2 characterized by green plants or foliage. 3 (G-) of or concerned with environmental issues. 4 unripe. 5 envious or jealous. 6 immature or gullible. ▷ *n* 7 colour between blue and yellow. 8 area of grass kept for a special purpose. ▷ *pl* 9 green vegetables. ▷ *v* 10 make or become green. greenness *n* greenery *n* vegetation. green belt protected area of open country around a town. green fingers skill in gardening. greenfly *n* green aphid, a common garden pest. greengage *n* sweet green plum. greengrocer *n* shopkeeper selling vegetables and fruit. greenhorn *n* novice. greenhouse *n* glass building for rearing plants. greenhouse effect rise in the temperature of the earth caused by heat

absorbed from the sun being unable to leave the atmosphere. green light 1 signal to go. 2 permission to proceed with something. greenroom *n* room for actors when offstage.
greet ❶ *v* 1 meet with expressions of welcome. 2 receive in a specified manner. 3 be immediately noticeable to. greeting *n*.
gregarious ❶ *adj* 1 fond of company. 2 (of animals) living in flocks or herds.
gremlin *n* imaginary being blamed for mechanical malfunctions.
grenade *n* small bomb thrown by hand or fired from a rifle. grenadier *n* soldier of a regiment formerly trained to throw grenades.
grenadine [gren-a-**deen**] *n* syrup made from pomegranates.
grey ❶ *adj* 1 of a colour between black and white. 2 (of hair) partly turned white. 3 dismal or dark. 4 dull or boring. ▷ *n* 5 grey colour. 6 grey or white horse. greying *adj* (of hair) turning grey. greyish *adj* greyness *n* grey matter *informal* brains.
greyhound *n* swift slender dog used in racing.
grid *n* 1 network of horizontal and vertical lines, bars, etc. 2 national network of electricity supply cables.

——————————————— THESAURUS ———————————————

great *adj* 1 = **large**, big, enormous, gigantic, huge, immense, prodigious, vast, voluminous 2 = **important**, critical, crucial, momentous, serious, significant 3 = **famous**, eminent, illustrious, noteworthy, outstanding, prominent, remarkable, renowned 4 *Inf* = **excellent**, fantastic (*inf*), fine, marvellous (*inf*), superb, terrific (*inf*), tremendous (*inf*), wonderful
greed *n* = **gluttony**, acquisitiveness, avarice, avidity, covetousness, craving, desire, edacity, esurience, gormandizing, hunger, longing, selfishness, voracity
green *adj* 2 = **leafy**, grassy, verdant 3 (with cap.) = **ecological**, conservationist,

environment-friendly, non-polluting, ozone-friendly 5 = **jealous**, covetous, envious, grudging, resentful 6 = **inexperienced**, gullible, immature, naive, new, raw, untrained, wet behind the ears (*inf*) ▷ *n* 8 = **lawn**, common, sward, turf
greet *v* 1, 2 = **welcome**, accost, address, compliment, hail, meet, receive, salute
gregarious *adj* 1 = **outgoing**, affable, companionable, convivial, cordial, friendly, sociable, social
grey *adj* 3 = **dismal**, dark, depressing, dim, drab, dreary, dull, gloomy 4 = **characterless**, anonymous, colourless, dull

griddle n flat iron plate for cooking.

gridiron n 1 frame of metal bars for grilling food. 2 American football pitch.

grief ❶ n deep sadness. **grieve** v (cause to) feel grief. **grievance** n real or imaginary cause for complaint. **grievous** adj 1 very severe or painful. 2 very serious.

grill n 1 device on a cooker that radiates heat downwards. 2 grilled food. 3 gridiron. ▷ v 4 cook under a grill. 5 question relentlessly. **grilling** n relentless questioning.

grille, grill n grating over an opening.

grim ❶ adj grimmer, grimmest 1 stern. 2 harsh or forbidding. 3 very unpleasant. **grimly** adv **grimness** n.

grimace ❶ n 1 ugly or distorted facial expression of pain, disgust, etc. ▷ v 2 make a grimace.

grime ❶ n 1 ingrained dirt. ▷ v 2 make very dirty. **grimy** adj **griminess** n.

grin v grinning, grinned 1 smile broadly, showing the teeth. ▷ n 2 broad smile.

grind ❶ v grinding, ground 1 crush or rub to a powder. 2 smooth or sharpen by friction. 3 scrape together with a harsh noise. 4 oppress. ▷ n 5 informal hard work. 6 act or sound of grinding. **grind out** v produce in a routine or uninspired manner.

grindstone n stone used for grinding.

grip ❶ n 1 firm hold or grasp. 2 way in which something is grasped. 3 mastery or understanding. 4 US travelling bag. 5 handle. ▷ v **gripping**, **gripped** 6 grasp or hold tightly. 7 hold the interest or attention of. **gripping** adj.

gripe v 1 informal complain persistently. ▷ n 2 informal complaint. 3 sudden intense bowel pain.

grisly ❶ adj -lier, -liest horrifying or ghastly.

grist n grain for grinding. **grist to one's mill** something which can be turned to advantage.

gristle n tough stringy animal tissue found in meat. **gristly** adj.

grit ❶ n 1 rough particles of sand. 2 courage. ▷ pl 3 coarsely ground grain. ▷ v **gritting**, **gritted** 4 spread grit on (an icy road etc.). 5 clench or grind (the teeth). **gritty** adj -tier, -tiest.

grizzle v informal whine or complain.

grizzled adj grey-haired.

grizzly n, pl -zlies large American bear (also **grizzly bear**).

groan ❶ n 1 deep sound of grief or pain. 2 informal complaint. ▷ v 3 utter a groan. 4 informal complain.

——— THESAURUS ———

grief n = **sadness**, anguish, distress, heartache, misery, regret, remorse, sorrow, suffering, woe

grim adj 1, 2 = **forbidding**, formidable, harsh, merciless, ruthless, severe, sinister, stern, terrible

grimace n 1 = **scowl**, face, frown, sneer ▷ v 2 = **scowl**, frown, lour or lower, make a face or faces, sneer

grime n 1 = **dirt**, filth, grot (sl), smut, soot

grind v 1 = **crush**, abrade, granulate, grate, mill, pound, powder, pulverize, triturate 2 = **smooth**, polish, sand, sharpen, whet 3 = **scrape**, gnash, grate ▷ n 5 Inf = **hard work**, chore, drudgery, labour, sweat (inf), toil

grip n 1 = **control**, clasp, clutches,

domination, hold, influence, mana (NZ), possession, power 3 = **understanding**, command, comprehension, grasp, mastery ▷ v 6 = **grasp**, clasp, clutch, hold, seize, take hold of 7 = **engross**, absorb, enthral, entrance, fascinate, hold, mesmerize, rivet

grisly adj = **gruesome**, appalling, awful, dreadful, ghastly, horrible, macabre, shocking, terrifying

grit n 1 = **gravel**, dust, pebbles, sand 2 = **courage**, backbone, determination, fortitude, guts (inf), perseverance, resolution, spirit, tenacity ▷ v 5 = **grind**, clench, gnash, grate

groan n 1 = **moan**, cry, sigh, whine 2 Inf = **complaint**, gripe (inf), grouse, grumble,

grocer *n* shopkeeper selling foodstuffs.
grocery *n*, *pl* **-ceries 1** business or
premises of a grocer. ▷ *pl* **2** goods sold by
a grocer.
grog *n* spirit, usu. rum, and water.
groin *n* **1** place where the legs join the
abdomen.
groom ⓸ *n* **1** person who looks after
horses. **2** bridegroom. **3** officer in a royal
household. ▷ *v* **4** make or keep one's
clothes and appearance neat and tidy.
5 brush or clean a horse. **6** train (someone)
for a future role.
groove ⓸ *n* long narrow channel in a
surface.
grope ⓸ *v* feel about or search uncertainly.
gross ⓸ *adj* **1** flagrant. **2** vulgar. **3** *slang*
disgusting or repulsive. **4** repulsively fat.
5 total, without deductions. ▷ *n* **6** twelve
dozen. ▷ *v* **7** make as total revenue before
deductions. **grossly** *adv*.
grotesque ⓸ [grow-**tesk**] *adj* **1** strangely
distorted. **2** absurd. ▷ *n* **3** grotesque
person or thing. **4** artistic style mixing
distorted human, animal, and plant forms.
grotesquely *adv*.
grotto *n*, *pl* **-toes**, **-tos** small picturesque
cave.

grotty *adj* **-tier**, **-tiest** *informal* nasty or in
bad condition.
grouch *informal* ▷ *v* **1** grumble or complain.
▷ *n* **2** person who is always complaining.
3 persistent complaint. **grouchy** *adj*.
ground ⓸ *n* **1** surface of the earth. **2** soil.
3 area used for a specific purpose, e.g.
rugby ground. **4** position in an argument
or controversy. **5** background colour of
a painting. ▷ *pl* **6** enclosed land round
a house. **7** reason or motive. **8** coffee
dregs. ▷ *adj* **9** on or of the ground. ▷ *v*
10 base or establish. **11** instruct in the
basics. **12** ban an aircraft or pilot from
flying. **13** run (a ship) aground. **14** place
on the ground. **groundless** *adj* without
reason. **grounding** *n* basic knowledge of a
subject. **ground-breaking** *adj* innovative.
ground floor floor of a building level
with the ground. **groundnut** *n* peanut.
groundsheet *n* waterproof sheet put on
the ground under a tent. **groundsman**
n person employed to maintain a sports
ground or park. **groundswell** *n* rapidly
developing general feeling or opinion.
groundwork *n* preliminary work.
group ⓸ *n* **1** number of people or things
regarded as a unit. **2** small band of

——————————————————————————— THESAURUS ———

objection, protest ▷ *v* **3** = **moan**, cry, sigh,
whine **4** *Inf* = **complain**, bemoan, gripe
(*inf*), grouse, grumble, lament, object
groom *n* **1** = **stableman**, hostler or ostler
(*arch*), stableboy ▷ *v* **4** = **smarten up**,
clean, preen, primp, spruce up, tidy
5 = **rub down**, brush, clean, curry, tend
6 = **train**, coach, drill, educate, make
ready, nurture, prepare, prime, ready
groove *n* = **indentation**, channel, cut,
flute, furrow, hollow, rut, trench, trough
grope *v* = **feel**, cast about, fish, flounder,
forage, fumble, scrabble, search
gross *adj* **1** = **blatant**, flagrant, grievous,
heinous, rank, sheer, unmitigated, utter
2 = **vulgar**, coarse, crude, indelicate,
obscene, offensive **4** = **fat**, corpulent,
hulking, obese, overweight **5** = **total**,

aggregate, before deductions, before tax,
entire, whole ▷ *v* **7** = **earn**, bring in, make,
rake in (*inf*), take
grotesque *adj* **1** = **deformed**, distorted
2 = **unnatural**, bizarre, fantastic, freakish,
outlandish, preposterous, strange
ground *n* **1, 2** = **earth**, dry land, land, soil,
terra firma, terrain, turf **3** = **stadium**,
arena, field, park (*inf*), pitch ▷ *pl*
6 = **land**, estate, fields, gardens, terrain,
territory **7** = **reason**, basis, cause,
excuse, foundation, justification,
motive, occasion, pretext, rationale
8 = **dregs**, deposit, lees, sediment ▷ *v*
10 = **base**, establish, fix, found, set, settle
11 = **instruct**, acquaint with, familiarize
with, initiate, teach, train, tutor
group *n* **1** = **set**, band, bunch, cluster,

musicians or singers. ▷ v **3** place or form into a group.

grouse¹ n **1** stocky game bird. **2** its flesh.

grouse² ❶ v **1** grumble or complain. ▷ n **2** complaint.

grout n **1** thin mortar. ▷ v **2** fill up with grout.

grove ❶ n small group of trees.

grovel ❶ [grov-el] v -**elling**, -**elled 1** behave humbly in order to win a superior's favour. **2** crawl on the floor.

grow ❶ v **growing**, **grew**, **grown 1** develop physically. **2** (of a plant) exist. **3** cultivate (plants). **4** increase in size or degree. **5** originate. **6** become gradually, e.g. *it was growing dark*. **growth** n **1** growing. **2** increase. **3** something grown or growing. **4** tumour. **grown-up** *adj, n* adult. **grow up** v mature.

growl v **1** make a low rumbling sound. **2** utter with a growl. ▷ n **3** growling sound.

grub ❶ n **1** legless insect larva. **2** *slang* food. ▷ v **grubbing**, **grubbed 3** search carefully for something by digging or by moving things about. **4** dig up the surface of (soil).

grubby ❶ adj -**bier**, -**biest** dirty. **grubbiness** n.

grudge ❶ v **1** be unwilling to give or allow. ▷ n **2** resentment.

gruel n thin porridge.

gruelling ❶ adj exhausting or severe.

gruesome ❶ adj causing horror and disgust.

gruff ❶ adj rough or surly in manner or voice. **gruffly** adv **gruffness** n.

grumble ❶ v **1** complain. **2** rumble. ▷ n **3** complaint. **4** rumble. **grumbling** adj, n.

collection, crowd, gang, pack, party ▷ v **3** = **arrange**, bracket, class, classify, marshal, order, sort

grouse² v **1** = **complain**, bellyache (*sl*), carp, gripe (*inf*), grumble, moan, whine, whinge (*inf*) ▷ n **2** = **complaint**, grievance, gripe (*inf*), grouch (*inf*), grumble, moan, objection, protest

grove n = **wood**, coppice, copse, covert, plantation, spinney, thicket

grovel v **1** = **humble oneself**, abase oneself, bow and scrape, crawl, creep, cringe, demean oneself, fawn, kowtow, toady **2** = **crawl**, creep

grow v **1** = **increase**, develop, enlarge, expand, get bigger, multiply, spread, stretch, swell **3** = **cultivate**, breed, farm, nurture, produce, propagate, raise **4** = **improve**, advance, flourish, progress, prosper, succeed, thrive **5** = **originate**, arise, issue, spring, stem **6** = **become**, come to be, get, turn

grub n **1** = **larva**, caterpillar, maggot **2** *Sl* = **food**, nosh (*sl*), rations, sustenance, tucker (*Aust & NZ inf*), victuals ▷ v **3** = **search**, ferret, forage, fossick (*Aust & NZ*), hunt, rummage, scour, uncover,

unearth **4** = **dig up**, burrow, pull up, root (*inf*)

grubby adj = **dirty**, filthy, grimy, messy, mucky, scruffy, scungy (*Aust & NZ inf*), seedy, shabby, sordid, squalid, unwashed

grudge v **1** = **resent**, begrudge, complain, covet, envy, mind ▷ n **2** = **resentment**, animosity, antipathy, bitterness, dislike, enmity, grievance, rancour

gruelling adj = **exhausting**, arduous, backbreaking, demanding, laborious, punishing, severe, strenuous, taxing, tiring

gruesome adj = **horrific**, ghastly, grim, grisly, horrible, macabre, shocking, terrible

gruff adj **a** = **surly**, bad-tempered, brusque, churlish, grumpy, rough, rude, sullen, ungracious **b** = **hoarse**, croaking, guttural, harsh, husky, low, rasping, rough, throaty

grumble v **1** = **complain**, bleat, carp, gripe (*inf*), grouch (*inf*), grouse, moan, whine, whinge (*inf*) **2** = **rumble**, growl, gurgle, murmur, mutter, roar ▷ n **3** = **complaint**, grievance, gripe (*inf*), grouch (*inf*), grouse, moan, objection, protest **4** = **rumble**,

grumpy ❶ *adj* **grumpier, grumpiest** bad-tempered. **grumpily** *adv* **grumpiness** *n*.

grunt *v* **1** make a low short gruff sound, like a pig. ▷ *n* **2** pig's sound. **3** gruff noise.

G-string *n* small strip of cloth covering the genitals and attached to a waistband.

guarantee ❶ *n* **1** formal assurance, esp. in writing, that a product will meet certain standards. **2** something that makes a specified condition or outcome certain. ▷ *v* **-teeing, -teed 3** give a guarantee. **4** secure against risk etc. **5** ensure. **guarantor** *n* person who gives or is bound by a guarantee.

guard ❶ *v* **1** watch over to protect or to prevent escape. ▷ *n* **2** person or group that guards. **3** official in charge of a train. **4** protection. **5** screen for enclosing anything dangerous. **6** posture of defence in sports such as boxing or fencing. ▷ *pl* **7 (G-)** regiment with ceremonial duties. **guarded** *adj* cautious or noncommittal. **guard against** *v* take precautions against. **guardian** *n* keeper or protector. **guardsman** *n* member of the Guards.

guava [**gwah**-va] *n* yellow-skinned tropical American fruit.

guerrilla, guerilla ❶ *n* member of an unofficial armed force fighting regular forces.

guess ❶ *v* **1** estimate or draw a conclusion without proper knowledge. **2** estimate correctly by guessing. **3** *US & Canad* suppose. ▷ *n* **4** estimate or conclusion reached by guessing. **guesswork** *n* process or results of guessing.

guest ❶ *n* **1** person entertained at another's house or at another's expense. **2** invited performer or speaker. **3** customer at a hotel or restaurant. ▷ *v* **4** appear as a visiting player or performer. **guesthouse** *n* boarding house.

guffaw *n* **1** crude noisy laugh. ▷ *v* **2** laugh in this way.

guide ❶ *n* **1** person who conducts tour expeditions. **2** person who shows the way. **3** book of instruction or information. **4** model for behaviour. **5** something used to gauge something or to help in planning one's actions. **6** (**G-**) member of an organization for girls equivalent to the Scouts. ▷ *v* **7** act as a guide for. **8** control, supervise, or influence. **guidance** *n* leadership, instruction, or advice. **guided missile** missile whose flight is controlled

———— THESAURUS ————

growl, gurgle, murmur, muttering, roar

grumpy *adj* = **irritable**, bad-tempered, cantankerous, crotchety (*inf*), peevish, sulky, sullen, surly, testy

guarantee *n* **1** = **assurance**, bond, certainty, pledge, promise, security, surety, warranty, word of honour ▷ *v* **3-5** = **ensure**, assure, certify, make certain, pledge, promise, secure, vouch for, warrant

guard *v* **1** = **watch over**, defend, mind, preserve, protect, safeguard, secure, shield ▷ *n* **2** = **protector**, custodian, defender, lookout, picket, sentinel, sentry, warder, watch, watchman **4, 5** = **protection**, buffer, defence, safeguard, screen, security, shield

guerrilla, guerilla *n* = **freedom fighter**, partisan, underground fighter

guess *v* **1** = **estimate**, conjecture, hypothesize, predict, speculate, work out **3** *Chiefly US* = **suppose**, believe, conjecture, fancy, imagine, judge, reckon, suspect, think *n* **4** = **supposition**, conjecture, hypothesis, prediction, shot in the dark, speculation, theory

guest *n* **1, 3** = **visitor**, boarder, caller, company, lodger, visitant

guide *n* **1, 2** = **escort**, adviser, conductor, counsellor, guru, leader, mentor, teacher, usher **3** = **guidebook**, catalogue, directory, handbook, instructions, key, manual **4** = **model**, example, ideal, inspiration, paradigm, standard **5** = **pointer**, beacon, guiding light, landmark, lodestar, marker, sign, signpost

electronically. **guide dog** dog trained to lead a blind person. **guideline** n set principle for doing something.

guild ❶ n 1 organization or club. 2 *Hist* society of men in the same trade or craft.

guile ❶ [**gile**] n cunning or deceit. **guileless** adj.

guillotine n 1 machine for beheading people. 2 device for cutting paper or sheet metal. 3 method of preventing lengthy debate in parliament by fixing a time for taking the vote. ▷ v 4 behead by guillotine. 5 limit debate by the guillotine.

guilt ❶ n 1 fact or state of having done wrong. 2 remorse for wrongdoing. **guiltless** adj innocent. **guilty** adj 1 responsible for an offence or misdeed. 2 feeling or showing guilt. **guiltily** adv.

guinea n 1 former British monetary unit worth 21 shillings (1.05 pounds). 2 former gold coin of this value. **guinea fowl** bird related to the pheasant. **guinea pig** 1 tailless S American rodent, commonly kept as a pet. 2 *informal* person used for experimentation.

guise ❶ [rhymes with **size**] n 1 false appearance. 2 external appearance.

guitar n stringed instrument with a flat back and a long neck, played by plucking or strumming. **guitarist** n.

gulf ❶ n 1 large deep bay. 2 chasm. 3 large difference in opinion or understanding.

gull n long-winged sea bird.

gullet n muscular tube through which food passes from the mouth to the stomach.

gullible ❶ adj easily tricked. **gullibility** n.

gully ❶ n, pl **-lies** channel cut by running water.

gulp ❶ v 1 swallow hastily. 2 gasp. ▷ n 3 gulping. 4 thing gulped.

gum¹ n firm flesh in which the teeth are set.

gum² ❶ n 1 sticky substance obtained from certain trees. 2 adhesive. 3 chewing gum. 4 gumdrop. 5 gumtree. ▷ v **gumming**, **gummed** 6 stick with gum. **gummy** adj **-mier**, **-miest**. **gumboots** pl n Wellington boots. **gumdrop** n hard jelly-like sweet. **gumtree** n eucalypt tree.

gumption ❶ n 1 *informal* resourcefulness. 2 courage.

gun ❶ n 1 weapon with a metal tube from

g

━━━━━━━━━ THESAURUS ━━━━━━━━━

▷ v 7 = **lead**, accompany, conduct, direct, escort, shepherd, show the way, usher 8 = **supervise**, advise, command, control, counsel, direct, handle, influence, instruct, manage, manoeuvre, oversee, steer, superintend, teach, train

guild n 1 = **society**, association, brotherhood, club, company, corporation, fellowship, fraternity, league, lodge, order, organization, union

guile n = **cunning**, artifice, cleverness, craft, deceit, slyness, trickery, wiliness

guilt n 1 = **culpability**, blame, guiltiness, misconduct, responsibility, sinfulness, wickedness, wrongdoing 2 = **remorse**, contrition, guilty conscience, regret, self-reproach, shame, stigma

guise n 1 = **disguise**, pretence, semblance 2 = **form**, appearance, aspect, demeanour, mode, shape

gulf n 1 = **bay**, bight, sea inlet 2 = **chasm**, abyss, gap, opening, rift, separation, split, void

gullible adj = **naive**, born yesterday, credulous, innocent, simple, trusting, unsuspecting, wet behind the ears (inf)

gully n = **channel**, ditch, gutter, watercourse

gulp v 1 = **swallow**, devour, gobble, guzzle, quaff, swig (inf), swill, wolf 2 = **gasp**, choke, swallow ▷ n 4 = **swallow**, draught, mouthful, swig (inf)

gum² n 1 = **resin** ▷ = **glue**, adhesive, cement, paste ▷ v 6 = **stick**, affix, cement, glue, paste

gumption n Inf 1 = **resourcefulness**, acumen, astuteness, common sense, enterprise, initiative, mother wit, savvy (sl), wit(s)

gun n 1 = **firearm**, handgun, piece (sl), shooter (sl)

which missiles are fired by explosion.
2 device from which a substance is ejected under pressure. ▷ v **gunning, gunned**
3 cause (an engine) to run at high speed.
jump the gun act prematurely. **gunner** n artillery soldier. **gunnery** n use or science of large guns. **gunboat** n small warship.
gun down v shoot (a person). **gun for** v seek or pursue vigorously. **gunman** n armed criminal. **gunmetal** n **1** alloy of copper, tin, and zinc. ▷ adj **2** dark grey.
gunpowder n explosive mixture of potassium nitrate, sulphur, and charcoal.
gunshot n shot or range of a gun.
gunge n informal sticky unpleasant substance. **gungy** adj **-gier, -giest**.
gunwale, gunnel [**gun**-nel] n top of a ship's side.
guppy n, pl **-pies** small colourful aquarium fish.
gurgle ❶ v, n (make) a bubbling noise.
guru ❶ n **1** Hindu or Sikh religious teacher or leader. **2** leader or adviser.
gush ❶ v **1** flow out suddenly and profusely.
2 express admiration effusively. ▷ n
3 sudden copious flow. **4** sudden surge of strong feeling.
gusset n piece of material sewn into a garment to strengthen it.

gust ❶ n **1** sudden blast of wind. ▷ v **2** blow in gusts. **gusty** adj.
gusto ❶ n enjoyment or zest.
gut ❶ n **1** intestine. **2** informal fat stomach.
3 short for CATGUT. ▷ pl **4** internal organs.
5 informal courage. ▷ v **gutting, gutted**
6 remove the guts from. **7** (of a fire) destroy the inside of (a building). ▷ adj **8** basic or instinctive, e.g. a gut reaction. **gutsy** adj **-sier, -siest** informal **1** courageous.
2 vigorous or robust, e.g. a gutsy performance.
gutted adj informal disappointed and upset.
gutter ❶ n **1** shallow channel for carrying away water from a roof or roadside. ▷ v **2** (of a candle) burn unsteadily, with wax running down the sides. **the gutter** degraded or criminal environment.
guttering n material for gutters.
gutter press newspapers that rely on sensationalism. **guttersnipe** n neglected slum child.
guttural ❶ adj **1** (of a sound) produced at the back of the throat. **2** (of a voice) harsh-sounding.
guy¹ ❶ n **1** informal man or boy. **2** effigy of Guy Fawkes burnt on November 5 (**Guy Fawkes Day**).
guy² n rope or chain to steady or secure something. **guyrope** n.

———————————————————— THESAURUS ————————————————————

gurgle v = **murmur**, babble, bubble, lap, plash, purl, ripple, splash ▷ n = **murmur**, babble, purl, ripple, ripple
guru n **2** = **teacher**, authority, leader, mana (NZ), master, mentor, sage, Svengali, tutor
gush v **1** = **flow**, cascade, flood, pour, run, rush, spout, spurt, stream **2** = **enthuse**, babble, chatter, effervesce, effuse, overstate, spout ▷ n **3, 4** = **stream**, cascade, flood, flow, jet, rush, spout, spurt, torrent
gust n **1** = **blast**, blow, breeze, puff, rush, squall ▷ v **3** = **blow**, blast, squall
gusto n = **relish**, delight, enjoyment, enthusiasm, fervour, pleasure, verve, zeal

gut n **2** Inf = **paunch**, belly, potbelly, spare tyre (Brit sl) ▷ pl **4** = **intestines**, belly, bowels, entrails, innards (inf), insides (inf), stomach, viscera **5** Inf = **courage**, audacity, backbone, bottle (sl), daring, mettle, nerve, pluck, spirit ▷ v **6** = **disembowel**, clean **7** = **ravage**, clean out, despoil, empty ▷ adj **8** = **instinctive**, basic, heartfelt, intuitive, involuntary, natural, spontaneous, unthinking, visceral
gutter n **1** = **drain**, channel, conduit, ditch, sluice, trench, trough
guttural adj = **throaty**, deep, gravelly, gruff, hoarse, husky, rasping, rough, thick
guy¹ n **1** Inf = **man**, bloke (Brit inf), chap, fellow, lad, person

guzzle ❶ v eat or drink greedily.

gym n 1 gymnasium. 2 gymnastics.

gymkhana [jim-**kah**-na] n horse-riding competition.

gymnasium n large room with equipment for physical training. **gymnast** n expert in gymnastics. **gymnastic** adj **gymnastics** pl n exercises to develop strength and agility.

gynaecology [guy-nee-**kol**-la-jee] n branch of medicine dealing with diseases and conditions specific to women. **gynaecologist** n.

gypsum n chalklike mineral used to make plaster of Paris.

Gypsy ❶ n, pl -**sies** member of a travelling people found throughout Europe.

gyrate [jire-**rate**] v rotate or spiral about a point or axis. **gyration** n.

gyroscope [**jire**-oh-skohp] n disc rotating on an axis that can turn in any direction, so the disc maintains the same position regardless of the movement of the surrounding structure.

g

——— THESAURUS ———

guzzle v = **devour**, bolt, cram, drink, gobble, stuff (oneself), swill, wolf

Gypsy n = **traveller**, Bohemian, nomad, rambler, roamer, Romany, rover, wanderer

haberdasher *n Brit, Aust & NZ* dealer in small articles used for sewing. **haberdashery** *n*.

habit ❶ *n* 1 established way of behaving. 2 addiction to a drug. 3 costume of a monk or nun. **habitual** *adj* done regularly and repeatedly.

habitable *adj* fit to be lived in. **habitat** *n* natural home of an animal or plant. **habitation** *n* (occupation of) a dwelling place.

hack¹ ❶ *v* cut or chop violently *Brit and NZ informal* tolerate.

hack² ❶ *n* 1 (inferior) writer or journalist. 2 horse kept for riding.

hackles *pl n* **make one's hackles rise** make one feel angry or hostile.

hackneyed ❶ *adj* (of a word or phrase) unoriginal and overused.

hacksaw *n* small saw for cutting metal.

haddock *n* edible sea fish.

haemoglobin [hee-moh-**globe**-in] *n* protein found in red blood cells which carries oxygen.

haemophilia [hee-moh-**fill**-lee-a] *n* hereditary illness in which the blood does not clot. **haemophiliac** *n*.

haemorrhage [**hem**-or-ij] *n* 1 heavy bleeding. ▷ *v* 2 bleed heavily.

- **SPELLING TIP**
- The Bank of English shows that the
- most usual mistake in spelling **haemorrhage** is to miss out the second *h*, which
- is silent.

haemorrhoids [**hem**-or-oydz] *pl n* swollen veins in the anus (also **piles**).

hag ❶ *n* ugly old woman. **hag-ridden** *adj* distressed or worried.

haggard ❶ *adj* looking tired and ill.

haggis *n* Scottish dish made from sheep's offal, oatmeal, suet, and seasonings, boiled in a bag made from the sheep's stomach.

haggle ❶ *v* bargain or wrangle over a price.

hail¹ ❶ *n* 1 (shower of) small pellets of ice. 2 large number of insults, missiles, blows, etc. ▷ *v* 3 fall as or like hail. **hailstone** *n*.

hail² ❶ *v* 1 call out to, greet. 2 stop (a taxi) by waving. 3 acknowledge publicly. **hail from** *v* come originally from.

hair ❶ *n* 1 threadlike growth on the skin. 2 such growths collectively, esp. on the head. **hairy** *adj* 1 covered with hair. 2 *slang* dangerous or exciting. **hairiness** *n* **hairdo** *n informal* hairstyle. **hairdresser** *n* person who cuts and styles hair. **hairgrip** *n* small,

——————————— THESAURUS ———————————

habit *n* 1 = **mannerism**, custom, practice, proclivity, propensity, quirk, tendency, way 2 = **addiction**, dependence

hack¹ *v* = **cut**, chop, hew, lacerate, mangle, mutilate, slash

hack² *n* 1 = **scribbler**, literary hack 2 = **horse**, crock, nag

hackneyed *adj* = **unoriginal**, clichéd, commonplace, overworked, stale, stereotyped, stock, threadbare, tired, trite

hag *n* = **witch**, crone, harridan

haggard *adj* = **gaunt**, careworn, drawn, emaciated, pinched, thin, wan

haggle *v* = **bargain**, barter, beat down

hail¹ *n* 1 = **shower**, rain, storm 2 = **barrage**, bombardment, downpour, volley ▷ *v* 3 = **shower**, batter, beat down upon, bombard, pelt, rain, rain down on

hail² *v* 1 = **salute**, greet, welcome 2 = **flag down**, signal to, wave down 3 = **acclaim**, acknowledge, applaud, cheer, honour ▷ *v* **hail from** = **come from**, be a native of, be born in, originate in

hair *n* 2 = **locks**, head of hair, mane, mop, shock, tresses

tightly bent metal hairpin. **hairline** *n*
1 edge of hair at the top of the forehead.
▷ *adj* 2 very fine or narrow. **hairpin** *n*
U-shaped wire used to hold the hair in
place. **hairpin bend** very sharp bend
in a road. **hair-raising** *adj* frightening
or exciting. **hairsplitting** *n, adj* making
petty distinctions. **hairstyle** *n* cut and
arrangement of a person's hair.

hale ❶ *adj* healthy, robust.

half ❶ *n, pl* **halves** 1 either of two equal
parts. 2 *informal* half-pint of beer etc.
3 half-price ticket. ▷ *adj* 4 denoting
one of two equal parts. ▷ *adv* 5 to the
extent of half. 6 partially. **half-baked**
adj informal not properly thought out.
half-brother, half-sister *n* brother *or*
sister related through one parent only.
half-caste *n offens* person with parents
of different races. **half-cocked** *adj* **go off
half-cocked, (at) half-cock** fail because
of inadequate preparation. **half-hearted**
adj unenthusiastic. **half-life** *n* time taken
for half the atoms in radioactive material
to decay. **half-pipe** large U-shaped ramp
used for skateboarding, snowboarding,
etc. **half-time** *n Sport* short rest period
between two halves of a game. **halfway**
adv, adj at or to half the distance. **halfwit** *n*
foolish or stupid person.

halibut *n* large edible flatfish.

halitosis *n* unpleasant-smelling breath.

hall ❶ *n* 1 (also **hallway**) entrance passage.
2 large room or building for public

meetings, dances, etc. 3 large country
house.

hallelujah [hal-ee-**loo**-ya] *interj*
exclamation of praise to God.

hallmark ❶ *n* 1 typical feature. 2 mark
indicating the standard of tested gold
and silver.

hallo *interj* same as HELLO.

hallowed *adj* regarded as holy.

hallucinate *v* seem to see something
that is not really there. **hallucination** *n*
hallucinatory *adj* **hallucinogenic** *adj*.

halo ❶ [**hay**-loh] *n, pl* **-loes, -los** 1 ring of
light round the head of a sacred figure.
2 circle of refracted light round the sun
or moon.

halt ❶ *v* 1 come or bring to a stop. ▷ *n*
2 temporary stop. 3 minor railway station
without a building. **halting** *adj* hesitant,
uncertain.

halter *n* strap round a horse's head with a
rope to lead it with. **halterneck** *n* woman's
top or dress with a strap fastened at the
back of the neck.

halve ❶ *v* 1 divide in half. 2 reduce by half.

ham¹ *n* smoked or salted meat from a pig's
thigh. **ham-fisted** *adj* clumsy.

ham² *informal* ▷ *n* 1 amateur radio operator.
2 actor who overacts. ▷ *v* **hamming,
hammed** 3 **ham it up** overact.

hamburger *n* minced beef shaped into
a flat disc, cooked and usu. served in a
bread roll.

hamlet *n* small village.

—————— THESAURUS ——————

hale *adj* = **healthy**, able-bodied, fit,
flourishing, in the pink, robust, sound,
strong, vigorous, well

half *n* 1 = **equal part**, fifty per cent,
hemisphere, portion, section ▷ *adj*
2 = **partial**, halved, limited, moderate
▷ *adv* 3 = **partially**, in part, partly

hall *n* 1 = **entrance hall**, corridor, entry,
foyer, lobby, passage, passageway,
vestibule 2 = **meeting place**, assembly
room, auditorium, chamber, concert hall

hallmark *n* 1 = **indication**, sure sign,

telltale sign 2 = **seal**, device, endorsement,
mark, sign, stamp, symbol

halo *n* = **ring of light**, aura, corona,
nimbus, radiance

halt *v* 1 **a** = **stop**, break off, cease, come
to an end, desist, rest, stand still, wait
b = **hold back**, block, bring to an end,
check, curb, cut short, end, nip in the bud,
terminate ▷ *n* 2 = **stop**, close, end, pause,
standstill, stoppage

halve *v* 1 = **bisect**, cut in half, divide
equally, share equally, split in two

hammer ❶ n **1** tool with a heavy metal head and a wooden handle, used to drive in nails etc. **2** part of a gun which causes the bullet to be fired. **3** heavy metal ball on a wire, thrown as a sport. **4** auctioneer's mallet. **5** striking mechanism in a piano. ▷ v **6** hit (as if) with a hammer. **7** informal punish or defeat utterly. **go at it hammer and tongs** do something, esp. argue, very vigorously. **hammerhead** n shark with a wide flattened head. **hammertoe** n condition in which a toe is permanently bent at the joint.

hammock n hanging bed made of canvas or net.

hamper¹ v make it difficult for (someone or something) to move or progress.

hamper² n **1** large basket with a lid. **2** selection of food and drink packed as a gift.

hamster n small rodent with a short tail and cheek pouches.

- ● **SPELLING TIP**
- ● The word **hamster** appears
- ● 750 times in the Bank of English. The
- ● misspelling *hampster*, with a *p*, appears
- ● 13 times.

hamstring n **1** tendon at the back of the knee. ▷ v **2** make it difficult for (someone) to take any action.

hand ❶ n **1** part of the body at the end of the arm, consisting of a palm, four fingers, and a thumb. **2** style of handwriting. **3** round of applause. **4** manual worker. **5** pointer on a dial, esp. on a clock. **6** cards dealt to a player in a card game. **7** unit of length of four inches used to measure horses. ▷ v **8** pass, give. **have a hand in** be involved in. **lend a hand** help. **out of hand 1** beyond control. **2** definitely and finally. **to hand, at hand, on hand** nearby. **win hands down** win easily. **handbag** n woman's small bag for carrying personal articles in. **handbook** n small reference or instruction book. **handcuff** n **1** one of a linked pair of metal rings designed to be locked round a prisoner's wrists by the police. ▷ v **2** put handcuffs on. **handheld** adj **1** (of a computer) small enough to be held in the hand. ▷ n **2** computer small enough to be held in the hand. **hand-out** n **1** clothing, food, or money given to a needy person. **2** written information given out at a talk etc. **hands-free** adj, n (of) a device allowing the user to make and receive phone calls without holding the handset. **hands-on** adj involving practical experience of equipment. **handstand** n act of supporting the body on the hands in an upside-down position. **handwriting** n (style of) writing by hand.

handicap ❶ n **1** physical or mental disability. **2** something that makes progress difficult. **3** contest in which the competitors are given advantages or disadvantages in an attempt to equalize their chances. **4** advantage or disadvantage given. ▷ v **5** make it difficult for (someone) to do something.

──────────────────────── THESAURUS ────────────────────────

hammer v **6** = **hit**, bang, beat, drive, knock, strike, tap **7** Inf = **defeat**, beat, drub, run rings around (inf), thrash, trounce, wipe the floor with (inf)

hamper¹ v = **hinder**, frustrate, hamstring, handicap, impede, interfere with, obstruct, prevent, restrict

hand n **1** = **palm**, fist, mitt (sl), paw (inf) **2** = **penmanship**, calligraphy, handwriting, script **3** = **round of applause**, clap, ovation **4** = **worker**, artisan, craftsman, employee, hired man, labourer, operative, workman ▷ v **8** = **give**, deliver, hand over, pass **to, at** or **on hand** = **nearby**, at one's fingertips, available, close, handy, near, ready, within reach

handicap n **1** = **disability**, defect, impairment **2** = **disadvantage**, barrier, drawback, hindrance, impediment, limitation, obstacle, restriction, stumbling block **3** = **advantage**, head start ▷ v **5** = **hinder**, burden, encumber, hamper, hamstring, hold back, impede, limit, restrict

handle ❶ n 1 part of an object that is held so that it can be used. ▷ v 2 hold, feel, or move with the hands. 3 control or deal with. **handler** n person who controls an animal. **handlebars** pl n curved metal bar used to steer a cycle.

handsome ❶ adj 1 (esp. of a man) good-looking. 2 large or generous, e.g. *a handsome profit*.

hang ❶ v hanging, hung 1 attach or be attached at the top with the lower part free. 2 past hanged suspend or be suspended by the neck until dead. 3 fasten to a wall. **get the hang of** informal begin to understand. **hanger** n curved piece of wood, wire, or plastic, with a hook, for hanging up clothes (also **coat hanger**). **hang back** v hesitate, be reluctant. **hangman** n man who executes people by hanging. **hangover** n headache and nausea as a result of drinking too much alcohol. **hang-up** n informal emotional or psychological problem.

hangar n large shed for storing aircraft.

hanker ❶ v (foll. by after) desire intensely.

hanky, hankie n, pl hankies informal handkerchief.

haphazard ❶ adj not organized or planned.

hapless adj unlucky.

happen ❶ v 1 take place, occur. 2 chance (to be or do something). **happening** n event, occurrence.

happy ❶ adj -pier, -piest 1 feeling or causing joy. 2 lucky, fortunate. **happily** adv **happiness** n **happy-go-lucky** adj carefree and cheerful.

harangue ❶ v 1 address angrily or forcefully. ▷ n 2 angry or forceful speech.

harass ❶ v annoy or trouble constantly. **harassed** adj **harassment** n.

- SPELLING TIP
- The commonest misspelling of **harass**
- is *harrass*. There should be only one r,
- but it's obviously difficult to remember:
- there are 232 instances of *harrassment* in
- the Bank of English and 10 of *harrasment*.
- The correct spelling is **harassment**.

harbour ❶ n 1 sheltered port. ▷ v 2 maintain secretly in the mind. 3 give shelter or protection to.

——— THESAURUS ———

handle n 1 = **grip**, haft, hilt, stock ▷ v 2 = **hold**, feel, finger, grasp, pick up, touch 3 = **control**, cope with, deal with, direct, guide, manage, manipulate, manoeuvre

handsome adj 1 = **good-looking**, attractive, comely, dishy (inf, chiefly Brit), elegant, gorgeous, personable 2 = **generous**, abundant, ample, considerable, large, liberal, plentiful, sizable or sizeable

hang v 1 = **suspend**, dangle, droop 2 = **execute**, lynch, string up (inf) **get the hang of** Inf = **grasp**, comprehend, understand

hanker v (foll. by after) = **desire**, crave, hunger, itch, long, lust, pine, thirst, yearn

haphazard adj = **unsystematic**, aimless, casual, disorganized, hit or miss (inf), indiscriminate, slapdash

happen v 1 = **occur**, come about, come to pass, develop, result, take place, transpire (inf) 2 = **chance**, turn out

happy adj 1 = **joyful**, blissful, cheerful, content, delighted, ecstatic, elated, glad, jubilant, merry, overjoyed, pleased, thrilled 2 = **fortunate**, advantageous, auspicious, favourable, lucky, timely

harangue v 1 = **rant**, address, declaim, exhort, hold forth, lecture, spout (inf) ▷ n 2 = **speech**, address, declamation, diatribe, exhortation, tirade

harass v = **annoy**, bother, harry, hassle (inf), hound, persecute, pester, plague, trouble, vex

harbour n 1 = **port**, anchorage, haven ▷ v 2 = **maintain**, cling to, entertain, foster, hold, nurse, nurture, retain 3 = **shelter**, hide, protect, provide refuge, shield

h

hard ❶ *adj* 1 firm, solid, or rigid. 2 difficult. 3 requiring a lot of effort. 4 unkind, unfeeling. 5 causing pain, sorrow, or hardship. 6 (of water) containing calcium salts which stop soap lathering freely. 7 (of a drug) strong and addictive. ▷ *adv* 8 with great energy or effort. 9 with great intensity. **hard drive** *Computers* mechanism that handles the reading, writing, and storage of data on the hard disk. **hard of hearing** unable to hear properly. **hard up** *informal* short of money. **harden** *v* **hardness** *n* **hardship** *n* 1 suffering. 2 difficult circumstances. **hard-bitten** *adj* tough and determined. **hard-boiled** *adj* 1 (of an egg) boiled until solid. 2 *informal* tough, unemotional. **hard copy** computer output printed on paper. **hard disk** *Computers* inflexible disk in a sealed container. **hard drive** *Computers* mechanism that handles the reading, writing, and storage of data on the hard disk. **hard-headed** *adj* shrewd, practical. **hardhearted** *adj* unsympathetic, uncaring. **hard sell** aggressive sales technique. **hard shoulder** surfaced verge at the edge of a motorway for emergency stops.

hardy ❶ *adj* **hardier**, **hardiest** able to stand difficult conditions. **hardiness** *n*.

hare *n* 1 animal like a large rabbit, with longer ears and legs. ▷ *v* 2 (usu. foll. by *off*) run (away) quickly. **harebell** *n* blue bell-shaped flower. **harebrained** *adj* foolish or impractical. **harelip** *n* slight split in the upper lip.

harem *n* (apartments of) a Muslim man's wives and concubines.

hark *v old-fashioned* listen. **hark back** *v* return (to an earlier subject).

harlequin *n* 1 stock comic character with a diamond-patterned costume and mask. ▷ *adj* 2 in many colours.

harlot *n lit* prostitute.

harm ❶ *v* 1 injure physically, mentally, or morally. ▷ *n* 2 physical, mental, or moral injury. **harmful** *adj* **harmless** *adj*.

harmony ❶ *n, pl* **-nies** 1 peaceful agreement and cooperation. 2 pleasant combination of notes sounded at the same time. **harmonious** *adj* **harmonic** *adj* of harmony. **harmonics** *n* science of musical sounds. **harmonize** *v* blend well together.

harness ❶ *n* 1 arrangement of straps for attaching a horse to a cart or plough. 2 set of straps fastened round someone's body to attach something, e.g. *a safety harness.* ▷ *v* 3 put a harness on. 4 control (something) in order to make use of it.

harp *n* large triangular stringed instrument played with the fingers. **harpist** *n* **harp on about** *v* talk about continuously.

————————————— THESAURUS —————————————

hard *adj* 1 = **tough**, firm, inflexible, rigid, rocklike, solid, stiff, strong, unyielding 2 = **difficult**, complicated, intricate, involved, knotty, perplexing, puzzling, thorny 3 = **strenuous**, arduous, backbreaking, exacting, exhausting, laborious, rigorous, tough 4 = **harsh**, callous, cold, cruel, hardhearted, pitiless, stern, unfeeling, unkind, unsympathetic 5 = **grim**, disagreeable, distressing, grievous, intolerable, painful, unpleasant ▷ *adv* 8, 9 = **energetically**, fiercely, forcefully, forcibly, heavily, intensely, powerfully, severely, sharply, strongly, vigorously, violently, with all one's might,

with might and main

hardy *adj* = **strong**, robust, rugged, sound, stout, sturdy, tough

harm *v* 1 = **injure**, abuse, damage, hurt, ill-treat, maltreat, ruin, spoil, wound *n* 2 = **injury**, abuse, damage, hurt, ill, loss, mischief, misfortune

harmony *n* 1 = **agreement**, accord, amicability, compatibility, concord, cooperation, friendship, peace, rapport, sympathy 2 = **tunefulness**, euphony, melody, tune, unison

harness *n* 1 = **tack** 2 = **equipment**, gear, tackle ▷ *v* 4 = **exploit**, channel, control, employ, mobilize, utilize

harpoon *n* **1** barbed spear attached to a rope used for hunting whales. ▷ *v* **2** spear with a harpoon.

harrier *n* cross-country runner.

harrow *n* **1** implement used to break up lumps of soil. ▷ *v* **2** draw a harrow over.

harry *v*-**rying**, -**ried** keep asking (someone) to do something, pester.

harsh ❶ *adj* **1** severe and difficult to cope with. **2** unkind, unsympathetic. **3** extremely hard, bright, or rough. **harshly** *adv* **harshness** *n*.

harvest ❶ *n* **1** (season for) the gathering of crops. **2** crops gathered. ▷ *v* **3** gather (a ripened crop). **harvester** *n*.

has *v* third person singular of the present tense of HAVE. **has-been** *n* *informal* person who is no longer popular or successful.

hash ❶ *n* dish of diced cooked meat and vegetables reheated. **make a hash of** *informal* spoil, do badly.

hashish [**hash**-eesh] *n* drug made from the cannabis plant, smoked for its intoxicating effects.

hassle ❶ *informal* ▷ *n* **1** trouble, bother. ▷ *v* **2** bother or annoy.

hassock *n* cushion for kneeling on in church.

haste ❶ *n* (excessive) quickness. **hasten** *v* (cause to) hurry. **hasty** *adj* (too) quick. **hastily** *adv*.

hat *n* covering for the head, often with a brim, usu. worn to give protection from the weather. **keep something under one's hat** keep something secret. **hat trick** any three successive achievements, esp. in sport.

hatch¹ ❶ *v* **1** (cause to) emerge from an egg. **2** devise (a plot).

hatch² *n* **1** hinged door covering an opening in a floor or wall. **2** opening in the wall between a kitchen and a dining area. **3** door in an aircraft or spacecraft. **hatchback** *n* car with a lifting door at the back. **hatchway** *n* opening in the deck of a ship.

hatchet *n* small axe. **bury the hatchet** become reconciled. **hatchet job** malicious verbal or written attack. **hatchet man** *informal* person carrying out unpleasant tasks for an employer.

hate ❶ *v* **1** dislike intensely. **2** be unwilling (to do something). ▷ *n* **3** intense dislike. **4** person or thing hated. **hateful** *adj* causing or deserving hate. **hater** *n* **hatred** *n* intense dislike.

haughty ❶ *adj*-**tier**, -**tiest** proud, arrogant. **haughtily** *adv* **haughtiness** *n*.

THESAURUS

---

harry *v* = **pester**, badger, bother, chivvy, harass, hassle (*inf*), plague

harsh *adj* **1, 2** = **severe**, austere, cruel, Draconian, drastic, hard, pitiless, punitive, ruthless, stern, tough **3** = **raucous**, discordant, dissonant, grating, guttural, rasping, rough, strident

harvest *n* **1 a** = **gathering**, harvesting, harvest-time, reaping **b** = **crop**, produce, yield ▷ *v* **2** = **gather**, mow, pick, pluck, reap

hash *n* **make a hash of** *Inf* = **mess up**, botch, bungle, make a pig's ear of (*inf*), mishandle, mismanage, muddle

hassle *Inf n* **1** = **trouble**, bother, difficulty, grief (*inf*), inconvenience, problem ▷ *v* **3** = **bother**, annoy, badger, bug (*inf*), harass, hound, pester

haste *n* = **speed**, alacrity, hurry, impetuosity, quickness, rapidity, rush, swiftness, urgency, velocity

hatch¹ *v* **1** = **incubate**, breed, bring forth, brood **2** = **devise**, conceive, concoct, contrive, cook up (*inf*), design, dream up (*inf*), think up

hate *v* **1** = **detest**, abhor, despise, dislike, loathe, recoil from **2** = **be unwilling**, be loath, be reluctant, be sorry, dislike, feel disinclined, shrink from ▷ *n* **3** = **dislike**, animosity, antipathy, aversion, detestation, enmity, hatred, hostility, loathing

haughty *adj* = **proud**, arrogant, conceited, contemptuous, disdainful, imperious, scornful, snooty (*inf*), stuck-up (*inf*), supercilious

haul ❶ v 1 pull or drag with effort. ▷ n
2 amount gained by effort or theft.
long haul something that takes a lot of
time and effort. **haulage** n (charge for)
transporting goods. **haulier** n firm or
person that transports goods by road.

haunch n human hip or fleshy hindquarter
of an animal.

haunt ❶ v 1 visit in the form of a ghost.
2 remain in the memory or thoughts of.
▷ n 3 place visited frequently. **haunted**
adj 1 frequented by ghosts. 2 worried.
haunting adj memorably beautiful or sad.

have ❶ v **has, having, had** 1 possess, hold.
2 receive, take, or obtain. 3 experience or
be affected by. 4 (foll. by to) be obliged,
must, e.g. I had to go. 5 cause to be done.
6 give birth to. 7 slang cheat or outwit.
8 used to form past tenses (with a past
participle), e.g. we have looked; she had
done enough. **have it out** informal settle a
matter by argument. **have on** v 1 wear.
2 informal tease or trick. **have up** v bring
to trial.

haven ❶ n place of safety.

haversack n canvas bag carried on the
back or shoulder.

havoc ❶ n disorder and confusion.

hawk¹ n 1 bird of prey with a short

hooked bill and very good eyesight.
2 Politics supporter or advocate of warlike
policies. **hawkish, hawklike** adj **hawk-
eyed** adj having very good eyesight.

hawk² v offer (goods) for sale in the street
or door-to-door. **hawker** n.

hawthorn n thorny shrub or tree.

hay n grass cut and dried as fodder.
hay fever allergy to pollen, causing
sneezing and watery eyes. **haystack** n
large pile of stored hay. **haywire** adj **go
haywire** informal not function properly.

hazard ❶ n 1 something that could be
dangerous. ▷ v 2 put in danger. 3 make (a
guess). **hazardous** adj.

haze ❶ n mist, often caused by heat. **hazy**
adj 1 not clear, misty. 2 confused or vague.

hazel n 1 small tree producing edible
nuts. ▷ adj 2 (of eyes) greenish-brown.
hazelnut n.

he pron refers to: 1 male person or animal.
2 person or animal of unspecified sex.

head ❶ n 1 upper or front part of the body,
containing the sense organs and the brain.
2 mind and mental abilities. 3 upper or
most forward part of anything. 4 person
in charge of a group, organization, or
school. 5 pus-filled tip of a spot or boil.
6 white froth on beer. 7 pl **head** person or

──────────────── THESAURUS ────────────────

haul v 1 = **drag**, draw, heave, lug, pull, tug
▷ n 2 = **yield**, booty, catch, gain, harvest,
loot, spoils, takings

haunt v 2 = **plague**, obsess, possess,
prey on, recur, stay with, torment,
trouble, weigh on ▷ n 3 = **meeting place**,
rendezvous, stamping ground

have v 1 = **possess**, hold, keep, obtain,
own, retain 2 = **receive**, accept, acquire,
gain, get, obtain, procure, secure, take
3 = **experience**, endure, enjoy, feel, meet
with, suffer, sustain, undergo 4 (foll. by to)
= **be obliged**, be bound, be compelled, be
forced, have got to, must, ought, should
6 = **give birth to**, bear, beget, bring forth,
deliver 7 Sl = **cheat**, deceive, dupe, fool,
outwit, swindle, take in (inf), trick

haven n = **sanctuary**, asylum, refuge,
retreat, sanctum, shelter

havoc n = **disorder**, chaos, confusion,
disruption, mayhem, shambles

hazard n 1 = **danger**, jeopardy, peril,
pitfall, risk, threat ▷ v 2 = **jeopardize**,
endanger, expose, imperil, risk, threaten
3 = **conjecture**, advance, offer, presume,
throw out, venture, volunteer

haze n = **mist**, cloud, fog, obscurity, vapour

head n 1 = **skull**, crown, loaf (sl), nut (sl),
pate 2 = **mind**, brain, brains (inf), intellect,
intelligence, thought, understanding
3 = **top**, crest, crown, peak, pinnacle,
summit, tip 4 = **leader**, boss (inf),
captain, chief, commander, director,
manager, master, principal, supervisor

animal considered as a unit. **8** headline or heading. **9** *informal* headache. ▷ *adj* **10** chief, principal. ▷ *v* **11** be at the top or front of. **12** be in charge of. **13** move (in a particular direction). **14** hit (a ball) with the head. **15** provide with a heading. **go to one's head** make one drunk or conceited. **head over heels (in love)** very much in love. **not make head nor tail of** not understand. **heads** *adv informal* with the side of a coin which has a portrait of a head on it uppermost. **header** *n* **1** striking a ball with the head. **2** headlong fall. **heading** *n* title written or printed at the top of a page. **heady** *adj* intoxicating or exciting. **headache** *n* **1** continuous pain in the head. **2** cause of worry or annoyance. **headboard** *n* vertical board at the top end of a bed. **headdress** *n* decorative head covering. **head-hunt** *v* (of a company) approach and offer a job to (a person working for a rival company). **head-hunter** *n* **headland** *n* area of land jutting out into the sea. **headlight** *n* powerful light on the front of a vehicle. **headline** *n* **1** title at the top of a newspaper article, esp. on the front page. ▷ *pl* **2** main points of a news broadcast. **headlong** *adv, adj* **1** with the

head first. **2** hastily. **headphones** *pl n* two small loudspeakers held against the ears by a strap. **headquarters** *pl n* centre from which operations are directed. **head start** advantage in a competition. **headstone** *n* memorial stone on a grave. **headstrong** *adj* self-willed, obstinate. **headway** *n* progress. **headwind** *n* wind blowing against the course of an aircraft or ship.

heal ❶ *v* make or become well.

health ❶ *n* normal (good) condition of someone's body. **healthy** *adj* **healthier**, **healthiest 1** having good health. **2** of or producing good health. **3** functioning well, sound.

heap ❶ *n* **1** pile of things one on top of another. **2** (also **heaps**) large number or quantity. ▷ *v* **3** gather into a pile. **4** (foll. by *on*) give liberally (to).

hear ❶ *v* **hearing, heard 1** perceive (a sound) by ear. **2** listen to. **3** learn or be informed. **4** *Law* try (a case). **hear! hear!** exclamation of approval or agreement. **hearing** *n* **1** ability to hear. **2** trial of a case. **within hearing** close enough to be heard.

hearken *v obs* listen.

hearse *n* funeral car used to carry a coffin.

heart ❶ *n* **1** organ that pumps blood round the body. **2** centre of emotions, esp.

▷ *adj* **10** = **chief**, arch, first, leading, main, pre-eminent, premier, prime, principal, supreme ▷ *v* **11** = **lead**, be *or* go first, cap, crown, lead the way, precede, top **12** = **be in charge of**, command, control, direct, govern, guide, head, lead, manage, run **13** = **make for**, aim, go to, make a beeline for, point, set off for, set out, start towards, steer, turn **go to one's head** = **excite**, intoxicate, make conceited, puff up **head over heels** = **completely**, intensely, thoroughly, uncontrollably, utterly, wholeheartedly

heal *v* = **cure**, make well, mend, regenerate, remedy, restore, treat

health *n* **a** = **condition**, constitution, fettle, shape, state **b** = **wellbeing**, fitness,

good condition, healthiness, robustness, soundness, strength, vigour

heap *n* **1** = **pile**, accumulation, collection, hoard, lot, mass, mound, stack **2** (also **heaps**) = **a lot**, great deal, load(s) (*inf*), lots (*inf*), mass, plenty, pot(s) (*inf*), stack(s), tons ▷ *v* **3** = **pile**, accumulate, amass, collect, gather, hoard, stack **4** (foll. by *on*) = **confer**, assign, bestow, load, shower upon

hear *v* **1** = **perceive**, catch, overhear **2** = **listen to 3** = **learn**, ascertain, discover, find out, gather, get wind of (*inf*), pick up **4** *Law* = **try**, examine, investigate, judge

heart *n* **2** = **nature**, character, disposition, soul, temperament **3** = **courage**, bravery, fortitude, pluck, purpose, resolution,

love. **3** courage, spirit. **4** central or most important part. **5** figure representing a heart. **6** playing card with red heart heart-shaped symbols. **break someone's heart** cause someone great grief. **by heart** from memory. **set one's heart on something** greatly desire something. **take something to heart** be upset about something. **hearten** v encourage, make cheerful. **heartless** adj cruel, unkind. **hearty** adj **1** substantial, nourishing. **2** friendly, enthusiastic. **heartily** adv **heart attack** sudden severe malfunction of the heart. **heart failure** sudden stopping of the heartbeat. **heart-rending** adj causing great sorrow. **heart-throb** n slang very attractive man, esp. a film or pop star.

hearth n floor of a fireplace.

heat ① v 1 make or become hot. ▷ n **2** state of being hot. **3** energy transferred as a result of a difference in temperature. **4** hot weather. **5** intensity of feeling. **6** preliminary eliminating contest in a competition. **on, in heat** (of some female animals) ready for mating. **heated** adj angry and excited. **heater** n.

heath n area of open uncultivated land.

heathen ① adj, n (of) a person who does not believe in an established religion.

heather n low-growing plant with small purple, pinkish, or white flowers, growing on heaths and mountains.

heave ① v 1 lift with effort. **2** throw (something heavy). **3** utter (a sigh). **4** rise and fall. **5** vomit. ▷ n **6** heaving.

heaven ① n 1 place believed to be the home of God, where good people go when they die. **2** place or state of bliss. **the heavens** sky. **heavenly** adj **1** of or like heaven. **2** of or occurring in space. **3** wonderful or beautiful.

heavy ① adj heavier, heaviest 1 of great weight. **2** having a high density. **3** great in degree or amount. **4** informal (of a situation) serious. **heavily** adv **heaviness** n **heavy industry** large-scale production of raw material or machinery. **heavy metal** very loud rock music featuring guitar riffs. **heavyweight** n boxer weighing over 175lb (professional) or 81kg (amateur).

heckle ① v interrupt (a public speaker) with comments, questions, or taunts. **heckler** n.

hectare n one hundred ares or 10 000 square metres (2.471 acres).

hectic ① adj rushed or busy.

hedge ① n 1 row of bushes forming a barrier or boundary. ▷ v **2** be evasive or noncommittal. **3** (foll. by against) protect

━━━━━━━━━━━━━━━━━━━━━━━ THESAURUS ━━━━━━━━━━━━━

spirit, will **4 = centre**, core, hub, middle, nucleus, quintessence **by heart = by memory**, by rote, off pat, parrot-fashion (inf), pat, word for word
heat v **1 = warm up**, make hot, reheat n **2 = hotness**, high temperature, warmth **5 = passion**, excitement, fervour, fury, intensity, vehemence
heathen adj **= pagan**, godless, idolatrous, irreligious ▷ n **= pagan**, infidel, unbeliever
heave v **1 = lift**, drag (up), haul (up), hoist, pull (up), raise, tug **2 = throw**, cast, fling, hurl, pitch, send, sling, toss **3 = sigh**, groan, puff **5 = vomit**, be sick, gag, retch, spew, throw up (inf)
heaven n **1 = paradise**, bliss, Elysium

or Elysian fields (Greek myth), hereafter, life everlasting, next world, nirvana (Buddhism, Hinduism), Zion (Christianity) **2 = happiness**, bliss, ecstasy, paradise, rapture, seventh heaven, utopia **the heavens = sky**, ether, firmament
heavy adj **1 = weighty**, bulky, hefty, massive, ponderous **3 = considerable**, abundant, copious, excessive, large, profuse
heckle v **= jeer**, barrack (inf), boo, disrupt, interrupt, shout down, taunt
hectic adj **= frantic**, animated, chaotic, feverish, frenetic, heated, turbulent
hedge n **1 = hedgerow** ▷ v **2 = dodge**, duck, equivocate, evade, flannel (Brit inf),

oneself (from). **hedgerow** n bushes forming a hedge.

hedonism n doctrine that pleasure is the most important thing in life. **hedonist** n **hedonistic** adj.

heed ⊕ n 1 careful attention. ▷ v 2 pay careful attention to. **heedless** adj **heedless of** taking no notice of.

heel¹ ⊕ n 1 back part of the foot. 2 part of a shoe supporting the heel. 3 slang contemptible person. ▷ v 4 repair the heel of (a shoe). **heeler** n Aust & NZ dog that herds cattle by biting at their heels.

heel² ⊕ v (foll. by over) lean to one side.

hefty ⊕ adj **heftier, heftiest** large, heavy, or strong.

heifer [**hef**-fer] n young cow.

height ⊕ n 1 distance from base to top. 2 distance above sea level. 3 highest degree or topmost point. **heighten** v make or become higher or more intense.

heinous adj evil and shocking.

heir ⊕ n person entitled to inherit property or rank. **heiress** n fem **heirloom** n object that has belonged to a family for generations.

helicopter n aircraft lifted and propelled by rotating overhead blades. **heliport** n airport for helicopters.

helium [**heel**-ee-um] n Chem very light colourless odourless gas.

helix [**heel**-iks] n, pl **helices, helixes** spiral.

hell ⊕ n 1 place believed to be where wicked people go when they die. 2 place or state of wickedness, suffering, or punishment. **hell for leather** at great speed. **hellish** adj **hellbent** adj (foll. by on) intent.

hello ⊕ interj expression of greeting or surprise.

helm ⊕ n tiller or wheel for steering a ship.

helmet n hard hat worn for protection.

help ⊕ v 1 make something easier, better, or quicker for (someone). 2 improve (a situation). 3 refrain from, e.g. I can't help smiling. ▷ n 4 assistance or support. **help oneself 1** take something, esp. food or drink, without being served. 2 informal steal something. **helper** n **helpful** adj **helping** n single portion of food. **helpless** adj weak or incapable. **helpline** n telephone line set aside for callers to contact an organization for help with a problem. **helpmate** n companion and helper, esp. a husband or wife.

h

— THESAURUS —

prevaricate, sidestep, temporize 3 (foll. by against) = **insure**, cover, guard, protect, safeguard, shield

heed n 1 = **care**, attention, caution, mind, notice, regard, respect, thought v 2 = **pay attention to**, bear in mind, consider, follow, listen to, note, obey, observe, take notice of

heel¹ n 3 Sl = **swine**, bounder (old-fashioned Brit sl), cad (Brit inf), rotter (sl, chiefly Brit)

heel² (foll. by over) v = **lean over**, keel over, list, tilt

hefty adj = **big**, burly, hulking, massive, muscular, robust, strapping, strong

height n 1, 2 = **altitude**, elevation, highness, loftiness, stature, tallness 3 **a** = **culmination**, climax, limit, maximum, ultimate **b** = **peak**, apex, crest, crown, pinnacle, summit, top, zenith

heir n = **successor**, beneficiary, heiress (fem), inheritor, next in line

hell n 1 = **underworld**, abyss, fire and brimstone, Hades (Greek myth), hellfire, inferno, nether world 2 = **torment**, agony, anguish, misery, nightmare, ordeal, suffering, wretchedness

hello interj = **hi** (inf), gidday (Aust & NZ), good afternoon, good evening, good morning, greetings, how do you do?, welcome

helm n = **tiller**, rudder, wheel **at the helm** = **in charge**, at the wheel, in command, in control, in the driving seat, in the saddle

help v 1 = **aid**, abet, assist, cooperate, lend a hand, succour, support 2 = **improve**, alleviate, ameliorate, ease, facilitate, mitigate, relieve 3 = **refrain from**, avoid, keep from, prevent, resist ▷ n

helter-skelter ❶ *adj* **1** haphazard and careless. ▷ *adv* **2** in a haphazard and careless manner. ▷ *n* **3** high spiral slide at a fairground.

hem ❶ *n* **1** bottom edge of a garment, folded under and stitched down. ▷ *v* **hemming, hemmed 2** provide with a hem. **hem in** *v* surround and prevent from moving.

hemisphere *n* half of a sphere, esp. the earth.

hemlock *n* poison made from a plant with spotted stems and small white flowers.

hemp *n* **1** (also **cannabis**) Asian plant with tough fibres. **2** its fibre, used to make canvas and rope. **3** narcotic drug obtained from hemp.

hen *n* **1** female domestic fowl. **2** female of any bird. **hen night, party** party for women only. **henpecked** *adj* (of a man) dominated by his wife.

hence ❶ *conj* **1** for this reason. ▷ *adv* **2** from this time. **henceforth** *adv* from now on.

henchman ❶ *n* attendant or follower.

henna *n* reddish dye made from a shrub or tree.

hepatitis *n* inflammation of the liver.

heptagon *n* geometric figure with seven sides.

her *pron* **1** refers to a female person or animal or anything personified as feminine when the object of a sentence or clause. ▷ *adj* **2** belonging to her.

herald ❶ *n* **1** person who announces important news. **2** forerunner. ▷ *v* **3** signal the approach of. **heraldry** *n* study of coats of arms and family trees. **heraldic** *adj*.

herb *n* plant used for flavouring in cookery, and in medicine. **herbal** *adj* **herbalist** *n* person who grows or specializes in the use of medicinal herbs. **herbaceous** *adj* (of a plant) soft-stemmed. **herbicide** *n* chemical used to destroy plants, esp. weeds. **herbivore** *n* animal that eats only plants. **herbivorous** [her-**biv**-or-uss] *adj*.

herd ❶ *n* **1** group of animals feeding and living together. **2** large crowd of people. ▷ *v* **3** collect into a herd. **herdsman** *n* man who looks after a herd of animals.

here *adv* in, at, or to this place or point. **hereabouts** *adv* near here. **hereafter** *adv* after this point or time. **the hereafter** life after death. **hereby** *adv* by means of or as a result of this. **herein** *adv* in this place, matter, or document. **herewith** *adv* with this.

heredity ❶ [hir-**red**-it-ee] *n* passing on of characteristics from one generation to another. **hereditary** *adj* **1** passed on genetically from one generation to another. **2** passed on by inheritance.

● **SPELLING TIP**
● There are several ways to misspell
● **hereditary**. The problems always come
● after the *t*, where there should be three
● more letters: -*ary*.

─────────────── THESAURUS ───────────

4 = **assistance**, advice, aid, cooperation, guidance, helping hand, support

helter-skelter *adj* **1** = **haphazard**, confused, disordered, higgledy-piggledy (*inf*), hit-or-miss, jumbled, muddled, random, topsy-turvy ▷ *adv* **2** = **carelessly**, anyhow, hastily, headlong, hurriedly, pell-mell, rashly, recklessly, wildly

hem *n* **1** = **edge**, border, fringe, margin, trimming

hence *conj* **1** = **therefore**, ergo, for this reason, on that account, thus

henchman *n* = **attendant**, associate,

bodyguard, follower, minder (*sl*), right-hand man, sidekick (*sl*), subordinate, supporter

herald *n* **1** = **messenger**, crier **2** = **forerunner**, harbinger, indication, omen, precursor, sign, signal, token ▷ *v* **3** = **indicate**, foretoken, portend, presage, promise, show, usher in

herd *n* **1** = **flock**, drove **2** = **crowd**, collection, horde, mass, mob, multitude, swarm, throng ▷ *v* **3** = **congregate**, assemble, collect, flock, gather, huddle, muster, rally

heredity *n* = **genetics**, constitution, genetic make-up, inheritance

heresy ❶ [**herr**-iss-ee] *n, pl* **-sies** opinion contrary to accepted opinion or belief. **heretic** [**herr**-it-ik] *n* person who holds unorthodox opinions. **heretical** [hir-**ret**-ik-al] *adj*.

heritage ❶ *n* 1 something inherited. 2 anything from the past, considered as the inheritance of present-day society.

hermaphrodite [her-**maf**-roe-dite] *n* animal, plant, or person with both male and female reproductive organs.

hermetic *adj* sealed so as to be airtight. **hermetically** *adv*.

hermit ❶ *n* person living in solitude, esp. for religious purposes. **hermitage** *n* home of a hermit.

hernia *n* protrusion of an organ or part through the lining of the surrounding body cavity.

hero ❶ *n, pl* **heroes** 1 principal character in a film, book, etc. 2 man greatly admired for his exceptional qualities or achievements. **heroine** *n fem* **heroic** *adj* 1 courageous. 2 of or like a hero. **heroics** *pl n* extravagant behaviour. **heroically** *adv* **heroism** [**herr**-oh-izz-um] *n*.

heroin *n* highly addictive drug derived from morphine.

heron *n* long-legged wading bird.

herring *n* important food fish of northern seas. **herringbone** *n* pattern of zigzag lines.

hertz *n, pl* **hertz** *Physics* unit of frequency.

hesitate ❶ *v* 1 be slow or uncertain in doing something. 2 be reluctant (to do something). **hesitation** *n* **hesitant** *adj* undecided or wavering. **hesitancy** *n*.

hessian *n* coarse jute fabric.

heterogeneous [het-er-oh-**jean**-ee-uss] *adj* composed of diverse elements. **heterogeneity** *n*.

heterosexual *n, adj* (person) sexually attracted to members of the opposite sex.

hew ❶ *v* **hewing, hewed, hewed** or **hewn** 1 cut with an axe. 2 carve from a substance.

hexagon *n* geometric figure with six sides. **hexagonal** *adj*.

hey *interj* expression of surprise or for catching attention.

heyday ❶ *n* time of greatest success, prime.

HI Hawaii.

hiatus ❶ [hie-**ay**-tuss] *n, pl* **-tuses, -tus** pause or interruption in continuity.

hibernate *v* (of an animal) pass the winter as if in a deep sleep. **hibernation** *n*.

hiccup, hiccough *n* 1 spasm of the breathing organs with a sharp coughlike sound. 2 *informal* small problem, hitch. ▷ *v* 3 make a hiccup.

hickory *n, pl* **-ries** 1 N American nut-bearing tree. 2 its wood.

hide ❶ *v* **hiding, hid, hidden** 1 put (oneself or an object) somewhere difficult to

heresy *n* = **unorthodoxy**, apostasy, dissidence, heterodoxy, iconoclasm

heritage *n* 1 = **inheritance**, bequest, birthright, endowment, legacy

hermit *n* = **recluse**, anchorite, loner (*inf*), monk

hero *n* 1 = **leading man**, protagonist 2 = **idol**, champion, conqueror, star, superstar, victor

hesitate *v* 1 = **waver**, delay, dither, doubt, hum and haw, pause, vacillate, wait 2 = **be reluctant**, balk, be unwilling, demur, hang back, scruple, shrink from, think twice

hew *v* 1 = **cut**, axe, chop, hack, lop, split

2 = **carve**, fashion, form, make, model, sculpt, sculpture, shape, smooth

heyday *n* = **prime**, bloom, pink, prime of life, salad days

hiatus *n* = **pause**, break, discontinuity, gap, interruption, interval, respite, space

hide¹ *v* 1 **a** = **go into hiding**, go to ground, go underground, hole up, lie low, take cover **b** = **conceal**, camouflage, cloak, cover, disguise, mask, obscure, secrete, shroud, stash (*inf*), veil 2 = **suppress**, draw a veil over, hush up, keep dark, keep secret, keep under one's hat, withhold

see or find. **2** keep secret. ▷ *n* **3** place of concealment, esp. for a bird-watcher. **hiding** *n* state of concealment, e.g. *in hiding*. **hide-out** *n* place to hide in.

hide² ❶ *n* skin of an animal. **hiding** *n slang* severe beating. **hidebound** *adj* unwilling to accept new ideas.

hideous ❶ [hid-ee-uss] *adj* ugly, revolting.

hierarchy ❶ [hire-ark-ee] *n, pl* **-chies** system of people or things arranged in a graded order. **hierarchical** *adj*.

hieroglyphic [hire-oh-**gliff**-ik] *adj* **1** of a form of writing using picture symbols, as used in ancient Egypt. ▷ *n* **2** symbol that is difficult to decipher. **3** (also **hieroglyph**) symbol representing an object, idea, or sound.

hi-fi *n* **1** set of high-quality sound-reproducing equipment. ▷ *adj* **2** high-fidelity.

high ❶ *adj* **1** of a great height. **2** far above ground or sea level. **3** being at its peak. **4** greater than usual in intensity or amount. **5** (of a sound) acute in pitch. **6** (of food) slightly decomposed. **7** of great importance, quality, or rank. **8** *informal* under the influence of alcohol or drugs. ▷ *adv* **9** at or to a high level. **highly** *adv* **highly strung** nervous and easily upset.

Highness *n* title used to address or refer to a royal person. **higher education** education at colleges and universities. **high-fidelity** *adj* able to reproduce sound with little or no distortion. **high-flown** *adj* (of language) extravagant or pretentious. **high-handed** *adj* excessively forceful. **high-rise** *adj* (of a building) having many storeys. **high tea** early evening meal consisting of a cooked dish, bread, cakes, and tea. **high time** latest possible time.

hijack ❶ *v* seize control of (an aircraft or other vehicle) while travelling. **hijacker** *n*.

hike ❶ *n* **1** long walk in the country, esp. for pleasure. ▷ *v* **2** go for a long walk. **3** (foll. by *up*) pull (up) or raise. **hiker** *n*.

hill ❶ *n* raised part of the earth's surface, less high than a mountain. **hilly** *adj* **hillock** *n* small hill. **hillbilly** *n US* unsophisticated country person.

hilt ❶ *n* handle of a sword or knife.

him *pron* refers to a male person or animal when the object of a sentence or clause.

hind¹ *adj* **hinder**, **hindmost** situated at the back.

hind² *n* female deer.

hinder ❶ *v* get in the way of. **hindrance** *n*.

hinge ❶ *n* **1** device for holding together two parts so that one can swing freely. ▷ *v*

──────────── THESAURUS ────────────

hide² *n* = **skin**, pelt

hideous *adj* = **ugly**, ghastly, grim, grisly, grotesque, gruesome, monstrous, repulsive, revolting, unsightly

hierarchy *n* = **grading**, pecking order, ranking

high *adj* **1, 2** = **tall**, elevated, lofty, soaring, steep, towering **4** = **extreme**, excessive, extraordinary, great, intensified, sharp, strong **5** = **high-pitched**, acute, penetrating, piercing, piping, sharp, shrill, strident **7** = **important**, arch, chief, eminent, exalted, powerful, superior, skookum (*Canad*) **8** *Inf* = **intoxicated**, stoned (*sl*), tripping (*inf*) ▷ *adv* **9** = **aloft**, at great height, far up, way up

hijack *v* = **seize**, commandeer, expropriate,

take over

hike *n* **1** = **walk**, march, ramble, tramp, trek ▷ *v* **2** = **walk**, back-pack, ramble, tramp **3** (foll. by *up*) = **raise**, hitch up, jack up, lift, pull up

hill *n* = **mount**, fell, height, hillock, hilltop, knoll, mound, tor

hilt *n* = **handle**, grip, haft, handgrip

hinder *v* = **obstruct**, block, check, delay, encumber, frustrate, hamper, handicap, hold up *or* back, impede, interrupt, stop

hinder, hindmost *adj* = **last**, final, furthest, furthest behind, rearmost, trailing

hinge *v* **2** (foll. by *on*) = **depend on**, be contingent on, hang on, pivot on, rest on, revolve around, turn on

2 (foll. by *on*) depend (on). 3 fit a hinge to.

hint ❶ *n* 1 indirect suggestion. 2 piece of advice. 3 small amount. ▷ *v* 4 suggest indirectly.

hinterland *n* land lying behind a coast or near a port, esp. a port.

hip[1] *n* either side of the body between the waist and the thigh.

hip[2] *n* rosehip.

hip[3] *adj* **hipper**, **hippest** *slang* aware of or following the latest trends.

hippie *adj, n* same as HIPPY.

hippopotamus *n, pl* **-muses**, **-mi** large African mammal with thick wrinkled skin, living near rivers.

hire ❶ *v* 1 pay to have temporary use of. 2 employ for wages. ▷ *n* 3 hiring. **for hire** available to be hired. **hireling** *n* person who works only for wages. **hire-purchase** *n* system of purchase by which the buyer pays for goods by instalments.

hirsute [**her**-suit] *adj* hairy.

his *pron, adj* (something) belonging to him.

hiss ❶ *n* 1 sound like that of a long *s* (as an expression of contempt). ▷ *v* 2 utter a hiss. 3 show derision or anger towards.

history ❶ *n, pl* **-ries** 1 (record or account of) past events and developments. 2 study of these. 3 record of someone's past. **historian** *n* writer of history. **historic** *adj* famous or significant in history. **historical** *adj* 1 occurring in the past. 2 based on history. **historically** *adv*.

histrionic *adj* excessively dramatic. **histrionics** *pl n* excessively dramatic behaviour.

hit ❶ *v* **hitting**, **hit** 1 strike, touch forcefully. 2 come into violent contact with. 3 affect badly. 4 reach (a point or place). ▷ *n* 5 hitting. 6 successful record, film, etc. 7 *Computers* single visit to a website. **hit it off** *informal* get on well together. **hit the road** *informal* start a journey. **hit-and-miss** *adj* sometimes successful and sometimes not. **hit man** hired assassin. **hit on** *v* think of (an idea).

hitch ❶ *n* 1 minor problem. ▷ *v* 2 *informal* obtain (a lift) by hitchhiking. 3 fasten with a knot or tie. 4 (foll. by *up*) pull up with a jerk. **hitchhike** *v* travel by obtaining free lifts. **hitchhiker** *n*.

hither *adv old-fashioned* to or towards this place. **hitherto** *adv* until this time.

hint *n* 1 = **indication**, allusion, clue, implication, innuendo, insinuation, intimation, suggestion 2 = **advice**, help, pointer, suggestion, tip 3 = **trace**, dash, suggestion, suspicion, tinge, touch, undertone ▷ *v* 4 = **suggest**, imply, indicate, insinuate, intimate

hire *v* 1 = **rent**, charter, engage, lease, let 2 = **employ**, appoint, commission, engage, sign up, take on ▷ *n* 3 = **rental**

hiss *n* 1 **a** = **sibilation**, buzz, hissing ▷ *n* **b** = **catcall**, boo, jeer ▷ *v* 2 = **whistle**, sibilate, wheeze, whirr, whiz 3 = **jeer**, boo, deride, hoot, mock

history *n* 1 **a** = **chronicle**, account, annals, narrative, recital, record, story **b** = **the past**, antiquity, olden days, yesterday, yesteryear

hit *v* 1 = **strike**, bang, beat, clout (*inf*),

knock, slap, smack, thump, wallop (*inf*), whack 2 = **collide with**, bang into, bump, clash with, crash against, run into, smash into 3 = **affect**, damage, devastate, impact on, influence, leave a mark on, overwhelm, touch 4 = **reach**, accomplish, achieve, arrive at, attain, gain ▷ *n* 5 = **stroke**, belt (*inf*), blow, clout (*inf*), knock, rap, slap, smack, wallop (*inf*) 6 = **success**, sensation, smash (*inf*), triumph, winner **hit it off** *Inf* = **get on (well) with**, be on good terms, click (*sl*), get on like a house on fire (*inf*)

hitch *n* 1 = **problem**, catch, difficulty, drawback, hindrance, hold-up, impediment, obstacle, snag ▷ *v* 2 *Inf* = **hitchhike**, thumb a lift 3 = **fasten**, attach, connect, couple, harness, join,

HIV human immunodeficiency virus, the cause of AIDS.

hive *n* same as BEEHIVE. **hive off** *v* separate from a larger group.

hives *n* allergic reaction in which itchy red or whitish patches appear on the skin.

HM Her (or His) Majesty.

HMS Her (or His) Majesty's Ship.

hoard ❶ *n* 1 store hidden away for future use. ▷ *v* 2 save or store. **hoarder** *n*.

hoarding *n* large board for displaying advertisements.

hoarse ❶ *adj* 1 (of a voice) rough and unclear. 2 having a rough and unclear voice. **hoarsely** *adv* **hoarseness** *n*.

hoary *adj* **hoarier, hoariest** 1 grey or white(-haired). 2 very old.

hoax ❶ *n* 1 deception or trick. ▷ *v* 2 deceive or play a trick upon.

hob *n* flat top part of a cooker, or a separate flat surface, containing gas or electric rings for cooking on.

hobble *v* 1 walk lamely. 2 tie the legs of (a horse) together.

hobby ❶ *n, pl* **-bies** activity pursued in one's spare time. **hobbyhorse** *n* 1 favourite topic. 2 toy horse.

hobgoblin *n* mischievous goblin.

hobnob ❶ *v* **-nobbing, -nobbed** (foll. by

with) be on friendly terms (with).

hobo *n, pl* **-bos** *US & Aust* tramp or vagrant.

hock¹ *n* joint in the back leg of an animal such as a horse that corresponds to the human ankle.

hock² *n* white German wine.

hockey *n* 1 team game played on a field with a ball and curved sticks. 2 *US & Canad* ice hockey.

hod *n* open wooden box attached to a pole, for carrying bricks or mortar.

hoe *n* 1 long-handled tool used for loosening soil or weeding. ▷ *v* 2 scrape or weed with a hoe.

hog *n* 1 castrated male pig. 2 *informal* greedy person. ▷ *v* **hogging, hogged** 3 *informal* take more than one's share of. **hogshead** *n* large cask. **hogwash** *n* *informal* nonsense.

hoist ❶ *v* 1 raise or lift up. ▷ *n* 2 device for lifting things.

hold¹ ❶ *v* **holding, held** 1 keep or support in or with the hands or arms. 2 arrange for (a meeting, party, etc.) to take place. 3 consider to be as specified, e.g. *who are you holding responsible?* 4 maintain in a specified position or state. 5 have the capacity for. 6 *informal* wait, esp. on the telephone. 7 reserve (a room etc.).

──────────────────────────── THESAURUS ────────────

tether, tie **4** (foll. by *up*) = **pull up**, jerk, tug, yank

hoard *n* 1 = **store**, accumulation, cache, fund, pile, reserve, stash, stockpile, supply, treasure-trove ▷ *v* 2 = **save**, accumulate, amass, collect, gather, lay up, put by, stash away (*inf*), stockpile, store

hoarse *adj* 1 = **rough**, croaky, grating, gravelly, gruff, guttural, husky, rasping, raucous, throaty

hoax *n* 1 = **trick**, con (*inf*), deception, fraud, practical joke, prank, spoof (*inf*), swindle ▷ *v* 2 = **deceive**, con (*sl*), dupe, fool, hoodwink, swindle, take in (*inf*), trick

hobby *n* = **pastime**, diversion, (leisure) activity, leisure pursuit, relaxation

hobnob *v* (foll. by *with*) = **socialize**,

associate, consort, fraternize, hang about, hang out (*inf*), keep company, mingle, mix

hoist *v* 1 = **raise**, elevate, erect, heave, lift ▷ *n* 2 = **lift**, crane, elevator, winch

hold¹ *v* 1 = **grasp**, clasp, cling, clutch, cradle, embrace, enfold, grip 2 = **convene**, call, conduct, preside over, run 5 = **accommodate**, contain, have a capacity for, seat, take 8 = **restrain**, confine, detain, impound, imprison 9 = **own**, have, keep, maintain, occupy, possess, retain 11 = **consider**, assume, believe, deem, judge, presume, reckon, regard, think *n* 12 = **grip**, clasp, grasp 13 = **control**, influence, mana (*NZ*), mastery 14 = **foothold**, footing, support

8 restrain or keep back. 9 own, possess. 10 (cause to) remain committed to (a promise etc.). 11 believe. ▷ n 12 act or way of holding. 13 controlling influence. 14 something to hold onto for support. **holder** n **holding** n property, such as land or stocks and shares. **holdall** n large strong travelling bag. **hold-up** n 1 armed robbery. 2 delay.

hold² n cargo compartment in a ship or aircraft.

hole ❶ n 1 area hollowed out in a solid. 2 opening or hollow. 3 animal's burrow. 4 *informal* unattractive place. 5 *informal* difficult situation. ▷ v 6 make holes in. 7 hit (a golf ball) into the target hole.

holiday ❶ n 1 time spent away from home for rest or recreation. 2 day or other period of rest from work or studies.

holistic adj considering the complete person, physically and mentally, in the treatment of an illness. **holism** n.

hollow ❶ adj 1 having a hole or space inside. 2 (of a sound) as if echoing in a hollow place. 3 without any real value or worth. ▷ n 4 cavity or space. 5 dip in the land. ▷ v 6 form a hollow in.

holly n evergreen tree with prickly leaves and red berries.

hollyhock n tall garden plant with spikes of colourful flowers.

holocaust ❶ n destruction or loss of life on a massive scale.

hologram n three-dimensional photographic image.

holster n leather case for a pistol, hung from a belt.

holy ❶ adj **-lier, -liest** 1 of God or a god. 2 devout or virtuous. **holier-than-thou** adj self-righteous. **Holy Grail** (in medieval legend) the bowl used by Jesus Christ at the Last Supper.

homage ❶ n show of respect or honour towards someone or something.

home ❶ n 1 place where one lives. 2 institution for the care of the elderly, orphans, etc. ▷ adj 3 of one's home, birthplace, or native country. 4 *Sport* played on one's own ground. ▷ adv 5 to or at home. ▷ v 6 (foll. by *in* or *in on*) direct towards (a point or target). **at home** at ease. **bring home to** make clear to. **home and dry** *informal* safe or successful. **homeless** adj 1 having nowhere to live. ▷ pl n 2 people who have nowhere to live. **homelessness** n **homely** adj 1 simple, ordinary, and comfortable. 2 *US* unattractive. **home page** *Computers* introductory information about a website with hyperlinks to further

—————— THESAURUS ——————

hole n 1 = **cavity**, cave, cavern, chamber, hollow, pit 2 = **opening**, aperture, breach, crack, fissure, gap, orifice, perforation, puncture, tear, vent 3 = **burrow**, den, earth, lair, shelter 4 *Inf* = **hovel**, dive (*sl*), dump (*inf*), slum *Inf* = **predicament**, dilemma, fix (*inf*), hot water (*inf*), jam (*inf*), mess, scrape (*inf*), spot (*inf*), tight spot

holiday n 1 = **vacation**, break, leave, recess, time off 2 = **festival**, celebration, feast, fete, gala

hollow adj 1 = **empty**, unfilled, vacant, void 2 = **toneless**, deep, dull, low, muted, reverberant 3 = **worthless**, fruitless, futile, meaningless, pointless, useless, vain n 4 = **cavity**, basin, bowl, crater, depression, hole, pit, trough 5 = **valley**, dale, dell, dingle, glen ▷ v 6 = **scoop**, dig, excavate, gouge

holocaust n = **genocide**, annihilation, conflagration, destruction, devastation, massacre

holy adj 1 = **sacred**, blessed, consecrated, hallowed, sacrosanct, sanctified, venerable 2 = **devout**, god-fearing, godly, pious, pure, religious, righteous, saintly, virtuous

homage n = **respect**, adoration, adulation, deference, devotion, honour, reverence, worship

home n 1 = **dwelling**, abode, domicile, habitation, house, pad (*sl*), residence ▷ adj

pages. **homeward** adj, adv **homewards**
adv **home-brew** n beer made at home.
home-made adj made at home or on the
premises. **home truths** unpleasant facts
told to a person about himself or herself.

homeopathy [home-ee-**op**-ath-ee] n
treatment of disease by small doses of
a drug that produces symptoms of the
disease in healthy people. **homeopath**
n person who practises homeopathy.
homeopathic adj.

homestead n 1 a house or estate and
the adjoining land and buildings, esp. on
a farm. 2 land assigned to a N American
settler.

homework n school work done at home.

homicide ❶ n 1 killing of a human being.
2 person who kills someone. **homicidal**
adj.

homily ❶ n, pl **-lies** speech telling people
how they should behave.

homogeneous ❶ [home-oh-**jean**-ee-uss]
adj formed of similar parts. **homogeneity**
n **homogenize** v 1 break up fat globules in
(milk or cream) to distribute them evenly.
2 make homogeneous.

homonym n word spelt or pronounced
the same as another, but with a different
meaning.

homosexual n, adj (person) sexually
attracted to members of the same sex.
homosexuality n.

hone ❶ v 1 sharpen 2 develop.

honest ❶ adj 1 truthful and moral. 2 open
and sincere. **honestly** adv **honesty** n.

honey n 1 sweet edible sticky substance
made by bees from nectar. 2 term
of endearment. **honeycomb** n waxy
structure of six-sided cells in which honey
is stored by bees in a beehive. **honey-
eater** n small Australasian songbird with
a brushlike tongue used for extracting
nectar from flowers. **honeymoon** n
holiday taken by a newly married couple.
honeysuckle n 1 climbing shrub with
sweet-smelling flowers. 2 Australian tree
or shrub with flowers in dense spikes.

honk n 1 sound made by a car horn.
2 sound made by a goose. ▷ v 3 (cause to)
make this sound.

honour ❶ n 1 sense of honesty and
fairness. 2 (award given out of) respect.
3 pleasure or privilege. ▷ pl 4 university
degree of a higher standard than an
ordinary degree. ▷ v 5 give praise
and attention to. 6 give an award to
(someone) out of respect. 7 accept or
pay (a cheque or bill). 8 keep (a promise).
do the honours act as host or hostess
by pouring drinks or giving out food.
honourable adj worthy of respect or
esteem. **honourably** adv **honorary**
adj 1 held or given only as an honour.
2 unpaid. **honorific** adj showing respect.

───── THESAURUS ─────

3 = **domestic**, familiar, internal, local,
native **at home** = **at ease**, comfortable,
familiar, relaxed **bring home to** = **make
clear**, drive home, emphasize, impress
upon, press home

homicide n 1 = **murder**, bloodshed,
killing, manslaughter, slaying
2 = **murderer**, killer, slayer

homily n = **sermon**, address, discourse,
lecture, preaching

homogeneous adj = **uniform**, akin,
alike, analogous, comparable, consistent,
identical, similar, unvarying

homosexual n = **gay**, lesbian ▷ adj = **gay**,

lesbian

hone v = **sharpen**, edge, file, grind, point,
polish, whet

honest adj 1 = **trustworthy**, ethical,
honourable, law-abiding, reputable,
scrupulous, truthful, upright, virtuous
2 = **open**, candid, direct, forthright,
frank, plain, sincere, upfront (inf)

honour n 1 = **integrity**, decency,
fairness, goodness, honesty, morality,
probity, rectitude 2 a = **tribute**,
accolade, commendation, homage,
praise, recognition b = **prestige**, credit,
dignity, distinction, fame, glory, renown,

hood n 1 head covering, often attached to a coat or jacket. 2 folding roof of a convertible car or a pram. 3 US & Aust car bonnet. **hooded** adj 1 (of a garment) having a hood. 2 (of eyes) having heavy eyelids that appear to be half-closed.

hoodie n informal 1 hooded sweatshirt. 2 young person who wears a hooded sweatshirt.

hoodlum n slang violent criminal, gangster.

hoof n, pl **hooves**, **hoofs** horny covering of the foot of a horse, deer, etc. **hoof it** slang walk.

hook ❶ n 1 curved piece of metal, plastic, etc., used to hang, hold, or pull something. 2 short swinging punch. ▷ v 3 fasten or catch (as if) with a hook. **hooked** adj 1 bent like a hook. 2 (foll. by on) slang addicted (to) or obsessed (with). **hooker** n 1 slang prostitute. 2 Rugby player who uses his feet to get the ball in a scrum. **hook-up** n linking of radio or television stations. **hookworm** n blood-sucking worm with hooked mouthparts.

hooligan ❶ n rowdy young person. **hooliganism** n.

hoon n Aust & NZ slang loutish youth who drives irresponsibly.

hoop ❶ n rigid circular band, used esp. as a child's toy or for animals to jump through in the circus. **hoop pine** Australian tree or shrub with flowers in dense spikes. **jump,**

be put through the hoops go through an ordeal or test.

hooray interj same as HURRAH.

hoot ❶ n 1 sound of a car horn. 2 cry of an owl. 3 cry of derision. 4 informal amusing person or thing. ▷ v 5 sound (a car horn). 6 jeer or yell contemptuously (at someone). **hooter** n 1 device that hoots. 2 slang nose.

Hoover n 1 ® vacuum cleaner. ▷ v 2 (h-) clean with a vacuum cleaner.

hop¹ v **hopping**, **hopped** 1 jump on one foot. 2 move in short jumps. 3 informal move quickly. ▷ n 4 instance of hopping. 5 informal dance. 6 short journey, esp. by air. **catch someone on the hop** informal catch someone unprepared.

hop² n (often pl) climbing plant, the dried flowers of which are used to make beer.

hope ❶ v 1 want (something) to happen or be true. ▷ n 2 expectation of something desired. 3 thing that gives cause for hope or is desired. **hopeful** adj 1 having, expressing, or inspiring hope. ▷ n 2 person considered to be on the brink of success. **hopefully** adv 1 in a hopeful manner. 2 it is hoped. **hopeless** adj.

hopper n container for storing substances such as grain or sand.

hopscotch n children's game of hopping in a pattern drawn on the ground.

horde ❶ n large crowd.

———— THESAURUS ————

reputation, respect 3 = **privilege**, compliment, credit, pleasure ▷ v 5 = **respect**, adore, appreciate, esteem, prize, value 6 = **acclaim**, commemorate, commend, decorate, praise 7 = **pay**, accept, acknowledge, pass, take 8 = **fulfil**, be true to, carry out, discharge, keep, live up to, observe

hook n 1 = **fastener**, catch, clasp, link, peg ▷ v 3 **a** = **fasten**, clasp, fix, secure **b** = **catch**, ensnare, entrap, snare, trap

hooligan n = **delinquent**, lager lout, ruffian, vandal, yob or yobbo (Brit sl)

hoop n = **ring**, band, circlet, girdle, loop,

round, wheel

hoot n 1 = **toot** 2 = **cry**, call 3 = **catcall**, boo, hiss, jeer ▷ v 6 = **jeer**, boo, hiss, howl down

hop¹ v 2 = **jump**, bound, caper, leap, skip, spring, trip, vault ▷ n 4 = **jump**, bounce, bound, leap, skip, spring, step, vault

hope v 1 = **desire**, aspire, cross one's fingers, long, look forward to, set one's heart on n 2 = **belief**, ambition, assumption, confidence, desire, dream, expectation, longing

horde n = **crowd**, band, drove, gang, host, mob, multitude, pack, swarm, throng

horizon ❶ *n* **1** apparent line that divides the earth and the sky. ▷ *pl* **2** limits of scope, interest, or knowledge. **horizontal** *adj* parallel to the horizon, level, flat.

hormone *n* **1** substance secreted by certain glands which stimulates certain organs of the body. **2** synthetic substance with the same effect. **hormonal** *adj*.

horn *n* **1** one of a pair of bony growths sticking out of the heads of cattle, sheep, etc. **2** substance of which horns are made. **3** musical instrument with a tube or pipe of brass fitted with a mouthpiece. **4** device on a vehicle sounded as a warning. **horned** *adj* **horny** *adj* **1** of or like horn. **2** *slang* (easily) sexually aroused. **hornpipe** *n* (music for) a solo dance, traditionally performed by sailors.

hornet *n* large wasp with a severe sting.

horoscope *n* **1** prediction of a person's future based on the positions of the planets, sun, and moon at his or her birth.

horrendous *adj* very unpleasant and shocking.

horror ❶ *n* (thing or person causing) terror or hatred. **horrible** *adj* disagreeable, unpleasant.

hors d'oeuvre [or **durv**] *n* appetizer served before a main meal.

horse ❶ *n* **1** large animal with hooves, a mane, and a tail, used for riding and pulling carts etc. **2** piece of gymnastic equipment used for vaulting over. **(straight) from the horse's mouth** from the original source. **horsey, horsy** *adj* **1** very keen on horses. **2** of or like a horse. **horse around** *v informal* play roughly or boisterously. **horse chestnut**

tree with broad leaves and inedible large brown shiny nuts in spiky cases. **horsefly** *n* large bloodsucking fly. **horsehair** *n* hair from the tail or mane of a horse. **horse laugh** loud coarse laugh. **horseman**, **horsewoman** *n* person riding a horse. **horseplay** *n* rough or rowdy play. **horsepower** *n* unit of power (equivalent to 745.7 watts), used to measure the power of an engine. **horseradish** *n* strong-tasting root of a plant, usu. made into a sauce. **horseshoe** *n* protective U-shaped piece of iron nailed to a horse's hoof, regarded as a symbol of good luck.

horticulture *n* art or science of cultivating gardens. **horticultural** *adj*.

hose¹ *n* **1** flexible pipe for conveying liquid. ▷ *v* **2** water with a hose.

hose² *n* stockings, socks, and tights. **hosiery** *n* stockings, socks, and tights collectively.

hoser *n* **1** *US sl* a person who swindles or deceives others. **2** *Canad sl* an unsophisticated, esp. rural, person.

hospice [**hoss**-piss] *n* nursing home for the terminally ill.

hospital *n* place where people who are ill are looked after and treated. **hospitalize** *v* send or admit to hospital. **hospitalization** *n*.

hospitality ❶ *n* kindness in welcoming strangers or guests. **hospitable** *adj* welcoming to strangers or guests.

host¹ ❶ *n* **1** (*fem* **hostess**) person who entertains guests, esp. in his own home. **2** place or country providing the facilities for an event. **3** compere of a show. **4** animal or plant on which a parasite lives. ▷ *v* **5** be the host of.

———————————— THESAURUS ————————————

horizon *n* **1** = **skyline**, vista

horror *n* = **terror**, alarm, aversion, consternation, detestation, disgust, dread, fear, fright, hatred, loathing, odium, panic, repugnance, revulsion

horse *n* **1** = **nag**, colt, filly, gee-gee (*sl*), mare, mount, stallion, steed (*arch or lit*)

hospitality *n* = **welcome**, conviviality,

cordiality, friendliness, neighbourliness, sociability, warmth

host¹ *n* **1** = **master of ceremonies**, entertainer, innkeeper, landlord *or* landlady, proprietor **3** = **presenter**, anchorman *or* anchorwoman, compere (*Brit*) ▷ *v* **5** = **present**, compere (*Brit*), front (*inf*), introduce

h

host² ❶ n large number.

hostage ❶ n person who is illegally held prisoner until certain demands are met by other people.

hostel n building providing accommodation at a low cost for travellers, homeless people, etc.

hostile ❶ adj 1 unfriendly. 2 (foll. by to) opposed (to). 3 of an enemy. **hostility** n, pl **-ties** 1 unfriendly and aggressive feelings or behaviour. ▷ pl 2 acts of warfare.

hot ❶ adj **hotter, hottest** 1 having a high temperature. 2 strong, spicy. 3 (of news) very recent. 4 (of a contest) fiercely fought. 5 (of a temper) quick to rouse. 6 liked very much, e.g. a hot favourite. 7 slang stolen. **in hot water** informal in trouble. **hotly** adv **hot air** informal empty talk. **hot-blooded** adj passionate or excitable. **hot dog** long roll split lengthways with a hot frankfurter inside. **hot-headed** adj rash, having a hot temper. **hotline** n direct telephone link for emergency use.

hotchpotch ❶ n jumbled mixture.

hotel n commercial establishment providing lodging and meals. **hotelier** n owner or manager of a hotel.

hound ❶ n 1 hunting dog. ▷ v 2 pursue relentlessly.

hour n 1 twenty-fourth part of a day, sixty minutes. 2 time of day. ▷ pl 3 period regularly appointed for work or business.

hourly adj, adv 1 (happening) every hour. 2 frequent(ly). **hourglass** n device with two glass compartments, containing a quantity of sand that takes an hour to trickle from the top section to the bottom one.

house ❶ n 1 building used as a home. 2 building used for some specific purpose, e.g. the opera house. 3 business firm. 4 law-making body or the hall where it meets. 5 family or dynasty. 6 theatre or cinema audience. ▷ v 7 give accommodation to. 8 contain or cover. **get on like a house on fire** informal get on very well together. **on the house** informal provided free by the management. **housing** n 1 (providing of) houses. 2 protective case or covering of a machine. **house arrest** confinement to one's home rather than in prison. **houseboat** n stationary boat used as a home. **housecoat** n woman's long loose coat-shaped garment for wearing at home. **household** n all the people living in a house. **householder** n person who owns or rents a house. **housekeeper** n person employed to run someone else's household. **housekeeping** n (money for) running a household. **housemaid** n female servant employed to do housework. **house-train** v train (a pet) to urinate and defecate outside. **house-warming** n party to celebrate moving into a new home. **housewife** n woman who runs her

h

──────────── THESAURUS ────────────

host² n = **multitude**, army, array, drove, horde, legion, myriad, swarm, throng

hostage n = **prisoner**, captive, pawn

hostile adj 1 = **unfriendly**, antagonistic, belligerent, contrary, ill-disposed, opposed, rancorous 2 (foll. by to) = **inhospitable**, adverse, unsympathetic, unwelcoming

hot adj 1 = **heated**, boiling, roasting, scalding, scorching, searing, steaming, sultry, sweltering, torrid, warm 2 = **spicy**, biting, peppery, piquant, pungent, sharp 3 = **new**, fresh, just out, latest, recent,

up to the minute 4 = **passionate**, fierce, fiery, intense, raging, stormy, violent 6 = **popular**, approved, favoured, in demand, in vogue, sought-after

hotchpotch n = **mixture**, farrago, jumble, medley, melange, mess, mishmash, potpourri

hound v 2 = **harass**, badger, goad, harry, impel, persecute, pester, provoke

house n 1 = **home**, abode, domicile, dwelling, habitation, homestead, pad (sl), residence 3 = **firm**, business, company, organization, outfit (inf) 4 = **assembly**,

own household and does not have a job.
housework n work of running a home,
such as cleaning, cooking, and shopping.
hovea n Australian plant with purple flowers.
hovel ❶ n small dirty house or hut.
hover ❶ v 1 (of a bird etc.) remain
suspended in one place in the air. 2 loiter.
3 be in a state of indecision. **hovercraft**
n vehicle which can travel over both land
and sea on a cushion of air.
how adv 1 in what way, by what means.
2 to what degree, e.g. I know how hard
it is. **however** adv 1 nevertheless. 2 by
whatever means. 3 no matter how, e.g.
however much it hurt, he could do it.
howl ❶ n 1 loud wailing cry. 2 loud burst
of laughter. ▷ v 3 utter a howl. **howler** n
informal stupid mistake.
HP, h.p. 1 hire-purchase. 2 horsepower.
HQ headquarters.
HRH Her (or His) Royal Highness.
HTML hypertext markup language: text
description language used on the Internet.
hub ❶ n 1 centre of a wheel, through which
the axle passes. 2 central point of activity.
hubbub n confused noise of many voices.
huddle ❶ v 1 hunch (oneself) through

cold or fear. 2 crowd closely together.
▷ n 3 small group. 4 informal impromptu
conference.
hue ❶ n colour, shade.
huff n 1 passing mood of anger or
resentment. ▷ v 2 blow or puff heavily.
huffy adj **huffily** adv.
hug ❶ v **hugging, hugged** 1 clasp tightly in
the arms, usu. with affection. 2 keep close
to (the ground, kerb, etc.). ▷ n 3 tight or
fond embrace.
huge ❶ adj very big. **hugely** adv.
hulk ❶ n 1 body of an abandoned ship.
2 offens large heavy person or thing.
hulking adj bulky, unwieldy.
hull ❶ n 1 main body of a boat. 2 leaves
round the stem of a strawberry, raspberry,
etc. ▷ v 3 remove the hulls from.
hullabaloo n, pl **-loos** loud confused noise
or clamour.
hum ❶ v **humming, hummed** 1 make a
low continuous vibrating sound. 2 sing
with the lips closed. 3 slang (of a place)
be very busy. ▷ n 4 humming sound.
hummingbird n very small American bird
whose powerful wings make a humming
noise as they vibrate.

——————————————————————————— THESAURUS ——————

Commons, legislative body, parliament
5 = **dynasty**, clan, family, tribe ▷ v
7 = **accommodate**, billet, harbour, lodge,
put up, quarter, take in 8 = **contain**, cover,
keep, protect, sheathe, shelter, store **on
the house** Inf = **free**, for nothing, gratis
hovel n = **hut**, cabin, den, hole, shack,
shanty, shed
hover v 1 = **float**, drift, flutter, fly, hang
2 = **linger**, hang about 3 = **waver**, dither,
fluctuate, oscillate, vacillate
howl n 1 = **cry**, bawl, bay, clamour, groan,
roar, scream, shriek, wail ▷ v 3 = **cry**,
bawl, bellow, roar, scream, shriek, wail,
weep, yell
hub n 2 = **centre**, core, focal point, focus,
heart, middle, nerve centre
huddle v 1 = **curl up**, crouch, hunch up
2 = **crowd**, cluster, converge, flock, gather,

press, throng ▷ n 4 Inf = **conference**,
confab (inf), discussion, meeting,
powwow
hue n = **colour**, dye, shade, tinge, tint, tone
hug v 1 = **clasp**, cuddle, embrace, enfold,
hold close, squeeze, take in one's arms ▷ n
3 = **embrace**, bear hug, clasp, clinch (sl),
squeeze
huge adj = **enormous**, colossal, gigantic,
immense, large, mammoth, massive,
monumental, tremendous, vast
hulk n 1 = **wreck**, frame, hull, shell,
shipwreck 2 Offens = **oaf**, lout, lubber,
lump (inf)
hull n 1 = **frame**, body, casing, covering,
framework
hum v 1 = **drone**, buzz, murmur, purr,
throb, thrum, vibrate, whir 3 Sl = **be busy**,
bustle, buzz, pulsate, pulse, stir

human ❶ adj **1** of or typical of people. ▷ n **2** human being. **humanly** adv by human powers or means. **human being** man, woman, or child. **humane** adj kind or merciful. **humanity** n human race.

humble ❶ adj **1** conscious of one's failings. **2** modest, unpretentious. **3** unimportant. ▷ v **4** cause to feel humble, humiliate. **humbly** adv.

humbug ❶ n **1** hard striped peppermint sweet. **2** nonsense. **3** dishonest person.

humdrum ❶ adj ordinary, dull.

humid ❶ adj damp and hot. **humidity** n **humidify** v **-fying, -fied. humidifier** n device for increasing the amount of water vapour in the air in a room.

humiliate ❶ v lower the dignity or hurt the pride of. **humiliating** adj **humiliation** n.

humility ❶ n quality of being humble.

hummock n very small hill.

humour ❶ n **1** ability to say or perceive things that are amusing. **2** amusing quality in a situation, film, etc. **3** state of mind, mood. **4** old-fashioned fluid in the body. ▷ v **5** be kind and indulgent to. **humorous** adj **humorist** n writer or entertainer who uses humour in his or her work.

● **SPELLING TIP**
● A lot of people simply add -ous to the
● noun **humour** to make **humourous**, but
● this is a mistake; you have to drop the
● second u when you write **humorous** or
● **humorist**.

hump ❶ n **1** raised piece of ground. **2** large lump on the back of an animal or person. ▷ v **3** slang carry or heave. **hump-back, humpbacked bridge** road bridge with a sharp slope on each side.

humus [**hew**-muss] n decomposing vegetable and animal mould in the soil.

hunch ❶ n **1** feeling or suspicion not based on facts. ▷ v **2** draw (one's shoulders) up or together. **hunchback** n offens person with an abnormal curvature of the spine.

hundred adj, n **1** ten times ten. ▷ n **2** (often pl) large but unspecified number. **hundredth** adj, n **hundredweight** n Brit unit of weight of 112 pounds (50.8 kilograms).

———————— THESAURUS ————————

human adj **1** = **mortal**, manlike n **2** = **human being**, creature, individual, man or woman, mortal, person, soul

humble adj **1** = **modest**, meek, self-effacing, unassuming, unostentatious, unpretentious **2** = **modest**, lowly, mean, obscure, ordinary, plebeian, poor, simple, undistinguished v **4** = **humiliate**, chasten, crush, disgrace, put (someone) in their place, subdue, take down a peg (inf)

humbug n **2** = **nonsense**, baloney (inf), cant, claptrap (inf), hypocrisy, kak (S Afr sl), quackery, rubbish **3** = **fraud**, charlatan, con man (inf), faker, impostor, phoney or phony (inf), swindler, trickster

humdrum adj = **dull**, banal, boring, dreary, monotonous, mundane, ordinary, tedious, tiresome, uneventful

humid adj = **damp**, clammy, dank, moist, muggy, steamy, sticky, sultry, wet

humiliate v = **embarrass**, bring low, chasten, crush, degrade, humble, mortify, put down, put (someone) in their place, shame

humility n = **modesty**, humbleness, lowliness, meekness, submissiveness, unpretentiousness

humour n **1, 2** = **funniness**, amusement, comedy, drollery, facetiousness, fun, jocularity, ludicrousness **3** = **mood**, disposition, frame of mind, spirits, temper ▷ v **5** = **indulge**, accommodate, flatter, go along with, gratify, mollify, pander to

hump n **1** = **lump**, bulge, bump, mound, projection, protrusion, protuberance, swelling ▷ v **3** Sl = **carry**, heave, hoist, lug, shoulder

hunch n **1** = **feeling**, idea, impression, inkling, intuition, premonition, presentiment, suspicion ▷ v **2** = **draw in**, arch, bend, curve

hunger 1 *n* **1** discomfort or weakness from lack of food. **2** desire or craving. ▷ *v* **3** (foll. by *for*) want very much. **hunger strike** refusal of all food, as a means of protest. **hungry** *adj* having a desire or craving (for).

hunk 1 *n* **1** large piece. **2** *slang* sexually attractive man.

hunt 1 *v* **1** seek out and kill (wild animals) for food or sport. **2** (foll. by *for*) search (for). ▷ *n* **3** hunting. **4** (party organized for) hunting wild animals for sport. **hunter** *n* person or animal that hunts wild animals for food or sport. **huntsman** *n* man who hunts animals, esp. foxes.

hurdle 1 *n* **1** *Sport* light barrier for jumping over in some races. **2** problem or difficulty. ▷ *pl* **3** race involving hurdles. ▷ *v* **4** jump over (something). **hurdler** *n*.

hurdy-gurdy *n*, *pl* **-dies** mechanical musical instrument, such as a barrel organ.

hurl 1 *v* throw or utter forcefully.

hurly-burly *n* loud confusion.

hurrah, hurray *interj* exclamation of joy or applause.

hurricane 1 *n* very strong, often destructive, wind or storm. **hurricane lamp** paraffin lamp with a glass covering.

hurry 1 *v* **-rying, -ried 1** (cause to) move or act very quickly. ▷ *n* **2** doing something quickly or the need to do something quickly. **hurriedly** *adv*.

hurt 1 *v* **hurting, hurt 1** cause physical or mental pain to. **2** be painful. **3** *informal* feel pain. ▷ *n* **4** physical or mental pain. **hurtful** *adj* unkind.

hurtle 1 *v* move quickly or violently.

husband 1 *n* **1** woman's partner in marriage. ▷ *v* **2** use economically. **husbandry** *n* **1** farming. **2** management of resources.

hush 1 *v* **1** make or be silent. ▷ *n* **2** stillness or silence. **hush-hush** *adj* *informal* secret. **hush up** *v* suppress information about.

husk *n* **1** outer covering of certain seeds and fruits. ▷ *v* **2** remove the husk from.

husky¹ *adj* **huskier, huskiest 1** slightly hoarse. **2** *informal* big and strong. **huskily** *adv*.

husky² *n*, *pl* **huskies** Arctic sledge dog with thick hair and a curled tail.

————————————————————————— THESAURUS —————————————————————————

hunger *n* **1** = **appetite**, emptiness, hungriness, ravenousness **2** = **desire**, ache, appetite, craving, itch, lust, thirst, yearning ▷ *v* **3** = **want**, ache, crave, desire, hanker, itch, long, thirst, wish, yearn

hunk *n* **1** = **lump**, block, chunk, mass, nugget, piece, slab, wedge

hunt *v* **1** = **stalk**, chase, hound, pursue, track, trail **2** (foll. by *for*) = **search**, ferret about, forage, fossick (*Aust & NZ*), look, scour, seek ▷ *n* **3** = **search**, chase, hunting, investigation, pursuit, quest

hurdle *n* **1** = **fence**, barricade, barrier **2** = **obstacle**, barrier, difficulty, handicap, hazard, hindrance, impediment, obstruction, stumbling block

hurl *v* = **throw**, cast, fling, heave, launch, let fly, pitch, propel, sling, toss

hurricane *n* = **storm**, cyclone, gale, tempest, tornado, twister (*US inf*), typhoon

hurry *v* **1** = **rush**, dash, fly, get a move on (*inf*), make haste, scoot, scurry, step on it (*inf*) ▷ *n* **2** = **haste**, flurry, quickness, rush, speed, urgency

hurt *v* **1 a** = **harm**, bruise, damage, disable, impair, injure, mar, spoil, wound **b** = **upset**, annoy, distress, grieve, pain, sadden, wound **2** = **ache**, be sore, be tender, burn, smart, sting, throb ▷ *n* **4** = **distress**, discomfort, pain, pang, soreness, suffering

hurtle *v* = **rush**, charge, crash, fly, plunge, race, shoot, speed, stampede, tear

husband *n* **1** = **partner**, better half (*hum*), mate, spouse ▷ *v* **2** = **economize**, budget, conserve, hoard, save, store

hush *v* **1** = **quieten**, mute, muzzle, shush, silence ▷ *n* **2** = **quiet**, calm, peace, silence, stillness, tranquillity

hussy *n, pl* **-sies** immodest or promiscuous woman.

hustings *pl n* political campaigns and speeches before an election.

hustle ❶ *v* **1** push about, jostle. ▷ *n* **2** lively activity or bustle.

hut ❶ *n* small house, shelter, or shed.

hutch *n* cage for pet rabbits etc.

hyacinth *n* sweet-smelling spring flower that grows from a bulb.

hybrid ❶ *n* **1** offspring of two plants or animals of different species. **2** anything of mixed origin. **3** vehicle powered by an internal-combustion engine and another source of power. ▷ *adj* **4** of mixed origin. **5** of a vehicle powered by more than one source.

hydrangea *n* ornamental shrub with clusters of pink, blue, or white flowers.

hydrant *n* outlet from a water main with a nozzle for a hose.

hydraulic *adj* operated by pressure forced through a pipe by a liquid such as water or oil. **hydraulics** *n* study of the mechanical properties of fluids as they apply to practical engineering.

hydrochloric acid *n* strong colourless acid used in many industrial and laboratory processes.

hydroelectric *adj* of the generation of electricity by water pressure.

hydrofoil *n* fast light boat with its hull raised out of the water on one or more pairs of fins.

hydrogen *n Chem* light flammable colourless gas that combines with oxygen to form water. **hydrogen bomb** extremely powerful bomb in which energy is released by fusion of hydrogen nuclei to give helium nuclei. **hydrogen peroxide** colourless liquid used as a hair bleach and as an antiseptic.

hydrophobia *n* **1** rabies. **2** fear of water.

hyena *n* scavenging doglike mammal of Africa and S Asia.

hygiene ❶ *n* principles and practice of health and cleanliness. **hygienic** *adj*.

hymen *n* membrane partly covering the opening of a girl's vagina, which breaks before puberty or at the first occurrence of sexual intercourse.

hymn ❶ *n* Christian song of praise sung to God or a saint. **hymnal** *n* book of hymns (also **hymn book**).

hype ❶ *n* **1** intensive or exaggerated publicity or sales promotion. ▷ *v* **2** promote (a product) using intensive or exaggerated publicity.

hyperbole [hie-**per**-bol-ee] *n* deliberate exaggeration for effect. **hyperbolic** *adj*.

hyperlink *Computers* ▷ *n* link from a hypertext file that gives users instant access to related material in another file.

hypermarket *n* huge self-service store.

hypertension *n* very high blood pressure.

hyphen *n* punctuation mark (-) indicating that two words or syllables are connected. **hyphenated** *adj* (of two words or syllables) having a hyphen between them. **hyphenation** *n*.

hypnosis *n* artificially induced state of relaxation in which the mind is more than usually receptive to suggestion. **hypnotic** *adj* of or (as if) producing hypnosis. **hypnotism** *n* inducing hypnosis in someone. **hypnotist** *n* **hypnotize** *v*.

hypochondria *n* undue preoccupation with one's health. **hypochondriac** *n*.

h

——————— THESAURUS ———————

hustle *v* **1** = **jostle**, elbow, force, jog, push, shove

hut *n* = **shed**, cabin, den, hovel, lean-to, shanty, shelter

hybrid *n* **1** = **crossbreed**, cross, half-breed, mongrel **2** = **mixture**, amalgam, composite, compound, cross

hygiene *n* = **cleanliness**, sanitation

hymn *n* = **song of praise**, anthem, carol, chant, paean, psalm

hype *n* **1** = **publicity**, ballyhoo (*inf*), brouhaha, build-up, plugging (*inf*),

hypocrisy ❶ [hip-**ok**-rass-ee] *n, pl*
-**sies** (instance of) pretence of having
standards or beliefs that are contrary to
one's real character or actual behaviour.
hypocrite [**hip**-oh-krit] *n* person who
pretends to be what he or she is not.
hypocritical *adj*.
hypodermic *adj, n* (denoting) a syringe
or needle used to inject a drug beneath
the skin.
hypotenuse [hie-**pot**-a-news] *n* side of
a right-angled triangle opposite the right
angle.
hypothermia *n* condition in which a

person's body temperature is dangerously
low as a result of prolonged exposure to
severe cold.
hypothesis ❶ [hie-**poth**-iss-iss] *n, pl*
-**ses** [-seez] suggested but unproved
explanation of something. **hypothetical**
adj based on assumption rather than fact
or reality.
hysterectomy *n, pl* -**mies** surgical
removal of the womb.
hysteria ❶ *n* state of uncontrolled
excitement, anger, or panic. **hysterical**
adj **hysterics** *pl n* **1** attack of hysteria.
2 *informal* uncontrollable laughter.

promotion, razzmatazz (*sl*)
hypocrisy *n* = **insincerity**, cant,
deceitfulness, deception, duplicity, pretence
hypothesis *n* = **assumption**, postulate,

premise, proposition, supposition, theory,
thesis
hysteria *n* = **frenzy**, agitation, delirium,
hysterics, madness, panic

Ii

I¹ *pron* used by a speaker or writer to refer to himself or herself as the subject of a verb.

I² the Roman numeral for one.

IA Iowa.

ibis [**ibe**-iss] *n* large wading bird with long legs.

ice *n* **1** frozen water. **2** portion of ice cream. ▷ *v* **3** (foll. by *up* or *over*) become covered with ice. **4** cover with icing. **break the ice** create a relaxed atmosphere, esp. between people meeting for the first time. **iced** *adj* **1** covered with icing. **2** (of a drink) containing ice. **icy** *adj* **icier**, **iciest 1** very cold. **2** covered with ice. **3** aloof and unfriendly. **icily** *adv* **iciness** *n* **iceberg** *n* large floating mass of ice. **icebox** *n* US refrigerator. **ice cream** sweet creamy frozen food. **ice floe** sheet of ice floating in the sea. **ice hockey** team game like hockey played on ice with a puck. **ice pick** pointed tool for breaking ice. **ice skate** boot with a steel blade fixed to the sole, to enable the wearer to glide over ice. **ice-skate** *v* **ice-skater** *n*.

icon *n* **1** picture of Christ or another religious figure, regarded as holy in the Orthodox Church. **2** picture on a computer screen representing a function that can be activated by moving the cursor over it.

ID 1 Idaho. **2** identification.

idea ❶ *n* **1** plan or thought formed in the mind. **2** thought of something. **3** belief or opinion. **ideal** *n* **1** idea of perfection. **2** perfect person or thing.

identity ❶ *n, pl* -**ties 1** state of being a specified person or thing. **2** individuality or personality. **3** state of being the same. **identical** *adj* very same. **identify** *v* establish identity of.

ideology *n, pl* -**gies** body of ideas and beliefs of a group, nation, etc. **ideological** *adj* **ideologist** *n*.

idiom ❶ *n* **1** group of words which when used together have a different meaning from the words individually, e.g. *raining cats and dogs*. **2** way of expression natural or peculiar to a language or group. **idiomatic** *adj* **idiomatically** *adv*.

idiosyncrasy ❶ *n, pl* -**sies** personal peculiarity of mind, habit, or behaviour.

idiot ❶ *n* **1** foolish or stupid person. **2** *offens* mentally retarded person. **idiotic** *adj* **idiotically** *adv*.

idle ❶ *adj* **1** not doing anything. **2** not willing to work, lazy. **3** not being used. **4** useless or meaningless, e.g. *an idle threat*. ▷ *v* **5** (usu. foll. by *away*) spend (time) doing

i

THESAURUS

idea *n* **1** = **intention**, aim, object, objective, plan, purpose **2** = **thought**, concept, impression, perception **3** = **belief**, conviction, notion, opinion, teaching, view

identity *n* **1, 2** = **existence**, individuality, personality, self **3** = **sameness**, correspondence, unity

idiom *n* **1** = **phrase**, expression, turn of phrase **2** = **language**, jargon, parlance, style, vernacular

idiosyncrasy *n* = **peculiarity**, characteristic, eccentricity, mannerism, oddity, quirk, trick

idiot *n* **1** = **fool**, chump, cretin, dunderhead, halfwit, imbecile, moron, nincompoop, numbskull *or* numskull, simpleton, twit (*inf, chiefly Brit*)

idle *adj* **1** = **inactive**, redundant, unemployed, unoccupied **2** = **lazy**, good-for-nothing, indolent, lackadaisical, shiftless, slothful, sluggish **3** = **unused**, vacant **4** = **useless**, fruitless, futile, groundless, ineffective, pointless, unavailing, unsuccessful, vain, worthless ▷ *v* **5** (usu. foll. by *away*) = **laze**, dally, dawdle, kill time, loaf, loiter, lounge, potter

very little. **6** (of an engine) run slowly with the gears disengaged. **idleness** n **idler** n **idly** adv.

idol ❶ n **1** object of excessive devotion. **2** image of a god as an object of worship. **idolatry** n worship of idols. **idolatrous** adj **idolize** v love or admire excessively.

idyll [**id**-ill] n scene or time of great peace and happiness. **idyllic** adj.

i.e. that is to say.

if ❶ conj **1** on the condition or supposition that. **2** whether. **3** even though. ▷ n **4** uncertainty or doubt, e.g. no ifs, ands, or buts. **iffy** adj informal doubtful, uncertain.

igloo n, pl **-loos** dome-shaped Inuit house made of snow and ice.

ignite v catch fire or set fire to.

ignoble adj dishonourable. **ignobly** adv.

ignominy ❶ [**ig**-nom-in-ee] n humiliating disgrace. **ignominious** adj.

ignore ❶ v refuse to notice, disregard deliberately. **ignorant** adj lacking knowledge.

iguana n large tropical American lizard.

IL Illinois.

ill ❶ adj **1** not in good health. **2** harmful or unpleasant, e.g. ill effects. ▷ n **3** evil, harm. ▷ adv **4** badly. **5** hardly, with difficulty, e.g. I can ill afford to lose him. **ill at ease** uncomfortable, unable to relax. **illness** n **ill-advised** adj **1** badly thought out. **2** unwise. **ill-disposed** adj (often foll. by towards) unfriendly, unsympathetic. **ill-fated** adj doomed to end unhappily. **ill-gotten** adj obtained dishonestly. **ill-health** n condition of being unwell. **ill-mannered** adj having bad manners. **ill-treat** v treat cruelly. **ill will** unkind feeling, hostility.

illegal ❶ adj against the law. **illegally** adv **illegality** n, pl **-ties**.

illegible ❶ adj unable to be read or deciphered.

illegitimate ❶ adj **1** born of parents not married to each other. **2** not lawful. **illegitimacy** n.

illicit ❶ adj **1** illegal. **2** forbidden or disapproved of by society.

illiterate ❶ n, adj (person) unable to read or write. **illiteracy** n.

illogical ❶ adj **1** unreasonable. **2** not logical.

━━━━━━━━━━━━━━━━━━━━━━━━━ THESAURUS ━━━━━━━

idol n **1** = **hero**, beloved, darling, favourite, pet, pin-up (sl) **2** = **graven image**, deity, god

if conj **1** = **provided**, assuming, on condition that, providing, supposing

ignite v **a** = **catch fire**, burn, burst into flames, flare up, inflame, take fire **b** = **set fire to**, kindle, light, set alight, torch

ignominy n = **disgrace**, discredit, dishonour, disrepute, humiliation, infamy, obloquy, shame, stigma

ignore v = **overlook**, discount, disregard, neglect, pass over, reject, take no notice of, turn a blind eye to

ill adj **1** = **unwell**, ailing, crook (Aust & NZ sl), diseased, indisposed, infirm, off-colour, poorly (inf), sick, under the weather (inf), unhealthy **2** = **harmful**, bad, damaging, deleterious, detrimental, evil, foul, injurious, unfortunate ▷ n **3** = **harm**, affliction, hardship, hurt, injury, misery,

misfortune, trouble, unpleasantness, woe adv **4** = **badly**, inauspiciously, poorly, unfavourably, unfortunately, unluckily **5** = **hardly**, barely, by no means, scantily

illegal adj = **unlawful**, banned, criminal, felonious, forbidden, illicit, outlawed, prohibited, unauthorized, unlicensed

illegible adj = **indecipherable**, obscure, scrawled, unreadable

illegitimate adj **1** = **born out of wedlock**, bastard **2** = **unlawful**, illegal, illicit, improper, unauthorized

illicit adj **1** = **illegal**, criminal, felonious, illegitimate, prohibited, unauthorized, unlawful, unlicensed **2** = **forbidden**, clandestine, furtive, guilty, immoral, improper

illiterate adj = **uneducated**, ignorant, uncultured, untaught, untutored

illogical adj = **irrational**, absurd, inconsistent, invalid, meaningless,

illuminate ❶ v **1** light up. **2** make clear, explain. **3** decorate with lights. **4** *Hist* decorate (a manuscript) with designs of gold and bright colours. **illumination** n **illuminating** adj.

illusion ❶ n deceptive appearance or belief. **illusionist** n conjuror. **illusory** adj seeming to be true, but actually false.

illustrate ❶ v **1** explain by use of examples. **2** provide (a book or text) with pictures. **3** be an example of. **illustration** n **1** picture or diagram. **2** example. **illustrative** adj **illustrator** n.

illustrious ❶ adj famous and distinguished.

image ❶ n **1** mental picture of someone or something. **2** impression people have of a person, organization, etc. **3** representation of a person or thing in a work of art. **4** optical reproduction of someone or something, for example in a mirror. **5** person or thing that looks almost exactly like another. **6** figure of speech, esp. a metaphor or simile. **imagery** n images collectively, esp. in the arts.

imagine ❶ v **1** form a mental image of.

2 think, believe, or guess. **imaginable** adj **imaginary** adj existing only in the imagination. **imagination** n **1** ability to make mental images of things that may not exist in real life. **2** creative mental ability. **imaginative** adj having or showing a lot of creative mental ability. **imaginatively** adv.

● **SPELLING TIP**
● Remembering that an e changes to an
● a to form **imagination** is a good way of
● getting **imaginary** right, because it has
● an a instead of an e too.

IMAX ® [**eye**-max] n film projection process which produces an image ten times larger than standard.

imbalance n lack of balance or proportion.

imbecile ❶ [**imb**-ess-eel] n **1** stupid person. ▷ adj **2** (also **imbecilic**) stupid or senseless. **imbecility** n.

imbibe ❶ v **1** drink (alcoholic drinks). **2** *lit* absorb (ideas etc.).

imbue v **-buing, -bued** (usu. foll. by *with*) fill or inspire with (ideals or principles).

imitate ❶ v **1** take as a model. **2** copy the voice and mannerisms of, esp. for

——— THESAURUS ———

senseless, shonky (Aust & NZ inf), unreasonable, unscientific, unsound

illuminate v **1** = **light up**, brighten **2** = **clarify**, clear up, elucidate, enlighten, explain, interpret, make clear, shed light on

illusion n **a** = **fantasy**, chimera, daydream, figment of the imagination, hallucination, mirage, will-o'-the-wisp **b** = **misconception**, deception, delusion, error, fallacy, misapprehension

illustrate v **1** = **demonstrate**, bring home, elucidate, emphasize, explain, point up, show

illustrious adj = **famous**, celebrated, distinguished, eminent, glorious, great, notable, prominent, renowned

image n **1, 2** = **concept**, idea, impression, mental picture, perception **3** = **representation**, effigy, figure, icon, idol, likeness, picture, portrait, statue

5 = **replica**, counterpart, (dead) ringer (sl), doppelgänger, double, facsimile, spitting image (inf)

imagine v **1** = **envisage**, conceive, conceptualize, conjure up, picture, plan, think of, think up, visualize **2** = **believe**, assume, conjecture, fancy, guess (inf, chiefly US & Canad), infer, suppose, surmise, suspect, take it, think

imbecile n **1** = **idiot**, chump, cretin, fool, halfwit, moron, numbskull or numskull, thickhead, twit (inf, chiefly Brit) ▷ adj **2** (also **imbecilic**) = **stupid**, asinine, fatuous, feeble-minded, foolish, idiotic, moronic, thick, witless

imbibe v **1** = **drink**, consume, knock back (inf), quaff, sink (inf), swallow, swig (inf) **2** Lit = **absorb**, acquire, assimilate, gain, gather, ingest, receive, take in

imitate v **1** = **follow**, emulate, mirror,

entertainment. **imitation** *n* **1** copy of an original. **2** imitating. **imitative** *adj* **imitator** *n*.

immaculate ❶ *adj* **1** completely clean or tidy. **2** completely flawless. **immaculately** *adv*.

immaterial ❶ *adj* not important, not relevant.

immature ❶ *adj* **1** not fully developed. **2** lacking wisdom or stability because of youth.

immediate ❶ *adj* **1** occurring at once. **2** next or nearest in time, space, or relationship. **immediately** *adv* **immediacy** *n*.

immense ❶ *adj* extremely large. **immensely** *adv* to a very great degree. **immensity** *n*.

immerse ❶ *v* **1** involve deeply, engross. **2** plunge (something or someone) into liquid. **immersion** *n*.

imminent ❶ *adj* about to happen. **imminence** *n*.

immobile ❶ *adj* **1** not moving. **2** unable to move. **immobility** *n* **immobilize** *v* make unable to move or work.

immolate *v* kill as a sacrifice.

immoral ❶ *adj* **1** morally wrong, corrupt. **2** sexually depraved or promiscuous. **immorality** *n*.

● **USAGE NOTE**
● Do not confuse *immoral* with
● *amoral*, which means 'having no moral
● standards'.

immortal ❶ *adj* **1** living forever. **2** famous for all time. ▷ *n* **3** person whose fame will last for all time. **4** immortal being. **immortality** *n* **immortalize** *v*.

immune ❶ *adj* **1** protected against a specific disease. **2** (foll. by *to*) secure (against). **3** (foll. by *from*) exempt (from). **immunity** *n*, *pl* **-ties 1** ability to resist disease. **2** freedom from prosecution, tax, etc. **immunize** *v* make immune to a disease. **immunization** *n*.

imp ❶ *n* **1** (in folklore) mischievous small creature with magical powers. **2** mischievous child.

——————————— THESAURUS ———————————

simulate **2** = **copy**, ape, echo, mimic, repeat

immaculate *adj* **1** = **clean**, neat, spick-and-span, spotless, spruce, squeaky-clean **2** = **pure**, above reproach, faultless, flawless, impeccable, perfect, unblemished, unexceptionable, untarnished

immaterial *adj* = **irrelevant**, extraneous, inconsequential, inessential, insignificant, of no importance, trivial, unimportant

immature *adj* **1** = **young**, adolescent, undeveloped, unformed, unripe **2** = **childish**, callow, inexperienced, infantile, juvenile, puerile

immediate *adj* **1** = **instant**, instantaneous **2** = **nearest**, close, direct, near, next

immense *adj* = **huge**, colossal, enormous, extensive, gigantic, great, massive, monumental, stupendous, tremendous, vast

immerse *v* **1** = **engross**, absorb, busy, engage, involve, occupy, take up **2** = **plunge**, bathe, dip, douse, duck, dunk, sink, submerge

imminent *adj* = **near**, at hand, close, coming, forthcoming, gathering, impending, in the pipeline, looming

immobile *adj* = **stationary**, at a standstill, at rest, fixed, immovable, motionless, rigid, rooted, static, still, stock-still, unmoving

immoral *adj* **1** = **wicked**, bad, corrupt, sinful, unethical, unprincipled, wrong **2** = **depraved**, debauched, dissolute, indecent

immortal *adj* **1** = **eternal**, deathless, enduring, everlasting, imperishable, lasting, perennial, undying *n* **3** = **great**, genius, hero **4** = **god**, goddess

immune *adj* **1** = **protected**, clear, free, resistant **2** = **invulnerable**, proof (against), safe, unaffected **3** = **exempt**

imp *n* **1** = **demon**, devil, sprite **2** = **rascal**,

impact ❶ *n* **1** strong effect. **2** (force of) a collision. ▷ *v* **3** press firmly into something.

impair ❶ *v* weaken or damage. **impairment** *n*.

impala [imp-**ah**-la] *n* southern African antelope.

impale *v* pierce with a sharp object.

impart ❶ *v* **1** communicate (information). **2** give.

impartial ❶ *adj* not favouring one side or the other. **impartially** *adv* **impartiality** *n*.

impassable ❶ *adj* (of a road etc.) impossible to travel through or over.

impasse ❶ [**am**-pass] *n* situation in which progress is impossible.

impassioned ❶ *adj* full of emotion.

impassive *adj* showing no emotion, calm.

impatient ❶ *adj* **1** irritable at any delay or difficulty. **2** restless (to have or do something). **impatience** *n*.

impeach ❶ *v* charge with a serious crime

against the state. **impeachment** *n*.

impeccable ❶ *adj* without fault, excellent. **impeccably** *adv*.

impede ❶ *v* hinder in action or progress. **impediment** *n* something that makes action, speech, or progress difficult. **impedimenta** *pl n* objects impeding progress, esp. baggage or equipment.

impel ❶ *v* **-pelling, -pelled** push or force (someone) to do something.

impending ❶ *adj* (esp. of something bad) about to happen.

imperative ❶ *adj* **1** extremely urgent, vital. **2** *Grammar* denoting a mood of verbs used in commands. ▷ *n* **3** *Grammar* imperative mood.

imperfect ❶ *adj* **1** having faults or mistakes. **2** not complete. **3** *Grammar* denoting a tense of verbs describing continuous, incomplete, or repeated past actions. ▷ *n* **4** *Grammar* imperfect tense. **imperfection** *n*.

──── THESAURUS ────

brat, minx, rogue, scamp

impact *n* **1** = **effect**, consequences, impression, influence, repercussions, significance **2** = **collision**, blow, bump, contact, crash, jolt, knock, smash, stroke, thump

impair *v* = **worsen**, blunt, damage, decrease, diminish, harm, hinder, injure, lessen, reduce, undermine, weaken

impart *v* **1** = **communicate**, convey, disclose, divulge, make known, pass on, relate, reveal, tell **2** = **give**, accord, afford, bestow, confer, grant, lend, yield

impartial *adj* = **neutral**, detached, disinterested, equitable, even-handed, fair, just, objective, open-minded, unbiased, unprejudiced

impassable *adj* = **blocked**, closed, impenetrable, obstructed

impasse *n* = **deadlock**, dead end, stalemate, standoff, standstill

impassioned *adj* = **intense**, animated, fervent, fiery, heated, inspired, passionate,

rousing, stirring

impatient *adj* **1** = **irritable**, demanding, hot-tempered, intolerant, quick-tempered, snappy, testy **2** = **restless**, eager, edgy, fretful, straining at the leash

impeach *v* = **charge**, accuse, arraign, indict

impeccable *adj* = **faultless**, blameless, flawless, immaculate, irreproachable, perfect, squeaky-clean, unblemished, unimpeachable

impede *v* = **hinder**, block, check, disrupt, hamper, hold up, obstruct, slow (down), thwart

impel *v* = **force**, compel, constrain, drive, induce, oblige, push, require

impending *adj* = **looming**, approaching, coming, forthcoming, gathering, imminent, in the pipeline, near, upcoming

imperative *adj* **1** = **urgent**, crucial, essential, pressing, vital

imperfect *adj* = **flawed**, damaged, defective, faulty, impaired, incomplete,

imperial ● *adj* **1** of or like an empire or emperor. **2** denoting a system of weights and measures formerly used in Britain. **imperialism** *n* rule by one country over many others. **imperialist** *adj*, *n*.

imperil ● *v* **-illing, -illed** put in danger.

imperious *adj* proud and domineering.

impersonal ● *adj* **1** not relating to any particular person, objective. **2** lacking human warmth or sympathy. **3** *Grammar* (of a verb) without a personal subject, e.g. *it is snowing*.

impersonate ● *v* **1** pretend to be (another person). **2** copy the voice and mannerisms of, esp. for entertainment. **impersonation** *n* **impersonator** *n*.

impertinent ● *adj* disrespectful or rude. **impertinence** *n*.

imperturbable ● *adj* calm, not excitable.

impervious ● *adj* (foll. by *to*) **1** not letting (water etc.) through. **2** not influenced by (a feeling, argument, etc.).

impetigo [imp-it-**tie**-go] *n* contagious skin disease.

impetuous ● *adj* done or acting without thought, rash. **impetuosity** *n*.

impetus ● [**imp**-it-uss] *n*, *pl* **-tuses** **1** incentive, impulse. **2** force that starts a body moving.

impinge ● *v* (foll. by *on*) affect or restrict.

impious ● [**imp**-ee-uss] *adj* showing a lack of respect or reverence.

implacable ● *adj* not prepared to be appeased, unyielding. **implacably** *adv*.

implant ● *n* **1** *Med* something put into someone's body, usu. by surgical operation. ▷ *v* **2** put (something) into someone's body, usu. by surgical operation. **3** fix firmly in someone's mind. **implantation** *n*.

implement ● *v* **1** carry out (instructions etc.). ▷ *n* **2** tool, instrument. **implementation** *n*.

implore ● *v* beg earnestly.

— THESAURUS —

limited, unfinished

imperial *adj* **2** = **royal**, kingly, majestic, princely, queenly, regal, sovereign

imperil *v* = **endanger**, expose, jeopardize, risk

impersonal *adj* **2** = **detached**, aloof, cold, dispassionate, formal, inhuman, neutral, remote

impersonate *v* **1** = **pretend to be**, masquerade as, pass oneself off as, pose as (*inf*) **2** = **imitate**, ape, do (*inf*), mimic, take off (*inf*)

impertinent *adj* = **rude**, brazen, cheeky (*inf*), disrespectful, impolite, impudent, insolent, presumptuous

imperturbable *adj* = **calm**, collected, composed, cool, nerveless, self-possessed, serene, unexcitable, unflappable (*inf*), unruffled

impervious *adj* **1** (foll. by *to*) = **sealed**, impassable, impenetrable, impermeable, resistant **2** = **unaffected**, immune, invulnerable, proof against, unmoved, untouched

impetuous *adj* = **rash**, hasty, impulsive, precipitate, unthinking

impetus *n* **1** = **incentive**, catalyst, goad, impulse, motivation, push, spur, stimulus **2** = **force**, energy, momentum, power

impinge *v* (foll. by *on*) = **affect**, bear upon, have a bearing on, impact, influence, relate to, touch

impious *adj* = **sacrilegious**, blasphemous, godless, irreligious, irreverent, profane, sinful, ungodly, unholy, wicked

implacable *adj* = **unyielding**, inflexible, intractable, merciless, pitiless, unbending, uncompromising, unforgiving

implant *v* **1** = **insert**, fix, graft **2** = **instil**, inculcate, infuse

implement *v* **1** = **carry out**, bring about, complete, effect, enforce, execute, fulfil, perform, realize ▷ *n* **2** = **tool**, apparatus, appliance, device, gadget, instrument, utensil

implore *v* = **beg**, beseech, entreat,

imply ❶ v -**plying**, -**plied** 1 indicate by hinting, suggest. 2 involve as a necessary consequence.

import ❶ v 1 bring in (goods) from another country. ▷ n 2 something imported. 3 importance. 4 meaning. **importation** n **importer** n.

important ❶ adj 1 of great significance or value. 2 having influence or power. **importance** n.

impose ❶ v 1 force the acceptance of. 2 (foll. by on) take unfair advantage (of). **imposing** adj grand, impressive. **imposition** n unreasonable demand.

impossible ❶ adj 1 not able to be done or to happen. 2 absurd or unreasonable. **impossibly** adv **impossibility** n, pl -**ties**.

impotent ❶ [imp-a-tent] adj 1 powerless. 2 (of a man) incapable of sexual intercourse. **impotence** n.

impound v take legal possession of, confiscate.

impoverish ❶ v make poor or weak.

impoverishment n.

impractical ❶ adj not sensible.

impregnable ❶ adj impossible to break into.

impregnate ❶ v 1 saturate, spread all through. 2 make pregnant. **impregnation** n.

impresario n, pl -**ios** person who runs theatre performances, concerts, etc.

● **SPELLING TIP**
● Don't be fooled into spelling **impresario**
● as *impressario*, which occurs 33 times in
● the Bank of English. The correct spelling
● has only one *s*.

impress ❶ v 1 affect strongly, usu. favourably. 2 stress, emphasize. 3 imprint, stamp. **impression** n 1 effect, esp. a strong or favourable one. 2 vague idea. 3 impersonation for entertainment. 4 mark made by pressing. **impressionable** adj easily impressed or influenced. **impressive** adj making a strong impression, esp. through size, importance, or quality.

—— THESAURUS ——

importune, plead with, pray

imply v 1 = **hint**, insinuate, intimate, signify, suggest 2 = **entail**, indicate, involve, mean, point to, presuppose

import v 1 = **bring in**, introduce ▷ n 3 = **importance**, consequence, magnitude, moment, significance, substance, weight 4 = **meaning**, drift, gist, implication, intention, sense, significance, thrust

important adj 1 = **significant**, far-reaching, momentous, seminal, serious, substantial, urgent, weighty 2 = **powerful**, eminent, high-ranking, influential, noteworthy, pre-eminent, prominent, skookum (*Canad*)

impose v 1 = **establish**, decree, fix, institute, introduce, levy, ordain 2 (foll. by on) = **inflict**, saddle (someone) with, take advantage of

impossible adj 1 = **inconceivable**, impracticable, out of the question,

unachievable, unattainable, unobtainable, unthinkable 2 = **absurd**, ludicrous, outrageous, preposterous, unreasonable

impotent adj 1 = **powerless**, feeble, frail, helpless, incapable, incapacitated, incompetent, ineffective, paralysed, weak

impoverish v = **bankrupt**, beggar, break, ruin

impractical adj = **unworkable**, impossible, impracticable, inoperable, nonviable, unrealistic, wild

impregnable adj = **invulnerable**, impenetrable, indestructible, invincible, secure, unassailable, unbeatable, unconquerable

impregnate v 1 = **saturate**, infuse, permeate, soak, steep, suffuse 2 = **fertilize**, inseminate, make pregnant

impress v 1 = **excite**, affect, inspire, make an impression, move, stir, strike, touch 2 = **stress**, bring home to, emphasize, fix, inculcate, instil into 3 = **imprint**, emboss,

imprint ❶ *n* 1 mark made by printing or stamping. 2 publisher's name and address on a book. ▷ *v* 3 produce (a mark) by printing or stamping.

imprison ❶ *v* put in prison. **imprisonment** *n*.

improbable ❶ *adj* not likely to be true or to happen. **improbability** *n*, *pl* -ties.

impromptu ❶ *adj* without planning or preparation.

improper ❶ *adj* 1 indecent. 2 incorrect or irregular. **improper fraction** fraction in which the numerator is larger than the denominator, as in 5/3.

improve ❶ *v* make or become better. **improvement** *n*.

improvident ❶ *adj* not planning for future needs. **improvidence** *n*.

improvise ❶ *v* 1 make use of whatever materials are available. 2 make up (a piece of music, speech, etc.) as one goes along. **improvisation** *n*.

impudent ❶ *adj* cheeky, disrespectful. **impudence** *n*.

impugn [imp-**yoon**] *v* challenge the truth

or validity of (something).

impulse ❶ *n* 1 sudden urge to do something. 2 short electrical signal passing along a wire or nerve or through the air. **on impulse** suddenly and without planning. **impulsive** *adj* acting or done without careful consideration. **impulsively** *adv*.

impunity ❶ [imp-**yoon**-it-ee] *n* **with impunity** without punishment.

impure ❶ *adj* 1 having dirty or unwanted substances mixed in. 2 immoral, obscene. **impurity** *n*.

impute *v* attribute responsibility to. **imputation** *n*.

in *prep* 1 indicating position inside, state or situation, etc. e.g. *in the net*; *in tears*. ▷ *adv* 2 indicating position inside, entry into, etc. e.g. *she stayed in*; *come in*. ▷ *adj* 3 fashionable. **inward** *adj* 1 directed towards the middle. 2 situated within. 3 spiritual or mental. ▷ *adv* 4 (also **inwards**) towards the inside or middle. **inwardly** *adv*.

───────────────────────────── THESAURUS ─────────

engrave, indent, mark, print, stamp

imprint *n* 1 = **mark**, impression, indentation, sign, stamp ▷ *v* 3 = **fix**, engrave, etch, impress, print, stamp

imprison *v* = **jail**, confine, detain, incarcerate, intern, lock up, put away, send down (*inf*)

improbable *adj* = **doubtful**, dubious, fanciful, far-fetched, implausible, questionable, unconvincing, unlikely, weak

impromptu *adj* = **unprepared**, ad-lib, extemporaneous, improvised, offhand, off the cuff (*inf*), spontaneous, unrehearsed, unscripted

improper *adj* 1 = **indecent**, risqué, smutty, suggestive, unbecoming, unseemly, untoward, vulgar 2 = **inappropriate**, out of place, uncalled-for, unfit, unsuitable, unwarranted

improve *v* a = **enhance**, ameliorate, better, correct, help, rectify, touch up, upgrade b = **progress**, advance, develop,

make strides, pick up, rally, rise

improvident *adj* = **imprudent**, careless, negligent, prodigal, profligate, reckless, short-sighted, spendthrift, thoughtless, wasteful

improvise *v* 1 = **concoct**, contrive, devise, throw together 2 = **extemporize**, ad-lib, busk, invent, play it by ear (*inf*), speak off the cuff (*inf*), wing it (*inf*)

impudent *adj* = **bold**, audacious, brazen, cheeky (*inf*), impertinent, insolent, presumptuous, rude, shameless

impulse *n* 1 = **urge**, caprice, feeling, inclination, notion, whim, wish

impunity *n* with impunity = **without punishment**, at liberty, with freedom, with immunity, with licence, with permission

impure *adj* 1 a = **unclean**, contaminated, defiled, dirty, infected, polluted, tainted b = **unrefined**, adulterated, debased, mixed 2 = **immoral**, corrupt, indecent, lascivious, lewd, licentious, obscene,

IN Indiana.

inability *n* lack of means or skill to do something.

inaccurate ① *adj* not correct. **inaccuracy** *n*, *pl* **-cies**.

inadequate ① *adj* **1** not enough. **2** not good enough. **inadequacy** *n*.

inane ① *adj* senseless, silly. **inanity** *n*.

inanimate ① *adj* not living.

inappropriate *adj* not suitable.

inarticulate *adj* unable to express oneself clearly or well.

inaugurate ① *v* **1** open or begin the use of, esp. with ceremony. **2** formally establish (a new leader) in office. **inaugural** *adj* **inauguration** *n*.

inborn ① *adj* existing from birth, natural.

inbox *n* Computers folder in a mailbox in which incoming messages are stored and displayed.

incalculable ① *adj* too great to be estimated.

incandescent *adj* glowing with heat. **incandescence** *n*.

incantation ① *n* ritual chanting of magic words or sounds.

incapable *adj* **1** (foll. by *of*) unable (to do something). **2** incompetent.

incapacitate ① *v* deprive of strength or ability. **incapacity** *n*.

incarcerate ① *v* imprison. **incarceration** *n*.

incarnate ① *adj* in human form. **incarnation** *n*.

incendiary [in-**send**-ya-ree] *adj* **1** (of a bomb, attack, etc.) designed to cause fires. ▷ *n*, *pl* **-aries 2** bomb designed to cause fires.

incense¹ ① *v* make very angry.

incense² *n* substance that gives off a sweet perfume when burned.

incentive ① *n* something that encourages effort or action.

inception ① *n* beginning.

incessant ① *adj* never stopping.

incest *n* sexual intercourse between two people too closely related to marry. **incestuous** *adj*.

inch *n* **1** unit of length equal to one twelfth

unchaste, x-rated (*inf*)

inaccurate *adj* = **incorrect**, defective, erroneous, faulty, imprecise, mistaken, out, shonky (*Aust & NZ inf*), unreliable, unsound, wrong

inadequate *adj* **1** = **insufficient**, meagre, scant, sketchy, sparse **2** = **deficient**, faulty, found wanting, incapable, incompetent, not up to scratch (*inf*), unqualified

inane *adj* = **senseless**, empty, fatuous, frivolous, futile, idiotic, mindless, silly, stupid, vacuous

inanimate *adj* = **lifeless**, cold, dead, defunct, extinct, inert

inaugurate *v* **1** = **launch**, begin, commence, get under way, initiate, institute, introduce, set in motion **2** = **invest**, induct, install

inborn *adj* = **natural**, congenital, hereditary, inbred, ingrained, inherent, innate, instinctive, intuitive, native

incalculable *adj* = **countless**, boundless, infinite, innumerable, limitless, numberless, untold, vast

incantation *n* = **chant**, charm, formula, invocation, spell

incapacitate *v* = **disable**, cripple, immobilize, lay up (*inf*), paralyse, put out of action (*inf*)

incarcerate *v* = **imprison**, confine, detain, impound, intern, jail *or* gaol, lock up, throw in jail

incarnate *adj* = **personified**, embodied, typified

incense¹ *v* = **anger**, enrage, inflame, infuriate, irritate, madden, make one's hackles rise, rile (*inf*)

incentive *n* = **encouragement**, bait, carrot (*inf*), enticement, inducement, lure, motivation, spur, stimulus

inception *n* = **beginning**, birth, commencement, dawn, initiation, origin, outset, start

incessant *adj* = **endless**, ceaseless,

of a foot or 2.54 centimetres. ▷ v **2** move
slowly and gradually.
incident ❶ n **1** something that happens.
2 event involving violence. **incidental** adj
occurring in connection with or resulting
from something more important.
incinerate ❶ v burn to ashes.
incineration n **incinerator** n furnace for
burning rubbish.
incipient ❶ adj just starting to appear or
happen.
incise v cut into with a sharp tool. **incision**
n **incisive** adj direct and forceful. **incisor** n
front tooth, used for biting into food.
incite ❶ v stir up, provoke. **incitement** n.
inclement ❶ adj (of weather) stormy or
severe. **inclemency** n.
incline ❶ v **1** lean, slope. **2** (cause to) have
a certain disposition or tendency. ▷ n
3 slope. **inclination** n **1** liking, tendency, or
preference. **2** slope.

include ❶ v **1** have as part of the whole.
2 put in as part of a set or group. **inclusion**
n **inclusive** adj including everything
(specified). **inclusively** adv.
incognito ❶ [in-kog-**nee**-toe] adj, adv
1 having adopted a false identity. ▷ n, pl
-tos 2 false identity.
incoherent ❶ adj unclear and impossible
to understand. **incoherence** n.
income ❶ n amount of money earned
from work, investments, etc. **income tax**
personal tax levied on annual income.
incoming ❶ adj **1** coming in. **2** about to
come into office.
incomparable ❶ adj beyond comparison,
unequalled. **incomparably** adv.
incompatible ❶ adj inconsistent or
conflicting. **incompatibility** n.
incompetent ❶ adj not having the
necessary ability or skill to do something.
incompetence n.

——————————— THESAURUS ———————————

constant, continual, eternal, interminable,
never-ending, nonstop, perpetual,
unceasing, unending
incident n **1** = **happening**, adventure,
episode, event, fact, matter, occasion,
occurrence **2** = **disturbance**, clash,
commotion, confrontation, contretemps,
scene
incinerate v = **burn up**, carbonize, char,
cremate, reduce to ashes
incipient adj = **beginning**, commencing,
developing, embryonic, inchoate, nascent,
starting
incite v = **provoke**, encourage, foment,
inflame, instigate, spur, stimulate, stir up,
urge, whip up
inclement adj = **stormy**, foul,
harsh, intemperate, rough, severe,
tempestuous
incline v **1** = **slope**, lean, slant, tilt, tip,
veer **2** = **predispose**, influence, persuade,
prejudice, sway ▷ n **3** = **slope**, ascent,
descent, dip, grade, gradient, rise
include v **1** = **contain**, comprise, cover,
embrace, encompass, incorporate,

involve, subsume, take in **2** = **introduce**,
add, enter, insert
incognito adj **1** = **in disguise**, disguised,
under an assumed name, unknown,
unrecognized
incoherent adj = **unintelligible**, confused,
disjointed, disordered, inarticulate,
inconsistent, jumbled, muddled, rambling,
stammering, stuttering
income n = **revenue**, earnings, pay,
proceeds, profits, receipts, salary, takings,
wages
incoming adj **1** = **arriving**, approaching,
entering, homeward, landing, returning
2 = **new**
incomparable adj = **unequalled**,
beyond compare, inimitable, matchless,
peerless, superlative, supreme,
transcendent, unmatched, unparalleled,
unrivalled
incompatible adj = **inconsistent**,
conflicting, contradictory, incongruous,
mismatched, unsuited
incompetent adj = **inept**, bungling,
floundering, incapable, ineffectual,

inconceivable ⓘ *adj* extremely unlikely, unimaginable.

inconclusive ⓘ *adj* not giving a final decision or result.

incongruous ⓘ *adj* inappropriate or out of place. **incongruity** *n*, *pl* -**ties**.

inconsequential *adj* unimportant, insignificant.

incontinent *adj* unable to control one's bladder or bowels. **incontinence** *n*.

incontrovertible ⓘ *adj* impossible to deny or disprove.

inconvenience ⓘ *n* **1** trouble or difficulty. ▷ *v* **2** cause trouble or difficulty to. **inconvenient** *adj*.

incorporate ⓘ *v* include or be included as part of a larger unit. **incorporation** *n*.

incorrigible ⓘ *adj* beyond correction or reform.

increase ⓘ *v* **1** make or become greater in size, number, etc. ▷ *n* **2** rise in number,

size, etc. **3** amount by which something increases. **increasingly** *adv*.

incredible ⓘ *adj* **1** hard to believe or imagine. **2** *informal* marvellous, amazing. **incredibly** *adv*.

incredulous ⓘ *adj* not willing to believe something. **incredulity** *n*.

increment ⓘ *n* increase in money or value, esp. a regular salary increase. **incremental** *adj*.

incriminate ⓘ *v* make (someone) seem guilty of a crime. **incriminating** *adj*.

incubate [in-cube-ate] *v* **1** (of a bird) hatch (eggs) by sitting on them. **2** grow (bacteria). **3** (of bacteria) remain inactive in an animal or person before causing disease. **incubation** *n* **incubator** *n* **1** heated enclosed apparatus for rearing premature babies. **2** apparatus for artificially hatching birds' eggs.

inculcate *v* fix in someone's mind by

inexpert, unfit, useless

inconceivable *adj* = **unimaginable**, beyond belief, incomprehensible, incredible, mind-boggling (*inf*), out of the question, unbelievable, unheard-of, unthinkable

inconclusive *adj* = **indecisive**, ambiguous, indeterminate, open, unconvincing, undecided, up in the air (*inf*), vague

incongruous *adj* = **inappropriate**, discordant, improper, incompatible, out of keeping, out of place, unbecoming, unsuitable

incontrovertible *adj* = **indisputable**, certain, established, incontestable, indubitable, irrefutable, positive, sure, undeniable, unquestionable

inconvenience *n* **1** = **trouble**, awkwardness, bother, difficulty, disadvantage, disruption, disturbance, fuss, hindrance, nuisance ▷ *v* **2** = **trouble**, bother, discommode, disrupt, disturb, put out, upset

incorporate *v* = **include**, absorb,

assimilate, blend, combine, integrate, merge, subsume

incorrigible *adj* = **incurable**, hardened, hopeless, intractable, inveterate, irredeemable, unreformed

increase *v* **1** = **grow**, advance, boost, develop, enlarge, escalate, expand, extend, multiply, raise, spread, swell ▷ *n* **2** = **growth**, development, enlargement, escalation, expansion, extension, gain, increment, rise, upturn

incredible *adj* **1** = **implausible**, beyond belief, far-fetched, improbable, inconceivable, preposterous, unbelievable, unimaginable, unthinkable **2** *Inf* = **amazing**, astonishing, astounding, extraordinary, prodigious, sensational (*inf*), wonderful

incredulous *adj* = **disbelieving**, distrustful, doubtful, dubious, sceptical, suspicious, unbelieving, unconvinced

increment *n* = **increase**, accrual, addition, advancement, augmentation, enlargement, gain, step up, supplement

incriminate *v* = **implicate**, accuse, blame,

constant repetition.

incumbent n **1** person holding a particular office or position. ▷ adj **2** **it is incumbent on** it is the duty of. **incumbency** n, pl -cies.

incur ❶ v -curring, -curred cause (something unpleasant) to happen.

indebted ❶ adj **1** owing gratitude for help or favours. **2** owing money. **indebtedness** n.

indecent ❶ adj **1** morally or sexually offensive. **2** unsuitable or unseemly, e.g. indecent haste. **indecency** n.

indeed adv **1** really, certainly. ▷ interj **2** expression of indignation or surprise.

indefatigable adj never getting tired.

indefensible ❶ adj **1** unable to be justified. **2** impossible to defend.

indefinite ❶ adj **1** without exact limits, e.g. for an indefinite period. **2** vague, unclear. **indefinite article** Grammar the word a or an. **indefinitely** adv.

indelible ❶ adj **1** impossible to erase or remove. **2** making indelible marks. **indelibly** adv.

indelicate ❶ adj crude, offensive, or

embarrassing.

indemnity ❶ n, pl -ties **1** insurance against loss or damage. **2** compensation for loss or damage.

indent v **1** start (a line of writing) further from the margin than the other lines. **2** order (goods) using a special order form. **indentation** n dent in a surface or edge.

independent ❶ adj **1** free from the control or influence of others. **2** separate. **3** financially self-reliant. **4** capable of acting for oneself or on one's own. ▷ n **5** politician who does represent any political party. **independence** n.

- ● **SPELLING TIP**
- ● People often get confused about how to
- ● spell **independent**. It is spelt independant
- ● 44 times in the Bank of English. It should
- ● be spelt with an e at the end in the
- ● same way as the noun it is related to:
- ● **independent** and **independence**.

indescribable ❶ adj too intense or extreme for words. **indescribably** adv.

indeterminate ❶ adj uncertain in extent, amount, or nature. **indeterminacy** n.

---

charge, impeach, inculpate, involve

incur v = **earn**, arouse, bring (upon oneself), draw, expose oneself to, gain, meet with, provoke

indebted adj **1** = **grateful**, beholden, obliged, obligated, under an obligation **2** = **in debt**, owing money

indecent adj **1** = **lewd**, crude, dirty, filthy, immodest, improper, impure, licentious, pornographic, salacious, scungy (Aust & NZ inf) **2** = **unbecoming**, in bad taste, indecorous, unseemly, vulgar

indeed adv **1** = **really**, actually, certainly, in truth, truly, undoubtedly

indefensible adj **1** = **unforgivable**, inexcusable, unjustifiable, unpardonable, untenable, unwarrantable, wrong

indefinite adj = **unclear**, doubtful, equivocal, ill-defined, imprecise, indeterminate, inexact, uncertain,

unfixed, vague

indelible adj **1** = **permanent**, enduring, indestructible, ineradicable, ingrained, lasting

indelicate adj = **offensive**, coarse, crude, embarrassing, immodest, risqué, rude, suggestive, tasteless, vulgar

indemnity n **1** = **insurance**, guarantee, protection, security **2** = **compensation**, redress, reimbursement, remuneration, reparation, restitution

independent adj **1** = **free**, autonomous, liberated, self-determining, self-governing, separate, sovereign, unconstrained, uncontrolled **3** = **self-sufficient**, liberated, self-contained, self-reliant, self-supporting

indescribable adj = **unutterable**, beyond description, beyond words, indefinable, inexpressible

indeterminate adj = **uncertain**, imprecise,

index *n, pl* **indices** [**in**-diss-eez]
1 alphabetical list of names or subjects
dealt with in a book. 2 file or catalogue
used to find things. ▷ *v* 3 provide (a book)
with an index. 4 enter in an index. 5 make
index-linked. **index finger** finger next to
the thumb. **index-linked** *adj* (of pensions,
wages, etc.) rising or falling in line with the
cost of living.

indicate ❶ *v* 1 be a sign or symptom
of. 2 point out. 3 state briefly. 4 (of a
measuring instrument) show a reading of.
indication *n* **indicative** *adj* 1 (foll. by *of*)
suggesting. 2 *Grammar* denoting a mood
of verbs used to make a statement. ▷ *n*
3 *Grammar* indicative mood. **indicator** *n*
1 something acting as a sign or indication.
2 flashing light on a vehicle showing the
driver's intention to turn. 3 dial or gauge.

indict ❶ [in-**dite**] *v* formally charge with a
crime. **indictable** *adj* **indictment** *n*.

indifferent ❶ *adj* 1 showing no interest or
concern. 2 of poor quality. **indifference** *n*.

indigenous [in-**dij**-in-uss] *adj* born in or
natural to a country.

indigent *adj* extremely poor. **indigence** *n*.

indigestion ❶ *n* (discomfort or pain

caused by) difficulty in digesting food.
indigestible *adj*.

indigo *adj* 1 deep violet-blue. ▷ *n* 2 dye of
this colour.

indirect ❶ *adj* 1 done or caused by someone
or something else. 2 not by a straight route.
indirect object *Grammar* person or thing
indirectly affected by the action of a verb,
e.g. *Amy* in *I bought Amy a bag*. **indirect
tax** tax, such as VAT, added to the price of
something.

indiscreet ❶ *adj* incautious or tactless in
revealing secrets. **indiscretion** *n*.

indiscriminate ❶ *adj* showing lack of
careful thought.

indispensable ❶ *adj* absolutely essential.

● **SPELLING TIP**
● For every twenty examples of the word
● **indispensable** in the Bank of English,
● there is one example of the misspelling
● *indispensible*. So remember that it ends
● in *-able*.

indisposed ❶ *adj* unwell, ill.
indisposition *n*.

indisputable ❶ *adj* beyond doubt.
indisputably *adv*.

indissoluble *adj* permanent.

i

indefinite, inexact, undefined, unfixed,
unspecified, unstipulated, vague

indicate *v* 1 = **signify**, betoken, denote,
imply, manifest, point to, reveal, suggest
2 = **point out**, designate, specify
4 = **show**, display, express, read, record,
register

indict *v* = **charge**, accuse, arraign, impeach,
prosecute, summon

indifferent *adj* 1 = **unconcerned**, aloof,
callous, cold, cool, detached, impervious,
inattentive, uninterested, unmoved,
unsympathetic 2 = **mediocre**, moderate,
no great shakes (*inf*), ordinary, passable,
so-so (*inf*), undistinguished

indigestion *n* = **heartburn**, dyspepsia,
upset stomach

indirect *adj* 1 = **incidental**, secondary,
subsidiary, unintended 2 = **circuitous**,

long-drawn-out, meandering, oblique,
rambling, roundabout, tortuous,
wandering

indiscreet *adj* = **tactless**, impolitic,
imprudent, incautious, injudicious, naive,
rash, reckless, unwise

indiscriminate *adj* = **random**,
careless, desultory, general, uncritical,
undiscriminating, unsystematic,
wholesale

indispensable *adj* = **essential**, crucial,
imperative, key, necessary, needed,
requisite, vital

indisposed *adj* = **ill**, ailing, crook (*Aust &
NZ sl*), poorly (*inf*), sick, under the weather,
unwell

indisputable *adj* = **undeniable**,
beyond doubt, certain, incontestable,
incontrovertible, indubitable, irrefutable,

individual ❶ *adj* **1** characteristic of or meant for a single person or thing. **2** separate, distinct. **3** distinctive, unusual. ▷ *n* **4** single person or thing. **individually** *adv* **individuality** *n* **individualism** *n* principle of living one's life in one's own way. **individualist** *n* **individualistic** *adj*.

indoctrinate ❶ *v* teach (someone) to accept a doctrine or belief uncritically. **indoctrination** *n*.

indolent ❶ *adj* lazy. **indolence** *n*.

indoor *adj* inside a building. **indoors** *adv*.

indubitable ❶ *adj* beyond doubt, certain. **indubitably** *adv*.

induce ❶ *v* **1** persuade or influence. **2** cause. **3** *Med* cause (a woman) to go into labour or bring on (labour) by the use of drugs etc. **inducement** *n* something used to persuade someone to do something.

induct *v* formally install (someone, esp. a clergyman) in office.

indulge ❶ *v* **1** allow oneself pleasure. **2** allow (someone) to have or do everything he or she wants. **indulgence** *n* **1** something allowed because it gives pleasure. **2** act of indulging oneself or someone else. **3** liberal or tolerant treatment. **indulgent** *adj* **indulgently** *adv*.

industry ❶ *n*, *pl* **-tries 1** manufacture of goods. **2** branch of this, e.g. *the music industry*. **3** quality of working hard. **industrial** *adj* of, used in, or employed in industry. **industrious** *adj* hard-working.

inedible *adj* not fit to be eaten.

ineffable *adj* too great for words.

ineligible ❶ *adj* not qualified for or entitled to something.

inept ❶ *adj* clumsy, lacking skill. **ineptitude** *n*.

inert ❶ *adj* **1** without the power of motion or resistance. **2** chemically unreactive.

inescapable ❶ *adj* unavoidable.

inestimable ❶ *adj* too great to be estimated.

inevitable ❶ *adj* unavoidable, sure to happen. **the inevitable** something that

unquestionable

individual *adj* **1** = **personal**, characteristic, exclusive, own, special, specific **3** = **distinctive**, idiosyncratic, munted (*NZ sl*), particular, peculiar, singular, unique ▷ *n* **4** = **person**, being, character, creature, soul, unit

indoctrinate *v* = **train**, brainwash, drill, ground, imbue, initiate, instruct, school, teach

indolent *adj* = **lazy**, idle, inactive, inert, languid, lethargic, listless, slothful, sluggish, workshy

indubitable *adj* = **certain**, incontestable, incontrovertible, indisputable, irrefutable, obvious, sure, undeniable, unquestionable

induce *v* **1** = **persuade**, convince, encourage, incite, influence, instigate, prevail upon, prompt, talk into **2** = **cause**, bring about, effect, engender, generate, give rise to, lead to, occasion, produce

indulge *v* **1** = **gratify**, feed, give way to, pander to, satisfy, yield to **2** = **spoil**, cosset, give in to, go along with, humour, mollycoddle, pamper

industry *n* **1, 2** = **business**, commerce, manufacturing, production, trade **3** = **effort**, activity, application, diligence, labour, tirelessness, toil, zeal

ineligible *adj* = **unqualified**, disqualified, ruled out, unacceptable, unfit, unsuitable

inept *adj* = **incompetent**, bumbling, bungling, clumsy, inexpert, maladroit

inert *adj* **1** = **inactive**, dead, dormant, immobile, lifeless, motionless, static, still, unresponsive **2** = **unreactive**

inescapable *adj* = **unavoidable**, certain, destined, fated, ineluctable, inevitable, inexorable, sure

inestimable *adj* = **incalculable**, immeasurable, invaluable, precious, priceless, prodigious

inevitable *adj* = **unavoidable**, assured, certain, destined, fixed, ineluctable,

cannot be prevented. **inevitably** adv
inevitability n.
inexorable ❶ adj unable to be prevented
from continuing or progressing.
inexorably adv.
inexplicable ❶ adj impossible to explain.
inexplicably adv.
infallible ❶ adj never wrong. **infallibly** adv
infallibility n.
infamous ❶ [in-fam-uss] adj well-known
for something bad. **infamy** n.
infant ❶ n very young child. **infancy**
n 1 early childhood. 2 early stage of
development. **infantile** adj childish.
infantry n soldiers who fight on foot.
infect ❶ v 1 affect with a disease. 2 affect
with a feeling. **infection** n **infectious** adj
1 (of a disease) spreading without actual
contact. 2 spreading from person to
person, e.g. infectious enthusiasm.
infer ❶ v -ferring, -ferred work out from
evidence. **inference** n.
inferior ❶ adj 1 lower in quality, position,
or status. ▷ n 2 person of lower position or

status. **inferiority** n.
infernal ❶ adj 1 of hell. 2 informal irritating.
inferno n, pl -nos intense raging fire.
infertile ❶ adj 1 unable to produce
offspring. 2 (of soil) barren, not productive.
infertility n.
infest ❶ v inhabit or overrun in unpleasantly
large numbers. **infestation** n.
infidelity n, pl -ties (act of) sexual
unfaithfulness to one's husband, wife, or
lover.
infiltrate ❶ v enter gradually and secretly.
infiltration n **infiltrator** n.
infinite ❶ [in-fin-it] adj without any limit
or end. **infinitely** adv **infinity** n endless
space, time, or number.
infinitive n Grammar form of a verb not
showing tense, person, or number, e.g.
to sleep.
infirm ❶ adj physically or mentally weak.
infirmity n, pl -ties.
inflame ❶ v make angry or excited.
inflamed adj (of part of the body)
red, swollen, and painful because of

——— THESAURUS ———

inescapable, inexorable, sure
inexorable adj = **unrelenting**,
inescapable, relentless, remorseless,
unbending, unyielding
inexplicable adj = **unaccountable**,
baffling, enigmatic, incomprehensible,
insoluble, mysterious, mystifying, strange,
unfathomable, unintelligible
infallible adj = **sure**, certain, dependable,
foolproof, reliable, sure-fire (inf),
trustworthy, unbeatable, unfailing
infamous adj = **notorious**, disreputable,
ignominious, ill-famed
infant n = **baby**, babe, bairn (Scot), child,
toddler, tot
infect v 1 = **contaminate**, affect, blight,
corrupt, defile, poison, pollute, taint
infer v = **deduce**, conclude, derive, gather,
presume, surmise, understand
inferior adj 1 = **lower**, lesser, menial,
minor, secondary, subordinate, subsidiary
▷ n 2 = **underling**, junior, menial,

subordinate
infernal adj 1 = **devilish**, accursed,
damnable, damned, diabolical, fiendish,
hellish, satanic
infertile adj = **barren**, sterile, unfruitful,
unproductive
infest v = **overrun**, beset, invade,
penetrate, permeate, ravage, swarm,
throng
infiltrate v = **penetrate**, filter through,
insinuate oneself, make inroads (into),
percolate, permeate, pervade, sneak in
(inf)
infinite adj = **never-ending**, boundless,
eternal, everlasting, illimitable,
immeasurable, inexhaustible, limitless,
measureless, unbounded
infirm adj = **frail**, ailing, debilitated,
decrepit, doddering, enfeebled, failing,
feeble, weak
inflame v = **enrage**, anger, arouse, excite,
incense, infuriate, madden, provoke,

infection. **inflammation** n.

inflate ❶ v 1 expand by filling with air or gas. 2 cause economic inflation in. **inflatable** adj 1 able to be inflated. ▷ n 2 plastic or rubber object which can be inflated.

inflection, inflexion n 1 change in the pitch of the voice. 2 Grammar change in the form of a word to show grammatical use.

inflexible ❶ adj 1 unwilling to be persuaded, obstinate. 2 (of a policy etc.) firmly fixed, unalterable. **inflexibly** adv **inflexibility** n.

inflict ❶ v impose (something unpleasant) on. **infliction** n.

influence ❶ n 1 effect of one person or thing on another. 2 (person with) the power to have such an effect. ▷ v 3 have an effect on. **influential** adj.

influenza n contagious viral disease causing headaches, muscle pains, and fever.

influx ❶ n arrival or entry of many people or things.

inform ❶ v 1 tell. 2 give incriminating information to the police. **informant** n person who gives information.

information n knowledge or facts.
informative adj giving useful information.
information superhighway worldwide network of computers transferring information at high speed. **information technology** use of computers and electronic technology to store and communicate information. **informer** n person who informs to the police.

informal ❶ adj 1 relaxed and friendly. 2 appropriate for everyday life or use. **informally** adv **informality** n.

infrared adj of or using rays below the red end of the visible spectrum.

infrastructure n basic facilities, services, and equipment needed for a country or organization to function properly.

infringe ❶ v break (a law or agreement). **infringement** n.

infuriate ❶ v make very angry.

infuse v 1 fill (with an emotion or quality). 2 soak to extract flavour. **infusion** n 1 infusing. 2 liquid obtained by infusing.

ingenious ❶ [in-**jean**-ee-uss] adj showing cleverness and originality. **ingenuity** [in-jen-**new**-it-ee] n.

ingenuous ❶ [in-**jen**-new-uss] adj unsophisticated and trusting.

━━━━━━━━━━━━━━━━━━━━━━━━ THESAURUS ━━━━━━━━━━━━━━━━━━━━━━

rouse, stimulate

inflate v 1 = **expand**, bloat, blow up, dilate, distend, enlarge, increase, puff up or out, pump up, swell

inflexible adj 1 = **obstinate**, implacable, intractable, obdurate, resolute, set in one's ways, steadfast, stubborn, unbending, uncompromising

inflict v = **impose**, administer, apply, deliver, levy, mete or deal out, visit, wreak

influence n 1 = **effect**, hold, magnetism, power, spell, sway, weight 2 = **power**, ascendancy, authority, clout (inf), control, domination, importance, leverage, mana (NZ), mastery, prestige, pull (inf) ▷ v 3 = **affect**, control, direct, guide, manipulate, sway

influx n = **arrival**, incursion, inrush,

inundation, invasion, rush

inform v 1 = **tell**, advise, communicate, enlighten, instruct, notify, teach, tip off 2 = **betray**, blow the whistle on (inf), denounce, grass (Brit sl), incriminate, inculpate, shop (sl, chiefly Brit), squeal (sl)

informal adj 1 = **relaxed**, casual, colloquial, cosy, easy, familiar, natural, simple, unofficial

infringe v = **break**, contravene, disobey, transgress, violate

infuriate v = **enrage**, anger, exasperate, incense, irritate, madden, provoke, rile

ingenious adj = **creative**, bright, brilliant, clever, crafty, inventive, original, resourceful, shrewd

ingenuous adj = **naive**, artless, guileless, honest, innocent, open, plain, simple,

ingot n oblong block of cast metal.
ingrained adj firmly fixed.
ingratiate ⊕ v try to make (oneself) popular with someone. **ingratiating** adj.
ingredient ⊕ n component of a mixture or compound.
inhabit ⊕ v-**habiting, -habited** live in. **inhabitant** n.
inhale ⊕ v breathe in (air, smoke, etc.). **inhalation** n **inhalant** n medical preparation inhaled to help breathing problems. **inhaler** n container for an inhalant.
inherent ⊕ adj existing as an inseparable part.
inherit ⊕ v-**heriting, -herited** 1 receive (money etc.) from someone who has died. 2 receive (a characteristic) from an earlier generation. 3 receive from a predecessor. **inheritance** n **inheritor** n.
inhibit ⊕ v-**hibiting, -hibited** 1 restrain (an impulse or desire). 2 hinder or prevent (action). **inhibited** adj **inhibition** n feeling

of fear or embarrassment that stops one from behaving naturally.
inhospitable ⊕ adj 1 not welcoming, unfriendly. 2 difficult to live in, harsh.
inhuman ⊕ adj 1 cruel or brutal. 2 not human.
inhumane ⊕ adj cruel or brutal. **inhumanity** n.
inimical ⊕ adj unfavourable or hostile.
inimitable ⊕ adj impossible to imitate, unique.
iniquity ⊕ n, pl -**ties** 1 injustice or wickedness. 2 wicked act. **iniquitous** adj.
initial ⊕ adj 1 first, at the beginning. ▷ n 2 first letter, esp. of a person's name. ▷ v -**tialling, -tialled** 3 sign with one's initials. **initially** adv.
initiate ⊕ v 1 begin or set going. 2 admit (someone) into a closed group. 3 instruct in the basics of something. ▷ n 4 recently initiated person. **initiation** n **initiator** n.

THESAURUS

---

sincere, trusting, unsophisticated
ingratiate v = **pander to**, crawl, curry favour, fawn, flatter, grovel, insinuate oneself, toady
ingredient n = **component**, constituent, element, part
inhabit v = **live**, abide, dwell, occupy, populate, reside
inhale v = **breathe in**, draw in, gasp, respire, suck in
inherent adj = **innate**, essential, hereditary, inborn, inbred, ingrained, inherited, intrinsic, native, natural
inherit v 1 = **be left**, come into, fall heir to, succeed to
inhibit v 1 = **restrain**, check, constrain, curb, discourage, hold back or in 2 = **hinder**, check, frustrate, hold back, impede, obstruct, prevent
inhospitable adj 1 = **unfriendly**, cool, uncongenial, unreceptive, unsociable, unwelcoming, xenophobic 2 = **bleak**, barren, desolate, forbidding, godforsaken, hostile

inhuman adj 1 = **cruel**, barbaric, brutal, cold-blooded, heartless, merciless, pitiless, ruthless, savage, unfeeling
inhumane adj = **cruel**, brutal, heartless, pitiless, unfeeling, unkind, unsympathetic
inimical adj = **hostile**, adverse, antagonistic, ill-disposed, opposed, unfavourable, unfriendly, unwelcoming
inimitable adj = **unique**, consummate, incomparable, matchless, peerless, unparalleled, unrivalled
iniquity n = **wickedness**, abomination, evil, injustice, sin, wrong
initial adj 1 = **first**, beginning, incipient, introductory, opening, primary
initiate v 1 = **begin**, commence, get under way, kick off (inf), launch, open, originate, set in motion, start 2 = **induct**, indoctrinate, introduce, invest 3 = **instruct**, acquaint with, coach, familiarize with, teach, train ▷ n 4 = **novice**, beginner, convert, entrant, learner, member, probationer

inject ❶ v 1 put (a fluid) into the body with a syringe. 2 introduce (a new element), e.g. *try to inject a bit of humour*. **injection** n.

injunction ❶ n court order not to do something.

injustice ❶ n 1 unfairness. 2 unfair action.

ink n 1 coloured liquid used for writing or printing. ▷ v 2 (foll. by *in*) mark in ink (something already marked in pencil). **inky** adj 1 dark or black. 2 covered in ink.

inkling ❶ n slight idea or suspicion.

inland ❶ adj, adv in or towards the interior of a country, away from the sea. **Inland Revenue** government department that collects taxes.

inlay n inlaid substance or pattern.

inlet ❶ n 1 narrow strip of water extending from the sea into the land. 2 valve etc. through which liquid or gas enters.

inmate n person living in an institution such as a prison.

inmost ❶ adj innermost.

inn n pub or small hotel, esp. in the country. **innkeeper** n.

innards pl n informal 1 internal organs. 2 working parts of a machine.

innate ❶ adj being part of someone's nature, inborn.

inner ❶ adj 1 happening or located inside. 2 relating to private feelings, e.g. *the inner self*. **innermost** adj furthest inside. **inner city** parts of a city near the centre, esp. having social and economic problems.

innings n 1 Sport player's or side's turn of batting. 2 period of opportunity.

innocent ❶ adj 1 not guilty of a crime. 2 without experience of evil. 3 without malicious intent. ▷ n 4 innocent person, esp. a child. **innocence** n.

innocuous adj not harmful. **innocuously** adv.

- ● SPELLING TIP
- ● Always make sure there are two *n*s in
- ● **innocuous**. It is more common to miss
- ● out an *n* than to double the *c* by mistake.

innuendo ❶ n, pl **-does** (remark making) an indirect reference to something rude or unpleasant.

innumerable ❶ adj too many to be counted.

inoculate v protect against disease by injecting with a vaccine. **inoculation** n.

——————————————— THESAURUS ——————

inject v 1 = **vaccinate**, inoculate 2 = **introduce**, bring in, infuse, insert, instil

injunction n = **order**, command, exhortation, instruction, mandate, precept, ruling

injustice n 1 = **unfairness**, bias, discrimination, inequality, inequity, iniquity, oppression, partisanship, prejudice, wrong

inkling n = **suspicion**, clue, conception, hint, idea, indication, intimation, notion, suggestion, whisper

inland adj = **interior**, domestic, internal, upcountry

inlet n 1 = **bay**, bight, creek, firth or frith (Scot), fjord, passage

inmost adj = **deepest**, basic, central, essential, innermost, intimate, personal, private, secret

innate adj = **inborn**, congenital, constitutional, essential, inbred, ingrained, inherent, instinctive, intuitive, native, natural

inner adj 1 = **inside**, central, interior, internal, inward, middle 2 = **hidden**, intimate, personal, private, repressed, secret, unrevealed

innocent adj 1 = **not guilty**, blameless, guiltless, honest, in the clear, uninvolved 2 = **naive**, artless, childlike, credulous, gullible, ingenuous, open, simple, unworldly 3 = **harmless**, innocuous, inoffensive, unobjectionable, well-intentioned, well-meant

innuendo n = **insinuation**, aspersion, hint, implication, imputation, intimation, overtone, suggestion, whisper

innumerable adj = **countless**, beyond number, incalculable, infinite, multitudinous, myriad, numberless,

● **SPELLING TIP**
● The verb **inoculate** has only one *n* and
● one *c*. There are 235 occurrences of the
● correct spelling of the noun **inoculation**
● in the Bank of English, with lots of
● different misspellings. The most popular
● one, *innoculation*, occurs 31 times.

inoperable *adj* (of a tumour or cancer)
unable to be surgically removed.
inordinate ⊕ *adj* excessive.
inorganic ⊕ *adj* **1** not having the
characteristics of living organisms. **2** of
chemical substances that do not contain
carbon.
input *n* **1** resources put into a project
etc. **2** data fed into a computer. ▷ *v*
-putting, -put 3 enter (data) in a
computer.
inquest ⊕ *n* official inquiry into a sudden
death.
inquire ⊕ *v* seek information or ask
(about). **inquirer** *n* **inquiry** *n, pl* **-ries**
1 question. **2** investigation.
inquisition ⊕ *n* thorough investigation.

inquisitor *n* **inquisitorial** *adj*.
inquisitive ⊕ *adj* excessively curious
about other people's affairs.
inquisitively *adv*.
insane ⊕ *adj* **1** mentally ill. **2** stupidly
irresponsible. **insanely** *adv* **insanity** *n*.
insatiable ⊕ [in-**saysh**-a-bl] *adj* unable to
be satisfied.
inscribe ⊕ *v* write or carve words on.
inscription *n* words inscribed.
inscrutable ⊕ *adj* mysterious,
enigmatic.
insect *n* small animal with six legs
and usu. wings, such as an ant or fly.
insecticide *n* substance for killing insects.
insectivorous *adj* insect-eating.
insecure ⊕ *adj* **1** anxious, not confident.
2 not safe or well-protected.
insensible ⊕ *adj* **1** unconscious, without
feeling. **2** (foll. by *to* or *of*) not aware (of) or
affected (by). **insensibility** *n*.
insensitive ⊕ *adj* unaware of or
ignoring other people's feelings.
insensitivity *n*.

——————————— THESAURUS ———————————

numerous, unnumbered, untold
inordinate *adj* = **excessive**,
disproportionate, extravagant,
immoderate, intemperate, preposterous,
unconscionable, undue, unreasonable,
unwarranted
inorganic *adj* **1** = **artificial**, chemical,
man-made
inquest *n* = **inquiry**, inquisition,
investigation, probe
inquire *v* = **investigate**, ask, examine,
explore, look into, make inquiries, probe,
query, question, research
inquisition *n* = **investigation**, cross-
examination, examination, grilling (*inf*),
inquest, inquiry, questioning, third degree
(*inf*)
inquisitive *adj* = **prying**, curious, nosy (*inf*),
probing
insane *adj* **1** = **mad**, crazed, crazy,
demented, deranged, mentally ill, out
of one's mind **2** = **stupid**, daft (*inf*),

foolish, idiotic, impractical, irrational,
irresponsible, preposterous, senseless
insatiable *adj* = **unquenchable**, greedy,
intemperate, rapacious, ravenous,
voracious
inscribe *v* = **carve**, cut, engrave, etch,
impress, imprint
inscrutable *adj* **a** = **mysterious**,
hidden, incomprehensible, inexplicable,
unexplainable, unfathomable,
unintelligible **b** = **enigmatic**, blank,
deadpan, impenetrable, poker-faced (*inf*),
unreadable
insecure *adj* **1** = **anxious**, afraid,
uncertain, unsure **2** = **unsafe**, defenceless,
exposed, unguarded, unprotected,
vulnerable, wide-open
insensible *adj* **2** (foll. by *to* or *of*)
= **unaware**, impervious, oblivious,
unaffected, unconscious, unmindful
insensitive *adj* = **unfeeling**, callous,
hardened, indifferent, thick-skinned,

insert ⓞ *v* **1** put inside or include. ▷ *n* **2** something inserted. **insertion** *n*.

inset *n* small picture inserted within a larger one.

inshore *adj* **1** close to the shore. ▷ *adj, adv* **2** towards the shore.

inside ⓞ *prep* **1** in or to the interior of. ▷ *adj* **2** on or of the inside. **3** by or from someone within an organization, e.g. *inside information*. ▷ *adv* **4** on, in, or to the inside, indoors. **5** *slang* in(to) prison. ▷ *n* **6** inner side, surface, or part. ▷ *pl* **7** *informal* stomach and bowels. **inside out** with the inside facing outwards. **know inside out** know thoroughly. **insider** *n* member of a group who has privileged knowledge about it.

insidious ⓞ *adj* subtle or unseen but dangerous.

insight ⓞ *n* deep understanding.

insignia ⓞ *n, pl* **-nias, -nia** badge or emblem of honour or office.

insignificant ⓞ *adj* not important. **insignificance** *n*.

insincere ⓞ *adj* showing false feelings, not genuine. **insincerely** *adv* **insincerity** *n, pl* **-ties**.

insinuate ⓞ *v* **1** suggest indirectly. **2** work (oneself) into a position by gradual manoeuvres. **insinuation** *n*.

insipid ⓞ *adj* lacking interest, spirit, or flavour.

insist ⓞ *v* demand or state firmly. **insistent** *adj* **1** making persistent demands. **2** demanding attention. **insistence** *n*.

insole *n* inner sole of a shoe or boot.

insolent ⓞ *adj* rude and disrespectful. **insolence** *n*.

insoluble ⓞ *adj* **1** incapable of being solved. **2** incapable of being dissolved.

insolvent ⓞ *adj* unable to pay one's debts. **insolvency** *n*.

insomnia ⓞ *n* inability to sleep.

                                               THESAURUS

tough, uncaring, unconcerned

insert *v* **1** = **enter**, embed, implant, introduce, place, put, stick in

inside *adj* **2** = **inner**, interior, internal, inward **3** = **confidential**, classified, exclusive, internal, private, restricted, secret ▷ *adv* **4** = **indoors**, under cover, within ▷ *n* **6** = **interior**, contents ▷ *pl* **7** *Inf* = **stomach**, belly, bowels, entrails, guts, innards (*inf*), viscera, vitals

insidious *adj* = **stealthy**, deceptive, sly, smooth, sneaking, subtle, surreptitious

insight *n* = **understanding**, awareness, comprehension, discernment, judgment, observation, penetration, perception, perspicacity, vision

insignia *n* = **badge**, crest, emblem, symbol

insignificant *adj* = **unimportant**, inconsequential, irrelevant, meaningless, minor, nondescript, paltry, petty, trifling, trivial

insincere *adj* = **deceitful**, dishonest, disingenuous, duplicitous, false, hollow, hypocritical, lying, two-faced, untruthful

insinuate *v* **1** = **imply**, allude, hint, indicate, intimate, suggest **2** = **ingratiate**, curry favour, get in with, worm *or* work one's way in

insipid *adj* **a** = **bland**, anaemic, characterless, colourless, prosaic, uninteresting, vapid, wishy-washy (*inf*) **b** = **tasteless**, bland, flavourless, unappetizing, watery

insist *v* **a** = **demand**, lay down the law, put one's foot down (*inf*), require **b** = **state**, assert, aver, claim, maintain, reiterate, repeat, swear, vow

insolent *adj* = **rude**, bold, contemptuous, impertinent, impudent, insubordinate, insulting

insoluble *adj* **1** = **inexplicable**, baffling, impenetrable, indecipherable, mysterious, unaccountable, unfathomable, unsolvable

insolvent *adj* = **bankrupt**, broke (*inf*), failed, gone bust (*inf*), gone to the wall, in receivership, munted (*NZ sl*), ruined

insomnia *n* = **sleeplessness**, wakefulness

insomniac n **insomnious** adj.

inspect ❶ v check closely or officially. **inspection** n **inspector** n **1** person who inspects. **2** high-ranking police officer.

inspire ❶ v **1** fill with enthusiasm, stimulate. **2** arouse (an emotion). **inspiration** n **1** creative influence or stimulus. **2** brilliant idea. **inspirational** adj.

install ❶ v **1** put in and prepare (equipment) for use. **2** place (a person) formally in a position or rank. **installation** n **1** installing. **2** equipment installed. **3** place containing equipment for a particular purpose, e.g. *oil installations*.

instalment ❶ n any of the portions of a thing presented or a debt paid in successive parts.

instance ❶ n **1** particular example. ▷ v **2** mention as an example. **for instance** as an example.

instant ❶ n **1** very brief time. **2** particular moment. ▷ adj **3** happening at once.

4 (of foods) requiring little preparation. **instantly** adv.

instead ❶ adv as a replacement or substitute.

instep n **1** part of the foot forming the arch between the ankle and toes. **2** part of a shoe etc. covering this.

instigate ❶ v cause to happen. **instigation** n **instigator** n.

instil ❶ v -**stilling**, -**stilled** introduce (an idea etc.) gradually into someone's mind.

instinct ❶ n inborn tendency to behave in a certain way. **instinctive** adj **instinctively** adv.

institute ❶ n **1** organization set up for a specific purpose, esp. research or teaching. ▷ v **2** start or establish. **institution** n large important organization such as a university or bank.

instruct ❶ v **1** order to do something. **2** teach (someone) how to do something. **instruction** n **1** order to do something. **2** teaching. ▷ pl **3** information on how

---
THESAURUS
---

inspect v = **examine**, check, go over or through, investigate, look over, scrutinize, survey, vet

inspire v **1** = **stimulate**, animate, encourage, enliven, galvanize, gee up, influence, spur **2** = **arouse**, enkindle, excite, give rise to, produce

install v **1** = **set up**, fix, lay, lodge, place, position, put in, station **2** = **induct**, establish, inaugurate, institute, introduce, invest

instalment n = **portion**, chapter, division, episode, part, repayment, section

instance n **1** = **example**, case, illustration, occasion, occurrence, situation ▷ v **2** = **quote**, adduce, cite, mention, name, specify

instant n **1** = **second**, flash, jiffy (inf), moment, split second, trice, twinkling of an eye (inf) **2** = **juncture**, moment, occasion, point, time ▷ adj **3** = **immediate**, direct, instantaneous, on-the-spot, prompt, quick, split-second

4 = **precooked**, convenience, fast, ready-mixed

instead adv = **rather**, alternatively, in lieu, in preference, on second thoughts, preferably **instead of** = **in place of**, in lieu of, rather than

instigate v = **provoke**, bring about, incite, influence, initiate, prompt, set off, start, stimulate, trigger

instil v = **introduce**, engender, imbue, implant, inculcate, infuse, insinuate

instinct n = **intuition**, faculty, gift, impulse, knack, predisposition, proclivity, talent, tendency

institute n **1** = **society**, academy, association, college, foundation, guild, institution, school ▷ v **2** = **establish**, fix, found, initiate, introduce, launch, organize, originate, pioneer, set up, start

instruct v **1** = **order**, bid, charge, command, direct, enjoin, tell **2** = **teach**, coach, drill, educate, ground, school, train, tutor

to do or use something. **instructive** *adj* informative or helpful. **instructor** *n*.

instrument ❶ *n* 1 tool used for particular work. 2 object played to produce a musical sound. 3 measuring device to show height, speed, etc. 4 *informal* someone or something used to achieve an aim. **instrumental** *adj* 1 (foll. by *in*) having an important function (in). 2 played by or composed for musical instruments. **instrumentalist** *n* player of a musical instrument. **instrumentation** *n* 1 set of instruments in a car etc. 2 arrangement of music for instruments.

insubordinate ❶ *adj* not submissive to authority. **insubordination** *n*.

insufferable ❶ *adj* unbearable.

insular ❶ *adj* not open to new ideas, narrow-minded. **insularity** *n*.

insulate ❶ *v* 1 prevent or reduce the transfer of electricity, heat, or sound by surrounding or lining with a nonconducting material. 2 isolate or set apart. **insulation** *n* **insulator** *n*.

insulin *n* hormone produced in the

pancreas that controls the amount of sugar in the blood.

insult ❶ *v* 1 behave rudely to, offend. ▷ *n* 2 insulting remark or action. **insulting** *adj*.

insuperable ❶ *adj* impossible to overcome.

insurrection ❶ *n* rebellion.

intact ❶ *adj* not changed or damaged in any way.

intake *n* amount or number taken in.

integer *n* positive or negative whole number or zero.

integral *adj* 1 being an essential part of a whole. ▷ *n* 2 *Maths* sum of a large number of very small quantities.

integrity ❶ *n* 1 quality of having high moral principles. 2 quality of being united.

intellect ❶ *n* power of thinking and reasoning. **intellectual** *adj* 1 of or appealing to the intellect. 2 clever, intelligent. ▷ *n* 3 intellectual person.

intelligent ❶ *adj* 1 able to understand, learn, and think things out quickly. 2 (of a computerized device) able to initiate

——————————————————————— THESAURUS ———————————

instrument *n* 1 = **tool**, apparatus, appliance, contraption (*inf*), device, gadget, implement, mechanism 4 *Inf* = **means**, agency, agent, mechanism, medium, organ, vehicle

insubordinate *adj* = **disobedient**, defiant, disorderly, mutinous, rebellious, recalcitrant, refractory, undisciplined, ungovernable, unruly

insufferable *adj* = **unbearable**, detestable, dreadful, impossible, insupportable, intolerable, unendurable

insular *adj* = **narrow-minded**, blinkered, circumscribed, inward-looking, limited, narrow, parochial, petty, provincial

insulate *v* 2 = **isolate**, close off, cocoon, cushion, cut off, protect, sequester, shield

insult *v* 1 = **offend**, abuse, affront, call names, put down, slander, slight, snub *n* 2 = **abuse**, affront, aspersion, insolence, offence, put-down, slap in the face (*inf*),

slight, snub

insuperable *adj* = **insurmountable**, impassable, invincible, unconquerable

insurrection *n* = **rebellion**, coup, insurgency, mutiny, revolt, revolution, riot, uprising

intact *adj* = **undamaged**, complete, entire, perfect, sound, unbroken, unharmed, unimpaired, unscathed, whole

integral *adj* 1 = **essential**, basic, component, constituent, fundamental, indispensable, intrinsic, necessary

integrity *n* 1 = **honesty**, goodness, honour, incorruptibility, principle, probity, purity, rectitude, uprightness, virtue 2 = **soundness**, coherence, cohesion, completeness, unity, wholeness

intellect *n* = **intelligence**, brains (*inf*), judgment, mind, reason, sense, understanding

intelligent *adj* 1 = **clever**, brainy (*inf*),

or modify action in the light of ongoing events. **intelligence** n 1 quality of being intelligent. 2 secret government or military information. 3 people or department collecting such information.

intemperate ● adj 1 unrestrained, uncontrolled. 2 drinking alcohol to excess. **intemperance** n.

intend ● v 1 propose or plan (to do something). 2 have as one's purpose.

intense ● adj 1 of great strength or degree. 2 deeply emotional. **intensity** n **intensify** v -**fying**, -**fied** make or become more intense. **intensification** n.

intent ● n 1 intention. ▷ adj 2 paying close attention. **intent on doing something** determined to do something.

inter ● [in-**ter**] v -**terring**, -**terred** bury (a corpse). **interment** n.

inter- prefix between or among, e.g. international.

interact v act on or in close relation with each other. **interaction** n **interactive** adj.

intercede ● v try to end a dispute between two people or groups. **intercession** n.

intercept ● v seize or stop in transit. **interception** n.

interchange ● v 1 (cause to) exchange places. ▷ n 2 motorway junction. **interchangeable** adj.

intercom n internal communication system with loudspeakers.

intercontinental adj travelling between or linking continents.

intercourse ● n 1 sexual intercourse. 2 communication or dealings between people or groups.

interest ● n 1 desire to know or hear more about something. 2 something in which one is interested. 3 (often pl) advantage, benefit. 4 sum paid for the use of borrowed money. 5 (often pl) right or share. ▷ v 6 arouse the interest of. **interested** adj 1 feeling or showing interest. 2 involved in or affected by something. **interesting** adj.

interface ● n 1 area where two things interact or link. 2 circuit linking a computer and another device.

interfere ● v 1 try to influence other

— THESAURUS —

bright, enlightened, perspicacious, quick-witted, sharp, smart, well-informed

intemperate adj 1 = **excessive**, extreme, immoderate, profligate, self-indulgent, unbridled, unrestrained, wild

intend v = **plan**, aim, have in mind or view, mean, propose, purpose

intense adj 1 = **extreme**, acute, deep, excessive, fierce, great, powerful, profound, severe 2 = **passionate**, ardent, fanatical, fervent, fierce, heightened, impassioned, vehement

intent n 1 = **intention**, aim, design, end, goal, meaning, object, objective, plan, purpose ▷ adj 2 = **intense**, absorbed, attentive, engrossed, preoccupied, rapt, steadfast, watchful

inter v = **bury**, entomb, lay to rest

intercede v = **mediate**, arbitrate, intervene, plead

intercept v = **seize**, block, catch, cut off,

head off, interrupt, obstruct, stop

interchange v 1 = **switch**, alternate, exchange, reciprocate, swap ▷ n 2 = **junction**, intersection

intercourse n 1 = **sexual intercourse**, carnal knowledge, coitus, copulation, sex (inf) 2 = **communication**, commerce, contact, dealings

interest n 1 = **curiosity**, attention, concern, notice, regard 2 = **hobby**, activity, diversion, pastime, preoccupation, pursuit 3 (often pl) = **advantage**, benefit, good, profit 5 (often pl) = **stake**, claim, investment, right, share ▷ v 6 = **arouse one's curiosity**, attract, catch one's eye, divert, engross, fascinate, intrigue

interface n 1 = **connection**, border, boundary, frontier, link

interfere v 1 = **intrude**, butt in, intervene, meddle, stick one's oar in (inf), tamper 2 (foll. by with) = **conflict**, clash, hamper,

people's affairs where one is not involved or wanted. **2** (foll. by *with*) clash (with). **3** (foll. by *with*) *euphemistic* abuse (a child) sexually. **interfering** *adj* **interference** *n* **1** interfering. **2** *Radio* interruption of reception by atmospherics or unwanted signals.

interim ❶ *adj* temporary or provisional.

interior ❶ *n* **1** inside. **2** inland region. ▷ *adj* **3** inside, inner. **4** mental or spiritual.

interject *v* make (a remark) suddenly or as an interruption. **interjection** *n*.

interlock *v* join firmly together.

interloper ❶ [in-ter-lope-er] *n* person in a place or situation where he or she has no right to be.

interlude ❶ *n* short rest or break in an activity or event.

intermarry *v* (of families, races, or religions) become linked by marriage. **intermarriage** *n*.

intermediate ❶ *adj* coming between two points or extremes.

interminable ❶ *adj* seemingly endless because boring.

intermission ❶ *n* interval between parts of a play, film, etc.

intern ❶ *v* **1** imprison, esp. during a war. ▷ *n* **2** *Chiefly US* trainee doctor in a hospital. **internment** *n* **internee** *n* person who is interned.

internal ❶ *adj* **1** of or on the inside. **2** within a country or organization. **3** spiritual or mental. **internal-combustion engine** engine powered by the explosion of a fuel-and-air mixture within the cylinders.

international ❶ *adj* **1** of or involving two or more countries. ▷ *n* **2** game or match between teams of different countries. **3** player in such a match.

internecine *adj* mutually destructive.

internet ❶ *n* large international computer network.

interplanetary *adj* of or linking planets.

interpolate [in-ter-pole-ate] *v* insert (a comment or passage) into (a conversation or text). **interpolation** *n*.

interpose ❶ *v* **1** insert between or among things. **2** say as an interruption.

interpret ❶ *v* **1** explain the meaning of. **2** translate orally from one language into another. **3** convey the meaning of (a poem, song, etc.) in performance. **interpretation** *n* **interpreter** *n*.

——————————————————————— THESAURUS ———————

handicap, hinder, impede, inhibit, obstruct

interim *adj* = **temporary**, acting, caretaker, improvised, makeshift, provisional, stopgap

interior *n* **1** = **inside**, centre, core, heart *adj* **3** = **inside**, inner, internal, inward **4** = **mental**, hidden, inner, intimate, personal, private, secret, spiritual

interloper *n* = **trespasser**, gate-crasher (*inf*), intruder, meddler

interlude *n* = **interval**, break, breathing space, delay, hiatus, intermission, pause, respite, rest, spell, stoppage

intermediate *adj* = **middle**, halfway, in-between (*inf*), intervening, mid, midway, transitional

interminable *adj* = **endless**, ceaseless, everlasting, infinite, long-drawn-out,

long-winded, never-ending, perpetual, protracted

intermission *n* = **interval**, break, interlude, pause, recess, respite, rest, stoppage

intern *v* **1** = **imprison**, confine, detain, hold, hold in custody

internal *adj* **1** = **inner**, inside, interior **2** = **domestic**, civic, home, in-house

international *adj* **1** = **universal**, cosmopolitan, global, intercontinental, worldwide

internet *n* = **the Net**, the cloud, the Web

interpose *v* **1** = **insert 2** = **interrupt**, interject, put one's oar in

interpret *v* **1** = **explain**, decipher, decode, elucidate, make sense of **2** = **translate**, construe **3** = **render**

interrogate ❶ v question closely.
interrogation n **interrogative** adj
1 questioning. ▷ n 2 word used in
asking a question, such as *how* or *why*.
interrogator n.

interrupt ❶ v 1 break into (a conversation
etc.). 2 stop (a process or activity)
temporarily. **interruption** n.

intersect v 1 (of roads) meet and cross.
2 divide by passing across or through.
intersection n.

interstellar adj between or among stars.

interstice [in-**ter**-stiss] n small crack or
gap between things.

intertwine v twist together.

interval ❶ n 1 time between two
particular moments or events. 2 break
between parts of a play, concert, etc.
3 difference in pitch between musical
notes. **at intervals** 1 repeatedly. 2 with
spaces left between.

intervene ❶ v 1 involve oneself in a
situation, esp. to prevent conflict.
2 happen so as to stop something.
intervention n.

interview ❶ n 1 formal discussion, esp.
between a job-seeker and an employer.
2 questioning of a well-known person

about his or her career, views, etc., by a
reporter. ▷ v 3 conduct an interview with.
interviewee n **interviewer** n.

intestate adj not having made a will.
intestacy n.

intestine n (often pl) lower part of the
alimentary canal between the stomach
and the anus. **intestinal** adj.

intimate[1] ❶ adj 1 having a close personal
relationship. 2 personal or private. 3 (of
knowledge) extensive and detailed.
4 (foll. by *with*) euphemistic having a sexual
relationship (with). 5 having a friendly
quiet atmosphere. ▷ n 6 close friend.
intimately adv **intimacy** n.

intimate[2] ❶ v 1 hint at or suggest.
2 announce. **intimation** n.

intimidate ❶ v subdue or influence by fear.
intimidating adj **intimidation** n.

into prep 1 indicating motion towards the
centre, result of a change, division, etc. e.g.
into the valley; *turned into a madman*; *cut into
pieces*. 2 informal interested in.

intolerable adj more than can be
endured.

intolerant adj refusing to accept practices
and beliefs different from one's own.
intolerance n.

---

interrogate v = **question**, cross-examine,
examine, grill (*inf*), investigate, pump, quiz

interrupt v 1 = **intrude**, barge in (*inf*),
break in, butt in, disturb, heckle, interfere
(with) 2 = **suspend**, break off, cut short,
delay, discontinue, hold up, lay aside, stop

interval n 1 = **break**, delay, gap, pause,
respite, rest, space, spell 2 = **interlude**,
intermission

intervene v 1 = **step in** (*inf*), arbitrate,
intercede, interfere, intrude, involve
oneself, mediate, take a hand (*inf*)
2 = **happen**, befall, come to pass, ensue,
occur, take place

interview n 2 = **meeting**, audience,
conference, consultation, dialogue,
press conference, talk ▷ v 3 = **question**,
examine, interrogate, talk to

intestine n (often pl) = **guts**, bowels,
entrails, innards (*inf*), insides (*inf*), viscera

intimate[1] adj 1 = **close**, bosom,
confidential, dear, near, thick (*inf*)
2 = **private**, confidential, personal, secret
3 = **detailed**, deep, exhaustive, first-hand,
immediate, in-depth, profound, thorough
5 = **snug**, comfy (*inf*), cosy, friendly,
warm ▷ n 6 = **friend**, close friend, cobber
(*Aust or old-fashioned NZ inf*), confidant or
confidante, (constant) companion, crony

intimate[2] v 1 = **suggest**, hint, imply,
indicate, insinuate 2 = **announce**,
communicate, declare, make known,
state

intimidate v = **frighten**, browbeat, bully,
coerce, daunt, overawe, scare, subdue,
terrorize, threaten

intone ⊕ v speak or recite in an unvarying tone of voice.

intoxicate v **1** make drunk. **2** excite to excess. **intoxicant** n intoxicating drink. **intoxication** n.

intractable adj **1** (of a person) difficult to control. **2** (of a problem or issue) difficult to deal with.

intranet n Computers internal network that makes use of Internet technology.

intransigent ⊕ adj refusing to change one's attitude. **intransigence** n.

intravenous [in-tra-**vee**-nuss] adj into a vein.

intrepid ⊕ adj fearless, bold. **intrepidity** n.

intricate ⊕ adj **1** involved or complicated. **2** full of fine detail. **intricately** adv **intricacy** n, pl -**cies**.

intrigue ⊕ v **1** make interested or curious. **2** plot secretly. ▷ n **3** secret plotting. **4** secret love affair. **intriguing** adj.

intrinsic ⊕ adj essential to the basic nature of something. **intrinsically** adv.

introduce ⊕ v **1** present (someone) by name (to another person). **2** present (a radio or television programme). **3** bring forward for discussion. **4** bring into use. **5** insert. **introduction** n **1** presentation of one person to another. **2** preliminary part or treatment. **introductory** adj.

introvert n person concerned more with his or her thoughts and feelings than with the outside world. **introverted** adj **introversion** n.

intrude ⊕ v come in or join in without being invited. **intruder** n **intrusion** n **intrusive** adj.

intuition ⊕ n instinctive knowledge or insight without conscious reasoning. **intuitive** adj **intuitively** adv **.**

Inuk n a member of any Inuit people.

Inuktitut n Canad the language of the Inuit.

inundate ⊕ v **1** flood. **2** overwhelm. **inundation** n.

inured adj accustomed, esp. to hardship or danger.

invade ⊕ v **1** enter (a country) by military force. **2** enter in large numbers. **3** disturb (someone's privacy). **invader** n.

────────── THESAURUS ──────────

intone v = **recite**, chant

intransigent adj = **uncompromising**, hard-line, intractable, obdurate, obstinate, stiff-necked, stubborn, unbending, unyielding

intrepid adj = **fearless**, audacious, bold, brave, courageous, daring, gallant, plucky, stouthearted, valiant

intricate adj **1** = **complicated**, complex, convoluted, involved, labyrinthine, tangled, tortuous **2** = **elaborate**, fancy

intrigue v **1** = **interest**, attract, fascinate, rivet, titillate **2** = **plot**, connive, conspire, machinate, manoeuvre, scheme ▷ n **3** = **plot**, chicanery, collusion, conspiracy, machination, manoeuvre, scheme, stratagem, wile **4** = **affair**, amour, intimacy, liaison, romance

intrinsic adj = **inborn**, basic, built-in, congenital, constitutional, essential, fundamental, inbred, inherent, native, natural

introduce v **1** = **present**, acquaint, familiarize, make known **3** = **bring up**, advance, air, broach, moot, put forward, submit **4** = **bring in**, establish, found, initiate, institute, launch, pioneer, set up, start **5** = **insert**, add, inject, put in, throw in (inf)

intrude v = **interfere**, butt in, encroach, infringe, interrupt, meddle, push in, trespass

intuition n = **instinct**, hunch, insight, perception, presentiment, sixth sense

inundate v **1** = **flood**, drown, engulf, immerse, overflow, submerge, swamp **2** = **overwhelm**, overrun

invade v **1** = **attack**, assault, burst in, descend upon, encroach, infringe, make inroads, occupy, raid, violate **2** = **infest**, overrun, permeate, pervade, swarm over

invalid¹ ❶ *adj, n* **1** disabled or chronically ill (person). ▷ *v* **2** (often foll. by *out*) dismiss from active service because of illness or injury. **invalidity** *n*.

invalid² ❶ *adj* **1** having no legal force. **2** (of an argument etc.) not valid because based on a mistake. **invalidate** *v* make or show to be invalid.

invaluable ❶ *adj* of very great value or worth.

invasion ❶ *n* **1** invading. **2** intrusion, e.g. *an invasion of privacy*.

invective ❶ *n* abusive speech or writing.

inveigle *v* coax by cunning or trickery.

invent ❶ *v* **1** think up or create (something new). **2** make up (a story, excuse, etc.). **invention** *n* **1** something invented. **2** ability to invent. **inventive** *adj* creative and resourceful. **inventiveness** *n* **inventor** *n*.

inventory ❶ *n, pl* **-tories** detailed list of goods or furnishings.

invert ❶ *v* turn upside down or inside out.

inversion *n* **inverted commas** quotation marks.

invertebrate *n* animal with no backbone.

invest ❶ *v* **1** spend (money, time, etc.) on something with the expectation of profit. **2** (foll. by *with*) give (power or rights) to. **investment** *n* **1** money invested. **2** something invested in. **investor** *n* **invest in** *v* buy.

investigate ❶ *v* inquire into, examine. **investigation** *n* **investigative** *adj* **investigator** *n*.

inveterate ❶ *adj* firmly established in a habit or condition.

invidious *adj* likely to cause resentment.

invigilate ❶ *v* supervise people sitting an examination. **invigilator** *n*.

invigorate ❶ *v* give energy to, refresh.

invincible ❶ *adj* impossible to defeat. **invincibility** *n*.

inviolable ❶ *adj* unable to be broken or violated.

——————— THESAURUS ———————

invalid¹ *adj* = **disabled**, ailing, bedridden, frail, ill, infirm, sick ▷ **= patient**, convalescent, valetudinarian

invalid² *adj* **1** = **null and void**, inoperative, void **2** = **unsound**, fallacious, false, illogical, irrational, shonky (*Aust & NZ inf*), unfounded, worthless

invaluable *adj* = **precious**, inestimable, priceless, valuable, worth one's or its weight in gold

invasion *n* **1** = **attack**, assault, campaign, foray, incursion, inroad, offensive, onslaught, raid **2** = **intrusion**, breach, encroachment, infraction, infringement, usurpation, violation

invective *n* = **abuse**, censure, denunciation, diatribe, tirade, tongue-lashing, vilification, vituperation

invent *v* **1** = **create**, coin, conceive, design, devise, discover, formulate, improvise, originate, think up **2** = **make up**, concoct, cook up (*inf*), fabricate, feign, forge, manufacture, trump up

inventory *n* = **list**, account, catalogue, file, record, register, roll, roster

invert *v* = **overturn**, reverse, transpose, upset, upturn

invest *v* **1** = **spend**, advance, devote, lay out, put in, sink **2** (foll. by *with*) = **empower**, authorize, charge, license, sanction, vest

investigate *v* = **examine**, explore, go into, inquire into, inspect, look into, probe, research, study

inveterate *adj* = **long-standing**, chronic, confirmed, deep-seated, dyed-in-the-wool, entrenched, habitual, hardened, incorrigible, incurable

invigilate *v* = **watch over**, conduct, keep an eye on, oversee, preside over, run, superintend, supervise

invigorate *v* = **refresh**, energize, enliven, exhilarate, fortify, galvanize, liven up, revitalize, stimulate

invincible *adj* = **unbeatable**, impregnable, indestructible, indomitable, insuperable, invulnerable, unassailable, unconquerable

inviolable *adj* = **sacrosanct**, hallowed, holy, inalienable, sacred, unalterable

invisible ❶ *adj* not able to be seen. **invisibility** *n*.

invite ❶ *v* 1 request the company of. 2 ask politely for. 3 encourage or provoke, e.g. *the two works inevitably invite comparison*. ▷ *n* 4 *informal* invitation. **inviting** *adj* tempting, attractive. **invitation** *n*.

invoice *v, n* (present with) a bill for goods or services supplied.

invoke ❶ *v* 1 put (a law or penalty) into operation. 2 prompt or cause (a certain feeling). 3 call on (a god or spirit) for help, inspiration, etc. **invocation** *n*.

involuntary ❶ *adj* not done consciously, unintentional. **involuntarily** *adv*.

involve ❶ *v* 1 include as a necessary part. 2 affect, concern. 3 implicate (a person). **involved** *adj* 1 complicated. 2 concerned, taking part. **involvement** *n*.

inward *adj, adv* see IN.

iodine *n Chem* bluish-black element used in medicine and photography. **iodize** *v* treat with iodine.

ion *n* electrically charged atom. **ionize** *v* change into ions. **ionosphere** *n* region of ionized air in the upper atmosphere that reflects radio waves.

IOU *n* signed paper acknowledging debt.

iPad *n* ® type of small portable computer activated by touching the screen.

iPhone *n* ® type of mobile phone which includes a music player and internet browser.

iPod *n* ® pocket-sized device used to play digital music files.

IQ intelligence quotient.

iridescent *adj* having shimmering changing colours like a rainbow.

iris *n* 1 coloured circular membrane of the eye containing the pupil. 2 tall plant with purple, yellow, or white flowers.

iron ❶ *n* 1 strong silvery-white metallic element, widely used for structural and engineering purposes. 2 appliance used, when heated, to press clothes. 3 metal-headed golf club. ▷ *pl* 4 chains, restraints. ▷ *adj* 5 made of iron. 6 strong, inflexible, e.g. *iron will*. ▷ *v* 7 smooth (clothes or fabric) with an iron. **ironbark** *n* Australian eucalyptus with hard rough bark. **ironing** *n* clothes to be ironed. **ironing board** long cloth-covered board with folding legs, for ironing clothes on. **iron out** *v* settle (a problem) through discussion.

irony ❶ *n, pl* **-nies** 1 mildly sarcastic use of words to imply the opposite of what is said. 2 aspect of a situation that is odd or amusing because the opposite of what one would expect.

irradiate *v* subject to or treat with radiation. **irradiation** *n*.

irrational ❶ *adj* not based on or not using logical reasoning.

irregular ❶ *adj* 1 not regular or even. 2 not conforming to accepted practice. 3 (of a

━━━━━━━━━━━━━━━━━ THESAURUS ━━━━━━━━━━━━━━━━━

invisible *adj* = **unseen**, imperceptible, indiscernible

invite *v* 1 = **request**, ask, beg, bid, summon 2 = **ask for** (*inf*) 3 = **encourage**, attract, court, entice, provoke, tempt

invoke *v* 1 = **apply**, implement, initiate, put into effect, resort to, use 3 = **call upon**, appeal to, beg, beseech, entreat, implore, petition, pray, supplicate

involuntary *adj* = **unintentional**, automatic, instinctive, reflex, spontaneous, unconscious, uncontrolled, unthinking

involve *v* 1 = **entail**, imply, mean,

necessitate, presuppose, require 2 = **concern**, affect, draw in, implicate, touch

iron *adj* 5 = **ferrous**, ferric 6 = **inflexible**, adamant, hard, implacable, indomitable, steely, strong, tough, unbending

irony *n* 1 = **sarcasm**, mockery, satire 2 = **paradox**, incongruity

irrational *adj* = **illogical**, absurd, crazy, nonsensical, preposterous, unreasonable

irregular *adj* 1 **a** *adj* = **variable**, erratic, fitful, haphazard, occasional, random, spasmodic, sporadic, unsystematic **b** = **uneven**, asymmetrical, bumpy,

word) not following the typical pattern of formation in a language. **irregularly** adv **irregularity** n, pl **-ties**.

irrelevant ❶ adj not connected with the matter in hand. **irrelevance** n.

irreparable ❶ adj not able to be repaired or put right.

irresistible ❶ adj too attractive or strong to resist. **irresistibly** adv.

irrevocable ❶ adj not possible to change or undo. **irrevocably** adv.

irrigate ❶ v supply (land) with water by artificial channels or pipes. **irrigation** n.

irritate ❶ v 1 annoy, anger. 2 cause (a body part) to itch or become inflamed. **irritable** adj easily annoyed. **irritably** adv **irritant** n, adj (person or thing) causing irritation. **irritation** n.

is v third person singular present tense of BE.

Islam n 1 Muslim religion teaching that there is one God and that Mohammed is his prophet. 2 Muslim countries and civilization. **Islamic** adj.

island ❶ n piece of land surrounded by water. **islander** n person who lives on an island.

isle n poetic island. **islet** n small island.

isobar [**ice**-oh-bar] n line on a map connecting places of equal atmospheric pressure.

isolate ❶ v 1 place apart or alone. 2 Chem obtain (a substance) in uncombined form. **isolation** n **isolationism** n policy of not participating in international affairs. **isolationist** n, adj.

isomer [**ice**-oh-mer] n substance whose molecules contain the same atoms as another but in a different arrangement.

isometric adj relating to muscular contraction without shortening of the muscle. **isometrics** pl n isometric exercises.

isotope n one of two or more atoms with the same number of protons in the nucleus but a different number of neutrons.

issue ❶ n 1 topic of interest or discussion. 2 reason for quarrelling. 3 particular edition of a magazine or newspaper. 4 outcome or result. 5 Law child or children. ▷ v 6 make (a statement etc.) publicly. 7 supply officially (with). 8 produce and make available. **take issue**

crooked, jagged, lopsided, ragged, rough 2 = **unconventional**, abnormal, exceptional, extraordinary, munted (NZ sl), peculiar, unofficial, unorthodox, unusual

irrelevant adj = **unconnected**, beside the point, extraneous, immaterial, impertinent, inapplicable, inappropriate, neither here nor there, unrelated

irreparable adj = **beyond repair**, incurable, irremediable, irretrievable, irreversible

irresistible adj = **overwhelming**, compelling, compulsive, overpowering, urgent

irrevocable adj = **fixed**, fated, immutable, irreversible, predestined, predetermined, settled, unalterable

irrigate v = **water**, flood, inundate, moisten, wet

irritate v 1 = **annoy**, anger, bother,

exasperate, get on one's nerves (inf), infuriate, needle (inf), nettle, rankle with, try one's patience 2 = **rub**, chafe, inflame, pain

island n = **isle**, ait or eyot (dial), atoll, cay or key, islet

isolate v 1 = **separate**, cut off, detach, disconnect, insulate, segregate, set apart

issue n 1 = **topic**, matter, point, question, subject 2 = **problem**, bone of contention 3 = **edition**, copy, number, printing 4 = **outcome**, consequence, effect, end result, result, upshot 5 Law = **children**, descendants, heirs, offspring, progeny ▷ v 6 = **announce**, broadcast 8 = **give out**, circulate, deliver, distribute, publish, put out, release **take issue with** = **disagree with**, challenge, dispute, object to, oppose, raise an objection to, take exception to

with disagree with.

isthmus [**iss**-muss] *n, pl* **-muses** narrow strip of land connecting two areas of land.

it *pron* **1** refers to a nonhuman, animal, plant, or inanimate object. **2** refers to a thing mentioned or being discussed. **3** used as the subject of impersonal verbs, e.g. *it's windy*. **4** *informal* crucial or ultimate point. **its** *adj, pron* belonging to it. **it's 1** it is. **2** it has. **itself** *pron* emphatic form of IT.

● **SPELLING TIP**
● Many people find **its** and **it's** confusing.
● But it's quite simple really. **It's** only
● needs an apostrophe when it is used as
● the informal short form of 'it is' or 'it has'.

italic *adj* (of printing type) sloping to the right. **italics** *pl n* this type, used for emphasis. **italicize** *v* put in italics.

itch ● *n* **1** skin irritation causing a desire to scratch. **2** restless desire. ▷ *v* **3** have an itch. **itchy** *adj*.

item ● *n* **1** single thing in a list or collection. **2** piece of information. **itemize** *v* make a list of.

itinerant ● *adj* travelling from place to place. **itinerary** *n* detailed plan of a journey.

ivory *n* **1** hard white bony substance forming the tusks of elephants. ▷ *adj* **2** yellowish-white. **ivory tower** remoteness from the realities of everyday life.

ivy *n, pl* **ivies** evergreen climbing plant.

——————————————————————— THESAURUS ———————

itch *n* **1** = **irritation**, itchiness, prickling, tingling **2** = **desire**, craving, hankering, hunger, longing, lust, passion, yearning, yen (*inf*) ▷ *v* **3 a** = **prickle**, irritate, tickle, tingle **b** = **long**, ache, crave, hanker, hunger, lust, pine, yearn

item *n* **1** = **detail**, article, component, entry, matter, particular, point, thing **2** = **report**, account, article, bulletin, dispatch, feature, note, notice, paragraph, piece

itinerant *adj* = **wandering**, migratory, nomadic, peripatetic, roaming, roving, travelling, vagrant

Jj

jab ❶ v **jabbing**, **jabbed** 1 poke sharply. ▷ n 2 quick punch or poke. 3 *informal* injection.

jabber ❶ v talk rapidly or incoherently.

jack n 1 device for raising a motor vehicle or other heavy object. 2 playing card with a picture of a pageboy. 3 *Bowls* small white bowl aimed at by the players. 4 socket in electrical equipment into which a plug fits. 5 flag flown at the bow of a ship, showing nationality.

jackal n doglike wild animal of Africa and Asia.

jackass n 1 fool. 2 male of the ass. **laughing jackass** same as KOOKABURRA.

jackboot n high military boot.

jackdaw n black-and-grey bird of the crow family.

jacket ❶ n 1 short coat. 2 skin of a baked potato. 3 outer paper cover on a hardback book.

jackknife v 1 (of an articulated lorry) go out of control so that the trailer swings round at a sharp angle to the cab. ▷ n 2 large clasp knife.

jackpot ❶ n largest prize that may be won in a game. **hit the jackpot** be very successful through luck.

Jacuzzi [jak-**oo**-zee] n ® circular bath with a device that swirls the water.

jade n 1 ornamental semiprecious stone, usu. dark green. ▷ adj 2 bluish-green.

jaded ❶ adj tired and unenthusiastic.

jaguar n large S American spotted cat.

jail ❶ n 1 prison. ▷ v 2 send to prison. **jailer** n **jailbird** n *informal* person who has often been in prison.

jam¹ ❶ v **jamming**, **jammed** 1 pack tightly into a place. 2 crowd or congest. 3 make or become stuck. 4 *Radio* block (another station) with impulses of equal wavelength. 5 play a jam session. ▷ n 6 hold-up of traffic. 7 *informal* awkward situation. **jam on the brakes** apply brakes fiercely. **jam-packed** adj filled to capacity. **jam session** informal rock or jazz performance.

jam² n food made from fruit boiled with sugar.

jamb n side post of a door or window frame.

jamboree ❶ n large gathering or celebration.

Jan. January.

jangle ❶ v 1 (cause to) make a harsh ringing noise. 2 (of nerves) be upset or irritated.

—————————— THESAURUS ——————————

jab v 1 = **poke**, dig, lunge, nudge, prod, punch, stab, thrust ▷ n 2 = **poke**, dig, lunge, nudge, prod, punch, stab, thrust

jabber v = **chatter**, babble, blether, gabble, mumble, prate, rabbit (on) (*Brit inf*), ramble, yap (*inf*)

jacket n 3 = **cover**, wrapper

jackpot n = **prize**, award, bonanza, reward, winnings

jaded adj = **tired**, exhausted, fatigued, spent, weary

jail n 1 = **prison**, nick (*Brit sl*), penitentiary (US), reformatory, slammer (*sl*) ▷ v 2 = **imprison**, confine, detain, incarcerate, lock up, send down

jam¹ v 1 = **pack**, cram, force, press, ram, squeeze, stuff, wedge 2 = **crowd**, congest, crush, throng 3 = **stick**, block, clog, obstruct, stall ▷ n 7 *Inf* = **predicament**, deep water, fix (*inf*), hole (*sl*), hot water, pickle (*inf*), tight spot, trouble

jamboree n = **festival**, carnival, celebration, festivity, fete, revelry

jangle v 1 = **rattle**, chime, clank, clash, clatter, jingle, vibrate

janitor ❶ n caretaker of a school or other building.

January n first month of the year.

jar¹ ❶ n wide-mouthed container, usu. round and made of glass.

jar² ❶ v **jarring, jarred 1** have a disturbing or unpleasant effect. **2** jolt or bump. ▷ n **3** jolt or shock.

jargon ❶ n specialized technical language of a particular subject.

jasmine n shrub with sweet-smelling yellow or white flowers.

jaundice n disease marked by yellowness of the skin. **jaundiced** adj **1** (of an attitude or opinion) bitter or cynical. **2** having jaundice.

jaunt ❶ n short journey for pleasure.

jaunty ❶ adj **-tier, -tiest 1** sprightly and cheerful. **2** smart. **jauntily** adv.

javelin n light spear thrown in sports competitions.

jaw ❶ n **1** one of the bones in which the teeth are set. ▷ pl **2** mouth. **3** gripping part of a tool. **4** narrow opening of a gorge or valley. ▷ v **5** slang talk lengthily.

jay n bird with a pinkish body and blue-and-black wings.

jazz n kind of music with an exciting rhythm, usu. involving improvisation. **jazzy** adj flashy or showy. **jazz up** v make more lively.

jealous ❶ adj **1** fearful of losing a partner or possession to a rival. **2** envious. **3** suspiciously watchful. **jealousy** n, pl **-sies**.

jeans pl n casual denim trousers.

Jeep n ® four-wheel-drive motor vehicle.

jeer ❶ v **1** scoff or deride. ▷ n **2** cry of derision.

jell ❶ v **1** form into a jelly-like substance. **2** take on a definite form.

jelly n, pl **-lies 1** soft food made of liquid set with gelatine. **2** jam made from fruit juice and sugar. **jellied** adj prepared in a jelly.

jemmy n, pl **-mies** short steel crowbar used by burglars.

jeopardy ❶ n danger. **jeopardize** v place in danger.

jerk ❶ v **1** move or throw abruptly. ▷ n **2** sharp or abruptly stopped movement. **3** slang contemptible person. **jerky** adj sudden or abrupt. **jerkily** adv **jerkiness** n.

jerkin n sleeveless jacket.

jersey n **1** knitted jumper. **2** machine-knitted fabric. **3** (J-) breed of cow.

jest ❶ n, v joke. **jester** n Hist professional clown at court.

━━━━━━━━━━━━━━━━━━━━━━━━━━━━━━━━━ THESAURUS ━━━

janitor n = **caretaker**, concierge, custodian, doorkeeper, porter

jar¹ n = **pot**, container, crock, jug, pitcher, urn, vase

jar² v **1** = **irritate**, annoy, get on one's nerves (inf), grate, irk, nettle, offend **2** = **jolt**, bump, convulse, rattle, rock, shake, vibrate ▷ n **3** = **jolt**, bump, convulsion, shock, vibration

jargon n = **parlance**, argot, idiom, usage

jaunt n = **outing**, airing, excursion, expedition, ramble, stroll, tour, trip

jaunty adj **1** = **sprightly**, buoyant, carefree, high-spirited, lively, perky, self-confident, sparky

jaw v **5** Sl = **talk**, chat, chatter, gossip, spout

jealous adj **1** = **possessive**, mistrustful, protective **2** = **envious**, covetous, desirous, green, grudging, resentful **3** = **suspicious**, vigilant, wary, watchful

jeans pl n = **denims**

jeer v **1** = **mock**, barrack, deride, gibe, heckle, ridicule, scoff, taunt ▷ n **2** = **mockery**, abuse, boo, catcall, derision, gibe, ridicule, taunt

jell v **1** = **solidify**, congeal, harden, set, thicken **2** = **take shape**, come together, crystallize, materialize

jeopardy n = **danger**, insecurity, peril, risk, vulnerability

jerk v **1** = **tug**, jolt, lurch, pull, thrust, twitch, wrench, yank ▷ n **2** = **tug**, jolt, lurch, pull, thrust, twitch, wrench, yank

jest n = **joke**, bon mot, crack (sl), jape, pleasantry, prank, quip, wisecrack (inf), witticism ▷ v = **joke**, kid (inf), mock, quip, tease

jet¹ ❶ *n* **1** aircraft driven by jet propulsion. **2** stream of liquid or gas, esp. one forced from a small hole. **3** nozzle from which gas or liquid is forced. ▷ *v* **jetting, jetted 4** fly by jet aircraft. **jet lag** fatigue caused by crossing time zones in an aircraft. **jet propulsion** propulsion by thrust provided by a jet of gas or liquid. **jet-propelled** *adj* **jet set** rich and fashionable people who travel the world for pleasure.

jet² *n* hard black mineral. **jet-black** *adj* glossy black.

jetsam *n* goods thrown overboard to lighten a ship.

jetty ❶ *n, pl* **-ties** small pier.

Jew *n* **1** person whose religion is Judaism. **2** descendant of the ancient Hebrews. **Jewish** *adj* **jew's-harp** *n* musical instrument held between the teeth and played by plucking a metal strip with one's finger.

jewel ❶ *n* **1** precious stone. **2** special person or thing. **jeweller** *n* dealer in jewels. **jewellery** *n* objects decorated with precious stones.

jewfish *n Aust* freshwater catfish.

jib¹ *n* triangular sail set in front of a mast.

jib² ❶ *v* **jibbing, jibbed** (of a horse, person, etc.) stop and refuse to go on. **jib at** *v* object to (a proposal etc.).

jib³ *n* projecting arm of a crane or derrick.

jibe¹ ❶ *n, v* taunt or jeer.

jibe² *v* same as GYBE.

jig ❶ *n* **1** type of lively dance. **2** music for it. **3** device that holds a component in place for cutting etc. ▷ *v* **jigging, jigged 4** make jerky up-and-down movements.

jilt *v* leave or reject (one's lover).

jingle ❶ *n* **1** catchy verse or song used in a radio or television advert. **2** gentle ringing noise. ▷ *v* **3** (cause to) make a gentle ringing sound.

jingoism *n* aggressive nationalism. **jingoistic** *adj.*

jinks *pl n* **high jinks** boisterous merrymaking.

jinx ❶ *n* **1** person or thing bringing bad luck. ▷ *v* **2** be or put a jinx on.

jitters ❶ *pl n* worried nervousness. **jittery** *adj* nervous.

jive *n* **1** lively dance of the 1940s and '50s. ▷ *v* **2** dance the jive.

job ❶ *n* **1** occupation or paid employment. **2** task to be done. **3** *informal* difficult task. **4** *informal* crime, esp. robbery. **jobbing** *adj* doing individual jobs for payment. **jobless** *adj, pl n* unemployed (people). **job lot** assortment sold together. **job sharing** splitting of one post between two people working part-time.

jet¹ *n* **2** = **stream**, flow, fountain, gush, spout, spray, spring **3** = **nozzle**, atomizer, sprayer, sprinkler ▷ *v* **4** = **fly**, soar, zoom

jetty *n* = **pier**, dock, quay, wharf

jewel *n* **1** = **gemstone**, ornament, rock (*sl*), sparkler (*inf*) **2** = **rarity**, collector's item, find, gem, humdinger (*sl*), pearl, treasure, wonder

jib² *v* = **refuse**, balk, recoil, retreat, shrink, stop short

jibe¹ *n* = **taunt**, jeering, mockery, ridicule, scoffing, scorn, sneering ▷ *v* = **taunt**, jeer, make fun of, mock, poke fun at, ridicule, scoff, scorn, sneer

jig *v* **4** = **skip**, bob, bounce, caper, prance, wiggle

jingle *n* **1** = **song**, chorus, ditty, melody, tune **2** = **rattle**, clink, reverberation, ringing, tinkle ▷ *v* **3** = **ring**, chime, clink, jangle, rattle, tinkle

jinx *n* **1** = **curse**, hex (*US & Canad inf*), hoodoo (*inf*), nemesis ▷ *v* **2** = **curse**, bewitch, hex (*US & Canad inf*)

jitters *pl n* = **nerves**, anxiety, butterflies (in one's stomach) (*inf*), cold feet (*inf*), fidgets, nervousness, the shakes (*inf*)

job *n* **1** = **occupation**, business, calling, career, employment, livelihood, profession, vocation **2** = **task**, assignment, chore, duty, enterprise, errand, undertaking, venture, work

jockey n 1 (professional) rider
of racehorses. ▷ v 2 **jockey for
position** manoeuvre to obtain an
advantage.

jockstrap n belt with a pouch to support
the genitals, worn by male athletes.

jocular ● adj 1 fond of joking. 2 meant as a
joke. **jocularity** n.

jodhpurs pl n riding trousers, loose-fitting
above the knee but tight below.

jog ● v **jogging, jogged** 1 run at a gentle
pace, esp. for exercise. 2 nudge slightly. ▷ n
3 slow run. **jogger** n **jogging** n.

John Dory n European dory with a deep
compressed body, spiny dorsal fins, and
massive jaws.

Johnny Canuck n Canad 1 an informal
name for a Canadian. 2 a personification
of Canada.

join ● v 1 become a member (of). 2 come
into someone's company. 3 take part (in).
4 come or bring together. ▷ n 5 place
where two things are joined. **join up** v
enlist in the armed services. **joined-up**
adj integrated by an overall strategy, e.g.
joined-up government.

joint ● adj 1 shared by two or more. ▷ n
2 place where bones meet but can move.
3 junction of two or more parts or objects.
4 piece of meat for roasting. 5 slang

house or place, esp. a disreputable bar or
nightclub. 6 slang marijuana cigarette.
▷ v 7 divide meat into joints. **out of joint**
1 disorganized. 2 dislocated. **jointly** adv.

joist n horizontal beam that helps support a
floor or ceiling.

joke ● n 1 thing said or done to cause
laughter. 2 amusing or ridiculous person
or thing. ▷ v 3 make jokes. **jokey** adj **joker**
n 1 person who jokes. 2 slang fellow.
3 extra card in a pack, counted as any other
in some games.

jolly ● adj -lier, -liest 1 (of a person)
happy and cheerful. 2 (of an occasion)
merry and festive. ▷ v -lying, -lied 3 **jolly
along** try to keep (someone) cheerful by
flattery or coaxing. **jollity** n **jollification** n
merrymaking.

jolt ● n 1 unpleasant surprise or shock.
2 sudden jerk or bump. ▷ v 3 surprise or
shock. 4 move or shake with a jerk.

joss stick n stick of incense giving off a
sweet smell when burnt.

jostle ● v knock or push against.

jot ● v **jotting, jotted** 1 write briefly. ▷ n
2 very small amount. **jotter** n notebook.
jottings pl n notes jotted down.

joual n nonstandard Canadian French
dialect, esp. as associated with ill-
educated speakers.

——————————————————————————— THESAURUS ——————

jocular adj 1, 2 = **humorous**, amusing, droll,
facetious, funny, joking, jovial, playful,
sportive, teasing, waggish

jog v 1 = **run**, canter, lope, trot 2 = **nudge**,
prod, push, shake, stir

join v 1 = **enrol**, enlist, enter, sign up

joint adj 1 = **shared**, collective, combined,
communal, cooperative, joined, mutual,
united ▷ n 3 = **junction**, connection,
hinge, intersection, nexus, node ▷ v
7 = **divide**, carve, cut up, dissect, segment,
sever

joke n 1 = **jest**, gag (inf), jape, prank,
pun, quip, wisecrack (inf), witticism
2 = **laughing stock**, buffoon, clown ▷ v
3 = **jest**, banter, kid (inf), mock, play the

fool, quip, taunt, tease

jolly adj 1 = **happy**, cheerful, chirpy (inf),
genial, jovial, merry, playful, sprightly,
upbeat (inf)

jolt n 1 = **surprise**, blow, bolt from the
blue, bombshell, setback, shock
2 = **jerk**, bump, jar, jog, jump,
lurch, shake, start ▷ v 3 = **surprise**,
discompose, disturb, perturb, stagger,
startle, stun 4 = **jerk**, jar, jog, jostle,
knock, push, shake, shove

jostle v = **push**, bump, elbow, hustle, jog,
jolt, shake, shove

jot v 1 = **note down**, list, record, scribble
▷ n 2 = **bit**, fraction, grain, morsel, scrap,
speck

joule [jool] n Physics unit of work or energy.

journal ❶ n **1** daily newspaper or magazine. **2** daily record of events. **journalese** n superficial style of writing, found in some newspapers. **journalism** n writing in or editing of newspapers and magazines. **journalist** n **journalistic** adj.

journey ❶ n **1** act or process of travelling from one place to another. ▷ v **2** travel.

journeyman n qualified craftsman employed by another.

jovial ❶ adj happy and cheerful. **jovially** adv **joviality** n.

joy ❶ n **1** feeling of great delight or pleasure. **2** cause of this feeling. **joyful** adj **joyless** adj **joyous** adj extremely happy and enthusiastic. **joyriding** n driving for pleasure, esp. in a stolen car. **joyride** n **joyrider** n **joystick** n control device for an aircraft or computer.

JP Justice of the Peace.

JPEG [jay-peg]Computing **1** standard compressed file format used for pictures. **2** picture held in this file format.

jubilant ❶ adj feeling or expressing great joy. **jubilation** n.

jubilee ❶ n special anniversary, esp. 25th (**silver jubilee**) or 50th (**golden jubilee**).

judder v **1** vibrate violently. ▷ n **2** violent vibration.

judge ❶ n **1** public official who tries cases and passes sentence in a court of law. **2** person who decides the outcome of a contest. ▷ v **3** act as a judge. **4** appraise critically. **5** consider something to be the case. **judgment**, **judgement** n **1** opinion reached after careful thought. **2** verdict of a judge. **3** ability to appraise critically. **judgmental**, **judgemental** adj.

judicial ❶ adj **1** of or by a court or judge. **2** showing or using judgment. **judicially** adv.

judo n sport in which two opponents try to throw each other to the ground.

jug ❶ n container for liquids, with a handle and small spout.

juggernaut n **1** large heavy lorry. **2** any irresistible destructive force.

juggle ❶ v **1** throw and catch (several objects) so that most are in the air at the same time. **2** manipulate (figures, situations, etc.) to suit one's purposes. **juggler** n.

juice ❶ n **1** liquid part of vegetables, fruit, or meat. **2** informal petrol. ▷ pl **3** fluids secreted by an organ of the body. **juicy** adj **1** full of juice. **2** interesting.

jujitsu n Japanese art of wrestling and self-defence.

jukebox n coin-operated machine on which records, CDs, or videos can be played.

THESAURUS

---

journal n **1** = **newspaper**, daily, gazette, magazine, monthly, periodical, weekly **2** = **diary**, chronicle, log, record

journey n **1** = **trip**, excursion, expedition, odyssey, pilgrimage, tour, trek, voyage ▷ v **2** = **travel**, go, proceed, roam, rove, tour, traverse, trek, voyage, wander

jovial adj = **cheerful**, animated, cheery, convivial, happy, jolly, merry, mirthful

joy n **1** = **delight**, bliss, ecstasy, elation, gaiety, glee, pleasure, rapture, satisfaction

jubilant adj = **overjoyed**, elated, enraptured, euphoric, exuberant, exultant, thrilled, triumphant

jubilee n = **celebration**, festival, festivity, holiday

judge n **1** = **magistrate**, beak (Brit sl), justice **2** = **referee**, adjudicator, arbiter, arbitrator, moderator, umpire ▷ v **3** = **adjudicate**, arbitrate, decide, mediate, referee, umpire **4** = **consider**, appraise, assess, esteem, estimate, evaluate, rate, value

judicial adj **1** = **legal**, official

jug n = **container**, carafe, crock, ewer, jar, pitcher, urn, vessel

juggle v **2** = **manipulate**, alter, change, manoeuvre, modify

juice n **1** = **liquid**, extract, fluid, liquor, nectar, sap

July *n* seventh month of the year.

jumble **❶** *n* **1** confused heap or state. **2** articles for a jumble sale. ▷ *v* **3** mix in a disordered way. **jumble sale** sale of miscellaneous second-hand items.

jumbo **❶** *adj* **1** *informal* very large. ▷ *n* **2** (also **jumbo jet**) large jet airliner.

jump **❶** *v* **1** leap or spring into the air using the leg muscles. **2** move quickly and suddenly. **3** jerk with surprise. **4** increase suddenly. **5** change the subject abruptly. **6** *informal* attack without warning. **7** pass over or miss out (intervening material). ▷ *n* **8** act of jumping. **9** sudden rise. **10** break in continuity. **jump the gun** act prematurely. **jump the queue** not wait one's turn. **jumpy** *adj* nervous. **jump at** *v* accept (a chance etc.) gladly. **jumped-up** *adj* arrogant because of recent promotion. **jump on** *v* attack suddenly and forcefully.

junction **❶** *n* place where routes, railway lines, or roads meet.

juncture **❶** *n* point in time, esp. a critical one.

June *n* sixth month of the year.

jungle *n* **1** tropical forest of dense tangled vegetation. **2** confusion or mess. **3** place of intense struggle for survival.

junior **❶** *adj* **1** of lower standing. **2** younger. ▷ *n* **3** junior person.

juniper *n* evergreen shrub with purple berries.

junk¹ **❶** *n* **1** discarded or useless objects. **2** *informal* rubbish. **3** *slang* narcotic drug, esp. heroin. **junkie, junky** *n, pl* **junkies** *slang* drug addict. **junk food** snack food of low nutritional value. **junk mail** unwanted mail advertising goods or services.

junk² *n* flat-bottomed Chinese sailing boat.

junket *n* **1** excursion by public officials paid for from public funds. **2** sweetened milk set with rennet.

junta *n* group of military officers holding power in a country, esp. after a coup.

jurisdiction **❶** *n* **1** right or power to administer justice and apply laws. **2** extent of this right or power.

jury *n, pl* **-ries** group of people sworn to deliver a verdict in a court of law. **juror** *n* member of a jury.

just **❶** *adv* **1** very recently. **2** at this instant. **3** merely, only. **4** exactly. **5** barely. **6** really. ▷ *adj* **7** fair or impartial in action or judgment. **8** proper or right. **justice**

━━━ THESAURUS ━━━

jumble *n* **1** = **muddle**, clutter, confusion, disarray, disorder, mess, mishmash, mixture ▷ *v* **3** = **mix**, confuse, disorder, disorganize, mistake, muddle, shuffle

jumbo *adj* **1** *Inf* = **giant**, gigantic, huge, immense, large, oversized

jump *v* **1** = **leap**, bounce, bound, hop, hurdle, skip, spring, vault **3** = **recoil**, flinch, jerk, start, wince **4** = **increase**, advance, ascend, escalate, rise, surge **7** = **miss**, avoid, evade, omit, skip ▷ *n* **8** = **leap**, bound, hop, skip, spring, vault **9** = **rise**, advance, increase, increment, upsurge, upturn **10** = **interruption**, break, gap, hiatus, lacuna, space

junction *n* = **connection**, coupling, linking, union

juncture *n* = **moment**, occasion, point, time

junior *adj* **1** = **lower**, inferior, lesser, minor, secondary, subordinate **2** = **younger**

junk¹ *n* **1, 2** = **rubbish**, clutter, debris, litter, odds and ends, refuse, scrap, trash, waste

jurisdiction *n* **1** = **authority**, command, control, influence, power, rule **2** = **range**, area, bounds, compass, field, province, scope, sphere

just *adv* **1** = **recently**, hardly, lately, only now, scarcely **3** = **merely**, by the skin of one's teeth, only, simply, solely **4** = **exactly**, absolutely, completely, entirely, perfectly, precisely ▷ *adj* **7** = **fair**, conscientious, equitable, fair-minded, good, honest, upright, virtuous **8** = **fitting**, appropriate, apt, deserved, due, justified, merited, proper, rightful

n **1** quality of being just. **2** judicial proceedings. **3** magistrate. **justify** *v* prove right or reasonable.

jut ❶ *v* **jutting, jutted** project or stick out.

jute *n* plant fibre, used for rope, canvas, etc.

juvenile ❶ *adj* **1** young. **2** of or suitable for young people. **3** immature and rather silly. ▷ *n* **4** young person or child. **juvenile delinquent** young person guilty of a crime.

juxtapose *v* put side by side. **juxtaposition** *n*.

————— THESAURUS —————

jut *v* = **stick out**, bulge, extend, overhang, poke, project, protrude

juvenile *adj* **1** = **young**, youthful

3 = **immature**, babyish, callow, childish, inexperienced, infantile, puerile ▷ *n* **4** = **child**, adolescent, boy, girl, infant, minor, youth

Kk

Kabloona *n* (in Canada) a person who is not of Inuit ancestry, esp. a White person.

kaftan *n* 1 long loose Eastern garment. 2 woman's dress resembling this.

kak *n S Afr slang* 1 faeces. 2 rubbish.

kaleidoscope *n* tube-shaped toy containing loose coloured pieces reflected by mirrors so that intricate patterns form when the tube is twisted. **kaleidoscopic** *adj*.

kamik *n Canad* a traditional Inuit boot made of caribou hide or sealskin.

kamikaze ❶ [kam-mee-**kah**-zee] *n* 1 (in World War II) Japanese pilot who performed a suicide mission. ▷ *adj* 2 (of an action) undertaken in the knowledge that it will kill or injure the person performing it.

kangaroo *n, pl* **-roos** Australian marsupial which moves by jumping with its powerful hind legs. **kangaroo court** unofficial court set up by a group to discipline its members. **kangaroo paw** Australian plant with green-and-red flowers.

karate *n* Japanese system of unarmed combat using blows with the feet, hands, elbows, and legs.

karma *n Buddhism, Hinduism* person's actions affecting his or her fate in the next reincarnation.

kayak *n* 1 Inuit canoe made of sealskins stretched over a frame. 2 fibreglass or canvas-covered canoe of this design.

kebab *n* 1 dish of small pieces of meat grilled on skewers. 2 (also **doner kebab**) grilled minced lamb served in a split slice of unleavened bread.

kedgeree *n* dish of fish with rice and eggs.

keel *n* main lengthways timber or steel support along the base of a ship. **keel over** *v* 1 turn upside down. 2 *informal* collapse suddenly.

keen¹ ❶ *adj* 1 eager or enthusiastic. 2 intense or strong. 3 intellectually acute. 4 (of the senses) capable of recognizing small distinctions. 5 sharp. 6 cold and penetrating. 7 competitive. **keenly** *adv* **keenness** *n*.

keep ❶ *v* **keeping**, **kept** 1 have or retain possession of. 2 take temporary charge of. 3 store. 4 stay or cause to stay (in, on, or at a place or position). 5 continue or persist. 6 support financially. 7 detain (someone). 8 look after or maintain. 9 (of food) remain good. ▷ *n* 10 cost of food and everyday expenses. 11 central tower of a castle. **keeper** *n* 1 person who looks after animals in a zoo. 2 person in charge of a museum or collection. 3 short for GOALKEEPER. **keeping** *n* care or charge. **in, out of keeping with** appropriate or inappropriate for. **keep fit** exercises designed to promote physical fitness. **keepsake** *n* gift treasured for the sake of the giver. **keep up** *v* maintain at the current level. **keep up with** *v* maintain a pace set by (someone).

———————————— THESAURUS ————————————

kamikaze *adj* 2 = **self-destructive**, foolhardy, suicidal

keen *adj* 1 = **eager**, ardent, avid, enthusiastic, impassioned, zealous 2 = **intense** 3 = **astute**, canny, clever, perceptive, quick, shrewd, wise 5 = **sharp**, cutting, incisive, razor-like

keep *v* 1 = **retain**, conserve, control, hold, maintain, possess, preserve

2 = **look after**, care for, guard, maintain, manage, mind, protect, tend, watch over 3 = **store**, carry, deposit, hold, place, stack, stock 6 = **support**, maintain, provide for, subsidize, sustain 7 = **detain**, delay, hinder, hold back, keep back, obstruct, prevent, restrain ▷ *n* 10 = **board**, food, living, maintenance 11 = **tower**, castle

keg ❶ *n* small metal beer barrel.
kelp *n* large brown seaweed.
ken *v* **kenning, kenned** *or* **kent** *Scot* know. **beyond one's ken** beyond one's range of knowledge.
kennel *n* **1** hutlike shelter for a dog. ▷ *pl* **2** place for breeding, boarding, or training dogs.
kerb *n* stone edging to a footpath.
kernel ❶ *n* **1** seed of a nut, cereal, or fruit stone. **2** central and essential part of something.
kerosene *n US & Canad* another name for PARAFFIN.
kestrel *n* type of small falcon.
ketchup *n* thick cold sauce, usu. made of tomatoes.
kettle *n* container with a spout and handle used for boiling water. **kettledrum** *n* large bowl-shaped metal drum.
key ❶ *n* **1** device for operating a lock by moving a bolt. **2** device turned to wind a clock, operate a machine, etc. **3** any of a set of levers or buttons pressed to operate a typewriter, computer, or musical keyboard instrument. **4** *Music* set of related notes. **5** something crucial in providing an explanation or interpretation. **6** means of achieving a desired end. **7** list of explanations of codes, symbols, etc. ▷ *adj* **8** of great importance. ▷ *v* **9** (also **key in**) enter (text) using a keyboard. **keyed up** very excited or nervous.
kg kilogram(s).

khaki *adj* **1** dull yellowish-brown. ▷ *n* **2** hard-wearing fabric of this colour used for military uniforms.
kibbutz *n, pl* **kibbutzim** communal farm or factory in Israel.
kick ❶ *v* **1** drive, push, or strike with the foot. **2** (of a gun) recoil when fired. **3** *informal* object or resist. **4** *informal* free oneself of (an addiction). **5** *Rugby* score with a kick. ▷ *n* **6** thrust or blow with the foot. **7** recoil of a gun. **8** *informal* excitement or thrill. **kickback** *n* money paid illegally for favours done. **kick off** *v* **1** start a game of football. **2** *informal* begin. **kick out** *v* dismiss or expel forcibly. **kick-start** *v* **1** start (a motorcycle) by kicking a pedal. **kick up** *v informal* create (a fuss).
kid¹ ❶ *n* **1** (also **kiddie**) *informal* child. **2** young goat. **3** leather made from the skin of a young goat. **treat, handle someone with kid gloves** treat someone with great tact in order not to upset them.
kid² ❶ *v* **kidding, kidded** *informal* tease or deceive (someone).
kidnap ❶ *v* **-napping, -napped** seize and hold (a person) to ransom. **kidnapper** *n*.
kidney *n* **1** either of the pair of organs that filter waste products from the blood to produce urine. **2** animal kidney used as food. **kidney bean** reddish-brown kidney-shaped bean, edible when cooked.
kill ❶ *v* **1** cause the death of. **2** *informal* cause (someone) pain or discomfort. **3** put an end to. **4** pass (time). ▷ *n* **5** act

keg *n* = **barrel**, cask, drum, vat
kernel *n* **2** = **essence**, core, germ, gist, nub, pith, substance
key¹ *n* **1** = **opener**, latchkey **5** = **answer**, explanation, solution ▷ *adj* **8** = **essential**, crucial, decisive, fundamental, important, leading, main, major, pivotal, principal ▷ *v* **9** (also **key in**) = **type**, enter, input, keyboard
kick *v* **1** = **boot**, punt **4** *Inf* = **give up**, abandon, desist from, leave off, quit, stop ▷ *n* **8** *Inf* = **thrill**, buzz (*sl*), pleasure, stimulation

kid¹ *n* **1** (also **kiddie**) *Inf* = **child**, baby, bairn, infant, teenager, tot, youngster, youth
kid² *v Inf* = **tease**, delude, fool, hoax, jest, joke, pretend, trick, wind up (*Brit sl*)
kidnap *v* = **abduct**, capture, hijack, hold to ransom, seize
kill *v* **1** = **slay**, assassinate, butcher, destroy, execute, exterminate, liquidate, massacre, murder, slaughter **3** = **suppress**, extinguish, halt, quash, quell, scotch, smother, stifle, stop

of killing. **6** animals or birds killed in a hunt. **killer** *n* **killing** *informal* ▷ *adj* **1** very tiring. **2** very funny. ▷ *n* **3** sudden financial success. **killjoy** *n* person who spoils others' pleasure.

kiln *n* oven for baking, drying, or processing pottery, bricks, etc.

kilo *n* short for KILOGRAM.

kilo- *combining form* one thousand, e.g. *kilometre*.

kilogram, kilogramme *n* one thousand grams.

kilohertz *n* one thousand hertz.

kilt *n* knee-length pleated tartan skirt worn orig. by Scottish Highlanders.

kimono *n, pl* -**nos 1** loose wide-sleeved Japanese robe, fastened with a sash. **2** European dressing gown resembling this.

kin, kinsfolk ❶ *n* person's relatives collectively. **kinship** *n*.

kind¹ ❶ *adj* considerate, friendly, and helpful. **kindness** *n* **kindly** *adj* **-lier**, **-liest 1** having a warm-hearted nature. **2** pleasant or agreeable. ▷ *adv* **3** in a considerate way. **4** please, e.g. *will you kindly be quiet!* **kindliness** *n* **kind-hearted** *adj*.

kind² ❶ *n* **1** class or group with common characteristics. **2** essential nature or character. **in kind 1** (of payment) in goods rather than money. **2** with something similar. **kind of** to a certain extent.

kindergarten *n* class or school for children of about four to six years old.

kindle ❶ *v* **1** set (a fire) alight. **2** (of a fire) start to burn. **3** arouse or be aroused.

kindling *n* dry wood or straw for starting fires.

Kindle *n* ® portable electronic device for downloading and reading books.

kindy, kindie *n, pl* -**dies** *Aust & NZ informal* kindergarten.

kinetic [kin-**net**-ik] *adj* relating to or caused by motion.

king ❶ *n* **1** male ruler of a monarchy. **2** ruler or chief. **3** best or most important of its kind. **4** piece in chess that must be defended. **5** playing card with a picture of a king on it. **kingship** *n* **kingdom** *n* **1** state ruled by a king or queen. **2** division of the natural world. **king prawn** large prawn, fished commercially in Australian waters. **king-size, king-sized** *adj* larger than standard size.

kingfisher *n* small bird with a bright greenish-blue and orange plumage, that dives for fish.

kink ❶ *n* **1** twist or bend in rope, wire, hair, etc. **2** *informal* quirk in someone's personality. **kinky** *adj* **1** *slang* given to unusual sexual practices. **2** full of kinks.

kiosk ❶ *n* **1** small booth selling drinks, cigarettes, newspapers, etc. **2** public telephone box.

kipper *n* cleaned, salted, and smoked herring.

kirk *n Scot* church.

kiss ❶ *v* **1** touch with the lips in affection or greeting. **2** join lips with a person in love or desire. ▷ *n* **3** touch with the lips. **kiss of life** mouth-to-mouth resuscitation.

kist *n S Afr* large wooden chest.

--- THESAURUS ---

kin, kinsfolk *n* = **family**, kindred, relations, relatives

kind¹ *adj* = **considerate**, benign, charitable, compassionate, courteous, friendly, generous, humane, kindly, obliging, philanthropic, tender-hearted

kind² *n* **1** = **class**, brand, breed, family, set, sort, species, variety

kindle *v* **1** = **set fire to**, ignite, inflame, light **3** = **arouse**, awaken, induce, inspire, provoke, rouse, stimulate, stir

king *n* **1** = **ruler**, emperor, monarch, sovereign

kink *n* **1** = **twist**, bend, coil, wrinkle **2** *Inf* = **quirk**, eccentricity, fetish, foible, idiosyncrasy, vagary, whim

kiosk *n* **1** = **booth**, bookstall, counter, newsstand, stall, stand

kiss *v* **1, 2** = **osculate**, neck (*inf*), peck (*inf*) ▷ *n* **3** = **osculation**, peck (*inf*), smacker (*sl*)

kit ❶ *n* **1** outfit or equipment for a specific purpose. **2** set of pieces of equipment sold ready to be assembled. **kit out** *v* **kitting**, **kitted** provide with clothes or equipment needed for a particular activity.

kitchen *n* room used for cooking. **kitchenette** *n* small kitchen. **kitchen garden** garden for growing vegetables, herbs, etc.

kite *n* **1** light frame covered with a thin material flown on a string in the wind. **2** large hawk with a forked tail.

kitsch *n* art or literature with popular sentimental appeal.

kitten *n* young cat. **kittenish** *adj* lively and flirtatious.

kitty *n*, *pl* **-ties** **1** communal fund. **2** total amount wagered in certain gambling games.

kiwi *n* **1** NZ flightless bird with a long beak and no tail. **2** *informal* New Zealander. **kiwi fruit** edible fruit with a fuzzy brownish skin and green flesh.

klaxon *n* loud horn used on emergency vehicles as a warning signal.

kleptomania *n* compulsive tendency to steal. **kleptomaniac** *n*.

kloof *n* S Afr mountain pass or gorge.

km kilometre(s).

knack ❶ *n* **1** skilful way of doing something. **2** innate ability.

knacker *n* buyer of old horses for killing.

knapsack *n* soldier's or traveller's bag worn strapped on the back.

knave ❶ *n* **1** jack at cards. **2** *obs* dishonest man.

knead ❶ *v* **1** work (dough) into a smooth mixture with the hands. **2** squeeze or press with the hands.

knee *n* **1** joint between thigh and lower leg. **2** lap. **3** part of a garment covering the knee. ▷ *v* **kneeing**, **kneed** **4** strike or push with the knee. **kneecap** *n* **1** bone in front of the knee. ▷ *v* **2** shoot in the kneecap. **kneejerk** *adj* (of a reply or reaction) automatic and predictable. **knees-up** *n informal* party.

kneel ❶ *v* **kneeling**, **kneeled** *or* **knelt** fall or rest on one's knees.

knell ❶ *n* **1** sound of a bell, esp. at a funeral or death. **2** portent of doom.

knickers ❶ *pl n* woman's or girl's undergarment covering the lower trunk and having legs or legholes.

knick-knack ❶ *n* trifle or trinket.

knife ❶ *n*, *pl* **knives** **1** cutting tool or weapon consisting of a sharp-edged blade with a handle. ▷ *v* **2** cut or stab with a knife.

knight *n* **1** man who has been given a knighthood. **2** *Hist* man who served his lord as a mounted armoured soldier. **3** chess piece shaped like a horse's head. ▷ *v* **4** award a knighthood to. **knighthood** *n* honorary title given to a man by the British sovereign.

knit ❶ *v* **knitting**, **knitted** *or* **knit** **1** make (a garment) by interlocking a series of loops in wool or other yarn. **2** join closely

k

——— THESAURUS ———

kit *n* **1** = **equipment**, apparatus, gear, paraphernalia, tackle, tools

knack *n* **1** = **skill**, trick **2** = **gift**, ability, aptitude, capacity, expertise, facility, propensity, skill, talent

knave *n* **2** Obs = **rogue**, blackguard, bounder (*old-fashioned Brit sl*), rascal, rotter (*sl, chiefly Brit*), scoundrel, villain

knead *v* **2** = **squeeze**, form, manipulate, massage, mould, press, rub, shape, work

kneel *v* = **genuflect**, stoop

knell *n* **1** = **ringing**, chime, peal, sound, toll

knickers *pl n* = **underwear**, bloomers, briefs, broekies (*S Afr inf*), drawers, panties, smalls

knick-knack *n* = **trinket**, bagatelle, bauble, bric-a-brac, plaything, trifle

knife *n* **1** = **blade**, cutter ▷ *v* **2** = **cut**, lacerate, pierce, slash, stab, wound

knit *v* **2** = **join**, bind, fasten, intertwine, link, tie, unite, weave **3** = **wrinkle**, crease, furrow, knot, pucker

together. **3** draw (one's eyebrows) together. **knitting** n **knitwear** n knitted clothes, such as sweaters.

knob ❶ n **1** rounded projection, such as a switch on a radio. **2** rounded handle on a door or drawer. **3** small amount of butter. **knobbly** adj covered with small bumps.

knock ❶ v **1** give a blow or push to. **2** rap audibly with the knuckles. **3** make or drive by striking. **4** informal criticize adversely. **5** (of an engine) make a regular banging noise as a result of a fault. ▷ n **6** blow or rap. **7** knocking sound. **knocker** n metal fitting for knocking on a door. **knock about, around** v **1** wander or spend time aimlessly. **2** hit or kick brutally. **knockabout** adj (of comedy) boisterous. **knock back** v informal **1** drink quickly. **2** cost. **3** reject or refuse. **knock down** v **1** demolish. **2** reduce the price of. **knockdown** adj (of a price) very low. **knock-knees** pl n legs that curve in at the knees. **knock off** v **1** informal cease work. **2** informal make or do (something) hurriedly or easily. **3** take (a specified amount) off a price. **4** informal steal. **knock out** v **1** render (someone) unconscious. **2** informal overwhelm or amaze. **3** defeat in a knockout competition. **knockout** n **1** blow that renders an opponent unconscious. **2** competition from which competitors are progressively eliminated. **3** informal overwhelmingly attractive person or thing. **knock up** v **1** informal assemble (something) quickly. **2** informal waken.

knoll n small rounded hill.

knot ❶ n **1** fastening made by looping and pulling tight strands of string, cord, or rope. **2** tangle (of hair). **3** small cluster or huddled group. **4** round lump or spot in timber. **5** feeling of tightness, caused by tension or nervousness. **6** unit of speed used by ships, equal to one nautical mile per hour. ▷ v **knotting, knotted 7** tie with or into a knot. **knotty** adj **1** full of knots. **2** puzzling or difficult.

know ❶ v **knowing, knew, known 1** be or feel certain of the truth of (information etc.). **2** be acquainted with. **3** have a grasp of or understand (a skill or language). **4** be aware of. **in the know** informal informed or aware. **knowing** adj suggesting secret knowledge. **knowingly** adv **1** deliberately. **2** in a way that suggests secret knowledge. **knowledge** n facts or experiences known by a person. **know-all** n offens person who acts as if knowing more than other people. **know-how** n informal ingenuity, aptitude, or skill.

knuckle n **1** bone at the finger joint. **2** knee joint of a calf or pig. **near the knuckle** informal rather rude or offensive. **knuckle-duster** n metal appliance worn on the knuckles to add force to a blow. **knuckle under** v yield or submit.

KO knockout.

koala n tree-dwelling Australian marsupial with dense grey fur (also **native bear**).

kohl n cosmetic powder used to darken the edges of the eyelids.

Koran n sacred book of Islam.

kosher [koh-sher] adj **1** conforming to Jewish religious law, esp. (of food) to

---

THESAURUS

knob n **1** = **lump**, bump, hump, knot, projection, protrusion, stud

knock v **1** = **hit**, belt (inf), cuff, punch, smack, strike, thump **2** = **rap 4** Inf = **criticize**, abuse, belittle, censure, condemn, denigrate, deprecate, disparage, find fault, run down ▷ n **6** = **blow**, clip, clout (inf), cuff, rap, slap, smack, thump

knot n **1** = **connection**, bond, joint,

ligature, loop, tie **3** = **cluster**, bunch, clump, collection ▷ v **7** = **tie**, bind, loop, secure, tether

know v **1** = **understand**, comprehend, feel certain, notice, perceive, realize, recognize, see **2** = **be acquainted with**, be familiar with, have dealings with, have knowledge of, recognize

k

Jewish dietary law. **2** *informal* legitimate or authentic. ▷ *n* **3** kosher food.

kowtow *v* be servile (towards).

krypton *n Chem* colourless gas present in the atmosphere and used in fluorescent lights.

KS Kansas.

kudos *n* fame or credit.

kugel [**koog**-el] *n S Afr* rich, fashion-conscious, materialistic young woman.

kumara *n NZ* tropical root vegetable with yellow flesh.

kung fu *n* Chinese martial art combining hand, foot, and weapon techniques.

kurrajong *n* Australian tree or shrub with tough fibrous bark.

KY Kentucky.

k

LI

l litre.
LA Louisiana.
lab *n informal* short for LABORATORY.
label ➊ *n* **1** piece of card or other material fixed to an object to show its ownership, destination, etc. ▷ *v* **-elling, -elled 2** give a label to.
laboratory *n, pl* **-ries** building or room designed for scientific research or for the teaching of practical science.
labrador *n* large retriever dog with a usu. gold or black coat.
laburnum *n* ornamental tree with yellow hanging flowers.
labyrinth ➊ [**lab**-er-inth] *n* **1** complicated network of passages. **2** interconnecting cavities in the internal ear. **labyrinthine** *adj.*
lace ➊ *n* **1** delicate decorative fabric made from threads woven into an open weblike pattern. **2** cord drawn through eyelets and tied. ▷ *v* **3** fasten with laces. **4** thread a cord or string through holes in something.
5 add a small amount of alcohol, a drug, etc. to (food or drink). **lacy** *adj* fine, like lace.
lacerate ➊ [**lass**-er-rate] *v* tear (flesh). **laceration** *n.*
lachrymose *adj* **1** tearful. **2** sad.
lack ➊ *n* **1** shortage or absence of something needed or wanted. ▷ *v* **2** need or be short of (something).
lackadaisical ➊ *adj* lazy and careless in a dreamy way.
lackey ➊ *n* **1** servile follower. **2** uniformed male servant.
lacklustre ➊ *adj* lacking brilliance or vitality.
laconic ➊ *adj* using only a few words, terse. **laconically** *adv.*
lacquer *n* **1** hard varnish for wood or metal. **2** clear sticky substance sprayed onto the hair to hold it in place.
lacrosse *n* sport in which teams catch and throw a ball using long sticks with a pouched net at the end, in an attempt to score goals.
lad ➊ *n* boy or young man.
ladder *n* **1** frame of two poles connected by horizontal steps used for climbing. **2** line of stitches that have come undone in tights or stockings. ▷ *v* **3** have or cause to have such a line of undone stitches.
laden ➊ *adj* **1** loaded. **2** burdened.
ladle *n* **1** spoon with a long handle and a

— THESAURUS —

label *n* **1 = tag**, marker, sticker, ticket ▷ *v* **2 = tag**, mark, stamp
labyrinth *n* **1 = maze**, intricacy, jungle, tangle
lace *n* **1 = netting**, filigree, openwork **2 = cord**, bootlace, shoelace, string, tie ▷ *v* **3 = fasten**, bind, do up, thread, tie **4 = intertwine**, interweave, twine **5 = mix in**, add to, fortify, spike
lacerate *v* **= tear**, claw, cut, gash, mangle, rip, slash, wound
lack *n* **1 = shortage**, absence, dearth, deficiency, need, scarcity, want ▷ *v* **2 = need**, be deficient in, be short of, be

without, miss, require, want
lackadaisical *adj* **= lazy**, abstracted, dreamy, idle, indolent, inert
lackey *n* **1 = hanger-on**, flatterer, minion, sycophant, toady, yes man **2 = manservant**, attendant, flunky, footman, valet
lacklustre *adj* **= flat**, drab, dull, leaden, lifeless, muted, prosaic, uninspired, vapid
laconic *adj* **= terse**, brief, concise, curt, monosyllabic, pithy, short, succinct
lad *n* **= boy**, fellow, guy (*inf*), juvenile, kid (*inf*), youngster, youth
laden *adj* **= loaded**, burdened, charged,

large bowl, used for serving soup etc. ▷ *v*
2 serve out.

lady ❶ *n, pl* **-dies 1** woman regarded as
having characteristics of good breeding
or high rank. **2** polite term of address
for a woman. **3** (**L-**) title of some female
members of the nobility. **lady-in-waiting**
n, pl **ladies-in-waiting** female servant of
a queen or princess. **ladykiller** *n informal*
man who is or thinks he is irresistible to
women. **ladylike** *adj* polite and dignified.

lag[1] ❶ *v* **lagging, lagged 1** go too slowly,
fall behind. ▷ *n* **2** delay between events.
laggard *n* person who lags behind.

lag[2] *v* **lagging, lagged** wrap (a boiler, pipes,
etc.) with insulating material. **lagging** *n*
insulating material.

lag[3] *n* **old lag** *slang* convict.

lager *n* light-bodied beer.

lagoon *n* body of water cut off from the
open sea by coral reefs or sand bars.

laid *v* past of LAY[1]. **laid-back** *adj informal*
relaxed.

lair ❶ *n* resting place of an animal.

laird *n* Scottish landowner.

laissez-faire [less-ay-**fair**] *n* principle of
nonintervention, esp. by a government in
commercial affairs.

laity [**lay**-it-ee] *n* people who are not
members of the clergy.

lake ❶ *n* expanse of water entirely
surrounded by land. **lakeside** *n*.

lama *n* Buddhist priest in Tibet or Mongolia.

lamb *n* **1** young sheep. **2** its meat. ▷ *v* **3** (of

sheep) give birth to a lamb or lambs.

lambast, lambaste *v* **1** beat or thrash.
2 reprimand severely.

lame ❶ *adj* **1** having an injured or disabled
leg or foot. **2** (of an excuse) unconvincing.
▷ *v* **3** make lame. **lamely** *adv* **lameness** *n*
lame duck person or thing unable to cope
without help.

lamé [**lah**-may] *n, adj* (fabric) interwoven
with gold or silver thread.

lament ❶ *v* **1** feel or express sorrow (for).
▷ *n* **2** passionate expression of grief.
lamentable *adj* very disappointing.
lamentation *n*.

laminate *v* **1** make (a sheet of material) by
sticking together thin sheets. **2** cover with
a thin sheet of material. ▷ *n* **3** laminated
sheet.

lamington *n Aust & NZ* sponge cake coated
with a sweet frosting.

lamp *n* device which produces light from
electricity, oil, or gas. **lamppost** *n* post
supporting a lamp in the street. **lampshade**
n.

lampoon ❶ *n* **1** humorous satire ridiculing
someone. ▷ *v* **2** satirize or ridicule.

lamprey *n* eel-like fish with a round
sucking mouth.

lance *n* **1** long spear used by a mounted
soldier. ▷ *v* **2** pierce (a boil or abscess)
with a lancet. **lancer** *n* formerly, cavalry
soldier armed with a lance. **lance corporal**
noncommissioned army officer of the
lowest rank.

—— THESAURUS ——

encumbered, full, weighed down

lady *n* **1** = **gentlewoman**, dame
2 = **woman**, female

lag[1] *v* **1** = **hang back**, dawdle, delay, linger,
loiter, straggle, tarry, trail

lair *n* = **nest**, burrow, den, earth, hole

laissez-faire *n* = **nonintervention**, free
enterprise, free trade

lake *n* = **pond**, lagoon, loch (*Scot*), lough
(*Irish*), mere, reservoir, tarn

lame *adj* **1** = **disabled**, crippled, game,
handicapped, hobbling, limping

2 = **unconvincing**, feeble, flimsy,
inadequate, pathetic, poor, thin,
unsatisfactory, weak

lament *v* **1** = **bemoan**, bewail, complain,
deplore, grieve, mourn, regret,
sorrow, wail, weep ▷ *n* **2** = **complaint**,
lamentation, moan, wailing

lampoon *n* **1** = **satire**, burlesque,
caricature, parody, send-up (*Brit inf*), skit,
takeoff (*inf*) ▷ *v* **2** = **ridicule**, caricature,
make fun of, mock, parody, satirize, send
up (*Brit inf*), take off (*inf*)

land ❶ *n* **1** solid part of the earth's surface. **2** ground, esp. with reference to its type or use. **3** rural or agricultural area. **4** property consisting of land. **5** country or region. ▷ *v* **6** come or bring to earth after a flight, jump, or fall. **7** go or take from a ship at the end of a voyage. **8** come to or touch shore. **9** come or bring to some point or condition. **10** *informal* obtain. **11** take (a hooked fish) from the water. **12** *informal* deliver (a punch). **landed** *adj* possessing or consisting of lands **landward** *adj* **1** nearest to or facing the land. ▷ *adv* **2** (also **landwards**) towards land. **landfall** *n* ship's first landing after a voyage. **landlocked** *adj* completely surrounded by land. **landlord** *n* person who rents out land, houses, etc. **landmark** *n* prominent object in or feature of a landscape. **landscape** *n* extensive piece of inland scenery seen from one place. **land up** *v* arrive at a final point or condition.

lane ❶ *n* **1** narrow road. **2** area of road for one stream of traffic. **3** specified route followed by ships or aircraft. **4** strip of a running track or swimming pool for use by one competitor.

language ❶ *n* **1** system of sounds, symbols, etc. for communicating thought. **2** particular system used by a nation or people. **3** system of words and symbols for computer programming.

languish ❶ *v* **1** suffer neglect or hardship. **2** lose or diminish in strength or vigour. **3** pine (for).

lank ❶ *adj* **1** (of hair) straight and limp. **2** thin or gaunt. **lanky** *adj* ungracefully tall and thin.

lantern *n* light in a transparent protective case.

lap¹ *n* part between the waist and knees of a person when sitting. **in the lap of luxury** in conditions of great comfort and wealth. **laptop** *adj* (of a computer) small enough to fit on a user's lap.

lap² ❶ *n* **1** single circuit of a racecourse or track. **2** stage of a journey. ▷ *v* **lapping**, **lapped 3** overtake an opponent so as to be one or more circuits ahead.

lap³ *v* **lapping, lapped** (of waves) beat softly against (a shore etc.). **lap up** *v* **1** drink by scooping up with the tongue. **2** accept (information or attention) eagerly.

lapel [lap-**pel**] *n* part of the front of a coat or jacket folded back towards the shoulders.

lapwing *n* plover with a tuft of feathers on the head.

larceny *n, pl* **-nies** *Law* theft.

larch *n* deciduous coniferous tree.

lard *n* **1** soft white fat obtained from a pig. ▷ *v* **2** insert strips of bacon in (meat) before cooking. **3** decorate (speech or writing) with strange words unnecessarily.

——————————————————————————————————————— THESAURUS ——————

land *n* **1** = **ground**, dry land, earth, terra firma **2** = **soil**, dirt, ground, loam **3** = **countryside**, farmland **4** = **property**, estate, grounds, realty, homestead (*US & Canad*) **5** = **country**, district, nation, province, region, territory, tract ▷ *v* **6** = **alight**, arrive, come to rest, touch down **7** = **disembark 8** = **dock 10** *Inf* = **obtain**, acquire, gain, get, secure, win

lane *n* **1** = **road**, alley, footpath, passageway, path, pathway, street, way

language *n* **1** = **speech**, communication, discourse, expression, parlance, talk

2 = **tongue**, dialect, patois, vernacular

languish *v* **1** = **waste away**, be abandoned, be neglected, rot, suffer **2** = **decline**, droop, fade, fail, faint, flag, weaken, wilt, wither **3** = **pine**, desire, hanker, hunger, long, yearn

lank *adj* **1** = **limp**, lifeless, straggling **2** = **thin**, emaciated, gaunt, lean, scrawny, skinny, slender, slim, spare

lap² *n* **1** = **circuit**, circle, loop, orbit, tour

lap³ *v* = **ripple**, gurgle, plash, purl, splash, swish, wash **lap up** *v* **1** = **drink**, lick, sip, sup

larder n storeroom for food.

large ❶ adj great in size, number, or extent. **at large 1** in general. **2** free, not confined. **3** fully. **largely** adv **largish** adj **large-scale** adj wide-ranging or extensive.

largo n, pl **-gos** adv Music (piece to be played) in a slow and dignified manner.

lark¹ n small brown songbird, skylark.

lark² ❶ n informal **1** harmless piece of mischief or fun. **2** unnecessary activity or job. **lark about** v play pranks.

larrikin n Aust or NZ old-fashioned slang mischievous or unruly person.

larva n, pl **-vae** insect in an immature stage, often resembling a worm. **larval** adj.

larynx n, pl **larynges** part of the throat containing the vocal cords. **laryngeal** adj **laryngitis** n inflammation of the larynx.

lasagne, lasagna [laz-**zan**-ya] n **1** pasta in wide flat sheets. **2** dish made from layers of lasagne, meat, and cheese.

lascivious [lass-**iv**-ee-uss] adj showing or producing sexual desire.

laser [**lay**-zer] n device that produces a very narrow intense beam of light, used for cutting very hard materials and in surgery etc.

lash¹ ❶ n **1** eyelash. **2** sharp blow with a whip. ▷ v **3** hit with a whip. **4** (of rain or waves) beat forcefully against. **5** attack verbally, scold. **6** flick or wave sharply to and fro. **lash out** v **1** make a sudden physical or verbal attack. **2** informal spend (money) extravagantly.

lash² ❶ v fasten or bind tightly with cord etc.

lashings pl n old-fashioned large amounts.

lass, lassie ❶ n girl.

lassitude n physical or mental weariness.

lasso [lass-**oo**] n, pl **-sos, -soes 1** rope with a noose for catching cattle and horses. ▷ v **-soing, -soed 2** catch with a lasso.

last¹ ❶ adj, adv **1** coming at the end or after all others. **2** most recent(ly). ▷ adj **3** only remaining. ▷ n **4** last person or thing. **lastly** adv **last-ditch** adj done as a final resort. **last post** army bugle-call played at sunset and funerals. **last straw** small irritation or setback that, coming after others, is too much to bear. **last word 1** final comment in an argument. **2** most recent or best example of something.

last² ❶ v **1** continue. **2** be sufficient for (a specified amount of time). **3** remain fresh, uninjured, or unaltered. **lasting** adj.

last³ n model of a foot on which shoes and boots are made or repaired.

latch ❶ n **1** fastening for a door with a bar and lever. **2** lock which can only be opened from the outside with a key. ▷ v

large adj = **big**, considerable, enormous, gigantic, great, huge, immense, massive, monumental, sizable or sizeable, substantial, vast **at large 1** = **in general**, as a whole, chiefly, generally, in the main, mainly **2** = **free**, at liberty, on the loose, on the run, unconfined **3** = **fully**, at length, exhaustively, greatly, in full detail

lark² n Inf = **prank**, caper, escapade, fun, game, jape, mischief **lark about** v = **play**, caper, cavort, have fun, make mischief

lash¹ n **2** = **blow**, hit, stripe, stroke, swipe (inf) ▷ v **3** = **whip**, beat, birch, flog, scourge, thrash **4** = **pound**, beat, buffet, dash, drum, hammer, smack, strike **5** = **censure**, attack, blast, criticize, put down, rouse on (Aust), scold, slate (inf, chiefly Brit), tear into (inf), upbraid

lash² v = **fasten**, bind, make fast, secure, strap, tie

lass, lassie n = **girl**, damsel, maid, maiden, young woman

last¹ adj **1** = **final**, at the end, closing, concluding, hindmost, rearmost, terminal, ultimate **2** = **most recent**, latest

last² v **1** = **continue**, abide, carry on, endure, keep on, persist, remain **3** = **survive**, stand up

latch n **1** = **fastening**, bar, bolt, catch, hasp, hook, lock ▷ v **3** = **fasten**, bar, bolt, make fast, secure

3 fasten with a latch. **latch onto** v become attached to (a person or idea).

late ❶ adj **1** after the normal or expected time. **2** towards the end of a period. **3** being at an advanced time. **4** recently dead. **5** recent. **6** former. ▷ adv **7** after the normal or expected time. **8** at a relatively advanced age. **9** recently. **lately** adv in recent times. **lateness** n **latish** adj, adv.

latent ❶ adj hidden and not yet developed. **latency** n.

lateral ❶ [**lat**-ter-al] adj of or relating to the side or sides.

latex n milky fluid found in some plants, esp. the rubber tree, used in making rubber.

lath n thin strip of wood used to support plaster, tiles, etc.

lathe n machine for turning wood or metal while it is being shaped.

lather ❶ n **1** froth of soap and water. **2** frothy sweat. **3** informal state of agitation. ▷ v **4** make frothy. **5** rub with soap until lather appears.

Latin n **1** language of the ancient Romans. ▷ adj **2** of or in Latin. **3** of a people whose language derives from Latin. **Latin America** parts of South and Central America whose official language is Spanish or Portuguese.

latitude ❶ n **1** angular distance measured in degrees N or S of the equator. **2** scope for freedom of action or thought. ▷ pl **3** regions considered in relation to their distance from the equator.

latrine n toilet in a barracks or camp.

latter ❶ adj **1** second of two. **2** later. **3** recent. **latterly** adv **latter-day** adj modern.

lattice ❶ [**lat**-iss] n **1** framework of intersecting strips of wood, metal, etc. **2** gate, screen, etc. formed of such a framework.

laud v praise or glorify. **laudable** adj praiseworthy. **laudatory** adj praising or glorifying.

laudanum [**lawd**-a-num] n opium-based sedative.

laugh ❶ v **1** make inarticulate sounds with the voice expressing amusement, merriment, or scorn. **2** utter or express with laughter. ▷ n **3** act or instance of laughing. **4** informal person or thing causing amusement. **laughable** adj ridiculously inadequate. **laughter** n sound or action of laughing. **laughing stock** object of general derision. **laugh off** v treat (something difficult or serious) lightly.

launch¹ ❶ v **1** put (a ship or boat) into the water, esp. for the first time. **2** begin (a campaign, project, etc.). **3** put a new product on the market. **4** send (a missile or spacecraft) into space or the air. ▷ n **5** launching. **launch into** v start doing

──────────────────── THESAURUS ────────

late adj **1** = **overdue**, behind, behindhand, belated, delayed, last-minute, tardy **4** = **dead**, deceased, defunct, departed, former, past **5** = **recent**, advanced, fresh, modern, new ▷ adv **7** = **belatedly**, at the last minute, behindhand, behind time, dilatorily, tardily

latent adj = **hidden**, concealed, dormant, invisible, potential, undeveloped, unrealized

lateral adj = **sideways**, edgeways, flanking

lather n **1** = **froth**, bubbles, foam, soapsuds, suds **3** Inf = **fluster**, dither, flap (inf), fuss, state (inf), sweat, tizzy (inf) ▷ v

4 = **froth**, foam **5** = **soap**

latitude n **2** = **scope**, elbowroom, freedom, laxity, leeway, liberty, licence, play, space

latter adj **1** = **second 2** = **later**, closing, concluding, last, last-mentioned

lattice n **1, 2** = **grid**, grating, grille, trellis

laugh v **1** = **chuckle**, be in stitches, chortle, giggle, guffaw, snigger, split one's sides, titter ▷ n **3** = **chuckle**, chortle, giggle, guffaw, snigger, titter **4** Inf **a** = **clown**, card (inf), entertainer, hoot (inf), scream (inf) **b** = **joke**, hoot (inf), lark

launch¹ v **2** = **begin**, commence, embark upon, inaugurate, initiate, instigate,

something enthusiastically.

launch² *n* open motorboat.

laureate [**lor**-ee-at] *adj* see POET LAUREATE.

laurel *n* 1 glossy-leaved shrub, bay tree. ▷ *pl* 2 wreath of laurel, an emblem of victory or merit.

lava *n* molten rock thrown out by volcanoes, which hardens as it cools.

lavatory ❶ *n*, *pl* -**ries** toilet.

lavender *n* 1 shrub with fragrant flowers. ▷ *adj* 2 bluish-purple.

lavish ❶ *adj* 1 great in quantity or richness. 2 giving or spending generously. 3 extravagant. ▷ *v* 4 give or spend generously.

law ❶ *n* 1 rule binding on a community. 2 system of such rules. 3 *informal* police. 4 invariable sequence of events in nature. 5 general principle deduced from facts. **lawful** *adj* allowed by law. **lawfully** *adv* **lawless** *adj* breaking the law, esp. in a violent way. **lawlessness** *n* **law-abiding** *adj* obeying the laws. **lawsuit** *n* court case brought by one person or group against another.

lawn *n* area of tended and mown grass.

lawn mower machine for cutting grass.

lawn tennis tennis, esp. when played on a grass court.

lawyer ❶ *n* professionally qualified legal expert.

lax ❶ *adj* not strict. **laxity** *n*.

lay¹ ❶ *v* **laying, laid** 1 cause to lie. 2 devise or prepare. 3 set in a particular place or position. 4 attribute (blame). 5 put forward (a plan, argument, etc.). 6 (of a bird or reptile) produce eggs. 7 place (a bet). 8 arrange (a table) for a meal. **lay-by** *n* stopping place for traffic beside a road. **lay off** *v* dismiss staff during a slack period. **lay-off** *n* **lay on** *v* provide or supply. **lay out** *v* 1 arrange or spread out. 2 prepare (a corpse) for burial. 3 *informal* spend money, esp. lavishly. 4 *informal* knock unconscious. **layout** *n* arrangement, esp. of matter for printing or of a building. **lay waste** devastate.

lay² *v* past tense of LIE². **layabout** *n* lazy person.

lay³ ❶ *adj* 1 of or involving people who are not clergymen. 2 nonspecialist. **layman** *n* 1 person who is not a member of the clergy.

introduce, open, start 4 = **propel**, discharge, dispatch, fire, project, send off, set in motion

lavatory *n* = **toilet**, bathroom, cloakroom (*Brit*), latrine, loo (*Brit inf*), powder room, privy, (public) convenience, washroom, water closet, W.C.

lavish *adj* 1 = **plentiful**, abundant, copious, profuse, prolific 2 = **generous**, bountiful, free, liberal, munificent, open-handed, unstinting 3 = **extravagant**, exaggerated, excessive, immoderate, prodigal, unrestrained, wasteful, wild ▷ *v* 4 = **spend**, deluge, dissipate, expend, heap, pour, shower, squander, waste

law *n* 1 = **rule**, act, command, commandment, decree, edict, order, ordinance, regulation, statute 2 = **constitution**, charter, code 5 = **principle**, axiom, canon, precept

lawyer *n* = **legal adviser**, advocate, attorney, barrister, counsel, counsellor, solicitor

lax *adj* = **slack**, careless, casual, lenient, negligent, overindulgent, remiss, slapdash, slipshod

lay¹ *v* 1, 3 = **place**, deposit, leave, plant, position, put, set, set down, spread 2 = **devise**, concoct, contrive, design, hatch, plan, plot, prepare, work out 4 = **attribute**, allocate, allot, ascribe, assign, impute 5 = **put forward**, advance, bring forward, lodge, offer, present, submit 6 = **produce**, bear, deposit 7 = **bet**, gamble, give odds, hazard, risk, stake, wager 8 = **arrange**, organize, set out

lay³ *adj* 1 = **nonclerical**, secular 2 = **nonspecialist**, amateur, inexpert, nonprofessional

2 person without specialist knowledge.

lay⁴ ❶ *n* short narrative poem designed to be sung.

layette *n* clothes for a newborn baby.

lazy ❶ *adj* **lazier**, **laziest** 1 not inclined to work or exert oneself. 2 done in a relaxed manner without much effort. 3 (of movement) slow and gentle. **lazily** *adv* **laziness** *n* **lazybones** *n informal* lazy person.

lbw *Cricket* leg before wicket.

lead¹ ❶ *v* **leading**, **led** 1 guide or conduct. 2 cause to feel, think, or behave in a certain way. 3 be the most important person or thing in. 4 be, go, or play first. 5 (of a road, path, etc.) go towards. 6 control or direct. 7 (foll. by *to*) result in. 8 pass or spend (one's life). ▷ *n* 9 first or most prominent place. 10 example or leadership. 11 amount by which a person or group is ahead of another. 12 clue. 13 length of leather or chain attached to a dog's collar to control it. 14 principal role or actor in a film, play, etc. 15 cable bringing current to an electrical device. ▷ *adj* 16 acting

as a leader or lead. **leader** *n* person who leads. **leading** *adj* 1 principal. 2 in the first position. **leading question** question worded to prompt the answer desired. **lead-in** *n* introduction to a subject.

lead² *n* 1 soft heavy grey metal. 2 (in a pencil) graphite. **leaded** *adj* (of windows) made from many small panes of glass held together with lead strips. **leaden** *adj* 1 heavy or sluggish. 2 dull grey. 3 made from lead.

leaf ❶ *n*, *pl* **leaves** 1 flat usu. green blade attached to the stem of a plant. 2 single sheet of paper in a book. 3 very thin sheet of metal. 4 extending flap on a table. **leafy** *adj* **leafless** *adj* **leaf through** *v* turn pages without reading them.

league¹ ❶ *n* 1 association promoting the interests of its members. 2 association of sports clubs organizing competitions between its members. 3 *informal* class or level.

league² *n obs* measure of distance, about three miles.

leak ❶ *n* 1 hole or defect that allows the escape or entrance of liquid, gas, radiation,

— THESAURUS —

lay⁴ *n* = **poem**, ballad, lyric, ode, song

lazy *adj* 1 = **idle**, inactive, indolent, inert, slack, slothful, slow, workshy 3 = **lethargic**, drowsy, languid, languorous, sleepy, slow-moving, sluggish, somnolent, torpid

lead¹ *v* 1 = **guide**, conduct, escort, pilot, precede, show the way, steer, usher 2 = **cause**, dispose, draw, incline, induce, influence, persuade, prevail, prompt 3 = **command**, direct, govern, head, manage, preside over, supervise 4 = **be ahead (of)**, blaze a trail, come first, exceed, excel, outdo, outstrip, surpass, transcend 7 (foll. by *to*) = **result in**, bring on, cause, contribute to, produce 8 = **live**, experience, have, pass, spend, undergo ▷ *n* 9 = **first place**, precedence, primacy, priority, supremacy, vanguard 10 = **example**, direction, guidance, leadership, model 11 = **advantage**, edge,

margin, start 12 = **clue**, hint, indication, suggestion 14 = **leading role**, principal, protagonist, title role ▷ *adj* 16 = **main**, chief, first, foremost, head, leading, premier, primary, prime, principal

leaf *n* 1 = **frond**, blade 2 = **page**, folio, sheet **leaf through** *v* = **skim**, browse, flip, glance, riffle, thumb (through)

league¹ *n* 1 = **association**, alliance, coalition, confederation, consortium, federation, fraternity, group, guild, partnership, union 3 *inf* = **class**, category, level

leak *n* 1 = **hole**, aperture, chink, crack, crevice, fissure, opening, puncture 2 = **leakage**, drip, percolation, seepage 3 = **disclosure**, divulgence ▷ *v* 5 = **escape**, drip, exude, ooze, pass, percolate, seep, spill, trickle 6 = **disclose**, divulge, give away, let slip, make known, make public, pass on, reveal, tell

etc. **2** liquid etc. that escapes or enters. **3** disclosure of secrets. ▷ v **4** let liquid etc. in or out. **5** (of liquid etc.) find its way through a leak. **6** disclose secret information. **leakage** n act or instance of leaking. **leaky** adj.

lean¹ ❶ v **leaning**, **leaned** or **leant 1** rest against. **2** bend or slope from an upright position. **3** tend (towards). **leaning** n tendency. **lean on** v **1** informal threaten or intimidate. **2** depend on for help or advice. **lean-to** n shed built against an existing wall.

lean² ❶ adj **1** thin but healthy-looking. **2** (of meat) lacking fat. **3** unproductive. ▷ n **4** lean part of meat. **leanness** n.

leap ❶ v **leaping**, **leapt** or **leaped 1** make a sudden powerful jump. ▷ n **2** sudden powerful jump. **3** abrupt increase, as in costs or prices. **leapfrog** n game in which a player vaults over another bending down. **leap year** year with February 29 as an extra day.

learn ❶ v **learning**, **learned** or **learnt 1** gain skill or knowledge by study, practice, or teaching. **2** memorize (something). **3** find

out or discover. **learned** adj **1** erudite, deeply read. **2** showing much learning. **learner** n **learning** n knowledge got by study.

lease ❶ n **1** contract by which land or property is rented for a stated time by the owner to a tenant. ▷ v **2** let or rent by lease. **leasehold** n, adj (land or property) held on lease. **leaseholder** n.

leash ❶ n lead for a dog.

least ❶ adj **1** superlative of LITTLE. **2** smallest. ▷ n **3** smallest one. ▷ adv **4** in the smallest degree.

leather n **1** material made from specially treated animal skins. ▷ adj **2** made of leather. ▷ v **3** beat or thrash. **leathery** adj like leather, tough.

leave¹ ❶ v **leaving**, **left 1** go away from. **2** allow to remain, accidentally or deliberately. **3** cause to be or remain in a specified state. **4** discontinue membership of. **5** permit. **6** entrust. **7** bequeath. **leave out** v exclude or omit.

leave² ❶ n **1** permission to be absent from work or duty. **2** period of such absence. **3** permission to do something. **4** formal parting.

lean¹ v **1** = **rest**, be supported, prop, recline, repose **2** = **bend**, heel, incline, slant, slope, tilt, tip **3** = **tend**, be disposed to, be prone to, favour, prefer **lean on 2** = **depend on**, count on, have faith in, rely on, trust

lean² adj **1** = **trim**, angular, bony, rangy, skinny, slender, slim, spare, thin, wiry **3** = **poor**, barren, meagre, scanty, unfruitful, unproductive

leap v **1** = **jump**, bounce, bound, hop, skip, spring ▷ n **2** = **jump**, bound, spring, vault **3** = **rise**, change, escalation, increase, surge, upsurge, upswing

learn v **1** = **master**, grasp, pick up **2** = **memorize**, commit to memory, get off pat, learn by heart **3** = **discover**, ascertain, detect, discern, find out, gather, hear, understand

lease v **2** = **hire**, charter, let, loan, rent

leash n = **lead**, rein, tether

least adj **1, 2** = **smallest**, fewest, lowest, meanest, minimum, poorest, slightest, tiniest

leave¹ v **1** = **depart**, decamp, disappear, exit, go, go away, make tracks, move, pull out, quit, retire, slope off, withdraw **2** = **forget**, leave behind, mislay **3** = **cause**, deposit, generate, produce, result in **4** = **give up**, abandon, drop, relinquish, renounce, surrender **6** = **entrust**, allot, assign, cede, commit, consign, give over, refer **7** = **bequeath**, hand down, will

leave² n **1, 2** = **holiday**, furlough, leave of absence, sabbatical, time off, vacation **3** = **permission**, allowance, authorization, concession, consent, dispensation, freedom, liberty, sanction **4** = **departure**, adieu, farewell, goodbye, leave-taking, parting, retirement, withdrawal

leaven [**lev**-ven] n 1 substance that causes dough to rise. 2 influence that produces a gradual change. ▷ v 3 raise with leaven. 4 spread through and influence (something).

lecherous ❶ [**letch**-er-uss] adj (of a man) having or showing excessive sexual desire. **lecher** n **lechery** n.

lectern n sloping reading desk, esp. in a church.

lecture ❶ n 1 informative talk to an audience on a subject. 2 lengthy rebuke or scolding. ▷ v 3 give a talk. 4 scold. **lecturer** n **lectureship** n appointment as a lecturer.

ledge ❶ n 1 narrow shelf sticking out from a wall. 2 shelflike projection from a cliff etc.

ledger n book of debit and credit accounts of a firm.

lee n sheltered part or side. **leeward** adj, n 1 (on) the lee side. ▷ adv 2 towards this side. **leeway** n room for free movement within limits.

leech n 1 species of bloodsucking worm. 2 person who lives off others.

leek n vegetable of the onion family with a long bulb and thick stem.

leer ❶ v 1 look or grin at in a sneering or suggestive manner. ▷ n 2 sneering or suggestive look or grin.

lees ❶ pl n sediment of wine.

left¹ ❶ adj 1 of the side that faces west when the front faces north. ▷ adv 2 on or towards the left. ▷ n 3 left hand or part. 4 Politics people supporting socialism rather than capitalism. **leftist** n, adj (person) of the political left. **left-handed** adj more adept with the left hand than with the right. **left-wing** adj 1 socialist. 2 belonging to the more radical part of a political party.

left² v past of LEAVE¹.

leg ❶ n 1 one of the limbs on which a person or animal walks, runs, or stands. 2 part of a garment covering the leg. 3 structure that supports, such as one of the legs of a table. 4 stage of a journey. 5 Sport (part of) one game or race in a series. **pull someone's leg** tease someone. **leggy** adj having long legs. **legless** adj 1 without legs. 2 slang very drunk. **leggings** pl n 1 covering of leather or other material for the legs. 2 close-fitting trousers for women or children.

legacy ❶ n, pl -**cies** 1 thing left in a will. 2 thing handed down to a successor.

legal ❶ adj 1 established or permitted by law. 2 relating to law or lawyers. **legally** adv **legality** n **legalize** v make legal. **legalization** n.

lecherous adj = **lustful**, lascivious, lewd, libidinous, licentious, prurient, randy (inf, chiefly Brit), salacious

lecture n 1 = **talk**, address, discourse, instruction, lesson, speech 2 = **telling off**, dressing-down (inf), rebuke, reprimand, reproof, scolding, talking-to (inf) ▷ v 3 = **talk**, address, discourse, expound, hold forth, speak, spout, teach 4 = **tell off**, admonish, berate, castigate, censure, reprimand, reprove, rouse on (Aust), scold (inf)

ledge n 1 = **shelf**, mantle, projection, sill 2 = **ridge**, step

leer n, v = **grin**, gloat, goggle, ogle, smirk, squint, stare

lees pl n = **sediment**, deposit, dregs, grounds

left¹ adj 1 = **left-hand**, larboard (Naut), port

leg n 1 = **limb**, lower limb, member, pin (inf), stump (inf) 3 = **support**, brace, prop, upright 4 = **stage**, lap, part, portion, section, segment, stretch **pull someone's leg** = **tease**, fool, kid (inf), make fun of, trick, wind up (Brit sl)

legacy n = **bequest**, estate, gift, heirloom, inheritance

legal adj 1 = **lawful**, allowed, authorized, constitutional, legitimate, licit, permissible, sanctioned, valid 2 = **judicial**, forensic, judiciary, juridical

legate n messenger or representative, esp. from the Pope. **legation** n 1 diplomatic minister and his staff. 2 official residence of a diplomatic minister.

legatee n recipient of a legacy.

legato [leg-**ah**-toe] n, pl **-tos** adv Music (piece to be played) smoothly.

legend ❶ n 1 traditional story or myth. 2 traditional literature. 3 famous person or event. 4 stories about such a person or event. 5 inscription. **legendary** adj 1 famous. 2 of or in legend.

legible ❶ adj easily read. **legibility** n **legibly** adv.

legion ❶ n 1 large military force. 2 large number. 3 association of veterans. 4 infantry unit in the Roman army. **legionary** adj, n **legionnaire** n member of a legion. **legionnaire's disease** serious bacterial disease similar to pneumonia.

legislate v make laws. **legislation** n 1 legislating. 2 laws made. **legislative** adj **legislator** n maker of laws. **legislature** n body of people that makes, amends, or repeals laws.

legitimate ❶ adj 1 authorized by or in accordance with law. 2 fairly deduced. 3 born to parents married to each other. ▷ v 4 make legitimate. **legitimacy** n **legitimately** adv **legitimize** v make legitimate, legalize. **legitimization** n.

legume n 1 pod of a plant of the pea

or bean family. ▷ pl 2 peas or beans. **leguminous** adj (of plants) pod-bearing.

leisure ❶ n time for relaxation or hobbies. **at one's leisure** when one has time. **leisurely** adj 1 deliberate, unhurried. ▷ adv 2 slowly.

lekker adj S Afr slang 1 attractive or nice. 2 tasty.

lemming n rodent of arctic regions, reputed to run into the sea and drown during mass migrations.

lemon n 1 yellow oval fruit that grows on trees. 2 slang useless or defective person or thing. ▷ adj 3 pale-yellow. **lemonade** n lemon-flavoured soft drink, often fizzy. **lemon curd** creamy spread made of lemons, butter, etc.

lemur n nocturnal animal like a small monkey, found in Madagascar.

length ❶ n 1 extent or measurement from end to end. 2 period of time for which something happens. 3 quality of being long. 4 piece of something narrow and long. **at length** 1 at last. 2 in full detail. **lengthy** adj very long or tiresome. **lengthily** adv **lengthen** v make or become longer. **lengthways, lengthwise** adj, adv.

lenient ❶ [lee-nee-ent] adj tolerant, not strict or severe. **leniency** n.

lens n, pl **lenses** 1 piece of glass or similar material with one or both sides curved, used to bring together or spread light rays

———— THESAURUS ————

legend n 1 = **myth**, fable, fiction, folk tale, saga, story, tale 3 = **celebrity**, luminary, megastar (inf), phenomenon, prodigy 5 = **inscription**, caption, motto

legible adj = **readable**, clear, decipherable, distinct, easy to read, neat

legion n 1 = **army**, brigade, company, division, force, troop 2 = **multitude**, drove, horde, host, mass, myriad, number, throng

legitimate adj 1 = **lawful**, authentic, authorized, genuine, kosher (inf), legal, licit, rightful 2 = **reasonable**, admissible, correct, justifiable, logical, sensible, valid, warranted, well-founded ▷ v

4 = **legitimize**, authorize, legalize, permit, pronounce lawful, sanction

leisure n = **spare time**, ease, freedom, free time, liberty, recreation, relaxation, rest

length n 1 = **distance**, extent, longitude, measure, reach, span 2 = **duration**, period, space, span, stretch, term 4 = **piece**, measure, portion, section, segment ▷ n **at length** 1 = **at last**, at long last, eventually, finally, in the end 2 = **in detail**, completely, fully, in depth, thoroughly, to the full

lenient adj = **merciful**, compassionate, forbearing, forgiving, indulgent, kind,

in cameras, spectacles, telescopes, etc.
2 transparent structure in the eye that
focuses light.

lent v past of LEND.

Lent n period from Ash Wednesday to Easter
Saturday.

lentil n edible seed of a leguminous Asian
plant.

leopard n large spotted carnivorous animal
of the cat family.

leotard n tight-fitting garment covering
most of the body, worn for dancing or
exercise.

leper n **1** person suffering from leprosy.
2 ignored or despised person.

leprechaun n mischievous elf of Irish
folklore.

lesbian ❶ n **1** homosexual woman. ▷ adj
2 of homosexual women. **lesbianism** n.

lesion n **1** structural change in an organ
of the body caused by illness or injury.
2 injury or wound.

less ❶ adj **1** smaller in extent, degree, or
duration. **2** not so much. **3** comparative of
LITTLE. ▷ pron **4** smaller part or quantity.
▷ adv **5** to a smaller extent or degree.
▷ prep **6** after deducting, minus. **lessen** v
make or become smaller or not as much.
lesser adj not as great in quantity, size,
or worth.

lesson ❶ n **1** single period of instruction in
a subject. **2** content of this. **3** experience
that teaches. **4** portion of Scripture read
in church.

lest conj **1** so as to prevent any possibility

that. **2** for fear that.

let¹ ❶ v letting, let **1** allow, enable, or cause.
2 used as an auxiliary to express a proposal,
command, threat, or assumption. **3** grant
use of for rent, lease. **4** allow to escape.
let alone not to mention. **let down** v
1 disappoint. **2** lower. **3** deflate. **letdown**
n disappointment. **let off** v **1** excuse from
(a duty or punishment). **2** fire or explode (a
weapon). **3** emit (gas, steam, etc.). **let on**
v informal reveal (a secret). **let out** v **1** emit.
2 release. **let up** v diminish or stop. **let-up**
n lessening.

let² n **1** Tennis minor infringement or
obstruction of the ball requiring a replay of
the point. **2** hindrance.

lethal ❶ adj deadly.

lethargy ❶ n **1** sluggishness or dullness.
2 abnormal lack of energy. **lethargic** adj
lethargically adv.

letter ❶ n **1** written message, usu. sent
by post. **2** alphabetical symbol. **3** strict
meaning (of a law etc.). ▷ pl **4** literary
knowledge or ability. **lettered** adj learned.
lettering n **letter box 1** slot in a door
through which letters are delivered. **2** box
in a street or post office where letters are
posted. **letterhead** n printed heading on
stationery giving the sender's name and
address.

lettuce n plant with large green leaves used
in salads.

leukaemia [loo-**kee**-mee-a] n disease
caused by uncontrolled overproduction of
white blood cells.

——————————————————————— THESAURUS ———————

sparing, tolerant

lesbian adj **2** = **homosexual**, gay

less adj **1** = **smaller**, shorter ▷ prep
6 = **minus**, excepting, lacking, subtracting,
without

lesson n **1** = **class**, coaching, instruction,
period, schooling, teaching, tutoring
3 = **example**, deterrent, message, moral

let¹ v **1** = **allow**, authorize, entitle, give
permission, give the go-ahead, permit,
sanction, tolerate **3** = **lease**, hire, rent

let² n **2** = **hindrance**, constraint,
impediment, interference, obstacle,
obstruction, prohibition, restriction

lethal adj = **deadly**, dangerous, destructive,
devastating, fatal, mortal, murderous,
virulent

lethargy n = **sluggishness**, apathy,
drowsiness, inertia, languor, lassitude,
listlessness, sleepiness, sloth

letter n **1** = **message**, communication,
dispatch, epistle, line, missive, note

level ❶ *adj* **1** horizontal. **2** having an even surface. **3** of the same height as something else. **4** equal to or even with (someone or something else). **5** not going above the top edge of (a spoon etc.). ▷ *v* **-elling, -elled** **6** make even or horizontal. **7** make equal in position or status. **8** direct (a gun, accusation, etc.) at. **9** raze to the ground. ▷ *n* **10** horizontal line or surface. **11** device for showing or testing if something is horizontal. **12** position on a scale. **13** standard or grade. **14** flat area of land. **on the level** *informal* honest or trustworthy. **level crossing** point where a railway line and road cross. **level-headed** *adj* not apt to be carried away by emotion.

lever ❶ *n* **1** handle used to operate machinery. **2** bar used to move a heavy object or to open something. **3** rigid bar pivoted about a fulcrum to transfer a force to a load. **4** means of exerting pressure to achieve an aim. ▷ *v* **5** prise or move with a lever. **leverage** *n* **1** action or power of a lever. **2** influence or strategic advantage.

leveret [**lev**-ver-it] *n* young hare.

leviathan [lev-**vie**-ath-an] *n* **1** sea monster. **2** anything huge or formidable.

levitation *n* raising of a solid body into the air supernaturally. **levitate** *v* rise or cause to rise into the air.

levity ❶ *n, pl* **-ties** inclination to make a joke of serious matters.

levy ❶ [**lev**-vee] *v* **levying, levied** **1** impose and collect (a tax). **2** raise (troops). ▷ *n, pl* **levies** **3** imposition or collection of taxes. **4** money levied.

lewd ❶ *adj* lustful or indecent.

lexicon *n* **1** dictionary. **2** vocabulary of a language. **lexical** *adj* relating to the vocabulary of a language. **lexicographer** *n* writer of dictionaries. **lexicography** *n*.

liable ❶ *adj* **1** legally obliged or responsible. **2** given to or at risk from a condition. **liability** *n* **1** hindrance or disadvantage. **2** state of being liable. **3** financial obligation.

liar ❶ *n* person who tells lies.

lib *n informal* short for LIBERATION.

libel ❶ *n* **1** published statement falsely damaging a person's reputation. ▷ *v* **-belling, -belled** **2** falsely damage the reputation of (someone). **libellous** *adj*.

liberal ❶ *adj* **1** having social and political views that favour progress and reform.

---

2 = **character**, sign, symbol

level *adj* **1** = **horizontal**, flat **2** = **even**, consistent, plain, smooth, uniform **4** = **equal**, balanced, commensurate, comparable, equivalent, even, neck and neck, on a par, proportionate ▷ *v* **6** = **flatten**, even off *or* out, plane, smooth **7** = **equalize**, balance, even up **8** = **direct**, aim, focus, point, train **9** = **destroy**, bulldoze, demolish, devastate, flatten, knock down, pull down, raze, tear down **13** = **position**, achievement, degree, grade, rank, stage, standard, standing, status **on the level** *Inf* = **honest**, above board, fair, genuine, square, straight

lever *n* **1, 2** = **handle**, bar ▷ *v* **5** = **prise**, force

levity *n* = **light-heartedness**, facetiousness, flippancy, frivolity, silliness, skittishness, triviality

levy *v* **1** = **impose**, charge, collect, demand, exact **2** = **conscript**, call up, mobilize, muster, raise ▷ *n* **3** = **imposition**, assessment, collection, exaction, gathering **4** = **tax**, duty, excise, fee, tariff, toll

lewd *adj* = **indecent**, bawdy, lascivious, libidinous, licentious, lustful, obscene, pornographic, smutty, wanton

liable *adj* **1** = **responsible**, accountable, answerable, obligated **2** = **vulnerable**, exposed, open, subject, susceptible

liar *n* = **falsifier**, fabricator, fibber, perjurer

libel *n* **1** = **defamation**, aspersion, calumny, denigration, smear ▷ *v* **2** = **defame**, blacken, malign, revile, slur, smear, vilify

liberal *adj* **1** = **progressive**, libertarian, radical, reformist **2** = **generous**, beneficent, bountiful, charitable, kind,

2 generous. **3** tolerant. **4** abundant. **5** (of education) designed to develop general cultural interests. ▷ *n* **6** person who has liberal ideas or opinions. **liberally** *adv* **liberalism** *n* belief in democratic reforms and individual freedom. **liberality** *n* generosity. **liberalize** *v* make (laws, a country, etc.) less restrictive. **liberalization** *n*.

liberate ❶ *v* set free. **liberation** *n* **liberator** *n*

libertine ❶ [lib-er-teen] *n* morally dissolute person.

liberty ❶ *n, pl* **-ties 1** freedom. **2** act or comment regarded as forward or socially unacceptable. **at liberty 1** free. **2** having the right. **take liberties** be presumptuous.

libido [lib-**ee**-doe] *n, pl* **-dos 1** psychic energy. **2** emotional drive, esp. of sexual origin. **libidinous** *adj* lustful.

library *n, pl* **-braries 1** room or building where books are kept. **2** collection of books, records, etc. for consultation or borrowing. **librarian** *n* keeper of or worker in a library. **librarianship** *n*.

libretto *n, pl* **-tos, -ti** words of an opera.

librettist *n*.

lice *n* a plural of LOUSE.

licence ❶ *n* **1** document giving official permission to do something. **2** formal permission. **3** disregard of conventions for effect, e.g. *poetic licence*. **4** excessive liberty. **license** *v* grant a licence to. **licensed** *adj* **licensee** *n* holder of a licence, esp. to sell alcohol.

license plate *n* the US and Canadian term for NUMBERPLATE.

licentious ❶ *adj* sexually unrestrained or promiscuous.

lichen *n* small flowerless plant forming a crust on rocks, trees, etc.

licit *adj* lawful, permitted.

lick ❶ *v* **1** pass the tongue over. **2** touch lightly or flicker round. **3** *slang* defeat. ▷ *n* **4** licking. **5** small amount (of paint etc.). **6** *informal* fast pace.

licorice *n* same as LIQUORICE.

lid *n* **1** movable cover. **2** short for EYELID.

lido [**lee**-doe] *n, pl* **-dos** open-air centre for swimming and water sports.

lie¹ ❶ *v* **lying, lied 1** make a deliberately false statement. ▷ *n* **2** deliberate falsehood.

━━━━━━━━ THESAURUS ━━━━━━

open-handed, open-hearted, unstinting **3** = **tolerant**, broad-minded, indulgent, permissive **4** = **abundant**, ample, bountiful, copious, handsome, lavish, munificent, plentiful, profuse, rich
liberate *v* = **free**, deliver, emancipate, let loose, let out, release, rescue, set free
libertine *n* = **reprobate**, debauchee, lecher, profligate, rake, roué, sensualist, voluptuary, womanizer
liberty *n* **1** = **freedom**, autonomy, emancipation, immunity, independence, liberation, release, self-determination, sovereignty **2** = **impertinence**, impropriety, impudence, insolence, presumption **at liberty 1** = **free**, on the loose **2** = **unrestricted**
licence *n* **1** = **certificate**, charter, permit, warrant **2** = **permission**, authority, authorization, blank cheque, carte

blanche, dispensation, entitlement, exemption, immunity, leave, liberty, right **3** = **freedom**, independence, latitude, leeway, liberty **4** = **laxity**, excess, immoderation, indulgence, irresponsibility
licentious *adj* = **promiscuous**, abandoned, debauched, dissolute, immoral, lascivious, lustful, sensual, wanton
lick *v* **1** = **taste**, lap, tongue **2** = **flicker**, dart, flick, play over, ripple, touch **3** *Inf* = **beat**, defeat, master, outdo, outstrip, overcome, rout, trounce, vanquish ▷ *n* **5** = **dab**, bit, stroke, touch **6** *Inf* = **pace**, clip (*inf*), rate, speed
lie¹ *v* **1** = **fib**, dissimulate, equivocate, fabricate, falsify, prevaricate, tell untruths ▷ *n* **2** = **falsehood**, deceit, fabrication, fib, fiction, invention,

white lie see WHITE.

lie² ❶ v **lying, lay, lain** 1 place oneself or be in a horizontal position. 2 be situated. 3 be or remain in a certain state or position. 4 exist or be found. ▷ n 5 way something lies. **lie-down** n rest. **lie in** v remain in bed late into the morning. **lie-in** n long stay in bed in the morning.

lieu [**lyew**] n **in lieu of** instead of.

lieutenant [lef-**ten**-ant] n 1 junior officer in the army or navy. 2 main assistant.

life ❶ n, pl **lives** 1 state of living beings, characterized by growth, reproduction, and response to stimuli. 2 period between birth and death or between birth and the present time. 3 way of living. 4 amount of time something is active or functions. 5 biography. 6 liveliness or high spirits. 7 living beings collectively. **lifeless** adj 1 dead. 2 not lively or exciting. 3 unconscious. **lifelike** adj **lifelong** adj lasting all of a person's life. **life belt, jacket** buoyant device to keep afloat a person in danger of drowning. **lifeboat** n boat used for rescuing people at sea. **life cycle** series of changes undergone by each generation of an animal or plant. **lifeline** n 1 means of contact or support. 2 rope used in rescuing a person in danger. **life science** any science concerned with living organisms, such

as biology, botany, or zoology. **lifestyle** n particular attitudes, habits, etc. **life-support** adj (of equipment or treatment) necessary to keep a person alive. **lifetime** n length of time a person is alive.

lift ❶ v 1 move upwards in position, status, volume, etc. 2 revoke or cancel. 3 take (plants) out of the ground for harvesting. 4 disappear. 5 make or become more cheerful. ▷ n 6 cage raised and lowered in a vertical shaft to transport people or goods. 7 ride in a car etc. as a passenger. 8 informal feeling of cheerfulness. 9 lifting. **liftoff** n moment a rocket leaves the ground.

ligament n band of tissue joining bones.

light¹ ❶ n 1 electromagnetic radiation by which things are visible. 2 source of this, lamp. 3 anything that lets in light, such as a window. 4 aspect or view. 5 mental vision. 6 means of setting fire to. ▷ pl 7 traffic lights. ▷ adj 8 bright. 9 (of a colour) pale. ▷ v **lighting, lighted** or **lit** 10 ignite. 11 illuminate or cause to illuminate. **lighten** v make less dark. **lighting** n apparatus for and use of artificial light in theatres, films, etc. **light bulb** glass part of an electric lamp. **lighthouse** n tower with a light to guide ships. **light year** Astronomy distance light

prevarication, untruth

lie² v 1 = **recline**, loll, lounge, repose, rest, sprawl, stretch out 2 = **be situated**, be, be placed, exist 3 = **be**, remain 4 = **exist**

life n 1 = **being**, sentience, vitality 2 = **existence**, being, lifetime, span, time 3 = **behaviour**, conduct, life style, way of life 5 = **biography**, autobiography, confessions, history, life story, memoirs, story 6 = **liveliness**, animation, energy, high spirits, spirit, verve, vigour, vitality, vivacity, zest

lift v 1 = **raise**, draw up, elevate, hoist, pick up, uplift, upraise 2 = **revoke**, annul, cancel, countermand, end, remove, rescind, stop, terminate 4 = **disappear**,

be dispelled, disperse, dissipate, vanish ▷ n 6 = **elevator** (chiefly US) 7 = **ride**, drive, run 8 Inf = **boost**, encouragement, fillip, gee-up, pick-me-up, shot in the arm (inf)

light¹ n 1 = **brightness**, brilliance, glare, gleam, glint, glow, illumination, luminosity, radiance, shine 2 = **lamp**, beacon, candle, flare, lantern, taper, torch 4 = **aspect**, angle, context, interpretation, point of view, slant, vantage point, viewpoint 6 = **match**, flame, lighter ▷ adj 8 = **bright**, brilliant, illuminated, luminous, lustrous, shining, well-lit 9 = **pale**, bleached, blond, blonde, faded, fair, pastel ▷ v 10 = **ignite**, inflame, kindle 11 = **illuminate**, brighten, light up

travels in one year, about six million million miles.

light² ❶ *adj* **1** not heavy, weighing relatively little. **2** relatively low in strength, amount, density, etc. **3** not clumsy. **4** not serious or profound. **5** easily digested. ▷ *adv* **6** with little equipment or luggage. ▷ *v* **lighting**, **lighted**, **lit 7** (esp. of birds) settle after flight. **8** come (upon) by chance. **lightly** *adv* **lightness** *n* **lighten** *v* **1** make less heavy or burdensome. **2** make more cheerful or lively. **light-fingered** *adj* skilful at stealing. **light-headed** *adj* feeling faint, dizzy. **light-hearted** *adj* carefree. **lightweight** *n*, *adj* **1** (person) of little importance. ▷ *n* **2** boxer weighing up to 135lb (professional) or 60kg (amateur).

lighter *n* device for lighting cigarettes etc.

like¹ ❶ *prep, conj adj, pron* indicating similarity, comparison, etc. **liken** *v* compare. **likeness** *n* **1** resemblance. **2** portrait. **likewise** *adv* similarly.

like² ❶ *v* **1** find enjoyable. **2** be fond of. **3** prefer, choose, or wish. **likeable, likable** *adj* **likely** *adj* probable. **liking** *n* **1** fondness. **2** preference.

lilac *n* **1** shrub with pale mauve or white flowers. ▷ *adj* **2** light-purple.

lilt *n* **1** pleasing musical quality in speaking. **2** jaunty rhythm. **3** graceful rhythmic motion. **lilting** *adj*.

lily *n, pl* **lilies** plant which grows from a bulb and has large, often white, flowers.

limb *n* **1** arm, leg, or wing. **2** main branch of a tree.

limber *adj* pliant or supple. **limber up** *v* loosen stiff muscles by exercising.

limbo¹ *n* **in limbo** not knowing the result or next stage of something and powerless to influence it.

limbo² *n, pl* **-bos** West Indian dance in which dancers lean backwards to pass under a bar.

lime¹ *n* calcium compound used as a fertilizer or in making cement. **limelight** *n* glare of publicity. **limestone** *n* sedimentary rock used in building.

lime² *n* small green citrus fruit. **lime-green** *adj* greenish-yellow.

lime³ *n* deciduous tree with heart-shaped leaves and fragrant flowers.

limerick [**lim**-mer-ik] *n* humorous verse of five lines.

limit ❶ *n* **1** ultimate extent, degree, or amount of something. **2** boundary or edge. ▷ *v* **-iting, -ited 3** restrict or confine. **limitation** *n* **limitless** *adj* **limited company** company whose shareholders' liability for debts is restricted.

limousine *n* large luxurious car.

limp¹ ❶ *v* **1** walk with an uneven step. ▷ *n* **2** limping walk.

━━━━━━━━━━━━━━━━━━━━━━━━━━━ THESAURUS ━━━━━━━━

light² *adj* **1** = **insubstantial**, airy, buoyant, flimsy, portable, slight **2** = **weak**, faint, gentle, indistinct, mild, moderate, slight, soft **3** = **nimble**, agile, graceful, lithe, sprightly, sylphlike **4** = **insignificant**, inconsequential, inconsiderable, scanty, slight, small, trifling, trivial **5** = **digestible**, frugal, modest ▷ *v* **7** = **settle**, alight, land, perch **8** = **come across**, chance upon, discover, encounter, find, happen upon, hit upon, stumble on

like¹ *adj* = **similar**, akin, alike, analogous, corresponding, equivalent, identical, parallel, same

like² *v* **1** = **enjoy**, be fond of, be keen on, be

partial to, delight in, go for, love, relish, revel in **2** = **admire**, appreciate, approve, cherish, esteem, hold dear, prize, take to **3** = **wish**, care to, choose, desire, fancy, feel inclined, prefer, want

limb *n* **1** = **part**, appendage, arm, extremity, leg, member, wing **2** = **branch**, bough, offshoot, projection, spur

limit *n* **1** = **end**, breaking point, deadline, ultimate **2** = **boundary**, border, edge, frontier, perimeter ▷ *v* **3** = **restrict**, bound, check, circumscribe, confine, curb, ration, restrain

limp¹ *v* **1** = **hobble**, falter, hop, shamble, shuffle ▷ *n* **2** = **lameness**, hobble

limp² **❶** *adj* without firmness or stiffness.

limpet *n* shellfish which sticks tightly to rocks.

limpid *adj* **1** clear or transparent. **2** easy to understand. **limpidity** *n*.

linchpin, lynchpin *n* **1** pin to hold a wheel on its axle. **2** essential person or thing.

linctus *n*, *pl* **-tuses** syrupy cough medicine.

line¹ **❶** *n* **1** long narrow mark. **2** indented mark or wrinkle. **3** continuous length without breadth. **4** boundary or limit. **5** mark on a sports ground showing divisions of a pitch or track. **6** edge or contour of a shape. **7** string or wire for a particular use. **8** telephone connection. **9** wire or cable for transmitting electricity. **10** shipping company. **11** railway track. **12** course or direction of movement. **13** course or method of action. **14** prescribed way of thinking. **15** field of interest or activity. **16** row or queue of people. **17** class of goods. **18** row of words. **19** unit of verse. **20** military formation. ▷ *pl* **21** words of a theatrical part. **22** school punishment of writing out a sentence a specified number of times. ▷ *v* **23** mark with lines. **24** be or form a border or edge. **in line for** likely to receive. **in line with** in accordance with. **line dancing** form of dancing performed by rows of people to country and western music. **line-up** *n* people or things assembled for a particular purpose. **line up** *v* form or organize a line-up.

line² **❶** *v* **1** give a lining to. **2** cover the inside of.

linen *n* **1** cloth or thread made from flax. **2** sheets, tablecloths, etc.

liner¹ *n* large passenger ship or aircraft.

liner² *n* something used as a lining.

linger **❶** *v* **1** delay or prolong departure. **2** continue in a weakened state for a long time before dying or disappearing. **3** spend a long time doing something.

lingerie [**lan**-zher-ee] *n* women's underwear or nightwear.

linguist *n* **1** person skilled in foreign languages. **2** person who studies linguistics. **linguistic** *adj* of languages. **linguistics** *n* scientific study of language.

liniment *n* medicated liquid rubbed on the skin to relieve pain or stiffness.

lining *n* **1** layer of cloth attached to the inside of a garment etc. **2** inner covering of anything.

link **❶** *n* **1** any of the rings forming a chain. **2** person or thing forming a connection. ▷ *v* **3** connect with or as if with links. **4** connect by association. **linkage** *n* **link-up** *n* joining together of two systems or groups.

links *pl n* golf course, esp. one by the sea.

linnet *n* songbird of the finch family.

lino *n* short for LINOLEUM.

linoleum *n* floor covering of hessian or

limp² *adj* = **floppy**, drooping, flabby, flaccid, pliable, slack, soft

line¹ *n* **1** = **stroke**, band, groove, mark, score, scratch, streak, stripe **2** = **wrinkle**, crease, crow's foot, furrow, mark **4** = **boundary**, border, borderline, edge, frontier, limit **7** = **string**, cable, cord, rope, thread, wire **12** = **trajectory**, course, direction, path, route, track **15** = **occupation**, area, business, calling, employment, field, job, profession, specialization, trade **16** = **row**, column, file, procession, queue, rank ▷ *pl n* **21** = **words**, part, script ▷ *v* **23** = **mark**, crease, furrow, rule, score **24** = **border**, bound, edge, fringe **in line for** = **due for**, in the running for

line² *v* = **fill**, ceil, cover, face, interline

linger *v* **1** = **stay**, hang around, loiter, remain, stop, tarry, wait **3** = **delay**, dally, dawdle, drag one's feet *or* heels, idle, take one's time

link *n* **2** = **connection**, affinity, association, attachment, bond, relationship, tie-up ▷ *v* **3** = **connect**, attach, bind, couple, fasten, join, tie, unite **4** = **associate**, bracket, connect, identify, relate

jute with a smooth decorative coating of powdered cork.

linseed *n* seed of the flax plant.

lint *n* soft material for dressing a wound.

lintel *n* horizontal beam at the top of a door or window.

lion *n* large animal of the cat family, the male of which has a shaggy mane. **lioness** *n fem* **the lion's share** the biggest part. **lionize** *v* treat as a celebrity.

lip ❶ *n* 1 either of the fleshy edges of the mouth. 2 rim of a jug etc. 3 *slang* impudence. **lip-reading** *n* method of understanding speech by interpreting lip movements. **lip service** insincere tribute or respect. **lipstick** *n* cosmetic in stick form, for colouring the lips.

liqueur [lik-**cure**] *n* flavoured and sweetened alcoholic spirit.

liquid ❶ *n* 1 substance in a physical state which can change shape but not size. ▷ *adj* 2 of or being a liquid. 3 flowing smoothly. 4 (of assets) in the form of money or easily converted into money. **liquidize** *v* make or become liquid. **liquidizer** *n* kitchen appliance that liquidizes food. **liquidity** *n* state of being able to meet financial obligations.

liquidate ❶ *v* 1 pay (a debt). 2 dissolve a company and share its assets among

creditors. 3 wipe out or kill. **liquidation** *n* **liquidator** *n* official appointed to liquidate a business.

liquor ❶ *n* 1 alcoholic drink, esp. spirits. 2 liquid in which food has been cooked.

liquorice [**lik**-ker-iss] *n* black substance used in medicine and as a sweet.

lira *n, pl* -**re**, -**ras** monetary unit of Italy and Turkey.

lisp *n* 1 speech defect in which *s* and *z* are pronounced *th*. ▷ *v* 2 speak or utter with a lisp.

lissom, lissome *adj* supple, agile.

list¹ ❶ *n* 1 item-by-item record of names or things, usu. written one below another. ▷ *v* 2 make a list of. 3 include in a list.

list² ❶ *v* 1 (of a ship) lean to one side. ▷ *n* 2 leaning to one side.

listen ❶ *v* 1 concentrate on hearing something. 2 heed or pay attention to. **listener** *n* **listen in** *v* listen secretly, eavesdrop.

listless ❶ *adj* lacking interest or energy.

litany *n, pl* -**nies** 1 prayer with responses from the congregation. 2 any tedious recital.

literal ❶ *adj* 1 according to the explicit meaning of a word or text, not figurative. 2 (of a translation) word for word. 3 actual, true. **literally** *adv*.

━━━━━━━━━━━━━━━━━━━ THESAURUS ━━━━━━━━━

lip *n* 2 = **edge**, brim, brink, margin, rim 3 *Sl* = **impudence**, backchat, (*inf*), cheek (*inf*), effrontery, impertinence, insolence

liquid *n* 1 = **fluid**, juice, solution ▷ *adj* 2 = **fluid**, aqueous, flowing, melted, molten, runny 4 *Of assets* = **convertible**, negotiable

liquidate *v* 1 = **pay**, clear, discharge, honour, pay off, settle, square 2 = **dissolve**, abolish, annul, cancel, terminate 3 = **kill**, destroy, dispatch, eliminate, exterminate, get rid of, murder, wipe out (*inf*)

liquor *n* 1 = **alcohol**, booze (*inf*), drink, hard stuff (*inf*), spirits, strong drink 2 = **juice**, broth, extract, liquid, stock

list¹ *n* 1 = **inventory**, catalogue, directory, index, record, register, roll, series, tally ▷ *v* 2, 3 = **itemize**, catalogue, enter, enumerate, record, register, tabulate

list² *v* 1 = **lean**, careen, heel over, incline, tilt, tip ▷ *n* 2 = **tilt**, cant, leaning, slant

listen *v* 1 = **hear**, attend, lend an ear, prick up one's ears 2 = **pay attention**, heed, mind, obey, observe, take notice

listless *adj* = **languid**, apathetic, indifferent, indolent, lethargic, sluggish

literal *adj* 1 = **explicit**, precise, strict 2 = **exact**, accurate, close, faithful, verbatim, word for word 3 = **actual**, bona fide, genuine, plain, real, simple, true, unvarnished

literate ❶ *adj* **1** able to read and write. **2** educated. **literati** *pl n* literary people.

literature ❶ *n* **1** written works such as novels, plays, and poetry. **2** books and writings of a country, period, or subject.

lithe ❶ *adj* flexible or supple, pliant.

lithium *n Chem* chemical element, the lightest known metal.

lithography [lith-**og**-ra-fee] *n* method of printing from a metal or stone surface in which the printing areas are made receptive to ink. **lithograph** *n* **1** print made by lithography. ▷ *v* **2** reproduce by lithography.

litmus *n* blue dye turned red by acids and restored to blue by alkalis. **litmus test** something which is regarded as a simple and accurate test of a particular thing.

litre *n* unit of liquid measure equal to 1.76 pints.

litter ❶ *n* **1** untidy rubbish dropped in public places. **2** group of young animals produced at one birth. **3** straw etc. as bedding for an animal. **4** dry material to absorb a cat's excrement. **5** bed or seat on parallel sticks for carrying people. ▷ *v* **6** strew with litter. **7** scatter or be scattered about untidily. **8** give birth to young.

little ❶ *adj* **1** small or smaller than average. **2** young. ▷ *adv* **3** not a lot. **4** hardly. **5** not much or often. ▷ *n* **6** small amount, extent, or duration.

liturgy *n, pl* -**gies** prescribed form of public worship. **liturgical** *adj*.

live¹ ❶ *v* **1** be alive. **2** remain in life or existence. **3** exist in a specified way, e.g. *we live well*. **4** reside. **5** continue or last. **6** subsist. **7** enjoy life to the full. **liver** *n* person who lives in a specified way. **live down** *v* wait till people forget a past mistake or misdeed. **live-in** *adj* resident. **live up to** *v* meet (expectations). **live with** *v* tolerate.

live² ❶ *adj* **1** living, alive. **2** (of a broadcast) transmitted during the actual performance. **3** (of a performance) done in front of an audience. **4** (of a wire, circuit, etc.) carrying an electric current. **5** causing interest or controversy. **6** capable of exploding. **7** glowing or burning. ▷ *adv* **8** in the form of a live performance. **lively** *adj* **1** full of life or vigour. **2** animated. **3** vivid. **liveliness** *n* **liven up** *v* make (more) lively.

livelihood ❶ *n* occupation or employment.

liver *n* **1** organ secreting bile. **2** animal liver as food. **liverish** *adj* **1** having a disorder of the liver. **2** touchy or irritable.

livery ❶ *n, pl* -**eries 1** distinctive dress,

literate *adj* **2** = **educated**, informed, knowledgeable

literature *n* = **writings**, lore

lithe *adj* = **supple**, flexible, limber, lissom(e), loose-limbed, pliable

litter *n* **1** = **rubbish**, debris, detritus, garbage (*chiefly US*), muck, refuse, trash **2** = **brood**, offspring, progeny, young ▷ *v* **6** = **clutter**, derange, disarrange, disorder, mess up, muss (*US & Canad*) **7** = **scatter**, strew

little *adj* **1** = **small**, diminutive, miniature, minute, petite, short, tiny, wee **2** = **young**, babyish, immature, infant, undeveloped ▷ *adv* **4** = **hardly**, barely **5** = **rarely**, hardly ever, not often, scarcely, seldom *n* **6** = **bit**, fragment, hint, particle, speck, spot, touch, trace

live¹ *v* **1** = **exist**, be, be alive, breathe **4** = **dwell**, abide, inhabit, lodge, occupy, reside, settle **5** = **persist**, last, prevail **6** = **survive**, endure, get along, make ends meet, subsist, support oneself **7** = **thrive**, flourish, prosper

live² *adj* **1** = **living**, alive, animate, breathing **5** = **topical**, burning, controversial, current, hot, pertinent, pressing, prevalent **7** = **burning**, active, alight, blazing, glowing, hot, ignited, smouldering

livelihood *n* = **occupation**, bread and butter (*inf*), employment, job, living, work, yakka (*Aust & NZ inf*)

livery *n* **1** = **costume**, attire, clothing, dress,

esp. of a servant or servants. **2** distinctive
design or colours of a company. **liveried**
adj **livery stable** stable where horses are
kept at a charge or hired out.

livestock *n* farm animals.

livid ❶ *adj* **1** *informal* angry or furious.
2 bluish-grey.

lizard *n* four-footed reptile with a long body
and tail.

llama *n* woolly animal of the camel family
used as a beast of burden in S America.

load ❶ *n* **1** burden or weight. **2** amount
carried. **3** source of worry. **4** amount of
electrical energy drawn from a source. ▷ *pl*
5 *informal* lots. ▷ *v* **6** put a load on or into.
7 burden or oppress. **8** cause to be biased.
9 put ammunition into (a weapon).
10 put film into (a camera). **11** transfer (a
program) into computer memory. **loaded**
adj **1** (of a question) containing a hidden
trap or implication. **2** (of dice) dishonestly
weighted. **3** *slang* wealthy.

loaf¹ ❶ *n*, *pl* **loaves 1** shaped mass of baked
bread. **2** shaped mass of food. **3** *slang*
head, esp. as the source of common sense,
e.g. *use your loaf*.

loaf² ❶ *v* idle, loiter. **loafer** *n*.

loam *n* fertile soil.

loan ❶ *n* **1** money lent at interest.
2 lending. **3** thing lent. ▷ *v* **4** lend. **loan
shark** person who lends money at an

extremely high interest rate.

loath, loth ❶ [rhymes with **both**] *adj*
unwilling or reluctant (to).
● **USAGE NOTE**
● Distinguish between *loath* 'reluctant'
● and *loathe* 'be disgusted by'.

lob *Sport* ▷ *n* **1** ball struck or thrown in a high
arc. ▷ *v* **lobbing**, **lobbed 2** strike or throw
(a ball) in a high arc.

lobby ❶ *n*, *pl* **-bies 1** corridor into which
rooms open. **2** group which tries to
influence legislators. **3** hall in a legislative
building to which the public has access.
▷ *v* **4** try to influence (legislators) in the
formulation of policy. **lobbyist** *n*.

lobe *n* **1** rounded projection. **2** soft hanging
part of the ear. **3** subdivision of a body
organ.

lobelia *n* garden plant with blue, red, or
white flowers.

lobster *n* shellfish with a long tail and
claws, which turns red when boiled.

local ❶ *adj* **1** of or existing in a particular
place. **2** confined to a particular place. ▷ *n*
3 person belonging to a particular district.
4 *informal* pub close to one's home. **locally**
adv **locality** *n* neighbourhood or area.
localize *v* restrict to a particular place.
locale [loh-**kahl**] *n* scene of an event. **local
anaesthetic** anaesthetic which produces
loss of feeling in one part of the body. **local**

———————————————————————————— **THESAURUS** ————————

garb, regalia, suit, uniform

livid *adj* **1** *Inf* = **angry**, beside oneself,
enraged, fuming, furious, incensed,
indignant, infuriated, outraged
2 = **discoloured**, black-and-blue, bruised,
contused, purple

load *n* **1** = **cargo**, consignment, freight,
shipment **3** = **burden**, albatross,
encumbrance, millstone, onus, trouble,
weight, worry ▷ *v* **6** = **fill**, cram, freight,
heap, pack, pile, stack, stuff **7** = **burden**,
encumber, oppress, saddle with, weigh
down, worry **9** *Firearms* = **make ready**,
charge, prime

loaf¹ *n* **2** = **lump**, block, cake, cube, slab

3 *Sl* = **head**, gumption (*Brit inf*), nous (*Brit
sl*), sense

loaf² *v* = **idle**, laze, lie around, loiter, lounge
around, take it easy

loan *n* **1-3** = **advance**, credit ▷ *v* **4** = **lend**,
advance, let out

loath, loth *adj* = **unwilling**, averse,
disinclined, opposed, reluctant

lobby *n* **1** = **corridor**, entrance hall,
foyer, hallway, passage, porch, vestibule
2 = **pressure group** ▷ *v* **2** = **campaign**,
influence, persuade, press, pressure,
promote, push, urge

local *adj* **1** = **regional**, provincial
2 = **restricted**, confined, limited ▷ *n*

authority governing body of a county or district. **local government** government of towns, counties, and districts by locally elected political bodies.

locate ❶ v 1 discover the whereabouts of. 2 situate or place. **location** n 1 site or position. 2 act of discovering where something is. 3 site of a film production away from the studio. 4 S Afr Black African or coloured township.

loch n Scot 1 lake. 2 long narrow bay.

lock¹ ❶ n 1 appliance for fastening a door, case, etc. 2 section of a canal shut off by gates between which the water level can be altered to aid boats moving from one level to another. 3 extent to which a vehicle's front wheels will turn. 4 interlocking of parts. 5 mechanism for firing a gun. 6 wrestling hold. ▷ v 7 fasten or become fastened securely. 8 become or cause to become fixed or united. 9 become or cause to become immovable. 10 embrace closely. **lockout** n closing of a workplace by an employer to force workers to accept terms. **locksmith** n person who makes and mends locks. **lockup** n 1 prison. 2 garage or storage place away from the main premises.

lock² ❶ n strand of hair.

locket n small hinged pendant for a portrait etc.

locomotive n 1 self-propelled engine for pulling trains. ▷ adj 2 of locomotion. **locomotion** n action or power of moving.

locum n temporary stand-in for a doctor or clergyman.

locus [**loh**-kuss] n, pl **loci** [**loh**-sigh] 1 area or place where something happens. 2 Maths set of points or lines satisfying one or more specified conditions.

locust n destructive African insect that flies in swarms and eats crops.

lodge ❶ n 1 gatekeeper's house. 2 house or cabin used occasionally by hunters, skiers, etc. 3 porters' room in a university or college. 4 local branch of some societies. ▷ v 5 live in another's house at a fixed charge. 6 stick or become stuck (in a place). 7 make (a complaint etc.) formally. **lodger** n **lodging** n 1 temporary residence. ▷ pl 2 rented room or rooms in another person's house.

loft n 1 space between the top storey and roof of a building. 2 gallery in a church etc. ▷ v 3 Sport strike, throw, or kick (a ball) high into the air.

log¹ ❶ n 1 portion of a felled tree stripped of branches. 2 detailed record of a journey of a ship, aircraft, etc. ▷ v **logging, logged** 3 saw logs from a tree. 4 record in a log. **logging** n work of cutting and transporting logs. **logbook** n book recording the details about a car or a ship's journeys. **log in, out** v gain entrance to or leave a computer system by keying in a special command.

log² n short for LOGARITHM.

loganberry n purplish-red fruit, similar to a raspberry.

logarithm n one of a series of arithmetical functions used to make certain calculations easier.

---

3 = **resident**, inhabitant, native

locate v 1 = **find**, come across, detect, discover, pin down, pinpoint, track down, unearth 2 = **place**, establish, fix, put, seat, set, settle, situate

lock¹ n 1 = **fastening**, bolt, clasp, padlock ▷ v 7 = **fasten**, bolt, close, seal, secure, shut 8 = **unite**, engage, entangle, entwine, join, link 9 = **clench**, freeze 10 = **embrace**, clasp, clutch, encircle,

enclose, grasp, hug, press

lock² n = **strand**, curl, ringlet, tress, tuft

lodge n 1 = **gatehouse** 2 = **cabin**, chalet, cottage, hut, shelter 4 = **society**, branch, chapter, club, group ▷ v 5 = **stay**, board, room 6 = **stick**, come to rest, imbed, implant 7 = **register**, file, put on record, submit

log¹ n 1 = **stump**, block, chunk, trunk 2 = **record**, account, journal, logbook ▷ v

loggerheads ❶ *pl n* **at loggerheads** quarrelling, disputing.

logic ❶ *n* **1** philosophy of reasoning. **2** reasoned thought or argument. **logical** *adj* **1** of logic. **2** capable of or using clear valid reasoning. **3** reasonable. **logically** *adv*.

logistics *n* detailed planning and organization of a large, esp. military, operation. **logistical**, **logistic** *adj*.

logo [**loh**-go] *n*, *pl* **-os** company emblem or similar device.

loin *n* **1** part of the body between the ribs and the hips. **2** cut of meat from this part of an animal. ▷ *pl* **3** hips and inner thighs. **loincloth** *n* piece of cloth covering the loins only.

loiter ❶ *v* stand or wait aimlessly or idly.

loll ❶ *v* **1** lounge lazily. **2** hang loosely.

lollipop *n* boiled sweet on a small wooden stick. **lollipop man**, **lady** *informal* person holding a circular sign on a pole, who controls traffic so that children may cross the road safely.

lolly *n*, *pl* **-ies 1** *informal* lollipop or ice lolly. **2** *Aust & NZ informal* sweet. **3** *slang* money.

lone ❶ *adj* solitary. **lonely** *adj* **1** sad because alone. **2** resulting from being alone. **3** unfrequented. **loneliness** *n* **loner** *n informal* person who prefers to be alone.

lonesome *adj Chiefly US & Canad* another word for LONELY.

long¹ ❶ *adj* **1** having length, esp. great length, in space or time. ▷ *adv* **2** for an extensive period. **long-distance** *adj* going between places far apart. **long face** glum expression. **longhand** *n* ordinary writing, not shorthand or typing. **long johns** *informal* long underpants. **long-life** *adj* (of milk, batteries, etc.) lasting longer than the regular kind. **long-lived** *adj* living or lasting for a long time. **long-range** *adj* **1** extending into the future. **2** (of vehicles, weapons, etc.) designed to cover great distances. **long shot** competitor, undertaking, or bet with little chance of success. **long-sighted** *adj* able to see distant objects in focus but not nearby ones. **long-standing** *adj* existing for a long time. **long-suffering** *adj* enduring trouble or unhappiness without complaint. **long-term** *adj* lasting or effective for a long time. **long wave** radio wave with a wavelength of over 1000 metres. **long-winded** *adj* speaking or writing at tedious length.

long² ❶ *v* have a strong desire (for). **longing** *n* yearning.

longevity [lon-**jev**-it-ee] *n* long life.

longitude *n* distance east or west from a standard meridian. **longitudinal** *adj* **1** of length or longitude. **2** lengthways.

longshoreman *n* a man employed in the loading or unloading of ships.

loo *n informal* toilet.

look ❶ *v* **1** direct the eyes or attention (towards). **2** have the appearance of being. **3** face in a particular direction. **4** search (for). **5** hope (for). ▷ *n* **6** instance

───────── THESAURUS ─────────

3 = **chop**, cut, fell, hew **4** = **record**, chart, note, register, set down

loggerheads *pl n* **at loggerheads** = **quarrelling**, at daggers drawn, at each other's throats, at odds, feuding, in dispute, opposed

logic *n* **2** = **reason**, good sense, sense

loiter *v* = **linger**, dally, dawdle, dilly-dally (*inf*), hang about *or* around, idle, loaf, skulk

loll *v* **1** = **lounge**, loaf, outspan (*S Afr*), recline, relax, slouch, slump, sprawl **2** = **droop**, dangle, drop, flap, flop, hang, sag

lone *adj* = **solitary**, one, only, single, sole, unaccompanied

long¹ *adj* **1 a** = **elongated**, expanded, extended, extensive, far-reaching, lengthy, spread out, stretched **b** = **prolonged**, interminable, lengthy, lingering, long-drawn-out, protracted, sustained

long² *v* = **desire**, crave, hanker, itch, lust, pine, want, wish, yearn

look *v* **1** = **see**, behold (*arch*), consider, contemplate, examine, eye, gaze, glance,

of looking. **7** (often pl) appearance. **look after** v take care of. **lookalike** n person who is the double of another. **look down on** v treat as inferior or unimportant. **look forward to** v anticipate with pleasure. **look on** v 1 be a spectator. **2** consider or regard. **lookout** n 1 guard. **2** place for watching. **3** informal worry or concern. **4** chances or prospect. **look out** v be careful. **look up** v 1 discover or confirm by checking in a book. **2** improve. **3** visit. **look up to** v respect.

loom¹ n machine for weaving cloth.

loom² ● v 1 appear dimly. **2** seem ominously close.

loonie n Canad sl 1 a Canadian dollar coin with a loon bird on one of its faces. **2** the Canadian currency.

loony slang ▷ adj **loonier**, **looniest** 1 foolish or insane. ▷ n, pl **loonies** 2 foolish or insane person.

loop ● n 1 rounded shape made by a curved line or rope crossing itself. ▷ v 2 form or fasten with a loop. **loophole** n means of evading a rule without breaking it.

loose ● adj 1 not tight, fastened, fixed, or tense. **2** vague. **3** dissolute or promiscuous. ▷ adv **4** in a loose manner. ▷ v **5** free. **6** unfasten. **7** slacken. **8** let fly (an arrow, bullet, etc.). **at a loose end** bored, with nothing to do. **loosely** adv **looseness** n **loosen** v make loose. **loosen up** v relax, stop worrying. **loose-leaf** adj allowing the addition or removal of pages.

loot ● n, v 1 plunder. ▷ n 2 informal money. **looting** n.

lop v lopping, **lopped** 1 cut away twigs and branches. **2** chop off.

lope v run with long easy strides.

lopsided ● adj greater in height, weight, or size on one side.

loquacious adj talkative. **loquacity** n.

lord ● n 1 person with power over others, such as a monarch or master. **2** male member of the nobility. **3** Hist feudal superior. **4** (L-) God or Jesus. **5** (L-) title given to certain male officials and peers. **lord it over** act in a superior manner towards. **lordly** adj imperious, proud. **Lordship** n title of some male officials and peers.

lore ● n body of traditions on a subject.

observe, scan, study, survey, view, watch **2 = seem**, appear, look like, strike one as **3 = face**, front, overlook **4 = search**, forage, fossick (Aust & NZ), hunt, seek **5 = hope**, anticipate, await, expect, reckon on ▷ n **7 = appearance**, air, aspect, bearing, countenance, demeanour, expression, manner, semblance

loom² v 1 = **appear**, bulk, emerge, hover, take shape **2 = threaten**, impend, menace

loop n 1 = **curve**, circle, coil, curl, ring, spiral, twirl, twist, whorl ▷ v 2 = **twist**, coil, curl, knot, roll, spiral, turn, wind round

loose adj 1 a = **slack**, easy, relaxed, sloppy adj b = **free**, insecure, unattached, unbound, unfastened, unfettered, unrestricted, untied **2 = vague**, ill-defined, imprecise, inaccurate, indistinct, inexact, rambling, random **3 = promiscuous**, abandoned, debauched, dissipated, dissolute, fast, immoral, profligate v **5, 6 = free**, detach, disconnect, liberate, release, set free, unfasten, unleash, untie

loot n 1 = **plunder**, booty, goods, haul, prize, spoils, swag (sl) ▷ v 1 = **plunder**, despoil, pillage, raid, ransack, ravage, rifle, rob, sack

lopsided adj = **crooked**, askew, asymmetrical, awry, cockeyed, disproportionate, skewwhiff (Brit inf), squint, unbalanced, uneven, warped

lord n 1 = **master**, commander, governor, leader, liege, overlord, ruler, superior **2 = nobleman**, earl, noble, peer, viscount **4** (with cap.) = **Jesus Christ**, Christ, God, Jehovah, the Almighty **lord it over = order around**, boss around (inf), domineer, pull rank, put on airs, swagger

lore n = **traditions**, beliefs, doctrine, sayings, teaching, wisdom

lorry *n, pl* **-ries** large vehicle for transporting loads by road.

lose ❶ *v* **losing, lost** 1 come to be without, esp. by accident or carelessness. 2 fail to keep or maintain. 3 be deprived of. 4 fail to get or make use of. 5 be defeated in a competition etc. 6 fail to perceive or understand. 7 go astray or allow to go astray. 8 be or become engrossed, e.g. *lost in thought.* 9 die or be destroyed. 10 (of a clock etc.) run slow (by a specified amount). **loser** *n* 1 person or thing that loses. 2 *informal* person who seems destined to fail. **loss** *n* 1 losing. 2 that which is lost. **lost** *adj* unable to find one's way.

● **SPELLING TIP**
● The verb **lose** (*I don't want to lose my hair*)
● should not be confused with **loose**,
● which, although existing as a verb, is
● more often used as an adjective (*a loose*
● *tooth*) or adverb (*to work loose*).

lot ❶ *pron* 1 great number. ▷ *n* 2 collection of people or things. 3 fate or destiny. 4 one of a set of objects drawn at random to make a selection or choice. 5 item at auction. ▷ *pl* 6 *informal* great numbers or quantities. **a lot** *informal* a great deal.

lotion ❶ *n* medical or cosmetic liquid for use on the skin.

lottery ❶ *n, pl* **-teries** 1 method of raising money by selling tickets that win prizes by chance. 2 gamble.

lotus *n* 1 legendary plant whose fruit induces forgetfulness. 2 Egyptian water lily.

loud ❶ *adj* 1 relatively great in volume. 2 capable of making much noise. 3 insistent and emphatic. 4 unpleasantly patterned or colourful. **loudly** *adv* **loudness** *n* **loudspeaker** *n* instrument for converting electrical signals into sound.

lounge ❶ *n* 1 living room in a private house. 2 more expensive bar in a pub. 3 area for waiting in an airport. ▷ *v* 4 sit, lie, or stand in a relaxed manner. **lounge suit** man's suit for daytime wear.

lour *v* same as LOWER².

louse *n* 1 *pl* **lice** wingless parasitic insect. 2 *pl* **louses** unpleasant person. **lousy** *adj* 1 *slang* mean or unpleasant. 2 bad, inferior. 3 unwell.

lout ❶ *n* crude, oafish, or aggressive person. **loutish** *adj*.

louvre [**loo**-ver] *n* one of a set of parallel slats slanted to admit air but not rain. **louvred** *adj*.

love ❶ *v* 1 have a great affection for. 2 feel sexual passion for. 3 enjoy (something) very much. ▷ *n* 4 great affection. 5 sexual

---

lose *v* 1 = **mislay**, drop, forget, misplace 2, 4 = **forfeit**, miss, pass up (*inf*), yield 3 = **be deprived of** 5 = **be defeated**, come to grief, lose out

lot *n* 2 = **collection**, assortment, batch, bunch (*inf*), consignment, crowd, group, quantity, set 3 = **destiny**, accident, chance, doom, fate, fortune **a lot** *Inf* = **plenty**, abundance, a great deal, heap(s), load(s) (*inf*), masses (*inf*), piles (*inf*), scores, stack(s)

lotion *n* = **cream**, balm, embrocation, liniment, salve, solution

lottery *n* 1 = **raffle**, draw, sweepstake 2 = **gamble**, chance, hazard, risk, toss-up (*inf*)

loud *adj* 1 = **noisy**, blaring, booming, clamorous, deafening, ear-splitting, forte (*Music*), resounding, thundering, tumultuous, vociferous 4 = **garish**, brash, flamboyant, flashy, gaudy, glaring, lurid, showy

lounge *v* 4 = **relax**, laze, lie about, loaf, loiter, loll, outspan (*S Afr*), sprawl, take it easy

lout *n* = **oaf**, boor, dolt, yob *or* yobbo (*Brit sl*)

love *v* 1 = **adore**, cherish, dote on, hold dear, idolize, prize, treasure, worship 3 = **enjoy**, appreciate, delight in, like, relish, savour, take pleasure in ▷ *n* 4 = **affection**, adoration, attachment, devotion, infatuation, tenderness, passion. **6** wholehearted liking for something. **7** beloved person. **8** *Tennis, squash, etc.* score of nothing. **fall in love** become in love. **in love (with)** feeling a strong emotional (and sexual) attraction (for). **make love (to)** have sexual intercourse (with). **lovable, loveable** *adj* **loveless** *adj* **lovely** *adj* **-lier, -liest 1** very attractive. **2** highly enjoyable. **lover** *n* **1** person having a sexual relationship outside marriage. **2** person in love. **3** someone who loves a specified person or thing. **loving** *adj* affectionate, tender. **love affair** romantic or sexual relationship between two people who are not married to each other. **lovebird** *n* small parrot. **love child** *euphemistic* child of an unmarried couple. **love life** person's romantic or sexual relationships. **lovelorn** *adj* miserable because of unhappiness in love. **lovemaking** *n*.

low¹ ⊕ *adj* **1** not tall, high, or elevated. **2** of little or less than the usual amount, degree, quality, or cost. **3** coarse or vulgar. **4** dejected. **5** ill. **6** not loud. **7** deep in pitch. **8** (of a gear) providing a relatively low speed. ▷ *adv* **9** in or to a low position, level, or degree. ▷ *n* **10** low position, level, or degree. **11** area of low atmospheric pressure, depression. **lowly** *adj* modest, humble. **lowliness** *n* **lowbrow** *n*, *adj* (person) with nonintellectual tastes and interests. **lowdown** *n* *informal* inside information. **low-down** *adj informal* mean, underhand, or dishonest. **low-key** *adj* subdued, restrained, not intense. **lowland** *n* **1** low-lying country. ▷ *pl* **2 (L-)** less mountainous parts of Scotland. **low profile** position or attitude avoiding prominence or publicity.

low² *n* **1** cry of cattle, moo. ▷ *v* **2** moo.

lower¹ ⊕ *adj* **1** below one or more other things. **2** smaller or reduced in amount or value. ▷ *v* **3** cause or allow to move down. **4** behave in a way that damages one's respect. **5** lessen. **lower case** small, as distinct from capital, letters.

lower², lour ⊕ *v* (of the sky or weather) look gloomy or threatening. **lowering** *adj*.

loyal ⊕ *adj* faithful to one's friends, country, or government. **loyally** *adv* **loyalty** *n* **loyalty card** swipe card issued by a supermarket or chain store to a cust omer, used to record credit points awarded for money spent in the s tore. **loyalist** *n*.

lozenge *n* **1** medicated tablet held in the mouth until it dissolves. **2** four-sided diamond-shaped figure.

LP *n* record playing approximately 20–25 minutes each side.

warmth **5 = passion**, ardour **6 = liking**, devotion, enjoyment, fondness, inclination, partiality, relish, soft spot, taste, weakness **7 = beloved**, darling, dear, dearest, lover, sweetheart, truelove **in love (with) = enamoured**, besotted, charmed, enraptured, infatuated, smitten

low¹ *adj* **1 = small**, little, short, squat, stunted **2 = inferior**, deficient, inadequate, poor, second-rate, shoddy **3 = coarse**, common, crude, disreputable, rough, rude, undignified, vulgar **4 = dejected**, depressed, despondent, disheartened, downcast, down in the dumps (*inf*), fed up, gloomy, glum, miserable **5 = ill**, debilitated, frail, stricken,

weak **6 = quiet**, gentle, hushed, muffled, muted, soft, subdued, whispered

lower¹ *adj* **1 = under**, inferior, junior, lesser, minor, secondary, second-class, smaller, subordinate **2 = reduced**, curtailed, decreased, diminished, lessened ▷ *v* **3 = drop**, depress, fall, let down, sink, submerge, take down **5 = lessen**, cut, decrease, diminish, minimize, prune, reduce, slash

lower², lour *v* **= darken**, be brewing, blacken, cloud up or over, loom, menace, threaten

loyal *adj* **= faithful**, constant, dependable, devoted, dutiful, staunch, steadfast, true, trustworthy, trusty, unwavering

L-plate *n* sign on a car being driven by a learner driver.

LSD lysergic acid diethylamide, a hallucinogenic drug.

lubricate ❶ [loo-brik-ate] *v* oil or grease to lessen friction. **lubricant** *n* lubricating substance, such as oil. **lubrication** *n*.

lucerne *n* fodder plant like clover, alfalfa.

lucid ❶ *adj* **1** clear and easily understood. **2** able to think clearly. **3** bright and clear. **lucidity** *n*.

luck ❶ *n* **1** fortune, good or bad. **2** good fortune. **lucky** *adj* having or bringing good luck. **lucky dip** game in which prizes are picked from a tub at random. **luckily** *adv* fortunately. **luckless** *adj* having bad luck.

lucrative ❶ *adj* very profitable.

luderick *n* Australian fish, usu. black or dark brown in colour.

ludicrous ❶ *adj* absurd or ridiculous.

lug¹ *v* **lugging, lugged** carry or drag with great effort.

lug² *n* **1** projection serving as a handle. **2** *informal* ear.

luggage ❶ *n* traveller's cases, bags, etc.

lugubrious ❶ *adj* mournful, gloomy.

lukewarm ❶ *adj* **1** moderately warm, tepid. **2** indifferent or half-hearted.

lull ❶ *v* **1** soothe (someone) by soft sounds or motions. **2** calm (fears or suspicions) by deception. ▷ *n* **3** brief time of quiet in a storm etc.

lumbago [lum-**bay**-go] *n* pain in the lower back. **lumbar** *adj* relating to the lower back.

lumber¹ ❶ *n* **1** unwanted disused household articles. **2** *Chiefly US* sawn timber. ▷ *v* **3** *informal* burden with something unpleasant. **lumberjack** *n* US man who fells trees and prepares logs for transport.

lumber² ❶ *v* move heavily and awkwardly. **lumbering** *adj*.

luminous ❶ *adj* reflecting or giving off light. **luminosity** *n* **luminary** *n* **1** famous person. **2** *lit* heavenly body giving off light. **luminescence** *n* emission of light at low temperatures by any process other than burning. **luminescent** *adj*.

lump¹ ❶ *n* **1** shapeless piece or mass. **2** swelling. **3** *informal* awkward or stupid

─────────────────────── THESAURUS ───────────────────

lubricate *v* = **oil**, grease, smear

lucid *adj* **1** = **clear**, comprehensible, explicit, intelligible, transparent **2** = **clear-headed**, *compos mentis*, all there, in one's right mind, rational, sane **3** = **translucent**, clear, crystalline, diaphanous, glassy, limpid, pellucid, transparent

luck *n* **1** = **fortune**, accident, chance, destiny, fate **2** = **good fortune**, advantage, blessing, godsend, prosperity, serendipity, success, windfall

lucrative *adj* = **profitable**, advantageous, fruitful, productive, remunerative, well-paid

ludicrous *adj* = **ridiculous**, absurd, crazy, farcical, laughable, nonsensical, outlandish, preposterous, silly

luggage *n* = **baggage**, bags, cases, gear, impedimenta, paraphernalia, suitcases, things

lugubrious *adj* = **gloomy**, doleful, melancholy, mournful, sad, serious, sombre, sorrowful, woebegone

lukewarm *adj* **1** = **tepid**, warm **2** = **half-hearted**, apathetic, cool, indifferent, unenthusiastic, unresponsive

lull *v* **1** = **calm**, allay, pacify, quell, soothe, subdue, tranquillize ▷ *n* **3** = **respite**, calm, hush, let-up (*inf*), pause, quiet, silence

lumber¹ *n* **1** = **junk**, clutter, jumble, refuse, rubbish, trash ▷ *v* **3** *Inf* = **burden**, encumber, land, load, saddle

lumber² *v* = **plod**, shamble, shuffle, stump, trudge, trundle, waddle

luminous *adj* = **bright**, glowing, illuminated, luminescent, lustrous, radiant, shining

lump¹ *n* **1** = **piece**, ball, chunk, hunk, mass, nugget **2** = **swelling**, bulge, bump, growth, hump, protrusion,

person. ▷ v **4** consider as a single group. **lump in one's throat** tight dry feeling in one's throat, usu. caused by great emotion. **lumpy** adj **lump sum** relatively large sum of money paid at one time.

lump² v **lump it** informal tolerate or put up with it.

lunar adj relating to the moon.

lunatic ❶ adj **1** foolish and irresponsible. ▷ n **2** foolish or annoying person. **3** old-fashioned insane person. **lunacy** n.

lunch n **1** meal taken in the middle of the day. ▷ v **2** eat lunch. **luncheon** n formal lunch. **luncheon meat** tinned ground mixture of meat and cereal.

lung n organ that allows an animal or bird to breathe air: humans have two lungs in the chest. **lungfish** n freshwater bony fish with an air-breathing lung of South America and Australia.

lunge ❶ n **1** sudden forward motion. **2** thrust with a sword. ▷ v **3** move with or make a lunge.

lupin n garden plant with tall spikes of flowers.

lurch¹ ❶ v **1** tilt or lean suddenly to one side.

2 stagger. ▷ n **3** lurching movement.

lurch² n **leave someone in the lurch** abandon someone in difficulties.

lure ❶ v **1** tempt or attract by the promise of reward. ▷ n **2** person or thing that lures. **3** brightly-coloured artificial angling bait.

lurid ❶ adj **1** vivid in shocking detail, sensational. **2** glaring in colour.

lurk ❶ v **1** lie hidden or move stealthily, esp. for sinister purposes. **2** be latent.

luscious ❶ [lush-uss] adj **1** extremely pleasurable to taste or smell. **2** very attractive.

lush ❶ adj **1** (of grass etc.) growing thickly and healthily. **2** opulent.

lust ❶ n **1** strong sexual desire. **2** any strong desire. ▷ v **3** have passionate desire (for). **lustful** adj **lusty** adj vigorous, healthy. **lustily** adv.

lustre ❶ n **1** gloss, sheen. **2** splendour or glory. **3** metallic pottery glaze. **lustrous** adj shining, luminous.

lute n ancient guitar-like musical instrument with a body shaped like a half pear.

tumour ▷ v **4** = **group**, collect, combine, conglomerate, consolidate, mass, pool

lunatic adj **1** = **irrational**, crackbrained, crackpot (inf), crazy, daft, deranged, insane, mad ▷ n **3** Old-fashioned = **madman**, maniac, nutcase (sl), psychopath

lunge n **1** = **pounce**, charge, spring, swing **2** = **thrust**, jab ▷ v **3 a** = **pounce**, charge, dive, leap **b** = **thrust**, jab

lurch¹ v **1** = **tilt**, heave, heel, lean, list, pitch, rock, roll **2** = **stagger**, reel, stumble, sway, totter, weave

lure v **1** = **tempt**, allure, attract, draw, ensnare, entice, invite, seduce ▷ n **2** = **temptation**, allurement, attraction, bait, carrot (inf), enticement, incentive, inducement

lurid adj **1** = **sensational**, graphic, melodramatic, shocking, vivid **2** = **glaring**, intense

lurk v **1** = **hide**, conceal oneself, lie in wait, prowl, skulk, slink, sneak

luscious adj **1** = **delicious**, appetizing, juicy, mouth-watering, palatable, succulent, sweet, toothsome

lush adj **1** = **abundant**, dense, flourishing, green, rank, verdant **2** = **luxurious**, elaborate, extravagant, grand, lavish, opulent, ornate, palatial, plush (inf), sumptuous

lust n **1** = **lechery**, lasciviousness, lewdness, sensuality **2** = **desire**, appetite, craving, greed, longing, passion, thirst ▷ v **3** = **desire**, covet, crave, hunger for or after, want, yearn

lustre n **1** = **sparkle**, gleam, glint, glitter, gloss, glow, sheen, shimmer, shine **2** = **glory**, distinction, fame, honour, prestige, renown

luxury ❶ *n, pl* **-ries 1** enjoyment of rich, very comfortable living. **2** enjoyable but not essential thing. ▷ *adj* **3** of or providing luxury. **luxurious** *adj* full of luxury, sumptuous.

lychee [lie-**chee**] *n* Chinese fruit with a whitish juicy pulp.

Lycra *n* ® elastic fabric used for tight-fitting garments, such as swimsuits.

lymph *n* colourless bodily fluid consisting mainly of white blood cells. **lymphatic** *adj*.

lynch *v* put to death without a trial.

lynx *n* animal of the cat family with tufted ears and a short tail.

lyre *n* ancient musical instrument like a U-shaped harp. **lyrebird** *n* pheasant-like Australian bird the male of which spreads its tail out into the shape of a lyre.

lyric *adj* **1** (of poetry) expressing personal emotion in songlike style. **2** like a song. ▷ *n* **3** short poem in a songlike style. ▷ *pl* **4** words of a popular song. **lyrical** *adj* **1** lyric. **2** enthusiastic. **lyricist** *n* person who writes the words of songs or musicals.

——————————— THESAURUS ———————————

luxury *n* **1** = **opulence**, affluence, hedonism, richness, splendour, sumptuousness **2** = **extravagance**, extra, frill, indulgence, treat

Mm

m 1 metre(s). 2 mile(s). 3 minute(s).

m 1 male. 2 married. 3 month.

MA 1 Master of Arts. 2 Massachusetts.

mac *n informal* mackintosh.

macabre [mak-**kahb**-ra] *adj* strange and horrible, gruesome.

macaroni *n* pasta in short tube shapes.

macaroon *n* small biscuit or cake made with ground almonds.

macaw *n* large tropical American parrot.

mace¹ *n* 1 ceremonial staff of office. 2 medieval weapon with a spiked metal head.

mace² *n* spice made from the dried husk of the nutmeg.

machete [mash-**ett**-ee] *n* broad heavy knife used for cutting or as a weapon.

Machiavellian ❶ [mak-ee-a-**vel**-yan] *adj* unprincipled, crafty, and opportunist.

machine ❶ *n* 1 apparatus, usu. powered by electricity, designed to perform a particular task. 2 vehicle, such as a car or aircraft. 3 controlling system of an organization. ▷ *v* 4 make or produce by machine. **machinery** *n* machines or machine parts collectively. **machinist** *n* person who operates a machine. **machine gun** automatic gun that fires rapidly and continuously. **machine-readable** *adj* (of data) in a form suitable for processing by a computer.

macho ❶ [**match**-oh] *adj* strongly or exaggeratedly masculine.

mackerel *n* edible sea fish with blue and silver stripes.

mackintosh *n* 1 waterproof raincoat of rubberized cloth. 2 any raincoat.

macramé [mak-**rah**-mee] *n* ornamental work of knotted cord.

macrocosm *n* 1 the universe. 2 any large complete system.

mad ❶ *adj* **madder**, **maddest** 1 mentally deranged, insane. 2 very foolish. 3 *informal* angry. 4 frantic. 5 (foll. by *about* or *on*) very enthusiastic (about). **like mad** *informal* with great energy, enthusiasm, or haste. **madly** *adv* **madness** *n* **madden** *v* infuriate or irritate. **maddening** *adj* **madman**, **madwoman** *n*.

madam *n* 1 polite form of address to a woman. 2 *informal* precocious or conceited girl.

m

THESAURUS

macabre *adj* = **gruesome**, dreadful, eerie, frightening, ghastly, ghostly, ghoulish, grim, grisly, morbid

Machiavellian *adj* = **scheming**, astute, crafty, cunning, cynical, double-dealing, opportunist, sly, underhand, unscrupulous

machine *n* 1 = **appliance**, apparatus, contraption, contrivance, device, engine, instrument, mechanism, tool 3 = **system**, machinery, organization, setup (*inf*), structure

macho *adj* = **manly**, chauvinist, masculine, virile

mad *adj* 1 = **insane**, *non compos mentis*, crazy (*inf*), demented, deranged, nuts

(*sl*), of unsound mind, out of one's mind, psychotic, raving, unhinged, unstable 2 = **foolish**, absurd, asinine, daft (*inf*), foolhardy, irrational, nonsensical, preposterous, senseless, wild 3 *Inf* = **angry**, berserk, enraged, furious, incensed, livid (*inf*), pissed (*taboo sl*), pissed off (*taboo sl*), wild 4 = **frenzied**, excited, frenetic, uncontrolled, unrestrained, wild 5 = **enthusiastic**, ardent, avid, crazy (*inf*), fanatical, impassioned, infatuated, wild **like mad** *Inf* = **energetically**, enthusiastically, excitedly, furiously, rapidly, speedily, violently, wildly

madcap ❶ *adj* foolish or reckless.

made *v* past of MAKE.

Madonna *n* 1 the Virgin Mary. 2 picture or statue of her.

madrigal *n* 16th–17th-century part song for unaccompanied voices.

maelstrom ❶ [**male**-strom] *n* 1 great whirlpool. 2 turmoil.

maestro ❶ [**my**-stroh] *n*, *pl* **-tri**, **-tros** 1 outstanding musician or conductor. 2 any master of an art.

magazine ❶ *n* 1 periodical publication with articles by different writers. 2 television or radio programme made up of short nonfictional items. 3 appliance for automatically supplying cartridges to a gun or slides to a projector. 4 storehouse for explosives or arms.

magenta [maj-**jen**-ta] *adj* deep purplish-red.

maggot *n* larva of an insect. **maggoty** *adj*.

magic ❶ *n* 1 supposed art of invoking supernatural powers to influence events. 2 mysterious quality or power. ▷ *adj* 3 (also **magical**) of, using, or like magic. 4 *informal* wonderful, marvellous. **magically** *adv* **magician** *n* 1 conjuror.

2 person with magic powers.

magistrate ❶ *n* 1 public officer administering the law. 2 justice of the peace. **magisterial** *adj* 1 commanding or authoritative. 2 of a magistrate.

magnanimous ❶ *adj* noble and generous. **magnanimity** *n*.

magnate ❶ *n* influential or wealthy person, esp. in industry.

magnesium *n* Chem silvery-white metallic element.

magnet *n* piece of iron or steel capable of attracting iron and pointing north when suspended. **magnetic** *adj* 1 having the properties of a magnet. 2 powerfully attractive. **magnetically** *adv* **magnetism** *n* 1 magnetic property. 2 powerful personal charm. 3 science of magnetic properties. **magnetize** *v* 1 make into a magnet. 2 attract strongly. **magnetic tape** plastic strip coated with a magnetic substance for recording sound or video signals.

magnificent ❶ *adj* 1 splendid or impressive. 2 excellent. **magnificently** *adv* **magnificence** *n*.

magnify ❶ *v* **-fying**, **-fied** 1 increase in apparent size, as with a lens. 2 exaggerate. **magnification** *n*.

━━━━━━━━━━━━━━━━━━━━━━ THESAURUS ━━━━━━━━━━

madcap *adj* = **reckless**, crazy, foolhardy, hare-brained, imprudent, impulsive, rash, thoughtless

maelstrom *n* 1 = **whirlpool**, vortex 2 = **turmoil**, chaos, confusion, disorder, tumult, upheaval

maestro *n* 1 = **virtuoso** 2 = **master**, expert, fundi (S Afr), genius

magazine *n* 1 = **journal**, pamphlet, periodical 4 = **storehouse**, arsenal, depot, store, warehouse

magic *n* 1 = **sorcery**, black art, enchantment, necromancy, witchcraft, wizardry 2 = **charm**, allurement, enchantment, fascination, glamour, magnetism, power ▷ *adj* 3 (also **magical**) = **miraculous**, bewitching, charming, enchanting, entrancing, fascinating,

spellbinding 4 *Inf* = **marvellous**

magistrate *n* 1 = **judge** 2 = **justice of the peace**, J.P., justice

magnanimous *adj* = **generous**, big-hearted, bountiful, charitable, kind, noble, selfless, unselfish

magnate *n* = **tycoon**, baron, big hitter (*inf*), captain of industry, heavy hitter (*inf*), mogul, plutocrat

magnificent *adj* 1 = **splendid**, glorious, gorgeous, imposing, impressive, majestic, regal, sublime, sumptuous 2 = **excellent**, brilliant, fine, outstanding, splendid, superb

magnify *v* 1 = **enlarge**, amplify, blow up (*inf*), boost, dilate, expand, heighten, increase 2 = **exaggerate**, inflate, intensify, overemphasize, overplay, overstate

magnitude ❶ *n* relative importance or size.

magnolia *n* shrub or tree with showy white or pink flowers.

magnum *n* large wine bottle holding about 1.5 litres.

magpie *n* **1** black-and-white bird. **2** any of various similar Australian birds, e.g. the butcherbird.

maharajah *n* former title of some Indian princes. **maharani** *n fem*.

mahogany *n* hard reddish-brown wood of several tropical trees.

maiden ❶ *n* **1** *lit* young unmarried woman. ▷ *adj* **2** unmarried. **3** first, e.g. *maiden voyage*. **maid** *n* female servant. **maidenly** *adj* **maidenhair** *n* fern with delicate fronds. **maiden name** woman's surname before marriage. **maiden over** *Cricket* over in which no runs are scored.

mail¹ *n* **1** letters and packages transported and delivered by the post office. **2** postal system. **3** single collection or delivery of mail. **4** train, ship, or aircraft carrying mail. **5** same as EMAIL. ▷ *v* **6** send by mail. ▷ *n* **mail order** system of buying goods by post. **mailshot** *n* posting of advertising material to many selected people at once.

mail² *n* flexible armour of interlaced rings or links.

mailbox *n* **1** *US & Canad* box into which letters are delivered or placed for collection. **2** computer directory in which email messages are stored.

mailman *n* person who collects or delivers mail.

maim ❶ *v* cripple or mutilate.

main ❶ *adj* **1** chief or principal. ▷ *n* **2** principal pipe or line carrying water, gas, or electricity. ▷ *pl* **3** main distribution network for water, gas, or electricity. **in the main** on the whole. **mainly** *adv* for the most part, chiefly. **mainframe** *n, adj Computers* (denoting) a high-speed general-purpose computer. **mainland** *n* stretch of land which forms the main part of a country. **mainmast** *n* chief mast of a ship. **mainsail** *n* largest sail on a mainmast. **mainspring** *n* **1** chief cause or motive. **2** chief spring of a watch or clock. **mainstay** *n* **1** chief support. **2** rope securing a mainmast. **mainstream** *adj* (of) a prevailing cultural trend.

maintain ❶ *v* **1** continue or keep in existence. **2** keep up or preserve. **3** support financially. **4** assert. **maintenance** *n* **1** maintaining. **2** upkeep of a building, car, etc. **3** provision of money for a separated or divorced spouse.

maisonette *n* flat with more than one floor.

maize *n* type of corn with spikes of yellow grains.

majesty ❶ *n, pl -ties* **1** stateliness or grandeur. **2** supreme power. **majestic** *adj* **majestically** *adv*.

magnitude *n* **a** = **importance**, consequence, greatness, moment, note, significance, weight **b** = **size**, amount, amplitude, extent, mass, quantity, volume

maiden *n* **1** *Lit* = **girl**, damsel, lass, lassie (*inf*), maid, virgin, wench ▷ *adj* **2** = **unmarried**, unwed **3** = **first**, inaugural, initial, introductory

mail¹ *n* **1** = **letters**, correspondence **1-3** = **post** **5** = **mail**, webmail, electronic mail ▷ *v* **6** = **post**, dispatch, forward, send

maim *v* = **cripple**, disable, hurt, injure, mutilate, wound

main *adj* **1** = **chief**, central, essential, foremost, head, leading, pre-eminent, primary, principal *n* **2** = **conduit**, cable, channel, duct, line, pipe **in the main** = **on the whole**, for the most part, generally, in general, mainly, mostly

maintain *v* **1** = **continue**, carry on, perpetuate, prolong, retain, sustain **2** = **keep up**, care for, preserve **3** = **look after**, provide for, support, take care of **4** = **assert**, avow, claim, contend, declare, insist, profess, state

majesty *n* **1** = **grandeur**, glory, magnificence, nobility, pomp, splendour, stateliness

major ❶ *adj* **1** greater in number, quality, or extent. **2** significant or serious. ▷ *n* **3** middle-ranking army officer. **4** scale in music. **5** *US & Canad* principal field of study at a university etc. ▷ *v* **6** (foll. by *in*) *US, Canad, Aust & NZ* do one's principal study in (a particular subject). **majority** *n* greater number.

make ❶ *v* **making, made 1** create, construct, or establish. **2** cause to do or be. **3** bring about or produce. **4** perform (an action). **5** serve as or become. **6** amount to. **7** earn. ▷ *n* **8** brand, type, or style. **make do** manage with an inferior alternative. **make it** *informal* be successful. **on the make** *informal* out for profit or conquest. **maker** *n* **making** *n* **1** creation or production. ▷ *pl* **2** necessary requirements or qualities. **make-believe** *n* fantasy or pretence. **make for** *v* head towards. **make off with** *v* steal or abduct. **makeshift** *adj* serving as a temporary substitute. **make up** *v* **1** form or constitute. **2** prepare. **3** invent. **4** supply what is lacking, complete. **5** (foll. by *for*) compensate (for). **6** settle a quarrel. **7** apply cosmetics. **make-up** *n* **1** cosmetics. **2** way something

is made. **3** mental or physical constitution. **makeweight** *n* something unimportant added to make up a lack.

mal- *combining form* bad or badly, e.g. *malformation.*

maladjusted ❶ *adj Psychol* unable to meet the demands of society. **maladjustment** *n.*

malady ❶ *n, pl* **-dies** disease or illness.

malaise ❶ [mal-*laze*] *n* vague feeling of unease, illness, or depression.

malapropism *n* comical misuse of a word by confusion with one which sounds similar.

malaria *n* infectious disease caused by the bite of some mosquitoes. **malarial** *adj.*

malcontent ❶ *n* discontented person.

male ❶ *adj* **1** of the sex which can fertilize female reproductive cells. ▷ *n* **2** male person or animal.

malevolent ❶ [mal-*lev*-a-lent] *adj* wishing evil to others. **malevolence** *n.*

malice ❶ [mal-*iss*] *n* desire to cause harm to others. **malicious** *adj* **maliciously** *adv.*

malign ❶ [mal-*line*] *v* **1** slander or defame. ▷ *adj* **2** evil in influence or effect.

malinger *v* feign illness to avoid work. **malingerer** *n.*

major *adj* **1** = **main**, bigger, chief, greater, higher, leading, senior, supreme **2** = **important**, critical, crucial, great, notable, outstanding, serious, significant

make *v* **1** = **create**, assemble, build, construct, fashion, form, manufacture, produce, put together, synthesize **2** = **force**, cause, compel, constrain, drive, impel, induce, oblige, prevail upon, require **3** = **produce**, accomplish, bring about, cause, create, effect, generate, give rise to, lead to **4** = **perform**, carry out, do, effect, execute **6** = **amount to**, add up to, compose, constitute, form **7** = **earn**, clear, gain, get, net, obtain, win ▷ *n* **8** = **brand**, kind, model, sort, style, type, variety

maladjusted *adj Psychol* = **disturbed**, alienated, neurotic, unstable

malady *n* = **disease**, affliction, ailment, complaint, disorder, illness, infirmity, sickness

malaise *n* = **unease**, anxiety, depression, disquiet, melancholy

malcontent *n* = **troublemaker**, agitator, mischief-maker, rebel, stirrer (*inf*)

male *adj* **1** = **masculine**, manly, virile

malevolent *adj* = **spiteful**, hostile, ill-natured, malicious, malign, vengeful, vindictive

malice *n* = **spite**, animosity, enmity, evil intent, hate, hatred, ill will, malevolence, vindictiveness

malign *v* **1** = **disparage**, abuse, defame, denigrate, libel, run down, slander, smear, vilify ▷ *adj* **2** = **evil**, bad, destructive, harmful, hostile, injurious, malevolent, malignant, pernicious, wicked

mall [**mawl**] n street or shopping area closed to vehicles.

mallard n wild duck.

malleable ⊕ [**mal**-lee-a-bl] adj **1** capable of being hammered or pressed into shape. **2** easily influenced. **malleability** n.

mallet n **1** (wooden) hammer. **2** stick with a head like a hammer, used in croquet or polo.

malnutrition n inadequate nutrition.

malodorous ⊕ [mal-**lode**-or-uss] adj bad-smelling.

malpractice ⊕ n immoral, illegal, or unethical professional conduct.

malt n **1** grain, such as barley, prepared for use in making beer or whisky.

maltreat ⊕ v treat badly. **maltreatment** n.

mammal n animal of the type that suckles its young. **mammalian** adj.

mammary adj of the breasts or milk-producing glands.

mammon n wealth regarded as a source of evil.

mammoth ⊕ n **1** extinct elephant-like mammal. ▷ adj **2** colossal.

man ⊕ n, pl **men 1** adult male. **2** human being or person. **3** mankind. **4** manservant. **5** piece used in chess etc. ▷ v **manning, manned 6** supply with

sufficient people for operation or defence. **manhood** n **mankind** n human beings collectively.

manly adj (possessing qualities) appropriate to a man. **manliness** n **mannish** adj like a man. **man-hour** n work done by one person in one hour. **man-made** adj made artificially.

mana n NZ authority, influence.

manacle ⊕ [**man**-a-kl] n, v handcuff or fetter.

manage ⊕ v **1** succeed in doing. **2** be in charge of, administer. **3** handle or control. **4** cope with (financial) difficulties. **manageable** adj **management** n **1** managers collectively. **2** administration or organization. **manager, manageress** n person in charge of a business, institution, actor, sports team, etc. **managerial** adj.

mandarin n **1** high-ranking government official. **2** kind of small orange.

mandate ⊕ n **1** official or authoritative command. **2** authorization or instruction from an electorate to its representative or government. ▷ v **3** give authority to. **mandatory** adj compulsory.

mandible n lower jawbone or jawlike part.

mandolin n musical instrument with four pairs of strings.

m

THESAURUS

---

malleable adj **1** = **workable**, ductile, plastic, soft, tensile **2** = **manageable**, adaptable, biddable, compliant, impressionable, pliable, tractable

malodorous adj = **smelly**, fetid, mephitic, nauseating, noisome, offensive, putrid, reeking, stinking

malpractice n = **misconduct**, abuse, dereliction, mismanagement, negligence

maltreat v = **abuse**, bully, harm, hurt, ill-treat, injure, mistreat

mammoth adj **2** = **colossal**, enormous, giant, gigantic, huge, immense, massive, monumental, mountainous, prodigious

man n **1** = **male**, bloke (Brit inf), chap (inf), gentleman, guy (inf) **2** = **human**, human being, individual, person, soul

3 = **mankind**, Homo sapiens, humanity, humankind, human race, people **4** = **manservant**, attendant, retainer, servant, valet ▷ v **6** = **staff**, crew, garrison, occupy, people

manacle n = **handcuff**, bond, chain, fetter, iron, shackle ▷ v = **handcuff**, bind, chain, fetter, put in chains, shackle

manage v **1** = **succeed**, accomplish, arrange, contrive, effect, engineer **2** = **administer**, be in charge (of), command, conduct, direct, handle, run, supervise **3** = **handle**, control, manipulate, operate, use **4** = **cope**, carry on, get by (inf), make do, muddle through, survive

mandate n **1** = **command**, commission, decree, directive, edict, instruction, order

mane n long hair on the neck of a horse, lion, etc.

manfully ❶ adv bravely and determinedly.

manganese n Chem brittle greyish-white metallic element.

mange n skin disease of domestic animals.

manger n eating trough in a stable or barn.

mangle¹ ❶ v 1 destroy by crushing and twisting. 2 spoil.

mangle² n 1 machine with rollers for squeezing water from washed clothes. ▷ v 2 put through a mangle.

mango n, pl -goes, -gos tropical fruit with sweet juicy yellow flesh.

mangrove n tropical tree with exposed roots, which grows beside water.

mania ❶ n 1 extreme enthusiasm. 2 madness. **maniac** n 1 mad person. 2 informal person who has an extreme enthusiasm for something. **maniacal** [man-**eye**-a-kl] adj.

manicure n 1 cosmetic care of the fingernails and hands. ▷ v 2 care for (the fingernails and hands) in this way. **manicurist** n.

manifest ❶ adj 1 easily noticed, obvious. ▷ v 2 show plainly. 3 be evidence of. ▷ n 4 list of cargo or passengers for customs. **manifestation** n.

manifold ❶ adj 1 numerous and varied.

▷ n 2 pipe with several outlets, esp. in an internal-combustion engine.

manila, manilla n strong brown paper used for envelopes.

manipulate ❶ v 1 handle skilfully. 2 control cleverly or deviously. **manipulation** n **manipulative** adj **manipulator** n.

manna n 1 Bible miraculous food which sustained the Israelites in the wilderness. 2 windfall.

mannequin n 1 woman who models clothes at a fashion show. 2 life-size dummy of the human body used to fit or display clothes.

manner ❶ n 1 way a thing happens or is done. 2 person's bearing or behaviour. 3 type or kind. ▷ pl 4 (polite) social behaviour. **mannered** adj affected. **mannerism** n person's distinctive habit or trait.

manoeuvre ❶ [man-**noo**-ver] n 1 skilful movement. 2 contrived, complicated, and possibly deceptive plan or action. ▷ pl 3 military or naval exercises. ▷ v 4 manipulate or contrive skilfully or cunningly. **manoeuvrable** adj.

manor n large country house and its lands. **manorial** adj.

———————— THESAURUS ————————

manfully adv = **bravely**, boldly, courageously, determinedly, gallantly, hard, resolutely, stoutly, valiantly

mangle v 1 = **crush**, deform, destroy, disfigure, distort, mutilate, tear 2 = **spoil**, ruin, wreck

mania n 1 = **obsession**, craze, fad (inf), fetish, fixation, passion, preoccupation, thing (inf) 2 = **madness**, delirium, dementia, derangement, insanity, lunacy

manifest adj 1 = **obvious**, apparent, blatant, clear, conspicuous, evident, glaring, noticeable, palpable, patent v 2 = **display**, demonstrate, exhibit, expose, express, reveal, show

manifold adj 1 = **numerous**, assorted, copious, diverse, many, multifarious, multiple, varied, various

manipulate v 1 = **work**, handle, operate, use 2 = **influence**, control, direct, engineer, manoeuvre

manner n 1 = **way**, method, mode 2 = **behaviour**, air, aspect, bearing, conduct, demeanour 3 = **type**, brand, category, form, kind, sort, variety

manoeuvre n 1 = **movement**, exercise, operation 2 = **stratagem**, dodge, intrigue, machination, ploy, ruse, scheme, subterfuge, tactic, trick ▷ v 4 = **manipulate**, contrive, engineer, machinate, pull strings, scheme, wangle (inf)

manse n house provided for a minister in some religious denominations.

mansion n large house.

mantle ❶ n 1 loose cloak. 2 covering. 3 responsibilities and duties which go with a particular job or position.

mantra n Hinduism, Buddhism any sacred word or syllable used as an object of concentration.

manual ❶ adj 1 of or done with the hands. 2 by human labour rather than automatic means. ▷ n 3 handbook. 4 organ keyboard. **manually** adv.

manufacture ❶ v 1 process or make (goods) on a large scale using machinery. 2 invent or concoct (an excuse etc.). ▷ n 3 process of manufacturing goods. **manufacturer** n.

manure ❶ n animal excrement used as a fertilizer.

manuscript n 1 book or document, orig. one written by hand. 2 copy for printing.

many ❶ adj **more**, **most** 1 numerous. ▷ n 2 large number.

map n 1 representation of the earth's surface or some part of it, showing geographical features. ▷ v **mapping**, **mapped** 2 make a map of. **map out** v plan.

maple n tree with broad leaves, a variety of which (**sugar maple**) yields sugar.

maple sugar n US & Canad sugar made from the sap of the sugar maple.

mar ❶ v **marring**, **marred** spoil or impair.

Mar. March.

maraca [mar-**rak**-a] n shaken percussion instrument made from a gourd containing dried seeds etc.

marathon n 1 long-distance race of 26 miles 385 yards (42.195 kilometres). 2 long or arduous task.

marble n 1 kind of limestone with a mottled appearance, which can be highly polished. 2 small glass ball used in playing marbles. ▷ pl 3 game of rolling these at one another. **marbled** adj having a mottled appearance like marble.

march ❶ v 1 walk with a military step. 2 make (a person or group) proceed. 3 progress steadily. ▷ n 4 action of marching. 5 steady progress. 6 distance covered by marching. 7 piece of music, as for a march. **marcher** n.

March n third month of the year.

marchioness [marsh-on-**ness**] n 1 woman holding the rank of marquis. 2 wife or widow of a marquis.

mare n female horse or zebra. **mare's nest** discovery which proves worthless.

margarine n butter substitute made from animal or vegetable fats.

margin ❶ n 1 edge or border. 2 blank space

——————— THESAURUS ———————

mansion n = **residence**, hall, manor, seat, villa

mantle n 1 = **cloak**, cape, hood, shawl, wrap 2 = **covering**, blanket, canopy, curtain, pall, screen, shroud, veil

manual adj 1 = **hand-operated** 2 = **human**, physical ▷ n 3 = **handbook**, bible, guide, instructions

manufacture v 1 = **make**, assemble, build, construct, create, mass-produce, produce, put together, turn out 2 = **concoct**, cook up (inf), devise, fabricate, invent, make up, think up, trump up ▷ n 3 = **making**, assembly, construction, creation, production

manure n = **compost**, droppings, dung, excrement, fertilizer, kak (S Afr sl), muck, ordure

many adj 1 = **numerous**, abundant, countless, innumerable, manifold, myriad, umpteen (inf), various ▷ n 2 = **a lot**, heaps (inf), lots (inf), plenty, scores

mar v = **spoil**, blemish, damage, detract from, disfigure, hurt, impair, ruin, scar, stain, taint, tarnish

march v 1 = **walk**, pace, parade, stride, strut 3 = **file** ▷ n 4 = **walk**, routemarch, trek 5 = **progress**, advance, development, evolution, progression

margin n 1 = **edge**, border, boundary,

round a printed page. **3** additional amount or one greater than necessary. **marginal** *adj* **1** insignificant, unimportant. **2** near a limit. **3** *Politics* (of a constituency) won by only a small margin. ▷ *n* **4** *Politics* marginal constituency. **marginally** *adv*.

marigold *n* plant with yellow or orange flowers.

marijuana ❶ [mar-ree-**wah**-na] *n* dried flowers and leaves of the cannabis plant, used as a drug, esp. in cigarettes.

marina *n* harbour for yachts and other pleasure boats.

marinade *n* **1** seasoned liquid in which fish or meat is soaked before cooking. ▷ *v* **2** same as MARINATE. **marinate** *v* soak in marinade.

marine ❶ *adj* **1** of the sea or shipping. ▷ *n* **2** soldier trained for land and sea combat. **3** country's shipping or fleet. **mariner** *n* sailor.

marionette *n* puppet worked with strings.

marital ❶ *adj* relating to marriage.

maritime ❶ *adj* **1** relating to shipping. **2** of, near, or living in the sea.

mark ❶ *n* **1** line, dot, scar, etc. visible on a surface. **2** distinguishing sign or symbol. **3** written or printed symbol. **4** letter or number used to grade academic work. **5** indication of position. **6** indication of some quality. **7** target or goal. ▷ *v* **8** make a mark on. **9** characterize or distinguish.

10 indicate. **11** pay attention to. **12** notice or watch. **13** grade (academic work). **14** stay close to (a sporting opponent) to hamper his or her play. **marked** *adj* noticeable. **markedly** *adv* **marker** *n*.

market ❶ *n* **1** assembly or place for buying and selling. **2** demand for goods. ▷ *v* **-keting, -keted 3** offer or produce for sale. **on the market** for sale. **marketable** *adj* **marketing** *n* part of a business that controls the way that goods or services are sold. **market garden** place where fruit and vegetables are grown for sale. **marketplace** *n* **1** market. **2** commercial world. **market research** research into consumers' needs and purchases.

marlin *n* large food and game fish of warm and tropical seas, with a very long upper jaw.

marmalade *n* jam made from citrus fruits.

marmoset *n* small bushy-tailed monkey.

maroon¹ *adj* reddish-purple.

maroon² ❶ *v* **1** abandon ashore, esp. on an island. **2** isolate without resources.

marquee *n* large tent used for a party or exhibition.

marquetry *n* ornamental inlaid work of wood.

marquis *n* (in various countries) nobleman of the rank above a count.

marrow *n* **1** fatty substance inside bones. **2** long thick striped green vegetable with whitish flesh.

---

brink, perimeter, periphery, rim, side, verge

marijuana *n* = **cannabis**, dope (*sl*), grass (*sl*), hemp, pot (*sl*)

marine *adj* **1** = **nautical**, maritime, naval, seafaring, seagoing

marital *adj* = **matrimonial**, conjugal, connubial, nuptial

maritime *adj* **1** = **nautical**, marine, naval, oceanic, seafaring **2** = **coastal**, littoral, seaside

mark *n* **1** = **spot**, blemish, blot, line, scar, scratch, smudge, stain, streak **2** = **sign**, badge, device, emblem, flag, hallmark, label, token **3** = **symbol**

6 = **criterion**, measure, norm, standard, yardstick **7** = **target**, aim, goal, object, objective, purpose ▷ *v* **8** = **scar**, blemish, blot, scratch, smudge, stain, streak **9** = **distinguish**, brand, characterize, denote, exemplify, flag, identify, illustrate, label, show, stamp **11** = **pay attention**, attend, mind, pay heed **12** = **observe**, note, notice, watch **13** = **grade**, appraise, assess, correct, evaluate

market *n* **1** = **fair**, bazaar, mart ▷ *v* **3** = **sell**, retail, vend

maroon² *v* **1** = **abandon**, desert, leave **2** = **strand**, leave high and dry (*inf*)

marry v -rying, -ried 1 take as a husband or wife. 2 join or give in marriage. 3 unite closely. **marriage** n 1 state of being married. 2 wedding. **marriageable** adj.

marsh n low-lying wet land. **marshy** adj.

marshal n 1 officer of the highest rank. 2 official who organizes ceremonies or events. 3 US law officer. ▷ v -shalling, -shalled 4 arrange in order. 5 assemble. 6 conduct with ceremony.

marshmallow n spongy pink or white sweet.

marsupial [mar-**soop**-ee-al] n animal that carries its young in a pouch, such as a kangaroo.

marten n 1 weasel-like animal.

martial adj of war, warlike. **martial art** any of various philosophies and techniques of self-defence, orig. Eastern, such as karate. **martial law** law enforced by military authorities in times of danger or emergency.

martin n bird with a slightly forked tail.

martinet n person who maintains strict discipline.

martyr n 1 person who dies or suffers for his or her beliefs. ▷ v 2 make a martyr of. **be a martyr to** be constantly suffering from. **martyrdom** n.

marvel v -velling, -velled 1 be filled with wonder. ▷ n 2 wonderful thing.

marvellous adj 1 amazing. 2 wonderful.

marzipan n paste of ground almonds, sugar, and egg whites.

mascara n cosmetic for darkening the eyelashes.

mascot n person, animal, or thing supposed to bring good luck.

masculine adj 1 relating to males. 2 manly. 3 Grammar of the gender of nouns that includes some male animate things. **masculinity** n.

mash n 1 informal mashed potatoes. 2 bran or meal mixed with warm water as food for horses etc. ▷ v 3 crush into a soft mass.

mask n 1 covering for the face, as a disguise or protection. 2 behaviour that hides one's true feelings. ▷ v 3 cover with a mask. 4 hide or disguise.

masochism [**mass**-oh-kiz-zum] n condition in which (sexual) pleasure is obtained from feeling pain or from being humiliated. **masochist** n **masochistic** adj.

mason n person who works with stone. **masonry** n stonework.

masquerade [mask-er-**aid**] n 1 deceptive show or pretence. 2 party at which masks and costumes are worn. ▷ v 3 pretend to be someone or something else.

mass n 1 coherent body of matter. 2 large quantity or number.

THESAURUS

---

marry v 1 = **wed**, get hitched (sl), tie the knot (inf) 3 = **unite**, ally, bond, join, knit, link, merge, unify, yoke

marsh n = **swamp**, bog, fen, morass, quagmire, slough, muskeg (Canad)

marshal v 4 = **arrange**, align, array, draw up, line up, order, organize 5 = **group**, deploy 6 = **conduct**, escort, guide, lead, shepherd, usher

martial adj = **military**, bellicose, belligerent, warlike

martinet n = **disciplinarian**, stickler

marvel v 1 = **wonder**, be amazed, be awed, gape ▷ n 2 = **wonder**, miracle, phenomenon, portent, prodigy

masculine adj 1 = **male**, manlike, mannish 2 = **manly**, virile

mask n 1 = **disguise**, camouflage, cover, veil 2 = **front**, facade, guise, screen ▷ v 4 = **disguise**, camouflage, cloak, conceal, cover, hide, obscure, screen, veil

masquerade n 1 = **pretence**, cloak, cover-up, deception, disguise, mask, pose, screen, subterfuge 2 = **masked ball**, fancy dress party, revel ▷ v 3 = **pose**, disguise, dissemble, dissimulate, impersonate, pass oneself off, pretend (to be)

mass n 1 = **piece**, block, chunk, hunk, lump 2 = **lot**, bunch, collection, heap, load, pile, quantity, stack 3 = **size**, bulk,

3 *Physics* amount of matter in a body. ▷ *adj*
4 large-scale. **5** involving many people.
▷ *v* **6** form into a mass. **the masses**
ordinary people. **massive** *adj* large and
heavy. **mass-market** *adj* for or appealing
to a large number of people. **mass media**
means of communication to many people,
such as television and newspapers. **mass-
produce** *v* manufacture (standardized
goods) in large quantities.

Mass *n* service of the Eucharist, esp. in the
RC Church.

massacre ❶ [mass-a-ker**]** *n*
1 indiscriminate killing of large numbers of
people. ▷ *v* **2** kill in large numbers.

massage ❶ [mass-ahzh**]** *n* **1** rubbing and
kneading of parts of the body to reduce
pain or stiffness. ▷ *v* **2** give a massage to.
masseur, *(fem)* **masseuse** *n* person who
gives massages.

mast *n* tall pole for supporting something,
esp. a ship's sails. **masthead** *n* **1** *Naut* head
of a mast. **2** name of a newspaper printed
at the top of the front page.

mastectomy [mass-tek-tom-ee**]** *n*, *pl*
-mies surgical removal of a breast.

master ❶ *n* **1** person in control, such as an
employer or an owner of slaves or animals.
2 expert. **3** great artist. **4** original thing
from which copies are made. **5** male
teacher. ▷ *adj* **6** overall or controlling.
7 main or principal. ▷ *v* **8** acquire

knowledge of or skill in. **9** overcome.
masterful *adj* **1** domineering. **2** showing
great skill. **masterly** *adj* showing great
skill. **mastery** *n* **1** expertise. **2** control or
command. **master key** key that opens all
the locks of a set. **mastermind** *v* **1** plan
and direct (a complex task). ▷ *n* **2** person
who plans and directs a complex task.
masterpiece *n* outstanding work of art.

masticate *v* chew. **mastication** *n*.

mastiff *n* large dog.

masturbate *v* fondle the genitals (of).
masturbation *n*.

mat *n* **1** piece of fabric used as a floor
covering or to protect a surface. **2** thick
tangled mass. ▷ *v* **matting, matted**
3 tangle or become tangled into a dense
mass.

matador *n* man who kills the bull in
bullfights.

match¹ ❶ *n* **1** contest in a game or sport.
2 person or thing exactly like, equal to, or
in harmony with another. **3** marriage. ▷ *v*
4 be exactly like, equal to, or in harmony
with. **5** put in competition (with). **6** find
a match for. **matchless** *adj* unequalled.
matchmaker *n* person who schemes to
bring about a marriage. **matchmaking**
n, adj.

match² *n* small stick with a tip which
ignites when scraped on a rough surface.
matchbox *n* **matchstick** *n* **1** wooden

———————————————————————————————— THESAURUS

greatness, magnitude ▷ *adj* **4** = **large-
scale**, extensive, general, indiscriminate,
wholesale, widespread ▷ *v* **6** = **gather**,
accumulate, assemble, collect,
congregate, rally, swarm, throng

massacre *n* **1** = **slaughter**, annihilation,
blood bath, butchery, carnage,
extermination, holocaust, murder ▷ *v*
2 = **slaughter**, butcher, cut to pieces,
exterminate, kill, mow down, murder,
wipe out

massage *n* **1** = **rub-down**, manipulation
▷ *v* **2** = **rub down**, knead, manipulate

master *n* **1** = **head**, boss *(inf)*, chief,

commander, controller, director,
governor, lord, manager, ruler
2 = **expert**, ace *(inf)*, doyen, fundi *(S Afr)*,
genius, maestro, past master, virtuoso,
wizard **5** = **teacher**, guide, guru,
instructor, tutor *adj* **7** = **main**, chief,
foremost, leading, predominant, prime,
principal ▷ *v* **8** = **learn**, get the hang
of *(inf)*, grasp **9** = **overcome**, conquer,
defeat, tame, triumph over, vanquish

match¹ *n* **1** = **game**, bout, competition,
contest, head-to-head, test, trial
2 = **equal**, counterpart, peer, rival
3 = **marriage**, alliance, pairing,

part of a match. ▷ *adj* **2** (of drawn figures) thin and straight. **matchwood** *n* small splinters.

mate[1] ❶ *n* **1** *informal* friend. **2** *informal* common British and Australian term of address between males. **3** associate or colleague, e.g. *running mate; team-mate*. **4** sexual partner of an animal. **5** officer in a merchant ship. **6** tradesman's assistant. ▷ *v* **7** pair (animals) or (of animals) be paired for reproduction.

mate[2] *n, v Chess* checkmate.

material ❶ *n* **1** substance of which a thing is made. **2** cloth. **3** information on which a piece of work may be based. ▷ *pl* **4** things needed for an activity. ▷ *adj* **5** of matter or substance. **6** not spiritual. **7** affecting physical wellbeing. **8** relevant. **materially** *adv* considerably. **materialism** *n* **1** excessive interest in or desire for money and possessions. **2** belief that only the material world exists. **materialist** *adj, n* **materialistic** *adj* **materialize** *v* **1** actually happen. **2** come into existence or view. **materialization** *n*.

maternal ❶ *adj* **1** of a mother. **2** related through one's mother. **maternity** *n* **1** motherhood. ▷ *adj* **2** of or for pregnant women.

math *n US & Canad* mathematics.

mathematics *n* science of number, quantity, shape, and space. **mathematical** *adj* **mathematically** *adv*

mathematician *n*.

maths *n informal* mathematics.

matinée [**mat**-in-nay] *n* afternoon performance in a theatre or cinema.

matins *pl n* early morning service in various Christian Churches.

matriarch [**mate**-ree-ark] *n* female head of a tribe or family. **matriarchal** *adj* **matriarchy** *n* society governed by a female, in which descent is traced through the female line.

matriculate *v* enrol or be enrolled in a college or university. **matriculation** *n*.

matrimony ❶ *n* marriage. **matrimonial** *adj*.

matrix [**may**-trix] *n, pl* **matrices** **1** substance or situation in which something originates, takes form, or is enclosed. **2** mould for casting. **3** *Maths* rectangular array of numbers or elements.

matron *n* **1** staid or dignified married woman. **2** woman who supervises the domestic or medical arrangements of an institution. **3** former name for NURSING OFFICER. **matronly** *adj*.

matter ❶ *n* **1** substance of which something is made. **2** event, situation, or subject. **3** written material in general. **4** pus. ▷ *v* **5** be of importance. **what's the matter?** what is wrong?

mattress *n* large stuffed flat case, often with springs, used on or as a bed.

partnership ▷ *v* **4** = **correspond**, accord, agree, fit, go with, harmonize, tally **5** = **rival**, compare, compete, emulate, equal, measure up to

mate[1] *n* **1** *Inf* = **friend**, buddy (*inf*), chum (*inf*), comrade, crony, pal (*inf*) **3** = **colleague**, associate, companion **6** = **assistant**, helper, subordinate ▷ *v* **7** = **pair**, breed, couple

material *n* **1** = **substance**, matter, stuff **2** = **cloth**, fabric **3** = **information**, data, evidence, facts, notes ▷ *adj* **5** = **tangible**, concrete, palpable, substantial **6** = **physical**, bodily, corporeal

8 = **relevant**, applicable, apposite, apropos, germane, pertinent

maternal *adj* **1** = **motherly**

matrimony *n* = **marriage**, nuptials, wedding ceremony, wedlock

matter *n* **1** = **substance**, material, stuff **2** = **situation**, affair, business, concern, event, incident, proceeding, question, subject, topic ▷ *v* **5** = **be important**, carry weight, count, make a difference, signify **what's the matter?** = **problem**, complication, difficulty, distress, trouble, worry

mature ❶ *adj* **1** fully developed or grown-up. **2** ripe. ▷ *v* **3** make or become mature. **4** (of a bill or bond) become due for payment. **maturity** *n* **maturation** *n*.

maudlin ❶ *adj* foolishly or tearfully sentimental.

maul ❶ *v* **1** handle roughly. **2** beat or tear.

mausoleum [maw-so-**lee**-um] *n* stately tomb.

mauve *adj* pale purple.

maverick ❶ *n, adj* independent and unorthodox (person).

maw *n* animal's mouth, throat, or stomach.

mawkish ❶ *adj* foolishly sentimental.

maxim ❶ *n* general truth or principle.

maximum ❶ *adj, n, pl* **-mums, -ma** greatest possible (amount or number). **maximal** *adj* **maximize** *v* increase to a maximum.

may *v, past tense* **might** used as an auxiliary to express possibility, permission, opportunity, etc. **maybe** *adv* perhaps, possibly.

May *n* **1** fifth month of the year. **2** (**m-**) same as HAWTHORN. **mayfly** *n* short-lived aquatic insect. **maypole** *n* pole set up for dancing round on the first day of May to celebrate spring.

Mayday *n* international radio distress signal.

mayhem ❶ *n* violent destruction or confusion.

mayonnaise *n* creamy sauce of egg yolks, oil, and vinegar.

● **SPELLING TIP**
● There are two *n*s to remember in the
● middle of **mayonnaise** - possibly a good
● reason for the increasing use of the ab-
● breviation 'mayo'.

mayor *n* head of a municipality. **mayoress** *n* **1** mayor's wife. **2** female mayor. **mayoralty** *n* (term of) office of a mayor.

maze ❶ *n* **1** complex network of paths or lines designed to puzzle. **2** any confusing network or system.

MBE Member of the Order of the British Empire.

MD 1 Doctor of Medicine. **2** Maryland.

me *pron* objective form of I.

mead *n* alcoholic drink made from honey.

meadow ❶ *n* piece of grassland.

meagre ❶ *adj* scanty or insufficient.

meal¹ *n* **1** occasion when food is served and eaten. **2** the food itself.

meal² *n* grain ground to powder. **mealy** *adj* **mealy-mouthed** *adj* not outspoken enough.

——————————— THESAURUS ———————————

mature *adj* **1** = **grown-up**, adult, full-grown, fully fledged, of age **2** = **ripe**, mellow, ready, seasoned ▷ *v* **3** = **develop**, age, bloom, blossom, come of age, grow up, mellow, ripen

maudlin *adj* = **sentimental**, mawkish, overemotional, slushy (*inf*), soppy (*Brit inf*), tearful, weepy (*inf*)

maul *v* **1** = **ill-treat**, abuse, batter, manhandle, molest **2** = **tear**, claw, lacerate, mangle

maverick *n* = **rebel**, dissenter, eccentric, heretic, iconoclast, individualist, nonconformist, protester, radical *adj* = **rebel**, dissenting, eccentric, heretical, iconoclastic, individualistic, nonconformist, radical

mawkish *adj* = **sentimental**, emotional,

maudlin, schmaltzy (*sl*), slushy (*inf*), soppy (*Brit inf*)

maxim *n* = **saying**, adage, aphorism, axiom, dictum, motto, proverb, rule

maximum *adj* = **greatest**, highest, most, paramount, supreme, topmost, utmost ▷ *n* = **top**, ceiling, height, peak, pinnacle, summit, upper limit, utmost, zenith

mayhem *n* = **chaos**, commotion, confusion, destruction, disorder, fracas, havoc, trouble, violence

maze *n* **1** = **labyrinth** **2** = **web**, confusion, imbroglio, tangle

meadow *n* = **field**, grassland, lea (*poet*), pasture

meagre *adj* = **insubstantial**, inadequate, measly, paltry, poor, puny, scanty, slight, small

mean¹ ⊕ v meaning, meant 1 intend to convey or express. 2 signify, denote, or portend. 3 intend. 4 have importance as specified. **meaning** n sense, significance. **meaningful** adj **meaningless** adj.

mean² ⊕ adj 1 miserly, ungenerous, or petty. 2 despicable or callous. 3 Chiefly US informal bad-tempered. **meanly** adv **meanness** n.

mean³ ⊕ n 1 middle point between two extremes. 2 average. ▷ pl 3 method by which something is done. 4 money. ▷ adj 5 intermediate in size or quantity. 6 average. **by all means** certainly. **by no means** in no way. **means test** inquiry into a person's means to decide on eligibility for financial aid.

meander ⊕ [mee-**and**-er] v 1 follow a winding course. 2 wander aimlessly. ▷ n 3 winding course.

measles n infectious disease producing red spots. **measly** adj informal meagre.

measure ⊕ n 1 size or quantity. 2 graduated scale etc. for measuring size or quantity. 3 unit of size or quantity. 4 extent. 5 action taken. 6 law. ▷ v 7 determine the size or quantity of. 8 be (a specified amount) in size or quantity.

measurable adj **measured** adj 1 slow and steady. 2 carefully considered. **measurement** n 1 measuring. 2 size. **measure up to** v fulfil (expectations or requirements).

meat ⊕ n animal flesh as food. **meaty** adj 1 (tasting) of or like meat. 2 brawny. 3 full of significance or interest.

mechanic n person skilled in repairing or operating machinery. **mechanics** n scientific study of motion and force. **mechanical** adj 1 of or done by machines. 2 (of an action) without thought or feeling. **mechanically** adv.

mechanism ⊕ n 1 way a machine works. 2 piece of machinery. 3 process or technique, e.g. defence mechanism. **mechanize** v 1 equip with machinery. 2 make mechanical or automatic. **mechanization** n.

medal n piece of metal with an inscription etc., given as a reward or memento. **medallion** n 1 disc-shaped ornament worn on a chain round the neck. 2 large medal. **medallist** n winner of a medal.

meddle ⊕ v interfere annoyingly. **meddlesome** adj.

media n 1 a plural of MEDIUM. 2 the mass media collectively.

mean¹ v 1 = **express**, convey, imply, indicate 2 = **signify**, denote, represent, spell, stand for, symbolize 3 = **intend**, aim, aspire, design, desire, plan, set out, want, wish

mean² adj 1 = **miserly**, mercenary, niggardly, parsimonious, penny-pinching, stingy, tight-fisted, ungenerous 2 = **dishonourable**, callous, contemptible, despicable, hard-hearted, petty, shabby, shameful, sordid, vile

mean³ n 1 = **middle**, balance, compromise, happy medium, midpoint ▷ adj 6 = **average**, norm, standard

meander v 1 = **wind**, snake, turn, zigzag 2 = **wander**, ramble, stroll ▷ n 3 = **curve**, bend, coil, loop, turn, twist, zigzag

measure n 1 = **quantity**, allotment, allowance, amount, portion, quota, ration, share 2 = **gauge**, metre, rule, scale, yardstick 5 = **action**, act, deed, expedient, manoeuvre, means, procedure, step 6 = **law**, act, bill, resolution, statute ▷ v 7 = **quantify**, assess, calculate, calibrate, compute, determine, evaluate, gauge, weigh

meat n = **food**, flesh, tucker (Aust & NZ inf)

mechanism n 2 = **machine**, apparatus, appliance, contrivance, device, instrument, tool 3 = **process**, agency, means, method, methodology, operation, procedure, system, technique, way

meddle v = **interfere**, butt in, intervene, intrude, pry, tamper

median *adj, n* middle (point or line).
mediate ❶ *v* intervene in a dispute to bring about agreement. **mediation** *n* **mediator** *n*.
medic *n informal* doctor or medical student.
medicine ❶ *n* 1 substance used to treat disease. 2 science of preventing, diagnosing, or curing disease. **medicinal** [med-**diss**-in-al] *adj* having therapeutic properties. **medical** *adj* **medicine man** witch doctor.
medieval [med-ee-**eve**-al] *adj* of the Middle Ages.
mediocre ❶ [mee-dee-**oak**-er] *adj* 1 average in quality. 2 second-rate. **mediocrity** [mee-dee-**ok**-rit-ee] *n*.
meditate ❶ *v* 1 reflect deeply, esp. on spiritual matters. 2 think about or plan. **meditation** *n* **meditative** *adj*.
medium ❶ *adj* 1 midway between extremes, average. ▷ *n, pl* **-dia, -diums** 2 middle state, degree, or condition. 3 intervening substance producing an effect. 4 means of communicating news or information to the public, such as radio or newspapers. 5 person who can supposedly communicate with the

dead. 6 surroundings or environment. **medium wave** radio wave with a wavelength between 100 and 1000 metres.
medley ❶ *n* 1 miscellaneous mixture. 2 musical sequence of different tunes.
meek ❶ *adj* submissive or humble. **meekly** *adv* **meekness** *n*.
meet ❶ *v* **meeting, met** 1 come together (with). 2 come into contact (with). 3 be at the place of arrival of. 4 make the acquaintance of. 5 satisfy (a need etc.). 6 experience. ▷ *n* 7 sports meeting. 8 assembly of a hunt. **meeting** *n* 1 coming together. 2 assembly.
meg *n Computers informal* short for MEGABYTE.
megabyte *n Computers* 2^{20} or 1 048 576 bytes.
megalith *n* great stone, esp. as part of a prehistoric monument. **megalithic** *adj*.
megalomania *n* craving for or mental delusions of power. **megalomaniac** *adj, n*.
megaphone *n* cone-shaped instrument used to amplify the voice.
megapode *n* bird of Australia, New Guinea, and adjacent islands.

━━━━━━━━━━━━━━━━━━━ THESAURUS ━━━━━━━

mediate *v* = **intervene**, arbitrate, conciliate, intercede, reconcile, referee, step in (*inf*), umpire
medicine *n* 1 = **remedy**, cure, drug, medicament, medication, nostrum
mediocre *adj* 1 = **average**, indifferent, middling, ordinary, passable, pedestrian, run-of-the-mill, so-so (*inf*), undistinguished 2 = **second-rate**, inferior
meditate *v* 1 = **reflect**, cogitate, consider, contemplate, deliberate, muse, ponder, ruminate, think 2 = **plan**, have in mind, intend, purpose, scheme
medium *adj* 1 = **average**, fair, intermediate, mean, median, mediocre, middle, middling, midway ▷ *n* 2 = **middle**, average, centre, compromise, mean, midpoint 3 = **means**, agency, channel, instrument, mode, organ, vehicle,

way 5 = **spiritualist**, channeller 6 = **environment**, atmosphere, conditions, milieu, setting, surroundings
medley *n* 1 = **mixture**, assortment, farrago, hotchpotch, jumble, *melange*, miscellany, mishmash, mixed bag (*inf*), potpourri
meek *adj* = **submissive**, acquiescent, compliant, deferential, docile, gentle, humble, mild, modest, timid, unassuming, unpretentious
meet *v* 1 = **gather**, assemble, collect, come together, congregate, convene, muster 2 **a** = **encounter**, bump into, chance on, come across, confront, contact, find, happen on, run across, run into **b** = **converge**, come together, connect, cross, intersect, join, link up, touch 5 = **fulfil**, answer, come up to, comply

megaton n explosive power equal to that of one million tons of TNT.

melancholy ❶ [**mel**-an-kol-lee] n **1** sadness or gloom. ▷ adj **2** sad or gloomy. **melancholia** [mel-an-**kole**-lee-a] n state of depression. **melancholic** adj, n.

melanin n dark pigment found in the hair, skin, and eyes of humans and animals.

mêlée [**mel**-lay] n noisy confused fight or crowd.

mellifluous ❶ [mel-**lif**-flew-uss] adj (of sound) smooth and sweet.

mellow ❶ adj **1** soft, not harsh. **2** kind-hearted, esp. through maturity. **3** (of fruit) ripe. ▷ v **4** make or become mellow.

melodrama n **1** play full of extravagant action and emotion. **2** overdramatic behaviour or emotion. **melodramatic** adj.

melody ❶ n, pl -**dies 1** series of musical notes which make a tune. **2** sweet sound. **melodic** [mel-**lod**-ik] adj **1** of melody. **2** melodious. **melodious** [mel-**lode**-ee-uss] adj **1** pleasing to the ear. **2** tuneful.

melon n large round juicy fruit with a hard rind.

melt ❶ v **1** (cause to) become liquid by heat. **2** dissolve. **3** disappear. **4** blend (into).

5 soften through emotion. **meltdown** n (in a nuclear reactor) melting of the fuel rods, with the possible release of radiation.

member ❶ n **1** individual making up a body or society. **2** limb. **membership** n.

membrane n thin flexible tissue in a plant or animal body. **membranous** adj.

memento ❶ n, pl -**tos, -toes** thing serving to remind, souvenir.

memo n, pl **memos** short for MEMORANDUM.

memoir ❶ [**mem**-wahr] n **1** biography or historical account based on personal knowledge. ▷ pl **2** collection of these. **3** autobiography.

memory ❶ n, pl -**ries 1** ability to remember. **2** sum of things remembered. **3** particular recollection. **4** length of time one can remember. **5** commemoration. **6** part of a computer which stores information. **memorable** adj **memorize** v commit to memory. **memorial** n **1** something serving to commemorate a person or thing. ▷ adj **2** serving as a memorial. **memory card** small removable data storage device, used in mobile phones, digital cameras, etc.

m

———————— THESAURUS ————————

with, discharge, match, measure up to, satisfy

melancholy n **1** = **sadness**, dejection, depression, despondency, gloom, low spirits, misery, sorrow, unhappiness adj **2** = **sad**, depressed, despondent, dispirited, downhearted, gloomy, glum, miserable, mournful, sorrowful

mêlée n = **fight**, brawl, fracas, free-for-all (inf), rumpus, scrimmage, scuffle, set-to (inf), skirmish, tussle

mellifluous adj = **sweet**, dulcet, euphonious, honeyed, silvery, smooth, soft, soothing, sweet-sounding

mellow adj **1** = **soft**, delicate **3** = **ripe**, full-flavoured, mature, rich, sweet ▷ v **4** = **mature**, develop, improve, ripen, season, soften, sweeten

melody n **1** = **tune**, air, music, song,

strain, theme **2** = **tunefulness**, euphony, harmony, melodiousness, musicality

melt v **1, 2** = **dissolve**, fuse, liquefy, soften, thaw **3** = **disappear**, disperse, dissolve, evanesce, evaporate, fade, vanish **5** = **soften**, disarm, mollify, outspan (SAfr), relax

member n **1** = **representative**, associate, fellow **2** = **limb**, appendage, arm, extremity, leg, part

memento n = **souvenir**, keepsake, memorial, relic, remembrance, reminder, token, trophy

memoir n **1** = **account**, biography, essay, journal, life, monograph, narrative, record

memory n **1** = **recall**, retention **3** = **recollection**, remembrance, reminiscence **5** = **commemoration**, honour, remembrance

men *n* plural of MAN.

menace ❶ *n* **1** threat. **2** *informal* nuisance. ▷ *v* **3** threaten, endanger. **menacing** *adj*.

menagerie [min-**naj**-er-ee] *n* collection of wild animals for exhibition.

mend ❶ *v* **1** repair or patch. **2** recover or heal. **3** make or become better. ▷ *n* **4** mended area. **on the mend** regaining health.

menial ❶ [**mean**-nee-al] *adj* **1** involving boring work of low status. ▷ *n* **2** domestic servant.

meningitis [men-in-**jite**-iss] *n* inflammation of the membranes of the brain.

menopause *n* time when a woman's menstrual cycle ceases. **menopausal** *adj*.

menstruation *n* approximately monthly discharge of blood and cellular debris from the womb of a nonpregnant woman. **menstruate** *v* **menstrual** *adj*.

mensuration *n* measuring, esp. in geometry.

mental ❶ *adj* **1** of, in, or done by the mind. **2** of or for mental illness. **3** *informal* insane. **mentally** *adv* **mentality** *n* way of thinking.

menthol *n* organic compound found in peppermint, used medicinally.

mention ❶ *v* **1** refer to briefly. **2** acknowledge. ▷ *n* **3** brief reference to a person or thing. **4** acknowledgment.

mentor ❶ *n* adviser or guide.

menu ❶ *n* **1** list of dishes to be served, or from which to order. **2** *Computers* list of options displayed on a screen.

mercantile ❶ *adj* of trade or traders.

mercenary ❶ *adj* **1** influenced by greed. **2** working merely for reward. ▷ *n, pl* **-aries** **3** hired soldier.

merchant ❶ *n* person engaged in trade, wholesale trader. **merchandise** *n* commodities. **merchant bank** bank dealing mainly with businesses and investment. **merchantman** *n* trading ship. **merchant navy** ships or crew engaged in a nation's commercial shipping.

mercury *n* *Chem* silvery liquid metal. **mercurial** *adj* lively, changeable.

mercy ❶ *n, pl* **-cies** **1** compassionate

---

menace *n* **1** = **threat**, intimidation, warning **2** *Inf* = **nuisance**, annoyance, pest, plague, troublemaker ▷ *v* **3** = **threaten**, bully, frighten, intimidate, loom, lour *or* lower, terrorize

mend *v* **1** = **repair**, darn, fix, patch, refit, renew, renovate, restore, retouch **2** = **heal**, convalesce, get better, recover, recuperate **3** = **improve**, ameliorate, amend, correct, emend, rectify, reform, revise ▷ *n* **4** = **repair**, darn, patch, stitch **on the mend** = **convalescent**, getting better, improving, recovering, recuperating

menial *adj* **1** = **unskilled**, boring, dull, humdrum, low-status, routine ▷ *n* **2** = **servant**, attendant, dogsbody (*inf*), drudge, flunky, lackey, skivvy (*chiefly Brit*), underling

mental *adj* **1** = **intellectual**, cerebral **3** *Inf* = **insane**, deranged, disturbed, mad, mentally ill, psychotic, unbalanced, unstable

mention *v* **1** = **refer to**, bring up, declare, disclose, divulge, intimate, point out, reveal, state, touch upon ▷ *n* **3** = **reference**, allusion, indication, observation, remark **4** = **acknowledgment**, citation, recognition, tribute

mentor *n* = **guide**, adviser, coach, counsellor, guru, instructor, teacher, tutor

menu *n* **1** = **bill of fare**, carte du jour, tariff (*chiefly Brit*)

mercantile *adj* = **commercial**, trading

mercenary *adj* **1** = **greedy**, acquisitive, avaricious, grasping, money-grubbing (*inf*), sordid, venal ▷ *n* **3** = **hireling**, soldier of fortune

merchant *n* = **tradesman**, broker, dealer, purveyor, retailer, salesman, seller, shopkeeper, supplier, trader, trafficker, vendor, wholesaler

mercy *n* **1** = **compassion**, clemency,

treatment of an offender or enemy who is in one's power. **2** merciful act. **merciful** *adj* **1** compassionate. **2** giving relief. **merciless** *adj*.

mere ❶ *adj* nothing more than, e.g. *mere chance*. **merely** *adv*.

merge ❶ *v* combine or blend. **merger** *n* combination of business firms into one.

meridian *n* imaginary circle of the earth passing through both poles.

meringue [mer-**rang**] *n* **1** baked mixture of egg whites and sugar. **2** small cake of this.

merit ❶ *n* **1** excellence or worth. ▷ *pl* **2** admirable qualities. ▷ *v* **-iting, -ited** **3** deserve. **meritorious** *adj* deserving praise. **meritocracy** [mer-it-**tok**-rass-ee] *n* rule by people of superior talent or intellect.

mermaid *n* imaginary sea creature with the upper part of a woman and the lower part of a fish.

merry ❶ *adj* **-rier, -riest 1** cheerful or jolly. **2** *informal* slightly drunk. **merrily** *adv* **merriment** *n* **merry-go-round** *n*

roundabout. **merrymaking** *n* noisy, cheerful celebrations or fun.

mesh ❶ *n* **1** network or net. **2** (open space between) strands forming a network. ▷ *v* **3** (of gear teeth) engage.

mesmerize ❶ *v* **1** hold spellbound. **2** *obs* hypnotize.

mess ❶ *n* **1** untidy or dirty confusion. **2** trouble or difficulty. **3** place where servicemen eat. **4** group of servicemen who regularly eat together. ▷ *v* **5** muddle or dirty. **6** (foll. by *about*) potter about. **7** (foll. by *with*) interfere with.

message ❶ *n* **1** communication sent. **2** meaning or moral. **messenger** *n* bearer of a message.

Messiah *n* **1** Jews' promised deliverer. **2** Christ. **Messianic** *adj*.

met *v* past of MEET¹.

metabolism [met-**tab**-oh-liz-zum] *n* chemical processes of a living body. **metabolic** *adj* **metabolize** *v* produce or be produced by metabolism.

metal *n* **1** chemical element, such as iron

m

forbearance, forgiveness, grace, kindness, leniency, pity **2 = blessing**, boon, godsend

mere *adj* **= simple**, bare, common, nothing more than, plain, pure, sheer

merge *v* **= combine**, amalgamate, blend, coalesce, converge, fuse, join, meet, mingle, mix, unite

merit *n* **1 = worth**, advantage, asset, excellence, goodness, integrity, quality, strong point, talent, value, virtue ▷ *v* **3 = deserve**, be entitled to, be worthy of, earn, have a right to, rate, warrant

merry *adj* **1 = cheerful**, blithe, carefree, convivial, festive, happy, jolly, joyous **2** *Inf* **= tipsy**, happy, mellow, squiffy (*Brit inf*), tiddly (*sl, chiefly Brit*)

mesh *n* **1 = net**, netting, network, tracery, web ▷ *v* **3 = engage**, combine, connect, coordinate, dovetail, interlock, knit

mesmerize *v* **1 = entrance**, captivate,

enthral, fascinate, grip, hold spellbound, hypnotize

mess *n* **1 = disorder**, chaos, clutter, confusion, disarray, disorganization, hotchpotch, jumble, litter, shambles, untidiness **2 = difficulty**, deep water, dilemma, fix (*inf*), hole (*inf*), jam (*inf*), muddle, pickle (*inf*), plight, predicament, tight spot ▷ *v* **5 = dirty**, clutter, disarrange, dishevel, muck up (*Brit sl*), muddle, pollute, scramble, muss (*US & Canad*) **6** (foll. by *about*) **= potter**, amuse oneself, dabble, fool (about or around), muck about (*inf*), play about or around, trifle **7** (foll. by *with*) **= interfere**, fiddle (*inf*), meddle, play, tamper, tinker

message *n* **1 = communication**, bulletin, communiqué, dispatch, email, letter, memorandum, note, SMS, text, text message, tidings, tweet, word **2 = point**, idea, import, meaning, moral, purport, theme

m

or copper, that is malleable and capable of conducting heat and electricity. **2 3 metallic** adj **metallurgy** n scientific study of the structure, properties, extraction, and refining of metals. **metallurgical** adj **metallurgist** n.

metamorphosis ❶ [met-a-**more**-foss-is] n, pl **-phoses** [-foss-eez] change of form or character. **metamorphic** adj (of rocks) changed in texture or structure by heat and pressure. **metamorphose** v transform.

metaphor ❶ n figure of speech in which a term is applied to something it does not literally denote in order to imply a resemblance, e.g. *he is a lion in battle.* **metaphorical** adj **metaphorically** adv.

mete ❶ v (usu. with *out*) deal out as punishment.

meteor n small fast-moving heavenly body, visible as a streak of incandescence if it enters the earth's atmosphere. **meteoric** [meet-ee-**or**-rik] adj **1** of a meteor. **2** brilliant and very rapid. **meteorite** n meteor that has fallen to earth.

meteorology n study of the earth's atmosphere, esp. for weather forecasting. **meteorological** adj **meteorologist** n.

meter n **1** instrument for measuring and recording something, such as the consumption of gas or electricity. ▷ v **2** measure by meter.

methamphetamine n variety of amphetamine used for its stimulant action.

methane n colourless inflammable gas.
method ❶ n **1** way or manner. **2** technique. **3** orderliness. **methodical** adj orderly. **methodically** adv **methodology** n particular method or procedure.

meths n informal methylated spirits.

methylated spirits n alcohol with methanol added, used as a solvent and for heating.

meticulous ❶ adj very careful about details. **meticulously** adv.

metre n **1** basic unit of length equal to about 1.094 yards (100 centimetres). **2** rhythm of poetry. **metric** adj of the decimal system of weights and measures based on the metre. **metrical** adj **1** of measurement. **2** of poetic metre. **metrication** n conversion to the metric system.

metronome n instrument which marks musical time by means of a ticking pendulum.

metropolis [mit-**trop**-oh-liss] n chief city of a country or region. **metropolitan** adj of a metropolis.

mettle ❶ n courage or spirit.

mew n **1** cry of a cat. ▷ v **2** utter this cry.

mews n yard or street orig. of stables, now often converted into houses.

mezzanine [**mez**-zan-een] n intermediate storey, esp. between the ground and first floor.

mezzo-soprano [**met**-so-] n voice or singer between a soprano and contralto (also **mezzo**).

mg milligram(s).

————————————— THESAURUS —————————————

metamorphosis n = **transformation**, alteration, change, conversion, mutation, transmutation

metaphor n = **figure of speech**, allegory, analogy, image, symbol, trope

mete v = **distribute**, administer, apportion, assign, deal, dispense, dole, portion

method n **1** = **manner**, approach, mode, modus operandi, procedure, process,
routine, style, system, way **2** = **technique 3** = **orderliness**, order, organization, pattern, planning, purpose, regularity, system

meticulous adj = **thorough**, exact, fastidious, fussy, painstaking, particular, precise, punctilious, scrupulous, strict

mettle n = **courage**, bravery, fortitude, gallantry, life, nerve, pluck, resolution, spirit, valour, vigour

MI Michigan.

miasma [mee-**azz**-ma] *n* unwholesome or foreboding atmosphere.

mica [**my**-ka] *n* glasslike mineral used as an electrical insulator.

microbe ❶ *n* minute organism, esp. one causing disease. **microbial** *adj*.

microchip *n* small wafer of silicon containing electronic circuits.

microcosm *n* **1** miniature representation of something.

microfiche [**my**-kroh-feesh] *n* microfilm in sheet form.

microfilm *n* miniaturized recording of books or documents on a roll of film.

microphone *n* instrument for amplifying or transmitting sounds.

microprocessor *n* integrated circuit acting as the central processing unit in a small computer.

microscope *n* instrument with lens(es) which produces a magnified image of a very small object. **microscopic** *adj* **1** too small to be seen except with a microscope. **2** very small. **3** of a microscope. **microscopically** *adv* **microscopy** *n* use of a microscope.

microwave *n* **1** electromagnetic wave with a wavelength of a few centimetres, used in radar and cooking. **2** microwave oven. ▷ *v* **3** cook in a microwave oven. **microwave oven** oven using microwaves to cook food quickly.

mid *adj* intermediate, middle. **midnight** *n* twelve o'clock at night. **midway** *adj*, *adv* halfway.

middle ❶ *adj* **1** equidistant from two extremes. **2** medium, intermediate. ▷ *n* **3** middle point or part. **middle age** period of life between youth and old age. **middle-aged** *adj* **Middle Ages** period from about 1000 AD to the 15th century. **middle class** social class of business and professional people. **middle-class** *adj* **Middle East** area around the eastern Mediterranean up to and including Iran. **middleman** *n* trader who buys from the producer and sells to the consumer. **middle-of-the-road** *adj* **1** politically moderate. **2** (of music) generally popular. **middleweight** *n* boxer weighing up to 160lb (professional) or 75kg (amateur).

midge *n* small mosquito-like insect.

midget ❶ *n* very small person or thing.

midriff *n* middle part of the body.

midst ❶ *n* **in the midst of 1** surrounded by. **2** at a point during.

midtown *n US & Canad* the centre of a town.

midwife *n* trained person who assists at childbirth. **midwifery** *n*.

mien [**mean**] *n lit* person's bearing, demeanour, or appearance.

might[1] *v* past tense of MAY.

might[2] ❶ *n* power or strength. **mighty** *adj* **1** powerful. **2** important. ▷ *adv* **3** *US & Aust informal* very. **mightily** *adv*.

migraine [**mee**-grain] *n* severe headache, often with nausea and visual disturbances.

migrate ❶ *v* **1** move from one place to settle in another. **2** (of animals) journey between different habitats at specific seasons. **migration** *n* **migrant** *n* **1** person or animal that moves from one place to

m

——— THESAURUS ———

microbe *n* = **microorganism**, bacillus, bacterium, bug (*inf*), germ, virus

middle *adj* **1** = **central**, halfway, intermediate, intervening, mean, median, mid **2** = **medium** ▷ *n* **3** = **centre**, focus, halfway point, heart, midpoint, midsection, midst

midget *n* = **dwarf**, pygmy *or* pigmy, shrimp (*inf*), Tom Thumb

midst *n* **in the midst of 1** = **among**, amidst, in the middle of, in the thick of, surrounded by **2** = **during**

might[2] *n* = **power**, energy, force, strength, vigour **with might and main** = **forcefully**, lustily, manfully, mightily, vigorously

migrate *v* **1** = **move**, emigrate, journey, roam, rove, travel, trek, voyage, wander

another. ▷ adj 2 moving from one place to another. **migratory** adj.

mike n informal microphone.

mild ❶ adj 1 not strongly flavoured. 2 gentle. 3 calm or temperate. **mildly** adv **mildness** n.

mildew n destructive fungus on plants or things exposed to damp.

mile n unit of length equal to 1760 yards or 1.609 kilometres. **mileage** n 1 distance travelled in miles. 2 miles travelled by a motor vehicle per gallon of petrol. 3 informal usefulness of something. **mileometer** n device that records the number of miles a vehicle has travelled. **milestone** n 1 significant event. 2 stone marker showing the distance to a certain place.

milieu ❶ [meal-**yer**] n, pl **milieux** [meal-**yerz**] environment or surroundings.

militant ❶ adj aggressive or vigorous in support of a cause. **militancy** n.

military ❶ adj 1 of or for soldiers, armies, or war. ▷ n 2 armed services. **militarism** n belief in the use of military force and methods. **militarized** adj.

militate ❶ v (usu. with against or for) have a strong influence or effect.

milk ❶ n 1 white fluid produced by female mammals to feed their young. 2 milk of cows, goats, etc., used by humans as food. 3 fluid in some plants. ▷ v 4 draw milk from. 5 exploit (a person or situation). **milky** adj **Milky Way**

luminous band of stars stretching across the night sky. **milkman** n man who delivers milk to people's houses. **milkshake** n frothy flavoured cold milk drink. **milksop** n feeble man. **milk teeth** first set of teeth in young children.

mill ❶ n 1 factory. 2 machine for grinding, processing, or rolling. ▷ v 3 grind, press, or process in or as if in a mill. 4 cut fine grooves across the edges of (coins). 5 move in a confused manner. **miller** n.

millennium n, pl -nia, -niums 1 period of a thousand years. 2 future period of peace and happiness.

- ● **SPELLING TIP**
- ● If you spell **millennium** with only one n,
- ● you are not alone: there are 338
- ● occurrences of this in the Bank of
- ● English. The correct spelling has two ls
- ● and two ns.

millet n a cereal grass.

milli- combining form denoting a thousandth part, e.g. millisecond.

milliner n maker or seller of women's hats. **millinery** n.

million n one thousand thousands. **millionth** adj, n **millionaire** n person who owns at least a million pounds, dollars, etc.

- ● **SPELLING TIP**
- ● Lots of people find it difficult to
- ● decide how many ls and ns to put in
- ● **millionaire**. They usually get the double
- ● l right, but remembering the single
- ● n is trickier.

──────────────── THESAURUS ────────────────

mild adj 1 = **bland**, smooth 2 = **gentle**, calm, docile, easy-going, equable, meek, peaceable, placid 3 = **temperate**, balmy, calm, moderate, tranquil, warm

milieu n = **surroundings**, background, element, environment, locale, location, scene, setting

militant adj = **aggressive**, active, assertive, combative, vigorous

military adj 1 = **warlike**, armed, martial, soldierly ▷ n 2 = **armed forces**, army,

forces, services

militate v militate against = **counteract**, be detrimental to, conflict with, counter, oppose, resist, tell against, weigh against

milk v 5 = **exploit**, extract, pump, take advantage of

mill n 1 = **factory**, foundry, plant, works 2 = **grinder**, crusher ▷ v 3 = **grind**, crush, grate, pound, powder 5 = **swarm**, crowd, throng

millipede n small animal with a jointed body and many pairs of legs.

mime ⊕ n **1** acting without the use of words. **2** performer who does this. ▷ v **3** act in mime.

mimic v **-icking, -icked 1** imitate (a person or manner), esp. for satirical effect. ▷ n **2** person or animal that is good at mimicking. **mimicry** n.

mimosa n shrub with fluffy yellow flowers and sensitive leaves.

minaret n tall slender tower of a mosque.

mince ⊕ v **1** cut or grind into very small pieces. **2** walk or speak in an affected manner. **3** soften or moderate (one's words). ▷ n **4** minced meat. **mincer** n machine for mincing meat. **mincing** adj affected in manner. **mincemeat** n sweet mixture of dried fruit and spices. **mince pie** pie containing mincemeat.

mind ⊕ n **1** thinking faculties. **2** memory or attention. **3** intention. **4** sanity. ▷ v **5** take offence at. **6** pay attention to. **7** take care of. **8** be cautious or careful about (something). **minded** adj

having an inclination as specified, e.g. *politically minded*. **minder** n informal aide or bodyguard. **mindful** adj **1** heedful. **2** keeping aware. **mindless** adj **1** stupid. **2** requiring no thought.

mine¹ pron belonging to me.

mine² ⊕ n **1** deep hole for digging out coal, ores, etc. **2** bomb placed under the ground or in water. **3** profitable source. ▷ v **4** dig for minerals. **5** dig (minerals) from a mine. **6** place explosive mines in or on. **miner** n **minefield** n area of land or water containing mines. **minesweeper** n ship for clearing away mines.

mineral n **1** naturally occurring inorganic substance, such as metal. ▷ adj **2** of, containing, or like minerals. **mineralogy** [min-er-**al**-a-jee] n study of minerals. **mineralogist** n **mineral water** water containing dissolved mineral salts or gases.

minestrone [min-ness-**strone**-ee] n soup containing vegetables and pasta.

mingle ⊕ v **1** mix or blend. **2** come into association (with).

mini n, adj **1** (something) small or miniature. **2** short (skirt).

m

mime v **3** = **act out**, gesture, represent, simulate

mimic v **1** = **imitate**, ape, caricature, do (inf), impersonate, parody, take off (inf) ▷ n **2** = **imitator**, caricaturist, copycat (inf), impersonator, impressionist

mince v **1** = **cut**, chop, crumble, grind, hash **3** = **tone down**, moderate, soften, spare, weaken

mind n **1** = **intelligence**, brain(s) (inf), grey matter (inf), intellect, reason, sense, understanding, wits **2** = **memory**, recollection, remembrance **3** = **intention**, desire, disposition, fancy, inclination, leaning, notion, urge, wish **4** = **sanity**, judgment, marbles (inf), mental balance, rationality, reason, senses, wits ▷ v **5** = **take offence**, be affronted, be bothered, care, disapprove, dislike, object,

resent **6** = **pay attention**, heed, listen to, mark, note, obey, observe, pay heed to, take heed **7** = **guard**, attend to, keep an eye on, look after, take care of, tend, watch **8** = **be careful**, be cautious, be on (one's) guard, be wary, take care, watch **make up one's mind** = **decide**, choose, determine, resolve

mine² n **1** = **pit**, colliery, deposit, excavation, shaft **3** = **source**, abundance, fund, hoard, reserve, stock, store, supply, treasury, wealth ▷ v **4, 5** = **dig up**, dig for, excavate, extract, hew, quarry, unearth

mingle v **1** = **mix**, blend, combine, intermingle, interweave, join, merge, unite **2** = **associate**, consort, fraternize, hang about or around, hobnob, rub shoulders (inf), socialize

miniature ❶ *n* **1** small portrait, model, or copy. ▷ *adj* **2** small-scale. **miniaturist** *n* **miniaturize** *v* make to a very small scale.

minidisc *n* small recordable compact disc.

minim *n Music* note half the length of a semibreve.

minimum ❶ *adj, n, pl* **-mums, -ma** least possible (amount or number). **minimal** *adj* minimum. **minimize** *v* **1** reduce to a minimum. **2** belittle.

minion ❶ *n* servile assistant.

minister ❶ *n* **1** head of a government department. **2** diplomatic representative. **3** clergyman. ▷ *v* **4** (foll. by *to*) attend to the needs of. **ministerial** *adj* **ministration** *n* giving of help. **ministry** *n, pl* **-tries** **1** profession or duties of a clergyman. **2** ministers collectively. **3** government department.

mink *n* **1** stoatlike animal. **2** its highly valued fur.

minnow *n* small freshwater fish.

minor ❶ *adj* **1** lesser. **2** *Music* (of a scale) having a semitone between the second and third notes. ▷ *n* **3** person regarded legally as a child. **4** *Music* minor scale. **minority** *n* **1** lesser number. **2** smaller party voting together. **3** group in a minority in any state.

minster *n* cathedral or large church.

minstrel ❶ *n* medieval singer or musician.

mint¹ *n* **1** plant with aromatic leaves used for seasoning and flavouring. **2** sweet flavoured with this.

mint² ❶ *n* **1** place where money is coined. ▷ *v* **2** make (coins).

minuet [min-new-**wet**] *n* **1** stately dance. **2** music for this.

minus *prep, adj* **1** indicating subtraction. ▷ *adj* **2** less than zero. ▷ *n* **3** sign (-) denoting subtraction or a number less than zero.

minuscule ❶ [**min**-niss-skyool] *adj* very small.

- **SPELLING TIP**
- The pronunciation of **minuscule** often
- influences the way people spell it. It's
- spelt *miniscule* 121 times in the Bank of
- English, but it should have only one *i*,
- and two *us*.

minute¹ ❶ [**min**-it] *n* **1** 60th part of an hour or degree. **2** moment. ▷ *pl* **3** record of the proceedings of a meeting. ▷ *v* **4** record in the minutes.

minute² ❶ [my-**newt**] *adj* **1** very small. **2** precise. **minutely** *adv* **minutiae** [my-**new**-shee-eye] *pl n* trifling or precise details.

minx ❶ *n* bold or flirtatious girl.

———————— THESAURUS ————————

miniature *adj* **2** = **small**, diminutive, little, minuscule, minute, scaled-down, tiny, toy

minimum *adj* = **least**, least possible, lowest, minimal, slightest, smallest ▷ *n* = **least**, lowest, nadir

minion *n* = **follower**, flunky, hanger-on, henchman, hireling, lackey, underling, yes man

minister *n* **3** = **clergyman**, cleric, parson, pastor, preacher, priest, rector, vicar ▷ *v* **4** = **attend to**, administer, cater to, pander to, serve, take care of, tend

minor *adj* **1** = **small**, inconsequential, insignificant, lesser, petty, slight, trivial, unimportant

minstrel *n* = **musician**, bard, singer,

songstress, troubadour

mint² *v* **2** = **make**, cast, coin, produce, punch, stamp, strike

minuscule *adj* = **tiny**, diminutive, infinitesimal, little, microscopic, miniature, minute

minute¹ *n* **2** = **moment**, flash, instant, jiffy (*inf*), second, tick (*Brit inf*), trice ▷ *pl* **3** = **record**, memorandum, notes, proceedings, transactions, transcript

minute² *adj* **1** = **small**, diminutive, infinitesimal, little, microscopic, miniature, minuscule, tiny **2** = **precise**, close, critical, detailed, exact, exhaustive, meticulous, painstaking, punctilious

minx *n* = **flirt**, coquette, hussy

miracle ❶ *n* 1 wonderful supernatural event. 2 marvel. **miraculous** *adj* **miraculously** *adv*.

mirage ❶ [mir-**rahzh**] *n* optical illusion, esp. one caused by hot air.

mire ❶ *n* 1 swampy ground. 2 mud.

mirror ❶ *n* 1 coated glass surface for reflecting images. ▷ *v* 2 reflect in or as if in a mirror.

mirth ❶ *n* laughter, merriment, or gaiety.

mis- *prefix* wrong(ly), bad(ly).

misadventure ❶ *n* unlucky chance.

misanthrope [**miz**-zan-thrope] *n* person who dislikes people in general. **misanthropic** [miz-zan-**throp**-ik] *adj* **misanthropy** [miz-**zan**-throp-ee] *n*.

misapprehension ❶ *n* misunderstanding.

misappropriate ❶ *v* take and use (money) dishonestly. **misappropriation** *n*.

miscellaneous ❶ [miss-sell-**lane**-ee-uss] *adj* mixed or assorted. **miscellany** [miss-**sell**-a-nee] *n* mixed assortment.

mischief ❶ *n* 1 annoying but not malicious behaviour. 2 inclination to tease. 3 harm. **mischievous** *adj* 1 full of mischief. 2 intended to cause harm.

misconception ❶ *n* wrong idea or belief.

misconduct ❶ *n* immoral or unethical behaviour.

miscreant ❶ [**miss**-kree-ant] *n* wrongdoer.

misdemeanour ❶ *n* minor wrongdoing.

miser ❶ *n* person who hoards money and hates spending it. **miserly** *adj*.

miserable ❶ *adj* 1 very unhappy, wretched. 2 causing misery. 3 squalid. 4 mean. **misery** *n*, *pl* **-eries** 1 great unhappiness. 2 *informal* complaining person.

— THESAURUS —

miracle *n* 2 = **wonder**, marvel, phenomenon, prodigy

mirage *n* = **illusion**, hallucination, optical illusion

mire *n* 1 = **swamp**, bog, marsh, morass, quagmire, muskeg (*Canad*) 2 = **mud**, dirt, muck, ooze, slime

mirror *n* 1 = **looking-glass**, glass, reflector ▷ *v* 2 = **reflect**, copy, echo, emulate, follow

mirth *n* = **merriment**, amusement, cheerfulness, fun, gaiety, glee, hilarity, jollity, joviality, laughter, revelry

misadventure *n* = **misfortune**, accident, bad luck, calamity, catastrophe, debacle, disaster, mishap, reverse, setback

misapprehension *n* = **misunderstanding**, delusion, error, fallacy, misconception, misinterpretation, mistake

misappropriate *v* = **steal**, embezzle, misspend, misuse, peculate, pocket

miscellaneous *adj* = **mixed**, assorted, diverse, jumbled, motley, sundry, varied, various

mischief *n* 1 = **misbehaviour**, impishness, monkey business (*inf*), naughtiness, shenanigans (*inf*), trouble, waywardness 3 = **harm**, damage, evil, hurt, injury, misfortune, trouble

misconception *n* = **delusion**, error, fallacy, misapprehension, misunderstanding

misconduct *n* = **immorality**, impropriety, malpractice, mismanagement, wrongdoing

miscreant *n* = **wrongdoer**, blackguard, criminal, rascal, reprobate, rogue, scoundrel, sinner, vagabond, villain

misdemeanour *n* = **offence**, fault, infringement, misdeed, peccadillo, transgression

miser *n* = **hoarder**, cheapskate (*inf*), niggard, penny-pincher (*inf*), Scrooge, skinflint

miserable *adj* 1 = **unhappy**, dejected, depressed, despondent, disconsolate, forlorn, gloomy, sorrowful, woebegone, wretched 2 = **despicable**, deplorable, lamentable, shameful, sordid, sorry 3 = **squalid**, wretched

m

misfire ❶ v **1** (of a firearm or engine) fail to fire correctly. **2** (of a plan) fail to turn out as intended.

misfit ❶ n person not suited to his or her social environment.

misfortune ❶ n (piece of) bad luck.

misgiving ❶ n feeling of fear or doubt.

misguided ❶ adj mistaken or unwise.

mishap ❶ n minor accident.

misjudge v judge wrongly or unfairly. **misjudgment**, **misjudgement** n.

mislay ❶ v lose (something) temporarily.

mislead ❶ v give false or confusing information to. **misleading** adj.

mismanage v organize or run (something) badly. **mismanagement** n.

misnomer [miss-**no**-mer] n **1** incorrect or unsuitable name. **2** use of this.

misogyny [miss-**oj**-in-ee] n hatred of women. **misogynist** n.

misprint ❶ n printing error.

miss ❶ v **1** fail to notice, hear, hit, reach, find, or catch. **2** not be in time for. **3** notice or regret the absence of. **4** avoid.

5 (of an engine) misfire. ▷ n **6** fact or instance of missing. **missing** adj lost or absent.

Miss n title of a girl or unmarried woman.

missal n book containing the prayers and rites of the Mass.

missile ❶ n object or weapon thrown, shot, or launched at a target.

mission ❶ n **1** specific task or duty. **2** group of people sent on a mission. **3** building in which missionaries work. **4** S Afr long and difficult process. **missionary** n, pl **-aries** person sent abroad to do religious and social work.

missive ❶ n letter.

mist ❶ n **1** thin fog. **2** fine spray of liquid. **misty** adj full of mist. **2** dim or obscure.

mistake ❶ n **1** error or blunder. ▷ v **-taking, -took, -taken 2** misunderstand. **3** confuse (a person or thing) with another.

mistletoe n evergreen plant with white berries growing as a parasite on trees.

———————————————————————— THESAURUS ————

misfire v = **fail**, fall through, go pear-shaped (inf), go wrong, miscarry

misfit n = **nonconformist**, eccentric, fish out of water (inf), oddball (inf), square peg (in a round hole) (inf)

misfortune n = **bad luck**, adversity, hard luck, ill luck, infelicity

misgiving n = **unease**, anxiety, apprehension, distrust, doubt, qualm, reservation, suspicion, trepidation, uncertainty, worry

misguided adj = **unwise**, deluded, erroneous, ill-advised, imprudent, injudicious, misplaced, mistaken, unwarranted

mishap n = **accident**, calamity, misadventure, mischance, misfortune

misjudge v = **miscalculate**, overestimate, overrate, underestimate, underrate

mislay v = **lose**, lose track of, misplace

mislead v = **deceive**, delude, fool, hoodwink, misdirect, misguide,

misinform, take in (inf)

misprint n = **mistake**, corrigendum, erratum, literal, typo (inf)

miss v **1** = **omit**, leave out, let go, overlook, pass over, skip **3** = **long for**, pine for, yearn for **4** = **avoid**, escape, evade ▷ n **6** = **mistake**, blunder, error, failure, omission, oversight

missile n = **rocket**, projectile, weapon

mission n **1** = **task**, assignment, commission, duty, errand, job, quest, undertaking

missive n = **letter**, communication, dispatch, epistle, memorandum, message, note, report

mist n **1** = **fog**, cloud, film, haze, smog, spray, steam, vapour

mistake n **1** = **error**, blunder, erratum, fault, faux pas, gaffe, howler (inf), miscalculation, oversight, slip ▷ v **2** = **misunderstand**, misapprehend, misconstrue, misinterpret, misjudge,

mistress ❶ n 1 woman who has a continuing sexual relationship with a married man. 2 woman in control of people or animals. 3 female teacher.

mistrust ❶ v 1 have doubts or suspicions about. ▷ n 2 lack of trust. **mistrustful** adj.

misunderstand ❶ v fail to understand properly. **misunderstanding** n.

misuse ❶ n 1 incorrect, improper, or careless use. ▷ v 2 use wrongly. 3 treat badly.

mite n 1 very small spider-like animal. 2 very small thing or amount.

mitigate ❶ v make less severe. **mitigation** n.

mitre [**my**-ter] n 1 bishop's pointed headdress. 2 joint between two pieces of wood bevelled to meet at right angles. ▷ v 3 join with a mitre joint.

mitt n 1 short for MITTEN. 2 baseball catcher's glove.

mitten n glove with one section for the thumb and one for the four fingers together.

mix ❶ v 1 combine or blend into one mass.

2 form (something) by mixing. 3 be sociable. ▷ n 4 mixture. **mixed** adj **mix up** v 1 confuse. 2 make into a mixture. **mixed up** adj **mix-up** n **mixer** n **mixture** n 1 something mixed. 2 combination.

mm millimetre(s).

mnemonic [nim-**on**-ik] n, adj (something, such as a rhyme) intended to help the memory.

moan ❶ n 1 low cry of pain. 2 informal grumble. ▷ v 3 make or utter with a moan. 4 informal grumble.

moat n deep wide ditch, esp. round a castle.

mob ❶ n 1 disorderly crowd. 2 slang gang. ▷ v **mobbing, mobbed** 3 surround in a mob to acclaim or attack.

mobile ❶ adj 1 able to move. ▷ n 2 same as MOBILE PHONE. 3 hanging structure designed to move in air currents. **mobile phone** cordless phone powered by batteries. **mobility** n.

mobilize ❶ v 1 (of the armed services) prepare for active service. 2 organize for a purpose. **mobilization** n.

misread 3 = **confuse with**, mix up with, take for

mistress n 1 = **lover**, concubine, girlfriend, kept woman, paramour

mistrust v 1 = **doubt**, be wary of, distrust, fear, suspect ▷ n 2 = **suspicion**, distrust, doubt, misgiving, scepticism, uncertainty, wariness

misunderstand v = **misinterpret**, be at cross-purposes, get the wrong end of the stick, misapprehend, misconstrue, misjudge, misread, mistake

misuse n 1 = **waste**, abuse, desecration, misapplication, squandering ▷ v 3 = **waste**, abuse, desecrate, misapply, prostitute, squander

mitigate v = **ease**, extenuate, lessen, lighten, moderate, soften, subdue, temper

mix v 1, 2 = **combine**, blend, cross, fuse, intermingle, interweave, join, jumble, merge, mingle 3 = **socialize**, associate,

consort, fraternize, hang out (inf), hobnob, mingle ▷ n 4 = **mixture**, alloy, amalgam, assortment, blend, combination, compound, fusion, medley

moan n 1 = **groan**, lament, sigh, sob, wail, whine 2 Inf = **grumble**, complaint, gripe (inf), grouch (inf), grouse, protest, whine ▷ v 3 = **groan**, lament, sigh, sob, whine 4 Inf = **grumble**, bleat, carp, complain, groan, grouse, whine, whinge (inf)

mob n 1 = **crowd**, drove, flock, horde, host, mass, multitude, pack, swarm, throng 2 Sl = **gang**, crew (inf), group, lot, set ▷ v 3 = **surround**, crowd around, jostle, set upon, swarm around

mobile adj 1 = **movable**, itinerant, moving, peripatetic, portable, travelling, wandering

mobilize v 1 = **call to arms**, activate, call up, marshal 2 = **prepare**, get or make ready, organize, rally, ready

moccasin *n* soft leather shoe.

● **SPELLING TIP**
● One **moccasin** has a double *c*, but only
● one *s*. The plural, **moccasins**, has two
● ss, but they are not together.

mocha [**mock**-a] *n* 1 kind of strong dark coffee. 2 flavouring made from coffee and chocolate.

mock ❶ *v* 1 make fun of. 2 mimic. ▷ *adj* 3 sham or imitation. **mocks** *pl n informal* (in England and Wales) practice exams taken before public exams. **mockery** *n* 1 derision. 2 inadequate or worthless attempt. **mockingbird** *n* N American bird which imitates other birds' songs. **mock-up** *n* full-scale model for test or study.

mode ❶ *n* 1 method or manner. 2 current fashion.

model ❶ *n* 1 (miniature) representation. 2 pattern. 3 person or thing worthy of imitation. 4 person who poses for an artist or photographer. 5 person who wears clothes to display them to prospective buyers. ▷ *v* -**elling**, -**elled** 6 make a model of. 7 mould. 8 display (clothing) as a model.

modem [**mode**-em] *n* device for connecting two computers by a telephone line.

moderate ❶ *adj* 1 not extreme. 2 self-restrained. 3 average. ▷ *n* 4 person of moderate views. ▷ *v* 5 make or become less violent or extreme. **moderately** *adv* **moderation** *n* **moderator** *n* 1 (Presbyterian Church) minister appointed to preside over a Church court, general assembly, etc. 2 person who presides over a public or legislative assembly.

modern ❶ *adj* 1 of present or recent times. 2 up-to-date. **modernity** *n* **modernism** *n* (support of) modern tendencies, thoughts, or styles. **modernist** *adj*, *n* **modernize** *v* bring up to date. **modernization** *n*.

modest ❶ *adj* 1 not vain or boastful. 2 not excessive. 3 not showy. 4 shy. **modestly** *adv* **modesty** *n*.

modicum ❶ *n* small quantity.

modify ❶ *v* -**fying**, -**fied** 1 change slightly. 2 tone down. 3 (of a word) qualify (another word). **modifier** *n* word that qualifies the sense of another. **modification** *n*.

━━━━━━━━━━━━━━━━━ THESAURUS ━━━━━━━━━━━

mock *v* 1 = **laugh at**, deride, jeer, make fun of, poke fun at, ridicule, scoff, scorn, sneer, taunt, tease 2 = **mimic**, ape, caricature, imitate, lampoon, parody, satirize, send up (*Brit inf*) ▷ *adj* 3 = **imitation**, artificial, dummy, fake, false, feigned, phoney *or* phony (*inf*), pretended, sham, spurious

mode *n* 1 = **method**, form, manner, procedure, process, style, system, technique, way 2 = **fashion**, craze, look, rage, style, trend, vogue

model *n* 1 = **representation**, copy, dummy, facsimile, image, imitation, miniature, mock-up, replica 2 = **pattern**, example, original, paradigm, prototype, standard 3 = **ideal**, archetype, paragon 4 = **sitter**, poser, subject ▷ *v* 7 = **shape**, carve, design, fashion, form, mould, sculpt 8 = **show off**, display, sport (*inf*), wear

moderate *adj* 1 = **middle-of-the-road**, limited 2 = **restrained**, controlled,

gentle, mild, modest, reasonable, steady 3 = **average**, fair, indifferent, mediocre, middling, ordinary, passable, so-so (*inf*), unexceptional ▷ *v* 5 = **lessen**, control, curb, ease, modulate, regulate, restrain, soften, subdue, temper, tone down

modern *adj* 1 = **current**, contemporary, present-day, recent 2 = **up-to-date**, fresh, new, newfangled, novel

modest *adj* 1, 4 = **shy**, bashful, coy, demure, diffident, reserved, reticent, retiring, self-effacing 2 = **moderate**, fair, limited, middling, small 3 = **unpretentious**, ordinary, unexceptional

modicum *n* = **little**, bit, crumb, drop, fragment, scrap, shred, touch

modify *v* 1 = **change**, adapt, adjust, alter, convert, reform, remodel, revise, rework 2 = **tone down**, ease, lessen, lower, moderate, qualify, restrain, soften, temper

modulate ❶ v **1** vary in tone.
2 adjust. **3** change the key of (music).
modulation n.

module n self-contained unit, section, or
component with a specific function.

mogul ❶ [**moh**-gl] n important or powerful
person.

mohair n **1** fine hair of the Angora goat.
2 yarn or fabric made from this.

moist ❶ adj slightly wet. **moisten** v
make or become moist. **moisture** n liquid
diffused as vapour or condensed in
drops. **moisturize** v add moisture to (the
skin etc.).

molar n large back tooth used for
grinding.

molasses n dark syrup, a by-product of
sugar refining.

mole[1] n small dark raised spot on the
skin.

mole[2] n **1** small burrowing mammal.
2 informal spy who has infiltrated
and become a trusted member of an
organization. **molehill** n small mound of
earth thrown up by a burrowing mole.
make a mountain out of a molehill
exaggerate an unimportant matter out of
all proportion.

molecule ❶ [**mol**-lik-kyool] n **1** simplest
freely existing chemical unit, composed
of two or more atoms. **2** very small

particle. **molecular** [mol-**lek**-yew-lar]
adj.

molest ❶ v **1** interfere with sexually.
2 annoy or injure. **molestation** n.

moll n slang gangster's female
accomplice.

mollify ❶ v **-fying, -fied** pacify or soothe.
mollification n.

mollusc n soft-bodied, usu. hard-shelled,
animal, such as a snail or oyster.

mollycoddle ❶ v pamper.

molten adj liquefied or melted.

mom n Chiefly US & Canada an informal word
for MOTHER.

moment ❶ n **1** short space of time.
2 (present) point in time. **momentary** adj
lasting only a moment. **momentarily** adv.

momentous ❶ [moh-**men**-tuss] adj of
great significance.

momentum ❶ n **1** impetus of a moving
body. **2** product of a body's mass and
velocity.

monarch ❶ n sovereign ruler of a state.
monarchical adj **monarchist** n supporter
of monarchy. **monarchy** n government by
or a state ruled by a sovereign.

monastery ❶ n, pl **-teries** residence of a
community of monks. **monastic** adj **1** of
monks, nuns, or monasteries. **2** simple
and austere. **monasticism** n.

Monday n second day of the week.

——— THESAURUS ———

modulate v **1** = **vary 2** = **adjust**, attune,
balance, regulate **3** = **tune**

mogul n = **tycoon**, baron, big hitter (inf),
big noise (inf), big shot (inf), heavy hitter
(inf), magnate, V.I.P.

moist adj = **damp**, clammy, dewy, humid,
soggy, wet

molecule n **2** = **particle**, jot, speck

molest v **1** = **abuse**, ill-treat, interfere
with, maltreat **2** = **annoy**, attack, badger,
beset, bother, disturb, harass, harm, hurt,
persecute, pester, plague, torment, worry

mollify v = **pacify**, appease, calm,
conciliate, placate, quiet, soothe, sweeten

mollycoddle v = **pamper**, baby, cosset,

indulge, spoil

moment n **1** = **instant**, flash, jiffy (inf),
second, split second, trice, twinkling
2 = **time**, juncture, point, stage

momentous adj = **significant**, critical,
crucial, fateful, historic, important,
pivotal, vital, weighty

momentum n **1, 2** = **impetus**, drive,
energy, force, power, propulsion, push,
strength, thrust

monarch n = **ruler**, emperor or empress,
king, potentate, prince or princess, queen,
sovereign

monastery n = **abbey**, cloister, convent,
friary, nunnery, priory

money ● n medium of exchange, coins or banknotes. **moneyed, monied** adj rich.

mongoose n, pl **-gooses** stoatlike mammal of Asia and Africa that kills snakes.

mongrel ● n 1 animal, esp. a dog, of mixed breed. 2 something arising from a variety of sources. ▷ adj 3 of mixed breed or origin.

monitor ● n 1 person or device that checks, controls, warns, or keeps a record of something. 2 pupil assisting a teacher with duties. 3 television set used in a studio to check what is being transmitted. ▷ v 4 watch and check on.

monk ● n member of an all-male religious community bound by vows. **monkish** adj.

monkey ● n 1 long-tailed primate. 2 mischievous child. ▷ v 3 (usu. foll. by *about* or *around*) meddle or fool. **monkey nut** peanut. **monkey puzzle** coniferous tree with sharp stiff leaves. **monkey wrench** wrench with adjustable jaws.

mono- combining form single, e.g. monosyllable.

monochrome adj 1 Photog black-and-white. 2 in only one colour.

monocle n eyeglass for one eye only.

monogamy n custom of being married to one person at a time.

monogram n design of combined letters, esp. a person's initials.

monograph n book or paper on a single subject.

monolith n large upright block of stone. **monolithic** adj.

monologue ● n 1 long speech by one person. 2 dramatic piece for one performer.

monopoly n 1 pl **-lies** exclusive possession of or right to do something. 2 (M-) ® board game for four to six players who deal in 'property' as they move around the board. **monopolize** v have or take exclusive possession of.

monotone n unvaried pitch in speech or sound. **monotonous** adj tedious due to lack of variety. **monotony** n.

monsoon n 1 seasonal wind of SE Asia. 2 rainy season accompanying this.

monster ● n 1 imaginary, usu. frightening, beast. 2 huge person, animal, or thing. 3 very wicked person. ▷ adj 4 huge. **monstrosity** n large ugly thing. **monstrous** adj 1 unnatural or ugly. 2 outrageous or shocking. 3 huge.

month n 1 one of the twelve divisions of the calendar year. 2 period of four weeks. **monthly** adj 1 happening or payable once a month. ▷ adv 2 once a month. ▷ n 3 monthly magazine.

monument ● n something, esp. a building or statue, that commemorates something. **monumental** adj 1 large, impressive, or lasting. 2 of or being a monument. 3 informal extreme. **monumentally** adv.

---

money n = **cash**, capital, coin, currency, hard cash, legal tender, lolly (Aust & NZ sl), readies (inf), riches, silver, wealth

mongrel n 1 = **crossbreed**, cross, half-breed 2 = **hybrid** ▷ adj 3 = **hybrid**, crossbred

monitor n 1 = **watchdog**, guide, invigilator, supervisor 2 = **prefect** (Brit) ▷ v 4 = **check**, follow, keep an eye on, keep tabs on, keep track of, observe, survey, watch

monk n = **friar**, brother (loosely)

monkey n 1 = **simian**, primate 2 = **rascal**, devil, imp, rogue, scamp ▷ v 3 (usu. foll.

by *about* or *around*) = **fool**, meddle, mess, play, tinker

monologue n 1 = **speech**, harangue, lecture, sermon 2 = **soliloquy**

monster n 1 = **freak**, monstrosity, mutant 2 = **giant**, colossus, mammoth, titan 3 = **brute**, beast, demon, devil, fiend, villain ▷ adj 4 = **huge**, colossal, enormous, gigantic, immense, mammoth, massive, stupendous, tremendous

monument n 1 = **memorial**, cairn, cenotaph, commemoration, gravestone, headstone, marker, mausoleum, shrine, tombstone

m

mooch v slang loiter about aimlessly.

mood¹ ⓘ n temporary (gloomy) state of mind. **moody** adj **1** sullen or gloomy. **2** changeable in mood. **moodily** adv.

mood² n Grammar form of a verb indicating whether it expresses a fact, wish, supposition, or command.

moon ⓘ n **1** natural satellite of the earth. **2** natural satellite of any planet. ▷ v **3** (foll. by about or around) be idle in a listless or dreamy way. **moonlight** n **1** light from the moon. ▷ v **2** informal work at a secondary job, esp. illegally. **moonshine** n **1** illicitly distilled whisky. **2** nonsense. **moonstone** n translucent semiprecious stone. **moonstruck** adj slightly mad or odd.

moor¹ ⓘ n tract of open uncultivated ground covered with grass and heather. **moorhen** n small black water bird.

moor² ⓘ v secure (a ship) with ropes etc. **mooring** n **1** place for mooring a ship. ▷ pl **2** ropes etc. used in mooring a ship.

moose n large N American deer.

moot ⓘ adj **1** debatable, e.g. a moot point. ▷ v **2** bring up for discussion.

mop ⓘ n **1** long stick with twists of cotton or a sponge on the end, used for cleaning. **2** thick mass of hair. ▷ v **mopping**, **mopped 3** clean or soak up with or as if with a mop.

mope ⓘ v be gloomy and apathetic.

moped n light motorized cycle.

mopoke n small spotted owl of Australia and New Zealand.

moral ⓘ adj **1** concerned with right and wrong conduct. **2** based on a sense of right and wrong. **3** (of support or a victory) psychological rather than practical. ▷ n **4** lesson to be obtained from a story or event. ▷ pl **5** principles of behaviour with respect to right and wrong. **morally** adv **moralist** n person with a strong sense of right and wrong. **morality** n **1** good moral conduct. **2** moral goodness or badness. **moralize** v make moral pronouncements.

morale ⓘ [mor-**rahl**] n degree of confidence or hope of a person or group.

morass ⓘ n **1** marsh. **2** mess.

moratorium ⓘ n, pl **-ria**, **-riums** legally authorized ban or delay.

morbid ⓘ adj **1** unduly interested in death or unpleasant events. **2** gruesome.

mordant ⓘ adj **1** sarcastic or scathing. ▷ n **2** substance used to fix dyes.

m

THESAURUS

---

mood¹ n = **state of mind**, disposition, frame of mind, humour, spirit, temper

moon n **1,2** = **satellite** ▷ v **3** (foll. by about or around) = **idle**, daydream, languish, mope, waste time

moor¹ n = **moorland**, fell (Brit), heath

moor² v = **tie up**, anchor, berth, dock, lash, make fast, secure

moot adj **1** = **debatable**, arguable, contestable, controversial, disputable, doubtful, undecided, unresolved, unsettled ▷ v **2** = **bring up**, broach, propose, put forward, suggest

mop n **1** = **squeegee**, sponge, swab **2** = **mane**, shock, tangle, thatch

mop v **3** = **clean up**, soak up, sponge, swab, wash, wipe

mope v = **brood**, fret, languish, moon, pine, pout, sulk

moral adj **1, 2** = **good**, decent, ethical, high-minded, honourable, just, noble, principled, right, virtuous n **4** = **lesson**, meaning, message, point, significance

morale n = **confidence**, esprit de corps, heart, self-esteem, spirit

morass n **1** = **marsh**, bog, fen, quagmire, slough, swamp, muskeg (Canad) **2** = **mess**, confusion, mix-up, muddle, tangle

moratorium n = **postponement**, freeze, halt, standstill, suspension

morbid adj **1** = **unwholesome**, ghoulish, gloomy, melancholy, sick, sombre, unhealthy **2** = **gruesome**, dreadful, ghastly, grisly, hideous, horrid, macabre

mordant adj **1** = **sarcastic**, biting, caustic, cutting, incisive, pungent, scathing, stinging, trenchant

more ❶ *adj* **1** greater in amount or degree. **2** comparative of MUCH or MANY **3** additional or further. ▷ *adv* **4** to a greater extent. **5** in addition. ▷ *pron* **6** greater or additional amount or number. **moreover** *adv* in addition to what has already been said.

mores [**more**-rayz] *pl n* customs and conventions embodying the fundamental values of a community.

Moreton Bay bug *n* Australian flattish edible shellfish.

morgue ❶ *n* mortuary.

moribund ❶ *adj* without force or vitality.

morning ❶ *n* part of the day before noon.

moron ❶ *n* **1** *informal* foolish or stupid person. **2** (formerly) person with a low intelligence quotient. **moronic** *adj*.

morose ❶ [mor-**rohss**] *adj* sullen or moody.

morphine, morphia *n* drug extracted from opium, used as an anaesthetic and sedative.

morrow *n* *poetic* next day.

Morse *n* former system of signalling in which letters of the alphabet are represented by combinations of short and long signals.

morsel ❶ *n* small piece, esp. of food.

mortal ❶ *adj* **1** subject to death. **2** causing death. ▷ *n* **3** human being. **mortally**

adv **mortality** *n* **1** state of being mortal. **2** great loss of life. **3** death rate. **mortal sin** *RC Church* sin meriting damnation.

mortar *n* **1** small cannon with a short range. **2** mixture of lime, sand, and water for holding bricks and stones together. **3** bowl in which substances are pounded. **mortarboard** *n* square academic cap.

mortgage *n* **1** conditional pledging of property, esp. a house, as security for the repayment of a loan. **2** the loan itself. ▷ *v* **3** pledge (property) as security thus. **mortgagee** *n* creditor in a mortgage. **mortgagor** *n* debtor in a mortgage.

mortify ❶ *v* -**fying, -fied 1** humiliate. **2** subdue by self-denial. **3** (of flesh) become gangrenous. **mortification** *n*.

mortuary ❶ *n*, *pl* -**aries** building where corpses are kept before burial or cremation.

mosaic [mow-**zay**-ik] *n* design or decoration using small pieces of coloured stone or glass.

mosque *n* Muslim temple.

mosquito *n*, *pl* -**toes, -tos** blood-sucking flying insect.

moss *n* small flowerless plant growing in masses on moist surfaces. **mossy** *adj*.

most *n* **1** greatest number or degree. ▷ *adj* **2** greatest in number or degree.

————————————————————————— THESAURUS —————————————————————————

more *adj* **1 = extra**, added, additional, further, new, new-found, other, supplementary ▷ *adv* **4 = to a greater extent**, better, further, longer

morgue *n* **= mortuary**

moribund *adj* **= declining**, on its last legs, stagnant, waning, weak

morning *n* **= dawn**, a.m., break of day, daybreak, forenoon, morn (*poet*), sunrise

moron *n* **1** *Inf* **= fool**, blockhead, cretin, dunce, dunderhead, halfwit, idiot, imbecile, oaf

morose *adj* **= sullen**, depressed, dour, gloomy, glum, ill-tempered, moody, sour, sulky, surly, taciturn

morsel *n* **= piece**, bit, bite, crumb,

mouthful, part, scrap, *soupçon*, taste, titbit

mortal *adj* **1 = human**, ephemeral, impermanent, passing, temporal, transient, worldly **2 = fatal**, deadly, death-dealing, destructive, killing, lethal, murderous, terminal ▷ *n* **3 = human being**, being, earthling, human, individual, man, person, woman

mortify *v* **1 = humiliate**, chagrin, chasten, crush, deflate, embarrass, humble, shame **2 = discipline**, abase, chasten, control, deny, subdue **3** *Of flesh* **= putrefy**, cark (*Aust & NZ sl*), deaden, die, fester

mortuary *n* **= morgue**, funeral parlour

3 superlative of MUCH or MANY. ▷ *adv* **4** in the greatest degree. **mostly** *adv* for the most part, generally.

motel *n* roadside hotel for motorists.

moth *n* nocturnal insect like a butterfly. **mothball** *n* **1** small ball of camphor or naphthalene used to repel moths from stored clothes. ▷ *v* **2** store (something operational) for future use. **3** postpone (a project etc.). **moth-eaten** *adj* **1** decayed or scruffy. **2** eaten or damaged by moth larvae.

mother ❶ *n* **1** female parent. **2** head of a female religious community. ▷ *adj* **3** native or inborn, e.g. *mother wit*. ▷ *v* **4** look after as a mother. **motherhood** *n* **motherly** *adj* **mother-in-law** *n* mother of one's husband or wife. **mother of pearl** iridescent lining of certain shells. **mother tongue** one's native language.

motif ❶ [moh-**teef**] *n* (recurring) theme or design.

motion ❶ *n* **1** process, action, or way of moving. **2** proposal in a meeting. **3** evacuation of the bowels. ▷ *v* **4** direct (someone) by gesture. **motionless** *adj* not moving. **motion picture** cinema film.

motive ❶ *n* **1** reason for a course of action. ▷ *adj* **2** causing motion. **motivate** *v* give incentive to. **motivation** *n*.

motley ❶ *adj* **1** miscellaneous. **2** multicoloured.

motocross *n* motorcycle race over a rough course.

motor *n* **1** engine, esp. of a vehicle. **2** machine that converts electrical energy into mechanical energy. **3** car. ▷ *v* **4** travel by car. **motorist** *n* driver of a car. **motorized** *adj* equipped with a motor or motor transport. **motorbike** *n* **motorcycle** *n* **motorcyclist** *n* **motorway** *n* main road for fast-moving traffic.

mottled ❶ *adj* marked with blotches.

motto ❶ *n*, *pl* **-toes**, **-tos** **1** saying expressing an ideal or rule of conduct. **2** verse or maxim in a paper cracker.

mould¹ ❶ *n* **1** hollow container in which metal etc. is cast. **2** shape, form, or pattern. **3** nature or character. ▷ *v* **4** shape. **5** influence or direct. **moulding** *n* moulded ornamental edging.

mould² ❶ *n* fungal growth caused by dampness. **mouldy** *adj* **1** stale or musty. **2** dull or boring.

mould³ ❶ *n* loose soil. **moulder** *v* decay into dust.

m

---

mother *n* **1** = **parent**, dam, ma (*inf*), mater, mum (*Brit inf*), mummy (*Brit inf*), mom (*US & Canad*) ▷ *adj* **3** = **native**, inborn, innate, natural ▷ *v* **4** = **nurture**, care for, cherish, nurse, protect, raise, rear, tend

motif *n* **a** = **theme**, concept, idea, leitmotif, subject **b** = **design**, decoration, ornament, shape

motion *n* **1** = **movement**, flow, locomotion, mobility, move, progress, travel **2** = **proposal**, proposition, recommendation, submission, suggestion ▷ *v* **4** = **gesture**, beckon, direct, gesticulate, nod, signal, wave

motive *n* **1** = **reason**, ground(s), incentive, inducement, inspiration, object, purpose, rationale, stimulus

motley *adj* **1** = **miscellaneous**, assorted,

disparate, heterogeneous, mixed, varied **2** = **multicoloured**, chequered, variegated

mottled *adj* = **blotchy**, dappled, flecked, piebald, speckled, spotted, stippled, streaked

motto *n* **1** = **saying**, adage, dictum, maxim, precept, proverb, rule, slogan, tag-line, watchword

mould¹ *n* **1** = **cast**, pattern, shape **2** = **design**, build, construction, fashion, form, format, kind, pattern, shape, style **3** = **nature**, calibre, character, kind, quality, sort, stamp, type ▷ *v* **4** = **shape**, construct, create, fashion, forge, form, make, model, sculpt, work **5** = **influence**, affect, control, direct, form, make, shape

mould² *n* = **fungus**, blight, mildew

mould³ *n* = **soil**, dirt, earth, humus, loam

moult v **1** shed feathers, hair, or skin to make way for new growth. ▷ n **2** process of moulting.

mound ❶ n **1** heap, esp. of earth or stones. **2** small hill.

mount ❶ v **1** climb or ascend. **2** get up on (a horse etc.). **3** increase or accumulate. **4** fix on a support or backing. **5** organize, e.g. *mount a campaign*. ▷ n **6** backing or support on which something is fixed. **7** horse for riding. **8** hill.

mountain ❶ n **1** hill of great size. **2** large heap. **mountainous** adj **1** full of mountains. **2** huge. **mountaineer** n person who climbs mountains. **mountaineering** n **mountain bike** bicycle with straight handlebars and heavy-duty tyres, for cycling over rough terrain.

mountebank n charlatan or fake.

mourn ❶ v feel or express sorrow for (a dead person or lost thing). **mourner** n **mournful** adj sad or dismal. **mournfully** adv **mourning** n **1** grieving. **2** conventional symbols of grief for death, such as the wearing of black.

mouse n, pl **mice 1** small long-tailed rodent. **2** timid person. **3** Computers hand-held device for moving the cursor without keying. **mousy** adj **1** like a mouse, esp. in hair colour. **2** meek and shy.

mousse n **1** dish of flavoured cream whipped and set.

moustache n hair on the upper lip.

mouth ❶ n **1** opening in the head for eating and issuing sounds. **2** entrance. **3** point where a river enters the sea. **4** opening. ▷ v **5** form (words) with the lips without speaking. **6** speak or utter insincerely, esp. in public. **mouthful** n **1** amount of food or drink put into the mouth at any one time when eating or drinking. **mouth organ** same as HARMONICA. **mouthpiece** n **1** part of a telephone into which a person speaks. **2** part of a wind instrument into which the player blows. **3** spokesperson.

move ❶ v **1** change in place or position. **2** change (one's house etc.). **3** take action. **4** stir the emotions of. **5** incite. **6** suggest (a proposal) formally. ▷ n **7** moving. **8** action towards some goal. **movable**, **moveable** adj **movement** n **1** action or process of moving. **2** group with a common aim. **3** division of a piece of music. **4** moving parts of a machine.

mow ❶ v **mowing**, **mowed**, **mowed** or **mown** cut (grass or crops). **mower** n **mow down** v kill in large numbers.

MP 1 Member of Parliament. **2** Military Police(man).

MP3 Computing Motion Picture Expert

——————————————————————— THESAURUS ——————

mound n **1** = **heap**, drift, pile, rick, stack **2** = **hill**, bank, dune, embankment, hillock, knoll, rise

mount v **1** = **ascend**, clamber up, climb, go up, scale **2** = **get (up) on**, bestride, climb onto, jump on **3** = **increase**, accumulate, build, escalate, grow, intensify, multiply, pile up, swell n **6** = **backing**, base, frame, setting, stand, support **7** = **horse**, steed (lit)

mountain n **1** = **peak**, alp, berg (S Afr), fell (Brit), mount **2** = **heap**, abundance, mass, mound, pile, stack, ton

mourn v = **grieve**, bemoan, bewail, deplore, lament, rue, wail, weep

mouth n **1** = **maw**, gob (sl, esp. Brit),

jaws **2** = **door**, entrance, gateway, inlet **4** = **opening**, aperture, orifice

move v **1** = **change**, advance, budge, go, proceed, progress, shift, stir, switch, transfer, transpose **2** = **relocate**, leave, migrate, pack one's bags (inf), quit, remove **3** = **drive**, activate, operate, propel, shift, start, turn **4** = **touch**, affect, excite, impress, inspire, rouse **5** = **prompt**, cause, incite, induce, influence, motivate, persuade **6** = **propose**, advocate, put forward, recommend, suggest, urge ▷ n **7** = **transfer**, relocation, removal, shift **8** = **action**, manoeuvre, measure, ploy, step, stratagem, stroke, turn

mow v = **cut**, crop, scythe, shear, trim

Group-1, Audio Layer-3: a digital com
pression format used to compress audio
files to a fraction of their original size
without loss of sound quality.

MPEG [**em**-peg] *Computing* Motion Picture
Expert Group: standard compressed file
format used for audio and video files.

mph miles per hour.

MT Montana.

much ● *adj* **more**, **most** 1 large amount or
degree of. ▷ *n* 2 large amount or degree.
▷ *adv* **more**, **most** 3 to a great degree.
4 nearly.

muck ● *n* 1 dirt, filth. 2 manure. **mucky**
adj.

mucus [**mew**-kuss] *n* slimy secretion of the
mucous membranes. **mucous membrane**
tissue lining body cavities or passages.

mud ● *n* wet soft earth. **muddy** *adj*
mudguard *n* cover over a wheel to
prevent mud or water being thrown up
by it. **cosmetic paste to improve the
complexion**.

muddle ● *v* 1 (often foll. by *up*) confuse.
2 mix up. ▷ *n* 3 state of confusion.

muesli [**mewz**-lee] *n* mixture of grain, nuts,
and dried fruit, eaten with milk.

muff¹ *n* tube-shaped covering to keep the

hands warm.

muff² *v* bungle (an action).

muffin *n* light round flat yeast cake.

muffle ● *v* wrap up for warmth or to
deaden sound. **muffler** *n* scarf.

mug¹ ● *n* large drinking cup.

mug² ● *n* 1 *slang* face. 2 *slang* gullible
person. ▷ *v* **mugging**, **mugged** 3 *informal*
attack in order to rob. **mugger** *n*.

mug³ ● *v* **mugging**, **mugged** (foll. by *up*)
informal study hard.

muggy ● *adj* **-gier**, **-giest** (of weather)
damp and stifling.

mulberry *n* 1 tree whose leaves are used to
feed silkworms. 2 purple fruit of this tree.

mulch *n* 1 mixture of wet straw, leaves,
etc., used to protect the roots of plants. ▷ *v*
2 cover (land) with mulch.

mule *n* offspring of a horse and a donkey.
mulish *adj* obstinate. **muleteer** *n* mule
driver.

mull ● *v* think (over) or ponder. **mulled** *adj*
(of wine or ale) flavoured with sugar and
spices and served hot.

mulloway *n* large Australian sea fish,
valued for sport and food.

multi- *combining form* many, e.g.
multicultural; *multistorey*.

——————— THESAURUS ———————

much *adj* 1 = **great**, abundant, a lot of,
ample, considerable, copious, plenty of,
sizable *or* sizeable, substantial ▷ *n* 2 = **a lot**,
a good deal, a great deal, heaps (*inf*), loads
(*inf*), lots (*inf*), plenty *adv* 3 = **greatly**, a
great deal, a lot, considerably, decidedly,
exceedingly

muck *n* 1 = **dirt**, filth, gunge (*inf*), mire,
mud, ooze, slime, sludge 2 = **manure**,
dung, kak (*S Afr sl*), ordure

mud *n* = **dirt**, clay, mire, ooze, silt, slime, sludge

muddle *v* 1 = **confuse**, befuddle, bewilder,
confound, daze, disorient, perplex,
stupefy 2 = **jumble**, disarrange, disorder,
disorganize, mess, mix up, scramble, spoil,
tangle ▷ *n* 3 = **confusion**, chaos, disarray,
disorder, disorganization, jumble, mess,
mix-up, predicament, tangle

muffle *v* a = **wrap up**, cloak, cover,
envelop, shroud, swaddle, swathe
b = **deaden**, muzzle, quieten, silence,
soften, stifle, suppress

mug¹ *n* = **cup**, beaker, pot, tankard

mug² *n* 1 *Sl* = **face**, countenance, features,
visage 2 *Sl* = **fool**, chump (*inf*), easy *or* soft
touch (*sl*), simpleton, sucker (*sl*) ▷ *v* 3 *Inf*
= **attack**, assault, beat up, rob, set about
or upon

mug³ *v* (foll. by *up*) *Inf* = **study**, bone up on
(*inf*), burn the midnight oil (*inf*), cram (*inf*),
swot (*Brit inf*)

muggy *adj* = **humid**, clammy, close, moist,
oppressive, sticky, stuffy, sultry

mull *v* = **ponder**, consider, contemplate,
deliberate, meditate, reflect on, ruminate,
think over, weigh

m

multifarious ❶ [mull-tee-**fare**-ee-uss] *adj* having many various parts.

multiple ❶ *adj* **1** having many parts. ▷ *n* **2** quantity which contains another an exact number of times. **multiply** *v* **1** increase in number, quantity, or degree. **2** add (a number) to itself a given number of times. **3** increase in number by reproduction.

multitude ❶ *n* **1** great number. **2** great crowd. **multitudinous** *adj* very numerous.

mum *n informal* mother.

mumble *v* speak indistinctly, mutter.

mummy¹ *n, pl* **-mies** body embalmed and wrapped for burial in ancient Egypt. **mummified** *adj* (of a body) preserved as a mummy.

mummy² *n, pl* **-mies** child's word for MOTHER.

mumps *n* infectious disease with swelling in the glands of the neck.

munch ❶ *v* chew noisily and steadily.

mundane ❶ *adj* **1** everyday. **2** earthly.

municipal ❶ *adj* relating to a city or town. **municipality** *n* **1** city or town with local self-government. **2** governing body of this.

munificent [mew-**niff**-fiss-sent] *adj* very generous. **munificence** *n*.

munted *adj NZ slang* **1** destroyed or ruined.

2 abnormal or peculiar.

mural *n* painting on a wall.

murder ❶ *n* **1** unlawful intentional killing of a human being. ▷ *v* **2** kill in this way. **murderer**, **murderess** *n* **murderous** *adj*.

murk *n* thick darkness. **murky** *adj* dark or gloomy.

murmur ❶ *v* **-muring, -mured 1** speak or say in a quiet indistinct way. **2** complain. ▷ *n* **3** continuous low indistinct sound.

muscle ❶ *n* **1** tissue in the body which produces movement by contracting. **2** strength or power. **muscular** *adj* **1** with well-developed muscles. **2** of muscles. **muscular dystrophy** disease with wasting of the muscles. **muscle in** *v informal* force one's way in.

muse ❶ *v* ponder quietly.

museum *n* building where natural, artistic, historical, or scientific objects are exhibited and preserved.

mush¹ *n* **1** soft pulpy mass. **2** *informal* cloying sentimentality. **mushy** *adj*.

mush² *interj* order to dogs in sled team to advance.

mushroom *n* **1** edible fungus with a stem and cap. ▷ *v* **2** grow rapidly.

music *n* **1** art form using a melodious and harmonious combination of notes. **2** written or printed form of this. **musical**

———————————— THESAURUS ————————————

multifarious *adj* = **diverse**, different, legion, manifold, many, miscellaneous, multiple, numerous, sundry, varied

multiple *adj* **1** = **many**, manifold, multitudinous, numerous, several, sundry, various

multitude *n* **2** = **mass**, army, crowd, horde, host, mob, myriad, swarm, throng

munch *v* = **chew**, champ, chomp, crunch

mundane *adj* **1** = **ordinary**, banal, commonplace, day-to-day, everyday, humdrum, prosaic, routine, workaday **2** = **earthly**, mortal, secular, temporal, terrestrial, worldly

municipal *adj* = **civic**, public, urban

murder *n* **1** = **killing**, assassination,

bloodshed, butchery, carnage, homicide, manslaughter, massacre, slaying ▷ *v* **2** = **kill**, assassinate, bump off (*sl*), butcher, eliminate (*sl*), massacre, slaughter, slay

murmur *v* **1** = **mumble**, mutter, whisper **2** = **grumble**, complain, moan (*inf*) ▷ *n* **3** = **drone**, buzzing, humming, purr, whisper

muscle *n* **1** = **tendon**, sinew **2** = **strength**, brawn, clout (*inf*), forcefulness, might, power, stamina, weight **muscle in** *v Inf* = **impose oneself**, butt in, force one's way in

muse *v* = **ponder**, brood, cogitate, consider, contemplate, deliberate, meditate, mull over, reflect, ruminate

adj **1** of or like music. **2** talented in or fond of music. **3** pleasant-sounding. ▷ *n* **4** play or film with songs and dancing. **musically** *adv* **musician** *n* **musicology** *n* scientific study of music. **musicologist** *n* **music hall** variety theatre.

musk *n* scent obtained from a gland of the musk deer or produced synthetically. **musky** *adj* **muskrat** *n* **1** N American beaver-like rodent. **2** its fur.

muskeg ❶ *n Canad* bog or swamp.

musket *n Hist* long-barrelled gun. **musketeer** *n*.

Muslim *n* **1** follower of the religion of Islam. ▷ *adj* **2** of or relating to Islam.

muslin *n* fine cotton fabric.

muss ❶ *v US & Canad inf* to make untidy.

mussel *n* edible shellfish with a dark hinged shell.

must ❶ *v* **1** used as an auxiliary to express obligation, certainty, or resolution. ▷ *n* **2** essential or necessary thing.

mustang *n* wild horse of SW USA.

mustard *n* **1** paste made from the powdered seeds of a plant, used as a condiment. **2** the plant. **mustard gas** poisonous gas causing blistering burns and blindness.

muster ❶ *v* **1** assemble. ▷ *n* **2** assembly of military personnel.

musty ❶ *adj* **mustier, mustiest** smelling mouldy and stale. **mustiness** *n*.

mute ❶ *adj* **1** silent. **2** unable to speak. ▷ *n* **3** person who is unable to speak. **4** *Music* device to soften the tone of an instrument. **muted** *adj* **1** (of sound or colour) softened. **2** (of a reaction) subdued. **mutely** *adv*.

mutilate ❶ [mew-till-ate] *v* **1** deprive of a limb or other part. **2** damage (a book or text). **mutilation** *n*.

mutiny ❶ [mew-tin-ee] *n, pl* **-nies 1** rebellion against authority, esp. by soldiers or sailors. ▷ *v* **-nying, -nied 2** commit mutiny. **mutineer** *n* **mutinous** *adj*.

mutter ❶ *v* **1** utter or speak indistinctly. **2** grumble. ▷ *n* **3** muttered sound or grumble.

mutton *n* flesh of sheep, used as food.

mutual ❶ [mew-chew-al] *adj* **1** felt or expressed by each of two people about the other. **2** common to both or all. **mutually** *adv*.

muzzle ❶ *n* **1** animal's mouth and nose. **2** cover for these to prevent biting. **3** open end of a gun. ▷ *v* **4** prevent from being heard or noticed. **5** put a muzzle on.

THESAURUS

muskeg *noun Canad* = **swamp**, bog, marsh, quagmire, slough, fen, mire, morass, pakihi (NZ)

muss *US & Canad verb* = **mess (up)**, disarrange, dishevel, ruffle, rumple, make untidy, tumble

must *n* = **necessity**, essential, fundamental, imperative, prerequisite, requirement, requisite, *sine qua non*

muster *v* **1** = **assemble**, call together, convene, gather, marshal, mobilize, rally, summon ▷ *n* **2** = **assembly**, collection, congregation, convention, gathering, meeting, rally, roundup

musty *adj* = **stale**, airless, dank, fusty, mildewed, mouldy, old, smelly, stuffy

mute *adj* **1, 2** = **silent**, dumb, mum, speechless, unspoken, voiceless, wordless

mutilate *v* **1** = **maim**, amputate, cut up, damage, disfigure, dismember, injure, lacerate, mangle **2** = **distort**, adulterate, bowdlerize, censor, cut, damage, expurgate

mutiny *n* **1** = **rebellion**, disobedience, insubordination, insurrection, revolt, revolution, riot, uprising ▷ *v* **2** = **rebel**, disobey, resist, revolt, rise up

mutter *v* **2** = **grumble**, complain, grouse, mumble, murmur, rumble

mutual *adj* **1** = **reciprocal**, requited, returned **2** = **shared**, common, interchangeable, joint

muzzle *n* **1** = **jaws**, mouth, nose, snout **2** = **gag**, guard ▷ *v* **4** = **suppress**, censor, curb, gag, restrain, silence, stifle

muzzy *adj* **-zier, -ziest** 1 confused or
muddled. 2 blurred or hazy.

my *adj* belonging to me.

myall *n* Australian acacia with hard scented
wood.

mynah *n* Asian bird which can mimic
human speech.

myopia [my-**oh**-pee-a] *n* short-
sightedness. **myopic** [my-**op**-ik] *adj*.

myriad ❶ [**mir**-ree-ad] *adj* 1 innumerable.
▷ *n* 2 large indefinite number.

myrrh [**mur**] *n* aromatic gum used in
perfume, incense, and medicine.

myrtle [**mur**-tl] *n* flowering evergreen shrub.

myself *pron* emphatic or reflexive form of
I *or* ME.

mystery ❶ *n, pl* **-teries** 1 strange or
inexplicable event or phenomenon.
2 obscure or secret thing. 3 story or film

that arouses suspense. **mysterious** *adj*
mysteriously *adv*.

mystic ❶ *n* 1 person who seeks spiritual
knowledge. ▷ *adj* 2 mystical. **mystical** *adj*
having a spiritual or religious significance
beyond human understanding. **mysticism** *n*.

mystify ❶ *v* **-fying, -fied** bewilder or
puzzle. **mystification** *n*.

mystique ❶ [miss-**steek**] *n* aura of
mystery or power.

myth ❶ *n* 1 tale with supernatural
characters, usu. of how the world
and mankind began. 2 untrue idea or
explanation. 3 imaginary person or
object. **mythical, mythic** *adj* **mythology**
n 1 myths collectively. 2 study of myths.
mythological *adj*.

myxomatosis [mix-a-mat-**oh**-siss] *n*
contagious fatal viral disease of rabbits.

————————————————————————————— THESAURUS ——————————

myriad *adj* 1 = **innumerable**,
countless, immeasurable, incalculable,
multitudinous, untold ▷ *n* 2 = **multitude**,
army, horde, host, swarm

mystery *n* 1 = **puzzle**, conundrum, enigma,
problem, question, riddle, secret, teaser

mystic *adj* 2 = **supernatural**, inscrutable,
metaphysical, mysterious, occult,
otherworldly, paranormal, preternatural,
transcendental

mystify *v* = **puzzle**, baffle, bewilder,
confound, confuse, flummox, nonplus,
perplex, stump

mystique *n* = **fascination**, awe, charisma,
charm, glamour, magic, spell

myth *n* 1 = **legend**, allegory, fable, fairy
story, fiction, folk tale, saga, story
2 = **illusion**, delusion, fancy, fantasy,
figment, imagination, superstition, tall
story

Nn

nab ⊕ v **nabbing, nabbed** informal
1 arrest (someone). 2 catch (someone) in
wrongdoing.

nadir ⊕ n 1 point in the sky opposite the
zenith. 2 lowest point.

naff ⊕ adj slang lacking quality or taste.

nag¹ ⊕ v **nagging, nagged** 1 scold or find
fault constantly. 2 be a constant source of
discomfort or worry to. ▷ n 3 person who
nags. **nagging** adj, n.

nag² ⊕ n informal old horse.

nail ⊕ n 1 pointed piece of metal with
a head, hit with a hammer to join two
objects together. 2 hard covering of the
upper tips of the fingers and toes. ▷ v
3 attach (something) with nails. 4 informal
catch or arrest. **hit the nail on the head**
say something exactly correct small metal

file used to smooth or shape the finger or
toe nails.

naive ⊕ [nye-**eev**] adj 1 innocent
and gullible. 2 simple and lacking
sophistication. **naively** adv **naivety,
naïveté** [nye-**eev**-tee] n.

naked ⊕ adj 1 without clothes. 2 without
any covering. **the naked eye** the eye
unassisted by any optical instrument.
nakedness n.

name ⊕ n 1 word by which a person or
thing is known. 2 reputation, esp. a
good one. ▷ v 3 give a name to. 4 refer
to by name. 5 fix or specify 6 insult
someone by using rude words to describe
him or her. **nameless** adj 1 without a
name. 2 unspecified. 3 too horrible to
be mentioned. **namely** adv that is to say.
namesake n person with the same name
as another.

nanny n, pl -**nies** woman whose job is
looking after young children. **nanny goat**
female goat.

nap¹ ⊕ n 1 short sleep. ▷ v **napping,
napped** 2 have a short sleep.

nap² ⊕ n raised fibres of velvet or similar
cloth.

THESAURUS

nab v Inf 1 = **apprehend**, arrest, capture,
catch, collar (inf) ▷ v 2 = **catch**,
apprehend, arrest, capture, collar (inf),
grab, seize

nadir n 2 = **bottom**, depths, lowest point,
minimum, rock bottom

naff adj Sl = **bad**, duff (Brit inf), inferior, low-
grade, poor, rubbishy, second-rate, shabby,
shoddy, worthless

nag¹ v 1 = **scold**, badger (inf), henpeck,
upbraid 2 = **worry**, annoy, harass, hassle,
irritate, pester, plague ▷ n 3 = **scold**, harpy,
shrew, tartar, virago

nag² n Inf = **horse**, hack

nail v 3 = **fasten**, attach, fix, hammer, join,
pin, secure, tack

naive adj 1 = **gullible**, callow,
credulous, green, innocent, trusting,
unsuspicious, wet behind the ears (inf)

2 = **unsophisticated**, artless,
guileless, ingenuous, innocent, simple,
unworldly

naked adj 1 = **nude**, bare, exposed, starkers
(inf), stripped, unclothed, undressed,
without a stitch on (inf)

name n 1 = **title**, designation, epithet,
handle (sl), nickname, sobriquet,
term 2 = **fame**, distinction, eminence,
esteem, honour, note, praise, renown,
repute ▷ v 4 = **call**, baptize, christen,
dub, entitle, label, style, term
5 = **nominate**, appoint, choose,
designate, select, specify

nap¹ n 1 = **sleep**, catnap, forty winks (inf),
kip (Brit sl), rest, siesta ▷ v 2 = **sleep**,
catnap, doze, drop off (inf), kip (Brit sl), nod
off (inf), rest, snooze (inf)

nap² n = **weave**, down, fibre, grain, pile

n

nape *n* back of the neck.

napkin ❶ *n* piece of cloth or paper for wiping the mouth or protecting the clothes while eating.

nappy *n, pl* **-pies** piece of absorbent material fastened round a baby's lower torso to absorb urine and faeces.

narcissism ❶ *n* exceptional interest in or admiration for oneself. **narcissistic** *adj*.

narcissus *n, pl* **-cissi** yellow, orange, or white flower related to the daffodil.

narcotic ❶ *n, adj* (of) a drug, such as morphine or opium, which produces numbness and drowsiness, used medicinally but addictive.

nark ❶ *slang* ▷ *v* 1 annoy. ▷ *n* 2 informer or spy. 3 someone who complains in an irritating manner. **narky** *adj slang* irritable or complaining.

narrate ❶ *v* 1 tell (a story). 2 speak the words accompanying and telling what is happening in a film or TV programme. **narration** *n* **narrator** *n* **narrative** *n* account, story.

narrow ❶ *adj* 1 small in breadth in comparison to length. 2 limited in range, extent, or outlook. 3 with little margin, e.g. *a narrow escape*. ▷ *v* 4 make or become narrow. **narrows** *pl n* narrow part of a strait, river, or current. **narrowly**

adv **narrowness** *n* **narrow-minded** *adj* intolerant or bigoted.

nasal *adj* 1 of the nose. 2 (of a sound) pronounced with air passing through the nose. **nasally** *adv*.

nasturtium *n* plant with yellow, red, or orange trumpet-shaped flowers.

nasty ❶ *adj* **-tier, -tiest** 1 unpleasant. 2 (of an injury) dangerous or painful. 3 spiteful or unkind. **nastily** *adv* **nastiness** *n*.

nation ❶ *n* people of one or more cultures or races organized as a single state. **national** *adj* 1 of or serving a national as a whole. 2 characteristic of a particular nation. **nationality** *n* fact of being a citizen of a particular nation.

native ❶ *adj* 1 relating to a place where a person was born. 2 born in a specified place. 3 (foll. by *to*) originating (in). 4 inborn. ▷ *n* 5 person born in a specified place. 6 indigenous animal or plant. 7 member of the original race of a country. **Native American** (person) descended from the original inhabitants of the American continent. **native bear** *Aust* same as KOALA. **native companion** *Aust* same as BROLGA. **native dog** *Aust* dingo.

NATO North Atlantic Treaty Organization.

───────────────── THESAURUS ─────────────

napkin *n* = **serviette**, cloth

narcissism *n* = **egotism**, self-love, vanity

narcotic *n* = **drug**, anaesthetic, analgesic, anodyne, opiate, painkiller, sedative, tranquillizer ▷ *adj* = **sedative**, analgesic, calming, hypnotic, painkilling, soporific

nark *Sl v* 1 = **annoy**, bother, exasperate, get on one's nerves (*inf*), irritate, nettle

narrate *v* 1 = **tell**, chronicle, describe, detail, recite, recount, relate, report

narrow *adj* 1 = **thin**, attenuated, fine, slender, slim, spare, tapering 2 = **insular**, dogmatic, illiberal, intolerant, narrow-minded, partial, prejudiced, small-minded 3 = **limited**, close, confined, constricted, contracted, meagre,

restricted, tight ▷ *v* 4 = **tighten**, constrict, limit, reduce

nasty *adj* 1 = **objectionable**, disagreeable, loathsome, obnoxious, offensive, unpleasant, vile 2 = **painful**, bad, critical, dangerous, serious, severe 3 = **spiteful**, despicable, disagreeable, distasteful, malicious, mean, unpleasant, vicious, vile

nation *n* = **country**, people, race, realm, society, state, tribe

native *adj* 1,2 = **local**, domestic, home, indigenous 3 (foll. by *to*) = **indigenous** 4 = **inborn**, congenital, hereditary, inbred, ingrained, innate, instinctive, intrinsic, natural ▷ *n* 5 = **inhabitant**, citizen, countryman, dweller, national, resident 7 = **aborigine**

natter ❶ *informal* ▷ *v* **1** talk idly or chatter. ▷ *n* **2** long idle chat.

natty ❶ *adj* **-tier, -tiest** *informal* smart and spruce.

nature ❶ *n* **1** whole system of the existence, forces, and events of the physical world that are not controlled by human beings. **2** fundamental or essential qualities. **3** kind or sort. **natural** *adj* normal or to be expected.

naturism *n* nudism. **naturist** *n*.

naughty ❶ *adj* **-tier, -tiest 1** disobedient or mischievous. **2** mildly indecent. **naughtily** *adv* **naughtiness** *n*.

nausea ❶ [naw-zee-a] *n* feeling of being about to vomit. **nauseate** *v* **1** make (someone) feel sick. **2** disgust. **nauseous** *adj* **1** as if about to vomit. **2** sickening.

nautical ❶ *adj* of the sea or ships. **nautical mile** 1852 metres (6076.12 feet).

nave *n* long central part of a church.

navel *n* hollow in the middle of the abdomen where the umbilical cord was attached.

navigate ❶ *v* **1** direct or plot the path or position of a ship, aircraft, or car. **2** travel over or through. **navigation** *n* **navigator**

n **navigable** *adj* **1** wide, deep, or safe enough to be sailed through. **2** able to be steered.

navvy ❶ *n, pl* **-vies** labourer employed on a road or a building site.

navy ❶ *n, pl* **-vies 1** branch of a country's armed services comprising warships with their crews and organization. **2** warships of a nation. ▷ *adj* **3** navy-blue. **naval** *adj* of or relating to a navy or ships. **navy-blue** *adj* very dark blue.

nay *interj obs* no.

NB 1 New Brunswick. **2** note well.

NC North Carolina.

ND North Dakota.

near ❶ *prep, adv adj* **1** indicating a place or time not far away. ▷ *adj* **2** almost being the thing specified, e.g. *a near disaster*. ▷ *v* **3** draw close (to). **nearly** *adv* almost. **nearness** *n* **nearby** *adj* not far away. **nearside** *n* side of a vehicle that is nearer the kerb.

neat ❶ *adj* **1** tidy and clean. **2** smoothly or competently done. **3** undiluted. **4** *US & Canad* good or pleasing. **neatly** *adv* **neatness** *n*.

nebulous ❶ *adj* vague, indistinct.

n

THESAURUS

---

natter *Inf v* **1 = gossip**, blether, chatter, gabble, jaw (*sl*), prattle, rabbit (on) (*Brit inf*), talk ▷ *n* **2 = gossip**, chat, chinwag (*Brit inf*), chitchat, conversation, gab (*inf*), jaw (*sl*), prattle, talk

natty *Inf adj* **= smart**, dapper, elegant, fashionable, neat, snazzy (*inf*), spruce, stylish, trim

nature *n* **1 = creation**, cosmos, earth, environment, universe, world **2 = make-up**, character, complexion, constitution, essence **3 = kind**, category, description, sort, species, style, type, variety

naughty *adj* **1 = disobedient**, bad, impish, misbehaved, mischievous, refractory, wayward, wicked, worthless **2 = obscene**, improper, lewd, ribald, risqué, smutty, vulgar

nausea *n* **= sickness**, biliousness,

queasiness, retching, squeamishness, vomiting

nautical *adj* **= maritime**, marine, naval

navigate *v* **1 = sail**, drive, guide, handle, manoeuvre, pilot, steer **2 = voyage**

navvy *n* **= labourer**, worker, workman

navy *n* **2 = fleet**, armada, flotilla

near *adj* **1 = close**, adjacent, adjoining, nearby, neighbouring **2 = forthcoming**, approaching, imminent, impending, in the offing, looming, nigh, upcoming

neat *adj* **1 = tidy**, orderly, shipshape, smart, spick-and-span, spruce, systematic, trim **2 = elegant**, adept, adroit, deft, dexterous, efficient, graceful, nimble, skilful, stylish **3 = undiluted**, pure, straight, unmixed

nebulous *adj* **= vague**, confused, dim, hazy, imprecise, indefinite, indistinct, shadowy, uncertain, unclear

necessary ❶ *adj* **1** needed to obtain the desired result, e.g. *the necessary skills.* **2** certain or unavoidable, e.g. *the necessary consequences.* **necessarily** *adv* **necessitate** *v* compel or require. **necessitous** *adj* very needy. **necessity** *n* **1** circumstances that inevitably require a certain result. **2** something needed.

- **SPELLING TIP**
- There are 41 examples of the misspelling
- *neccessary* in the Bank of English; single
- letters throughout (*necesary*) are also
- popular. The correct spelling, **neces-**
- **sary**, has one *c* and two *s*s. When you
- add *un-* at the beginning, you end up
- with a double *n* too: **unnecessary.**

neck *n* **1** part of the body joining the head to the shoulders. **2** part of a garment round the neck. **3** long narrow part of a bottle or violin. ▷ *v* **4** *slang* kiss and cuddle. **neck and neck** absolutely level in a race or competition. **neckerchief** *n* piece of cloth worn tied round the neck. **necklace** *n* decorative piece of jewellery worn around the neck.

nectar *n* **1** sweet liquid collected from flowers by bees. **2** drink of the gods.

nectarine *n* smooth-skinned peach.

née [**nay**] *prep* indicating the maiden name of a married woman.

need ❶ *v* **1** require or be in want of. ▷ *n* **2** condition of lacking something. **3** requirement or necessity. **4** poverty. **needs** *adv* (preceded or foll. by *must*) necessarily. **needy** *adj* poor, in need of financial support. **needful** *adj* necessary or required. **needless** *adj* unnecessary.

needle ❶ *n* **1** thin pointed piece of metal with an eye through which thread is passed for sewing. **2** long pointed rod used in knitting. **3** pointed part of a hypodermic syringe. **4** small pointed part in a record player that touches the record and picks up the sound signals, stylus. **5** pointer on a measuring instrument or compass. **6** long narrow stiff leaf. ▷ *v* **7** *informal* goad or provoke. **needlework** *n* sewing and embroidery.

ne'er-do-well ❶ *n* useless or lazy person.

nefarious ❶ [nif-**fair**-ee-uss] *adj* wicked.

negate ❶ *v* **1** invalidate. **2** deny the existence of. **negation** *n*.

negative ❶ *adj* **1** expressing a denial or refusal. **2** lacking positive qualities. **3** (of an electrical charge) having the same electrical charge as an electron. ▷ *n* **4** negative word or statement. **5** *Photog* image with a reversal of tones or colours from which positive prints are made.

necessary *adj* **1** = **needed**, compulsory, essential, imperative, indispensable, mandatory, obligatory, required, requisite, vital **2** = **certain**, fated, inescapable, inevitable, inexorable, unavoidable

need *v* **1** = **require**, call for, demand, entail, lack, miss, necessitate, want ▷ *n* **2** = **lack**, inadequacy, insufficiency, paucity, shortage **3** = **requirement**, demand, desideratum, essential, necessity, requisite **4** = **poverty**, deprivation, destitution, penury

needle *v* **7** *Inf* = **irritate**, annoy, get on one's nerves (*inf*), goad, harass, nag, pester, provoke, rile, taunt

ne'er-do-well *n* = **layabout**, black sheep,

good-for-nothing, idler, loafer, loser, skiver (*Brit sl*), wastrel

nefarious *adj* = **wicked**, criminal, depraved, evil, foul, heinous, infernal, villainous

negate *v* **1** = **invalidate**, annul, cancel, countermand, neutralize, nullify, obviate, reverse, wipe out **2** = **deny**, contradict, disallow, disprove, gainsay (*arch or lit*), oppose, rebut, refute

negative *adj* **1** = **contradictory**, contrary, denying, dissenting, opposing, refusing, rejecting, resisting **2** = **pessimistic**, cynical, gloomy, jaundiced, uncooperative, unenthusiastic, unwilling *n*
4 = **contradiction**, denial, refusal

neglect ❶ v 1 take no care of. 2 fail (to do something) through carelessness. 3 disregard. ▷ n 4 neglecting or being neglected. **neglectful** adj.

negligee [neg-lee-zhay] n woman's lightweight usu. lace-trimmed dressing gown.

negligence ❶ n neglect or carelessness. **negligent** adj **negligently** adv.

negotiate ❶ v 1 discuss in order to reach (an agreement). 2 succeed in passing round or over (a place or problem). **negotiation** n **negotiator** n **negotiable** adj.

neigh n 1 loud high-pitched sound made by a horse. ▷ v 2 make this sound.

neighbour n person who lives or is situated near another. **neighbouring** adj situated nearby. **neighbourhood** n 1 district. 2 surroundings. 3 people of a district. **neighbourly** adj kind, friendly, and helpful.

neither adj, pron 1 not one nor the other. ▷ conj 2 not.

nemesis ❶ [nem-miss-iss] n, pl -ses retribution or vengeance.

neologism [nee-ol-a-jiz-zum] n newly-coined word or an established word used in a new sense.

neon n Chem colourless odourless gaseous element used in illuminated signs and lights.

nephew n son of one's sister or brother.

nepotism ❶ [nep-a-tiz-zum] n favouritism in business shown to relatives and friends.

nerve ❶ n 1 cordlike bundle of fibres that conducts impulses between the brain and other parts of the body. 2 bravery and determination. 3 impudence. ▷ pl 4 anxiety or tension. **get on someone's nerves** irritate someone. **nerve oneself** prepare oneself (to do something difficult or unpleasant). **nervy** adj excitable or nervous. **nerve centre** place from which a system or organization is controlled. **nerve-racking** adj very distressing or harrowing.

nestle ❶ v 1 snuggle. 2 be in a sheltered position.

net¹ ❶ n 1 fabric of meshes of string, thread, or wire with many openings. 2 piece of net used to protect or hold things or to trap animals. 3 informal short for INTERNET. ▷ v **netting, netted** 4 catch (a fish or animal) in a net. **netting** n material made of net. **netball** n team game in which a ball has to be thrown through a net hanging from a ring at the top of a pole.

net², nett ❶ adj 1 left after all deductions. 2 (of weight) excluding the wrapping or

---

neglect v 2 = **forget**, be remiss, evade, omit, pass over, shirk, skimp 3 = **disregard**, disdain, ignore, overlook, rebuff, scorn, slight, spurn ▷ n 4 = **negligence**, carelessness, dereliction, failure, laxity, oversight, slackness

negligence n = **carelessness**, dereliction, disregard, inattention, indifference, laxity, neglect, slackness, thoughtlessness

negotiate v 1 = **deal**, arrange, bargain, conciliate, cut a deal, debate, discuss, mediate, transact, work out 2 = **get round**, clear, cross, get over, get past, pass, surmount

nemesis n = **retribution**, destiny, destruction, fate, vengeance

nepotism n = **favouritism**, bias, partiality, patronage, preferential treatment

nerve n 2 = **bravery**, bottle (Brit sl), courage, daring, fearlessness, grit, guts (inf), pluck, resolution, will 3 Inf = **impudence**, audacity, boldness, brazenness, cheek (inf), impertinence, insolence, temerity ▷ **nerve oneself** = **brace oneself**, fortify oneself, gee oneself up, steel oneself

nestle v 1 = **snuggle**, cuddle, curl up, huddle, nuzzle

net¹ n 1 = **mesh**, lattice, netting, network, openwork, tracery, web ▷ v 4 = **catch**, bag, capture, enmesh, ensnare, entangle, trap

net², nett adj 1 = **take-home**, after taxes,

n

container. ▷ v **netting**, **netted** 3 yield or
earn as a clear profit.

nether ❶ adj lower.

nettle n plant with stinging hairs on the
leaves. **nettled** adj irritated or annoyed.

network ❶ n 1 system of intersecting
lines, roads, etc. 2 interconnecting group
or system. 3 (in broadcasting) group
of stations that all transmit the same
programmes simultaneously.

neural adj of a nerve or the nervous system.

neuralgia n severe pain along a nerve.

neurosis ❶ n, pl **-ses** mental disorder
producing hysteria, anxiety, depression,
or obsessive behaviour. **neurotic** adj
1 emotionally unstable. 2 suffering from
neurosis. ▷ n 3 neurotic person.

neuter ❶ adj 1 belonging to a particular
class of grammatical inflections in some
languages. ▷ v 2 castrate (an animal).

neutral ❶ adj 1 taking neither side in a war
or dispute. 2 of or belonging to a neutral
party or country. 3 (of a colour) not
definite or striking. ▷ n 4 neutral person
or nation. 5 neutral gear. **neutrality** n
neutralize v make ineffective or neutral.
neutral gear position of the controls
of a gearbox that leaves the gears
unconnected to the engine.

neutron n electrically neutral elementary

particle of about the same mass as a
proton.

never ❶ adv at no time. **nevertheless** adv
in spite of that.

new ❶ adj 1 not existing before. 2 recently
acquired. 3 having lately come into
some state. 4 additional. 5 (foll.
by to) unfamiliar. ▷ adv 6 recently.
newness n **New Age** late 1980s
philosophy characterized by a belief in
alternative medicine and spiritualism.
newbie informal ▷ n person new to a
job, club, etc. **newborn** adj recently or
just born. **newcomer** n recent arrival or
participant. **newfangled** adj objectionably
or unnecessarily modern. **newlyweds** pl n
recently married couple. **new moon** moon
when it appears as a narrow crescent at
the beginning of its cycle.

news ❶ n 1 important or interesting new
happenings. 2 information about such
events reported in the mass media. **newsy**
adj full of news. **newsagent** n shopkeeper
who sells newspapers and magazines.
newsflash n brief important news item,
which interrupts a radio or television
programme. **newsletter** n bulletin issued
periodically to members of a group.
newspaper n weekly or daily publication
containing news. **newsprint** n inexpensive

───────────────── THESAURUS ─────────────

clear, final ▷ v 3 = **earn**, accumulate, bring
in, clear, gain, make, realize, reap

nether adj = **lower**, below, beneath,
bottom, inferior, under, underground

network n 1, 2 = **system**, arrangement,
complex, grid, labyrinth, lattice, maze,
organization, structure, web

neurosis n = **obsession**, abnormality,
affliction, derangement, instability,
maladjustment, mental illness,
phobia

neuter v 2 = **castrate**, doctor (inf),
emasculate, fix (inf), geld, spay

neutral adj 1 = **unbiased**, even-handed,
impartial, nonaligned, nonpartisan,
uncommitted, uninvolved, unprejudiced

3 = **indeterminate**, dull, indistinct,
intermediate, undefined

never adv = **at no time**, not at all, on no
account, under no circumstances

new adj 1 = **modern**, contemporary,
current, fresh, ground-breaking, latest,
novel, original, recent, state-of-the-art,
unfamiliar, up-to-date 3 = **changed**,
altered, improved, modernized,
redesigned, renewed, restored
4 = **extra**, added, more, new-found,
supplementary

news n 1, 2 = **information**, bulletin,
communiqué, exposé, gossip, hearsay,
intelligence, latest (inf), report, revelation,
rumour, story

paper used for newspapers. **newsreader**, **newscaster** n person who reads the news on the television or radio. **newsreel** n short film giving news. **newsroom** n room where news is received and prepared for publication or broadcasting. **newsworthy** adj sufficiently interesting to be reported as news.

newt n small amphibious creature with a long slender body and tail.

newton n unit of force.

next 🟊 adj, adv **1** immediately following. **2** nearest. **next-of-kin** n closest relative.

NF Newfoundland.

NH New Hampshire.

NHS National Health Service.

nib n writing point of a pen.

nibble 🟊 v **1** take little bites (of). ▷ n **2** little bite.

nice 🟊 adj **1** pleasant. **2** kind. **3** good or satisfactory. **4** subtle, e.g. a nice distinction. **nicely** adv **niceness** n.

niche 🟊 [neesh] n **1** hollow area in a wall. **2** suitable position for a particular person.

nick 🟊 v **1** make a small cut in. **2** slang steal. **3** slang arrest. ▷ n **4** small cut. **5** slang prison or police station. **in good nick** informal in good condition. **in the nick of time** just in time.

nickel n **1** Chem silvery-white metal often

used in alloys. **2** US coin worth five cents.

nickname 🟊 n **1** familiar name given to a person or place. ▷ v **2** call by a nickname.

nicotine n poisonous substance found in tobacco.

niece n daughter of one's sister or brother.

nifty 🟊 adj **-tier, -tiest** informal neat or smart.

niggard 🟊 n stingy person. **niggardly** adj.

niggle 🟊 v **1** worry slightly. **2** continually find fault (with). ▷ n **3** small worry or doubt.

nigh adv, prep lit near.

night 🟊 n **1** time of darkness between sunset and sunrise. **2** evening. **3** period between going to bed and morning. **4** nightfall or dusk. **5** an evening designated for a specified activity, e.g. parents' night. ▷ adj **6** of, occurring, or working at night, e.g. the night shift. **nightly** adj, adv (happening) each night. **nightcap** n **1** drink taken just before bedtime. **2** soft cap formerly worn in bed. **nightclub** n establishment for dancing, music, etc., open late at night. **nightdress** n woman's loose dress worn in bed. **nightfall** n approach of darkness. **nightie** n informal nightdress. **nightingale** n small bird with a musical song usu. heard at night. **nightjar** n nocturnal bird with a

next adj **1** = **following**, consequent, ensuing, later, subsequent, succeeding **2** = **nearest**, adjacent, adjoining, closest, neighbouring ▷ adv **1** = **afterwards**, following, later, subsequently, thereafter

nibble v **1** = **bite**, eat, gnaw, munch, nip, peck, pick at ▷ n **2** = **taste**, crumb, morsel, peck, soupçon, titbit

nice adj **1** = **pleasant**, agreeable, attractive, charming, delightful, good, pleasurable **2** = **kind**, courteous, friendly, likable or likeable, polite, well-mannered **3** = **neat**, dainty, fine, tidy, trim **4** = **subtle**, careful, delicate, fastidious, fine, meticulous, precise, strict

niche n **1** = **alcove**, corner, hollow, nook,

opening, recess **2** = **position**, calling, pigeonhole (inf), place, slot (inf), vocation

nick v **1** = **cut**, chip, dent, mark, notch, scar, score, scratch, snick **2** Sl = **steal**, pilfer, pinch (inf), swipe (sl) ▷ n **4** = **cut**, chip, dent, mark, notch, scar, scratch

nickname n **1** = **pet name**, diminutive, epithet, label, sobriquet

nifty adj Inf = **neat**, attractive, chic, deft, pleasing, smart, stylish

niggard n = **miser**, cheapskate (inf), Scrooge, skinflint

niggle v **1** = **worry**, annoy, irritate, rankle **2** = **criticize**, carp, cavil, find fault, fuss

night n **1** = **darkness**, dark, night-time **3** = **night-time**

harsh cry. **nightlife** n entertainment and social activities available at night in a town or city. **nightmare** n **1** very bad dream. **2** very unpleasant experience. **night school** place where adults can attend educational courses in the evenings. **nightshade** n plant with bell-shaped flowers which are often poisonous. **night-time** n time from sunset to sunrise.

nil ❶ n nothing, zero.

nimble ❶ adj agile and quick. **nimbly** adv.

nimbus n, pl -**bi**, -**buses** dark grey rain cloud.

nincompoop ❶ n informal stupid person.

nine adj, n one more than eight. **ninth** adj, n (of) number nine in a series. **ninepins** n game of skittles.

nip¹ ❶ v **nipping**, **nipped 1** informal hurry. **2** pinch or squeeze. **3** bite lightly. **4** (of the cold) cause pain. ▷ n **5** pinch or light bite. **6** sharp coldness, e.g. a nip in the air. **nippy** adj -**pier**, -**piest 1** frosty or chilly. **2** informal quick or nimble. **nipper** n informal small child.

nip² ❶ n small alcoholic drink.

nipple n projection in the centre of a breast.

nit n **1** egg or larva of a louse. **2** informal short for NITWIT. **nit-picking** adj informal overconcerned with insignificant detail, esp. to find fault. **nitwit** n informal stupid person.

nitrogen [**nite**-roj-jen] n Chem colourless odourless gas that forms four fifths of the air. **nitric**, **nitrous**, **nitrogenous**

adj of or containing nitrogen. **nitrate** n compound of nitric acid, used as a fertilizer. **nitroglycerine**, **nitroglycerin** n explosive liquid.

NJ New Jersey.

NM New Mexico.

no ❶ interj **1** expresses denial, disagreement, or refusal. ▷ adj **2** not any, not a. ▷ adv **3** not at all. ▷ n, pl **noes**, **nos 4** answer or vote of 'no'. **5** person who answers or votes 'no'. **no-go area** district barricaded off so that the police or army can enter only by force. **no-man's-land** n land between boundaries, esp. contested land between two opposing forces. **no-one**, **no one** pron nobody.

no. number.

noble ❶ adj **1** showing or having high moral qualities. **2** of the nobility. **3** impressive and magnificent. ▷ n **4** member of the nobility. **nobility** n **1** quality of being noble. **2** class of people holding titles and high social rank. **nobly** adv **nobleman**, **noblewoman** n.

nobody ❶ pron **1** no person. ▷ n, pl -**bodies 2** person of no importance.

nocturnal ❶ adj **1** of the night. **2** active at night.

nod ❶ v **nodding**, **nodded 1** lower and raise (one's head) briefly in agreement or greeting. **2** let one's head fall forward with sleep. ▷ n **3** act of nodding. **nod off** v informal fall asleep.

─────────── THESAURUS ───────────

nil n = **nothing**, love, naught, none, zero

nimble adj = **agile**, brisk, deft, dexterous, lively, quick, sprightly, spry, swift

nincompoop n Inf = **idiot**, blockhead, chump, fool, nitwit (inf), numbskull or numskull, twit (inf, chiefly Brit)

nip¹ v **2** = **pinch**, squeeze, tweak **3** = **bite**

nip² n = **dram**, draught, drop, mouthful, shot (inf), sip, snifter (inf)

no interj **1** = **never**, nay, not at all, no way ▷ n **4** = **refusal**, denial, negation, rejection

noble adj **1** = **worthy**, generous, honourable, magnanimous, upright,

virtuous **2** = **aristocratic**, blue-blooded, highborn, lordly, patrician, titled **3** = **impressive**, dignified, distinguished, grand, great, imposing, lofty, splendid, stately ▷ n **4** = **lord**, aristocrat, nobleman, peer

nobody pron **1** = **no-one** ▷ n **2** = **nonentity**, cipher, lightweight (inf), menial

nocturnal adj = **nightly**, night-time

nod v **1** = **acknowledge**, bow, gesture, indicate, signal **2** = **sleep**, doze, drowse, nap ▷ n **3** = **gesture**, acknowledgment, greeting, indication, sign, signal

node *n* **1** point on a plant stem from which leaves grow. **2** point at which a curve crosses itself.

nodule *n* **1** small knot or lump. **2** rounded mineral growth on the root of a plant.

noise ● *n* sound, usu. a loud or disturbing one. **noisy** *adj* **1** making a lot of noise. **2** full of noise. **noisily** *adv* **noiseless** *adj*.

nomad ● *n* member of a tribe with no fixed dwelling place, wanderer. **nomadic** *adj*.

nomenclature ● *n* system of names used in a particular subject.

nominal ● *adj* **1** in name only. **2** very small in comparison with real worth. **nominally** *adv*.

nominate ● *v* **1** suggest as a candidate. **2** appoint to an office or position. **nomination** *n* **nominee** *n* candidate. **nominative** *n* form of a noun indicating the subject of a verb.

non- *prefix* indicating: **1** negation, e.g. *nonexistent*. **2** refusal or failure, e.g. *noncooperation*. **3** exclusion from a specified class, e.g. *nonfiction*. **4** lack or absence, e.g. *nonevent*.

nonchalant ● *adj* casually unconcerned or indifferent. **nonchalantly** *adv* **nonchalance** *n*.

noncommissioned officer *n* (in the armed forces) a subordinate officer, risen from the ranks.

noncommittal ● *adj* not committing oneself to any particular opinion.

nonconformist ● *n* **1** person who does not conform to generally accepted patterns of behaviour or thought. **2** (N-) member of a Protestant group separated from the Church of England.

nondescript ● *adj* lacking outstanding features.

none ● *pron* **1** not any. **2** no-one. **nonetheless** *adv* despite that, however.

nonentity ● [non-**enn**-tit-tee] *n, pl* **-ties** insignificant person or thing.

nonevent ● *n* disappointing or insignificant occurrence.

nonflammable *adj* not easily set on fire.

nonpareil [non-par-**rail**] *n* person or thing that is unsurpassed.

nonplussed *adj* perplexed.

nonsense ● *n* **1** something that has or makes no sense. **2** absurd language. **3** foolish behaviour. **nonsensical** *adj*.

non sequitur [**sek**-wit-tur] *n* statement with little or no relation to what preceded it.

n

THESAURUS

---

noise *n* = **sound**, clamour, commotion, din, hubbub, racket, row, uproar

nomad *n* = **wanderer**, drifter, itinerant, migrant, rambler, rover, vagabond

nomenclature *n* = **terminology**, classification, codification, phraseology, taxonomy, vocabulary

nominal *adj* **1** = **so-called**, formal, ostensible, professed, puppet, purported, supposed, theoretical, titular **2** = **small**, inconsiderable, insignificant, minimal, symbolic, token, trifling, trivial

nominate *v* **1** = **suggest**, propose, recommend **2** = **name**, appoint, assign, choose, designate, elect, select

nonchalant *adj* = **casual**, blasé, calm, careless, indifferent, insouciant, laid-back (*inf*), offhand, unconcerned, unperturbed

noncommittal *adj* = **evasive**, cautious, circumspect, equivocal, guarded, neutral, politic, temporizing, tentative, vague, wary

nonconformist *n* **1** = **maverick**, dissenter, eccentric, heretic, iconoclast, individualist, protester, radical, rebel

nondescript *adj* = **ordinary**, commonplace, dull, featureless, run-of-the-mill, undistinguished, unexceptional, unremarkable

none *pron* = **not any**, nil, nobody, no-one, nothing, not one, zero

nonentity *n* = **nobody**, cipher, lightweight (*inf*), mediocrity, small fry

nonevent *n* = **flop** (*inf*), disappointment, dud (*inf*), failure, fiasco, washout

nonsense *n* **1, 2** = **rubbish**, balderdash, claptrap (*inf*), double Dutch (*Brit inf*),

nook ❶ n sheltered place.

noon ❶ n twelve o'clock midday. **noonday** adj happening at noon.

noose n loop in the end of a rope, tied with a slipknot.

nor conj and not.

norm ❶ n standard that is regarded as usual. **normal** adj usual, regular, or typical.

north ❶ n **1** direction towards the North Pole, opposite south. **2** area lying in or towards the north. ▷ adj **3** to or in the north. **4** (of a wind) from the north. ▷ adv **5** in, to, or towards the north. **northerly** adj **northern** adj **northerner** n person from the north of a country or area. **northward** adj, adv **northwards** adv **North Pole** northernmost point on the earth's axis.

nose ❶ n **1** organ of smell, used also in breathing. **2** front part of a vehicle. ▷ v **3** move forward slowly and carefully. **4** pry or snoop. **nose dive** sudden drop. **nosey, nosy** adj informal prying or inquisitive. **nosiness** n.

nosh slang ▷ n **1** food. ▷ v **2** eat.

nostalgia ❶ n sentimental longing for the past. **nostalgic** adj.

nostril n one of the two openings at the end of the nose.

not adv expressing negation, refusal, or denial.

notable ❶ adj **1** worthy of being noted, remarkable. ▷ n **2** person of distinction. **notably** adv **notability** n.

notary n, pl **-ries** person authorized to witness the signing of legal documents.

notation ❶ n **1** representation of numbers or quantities in a system by a series of symbols. **2** set of such symbols.

notch ❶ n **1** V-shaped cut. **2** informal step or level. ▷ v **3** make a notch in. **4** (foll. by up) score or achieve.

note ❶ n **1** short letter. **2** brief comment or record. **3** banknote. **4** (symbol for) a musical sound. **5** hint or mood. ▷ v **6** notice, pay attention to. **7** record in writing. **8** remark upon. **noted** adj well-known. **notebook** n book for writing in. **noteworthy** adj worth noting, remarkable.

nothing ❶ pron **1** not anything. **2** matter of no importance. **3** figure o. ▷ adv **4** not at all. **nothingness** n **1** nonexistence. **2** insignificance.

drivel, gibberish, hot air (inf), stupidity, tripe (inf), twaddle

nook n = **niche**, alcove, corner, cubbyhole, hide-out, opening, recess, retreat

noon n = **midday**, high noon, noonday, noontide, twelve noon

norm n = **standard**, average, benchmark, criterion, par, pattern, rule, yardstick

north adj **3** = **northern**, Arctic, boreal, northerly, polar ▷ adv **5** = **northward(s)**, northerly

nose n **1** = **snout**, beak, bill, hooter (sl), proboscis ▷ v **3** = **ease forward**, nudge, nuzzle, push, shove **4** = **pry**, meddle, snoop (inf)

nostalgia n = **reminiscence**, homesickness, longing, pining, regretfulness, remembrance, wistfulness, yearning

notable adj **1** = **remarkable**, conspicuous,

extraordinary, memorable, noteworthy, outstanding, rare, striking, uncommon, unusual ▷ n **2** = **celebrity**, big name, dignitary, luminary, personage, V.I.P.

notation n **2** = **signs**, characters, code, script, symbols, system

notch n **1** = **cut**, cleft, incision, indentation, mark, nick, score **2** Inf = **level**, degree, grade, step ▷ v **3** = **cut**, indent, mark, nick, score, scratch

note n **1, 2** = **message**, comment, communication, epistle, jotting, letter, memo, memorandum, minute, remark, reminder ▷ v **6** = **see**, notice, observe, perceive **7** = **mark**, denote, designate, indicate, record, register **8** = **mention**, remark

nothing pron **1** = **nothingness**, emptiness, nullity, void **3** = **nought**, nil, zero

notice ① *n* **1** observation or attention. **2** sign giving warning or an announcement. **3** advance notification of intention to end a contract of employment. ▷ *v* **4** observe, become aware of. **5** point out or remark upon.

noticeable ① *adj* easily seen or detected, appreciable.

notify ① *v* **-fying, -fied** inform. **notification** *n* **notifiable** *adj* having to be reported to the authorities.

notion ① *n* **1** idea or opinion. **2** whim.

notorious ① *adj* well known for something bad. **notoriously** *adv* **notoriety** *n*.

notwithstanding ① *prep* in spite of.

nougat *n* chewy sweet containing nuts and fruit.

nought ① *n* **1** figure o. **2** nothing. **noughties** *pl n informal* decade from 2000 to 2009.

noun *n* word that refers to a person, place, or thing.

nourish ① *v* **1** feed. **2** encourage or foster (an idea or feeling). **nourishment** *n* **nourishing** *adj* providing the food necessary for life and growth.

Nov. November.

novel¹ ① *n* long fictitious story in book form. **novelist** *n* writer of novels.

novel² ① *adj* fresh, new, or original. **novelty** *n* **1** newness. **2** something new or unusual. **3** cheap toy or trinket.

November *n* eleventh month of the year.

novice ① *n* **1** beginner. **2** person who has entered a religious order but has not yet taken vows.

now ① *adv* **1** at or for the present time. **2** immediately. ▷ *conj* **3** seeing that, since. **now and again** *or* **then** occasionally. **nowadays** *adv* in these times.

nowhere *adv* not anywhere.

noxious ① *adj* **1** poisonous or harmful. **2** extremely unpleasant.

nozzle *n* projecting spout through which fluid is discharged.

NS Nova Scotia.

THESAURUS

notice *n* **1 = interest**, cognizance, consideration, heed, note, observation, regard **2 = announcement**, advice, communication, instruction, intimation, news, notification, order, warning ▷ *v* **4 = observe**, detect, discern, distinguish, mark, note, perceive, see, spot

noticeable *adj* **= obvious**, appreciable, clear, conspicuous, evident, manifest, perceptible, plain, striking

notify *v* **= inform**, advise, alert, announce, declare, make known, publish, tell, warn

notion *n* **1 = idea**, belief, concept, impression, inkling, opinion, sentiment, view **2 = whim**, caprice, desire, fancy, impulse, inclination, wish

notional *adj* **= speculative**, abstract, conceptual, hypothetical, imaginary, theoretical, unreal

notorious *adj* **= infamous**, dishonourable, disreputable, opprobrious, scandalous

notwithstanding *prep* **= despite**, in spite of

nought *n* **1 = zero**, nil **2 = nothing**, nil, zero

nourish *v* **1 = feed**, nurse, nurture, supply, sustain, tend **2 = encourage**, comfort, cultivate, foster, maintain, promote, support

novel¹ *n* **= story**, fiction, narrative, romance, tale

novel² *adj* **= new**, different, fresh, innovative, original, strange, uncommon, unfamiliar, unusual

novice *n* **1 = beginner**, amateur, apprentice, learner, newcomer, probationer, pupil, trainee

now *adv* **1 = nowadays**, any more, at the moment **2 = immediately**, at once, instantly, promptly, straightaway **now and again** *or* **then = occasionally**, from time to time, infrequently, intermittently, on and off, sometimes, sporadically

noxious *adj* **1 = harmful**, deadly, destructive, foul, hurtful, injurious, poisonous, unhealthy, unwholesome

n

NSW New South Wales.

nuance ❶ [**new**-ahnss] n subtle difference in colour, meaning, or tone.

nub n point or gist (of a story etc.).

nubile ❶ [**new**-bile] adj (of a young woman) 1 sexually attractive. 2 old enough to get married.

nucleus ❶ n, pl -**clei** 1 centre, esp. of an atom or cell. 2 central thing around which others are grouped.

nude ❶ adj 1 naked. ▷ n 2 naked figure in painting, sculpture, or photography. **nudity** n **nudism** n practice of not wearing clothes. **nudist** n.

nudge ❶ v 1 push gently, esp. with the elbow. ▷ n 2 gentle push or touch.

nugget ❶ n 1 small lump of gold in its natural state. 2 something small but valuable. ▷ v 3 NZ & S Afr polish footwear.

nuisance ❶ n something or someone that causes annoyance or bother.

nuke slang ▷ v 1 attack with nuclear weapons. ▷ n 2 nuclear weapon.

null ❶ adj **null and void** not legally valid. **nullity** n **nullify** v 1 make ineffective. 2 cancel.

numb ❶ adj 1 without feeling, as through cold, shock, or fear. ▷ v 2 make numb.

numbness n **numbskull** n stupid person.

number ❶ n 1 sum or quantity. 2 word or symbol used to express a sum or quantity, numeral. 3 numeral or string of numerals used to identify a person or thing. 4 one of a series, such as a copy of a magazine. 5 song or piece of music. 6 group of people. 7 Grammar classification of words depending on how many persons or things are referred to. ▷ v 8 count. 9 give a number to. 10 amount to. 11 include in a group. **numberless** adj too many to be counted. **number crunching** Computers large-scale processing of numerical data. **number one** n informal 1 oneself. 2 bestselling pop record in any one week. **numberplate** n plate on a car showing the registration number.

numeral ❶ n word or symbol used to express a sum or quantity.

numskull n same as NUMBSKULL.

nun n female member of a religious order. **nunnery** n convent.

nuptial ❶ adj relating to marriage. **nuptials** pl n wedding.

nurse ❶ n 1 person employed to look after sick people, usu. in a hospital. 2 woman employed to look after children. ▷ v

n

               THESAURUS

nuance n = **subtlety**, degree, distinction, gradation, nicety, refinement, shade, tinge

nubile adj 2 = **marriageable**, ripe (inf)

nucleus n 2 = **centre**, basis, core, focus, heart, kernel, nub, pivot

nude adj 1 = **naked**, bare, disrobed, stark-naked, stripped, unclad, unclothed, undressed, without a stitch on (inf)

nudge v, n = **push**, bump, dig, elbow, jog, poke, prod, shove, touch

nugget n 2 = **lump**, chunk, clump, hunk, mass, piece

nuisance n = **problem**, annoyance, bother, drag (inf), hassle (inf), inconvenience, irritation, pain in the neck, pest, trouble

null adj **null and void** = **invalid**, inoperative, useless, valueless, void, worthless

numb adj 1 = **unfeeling**, benumbed, dead, deadened, frozen, immobilized, insensitive, paralysed, torpid v 2 = **deaden**, benumb, dull, freeze, immobilize, paralyse

number n 1 = **quantity**, aggregate, amount, collection 2 = **numeral**, character, digit, figure, integer 4 = **issue**, copy, edition, imprint, printing 6 = **throng**, collection, crowd, horde, multitude ▷ v 8 = **calculate**, account, add, compute, count, enumerate, include, reckon, total

numeral n = **number**, digit, figure, integer

nuptial adj = **marital**, bridal, conjugal, connubial, matrimonial

nurse v 3 = **look after**, care for, minister to, tend, treat 4 = **breast-feed**, feed, nourish,

3 look after (a sick person). **4** breast-feed (a baby). **5** try to cure (an ailment). **6** harbour or foster (a feeling). **nursing home** private hospital or home for old people. **nursing officer** administrative head of the nursing staff of a hospital.

nurture ❶ *n* **1** act or process of promoting the development of a child or young plant. ▷ *v* **2** promote or encourage the development of.

nut ❶ *n* **1** fruit consisting of a hard shell and a kernel. **2** small piece of metal that screws onto a bolt. **3** (also **nutcase**) *slang* insane or eccentric person. **4** *slang* head. **nutty** *adj* **1** containing or resembling nuts. **2** *slang* insane or eccentric. **nutter** *n* *slang* insane person. **nutcracker** *n* device for cracking the shells of nuts. **nuthatch** *n* small songbird. **nutmeg** *n* spice made from the seed of a tropical tree.

nutrient *n* substance that provides nourishment.

nutrition ❶ *n* **1** process of taking in and absorbing nutrients. **2** process of being nourished. **nutritional** *adj* **nutritious**, **nutritive** *adj* nourishing.

nuzzle ❶ *v* push or rub gently with the nose or snout.

NV Nevada.

NWT Northwest Territories.

NY New York.

nylon *n* **1** synthetic material used for clothing etc. ▷ *pl* **2** stockings made of nylon.

nymph ❶ *n* **1** mythical spirit of nature, represented as a beautiful young woman. **2** larva of certain insects, resembling the adult form.

nymphomaniac *n* woman with an abnormally intense sexual desire.

THESAURUS

---

nurture, suckle, wet-nurse **6** = **foster**, cherish, cultivate, encourage, harbour, preserve, promote, succour, support

nurture *n* **1** = **development**, discipline, education, instruction, rearing, training, upbringing ▷ *v* **2** = **develop**, bring up, discipline, educate, instruct, rear, school, train

nut *n* **3** (also **nutcase**) *Sl* = **madman**, crank (*inf*), lunatic, maniac, nutcase (*sl*), psycho (*sl*) **4** *Sl* = **head**, brain, mind, reason, senses

nutrition *n* **1, 2** = **food**, nourishment, nutriment, sustenance

nuzzle *v* = **snuggle**, burrow, cuddle, fondle, nestle, pet

nymph *n* **1** = **sylph**, dryad, naiad

n

oaf ❶ *n* stupid or clumsy person. **oafish** *adj*.
oak *n* **1** deciduous forest tree. **2** its wood, used for furniture. **oak apple** brownish lump found on oak trees.
OAP old-age pensioner.
oar *n* pole with a broad blade, used for rowing a boat.
oasis *n*, *pl* **-ses** fertile area in a desert.
oat *n* **1** hard cereal grown as food. ▷ *pl* **2** grain of this cereal. **sow one's wild oats** have many sexual relationships when young. **oatmeal** *adj* **1** pale brownish-cream.
oath ❶ *n* **1** solemn promise, esp. to be truthful in court. **2** swearword.
obdurate ❶ *adj* hardhearted or stubborn. **obduracy** *n*.
OBE Officer of the Order of the British Empire.

obelisk ❶ [**ob**-bill-isk] *n* four-sided stone column tapering to a pyramid at the top.
obese ❶ [oh-**beess**] *adj* very fat. **obesity** *n*.
obey ❶ *v* carry out instructions or orders.
obituary *n*, *pl* **-aries** announcement of someone's death, esp. in a newspaper.
object¹ ❶ *n* **1** physical thing. **2** focus of thoughts or action. **3** aim or purpose. **4** *Grammar* word that a verb or preposition affects. **no object** not a hindrance.
object² ❶ *v* express disapproval. **objection** *n* **objectionable** *adj* unpleasant. **objector** *n*.
objective ❶ *n* **1** aim or purpose. ▷ *adj* **2** not biased. **3** existing in the real world outside the human mind. **objectively** *adv* **objectivity** *n*.
oblige ❶ *v* **1** compel (someone) morally or by law to do something. **2** do a favour for (someone). **obliging** *adj* ready to help other people. **obligated** *adj* obliged to do something. **obligation** *n* duty. **obligatory** *adj* required by a rule or law.
oblique ❶ [oh-**bleak**] *adj* **1** slanting. **2** indirect. ▷ *n* **3** the symbol (/). **obliquely** *adv* **oblique angle** angle that is not a right angle.

——————————————————————————————— THESAURUS ———

oaf *n* = **dolt**, blockhead, clod, dunce, fool, goon, idiot, lout, moron, numbskull *or* numskull
oath *n* **1** = **promise**, affirmation, avowal, bond, pledge, vow, word **2** = **swearword**, blasphemy, curse, expletive, profanity
obdurate *adj* = **stubborn**, dogged, hard-hearted, immovable, implacable, inflexible, obstinate, pig-headed, unyielding
obelisk *n* = **column**, monolith, monument, needle, pillar, shaft
obese *adj* = **fat**, corpulent, gross, heavy, overweight, paunchy, plump, portly, rotund, stout, tubby
obey *v* = **carry out**, abide by, act upon, adhere to, comply, conform, follow, heed, keep, observe
object¹ *n* **1** = **thing**, article, body, entity, item, phenomenon **2** = **target**, focus,

recipient, victim **3** = **purpose**, aim, design, end, goal, idea, intention, objective, point
object² *v* = **protest**, argue against, demur, draw the line (at something), expostulate, oppose, take exception
objective *n* **1** = **purpose**, aim, ambition, end, goal, intention, mark, object, target ▷ *adj* **2** = **unbiased**, detached, disinterested, dispassionate, even-handed, fair, impartial, impersonal, open-minded, unprejudiced
oblige *v* **1** = **compel**, bind, constrain, force, impel, make, necessitate, require **2** = **do (someone) a favour** *or* **a kindness**, accommodate, benefit, gratify, indulge, please
oblique *adj* **1** = **slanting**, angled, aslant, sloping, tilted **2** = **indirect**, backhanded, circuitous, implied, roundabout, sidelong

o

obliterate ❶ v wipe out, destroy. **obliteration** n.

oblong adj **1** having two long sides, two short sides, and four right angles. ▷ n **2** oblong figure.

obnoxious ❶ adj offensive.

oboe n double-reeded woodwind instrument. **oboist** n.

obscene ❶ adj **1** portraying sex offensively. **2** disgusting. **obscenity** n.

obscure ❶ adj **1** not well known. **2** hard to understand. **3** indistinct. ▷ v **4** make (something) obscure. **obscurity** n.

obsequious ❶ [ob-**seek**-wee-uss] adj overattentive in order to gain favour. **obsequiousness** n.

observe ❶ v **1** see or notice. **2** watch (someone or something) carefully. **3** remark. **4** act according to (a law or custom). **observation** n **1** action or habit of observing. **2** remark. **observer** n **observance** n observing of a custom. **observant** adj quick to notice things. **observatory** n building equipped for studying the weather and the stars.

obsess v preoccupy (someone) compulsively. **obsessed** adj **obsessive** adj **obsession** n.

obsolete ❶ adj no longer in use; out of date. **obsolescent** adj becoming obsolete. **obsolescence** n.

obstacle ❶ n something that makes progress difficult.

obstetrics n branch of medicine concerned with pregnancy and childbirth. **obstetric** adj **obstetrician** n.

obstinate ❶ adj **1** stubborn. **2** difficult to remove or change. **obstinacy** n.

obstreperous ❶ adj unruly, noisy.

obstruct ❶ v block with an obstacle. **obstruction** n **obstructive** adj.

THESAURUS
---

obliterate v = **destroy**, annihilate, blot out, efface, eradicate, erase, expunge, extirpate, root out, wipe out

obnoxious adj = **offensive**, disagreeable, insufferable, loathsome, nasty, nauseating, objectionable, odious, repulsive, revolting, unpleasant

obscene adj **1** = **indecent**, dirty, filthy, immoral, improper, lewd, offensive, pornographic, salacious, scungy (Aust & NZ inf) **2** = **disgusting**, atrocious, evil, heinous, loathsome, outrageous, shocking, sickening, vile, wicked

obscure adj **1** = **little-known**, humble, lowly, out-of-the-way, remote, undistinguished, unheard-of, unknown **2** = **vague**, ambiguous, arcane, confusing, cryptic, enigmatic, esoteric, mysterious, opaque, recondite, unclear **3** = **dark**, blurred, cloudy, dim, faint, gloomy, indistinct, murky, shadowy ▷ v **4** = **conceal**, cover, disguise, hide, obfuscate, screen, veil

obsequious adj = **sycophantic**, cringing, deferential, fawning, flattering, grovelling, ingratiating, servile, submissive, unctuous

observe v **1** = **see**, detect, discern, discover, note, notice, perceive, spot, witness **2** = **watch**, check, keep an eye on (inf), keep track of, look at, monitor, scrutinize, study, survey, view **3** = **remark**, comment, mention, note, opine, say, state **4** = **carry out**, abide by, adhere to, comply, conform to, follow, heed, honour, keep, obey, respect

obsolete adj = **out of date**, antiquated, archaic, discarded, disused, extinct, old, old-fashioned, outmoded, passé

obstacle n = **difficulty**, bar, barrier, block, hindrance, hitch, hurdle, impediment, obstruction, snag, stumbling block

obstinate adj **1** = **stubborn**, determined, dogged, inflexible, intractable, intransigent, pig-headed, refractory, self-willed, strong-minded, wilful

obstreperous adj = **unruly**, disorderly, loud, noisy, riotous, rowdy, turbulent, unmanageable, wild

obstruct v = **block**, bar, barricade

obtain ⊙ v 1 acquire intentionally. 2 be customary. **obtainable** adj.

obtrude v push oneself or one's ideas on others. **obtrusion** n **obtrusive** adj unpleasantly noticeable.

obtuse ⊙ adj 1 mentally slow. 2 Maths (of an angle) between 90° and 180° 3 not pointed. **obtuseness** n.

obverse n 1 opposite way of looking at an idea. 2 main side of a coin or medal.

obviate ⊙ v make unnecessary.

obvious ⊙ adj easy to see or understand, evident. **obviously** adv.

occasion ⊙ n 1 time at which a particular thing happens. 2 reason, e.g. no occasion for complaint. 3 special event. ▷ v 4 cause. **occasional** adj happening sometimes. **occasionally** adv.

● **SPELLING TIP**
● The commonest misspelling of **occasion**
● is occassion, with 44 occurrences in the
● Bank of English. There are also examples
● of ocasion and ocassion. The correct
● spelling has two cs and one s.

Occident n lit the West. **Occidental** adj.

occult ⊙ adj relating to the supernatural.

occupy ⊙ v -pying, -pied 1 live or work in (a building). 2 take up the attention

of (someone). 3 take up (space or time). 4 take possession of (a place) by force. **occupant** n **occupation** n profession. **occupier** n.

occur ⊙ v -curring, -curred 1 happen. 2 exist. **occur to** to come to the mind of. **occurrence** n 1 something that occurs. 2 fact of occurring.

● **SPELLING TIP**
● Rather surprisingly, there are no
● examples in the Bank of English where
● **occurrence** has been spelt with only
● one c. However, there are 85 examples of
● occurence, with only one r, as opposed to
● 2013 instances where the word is spelt
● correctly: **occurrence**.

ocean n vast area of sea between continents. **oceanic** adj **oceanography** n scientific study of the oceans.

ochre [oak-er] adj, n brownish-yellow (earth).

o'clock adv used after a number to specify an hour.

Oct. October.

octagon n geometric figure with eight sides. **octagonal** adj.

octane n hydrocarbon found in petrol.

octave n Music (interval between the first and) eighth note of a scale.

                             THESAURUS

obtain v 1 = **get**, achieve, acquire, attain, earn, gain, land, procure, secure 2 = **exist**, be in force, be prevalent, be the case, hold, prevail

obtuse adj 1 = **stupid**, dense, dull, dumb (inf), slow, stolid, thick, uncomprehending

obviate v = **preclude**, avert, prevent, remove

obvious adj = **evident**, apparent, clear, conspicuous, distinct, indisputable, manifest, noticeable, plain, self-evident, undeniable, unmistakable

occasion n 1 = **time**, moment 2 = **reason**, call, cause, excuse, ground(s), justification, motive, prompting, provocation 3 = **event**, affair, celebration, experience, happening, occurrence

▷ v 4 = **cause**, bring about, engender, generate, give rise to, induce, inspire, lead to, produce, prompt, provoke

occult adj = **supernatural**, arcane, esoteric, magical, mysterious, mystical

occupy v 1 = **live in**, dwell in, inhabit, own, possess, reside in 2 = **take up**, divert, employ, engage, engross, involve, monopolize, preoccupy, tie up 3 = **fill**, cover, permeate, pervade, take up 4 = **invade**, capture, overrun, seize, take over

occur v 1 = **happen**, befall, come about, crop up (inf), take place, turn up (inf) 2 = **exist**, appear, be found, be present, develop, manifest itself, show itself **occur to** = **come to mind**, cross one's mind, dawn on, enter one's head, spring to mind, strike one, suggest itself

octet n 1 group of eight performers.
2 music for such a group.

October n tenth month of the year.

octopus n, pl **-puses** sea creature with a
soft body and eight tentacles.

odd ❶ adj 1 unusual. 2 occasional. 3 not
divisible by two. 4 not part of a set. **odds**
pl n (ratio showing) the probability of
something happening. **at odds** in conflict.
odds and ends small miscellaneous items.
oddity n odd person or thing. **oddments** pl
n things left over.

ode n lyric poem, usu. addressed to a
particular subject.

odium [**oh**-dee-um] n widespread dislike.
odious adj offensive.

odour ❶ n particular smell. **odorous** adj
odourless adj.

odyssey [**odd**-iss-ee] n long eventful
journey.

oesophagus [ee-**soff**-a-guss] n, pl **-gi**
passage between the mouth and
stomach.

of prep 1 belonging to. 2 consisting of.
3 connected with. 4 characteristic of.

off ❶ prep 1 away from. ▷ adv 2 away. ▷ adj
3 not operating. 4 cancelled. 5 (of food)
gone bad. ▷ n 6 Cricket side of the field to
which the batsman's feet point. **off colour**
slightly ill. **off-line** adj (of a computer) not

directly controlled by a central processor.
off-message adj (esp. of a politician) not
following the official Party line.

offal n edible organs of an animal, such as
liver or kidneys.

offend ❶ v 1 hurt the feelings of, insult.
2 commit a crime. **offender** n **offence** n
1 (cause of) hurt feelings or annoyance.
2 illegal act. **offensive** adj 1 disagreeable.
2 insulting. 3 aggressive. ▷ n 4 position or
action of attack.

offer ❶ v 1 present (something) for
acceptance or rejection. 2 provide. 3 be
willing (to do something). 4 propose
as payment. ▷ n 5 instance of offering
something. **offering** n thing offered.

office ❶ n 1 room or building where
people work at desks. 2 department of
a commercial organization. 3 formal
position of responsibility. 4 place where
tickets or information can be obtained.
officer n 1 person in authority in the
armed services. 2 member of the police
force. 3 person with special responsibility
in an organization.

official ❶ adj 1 of a position of authority.
2 approved or arranged by someone
in authority. ▷ n 3 person who holds
a position of authority. **officially** adv
officialdom n officials collectively.

o

————————————————— THESAURUS —————————————————

odd adj 1 = **unusual**, bizarre,
extraordinary, freakish, irregular, munted
(NZ sl), peculiar, rare, remarkable,
singular, strange 2 = **occasional**, casual,
incidental, irregular, periodic, random,
sundry, various 4 = **unmatched**,
unpaired

odour n = **smell**, aroma, bouquet, essence,
fragrance, perfume, redolence, scent,
stench, stink

odyssey n = **journey**, crusade, pilgrimage,
quest, trek, voyage

off adv 2 = **away**, apart, aside, elsewhere,
out ▷ adj 4 = **cancelled**, finished, gone,
postponed, unavailable 5 = **bad**, mouldy,
rancid, rotten, sour, turned

offend v 1 = **insult**, affront, annoy,
displease, hurt (someone's) feelings,
outrage, slight, snub, upset, wound

offer v 1 = **propose**, advance, submit,
suggest 2 = **provide**, afford, furnish,
present 3 = **volunteer**, come forward,
offer one's services ▷ n 5 = **proposal**, bid,
tender

office n 3 = **post**, function, occupation,
place, responsibility, role, situation

official adj 2 = **authorized**, accredited,
authentic, certified, legitimate,
licensed, sanctioned ▷ n 3 = **officer**,
agent, bureaucrat, executive,
functionary, office bearer,
representative

officiate **①** *v* act in an official role.

officious **①** *adj* interfering unnecessarily.

offside *adj, adv Sport* (positioned) illegally ahead of the ball.

often **①** *adv* frequently, much of the time. **oft** *adv poetic* often.

ogle **①** *v* stare at (someone) lustfully.

ogre **①** *n* 1 giant that eats human flesh. 2 monstrous or cruel person.

oh *interj* exclamation of surprise, pain, etc.

OH Ohio.

ohm *n* unit of electrical resistance.

oil **①** *n* 1 viscous liquid, insoluble in water and usu. flammable. 2 same as PETROLEUM. 3 petroleum derivative, used as a fuel or lubricant. ▷ *pl* 4 oil-based paints used in art. ▷ *v* 5 lubricate (a machine) with oil. **oily** *adj* **oilskin** *n* (garment made from) waterproof material.

ointment **①** *n* greasy substance used for healing skin or as a cosmetic.

OK Oklahoma.

O.K., okay *informal* ▷ *interj* 1 expression of approval. ▷ *adj, adv* 2 acceptable; in an acceptable way. ▷ *v* 3 approve (something). ▷ *n* 4 approval.

old **①** *adj* 1 having lived or existed for a long time. 2 of a specified age, e.g. *two years old*. 3 former. **olden** *adj* old, e.g. *in the olden days*. **oldie** *n informal* old but popular song or film.

old-fashioned *adj* no longer commonly used or valued. **old guard** group of people in an organization who have traditional values. **old hat** boring because so familiar. **old master** European painter or painting from the period 1500–1800. **old school tie** system of mutual help between former pupils of public schools. **Old Testament** part of the Bible recording Hebrew history. **Old World** world as it was known before the discovery of the Americas.

olfactory *adj* relating to the sense of smell.

oligarchy [ol-lee-gark-ee] *n, pl* -chies 1 government by a small group of people. 2 state governed this way. **oligarchic, oligarchical** *adj*.

olive *n* 1 small green or black fruit used as food or pressed for its oil. 2 tree on which this fruit grows. ▷ *adj* 3 greyish-green. **olive branch** peace offering.

ombudsman *n* official who investigates complaints against government organizations.

omelette *n* dish of eggs beaten and fried.

● **SPELLING TIP**
● You don't hear it in the pronunciation,
● but there is an *e* after the *m* in **omelette**.

omen **①** *n* happening or object thought to foretell success or misfortune. **ominous** *adj* worrying, seeming to foretell misfortune.

——————————————————— THESAURUS ———————

officiate *v* = **preside**, chair, conduct, manage, oversee, serve, superintend

officious *adj* = **interfering**, dictatorial, intrusive, meddlesome, obtrusive, overzealous, pushy (*inf*), self-important

often *adv* = **frequently**, generally, repeatedly, time and again

ogle *v* = **leer**, eye up (*inf*)

ogre *n* 1 = **giant** 2 = **monster**, bogeyman, bugbear, demon, devil, spectre

oil *v* 5 = **lubricate**, grease

ointment *n* = **lotion**, balm, cream, embrocation, emollient, liniment, salve, unguent

O.K., okay *Inf interj* 1 = **all right**, agreed, right, roger, very good, very well, ya (S

Afr), yebo (*S Afr inf*), yes ▷ *adj, adv* 2 = **fine**, acceptable, adequate, all right, good, in order, permitted, satisfactory, up to scratch (*inf*) ▷ *v* 3 = **approve**, agree to, authorize, endorse, give the green light, rubber-stamp (*inf*), sanction ▷ *n* 4 = **approval**, agreement, assent, authorization, consent, go-ahead (*inf*), green light, permission, sanction, say-so (*inf*), seal of approval

old *adj* 1 = **aged**, ancient, antediluvian, antiquated, antique, decrepit, elderly, mature, senile, timeworn, venerable 3 = **former**, earlier, erstwhile, one-time, previous

omen *n* = **sign**, foreboding, indication, portent, premonition, presage, warning

omit ❶ v omitting, omitted **1** leave out. **2** neglect (to do something). **omission** n.

omnibus n **1** several books or TV or radio programmes made into one. **2** old-fashioned bus.

omnipotent ❶ adj having unlimited power. **omnipotence** n.

omniscient ❶ [om-**niss**-ee-ent] adj knowing or seeming to know everything. **omniscience** n.

omnivorous [om-**niv**-vor-uss] adj eating food obtained from both animals and plants. **omnivore** n animal that eats any type of food.

on prep **1** indicating position above, attachment, closeness, etc. e.g. lying on the ground; a puppet on a string; on the coast. ▷ adv **2** in operation. **3** continuing. **4** forwards. ▷ adj **5** operating. **6** taking place. ▷ n **7** Cricket side of the field on which the batsman stands. **on line, online** adj **1** (of a computer) directly controlled by a central processor. **2** relating to the Internet, e.g. online shopping. **on-message** adj (esp. of a politician) following the official Party line.

ON Ontario.

once ❶ adv **1** on one occasion. **2** formerly. ▷ conj **3** as soon as. **at once 1** immediately. **2** simultaneously. **once-over** n informal quick, casual examination.

one adj **1** single, lone. ▷ n **2** number or figure 1. **3** single unit. ▷ pron **4** any person. **oneness** n unity. **oneself** pron reflexive form of ONE. **one-liner** n witty remark. **one-night stand** sexual encounter lasting one night. **one-sided** adj considering only one point of view. **one-way** adj allowing movement in one direction only.

onerous ❶ [**own**-er-uss] adj (of a task) difficult to carry out.

onion n strongly flavoured edible bulb.

onlooker ❶ n person who watches without taking part.

only ❶ adj **1** alone of its kind. ▷ adv **2** exclusively. **3** merely. **4** no more than. ▷ conj **5** but.

onset ❶ n beginning.

onslaught ❶ n violent attack.

onto prep **1** to a position on. **2** aware of, e.g. she's onto us.

onus ❶ [**own**-uss] n, pl **onuses** responsibility or burden.

onward ❶ adj **1** directed or moving forward. ▷ adv **2** (also **onwards**) ahead, forward.

onyx n type of quartz with coloured layers.

ooze¹ ❶ v **1** flow slowly. **2** overflow with (a quality). ▷ n **3** sluggish flow. **oozy** adj.

o

——————— THESAURUS ———————

omit v **1** = **leave out**, drop, eliminate, exclude, pass over, skip **2** = **forget**, neglect, overlook

omnipotent adj = **almighty**, all-powerful, supreme

omniscient adj = **all-knowing**, all-wise

once adv **2** = **at one time**, formerly, long ago, once upon a time, previously **at once 1** = **immediately**, directly, forthwith, instantly, now, right away, straight away, this (very) minute **2** = **simultaneously**, at the same time, together

onerous adj = **difficult**, burdensome, demanding, exacting, hard, heavy, laborious, oppressive, taxing

onlooker n = **observer**, bystander,

eyewitness, looker-on, spectator, viewer, watcher, witness

only adj **1** = **sole**, exclusive, individual, lone, single, solitary, unique ▷ adv **3** = **merely**, barely, just, purely, simply

onset n = **beginning**, inception, outbreak, start

onslaught n = **attack**, assault, blitz, charge, offensive, onrush, onset

onus n = **burden**, liability, load, obligation, responsibility, task

onward adv **2** (also **onwards**) = **ahead**, beyond, forth, forward, in front, on

ooze¹ v **1** = **seep**, drain, dribble, drip, escape, filter, leak

ooze² ⊙ *n* soft mud at the bottom of a lake or river.

opal *n* iridescent precious stone.
opalescent *adj* iridescent like an opal.

opaque ⊙ *adj* not able to be seen through, not transparent. **opacity** *n*.

open ⊙ *adj* **1** not closed. **2** not covered.
3 unfolded. **4** ready for business.
5 free from obstruction, accessible.
6 unrestricted. **7** not finalized. **8** frank.
▷ *v* **9** (cause to) become open. **10** begin.
▷ *n* **11** *Sport* competition which all may enter. **in the open** outdoors. **openly** *adv* without concealment. **opening** *n* **1** opportunity. **2** hole. ▷ *adj* **3** first. **opencast mining** mining at the surface and not underground. **open day** day on which a school or college is open to the public. **open-handed** *adj* generous. **open house** hospitality to visitors at any time. **open letter** letter to an individual that the writer makes public in a newspaper or magazine. **open-minded** *adj* receptive to new ideas. **open-plan** *adj* (of a house or office) having few interior walls. **open prison** prison with minimal security.

opera *n* drama in which the text is sung to an orchestral accompaniment. **operatic** *adj* **operetta** *n* light-hearted comic opera. **opera glasses** small binoculars used by theatre audiences to see the stage.

ophthalmic *adj* relating to the eye.
ophthalmology *n* study of the eye and its diseases. **ophthalmologist** *n*.

opinion ⊙ *n* personal belief or judgment.
opinionated *adj* having strong opinions.
opine *v* old-fashioned express an opinion.
opinion poll see POLL.

opium *n* addictive narcotic drug made from poppy seeds.

opossum *n* small marsupial of America or Australia.

opponent ⊙ *n* person one is working against in a contest, battle, or argument.

opportunity ⊙ *n*, *pl* **-ties 1** favourable time or condition. **2** good chance.
opportunity shop *Aust & NZ* shop selling second-hand clothes, sometimes for charity (also **op-shop**).

  ● **SPELLING TIP**
  ● Lots of people forget that **opportunity**,
  ● which is a very common word, has
  ● two *p*s.

oppose ⊙ *v* work against. **be opposed to** disagree with or disapprove of. **opposite** *adj* situated on the other side. **opposition** *n* **1** obstruction or hostility. **2** group opposing another. **3** political party not in power.

oppress ⊙ *v* **1** control by cruelty or force.

——————————————————————————————— THESAURUS ——————

ooze² *n* = **mud**, alluvium, mire, silt, slime, sludge

opaque *adj* = **cloudy**, dim, dull, filmy, hazy, impenetrable, murky

open *adj* **1** = **unclosed**, agape, ajar, gaping, uncovered, unfastened, unlocked, yawning **3** = **extended**, unfolded, unfurled **5** = **accessible**, available, free, public, unoccupied, vacant **6** = **unrestricted** **7** = **unresolved**, arguable, debatable, moot, undecided, unsettled **8** = **frank**, candid, guileless, honest, sincere, transparent ▷ *v* **9** = **unfasten**, expand, spread (out), unblock, uncork, uncover, undo, unfold, unfurl, unlock, unroll, untie, unwrap **10** = **start**, begin, commence,

inaugurate, initiate, kick off (*inf*), launch, set in motion

opinion *n* = **belief**, assessment, feeling, idea, impression, judgment, point of view, sentiment, theory, view

opponent *n* = **adversary**, antagonist, challenger, competitor, contestant, enemy, foe, rival

opportunity *n* = **chance**, moment, occasion, opening, scope, time

oppose *v* = **fight**, block, combat, counter, defy, resist, take issue with, take on, thwart, withstand

oppress *v* **1** = **subjugate**, abuse, maltreat, persecute, subdue, suppress, wrong **2** = **depress**, afflict, burden, dispirit,

2 depress. **oppression** n **oppressor**
n **oppressive** adj 1 tyrannical. 2 (of
weather) hot and humid.

opt ❶ v show a preference, choose.

optic adj relating to the eyes or sight.
optics n science of sight and light.
optical adj.

optimism n tendency to take the most
hopeful view. **optimist** n **optimistic** adj
optimistically adv.

optimum ❶ n, pl **-ma, -mums** 1 best
possible conditions. ▷ adj 2 most
favourable. **optimal** adj **optimize** v make
the most of.

option ❶ n 1 choice. 2 thing chosen.
3 right to buy or sell something at a
specified price within a given time.
optional adj possible but not compulsory.

optometrist n person qualified to
prescribe glasses. **optometry** n.

opulent ❶ [**op**-pew-lent] adj having or
indicating wealth. **opulence** n.

opus ❶ n, pl **opuses, opera** artistic
creation, esp. a musical work.

or conj used to join alternatives, e.g. tea or
coffee.

OR Oregon.

oracle ❶ n 1 shrine of an ancient god.
2 prophecy, often obscure, revealed at a
shrine. 3 person believed to make infallible
predictions. **oracular** adj.

oral ❶ adj 1 spoken. 2 (of a drug) to be taken
by mouth. ▷ n 3 spoken examination.
orally adv.

orange n 1 reddish-yellow citrus fruit. ▷ adj
2 reddish-yellow.

orang-utan, orang-utang n large
reddish-brown ape with long arms.

orator ❶ [**or**-rat-tor] n skilful public
speaker. **oration** n formal speech.

oratory ❶ [**or**-rat-tree] n art of making
speeches. **oratorical** adj.

orb n ceremonial decorated sphere with a
cross on top, carried by a monarch.

orbit ❶ n 1 curved path of a planet,
satellite, or spacecraft around another
body. 2 sphere of influence. ▷ v **orbiting,
orbited** 3 move in an orbit around. 4 put
(a satellite or spacecraft) into orbit.
orbital adj.

orchard n area where fruit trees are
grown.

orchestra n 1 large group of musicians,
esp. playing a variety of instruments.
2 (also **orchestra pit**) area of a theatre
in front of the stage, reserved for the
musicians. **orchestral** adj **orchestrate** v
1 arrange (music) for orchestra. 2 organize
(something) to produce a particular result.
orchestration n.

orchid n plant with flowers that have
unusual lip-shaped petals.

harass, sadden, torment, vex

opt v = **choose**, decide (on), elect, go for,
plump for, prefer

optimum adj 2 = **ideal**, best, highest,
optimal, peak, perfect, superlative

option n 1 = **choice**, alternative,
preference, selection

opulent adj = **rich**, affluent,
lavish, luxurious, moneyed,
prosperous, sumptuous, wealthy,
well-off, well-to-do

opus n = **work**, brainchild, composition,
creation, oeuvre, piece, production

oracle n 2 = **prophecy**, divination,
prediction, prognostication, revelation

3 = **authority**, adviser, guru, mana (NZ),
mastermind, mentor, pundit, wizard

oral adj 1 = **spoken**, verbal, vocal

orator n = **public speaker**, declaimer,
lecturer, rhetorician, speaker

oratory n = **eloquence**, declamation,
elocution, grandiloquence, public
speaking, rhetoric, speech-making

orbit n 1 = **path**, circle, course, cycle,
revolution, rotation, trajectory
2 = **sphere of influence**, ambit,
compass, domain, influence, range,
reach, scope, sweep ▷ v 3 = **circle**,
circumnavigate, encircle, revolve
around

ordain ❶ v 1 make (someone) a member of the clergy. 2 order or establish with authority.

ordeal ❶ n painful or difficult experience.

ordinal number n number showing a position in a series, e.g. *first*; *second*.

ordinance n official rule or order.

ordinary ❶ adj 1 usual or normal. 2 dull or commonplace. **ordinarily** adv.

ordnance n weapons and military supplies. **Ordnance Survey** n official organization making maps of Britain.

ore n (rock containing) a mineral which yields metal.

oregano [or-rig-**gah**-no] n sweet-smelling herb used in cooking.

organ ❶ n 1 part of an animal or plant that has a particular function, such as the heart or lungs. 2 musical keyboard instrument in which notes are produced by forcing air through pipes. 3 means of conveying information, esp. a newspaper. **organist** n organ player.

organism ❶ n any living animal or plant.

organize ❶ v 1 make arrangements for. 2 arrange systematically. **organization** n 1 group of people working together. 2 act of organizing. **organizational** adj **organizer** n.

orgasm n most intense point of sexual pleasure. **orgasmic** adj.

orgy ❶ n, pl -gies 1 party involving promiscuous sexual activity. 2 unrestrained indulgence, e.g. *an orgy of destruction*.

orient, orientate ❶ v 1 position (oneself) according to one's surroundings. 2 position (a map) in relation to the points of the compass. **orientation** n **orienteering** n sport in which competitors hike over a course using a compass and map.

orifice ❶ [or-rif-fiss] n opening or hole.

origami [or-rig-**gah**-mee] n Japanese decorative art of paper folding.

origin ❶ n point from which something develops. **original** adj 1 first or earliest. 2 new, not copied or based on something else. 3 able to think up new ideas. ▷ n 4 first version, from which others are copied. **original sin** human imperfection and mortality as a result of Adam's disobedience. **originality** n **originally** adv **originate** v come or bring into existence. **origination** n **originator** n.

ornament ❶ n 1 decorative object. ▷ v 2 decorate. **ornamental** adj

———————————————————————— THESAURUS ————

ordain v 1 = **appoint**, anoint, consecrate, invest, nominate 2 = **order**, decree, demand, dictate, fix, lay down, legislate, prescribe, rule, will

ordeal n = **hardship**, agony, anguish, baptism of fire, nightmare, suffering, test, torture, trial, tribulation(s)

ordinary adj 1 = **usual**, common, conventional, everyday, normal, regular, routine, standard, stock, typical 2 = **commonplace**, banal, humble, humdrum, modest, mundane, plain, run-of-the-mill, unremarkable, workaday

organ n 1 = **part**, element, structure, unit 3 = **medium**, forum, mouthpiece, vehicle, voice

organism n = **creature**, animal, being,

body, entity

organize v 1 = **plan**, arrange, coordinate, marshal, put together, run, set up, take care of 2 = **put in order**, arrange, classify, group, systematize

orgy n 1 = **revel**, bacchanalia, carousal, debauch, revelry, Saturnalia 2 = **spree**, binge (*inf*), bout, excess, indulgence, overindulgence, splurge, surfeit

orient, orientate v 1 = **adjust**, acclimatize, adapt, align, familiarize

orifice n = **opening**, aperture, cleft, hole, mouth, pore, rent, vent

origin n = **root**, base, basis, derivation, foundation, fount, fountainhead, inception, launch, source, start, wellspring

ornament n 1 = **decoration**, accessory,

ornamental *adj* ornamentation *n*.
ornate ❶ *adj* highly decorated, elaborate.
ornithology *n* study of birds.
ornithological *adj* ornithologist *n*.
orphan *n* child whose parents are dead.
orphanage *n* children's home for orphans.
orphaned *adj* having no living parents.
orthodox ❶ *adj* conforming to established views. orthodoxy *n* Orthodox Church dominant Christian Church in Eastern Europe.
oscillate ❶ [oss-ill-late] *v* swing back and forth. oscillation *n* oscilloscope [oss-sill-oh-scope] *n* instrument that shows the shape of a wave on a cathode-ray tube.
osmosis *n* 1 movement of a liquid through a membrane from a lower to a higher concentration. 2 process of subtle influence. osmotic *adj*.
osprey *n* large fish-eating bird of prey.
ossify ❶ *v* -fying, -fied 1 (cause to) become bone, harden. 2 become inflexible. ossification *n*.
ostensible ❶ *adj* apparent, seeming. ostensibly *adv*.
ostentation ❶ *n* pretentious display. ostentatious *adj*.
osteopathy *n* medical treatment involving manipulation of the joints.

osteopath *n* osteopathic *adj*.
ostracize ❶ *v* exclude (a person) from a group. ostracism *n*.
ostrich *n* large African bird that runs fast but cannot fly.
other ❶ *adj* 1 remaining in a group of which one or some have been specified. 2 different from the ones specified or understood. 3 additional. ▷ *n* 4 other person or thing. otherwise *conj* 1 or else, if not. ▷ *adv* 2 differently, in another way. otherworldly *adj* concerned with spiritual rather than practical matters.
otter *n* small brown freshwater mammal that eats fish.
ouch *interj* exclamation of sudden pain.
ought *v* used to express: 1 obligation, e.g. *you ought to pay*. 2 advisability, e.g. *you ought to diet*. 3 probability, e.g. *you ought to know by then*.
ounce *n* unit of weight equal to one sixteenth of a pound (28.4 grams).
our *adj* belonging to us. ours *pron* thing(s) belonging to us. ourselves *pron* emphatic and reflexive form of WE or US.
oust ❶ *v* force (someone) out, expel.
out ❶ *adv, adj* 1 denoting movement or distance away from, a state of being used up or extinguished, public availability, etc.

o

bauble, knick-knack, trinket ▷ *v*
2 = **decorate**, adorn, beautify, embellish, festoon, grace, prettify
ornate *adj* = **elaborate**, baroque, busy, decorated, fancy, florid, fussy, ornamented, overelaborate, rococo
orthodox *adj* = **established**, accepted, approved, conventional, customary, official, received, traditional, well-established
oscillate *v* = **swing**, seesaw, sway, vibrate
ossify *v* 2 = **harden**, solidify, stiffen
ostensible *adj* = **apparent**, outward, pretended, professed, purported, seeming, so-called, superficial, supposed
ostentation *n* = **display**, affectation,

exhibitionism, flamboyance, flashiness, flaunting, parade, pomp, pretentiousness, show, showing off (*inf*)
ostracize *v* = **exclude**, banish, cast out, cold-shoulder, exile, give (someone) the cold shoulder, reject, send to Coventry, shun
other *adj* 1 = **spare** 2 = **different**, alternative, contrasting, dissimilar, distinct, diverse, separate, unrelated, variant 3 = **additional**, added, auxiliary, extra, further, more, supplementary
oust *v* = **expel**, depose, dislodge, displace, dispossess, eject, throw out, topple, turn out, unseat
out *adj* 1 a = **away**, abroad, absent, elsewhere, gone, not at home, outside

e.g. *oil was pouring out*; *turn the light out*; *her new book is out*. ▷ **v 2** *informal* name (a public figure) as being homosexual. **out of** at or to a point outside. **out-of-date** *adj* old-fashioned. **outer** *adj* on the outside. **outermost** *adj* furthest out. **outing** *n* leisure trip. **outward** *adj* **1** apparent. ▷ *adv* **2** (also **outwards**) away from somewhere. **outwardly** *adv*.

outbreak ❶ *n* sudden occurrence (of something unpleasant).

outburst ❶ *n* sudden expression of emotion.

outcast ❶ *n* person rejected by a particular group.

outcome ❶ *n* result.

outcry ❶ *n*, *pl* **-cries** vehement or widespread protest.

outdoors *adv* **1** in(to) the open air. ▷ *n* **2** the open air. **outdoor** *adj*.

outfit ❶ *n* **1** matching set of clothes. **2** *informal* group of people working together. **outfitter** *n* supplier of men's clothes.

outgoing ❶ *adj* **1** leaving. **2** sociable. **outgoings** *pl n* expenses.

outlandish ❶ *adj* extremely unconventional.

outlaw ❶ *n* **1** *Hist* criminal deprived of legal protection, bandit. ▷ *v* **2** make illegal. **3** *Hist* make (someone) an outlaw.

outlay ❶ *n* expenditure.

outline ❶ *n* **1** short general explanation. **2** line defining the shape of something. ▷ *v* **3** summarize. **4** show the general shape of.

outlook ❶ *n* **1** attitude. **2** probable outcome.

outlying ❶ *adj* distant from the main area.

outmoded ❶ *adj* no longer fashionable or accepted.

——————————————— THESAURUS ———————————————

b = **extinguished**, at an end, dead, ended, exhausted, expired, finished, used up

outbreak *n* = **eruption**, burst, epidemic, explosion, flare-up, outburst, rash, upsurge

outburst *n* = **outpouring**, paroxysm, spasm, surge

outcast *n* = **pariah**, *persona non grata*, castaway, exile, leper, refugee, vagabond, wretch

outcome *n* = **result**, conclusion, consequence, end, issue, payoff (*inf*), upshot

outcry *n* = **protest**, clamour, commotion, complaint, hue and cry, hullabaloo, outburst, uproar

outfit *n* **1** = **costume**, clothes, ensemble, garb, get-up (*inf*), kit, suit **2** *Inf* = **group**, company, crew, organization, setup (*inf*), squad, team, unit

outgoing *adj* **1** = **leaving**, departing, former, retiring, withdrawing **2** = **sociable**, approachable, communicative, expansive, extrovert, friendly, gregarious, open, warm

outlandish *adj* = **strange**, bizarre, exotic, fantastic, far-out (*sl*), freakish, outré,

preposterous, unheard-of, weird

outlaw *n* **1** *Hist* = **bandit**, brigand, desperado, fugitive, highwayman, marauder, outcast, robber ▷ *v* **2** = **forbid**, ban, bar, disallow, exclude, prohibit, proscribe **3** *Hist* = **put a price on (someone's) head**

outlay *n* = **expenditure**, cost, expenses, investment, outgoings, spending

outline *n* **1** = **summary**, recapitulation, résumé, rundown, synopsis, thumbnail sketch **2** = **shape**, configuration, contour, delineation, figure, form, profile, silhouette ▷ *v* **3** = **summarize**, adumbrate **4** = **draft**, delineate, plan, rough out, sketch (in), trace

outlook *n* **1** = **attitude**, angle, frame of mind, perspective, point of view, slant, standpoint, viewpoint **2** = **prospect**, expectations, forecast, future

outlying *adj* = **remote**, distant, far-flung, out-of-the-way, peripheral, provincial

outmoded *adj* = **old-fashioned**, anachronistic, antiquated, archaic, obsolete, out-of-date, outworn, passé, unfashionable

outpatient n patient who does not stay in hospital overnight.

outport n Canad isolated fishing village, esp. in Newfoundland.

outpost n outlying settlement.

output ❶ n 1 amount produced. 2 power, voltage, or current delivered by an electrical circuit. 3 Computers data produced. ▷ v 4 Computers produce (data) at the end of a process.

outrage ❶ n 1 great moral indignation. 2 gross violation of morality. ▷ v 3 offend morally. **outrageous** adj 1 shocking. 2 offensive.

outright ❶ adj, adv 1 absolute(ly). 2 open(ly) and direct(ly).

outset ❶ n beginning.

outside ❶ prep, adj adv 1 indicating movement to or position on the exterior. ▷ adj 2 unlikely, e.g. an outside chance. 3 coming from outside. ▷ n 4 external area or surface. **outsider** n 1 person outside a specific group. 2 contestant thought unlikely to win.

outsize, outsized ❶ adj larger than normal.

outskirts ❶ pl n outer areas, esp. of a town.

outspan v S Afr relax.

outspoken ❶ adj 1 tending to say what one thinks. 2 said openly.

outstanding ❶ adj 1 excellent. 2 still to be dealt with or paid.

outweigh ❶ v be more important, significant, or influential than.

outwit ❶ v -witting, -witted get the better of (someone) by cunning.

oval ❶ adj 1 egg-shaped. ▷ n 2 anything that is oval in shape.

ovary n, pl -ries female egg-producing organ. **ovarian** adj.

ovation ❶ n enthusiastic round of applause.

—————— THESAURUS ——————

output n 1 = **production**, achievement, manufacture, productivity, yield

outrage n 1 = **indignation**, anger, fury, hurt, resentment, shock, wrath 2 = **violation**, abuse, affront, desecration, indignity, insult, offence, sacrilege, violence ▷ v 3 = **offend**, affront, incense, infuriate, madden, scandalize, shock

outright adj 1 = **absolute**, complete, out-and-out, perfect, thorough, thoroughgoing, total, unconditional, unmitigated, unqualified 2 = **direct**, definite, flat, straightforward, unequivocal, unqualified ▷ adv 1 = **absolutely**, completely, straightforwardly, thoroughly, to the full 2 = **openly**, overtly

outset n = **beginning**, commencement, inauguration, inception, kickoff (inf), onset, opening, start

outside adj 1 = **external**, exterior, extraneous, outer, outward 2 = **remote**, distant, faint, marginal, slight, slim, small, unlikely ▷ n 4 = **exterior**, facade, face, front, skin, surface, topside

outsize, outsized adj = **extra-large**, giant, gigantic, huge, jumbo (inf), mammoth, monster, oversized

outskirts pl n = **edge**, boundary, environs, periphery, suburbia, suburbs

outspoken adj 1 = **plain-spoken**, unequivocal 2 = **forthright**, abrupt, blunt, explicit, frank, open, unceremonious

outstanding adj 1 = **excellent**, exceptional, great, important, impressive, special, superior, superlative 2 = **unpaid**, due, payable, pending, remaining, uncollected, unsettled

outweigh v = **override**, cancel (out), compensate for, eclipse, prevail over, take precedence over, tip the scales

outwit v = **outsmart** (inf), cheat, dupe, get the better of, outfox, outmanoeuvre, outthink, put one over on (inf), swindle, take in (inf)

oval adj 1 = **elliptical**, egg-shaped, ovoid

ovation n = **applause**, acclaim, acclamation, big hand, cheers, clapping, plaudits, tribute

O

oven *n* heated compartment or container for cooking or for drying or firing ceramics.

over ❶ *prep, adv* **1** indicating position on the top of, movement to the other side of, amount greater than, etc. e.g. *a room over the garage; climbing over the fence; over fifty pounds.* ▷ *adj* **2** finished. ▷ *n* **3** Cricket series of six balls bowled from one end. **overly** *adv* excessively.

over- *prefix* **1** too much, e.g. *overeat.* **2** above, e.g. *overlord.* **3** on top, e.g. *overshoe.*

overall ❶ *adj, adv* **1** in total. ▷ *n* **2** coat-shaped protective garment. ▷ *pl* **3** protective garment consisting of trousers with a jacket or bib and braces attached.

overbearing ❶ *adj* unpleasantly forceful.

overboard *adv* from a boat into the water. **go overboard** go to extremes, esp. in enthusiasm.

overcast ❶ *adj* (of the sky) covered by clouds.

overcome ❶ *v* **1** gain control over after an effort. **2** (of an emotion) affect strongly.

overdose *n* **1** excessive dose of a drug. ▷ *v* **2** take an overdose.

overdraft *n* **1** overdrawing. **2** amount overdrawn.

overdrive *n* very high gear in a motor vehicle.

overgrown *adj* thickly covered with plants and weeds.

overhaul ❶ *v* **1** examine and repair. ▷ *n* **2** examination and repair.

overhead ❶ *adv, adj* above one's head. **overheads** *pl n* general cost of maintaining a business.

overland *adj, adv* by land.

overlap *v* **1** share part of the same space or period of time (as). ▷ *n* **2** area overlapping.

overlook ❶ *v* **1** fail to notice. **2** ignore. **3** look at from above.

overseas *adv, adj* to, of, or from a distant country.

overshadow ❶ *v* **1** reduce the significance of (a person or thing) by comparison. **2** sadden the atmosphere of.

oversight ❶ *n* mistake caused by not noticing something.

overt ❶ *adj* open, not hidden. **overtly** *adv*.

— THESAURUS —

over *prep* **1 a = on top of**, above, on, upon **b = more than**, above, exceeding, in excess of ▷ *adv* **1 c = above**, aloft, on high, overhead **d = extra**, beyond, in addition, in excess, left over **2 = finished**, bygone, closed, completed, concluded, done (with), ended, gone, past

overall *adj* **1 = total**, all-embracing, blanket, complete, comprehensive, general, global, inclusive, overarching ▷ *adv* **1 = in general**, on the whole

overbearing *adj* **= dictatorial**, arrogant, bossy (*inf*), domineering, haughty, high-handed, imperious, supercilious, superior

overcast *adj* **= cloudy**, dismal, dreary, dull, grey, leaden, louring *or* lowering, murky

overcome *v* **1 = surmount**, master, overpower, overwhelm, prevail, subdue, subjugate, triumph over **2 = conquer**, beat, defeat, vanquish

overhaul *v* **1 = check**, do up (*inf*), examine, inspect, recondition, repair, restore, service ▷ *n* **2 = checkup**, check, examination, going-over (*inf*), inspection, reconditioning, service

overhead *adv* **= above**, aloft, in the sky, on high, skyward, up above, upward ▷ *adj* **= aerial**, overhanging, upper

overlook *v* **1 = miss**, disregard, forget, neglect, omit, pass **2 = ignore**, condone, disregard, excuse, forgive, make allowances for, pardon, turn a blind eye to, wink at **3 = have a view of**, look over *or* out on

overshadow *v* **1 = outshine**, dominate, dwarf, eclipse, leave *or* put in the shade, surpass, tower above **2 = spoil**, blight, mar, put a damper on, ruin, temper

oversight *n* **= mistake**, blunder, carelessness, error, fault, lapse, neglect, omission, slip

overt *adj* **= open**, blatant, manifest,

overtake ❶ v move past (a vehicle or person) travelling in the same direction.

overthrow ❶ v 1 defeat and replace. ▷ n 2 downfall, destruction.

overtime n, adv 1 (paid work done) in addition to one's normal working hours. ▷ n 2 period of extra time in a contest or game.

overtone ❶ n additional meaning.

overture ❶ n 1 Music orchestral introduction. ▷ pl 2 opening moves in a new relationship.

overwhelm ❶ v 1 overpower, esp. emotionally. 2 defeat by force. **overwhelming** adj.

overwrought ❶ adj nervous and agitated.

owe ❶ v be obliged to pay (a sum of money) to (a person). **owing to** as a result of.

owl n night bird of prey. **owlish** adj.

own ❶ adj 1 used to emphasize possession, e.g. my own idea. ▷ v 2 possess. **owner** n **ownership** n **own up** v confess.

ox n, pl **oxen** castrated bull.

oxide n compound of oxygen and one other element. **oxidize** v combine chemically with oxygen, as in burning or rusting. ·

oxygen n Chem gaseous element essential to life and combustion. **oxygenate** v add oxygen to.

oyster n edible shellfish.

oz. ounce.

Oz n slang Australia.

ozone n strong-smelling form of oxygen. **ozone layer** layer of ozone in the upper atmosphere that filters out ultraviolet radiation.

THESAURUS

---

observable, obvious, plain, public, unconcealed, undisguised

overtake v = **pass**, catch up with, get past, leave behind, outdistance, outdo, outstrip, overhaul

overthrow v 1 = **defeat**, bring down, conquer, depose, dethrone, oust, overcome, overpower, topple, unseat, vanquish n 2 = **downfall**, defeat, destruction, dethronement, fall, ousting, undoing, unseating

overtone n = **hint**, connotation, implication, innuendo, intimation, nuance, sense, suggestion, undercurrent

overture n 1 Music = **introduction**, opening, prelude ▷ pl 2 = **approach**, advance, invitation, offer, proposal,

proposition

overwhelm v 1 = **overcome**, bowl over (inf), devastate, knock (someone) for six (inf), stagger, sweep (someone) off his or her feet, take (someone's) breath away 2 = **destroy**, crush, cut to pieces, massacre, overpower, overrun, rout

overwrought adj = **agitated**, distracted, excited, frantic, keyed up, on edge, overexcited, tense, uptight (inf), wired (sl)

owe v = **be in debt**, be in arrears

own adj 1 = **personal**, individual, particular, private ▷ v 2 = **possess**, be in possession of, enjoy, have, hold, keep, retain **own up** v = **confess**, admit, come clean, tell the truth

o

Pp

p penny *or* pence.
pace ❶ *n* **1** single step in walking. **2** length of a step. **3** rate of progress. ▷ *v* **4** walk up and down, esp. in anxiety. **5** (foll. by *out*) cross or measure with steps. **pacemaker** *n* **1** electronic device surgically implanted in a person with heart disease to regulate the heartbeat. **2** person who, by taking the lead early in a race, sets the pace for the rest of the competitors.
pacifier *n US & Canad* a baby's dummy or teething ring.
pacify ❶ *v* **-fying, -fied** soothe, calm. **pacification** *n*.
pack ❶ *v* **1** put (clothes etc.) together in a suitcase or bag. **2** put (goods) into containers or parcels. **3** fill with people or things. ▷ *n* **4** bag carried on a person's or animal's back. **5** *Chiefly US* same as PACKET. **6** set of playing cards. **7** group of dogs or wolves that hunt together. **pack in** *v informal* stop doing. **pack off** *v* send away.
packsack *n* a US and Canadian word for HAVERSACK.

pact ❶ *n* formal agreement.
pad ❶ *n* **1** piece of soft material used for protection, support, absorption of liquid, etc. **2** number of sheets of paper fastened at the edge. **3** fleshy underpart of an animal's paw. **4** place for launching rockets. **5** *slang* home. ▷ *v* **padding, padded 6** protect or fill with soft material. **7** walk with soft steps. **padding** *n* **1** soft material used to pad something. **2** unnecessary words put into a speech or written work to make it longer.
paddle¹ ❶ *n* **1** short oar with a broad blade at one or each end. ▷ *v* **2** move (a canoe etc.) with a paddle. **paddle steamer** ship propelled by paddle wheels.
paddle² ❶ *v* walk barefoot in shallow water.
paddock *n* small field or enclosure for horses.
paddy field *n* field where rice is grown (also **paddy**).
pademelon, paddymelon [pad-ee-mel-an] *n* small Australian wallaby.
padlock *n* detachable lock with a hinged hoop fastened over a ring on the object to be secured.
paediatrics *n* branch of medicine concerned with diseases of children. **paediatrician** *n*.
paedophile *n* person who is sexually attracted to children.
paella [pie-**ell**-a] *n* Spanish dish of rice, chicken, shellfish, and vegetables.

———————————————————————— THESAURUS ————————

pace *n* **1** = **step**, gait, stride, tread, walk **3** = **speed**, rate, tempo, velocity ▷ *v* **4** = **stride**, march, patrol, pound **5** (foll. by *out*) = **measure**, count, mark out, step
pacify *v* = **calm**, allay, appease, assuage, mollify, placate, propitiate, soothe
pack *v* **1** = **package**, bundle, load, store, stow **2, 3** = **cram**, compress, crowd, fill, jam, press, ram, stuff ▷ *n* **4** = **bundle**, back pack, burden, kitbag, knapsack, load, parcel, rucksack **5** *Chiefly US* = **packet**, package **pack in** *v Inf* = **stop**, cease, chuck (*inf*), give up *or* over, kick

(*inf*) **pack off** *v* = **send away**, dismiss, send packing (*inf*)
pact *n* = **agreement**, alliance, bargain, covenant, deal, treaty, understanding
pad *n* **1** = **cushion**, buffer, protection, stuffing, wad **2** = **writing pad**, block, jotter **3** = **paw**, foot, sole **5** *Sl* = **home**, apartment, flat, place ▷ *v* **6** = **pack**, cushion, fill, protect, stuff **7** = **sneak**, creep, go barefoot, steal
paddle¹ *n* **1** = **oar**, scull ▷ *v* **2** = **row**, propel, pull, scull
paddle² *v* = **wade**, slop, splash (about)

pagan ● *n, adj* (person) not belonging to one of the world's main religions.

page¹ ● *n* **1** (one side of) a sheet of paper forming a book etc. **2** screenful of information from a website or teletext service.

page² ● *n* **1** (also **pageboy**) small boy who attends a bride at her wedding. **2** *Hist* boy in training for knighthood. ▷ *v* **3** summon (someone) by bleeper or loudspeaker, in order to pass on a message.

pageant ● *n* parade or display of people in costume, usu. illustrating a scene from history. **pageantry** *n*.

pagoda *n* pyramid-shaped Asian temple or tower.

pail *n* (contents of) a bucket.

pain ● *n* **1** physical or mental suffering. ▷ *pl* **2** trouble, effort. **on pain of** subject to the penalty of. **painful** *adj* **painfully** *adv* **painless** *adj* **painlessly** *adv* **painkiller** *n* drug that relieves pain.

paint ● *n* **1** coloured substance, spread on a surface with a brush or roller. ▷ *v* **2** colour or coat with paint. **3** use paint to make a picture of. **painter** *n* **painting** *n*.

pair ● *n* **1** set of two things matched for use together. ▷ *v* **2** group or be grouped in twos.

pal ● *n informal* friend.

palace *n* **1** residence of a king, bishop, etc. **2** large grand building.

palate ● *n* **1** roof of the mouth. **2** sense of taste.

palaver ● [pal-**lah**-ver] *n* time-wasting fuss.

pale¹ ● *adj* **1** light, whitish. **2** whitish in the face, esp. through illness or shock. ▷ *v* **3** become pale. **pale in, by comparison with** appear inferior when compared with.

pale² ● *n* wooden or metal post used in fences. **beyond the pale** outside the limits of social convention.

palette *n* artist's flat board for mixing colours on.

palindrome *n* word or phrase that reads the same backwards as forwards.

paling *n* wooden or metal post used in fences.

pall¹ ● *n* **1** cloth spread over a coffin. **2** dark cloud (of smoke). **3** depressing oppressive

pagan *n* = **heathen**, idolater, infidel, polytheist ▷ *adj* = **heathen**, idolatrous, infidel, polytheistic

page¹ *n* **1** = **folio**, leaf, sheet, side

page² *n* **1** = **attendant**, pageboy **2** *Hist* = **squire** ▷ *v* **3** = **call**, send for, summon

pageant *n* = **show**, display, parade, procession, spectacle, tableau

pain *n* **1 a** = **hurt**, ache, discomfort, irritation, pang, soreness, tenderness, throb, twinge **b** = **suffering**, agony, anguish, distress, heartache, misery, torment, torture ▷ *pl* **2** = **trouble**, bother, care, diligence, effort

paint *n* **1** = **colouring**, colour, dye, pigment, stain, tint ▷ *v* **2** = **coat**, apply, colour, cover, daub **3** = **depict**, draw, picture, portray, represent, sketch

pair *n* **2** = **couple**, brace, duo, twins ▷ *v* **2** = **couple**, bracket, join, match (up)

team, twin

pal *n Inf* = **friend**, buddy (*inf*), chum (*inf*), cobber (*Aust or old-fashioned NZ inf*), companion, comrade, crony, mate (*inf*)

palate *n* **2** = **taste**, appetite, stomach

palaver *n* = **fuss**, business (*inf*), carry-on (*inf, chiefly Brit*), pantomime (*inf, chiefly Brit*), performance (*inf*), rigmarole, song and dance (*Brit inf*), to-do

pale¹ *adj* **1** = **white**, ashen, bleached, colourless, faded, light **2** = **ashen**, pallid, pasty, wan, white *v* **3** = **become pale**, blanch, go white, lose colour, whiten

pale² *n* = **post**, paling, palisade, picket, slat, stake, upright **beyond the pale** = **unacceptable**, barbaric, forbidden, improper, inadmissible, indecent, irregular, not done, out of line, unseemly, unspeakable, unsuitable

pall¹ *n* **2** = **cloud**, mantle, shadow, shroud,

P

atmosphere. **pallbearer** n person who helps to carry the coffin at a funeral.

pall² ● v become boring.

pallet n portable platform for storing and moving goods.

palliate v lessen the severity of (something) without curing it. **palliative** adj **1** giving temporary or partial relief. ▷ n **2** something, for example a drug, that palliates.

pallid ● adj pale, esp. because ill or weak. **pallor** n.

palm¹ n inner surface of the hand. **palm off** v get rid of (an unwanted thing or person), esp. by deceit. **palmtop** n computer small enough to be held in the hand.

palm² n tropical tree with long pointed leaves growing out of the top of a straight trunk. **Palm Sunday** Sunday before Easter.

palomino n, pl **-nos** gold-coloured horse with a white mane and tail.

palpable ● adj **1** obvious, e.g. a palpable hit. **2** so intense as to seem capable of being touched, e.g. the tension is almost palpable. **palpably** adv.

palpitate ● v **1** (of the heart) beat rapidly. **2** flutter or tremble. **palpitation** n.

palsy [**pawl**-zee] n paralysis. **palsied** adj affected with palsy.

paltry ● adj **-trier, -triest** insignificant.

pamper ● v treat (someone) with great indulgence, spoil.

pamphlet ● n thin paper-covered booklet. **pamphleteer** n writer of pamphlets.

pan¹ ● n **1** wide long-handled metal container used in cooking. **2** bowl of a toilet. ▷ v **panning, panned 3** sift gravel from (a river) in a pan to search for gold. **4** informal criticize harshly. **pan out** v result.

pan² ● v **panning, panned** (of a film camera) be moved slowly so as to cover a whole scene or follow a moving object.

pan- combining form all, e.g. pan-American.

panacea ● [pan-a-**see**-a] n remedy for all diseases or problems.

panache ● [pan-**ash**] n confident elegant style.

pancake n thin flat circle of fried batter.

pancreas [**pang**-kree-ass] n large gland behind the stomach that produces insulin and helps digestion. **pancreatic** adj.

panda n large black-and-white bearlike mammal from China.

pandemonium ● n wild confusion, uproar.

pander n person who procures a sexual partner for someone. **pander to** v indulge (a person or his or her desires).

veil **3** = **gloom**, check, damp, damper

pall² v = **become boring**, become dull, become tedious, cloy, jade, sicken, tire, weary

pallid adj = **pale**, anaemic, ashen, colourless, pasty, wan

palpable adj **1** = **obvious**, clear, conspicuous, evident, manifest, plain, unmistakable, visible

palpitate v = **beat**, flutter, pound, pulsate, throb, tremble

paltry adj = **insignificant**, contemptible, despicable, inconsiderable, meagre, mean, measly, minor, miserable, petty, poor, puny, slight, small, trifling, trivial, unimportant, worthless

pamper v = **spoil**, coddle, cosset, indulge, mollycoddle, pet

pamphlet n = **booklet**, brochure, circular, leaflet, tract

pan¹ n **1** = **pot**, container, saucepan ▷ v **3** = **sift out**, look for, search for **4** Inf = **criticize**, censure, knock (inf), slam (sl), tear into (inf)

pan² v = **move**, follow, sweep, track

panacea n = **cure-all**, nostrum, universal cure

panache n = **style**, dash, élan, flamboyance

pandemonium n = **uproar**, bedlam, chaos, confusion, din, hullabaloo, racket, rumpus, turmoil

pane n sheet of glass in a window or door.

panegyric [pan-ee-**jire**-ik] n formal speech or piece of writing in praise of someone or something.

panel n 1 flat distinct section of a larger surface, for example in a door. 2 group of people as a team in a quiz etc. 3 list of jurors, doctors, etc. 4 board or surface containing switches and controls to operate equipment. ▷ v **-elling, -elled** 5 cover or decorate with panels. **panelling** n panels collectively, esp. on a wall. **panellist** n member of a panel.

pang ❶ n sudden sharp feeling of pain or sadness.

panic ❶ n 1 sudden overwhelming fear, often affecting a whole group of people. ▷ v **-icking, -icked** 2 feel or cause to feel panic. **panicky** adj **panic-stricken** adj.

panini n, pl **-ni** or **-nis** Italian bread usu. served grilled with a filling.

pannier n 1 bag fixed on the back of a cycle. 2 basket carried by a beast of burden.

panoply ❶ n magnificent array.

panorama ❶ n wide unbroken view of a scene. **panoramic** adj.

pansy n, pl **-sies** 1 small garden flower with velvety purple, yellow, or white petals. 2 offens effeminate or homosexual man.

pant ❶ v breathe quickly and noisily after exertion.

pantechnicon n large van for furniture removals.

panther n leopard, esp. a black one.

pantomime n play based on a fairy tale, performed at Christmas time.

pantry n, pl **-tries** small room or cupboard for storing food.

pants ❶ pl n 1 undergarment for the lower part of the body. 2 US, Canad, Aust & NZ trousers.

pap n 1 soft food for babies or invalids. 2 worthless entertainment or information.

papacy [**pay**-pa-see] n, pl **-cies** position or term of office of a pope. **papal** adj of the pope.

paper ❶ n 1 material made in sheets from wood pulp or other fibres. 2 printed sheet of this. 3 newspaper. 4 set of examination questions. 5 article or essay. ▷ pl 6 personal documents. ▷ v 7 cover (walls) with wallpaper. **paperback** n book with covers made of flexible card. **paperweight** n heavy decorative object placed on top of loose papers. **paperwork** n clerical work, such as writing reports and letters.

papier-mâché [**pap**-yay **mash**-ay] n material made from paper mixed with paste and moulded when moist.

paprika n mild powdered seasoning made from red peppers.

papyrus [pap-**ire**-uss] n, pl **-ri, -ruses** 1 tall water plant. 2 (manuscript written on) a kind of paper made from this plant.

par ❶ n 1 usual or average condition, e.g. feeling under par. 2 Golf expected standard score. 3 face value of stocks and shares. **on a par with** equal to.

P

pang n = **twinge**, ache, pain, prick, spasm, stab, sting

panic n 1 = **fear**, alarm, fright, hysteria, scare, terror ▷ v 2 = **go to pieces**, alarm, become hysterical, lose one's nerve, scare, unnerve

panoply n = **array**, attire, dress, garb, regalia, trappings

panorama n = **view**, prospect, vista

pant v = **puff**, blow, breathe, gasp, heave, wheeze

pants pl n 1 = **underpants**, boxer shorts, briefs, broekies (S Afr inf), drawers, knickers, panties 2 US, Canad, Aust & NZ = **trousers**, slacks

paper n 3 = **newspaper**, daily, gazette, journal 5 = **essay**, article, dissertation, report, treatise ▷ pl 6 = **documents**, archive, certificates, deeds, diaries, dossier, file, letters, records ▷ v 7 = **wallpaper**, hang

par n 1 = **average**, level, mean, norm, standard, usual

parable ❶ n story that illustrates a religious teaching.

parachute n 1 large fabric canopy that slows the descent of a person or object from an aircraft. ▷ v 2 land or drop by parachute. **parachutist** n.

parade ❶ n 1 procession or march. 2 street or promenade. ▷ v 3 display or flaunt. 4 march in procession.

paradise ❶ n 1 heaven. 2 place or situation that is near-perfect.

paradox ❶ n statement that seems self-contradictory but may be true. **paradoxical** adj **paradoxically** adv.

paraffin n liquid mixture distilled from petroleum and used as a fuel or solvent.

● SPELLING TIP
● People have trouble remembering
● whether the r or the f is doubled in
● **paraffin**, but according to the Bank of
● English, the most popular mistake is to
● decide on neither, as in *parafin*.

paragon ❶ n model of perfection.

paragraph ❶ n section of a piece of writing starting on a new line.

parakeet n small long-tailed parrot.

parallel ❶ adj 1 separated by an equal distance at every point. 2 exactly corresponding. ▷ n 3 line separated from another by an equal distance

at every point. 4 thing with similar features to another. 5 line of latitude. ▷ v 6 correspond to.

paralysis ❶ n inability to move or feel, because of damage to the nervous system. **paralyse** v 1 affect with paralysis. 2 make temporarily unable to move or take action. **paralytic** n, adj (person) affected with paralysis.

paramedic n person working in support of the medical profession.

parameter ❶ [par-**am**-it-er] n limiting factor, boundary.

paramilitary adj organized on military lines.

paramount ❶ adj of the greatest importance.

paranoia n 1 mental illness causing delusions of grandeur or persecution. 2 informal intense fear or suspicion. **paranoid, paranoiac** adj, n.

parapet n low wall or railing along the edge of a balcony or roof.

paraphernalia ❶ n personal belongings or bits of equipment.

paraphrase ❶ v put (a statement or text) into other words.

paraplegia [par-a-**pleej**-ya] n paralysis of the lower half of the body. **paraplegic** adj, n.

parable n = **lesson**, allegory, fable, moral tale, story

parade n 1 = **procession**, array, cavalcade, march, pageant ▷ v 3 = **flaunt**, display, exhibit, show off (inf) 4 = **march**, process

paradise n 1 = **heaven**, Elysian fields, Happy Valley (Islam), Promised Land 2 = **bliss**, delight, felicity, heaven, utopia

paradox n = **contradiction**, anomaly, enigma, oddity, puzzle

paragon n = **model**, epitome, exemplar, ideal, nonpareil, pattern, quintessence

paragraph n = **section**, clause, item, part, passage, subdivision

parallel adj 1 = **equidistant**, alongside, side by side 2 = **matching**, analogous,

corresponding, like, resembling, similar ▷ n 4 = **similarity**, analogy, comparison, likeness, resemblance

paralysis n = **immobility**, palsy

parameter n = **limit**, framework, limitation, restriction, specification

paramount adj = **principal**, cardinal, chief, first, foremost, main, primary, prime, supreme

paraphernalia n = **equipment**, apparatus, baggage, belongings, effects, gear, stuff, tackle, things, trappings

paraphrase v = **reword**, express in other words or one's own words, rephrase, restate

parasite ❶ n 1 animal or plant living in or on another. 2 person who lives at the expense of others. **parasitic** adj.

parasol n umbrella-like sunshade.

paratroops pl n troops trained to be dropped by parachute into a battle area. **paratrooper** n member of the paratroops.

parboil v boil until partly cooked.

parcel ❶ n 1 something wrapped up, package. ▷ v -celling, -celled 2 (often foll. by up) wrap up.

parch ❶ v 1 make very hot and dry. 2 make thirsty.

parchment n thick smooth writing material made from animal skin.

pardon ❶ v 1 forgive, excuse. ▷ n 2 forgiveness. 3 official release from punishment for a crime. **pardonable** adj.

pare ❶ v 1 cut off the skin or top layer of. 2 (often foll. by down) reduce in size or amount. **paring** n piece pared off.

parent ❶ n father or mother. **parental** adj **parenthood** n **parentage** n ancestry or family. **parenting** n activity of bringing up children.

parenthesis [par-**en**-thiss-iss] n, pl **-ses** 1 word or sentence inserted into a passage, marked off by brackets or dashes. ▷ pl 2 round brackets, ( ). **parenthetical** adj.

pariah ❶ [par-**rye**-a] n social outcast.

parish ❶ n area that has its own church and clergyman. **parishioner** n inhabitant of a parish.

parity ❶ n equality or equivalence.

park ❶ n 1 area of open land for recreational use by the public. 2 area containing a number of related enterprises, e.g. a business park. 3 area of private land around a large country house. ▷ v 4 stop and leave (a vehicle) temporarily.

parka n long jacket with a quilted lining and a fur-trimmed hood.

parkade n Canad a building used as a car park.

parkette n Canad a small public park.

parking lot n US & Canad area or building where vehicles may be left for a time.

parlance ❶ n particular way of speaking, idiom.

parley n 1 meeting between leaders or representatives of opposing forces to discuss terms. ▷ v 2 have a parley.

parliament ❶ n law-making assembly of a country. **parliamentary** adj.

parlour ❶ n old-fashioned living room for receiving visitors.

parochial ❶ adj 1 narrow in outlook. 2 of a parish. **parochialism** n.

parasite n 2 = **sponger**, bloodsucker (inf), hanger-on, leech, scrounger (inf)

parcel n 1 = **package**, bundle, pack ▷ v 2 (often foll. by up) = **wrap**, do up, pack, package, tie up

parch v 1 = **dry up**, dehydrate, desiccate, evaporate, shrivel, wither

pardon v 1 = **forgive**, absolve, acquit, excuse, exonerate, let off (inf), overlook n 2 = **forgiveness**, absolution, exoneration 3 = **acquittal**, amnesty

pare v 1 = **peel**, clip, cut, shave, skin, trim 2 (often foll. by down) = **cut back**, crop, cut, decrease, dock, reduce

parent n = **father** or **mother**, procreator, progenitor, sire

pariah n = **outcast**, exile, undesirable, untouchable

parish n = **community**, church, congregation, flock

parity n = **equality**, consistency, equivalence, uniformity, unity

park n 3 = **parkland**, estate, garden, grounds, woodland

parlance n = **language**, idiom, jargon, phraseology, speech, talk, tongue

parliament n = **assembly**, congress, convention, council, legislature, senate

parlour n Old-fashioned = **sitting room**, drawing room, front room, living room, lounge

parochial adj 1 = **provincial**, insular,

parody ❶ *n, pl* **-dies 1** exaggerated and amusing imitation of someone else's style. ▷ *v* **-dying, -died 2** make a parody of.

parole *n* **1** early freeing of a prisoner on condition that he or she behaves well. ▷ *v* **2** put on parole. **on parole** (of a prisoner) released on condition that he or she behaves well.

paroxysm ❶ *n* **1** uncontrollable outburst of rage, delight, etc. **2** spasm or convulsion of coughing, pain, etc.

parquet [par-kay] *n* floor covering made of wooden blocks arranged in a geometric pattern. **parquetry** *n*.

parrot ❶ *n* **1** tropical bird with a short hooked beak and an ability to imitate human speech. ▷ *v* **-roting, -roted 2** repeat (someone else's words) without thinking.

parry ❶ *v* **-rying, -ried 1** ward off (an attack). **2** cleverly avoid (an awkward question).

parsimony *n* extreme caution in spending money. **parsimonious** *adj*.

parsley *n* herb used for seasoning and decorating food.

parsnip *n* long tapering cream-coloured root vegetable.

parson ❶ *n* parish priest in the Church of England. **parsonage** *n* parson's house.

part ❶ *n* **1** one of the pieces that make up a whole. **2** one of several equal divisions. **3** actor's role. **4** (often *pl*) region, area. **5** component of a vehicle or machine. ▷ *v* **6** divide or separate. **7** (of people) leave each other. **take someone's part** support someone in an argument etc. **take (something) in good part** respond to (teasing or criticism) with good humour. **parting** *n* **1** occasion when one person leaves another. **2** line of scalp between sections of hair combed in opposite directions. **3** dividing or separating. **partly** *adv* not completely. **part of speech** particular grammatical class of words, such as noun or verb. **part-time** *adj* occupying or working less than the full working week. **part with** *v* give away, hand over.

partake ❶ *v* **-taking, -took, -taken 1** (foll. by *of*) take (food or drink). **2** (foll. by *in*) take part in.

partial ❶ *adj* **1** not complete. **2** prejudiced. **partial to** having a liking for. **partiality** *n* **partially** *adv*.

participate ❶ *v* become actively involved. **participant** *n* **participation** *n*.

participle *n* form of a verb used in

——————————————————— THESAURUS ——————

limited, narrow, narrow-minded, petty, small-minded

parody *n* **1** = **takeoff**, burlesque, caricature, satire, send-up (*Brit inf*), skit, spoof (*inf*) (*inf*) ▷ *v* **2** = **take off**, burlesque, caricature, do a takeoff of (*inf*), satirize, send up (*Brit inf*)

paroxysm *n* **2** = **outburst**, attack, convulsion, fit, seizure, spasm

parrot *v* **2** = **repeat**, copy, echo, imitate, mimic

parry *v* **1** = **ward off**, block, deflect, rebuff, repel, repulse **2** = **evade**, avoid, dodge, sidestep

parson *n* = **clergyman**, churchman, cleric, minister, pastor, preacher, priest, vicar

part *n* **1** = **piece**, bit, fraction, fragment, portion, scrap, section, share **2** = **division**, branch, component, constituent, member, unit **3** = **role**, character, lines **4** (often *pl*) = **region**, area, district, neighbourhood, quarter, vicinity ▷ *v* **6** = **divide**, break, come apart, detach, rend, separate, sever, split, tear **7** = **leave**, depart, go, go away, separate, split up, withdraw

partake *v* **1** (foll. by *of*) = **consume**, eat, take **2** (foll. by *in*) = **participate in**, engage in, share in, take part in

partial *adj* **1** = **incomplete**, imperfect, uncompleted, unfinished **2** = **biased**, discriminatory, one-sided, partisan, prejudiced, unfair, unjust

participate *v* = **take part**, be involved in, join in, partake, perform, share

compound tenses or as an adjective, e.g. *worried*; *worrying*.

particle ❶ *n* **1** extremely small piece or amount. **2** *Physics* minute piece of matter, such as a proton or electron.

particular ❶ *adj* **1** relating to one person or thing, not general. **2** exceptional or special. **3** very exact. **4** difficult to please, fastidious. ▷ *n* **5** item of information, detail. **particularly** *adv*.

partisan ❶ *n* **1** strong supporter of a party or group. **2** guerrilla, member of a resistance movement. ▷ *adj* **3** prejudiced or one-sided.

partition ❶ *n* **1** screen or thin wall that divides a room. **2** division of a country into independent parts. ▷ *v* **3** divide with a partition.

partner ❶ *n* **1** either member of a couple in a relationship or activity. **2** member of a business partnership. ▷ *v* **3** be the partner of. **partnership** *n* joint business venture between two or more people.

partridge *n* game bird of the grouse family.

party ❶ *n, pl* **-ties 1** social gathering for pleasure. **2** group of people travelling or working together. **3** group of people with a common political aim. **4** person or people forming one side in a lawsuit or dispute. **party line 1** official view of a political party. **2** telephone line shared by two or more subscribers.

pass ❶ *v* **1** go by, past, or through. **2** be successful in (a test or examination). **3** spend (time) or (of time) go by. **4** give, hand. **5** be inherited by. **6** *Sport* hit, kick, or throw (the ball) to another player. **7** (of a law-making body) agree to (a law). **8** exceed. **9** choose not to answer a question or not to take one's turn in a game. **10** come to an end. ▷ *n* **11** successful result in a test or examination. **12** *Sport* transfer of a ball. **13** narrow gap through mountains. **14** permit or licence. **make a pass at** *informal* make sexual advances to. **passable** *adj* **1** (just) acceptable. **2** (of a road) capable of being travelled along. **passing** *adj* **1** brief or transitory. **2** cursory or casual. **pass away** *v* die. **pass out** *v* *informal* faint. **pass up** *v* *informal* fail to take advantage of (something).

particle *n* **1** = **bit**, grain, iota, jot, mite, piece, scrap, shred, speck

particular *adj* **1** = **specific**, distinct, exact, peculiar, precise, special **2** = **special**, especial, exceptional, marked, notable, noteworthy, remarkable, singular, uncommon, unusual **4** = **fussy**, choosy (*inf*), demanding, fastidious, finicky, pernickety (*inf*), picky (*inf*) ▷ *n* **5** = **detail**, circumstance, fact, feature, item, specification

partisan *n* **1** = **supporter**, adherent, devotee, upholder **2** = **underground fighter**, guerrilla, resistance fighter ▷ *adj* **3** = **prejudiced**, biased, interested, one-sided, partial, sectarian

partition *n* **1** = **screen**, barrier, wall **2** = **division**, segregation, separation ▷ *v* **3** = **separate**, divide, screen

partner *n* **1** = **spouse**, consort, husband or wife, mate, significant other (*US inf*) **2** = **associate**, colleague

party *n* **1** = **get-together** (*inf*), celebration, do (*inf*), festivity, function, gathering, reception, social gathering **2** = **group**, band, company, crew, gang, squad, team, unit **3** = **faction**, camp, clique, coterie, league, set, side

pass *v* **1** = **go by** or **past**, elapse, go, lapse, move, proceed, run **2** = **qualify**, do, get through, graduate, succeed **3** = **spend**, fill, occupy, while away **4** = **give**, convey, deliver, hand, send, transfer **7** = **approve**, accept, decree, enact, legislate, ordain, ratify **8** = **exceed**, beat, go beyond, outdo, outstrip, overtake, surpass **10** = **end**, blow over, cease, go ▷ *n* **13** = **gap**, canyon, gorge, ravine, route **14** = **licence**, authorization, passport, permit, ticket, warrant

P

passage ❶ *n* **1** channel or opening providing a way through. **2** hall or corridor. **3** section of a book etc. **4** journey by sea. **5** right or freedom to pass.
passageway *n* passage or corridor.

passé [**pas**-say] *adj* out-of-date.

passenger ❶ *n* **1** person travelling in a vehicle driven by someone else. **2** member of a team who does not pull his or her weight.

passion ❶ *n* **1** intense sexual love. **2** any strong emotion. **3** great enthusiasm. **4** (**P-**) *Christianity* the suffering of Christ.
passionate *adj*.

passive ❶ *adj* **1** not playing an active part. **2** submissive and receptive to outside forces. **3** *Grammar* (of a verb) in a form indicating that the subject receives the action, e.g. *was jeered* in *he was jeered by the crowd*. **passivity** *n* **passive smoking** inhalation of smoke from others' cigarettes by a nonsmoker.

passport *n* official document granting permission to travel abroad.

password ❶ *n* secret word or phrase that ensures admission.

past ❶ *adj* **1** of the time before the present. **2** ended, gone by. **3** *Grammar* (of a verb tense) indicating that the action

specified took place earlier. ▷ *n* **4** period of time before the present. **5** person's earlier life, esp. a disreputable period. **6** *Grammar* past tense. ▷ *adv* **7** by, along. ▷ *prep* **8** beyond. **past it** *informal* unable to do the things one could do when younger. **past master** person with great talent or experience in a particular subject.

pasta *n* type of food, such as spaghetti, that is made in different shapes from flour and water.

paste ❶ *n* **1** moist soft mixture, such as toothpaste. **2** adhesive, esp. for paper. **3** pastry dough. **4** shiny glass used to make imitation jewellery. ▷ *v* **5** fasten with paste. **pasting** *n informal* **1** heavy defeat. **2** strong criticism.

pastel ❶ *n* **1** coloured chalk crayon for drawing. **2** picture drawn in pastels. **3** pale delicate colour. ▷ *adj* **4** pale and delicate in colour.

pasteurize *v* sterilize by heating. **pasteurization** *n*.

pastiche ❶ [pass-**teesh**] *n* work of art that mixes styles or copies the style of another artist.

pastille *n* small fruit-flavoured and sometimes medicated sweet.

━━━━━━━━━━━━━━━━━━━━━━━━━━━━━━━━━━━ THESAURUS ━━━━━━

passage *n* **1** = **way**, alley, avenue, channel, course, path, road, route **2** = **corridor**, hall, lobby, vestibule **3** = **extract**, excerpt, piece, quotation, reading, section, text **4** = **journey**, crossing, trek, trip, voyage **5** = **safe-conduct**, freedom, permission, right

passé *adj* = **out-of-date**, dated, obsolete, old-fashioned, old hat, outdated, outmoded, unfashionable

passenger *n* **1** = **traveller**, fare, rider

passion *n* **1** = **love**, ardour, desire, infatuation, lust **2** = **emotion**, ardour, excitement, feeling, fervour, fire, heat, intensity, warmth, zeal **3** = **mania**, bug (*inf*), craving, craze, enthusiasm, fascination, obsession

passive *adj* **1, 2** = **submissive**, compliant, docile, inactive, quiescent, receptive

password *n* = **signal**, key word, watchword

past *adj* **1** = **former**, ancient, bygone, early, olden, previous **2** = **over**, done, ended, finished, gone ▷ *n* **4** = **former times**, days gone by, long ago, olden days **5** = **background**, history, life, past life ▷ *prep* **8** = **beyond**, across, by, over

paste *n* **2** = **adhesive**, cement, glue, gum ▷ *v* **5** = **stick**, cement, glue, gum

pastel *adj* **4** = **pale**, delicate, light, muted, soft

pastiche *n* = **medley**, melange, blend, hotchpotch, miscellany, mixture

pastime ❶ *n* activity that makes time pass pleasantly.

pastor ❶ *n* clergyman in charge of a congregation. **pastoral** *adj* **1** of or depicting country life. **2** of a clergyman or his duties.

pastry *n, pl* **-ries 1** baking dough made of flour, fat, and water. **2** cake or pie.

pasture ❶ *n* grassy land for farm animals to graze on.

pasty¹ ❶ [**pay**-stee] *adj* **pastier, pastiest** (of a complexion) pale and unhealthy.

pasty² [**pass**-tee] *n, pl* **pasties** round of pastry folded over a savoury filling.

pat¹ ❶ *v* **patting, patted 1** tap lightly. ▷ *n* **2** gentle tap or stroke. **3** small shaped mass of butter etc.

pat² ❶ *adj* quick, ready, or glib. **off pat** learned thoroughly.

patch ❶ *n* **1** piece of material sewn on a garment. **2** small contrasting section. **3** plot of ground. **4** protective pad for the eye. ▷ *v* **5** mend with a patch. **patchy** *adj* of uneven quality or intensity. **patch up** *v* **1** repair clumsily. **2** make up (a quarrel). **patchwork** *n* needlework made of pieces of different materials sewn together.

pate *n* old-fashioned head.

pâté [**pat**-ay] *n* spread of finely minced liver, poultry, etc.

patent ❶ *n* **1** document giving the exclusive right to make or sell an invention. ▷ *adj* **2** open to public inspection, e.g. *letters patent*. **3** obvious. **4** protected by a patent. ▷ *v* **5** obtain a patent for. **patently** *adv* obviously. **patent leather** leather processed to give a hard glossy surface.

paternal ❶ *adj* **1** fatherly. **2** related through one's father. **paternity** *n* fact or state of being a father. **paternalism** *n* authority exercised in a way that limits individual responsibility. **paternalistic** *adj*.

path ❶ *n* **1** surfaced walk or track. **2** course of action.

pathetic ❶ *adj* **1** causing feelings of pity or sadness. **2** distressingly inadequate. **pathetically** *adv*.

pathology *n* scientific study of diseases. **pathological** *adj* **1** of pathology. **2** *informal* compulsively motivated. **pathologist** *n*.

pathos ❶ *n* power of arousing pity or sadness.

patient ❶ *adj* **1** enduring difficulties or delays calmly. ▷ *n* **2** person receiving medical treatment. **patience** *n* **1** quality of being patient. **2** card game for one.

———— THESAURUS ————

pastime *n* = **activity**, amusement, diversion, entertainment, game, hobby, recreation

pastor *n* = **clergyman**, churchman, ecclesiastic, minister, parson, priest, rector, vicar

pasture *n* = **grassland**, grass, grazing, meadow

pasty¹ *adj* = **pale**, anaemic, pallid, sickly, wan

pat¹ *v* **1** = **stroke**, caress, fondle, pet, tap, touch ▷ *n* **2** = **stroke**, clap, tap

pat² *adj* = **glib**, automatic, easy, facile, ready, simplistic, slick, smooth **off pat** = **perfectly**, exactly, faultlessly, flawlessly, precisely

patch *n* **1** = **reinforcement**, piece of material **2** = **spot**, bit, scrap, shred, small piece **3** = **plot**, area, ground, land, tract ▷ *v* **5** = **mend**, cover, reinforce, repair, sew up

patent *n* **1** = **copyright**, licence ▷ *adj* **3** = **obvious**, apparent, clear, evident, glaring, manifest

paternal *adj* **1** = **fatherly**, concerned, protective, solicitous

path *n* **1** = **way**, footpath, road, track, trail **2** = **course**, direction, road, route, way

pathetic *adj* **1** = **sad**, affecting, distressing, gut-wrenching, heart-rending, moving, pitiable, plaintive, poignant, tender, touching

pathos *n* = **sadness**, pitifulness, plaintiveness, poignancy

patient *adj* **1** = **long-suffering**, calm, enduring, persevering, philosophical,

patio *n, pl* **-tios** paved area adjoining a house.

patriarch *n* **1** male head of a family or tribe. **2** highest-ranking bishop in Orthodox Churches. **patriarchal** *adj* **patriarchy** *n, pl* **-chies** society in which men have most of the power.

patrician *n* **1** member of the nobility. ▷ *adj* **2** of noble birth.

patriot ❶ *n* person who loves his or her country and supports its interests. **patriotic** *adj* **patriotism** *n*.

patrol ❶ *n* **1** regular circuit by a guard. **2** person or small group patrolling. **3** unit of Scouts or Guides. ▷ *v* **-trolling, -trolled** **4** go round on guard, or reconnoitring.

patron ❶ *n* **1** person who gives financial support to charities, artists, etc. **2** regular customer of a shop, pub, etc. **patronage** *n* support given by a patron. **patronize** *v* **1** treat in a condescending way. **2** be a patron of. **patron saint** saint regarded as the guardian of a country or group.

patter¹ ❶ *v* **1** make repeated soft tapping sounds. ▷ *n* **2** quick succession of taps.

patter² ❶ *n* glib rapid speech.

pattern ❶ *n* **1** arrangement of repeated parts or decorative designs. **2** regular way that something is done. **3** diagram or shape used as a guide to make something. **patterned** *adj* decorated with a pattern.

paunch ❶ *n* protruding belly.

pauper ❶ *n* very poor person.

pause ❶ *v* **1** stop for a time. ▷ *n* **2** stop or rest in speech or action.

pave ❶ *v* form (a surface) with stone or brick. **pavement** *n* paved path for pedestrians.

pavilion *n* **1** building on a playing field etc. **2** building for housing an exhibition etc.

paw ❶ *n* **1** animal's foot with claws and pads. ▷ *v* **2** scrape with the paw or hoof. **3** *informal* touch in a rough or overfamiliar way.

pawn¹ ❶ *v* deposit (an article) as security for money borrowed. **in pawn** deposited as security with a pawnbroker. **pawnbroker** *n* lender of money on goods deposited.

pawn² ❶ *n* **1** chessman of the lowest value. **2** person manipulated by someone else.

pay ❶ *v* **paying, paid 1** give money etc.

——————————————— THESAURUS ———————————————

resigned, stoical, submissive, uncomplaining ▷ *n* **2** = **sick person**, case, invalid, sufferer

patriot *n* = **nationalist**, chauvinist, loyalist

patrol *n* **1** = **policing**, guarding, protecting, vigilance, watching **2** = **guard**, patrolman, sentinel, watch, watchman ▷ *v* **4** = **police**, guard, inspect, keep guard, keep watch, safeguard

patron *n* **1** = **supporter**, backer, benefactor, champion, friend, helper, philanthropist, sponsor **2** = **customer**, buyer, client, frequenter, habitué, shopper

patter¹ *v* **1** = **tap**, beat, pat, pitter-patter ▷ *n* **2** = **tapping**, pattering, pitter-patter

patter² *n* = **spiel**, line, pitch (*inf*)

pattern *n* **1** = **design**, arrangement, decoration, device, figure, motif **2** = **order**, method, plan, sequence, system **3** = **plan**, design, diagram, guide,

original, stencil, template

paunch *n* = **belly**, pot, potbelly, spare tyre (*Brit sl*)

pauper *n* = **down-and-out**, bankrupt, beggar, mendicant, poor person

pause *v* **1** = **stop briefly**, break, cease, delay, halt, have a breather (*inf*), interrupt, rest, take a break, wait ▷ *n* **2** = **stop**, break, breather (*inf*), cessation, gap, halt, interlude, intermission, interval, lull, respite, rest, stoppage

pave *v* = **cover**, concrete, floor, surface, tile

paw *v* **3** *Inf* = **manhandle**, grab, handle roughly, maul, molest

pawn¹ *v* = **hock** (*inf, chiefly US*), deposit, mortgage, pledge

pawn² *n* **2** = **tool**, cat's-paw, instrument, plaything, puppet, stooge (*sl*)

pay *v* **1, 2** = **reimburse**, give, remit, remunerate, requite, reward, settle

p

in return for goods or services. **2** settle a debt or obligation. **3** compensate (for). **4** give. **5** be profitable to. ▷ *n* **6** wages or salary. **payment** *n* **1** act of paying. **2** money paid. **payable** *adj* due to be paid. **payee** *n* person to whom money is paid or due. **pay off** *v* **1** pay (debt) in full. **2** turn out successfully. **pay out** *v* **1** spend. **2** release (a rope) bit by bit.

PC 1 personal computer. **2** Police Constable. **3** politically correct. **4** Privy Councillor.

PDA personal digital assistant.

PE 1 physical education. **2** Prince Edward Island.

pea *n* **1** climbing plant with seeds growing in pods. **2** its seed, eaten as a vegetable.

peace ❶ *n* **1** calm, quietness. **2** absence of anxiety. **3** freedom from war. **4** harmony between people. **peaceable** *adj* inclined towards peace. **peaceably** *adv* **peaceful** *adj* **peacefully** *adv*.

peach *n* **1** soft juicy fruit with a stone and a downy skin. **2** *informal* very pleasing person or thing. ▷ *adj* **3** pinkish-orange.

peacock *n* (*fem* **peahen**) large male bird with a brilliantly coloured fanlike tail.

peak ❶ *n* **1** pointed top, esp. of a mountain. **2** point of greatest development etc. **3** projecting piece on the front of a cap. ▷ *v* **4** form or reach a peak. ▷ *adj* **5** of or at the point of greatest demand. **peaked** *adj* **peaky** *adj* pale and sickly.

peal ❶ *n* **1** long loud echoing sound, esp. of bells or thunder. ▷ *v* **2** sound with a peal or peals.

peanut *n* **1** pea-shaped nut that ripens underground. ▷ *pl* **2** *informal* trifling amount of money.

pear *n* sweet juicy fruit with a narrow top and rounded base.

pearl *n* hard round shiny object found inside some oyster shells and used as a jewel. **pearly** *adj*.

peasant ❶ *n* farmer or farmworker of a low social class. **peasantry** *n* peasants collectively.

peat *n* decayed vegetable material found in bogs, used as fertilizer or fuel.

pebble *n* small roundish stone. **pebbly** *adj* **pebble dash** coating for exterior walls consisting of small stones set in plaster.

peccadillo ❶ *n*, *pl* **-loes, -los** trivial misdeed.

peck ❶ *v* **1** strike or pick up with the beak. **2** *informal* kiss quickly. ▷ *n* **3** pecking movement. **peckish** *adj informal* slightly hungry. **peck at** *v* nibble, eat reluctantly.

pectoral *adj* **1** of the chest or thorax. ▷ *n* **2** pectoral muscle or fin.

peculiar ❶ *adj* **1** strange. **2** distinct, special. **3** belonging exclusively

P

3 = **compensate**, recompense **4** = **give**, bestow, extend, grant, hand out, present **5** = **be profitable**, benefit, be worthwhile, make a return, make money, repay ▷ *n* **6** = **wages**, allowance, earnings, fee, income, payment, recompense, reimbursement, remuneration, reward, salary, stipend

peace *n* **1** = **stillness**, calm, calmness, hush, quiet, repose, rest, silence, tranquillity **2** = **serenity**, calm, composure, contentment, repose **3** = **truce**, armistice, treaty **4** = **harmony**, accord, agreement, concord

peak *n* **1** = **point**, apex, brow, crest, pinnacle, summit, tip, top **2** = **high point**, acme, climax, crown, culmination, zenith ▷ *v* **4** = **culminate**, climax, come to a head

peal *n* **1** = **ring**, blast, chime, clang, clap, crash, reverberation, roar, rumble ▷ *v* **2** = **ring**, chime, crash, resound, roar, rumble

peasant *n* = **rustic**, countryman

peccadillo *n* = **misdeed**, error, indiscretion, lapse, misdemeanour, slip

peck *v* **1** = **pick**, dig, hit, jab, poke, prick, strike, tap

peculiar *adj* **1** = **odd**, abnormal, bizarre, curious, eccentric, extraordinary, freakish, funny, munted (*NZ sl*), offbeat, outlandish,

to. **peculiarity** n, pl **-ties 1** oddity, eccentricity. **2** distinguishing trait.

pedal n **1** foot-operated lever used to control a vehicle or machine, or to modify the tone of a musical instrument. ▷ v **-alling, -alled 2** propel (a bicycle) by using its pedals.

pedant ❶ n person who is excessively concerned with details and rules, esp. in academic work. **pedantic** adj **pedantry** n.

peddle v sell (goods) from door to door. **peddler** n person who sells illegal drugs.

pedestal ❶ n base supporting a column, statue, etc.

pedestrian ❶ n **1** person who walks. ▷ adj **2** dull, uninspiring. **pedestrian crossing** place marked where pedestrians may cross a road.

pedigree ❶ n register of ancestors, esp. of a purebred animal.

pedlar ❶ n person who sells goods from door to door.

peek ❶ v, n peep or glance.

peel ❶ v **1** remove the skin or rind of (a vegetable or fruit). **2** (of skin or a surface) come off in flakes. ▷ n **3** rind or skin.

peep¹ ❶ v **1** look slyly or quickly. ▷ n **2** peeping look. **Peeping Tom** man who furtively watches women undressing.

peep² ❶ v **1** make a small shrill noise. ▷ n **2** small shrill noise.

peer¹ ❶ n **1** (fem **peeress**) member of the nobility. **2** person of the same status, age, etc. **peerage** n **1** whole body of peers. **2** rank of a peer. **peerless** adj unequalled, unsurpassed. **peer group** group of people of similar age, status, etc.

peer² ❶ v look closely and intently.

peeved adj informal annoyed.

peevish ❶ adj fretful or irritable.

peewit n same as LAPWING.

peg ❶ n **1** pin or clip for joining, fastening, marking, etc. **2** hook or knob for hanging things on. ▷ v **pegging, pegged 3** fasten with pegs. **4** stabilize (prices). **off the peg** (of clothes) ready-to-wear, not tailor-made.

pejorative ❶ [pij-**jor**-a-tiv] adj (of words etc.) with an insulting or critical meaning.

pelican n large water bird with a pouch beneath its bill for storing fish. **pelican crossing** road crossing with pedestrian-operated traffic lights.

━━━━━━━━━━━━━━━━━━━━━━━━━━━━━━━━━━ THESAURUS ━━━━

outré, quaint, queer, singular, strange, uncommon, unconventional, unusual, weird **2** = **specific**, characteristic, distinctive, particular, special, unique

pedant n = **hairsplitter**, nit-picker (inf), quibbler

peddle v = **sell**, flog (sl), hawk, market, push (inf), trade

pedestal n = **support**, base, foot, mounting, plinth, stand

pedestrian n **1** = **walker**, foot-traveller adj **2** = **dull**, banal, boring, commonplace, humdrum, mediocre, mundane, ordinary, prosaic, run-of-the-mill, uninspired

pedigree n = **lineage**, ancestry, blood, breed, descent, extraction, family, family tree, genealogy, line, race, stock

pedlar n = **seller**, door-to-door salesman, hawker, huckster, vendor

peek v = **glance**, eyeball (sl), look, peep ▷ n

= **glance**, glimpse, look, look-see (sl), peep

peel v **1** = **skin**, pare, strip off **2** = **flake off**, scale ▷ n **3** = **skin**, peeling, rind

peep¹ v **1** = **peek**, eyeball (sl), look, sneak a look, steal a look ▷ n **2** = **look**, glimpse, look-see (sl), peek

peep² v **1** = **tweet**, cheep, chirp, squeak ▷ n **2** = **tweet**, cheep, chirp, squeak

peer¹ n **1** = **noble**, aristocrat, lord, nobleman **2** = **equal**, compeer, fellow, like

peer² v = **squint**, gaze, inspect, peep, scan, snoop, spy

peevish adj = **irritable**, cantankerous, childish, churlish, cross, crotchety (inf), fractious, fretful, grumpy, petulant, querulous, snappy, sulky, sullen, surly

peg v **3** = **fasten**, attach, fix, join, secure

pejorative adj = **derogatory**, deprecatory, depreciatory, disparaging, negative, uncomplimentary, unpleasant

p

pellet n small ball of something.

pelmet n ornamental drapery or board, concealing a curtain rail.

pelt¹ ❶ v 1 throw missiles at. 2 run fast, rush. 3 rain heavily. **at full pelt** at top speed.

pelt² ❶ n skin of a fur-bearing animal.

pelvis n framework of bones at the base of the spine, to which the hips are attached. **pelvic** adj.

pen¹ ❶ n 1 instrument for writing in ink. ▷ v **penning, penned** 2 write or compose. **pen friend** friend with whom a person corresponds without meeting. **penknife** n small knife with blade(s) that fold into the handle. **pen name** name used by a writer instead of his or her real name.

pen² ❶ n 1 small enclosure for domestic animals. ▷ v **penning, penned** 2 put or keep in a pen. **penned in** trapped or confined.

penal ❶ [**pee**-nal] adj of or used in punishment. **penalize** v 1 impose a penalty on. 2 handicap, hinder. **penalty** n, pl **-ties** 1 punishment for a crime or offence. 2 Sport handicap or disadvantage imposed for breaking a rule.

penance ❶ n voluntary self-punishment to make amends for wrongdoing.

pence n a plural of PENNY.

penchant ❶ [**pon**-shon] n inclination or liking.

pencil n 1 thin cylindrical instrument containing graphite, for writing or drawing. ▷ v **-cilling, -cilled** 2 draw, write, or mark with a pencil.

pendant n ornament worn on a chain round the neck.

pending ❶ prep 1 while waiting for. ▷ adj 2 not yet decided or settled.

pendulous adj hanging, swinging.

penetrate ❶ v 1 find or force a way into or through. 2 arrive at the meaning of. **penetrable** adj capable of being penetrated. **penetrating** adj 1 (of a sound) loud and unpleasant. 2 quick to understand. **penetration** n.

penguin n flightless black-and-white Antarctic sea bird.

penicillin n antibiotic drug effective against a wide range of diseases and infections.

peninsula n strip of land nearly surrounded by water. **peninsular** adj.

penis n organ of copulation and urination in male mammals.

penitent ❶ adj 1 feeling sorry for having done wrong. ▷ n 2 someone who is penitent. **penitence** n **penitentiary** n, pl **-ries** 1 US prison. ▷ adj 2 (also **penitential**) relating to penance.

———— THESAURUS ————

pelt¹ v 1 = **throw**, batter, bombard, cast, hurl, pepper, shower, sling, strike 2 = **rush**, belt (sl), charge, dash, hurry, run fast, shoot, speed, tear 3 = **pour**, bucket down (inf), rain cats and dogs (inf), rain hard, teem

pelt² n = **coat**, fell, hide, skin

pen¹ v 1 = **write**, compose, draft, draw up, jot down **pen name** = **pseudonym**, nom de plume

pen² n 1 = **enclosure**, cage, coop, fold, hutch, pound, sty ▷ v 2 = **enclose**, cage, confine, coop up, fence in, hedge, shut up or in

penal adj = **disciplinary**, corrective, punitive

penance n = **atonement**, penalty,

reparation, sackcloth and ashes

penchant n = **liking**, bent, bias, fondness, inclination, leaning, partiality, predilection, proclivity, propensity, taste, tendency

pending adj 2 = **undecided**, awaiting, imminent, impending, in the balance, undetermined, unsettled

penetrate v 1 = **pierce**, bore, enter, go through, prick, stab 2 = **grasp**, comprehend, decipher, fathom, figure out (inf), get to the bottom of, suss (out) (sl), work out

penitent adj 1 = **repentant**, abject, apologetic, conscience-stricken, contrite, regretful, remorseful, sorry

pennant ❶ *n* long narrow flag.

penny *n, pl* **pence**, **pennies** 1 British bronze coin worth one hundredth of a pound. 2 former British coin worth one twelfth of a shilling. **penniless** *adj* very poor.

pension¹ ❶ *n* regular payment to people above a certain age, retired employees, widows, etc. **pensionable** *adj* **pensioner** *n* person receiving a pension. **pension off** *v* force (someone) to retire from a job and pay him or her a pension.

pension² [**pon-syon**] *n* boarding house in Europe.

pensive ❶ *adj* deeply thoughtful, often with a tinge of sadness.

pentagon *n* 1 geometric figure with five sides. 2 (**P-**) headquarters of the US military. **pentagonal** *adj*.

penthouse *n* flat built on the roof or top floor of a building.

penultimate *adj* second last.

penury ❶ *n* extreme poverty.

peony *n, pl* **-nies** garden plant with showy red, pink, or white flowers.

people ❶ *pl n* 1 persons generally. 2 the community. 3 one's family. ▷ *n* 4 race or nation. ▷ *v* 5 provide with inhabitants.

pep *n informal* high spirits, energy, or enthusiasm. **pep talk** *informal* talk designed to increase confidence and enthusiasm. **pep up** *v* **pepping**, **pepped** stimulate, invigorate.

pepper ❶ *n* 1 sharp hot condiment made from the fruit of an East Indian climbing plant. 2 colourful tropical fruit used as a vegetable, capsicum. ▷ *v* 3 season with pepper. 4 sprinkle, dot. 5 pelt with missiles. **peppery** *adj* 1 tasting of pepper. 2 irritable. **peppercorn** *n* dried berry of the pepper plant.

per *prep* for each. **as per** in accordance with.

perambulate *v* walk through or about (a place). **perambulator** *n* pram.

per annum *adv Latin* in each year.

per capita *adj, adv Latin* of or for each person.

perceive ❶ *v* 1 become aware of (something) through the senses. 2 understand. **perception** *n*.

percentage *n* proportion or rate per hundred. **per cent** in each hundred.

perch¹ ❶ *n* 1 resting place for a bird. ▷ *v* 2 alight, rest, or place on or as if on a perch.

perch² *n* edible freshwater fish.

perchance *adv old-fashioned* perhaps.

percolate *v* 1 pass or filter through small holes. 2 spread gradually. 3 make (coffee) or (of coffee) be made in a percolator. **percolator** *n* coffeepot in which boiling water is forced through a tube and filters down through coffee.

percussion ❶ *n* striking of one thing against another. **percussion instrument**

——————————————— THESAURUS ———————

pennant *n* = **flag**, banner, ensign, pennon, streamer

pension¹ *n* = **allowance**, annuity, benefit, superannuation

pensive *adj* = **thoughtful**, contemplative, dreamy, meditative, musing, preoccupied, reflective, sad, serious, solemn, wistful

penury *n* = **poverty**, beggary, destitution, indigence, need, privation, want

people *pl n* 1 = **persons**, humanity, mankind, men and women, mortals 2 = **nation**, citizens, community, folk, inhabitants, population, public 3 = **family**, clan, race, tribe ▷ *v* 5 = **inhabit**, colonize,

occupy, populate, settle

pepper *n* 1 = **seasoning**, flavour, spice ▷ *v* 4 = **sprinkle**, dot, fleck, spatter, speck 5 = **pelt**, bombard, shower

perceive *v* 1 = **see**, behold, discern, discover, espy, make out, note, notice, observe, recognize, spot 2 = **understand**, comprehend, gather, grasp, learn, realize, see, suss (out) (*sl*)

perch¹ *n* 1 = **resting place**, branch, pole, post ▷ *v* 2 = **sit**, alight, balance, land, rest, roost, settle

percussion *n* = **impact**, blow, bump, clash, collision, crash, knock, smash, thump

musical instrument played by being struck, such as drums or cymbals.

peremptory ❶ *adj* authoritative, imperious.

perennial ❶ *adj* **1** lasting through many years. ▷ *n* **2** plant lasting more than two years. **perennially** *adv*.

perfect ❶ *adj* **1** having all the essential elements. **2** faultless. **3** correct, precise. **4** utter or absolute. ▷ *v* **5** improve. **6** make fully correct. **perfectly** *adv* **perfection** *n* state of being perfect. **perfectionist** *n* person who demands the highest standards of excellence. **perfectionism** *n*.

perforate ❶ *v* make holes in. **perforation** *n*.

perform ❶ *v* **1** carry out (an action). **2** act, sing, or present a play before an audience. **3** fulfil (a request etc.). **performance** *n* **performer** *n*.

perfume ❶ *n* **1** liquid cosmetic worn for its pleasant smell. **2** fragrance. ▷ *v* **3** give a pleasant smell to. **perfumery** *n* perfumes in general.

perfunctory ❶ *adj* done only as a matter of routine, superficial. **perfunctorily** *adv*.

perhaps ❶ *adv* possibly, maybe.

peril ❶ *n* great danger. **perilous** *adj*.

perimeter ❶ [per-**rim**-it-er] *n* (length of) the outer edge of an area.

period ❶ *n* **1** particular portion of time. **2** single occurrence of menstruation. **3** division of time at school etc. when a particular subject is taught. **4** *US* full stop. ▷ *adj* **5** (of furniture, dress, a play, etc.) dating from or in the style of an earlier time. **periodic** *adj* recurring at intervals. **periodic table** *Chem* chart of the elements, arranged to show their relationship to each other. **periodical** *n* **1** magazine issued at regular intervals. ▷ *adj* **2** periodic.

peripatetic [per-rip-a-**tet**-ik] *adj* travelling about from place to place.

periphery [per-**if**-er-ee] *n, pl* **-eries** **1** boundary or edge. **2** fringes of a field of activity. **peripheral** [per-**if**-er-al] *adj* **1** unimportant, not central. **2** of or on the periphery.

periscope *n* instrument used, esp. in submarines, to give a view of objects on a different level.

perish ❶ *v* **1** be destroyed or die. **2** decay, rot. **perishable** *adj* liable to rot quickly. **perishing** *adj informal* very cold.

THESAURUS

peremptory *adj* = **imperious**, authoritative, bossy (*inf*), dictatorial, dogmatic, domineering, overbearing

perennial *adj* **1** = **lasting**, abiding, constant, continual, enduring, incessant, persistent, recurrent

perfect *adj* **1** = **complete**, absolute, consummate, entire, finished, full, sheer, unmitigated, utter, whole **2** = **faultless**, flawless, immaculate, impeccable, pure, spotless, unblemished **3** = **exact**, accurate, correct, faithful, precise, true, unerring ▷ *v* **5** = **improve**, develop, polish, refine

perforate *v* = **pierce**, bore, drill, penetrate, punch, puncture

perform *v* **1, 3** = **carry out**, accomplish, achieve, complete, discharge, do, execute, fulfil, pull off, work **2** = **present**, act,

enact, play, produce, put on, represent, stage

perfume *n* **2** = **fragrance**, aroma, bouquet, odour, scent, smell

perfunctory *adj* = **offhand**, cursory, heedless, indifferent, mechanical, routine, sketchy, superficial

perhaps *adv* = **maybe**, conceivably, feasibly, it may be, perchance (*arch*), possibly

peril *n* = **danger**, hazard, jeopardy, menace, risk, uncertainty

perimeter *n* = **boundary**, ambit, border, bounds, circumference, confines, edge, limit, margin, periphery

period *n* **1** = **time**, interval, season, space, span, spell, stretch, term, while

perish *v* **1 a** = **be destroyed**, cark (*Aust & NZ sl*), collapse, decline, disappear, fall,

perk ❶ *n informal* incidental benefit gained from a job, such as a company car.

perm *n* **1** long-lasting curly hairstyle produced by treating the hair with chemicals. ▷ *v* **2** give (hair) a perm.

permanent ❶ *adj* lasting forever. **permanence** *n*.

permeate ❶ *v* pervade or pass through the whole of (something). **permeable** *adj* able to be permeated, esp. by liquid.

permit ❶ *v* **-mitting, -mitted 1** give permission, allow. ▷ *n* **2** document giving permission to do something. **permission** *n* authorization to do something. **permissible** *adj* **permissive** *adj* (excessively) tolerant, esp. in sexual matters.

permutation *n* any of the ways a number of things can be arranged or combined.

pernicious ❶ *adj* **1** wicked. **2** extremely harmful, deadly.

pernickety ❶ *adj informal* (excessively) fussy about details.

peroxide *n* **1** hydrogen peroxide used as a hair bleach. **2** oxide containing a high proportion of oxygen.

perpendicular ❶ *adj* **1** at right angles to a line or surface. **2** upright or vertical. ▷ *n* **3** line or plane at right angles to another.

perpetrate ❶ *v* commit or be responsible for (a wrongdoing). **perpetration** *n* **perpetrator** *n*.

perpetual ❶ *adj* **1** lasting forever. **2** continually repeated. **perpetually** *adv* **perpetuate** *v* cause to continue or be remembered. **perpetuation** *n* **in perpetuity** forever.

perplex ❶ *v* puzzle, bewilder. **perplexity** *n, pl* **-ties**.

persecute ❶ *v* **1** treat cruelly because of race, religion, etc. **2** subject to persistent harassment. **persecution** *n* **persecutor** *n*.

persevere ❶ *v* keep making an effort despite difficulties. **perseverance** *n*.

persist ❶ *v* **1** continue to be or happen, last. **2** continue in spite of obstacles or

———————————————————————————— THESAURUS ————

vanish **b = die**, be killed, expire, lose one's life, pass away **2 = rot**, decay, decompose, disintegrate, moulder, waste

perk *n Inf* **= bonus**, benefit, extra, fringe benefit, perquisite, plus

permanent *adj* **= lasting**, abiding, constant, enduring, eternal, everlasting, immutable, perpetual, persistent, stable, steadfast, unchanging

permeate *v* **= pervade**, charge, fill, imbue, impregnate, infiltrate, penetrate, saturate, spread through

permit *v* **1 = allow**, authorize, consent, enable, entitle, give leave *or* permission, give the green light to, grant, let, license, sanction ▷ *n* **2 = licence**, authorization, pass, passport, permission, warrant

pernicious *adj* **1 = wicked**, bad, evil **2 = deadly**, damaging, dangerous, destructive, detrimental, fatal, harmful, hurtful, malign, poisonous

pernickety *adj Inf* **= fussy**, exacting, fastidious, finicky, overprecise,

particular, picky (*inf*)

perpendicular *adj* **1, 2 = upright**, at right angles to, on end, plumb, straight, vertical

perpetrate *v* **= commit**, carry out, do, enact, execute, perform, wreak

perpetual *adj* **1 = everlasting**, endless, eternal, infinite, lasting, never-ending, perennial, permanent, unchanging, unending **2 = continual**, constant, continuous, endless, incessant, interminable, never-ending, persistent, recurrent, repeated

perplex *v* **= puzzle**, baffle, bewilder, confound, confuse, mystify, stump

persecute *v* **1 = victimize**, afflict, ill-treat, maltreat, oppress, pick on, torment, torture **2 = harass**, annoy, badger, bother, hassle (*inf*), pester, tease

persevere *v* **= keep going**, carry on, continue, go on, hang on, persist, remain, stick at *or* to

persist *v* **1 = continue**, carry on, keep up, last, linger, remain **2 = persevere**,

objections. **persistent** *adj* **persistently** *adv* **persistence** *n*.

person ❶ *n* 1 human being. 2 body of a human being. 3 *Grammar* form of pronouns and verbs that shows if a person is speaking, spoken to, or spoken of. **personal** *adj* individual, private. **personality** *n* distinctive character. **in person** actually present.

persona [per-**soh**-na] *n, pl* -**nae** [-nee] someone's personality as presented to others.

personify ❶ *v* -**fying, -fied** 1 give human characteristics to. 2 be an example of, typify. **personification** *n*.

personnel ❶ *n* people employed in an organization.

perspective ❶ *n* 1 view of the relative importance of situations or facts. 2 method of drawing that gives the effect of solidity and relative distances and sizes.

Perspex *n* ® transparent acrylic substitute for glass.

perspicacious ❶ *adj* having quick mental insight. **perspicacity** *n*.

perspire ❶ *v* sweat. **perspiration** *n*.

persuade ❶ *v* 1 make (someone) do something by argument, charm, etc. 2 convince. **persuasion** *n* 1 act of persuading. 2 way of thinking or belief. **persuasive** *adj*.

pert ❶ *adj* saucy and cheeky.

pertain ❶ *v* belong or be relevant (to).

pertinacious *adj* very persistent and determined. **pertinacity** *n*.

pertinent ❶ *adj* relevant. **pertinence** *n*.

perturb ❶ *v* disturb greatly. **perturbation** *n*.

peruse ❶ *v* read in a careful or leisurely manner. **perusal** *n*.

pervade ❶ *v* spread right through (something). **pervasive** *adj*.

pervert ❶ *v* 1 use or alter for a wrong purpose. 2 lead into abnormal (sexual) behaviour. ▷ *n* 3 person who practises sexual perversion. **perversion** *n* 1 sexual act or desire considered abnormal. 2 act of perverting.

peseta [pa-**say**-ta] *n* former monetary unit of Spain.

---

continue, insist, stand firm

person *n* 1 = **individual**, being, body, human, soul **in person** = **personally**, bodily, in the flesh, oneself

personify *v* 2 = **embody**, epitomize, exemplify, represent, symbolize, typify

personnel *n* = **employees**, helpers, human resources, people, staff, workers, workforce

perspective *n* 1 = **objectivity**, proportion, relation, relative importance, relativity

perspicacious *adj* = **perceptive**, acute, alert, astute, discerning, keen, percipient, sharp, shrewd

perspire *v* = **sweat**, exude, glow, pour with sweat, secrete, swelter

persuade *v* 1 = **talk into**, bring round (*inf*), coax, entice, impel, incite, induce, influence, sway, urge, win over 2 = **convince**, cause to believe, satisfy

pert *adj* = **impudent**, bold, cheeky, forward, impertinent, insolent, sassy (*US inf*), saucy

pertain *v* = **relate**, apply, befit, belong, be relevant, concern, refer, regard

pertinent *adj* = **relevant**, applicable, apposite, appropriate, apt, fit, fitting, germane, material, proper, to the point

perturb *v* = **disturb**, agitate, bother, disconcert, faze, fluster, ruffle, trouble, unsettle, vex, worry

peruse *v* = **read**, browse, check, examine, eyeball (*sl*), inspect, scan, scrutinize, study

pervade *v* = **spread through**, charge, fill, imbue, infuse, penetrate, permeate, suffuse

pervert *v* 1 = **distort**, abuse, falsify, garble, misrepresent, misuse, twist, warp 2 = **corrupt**, debase, debauch, degrade, deprave, lead astray ▷ *n* 3 = **deviant**, degenerate, weirdo or weirdie (*inf*)

P

pessimism ❶ n tendency to expect the worst in all things. **pessimist** n **pessimistic** adj.

pest ❶ n 1 annoying person. 2 insect or animal that damages crops. **pesticide** n chemical for killing insect pests.

pester ❶ v annoy or nag continually.

pestilence ❶ n deadly epidemic disease. **pestilent** adj 1 annoying, troublesome. 2 deadly. **pestilential** adj.

pestle n club-shaped implement for grinding things to powder in a mortar.

pet ❶ n 1 animal kept for pleasure and companionship. 2 person favoured or indulged. ▷ adj 3 particularly cherished. ▷ v **petting, petted** 4 treat as a pet. 5 pat or stroke affectionately. 6 informal kiss and caress erotically.

petal n one of the brightly coloured outer parts of a flower.

petite ❶ adj (of a woman) small and dainty.

petition ❶ n 1 formal request, esp. one signed by many people and presented to parliament. ▷ v 2 present a petition to. **petitioner** n.

petrel n sea bird with a hooked bill and tubular nostrils.

petrify ❶ v -fying, -fied 1 frighten severely. 2 turn to stone. **petrification** n.

petroleum n thick dark oil found underground.

petticoat n woman's skirt-shaped undergarment.

pettifogging adj excessively concerned with unimportant detail.

petty ❶ adj -tier, -tiest 1 unimportant, trivial. 2 small-minded. 3 on a small scale, e.g. petty crime. **pettiness** n **petty cash** cash kept by a firm to pay minor expenses. **petty officer** noncommissioned officer in the navy.

petulant ❶ adj childishly irritable or peevish. **petulance** n **petulantly** adv.

petunia n garden plant with funnel-shaped flowers.

pew n 1 fixed benchlike seat in a church. 2 informal chair, seat.

pewter n greyish metal made of tin and lead.

phallus n, pl -luses, -li penis, esp. as a symbol of reproductive power in primitive rites. **phallic** adj.

phantom ❶ n 1 ghost. 2 unreal vision.

Pharaoh [**fare**-oh] n title of the ancient Egyptian kings.

——————— THESAURUS ———————

pessimism n = **gloominess**, dejection, depression, despair, despondency, distrust, gloom, hopelessness, melancholy

pest n = **nuisance**, annoyance, bane, bother, drag (inf), irritation, pain (inf), thorn in one's flesh, trial, vexation

pester v = **annoy**, badger, bedevil, be on one's back (sl), bother, bug (inf), harass, harry, hassle (inf), nag, plague, torment

pestilence n = **plague**, epidemic, visitation

pet n 2 = **favourite**, darling, idol, jewel, treasure ▷ adj 3 = **favourite**, cherished, dearest, dear to one's heart, favoured ▷ v 4 = **pamper**, baby, coddle, cosset, mollycoddle, spoil 5 = **fondle**, caress, pat, stroke 6 Inf = **cuddle**, canoodle (sl), kiss, neck (inf), smooch (inf), snog (Brit sl)

petite adj = **small**, dainty, delicate, elfin,

little, slight

petition n 1 = **appeal**, entreaty, plea, prayer, request, solicitation, suit, supplication ▷ v 2 = **appeal**, adjure, ask, beg, beseech, entreat, plead, pray, solicit, supplicate

petrify v 1 = **terrify**, horrify, immobilize, paralyse, stun, stupefy, transfix 2 = **fossilize**, calcify, harden, turn to stone

petty adj 1 = **trivial**, contemptible, inconsiderable, insignificant, little, measly (inf), negligible, paltry, slight, small, trifling, unimportant 2 = **small-minded**, mean, mean-minded, shabby, spiteful, ungenerous

petulant adj = **sulky**, bad-tempered, huffy, ill-humoured, moody, peevish, sullen

phantom n 1 = **spectre**, apparition, ghost, phantasm, shade (lit), spirit, spook

pharmaceutical *adj* of pharmacy.
pharmacy *n* 1 preparation and dispensing of drugs and medicines. 2 pharmacist's shop.
phase ❶ *n* 1 any distinct or characteristic stage in a development or chain of events. ▷ *v* 2 arrange or carry out in stages or to coincide with something else. **phase in, out** *v* introduce *or* discontinue gradually.
PhD Doctor of Philosophy.
pheasant *n* game bird with bright plumage.
phenomenon ❶ *n, pl* **-ena** 1 anything appearing or observed. 2 remarkable person or thing. **phenomenal** *adj* extraordinary, outstanding. **phenomenally** *adv*.
phial *n* small bottle for medicine etc.
philanthropy ❶ *n* practice of helping people less well-off than oneself. **philanthropic** *adj* **philanthropist** *n*.
philately [fill-**lat**-a-lee] *n* stamp collecting. **philatelist** *n*.
philistine ❶ *adj, n* boorishly uncultivated (person). **philistinism** *n*.
philosophy ❶ *n, pl* **-phies** 1 study of the meaning of life, knowledge, thought, etc. 2 theory or set of ideas held by a particular philosopher. 3 person's outlook on life. **philosopher** *n* person who studies philosophy. **philosophical, philosophic** *adj* 1 of philosophy. 2 calm in the face of difficulties or disappointments. **philosophize** *v* discuss in a philosophical manner.
phlegm [**flem**] *n* thick yellowish substance formed in the nose and throat during a cold.
phobia ❶ *n* intense and unreasoning fear or dislike.
phoenix *n* legendary bird said to set fire to itself and rise anew from its ashes.
phone ❶ *n, v* informal telephone. **phonecard** *n* card used to operate certain public telephones. **phone-in** *n* broadcast in which telephone comments or questions from the public are transmitted live.
phonetic *adj* 1 of speech sounds. 2 (of spelling) written as it is sounded. **phonetics** *n* science of speech sounds. **phonetically** *adv*.
phoney, phony ❶ informal ▷ *adj* **phonier, phoniest** 1 not genuine. 2 insincere. ▷ *n, pl* **phoneys, phonies** 3 phoney person or thing.

— THESAURUS —

(*inf*), wraith 2 = **illusion**, figment of the imagination, hallucination, vision
phase *n* 1 = **stage**, chapter, development, juncture, period, point, position, step, time
phenomenon *n* 1 = **occurrence**, circumstance, episode, event, fact, happening, incident 2 = **wonder**, exception, marvel, miracle, prodigy, rarity, sensation
philanthropy *n* = **humanitarianism**, beneficence, benevolence, brotherly love, charitableness, charity, generosity, kind-heartedness
philistine *adj* = **uncultured**, boorish, ignorant, lowbrow, tasteless, uncultivated, uneducated, unrefined ▷ *n* = **boor**, barbarian, ignoramus, lout, lowbrow, vulgarian, yahoo
philosophy *n* 1 = **thought**, knowledge, logic, metaphysics, rationalism, reasoning, thinking, wisdom 2, 3 = **outlook**, beliefs, convictions, doctrine, ideology, principles, tenets, thinking, values, viewpoint, world view
phobia *n* = **terror**, aversion, detestation, dread, fear, hatred, horror, loathing, repulsion, revulsion, thing (*inf*)
phone *n* *Inf* = **telephone**, blower (*inf*), iPhone®, smartphone ▷ *v* *Inf* = **call**, get on the blower (*inf*), give someone a call, give someone a ring (*inf, chiefly Brit*), give someone a tinkle (*Brit inf*), make a call, ring (up) (*inf, chiefly Brit*), telephone
phoney, phony *Inf adj* 1 = **fake**, bogus, counterfeit, ersatz, false, imitation,

phosphorus *n Chem* toxic flammable nonmetallic element which appears luminous in the dark. **phosphate** *n* 1 compound of phosphorus. 2 fertilizer containing phosphorus.

photo *n, pl* **photos** short for PHOTOGRAPH. **photo finish** finish of a race in which the contestants are so close that a photograph is needed to decide the result.

photocopy *n, pl* **-copies** 1 photographic reproduction. ▷ *v* **-copying, -copied** 2 make a photocopy of. **photocopier** *n*.

photogenic *adj* always looking attractive in photographs.

photograph **❶** *n* 1 picture made by the chemical action of light on sensitive film. ▷ *v* 2 take a photograph of. **photographer** *n* **photographic** *adj* **photography** *n*.

photosynthesis *n* process by which a green plant uses sunlight to build up carbohydrate reserves.

phrase **❶** *n* 1 group of words forming a unit of meaning, esp. within a sentence. 2 short effective expression. ▷ *v* 3 express in words. **phrasal verb** phrase consisting of a verb and an adverb or preposition, with a meaning different from the parts, such as *take in* meaning *deceive*.

phylum *n, pl* **-la** major taxonomic division of animals and plants that contains one or more classes.

physical **❶** *adj* 1 of the body, as contrasted with the mind or spirit. 2 of material things or nature.

physician **❶** *n* doctor of medicine.

physics *n* science of the properties of matter and energy. **physicist** *n*.

physiognomy [fiz-ee-**on**-om-ee] *n* face.

physiology *n* science of the normal function of living things. **physiological** *adj* **physiologist** *n*.

physiotherapy *n* treatment of disease or injury by physical means such as massage, rather than by drugs. **physiotherapist** *n*.

physique **❶** *n* person's bodily build and muscular development.

pi *n Maths* ratio of the circumference of a circle to its diameter.

piano¹ *n, pl* **pianos** musical instrument with strings which are struck by hammers worked by a keyboard (also **pianoforte**). **pianist** *n* **Pianola** *n* ® mechanically played piano.

piano² *adv Music* quietly.

picador *n* mounted bullfighter with a lance.

piccalilli *n* pickle of vegetables in mustard sauce.

piccolo *n, pl* **-los** small flute.

pick¹ **❶** *v* 1 choose. 2 remove (flowers or fruit) from a plant. 3 take hold of and move with the fingers. 4 provoke (a fight etc.) deliberately. 5 open (a lock) by means

———————————— THESAURUS ————————————

pseudo (*inf*), sham ▷ *n* 3 = **fake**, counterfeit, forgery, fraud, impostor, pseud (*inf*), sham

photograph *n* 1 = **picture**, photo (*inf*), print, shot, snap (*inf*), snapshot, transparency ▷ *v* 2 = **take a picture of**, film, record, shoot, snap (*inf*), take (someone's) picture

phrase *n* 1 = **expression**, group of words, idiom, remark, saying ▷ *v* 3 = **express**, put, put into words, say, voice, word

physical *adj* 1 = **bodily**, corporal, corporeal, earthly, fleshly, incarnate, mortal 2 = **material**, natural, palpable,

real, solid, substantial, tangible

physician *n* = **doctor**, doc (*inf*), doctor of medicine, general practitioner, G.P., M.D., medic (*inf*), medical practitioner

physique *n* = **build**, body, constitution, figure, form, frame, shape, structure

pick¹ *v* 1 = **select**, choose, decide upon, elect, fix upon, hand-pick, opt for, settle upon, single out 2 = **gather**, collect, harvest, pluck, pull 4 = **provoke**, incite, instigate, start 5 = **open**, break into, break open, crack, force ▷ *n* 6 = **choice**, decision, option, preference, selection 7 = **the best**, elect, elite, the cream

other than a key. ▷ *n* **6** choice. **7** best part.
pick-me-up *n informal* stimulating drink,
tonic. **pick on** *v* continually treat unfairly.
pick out *v* recognize, distinguish. **pick
up** *v* **1** raise, lift. **2** collect. **3** improve,
get better. **4** become acquainted with
for a sexual purpose. **pick-up** *n* **1** small
truck. **2** casual acquaintance made for a
sexual purpose. **3** device for conversion
of vibrations into electrical signals, as in a
record player.

pick² *n* tool with a curved iron crossbar
and wooden shaft, for breaking up hard
ground or rocks.

picket ❶ *n* **1** person or group standing
outside a workplace to deter would-be
workers during a strike. **2** sentry or
sentries posted to give warning of an
attack. **3** pointed stick used as part of
a fence. ▷ *v* **4** form a picket outside (a
workplace). **picket line** line of people
acting as pickets.

pickle ❶ *n* **1** food preserved in vinegar or
salt water. **2** *informal* awkward situation.
▷ *v* **3** preserve in vinegar or salt water.
pickled *adj informal* drunk.

picnic ❶ *n* **1** informal meal out of doors. ▷ *v*
-nicking, -nicked 2 have a picnic.

picture ❶ *n* **1** drawing or painting.

2 photograph. **3** mental image. **4** image
on a TV screen. ▷ *pl* **5** cinema. ▷ *v*
6 visualize, imagine. **7** represent in a
picture. **picturesque** *adj* **1** (of a place or
view) pleasant to look at. **2** (of language)
forceful, vivid.

pidgin *n* language, not a mother tongue,
made up of elements of two or more other
languages.

pie *n* dish of meat, fruit, etc. baked in pastry.
pie chart circular diagram with sectors
representing quantities.

piebald ❶ *n*, *adj* (horse) with irregular
black-and-white markings.

piece ❶ *n* **1** separate bit or part. **2** instance,
e.g. *a piece of luck*. **3** example, specimen.
4 literary or musical composition. **5** coin.
6 small object used in draughts, chess,
etc. **piece together** *v* make or assemble
bit by bit.

pier ❶ *n* **1** platform on stilts sticking out
into the sea. **2** pillar, esp. one supporting
a bridge.

pierce ❶ *v* **1** make a hole in or through
with a sharp instrument. **2** make a way
through. **piercing** *adj* **1** (of a sound) shrill
and high-pitched.

piety ❶ *n*, *pl* **-ties** deep devotion to God
and religion.

p

picket *n* **1** = **protester**, demonstrator,
picketer **2** = **lookout**, guard, patrol,
sentinel, sentry, watch **3** = **stake**, pale,
paling, post, stanchion, upright ▷ *v*
4 = **blockade**, boycott, demonstrate
pickle *n* **2** *Inf* = **predicament**, bind (*inf*),
difficulty, dilemma, fix (*inf*), hot water
(*inf*), jam (*inf*), quandary, scrape (*inf*), tight
spot ▷ *v* **3** = **preserve**, marinade, steep
picnic *n* **1** = **excursion**, outdoor meal,
outing
picture *n* **1** = **representation**, drawing,
engraving, illustration, image, likeness,
painting, portrait, print, sketch
2 = **photograph** ▷ *n*, *pl* **5** = **flicks** (*sl*),
movies (*US inf*) ▷ *v* **6** = **imagine**, conceive
of, envision, see, visualize **7** = **represent**,

depict, draw, illustrate, paint, photograph,
show, sketch
piebald *adj* = **pied**, black and white,
brindled, dappled, flecked, mottled,
speckled, spotted
piece *n* **1** = **bit**, chunk, fragment, morsel,
part, portion, quantity, segment, slice
4 = **work**, article, composition, creation,
item, study, work of art
pier *n* **1** = **jetty**, landing place, promenade,
quay, wharf **2** = **pillar**, buttress, column,
pile, post, support, upright
pierce *v* **1** = **penetrate**, bore, drill, enter,
perforate, prick, puncture, spike, stab,
stick into
piety *n* = **holiness**, faith, godliness,
piousness, religion, reverence

pig ❶ n 1 animal kept and killed for pork, ham, and bacon. 2 *informal* greedy, dirty, or rude person. **piggish, piggy** adj 1 *informal* dirty. 2 greedy. 3 stubborn. **piggery** n, pl **-geries** place for keeping and breeding pigs. **pig-headed** adj obstinate.

pigeon n bird with a heavy body and short legs, sometimes trained to carry messages. **pigeonhole** n 1 compartment for papers in a desk etc. ▷ v 2 classify. 3 put aside and do nothing about. **pigeon-toed** adj with the feet or toes turned inwards.

piggyback n 1 ride on someone's shoulders. ▷ adv 2 carried on someone's shoulders.

pigment ❶ n colouring matter, paint or dye. **pigmentation** n.

pigtail n plait of hair hanging from the back or either side of the head.

pike¹ n large predatory freshwater fish.

pike² n *Hist* long-handled spear.

pikelet n *Aust & NZ* small thick pancake.

piker n *Aust & NZ slang* shirker.

pilau, pilaf or **pilaff** n Middle Eastern dish of meat, fish, or poultry boiled with rice, spices, etc.

pilchard n small edible sea fish of the herring family.

pile¹ ❶ n 1 number of things lying on top of each other. 2 *informal* large amount. 3 large building. ▷ v 4 collect into a pile. 5 (foll. by *in* or *out*) move in a group. **pile-up** n *informal* traffic accident involving several vehicles.

pile² ❶ n beam driven into the ground, esp. as a foundation for building.

pile³ ❶ n fibres of a carpet or a fabric, esp. velvet, that stand up from the weave.

piles pl n swollen veins in the rectum, haemorrhoids.

pilfer ❶ v steal in small quantities.

pilgrim ❶ n person who journeys to a holy place. **pilgrimage** n.

pill ❶ n small ball of medicine swallowed whole. **the pill** pill taken by a woman to prevent pregnancy.

pillage ❶ v 1 steal property by violence in war. ▷ n 2 violent seizure of goods, esp. in war.

pillar ❶ n 1 upright post, usu. supporting a roof. 2 strong supporter. **pillar box** red pillar-shaped letter box in the street.

pillion n seat for a passenger behind the rider of a motorcycle.

pillory ❶ n, pl **-ries** 1 *Hist* frame with holes for the head and hands in which an

---

THESAURUS

pig n 1 = **hog**, boar, porker, sow, swine 2 *Inf* = **slob** (*sl*), boor, brute, glutton, swine

pigment n = **colour**, colouring, dye, paint, stain, tincture, tint

pile¹ n 1 = **heap**, accumulation, berg (*S Afr*), collection, hoard, mass, mound, mountain, stack 2 *Inf* = **a lot**, great deal, ocean, quantity, stacks 3 = **building**, edifice, erection, structure ▷ v 4 = **collect**, accumulate, amass, assemble, gather, heap, hoard, stack 5 (foll. by *in* or *out*) = **crowd**, crush, flock, flood, jam, pack, rush, stream

pile² n = **foundation**, beam, column, pillar, post, support, upright

pile³ n = **nap**, down, fibre, fur, hair, plush

pilfer v = **steal**, appropriate, embezzle, filch, knock off (*sl*), lift (*inf*), nick (*sl, chiefly Brit*), pinch (*inf*), purloin, snaffle (*Brit inf*), swipe (*sl*), take

pilgrim n = **traveller**, wanderer, wayfarer

pill n = **tablet**, capsule, pellet **the pill** = **oral contraceptive**

pillage v 1 = **plunder**, despoil, loot, maraud, raid, ransack, ravage, sack ▷ n 2 = **plunder**, marauding, robbery, sack, spoliation

pillar n 1 = **support**, column, pier, post, prop, shaft, stanchion, upright 2 = **supporter**, leader, leading light (*inf*), mainstay, upholder

pillory v 2 = **ridicule**, brand, denounce, stigmatize

offender was locked and exposed to public abuse. ▷ v **-rying, -ried 2** ridicule publicly.

pillow n **1** stuffed cloth bag for supporting the head in bed. ▷ v **2** rest as if on a pillow. **pillowcase, pillowslip** n removable cover for a pillow.

pilot ⊕ n **1** person qualified to fly an aircraft or spacecraft. **2** person employed to steer a ship entering or leaving a harbour. ▷ adj **3** experimental and preliminary. ▷ v **4** act as the pilot of. **5** guide, steer. **pilot light** small flame lighting the main one in a gas appliance.

pimento n, pl **-tos** mild-tasting red pepper.

pimp n **1** man who gets customers for a prostitute in return for a share of his or her earnings. ▷ v **2** act as a pimp.

pimpernel n wild plant with small star-shaped flowers.

pimple ⊕ n small pus-filled spot on the skin. **pimply** adj.

pin ⊕ n **1** short thin piece of stiff wire with a point and head, for fastening things. **2** wooden or metal peg or stake. ▷ v **pinning, pinned 3** fasten with a pin. **4** seize and hold fast. **pin down** v **1** force (someone) to make a decision, take action, etc. **2** define clearly. **pin money** small amount earned to buy small luxuries. **pin-up** n picture of a sexually attractive person, esp. (partly) naked.

PIN personal identification number:

number used with a credit or debit card to withdraw money, confirm a purchase, etc.

pinafore n **1** apron. **2** dress with a bib top.

pincers pl n **1** tool consisting of two hinged arms, for gripping. **2** claws of a lobster etc.

pinch ⊕ v **1** squeeze between finger and thumb. **2** cause pain by being too tight. **3** informal steal. ▷ n **4** act of pinching. **5** as much as can be taken up between the finger and thumb. **at a pinch** if absolutely necessary. **feel the pinch** have to economize.

pine¹ n **1** evergreen coniferous tree. **2** its wood.

pine² **⊕** v **1** (foll. by for) feel great longing (for). **2** become thin and ill through grief etc.

pineapple n large tropical fruit with juicy yellow flesh and a hard skin.

pinion ⊕ n **1** bird's wing. ▷ v **2** immobilize (someone) by tying or holding his or her arms.

pink ⊕ n **1** pale reddish colour. **2** fragrant garden plant. ▷ adj **3** of the colour pink. ▷ v **4** (of an engine) make a metallic noise because not working properly, knock. **in the pink** in good health.

pinnacle ⊕ n **1** highest point of success etc. **2** mountain peak. **3** small slender spire.

pint n liquid measure, 1/8 gallon (.568 litre).

P

pilot n **1** = **airman**, aviator, flyer
2 = **helmsman**, navigator, steersman
▷ adj **3** = **trial**, experimental, model, test
▷ v **4, 5** = **fly**, conduct, direct, drive, guide, handle, navigate, operate, steer

pimple n = **spot**, boil, plook (Scot), pustule, zit (sl)

pin v **3** = **fasten**, affix, attach, fix, join, secure **4** = **hold fast**, fix, hold down, immobilize, pinion

pinch v **1** = **squeeze**, compress, grasp, nip, press **2** = **hurt**, cramp, crush, pain **3** Inf = **steal**, filch, knock off (sl), lift (inf),

nick (sl, chiefly Brit), pilfer, purloin, snaffle (Brit inf), swipe (sl) ▷ n
4 = **squeeze**, nip

pine² v **1** (foll. by for) = **long**, ache, crave, desire, eat one's heart out over, hanker, hunger for, thirst for, wish for, yearn for
2 = **waste**, decline, fade, languish, sicken

pinion v **2** = **immobilize**, bind, chain, fasten, fetter, manacle, shackle, tie

pink adj **3** = **rosy**, flushed, reddish, rose, roseate, salmon

pinnacle n **1** = **peak**, apex, crest, crown, height, summit, top, vertex, zenith

pioneer ❶ *n* **1** explorer or early settler of a new country. **2** originator or developer of something new. ▷ *v* **3** be the pioneer or leader of.

pious ❶ *adj* deeply religious, devout.

pip¹ *n* small seed in a fruit.

pip² *n* **1** high-pitched sound used as a time signal on radio. **2** *informal* star on a junior army officer's shoulder showing rank.

pip³ *n* **give someone the pip** *Brit, NZ & S Afr slang* annoy.

pipe ❶ *n* **1** tube for conveying liquid or gas. **2** tube with a small bowl at the end for smoking tobacco. **3** tubular musical instrument. ▷ *pl* **4** bagpipes. ▷ *v* **5** play on a pipe. **6** utter in a shrill tone. **7** convey by pipe. **8** decorate with piping. **piper** *n* player on a pipe or bagpipes. **piping** *n* **1** system of pipes. **2** decoration of icing on a cake etc. **3** fancy edging on clothes etc. **pipe down** *v informal* stop talking. **pipe dream** fanciful impossible plan. **pipeline** *n* **1** long pipe for transporting oil, water, etc. **2** means of communication. **in the pipeline** in preparation. **pipe up** *v* speak suddenly or shrilly.

piquant ❶ [pee-kant] *adj* **1** having a pleasant spicy taste. **2** mentally stimulating. **piquancy** *n*.

pique ❶ [peek] *n* **1** feeling of hurt pride, baffled curiosity, or resentment. ▷ *v* **2** hurt the pride of. **3** arouse (curiosity).

piranha *n* small fierce freshwater fish of tropical America.

pirate ❶ *n* **1** sea robber. **2** person who illegally publishes or sells work owned by someone else. **3** person or company that broadcasts illegally. ▷ *v* **4** sell or reproduce (artistic work etc.) illegally. **piracy** *n* **piratical** *adj*.

pirouette *v, n* (make) a spinning turn balanced on the toes of one foot.

pistachio *n, pl* **-chios** edible nut of a Mediterranean tree.

piste [peest] *n* ski slope.

pistol *n* short-barrelled handgun.

piston *n* cylindrical part in an engine that slides to and fro in a cylinder.

pit ❶ *n* **1** deep hole in the ground. **2** coal mine. **3** dent or depression. **4** servicing and refuelling area on a motor-racing track. **5** same as ORCHESTRA PIT. ▷ *v* **pitting, pitted 6** mark with small dents or scars. **pit one's wits against** compete against in a test or contest.

pitch¹ ❶ *v* **1** throw, hurl. **2** set up (a tent). **3** fall headlong. **4** (of a ship or plane) move with the front and back going up

────────── THESAURUS ──────────

pioneer *n* **1** = **settler**, colonist, explorer **2** = **founder**, developer, innovator, leader, trailblazer ▷ *v* **3** = **develop**, create, discover, establish, initiate, instigate, institute, invent, originate, show the way, start

pious *adj* = **religious**, devout, God-fearing, godly, holy, reverent, righteous, saintly

pipe *n* **1** = **tube**, conduit, duct, hose, line, main, passage, pipeline ▷ *v* **5** = **play**, sound **7** = **whistle**, cheep, peep, sing, warble **7** = **convey**, channel, conduct

piquant *adj* **1** = **spicy**, biting, pungent, savoury, sharp, tangy, tart, zesty **2** = **interesting**, lively, provocative, scintillating, sparkling, stimulating

pique *n* **1** = **resentment**, annoyance, displeasure, huff, hurt feelings, irritation, offence, umbrage, wounded pride ▷ *v* **2** = **displease**, affront, annoy, get (*inf*), irk, irritate, nettle, offend, rile, sting **3** = **arouse**, excite, rouse, spur, stimulate, stir, whet

pirate *n* **1** = **buccaneer**, corsair, freebooter, marauder, raider **2** = **plagiarist**, cribber (*inf*), infringer, plagiarizer ▷ *v* **4** = **copy**, appropriate, crib (*inf*), plagiarize, poach, reproduce, steal

pit *n* **1** = **hole**, abyss, cavity, chasm, crater, dent, depression, hollow ▷ *v* **6** = **scar**, dent, indent, mark, pockmark

pitch¹ *v* **1** = **throw**, cast, chuck (*inf*), fling, heave, hurl, lob (*inf*), sling, toss **2** = **set up**, erect, put up, raise, settle **3** = **fall**,

and down alternately. **5** set the level or tone of. ▷ *n* **6** area marked out for playing sport. **7** degree or angle of slope. **8** degree of highness or lowness of a (musical) sound. **9** place where a street or market trader regularly sells. **10** *informal* persuasive sales talk. **pitch in** *v* join in enthusiastically. **pitch into** *v informal* attack.

pitch² **ⓘ** *n* dark sticky substance obtained from tar. **pitch-black**, **pitch-dark** *adj* very dark.

pitcher *n* large jug with a narrow neck.

pith **ⓘ** *n* **1** soft white lining of the rind of oranges etc. **2** essential part. **3** soft tissue in the stems of certain plants. **pithy** *adj* short and full of meaning.

pittance **ⓘ** *n* very small amount of money.

pituitary *n, pl* **-taries** gland at the base of the brain, that helps to control growth (also **pituitary gland**).

pity **ⓘ** *n, pl* **pities 1** sympathy or sorrow for others' suffering. **2** regrettable fact. ▷ *v* **pitying**, **pitied 3** feel pity for. **piteous**, **pitiable** *adj* arousing pity. **pitiful** *adj* **1** arousing pity. **2** woeful, contemptible.

pitifully *adv* **pitiless** *adj* feeling no pity or mercy.

pivot **ⓘ** *n* **1** central shaft on which something turns. ▷ *v* **2** provide with or turn on a pivot. **pivotal** *adj* of crucial importance.

pixel *n* smallest constituent element of an image, as on a visual display unit.

pixie **ⓘ** *n* (in folklore) fairy.

pizza *n* flat disc of dough covered with a wide variety of savoury toppings and baked.

pizzicato [pit-see-**kah**-toe] *adj* *Music* played by plucking the string of a violin etc. with the finger.

placard **ⓘ** *n* notice that is carried or displayed in public.

placate **ⓘ** *v* make (someone) stop feeling angry or upset. **placatory** *adj*.

place **ⓘ** *n* **1** particular part of an area or space. **2** particular town, building, etc. **3** position or point reached. **4** seat or space. **5** duty or right. **6** position of employment. **7** usual position. ▷ *v* **8** put in a particular place. **9** identify, put in context. **10** make (an order, bet, etc.).

THESAURUS

---

dive, drop, topple, tumble **4 = toss**, lurch, plunge, roll ▷ *n* **6 = sports field**, field of play, ground, park (*US & Canad*) **7 = slope**, angle, degree, dip, gradient, height, highest point, incline, level, point, summit, tilt **8 = tone**, modulation, sound, timbre **10** *Inf* **= sales talk**, patter, spiel (*inf*)

pith *n* **2 = essence**, core, crux, gist, heart, kernel, nub, point, quintessence, salient point

pittance *n* **= peanuts** (*sl*), chicken feed (*sl*), drop, mite, slave wages, trifle

pity *n* **1 = compassion**, charity, clemency, fellow feeling, forbearance, kindness, mercy, sympathy **2 = shame**, bummer (*sl*), crying shame, misfortune, sin ▷ *v* **3 = feel sorry for**, bleed for, feel for, grieve for, have compassion for, sympathize with, weep for

pivot *n* **1 = axis**, axle, centre, fulcrum, heart, hinge, hub, kingpin, spindle, swivel

▷ *v* **2 = turn**, revolve, rotate, spin, swivel, twirl

pixie *n* **= elf**, brownie, fairy, sprite

placard *n* **= notice**, advertisement, bill, poster

placate *v* **= calm**, appease, assuage, conciliate, humour, mollify, pacify, propitiate, soothe

place *n* **1 = spot**, area, location, point, position, site, venue, whereabouts **3 = position**, grade, rank, station, status **5 = duty**, affair, charge, concern, function, prerogative, responsibility, right, role **6 = job**, appointment, employment, position, post ▷ *v* **8 = put**, deposit, install, lay, locate, position, rest, set, situate, stand, station, stick (*inf*) **9 = identify**, know, put one's finger on, recognize, remember **take place = happen**, come about, go on, occur, transpire (*inf*)

P

be placed (of a competitor in a race) be among the first three. **take place** happen, occur.

placebo [plas-**see**-bo] *n*, *pl* **-bos**, **-boes** sugar pill etc. given to an unsuspecting patient instead of an active drug.

placenta [plass-**ent**-a] *n*, *pl* **-tas**, **-tae** organ formed in the womb during pregnancy, providing nutrients for the fetus.
placental *adj*.

placid ● *adj* not easily excited or upset, calm. **placidity** *n*.

plague ● *n* 1 fast-spreading fatal disease. 2 *Hist* bubonic plague. 3 widespread infestation. ▷ *v* **plaguing**, **plagued** 4 trouble or annoy continually.

plaice *n* edible European flatfish.

plaid *n* 1 long piece of tartan cloth worn as part of Highland dress. 2 tartan cloth or pattern.

plain ● *adj* 1 easy to see or understand. 2 expressed honestly and clearly. 3 without decoration or pattern. 4 not beautiful. 5 simple, ordinary. ▷ *n* 6 large

stretch of level country. **plainly** *adv* **plainness** *n* **plain clothes** ordinary clothes, as opposed to uniform. **plain sailing** easy progress.

plaintiff *n* person who sues in a court of law.

plaintive ● *adj* sad, mournful. **plaintively** *adv*.

plait [**platt**] *n* 1 intertwined length of hair. ▷ *v* 2 intertwine separate strands in a pattern.

plan ● *n* 1 way thought out to do or achieve something. 2 diagram showing the layout or design of something. ▷ *v* **planning**, **planned** 3 arrange beforehand. 4 make a diagram of. **planner** *n*.

plane¹ ● *n* 1 an aircraft. 2 *Maths* flat surface. 3 level of attainment etc. ▷ *adj* 4 perfectly flat or level. ▷ *v* 5 glide or skim.

plane² *n* 1 tool for smoothing wood. ▷ *v* 2 smooth (wood) with a plane.

plane³ *n* tree with broad leaves.

planet *n* large body in space that revolves round the sun or another star. **planetary** *adj*.

──────── THESAURUS ────────

placid *adj* = **calm**, collected, composed, equable, even-tempered, imperturbable, serene, tranquil, unexcitable, unruffled, untroubled

plague *n* 1 = **disease**, epidemic, infection, pestilence 3 = **affliction**, bane, blight, curse, evil, scourge, torment ▷ *v* 4 = **pester**, annoy, badger, bother, harass, harry, hassle (*inf*), tease, torment, torture, trouble, vex

plain *adj* 1 = **clear**, comprehensible, distinct, evident, manifest, obvious, overt, patent, unambiguous, understandable, unmistakable, visible 2 = **straightforward**, blunt, candid, direct, downright, forthright, frank, honest, open, outspoken, upfront (*inf*) 3 = **unadorned**, austere, bare, basic, severe, simple, Spartan, stark, unembellished, unfussy, unornamented 4 = **ugly**, ill-favoured, no oil painting

(*inf*), not beautiful, unattractive, unlovely, unprepossessing 5 = **ordinary**, common, commonplace, everyday, simple, unaffected, unpretentious ▷ *n* 6 = **flatland**, grassland, plateau, prairie, steppe, veld

plaintive *adj* = **sorrowful**, heart-rending, mournful, pathetic, piteous, pitiful, sad

plan *n* 1 = **scheme**, design, method, plot, programme, proposal, strategy, suggestion, system 2 = **diagram**, blueprint, chart, drawing, layout, map, representation, sketch ▷ *v* 3 = **devise**, arrange, contrive, design, draft, formulate, organize, outline, plot, scheme, think out

plane¹ *n* 1 = **aeroplane**, aircraft, jet 2 *Maths* = **flat surface**, level surface 3 = **level**, condition, degree, position ▷ *adj* 4 = **level**, even, flat, horizontal, regular, smooth ▷ *v* 5 = **skim**, glide, sail, skate

p

planetarium n, pl **-iums**, **-ia** building where the movements of the stars, planets, etc. are shown by projecting lights on the inside of a dome.

plank n long flat piece of sawn timber.

plankton n minute animals and plants floating in the surface water of a sea or lake.

plant ❶ n 1 living organism that grows in the ground and has no power to move. 2 equipment or machinery used in industrial processes. 3 factory or other industrial premises. ▷ v 4 put in the ground to grow. 5 place firmly in position. 6 informal put (a person) secretly in an organization to spy. 7 informal hide (stolen goods etc.) on a person to make him or her seem guilty. **planter** n 1 owner of a plantation.

plantation n 1 estate for the cultivation of tea, tobacco, etc. 2 wood of cultivated trees.

plaque n 1 inscribed commemorative stone or metal plate. 2 filmy deposit on teeth that causes decay.

plasma n clear liquid part of blood. **plasma screen** type of high-resolution flat screen on a television or visual display unit.

plaster ❶ n 1 mixture of lime, sand, etc. for coating walls. 2 adhesive strip of material for dressing cuts etc. ▷ v 3 cover with plaster. 4 coat thickly. **plastered** adj slang drunk. **plaster of Paris** white powder which dries to form a hard solid when

mixed with water, used for sculptures and casts for broken limbs.

plastic ❶ n 1 synthetic material that can be moulded when soft but sets in a hard long-lasting shape. 2 credit cards etc. as opposed to cash. ▷ adj 3 made of plastic. 4 easily moulded, pliant. **plasticity** n ability to be moulded. **plastic surgery** repair or reconstruction of missing or malformed parts of the body.

Plasticine n ® soft coloured modelling material used esp. by children.

plate ❶ n 1 shallow dish for holding food. 2 flat thin sheet of metal, glass, etc. 3 thin coating of metal on another metal. 4 dishes or cutlery made of gold or silver. 5 illustration, usu. on fine quality paper, in a book. 6 informal set of false teeth. ▷ v 7 cover with a thin coating of gold, silver, or other metal. **plateful** n **plate glass** glass in thin sheets, used for mirrors and windows.

plateau ❶ n, pl **-teaus**, **-teaux** 1 area of level high land. 2 stage when there is no change or development.

platform ❶ n 1 raised floor. 2 raised area in a station from which passengers board trains. 3 structure in the sea which holds machinery, stores, etc. for drilling an oil well. 4 programme of a political party.

platinum n Chem valuable silvery-white metal. **platinum blonde** woman with silvery-blonde hair.

P

—————— THESAURUS ——————

plant n 1 = **vegetable**, bush, flower, herb, shrub, weed 2 = **machinery**, apparatus, equipment, gear 3 = **factory**, foundry, mill, shop, works, yard ▷ v 4 = **sow**, put in the ground, scatter, seed, transplant 5 = **place**, establish, fix, found, insert, put, set

plaster n 1 = **mortar**, gypsum, plaster of Paris, stucco 2 = **bandage**, adhesive plaster, dressing, Elastoplast, sticking plaster ▷ v 4 = **cover**, coat, daub, overlay, smear, spread

plastic adj 4 = **pliant**, ductile, flexible, mouldable, pliable, soft, supple

plate n 1 = **platter**, dish, trencher (arch) 2 = **layer**, panel, sheet, slab 5 = **illustration**, lithograph, print ▷ v 7 = **coat**, cover, gild, laminate, overlay

plateau n 1 = **upland**, highland, table, tableland 2 = **levelling off**, level, stability, stage

platform n 1 = **stage**, dais, podium, rostrum, stand 4 = **policy**, manifesto, objective(s), party line, principle, programme

platitude ⊙ *n* remark that is true but not interesting or original. **platitudinous** *adj*.

platonic *adj* friendly or affectionate but not sexual.

platoon ⊙ *n* smaller unit within a company of soldiers.

platter ⊙ *n* large dish.

platypus *n* Australian egg-laying amphibious mammal, with dense fur, webbed feet, and a ducklike bill (also **duck-billed platypus, duckbill**).

plausible ⊙ *adj* 1 apparently true or reasonable. 2 persuasive but insincere. **plausibly** *adv* **plausibility** *n*.

play ⊙ *v* 1 occupy oneself in (a game or recreation). 2 compete against in a game or sport. 3 behave carelessly. 4 act (a part) on the stage. 5 perform on (a musical instrument). 6 cause (a radio, record player, etc.) to give out sound. 7 move lightly or irregularly, flicker. ▷ *n* 8 story performed on stage or broadcast. 9 activities children take part in for amusement. 10 playing of a game. 11 conduct, e.g. *fair play*. 12 (scope for) freedom of movement. **player** *n* **playful** *adj* lively. **play back** *v* listen to or watch (something recorded). **play down** *v* minimize the importance of. **playing card** one of a set of 52 cards used in card

games. **playing field** extensive piece of ground for sport. **play-lunch** *n Aust & NZ* child's mid-morning snack at school. **play off** *v* set (two people) against each other for one's own ends. **play on** *v* exploit or encourage (someone's sympathy or weakness). **plaything** *n* 1 toy. 2 person regarded or treated as a toy. **play up** *v* 1 give prominence to. 2 cause trouble. **playwright** *n* author of plays.

plaza *n* open space or square.

plea ⊙ *n* 1 serious or urgent request, entreaty. 2 statement of a prisoner or defendant. 3 excuse.

please ⊙ *v* 1 give pleasure or satisfaction to. ▷ *adv* 2 polite word of request. **pleasant** *adj* pleasing, enjoyable. **please oneself** do as one likes. **pleased** *adj* **pleasing** *adj* **pleasure** *n* 1 feeling of happiness and satisfaction. 2 something that causes this.

pleat *n* 1 fold made by doubling material back on itself. ▷ *v* 2 arrange (material) in pleats.

plebeian ⊙ [pleb-**ee**-an] *adj* 1 of the lower social classes. 2 vulgar or rough. ▷ *n* 3 (also **pleb**) member of the lower social classes.

plectrum *n*, *pl* **-trums, -tra** small implement for plucking the strings of a guitar etc.

——————————————— THESAURUS ———————————————

platitude *n* = **cliché**, banality, commonplace, truism

platoon *n* = **squad**, company, group, outfit (*inf*), patrol, squadron, team

platter *n* = **plate**, dish, salver, tray, trencher (*arch*)

plausible *adj* 1 = **believable**, conceivable, credible, likely, persuasive, possible, probable, reasonable, tenable 2 = **glib**, smooth, smooth-talking, smooth-tongued, specious

play *v* 1 = **amuse oneself**, entertain oneself, fool, have fun, revel, romp, sport, trifle 2 = **compete**, challenge, contend against, participate, take

on, take part 4 = **act**, act the part of, perform, portray, represent ▷ *n* 8 = **drama**, comedy, dramatic piece, farce, pantomime, piece, show, stage show, tragedy 9 = **amusement**, diversion, entertainment, fun, game, pastime, recreation, sport 12 = **space**, elbowroom, latitude, leeway, margin, room, scope

plea *n* 1 = **appeal**, entreaty, intercession, petition, prayer, request, suit, supplication 3 = **excuse**, defence, explanation, justification

please *v* 1 = **delight**, amuse, entertain, gladden, gratify, humour, indulge, satisfy, suit

pledge ❶ *n* **1** solemn promise.
2 something valuable given as a guarantee that a promise will be kept or a debt paid.
▷ *v* **3** promise solemnly. **4** bind by or as if by a pledge.

plenary *adj* (of a meeting) attended by all members.

plenipotentiary *adj* **1** having full powers. ▷ *n, pl* **-aries 2** diplomat or representative having full powers.

plenitude *n* completeness, abundance.

plenty ❶ *n* **1** large amount or number.
2 quite enough. **plentiful** *adj* existing in large amounts or numbers. **plentifully** *adv*.

plethora ❶ *n* excess.

pleurisy *n* inflammation of the membrane covering the lungs.

pliable ❶ *adj* **1** easily bent. **2** easily influenced. **pliability** *n*.

pliers *pl n* tool with hinged arms and jaws for gripping.

plight¹ ❶ *n* difficult or dangerous situation.

plight² *v* **plight one's troth** *old-fashioned* promise to marry.

plimsolls *pl n* rubber-soled canvas shoes.

plinth *n* slab forming the base of a statue, column, pedestal, etc.

plod ❶ *v* **plodding, plodded 1** walk with slow heavy steps. **2** work slowly but determinedly. **plodder** *n*.

plonk¹ *v* put (something) down heavily and carelessly.

plonk² *n informal* cheap inferior wine.

plop *n* **1** sound of an object falling into water without a splash. ▷ *v* **plopping, plopped 2** make this sound.

plot¹ ❶ *n* **1** secret plan to do something illegal or wrong. **2** story of a film, novel, etc. ▷ *v* **plotting, plotted 3** plan secretly, conspire. **4** mark the position or course of (a ship or aircraft) on a map. **5** mark and join up (points on a graph).

plot² ❶ *n* small piece of land.

plough ❶ *n* **1** agricultural tool for turning over soil. ▷ *v* **2** turn over (earth) with a plough. **3** (usu with *through*) move or work through slowly and laboriously. **ploughman** *n* **ploughshare** *n* blade of a plough.

plover *n* shore bird with a straight bill and long pointed wings.

ploy ❶ *n* manoeuvre designed to gain an advantage.

— THESAURUS —

pledge *n* **1** = **promise**, assurance, covenant, oath, undertaking, vow, warrant, word **2** = **guarantee**, bail, collateral, deposit, pawn, security, surety ▷ *v* **3** = **promise**, contract, engage, give one's oath, give one's word, swear, vow

plenty *n* **1** = **lots** (*inf*), abundance, enough, great deal, heap(s) (*inf*), masses, pile(s) (*inf*), plethora, quantity, stack(s)

plethora *n* = **excess**, glut, overabundance, profusion, superabundance, surfeit, surplus

pliable *adj* **1** = **flexible**, bendable, bendy, malleable, plastic, pliant, supple **2** = **compliant**, adaptable, docile, easily led, impressionable, pliant, receptive, responsive, susceptible, tractable

plight¹ *n* = **difficulty**, condition, jam (*inf*), predicament, scrape (*inf*), situation, spot (*inf*), state, trouble

plod *v* **1** = **trudge**, clump, drag, lumber, tramp, tread **2** = **slog**, grind (*inf*), labour, persevere, plough through, plug away (*inf*), soldier on, toil

plot¹ *n* **1** = **plan**, cabal, conspiracy, intrigue, machination, scheme, stratagem **2** = **story**, action, narrative, outline, scenario, story line, subject, theme ▷ *v* **3** = **devise**, collude, conceive, concoct, conspire, contrive, cook up, design, hatch, intrigue, lay (*inf*), machinate, manoeuvre, plan, scheme **4** = **chart**, calculate, locate, map, mark, outline

plot² *n* = **patch**, allotment, area, ground, lot, parcel, tract

plough *v* **2** = **turn over**, cultivate, dig, till **3** (usu. with *through*) = **forge**, cut, drive, plunge, press, push, wade

ploy *n* = **tactic**, device, dodge, manoeuvre, move, ruse, scheme, stratagem, trick, wile

P

pluck ❶ v 1 pull or pick off. 2 pull out the feathers of (a bird for cooking). 3 sound the strings of (a guitar etc.) with the fingers or a plectrum. ▷ n 4 courage. **plucky** adj brave. **pluckily** adv **pluck up** v summon up (courage).

plug ❶ n 1 thing fitting into and filling a hole. 2 device connecting an appliance to an electricity supply. 3 informal favourable mention of a product etc., to encourage people to buy it. ▷ v **plugging**, **plugged** 4 block or seal (a hole or gap) with a plug. 5 informal advertise (a product etc.) by constant repetition. **plug away** v informal work steadily. **plug in** v connect (an electrical appliance) to a power source by pushing a plug into a socket.

plum ❶ n 1 oval usu. dark red fruit with a stone in the middle. ▷ adj 2 dark purplish-red. 3 very desirable.

plumb ❶ v 1 understand (something obscure). 2 test with a plumb line. ▷ adv 3 exactly. **plumb the depths** of experience the worst extremes of (an unpleasant quality or emotion). **plumber** n person who fits and repairs pipes and fixtures for water and drainage systems.

plumbing n pipes and fixtures used in water and drainage systems. **plumb in** v connect (an appliance such as a washing machine) to a water supply. **plumb line** string with a weight at the end, used to test the depth of water or to test whether something is vertical.

plume ❶ n feather, esp. one worn as an ornament.

plummet ❶ v **-meting**, **-meted** plunge downward.

plump¹ ❶ adj moderately or attractively fat. **plump up** v make (a pillow) fuller or rounded.

plump² ❶ v sit or fall heavily and suddenly. **plump for** v choose, vote for.

plunder ❶ v 1 take by force, esp. in time of war. ▷ n 2 things plundered, spoils.

plunge ❶ v 1 put or throw forcibly or suddenly (into). 2 descend steeply. ▷ n 3 plunging, dive. **take the plunge** informal embark on a risky enterprise. **plunger** n rubber suction cup used to clear blocked pipes. **plunge into** v become deeply involved in.

plural adj 1 of or consisting of more than one. ▷ n 2 word indicating more than one.

━━━━━━━━━━━━━━ THESAURUS ━━━━━━━━━━━━━━

pluck v 1 = **pull out** or **off**, collect, draw, gather, harvest, pick 3 = **strum**, finger, pick, twang ▷ n 4 = **courage**, backbone, boldness, bottle (Brit sl), bravery, grit, guts (inf), nerve

plug n 1 = **stopper**, bung, cork, spigot 3 Inf = **mention**, advert (Brit inf), advertisement, hype, publicity, push ▷ v 4 = **seal**, block, bung, close, cork, fill, pack, stop, stopper, stop up, stuff 5 Inf = **mention**, advertise, build up, hype, promote, publicize, push **plug away** v Inf = **slog**, grind (inf), labour, peg away, plod, toil

plum adj 3 = **choice**, best, first-class, prize

plumb v 1 = **delve**, explore, fathom, gauge, go into, penetrate, probe, unravel ▷ adv 3 = **exactly**, bang, precisely, slap, spot-on (Brit inf) **plumb line** = **weight**, lead, plumb bob, plummet

plume n = **feather**, crest, pinion, quill

plummet v = **plunge**, crash, descend, dive, drop down, fall, nose-dive, tumble

plump¹ adj = **chubby**, corpulent, dumpy, fat, podgy, roly-poly, rotund, round, stout, tubby

plump² v = **flop**, drop, dump, fall, sink, slump **plump for** v = **choose**, back, come down in favour of, favour, opt for, side with, support

plunder v 1 = **loot**, pillage, raid, ransack, rifle, rob, sack, strip ▷ n 2 = **loot**, booty, ill-gotten gains, pillage, prize, spoils, swag (sl)

plunge v 1 = **throw**, career, cast, charge, dash, hurtle, jump, pitch, rush, tear 2 = **descend**, dip, dive, drop, fall, nose-dive, plummet, sink, tumble ▷ n 3 = **dive**, descent, drop, fall, jump

plus ❶ *prep, adj* 1 indicating addition.
▷ *adj* 2 more than zero. 3 positive.
4 advantageous. ▷ *n* 5 sign (+) denoting
addition. 6 advantage.

plush ❶ *n* 1 fabric with long velvety pile.
▷ *adj* 2 (also **plushy**) luxurious.

ply¹ ❶ *v* **plying**, **plied** 1 work at (a job or
trade). 2 use (a tool). 3 (of a ship) travel
regularly along or between. **ply with** *v*
supply with or subject to persistently.

ply² ❶ *n* thickness of wool, fabric, etc.

PM prime minister.

p.m. 1 after noon. 2 postmortem.

pneumatic *adj* worked by or inflated with
wind or air.

pneumonia *n* inflammation of the lungs.

PO 1 postal order. 2 Post Office.

poach¹ ❶ *v* 1 catch (animals) illegally on
someone else's land. 2 encroach on or
steal something belonging to someone
else. **poacher** *n*.

poach² *v* simmer (food) gently in liquid.

pocket ❶ *n* 1 small bag sewn into clothing
for carrying things. 2 pouchlike container,
esp. for catching balls at the edge of
a snooker table. 3 isolated or distinct
group or area. ▷ *v* **pocketing**, **pocketed**
4 put into one's pocket. 5 take secretly or
dishonestly. ▷ *adj* 6 small. **out of pocket**

having made a loss. **pocket money**
1 small regular allowance given to children
by parents. 2 money for small personal
expenses.

pod ❶ *n* long narrow seed case of peas,
beans, etc.

podcast *n* 1 audio file that can be
downloaded to a computer, music player,
etc. ▷ *v* 2 create such files and make them
available for downloading.

podgy ❶ *adj* **podgier, podgiest** short
and fat.

podium ❶ *n, pl* **-diums, -dia** small raised
platform for a conductor or speaker.

poem ❶ *n* imaginative piece of writing in
rhythmic lines.

poep *n Aust & NZ slang* emission of gas from
the anus.

poet ❶ *n* writer of poems. **poetry**
n 1 poems. 2 art of writing poems.
3 beautiful or pleasing quality.

pogey ❶ *n Canad sl* money received from
the state while out of work.

poignant ❶ *adj* sharply painful to the
feelings. **poignancy** *n*.

point ❶ *n* 1 main idea in a discussion,
argument, etc. 2 aim or purpose. 3 detail
or item. 4 characteristic. 5 particular
position, stage, or time. 6 dot indicating

---

plus *prep* 1 = **and**, added to, coupled with,
with ▷ *n* 6 = **advantage**, asset, benefit,
bonus, extra, gain, good point

plush *adj* 2 = **luxurious**, de luxe, lavish,
luxury, opulent, rich, sumptuous

ply¹ *v* 1 = **work at**, carry on, exercise, follow,
practise, pursue 2 = **use**, employ, handle,
manipulate, wield

ply² *n* = **thickness**, fold, layer, leaf, sheet,
strand

poach¹ *v* 2 = **encroach**, appropriate,
infringe, intrude, trespass

pocket *n* 2 = **pouch**, bag, compartment,
receptacle, sack ▷ *v* 5 = **steal**, appropriate,
filch, lift (*inf*), pilfer, purloin, take ▷ *adj*
6 = **small**, abridged, compact, concise,
little, miniature, portable

pod *n* = **shell**, hull, husk, shuck

podgy *adj* = **tubby**, chubby, dumpy, fat,
plump, roly-poly, rotund, stout

podium *n* = **platform**, dais, rostrum, stage

poem *n* = **verse**, lyric, ode, rhyme, song,
sonnet

poet *n* = **bard**, lyricist, rhymer, versifier

pogey *Canad* = **benefits**, the dole (*Brit
& Austral*), welfare, social security,
unemployment benefit, state benefit,
allowance

poignant *adj* = **moving**, bitter, distressing,
gut-wrenching, heart-rending, intense,
painful, pathetic, sad, touching

point *n* 1 = **essence**, crux, drift, gist, heart,
import, meaning, nub, pith, question,
subject, thrust 2 = **aim**, end, goal, intent,

p

decimals. **7** full stop. **8** sharp end.
9 headland. **10** unit for recording a value
or score. **11** one of the direction marks
of a compass. **12** movable rail used to
change a train to other rails. **13** electrical
socket. ▷ *pl* **14** electrical contacts in the
distributor of an engine. ▷ *v* **15** show the
direction or position of something or draw
attention to it by extending a finger or
other pointed object towards it. **16** direct
or face towards. **17** finish or repair the
joints in brickwork with mortar. **18** (of a
gun dog) show where game is by standing
rigidly with the muzzle towards it. **on the
point of** very shortly going to. **pointed**
adj **1** having a sharp end. **2** (of a remark)
obviously directed at a particular person.
pointedly *adv* **pointer** *n* **1** helpful hint.
2 indicator on a measuring instrument.
3 breed of gun dog. **pointless** *adj*
meaningless, irrelevant. **point-blank** *adj*
1 fired at a very close target. **2** (of a remark
or question) direct, blunt. ▷ *adv* **3** directly
or bluntly. **point duty** control of traffic
by a policeman at a road junction. **point
of view** way of considering something.
point-to-point *n* horse race across open
country.

poise ❶ *n* calm dignified manner. **poised**
adj **1** absolutely ready. **2** behaving with or
showing poise.
poison ❶ *n* **1** substance that kills or injures
when swallowed or absorbed. ▷ *v* **2** give
poison to. **3** have a harmful or evil effect
on, spoil. **poisoner** *n* **poisonous** *adj*
poison-pen letter malicious anonymous
letter.
poke ❶ *v* **1** jab or prod with one's finger,
a stick, etc. **2** thrust forward or out. ▷ *n*
3 poking. **poky** *adj* small and cramped.
poker *n* card game in which players bet
on the hands dealt. **poker-faced** *adj*
expressionless.
pole¹ ❶ *n* long rounded piece of wood etc.
pole² ❶ *n* **1** point furthest north or south on
the earth's axis of rotation. **2** either of the
opposite ends of a magnet or electric cell.
poleaxe *v* hit or stun with a heavy blow.
polecat *n* small animal of the weasel family.
police ❶ *n* **1** organized force in a state
which keeps law and order. ▷ *v* **2** control
or watch over with police or a similar body.
policeman, **policewoman** *n* member of a
police force.
policy¹ ❶ *n*, *pl* **-cies** plan of action adopted
by a person, group, or state.

intention, motive, object, objective,
purpose, reason **3** = **item**, aspect, detail,
feature, particular **4** = **characteristic**,
aspect, attribute, quality, respect, trait
5 = **place**, instant, juncture, location,
moment, position, site, spot, stage,
time, very minute **7** = **full stop**, dot,
mark, period, stop **8** = **end**, apex, prong,
sharp end, spike, spur, summit, tip, top
9 = **headland**, cape, head, promontory
10 = **unit**, score, tally ▷ *v* **15** = **indicate**,
call attention to, denote, designate,
direct, show, signify **16** = **aim**, direct,
level, train
poise *n* = **composure**, aplomb, assurance,
calmness, cool (*sl*), dignity, presence,
sang-froid, self-possession
poison *n* **1** = **toxin**, bane, venom ▷ *v*

2 = **murder**, give (someone) poison, kill
3 = **corrupt**, contaminate, defile, deprave,
infect, pervert, pollute, subvert, taint,
undermine, warp
poke *v* **1** = **jab**, dig, nudge, prod, push,
shove, stab, stick, thrust ▷ *n* **3** = **jab**, dig,
nudge, prod, thrust
pole¹ *n* = **rod**, bar, mast, post, shaft, spar,
staff, stick
pole² *n* **1** = **extremity**, antipode, limit,
terminus
police *n* **1** = **the law** (*inf*), boys in blue (*inf*),
constabulary, fuzz (*sl*), police force, the
Old Bill (*sl*) ▷ *v* **2** = **control**, guard, patrol,
protect, regulate, watch
policy¹ *n* = **procedure**, action, approach,
code, course, custom, plan, practice, rule,
scheme

p

policy² *n, pl* **-cies** document containing an insurance contract.

polio *n* disease affecting the spinal cord, which often causes paralysis (also **poliomyelitis**).

polish ❶ *v* **1** make smooth and shiny by rubbing. **2** make more nearly perfect. ▷ *n* **3** substance used for polishing. **4** pleasing elegant style. **polished** *adj* **1** accomplished. **2** done or performed well or professionally. **polish off** *v* finish completely, dispose of.

polite ❶ *adj* **1** showing consideration for others in one's manners, speech, etc. **2** socially correct or refined. **politely** *adv* **politeness** *n*.

politics ❶ *n* **1** winning and using of power to govern society. **2** (study of) the art of government. **3** person's beliefs about how a country should be governed. **political** *adj* of the state, government, or public administration. **politically** *adv* **politically correct** (of language) intended to avoid any implied prejudice. **political prisoner** person imprisoned because of his or her political beliefs. **politician** *n* person actively engaged in politics, esp. a member of parliament.

polka *n* **1** lively 19th-century dance. **2** music for this. **polka dots** pattern of bold spots on fabric.

poll ❶ *n* **1** (also **opinion poll**) questioning of a random sample of people to find out general opinion. **2** voting. **3** number of votes recorded. ▷ *v* **4** receive (votes). **5** question in an opinion poll. **pollster**

n person who conducts opinion polls. **polling station** building where people vote in an election.

pollen *n* fine dust produced by flowers to fertilize other flowers. **pollinate** *v* fertilize with pollen. **pollen count** measure of the amount of pollen in the air, esp. as a warning to people with hay fever.

pollute ❶ *v* contaminate with something poisonous or harmful. **pollution** *n* **pollutant** *n* something that pollutes.

polo *n* game like hockey played by teams of players on horseback. **polo neck** sweater with tight turned-over collar.

poltergeist *n* spirit believed to move furniture and throw objects around.

polyester *n* synthetic material used to make plastics and textile fibres.

polygamy [pol-**ig**-a-mee] *n* practice of having more than one husband or wife at the same time. **polygamous** *adj* **polygamist** *n*.

polygon *n* geometrical figure with three or more angles and sides. **polygonal** *adj*.

polystyrene *n* synthetic material used esp. as white rigid foam for packing and insulation.

polythene *n* light plastic used for bags etc.

polyunsaturated *adj* of a group of fats that do not form cholesterol in the blood.

polyurethane *n* synthetic material used esp. in paints.

pom *n Aust & NZ slang* person from England (also **pommy**).

polish *v* **1** = **shine**, brighten, buff, burnish, rub, smooth, wax **2** = **perfect**, brush up, enhance, finish, improve, refine, touch up ▷ *n* **3** = **varnish**, wax **4** = **style**, breeding, class (*inf*), elegance, finesse, finish, grace, refinement

polite *adj* **1** = **mannerly**, civil, complaisant, courteous, gracious, respectful, well-behaved, well-mannered **2** = **refined**, civilized, cultured, elegant, genteel,

polished, sophisticated, well-bred

politics *n* **2** = **statesmanship**, affairs of state, civics, government, political science

poll *n* **1** (also **opinion poll**) = **canvass**, census, sampling, survey **2** = **vote**, ballot, count, voting **3** = **figures**, returns, tally ▷ *v* **4** = **tally**, register **5** = **question**, ballot, canvass, interview, sample, survey

pollute *v* = **contaminate**, dirty, foul, infect, poison, soil, spoil, stain, taint

pomegranate n round tropical fruit with a thick rind containing many seeds in a red pulp.

pommel n 1 raised part on the front of a saddle. 2 knob at the top of a sword hilt.

pomp ❶ n stately display or ceremony.

pompom n decorative ball of tufted wool, silk, etc.

pompous ❶ adj foolishly serious and grand, self-important. **pomposity** n.

pond ❶ n small area of still water.

ponder ❶ v think thoroughly or deeply (about).

ponderous ❶ adj 1 serious and dull. 2 heavy and unwieldy. 3 (of movement) slow and clumsy.

pong v, n informal (give off) a strong unpleasant smell.

pontiff n the Pope. **pontificate** v 1 state one's opinions as if they were the only possible correct ones. ▷ n 2 period of office of a Pope.

pontoon¹ n floating platform supporting a temporary bridge.

pontoon² n gambling card game.

pony n, pl **ponies** small horse. **ponytail** n long hair tied in one bunch at the back of the head.

poodle n dog with curly hair often clipped fancifully.

pool¹ ❶ n 1 small body of still water. 2 puddle of spilt liquid. 3 swimming pool.

pool² ❶ n 1 shared fund or group of workers or resources. 2 game like snooker. ▷ pl 3 short for FOOTBALL POOLS. ▷ v 4 put in a common fund.

poop n raised part at the back of a sailing ship.

poor ❶ adj 1 having little money and few possessions. 2 less, smaller, or weaker than is needed or expected. 3 inferior. 4 unlucky, pitiable. **poorly** adv 1 in a poor manner. ▷ adj 2 not in good health.

pop¹ ❶ v popping, popped 1 make or cause to make a small explosive sound. 2 informal go, put, or come unexpectedly or suddenly. ▷ n 3 small explosive sound. 4 nonalcoholic fizzy drink. **popcorn** n grains of maize heated until they puff up and burst.

pomp n **a** = **show**, display, grandiosity, ostentation **b** = **ceremony**, flourish, grandeur, magnificence, pageant, pageantry, splendour, state

pompous adj **a** = **grandiloquent**, boastful, bombastic, high-flown, inflated **b** = **self-important**, arrogant, grandiose, ostentatious, pretentious, puffed up, showy

pond n = **pool**, duck pond, fish pond, millpond, small lake, tarn

ponder v = **think**, brood, cogitate, consider, contemplate, deliberate, meditate, mull over, muse, reflect, ruminate

ponderous adj 1 = **dull**, heavy, long-winded, pedantic, tedious 2 = **unwieldy**, bulky, cumbersome, heavy, huge, massive, weighty 3 = **clumsy**, awkward, heavy-footed, lumbering

pool¹ n 1 = **pond**, lake, mere, puddle, tarn 3 = **swimming pool**, swimming bath

pool² n 1 **a** = **kitty**, bank, funds, jackpot, pot **b** = **syndicate**, collective, consortium, group, team, trust ▷ v 4 = **combine**, amalgamate, join forces, league, merge, put together, share

poor adj 1 = **impoverished**, broke (inf), destitute, down and out, hard up (inf), impecunious, indigent, needy, on the breadline, penniless, poverty-stricken, short, skint (Brit sl), stony-broke (Brit sl) 2 = **meagre**, deficient, inadequate, incomplete, insufficient, lacking, measly, scant, scanty, skimpy 3 = **inferior**, below par, low-grade, mediocre, no great shakes (inf), rotten (inf), rubbishy, second-rate, substandard, unsatisfactory 4 = **unfortunate**, hapless, ill-fated, pitiable, unlucky, wretched

pop¹ v 1 = **burst**, bang, crack, explode, go off, snap ▷ n 3 = **bang**, burst, crack, explosion, noise, report

pop² n **1** music of general appeal, esp. to young people. ▷ adj **2** popular. **pop art** movement in modern art that uses the methods, styles, and themes of popular culture and mass media.

Pope n head of the Roman Catholic Church.

poplar n tall slender tree.

poplin n ribbed cotton material.

poppadom n thin round crisp Indian bread.

poppy n, pl **-pies** plant with a large red flower.

Popsicle ® n US & Canad an ice lolly.

populace ❶ n the ordinary people.

popular ❶ adj **1** widely liked and admired. **2** of or for the public in general. **popularly** adv **popularity** n **popularize** v **1** make popular. **2** make (something technical or specialist) easily understood.

populate ❶ v **1** live in, inhabit. **2** fill with inhabitants. **population** n **1** all the people who live in a particular place. **2** the number of people living in a particular place. **populous** adj densely populated.

porcelain n **1** fine china. **2** objects made of it.

porch n covered approach to the entrance of a building.

porcupine n animal covered with long pointed quills.

pore ❶ n tiny opening in the skin or in the surface of a plant.

pork n pig meat. **porker** n pig weighing 40 to 67 kg, raised for food.

pornography ❶ n writing, films, or pictures designed to be sexually exciting. **pornographer** n producer of pornography. **pornographic** adj.

porpoise n fishlike sea mammal.

porridge n **1** breakfast food made of oatmeal cooked in water or milk. **2** slang term in prison.

port¹ ❶ n (town with) a harbour.

port² n left side of a ship or aircraft when facing the front of it.

port³ n strong sweet wine, usu. red.

port⁴ n **1** opening in the side of a ship. **2** porthole.

portable ❶ adj easily carried. **portability** n.

portcullis n grating suspended above a castle gateway, that can be lowered to block the entrance.

portend ❶ v be a sign of.

porter¹ ❶ n **1** man who carries luggage. **2** hospital worker who transfers patients between rooms etc.

porter² ❶ n doorman or gatekeeper of a building.

portfolio n, pl **-os 1** (flat case for carrying) examples of an artist's work. **2** area of responsibility of a government minister. **3** list of investments held by an investor.

portico n, pl **-coes, -cos** porch or covered walkway with columns supporting the roof.

P

—————— THESAURUS ——————

Pope n = **Holy Father**, Bishop of Rome, pontiff, Vicar of Christ

populace n = **people**, general public, hoi polloi, masses, mob, multitude

popular adj **1** = **well-liked**, accepted, approved, fashionable, favourite, in, in demand, in favour, liked, sought-after **2** = **common**, conventional, current, general, prevailing, prevalent, universal

populate v **1** = **inhabit**, colonize, live in, occupy, settle

pore n = **opening**, hole, orifice, outlet

pornography n = **obscenity**, dirt, filth, indecency, porn (inf), smut

port¹ n = **harbour**, anchorage, haven, seaport

portable adj = **light**, compact, convenient, easily carried, handy, manageable, movable

portend v = **foretell**, augur, betoken, bode, foreshadow, herald, indicate, predict, prognosticate, promise, warn of

porter¹ n **1** = **baggage attendant**, bearer, carrier

porter² n = **doorman**, caretaker, concierge, gatekeeper, janitor

portion ⊕ *n* 1 part or share. 2 helping of food for one person. 3 destiny or fate.

portly ⊕ *adj* **-lier, -liest** rather fat.

portmanteau *n, pl* **-teaus, -teaux** *old-fashioned* large suitcase that opens into two compartments. ▷ *adj* 2 combining aspects of different things.

portray ⊕ *v* describe or represent by artistic means, as in writing or film. **portrait** *n* picture of a person. **portrayal** *n*.

pose ⊕ *v* 1 place in or take up a particular position to be photographed or drawn. 2 raise (a problem). 3 ask (a question). ▷ *n* 4 position while posing. 5 behaviour adopted for effect. **pose as** pretend to be. **poser** *n* 1 puzzling question. 2 poseur. **poseur** *n* person who behaves in an affected way to impress others.

posh ⊕ *adj informal* 1 smart, luxurious. 2 affectedly upper-class.

position ⊕ *n* 1 place. 2 usual or expected place. 3 way in which something is placed

or arranged. 4 attitude, point of view. 5 social standing. 6 job. ▷ *v* 7 place.

positive ⊕ *adj* 1 feeling no doubts, certain. 2 confident, hopeful. 3 helpful, providing encouragement. 4 absolute, downright. 5 *Maths* greater than zero. 6 (of an electrical charge) having a deficiency of electrons. **positively** *adv* **positive discrimination** provision of special opportunities for a disadvantaged group.

possess ⊕ *v* 1 have as one's property. 2 (of a feeling, belief, etc.) have complete control of, dominate. **possessor** *n* **possession** *n* 1 state of possessing, ownership. ▷ *pl* 2 things a person possesses. **possessive** *adj* 1 wanting all the attention or love of another person. 2 (of a word) indicating the person or thing that something belongs to. **possessiveness** *n*.

possible ⊕ *adj* 1 able to exist, happen, or be done. 2 worthy of consideration. ▷ *n*

THESAURUS

portion *n* 1 **a = part**, bit, fragment, morsel, piece, scrap, section, segment **b = share**, allocation, allotment, allowance, lot, measure, quantity, quota, ration 2 = **helping**, piece, serving 3 = **destiny**, fate, fortune, lot, luck

portly *adj* = **stout**, burly, corpulent, fat, fleshy, heavy, large, plump

portray *v* **a = represent**, depict, draw, figure, illustrate, paint, picture, sketch **b = describe**, characterize, depict, put in words **c = play**, act the part of, represent

pose *v* 1 = **position**, model, sit ▷ *n* 4 = **posture**, attitude, bearing, position, stance 5 = **act**, affectation, air, facade, front, mannerism, posturing, pretence **pose as** *v* = **impersonate**, masquerade as, pass oneself off as, pretend to be, profess to be

posh *adj Inf* 1 = **smart**, classy (*sl*), grand, luxurious, ritzy (*sl*), stylish, swanky (*inf*), swish (*inf, chiefly Brit*) ▷ *adj* 2 = **upper-class**, high-class, up-market

position *n* 1 = **place**, area, bearings,

locale, location, point, post, situation, spot, station, whereabouts 3 = **posture**, arrangement, attitude, pose, stance 4 = **attitude**, belief, opinion, outlook, point of view, slant, stance, view, viewpoint 5 = **status**, importance, place, prestige, rank, reputation, standing, station, stature 6 = **job**, duty, employment, occupation, office, place, post, role, situation ▷ *v* 7 = **place**, arrange, lay out, locate, put, set, stand

positive *adj* 1, 2 = **certain**, assured, confident, convinced, sure 3 = **helpful**, beneficial, constructive, practical, productive, progressive, useful 4 **a = definite**, absolute, categorical, certain, clear, conclusive, decisive, explicit, express, firm, real **b = absolute**, complete, consummate, downright, out-and-out, perfect, thorough, utter

possess *v* 1 = **have**, enjoy, hold, own 2 = **dominate**, control, seize, take over

possible *adj* 1 **a = conceivable**, credible, hypothetical, imaginable, likely, potential

3 person or thing that might be suitable or chosen. **possibility** n, pl **-ties**. **possibly** adv perhaps, not necessarily.

possum n **1** same as OPOSSUM. **2** Aust & NZ same as PHALANGER. **play possum** pretend
to be dead or asleep to deceive an opponent.

post¹ ❶ n **1** official system of delivering letters and parcels. **2** (single collection or delivery of) letters and parcels sent by this system. ▷ v **3** send by post. **keep someone posted** supply someone regularly with the latest information. **postage** n charge for sending a letter or parcel by post. **postal** adj **postal order** written money order sent by post and cashed at a post office by the person who receives it. **postbag** n **1** postman's bag. **2** post received by a magazine, famous person, etc. **postbox** n same as LETTER BOX (sense 2). **postcode** n system of letters and numbers used to aid the sorting of mail. **postie** Aust, NZ & Scot informal postman. **postman**, **postwoman** n person who collects and delivers post. **postmark** n official mark stamped on letters showing place and date of posting. **postmaster**, **postmistress** n official in charge of a post office. **post office** place where postal business is conducted. **post**

shop NZ shop providing postal services.

post² ❶ n **1** length of wood, concrete, etc. fixed upright to support or mark something. ▷ v **2** put up (a notice) in a public place.

post³ ❶ n **1** job. **2** position to which someone, esp. a soldier, is assigned for duty. **3** military establishment. ▷ v **4** send (a person) to a new place to work. **5** put (a guard etc.) on duty.

post- prefix after, later than, e.g. postwar.

posterior n **1** buttocks. ▷ adj **2** behind, at the back of.

posterity ❶ n future generations, descendants.

posthaste adv with great speed.

posthumous [**poss**-tume-uss] adj **1** occurring after one's death. **posthumously** adv.

postmortem n medical examination of a body to establish the cause of death.

postpone ❶ v put off to a later time. **postponement** n.

postscript ❶ n passage added at the end of a letter.

postulate ❶ v assume to be true as the basis of an argument or theory.

posture ❶ n **1** position or way in which someone stands, walks, etc. ▷ v **2** behave in an exaggerated way to get attention.

posy n, pl **-sies** small bunch of flowers.

—————— THESAURUS ——————

b = **likely**, hopeful, potential, probable, promising **c** = **feasible**, attainable, doable, practicable, realizable, viable, workable

post¹ n **1** = **mail**, collection, delivery, postal service ▷ v **3** = **send**, dispatch, mail, transmit **keep someone posted** = **notify**, advise, brief, fill in on (inf), inform, report to

post² n **1** = **support**, column, picket, pillar, pole, shaft, stake, upright ▷ v **2** = **put up**, affix, display, pin up

post³ n **1** = **job**, appointment, assignment, employment, office, place, position, situation **2** = **station**, beat, place, position ▷ v **4** = **station**, assign, place,

position, put, situate

posterity n **a** = **future**, succeeding generations **b** = **descendants**, children, family, heirs, issue, offspring, progeny

postpone v = **put off**, adjourn, defer, delay, put back, put on the back burner (inf), shelve, suspend

postscript n = **P.S.**, addition, afterthought, supplement

postulate v = **presuppose**, assume, hypothesize, posit, propose, suppose, take for granted, theorize

posture n **1** = **bearing**, attitude, carriage, disposition, set, stance ▷ v **2** = **show off**, affect, pose, put on airs (inf)

pot¹ ❶ *n* **1** round deep container. **2** teapot. ▷ *pl* **3** *informal* a lot. ▷ *v* **potting, potted** **4** plant in a pot. **5** *Snooker* hit (a ball) into a pocket. **potted** *adj* **1** grown in a pot. **2** (of meat or fish) cooked or preserved in a pot. **3** *informal* abridged. **potbelly** *n* bulging belly. **potsherd** *n* broken fragment of pottery. **pot shot** shot taken without aiming carefully. **potting shed** shed where plants are potted.

pot² *n slang* cannabis.

potassium *n Chem* silvery metallic element.

potato *n, pl* **-toes** roundish starchy vegetable that grows underground.

potato chip *n* the US and Canadian term for CRISP.

potent ❶ *adj* **1** having great power or influence. **2** (of a male) capable of having sexual intercourse. **potency** *n*.

potentate *n* ruler or monarch.

potential ❶ *adj* **1** possible but not yet actual. ▷ *n* **2** ability or talent not yet fully used. **3** *Electricity* level of electric pressure. **potentially** *adv* **potentiality** *n, pl* **-ties**.

pothole *n* **1** hole in the surface of a road. **2** deep hole in a limestone area. **potholing** *n* sport of exploring underground caves. **potholer** *n*.

potion ❶ *n* dose of medicine or poison.

potoroo *n, pl* **-roos** Australian leaping rodent.

potpourri [po-**poor**-ee] *n* **1** fragrant mixture of dried flower petals. **2** assortment or medley.

potter¹ *n* person who makes pottery.

potter² ❶ *v* be busy in a pleasant but aimless way.

potty¹ *adj* **-tier, -tiest** *informal* crazy or silly.

potty² *n, pl* **-ties** bowl used by a small child as a toilet.

pouch ❶ *n* **1** small bag. **2** baglike pocket of skin on an animal.

poultice [**pole**-tiss] *n* moist dressing, often heated, applied to inflamed skin.

poultry *n* domestic fowls.

pounce ❶ *v* **1** spring upon suddenly to attack or capture. ▷ *n* **2** pouncing.

pound¹ *n* **1** monetary unit of Britain and some other countries. **2** unit of weight equal to 0.454 kg.

pound² ❶ *v* **1** hit heavily and repeatedly. **2** crush to pieces or powder. **3** (of the heart) throb heavily. **4** run heavily.

pound³ ❶ *n* enclosure for stray animals or officially removed vehicles.

pour ❶ *v* **1** flow or cause to flow out in a stream. **2** rain heavily. **3** come or go in large numbers.

pot¹ *n* **1** = **container**, bowl, pan, vessel
potent *adj* **1** = **powerful**, authoritative, commanding, dominant, dynamic, forceful, influential, mighty, strong, vigorous
potential *adj* **1** = **possible**, dormant, future, hidden, inherent, latent, likely, promising ▷ *n* **2** = **ability**, aptitude, capability, capacity, possibility, potentiality, power, wherewithal
potion *n* = **concoction**, brew, dose, draught, elixir, mixture, philtre
potter² *v* = **mess about**, dabble, footle (*inf*), tinker
pouch *n* **1** = **bag**, container, pocket, purse, sack
pounce *v* **1** = **spring**, attack, fall

upon, jump, leap at, strike, swoop ▷ *n* **2** = **spring**, assault, attack, bound, jump, leap, swoop
pound² *v* **1** = **beat**, batter, belabour, clobber (*sl*), hammer, pummel, strike, thrash, thump **2** = **crush**, powder, pulverize **3** = **pulsate**, beat, palpitate, pulse, throb **4** = **stomp** (*inf*), march, thunder, tramp
pound³ *n* = **enclosure**, compound, pen, yard
pour *v* **1** = **flow**, course, decant, emit, gush, let flow, run, rush, spew, spill, splash, spout, stream **2** = **rain**, bucket down (*inf*), pelt (down), teem **3** = **stream**, crowd, swarm, teem, throng

pout ❶ v **1** thrust out one's lips, look sulky. ▷ n **2** pouting look.

poverty ❶ n **1** state of being without enough food or money. **2** lack of, scarcity.

powder ❶ n **1** substance in the form of tiny loose particles. **2** medicine or cosmetic in this form. ▷ v **3** apply powder to. **powdery** adj.

power ❶ n **1** ability to do or act. **2** strength. **3** position of authority or control. **4** person or thing having authority. **5** Maths product from continuous multiplication of a number by itself. **6** Physics rate at which work is done. **7** electricity supply. **8** particular form of energy, e.g. nuclear power. **powered** adj having or operated by mechanical or electrical power. **powerful** adj **powerless** adj **power cut** temporary interruption in the supply of electricity. **power station** installation for generating and distributing electric power.

PP (in signing a document) for and on behalf of.

PQ Province of Quebec.

PR 1 proportional representation. **2** public relations.

practical ❶ adj **1** involving experience or actual use rather than theory. **2** sensible, useful, and effective. **3** good at making or doing things. **4** in effect though not in name. ▷ n **5** examination in which something has to be done or made. **practically** adv **practical joke** trick intended to make someone look foolish.

practise ❶ v **1** do repeatedly so as to gain skill. **2** take part in, follow (a religion etc.). **3** work at, e.g. practise medicine. **4** do habitually. **practice** n something done regularly or habitually.

pragmatic ❶ adj concerned with practical consequences rather than theory. **pragmatism** n **pragmatist** n.

prairie n a treeless grassy plain of the central US and S Canada.

praise ❶ v **1** express approval or admiration of (someone or something). **2** express honour and thanks to (one's

---

THESAURUS

---

pout v **1** = **sulk**, glower, look petulant, pull a long face ▷ n **2** = **sullen look**, glower, long face

poverty n **1** = **pennilessness**, beggary, destitution, hardship, indigence, insolvency, need, penury, privation, want **2** = **scarcity**, dearth, deficiency, insufficiency, lack, paucity, shortage

powder n **1** = **dust**, fine grains, loose particles, talc ▷ v **3** = **dust**, cover, dredge, scatter, sprinkle, strew

power n **1** = **ability**, capability, capacity, competence, competency, faculty, potential **2** = **strength**, brawn, energy, force, forcefulness, intensity, might, muscle, potency, vigour **3** = **control**, ascendancy, authority, command, dominance, domination, dominion, influence, mana (NZ), mastery, prerogative, privilege, rule, skookum

practical adj **1** = **functional**, applied, empirical, experimental, factual, pragmatic, realistic, utilitarian **2** = **ordinary**, businesslike, down-to-earth, hard-headed, matter-of-fact, realistic **3** = **skilled**, accomplished, efficient, experienced, proficient

practise v **1** = **rehearse**, drill, exercise, go over, go through, prepare, repeat, study, train **2** = **follow**, observe, perform **3** = **work at**, carry on, engage in, pursue

pragmatic adj = **practical**, businesslike, down-to-earth, hard-headed, realistic, sensible, utilitarian

praise v **1** = **approve**, acclaim, admire, applaud, cheer, compliment, congratulate, eulogize, extol, honour, laud **2** = **give thanks to**, adore, bless, exalt, glorify, worship ▷ n **3 a** = **approval**, acclaim, acclamation, approbation, commendation, compliment, congratulation, eulogy, plaudit, tribute **b** = **thanks**, adoration, glory, homage, worship

P

God). ▷ *n* **3** something said or written to show approval or admiration. **sing someone's praises** praise someone highly. **praiseworthy** *adj*.

pram *n* four-wheeled carriage for a baby, pushed by hand.

prance ❶ *v* walk with exaggerated bouncing steps.

prank *n* mischievous trick.

prattle ❶ *v* **1** chatter in a childish or foolish way. ▷ *n* **2** childish or foolish talk.

prawn *n* edible shellfish like a large shrimp.

pray ❶ *v* **1** say prayers. **2** ask earnestly, entreat. **prayer** *n* **1** thanks or appeal addressed to one's God. **2** set form of words used in praying. **3** earnest request.

pre- *prefix* before, beforehand, e.g. *prenatal*; *prerecorded*; *preshrunk*.

preach ❶ *v* **1** give a talk on a religious theme as part of a church service. **2** speak in support of (an idea, principle, etc.). **preacher** *n*.

preamble ❶ *n* introductory part to something said or written.

precarious ❶ *adj* insecure, unsafe, likely to fall or collapse.

precaution ❶ *n* action taken in advance to prevent something bad happening. **precautionary** *adj*.

precede ❶ *v* go or be before. **precedence** [**press**-ee-denss] *n* formal order of rank or position. **take precedence over** be more important than. **precedent** *n* previous case or occurrence regarded as an example to be followed.

precept ❶ *n* rule of behaviour.

precinct ❶ *n* **1** area in a town closed to traffic. **2** enclosed area round a building. **3** *US* administrative area of a city. ▷ *pl* **4** surrounding region.

precious ❶ *adj* **1** of great value and importance. **2** loved and treasured. **3** (of behaviour) affected, unnatural. **precious metal** gold, silver, or platinum. **precious stone** rare mineral, such as a ruby, valued as a gem.

precipice ❶ *n* very steep cliff or rockface. **precipitous** *adj* sheer.

prance *v* = **dance**, caper, cavort, frisk, gambol, parade, romp, show off (*inf*), skip, stalk, strut, swagger, swank (*inf*)

prank *n* = **trick**, escapade, jape, lark (*inf*), practical joke

prattle *v* **1** = **chatter**, babble, blather, blether, gabble, jabber, rabbit (on) (*Brit inf*), waffle (*inf, chiefly Brit*), witter (*inf*)

pray *v* **1** = **say one's prayers**, offer a prayer, recite the rosary **2** = **beg**, adjure, ask, beseech, entreat, implore, petition, plead, request, solicit

preach *v* **1** = **deliver a sermon**, address, evangelize **2** = **lecture**, advocate, exhort, moralize, sermonize

preamble *n* = **introduction**, foreword, opening statement *or* remarks, preface, prelude

precarious *adj* = **dangerous**, dodgy (*Brit, Aust & NZ inf*), hazardous, insecure, perilous, risky, shaky, shonky (*Aust & NZ*

inf), tricky, unreliable, unsafe, unsure

precaution *n* = **safeguard**, care, caution, forethought, protection, safety measure, wariness

precede *v* = **go before**, antedate, come first, head, introduce, lead, preface

precept *n* = **rule**, canon, command, commandment, decree, instruction, law, order, principle, regulation, statute

precinct *n* **1** = **area**, district, quarter, section, sector, zone **2** = **enclosure**, confine, limit

precious *adj* **1** = **valuable**, costly, dear, expensive, fine, invaluable, priceless, prized **2** = **loved**, adored, beloved, cherished, darling, dear, prized, treasured **3** = **affected**, artificial, overnice, overrefined, twee (*Brit inf*)

precipice *n* = **cliff**, bluff, crag, height, rock face

P

precipitate ❶ v **1** cause to happen suddenly. **2** *Chem* cause to be deposited in solid form from a solution. **3** throw headlong. ▷ *adj* **4** done rashly or hastily. **precipitately** *adv* **precipitation** *n* rain, snow, etc.

précis [**pray**-see] *n, pl* **précis 1** short written summary of a longer piece. ▷ *v* **2** make a précis of.

precise ❶ *adj* **1** exact, accurate in every detail. **2** strict in observing rules or standards. **precisely** *adv* **precision** *n*.

preclude ❶ v make impossible to happen.

precocious ❶ *adj* having developed or matured early or too soon. **precocity** *n*.

precursor ❶ *n* something that precedes and is a signal of something else, forerunner.

predatory ❶ [**pred**-a-tree] *adj* habitually hunting and killing other animals for food. **predator** *n* predatory animal.

predecessor ❶ *n* **1** person who precedes another in an office or position. **2** ancestor.

predicament ❶ *n* embarrassing or difficult situation.

predict ❶ v tell about in advance, prophesy. **predictable** *adj* **predictive** *adj* (of a word processer or cell phone) able to complete words after only part of a word has been keyed. **prediction** *n*.

predispose ❶ v **1** influence (someone) in favour of something. **2** make (someone) susceptible to something. **predisposition** *n*.

predominate ❶ v be the main or controlling element. **predominance** *n* **predominant** *adj*.

pre-eminent ❶ *adj* excelling all others, outstanding. **pre-eminence** *n*.

pre-empt ❶ v prevent an action by doing something which makes it pointless or impossible. **pre-emptive** *adj*.

THESAURUS

precipitate v **1** = **quicken**, accelerate, advance, bring on, expedite, hasten, hurry, speed up, trigger **3** = **throw**, cast, fling, hurl, launch, let fly ▷ *adj* **4** = **hasty**, abrupt, breakneck, brief, headlong, heedless, impetuous, impulsive, precipitous, quick, rapid, rash, reckless, rushing, sudden, swift, unexpected, without warning

précis *n* **1** = **summary**, abridgment, outline, résumé, synopsis ▷ *v* **2** = **summarize**, abridge, outline, shorten, sum up

precise *adj* **1** = **exact**, absolute, accurate, correct, definite, explicit, express, particular, specific, strict **2** = **strict**, careful, exact, fastidious, finicky, formal, meticulous, particular, punctilious, rigid, scrupulous, stiff

preclude v = **prevent**, check, debar, exclude, forestall, inhibit, obviate, prohibit, rule out, stop

precocious *adj* = **advanced**, ahead, bright, developed, forward, quick, smart

precursor *n* **a** = **herald**, forerunner,

harbinger, vanguard **b** = **forerunner**, antecedent, forebear, predecessor

predatory *adj* = **hunting**, carnivorous, predacious, raptorial

predecessor *n* **1** = **previous job holder**, antecedent, forerunner, precursor **2** = **ancestor**, antecedent, forebear, forefather

predicament *n* = **fix** (*inf*), dilemma, hole (*sl*), jam (*inf*), mess, pinch, plight, quandary, scrape (*inf*), situation, spot (*inf*)

predict v = **foretell**, augur, divine, forecast, portend, prophesy

predispose v **1** = **incline**, affect, bias, dispose, influence, lead, prejudice, prompt

predominate v = **prevail**, be most noticeable, carry weight, hold sway, outweigh, overrule, overshadow

pre-eminent *adj* = **outstanding**, chief, distinguished, excellent, foremost, incomparable, matchless, predominant, renowned, superior, supreme

pre-empt v = **anticipate**, appropriate, assume, usurp

P

preen ❶ v (of a bird) clean or trim (feathers) with the beak. **preen oneself 1** smarten oneself. **2** show self-satisfaction.

prefabricated adj (of a building) manufactured in shaped sections for rapid assembly on site.

preface ❶ [**pref**-iss] n **1** introduction to a book. ▷ v **2** serve as an introduction to (a book, speech, etc.).

prefect n **1** senior pupil in a school, with limited power over others. **2** senior administrative officer in some countries. **prefecture** n office or area of authority of a prefect.

prefer ❶ v **-ferring, -ferred 1** like better. **2** Law bring (charges) before a court. **preferable** adj more desirable. **preferably** adv **preference** n **preferential** adj showing preference. **preferment** n promotion or advancement.

prefix n **1** letter or group of letters put at the beginning of a word to make a new word, such as un- in unhappy. v **2** put as an introduction or prefix (to).

pregnant ❶ adj **1** carrying a fetus in the womb. **2** full of meaning or significance,

e.g. a pregnant pause. **pregnancy** n, pl **-cies**

prehistoric ❶ adj of the period before written history begins. **prehistory** n.

prejudice ❶ n **1** unreasonable or unfair dislike or preference. ▷ v **2** cause (someone) to have a prejudice. **3** harm, cause disadvantage to. **prejudicial** adj harmful, disadvantageous.

● **SPELLING TIP**
● There are examples in the Bank of
● English of **prejudice** being misspelt as
● predjudice, with an extra d. Although d
● often combines with g in English, it is
● not necessary before j.

preliminary ❶ adj **1** happening before and in preparation, introductory. ▷ n, pl **-naries 2** preliminary remark, contest, etc.

prelude ❶ n **1** introductory movement in music. **2** event preceding and introducing something else.

premature ❶ adj **1** happening or done before the normal or expected time. **2** (of a baby) born before the end of the normal period of pregnancy. **prematurely** adv.

premeditated ❶ adj planned in advance. **premeditation** n.

────────────────────────── THESAURUS ──────────────

preen v = **clean**, plume **preen oneself 1** = **smarten**, dress up, spruce up, titivate **2** = **pride oneself**, congratulate oneself

preface n **1** = **introduction**, foreword, preamble, preliminary, prelude, prologue ▷ v **2** = **introduce**, begin, open, prefix

prefer v **1** = **like better**, be partial to, choose, desire, fancy, favour, go for, incline towards, opt for, pick

pregnant adj **1** = **expectant**, big or heavy with child, expecting (inf), in the club (Brit sl), with child **2** = **meaningful**, charged, eloquent, expressive, loaded, pointed, significant, telling, weighty

prehistoric adj = **earliest**, early, primeval, primitive, primordial

prejudice n **1 a** = **discrimination**, bigotry, chauvinism, injustice, intolerance, narrow-mindedness, unfairness **b** = **bias**, partiality, preconceived notion,

preconception, prejudgment ▷ v **2** = **bias**, colour, distort, influence, poison, predispose, slant **3** = **harm**, damage, hinder, hurt, impair, injure, mar, spoil, undermine

preliminary adj **1** = **first**, initial, introductory, opening, pilot, prefatory, preparatory, prior, test, trial ▷ n **2** = **introduction**, beginning, opening, overture, preamble, preface, prelude, start

prelude n **1** = **overture 2** = **introduction**, beginning, foreword, preamble, preface, prologue, start

premature adj **1 a** = **hasty**, ill-timed, overhasty, previous (inf), rash, too soon, untimely **b** = **early**

premeditated adj = **planned**, calculated, conscious, considered, deliberate, intentional, wilful

premier ❶ *n* 1 prime minister. ▷ *adj*
2 chief, leading. **premiership** *n*.

première ❶ *n* first performance of a play,
film, etc.

premise, premiss ❶ *n* statement
assumed to be true and used as the basis
of reasoning.

premises ❶ *pl n* house or other building
and its land.

premium ❶ *n* 1 additional sum of money,
as on a wage or charge. 2 (regular) sum
paid for insurance. **at a premium** in great
demand because scarce.

premonition ❶ *n* feeling that something
unpleasant is going to happen;
foreboding. **premonitory** *adj*.

preoccupy *v* **-pying, -pied** fill the thoughts
or attention of (someone) to the exclusion
of other things. **preoccupation** *n*.

preordained *adj* decreed or determined
in advance.

prepare ❶ *v* make or get ready. **prepared**
adj 1 willing. 2 ready. **preparation** *n*
1 preparing. 2 something done in readiness
for something else. 3 mixture prepared

for use as a cosmetic, medicine, etc.

preparatory [prip-**par**-a-tree] *adj* preparing
for. **preparatory school** private school for
children going on to public school.

preposition *n* word used before a noun
or pronoun to show its relationship
with other words, such as *by* in *go by bus.*
prepositional *adj*.

prepossessing ❶ *adj* making a favourable
impression, attractive.

preposterous ❶ *adj* utterly absurd.

prerequisite ❶ *n, adj* (something)
required before something else is possible.

prerogative ❶ *n* special power or privilege.

- ● SPELLING TIP
- ● The way **prerogative** is often pro-
- ● nounced is presumably the reason
- ● why *perogative* is a common way of
- ● misspelling it.

prescribe ❶ *v* 1 recommend the use
of (a medicine). 2 lay down as a rule.
prescription *n* written instructions from
a doctor for the making up and use of a
medicine. **prescriptive** *adj* laying down
rules.

THESAURUS

---

premier *n* 1 = **head of government**,
chancellor, chief minister, P.M., prime
minister ▷ *adj* 2 = **chief**, first, foremost,
head, highest, leading, main, primary,
prime, principal

première *n* = **first night**, debut, opening

premise, premiss *n* = **assumption**,
argument, assertion, hypothesis,
postulation, presupposition, proposition,
supposition

premises *pl n* = **building**, establishment,
place, property, site

premium *n* 1 = **bonus**, bounty, fee, perk
(*Brit inf*) perquisite, prize, reward **at a
premium** = **in great demand**, hard to
come by, in short supply, rare, scarce

premonition *n* = **feeling**, foreboding,
hunch, idea, intuition, presentiment,
suspicion

prepare *v* = **make** *or* **get ready**,
adapt, adjust, arrange, practise, prime,

train, warm up

prepossessing *adj* = **attractive**,
appealing, charming, engaging, fetching,
good-looking, handsome, likable *or*
likeable, pleasing

preposterous *adj* = **ridiculous**, absurd,
crazy, incredible, insane, laughable,
ludicrous, nonsensical, out of the
question, outrageous, unthinkable

prerequisite *n* = **requirement**, condition,
essential, must, necessity, precondition,
qualification, requisite, *sine qua non* ▷ *adj*
= **required**, essential, indispensable,
mandatory, necessary, obligatory,
requisite, vital

prerogative *n* = **right**, advantage,
due, exemption, immunity, liberty,
privilege

prescribe *v* 2 = **order**, decree, dictate,
direct, lay down, ordain, recommend, rule,
set, specify, stipulate

P

present¹ ❶ *adj* **1** being in a specified place. **2** existing or happening now. **3** *Grammar* (of a verb tense) indicating that the action specified is taking place now. ▷ *n* **4** present time or tense. **presence** *n* **1** fact of being in a specified place. **2** impressive dignified appearance. **presently** *adv* **1** soon. **2** *US & Scot* now.

present² ❶ *n* **1** something given to bring pleasure to another person. ▷ *v* **2** introduce formally or publicly. **3** introduce and compère (a TV or radio show). **4** cause, e.g. *present a difficulty*. **5** give, award. **presentation** *n* **presentable** *adj* attractive, neat, fit for people to see. **presenter** *n* person introducing a TV or radio show.

presentiment [priz-**zen**-tim-ent] *n* sense of something unpleasant about to happen.

preserve ❶ *v* **1** keep from being damaged, changed, or ended. **2** treat (food) to prevent it decaying. ▷ *n* **3** area of interest restricted to a particular person or group. **4** fruit preserved by cooking in sugar. **preservation** *n* **preservative** *n* chemical that prevents decay.

preside ❶ *v* be in charge, esp. of a meeting. **president** *n* **1** head of state in countries without a king or queen. **2** head of a society, institution, etc.

press ❶ *v* **1** apply force or weight to. **2** squeeze. **3** smooth by applying pressure or heat. **4** urge insistently. **5** crowd, push. ▷ *n* **6** printing machine. **pressed for** short of, e.g. *pressed for time*. **the press 1** news media collectively, esp. newspapers. **2** reporters, journalists. **pressing** *adj* urgent. **press box** room at a sports ground reserved for reporters. **press conference** interview for reporters given by a celebrity. **press release** official announcement or account of a news item supplied to the press. **press stud** fastener in which one part with a projecting knob snaps into a hole on another part.

pressure ❶ *n* **1** force produced by pressing. **2** urgent claims or demands. **3** *Physics* force applied to a surface per unit of area. **pressure cooker** airtight pot which cooks food quickly by steam under pressure. **pressure group** group that tries to influence policies, public opinion, etc.

─────────────── THESAURUS ───────────────

present¹ *adj* **1** = **here**, at hand, near, nearby, ready, there **2** = **current**, contemporary, existent, existing, immediate, present-day ▷ *n* **4** = **now**, here and now, the present moment, the time being, today

present² *n* **1** = **gift**, boon, donation, endowment, grant, gratuity, hand-out, offering, prezzie (*inf*) **2** = **introduce**, acquaint with, make known **3** = **put on**, display, exhibit, give, show, stage **5** = **give**, award, bestow, confer, grant, hand out, hand over

preserve *v* **1 a** = **protect**, care for, conserve, defend, keep, safeguard, save, shelter, shield **b** = **maintain**, continue, keep, keep up, perpetuate, sustain, uphold ▷ *n* **3** = **area**, domain, field, realm, sphere

preside *v* = **run**, administer, chair, conduct, control, direct, govern, head, lead, manage, officiate

press *v* **1** = **compress**, crush, depress, force down, jam, mash, push, squeeze **2** = **hug**, clasp, crush, embrace, fold in one's arms, hold close, squeeze **3** = **smooth**, flatten, iron **4** = **urge**, beg, entreat, exhort, implore, petition, plead, pressurize **5** = **crowd**, flock, gather, herd, push, seethe, surge, swarm, throng **the press 1** = **newspapers**, Fleet Street, fourth estate, news media, the papers **2** = **journalists**, columnists, correspondents, reporters

pressure *n* **1** = **force**, compressing, compression, crushing, squeezing, weight **2 a** = **power**, coercion, compulsion, constraint, force, influence, mana (NZ), sway **b** = **stress**, burden, demands, hassle (*inf*), heat, load, strain, urgency

prestige ❶ *n* high status or respect resulting from success or achievements. **prestigious** *adj.*

presto *adv Music* very quickly.

presume ❶ *v* **1** suppose to be the case. **2** dare (to). **presumably** *adv* one supposes (that). **presumption** *n* **1** bold insolent behaviour. **2** strong probability. **presumptuous** *adj* doing things one has no right or authority to do. **presumptive** *adj* assumed to be true or valid until the contrary is proved.

presuppose ❶ *v* need as a previous condition in order to be true. **presupposition** *n.*

pretend ❶ *v* claim or give the appearance of (something untrue) to deceive or in play. **pretender** *n* person who makes a false or disputed claim to a position of power. **pretence** *n* behaviour intended to deceive, pretending. **pretentious** *adj* making (unjustified) claims to special merit or importance. **pretension** *n.*

pretext ❶ *n* false reason given to hide the real one.

pretty ❶ *adj* **-tier, -tiest 1** pleasing to look at. ▷ *adv* **2** fairly, moderately, e.g. *I'm pretty certain.* **prettily** *adv* **prettiness** *n.*

prevail ❶ *v* **1** gain mastery. **2** be generally established. **prevailing** *adj* **1** widespread. **2** predominant. **prevalence** *n* **prevalent** *adj* widespread, common.

prevaricate ❶ *v* avoid giving a direct or truthful answer. **prevarication** *n.*

prevent ❶ *v* keep from happening or doing. **preventable** *adj* **prevention** *n* **preventive** *adj, n.*

preview ❶ *n* advance showing of a film or exhibition before it is shown to the public.

previous ❶ *adj* coming or happening before. **previously** *adv.*

prey ❶ *n* **1** animal hunted and killed for food by another animal. **2** victim. **bird of prey** bird that kills and eats other birds or animals. **prey on** *v* **1** hunt and kill for food. **2** worry, obsess.

price ❶ *n* **1** amount of money for which a thing is bought or sold. **2** unpleasant thing that must be endured to get something desirable. ▷ *v* **3** fix or ask the

---
THESAURUS
---

prestige *n* = **status**, credit, distinction, eminence, fame, honour, importance, kudos, renown, reputation, standing

presume *v* **1** = **believe**, assume, conjecture, guess (*inf, chiefly US & Canad*), infer, postulate, suppose, surmise, take for granted, think **2** = **dare**, go so far, make so bold, take the liberty, venture

presuppose *v* = **presume**, assume, imply, posit, postulate, take as read, take for granted

pretend *v* **a** = **feign**, affect, allege, assume, fake, falsify, impersonate, profess, sham, simulate **b** = **make believe**, act, imagine, make up, suppose

pretext *n* = **guise**, cloak, cover, excuse, ploy, pretence, ruse, show

pretty *adj* **1** = **attractive**, beautiful, bonny, charming, comely, fair, good-looking, lekker (*S Afr sl*), lovely ▷ *adv* **2** = **fairly**, kind of (*inf*), moderately, quite, rather,

reasonably, somewhat

prevail *v* **1** = **win**, be victorious, overcome, overrule, succeed, triumph **2** = **be widespread**, abound, be current, be prevalent, exist generally, predominate

prevaricate *v* = **evade**, beat about the bush, cavil, deceive, dodge, equivocate, flannel (*Brit inf*), hedge

prevent *v* = **stop**, avert, avoid, foil, forestall, frustrate, hamper, hinder, impede, inhibit, obstruct, obviate, preclude, thwart

preview *n* = **sample**, advance showing, foretaste, sneak preview, taster, trailer

previous *adj* = **earlier**, erstwhile, foregoing, former, past, preceding, prior

prey *n* **1** = **quarry**, game, kill **2** = **victim**, dupe, fall guy (*inf*), mug (*Brit sl*), target

price *n* **1** = **cost**, amount, charge, damage (*inf*), estimate, expense, fee, figure, rate, value, worth **2** = **consequences**, cost,

P

price of. **priceless** *adj* **1** very valuable.
2 *informal* very funny. **pricey** *adj* **pricier**,
priciest *informal* expensive.
prick ❶ *v* **1** pierce lightly with a sharp
point. **2** cause to feel mental pain. **3** (of an
animal) make (the ears) stand erect. ▷ *n*
4 sudden sharp pain caused by pricking.
5 mark made by pricking. **6** remorse.
prick up one's ears listen intently.
pride ❶ *n* **1** feeling of pleasure and
satisfaction when one has done well.
2 too high an opinion of oneself. **3** sense of
dignity and self-respect. **4** something that
causes one to feel pride. **5** group of lions.
pride of place most important position.
pride oneself on feel pride about.
priest ❶ *n* **1** (in the Christian church)
a person who can administer the
sacraments and preach. **2** (in some
other religions) an official who performs
religious ceremonies. **priestess** *n fem*
priesthood *n* **priestly** *adj*.
prig ❶ *n* self-righteous person who acts
as if superior to others. **priggish** *adj*
priggishness *n*.
prim ❶ *adj* **primmer**, **primmest** formal,
proper, and rather prudish.
primacy *n*, *pl* **-cies 1** state of being
first in rank, grade, etc. **2** office of

an archbishop or the pope.
prima donna *n* **1** leading female opera
singer. **2** *informal* temperamental
person.
primary ❶ *adj* **1** chief, most important.
2 being the first stage, elementary.
primarily *adv* **primary colours** (in
physics) red, green, and blue or (in art)
red, yellow, and blue, from which all
other colours can be produced by mixing.
primary school school for children from
five to eleven years.
primate¹ *n* member of an order of mammals
including monkeys and humans.
primate² *n* archbishop.
prime ❶ *adj* **1** main, most important.
2 of the highest quality. ▷ *n* **3** time
when someone is at his or her best or
most vigorous. ▷ *v* **4** give (someone)
information in advance to prepare them
for something. **5** prepare (a surface) for
painting. **6** prepare (a gun, pump, etc.) for
use. **primer** *n* special paint applied to bare
wood etc. before the main paint. **Prime
Minister** leader of a government. **prime
number** number that can be divided
exactly only by itself and one.
primeval ❶ [prime-**ee**-val] *adj* of the
earliest age of the world.

---

penalty, toll ▷ *v* **3** = **evaluate**, assess, cost,
estimate, rate, value
prick *v* **1** = **pierce**, jab, lance, perforate,
punch, puncture, stab ▷ *n* **5** = **puncture**,
hole, perforation, pinhole, wound
pride *n* **1** = **satisfaction**, delight,
gratification, joy, pleasure **2** = **conceit**,
arrogance, egotism, hubris, self-
importance, vanity **3** = **self-respect**,
dignity, honour, self-esteem, self-worth
4 = **gem**, jewel, pride and joy, treasure
priest *n* **1** = **clergyman**, cleric, curate,
divine, ecclesiastic, father, minister,
pastor, vicar
prig *n* = **goody-goody** (*inf*), prude, puritan,
stuffed shirt (*inf*)
prim *adj* = **prudish**, demure, fastidious,

fussy, priggish, prissy (*inf*), proper,
puritanical, strait-laced
primary *adj* **1** = **chief**, cardinal, first,
greatest, highest, main, paramount,
prime, principal **2** = **elementary**,
introductory, rudimentary, simple
prime *adj* **1** = **main**, chief, leading,
predominant, pre-eminent, primary,
principal **2** = **best**, choice, excellent, first-
class, first-rate, highest, quality, select,
top ▷ *n* **3** = **peak**, bloom, flower, height,
heyday, zenith ▷ *v* **4** = **inform**, brief, clue
in (*inf*), coach, fill in (*inf*), get ready, make
ready, notify, prepare, tell, train
primeval *adj* = **earliest**, ancient, early,
first, old, prehistoric, primal, primitive,
primordial

primitive ❶ *adj* **1** of an early simple stage of development. **2** basic, crude.

primrose *n* pale yellow spring flower.

prince ❶ *n* **1** male member of a royal family, esp. the son of the king or queen. **2** male ruler of a small country. **princely** *adj* **1** of or like a prince. **2** generous, lavish, or magnificent. **princess** *n* female member of a royal family, esp. the daughter of the king or queen.

principal ❶ *adj* **1** main, most important. ▷ *n* **2** head of a school or college. **3** person taking a leading part in something. **4** sum of money lent on which interest is paid. **principally** *adv*.

principle ❶ *n* **1** moral rule guiding behaviour. **2** general or basic truth. **3** scientific law concerning the working of something. **in principle** in theory but not always in practice. **on principle** because of one's beliefs.

print ❶ *v* **1** reproduce (a newspaper, book, etc.) in large quantities by mechanical or electronic means. **2** reproduce (text or pictures) by pressing ink onto paper etc. **3** write in letters that are not joined up. **4** stamp (fabric) with a design. **5** *Photog* produce (pictures) from negatives. ▷ *n* **6** printed words etc.

7 printed copy of a painting. **8** printed lettering. **9** photograph. **10** printed fabric. **11** mark left on a surface by something that has pressed against it. **out of print** no longer available from a publisher.

printer *n* **1** person or company engaged in printing. **2** machine that prints. **printing** *n* **printed circuit** electronic circuit with wiring printed on an insulating base. **print-out** *n* printed information from a computer.

prior¹ ❶ *adj* earlier. **prior to** before.

prior² *n* head monk in a priory. **prioress** *n* deputy head nun in a convent. **priory** *n, pl* **-ries** place where certain orders of monks or nuns live.

prise *v* force open by levering.

prism *n* transparent block usu. with triangular ends and rectangular sides, used to disperse light into a spectrum or refract it in optical instruments. **prismatic** *adj* **1** of or shaped like a prism. **2** (of colour) as if produced by refraction through a prism, rainbow-like.

prison ❶ *n* building where criminals and accused people are held. **prisoner** *n* person held captive. **prisoner of war** serviceman captured by an enemy in wartime.

P

primitive *adj* **1** = **early**, elementary, first, original, primary, primeval, primordial **2** = **crude**, rough, rudimentary, simple, unrefined

prince *n* **2** = **ruler**, lord, monarch, sovereign

principal *adj* **1** = **main**, cardinal, chief, essential, first, foremost, key, leading, paramount, pre-eminent, primary, prime ▷ *n* **2** = **headmaster** or **headmistress**, dean, head (*inf*), head teacher, master or mistress, rector **3** = **star**, lead, leader **4** = **capital**, assets, money

principle *n* **1** = **morals**, conscience, integrity, probity, scruples, sense of honour **2** = **rule**, canon, criterion, doctrine, dogma, fundamental, law,

maxim, precept, standard, truth **in principle** = **in theory**, ideally, theoretically

print *v* **1** = **publish** **2** = **imprint**, impress, issue, mark, stamp ▷ *n* **6** = **publication**, book, magazine, newspaper, newsprint, periodical, printed matter **7** = **reproduction**, copy **9** = **photograph**, photo (*inf*), picture

prior¹ *adj* = **earlier**, foregoing, former, preceding, pre-existing, previous **prior to** = **before**, earlier than, preceding, previous to

prison *n* = **jail**, clink (*sl*), confinement, cooler (*sl*), dungeon, jug (*sl*), lockup, nick (*Brit sl*), penitentiary (*US*), slammer (*sl*)

pristine ❶ *adj* clean, new, and unused.

private ❶ *adj* 1 for the use of one person or group only. 2 secret. 3 personal, unconnected with one's work. 4 owned or paid for by individuals rather than by the government. 5 quiet, not likely to be disturbed. ▷ *n* 6 soldier of the lowest rank. **privately** *adv* **privacy** *n*.

privation *n* loss or lack of the necessities of life.

privet *n* bushy evergreen shrub used for hedges.

privilege ❶ *n* advantage or favour that only some people have. **privileged** *adj* enjoying a special right or immunity

  ● SPELLING TIP
  ● Although the Bank of English shows
  ● that people find it difficult to decide
  ● whether to use *is* or *es* when spelling
  ● **privilege**, the commonest mistake is to
  ● insert an extra *d* to make *priviledge*. The
  ● adjective, **privileged**, should not have a
  ● *d* in the middle either

privy ❶ *adj* 1 sharing knowledge of something secret. ▷ *n*, *pl* **privies** 2 *obs* toilet, esp. an outside one. **privy council** private council of the British monarch.

prize¹ ❶ *n* 1 reward given for success in a competition etc. ▷ *adj* 2 winning or likely to win a prize. **prizefighter** *n* boxer who fights for money. **prizefight** *n*.

prize² ❶ *v* value highly.

pro¹ *adv*, *prep* in favour of. **pros and cons** arguments for and against.

pro² *n*, *pl* **pros** *informal* 1 professional. 2 prostitute.

pro- *prefix* 1 in favour of, e.g. *pro-Russian*. 2 instead of, e.g. *pronoun*.

proactive *adj* tending to initiate change rather than reacting to events.

probable ❶ *adj* likely to happen or be true. **probably** *adv* **probability** *n*, *pl* **-ties**.

probate *n* 1 process of proving the validity of a will. 2 certificate stating that a will is genuine.

probation ❶ *n* 1 system of dealing with law-breakers, esp. juvenile ones, by placing them under supervision. 2 period when someone is assessed for suitability for a job etc. **probationer** *n* person on probation.

probe ❶ *v* 1 search into or examine closely. ▷ *n* 2 surgical instrument used to examine a wound, cavity, etc.

probiotic *n* 1 bacterium that protects the body from harmful bacteria. ▷ *adj* 2 relating to probiotics, e.g. *probiotic yogurts*.

probity *n* honesty, integrity.

problem ❶ *n* 1 something difficult to deal with or solve. 2 question or puzzle set for solution. **problematic**, **problematical** *adj*.

THESAURUS

pristine *adj* = **new**, immaculate, pure, uncorrupted, undefiled, unspoiled, unsullied, untouched, virginal

private *adj* 1 = **exclusive**, individual, intimate, own, personal, reserved, special 2 = **secret**, clandestine, confidential, covert, hush-hush (*inf*), off the record, unofficial 5 = **separate**, isolated, secluded, secret, sequestered, solitary, withdrawn

privilege *n* = **right**, advantage, claim, concession, due, entitlement, freedom, liberty, prerogative

privy *adj* 1 = **secret**, confidential, private ▷ *n* 2 *Obs* = **lavatory**, latrine, outside toilet

prize¹ *n* 1 = **reward**, accolade, award, haul, honour, jackpot, purse, stakes, trophy, winnings ▷ *adj* 2 = **champion**, award-winning, best, first-rate, outstanding, top, winning

prize² *v* = **value**, cherish, esteem, hold dear, treasure

probable *adj* = **likely**, apparent, credible, feasible, plausible, possible, presumable, reasonable

probation *n* 2 = **trial period**, apprenticeship, trial

probe *v* 1 a = **examine**, explore, go into, investigate, look into, scrutinize, search b = **explore**, feel around, poke, prod ▷ *n*

problem *n* 1 = **difficulty**, complication, dilemma, dispute, predicament, quandary,

proceed ❶ *v* **1** start or continue doing.
2 *formal* walk, go. **3** start a legal action.
4 arise from. **proceeds** *pl n* money
obtained from an event or activity.
proceedings *pl n* **1** organized or related
series of events. **2** minutes of a meeting.
3 legal action. **procedure** *n* way of doing
something, esp. the correct or usual one.

process ❶ *n* **1** series of actions or
changes. **2** method of doing or producing
something. ▷ *v* **3** handle or prepare
by a special method of manufacture.
processed *adj* (of food) treated to prevent
it decaying. **processor** *n*.

proclaim ❶ *v* declare publicly.
proclamation *n*.

procrastinate ❶ *v* put off taking action,
delay. **procrastination** *n*.

procreate *v* *formal* produce offspring.
procreation *n*.

procure ❶ *v* **1** get, provide. **2** obtain
(people) to act as prostitutes. **procurement**
n **procurer, procuress** *n* person who

obtains people to act as prostitutes.

prod ❶ *v* **prodding, prodded 1** poke with
something pointed. **2** goad (someone) to
take action. ▷ *n* **3** prodding.

prodigal ❶ *adj* recklessly extravagant,
wasteful.

prodigy ❶ *n, pl* **-gies 1** person with some
marvellous talent. **2** wonderful thing.
prodigious *adj* **1** very large, immense.
2 wonderful.

produce ❶ *v* **1** bring into existence.
2 present to view, show. **3** make,
manufacture. **4** present on stage, film,
or television. ▷ *n* **5** food grown for sale.
producer *n* **1** person with control over the
making of a film, record, etc. **2** person or
company that produces something.

profane ❶ *adj* **1** showing disrespect for
religion or holy things. **2** (of language)
coarse, blasphemous. ▷ *v* **3** treat
(something sacred) irreverently,
desecrate. **profanity** *n, pl* **-ties** profane
talk or behaviour, blasphemy.

— THESAURUS —

trouble **2** = **puzzle**, conundrum, enigma,
poser, question, riddle
proceed *v* **1** = **go on**, carry on, continue,
go ahead, move on, press on, progress
4 = **arise**, come, derive, emanate, flow,
issue, originate, result, spring, stem
process *n* **1** = **development**, advance,
evolution, growth, movement, progress,
progression **2** = **procedure**, action,
course, manner, means, measure,
method, operation, performance,
practice, system ▷ *v* **3** = **handle**
proclaim *v* = **declare**, advertise,
announce, circulate, herald, indicate,
make known, profess, publish
procrastinate *v* = **delay**, dally, drag
one's feet (*inf*), gain time, play for time,
postpone, put off, stall, temporize
procure *v* **1** = **obtain**, acquire, buy, come
by, find, gain, get, pick up, purchase, score
(*sl*), secure, win
prod *v* **1** = **poke**, dig, drive, jab, nudge,
push, shove **2** = **prompt**, egg on, goad,

impel, incite, motivate, move, rouse, spur,
stimulate, urge ▷ *n* **3 a** = **poke**, dig, jab,
nudge, push, shove **b** = **prompt**, cue,
reminder, signal, stimulus
prodigal *adj* = **extravagant**, excessive,
immoderate, improvident, profligate,
reckless, spendthrift, wasteful
prodigy *n* **1** = **genius**, mastermind, talent,
whizz (*inf*), wizard **2** = **wonder**, marvel,
miracle, phenomenon, sensation
produce *v* **1** = **bring forth**, bear, beget,
breed, bring about, cause, deliver, effect,
generate, give rise to **2** = **show**, advance,
demonstrate, exhibit, offer, present
3 = **make**, compose, construct, create,
develop, fabricate, invent, manufacture
4 = **present**, direct, do, exhibit, mount,
put on, show, stage ▷ *n* **5** = **fruit and
vegetables**, crop, greengrocery, harvest,
product, yield
profane *adj* **1** = **sacrilegious**,
disrespectful, godless, impious, impure,
irreligious, irreverent, sinful, ungodly,

P

profess ❶ v 1 state or claim (something as true), sometimes falsely. 2 have as one's belief or religion. **professed** adj supposed.
proffer v offer.
proficient ❶ adj skilled, expert. **proficiency** n.
profile ❶ n 1 outline, esp. of the face, as seen from the side. 2 brief biographical sketch.
profit ❶ n 1 money gained. 2 benefit obtained. ▷ v 3 gain or benefit. **profitable** adj making profit. **profitably** adv **profitability** n **profiteer** n person who makes excessive profits at the expense of the public. **profiteering** n.
profligate ❶ adj 1 recklessly extravagant. 2 shamelessly immoral. ▷ n 3 profligate person. **profligacy** n.
profound ❶ adj 1 showing or needing

great knowledge. 2 strongly felt, intense. **profundity** n, pl **-ties**.
profuse ❶ adj plentiful. **profusion** n.
progeny ❶ [**proj**-in-ee] n, pl **-nies** children. **progenitor** [pro-**jen**-it-er] n ancestor.
prognosis ❶ n, pl **-noses** 1 doctor's forecast about the progress of an illness. 2 any forecast.
programme ❶ n 1 planned series of events. 2 broadcast on radio or television. 3 list of items or performers in an entertainment.
progress ❶ n 1 improvement, development. 2 movement forward. ▷ v 3 become more advanced or skilful. 4 move forward. **in progress** taking place. **progression** n **progressive** adj 1 favouring political or social reform. 2 happening gradually. **progressively** adv.

wicked 2 = **crude**, blasphemous, coarse, filthy, foul, obscene, vulgar ▷ v 3 = **desecrate**, commit sacrilege, debase, defile, violate
profess v 1 a = **state**, admit, affirm, announce, assert, avow, confess, declare, proclaim, vouch b = **claim**, allege, fake, feign, make out, pretend, purport
proficient adj = **skilled**, able, accomplished, adept, capable, competent, efficient, expert, gifted, masterly, skilful
profile n 1 = **outline**, contour, drawing, figure, form, side view, silhouette, sketch 2 = **biography**, characterization, sketch, thumbnail sketch, vignette
profit n 1 = **earnings**, gain, proceeds, receipts, return, revenue, takings, yield 2 = **benefit**, advancement, advantage, gain, good, use, value ▷ v 3 a = **make money**, earn, gain b = **benefit**, be of advantage to, gain, help, improve, promote, serve
profligate adj 1 = **extravagant**, immoderate, improvident, prodigal, reckless, spendthrift, wasteful 2 = **depraved**, debauched, degenerate,

dissolute, immoral, licentious, shameless, wanton, wicked, wild ▷ n 3 a = **spendthrift**, squanderer, waster, wastrel b = **degenerate**, debauchee, libertine, rake, reprobate, roué
profound adj 1 = **wise**, abstruse, deep, learned, penetrating, philosophical, sagacious, sage 2 = **sincere**, acute, deeply felt, extreme, great, heartfelt, intense, keen
profuse adj = **plentiful**, abundant, ample, bountiful, copious, luxuriant, overflowing, prolific
progeny n = **children**, descendants, family, issue, lineage, offspring, race, stock, young
prognosis n 1 = **diagnosis** 2 = **forecast**, prediction, prognostication, projection
programme n 1 = **schedule**, agenda, curriculum, line-up, list, listing, order of events, plan, syllabus, timetable 2 = **show**, broadcast, performance, presentation, production
progress n 1 = **development**, advance, breakthrough, gain, growth, headway, improvement 2 = **movement**, advance, course, headway, passage ▷ v

prohibit ❶ v forbid or prevent from happening. **prohibition** n **1** act of forbidding. **2** ban on the sale or drinking of alcohol. **prohibitive** adj (of prices) too high to be affordable. **prohibitively** adv.

project ❶ n **1** planned scheme to do or examine something over a period. ▷ v **2** make a forecast based on known data. **3** make (a film or slide) appear on a screen. **4** communicate (an impression). **5** stick out beyond a surface or edge. **projector** n apparatus for projecting photographic images, films, or slides on a screen. **projection** n **projectionist** n person who operates a projector.

proletariat ❶ [pro-lit-**air**-ee-at] n working class. **proletarian** adj, n.

proliferate ❶ v grow or reproduce rapidly. **proliferation** n.

prolific ❶ adj very productive. **prolifically** adv.

prologue ❶ n introduction to a play or book.

prolong ❶ v make (something) last longer. **prolongation** n.

promenade ❶ n **1** paved walkway along the seafront at a holiday resort. ▷ v, n **2** old-fashioned (take) a leisurely walk.

prominent ❶ adj **1** very noticeable. **2** famous, widely known. **prominence** n.

promiscuous ❶ adj having many casual sexual relationships. **promiscuity** n.

promise ❶ v **1** say that one will definitely do or not do something. **2** show signs of, seem likely. ▷ n **3** undertaking to do or not to do something. **4** indication of future success. **promising** adj likely to succeed or turn out well.

3 = **develop**, advance, gain, grow, improve
4 = **move on**, advance, continue, go forward, make headway, proceed, travel
in progress = **going on**, being done, happening, occurring, proceeding, taking place, under way
prohibit v a = **forbid**, ban, debar, disallow, outlaw, proscribe, veto b = **prevent**, hamper, hinder, impede, restrict, stop
project n **1** = **scheme**, activity, assignment, enterprise, job, occupation, plan, task, undertaking, venture, work ▷ v **2** = **forecast**, calculate, estimate, extrapolate, gauge, predict, reckon **5** = **stick out**, bulge, extend, jut, overhang, protrude, stand out
proletariat n = **working class**, commoners, hoi polloi, labouring classes, lower classes, plebs, proles (offens), the common people, the masses
proliferate v = **increase**, breed, expand, grow rapidly, multiply
prolific adj = **productive**, abundant, copious, fecund, fertile, fruitful, luxuriant, profuse
prologue n = **introduction**, foreword,

preamble, preface, prelude
prolong v = **lengthen**, continue, delay, drag out, draw out, extend, perpetuate, protract, spin out, stretch
promenade n **1** = **walkway**, esplanade, parade, prom ▷ v **2** Old-fashioned = **stroll**, saunter, walk
prominent adj **1** = **noticeable**, conspicuous, eye-catching, obtrusive, obvious, outstanding, pronounced **2** = **famous**, distinguished, eminent, foremost, important, leading, main, notable, renowned, top, well-known
promiscuous adj = **licentious**, abandoned, debauched, fast, immoral, libertine, loose, wanton, wild
promise v **1** = **guarantee**, assure, contract, give one's word, pledge, swear, take an oath, undertake, vow, warrant **2** = **seem likely**, augur, betoken, indicate, look like, show signs of, suggest ▷ n **3** = **guarantee**, assurance, bond, commitment, oath, pledge, undertaking, vow, word **4** = **potential**, ability, aptitude, capability, capacity, talent

P

promontory ❶ *n, pl* **-ries** point of high land jutting out into the sea.

promote ❶ *v* **1** help to make (something) happen or increase. **2** raise to a higher rank or position. **3** encourage the sale of by advertising. **promoter** *n* person who organizes or finances an event etc. **promotion** *n* **promotional** *adj*.

prompt ❶ *v* **1** cause (an action). **2** remind (an actor or speaker) of words that he or she has forgotten. ▷ *adj* **3** done without delay. ▷ *adv* **4** exactly, e.g. *six o'clock prompt*. **promptly** *adv* immediately, without delay. **promptness** *n* **prompter** *n* person offstage who prompts actors.

promulgate ❶ *v* **1** put (a law etc.) into effect by announcing it officially. **2** make widely known. **promulgation** *n*.

prone ❶ *adj* **1** (foll. by *to*) likely to do or be affected by (something). **2** lying face downwards.

prong ❶ *n* one spike of a fork or similar instrument.

pronoun *n* word, such as *she* or *it*, used to replace a noun.

pronounce ❶ *v* **1** form the sounds of (words or letters), esp. clearly or in a particular

way. **2** declare formally or officially. **pronounceable** *adj* **pronounced** *adj* very noticeable. **pronouncement** *n* formal announcement. **pronunciation** *n* way in which a word or language is pronounced.

● **SPELLING TIP**
● The noun **pronunciation**, which
● appears in the Bank of English 823 times,
● is spelt *pronounciation* 21 times, probably
● because of the way **pronounce** is spelt.
● Remember, there is no *o* between the *n*
● and the *u*.

proof ❶ *n* **1** evidence that shows that something is true or has happened. **2** copy of something printed, such as the pages of a book, for checking before final production. ▷ *adj* **3** able to withstand, e.g. *proof against criticism*. **4** denoting the strength of an alcoholic drink, e.g. *seventy proof*. **proofread** *v* read and correct (printer's proofs).

prop¹ ❶ *v* **propping, propped** **1** support (something) so that it stays upright or in place. ▷ *n* **2** pole, beam, etc. used as a support.

prop² *n* movable object used on the set of a film or play.

propaganda ❶ *n* (organized promotion

promontory *n* = **point**, cape, foreland, head, headland

promote *v* **1** = **help**, advance, aid, assist, back, boost, encourage, forward, foster, gee up, support **2** = **raise**, elevate, exalt, upgrade **3** = **advertise**, hype, plug (*inf*), publicize, push, sell

prompt *v* **1** = **cause**, elicit, give rise to, occasion, provoke **2** = **remind**, assist, cue, help out ▷ *adj* **3** = **immediate**, early, instant, quick, rapid, speedy, swift, timely *adv* **4** = **exactly**, on the dot, promptly, punctually, sharp

promulgate *v* **2** = **make known**, broadcast, circulate, communicate, disseminate, make public, proclaim, promote, publish, spread

prone *adj* **1** (foll. by *to*) = **liable**, apt, bent, disposed, given, inclined, likely,

predisposed, subject, susceptible, tending **2** = **face down**, flat, horizontal, prostrate, recumbent

prong *n* = **point**, spike, tine

pronounce *v* **1** = **say**, accent, articulate, enunciate, sound, speak **2** = **declare**, affirm, announce, decree, deliver, proclaim

proof *n* **1** = **evidence**, authentication, confirmation, corroboration, demonstration, substantiation, testimony, verification ▷ *adj* **4** = **impervious**, impenetrable, repellent, resistant, strong

prop¹ *v* **1** = **support**, bolster, brace, buttress, hold up, stay, sustain, uphold ▷ *n* **2** = **support**, brace, buttress, mainstay, stanchion, stay

propaganda *n* = **information**, advertising, disinformation, hype, promotion, publicity

of) information to assist or damage the
cause of a government or movement.
propagandist n.

propagate ❶ v 1 spread (information
and ideas). 2 reproduce, breed, or grow.
propagation n.

propel ❶ v -pelling, -pelled cause to move
forward. **propellant** n 1 something that
provides or causes propulsion. 2 gas used
in an aerosol spray. **propeller** n revolving
shaft with blades for driving a ship or
aircraft. **propulsion** n 1 method by which
something is propelled. 2 act of propelling
or state of being propelled.

propensity ❶ n, pl -ties natural
tendency.

proper ❶ adj 1 real or genuine. 2 suited
to a particular purpose. 3 correct in
behaviour. 4 excessively moral. 5 informal
complete. **properly** adv.

property ❶ n, pl -ties 1 something owned.
2 possessions collectively. 3 land or
buildings owned by somebody. 4 quality
or attribute.

prophet ❶ n 1 person supposedly chosen
by God to spread His word. 2 person

who predicts the future. **prophetic** adj
prophetically adv **prophecy** n, pl -cies
1 prediction. 2 message revealing God's
will. **prophesy** v -sying, -sied foretell.

proponent n person who argues in favour
of something.

proportion ❶ n 1 relative size or extent.
2 correct relation between connected
parts. 3 part considered with respect
to the whole. ▷ pl 4 dimensions or size.
▷ v 5 adjust in relative amount or size. **in
proportion** 1 comparable in size, rate of
increase, etc. 2 without exaggerating.
proportional, **proportionate** adj
being in proportion. **proportionally**,
proportionately adv.

propose ❶ v 1 put forward for
consideration. 2 nominate. 3 intend
or plan (to do). 4 make an offer of
marriage. **proposal** n **proposition**
n 1 offer. 2 statement or assertion.
3 Maths theorem. 4 informal thing to be
dealt with. ▷ v 5 informal ask (someone) to
have sexual intercourse.

propound v put forward for
consideration.

propagate v 1 = **spread**, broadcast,
circulate, disseminate, promote,
promulgate, publish, transmit
2 = **reproduce**, beget, breed, engender,
generate, increase, multiply, procreate,
produce

propel v = **drive**, force, impel, launch, push,
send, shoot, shove, thrust

propensity n = **tendency**, bent,
inclination, liability, penchant,
predisposition, proclivity

proper adj 2 = **suitable**, appropriate, apt,
becoming, befitting, fit, fitting, right
3 = **correct**, accepted, conventional,
established, formal, orthodox, precise,
right 4 = **polite**, decent, decorous,
genteel, gentlemanly, ladylike, mannerly,
respectable, seemly

property n 2 = **possessions**, assets,
belongings, capital, effects, estate, goods,

holdings, riches, wealth 3 = **land**, estate,
freehold, holding, real estate 4 = **quality**,
attribute, characteristic, feature,
hallmark, trait

prophet n 2 = **soothsayer**, diviner,
forecaster, oracle, prophesier, seer, sibyl

proportion n 1 = **relative amount**, ratio,
relationship 2 = **balance**, congruity,
correspondence, harmony, symmetry
3 = **part**, amount, division, fraction,
percentage, quota, segment, share ▷ pl
n 4 = **dimensions**, capacity, expanse,
extent, size, volume

propose v 1 = **put forward**, advance,
present, submit, suggest 2 = **nominate**,
name, present, recommend 3 = **intend**,
aim, design, have in mind, mean, plan,
scheme 4 = **offer marriage**, ask for
someone's hand (in marriage), pop the
question (inf)

P

proprietor ❶ n owner of a business establishment. **proprietress** n fem

proprietary adj 1 made and distributed under a trade name. 2 denoting or suggesting ownership.

propriety ❶ n, pl -ties correct conduct.

propulsion ❶ n see PROPEL.

prosaic ❶ [pro-**zay**-ik] adj lacking imagination, dull.

proscribe ❶ v prohibit, outlaw. **proscription** n **proscriptive** adj.

prose n ordinary speech or writing in contrast to poetry.

prosecute ❶ v 1 bring a criminal charge against. 2 continue to do. **prosecution** n **prosecutor** n.

prospect ❶ n 1 something anticipated. 2 old-fashioned view from a place. ▷ pl 3 probability of future success. ▷ v 4 explore, esp. for gold. **prospective** adj 1 future. 2 expected. **prospector** n **prospectus** n booklet giving details of a university, company, etc.

prosper ❶ v be successful. **prosperity** n

success and wealth. **prosperous** adj.

prostate n gland in male mammals that surrounds the neck of the bladder.

prostitute ❶ n 1 person who offers sexual intercourse in return for payment. ▷ v 2 make a prostitute of. 3 offer (oneself or one's talents) for unworthy purposes. **prostitution** n.

prostrate ❶ adj 1 lying face downwards. 2 physically or emotionally exhausted. ▷ v 3 lie face downwards. 4 exhaust physically or emotionally. **prostration** n.

protagonist ❶ n 1 supporter of a cause. 2 leading character in a play or a story.

protect ❶ v defend from trouble, harm, or loss. **protection** n **protectionism** n policy of protecting industries by taxing competing imports. **protectionist** n, adj **protective** adj 1 giving protection, e.g. protective clothing. 2 tending or wishing to protect someone. **protector** n 1 person or thing that protects. 2 regent. **protectorate** n 1 territory largely

——————————— THESAURUS ———————————

propriety n = **correctness**, aptness, fitness, rightness, seemliness

propulsion n = **drive**, impetus, impulse, propelling force, push, thrust

prosaic adj = **dull**, boring, everyday, humdrum, matter-of-fact, mundane, ordinary, pedestrian, routine, trite, unimaginative

proscribe v a = **prohibit**, ban, embargo, forbid, interdict b = **outlaw**, banish, deport, exclude, exile, expatriate, expel, ostracize

prosecute v 1 = **put on trial**, arraign, bring to trial, indict, litigate, sue, take to court, try

prospect n 1 = **expectation**, anticipation, future, hope, odds, outlook, probability, promise 2 Old-fashioned = **view**, landscape, outlook, scene, sight, spectacle, vista ▷ pl n 3 = **likelihood**, chance, possibility ▷ v 4 = **look for**, fossick (Aust & NZ), search for, seek

prosper v = **succeed**, advance, do well, flourish, get on, progress, thrive

prostitute n 1 = **whore**, call girl, fallen woman, harlot, hooker (US sl), loose woman, pro (sl), scrubber (Brit & Aust sl), streetwalker, strumpet, tart (inf), trollop ▷ v 3 = **cheapen**, debase, degrade, demean, devalue, misapply, pervert, profane

prostrate adj 1 = **prone**, flat, horizontal 2 = **exhausted**, dejected, depressed, desolate, drained, inconsolable, overcome, spent, worn out ▷ v 4 = **exhaust**, drain, fatigue, sap, tire, wear out, weary

protagonist n 1 = **supporter**, advocate, champion, exponent 2 = **leading character**, central character, hero or heroine, principal

protect v = **keep safe**, defend, guard, look after, preserve, safeguard, save, screen, shelter, shield, stick up for (inf), support, watch over

controlled by a stronger state. **2** (period of) rule of a regent.

protégé (*fem*) **protégée** [**pro**-ti-zhay] *n* person who is protected and helped by another.

protein *n* any of a group of complex organic compounds that are essential for life.

protest ❶ *n* **1** declaration or demonstration of objection. ▷ *v* **2** object, disagree. **3** assert formally. **protestation** *n* strong declaration.

Protestant *n* **1** follower of any of the Christian churches that split from the Roman Catholic Church in the sixteenth century. ▷ *adj* **2** of or relating to such a church. **Protestantism** *n*.

protocol ❶ *n* rules of behaviour for formal occasions.

proton *n* positively charged particle in the nucleus of an atom.

prototype ❶ *n* original or model to be copied or developed.

protract *v* lengthen or extend. **protracted** *adj* **protractor** *n* instrument for measuring angles.

protrude ❶ *v* stick out, project. **protrusion** *n*.

protuberant ❶ *adj* swelling out, bulging. **protuberance** *n*.

proud ❶ *adj* **1** feeling pleasure and satisfaction. **2** feeling honoured. **3** thinking oneself superior to other people. **4** dignified. **proudly** *adv*.

prove ❶ *v* **proving**, **proved**, **proved** or **proven 1** establish the validity of. **2** demonstrate, test. **3** be found to be. **proven** *adj* known from experience to work.

proverb ❶ *n* short saying that expresses a truth or gives a warning. **proverbial** *adj*

provide ❶ *v* make available. **provider** *n* **provided that**, **providing** on condition that. **provide for** *v* **1** take precautions (against). **2** support financially.

province ❶ *n* **1** area governed as a unit of a country or empire. **2** area of learning, activity, etc. ▷ *pl* **3** parts of a country outside the capital. **provincial** *adj* **1** of a province or the provinces. **2** unsophisticated and narrow-minded. ▷ *n* **3** unsophisticated person. **4** person from a province or the provinces. **provincialism** *n* narrow-mindedness and lack of sophistication.

protest *n* **1** = **objection**, complaint, dissent, outcry, protestation, remonstrance ▷ *v* **2** = **object**, complain, cry out, demonstrate, demur, disagree, disapprove, express disapproval, oppose, remonstrate **3** = **assert**, affirm, attest, avow, declare, insist, maintain, profess

protocol *n* = **code of behaviour**, conventions, customs, decorum, etiquette, manners, propriety

prototype *n* = **original**, example, first, model, pattern, standard, type

protrude *v* = **stick out**, bulge, come through, extend, jut, obtrude, project, stand out

proud *adj* **1** = **satisfied**, content, glad, gratified, pleased, well-pleased **3** = **conceited**, arrogant, boastful, disdainful, haughty, imperious, lordly,

overbearing, self-satisfied, snobbish, supercilious

prove *v* **1** = **verify**, authenticate, confirm, demonstrate, determine, establish, justify, show, substantiate **2** = **test**, analyse, assay, check, examine, try **3** = **turn out**, come out, end up, result

proverb *n* = **saying**, adage, dictum, maxim, saw

provide *v* **1** = **supply**, add, afford, bring, cater, equip, furnish, give, impart, lend, outfit, present, produce, purvey, render, serve, stock up, yield **provide for** *v* **1** = **take precautions**, anticipate, forearm, plan ahead, plan for, prepare for **2** = **support**, care for, keep, maintain, sustain, take care of

province *n* **1** = **region**, colony, department, district, division, domain,

P

provision ❶ n 1 act of supplying something. 2 something supplied. 3 *Law* condition incorporated in a document. ▷ pl 4 food. ▷ v 5 supply with food. **provisional** *adj* temporary or conditional. **provisionally** *adv*.

proviso ❶ [pro-**vize**-oh] n, pl -**sos**, -**soes** condition, stipulation.

provoke ❶ v 1 deliberately anger. 2 cause (an adverse reaction). **provocation** n **provocative** *adj*.

prow n bow of a vessel.

prowess ❶ n 1 superior skill or ability. 2 bravery, fearlessness.

prowl ❶ v 1 move stealthily around a place as if in search of prey or plunder. ▷ n 2 prowling. **prowler** n.

proximity ❶ n 1 nearness in space or time. 2 nearness or closeness in a series.

proxy ❶ n, pl **proxies** 1 person authorized to act on behalf of someone else. 2 authority to act on behalf of someone else.

prude n person who is excessively modest, prim, or proper. **prudish** *adj* **prudery** n.

prudent ❶ *adj* cautious, discreet, and sensible. **prudence** n **prudential** *adj* old-fashioned prudent.

prune¹ n dried plum.

prune² ❶ v 1 cut off dead parts or excessive branches from (a tree or plant). 2 shorten, reduce.

pry ❶ v **prying**, **pried** make an impertinent or uninvited inquiry into a private matter.

PS postscript.

psalm ❶ n sacred song. **psalmist** n writer of psalms.

pseudo- *combining form* false, pretending, or unauthentic, e.g. *pseudoclassical*.

pseudonym ❶ n fictitious name adopted esp. by an author.

psychic ❶ *adj* (also **psychical**) 1 having mental powers which cannot be explained by natural laws. 2 relating to the mind. ▷ n 3 person with psychic powers.

PTO please turn over.

——————————— THESAURUS ———————————

patch, section, zone 2 = **area**, business, capacity, concern, duty, field, function, line, responsibility, role, sphere

provision n 1 = **supplying**, catering, equipping, furnishing, providing 3 *Law* = **condition**, clause, demand, proviso, requirement, rider, stipulation, term ▷ pl 4 = **food**, comestibles, eatables, edibles, fare, foodstuffs, rations, stores, supplies, tucker (*Aust & NZ inf*), victuals

proviso n = **condition**, clause, qualification, requirement, rider, stipulation

provoke v 1 = **anger**, aggravate (*inf*), annoy, enrage, hassle (*inf*), incense, infuriate, irk, irritate, madden, rile 2 = **rouse**, bring about, cause, elicit, evoke, incite, induce, occasion, produce, promote, prompt, stir

prowess n 1 = **skill**, ability, accomplishment, adeptness, aptitude, excellence, expertise, genius, mastery, talent 2 = **bravery**, courage, daring, fearlessness, heroism,

mettle, valiance, valour

prowl v 1 = **move stealthily**, skulk, slink, sneak, stalk, steal

proximity n = **nearness**, closeness

proxy n 1 = **representative**, agent, delegate, deputy, factor, substitute

prudent *adj* **a** = **careful**, canny, cautious, discerning, judicious, shrewd, vigilant, wary **b** = **discreet**, politic **c** = **sensible**, wise

prune² v 1 = **cut**, clip, dock, shape, snip, trim 2 = **reduce**, shorten

pry v = **be inquisitive**, be nosy (*inf*), interfere, intrude, meddle, poke, snoop (*inf*)

psalm n = **hymn**, chant

pseudo- *combining form* = **false**, artificial, fake, imitation, mock, phoney or phony (*inf*), pretended, sham, spurious

pseudonym n = **false name**, alias, assumed name, incognito, nom de plume, pen name

psychic *adj* (also **psychical**) 1 = **supernatural**, mystic, occult ▷ *adj* 2 = **mental**, psychological, spiritual

pub ❶ *n* building with a bar licensed to sell alcoholic drinks.

puberty ❶ *n* beginning of sexual maturity. **pubertal** *adj*.

pubic *adj* of the lower abdomen, e.g. *pubic hair*.

public ❶ *adj* 1 of or concerning the people as a whole. 2 for use by everyone. 3 well-known. 4 performed or made openly. ▷ *n* 5 the community, people in general. **publicly** *adv* **public house** pub. **public relations** promotion of a favourable opinion towards an organization among the public. **public school** private fee-paying school in Britain. **public-spirited** *adj* having or showing an active interest in the good of the community.

publicity ❶ *n* 1 process or information used to arouse public attention. 2 public interest so aroused. **publicize** *v* advertise. **publicist** *n* person, esp. a press agent or journalist, who publicizes something.

publish ❶ *v* 1 produce and issue (printed matter) for sale. 2 announce formally or in public. **publication** *n* **publisher** *n*.

puck *n* small rubber disc used in ice hockey.

pucker ❶ *v* 1 gather into wrinkles. ▷ *n* 2 wrinkle or crease.

pudding ❶ *n* 1 dessert, esp. a cooked one served hot. 2 savoury dish with pastry or batter, e.g. *steak-and-kidney pudding*. 3 sausage-like mass of meat, e.g. *black pudding*.

puddle *n* small pool of water, esp. of rain.

puerile ❶ *adj* silly and childish.

puff ❶ *n* 1 (sound of) a short blast of breath, wind, etc. 2 act of inhaling cigarette smoke. ▷ *v* 3 blow or breathe in short quick draughts. 4 take draws at (a cigarette). 5 send out in small clouds. 6 swell. **out of puff** out of breath. **puffy** *adj*.

puffin *n* black-and-white sea bird with a brightly-coloured beak.

pug *n* small snub-nosed dog.

pugnacious *adj* ready and eager to fight. **pugnacity** *n*.

pull ❶ *v* 1 exert force on (an object) to move it towards the source of the force. 2 strain or stretch. 3 remove or extract. 4 attract. ▷ *n* 5 act of pulling. 6 force used in pulling. 7 act of taking in drink or smoke. 8 *informal* power, influence. **pull in** *v* 1 (of a vehicle or driver) draw in to the side of

---

THESAURUS

pub *n* = **tavern**, bar, inn, beer parlour (*Canad*), beverage room (*Canad*)

puberty *n* = **adolescence**, pubescence, teens

public *adj* 1 = **general**, civic, common, national, popular, social, state, universal, widespread 2 = **open**, accessible, communal, unrestricted 3 = **well-known**, important, prominent, respected 4 = **known**, acknowledged, obvious, open, overt, patent, plain *n* 5 = **people**, citizens, community, electorate, everyone, nation, populace, society

publicity *n* 1 = **advertising**, attention, boost, hype, plug (*inf*), press, promotion

publish *v* 1 = **put out**, issue, print, produce 2 = **announce**, advertise, broadcast, circulate, disclose, divulge, proclaim, publicize, reveal, spread

pucker *v* 1 = **wrinkle**, contract, crease, draw together, gather, knit, purse, screw up, tighten ▷ *n* 2 = **wrinkle**, crease, fold

pudding *n* 1 = **dessert**, afters (*Brit inf*), pud (*inf*), sweet

puerile *adj* = **childish**, babyish, foolish, immature, juvenile, silly, trivial

puff *n* 1 = **blast**, breath, draught, gust, whiff 2 = **smoke**, drag (*sl*), pull ▷ *v* 3 = **blow**, breathe, exhale, gasp, gulp, pant, wheeze 4 = **smoke**, drag (*sl*), draw, inhale, pull at *or* on, suck 6 = **swell**, bloat, dilate, distend, expand, inflate

pull *v* 1 = **draw**, drag, haul, jerk, tow, trail, tug, yank 2 = **strain**, dislocate, rip, sprain, stretch, tear, wrench 3 = **extract**, draw out, gather, pick, pluck, remove, take out, uproot 4 = **attract**, draw, entice, lure, magnetize ▷ *n* 5 = **tug**, jerk, twitch,

the road or stop. **2** reach a destination. **3** attract in large numbers. **4** *slang* arrest. **pull off** *v informal* succeed in performing. **pull out** *v* **1** (of a vehicle or driver) move away from the side of the road or move out to overtake. **2** (of a train) depart. **3** withdraw. **4** remove by pulling. **pull up 1** (of a vehicle or driver) stop. **2** remove by the roots. **3** reprimand.

pulley *n* wheel with a grooved rim in which a belt, chain, or piece of rope runs in order to lift weights by a downward pull.

pullover *n* sweater that is pulled on over the head.

pulmonary *adj* of the lungs.

pulp ❶ *n* **1** soft wet substance made from crushed or beaten matter. **2** flesh of a fruit. **3** poor-quality books and magazines. ▷ *v* **4** reduce to pulp.

pulpit *n* raised platform for a preacher.

pulse¹ ❶ *n* **1** regular beating of blood through the arteries at each heartbeat. **2** any regular beat or vibration. **pulsate** *v* throb, quiver. **pulsation** *n*.

pulse² *n* edible seed of a pod-bearing plant such as a bean or pea.

pulverize ❶ *v* **1** reduce to fine pieces. **2** destroy completely. **pulverization** *n*.

puma *n* large American wild cat with a greyish-brown coat.

pumice [**pumm**-iss] *n* light porous stone used for scouring and polishing.

pummel ❶ *v* **-melling, -melled** strike repeatedly with or as if with the fists.

pump¹ ❶ *n* **1** machine used to force a liquid or gas to move in a particular direction. ▷ *v* **2** raise or drive with a pump. **3** supply in large amounts. **4** operate or work in the manner of a pump. **5** extract information from.

pump² *n* light flat-soled shoe.

pumpkin *n* large round fruit with an orange rind, soft flesh, and many seeds.

pun ❶ *n* **1** use of words to exploit double meanings for humorous effect. ▷ *v* **punning, punned 2** make puns.

punch¹ ❶ *v* **1** strike at with a clenched fist. ▷ *n* **2** blow with a clenched fist. **3** *informal* effectiveness or vigour. **punchy** *adj* forceful. **punch-drunk** *adj* dazed by or as if by repeated blows to the head. **punch line** line of a joke or funny story that gives it its point. **punch-up** *n informal* fight or brawl.

punch² ❶ *n* **1** tool or machine for shaping, piercing, or engraving. ▷ *v* **2** pierce, cut, stamp, shape, or drive with a punch.

punch³ *n* drink made from a mixture of wine, spirits, fruit, sugar, and spices.

punctilious ❶ *adj* **1** paying great attention to correctness in etiquette. **2** careful about small details.

yank **7** = **puff**, drag (*sl*), inhalation **8** *Inf* = **influence**, clout (*inf*), mana (*NZ*), muscle, power, weight

pulp *n* **1** = **paste**, mash, mush **2** = **flesh**, soft part ▷ *v* **4** = **crush**, mash, pulverize, squash

pulse¹ *n* **1** = **beat**, beating, pulsation, throb, throbbing **2** = **vibration**, rhythm

pulverize *v* **1** = **crush**, granulate, grind, mill, pound **2** = **defeat**, annihilate, crush, demolish, destroy, flatten, smash, wreck

pummel *v* = **beat**, batter, hammer, pound, punch, strike, thump

pump¹ *v* **2** = **drive**, force, inject, push

3 = **supply**, pour, send **5** = **interrogate**, cross-examine, probe, quiz

pun *n* **1** = **play on words**, double entendre, quip, witticism

punch¹ *v* **1** = **hit**, belt (*inf*), bop (*inf*), box, pummel, smash, sock (*sl*), strike, swipe (*inf*) ▷ *n* **2** = **blow**, bop (*inf*), hit, jab, sock (*sl*), swipe (*inf*) **3** *Inf* = **effectiveness**, bite, drive, forcefulness, impact, verve, vigour

punch² *v* **2** = **pierce**, bore, cut, drill, perforate, prick, puncture, stamp

punctilious *adj* **1** = **formal**, proper **2** = **particular**, exact, finicky, fussy, meticulous, nice, precise, strict

punctual ● *adj* arriving or taking place at the correct time. **punctuality** *n* **punctually** *adv*.

punctuate ● *v* 1 put punctuation marks in. 2 interrupt at frequent intervals. **punctuation** *n* (use of) marks such as commas, colons, etc. in writing, to assist in making the sense clear.

puncture ● *n* 1 small hole made by a sharp object, esp. in a tyre. ▷ *v* 2 pierce a hole in.

pundit *n* expert who speaks publicly on a subject.

pungent ● *adj* having a strong sharp bitter flavour. **pungency** *n*.

punish ● *v* cause (someone) to suffer or undergo a penalty for some wrongdoing. **punishing** *adj* harsh or difficult. **punishment** *n*.

punitive [pew-nit-tiv] *adj* relating to punishment.

punnet *n* small basket for fruit.

punter ● *n* 1 person who bets. 2 any member of the public.

puny ● *adj* -nier, -niest small and feeble.

pup *n* young of certain animals, such as dogs and seals.

pupa *n*, *pl* -pae, -pas insect at the stage of development between a larva and an adult.

pupil¹ ● *n* person who is taught by a teacher.

pupil² *n* round dark opening in the centre of the eye.

puppet ● *n* 1 small doll or figure moved by strings or by the operator's hand. 2 person or country controlled by another. **puppeteer** *n*.

puppy *n*, *pl* -pies young dog.

purchase ● *v* 1 obtain by payment. ▷ *n* 2 thing that is bought. 3 act of buying. 4 leverage, grip. **purchaser** *n*.

pure ● *adj* 1 unmixed, untainted. 2 innocent. 3 complete, e.g. *pure delight*. 4 concerned with theory only, e.g. *pure mathematics*. **purely** *adv* **purity** *n* **purify** *v* -fying, -fied make or become pure. **purification** *n* **purist** *n* person obsessed with strict obedience to the traditions of a subject.

purée [pure-ray] *n* 1 pulp of cooked food. ▷ *v* -réeing, -réed 2 make into a purée.

purgatory *n* 1 place or state of temporary suffering. 2 (P-) RC Church place where

---

punctual *adj* = **on time**, exact, on the dot, precise, prompt, timely

punctuate *v* 2 = **interrupt**, break, intersperse, pepper, sprinkle

puncture *n* 1 **a** = **hole**, break, cut, damage, leak, nick, opening, slit **b** = **flat tyre**, flat ▷ *v* 2 = **pierce**, bore, cut, nick, penetrate, perforate, prick, rupture

pungent *adj* = **strong**, acrid, bitter, hot, peppery, piquant, sharp, sour, spicy, tart

punish *v* = **discipline**, castigate, chasten, chastise, correct, penalize, sentence

punitive *adj* = **retaliatory**, in reprisal, retaliative

punter *n* 1 = **gambler**, backer, better 2 = **person**, man in the street

puny *adj* = **feeble**, frail, little, sickly, stunted, tiny, weak

pupil¹ *n* = **learner**, beginner, disciple, novice, schoolboy or schoolgirl, student

puppet *n* 1 = **marionette**, doll 2 = **pawn**, cat's-paw, instrument, mouthpiece, stooge, tool

purchase *v* 1 = **buy**, acquire, come by, gain, get, obtain, pay for, pick up, score (*sl*) ▷ *n* 2 = **buy**, acquisition, asset, gain, investment, possession, property 4 = **grip**, foothold, hold, leverage, support

pure *adj* 1 **a** = **unmixed**, authentic, flawless, genuine, natural, real, simple, straight, unalloyed **b** = **clean**, germ-free, neat, sanitary, spotless, squeaky-clean, sterilized, uncontaminated, unpolluted, untainted, wholesome 2 = **innocent**, blameless, chaste, impeccable, modest, squeaky-clean, uncorrupted, unsullied, virginal, virtuous 3 = **complete**, absolute,

P

souls of the dead undergo punishment
for their sins before being admitted to
Heaven.
purge ❶ v **1** rid (a thing or place) of
(unwanted things or people). ▷ n
2 purging. **purgative** n, adj (medicine)
designed to cause defecation.
purl n **1** stitch made by knitting a plain
stitch backwards. ▷ v **2** knit in purl.
purloin ❶ v steal.
purple adj, n (of) a colour between red
and blue.
purport ❶ v **1** claim (to be or do
something). ▷ n **2** apparent meaning,
significance.
purpose ❶ n **1** reason for which something
is done or exists. **2** determination.
3 practical advantage or use, e.g. use
the time to good purpose. **purposely** adv
intentionally (also **on purpose**).
purr v **1** (of cats) make low vibrant sound,
usu. when pleased. ▷ n **2** this sound.
purse ❶ n **1** small bag for money. **2** US &
Canad handbag. **3** financial resources.
4 prize money. ▷ v **5** draw (one's lips)
together into a small round shape. **purser**
n ship's officer who keeps the accounts.

pursue ❶ v **1** chase. **2** follow (a goal).
3 engage in. **4** continue to discuss or ask
about (something). **pursuer** n **pursuit** n
1 pursuing. **2** occupation or pastime.
- **SPELLING TIP**
- The misspelling *persue* is very common,
- occurring in the Bank of English 52
- times. It should, of course, be spelt with
- a *u* in each half of the word, as in
- **pursuing** and **pursued**.
purvey ❶ v supply (provisions).
purveyor n.
pus n yellowish matter produced by
infected tissue.
push ❶ v **1** move or try to move by steady
force. **2** drive or spur (oneself or another
person) to do something. **3** informal sell
(drugs) illegally. ▷ n **4** act of pushing.
5 special effort. **the push** slang dismissal
from a job or relationship. **pusher** n
person who sells illegal drugs. **pushy** adj
too assertive or ambitious.
pushchair n folding chair on wheels
for a baby.
puss, pussy n, pl **pusses, pussies** informal
cat.
pustule n pimple containing pus.

——————————————————————————— THESAURUS —————————

outright, sheer, thorough, unmitigated,
unqualified, utter
purge v **1** = **get rid of**, do away with,
eradicate, expel, exterminate, remove,
wipe out ▷ n **2** = **removal**, ejection,
elimination, eradication, expulsion
purloin v = **steal**, appropriate, filch, nick
(sl, chiefly Brit), pilfer, pinch (inf), swipe
(sl), thieve
purport v **1** = **claim**, allege, assert, profess
▷ n **2** = **significance**, drift, gist, idea,
implication, import, meaning
purpose n **1 a** = **aim**, ambition, desire,
end, goal, hope, intention, object, plan,
wish **b** = **reason**, aim, idea, intention,
object, point **2** = **determination**,
firmness, persistence, resolution, resolve,
single-mindedness, tenacity, will
purse n **1** = **pouch**, money-bag, wallet

3 = **money**, exchequer, funds, lolly (Aust
& NZ inf), means, resources, treasury,
wealth ▷ v **5** = **pucker**, contract, pout,
press together, tighten
pursue v **1** = **follow**, chase, dog, hound,
hunt, hunt down, run after, shadow,
stalk, tail (inf), track **2** = **try for**, aim for,
desire, seek, strive for, work towards
3 = **engage in**, carry on, conduct, perform,
practise **4** = **continue**, carry on, keep on,
maintain, persevere in, persist in, proceed
purvey v = **supply**, cater, deal in, furnish,
provide, sell, trade in
push v **1** = **shove**, depress, drive, press,
propel, ram, thrust **2** = **urge**, encourage,
gee up, hurry, impel, incite, persuade,
press, spur ▷ n **4** = **shove**, butt, nudge,
thrust **5** = **drive**, ambition, dynamism,
energy, enterprise, go (inf), initiative,

put ❶ *v* **putting, put 1** cause to be (in a position, state, or place). **2** express. **3** throw (the shot) in the shot put. ▷ *n* **4** throw in putting the shot. **put across** *v* express successfully. **put off** *v* **1** postpone. **2** disconcert. **3** repel. **put up** *v* **1** erect. **2** accommodate. **3** nominate. **put-upon** *adj* taken advantage of.

putrid ❶ *adj* rotten and foul-smelling. **putrefy** *v* **-fying, -fied** rot and produce an offensive smell. **putrefaction** *n* **putrescent** *adj* rotting.

putt *Golf* ▷ *n* **1** stroke on the putting green to roll the ball into or near the hole. ▷ *v* **2** strike (the ball) in this way. **putter** *n* golf club for putting.

putty *n* paste used to fix glass into frames and fill cracks in woodwork.

puzzle ❶ *v* **1** perplex and confuse or be perplexed or confused. ▷ *n* **2** problem that cannot be easily solved. **3** toy, game, or question that requires skill or ingenuity to solve. **puzzlement** *n* **puzzling** *adj*.

PVC polyvinyl chloride: plastic material used in clothes etc.

pygmy *adj* very small. ▷ *n, pl* **-mies** very small person or thing.

pyjamas *pl n* loose-fitting trousers and top worn in bed.

pylon *n* steel tower-like structure supporting electrical cables.

pyramid *n* **1** solid figure with a flat base and triangular sides sloping upwards to a point. **2** building of this shape, esp. an ancient Egyptian one. **pyramidal** *adj*.

pyre *n* pile of wood for burning a corpse on.

pyromania *n* uncontrollable urge to set things on fire. **pyromaniac** *n*.

pyrotechnics *n* **1** art of making fireworks. **2** firework display. **pyrotechnic** *adj*.

python *n* large nonpoisonous snake that crushes its prey.

——— THESAURUS ———————————

vigour, vitality **the push** *Sl* = **dismissal**, discharge, one's cards (*inf*), the boot (*sl*), the sack (*inf*)

put *v* **1** = **place**, deposit, lay, position, rest, set, settle, situate **2** = **express**, phrase, state, utter, word **3** = **throw**, cast, fling, heave, hurl, lob, pitch, toss

putrid *adj* = **rotten**, bad, decayed, decomposed, off, putrefied, rancid, rotting, spoiled

puzzle *v* **1** = **perplex**, baffle, bewilder, confound, confuse, mystify, stump ▷ *n* **2, 3** = **problem**, conundrum, enigma, mystery, paradox, poser, question, riddle

P

Qq

QC Queen's Counsel.

QLD Queensland.

quack¹ v 1 (of a duck) utter a harsh guttural sound. 2 make a noise like a duck. ▷ n 3 sound made by a duck.

quack² ❶ n 1 unqualified person who claims medical knowledge. 2 *informal* doctor.

quadrangle n 1 (also **quad**) rectangular courtyard with buildings on all four sides. 2 geometric figure consisting of four points connected by four lines.

quadrant n 1 quarter of a circle. 2 quarter of a circle's circumference. 3 instrument for measuring the altitude of the stars.

quadrilateral adj 1 having four sides. ▷ n 2 polygon with four sides.

quadruped [**kwod**-roo-ped] n any animal with four legs.

quadruple v 1 multiply by four. ▷ adj 2 four times as much or as many.

3 consisting of four parts.

quadruplet n one of four offspring born at one birth.

quaff ❶ [**kwoff**] v drink heartily or in one draught.

quagmire ❶ [**kwog**-mire] n soft wet area of land.

quail¹ n small game bird of the partridge family.

quail² ❶ v shrink back with fear.

quaint ❶ adj attractively unusual, esp. in an old-fashioned style.

quake ❶ v 1 shake or tremble with or as if with fear. ▷ n 2 *informal* earthquake.

qualify ❶ v -fying, -fied 1 provide or be provided with the abilities necessary for a task, office, or duty. 2 moderate or restrict (a statement). **qualified** adj **qualification** n 1 official record of achievement in a course or examination. 2 quality or skill needed for a particular activity. 3 condition that modifies or limits. 4 act of qualifying.

quality ❶ n, pl -ties 1 degree or standard of excellence. 2 distinguishing characteristic or attribute. 3 basic character or nature of something. ▷ adj 4 excellent or superior. **qualitative** adj of or relating to quality.

qualm ❶ [**kwahm**] n 1 pang of conscience. 2 sudden sensation of misgiving.

———————————————— THESAURUS ————————————————

quack² n 1 = **charlatan**, fake, fraud, humbug, impostor, mountebank, phoney or phony (inf)

quaff v = **drink**, down, gulp, imbibe, swallow, swig (inf)

quagmire n = **bog**, fen, marsh, mire, morass, quicksand, slough, swamp, muskeg (Canad)

quail² v = **shrink**, blanch, blench, cower, cringe, falter, flinch, have cold feet (inf), recoil, shudder

quaint adj = **old-fashioned**, antiquated, old-world, picturesque

quake v 1 = **shake**, move, quiver, rock, shiver, shudder, tremble, vibrate

qualify v 1 = **certify**, empower, equip, fit, permit, prepare, ready, train 2 = **moderate**, diminish, ease, lessen, limit, reduce, regulate, restrain, restrict, soften, temper

quality n 1 = **excellence**, calibre, distinction, grade, merit, position, rank, standing, status 2 = **characteristic**, aspect, attribute, condition, feature, mark, property, trait 3 = **nature**, character, kind, make, sort

qualm n 1 = **compunction**, scruple, twinge or pang of conscience 2 = **misgiving**, anxiety, apprehension, disquiet, doubt, hesitation, uneasiness

q

quandary ❶ *n, pl* **-ries** difficult situation or dilemma.

quandong [**kwon**-dong] *n* **1** small Australian tree with edible fruit and nuts used in preserves. **2** Australian tree with pale timber.

quango *n, pl* **-gos** quasi-autonomous nongovernmental organization: any partly independent official body set up by a government.

quantify *v* **-fying, -fied** discover or express the quantity of. **quantifiable** *adj*.

quantity ❶ *n, pl* **-ties 1** specified or definite amount or number. **2** aspect of anything that can be measured, weighed, or counted. **quantitative** *adj* of or relating to quantity. **quantity surveyor** person who estimates the cost of the materials and labour necessary for a construction job.

quarantine *n* **1** period of isolation of people or animals to prevent the spread of disease. ▷ *v* **2** isolate in or as if in quarantine.

quarrel ❶ *n* **1** angry disagreement. **2** cause of dispute. ▷ *v* **-relling, -relled 3** have a disagreement or dispute. **quarrelsome** *adj*.

quarry¹ *n, pl* **-ries 1** place where stone is dug from the surface of the earth. ▷ *v* **-rying, -ried 2** extract (stone) from a quarry.

quarry² ❶ *n, pl* **-ries** person or animal that is being hunted.

quart *n* unit of liquid measure equal to two pints.

quarter ❶ *n* **1** one of four equal parts of something. **2** fourth part of a year. **3** *informal* unit of weight equal to 4 ounces. **4** region or district of a town or city. **5** *US* 25-cent piece. **6** mercy or pity, as shown towards a defeated opponent. ▷ *pl* **7** lodgings. ▷ *v* **8** divide into four equal parts. **9** billet or be billeted in lodgings. **quarterly** *adj* **1** occurring, due, or issued at intervals of three months. ▷ *n* **2** magazine issued every three months. ▷ *adv* **3** once every three months. **quarterdeck** *n Naut* rear part of the upper deck of a ship. **quarterfinal** *n* round before the semifinal in a competition. **quartermaster** *n* military officer responsible for accommodation, food, and equipment.

quartet *n* **1** group of four performers. **2** music for such a group.

quartz *n* hard glossy mineral.

quash ❶ *v* **1** annul or make void. **2** subdue forcefully and completely.

quasi- [**kway**-zie] *combining form* almost but not really, e.g. *quasi-religious; a quasi-scholar*.

quaver ❶ *v* **1** (of a voice) quiver or tremble. ▷ *n* **2** *Music* note half the length of a

quandary *n* = **difficulty**, cleft stick, dilemma, impasse, plight, predicament, puzzle, strait

quantity *n* **1** = **amount**, lot, number, part, sum, total **2** = **size**, bulk, capacity, extent, length, magnitude, mass, measure, volume

quarrel *n* **1** = **disagreement**, argument, brawl, breach, contention, controversy, dispute, dissension, feud, fight, row, squabble, tiff ▷ *v* **3** = **disagree**, argue, bicker, brawl, clash, differ, dispute, fall out (*inf*), fight, row, squabble

quarry² *n* = **prey**, aim, game, goal, objective, prize, victim

quarter *n* **4** = **district**, area, locality, neighbourhood, part, place, province, region, side, zone **6** = **mercy**, clemency, compassion, forgiveness, leniency, pity ▷ *pl* **7** = **lodgings**, abode, barracks, billet, chambers, dwelling, habitation, residence, rooms ▷ *v* **9** = **accommodate**, billet, board, house, lodge, place, post, station

quash *v* **1** = **annul**, cancel, invalidate, overrule, overthrow, rescind, reverse, revoke **2** = **suppress**, beat, crush, overthrow, put down, quell, repress, squash, subdue

quasi- *combining form* = **pseudo-**, apparent, seeming, semi-, so-called, would-be

quaver *v* **1** = **tremble**, flicker, flutter, quake, quiver, shake, vibrate, waver ▷ *n*

q

crotchet. **3** tremulous sound or note.

quay [kee] *n* wharf built parallel to the shore.

queasy ❶ *adj* **-sier, -siest 1** having the feeling that one is about to vomit. **2** feeling or causing uneasiness. **queasiness** *n*.

queen ❶ *n* **1** female sovereign who is the official ruler or head of state. **2** wife of a king. **3** woman, place, or thing considered to be the best of her or its kind. **4** *slang* effeminate male homosexual. **5** only fertile female in a colony of bees, wasps, or ants. **6** the most powerful piece in chess. **queenly** *adj* **Queen's Counsel** barrister or advocate appointed Counsel to the Crown.

queer ❶ *adj* **1** not normal or usual. **2** faint, giddy, or queasy. **3** *offens* homosexual. ▷ *n* **4** *offens* homosexual. **queer someone's pitch** *informal* spoil someone's chances of something.

quell ❶ *v* **1** suppress. **2** overcome.

quench ❶ *v* **1** satisfy (one's thirst). **2** put out or extinguish.

querulous ❶ [kwer-yoo-luss] *adj* complaining or whining.

query ❶ *n, pl* **-ries 1** question, esp. one raising doubt. **2** question mark. ▷ *v* **-rying, -ried 3** express uncertainty, doubt, or an objection concerning (something).

quest ❶ *n* **1** long and difficult search. ▷ *v* **2** (foll. by *for* or *after*) go in search of.

question ❶ *n* **1** form of words addressed to a person in order to obtain an answer. **2** point at issue. **3** difficulty or uncertainty. ▷ *v* **4** put a question or questions to (a person). **5** express uncertainty about. **in question** under discussion. **out of the question** impossible. **questionable** *adj* of disputable value or authority. **questionnaire** *n* set of questions on a form, used to collect information from people. **question mark** punctuation mark (?) written at the end of questions.

● **SPELLING TIP**
● There are 28 occurrences of the
● misspelling *questionaire* (with only one
● n), in the Bank of English. The correct
● spelling, **questionnaire**, has two ns,
● and appears in the Bank of English over
● 3000 times.

———————————————— THESAURUS ————————————————

3 = **trembling**, quiver, shake, tremble, tremor, vibration

queasy *adj* **1** = **sick**, bilious, green around the gills (*inf*), ill, nauseated, off colour, squeamish, upset **2** = **uneasy**, anxious, fidgety, ill at ease, restless, troubled, uncertain, worried

queen *n* **1** = **sovereign**, consort, monarch, ruler **3** = **ideal**, model, star

queer *adj* **1** = **strange**, abnormal, curious, droll, extraordinary, funny, munted (*NZ sl*), odd, peculiar, uncommon, unusual, weird **2** = **faint**, dizzy, giddy, light-headed, queasy

quell *v* **1, 2** = **suppress**, conquer, crush, defeat, overcome, overpower, put down, quash, subdue, vanquish

quench *v* **1** = **satisfy**, allay, appease, sate, satiate, slake **2** = **put out**, crush, douse, extinguish, smother, stifle, suppress

querulous *adj* = **complaining**, captious,

carping, critical, discontented, dissatisfied, fault-finding, grumbling, peevish, whining

query *n* **1** = **question**, doubt, inquiry, objection, problem, suspicion ▷ *v*
3 = **doubt**, challenge, disbelieve, dispute, distrust, mistrust, question, suspect

quest *n* **1** = **search**, adventure, crusade, enterprise, expedition, fossick (*Aust & NZ*), hunt, journey, mission

question *n* **2** = **issue**, motion, point, point at issue, proposal, proposition, subject, theme, topic **3** = **difficulty**, argument, contention, controversy, dispute, doubt, problem, query ▷ *v* **4** = **ask**, cross-examine, examine, inquire, interrogate, interview, probe, quiz **5** = **dispute**, challenge, disbelieve, doubt, mistrust, oppose, query, suspect **in question** = **under discussion**, at issue, in doubt, open to debate **out of the question** = **impossible**, inconceivable, unthinkable

q

queue ❶ n 1 line of people or vehicles waiting for something. ▷ v **queuing** or **queueing**, **queued** 2 (often foll. by *up*) form or remain in a line while waiting.

quibble ❶ v 1 make trivial objections. ▷ n 2 trivial objection.

quiche [**keesh**] n savoury flan with an egg custard filling to which vegetables etc. are added.

quick ❶ adj 1 speedy, fast. 2 lasting or taking a short time. 3 alert and responsive. 4 easily excited or aroused. ▷ n 5 area of sensitive flesh under a nail. ▷ adv 6 *informal* in a rapid manner. **cut someone to the quick** hurt someone's feelings deeply. **quickly** adv **quicken** v 1 make or become faster. 2 make or become more lively. **quicksand** n deep mass of loose wet sand that sucks anything on top of it into it. **quicksilver** n mercury. **quickstep** n fast modern ballroom dance.

quiet ❶ adj 1 with little noise. 2 calm or tranquil. 3 untroubled. ▷ n 4 quietness. ▷ v 5 make or become quiet. **on the quiet** without other people knowing, secretly. **quietly** adv **quietness** n **quieten** v (often foll. by *down*) make or become quiet.

quiff n prominent tuft of hair brushed up above the forehead.

quill n 1 pen made from the feather of a bird's wing or tail. 2 stiff hollow spine of a hedgehog or porcupine.

quilt ❶ n padded covering for a bed. **quilted** adj consisting of two layers of fabric with a layer of soft material between them.

quinine n bitter drug used as a tonic and formerly to treat malaria.

quintessence ❶ n most perfect representation of a quality or state. **quintessential** adj.

quintet n 1 group of five performers. 2 music for such a group.

quintuplet n one of five offspring born at one birth.

quip ❶ n 1 witty saying. ▷ v **quipping**, **quipped** 2 make a quip.

quirk ❶ n 1 peculiarity of character. 2 unexpected twist or turn, e.g. *a quirk of fate*. **quirky** adj.

quit ❶ v **quitting**, **quit** 1 stop (doing something). 2 give up (a job). 3 depart from. **quitter** n person who lacks perseverance. **quits** adj *informal* on an equal footing.

quite ❶ adv 1 somewhat, e.g. *she's quite pretty.* 2 absolutely, e.g. *you're quite right.*

——— **THESAURUS** ———

queue n 1 = **line**, chain, file, sequence, series, string, train

quibble v 1 = **split hairs**, carp, cavil ▷ n 2 = **objection**, cavil, complaint, criticism, nicety, niggle

quick adj 1 = **fast**, brisk, express, fleet, hasty, rapid, speedy, swift 2 = **brief**, cursory, hasty, hurried, perfunctory 3 = **intelligent**, acute, alert, astute, bright (*inf*), clever, perceptive, quick-witted, sharp, shrewd, smart 4 = **excitable**, irascible, irritable, passionate, testy, touchy

quiet adj 1 = **silent**, hushed, inaudible, low, noiseless, peaceful, soft, soundless 2, 3 = **calm**, mild, peaceful, placid, restful, serene, smooth, tranquil ▷ n 4 = **peace**, calmness, ease, quietness, repose, rest, serenity, silence, stillness, tranquillity

quilt n = **bedspread**, continental quilt, counterpane, coverlet, duvet, eiderdown

quintessence n = **essence**, distillation, soul, spirit

quip n 1 = **joke**, gibe, jest, pleasantry, retort, riposte, sally, wisecrack (*inf*), witticism

quirk n 1 = **peculiarity**, aberration, characteristic, eccentricity, foible, habit, idiosyncrasy, kink, mannerism, oddity, trait

quit v 1 = **stop**, abandon, cease, discontinue, drop, end, give up, halt 2 = **resign**, abdicate, go, leave, pull out, retire, step down (*inf*) 3 = **depart**, go, leave, pull out

quite adv 1 = **somewhat**, fairly, moderately, rather, reasonably, relatively

q

3 in actuality, truly. ▷ *interj* **4** expression of agreement.

quiver¹ ❶ *v* **1** shake with a tremulous movement. ▷ *n* **2** shaking or trembling.

quiver² *n* case for arrows.

quiz ❶ *n, pl* **quizzes 1** entertainment in which the knowledge of the players is tested by a series of questions. ▷ *v* **quizzing, quizzed 2** investigate by close questioning. **quizzical** *adj* questioning and mocking. **quizzically** *adv*.

quoit *n* **1** large ring used in the game of quoits. ▷ *pl* **2** game in which quoits are tossed at a stake in the ground in attempts to encircle it.

quorum *n* minimum number of people required to be present at a meeting before

any transactions can take place. **quorate** *adj* having or being a quorum.

quota ❶ *n* **1** share that is due from, due to, or allocated to a group or person. **2** prescribed number or quantity allowed, required, or admitted.

quote ❶ *v* **1** repeat (words) exactly from (an earlier work, speech, or conversation). **2** state (a price) for goods or a job of work. ▷ *n* **3** *informal* quotation. **quotable** *adj* **quotation** *n* **1** written or spoken passage repeated exactly in a later work, speech, or conversation. **2** act of quoting. **3** estimate of costs submitted by a contractor to a prospective client.

quotient *n* result of the division of one number or quantity by another.

───────────────────── THESAURUS ─────

2 = **absolutely**, completely, entirely, fully, perfectly, totally, wholly **3** = **truly**, in fact, in reality, in truth, really

quiver¹ *v* **1** = **shake**, oscillate, quake, quaver, shiver, shudder, tremble, vibrate ▷ *n* **2** = **shake**, oscillation, shiver, shudder, tremble, tremor, vibration

quiz *n* **1** = **examination**, investigation,

questioning, test ▷ *v* **2** = **question**, ask, examine, interrogate, investigate

quota *n* **1** = **share**, allowance, assignment, part, portion, ration, slice, whack (*inf*)

quote *v* **1** = **repeat**, cite, detail, instance, name, recall, recite, recollect, refer to

Rr

R 1 Queen. **2** King. **3** River.

rabbi [**rab**-bye] *n*, *pl* **-bis** Jewish spiritual leader. **rabbinical** *adj*.

rabbit *n* small burrowing mammal with long ears. **rabbit on** *v* **rabbiting, rabbited** *informal* talk too much.

rabble ❶ *n* disorderly crowd of noisy people.

rabid ❶ *adj* **1** fanatical. **2** having rabies.

rabies [**ray**-beez] *n* usu. fatal viral disease transmitted by dogs and certain other animals.

raccoon *n* small N American mammal with a long striped tail.

race¹ ❶ *n* **1** contest of speed. ▷ *pl* **2** meeting for horse racing. ▷ *v* **3** compete with in a race. **4** run swiftly. **5** (of an engine) run faster than normal. **racer** *n* **racecourse** *n* **racehorse** *n* **racetrack** *n*.

race² ❶ *n* group of people of common ancestry with distinguishing physical features, such as skin colour. **racial** *adj* **racism, racialism** *n* hostile attitude or behaviour to members of other races,

based on a belief in the innate superiority of one's own race. **racist, racialist** *adj*, *n*.

rack ❶ *n* **1** framework for holding particular articles, such as coats or luggage. **2** straight bar with teeth on its edge, to work with a cogwheel. **3** *Hist* instrument of torture that stretched the victim's body. ▷ *v* **4** cause great suffering to. **rack one's brains** try very hard to remember.

racket¹ ❶ *n* **1** noisy disturbance. **2** occupation by which money is made illegally.

racket², racquet *n* bat with strings stretched in an oval frame, used in tennis etc. **rackets** *n* ball game played in a paved walled court.

raconteur [rak-on-**tur**] *n* skilled storyteller.

racy ❶ *adj* **racier, raciest 1** slightly shocking. **2** spirited or lively.

radar *n* device for tracking distant objects by bouncing high-frequency radio pulses off them.

radial *adj* **1** spreading out from a common central point. **2** of a radius. **3** (also **radial-ply**) (of a tyre) having flexible sides strengthened with radial cords.

radiate ❶ *v* **1** spread out from a centre. **2** emit or be emitted as radiation. **radiator** *n* **1** arrangement of pipes containing hot water or steam to heat a room. **2** tubes containing water as cooling apparatus for a car engine.

r

THESAURUS

---

rabble *n* = **mob**, canaille, crowd, herd, horde, swarm, throng

rabid *adj* **1** = **fanatical**, extreme, fervent, irrational, narrow-minded, zealous **2** = **mad**, hydrophobic

race¹ *n* **1** = **contest**, chase, competition, dash, pursuit, rivalry ▷ *v* **3** = **compete**, contest, run **4** = **run**, career, dart, dash, fly, gallop, hurry, speed, tear, zoom

race² *n* = **people**, blood, folk, nation, stock, tribe, type

rack *n* **1** = **frame**, framework, stand, structure ▷ *v* **4** = **torture**, afflict, agonize,

crucify, harrow, oppress, pain, torment

racket¹ *n* **1** = **noise**, clamour, din, disturbance, fuss, outcry, pandemonium, row **2** = **fraud**, scheme

racy *adj* **1** = **risqué**, bawdy, blue, naughty, near the knuckle (*inf*), smutty, suggestive **2** = **lively**, animated, energetic, entertaining, exciting, sparkling, spirited

radiate *v* **1** = **spread out**, branch out, diverge, issue **2** = **emit**, diffuse, give off *or* out, pour, scatter, send out, shed, spread

radical ❶ adj 1 fundamental. 2 thorough. 3 advocating fundamental change. ▷ n 4 person advocating fundamental (political) change. 5 number expressed as the root of another. **radically** adv **radicalism** n.

radio n, pl **-dios** 1 use of electromagnetic waves for broadcasting, communication, etc. 2 device for receiving and amplifying radio signals. 3 sound broadcasting. ▷ v 4 transmit (a message) by radio.

radioactive adj emitting radiation as a result of nuclear decay. **radioactivity** n.

radiography [ray-dee-**og**-ra-fee] n production of an image on a film or plate by radiation. **radiographer** n.

radiology [ray-dee-**ol**-a-jee] n science of using x-rays in medicine. **radiologist** n.

radiotherapy n treatment of disease, esp. cancer, by radiation. **radiotherapist** n.

radish n small hot-flavoured root vegetable eaten raw in salads.

radium n Chem radioactive metallic element.

radius n, pl **radii, radiuses** 1 (length of) a straight line from the centre to the circumference of a circle. 2 outer of two bones in the forearm.

RAF Royal Air Force.

raffia n prepared palm fibre for weaving mats etc.

raffle ❶ n 1 lottery with goods as prizes. ▷ v 2 offer as a prize in a raffle.

raft n floating platform of logs, planks, etc.

rafter n one of the main beams of a roof.

rag n 1 fragment of cloth. 2 informal newspaper. ▷ pl 3 tattered clothing. **from rags to riches** from being extremely poor to being extremely wealthy. **ragged** [**rag**-gid] adj 1 dressed in shabby or torn clothes. 2 torn. 3 lacking smoothness. **ragbag** n confused assortment, jumble.

ragamuffin ❶ n ragged dirty child.

rage ❶ n 1 violent anger or passion. ▷ v 2 speak or act with fury. 3 proceed violently and without check. **all the rage** very popular.

raglan adj (of a sleeve) joined to a garment by diagonal seams from the neck to the underarm.

raid ❶ n 1 sudden surprise attack or search. ▷ v 2 make a raid on. **raider** n.

rail¹ n 1 horizontal bar, esp. as part of a fence or track. 2 railway. **go off the rails** start behaving eccentrically or improperly. **railing** n fence made of rails supported by posts. **railcard** n card which pensioners, young people, etc. can buy, entitling them to cheaper rail travel. **railroad** n 1 US railway. ▷ v 2 informal force (a person) into an action with haste or by unfair means. **railway** n 1 track of iron rails on which trains run. 2 company operating a railway.

rail² v (foll. by at) (against) complain bitterly or loudly. **raillery** n teasing or joking.

rain ❶ n 1 water falling in drops from the

━━━━━━━━━━━━━━━━━━━━━━━━━ THESAURUS ━━━━━━━━━━━

radical adj 1 = **fundamental**, basic, deep-seated, innate, natural, profound 2 = **extreme**, complete, drastic, entire, severe, sweeping, thorough 3 = **revolutionary**, extremist, fanatical ▷ n 4 = **extremist**, fanatic, militant, revolutionary

raffle n 1 = **draw**, lottery, sweep, sweepstake

ragamuffin n = **urchin**, guttersnipe

rage n 1 = **fury**, anger, frenzy, ire, madness, passion, rampage, wrath v 2 = **be**

furious, blow one's top, blow up (inf), fly off the handle (inf), fume, go ballistic (sl, chiefly US), go up the wall (sl), lose it (inf), lose one's temper, lose the plot (inf), seethe, storm

raid n 1 = **attack**, foray, incursion, inroad, invasion, sally, sortie ▷ v 2 = **attack**, assault, foray, invade, pillage, plunder, sack

rain n 1 = **rainfall**, cloudburst, deluge, downpour, drizzle, fall, raindrops, showers ▷ v 2 = **pour**, bucket down (inf),

clouds. ▷ v **2** fall or pour down as rain.
3 fall rapidly and in large quantities. **rainy**
adj **rainbow** n arch of colours in the sky.
rainfall n amount of rain. **rainforest** n
dense forest in the tropics.

raise ❶ v **1** lift up. **2** set upright. **3** increase
in amount or intensity. **4** collect or levy.
5 bring up (a family). **6** put forward for
consideration. **7** build. **8** end, e.g. *raise a
siege*.

raisin n dried grape.

rake[1] ❶ n **1** tool with a long handle and a
crosspiece with teeth, used for smoothing
earth or gathering leaves, hay, etc. ▷ v
2 gather or smooth with a rake. **3** search
(through). **4** sweep (with gunfire). **rake it
in** *informal* make a large amount of money.
rake up v revive memories of (a forgotten
unpleasant event).

rake[2] n dissolute or immoral man.

rakish ❶ adj dashing or jaunty.

rally ❶ n, pl **-lies 1** large gathering of
people for a meeting. **2** marked recovery

of strength. **3** *Tennis etc.* lively exchange
of strokes. **4** car-driving competition
on public roads. ▷ v **-lying**, **-lied 5** bring
or come together after dispersal or for
a common cause. **6** regain health or
strength, revive.

ram ❶ n **1** male sheep. **2** hydraulic
machine. ▷ v **ramming**, **rammed 3** strike
against with force. **4** force or drive.

ramble ❶ v **1** walk without a definite
route. **2** talk incoherently. ▷ n **3** walk, esp.
in the country. **rambler** n **1** person who
rambles. **2** climbing rose.

ramp ❶ n slope joining two level surfaces.

rampage ❶ v dash about violently. **on
the rampage** behaving violently or
destructively.

rampant ❶ adj **1** growing or spreading
uncontrollably. **2** (of a heraldic beast) on
its hind legs.

rampart ❶ n mound or wall for defence.

ramshackle ❶ adj tumbledown, rickety,
or makeshift.

come down in buckets (*inf*), drizzle, pelt
(down), teem **3** = **fall**, deposit, drop,
shower, sprinkle

raise v **1** = **lift**, elevate, heave, hoist, rear,
uplift **3** = **increase**, advance, amplify,
boost, enhance, enlarge, heighten,
inflate, intensify, magnify, strengthen
4 = **collect**, assemble, form, gather,
mass, obtain, rally, recruit **5** = **bring up**,
develop, nurture, rear **6** = **put forward**,
advance, broach, introduce, moot,
suggest **7** = **build**, construct, erect,
put up

rake[1] v **2** = **gather**, collect, remove
3 = **search**, comb, scour, scrutinize

rake[2] n = **libertine**, debauchee, lecher,
playboy, roué, swinger (*sl*)

rakish adj = **dashing**, dapper, debonair,
devil-may-care, jaunty, natty (*inf*), raffish,
smart

rally n **1** = **gathering**, assembly, congress,
convention, meeting **2** = **recovery**,
improvement, recuperation, revival ▷ v

5 = **reassemble**, regroup, reorganize,
unite **6** = **recover**, get better, improve,
recuperate, revive

ram v **3** = **hit**, butt, crash, dash, drive, force,
impact, smash **4** = **cram**, crowd, force,
jam, stuff, thrust

ramble v **1** = **walk**, range, roam, rove,
saunter, stray, stroll, wander **3** = **babble**,
rabbit (on) (*Brit inf*), waffle (*inf, chiefly
Brit*), witter on (*inf*) ▷ n **3** = **walk**, hike,
roaming, roving, saunter, stroll, tour

ramp n = **slope**, gradient, incline, rise

rampage v = **go berserk**, rage, run amok,
run riot, storm ▷ n **on the rampage**
= **berserk**, amok, out of control, raging,
riotous, violent, wild

rampant adj **1** = **widespread**, prevalent,
profuse, rife, spreading like wildfire,
unchecked, uncontrolled, unrestrained
2 = **upright**, erect, rearing, standing

rampart n = **defence**, bastion, bulwark,
fence, fortification, wall

ramshackle adj = **rickety**, crumbling,

r

ran v past tense of RUN.

ranch n large cattle farm in the American West. **rancher** n.

rancid ❶ adj (of butter, bacon, etc.) stale and having an offensive smell. **rancidity** n.

rancour ❶ n deep bitter hate. **rancorous** adj.

random ❶ adj made or done by chance or without plan. **at random** haphazard(ly).

randy ❶ adj **randier**, **randiest** informal sexually aroused.

rang v past tense of RING¹.

range ❶ n 1 limits of effectiveness or variation. 2 distance that a missile or plane can travel. 3 distance of a mark shot at. 4 whole set of related things. 5 chain of mountains. 6 place for shooting practice or rocket testing. 7 kitchen stove. ▷ v 8 vary between one point and another. 9 cover or extend over. 10 roam. **ranger** n official in charge of a nature reserve etc.

rank¹ ❶ n 1 relative place or position. 2 status. 3 social class. 4 row or line. ▷ v 5 have a specific rank or position. 6 arrange in rows or lines. **rank and file** ordinary people or members. **the ranks** common soldiers.

rank² ❶ adj 1 complete or absolute, e.g. rank favouritism. 2 smelling offensively strong. 3 growing too thickly.

rankle ❶ v continue to cause resentment or bitterness.

ransack ❶ v 1 search thoroughly. 2 pillage, plunder.

ransom ❶ n money demanded in return for the release of someone who has been kidnapped.

rant ❶ v talk in a loud and excited way.

rap ❶ v **rapping**, **rapped** 1 hit with a sharp quick blow. 2 utter (a command) abruptly. 3 perform a rhythmic monologue with musical backing. ▷ n 4 quick sharp blow. 5 rhythmic monologue performed to music. **take**

──────────── THESAURUS ────────────

decrepit, derelict, flimsy, shaky, tumbledown, unsafe, unsteady

rancid adj = **rotten**, bad, fetid, foul, off, putrid, rank, sour, stale, strong-smelling, tainted

rancour n = **hatred**, animosity, bad blood, bitterness, hate, ill feeling, ill will

random adj = **chance**, accidental, adventitious, casual, fortuitous, haphazard, hit or miss, incidental **at random** = **haphazardly**, arbitrarily, by chance, randomly, unsystematically, willy-nilly

randy adj Inf = **lustful**, amorous, aroused, horny (sl), hot, lascivious, turned-on (sl)

range n 1 = **limits**, area, bounds, orbit, province, radius, reach, scope, sphere 4 = **series**, assortment, collection, gamut, lot, selection, variety ▷ v 8 = **vary** 9 = **extend**, reach, run, stretch 10 = **roam**, ramble, rove, traverse, wander

rank¹ n 1, 2 = **status**, caste, class, degree,

division, grade, level, order, position, sort, type 3 = **class**, caste 4 = **row**, column, file, group, line, range, series, tier ▷ v 6 = **arrange**, align, array, dispose, line up, order, sort **rank and file** = **general public**, majority, mass, masses

rank² adj 1 = **absolute**, arrant, blatant, complete, downright, flagrant, gross, sheer, thorough, total, utter 2 = **foul**, bad, disgusting, noisome, noxious, offensive, rancid, revolting, stinking 3 = **abundant**, dense, lush, luxuriant, profuse

rankle v = **annoy**, anger, gall, get on one's nerves (inf), irk, irritate, rile

ransack v 1 = **search**, comb, explore, go through, rummage, scour, turn inside out 2 = **plunder**, loot, pillage, raid, strip

ransom n = **payment**, money, payoff, price

rant v = **shout**, cry, declaim, rave, roar, yell

rap v 1 = **hit**, crack, knock, strike, tap ▷ n 4 = **blow**, clout (inf), crack, knock, tap

the rap *slang* suffer punishment for something whether guilty or not. **rapper** *n*.

rapacious ❶ *adj* greedy or grasping.

rape¹ ❶ *v* **1** force to submit to sexual intercourse. ▷ *n* **2** act of raping. **3** any violation or abuse. **rapist** *n*.

rape² *n* plant with oil-yielding seeds, also used as fodder.

rapid ❶ *adj* quick, swift. **rapids** *pl n* part of a river with a fast turbulent current. **rapidity** *n*.

rapier [**ray**-pyer] *n* fine-bladed sword.

rapport ❶ [rap-**pore**] *n* harmony or agreement.

rapt ❶ *adj* engrossed or spellbound. **rapture** *n* ecstasy. **rapturous** *adj*.

rare¹ ❶ *adj* **1** uncommon. **2** infrequent. **3** of uncommonly high quality. **4** (of air at high altitudes) having low density, thin. **rarely** *adv* seldom. **rarity** *n*.

rare² ❶ *adj* (of meat) lightly cooked.

raring ❶ *adj* **raring to** enthusiastic, willing, or ready to.

rascal ❶ *n* **1** rogue. **2** naughty (young) person. **rascally** *adj*.

rash¹ ❶ *adj* hasty, reckless, or incautious. **rashly** *adv*.

rash² ❶ *n* **1** eruption of spots or patches on the skin. **2** outbreak of (unpleasant) occurrences.

rasher *n* thin slice of bacon.

rasp *n* **1** harsh grating noise. **2** coarse file. ▷ *v* **3** speak in a grating voice. **4** make a scraping noise.

raspberry *n* **1** red juicy edible berry. **2** *informal* spluttering noise made with the tongue and lips, to show contempt.

Rastafarian *n, adj* (member) of a religion originating in Jamaica and regarding Haile Selassie as God (also **Rasta**).

rat *n* **1** small rodent. **2** *informal* contemptible person, esp. a deserter or informer. ▷ *v* **ratting, ratted 3** *informal* inform (on). **4** hunt rats. **ratty** *adj* *informal* bad-tempered, irritable. **rat race** continual hectic competitive activity.

ratchet *n* set of teeth on a bar or wheel allowing motion in one direction only.

rate ❶ *n* **1** degree of speed or progress. **2** proportion between two things. **3** charge. ▷ *pl* **4** local tax on business. ▷ *v*

rapacious *adj* = **greedy**, avaricious, grasping, insatiable, predatory, preying, voracious

rape¹ *v* **1** = **sexually assault**, abuse, force, outrage, ravish, violate ▷ *n* **2** = **sexual assault**, outrage, ravishment, violation **3** = **desecration**, abuse, defilement, violation

rapid *adj* = **quick**, brisk, express, fast, hasty, hurried, prompt, speedy, swift

rapport *n* = **bond**, affinity, empathy, harmony, link, relationship, sympathy, tie, understanding

rapt *adj* = **spellbound**, absorbed, engrossed, enthralled, entranced, fascinated, gripped

rare¹ *adj* **1** = **uncommon**, few, infrequent, scarce, singular, sparse, strange, unusual **2** = **infrequent**, few, uncommon, unusual **3** = **superb**, choice, excellent, fine, great,

peerless, superlative

rare² *adj* = **underdone**, bloody, half-cooked, half-raw, undercooked

raring *adj* = **eager**, desperate, enthusiastic, impatient, keen, longing, ready

rascal *n* **1** = **rogue**, blackguard, devil, good-for-nothing, ne'er-do-well, scoundrel, villain **2** = **imp**, scamp

rash¹ *adj* = **reckless**, careless, foolhardy, hasty, heedless, ill-advised, impetuous, imprudent, impulsive, incautious

rash² *n* **1** = **outbreak**, eruption **2** = **spate**, flood, outbreak, plague, series, wave

rate *n* **1** = **speed**, pace, tempo, velocity **2** = **degree**, proportion, ratio, scale, standard **3** = **charge**, cost, fee, figure, price ▷ *v* **5** = **evaluate**, consider, count, estimate, grade, measure, rank, reckon, value **6** = **estimate**, evaluate, value, merit **at any rate** = **in any case**, anyhow,

r

5 consider or value. **6** estimate the value of. **at any rate** in any case. **rateable** *adj* **1** able to be rated. **2** (of property) liable to payment of rates.

rather ❶ *adv* **1** to some extent. **2** more truly or appropriately. **3** more willingly.

ratify ❶ *v* **-fying, -fied** give formal approval to. **ratification** *n*.

rating ❶ *n* **1** valuation or assessment. **2** classification. **3** noncommissioned sailor. ▷ *pl* **4** size of the audience for a TV programme.

ratio ❶ *n, pl* **-tios** relationship between two numbers or amounts expressed as a proportion.

ration ❶ *n* **1** fixed allowance of food etc. ▷ *v* **2** limit to a certain amount per person.

rational ❶ *adj* **1** reasonable, sensible. **2** capable of reasoning. **rationally** *adv* **rationality** *n* **rationale** [rash-a-**nahl**] *n* reason for an action or decision. **rationalism** *n* philosophy that regards reason as the only basis for beliefs or actions. **rationalist** *n* **rationalize** *v* **1** justify by plausible reasoning. **2** reorganize to improve efficiency or profitability. **rationalization** *n*.

rattle ❶ *v* **1** give out a succession of short sharp sounds. **2** shake briskly causing sharp sounds. **3** *informal* confuse or fluster. ▷ *n* **4** short sharp sound. **5** instrument for making such a sound. **rattlesnake** *n* poisonous snake with loose horny segments on the tail that make a rattling sound.

raucous ❶ *adj* hoarse or harsh.

raunchy ❶ *adj* **-chier, -chiest** *slang* earthy, sexy.

ravage ❶ *v* cause extensive damage to. **ravages** *pl n* damaging effects.

rave ❶ *v* **1** talk wildly or with enthusiasm. ▷ *n* **2** *slang* large-scale party with electronic dance music. **raving** *adj* **1** delirious. **2** *informal* exceptional, e.g. *a raving beauty.*

raven *n* **1** black bird like a large crow. ▷ *adj* **2** (of hair) shiny black.

ravenous ❶ *adj* very hungry.

ravine ❶ [rav-**veen**] *n* narrow steep-sided valley worn by a stream.

ravioli *pl n* small squares of pasta with a savoury filling.

ravish ❶ *v* **1** enrapture. **2** *lit* rape. **ravishing** *adj* lovely or entrancing.

━━━━━━━━━━━━━━━━━━━━━ THESAURUS ━━━━━━━━

anyway, at all events

rather *adv* **1** = **to some extent**, a little, fairly, moderately, quite, relatively, somewhat, to some degree **3** = **preferably**, more readily, more willingly, sooner

ratify *v* = **approve**, affirm, authorize, confirm, endorse, establish, sanction, uphold

rating *n* **2** = **position**, class, degree, grade, order, placing, rank, rate, status

ratio *n* = **proportion**, fraction, percentage, rate, relation

ration *n* **1** = **allowance**, allotment, helping, measure, part, portion, quota, share ▷ *v* **2** = **limit**, budget, control, restrict

rational *adj* **1, 2** = **sensible**, intelligent, logical, lucid, realistic, reasonable, sane,

sound, wise

rattle *v* **1** = **clatter**, bang, jangle **2** = **shake**, bounce, jar, jolt, vibrate **3** *Inf* = **fluster**, disconcert, disturb, faze, perturb, shake, upset

raucous *adj* = **harsh**, grating, hoarse, loud, noisy, rough, strident

raunchy *adj Sl* = **sexy**, coarse, earthy, lusty, sexual, steamy (*inf*)

ravage *v* = **destroy**, demolish, despoil, devastate, lay waste, ransack, ruin, spoil

rave *v* **1 a** = **rant**, babble, be delirious, rage, roar **b** = **enthuse**, be mad about (*inf*), be wild about (*inf*), gush, praise

ravenous *adj* = **starving**, famished, starved

ravine *n* = **canyon**, defile, gorge, gulch (*US & Canad*), gully, pass

ravish *v* **1** = **enchant**, captivate, charm, delight, enrapture, entrance, fascinate,

raw ❶ *adj* **1** uncooked. **2** not manufactured or refined. **3** inexperienced. **4** chilly. **raw deal** unfair or dishonest treatment. **rawhide** *n* untanned hide.

ray¹ ❶ *n* **1** single line or narrow beam of light.

ray² *n* large sea fish with a flat body and a whiplike tail.

rayon *n* (fabric made of) a synthetic fibre.

raze ❶ *v* destroy (buildings or a town) completely.

razor *n* sharp instrument for shaving.

razzle-dazzle, razzmatazz *n slang* showy activity.

RC 1 Roman Catholic. **2** Red Cross.

re ❶ *prep* with reference to, concerning.

RE religious education.

re- *prefix* again, e.g. *re-enter; retrial.*

reach ❶ *v* **1** arrive at. **2** make a movement in order to grasp or touch. **3** succeed in touching. **4** make contact or communication with. **5** extend as far as. ▷ *n* **6** distance that one can reach. **7** range of influence. ▷ *pl* **8** stretch of a river.

react ❶ *v* **1** act in response (to). **2** (foll. by *against*) act in an opposing or contrary manner. **reaction** *n* **1** physical or emotional response to a stimulus. **2** any action resisting another. **3** opposition

to change. **4** chemical or nuclear change, combination, or decomposition. **reactionary** *n, adj* (person) opposed to change, esp. in politics. **reactive** *adj* chemically active. **reactor** *n* apparatus in which a nuclear reaction is maintained and controlled to produce nuclear energy.

read ❶ *v* **reading, read 1** look at and understand or take in (written or printed matter). **2** look at and say aloud. **3** interpret the significance or meaning of. **4** (of an instrument) register. **5** study. ▷ *n* **6** matter suitable for reading, e.g. *a good read.* **readable** *adj* **1** enjoyable to read. **2** legible. **reader** *n* **1** person who reads. **2** textbook. **3** senior university lecturer. **readership** *n* readers of a publication collectively. **reading** *n.*

ready ❶ *adj* **readier, readiest 1** prepared for use or action. **2** willing, prompt. **readily** *adv* **readiness** *n* **ready-made** *adj* for immediate use by any customer.

real ❶ *adj* **1** existing in fact. **2** actual. **3** genuine. **really** *adv* **1** very. **2** truly. ▷ *interj* **3** exclamation of dismay, doubt, or surprise. **reality** *n* state of things as they are. **reality TV** television programmes focusing on members of the public living in conditions created especially by the

— THESAURUS —

spellbind **2** *Lit* = **rape**, abuse, force, sexually assault, violate

raw *adj* **1** = **uncooked**, fresh, natural **2** = **unrefined**, basic, coarse, crude, natural, rough, unfinished, unprocessed **3** = **inexperienced**, callow, green, immature, new **4** = **chilly**, biting, bitter, cold, freezing, parky (*Brit inf*), piercing

ray¹ *n* **1** = **beam**, bar, flash, gleam, shaft

raze *v* = **destroy**, demolish, flatten, knock down, level, pull down, ruin

re *prep* = **concerning**, about, apropos, regarding, with reference to, with regard to

reach *v* **1** = **arrive at**, attain, get to, make **3, 5** = **touch**, contact, extend to, grasp, stretch to **4** = **contact**, communicate with, get hold of, get in touch with, get

through to ▷ *n* **6** = **range**, distance, extension, extent, grasp, stretch **7** = **power**, capacity, influence, mana (*NZ*), scope

react *v* **1** = **respond**, answer, reply

read *v* **1** = **look at**, comprehend, construe, decipher, discover, follow, interpret, peruse, pore over, scan, see, study, understand **4** = **register**, display, indicate, record, show **5** = **study**, pore over

ready *adj* **1** = **prepared**, accessible, arranged, available, convenient, fit, handy, near, organized, present, primed, ripe, set **2** = **willing**, agreeable, alert, bright, clever, disposed, eager, glad, happy, inclined, keen, prompt, prone, quick

real *adj* = **genuine**, actual, authentic, factual, rightful, sincere, true, unfeigned, valid

programme makers. **real ale** beer allowed to ferment in the barrel. **real estate** property consisting of land and houses.

realize ❶ v 1 become aware or grasp the significance of. 2 achieve (a plan, hopes, etc.). 3 convert into money. **realization** n.

realm ❶ n 1 kingdom. 2 sphere of interest.

realtor n US & Canad agent, esp. accredited one who sells houses, etc. for others.

ream n 1 twenty quires of paper, generally 500 sheets. ▷ pl 2 informal large quantity (of written matter).

reap ❶ v 1 cut and gather (a harvest). 2 receive as the result of a previous activity. **reaper** n.

rear¹ ❶ n 1 back part. 2 part of an army, procession, etc. behind the others. **bring up the rear** come last. **rearmost** adj **rear admiral** high-ranking naval officer. **rearguard** n troops protecting the rear of an army.

rear² ❶ v 1 care for and educate (children). 2 breed (animals). 3 (of a horse) rise on its hind feet.

reason ❶ n 1 cause or motive. 2 faculty of rational thought. 3 sanity. ▷ v 4 think logically in forming conclusions. **reason with** persuade by logical argument into doing something. **reasonable** adj 1 sensible. 2 not excessive. 3 logical. **reasonably** adv.

reassure ❶ v restore confidence to. **reassurance** n.

rebate ❶ n discount or refund.

rebel ❶ v -belling, -belled 1 revolt against the ruling power. 2 reject accepted conventions. ▷ n 3 person who rebels. **rebellion** n 1 organized open resistance to authority. 2 rejection of conventions. **rebellious** adj.

rebound ❶ v 1 spring back. 2 misfire so as to hurt the perpetrator of a plan or deed. **on the rebound** informal while recovering from rejection.

rebuff ❶ v 1 reject or snub. ▷ n 2 blunt refusal, snub.

rebuke ❶ v 1 scold sternly. ▷ n 2 stern scolding.

———————————————————————— THESAURUS ——————

realize v 1 = **become aware of**, comprehend, get the message, grasp, take in, understand 2 = **achieve**, accomplish, carry out or through, complete, do, effect, fulfil, perform

realm n 1 = **kingdom**, country, domain, dominion, empire, land 2 = **field**, area, branch, department, province, sphere, territory, world

reap v 1 = **collect**, bring in, cut, garner, gather, harvest 2 = **get**, acquire, derive, gain, obtain

rear¹ n 1 = **back**, end, rearguard, stern, tail, tail end

rear² v 1 = **bring up**, educate, foster, nurture, raise, train 2 = **breed** 3 = **rise**

reason n 1 = **cause**, aim, goal, grounds, incentive, intention, motive, object, purpose 2 = **sense**, intellect, judgment, logic, understanding 3 = **sanity**, mind, rationality, soundness ▷ v 4 = **deduce**, conclude, infer, make out, think, work

out **reason with** = **persuade**, bring round (inf), prevail upon, talk into or out of, urge, win over

reassure v = **encourage**, comfort, gee up, hearten, put or set one's mind at rest, restore confidence to

rebate n = **refund**, allowance, bonus, deduction, discount, reduction

rebel v 1 = **revolt**, mutiny, resist, rise up 2 = **defy** ▷ n 3 = **revolutionary**, insurgent, revolutionist, secessionist

rebound v 1 = **bounce**, recoil, ricochet 2 = **misfire**, backfire, boomerang, recoil

rebuff v 1 = **reject**, cold-shoulder, cut, knock back (sl), refuse, repulse, slight, snub, spurn, turn down ▷ n 2 = **rejection**, cold shoulder, kick in the teeth (sl), knock-back (sl), refusal, repulse, slap in the face (inf), slight, snub

rebuke v 1 = **scold**, admonish, castigate, censure, chide, dress down (inf), give a rocket (Brit & NZ inf), haul (someone) over

rebut ❶ v **-butting, -butted** prove that (a claim) is untrue. **rebuttal** n.

recalcitrant adj wilfully disobedient. **recalcitrance** n.

recall ❶ v **1** recollect or remember. **2** order to return. **3** annul or cancel. ▷ n **4** ability to remember. **5** order to return.

recant ❶ v withdraw (a statement or belief) publicly. **recantation** n.

recap informal ▷ v **-capping, -capped** **1** recapitulate. ▷ n **2** recapitulation.

recapitulate ❶ v state again briefly, repeat. **recapitulation** n.

recede ❶ v **1** move to a more distant place. **2** (of the hair) stop growing at the front.

receipt ❶ n **1** written acknowledgment of money or goods received. **2** receiving or being received.

receive ❶ v **1** take, accept, or get. **2** experience. **3** greet (guests). **received** adj generally accepted. **receiver** n **1** part of telephone that is held to the ear. **2** equipment in a telephone, radio, or television that converts electrical signals into sound. **3** person appointed by a court to manage the property of a bankrupt. **receivership** n state of being administered by a receiver.

recent ❶ adj **1** having happened lately. **2** new. **recently** adv.

receptacle ❶ n object used to contain something.

reception ❶ n **1** area for receiving guests, clients, etc. **2** formal party. **3** manner of receiving. **4** welcome. **5** (in broadcasting) quality of signals received. **receptionist** n person who receives guests, clients, etc.

receptive ❶ adj willing to accept new ideas, suggestions, etc. **receptivity** n.

recess ❶ n **1** niche or alcove. **2** holiday between sessions of work. **3** secret hidden place.

recession ❶ n period of economic difficulty when little is being bought or

—————— THESAURUS ——————

the coals (*inf*), reprimand, reprove, rouse on (*Aust*), tear (someone) off a strip (*inf*), tell off (*inf*) ▷ n **2** = **scolding**, admonition, censure, dressing down (*inf*), reprimand, row, telling-off (*inf*)

rebut v = **disprove**, confute, invalidate, negate, overturn, prove wrong, refute

recall v **1** = **recollect**, bring *or* call to mind, evoke, remember **3** = **annul**, cancel, countermand, repeal, retract, revoke, withdraw ▷ n **4** = **recollection**, memory, remembrance **5** = **repeal**, rescindment, retraction, withdrawal

recant v = **withdraw**, disclaim, forswear, renege, repudiate, retract, revoke, take back

recapitulate v = **restate**, outline, recap (*inf*), recount, repeat, summarize

recede v **1** = **fall back**, abate, ebb, regress, retire, retreat, return, subside, withdraw

receipt n **1** = **sales slip**, counterfoil, proof of purchase **2** = **receiving**, acceptance, delivery, reception

receive v **1** = **get**, accept, acquire, be given, collect, obtain, pick up, take **2** = **experience**, bear, encounter, suffer, sustain, undergo **3** = **greet**, accommodate, admit, entertain, meet, welcome

recent adj **1** = **late 2** = **new**, current, fresh, modern, novel, present-day, up-to-date

receptacle n = **container**, holder, repository

reception n **2** = **party**, function, soiree **3** = **response**, acknowledgment, greeting, reaction, treatment, welcome **4** = **welcome**, greeting

receptive adj = **open**, amenable, interested, open-minded, open to suggestions, susceptible, sympathetic

recess n **1** = **alcove**, bay, corner, hollow, niche, nook **2** = **break**, holiday, intermission, interval, respite, rest, vacation

recession n = **depression**, decline, drop, slump

sold. **recessive** *adj* receding.

recipe ❶ *n* **1** directions for cooking a dish.
2 method for achieving something.

recipient *n* person who receives something.

reciprocal ❶ [ris-**sip**-pro-kl] *adj* **1** mutual.
2 given or done in return. **reciprocate**
v **1** give or feel in return. **2** (of a machine
part) move backwards and forwards.
reciprocation *n* **reciprocity** *n*.

recite ❶ *v* repeat (a poem etc.) aloud to an
audience. **recital** *n* **1** musical performance
by a soloist or soloists. **2** act of reciting.
recitation *n* recital, usu. from memory, of
poetry or prose.

reckless ❶ *adj* heedless of danger.
recklessly *adv* **recklessness** *n*.

reckon ❶ *v* **1** consider or think.
2 make calculations, count. **3** expect.
reckoning *n*.

reclaim ❶ *v* **1** regain possession of. **2** make
fit for cultivation. **reclamation** *n*.

recline ❶ *v* rest in a leaning position.
reclining *adj*.

recluse ❶ *n* person who avoids other

people. **reclusive** *adj*.

recognize ❶ *v* **1** identify as (a person or
thing) already known. **2** accept as true
or existing. **3** treat as valid. **4** notice,
show appreciation of. **recognition** *n*
recognizable *adj*.

recoil ❶ *v* **1** jerk or spring back. **2** draw
back in horror. **3** (of an action) go wrong
so as to hurt the doer. ▷ *n* **4** backward
jerk. **5** recoiling.

recollect ❶ *v* call back to mind, remember.
recollection *n*.

recommend ❶ *v* **1** advise or counsel.
2 praise or commend. **3** make acceptable.
recommendation *n*.

- **SPELLING TIP**
- If you wonder how many *c*s and *m*s to
- put in **recomme nd**, you are not alone.
- Most people who make the wrong
- decision go for single letters throughout
- (*recomend* and *recomendation*); they
- should, of course, double the *m*, as in
- **recommendation**.

recompense ❶ *v* **1** pay or reward.

——————————— THESAURUS ———————————

recipe *n* **1** = **directions**, ingredients,
instructions **2** = **method**, formula,
prescription, procedure, process, technique

reciprocal *adj* **1, 2** = **mutual**,
alternate, complementary, correlative,
corresponding, equivalent, exchanged,
interchangeable

recite *v* = **repeat**, declaim, deliver, narrate,
perform, speak

reckless *adj* = **careless**, hasty, headlong,
heedless, imprudent, mindless,
precipitate, rash, thoughtless, wild

reckon *v* **1** = **consider**, account, assume,
believe, count, deem, esteem, guess (*inf,
chiefly US & Canad*), imagine, judge, rate,
regard, suppose, think **2** = **count**, add
up, calculate, compute, figure, number,
tally, total

reclaim *v* **1** = **regain**, recapture, recover,
redeem, retrieve

recline *v* = **lean**, lie (down), loll, lounge,
repose, rest, sprawl

recluse *n* = **hermit**, anchoress, anchorite,
monk, solitary

recognize *v* **1** = **identify**, know, notice,
place, recall, recollect, remember, spot
2 = **acknowledge**, accept, admit, allow,
concede, grant **4** = **appreciate**, notice,
respect

recoil *v* **1** = **jerk back**, kick, react, rebound,
spring back **2** = **draw back**, falter, quail,
shrink **3** = **backfire**, boomerang, go
pear-shaped (*inf*), misfire, rebound ▷ *n*
4 = **reaction**, backlash, kick, rebound,
repercussion

recollect *v* = **remember**, place, recall,
summon up

recommend *v* **1** = **advise**, advance,
advocate, counsel, prescribe, propose, put
forward, suggest **2** = **commend**, approve,
endorse, praise

recompense *v* **1** = **reward**, pay,
remunerate **2** = **compensate**, make up
for, pay for, reimburse, repay, requite,

2 compensate or make up for. ▷ *n* **3** compensation. **4** reward or remuneration.

reconcile ❶ *v* **1** harmonize (conflicting beliefs etc.). **2** bring back into friendship. **3** accept or cause to accept (an unpleasant situation). **reconciliation** *n*.

- ● SPELLING TIP
- ● The Bank of English shows that
- ● the most common way to misspell
- ● **reconnaissance** is to miss out an *s*,
- ● although there are examples where
- ● an *n* has been missed out instead.
- ● Remember, there are two *n*s in the
- ● middle and two *ss*.

reconnoitre ❶ [rek-a-**noy**-ter] *v* make a reconnaissance of.

reconstitute *v* **1** reorganize. **2** restore (dried food) to its former state by adding water. **reconstitution** *n*.

record ❶ *n* [**rek**-ord] **1** document or other thing that preserves information. **2** disc with indentations which a record player transforms into sound. **3** best recorded achievement. **4** known facts

about a person's past. ▷ *v* [rik-**kord**] **5** put in writing. **6** preserve (sound, TV programmes, etc.) on plastic disc, magnetic tape, etc., for reproduction on a playback device. **7** show or register. **off the record** not for publication. **recorder** *n* **1** person or machine that records, esp. a video, cassette, or tape recorder. **2** type of flute, held vertically. **3** judge in certain courts. **recording** *n* **record player** instrument for reproducing sound on records.

recount ❶ *v* tell in detail.

recoup ❶ [rik-**koop**] *v* **1** regain or make good (a loss). **2** recompense or compensate.

recourse ❶ *n* source of help. **have recourse to** turn to a source of help or course of action.

recover ❶ *v* **1** become healthy again. **2** regain a former condition. **3** find again. **4** get back (a loss or expense). **recovery** *n*.

recreation ❶ *n* agreeable or refreshing occupation, relaxation, or amusement. **recreational** *adj* **recreational vehicle** *n*

THESAURUS
---

ress ▷ *n* **3** = **compensation**, amends, damages, payment, remuneration, reparation, repayment, requital, restitution **4** = **reward**, payment, return, wages

reconcile *v* **1** = **resolve**, adjust, compose, put to rights, rectify, settle, square **2** = **make peace between**, appease, conciliate, propitiate, reunite **3** = **accept**, put up with (*inf*), resign oneself, submit, yield

reconnoitre *v* = **inspect**, case (*sl*), explore, investigate, observe, scan, spy out, survey

record *n* **1** = **document**, account, chronicle, diary, entry, file, journal, log, register, report **2** = **disc**, album, LP, single, vinyl **4** = **background**, career, history, performance ▷ *v* **5** = **set down**, chronicle, document, enter, log, minute, note, register, take down, write down

6 = **make a recording of**, tape, tape-record, video, video-tape **7** = **register**, give evidence of, indicate, say, show **off the record** = **not for publication**, confidential, private, unofficial

recount *v* = **tell**, depict, describe, narrate, recite, relate, repeat, report

recoup *v* **1** = **regain**, recover, retrieve, win back **2** = **compensate**, make up for, refund, reimburse, repay, requite

recourse *n* = **option**, alternative, choice, expedient, remedy, resort, resource, way out

recover *v* **1** = **get better**, convalesce, get well, heal, improve, mend, rally, recuperate, revive **2-4** = **regain**, get back, recapture, reclaim, redeem, repossess, restore, retrieve

recreation *n* = **pastime**, amusement, diversion, enjoyment, entertainment, fun, hobby, leisure activity, play, relaxation, sport

r

chiefly US a large vanlike vehicle equipped to be lived in.

recrimination ❶ *n* mutual blame.

recruit ❶ *v* 1 enlist (new soldiers, members, etc.). ▷ *n* 2 newly enlisted soldier. 3 new member or supporter. **recruitment** *n*.

rectangle *n* oblong four-sided figure with four right angles. **rectangular** *adj*.

rectify ❶ *v* **-fying, -fied** put right, correct. **rectification** *n*.

rectitude ❶ *n* moral correctness.

rector *n* 1 clergyman in charge of a parish. 2 head of certain academic institutions. **rectory** *n* rector's house.

rectum *n*, *pl* **-tums, -ta** final section of the large intestine.

recumbent *adj* lying down.

recuperate ❶ *v* recover from illness. **recuperation** *n* **recuperative** *adj*.

recur ❶ *v* **-curring, -curred** happen again. **recurrence** *n* repetition. **recurrent** *adj*.

recycle ❶ *v* reprocess (used materials) for further use.

red ❶ *adj* **redder, reddest** 1 of a colour varying from crimson to orange and seen in blood, fire, etc. 2 flushed in the face from anger, shame, etc. ▷ *n* 3 red

colour. 4 (**R-**) *informal* communist. **in the red** *informal* in debt. **see red** *informal* be angry. **redness** *n* **redden** *v* make or become red. **reddish** *adj* **redback spider** small venomous Australian spider with a red stripe on the back of the abdomen. **red-blooded** *adj informal* vigorous or virile. **red carpet** very special welcome for an important guest. **redcurrant** *n* small round edible red berry. **red-handed** *adj informal* (caught) in the act of doing something wrong or illegal. **red herring** something which diverts attention from the main issue. **red-hot** *adj* 1 glowing red. 2 extremely hot. 3 very keen **danger signal**. **red tape** excessive adherence to official rules.

redeem ❶ *v* 1 make up for. 2 reinstate (oneself) in someone's good opinion. 3 free from sin. 4 buy back. 5 pay off (a loan or debt). **redeemable** *adj* **redemption** *n* **redemptive** *adj*.

redolent *adj* 1 reminiscent (of). 2 smelling strongly (of).

redouble *v* increase, multiply, or intensify.

redoubtable ❶ *adj* formidable.

redress ❶ *v* 1 make amends for. ▷ *n* 2 compensation or amends.

——————————— THESAURUS ———————————

recrimination *n* = **bickering**, counterattack, mutual accusation, quarrel, squabbling

recruit *v* 1 = **enlist**, draft, enrol, levy, mobilize, muster, raise ▷ *n* 3 = **beginner**, apprentice, convert, helper, initiate, learner, novice, trainee

rectify *v* = **correct**, adjust, emend, fix, improve, redress, remedy, repair, right

rectitude *n* = **morality**, decency, goodness, honesty, honour, integrity, principle, probity, virtue

recuperate *v* = **recover**, convalesce, get better, improve, mend

recur *v* = **happen again**, come again, persist, reappear, repeat, return, revert

recycle *v* = **reprocess**, reclaim, reuse, salvage, save

red *adj* 1 = **crimson**, carmine, cherry, coral, ruby, scarlet, vermilion 2 = **flushed**, blushing, embarrassed, florid, shamefaced **in the red** *Inf* = **in debt**, in arrears, insolvent, overdrawn **see red** *Inf* = **lose one's temper**, be *or* get pissed (off) (*taboo sl*), blow one's top, crack up (*inf*), fly off the handle (*inf*), go ballistic (*sl, chiefly US*), go mad (*inf*), lose it (*inf*)

redeem *v* 1 = **make up for**, atone for, compensate for, make amends for 2 = **reinstate**, absolve, restore to favour 3 = **save**, deliver, free 4 = **buy back**, reclaim, recover, regain, repurchase, retrieve

redoubtable *adj* = **formidable**, fearful, fearsome, mighty, powerful, strong

redress *v* 1 = **make amends for**,

reduce ❶ v **1** bring down, lower. **2** lessen, weaken. **3** bring by force or necessity to some state or action. **4** slim. **5** simplify. **6** make (a sauce) more concentrated. **reducible** adj **reduction** n.

redundant ❶ adj **1** (of a worker) no longer needed. **2** superfluous. **redundancy** n.

reed n **1** tall grass that grows in swamps and shallow water. **2** tall straight stem of this plant. **3** Music vibrating cane or metal strip in certain wind instruments. **reedy** adj harsh and thin in tone.

reef n **1** ridge of rock or coral near the surface of the sea. **2** vein of ore.

reek ❶ v **1** smell strongly. ▷ n **2** strong unpleasant smell. **reek of** give a strong suggestion of.

reel¹ n **1** cylindrical object on which film, tape, thread, or wire is wound. **2** winding apparatus, as of a fishing rod. **3** roll of film. **reel in** v draw in by means of a reel. **reel off** v recite or write fluently or quickly.

reel² ❶ v stagger, sway, or whirl.

reel³ n lively Scottish dance.

refectory n, pl **-tories** room for meals in a college etc.

refer ❶ v **-ferring, -ferred** (foll. by to) **1** allude (to). **2** be relevant (to). **3** send (to) for information. **4** submit (to) for

decision. **referral** n **reference** n **1** act of referring. **2** citation or direction in a book. **3** written testimonial regarding character or capabilities. **with reference to** concerning.

referee ❶ n **1** umpire in sports, esp. football or boxing. **2** person willing to testify to someone's character etc. **3** arbitrator. ▷ v **-eeing, -eed 4** act as referee of.

referendum ❶ n, pl **-dums, -da** direct vote of the electorate on an important question.

refill v **1** fill again. ▷ n **2** second or subsequent filling. **3** replacement supply of something in a permanent container.

refine ❶ v **1** purify. **2** improve. **refined** adj **1** cultured or polite. **2** purified. **refinement** n **1** improvement or elaboration. **2** fineness of taste or manners. **3** subtlety. **refinery** n place where sugar, oil, etc. is refined.

reflect ❶ v **1** throw back, esp. rays of light, heat, etc. **2** form an image of. **3** show. **4** consider at length. **5** bring credit or discredit upon. **reflection** n **1** act of reflecting. **2** return of rays of heat, light, etc. from a surface. **3** image of an object given back by a mirror etc. **4** conscious thought or meditation. **5** attribution of

────── THESAURUS ──────

compensate for, make up for ▷ n **2 = amends**, atonement, compensation, payment, recompense, reparation

reduce v **1, 2 = lessen**, abate, curtail, cut, cut down, decrease, diminish, lower, moderate, shorten, weaken

redundant adj **1 = unemployed**, jobless, out of work **2 = superfluous**, extra, inessential, supernumerary, surplus, unnecessary, unwanted

reek v **1 = stink**, pong (Brit inf), smell ▷ n **2 = stink**, fetor, odour, pong (Brit inf), smell, stench

reel² v **= stagger**, lurch, pitch, revolve, rock, roll, spin, sway, swirl, whirl

refer v (foll. by to) **1 = allude**, bring up,

cite, mention, speak of **2 = relate**, apply, belong, be relevant to, concern, pertain **3 = consult**, apply, go, look up, turn to **4 = direct**, guide, point, send

referee n **1 = umpire**, adjudicator, judge, ref (inf) **3 = arbitrator**, arbiter ▷ v **5 a = umpire**, adjudicate, judge **b = arbitrate**, mediate

referendum n **= public vote**, plebiscite

refine v **1 = purify**, clarify, cleanse, distil, filter, process **2 = improve**, hone, perfect, polish

reflect v **1 = throw back**, echo, return **2 = mirror**, reproduce **3 = show**, demonstrate, display, indicate, manifest, reveal **4 = consider**, cogitate, meditate,

r

discredit or blame. **reflective** *adj* **1** quiet, contemplative. **2** capable of reflecting images. **reflector** *n* polished surface for reflecting light etc.

reflex *n* **1** involuntary response to a stimulus or situation. ▷ *adj* **2** (of a muscular action) involuntary. **3** reflected. **4** (of an angle) more than 180° **reflexive** *adj Grammar* denoting a verb whose subject is the same as its object, e.g. *dress oneself*.

reform ❶ *n* **1** improvement. ▷ *v* **2** improve. **3** abandon evil practices. **reformer** *n* **reformation** *n* **1** a reforming. **2** (R-) religious movement in 16th-century Europe that resulted in the establishment of the Protestant Churches. **reformatory** *n* (formerly) institution for reforming young offenders.

refract *v* change the course of (light etc.) passing from one medium to another. **refraction** *n* **refractive** *adj*.

refractory *adj* **1** unmanageable or rebellious. **2** *Med* resistant to treatment. **3** resistant to heat.

refrain¹ ❶ *v* **refrain from** keep oneself from doing.

refrain² ❶ *n* frequently repeated part of a song.

refresh ❶ *v* **1** revive or reinvigorate, as through food, drink, or rest. **2** stimulate (the memory). **refresher** *n* **refreshing** *adj* **1** having a reviving effect. **2** pleasantly different or new. **refreshment** *n* something that refreshes, esp. food or drink.

refrigerate ❶ *v* cool or freeze in order to preserve. **refrigeration** *n* **refrigerator** *n* full name for FRIDGE.

refuge ❶ *n* (source of) shelter or protection. **refugee** *n* person who seeks refuge, esp. in a foreign country.

refund ❶ *v* **1** pay back. ▷ *n* **2** return of money. **3** amount returned.

refurbish ❶ *v* renovate and brighten up.

refuse¹ ❶ *v* decline, deny, or reject. **refusal** *n* denial of anything demanded or offered.

refuse² ❶ *n* rubbish or useless matter.

refute ❶ *v* disprove. **refutation** *n*.

regain ❶ *v* **1** get back or recover. **2** reach again.

regal ❶ *adj* of or like a king or queen. **regally** *adv* **regalia** *pl n* ceremonial emblems of royalty or high office.

regale ❶ *v* entertain (someone) with stories etc.

━━━━━━━━━━━━━━━━━━━━━━━━ THESAURUS ━━━━━━

muse, ponder, ruminate, think, wonder
reform *n* **1** = **improvement**, amendment, betterment, rehabilitation ▷ *v* **2** = **improve**, amend, correct, mend, rectify, restore **3** = **mend one's ways**, clean up one's act (*inf*), go straight (*inf*), pull one's socks up (*Brit inf*), shape up (*inf*), turn over a new leaf
refrain¹ *v* = **stop**, abstain, avoid, cease, desist, forbear, leave off, renounce
refrain² *n* = **chorus**, melody, tune
refresh *v* **1** = **revive**, brace, enliven, freshen, invigorate, revitalize, stimulate **2** = **stimulate**, jog, prompt, renew
refrigerate *v* = **cool**, chill, freeze, keep cold
refuge *n* = **shelter**, asylum, haven, hide-out, protection, retreat, sanctuary

refund *v* **1** = **repay**, pay back, reimburse, restore, return ▷ *n* **2, 3** = **repayment**, reimbursement, return
refurbish *v* = **renovate**, clean up, do up (*inf*), mend, overhaul, repair, restore, revamp
refuse¹ *v* = **reject**, decline, deny, say no, spurn, turn down, withhold
refuse² *n* = **rubbish**, garbage, junk (*inf*), litter, trash, waste
refute *v* = **disprove**, discredit, negate, overthrow, prove false, rebut
regain *v* **1** = **recover**, get back, recapture, recoup, retrieve, take back, win back **2** = **get back to**, reach again, return to
regal *adj* = **royal**, kingly *or* queenly, magnificent, majestic, noble, princely
regale *v* = **entertain**, amuse, delight, divert

regard ❶ v 1 consider. 2 look at. 3 heed. ▷ n 4 respect or esteem. 5 attention. 6 look. ▷ pl 7 expression of goodwill. **as regards, regarding** in respect of, concerning. **regardless** adj 1 heedless. ▷ adv 2 in spite of everything.

regatta n meeting for yacht or boat races.

regenerate ❶ v 1 (cause to) undergo spiritual, moral, or physical renewal. 2 reproduce or re-create. **regeneration** n **regenerative** adj.

regent n 1 ruler of a kingdom during the absence, childhood, or illness of its monarch. ▷ adj 2 ruling as a regent, e.g. prince regent. **regency** n status or period of office of a regent.

reggae n style of Jamaican popular music with a strong beat.

regime ❶ [ray-**zheem**] n 1 system of government. 2 particular administration.

regiment n organized body of troops as a unit of the army. **regimental** adj **regimentation** n **regimented** adj very strictly controlled.

region ❶ n 1 administrative division of a country. 2 area considered as a unit but with no definite boundaries. 3 part of the body. **regional** adj.

register ❶ n 1 (book containing) an official list or record of things. 2 range of a voice or instrument. ▷ v 3 enter in a register or set down in writing. 4 show or be shown on a meter or the face. **registration** n **registration number** numbers and letters displayed on a vehicle to identify it. **registrar** n 1 keeper of official records. 2 senior hospital doctor, junior to a consultant. **register office, registry office** place where births, marriages, and deaths are recorded.

regress ❶ v revert to a former worse condition. **regression** n 1 act of regressing. 2 Psychol use of an earlier (inappropriate) mode of behaviour. **regressive** adj.

regret ❶ v **-gretting, -gretted** 1 feel sorry about. 2 express apology or distress. ▷ n 3 feeling of repentance, guilt, or sorrow. **regretful** adj **regrettable** adj.

regular ❶ adj 1 normal, customary, or

regard v 1 = **consider**, believe, deem, esteem, judge, rate, see, suppose, think, view 2 = **look at**, behold, check out (inf), clock (Brit sl), eye, eyeball (US sl), gaze at, observe, scrutinize, view, watch 3 = **heed**, attend, listen to, mind, pay attention to, take notice of ▷ n 4 = **respect**, care, concern, consideration, esteem, thought 5 = **heed**, attention, interest, mind, notice 6 = **look**, gaze, glance, scrutiny, stare ▷ pl 7 = **good wishes**, best wishes, compliments, greetings, respects **as regards, regarding** = **concerning**, about, in or with regard to, on the subject of, pertaining to, re, relating to, respecting, with reference to

regenerate v 1 = **renew**, breathe new life into, invigorate, reawaken, reinvigorate, rejuvenate, restore, revive

regime n 1, 2 = **government**, leadership, management, reign, rule, system

region n 1 = **area**, district, locality, part, place, quarter, section, sector, territory, tract, zone

register n 1 = **list**, archives, catalogue, chronicle, diary, file, log, record, roll, roster ▷ v 3 = **record**, catalogue, chronicle, enlist, enrol, enter, list, note 4 = **show**, display, exhibit, express, indicate, manifest, mark, reveal

regress v = **revert**, backslide, degenerate, deteriorate, fall away or off, go back, lapse, relapse, return

regret v 1 = **feel sorry about**, bewail, deplore, lament 2 = **grieve**, bemoan, miss, mourn, repent, rue ▷ n 3 = **sorrow**, bitterness, compunction, contrition, penitence, remorse, repentance, ruefulness

regular adj 1 = **normal**, common, customary, habitual, ordinary, routine, typical, usual 2 = **even**, balanced, flat,

r

usual. **2** symmetrical or even. **3** done or occurring according to a rule. **4** periodical. **5** employed continuously in the armed forces. ▷ *n* **6** regular soldier. **7** *informal* frequent customer. **regularity** *n* **regularize** *v* **regularly** *adv*.

regulate ❶ *v* **1** control, esp. by rules. **2** adjust slightly. **regulation** *n* **1** rule. **2** regulating. **regulator** *n* device that automatically controls pressure, temperature, etc.

regurgitate ❶ *v* **1** vomit. **2** (of some birds and animals) bring back (partly digested food) into the mouth. **3** reproduce (ideas, facts, etc.) without understanding them. **regurgitation** *n*.

rehabilitate ❶ *v* **1** help (a person) to readjust to society after illness, imprisonment, etc. **2** restore to a former position or rank. **3** restore the good reputation of. **rehabilitation** *n*.

rehash ❶ *v* **1** rework or reuse. ▷ *n* **2** old ideas presented in a new form.

rehearse ❶ *v* **1** practise (a play, concert, etc.). **2** repeat aloud. **rehearsal** *n*.

reign ❶ *n* **1** period of a sovereign's rule. ▷ *v* **2** rule (a country). **3** be supreme.

reimburse ❶ *v* refund, pay back. **reimbursement** *n*.

rein ❶ *v* **1** check or manage with reins. **2** control or limit. **reins** *pl n* **1** narrow straps attached to a bit to guide a horse. **2** means of control.

reincarnation *n* **1** rebirth of a soul in successive bodies. **2** one of a series of such transmigrations. **reincarnate** *v*.

reindeer *n*, *pl* -**deer**, -**deers** deer of arctic regions with large branched antlers.

reinforce ❶ *v* **1** strengthen with new support, material, or force. **2** strengthen with additional troops, ships, etc. **reinforcement** *n*.

reinstate ❶ *v* restore to a former position. **reinstatement** *n*.

reiterate ❶ *v* repeat again and again. **reiteration** *n*.

reject ❶ *v* **1** refuse to accept or believe. **2** rebuff (a person). **3** discard as useless. ▷ *n* **4** person or thing rejected as not up to standard. **rejection** *n*.

——————————————————————— THESAURUS ———————

level, smooth, straight, symmetrical, uniform **3** = **systematic**, consistent, constant, even, fixed, ordered, set, stated, steady, uniform

regulate *v* **1** = **control**, direct, govern, guide, handle, manage, rule, run, supervise **2** = **adjust**, balance, fit, moderate, modulate, tune

regurgitate *v* **1** = **vomit**, disgorge, puke (*sl*), sick up (*inf*), spew (out *or* up), throw up (*inf*)

rehabilitate *v* **1** = **reintegrate**, adjust **3** = **redeem**, clear, reform, restore, save

rehash *v* **1** = **rework**, refashion, rejig (*inf*), reuse, rewrite ▷ *n* **2** = **reworking**, new version, rearrangement, rewrite

rehearse *v* **1** = **practise**, drill, go over, prepare, run through, train **2** = **repeat**, recite

reign *n* **1** = **rule**, command, control, dominion, monarchy, power ▷ *v* **2** = **rule**,

be in power, command, govern, influence **3** = **be supreme**, hold sway, predominate, prevail

reimburse *v* = **pay back**, compensate, recompense, refund, remunerate, repay, return

rein *v* = **control**, check, curb, halt, hold back, limit, restrain, restrict ▷ *pl n* **1** = **control**, brake, bridle, check, curb, harness, hold, restraint

reinforce *v* **1** = **emphasize**, stress **2** = **support**, bolster, fortify, prop, strengthen, supplement, toughen

reinstate *v* = **restore**, recall, re-establish, replace, return

reiterate *v* = **repeat**, do again, restate, say again

reject *v* **1** = **deny**, decline, disallow, exclude, renounce, repudiate, veto **2** = **rebuff**, jilt, refuse, repulse, say no to, spurn, turn down **3** = **discard**, eliminate,

rejig ⊕ v -jigging, -jigged 1 re-equip (a factory or plant). 2 rearrange.

rejoice ⊕ v feel or express great happiness.

rejoin ⊕ v reply. **rejoinder** n answer, retort.

rejuvenate ⊕ v restore youth or vitality to. **rejuvenation** n.

relapse ⊕ v 1 fall back into bad habits, illness, etc. ▷ n 2 return of bad habits, illness, etc.

relate ⊕ v 1 establish a relation between. 2 have reference or relation to. 3 have an understanding (of people or ideas). 4 tell (a story) or describe (an event). **related** adj.

relation ⊕ n 1 connection between things. 2 relative. 3 connection by blood or marriage. 4 act of relating (a story). ▷ pl 5 social or political dealings. 6 family. **relationship** n 1 dealings and feelings between people or countries. 2 emotional or sexual affair. 3 connection between two things. 4 association by blood or marriage, kinship. **relative** adj true to a certain degree or extent.

relax ⊕ v 1 make or become looser, less tense, or less rigid. 2 ease up from effort or attention, rest. 3 be less strict about. 4 become more friendly. **relaxing** adj **relaxation** n.

relay ⊕ n 1 fresh set of people or animals relieving others. 2 Electricity device for making or breaking a local circuit. 3 broadcasting station receiving and retransmitting programmes. ▷ v -laying, -layed 4 pass on (a message). **relay race** race between teams in which each runner races part of the distance.

release ⊕ v 1 set free. 2 let go or fall. 3 issue (a record, film, etc.) for sale or public showing. 4 emit heat, energy, etc. ▷ n 5 setting free. 6 statement to the press. 7 act of issuing for sale or publication. 8 newly issued film, record, etc.

—— THESAURUS ——

jettison, scrap, throw away or out ▷ n 4 = **castoff**, discard, failure, second

rejig v 2 = **rearrange**, alter, juggle, manipulate, reorganize, tweak

rejoice v = **be glad**, be happy, be overjoyed, celebrate, exult, glory

rejoin v = **reply**, answer, respond, retort, riposte

rejuvenate v = **revitalize**, breathe new life into, refresh, regenerate, renew, restore

relapse v 1 a = **lapse**, backslide, degenerate, fail, regress, revert, slip back b = **worsen**, deteriorate, fade, fail, sicken, sink, weaken ▷ n 2 c = **lapse**, backsliding, regression, retrogression d = **worsening**, deterioration, turn for the worse, weakening

relate v 1 = **connect**, associate, correlate, couple, join, link 2 = **concern**, apply, be relevant to, have to do with, pertain, refer 4 = **tell**, describe, detail, narrate, recite, recount, report

relation n 1 = **connection**, bearing, bond, comparison, correlation, link

2 = **relative**, kin, kinsman or kinswoman 3 = **kinship**, affinity, kindred ▷ pl 5 = **dealings**, affairs, connections, contact, interaction, intercourse, relationship 6 = **family**, clan, kin, kindred, kinsfolk, kinsmen, relatives, tribe

relax v 1 = **lessen**, abate, ease, ebb, let up, loosen, lower, moderate, reduce, relieve, slacken, weaken 2 = **be or feel at ease**, calm, chill out (sl, chiefly US), outspan (S Afr), rest, take it easy, unwind 3 = **lighten up** (sl), chill out (sl, chiefly US), take it easy

relay n 1 = **shift**, relief, turn ▷ v 4 = **pass on**, broadcast, carry, communicate, send, spread, transmit

release v 1 = **set free**, discharge, drop, extricate, free, liberate, loose, unbridle, undo, unfasten 3 = **issue**, circulate, distribute, launch, make known, make public, publish, put out ▷ n 5 = **liberation**, deliverance, discharge, emancipation, freedom, liberty 6 = **proclamation** 7 = **issue**, publication

r

relegate ⊙ v 1 put in a less important position. 2 demote (a sports team) to a lower league. **relegation** n.

relent ⊙ v give up a harsh intention, become less severe. **relentless** adj 1 unremitting. 2 merciless.

relevant ⊙ adj to do with the matter in hand. **relevance** n.

> ● SPELLING TIP
> ● A common word in English, **relevant**
> ● is not always spelt correctly. The final
> ● syllable is the problem and sometimes
> ● appears incorrectly in the Bank of
> ● English as -ent.

reliable ⊙ adj able to be trusted, dependable. **reliably** adv **reliability** n.

relic ⊙ n 1 something that has survived from the past. 2 body or possession of a saint, regarded as holy. ▷ pl 3 remains or traces.

relief ⊙ n 1 gladness at the end or removal of pain, distress, etc. 2 release from monotony or duty. 3 money or food given to victims of disaster, poverty, etc. 4 freeing of a besieged city etc. 5 person who replaces another. 6 projection of a carved design from the surface. 7 any vivid effect resulting from contrast, e.g. *comic relief*. **relieve** v bring relief to.

relieve oneself urinate or defecate. **relief map** map showing the shape and height of land by shading.

religion ⊙ n system of belief in and worship of a supernatural power or god. **religious** adj 1 of religion. 2 pious or devout. 3 scrupulous or conscientious.

relinquish ⊙ v give up or abandon.

relish ⊙ v 1 enjoy, like very much. ▷ n 2 liking or enjoyment. 3 appetizing savoury food, such as pickle. 4 zestful quality or flavour.

relocate v move to a new place to live or work. **relocation** n.

reluctant ⊙ adj unwilling or disinclined. **reluctance** n.

rely ⊙ v **-lying**, **-lied** 1 depend (on). 2 trust. **reliable** adj able to be trusted.

remain ⊙ v 1 continue. 2 stay, be left behind. 3 be left (over). 4 be left to be done, said, etc. **remains** pl n 1 relics, esp. of ancient buildings. 2 dead body. **remainder** n 1 part which is left. 2 amount left over after subtraction or division. ▷ v 3 offer (copies of a poorly selling book) at reduced prices.

remand v send back into custody or put on bail before trial. **on remand** in custody or on bail before trial. **remand centre**

r

relegate v = **demote**, downgrade
relent v = **be merciful**, capitulate, change one's mind, come round, have pity, show mercy, soften, yield
relevant adj = **significant**, apposite, appropriate, apt, fitting, germane, pertinent, related, to the point
reliable adj = **dependable**, faithful, safe, sound, staunch, sure, true, trustworthy
relic n 1 = **remnant**, fragment, keepsake, memento, souvenir, trace, vestige
relief n 1 = **ease**, comfort, cure, deliverance, mitigation, release, remedy, solace 2 = **rest**, break, breather (*inf*), relaxation, respite 3 = **aid**, assistance, help, succour, support
relinquish v = **give up**, abandon,

abdicate, cede, drop, forsake, leave, let go, renounce, surrender
relish v 1 = **enjoy**, delight in, fancy, like, revel in, savour ▷ n 2 = **enjoyment**, fancy, fondness, gusto, liking, love, partiality, penchant, predilection, taste 3 = **condiment**, sauce, seasoning 4 = **flavour**, piquancy, smack, spice, tang, taste, trace
reluctant adj = **unwilling**, disinclined, hesitant, loath, unenthusiastic
rely v 1 = **depend**, bank, bet, count ▷ n 2 = **trust**
remain v 1 = **continue**, abide, dwell, endure, go on, last, persist, stand, stay, survive 2 = **stay behind**, be left, delay, linger, wait

place where accused people are detained awaiting trial.

remark ❶ v 1 make a casual comment (on). 2 say. 3 observe or notice. ▷ n 4 observation or comment. **remarkable** adj 1 worthy of note or attention. 2 striking or unusual. **remarkably** adv.

remedy ❶ n, pl **-edies** 1 means of curing pain or disease. 2 means of solving a problem. ▷ v **-edying, -edied** 3 put right. **remedial** adj intended to correct a specific disability, handicap, etc.

remember ❶ v 1 retain in or recall to one's memory. 2 keep in mind. **remembrance** n 1 memory. 2 token or souvenir. 3 honouring of the memory of a person or event.

remind ❶ v 1 cause to remember. 2 put in mind (of). **reminder** n 1 something that recalls the past. 2 note to remind a person of something not done.

reminisce ❶ v talk or write of past times, experiences, etc. **reminiscence** n 1 remembering. 2 thing recollected. ▷ pl 3 memoirs. **reminiscent** adj reminding or suggestive (of).

remiss ❶ adj negligent or careless.

remit ❶ v [rim-**mitt**]-**mitting, -mitted** 1 send (money) for goods, services, etc., esp. by post. 2 cancel (a punishment or debt). 3 refer (a decision) to a higher authority or later date. ▷ n [**ree**-mitt] 4 area of competence or authority. **remittance** n money sent as payment.

remnant ❶ n 1 small piece, esp. of fabric, left over. 2 surviving trace.

remonstrate ❶ v argue in protest.

remorse ❶ n feeling of sorrow and regret for something one did. **remorseful** adj **remorseless** adj 1 pitiless. 2 persistent.

remote ❶ adj 1 far away, distant. 2 aloof. 3 slight or faint. **remotely** adv **remote control** control of an apparatus from a distance by an electrical device.

remove ❶ v 1 take away or off. 2 get rid of. 3 dismiss from office. ▷ n 4 degree of difference. **removable** adj **removal** n removing, esp. changing residence.

——— THESAURUS ———

remark v 1, 2 = **comment**, declare, mention, observe, pass comment, reflect, say, state 3 = **notice**, espy, make out, mark, note, observe, perceive, see ▷ n 4 = **comment**, observation, reflection, statement, utterance

remedy n 1 = **cure**, medicine, nostrum, treatment ▷ v 3 = **put right**, correct, fix, rectify

remember v 1 = **recall**, call to mind, commemorate, look back (on), recollect, reminisce, think back 2 = **bear in mind**, keep in mind

remind v = **call to mind**, jog one's memory, make (someone) remember, prompt

reminisce v = **recall**, hark back, look back, recollect, remember, think back

remiss adj = **careless**, forgetful, heedless, lax, neglectful, negligent, thoughtless

remit v 1 = **send**, dispatch, forward, mail, post, transmit 2 = **cancel**, halt, repeal, rescind, stop 3 = **postpone**, defer, delay, put off, shelve, suspend

remnant n = **remainder**, end, fragment, leftovers, remains, residue, rest, trace, vestige

remonstrate v = **protest**, argue, dispute, dissent, object, take issue

remorse n = **regret**, anguish, compunction, contrition, grief, guilt, penitence, repentance, shame, sorrow

remote adj 1 = **distant**, far, inaccessible, in the middle of nowhere, isolated, out-of-the-way, secluded 2 = **aloof**, abstracted, cold, detached, distant, reserved, standoffish, uncommunicative, withdrawn 3 = **slight**, doubtful, dubious, faint, outside, slender, slim, small, unlikely

remove v 1, 2 = **take away** or **off** or **out**, abolish, delete, detach, displace, eject, eliminate, erase, excise, extract, get rid of, wipe from the face of the earth, withdraw 3 = **dismiss**, depose, dethrone, discharge, expel, oust, throw out

r

remunerate ① v reward or pay. **remuneration** n **remunerative** adj.
renaissance ① n 1 revival or rebirth. 2 (R-) revival of learning in the 14th–16th centuries.
renal [**ree**-nal] adj of the kidneys.
rend ① v **rending, rent 1** tear or wrench apart. 2 (of a sound) break (the silence) violently.
render ① v 1 cause to become. 2 give or provide (aid, a service, etc.). 3 submit or present (a bill). 4 portray or represent. 5 cover with plaster. 6 melt down (fat).
rendezvous ① [**ron**-day-voo] n, pl -**vous** 1 appointment. 2 meeting place. ▷ v 3 meet as arranged.
rendition ① n 1 performance. 2 translation.
renegade ① n person who deserts a cause.
renege ① [rin-**nayg**] v go back (on a promise etc.).
renew ① v 1 begin again. 2 make valid

again. 3 grow again. 4 restore to a former state. 5 replace (a worn part). 6 restate or reaffirm. **renewable** adj **renewal** n.
renounce ① v 1 give up (a belief, habit, etc.) voluntarily. 2 give up (a title or claim) formally. **renunciation** n.
renovate ① v restore to good condition. **renovation** n.
renown ① n widespread good reputation. **renowned** adj famous.
rent¹ ① v 1 give or have use of in return for regular payments. ▷ n 2 regular payment for use of land, a building, machine, etc. **rental** n sum payable as rent.
rent² ① n 1 tear or fissure. ▷ v 2 past of REND.
reorganize v organize in a new and more efficient way. **reorganization** n.
repair¹ ① v 1 restore to good condition, mend. ▷ n 2 act of repairing. 3 repaired part. 4 state or condition, e.g. in good repair. **reparation** n something done or

────────── THESAURUS ──────────

remunerate v = **pay**, compensate, recompense, reimburse, repay, requite, reward
renaissance n 1 = **rebirth**, reappearance, reawakening, renewal, restoration, resurgence, revival
rend v 1 = **tear**, rip, rupture, separate, wrench
render v 1 = **make**, cause to become, leave 2 = **provide**, furnish, give, hand out, pay, present, submit, supply, tender 4 = **represent**, act, depict, do, give, perform, play, portray
rendezvous n 1 = **appointment**, assignation, date, engagement, meeting, tryst (arch) 2 = **meeting place**, gathering point, venue ▷ v 3 = **meet**, assemble, come together, gather, join up
rendition n 1 = **performance**, arrangement, interpretation, portrayal, presentation, reading, rendering, version 2 = **translation**, interpretation, reading, transcription, version
renegade n = **deserter**, apostate,

defector, traitor, turncoat
renege v = **break one's word**, back out, break a promise, default, go back
renew v 1 = **recommence**, continue, extend, recreate, reopen, repeat, resume 4 = **restore**, mend, modernize, overhaul, refit, refurbish, renovate, repair 5 = **replace**, refresh, replenish, restock 6 = **reaffirm**
renounce v = **give up**, abjure, deny, disown, forsake, forswear, quit, recant, relinquish, waive
renovate v = **restore**, do up (inf), modernize, overhaul, recondition, refit, refurbish, renew, repair
renown n = **fame**, distinction, eminence, note, reputation, repute
rent¹ v 1 = **hire**, charter, lease, let ▷ n 2 = **hire**, fee, lease, payment, rental
rent² n 1 = **tear**, gash, hole, opening, rip, slash, slit, split
repair¹ v 1 = **mend**, fix, heal, patch, patch up, renovate, restore ▷ n 2, 3 = **mend**, darn, overhaul, patch, restoration

given as compensation.

repair² ❶ *v* go (to).

repartee ❶ *n* 1 interchange of witty retorts. 2 witty retort.

repatriate *v* send (someone) back to his or her own country. **repatriation** *n*.

repay ❶ *v* **repaying, repaid** 1 pay back, refund. 2 do something in return for, e.g. *repay hospitality*. **repayable** *adj* **repayment** *n*.

repeal ❶ *v* 1 cancel (a law) officially. ▷ *n* 2 act of repealing.

repeat ❶ *v* 1 say or do again. 2 happen again, recur. ▷ *n* 3 act or instance of repeating. 4 programme broadcast again. **repeatedly** *adv* **repetition** *n* act of repeating.

repel ❶ *v* **-pelling, -pelled** 1 be disgusting to. 2 drive back, ward off. 3 resist. **repellent** *adj* 1 distasteful. 2 resisting water etc. ▷ *n* 3 something that repels, esp. a chemical to repel insects.

repent ❶ *v* feel regret for (a deed or

omission). **repentance** *n* **repentant** *adj*.

repertoire ❶ *n* stock of plays, songs, etc. that a player or company can give.

repetition ❶ *n* 1 act of repeating. 2 thing repeated. **repetitive, repetitious** *adj* full of repetition.

replace ❶ *v* 1 substitute for. 2 put back. **replacement** *n*.

replay *n* 1 (also **action replay**) immediate reshowing on TV of an incident in sport, esp. in slow motion. 2 second sports match, esp. one following an earlier draw. ▷ *v* 3 play (a match, recording, etc.) again.

replenish ❶ *v* fill up again, resupply. **replenishment** *n*.

replete ❶ *adj* filled or gorged.

replica ❶ *n* exact copy. **replicate** *v* make or be a copy of.

reply ❶ *v* **-plying, -plied** 1 answer or respond. ▷ *n*, *pl* **-plies** 2 answer or response.

report ❶ *v* 1 give an account of. 2 make a report (on). 3 make a formal complaint

---

THESAURUS

4 = **condition**, form, shape (*inf*), state

repair² *v* = **go**, betake oneself, head for, leave for, move, remove, retire, set off for, withdraw

repartee *n* 1 = **wit**, badinage, banter, wittiness, wordplay 2 = **riposte**

repay *v* 1 = **pay back**, compensate, recompense, refund, reimburse, requite, return, square 2 = **reciprocate**, avenge, get even with (*inf*), get one's own back on (*inf*), hit back, retaliate, revenge

repeal *v* 1 = **abolish**, annul, cancel, invalidate, nullify, recall, reverse, revoke ▷ *n* 2 = **abolition**, annulment, cancellation, invalidation, rescindment

repeat *v* 1 = **reiterate**, echo, replay, reproduce, rerun, restate, retell ▷ *n* 3 = **repetition**, echo, reiteration, replay, rerun

repel *v* 1 = **disgust**, gross out (*US sl*), nauseate, offend, revolt, sicken 2, 3 = **drive off**, fight, hold off, parry, rebuff, repulse, resist, ward off

repent *v* = **regret**, be sorry, feel remorse, rue

repertoire *n* = **range**, collection, list, repertory, stock, store, supply

repetition *n* = **repeating**, echo, recurrence, reiteration, renewal, replication, restatement, tautology

replace *v* 1 = **take the place of**, follow, oust, substitute, succeed, supersede, supplant, take over from 2 = **put back**, re-establish, reinstate, restore

replenish *v* = **refill**, fill, provide, reload, replace, restore, top up

replete *adj* = **filled**, crammed, full, full up, glutted, gorged, sated, stuffed

replica *n* = **duplicate**, carbon copy (*inf*), copy, facsimile, imitation, model, reproduction

reply *v* 1 = **answer**, counter, reciprocate, rejoin, respond, retaliate, retort ▷ *n* 2 = **answer**, counter, counterattack, reaction, rejoinder, response, retaliation, retort

report *v* 1, 2 = **communicate**, broadcast,

about. **4** present oneself (to). **5** be responsible (to). ▷ *n* **6** account or statement. **7** rumour. **8** written statement of a child's progress at school. **9** bang. **reportedly** *adv* according to rumour. **reporter** *n* person who gathers news for a newspaper, TV, etc.

repose ❶ *n* **1** peace. **2** composure. **3** sleep. ▷ *v* **4** lie or lay at rest.

repossess *v* (of a lender) take back property from a customer who is behind with payments. **repossession** *n*.

reprehensible ❶ *adj* open to criticism, unworthy.

represent ❶ *v* **1** act as a delegate or substitute for. **2** stand for. **3** symbolize. **4** make out to be. **5** portray, as in art. **representation** *n* **representative** *n* **1** person chosen to stand for a group. **2** (travelling) salesperson.

▷ *adj* **3** typical.

repress ❶ *v* **1** keep (feelings) in check. **2** restrict the freedom of. **repression** *n* **repressive** *adj*.

reprieve ❶ *v* **1** postpone the execution of (a condemned person). **2** give temporary relief to. ▷ *n* **3** (document granting) postponement or cancellation of a punishment. **4** temporary relief.

reprimand ❶ *v* **1** blame (someone) officially for a fault. ▷ *n* **2** official blame.

reprisal ❶ *n* retaliation.

reproach ❶ *n, v* blame, rebuke. **reproachful** *adj*.

reprobate *adj, n* depraved or disreputable (person).

reproduce ❶ *v* **1** produce a copy of. **2** bring new individuals into existence. **3** re-create. **reproduction** *n* **1** process of

——————————————————————— THESAURUS ———————————

cover, describe, detail, inform of, narrate, pass on, recount, relate, state, tell **4** = **present oneself**, appear, arrive, come, turn up ▷ *n* **6** = **account**, communication, description, narrative, news, record, statement, word **7** = **rumour**, buzz, gossip, hearsay, talk **9** = **bang**, blast, boom, crack, detonation, discharge, explosion, noise, sound

repose *n* **1** = **peace**, ease, quietness, relaxation, respite, rest, stillness, tranquillity **2** = **composure**, calmness, poise, self-possession **3** = **sleep**, slumber ▷ *v* **4** = **rest**, lie, lie down, recline, rest upon

reprehensible *adj* = **blameworthy**, bad, culpable, disgraceful, objectionable, shameful, unworthy

represent *v* **1, 2** = **stand for**, act for, betoken, mean, serve as, speak for, symbolize **3** = **exemplify**, embody, epitomize, personify, symbolize, typify **5** = **depict**, denote, describe, illustrate, outline, picture, portray, show

repress *v* **1** = **control**, bottle up, check, curb, hold back, inhibit, restrain, stifle,

suppress **2** = **subdue**, quell, subjugate

reprieve *v* **1** = **grant a stay of execution to**, let off the hook (*sl*), pardon **2** = **relieve**, abate, allay, alleviate, mitigate, palliate ▷ *n* **3** = **stay of execution**, amnesty, deferment, pardon, postponement, remission **4** = **relief**, alleviation, mitigation, palliation, respite

reprimand *v* **1** = **blame**, censure, dress down (*inf*), haul over the coals (*inf*), rap over the knuckles, rebuke, rouse on (*Aust*), scold, tear (someone) off a strip (*Brit inf*) ▷ *n* **2** = **blame**, censure, dressing-down (*inf*), rebuke, reproach, reproof, talking-to (*inf*)

reprisal *n* = **retaliation**, retribution, revenge, vengeance

reproach *n* = **blame**, censure, condemnation, disapproval, opprobrium, rebuke ▷ *v* = **blame**, censure, condemn, criticize, lambast(e), read the riot act, rebuke, reprimand, rouse on (*Aust*), scold, upbraid

reproduce *v* **1** = **copy**, duplicate, echo, imitate, match, mirror, recreate, repeat, replicate **2** = **breed**, multiply, procreate,

r

reproducing. **2** facsimile, as of a painting
etc. **3** quality of sound from an audio
system. **reproductive** adj.

reprove ❶ v speak severely to (someone)
about a fault. **reproof** n severe blaming of
someone for a fault.

reptile n cold-blooded egg-laying
vertebrate with horny scales or plates,
such as a snake or tortoise. **reptilian** adj.

republic n **1** form of government in
which the people or their elected
representatives possess the supreme
power. **2** country in which a president
is the head of state. **Republican** n,
adj **1** (member or supporter) of the
Republican Party, the more conservative
of the two main political parties in the US.
Republicanism n.

repudiate ❶ [rip-**pew**-dee-ate] v **1** reject
the authority or validity of. **2** disown.
repudiation n.

repugnant ❶ adj offensive or distasteful.
repugnance n.

repulse ❶ v **1** be disgusting to. **2** drive

(an army) back. **3** rebuff or reject. ▷ n
4 driving back. **5** rejection or rebuff.
repulsion n **1** distaste or aversion.
2 Physics force separating two objects.
repulsive adj loathsome, disgusting.

reputation ❶ n estimation in which a
person is held.

request ❶ v **1** ask. ▷ n **2** asking. **3** thing
asked for.

Requiem [**rek**-wee-em] n **1** Mass for the
dead. **2** music for this.

require ❶ v **1** want or need. **2** demand.
requirement n **1** essential condition.
2 specific need or want.

requisite ❶ [**rek**-wizz-it] adj **1** necessary,
essential. ▷ n **2** essential thing.

requisition ❶ v **1** demand (supplies). ▷ n
2 formal demand, such as for materials
or supplies.

requite ❶ v return to someone (the
same treatment or feeling as received).
requital n.

rescind ❶ v annul or repeal.

rescue ❶ v **-cuing, -cued 1** deliver from

— THESAURUS —

propagate, spawn

reprove v = **rebuke**, berate, blame,
censure, condemn, read the riot act,
reprimand, rouse on (Aust), scold, tear into
(inf), tear (someone) off a strip (Brit inf),
tell off (inf)

repudiate v **1** = **reject**, deny, disavow,
disclaim, renounce **2** = **disown**

repugnant adj = **distasteful**, abhorrent,
disgusting, loathsome, nauseating,
offensive, repellent, revolting, sickening,
vile

repulse v **1** = **disgust**, nauseate, offend,
put off, repel, revolt, sicken, turn one's
stomach **2** = **drive back**, beat off, fight off,
rebuff, repel, ward off **3** = **reject**, rebuff,
refuse, snub, spurn, turn down

reputation n = **name**, character, esteem,
estimation, renown, repute, standing,
stature

request v **1** = **ask (for)**, appeal for,
demand, desire, entreat, invite, seek,

solicit ▷ n **2** = **asking**, appeal, call,
demand, desire, entreaty, suit

require v **1** = **need**, crave, desire, lack,
miss, want, wish **2** = **order**, ask, bid, call
upon, command, demand, exact,
insist upon

requisite adj **1** = **necessary**, called for,
essential, indispensable, needed, needful,
obligatory, required ▷ n **2** = **necessity**,
condition, essential, must, need,
prerequisite, requirement

requisition v **1** = **demand**, call for,
request ▷ n **2** = **demand**, call, request,
summons

requite v = **return**, get even, give in return,
pay (someone) back in his or her own coin,
reciprocate, repay, respond, retaliate

rescind v = **annul**, cancel, countermand,
declare null and void, invalidate, repeal,
set aside

rescue v **1** = **save**, deliver, get out, liberate,
recover, redeem, release, salvage ▷ n

r

danger or trouble, save. ▷ n 2 rescuing. **rescuer** n.

research ⓿ n 1 systematic investigation to discover facts or collect information. ▷ v 2 carry out investigations. **researcher** n.

resemble ⓿ v be or look like. **resemblance** n.

resent ⓿ v feel indignant or bitter about. **resentful** adj **resentment** n.

reserve ⓿ v 1 set aside, keep for future use. 2 obtain by arranging beforehand, book. 3 retain. ▷ n 4 something, esp. money or troops, kept for emergencies. 5 area of land reserved for a particular purpose. 6 Sport substitute. 7 concealment of feelings or friendliness. **reservation** n 1 doubt. 2 exception or limitation. 3 seat, room, etc. that has been reserved. **reserved** adj 1 not showing one's feelings, lacking friendliness. 2 set aside for use by a particular person. **reservist** n member of a military reserve.

reservoir ⓿ n 1 natural or artificial lake storing water for community supplies. 2 store or supply of something.

reshuffle n 1 reorganization. ▷ v

2 reorganize.

reside ⓿ v dwell permanently. **residence** n home or house. **resident** n, adj **residential** adj 1 (of part of a town) consisting mainly of houses. 2 providing living accommodation.

residue ⓿ n what is left, remainder. **residual** adj.

resign ⓿ v 1 give up office, a job, etc. 2 reconcile (oneself) to. **resigned** adj content to endure. **resignation** n 1 resigning. 2 passive endurance of difficulties.

resilient ⓿ adj 1 (of a person) recovering quickly from a shock etc. 2 able to return to normal shape after stretching etc. **resilience** n.

resin [**rezz**-in] n 1 sticky substance from plants, esp. pines. 2 similar synthetic substance. **resinous** adj.

resist ⓿ v 1 withstand or oppose. 2 refrain from despite temptation. 3 be proof against. **resistance** n 1 act of resisting. 2 capacity to withstand something. 3 Electricity opposition offered by a circuit to the passage of a current through it.

─────────────────────────────── THESAURUS ───────────────────────────────

2 = **liberation**, deliverance, recovery, redemption, release, salvage, salvation, saving

research n 1 = **investigation**, analysis, examination, exploration, probe, study ▷ v 2 = **investigate**, analyse, examine, explore, probe, study

resemble v = **be like**, bear a resemblance to, be similar to, look like, mirror, parallel

resent v = **be bitter about**, begrudge, be pissed (off) about (taboo sl), grudge, object to, take exception to, take offence at

reserve v 1 = **keep**, hoard, hold, put by, retain, save, set aside, stockpile, store 2 = **book**, engage, prearrange, secure ▷ n 4 = **store**, cache, fund, hoard, reservoir, savings, stock, supply 5 = **reservation**, park, preserve, sanctuary, tract 6 Sport = **substitute** 7 = **shyness**, constraint,

reservation, restraint, reticence, secretiveness, silence, taciturnity

reservoir n 1 = **lake**, basin, pond, tank 2 = **store**, pool, reserves, source, stock, supply

reside v = **live**, abide, dwell, inhabit, lodge, stay

residue n = **remainder**, dregs, excess, extra, leftovers, remains, remnant, rest, surplus

resign v 1 = **quit**, abdicate, give in one's notice, leave, step down (inf), vacate 2 = **accept**, acquiesce, give in, resign oneself, succumb, yield

resilient adj 1 = **tough**, buoyant, hardy, irrepressible, strong 2 = **flexible**, elastic, plastic, pliable, rubbery, springy, supple

resist v 1 = **oppose**, battle, combat, defy, hinder, stand up to 2 = **refrain from**, abstain from, avoid, forbear, forgo, keep from 3 = **withstand**, be proof against

resistant *adj* **resistible** *adj* **resistor** *n* component of an electrical circuit producing resistance.

resit *v* **1** take (an exam) again. ▷ *n* **2** exam that has to be taken again.

resolute ❶ *adj* firm in purpose. **resolutely** *adv* **resolution** *n* **1** firmness of conduct or character. **2** thing resolved upon. **3** decision of a court or vote of an assembly. **4** act of resolving.

resolve ❶ *v* **1** decide with an effort of will. **2** form (a resolution) by a vote. **3** separate the component parts of. **4** make clear, settle. **resolved** *adj* determined.

resonance ❶ *n* **1** echoing, esp. with a deep sound. **2** sound produced in one object by sound waves coming from another object. **resonant** *adj* **resonate** *v*.

resort ❶ *v* **1** have recourse (to) for help etc. ▷ *n* **2** place for holidays. **3** recourse.

resound ❶ [riz-**zownd**] *v* echo or ring with sound. **resounding** *adj* **1** echoing. **2** clear and emphatic.

resource ❶ *n* **1** thing resorted to for support. **2** ingenuity. **3** means of achieving something. ▷ *pl* **4** sources of economic wealth. **5** stock that can be drawn on, funds. **resourceful** *adj* **resourcefulness** *n*.

respect ❶ *n* **1** consideration. **2** deference or esteem. **3** point or aspect. **4** reference or relation, e.g. *with respect to*. ▷ *v* **5** treat with esteem. **6** show consideration for. **respecter** *n* **respectful** *adj* **respecting** *prep* concerning.

respiration [ress-per-**ray**-shun] *n* breathing. **respirator** *n* apparatus worn over the mouth and breathed through as protection against dust, poison gas, etc., or to provide artificial respiration. **respiratory** *adj* **respire** *v* breathe.

respite ❶ *n* **1** pause, interval of rest. **2** delay.

resplendent ❶ *adj* **1** brilliant or splendid. **2** shining.

respond ❶ *v* **1** answer. **2** act in answer to any stimulus. **3** react favourably. **respondent** *n* *Law* defendant. **response** *n* **1** answer. **2** reaction to a stimulus. **responsive** *adj* readily reacting to some influence. **responsiveness** *n*.

--- THESAURUS ---

resolute *adj* = **determined**, dogged, firm, fixed, immovable, inflexible, set, steadfast, strong-willed, tenacious, unshakable, unwavering

resolve *v* **1** = **decide**, agree, conclude, determine, fix, intend, purpose **3** = **break down**, analyse, reduce, separate **4** = **work out**, answer, clear up, crack, fathom

resort *v* **1** = **have recourse to**, employ, fall back on, turn to, use, utilize ▷ *n* **2** = **holiday centre**, haunt, retreat, spot, tourist centre **3** = **recourse**, reference

resound *v* = **echo**, re-echo, resonate, reverberate, ring

resource *n* **2** = **ingenuity**, ability, capability, cleverness, initiative, inventiveness **3** = **means**, course, device, expedient, resort ▷ *pl* **4** = **assets**, capital, holdings, lolly (*Aust & NZ sl*), money, riches, wealth **5** = **funds**, reserves, supplies

respect *n* **1** = **consideration** **2** = **regard**, admiration, deference, esteem, estimation, honour, recognition **3** = **particular**, aspect, characteristic, detail, feature, matter, point, sense, way **4** = **relation**, bearing, connection, reference, regard ▷ *v* **5** = **think highly of**, admire, defer to, esteem, have a good or high opinion of, honour, look up to, value **6** = **abide by**, adhere to, comply with, follow, heed, honour, obey, observe, show consideration for

respite *n* **1** = **pause**, break, cessation, halt, interval, lull, recess, relief, rest

resplendent *adj* = **brilliant**, bright, dazzling, glorious, radiant, shining, splendid

respond *v* **1** = **answer**, counter, reciprocate, rejoin, reply, retort, return **2** = **react**

r

responsible ❶ *adj* 1 having control and
authority. 2 reporting or accountable
(to). 3 sensible and dependable.
4 involving responsibility. **responsibly** *adv*
responsibility *n, pl* **-ties** 1 state of being
responsible. 2 person or thing for which
one is responsible.

rest¹ ❶ *n* 1 freedom from exertion etc.
2 repose. 3 pause, esp. in music. 4 object
used for support. ▷ *v* 5 take a rest. 6 give
a rest (to). 7 be supported. 8 place on a
support. **restful** *adj* **restless** *adj*.

rest² ❶ *n* 1 what is left. 2 others. ▷ *v*
3 remain, continue to be.

restaurant ❶ *n* commercial
establishment serving meals.
restaurateur [rest-er-a-**tur**] *n* person who
owns or runs a restaurant.

restitution ❶ *n* 1 giving back.
2 reparation or compensation.

restive ❶ *adj* restless or impatient.

restore ❶ *v* 1 return (a building, painting,

etc.) to its original condition. 2 cause
to recover health or spirits. 3 give back,
return. 4 re-establish. **restoration** *n*
restorative *adj* 1 restoring. ▷ *n* 2 food or
medicine to strengthen etc. **restorer** *n*.

restrain ❶ *v* 1 hold (someone) back
from action. 2 control or restrict.
restraint *n* 1 control, esp. self-control.
2 restraining. **restrained** *adj* not
displaying emotion.

restrict ❶ *v* confine to certain limits.
restriction *n* **restrictive** *adj*.

result ❶ *n* 1 outcome or consequence.
2 score. 3 number obtained from a
calculation. 4 exam mark or grade.
▷ *v* 5 (foll. by *from*) be the outcome or
consequence (of). 6 (foll. by *in*) end (in).
resultant *adj*.

resume ❶ *v* 1 begin again. 2 occupy or
take again. **resumption** *n*.

resurgence ❶ *n* rising again to vigour.
resurgent *adj*.

responsible *adj* 1 = **in charge**, in
authority, in control 2 = **accountable**,
answerable, liable 3 = **sensible**,
dependable, level-headed, rational,
reliable, trustworthy

rest¹ *n* 1 = **inactivity** 2 = **relaxation**,
leisure, repose 3 = **pause**, break,
cessation, halt, interlude, intermission,
interval, lull, respite, stop 4 = **support**,
base, holder, prop, stand ▷ *v* 5 **a** = **relax**,
be at ease, put one's feet up, sit down, take
it easy **b** = **stop**, break off, cease, halt,
have a break, take a breather (*inf*) 7 = **be
supported**, lean, lie, recline, repose, sit
8 = **place**, lean, lie, prop, sit

rest² *n* 1 = **remainder**, balance, excess,
remains, remnants, residue, surplus
2 = **others**

restaurant *n* = **café**, bistro, cafeteria,
diner (*chiefly US & Canad*), tearoom

restitution *n* 1 = **return**, restoration
2 = **compensation**, amends, recompense,
reparation, requital

restive *adj* = **restless**, edgy, fidgety,

impatient, jumpy, nervous, on edge,
wired (*sl*)

restore *v* 1 = **repair**, fix, mend, rebuild,
recondition, reconstruct, refurbish, renew,
renovate 2 = **revive**, build up, refresh,
revitalize, strengthen 3 = **return**, bring
back, give back, recover, reinstate, replace
4 = **reinstate**, re-establish, reintroduce

restrain *v* 1, 2 = **hold back**, check,
constrain, contain, control, curb, curtail,
hamper, hinder, inhibit, restrict

restrict *v* = **limit**, bound, confine, contain,
hamper, handicap, inhibit, regulate,
restrain

result *n* 1 = **consequence**, effect, end, end
result, outcome, product, sequel, upshot
▷ *v* 5 (foll. by *from*) = **arise**, appear, derive,
develop, ensue, follow, happen, issue,
spring 6 (foll. by *in*) = **end**, culminate

resume *v* 1 = **begin again**, carry on,
continue, go on, proceed, reopen, restart

resurgence *n* = **revival**, rebirth, re-
emergence, renaissance, resumption,
resurrection, return

resurrect ❶ v 1 restore to life. 2 use once more (something discarded etc.), revive. **resurrection** n 1 rising again (esp. from the dead). 2 revival.

resuscitate ❶ [ris-**suss**-it-tate] v restore to consciousness. **resuscitation** n.

● **SPELLING TIP**
● There is a silent c in **resuscitate**, but
● only one: it comes after the second s,
● not after the first one.

retail n 1 selling of goods individually or in small amounts to the public. ▷ adv 2 by retail. ▷ v 3 sell or be sold retail. 4 recount in detail. **retailer** n.

retain ❶ v 1 keep in one's possession. 2 engage the services of. **retainer** n 1 fee to retain someone's services. 2 old-established servant of a family.

retaliate ❶ v repay an injury or wrong in kind. **retaliation** n **retaliatory** adj.

retard ❶ v delay or slow (progress or development). **retarded** adj underdeveloped, esp. mentally. **retardation** n.

retch ❶ v try to vomit.

reticent ❶ adj uncommunicative, reserved. **reticence** n.

retina n, pl **-nas, -nae** light-sensitive membrane at the back of the eye.

retinue ❶ n band of attendants.

retire ❶ v 1 (cause to) give up office or work, esp. through age. 2 go away or withdraw. 3 go to bed. **retired** adj having retired from work etc. **retirement** n **retiring** adj shy.

retort¹ ❶ v 1 reply quickly, wittily, or angrily. ▷ n 2 quick, witty, or angry reply.

retort² n glass container with a bent neck used for distilling.

retrace v go back over (a route etc.) again.

retract ❶ v 1 withdraw (a statement etc.). 2 draw in or back. **retractable, retractile** adj able to be retracted. **retraction** n.

retreat ❶ v 1 move back from a position, withdraw. ▷ n 2 act of or military signal for retiring or withdrawal. 3 place to which anyone retires, refuge.

retrench v reduce expenditure, cut back. **retrenchment** n.

retribution ❶ n punishment or vengeance

THESAURUS

resurrect v 1 = **restore to life**, raise from the dead 2 = **revive**, bring back, reintroduce, renew

resuscitate v = **revive**, bring round, resurrect, revitalize, save

retain v 1 = **keep**, hold, maintain, preserve, reserve, save 2 = **hire**, commission, employ, engage, pay, reserve

retaliate v = **pay (someone) back**, get even with (inf), get one's own back (inf), hit back, reciprocate, strike back, take revenge

retard v = **slow down**, arrest, check, delay, handicap, hinder, hold back or up, impede, set back

retch v = **gag**, be sick, heave, puke (sl), regurgitate, spew, throw up (inf), vomit

reticent adj = **uncommunicative**, close-lipped, quiet, reserved, silent, taciturn, tight-lipped, unforthcoming

retinue n = **attendants**, aides, entourage,

escort, followers, servants

retire v 1 = **stop working**, give up work 2 = **withdraw**, depart, exit, go away, leave 3 = **go to bed**, hit the hay (sl), hit the sack (sl), turn in (inf)

retort¹ v 1 = **reply**, answer, come back with, counter, respond, return, riposte ▷ n 2 = **reply**, answer, comeback (inf), rejoinder, response, riposte

retract v 1 = **withdraw**, deny, disavow, disclaim, eat one's words, recant, renege, renounce, revoke, take back 2 = **draw in**, pull back, pull in, sheathe

retreat v 1 = **withdraw**, back away, back off, depart, draw back, fall back, go back, leave, pull back ▷ n 2 = **withdrawal**, departure, evacuation, flight, retirement 3 = **refuge**, haven, hideaway, sanctuary, seclusion, shelter

retribution n = **punishment**, justice, Nemesis, reckoning, reprisal, retaliation,

r

for wrongdoing or evil deeds.

retrieve ❶ v **1** fetch back again. **2** restore to a better state. **3** recover (information) from a computer. **retrieval** n **retriever** n dog trained to retrieve shot game.

retroactive adj effective from a date in the past.

retrograde ❶ adj tending towards an earlier worse condition.

retrospect n **in retrospect** when looking back on the past. **retrospective** adj **1** looking back in time. **2** applying from a date in the past. ▷ n **3** exhibition of an artist's life's work.

return ❶ v **1** go or come back. **2** give, put, or send back. **3** reply. **4** elect. ▷ n **5** returning. **6** (thing) being returned. **7** profit. **8** official report, as of taxable income. **9** return ticket. **return ticket** ticket allowing a passenger to travel to a place and back.

reunion n meeting of people who have been apart. **reunite** v bring or come together again after a separation.

rev informal ▷ n **1** revolution (of an engine). ▷ v **revving, revved 2** (foll. by up)

increase the speed of revolution of (an engine).

Rev., Revd. Reverend.

revalue v adjust the exchange value of (a currency) upwards. **revaluation** n.

revamp ❶ v renovate or restore.

reveal ❶ v **1** make known. **2** expose or show. **revelation** n.

reveille [riv-**val**-ee] n morning bugle call to waken soldiers.

revel ❶ v **-elling, -elled 1** take pleasure (in). **2** make merry. **reveller** n **revelry** n festivity.

revenge ❶ n **1** retaliation for wrong done. ▷ v **2** make retaliation for. **3** avenge (oneself or another). **revengeful** adj.

revenue ❶ n income, esp. of a state.

reverberate ❶ v echo or resound. **reverberation** n.

revere ❶ v be in awe of and respect greatly. **reverence** n awe mingled with respect and esteem. **Reverend** adj title of respect for a clergyman. **reverent** adj showing reverence. **reverential** adj marked by reverence.

reverie ❶ n absent-minded daydream.

                                       THESAURUS

revenge, vengeance

retrieve v **1 = get back**, recapture, recoup, recover, redeem, regain, restore, save, win back

retrograde adj **1 = deteriorating**, backward, declining, degenerative, downward, regressive, retrogressive, worsening

return v **1 = come back**, go back, reappear, rebound, recur, retreat, revert, turn back **2 = put back**, re-establish, reinstate, replace, restore **3 = reply**, answer, respond, retort **4 = elect**, choose, vote in ▷ n **7 = profit**, gain, income, interest, proceeds, revenue, takings, yield **8 = statement**, account, form, list, report, summary

revamp v **= renovate**, do up (inf), overhaul, recondition, refurbish, restore

reveal v **1 = make known**, announce, disclose, divulge, give away, impart,

let out, let slip, make public, proclaim, tell **2 = show**, display, exhibit, manifest, uncover, unearth, unmask, unveil

revel v **1 = revel in = enjoy**, delight in, indulge in, lap up, luxuriate in, relish, take pleasure in, thrive on **2 = celebrate**, carouse, live it up (inf), make merry

revenge n **1 = retaliation**, an eye for an eye, reprisal, retribution, vengeance ▷ v **2, 3 = avenge**, get even, get one's own back for (inf), repay, retaliate, take revenge for

revenue n **= income**, gain, proceeds, profits, receipts, returns, takings, yield

reverberate v **= echo**, re-echo, resound, ring, vibrate

revere v **= be in awe of**, exalt, honour, look up to, respect, reverence, venerate, worship

reverie n **= daydream**, abstraction, brown

reverse ⊘ v **1** turn upside down or the other way round. **2** change completely. **3** move (a vehicle) backwards. ▷ n **4** opposite. **5** back side. **6** change for the worse. **7** reverse gear. ▷ adj **8** opposite or contrary. **reversal** n **reversible** adj **reverse gear** mechanism enabling a vehicle to move backwards.

revert ⊘ v **1** return to a former state. **2** come back to a subject. **3** (of property) return to its former owner. **reversion** n.

review ⊘ n **1** critical assessment of a book, concert, etc. **2** publication with critical articles. **3** general survey. **4** formal inspection. ▷ v **5** hold or write a review of. **6** examine, reconsider, or look back on. **7** inspect formally. **reviewer** n writer of reviews.

revile ⊘ v be abusively scornful of.

revise ⊘ v **1** change or alter. **2** restudy (work) in preparation for an examination. **revision** n.

revive ⊘ v bring or come back to life, vigour, use, etc. **revival** n **1** reviving or renewal. **2** movement seeking to restore religious faith. **revivalism** n **revivalist** n.

revoke ⊘ v cancel (a will, agreement, etc.). **revocation** n.

revolt ⊘ n **1** uprising against authority. ▷ v **2** rise in rebellion. **3** cause to feel disgust. **revolting** adj disgusting, horrible.

revolve ⊘ v turn round, rotate. **revolve around** be centred on. **revolver** n repeating pistol.

revue n theatrical entertainment with topical sketches and songs.

revulsion ⊘ n strong disgust.

reward ⊘ n **1** something given in return for a service. **2** sum of money offered for finding a criminal or missing property. ▷ v

————————————— THESAURUS —————————————

study, woolgathering

reverse v **1** = **turn round**, invert, transpose, turn back, turn over, turn upside down, upend **2** = **change**, overthrow, overturn **3** = **go backwards**, back, back up, move backwards, retreat ▷ n **4** = **opposite**, contrary, converse, inverse **5** = **back**, other side, rear, underside, wrong side **6** = **misfortune**, adversity, affliction, blow, disappointment, failure, hardship, misadventure, mishap, reversal, setback ▷ adj **8** = **opposite**, contrary, converse

revert v **1,2** = **return**, come back, go back, resume

review n **1** = **critique**, commentary, criticism, evaluation, judgment, notice **2** = **magazine**, journal, periodical **3** = **survey**, analysis, examination, scrutiny, study **4** = **inspection**, march past, parade ▷ v **5** = **assess**, criticize, evaluate, judge, study **6** = **look back on**, examine, inspect, reassess, recall, recollect, reconsider, re-evaluate, re-examine, reflect on, remember, rethink, revise, think over

revile v = **malign**, abuse, bad-mouth (sl, chiefly US & Canad), denigrate, knock (inf), reproach, run down, slag (off) (sl), vilify

revise v **1** = **change**, alter, amend, correct, edit, emend, redo, review, rework, update **2** = **study**, cram (inf), go over, run through, swot up (Brit inf)

revive v = **revitalize**, awaken, bring round, come round, invigorate, reanimate, recover, refresh, rekindle, renew, restore

revoke v = **cancel**, annul, countermand, disclaim, invalidate, negate, nullify, obviate, quash, repeal, rescind, retract, reverse, set aside, withdraw

revolt n **1** = **uprising**, insurgency, insurrection, mutiny, rebellion, revolution, rising ▷ v **2** = **rebel**, mutiny, resist, rise **3** = **disgust**, gross out (US sl), make one's flesh creep, nauseate, repel, repulse, sicken, turn one's stomach

revolve v = **go round**, circle, orbit, rotate, spin, turn, twist, wheel, whirl

revulsion n = **disgust**, abhorrence, detestation, loathing, repugnance, repulsion

reward n **1** = **payment**, bonus, bounty,

r

3 pay or give something to (someone) for a service, information, etc. **rewarding** adj giving personal satisfaction, worthwhile.

rewind v run (a tape or film) back to an earlier point in order to replay.

rewire v provide (a house, engine, etc.) with new wiring.

rhapsody ❶ n, pl -dies **1** freely structured emotional piece of music. **2** expression of ecstatic enthusiasm. **rhapsodic** adj **rhapsodize** v speak or write with extravagant enthusiasm.

rhesus [ree-suss] n small long-tailed monkey of S Asia. **rhesus factor, Rh factor** antigen commonly found in human blood: the terms **Rh positive** and **Rh negative** are used to indicate its presence or absence.

rhetoric ❶ n **1** art of effective speaking or writing. **2** artificial or exaggerated language. **rhetorical** adj (of a question) not requiring an answer. **rhetorically** adv.

rheumatism n painful inflammation of joints or muscles. **rheumatic** n, adj (person) affected by rheumatism. **rheumatoid** adj of or like rheumatism.

rhinoceros n, pl -oses, -os large thick-skinned animal with one or two horns on its nose.

● **SPELLING TIP**
● The pronunciation of **rhinoceros**
● probably misleads some people into
● adding a u before the final s (rhinocerous).

rhododendron n evergreen flowering shrub.

rhombus n, pl -buses, -bi parallelogram with sides of equal length but no right angles, diamond-shaped figure.

rhomboid n parallelogram with adjacent sides of unequal length.

rhubarb n garden plant of which the fleshy stalks are cooked as fruit.

rhyme ❶ n **1** sameness of the final sounds at the ends of lines of verse, or in words. **2** word identical in sound to another in its final sounds. **3** verse marked by rhyme. ▷ v **4** make a rhyme.

rhythm ❶ n **1** any regular movement or beat. **2** arrangement of the durations of and stress on the notes of a piece of music, usu. grouped into a regular pattern. **3** (in poetry) arrangement of words to form a regular pattern of stresses. **rhythmic, rhythmical** adj **rhythmically** adv **rhythm and blues** popular music, orig. Black American, influenced by the blues.

● **SPELLING TIP**
● The second letter of **rhythm** is a silent h,
● which people often forget in writing.

RI Rhode Island.

rib n **1** one of the curved bones forming the framework of the upper part of the body. **2** cut of meat including the rib(s). **3** curved supporting part, as in the hull of a boat. **4** raised series of rows in knitting. ▷ v **ribbing, ribbed 5** provide or mark with ribs. **6** knit to form a rib pattern. **ribbed** adj **ribbing** n **ribcage** n bony structure of ribs enclosing the lungs.

ribald ❶ adj humorously or mockingly rude or obscene. **ribaldry** n.

ribbon n **1** narrow band of fabric used for trimming, tying, etc. **2** any long strip, for example of inked tape in a typewriter.

rice n **1** cereal plant grown on wet ground in warm countries. **2** its seeds as food.

compensation, premium, prize, recompense, repayment, return, wages ▷ v **3** = **compensate**, pay, recompense, remunerate, repay
rhetoric n **1** = **oratory**, eloquence **2** = **hyperbole**, bombast, grandiloquence, magniloquence, verbosity, wordiness

rhyme n **3** = **poetry**, ode, poem, song, verse ▷ v **4** = **sound like**, harmonize
rhythm n **1** = **beat**, accent, cadence, lilt, metre, pulse, swing, tempo, time
ribald adj = **coarse**, bawdy, blue, broad, earthy, naughty, near the knuckle (inf), obscene, racy, rude, smutty, vulgar

rich ⓘ *adj* 1 owning a lot of money or property, wealthy. 2 abounding. 3 fertile. 4 (of food) containing much fat or sugar. 5 mellow. 6 amusing. **riches** *pl n* wealth. **richly** *adv* 1 elaborately. 2 fully. **richness** *n*.

rick¹ *n* stack of hay etc.

rick² *v, n* sprain or wrench.

rickets *n* disease of children marked by softening of the bones, bow legs, etc., caused by vitamin D deficiency.

rickshaw *n* light two-wheeled man-drawn Asian vehicle.

ricochet [rik-osh-ay] *v* 1 (of a bullet) rebound from a solid surface. ▷ *n* 2 such a rebound.

rid ⓘ *v* **ridding, rid** clear or relieve (of). **get rid of** free oneself of (something undesirable). **good riddance** relief at getting rid of something or someone.

ridden *v* 1 past participle of RIDE. ▷ *adj* 2 afflicted or affected by the thing specified, e.g. *disease-ridden*.

riddle¹ ⓘ *n* 1 question made puzzling to test one's ingenuity. 2 puzzling person or thing.

riddle² ⓘ *v* 1 pierce with many holes. ▷ *n* 2 coarse sieve for gravel etc. **riddled with** full of.

ride ⓘ *v* **riding, rode, ridden** 1 sit on and control or propel (a horse, bicycle, etc.). 2 go on horseback or in a vehicle. 3 travel over. 4 be carried on or across. 5 lie at anchor. ▷ *n* 6 journey on a horse etc., or in a vehicle. 7 type of movement experienced in a vehicle. **rider** *n* 1 person who rides. 2 supplementary clause added to a document. **ride up** *v* (of a garment) move up from the proper position.

ridge *n* 1 long narrow hill. 2 long narrow raised part on a surface. 3 line where two sloping surfaces meet. 4 *Meteorol* elongated area of high pressure. **ridged** *adj*.

ridiculous ⓘ *adj* deserving to be laughed at, absurd. **ridicule** *n* 1 treatment of a person or thing as ridiculous. ▷ *v* 2 laugh at, make fun of.

rife ⓘ *adj* widespread or common. **rife with** full of.

riff *n Jazz, rock* short repeated melodic figure.

riffraff ⓘ *n* rabble, disreputable people.·

rifle¹ *n* 1 firearm with a long barrel. ▷ *v* 2 cut spiral grooves inside the barrel of a gun.

rifle² ⓘ *v* 1 search and rob. 2 steal.

rift ⓘ *n* 1 break in friendly relations.

rich *adj* 1 = **wealthy**, affluent, loaded (*sl*), moneyed, prosperous, well-heeled (*inf*), well-off, well-to-do 2 = **well-stocked**, full, productive, well-supplied 3 = **fruitful**, abounding, abundant, ample, copious, fertile, lush, luxurious, plentiful, productive, prolific 4 = **full-bodied**, creamy, fatty, luscious, succulent, sweet, tasty

rid *v* = **free**, clear, deliver, disburden, disencumber, make free, purge, relieve, unburden **get rid of** = **dispose of**, dump, eject, eliminate, expel, remove, throw away *or* out

riddle¹ *n* 1, 2 = **puzzle**, conundrum, enigma, mystery, poser, problem

riddle² *v* 1 = **pierce**, honeycomb, pepper, perforate, puncture ▷ *n* 2 = **sieve**, filter, screen, strainer

ride *v* 1 = **control**, handle, manage 2 = **travel**, be carried, go, move ▷ *n* 6 = **journey**, drive, jaunt, lift, outing, trip

ridiculous *adj* = **laughable**, absurd, comical, farcical, funny, ludicrous, risible, silly, stupid

rife *adj* = **widespread**, common, frequent, general, prevalent, rampant, ubiquitous, universal

riffraff *n* = **rabble**, hoi polloi, ragtag and bobtail

rifle² *v* = **ransack**, burgle, go through, loot, pillage, plunder, rob, sack, strip

rift *n* 1 = **breach**, disagreement, division, falling out (*inf*), quarrel, separation,

r

2 crack, split, or cleft.

rig ❶ *v* **rigging**, **rigged** **1** arrange in a dishonest way. **2** equip, esp. a ship. ▷ *n* **3** apparatus for drilling for oil and gas. **4** way a ship's masts and sails are arranged. **5** *informal* outfit of clothes. **rigging** *n* ship's spars and ropes. **rig up** *v* set up or build temporarily.

right ❶ *adj* **1** just. **2** true or correct. **3** proper. **4** in a satisfactory condition. **5** of the side that faces east when the front is turned to the north. **6** of the outer side of a fabric. ▷ *adv* **7** properly. **8** straight or directly. **9** on or to the right side. ▷ *n* **10** claim, title, etc. allowed or due. **11** what is just or due. **12** (**R-**) conservative political party or group. ▷ *v* **13** bring or come back to a normal or correct state. **14** bring or come back to a vertical position. **in the right** morally or legally correct. **right away** immediately. **rightly** *adv* **rightful** *adj* **rightist** *n*, *adj* (person) on the political right. **right angle** angle of 90°. **right-handed** *adj* using or for the right hand. **right-hand man** person's most valuable assistant. **right of way 1** right of one vehicle to go before another. **2** legal right to pass over someone's land.

righteous ❶ [**rye**-chuss] *adj* **1** upright, godly, or virtuous. **2** morally justified. **righteousness** *n*.

rigid ❶ *adj* **1** inflexible or strict. **2** unyielding or stiff. **rigidly** *adv* **rigidity** *n*.

rigmarole ❶ *n* long complicated procedure.

rigor mortis *n* stiffening of the body after death.

rigour ❶ *n* **1** harshness, severity, or strictness. **2** hardship. **rigorous** *adj* harsh, severe, or stern.

rile ❶ *v* anger or annoy.

rim ❶ *n* **1** edge or border. **2** outer ring of a wheel.

rind ❶ *n* tough outer coating of fruits,

---

split **2** = **split**, break, cleft, crack, crevice, fault, fissure, flaw, gap, opening

rig *v* **1** = **fix** (*inf*), arrange, engineer, gerrymander, manipulate, tamper with **2** = **equip**, fit out, furnish, kit out, outfit, supply ▷ *n* **3** = **apparatus**, equipment, fittings, fixtures, gear, tackle **5** *Inf* = **outfit**, costume, dress, garb, gear (*inf*), get-up (*inf*), togs

right *adj* **1** = **just**, equitable, ethical, fair, good, honest, lawful, moral, proper **2** = **correct**, accurate, exact, factual, genuine, precise, true, valid **3** = **proper**, appropriate, becoming, desirable, done, fit, fitting, seemly, suitable ▷ *adv* **7** = **suitably**, appropriately, aptly, fittingly, properly **8** = **straight**, directly, promptly, quickly, straightaway ▷ *n* **10** = **prerogative**, authority, business, claim, due, freedom, liberty, licence, mana (*NZ*), permission, power, privilege **11** = **justice**, fairness, lawfulness, legality, righteousness, truth ▷ *v* **13** = **rectify**, correct, fix, put right, redress, settle, sort out, straighten **right away** = **immediately**, at once, directly, forthwith, instantly, now, pronto (*inf*), straightaway

righteous *adj* = **virtuous**, ethical, fair, good, honest, honourable, just, moral, pure, upright

rigid *adj* **1** = **strict**, exact, fixed, inflexible, rigorous, set, stringent, unbending, uncompromising **2** = **stiff**, inflexible, unyielding

rigmarole *n* = **procedure**, bother, carry-on (*inf, chiefly Brit*), fuss, hassle (*inf*), nonsense, palaver, pantomime (*inf*), performance (*inf*)

rigour *n* **1** = **strictness**, harshness, inflexibility, rigidity, sternness, stringency **2** = **hardship**, ordeal, privation, suffering, trial

rile *v* = **anger**, aggravate (*inf*), annoy, get or put one's back up, irk, irritate

rim *n* **1** = **edge**, border, brim, brink, lip, margin, verge

rind *n* = **skin**, crust, husk, outer layer, peel

cheese, or bacon.

ring¹ ❶ v **ringing**, **rang**, **rung 1** give out a clear resonant sound, as a bell. **2** cause (a bell) to sound. **3** telephone. **4** resound. ▷ n **5** ringing. **6** telephone call. **ring off** v end a telephone call. **ringtone** n tune played by a cell phone when it receives a call. **ring up** v telephone.

ring² ❶ n **1** circle of gold etc., esp. for a finger. **2** any circular band, coil, or rim. **3** circle of people. **4** enclosed area, esp. a circle for a circus or a roped-in square for boxing. **5** group operating (illegal) control of a market. ▷ v **6** put a ring round. **7** mark (a bird) with a ring. **8** kill (a tree) by cutting the bark round the trunk. **ringer** n slang person or thing apparently identical to another (also **dead ringer**). **ringlet** n curly lock of hair. **ringleader** n instigator of a mutiny, riot, etc. **ring road** main road that bypasses a town (centre). **ringside** n row of seats nearest a boxing or circus ring. **ringtail** n Aust possum with a curling tail used to grip branches while climbing. **ringtone** n tune played by a mobile phone when it receives a call. **ringworm** n fungal skin disease in circular patches.

rink n **1** sheet of ice for skating or curling. **2** floor for roller-skating.

rinse ❶ v **1** remove soap from (washed clothes, hair, etc.) by applying clean water. **2** wash lightly. ▷ n **3** rinsing. **4** liquid to tint hair.

riot ❶ n **1** disorderly unruly disturbance. **2** loud revelry. **3** profusion. **4** slang very amusing person or thing. ▷ v **5** take part in a riot. **read the riot act** reprimand severely. **run riot 1** behave without restraint. **2** grow profusely. **riotous** adj **1** unrestrained. **2** unruly or rebellious.

rip ❶ v **ripping**, **ripped 1** tear violently. **2** tear away. **3** informal rush. ▷ n **4** split or tear. **let rip** act or speak without restraint. **ripcord** n cord pulled to open a parachute. **rip off** v slang cheat by overcharging. **rip-off** n slang cheat or swindle. **rip-roaring** adj informal boisterous and exciting.

RIP rest in peace.

ripe ❶ adj **1** ready to be reaped, eaten, etc. **2** matured. **3** ready or suitable. **ripen** v **1** grow ripe. **2** mature.

riposte ❶ [rip-**posst**] n **1** verbal retort. **2** counterattack, esp. in fencing. ▷ v **3** make a riposte.

ripple n **1** slight wave or ruffling of a surface. **2** sound like ripples of water. ▷ v **3** flow or form into little waves (on). **4** (of sounds) rise and fall gently.

ring¹ v **1, 2** = **chime**, clang, peal, reverberate, sound, toll **3** = **phone**, buzz (inf, chiefly Brit), call, telephone ▷ n **5** = **chime**, knell, peal **6** = **call**, buzz (inf, chiefly Brit), phone call

ring² n **1, 2** = **circle**, band, circuit, halo, hoop, loop, round **4** = **arena**, circus, enclosure, rink **5** = **gang**, association, band, cartel, circle, group, mob, syndicate ▷ v **6** = **encircle**, enclose, gird, girdle, surround

rinse v **1, 2** = **wash**, bathe, clean, cleanse, dip, splash ▷ n **3** = **wash**, bath, dip, splash

riot n **1** = **disturbance**, anarchy, confusion, disorder, lawlessness, strife, tumult, turbulence, turmoil, upheaval **2** = **merrymaking**, carousal, festivity,

frolic, high jinks, revelry **3** = **display**, extravaganza, profusion, show, splash ▷ v **5** = **rampage**, go on the rampage **run riot 1** = **rampage**, be out of control, go wild **2** = **grow profusely**, spread like wildfire

rip v **1** = **tear**, burst, claw, cut, gash, lacerate, rend, slash, slit, split ▷ n **4** = **tear**, cut, gash, hole, laceration, rent, slash, slit, split

ripe adj **1, 2** = **mature**, mellow, ready, ripened, seasoned **3** = **suitable**, auspicious, favourable, ideal, opportune, right, timely

riposte n **1** = **retort**, answer, comeback (inf), rejoinder, reply, response, sally ▷ v **3** = **retort**, answer, come back, reply, respond

r

rise ⓥ *v* **rising, rose, risen 1** get up from a lying, sitting, or kneeling position. **2** move upwards. **3** (of the sun or moon) appear above the horizon. **4** reach a higher level. **5** (of an amount or price) increase. **6** rebel. **7** (of a court) adjourn. ▷ *n* **8** rising. **9** upward slope. **10** increase, esp. of wages. **give rise to** cause. **riser** *n* **1** person who rises, esp. from bed. **2** vertical part of a step. **rising** *n* **1** revolt. ▷ *adj* **2** increasing in rank or maturity.

risk ⓥ *n* **1** chance of disaster or loss. **2** person or thing considered as a potential hazard. ▷ *v* **3** act in spite of the possibility of (injury or loss). **4** expose to danger or loss. **risky** *adj* full of risk, dangerous.

risotto *n, pl* **-tos** dish of rice cooked in stock with vegetables, meat, etc.

risqué [**risk**-ay] *adj* bordering on indecency.

rissole *n* cake of minced meat, coated with breadcrumbs and fried.

rite ⓥ *n* formal practice or custom, esp. religious.

rival ⓥ *n* **1** person or thing that competes with or equals another for favour, success, etc. ▷ *adj* **2** in the position of a rival. ▷ *v* **-valling, -valled 3** (try to) equal. **rivalry** *n* keen competition.

river ⓥ *n* **1** large natural stream of water.

2 plentiful flow.

rivet ⓥ [**riv**-vit] *n* **1** bolt for fastening metal plates, the end being put through holes and then beaten flat. ▷ *v* **riveting, riveted 2** fasten with rivets. **3** cause to be fixed, as in fascination. **riveting** *adj* very interesting and exciting.

rivulet *n* small stream.

RN Royal Navy.

road ⓥ *n* **1** way prepared for passengers, vehicles, etc. **2** route in a town or city with houses along it. **3** way or course, e.g. *the road to fame*. **on the road** travelling. **roadie** *n* *informal* person who transports and sets up equipment for a band. **roadblock** *n* barricade across a road to stop traffic for inspection etc. **road hog** *informal* selfish aggressive driver. **roadhouse** *n* pub or restaurant on a country road. **roadside** *n, adj* **road test** test of a vehicle etc. in actual use. **roadway** *n* the part of a road used by vehicles. **roadworks** *pl n* repairs to a road, esp. blocking part of the road. **roadworthy** *adj* (of a vehicle) mechanically sound.

roam ⓥ *v* wander about.

roar ⓥ *v* **1** make or utter a loud deep hoarse sound like that of a lion. **2** shout

---

THESAURUS

rise *v* **1** = **get up**, arise, get to one's feet, stand up **2** = **go up**, ascend, climb **4** = **advance**, get on, progress, prosper **5** = **increase**, go up, grow, intensify, mount **6** = **rebel**, mutiny, revolt ▷ *n* **10** = **advancement**, climb, progress, promotion **11** = **upward slope**, ascent, elevation, incline **12** = **increase**, increment, pay increase, raise (*US*), upsurge, upswing, upturn **give rise to** = **cause**, bring about, effect, produce, result in

risk *n* **1** = **danger**, chance, gamble, hazard, jeopardy, peril, pitfall, possibility ▷ *v* **3, 4** = **dare**, chance, endanger, gamble, hazard, imperil, jeopardize, venture

risqué *adj* = **suggestive**, bawdy, blue, improper, indelicate, naughty, near the

knuckle (*inf*), racy, ribald

rite *n* = **ceremony**, custom, observance, practice, procedure, ritual

rival *n* **1** = **opponent**, adversary, competitor, contender, contestant *adj* **2** = **competing**, conflicting, opposing ▷ *v* **3** = **compete**, be a match for, compare with, equal, match

river *n* **1** = **stream**, brook, burn (*Scot*), creek, tributary, waterway **2** = **flow**, flood, rush, spate, torrent

road *n* **1** = **way**, course, highway, lane, motorway, path, pathway, roadway, route, track

roam *v* = **wander**, prowl, ramble, range, rove, stray, travel, walk

roar *v* **2** = **cry**, bawl, bellow, howl, shout,

(something) as in anger. **3** laugh loudly. ▷ *n* **4** such a sound. **a roaring trade** *informal* brisk and profitable business.

roast *v* **1** cook by dry heat, as in an oven. **2** make or be very hot. ▷ *n* **3** roasted joint of meat. ▷ *adj* **4** roasted. **roasting** *informal* ▷ *adj* **1** extremely hot. ▷ *n* **2** severe criticism or scolding.

rob ❶ *v* **robbing, robbed** **1** steal from. **2** deprive. **robber** *n* **robbery** *n*.

robe ❶ *n* **1** long loose outer garment. ▷ *v* **2** put a robe on.

robin *n* small brown bird with a red breast.

robot ❶ *n* **1** automated machine, esp. one performing functions in a human manner. **2** person of machine-like efficiency. **3** *S Afr* set of coloured lights at a junction to control the traffic flow. **robotic** *adj* **robotics** *n* science of designing and using robots.

robust ❶ *adj* very strong and healthy. **robustness** *n*.

rock¹ ❶ *n* **1** hard mineral substance that makes up part of the earth's crust, stone. **2** large rugged mass of stone. **3** hard sweet in sticks. **on the rocks 1** (of a marriage) about to end. **2** (of an alcoholic drink) served with ice. **rocky** *adj* having many rocks. **rockery** *n* mound of stones in a garden for rock plants. **rock bottom** lowest possible level.

rock² ❶ *v* **1** (cause to) sway to and fro. ▷ *n* **2** (also **rock music**) style of pop music with a heavy beat. **rocky** *adj* shaky or unstable. **rock and roll, rock'n'roll** style of pop music blending rhythm and blues and country music. **rocking chair** chair allowing the sitter to rock backwards and forwards.

rocket *n* **1** self-propelling device powered by the burning of explosive contents (used as a firework, weapon, etc.). **2** vehicle propelled by a rocket engine, as a weapon or carrying a spacecraft. ▷ *v* **-eting, -eted** **3** move fast, esp. upwards, like a rocket.

rock melon *n Aust, NZ & US* type of melon with sweet orange flesh.

rod ❶ *n* **1** slender straight bar, stick. **2** cane.

rodent *n* animal with teeth specialized for gnawing, such as a rat, mouse, or squirrel.

rodeo *n, pl* **-deos** display of skill by cowboys, such as bareback riding.

roe¹ *n* mass of eggs in a fish, sometimes eaten as food.

roe² *n* small species of deer.

rogue ❶ *n* **1** dishonest or unprincipled person. **2** mischief-loving person. ▷ *adj* **3** (of a wild beast) having a savage temper and living apart from the herd. **roguish** *adj*.

role, rôle ❶ *n* **1** task or function. **2** actor's part.

roll ❶ *v* **1** move by turning over and over. **2** move or sweep along. **3** wind round.

r

yell **3** = **guffaw**, hoot, laugh heartily, split one's sides (*inf*) ▷ *n* **4** = **cry**, bellow, hoot, howl, outcry, shout, yell

rob *v* **1** = **steal from**, burgle, cheat, con (*inf*), defraud, dispossess, do out of (*inf*), hold up, loot, mug (*inf*), pillage, plunder, raid **2** = **deprive**, do out of

robe *n* **1** = **gown**, costume, habit ▷ *v* **2** = **clothe**, dress, garb

robot *n* **1** = **machine**, android, automaton, mechanical man

robust *adj* = **strong**, fit, hale, hardy, healthy, muscular, powerful, stout, strapping, sturdy, tough, vigorous

rock¹ *n* **2** = **stone**, boulder

rock² *v* **1** = **sway**, lurch, pitch, reel, roll, swing, toss

rod *n* = **stick**, bar, baton, cane, pole, shaft, staff, wand

rogue *n* **1** = **scoundrel**, blackguard, crook (*inf*), fraud, rascal, scally (*NW Eng dial*), villain **2** = **scamp**, rascal

role, rôle *n* **1** = **job**, capacity, duty, function, part, position, post, task **2** = **part**, character, portrayal, representation

roll *v* **1** = **turn**, go round, revolve, rotate, spin, swivel, trundle, twirl, wheel, whirl

4 undulate. **5** smooth out with a roller. **6** (of a ship or aircraft) turn from side to side about a line from nose to tail. ▷ *n* **7** act of rolling over or from side to side. **8** piece of paper etc. rolled up. **9** small round individually baked piece of bread. **10** list or register. **11** continuous sound, as of drums, thunder, etc. **12** swaying unsteady movement or gait. **roll call** calling out of a list of names, as in a school or the army, to check who is present. **rolling pin** cylindrical roller for flattening pastry. **rolling stock** locomotives and coaches of a railway. **rolling stone** restless wandering person. **roll up** *v* *informal* appear or arrive.

rollicking *adj* boisterously carefree.

roly-poly ❶ *adj* round or plump.

ROM *Computers* read only memory.

Roman *adj* of Rome or the Roman Catholic Church. **Roman Catholic** (member) of that section of the Christian Church that acknowledges the supremacy of the Pope. **Roman numerals** the letters I, V, X, L, C, D, M, used to represent numbers. **roman type** plain upright letters in printing.

romance ❶ *n* **1** love affair. **2** mysterious or exciting quality. **3** novel or film dealing with love, esp. sentimentally. **4** story with scenes remote from ordinary life. **romantic** *adj*.

Romany *n*, *pl* **-nies**, *adj* Gypsy.

romp ❶ *v* **1** play wildly and joyfully. ▷ *n* **2** boisterous activity. **rompers** *pl n* child's overalls.

roof *n*, *pl* **roofs** **1** outside upper covering of a building, car, etc. ▷ *v* **2** put a roof on.

rooibos *n S Afr* tea prepared from the dried leaves of an African plant.

rook *n* **1** bird of the crow family. ▷ *v* **2** *old-fashioned slang* swindle. **rookery** *n*, *pl* **-eries** colony of rooks, penguins, or seals.

rookie *n informal* new recruit.

room ❶ *n* **1** enclosed area in a building. **2** unoccupied space. **3** scope or opportunity. ▷ *pl* **4** lodgings. **roomy** *adj* spacious.

roost *n* **1** perch for fowls. ▷ *v* **2** perch.

rooster *n US & Canad* domestic cock.

root¹ ❶ *n* **1** part of a plant that grows down into the earth obtaining nourishment. **2** plant with an edible root, such as a carrot. **3** part of a tooth, hair, etc. below the skin. **4** source or origin. **5** form of a word from which other words and forms are derived. **6** *Maths* factor of a quantity which, when multiplied by itself the number of times indicated, gives the quantity. ▷ *pl* **7** person's sense of belonging. ▷ *v* **8** establish a root and start to grow. **rootless** *adj* having no sense of belonging. **root for** *v informal*

————————————————————————————— THESAURUS —————————————————————————————

3 = **wind**, bind, enfold, envelop, furl, swathe, wrap **4** = **flow**, run, undulate **5** = **level**, even, flatten, press, smooth **6** = **toss**, lurch, reel, rock, sway, tumble ▷ *n* **7** = **turn**, cycle, reel, revolution, rotation, spin, twirl, wheel, whirl **10** = **register**, census, index, list, record **11** = **rumble**, boom, reverberation, roar, thunder

roly-poly *adj* = **plump**, buxom, chubby, fat, podgy, rounded, tubby

romance *n* **1** = **love affair**, affair, amour, attachment, liaison, relationship **2** = **excitement**, charm, colour, fascination, glamour, mystery **3**, **4** = **story**, fairy tale, fantasy, legend, love

story, melodrama, tale

romp *v* **1** = **frolic**, caper, cavort, frisk, gambol, have fun, sport ▷ *n* **2** = **frolic**, caper, lark (*inf*)

room *n* **1** = **chamber**, apartment, office **2** = **space**, area, capacity, expanse, extent, leeway, margin, range, scope **3** = **opportunity**, chance, occasion, scope

root¹ *n* **1** = **stem**, rhizome, tuber **4** = **source**, base, bottom, cause, core, foundation, heart, nucleus, origin, seat, seed ▷ *pl* **7** = **sense of belonging**, heritage, origins ▷ *v* **8** = **become established**, anchor, establish, fasten, fix, ground, implant, moor, set, stick

cheer on. **root out** v get rid of completely. **rootstock** n rhizome.

root², **rootle** ❶ v 1 dig or burrow. 2 *informal* search vigorously but unsystematically.

rope ❶ n thick cord. **know the ropes** be thoroughly familiar with an activity. **rope in** v persuade to join in.

rort n *Aust informal* dishonest scheme.

rosary n, pl **-saries** 1 series of prayers. 2 string of beads for counting these prayers.

rose n 1 shrub or climbing plant with prickly stems and fragrant flowers. 2 flower of this plant. 3 perforated flat nozzle for a hose. 4 pink colour. ▷ *adj* 5 pink. **roseate** [roe-zee-ate] *adj* rose-coloured. **rose window** circular window with spokes branching from the centre. **rosewood** n fragrant wood used to make furniture.

rosé [roe-zay] n pink wine.

rosemary n 1 fragrant flowering shrub. 2 its leaves as a herb.

roster ❶ n list of people and their turns of duty.

rostrum ❶ n, pl **-trums**, **-tra** platform or stage.

rot ❶ v **rotting**, **rotted** 1 decompose or decay. 2 slowly deteriorate physically or mentally. ▷ n 3 decay. 4 *informal* nonsense. **rotten** *adj*.

rota n list of people who take it in turn to do a particular task.

rotary ❶ *adj* 1 revolving. 2 operated by rotation.

rote n mechanical repetition. **by rote** by memory.

rotor n 1 revolving portion of a dynamo, motor, or turbine. 2 rotating device with long blades that provides thrust to lift a helicopter.

rotund ❶ [roe-**tund**] *adj* 1 round and plump. 2 sonorous. **rotundity** n.

rouge n red cosmetic used to colour the cheeks.

rough ❶ *adj* 1 uneven or irregular. 2 not careful or gentle. 3 difficult or unpleasant. 4 approximate. 5 violent, stormy, or boisterous. 6 in preliminary form. 7 lacking refinement. ▷ v 8 make rough. ▷ n 9 rough state or area. **rough it** live without the usual comforts etc. **roughen** v **roughly** *adv* **roughness** n **roughage** n indigestible constituents of food which aid digestion. **rough-and-ready** *adj* hastily

root², **rootle** v 1 = **dig**, burrow, ferret

rope n = **cord**, cable, hawser, line, strand **know the ropes** = **be experienced**, be an old hand, be knowledgeable

roster n = **rota**, agenda, catalogue, list, register, roll, schedule, table

rostrum n = **stage**, dais, platform, podium, stand

rot v 1 = **decay**, crumble, decompose, go bad, moulder, perish, putrefy, spoil 2 = **deteriorate**, decline, waste away ▷ n 3 = **decay**, blight, canker, corruption, decomposition, mould, putrefaction 4 *Inf* = **nonsense**, claptrap (*inf*), codswallop (*Brit sl*), drivel, garbage (*chiefly US*), hogwash, kak (*S Afr sl*), poppycock (*inf*), rubbish, trash, tripe (*inf*), twaddle

rotary *adj* = **revolving**, rotating, spinning, turning

rotund *adj* 1 = **plump**, chubby, corpulent, fat, fleshy, globular, podgy, portly, rounded, spherical, stout, tubby

rough *adj* 1 = **uneven**, broken, bumpy, craggy, irregular, jagged, rocky, stony 2 = **harsh**, cruel, hard, nasty, tough, unfeeling, unpleasant, violent 3 = **unpleasant**, arduous, difficult, hard, tough, uncomfortable 4 = **approximate**, estimated, general, imprecise, inexact, sketchy, vague 5 = **stormy**, choppy, squally, turbulent, wild 6 = **basic**, crude, imperfect, incomplete, rudimentary, sketchy, unfinished, unpolished, unrefined 7 = **ungracious**, blunt, brusque, coarse, impolite, rude, unceremonious, uncivil, uncouth, unmannerly

r

prepared but adequate. **rough-and-tumble** n playful fight. **roughhouse** n slang fight. **rough out** v prepare (a sketch or report) in preliminary form.

roulette n gambling game played with a revolving wheel and a ball.

round ⊕ adj 1 spherical, cylindrical, circular, or curved. 2 complete or whole, e.g. round numbers. ▷ adv, prep 3 indicating an encircling movement, presence on all sides, etc. e.g. tied round the waist; books scattered round the room. ▷ v 4 move round. ▷ n 5 round shape. 6 recurrent duties. 7 customary course, as of a milkman. 8 game (of golf). 9 stage in a competition. 10 one of several periods in a boxing match etc. 11 number of drinks bought at one time. 12 bullet or shell for a gun. 13 part song in which singers join at equal intervals. 14 circular movement. 15 set of sandwiches. **roundly** adv thoroughly. **rounders** n bat-and-ball team game. **round robin** petition signed with names in a circle to conceal the order. **round-the-clock** adj throughout the day and night. **round trip** journey out and back again. **round up** v gather (people or animals) together. **roundup** n.

rouse¹ ⊕ v 1 wake up. 2 provoke or excite. **rousing** adj lively, vigorous.

rouse² [rhymes with **mouse**] v (foll. by on) Aust scold or rebuke.

rout ⊕ n 1 overwhelming defeat. 2 disorderly retreat. ▷ v 3 defeat and put to flight.

route ⊕ n 1 roads taken to reach a destination. 2 chosen way. **routemarch** n long military training march.

routine ⊕ n 1 usual or regular method of procedure. 2 set sequence. ▷ adj 3 ordinary or regular.

rove ⊕ v wander. **rover** n.

row¹ ⊕ [rhymes with **go**] n straight line of people or things. **in a row** in succession.

row² [rhymes with **go**] v 1 propel (a boat) by oars. ▷ n 2 spell of rowing. **rowing boat** boat propelled by oars.

row³ ⊕ [rhymes with **now**] informal ▷ n 1 dispute. 2 disturbance. 3 reprimand. ▷ v 4 quarrel noisily.

rowan n tree producing bright red berries, mountain ash.

rowdy ⊕ adj **-dier**, **-diest** 1 disorderly, noisy, and rough. ▷ n, pl **-dies** 2 person like this.

rowlock [**rol**-luk] n device on a boat that

─────────────────────────────── THESAURUS ───────────────────────────────

round adj 1 = **spherical**, circular, curved, cylindrical, globular, rotund, rounded ▷ v 4 = **go round**, bypass, circle, encircle, flank, skirt, turn ▷ n 5 = **sphere**, ball, band, circle, disc, globe, orb, ring 7 = **course**, beat, circuit, routine, schedule, series, tour 9 = **stage**, division, lap, level, period, session, turn

rouse¹ v 1 = **wake up**, awaken, call, rise, wake 2 = **excite**, agitate, anger, animate, incite, inflame, move, provoke, stimulate, stir

rout n 1 = **defeat**, beating, debacle, drubbing, overthrow, pasting (sl), thrashing ▷ v 3 = **defeat**, beat, conquer, crush, destroy, drub, overthrow, thrash, wipe the floor with (inf)

route n 2 = **way**, beat, circuit, course,

direction, itinerary, journey, path, road

routine n 1 = **procedure**, custom, method, order, pattern, practice, programme ▷ adj 3 = **usual**, customary, everyday, habitual, normal, ordinary, standard, typical

rove v = **wander**, drift, ramble, range, roam, stray, traipse (inf)

row¹ n = **line**, bank, column, file, range, series, string **in a row** = **consecutively**, one after the other, successively

row³ Inf n 1 = **quarrel**, brawl, dispute, squabble, tiff, trouble 2 = **disturbance**, commotion, noise, racket, rumpus, tumult, uproar ▷ v 4 = **quarrel**, argue, dispute, fight, squabble, wrangle

rowdy adj 1 = **disorderly**, loud, noisy, rough, unruly, wild n 2 = **hooligan**, lout, ruffian, tearaway (Brit), yob or yobbo (Brit sl)

r

holds an oar in place.

royal ❶ *adj* **1** of, befitting, or supported by a king or queen. **2** splendid. ▷ *n* **3** *informal* member of a royal family. **royally** *adv* **royalist** *n* supporter of monarchy. **royalty** *n* **1** royal people. **2** rank or power of a monarch. **3** *pl* **-ties** payment to an author, musician, inventor, etc. **royal blue** deep blue.

rpm revolutions per minute.

RSVP please reply.

rub ❶ *v* **rubbing, rubbed** **1** apply pressure and friction to (something) with a circular or backwards-and-forwards movement. **2** clean, polish, or dry by rubbing. **3** chafe or fray through rubbing. ▷ *n* **4** act of rubbing. **rub it in** emphasize an unpleasant fact. **rub out** *v* remove with a rubber.

rubber *n* **1** strong waterproof elastic material, orig. made from the dried sap of a tropical tree, now usu. synthetic. **2** piece of rubber used for erasing writing. ▷ *adj* **3** made of or producing rubber. **rubberize** *v* coat or treat with rubber. **rubbery** *adj* **rubberneck** *v* US stare with unthinking curiosity. **rubber plant** house plant with glossy leaves. **rubber stamp** **1** device for imprinting the date, a name, etc.

2 automatic authorization.

rubbish ❶ *n* **1** waste matter. **2** anything worthless. **3** nonsense. **rubbishy** *adj*.

rubble *n* fragments of broken stone, brick, etc.

rubella *n* same as GERMAN MEASLES.

ruby *n, pl* **-bies** **1** red precious gemstone. ▷ *adj* **2** deep red.

ruck[1] *n* **1** rough crowd of common people. **2** *Rugby* loose scrummage.

ruck[2] *n, v* wrinkle or crease.

rucksack *n* large pack carried on the back.

rudder *n* vertical hinged piece at the stern of a boat or at the rear of an aircraft, for steering.

ruddy ❶ *adj* **-dier, -diest** of a fresh healthy red colour.

rude ❶ *adj* **1** impolite or insulting. **2** coarse, vulgar, or obscene. **3** unexpected and unpleasant. **4** roughly made. **5** robust. **rudely** *adv* **rudeness** *n*.

rudiments ❶ *pl n* simplest and most basic stages of a subject. **rudimentary** *adj* basic, elementary.

rue ❶ *v* **ruing, rued** feel regret for. **rueful** *adj* regretful or sorry. **ruefully** *adv*.

ruff *n* **1** starched and frilled collar. **2** natural collar of feathers, fur, etc. on certain birds and animals.

——— THESAURUS ———

royal *adj* **1** = **regal**, imperial, kingly, princely, queenly, sovereign **2** = **splendid**, grand, impressive, magnificent, majestic, stately

rub *v* **1** = **stroke**, caress, massage **2** = **polish**, clean, scour, shine, wipe **3** = **chafe**, abrade, fray, grate, scrape ▷ *n* **4** = **massage**, caress, kneading, polish, shine, stroke, wipe

rubbish *n* **1, 2** = **waste**, garbage (*chiefly US*), junk (*inf*), litter, lumber, refuse, scrap, trash **3** = **nonsense**, claptrap (*inf*), codswallop (*Brit sl*), garbage (*chiefly US*), hogwash, hot air (*inf*), kak (*S Afr sl*), rot, tommyrot, trash, tripe (*inf*), twaddle

ruddy *adj* = **rosy**, blooming, fresh, glowing, healthy, radiant, red, reddish,

rosy-cheeked

rude *adj* **1** = **impolite**, abusive, cheeky, discourteous, disrespectful, ill-mannered, impertinent, impudent, insolent, insulting, uncivil, unmannerly **2** = **vulgar**, boorish, brutish, coarse, graceless, loutish, oafish, rough, uncivilized, uncouth, uncultured **3** = **unpleasant**, abrupt, harsh, sharp, startling, sudden **4** = **roughly-made**, artless, crude, inartistic, inelegant, makeshift, primitive, raw, rough, simple

rudiments *pl n* = **basics**, beginnings, elements, essentials, foundation, fundamentals

rue *v* = **regret**, be sorry for, kick oneself for, lament, mourn, repent

r

ruffian ❶ *n* violent lawless person.
rug *n* **1** small carpet. **2** thick woollen blanket.
rugby *n* form of football played with an oval ball which may be handled by the players.
rugged ❶ [**rug**-gid] *adj* **1** rocky or steep. **2** uneven and jagged. **3** strong-featured. **4** tough and sturdy.
ruin ❶ *v* **1** destroy or spoil completely. **2** impoverish. ▷ *n* **3** destruction or decay. **4** loss of wealth, position, etc. **5** broken-down unused building. **ruination** *n* **1** act of ruining. **2** state of being ruined. **3** cause of ruin. **ruinous** *adj* **1** causing ruin. **2** more expensive than can be afforded. **ruinously** *adv*.
rule ❶ *n* **1** statement of what is allowed, for example in a game or procedure. **2** what is usual. **3** government, authority, or control. **4** measuring device with a straight edge. ▷ *v* **5** govern. **6** be pre-eminent. **7** give a formal decision. **8** mark with straight line(s). **9** restrain. **as a rule** usually. **ruler** *n* **1** person who governs. **2** measuring device with a straight edge. **ruling** *n* formal decision. **rule of thumb** practical but imprecise approach. **rule out** *v* exclude.
rum *n* alcoholic drink distilled from sugar cane.
rumba *n* lively ballroom dance of Cuban origin.
rumble *v* **1** make a low continuous noise. **2** *informal* discover the (disreputable) truth about. ▷ *n* **3** deep resonant sound.
ruminate ❶ *v* **1** chew the cud. **2** ponder or meditate. **ruminant** *adj, n* cud-chewing (animal, such as a cow, sheep, or deer). **rumination** *n* quiet meditation and reflection. **ruminative** *adj*.
rummage ❶ *v* **1** search untidily and at length. ▷ *n* **2** untidy search through a collection of things.
rummy *n* card game in which players try to collect sets or sequences.
rumour ❶ *n* **1** unproved statement. **2** gossip or common talk. **rumoured** *adj* suggested by rumour.
rump ❶ *n* **1** buttocks. **2** rear of an animal.

━━ THESAURUS ━━━━━

ruffian *n* = **thug**, brute, bully, heavy (*sl*), hoodlum, hooligan, rough (*inf*), tough
rugged *adj* **1** = **rocky**, craggy **2** = **uneven**, broken, bumpy, craggy, difficult, irregular, jagged, ragged, rough **3** = **strong-featured**, rough-hewn, weather-beaten **4** = **tough**, brawny, burly, husky (*inf*), muscular, robust, strong, sturdy, well-built
ruin *v* **1** = **destroy**, blow (*sl*), botch, crush, damage, defeat, demolish, devastate, lay waste, make a mess of, mess up, screw up (*inf*), smash, spoil, wreck **2** = **bankrupt**, impoverish, pauperize ▷ *n* **3** = **disrepair**, decay, disintegration, ruination, wreckage **4 a** = **destruction**, breakdown, collapse, defeat, devastation, downfall, fall, undoing, wreck **b** = **bankruptcy**, destitution, insolvency
rule *n* **1** = **regulation**, axiom, canon, decree, direction, guideline, law, maxim, precept, principle, tenet **2** = **custom**, convention, habit, practice, procedure, routine, tradition **3** = **government**, authority, command, control, dominion, jurisdiction, mana (*NZ*), mastery, power, regime, reign ▷ *v* **5** = **govern**, be in authority, be in power, command, control, direct, reign **7** = **decree**, decide, judge, pronounce, settle **as a rule** = **usually**, generally, mainly, normally, on the whole, ordinarily
ruminate *v* **2** = **ponder**, cogitate, consider, contemplate, deliberate, mull over, muse, reflect, think, turn over in one's mind
rummage *v* **1** = **search**, delve, forage, hunt, ransack, root
rumour *n* **2** = **story**, buzz, dirt (*US sl*), gossip, hearsay, news, report, talk, whisper, word
rump *n* = **buttocks**, backside (*inf*), bottom, bum (*Brit sl*), butt (*US & Canad*

r

rumple v make untidy, crumpled, or dishevelled.

rumpus ❶ n, pl **-puses** noisy commotion.

run ❶ v **running**, **ran**, **run 1** move with a more rapid gait than walking. **2** go quickly (across). **3** compete in a race, election, etc. **4** travel according to schedule. **5** function. **6** manage. **7** continue in a particular direction or for a specified period. **8** expose oneself to (a risk). **9** flow. **10** spread. **11** (of stitches) unravel. **12** (of a newspaper) publish (a story). **13** smuggle (goods, esp. arms). ▷ n **14** act or spell of running. **15** ride in a car. **16** unrestricted access. **17** continuous period. **18** sequence. **19** heavy demand. **20** series of unravelled stitches, ladder. **21** steep snow-covered course for skiing. **22** enclosure for domestic fowls. **23** score of one at cricket. **run away** v make one's escape, flee. **run down** v **1** be rude about. **2** reduce in number or size. **3** stop working. **rundown** n **run-down** adj exhausted. **run into** v meet. **run-of-the-mill** adj ordinary. **run out** v be completely used up. **run over** v knock down (a person) with a moving vehicle. **run up** v incur (a debt).

rune n any character of the earliest Germanic alphabet. **runic** adj.

rung n crossbar on a ladder.

runt n **1** smallest animal in a litter. **2** undersized person.

rupture ❶ n **1** breaking, breach. **2** hernia. ▷ v **3** break, burst, or sever.

rural ❶ adj in or of the countryside.

ruse ❶ [rooz] n stratagem or trick.

rush¹ ❶ v **1** move or do very quickly. **2** force (someone) to act hastily. **3** make a sudden attack upon (a person or place). ▷ n **4** sudden quick or violent movement. ▷ pl **5** first unedited prints of a scene for a film. ▷ adj **6** done with speed, hasty. **rush hour** period at the beginning and end of the working day, when many people are travelling to or from work.

rush² n marsh plant with a slender pithy stem.

rusk n hard brown crisp biscuit, used esp. for feeding babies.

russet adj **1** reddish-brown. ▷ n **2** apple with rough reddish-brown skin.

rust ❶ n **1** reddish-brown coating formed on

inf), hindquarters, posterior, rear, rear end, seat

rumpus n = **commotion**, disturbance, furore, fuss, hue and cry, noise, row, uproar

run v **1** = **race**, bolt, dash, gallop, hare (Brit inf), hurry, jog, leg it (inf), lope, rush, scurry, sprint **2** = **move**, course, glide, go, pass, roll, skim **3** = **compete**, be a candidate, contend, put oneself up for, stand, take part **5** = **work**, function, go, operate, perform **6** = **manage**, administer, be in charge of, control, direct, handle, head, lead, operate **7** = **continue**, extend, go, proceed, reach, stretch **9** = **flow**, discharge, go, gush, leak, pour, spill, spout, stream **12** = **publish**, display, feature, print **13** = **smuggle**, bootleg, traffic in ▷ n **14** = **race**, dash, gallop, jog, rush, sprint, spurt **15** = **ride**,

drive, excursion, jaunt, outing, spin (inf), trip **18** = **sequence**, course, period, season, series, spell, stretch, string **22** = **enclosure**, coop, pen

rupture n **1** = **break**, breach, burst, crack, fissure, rent, split, tear ▷ v **3** = **break**, burst, crack, separate, sever, split, tear

rural adj = **rustic**, agricultural, country, pastoral, sylvan

ruse n = **trick**, device, dodge, hoax, manoeuvre, ploy, stratagem, subterfuge

rush¹ v **1** = **hurry**, bolt, career, dash, fly, hasten, race, run, shoot, speed, tear **2** = **push**, hurry, hustle, press **3** = **attack**, charge, storm ▷ n **4 a** = **hurry**, charge, dash, haste, race, scramble, stampede, surge **b** = **attack**, assault, charge, onslaught ▷ adj **6** = **hasty**, fast, hurried, quick, rapid, swift, urgent

rust n **1** = **corrosion**, oxidation

iron etc. that has been exposed to moisture.
2 disease of plants which produces rust-
coloured spots. ▷ *adj* **3** reddish-brown.
▷ *v* **4** become coated with rust. **rusty** *adj*
1 coated with rust. **2** of a rust colour. **3** out
of practice.

rustic ❶ *adj* **1** of or resembling country
people. **2** rural. **3** crude, awkward,
or uncouth. **4** (of furniture) made of
untrimmed branches. ▷ *n* **5** person from
the country.

rustle¹ ❶ *v, n* (make) a low whispering

sound, as of dry leaves or paper .

rustle² *v US* steal (cattle). **rustler** *n*
US cattle thief. **rustle up** *v* prepare at
short notice.

rut ❶ *n* **1** furrow made by wheels. **2** dull
settled habits or way of living.

rutabaga *n* the US and Canadian name
for SWEDE.

ruthless ❶ *adj* pitiless, merciless.
ruthlessness *n*.

rye *n* **1** kind of grain used for fodder and
bread. **2** *US* whiskey made from rye.

——————————————————————————————— THESAURUS ———————————

2 = **mildew**, blight, mould, must, rot ▷ *v*
4 = **corrode**, oxidize
rustic *adj* **1, 2** = **rural**, country,
pastoral, sylvan **3** = **uncouth**,
awkward, coarse, crude, rough
▷ *n* **5** = **yokel**, boor, bumpkin, clod,
clodhopper (*inf*), hick (*inf, chiefly US &
Canad*), peasant

rustle¹ *v* = **crackle**, crinkle, whisper ▷ *n*
= **crackle**, crinkling, rustling, whisper
rut *n* **1** = **groove**, furrow, indentation,
track, trough, wheel mark **2** = **habit**, dead
end, pattern, routine, system
ruthless *adj* = **merciless**, brutal, callous,
cruel, harsh, heartless, pitiless, relentless,
remorseless

r

Ss

Sabbath n day of worship and rest: Saturday for Jews, Sunday for Christians. **sabbatical** adj, n (denoting) leave for study.

sabotage ❶ n 1 intentional damage done to machinery, systems, etc. ▷ v 2 damage intentionally. **saboteur** n person who commits sabotage.

sabre n curved cavalry sword.

sac n pouchlike structure in an animal or plant.

saccharin n artificial sweetener. **saccharine** adj excessively sweet.

sachet n small envelope or bag containing a single portion.

sack¹ ❶ n 1 large bag made of coarse material. 2 informal dismissal. 3 slang bed. ▷ v 4 informal dismiss. **sacking** n rough woven material used for sacks. **sackcloth** n coarse fabric used for sacks, formerly worn as a penance.

sack² ❶ n 1 plundering of a captured town. ▷ v 2 plunder (a captured town).

sacrament n ceremony of the Christian Church, esp. Communion. **sacramental** adj.

sacred ❶ adj 1 holy. 2 connected with religion. 3 set apart, reserved.

sacrifice ❶ n 1 giving something up. 2 thing given up. 3 making of an offering to a god. 4 thing offered. ▷ v 5 offer as a sacrifice. 6 give (something) up. **sacrificial** adj.

sacrilege ❶ n misuse or desecration of something sacred. **sacrilegious** adj.

● **SPELLING TIP**
● It may sound as if **sacrilegious** has
● something to do with the word
● 'religious', which might explain why the
● most common misspelling of the word
● in the Bank of English is *sacriligious*. But
● it should be spelt **sacrilegious**.

sacristy n, pl **-ties** room in a church where sacred objects are kept.

sacrosanct ❶ adj regarded as sacred, inviolable.

sad ❶ adj **sadder**, **saddest** 1 sorrowful, unhappy. 2 deplorably bad. **sadden** v make sad. **sadly** adv **sadness** n.

THESAURUS

---

sabotage n 1 = **damage**, destruction, disruption, subversion, wrecking ▷ v 2 = **damage**, destroy, disable, disrupt, incapacitate, subvert, vandalize, wreck

sack¹ n 2 Inf = **dismissal**, discharge, the axe (inf), the boot (sl), the push (sl) ▷ v 4 Inf = **dismiss**, axe (inf), discharge, fire (inf), give (someone) the push (inf)

sack² n 1 = **plundering**, looting, pillage ▷ v 2 = **plunder**, loot, pillage, raid, rob, ruin, strip

sacred adj 1 = **holy**, blessed, divine, hallowed, revered, sanctified
2 = **religious**, ecclesiastical, holy
3 = **inviolable**, protected, sacrosanct

sacrifice n 1 = **surrender**, loss, renunciation 3, 4 = **offering**, oblation ▷ v
5 = **offer**, immolate, offer up 6 = **give up**, forego, forfeit, let go, lose, say goodbye to, surrender

sacrilege n = **desecration**, blasphemy, heresy, impiety, irreverence, profanation, violation

sacrosanct adj = **inviolable**, hallowed, inviolate, sacred, sanctified, set apart, untouchable

sad adj 1 = **unhappy**, blue, dejected, depressed, doleful, down, low, low-spirited, melancholy, mournful, woebegone 2 = **tragic**, depressing, dismal, grievous, harrowing, heart-rending, moving, pathetic, pitiful, poignant, upsetting 3 = **deplorable**, bad, lamentable, sorry, wretched

saddle ⊙ *n* **1** rider's seat on a horse or bicycle. **2** joint of meat. ▷ *v* **3** put a saddle on (a horse). **4** burden (with a responsibility). **saddler** *n* maker or seller of saddles.

sadism [**say**-dizz-um] *n* gaining of (sexual) pleasure from inflicting pain. **sadist** *n* **sadistic** *adj* **sadistically** *adv*.

safari *n*, *pl* **-ris** expedition to hunt or observe wild animals, esp. in Africa. **safari park** park where lions, elephants, etc. are kept uncaged so that people can see them from cars.

safe ⊙ *adj* **1** secure, protected. **2** uninjured, out of danger. **3** not involving risk. ▷ *n* **4** strong lockable container. **safely** *adv* **safe-conduct** *n* permit allowing travel through a dangerous area. **safekeeping** *n* protection. **safety** *n*.

saffron *n* **1** orange-coloured flavouring obtained from a crocus. ▷ *adj* **2** orange.

sag ⊙ *v* **sagging, sagged 1** sink in the middle. **2** tire. **3** (of clothes) hang loosely. ▷ *n* **4** droop.

saga ⊙ [**sah**-ga] *n* **1** legend of Norse heroes. **2** any long story.

sage¹ ⊙ *n* **1** very wise man. ▷ *adj* **2** *lit* wise. **sagely** *adv*.

sage² *n* aromatic herb with grey-green leaves.

sago *n* starchy cereal from the powdered pith of the sago palm tree.

said *v* past of SAY.

sail ⊙ *n* **1** sheet of fabric stretched to catch the wind for propelling a sailing boat. **2** arm of a windmill. ▷ *v* **3** travel by water. **4** begin a voyage. **5** move smoothly. **sailor** *n* member of a ship's crew.

saint *n* **1** *Christianity* person venerated after death as especially holy. **2** exceptionally good person. **saintly** *adj* **saintliness** *n*.

sake ⊙ *n* **1** benefit. **2** purpose. **for the sake of 1** for the purpose of. **2** to please or benefit (someone).

salad *n* dish of raw vegetables, eaten as a meal or part of a meal.

salami *n* highly spiced sausage.

salary ⊙ *n*, *pl* **-ries** fixed regular payment, usu. monthly, to an employee.

sale ⊙ *n* **1** exchange of goods for money. **2** selling of goods at unusually low prices. **3** auction. **saleable** *adj* fit or likely to be sold. **salesman, saleswoman, salesperson** *n* person who sells goods. **salesmanship** *n* skill in selling.

salient ⊙ [**say**-lee-ent] *adj* **1** prominent, noticeable. ▷ *n* **2** *Mil* projecting part of a front line.

saline [**say**-line] *adj* containing salt. **salinity** *n*.

saliva *n* liquid that forms in the mouth, spittle. **salivary** *adj* **salivate** *v* produce saliva.

—————————————————————————— THESAURUS ——————————

s

saddle *v* **4** = **burden**, encumber, load, lumber (*Brit inf*)

safe *adj* **1** = **secure**, impregnable, in safe hands, out of danger, out of harm's way, protected, safe and sound **2** = **unharmed**, all right, intact, O.K. or okay (*inf*), undamaged, unhurt, unscathed **3** = **risk-free**, certain, impregnable, secure, sound ▷ *n* **4** = **strongbox**, coffer, deposit box, repository, safe-deposit box, vault

sag *v* **1** = **sink**, bag, dip, droop, fall, give way, hang loosely, slump **2** = **tire**, droop, flag, wane, weaken, wilt

saga *n* **2** = **tale**, epic, narrative, story, yarn

sage¹ *n* **1** = **wise man**, elder, guru, master, philosopher ▷ *adj* **2** *Lit* = **wise**, judicious, sagacious, sapient, sensible

sail *v* **3** = **embark**, set sail **5** = **glide**, drift, float, fly, skim, soar, sweep, wing

sake *n* **1** = **benefit**, account, behalf, good, interest, welfare **2** = **purpose**, aim, end, motive, objective, reason

salary *n* = **pay**, earnings, income, wage, wages

sale *n* **1** = **selling**, deal, disposal, marketing, transaction

salient *adj* **1** = **prominent**, conspicuous, important, noticeable, outstanding, pronounced, striking

sallee n *Aust* (also **snow gum**) **1** SE Australian eucalyptus with a pale grey bark. **2** acacia tree.

sallow ❶ *adj* of an unhealthy pale or yellowish colour.

sally n, pl **-lies 1** witty remark. **2** sudden brief attack by troops. ▷ v **-lying, -lied** (foll. by *forth*) **3** rush out. **4** go out.

salmon n **1** large fish with orange-pink flesh valued as food. **2** any of several unrelated fish. ▷ adj **3** orange-pink.

salmonella n, pl **-lae** bacterium causing food poisoning.

salon n **1** commercial premises of a hairdresser, beautician, etc. **2** elegant reception room for guests.

saloon n **1** car with a fixed roof. **2** large public room, as on a ship. **3** *US* bar serving alcoholic drinks. **saloon bar** more expensive bar in a pub.

salt ❶ n **1** white crystalline substance used to season food. **2** chemical compound of acid and metal. ▷ v **3** season or preserve with salt. **with a pinch of salt** allowing for exaggeration. **worth one's salt** efficient. **salty** adj **saltbush** n shrub that grows in alkaline desert regions. **saltcellar** n small container for salt at table.

salubrious ❶ adj favourable to health.

salutary ❶ adj producing a beneficial result.

salute ❶ n **1** motion of the arm as a formal military sign of respect. **2** firing of guns as a military greeting of honour. ▷ v **3** greet with a salute. **4** make a salute. **5** acknowledge with praise. **salutation** n greeting by words or actions.

salvation ❶ n fact or state of being saved from harm or the consequences of sin.

salve ❶ n **1** healing or soothing ointment. ▷ v **2** soothe or appease.

salver n (silver) tray on which something is presented.

salvo n, pl **-vos, -voes 1** simultaneous discharge of guns etc. **2** burst of applause or questions.

same ❶ adj **1** identical, not different, unchanged. **2** just mentioned. **sameness** n.

sample ❶ n **1** part taken as representative of a whole. ▷ n **2** *Music* short extract from an existing recording mixed into a backing track to produce a new recording. ▷ v **3** take and test a sample of. **sampler** n piece of embroidery showing the embroiderer's skill.

sanatorium n, pl **-riums, -ria 1** institution for invalids or convalescents. **2** room for sick pupils at a boarding school.

sanctify ❶ v **-fying, -fied** make holy.

sanctimonious ❶ adj pretending to be religious and virtuous.

sanction ❶ n **1** permission, authorization. **2** coercive measure or penalty. ▷ v **3** allow, authorize.

THESAURUS

---

sallow adj = **wan**, anaemic, pale, pallid, pasty, sickly, unhealthy, yellowish

salt n **1** = **seasoning**, flavour, relish, savour, taste **with a pinch of salt** = **sceptically**, cynically, disbelievingly, suspiciously, with reservations

salubrious adj = **health-giving**, beneficial, good for one, healthy, wholesome

salutary adj = **beneficial**, advantageous, good for one, profitable, useful, valuable

salute n **1** = **salutation** ▷ v **3** = **greet**, acknowledge, address, hail, welcome **5** = **honour**, acknowledge, pay tribute or homage to, recognize

salvation n = **saving**, deliverance, escape, preservation, redemption, rescue

salve n = **ointment**, balm, cream, lotion

same adj **1 a** = **identical**, alike, corresponding, duplicate, equal, twin adj **b** = **unchanged**, changeless, consistent, constant, invariable, unaltered, unvarying **2** = **aforementioned**, aforesaid

sample n **1** = **specimen**, example, instance, model, pattern ▷ v **3** = **test**, experience, inspect, taste, try

sanctify v = **consecrate**, cleanse, hallow

sanctimonious adj = **holier-than-thou**, hypocritical, pious, self-righteous, smug

sanction n **1** = **permission**, approval, authority, authorization, backing (*inf*),

S

sand n 1 substance consisting of small grains of rock, esp. on a beach or in a desert. ▷ pl 2 stretches of sand forming a beach or desert. ▷ v 3 smooth with sandpaper. **sander** n power tool for smoothing surfaces. **sandy** adj 1 covered with sand. 2 (of hair) reddish-fair. **sandbag** n bag filled with sand, used as protection against gunfire or flood water. **sandpaper** n paper coated with sand for smoothing a surface. **sandpiper** n shore bird with a long bill and slender legs. **sandstone** n rock composed of sand.

sandal n light shoe consisting of a sole attached by straps.

sandwich n 1 two slices of bread with a layer of food between. ▷ v 2 insert between two other things. **sandwich board** pair of boards hung over a person's shoulders to display advertisements in front and behind.

sane ❶ adj 1 of sound mind. 2 sensible, rational. **sanity** n.

sang v past tense of SING.

sanguine ❶ adj cheerful, optimistic.

sanitary ❶ adj promoting health by getting rid of dirt and germs. **sanitation** n sanitary measures, esp. drainage or sewerage.

sap¹ ❶ n 1 moisture that circulates in plants. 2 informal gullible person.

sap² ❶ v sapping, sapped 1 undermine. 2 weaken. **sapper** n soldier in an engineering unit.

sapphire n 1 blue precious stone. ▷ adj 2 deep blue.

sarcasm ❶ n (use of) bitter or wounding ironic language. **sarcastic** adj **sarcastically** adv.

sarcophagus n, pl -gi, -guses stone coffin.

sardine n small fish of the herring family, usu. preserved in tightly packed tins.

sardonic ❶ adj mocking or scornful. **sardonically** adv.

sargassum, sargasso n type of floating seaweed.

sari, saree n long piece of cloth draped around the body and over one shoulder, worn by Hindu women.

sarmie n S Afr slang sandwich.

sartorial adj of men's clothes or tailoring.

sash n decorative strip of cloth worn round the waist or over one shoulder.

Satan ❶ n the Devil. **satanic** adj 1 of Satan. 2 supremely evil. **Satanism** n worship of Satan.

satay, saté [**sat**-ay] n Indonesian and Malaysian dish consisting of pieces of chicken, pork, etc., grilled on skewers and served with peanut sauce.

satchel n bag, usu. with a shoulder strap, for carrying school books.

satellite n 1 man-made device orbiting in space. 2 heavenly body that orbits another. 3 country that is dependent on a more powerful one. ▷ adj 4 of or used in the transmission of television signals from a satellite to the home.

S

———————————— THESAURUS ————————————

mana (NZ), O.K. or okay, stamp or seal of approval 2 = **ban**, boycott, coercive measures, embargo, penalty v 3 = **permit**, allow, approve, authorize, endorse

sane adj 1 = **of sound mind**, all there (sl), compos mentis, in one's right mind, mentally sound 2 = **sensible**, balanced, judicious, level-headed, rational, reasonable, sound

sanguine adj = **cheerful**, buoyant, confident, hopeful, optimistic

sanitary adj = **hygienic**, clean, germ-free, healthy, wholesome

sap¹ n 1 = **vital fluid**, essence, lifeblood 2 Inf = **fool**, idiot, jerk (sl, chiefly US & Canad), ninny, simpleton, twit (inf), wally (sl)

sap² v 1 = **undermine** 2 = **weaken**, deplete, drain, exhaust

sarcasm n = **irony**, bitterness, cynicism, derision, mockery, ridicule, satire

sardonic adj = **mocking**, cynical, derisive, dry, ironical, sarcastic, sneering, wry

Satan n = **The Devil**, Beelzebub, Lord of the Flies, Lucifer, Mephistopheles, Old Nick (inf), Prince of Darkness, The Evil One

satin n silky fabric with a glossy surface on one side. **satiny** adj of or like satin.

satire ① ** n 1 use of ridicule to expose vice or folly. 2 poem or other work that does this. **satirical adj **satirist** n **satirize** v ridicule by means of satire.

satisfy ① ** v **-fying, -fied 1 please, content. 2 provide amply for (a need or desire). 3 convince, persuade. **satisfaction** n **satisfactory** adj.

satnav n Motoring informal satellite navigation.

satsuma n kind of small orange.

saturate ① ** v 1 soak thoroughly. 2 cause to absorb the maximum amount of something. **saturation n.

Saturday n seventh day of the week.

**saturnine ① ** adj gloomy in temperament or appearance.

satyr n 1 woodland god, part man, part goat. 2 lustful man.

sauce n 1 liquid added to food to enhance flavour. 2 informal impudence. **saucy** adj 1 impudent. 2 pert, jaunty. **saucily** adv **saucepan** n cooking pot with a long handle.

saucer n small round dish put under a cup.

sauerkraut n shredded cabbage fermented in brine.

sauna n Finnish-style steam bath.

**saunter ① ** v 1 walk in a leisurely manner, stroll. ▷ n 2 leisurely walk.

sausage n minced meat in an edible tube-shaped skin. **sausage roll** skinless sausage covered in pastry.

sauté [**so**-tay] v **-téing** or **-téeing, -téed** fry quickly in a little fat.

savage ① ** adj 1 wild, untamed. 2 cruel and violent. 3 uncivilized, primitive. ▷ n 4 uncivilized person. ▷ v 5 attack ferociously. **savagely adv **savagery** n.

save ① ** v 1 rescue or preserve from harm, protect. 2 keep for the future. 3 set aside (money). 4 Sport prevent the scoring of (a goal). ▷ n 5 Sport act of preventing a goal. **saver n **saving** n 1 economy. ▷ pl 2 money put by for future use.

saviour ① ** n 1 person who rescues another. 2 (S-**) Christ.

savour ① ** v 1 enjoy, relish. 2 (foll. by of) have a flavour or suggestion of. ▷ n 3 characteristic taste or odour. 4 slight but distinctive quality. **savoury adj 1 salty or spicy. ▷ n, pl **-vouries** 2 savoury dish served before or after a meal.

saw¹ n 1 cutting tool with a toothed metal blade. ▷ v **sawing, sawed, sawed** or **sawn** 2 cut with a saw. 3 move (something)

---

satire n 1 = **mockery**, irony, ridicule 2 = **parody**, burlesque, caricature, lampoon

satisfy v 1 = **content**, assuage, gratify, indulge, pacify, pander to, please, quench, sate, slake 2 = **be sufficient**, answer, be enough, do, fulfil, meet, serve, suffice 3 = **convince**, assure, persuade, reassure

saturate v = **soak**, drench, imbue, souse, steep, suffuse, waterlog, wet through

saturnine adj = **gloomy**, dour, glum, grave, morose, sombre

saunter v 1 = **stroll**, amble, meander, mosey (inf), ramble, roam, wander ▷ n 2 = **stroll**, airing, amble, ramble, turn, walk

savage adj 1 = **wild**, feral, rough, rugged, uncultivated, undomesticated, untamed

2 = **cruel**, barbarous, bestial, bloodthirsty, brutal, ferocious, fierce, harsh, ruthless, sadistic, vicious 3 = **primitive**, rude, uncivilized, unspoilt ▷n 4 = **lout**, boor, yahoo, yob (Brit sl) ▷ v 5 = **attack**, lacerate, mangle, maul

save v 1 a = **rescue**, deliver, free, liberate, recover, redeem, salvage b = **protect**, conserve, guard, keep safe, look after, preserve, safeguard 2, 3 = **keep**, collect, gather, hoard, hold, husband, lay by, put by, reserve, set aside, store

saviour n 1 = **rescuer**, defender, deliverer, liberator, preserver, protector, redeemer

savour v 1 = **enjoy**, appreciate, delight in, luxuriate in, relish, revel in 2 (foll. by of) = **suggest**, be suggestive of, show signs

S

back and forth. **sawyer** n person who
saws timber for a living. **sawdust** n fine
wood fragments made in sawing. **sawmill**
n mill where timber is sawn into planks.

saw² v past tense of SEE¹.

saxophone n brass wind instrument with
keys and a curved body. **saxophonist** n.

say 🟊 v **saying, said 1** speak or utter.
2 express (an idea) in words. **3** give as
one's opinion. **4** suppose as an example or
possibility. ▷ n **5** right or chance to speak.
6 share in a decision. **saying** n maxim,
proverb.

scab n **1** crust formed over a wound.
2 offens blackleg. **scabby** adj **1** covered
with scabs. **2** informal despicable.

scabbard n sheath for a sword or dagger.

scaffold n **1** temporary platform for
workmen. **2** gallows. **scaffolding** n
(materials for building) scaffolds.

scald v **1** burn with hot liquid or steam.
2 sterilize with boiling water. **3** heat
(liquid) almost to boiling point. ▷ n
4 injury by scalding.

scale¹ 🟊 n **1** one of the thin overlapping
plates covering fishes and reptiles. **2** thin
flake. **3** coating which forms in kettles etc.
due to hard water. **4** tartar formed on the
teeth. ▷ v **5** remove scales from. **6** come
off in scales. **scaly** adj.

scale² n (often pl) weighing instrument.

scale³ 🟊 n **1** graduated table or sequence
of marks at regular intervals, used as
a reference in making measurements.
2 ratio of size between a thing and a
representation of it. **3** relative degree or
extent. **4** fixed series of notes in music.
▷ v **5** climb. **scale up, down** v increase or
decrease proportionally in size.

scallop n **1** edible shellfish with two fan-
shaped shells. **2** one of a series of small
curves along an edge.

scalp n **1** skin and hair on top of the head.
▷ v **2** cut off the scalp of.

scalpel n small surgical knife.

scamp 🟊 n mischievous child.

scamper 🟊 v **1** run about hurriedly or in
play. ▷ n **2** scampering.

scampi pl n large prawns.

scan 🟊 v **scanning, scanned 1** scrutinize
carefully. **2** glance over quickly.
3 examine or search (an area) by passing
a radar or sonar beam over it. **4** (of verse)
conform to metrical rules. ▷ n **5** scanning.
scanner n electronic device used for
scanning. **scansion** n metrical scanning
of verse.

scandal 🟊 n **1** disgraceful action or event.
2 malicious gossip. **scandalize** v shock by
scandal. **scandalous** adj.

───────── THESAURUS ─────────

of, smack of ▷ n **3** = **flavour**, piquancy,
relish, smack, smell, tang, taste **4** = **trace**,
distinctive quality

say v **1** = **speak**, announce, express,
mention, pronounce, remark, state,
utter, voice **2** = **express**, communicate,
convey, imply **3** = **declare**, affirm,
assert, maintain **4** = **suppose**, assume,
conjecture, estimate, guess, imagine,
presume, surmise ▷ n **5** = **chance
to speak**, voice, vote **6** = **influence**,
authority, clout (inf), mana (NZ), power,
weight

scale¹ n = **flake**, lamina, layer, plate

scale³ n **1** = **graduation**, gradation,
hierarchy, ladder, progression, ranking,

sequence, series, steps **2** = **ratio**,
proportion **3** = **degree**, extent, range,
reach, scope ▷ v **5** = **climb**, ascend,
clamber, escalade, mount, surmount **scale
up, down** v = **adjust**, proportion, regulate

scamp n = **rascal**, devil, imp, monkey,
rogue, scallywag (inf)

scamper v **1** = **run**, dart, dash, hasten,
hurry, romp, scoot, scurry, scuttle

scan v **1** = **scrutinize**, check, check out
(inf), examine, eye, eyeball (sl), investigate
2 = **glance over**, look through, run one's
eye over, run over, skim **3** = **survey**, scour,
search, sweep

scandal n **1 a** = **crime**, disgrace,
embarrassment, offence, sin, wrongdoing

S

scant ❶ *adj* barely sufficient, meagre.

scapegoat ❶ *n* person made to bear the blame for others.

scar ❶ *n* **1** mark left by a healed wound. **2** permanent emotional damage left by an unpleasant experience. ▷ *v* **scarring**, **scarred 3** mark or become marked with a scar.

scarce ❶ *adj* **1** insufficient to meet demand. **2** not common, rarely found. **make oneself scarce** *informal* go away. **scarcely** *adv* **1** hardly at all. **2** definitely or probably not. **scarcity** *n*.

scare ❶ *v* **1** frighten or be frightened. ▷ *n* **2** fright, sudden panic. **scary** *adj informal* frightening. **scarecrow** *n* **1** figure dressed in old clothes, set up to scare birds away from crops. **2** raggedly dressed person. **scaremonger** *n* person who spreads alarming rumours.

scarf *n*, *pl* **scarves**, **scarfs** piece of material worn round the neck, head, or shoulders.

scarlet *adj*, *n* brilliant red. **scarlet fever** infectious fever with a scarlet rash.

scathing ❶ *adj* harshly critical.

scatter ❶ *v* **1** throw about in various directions. **2** disperse. **scatterbrain** *n*

empty-headed person.

scavenge *v* search for (anything usable) among discarded material. **scavenger** *n* **1** person who scavenges. **2** animal that feeds on decaying matter.

scenario ❶ *n*, *pl* **-rios 1** summary of the plot of a play or film. **2** imagined sequence of future events.

scene ❶ *n* **1** place of action of a real or imaginary event. **2** subdivision of a play or film in which the action is continuous. **3** view of a place. **4** display of emotion. **5** *informal* specific activity or interest, e.g. *the fashion scene*. **behind the scenes 1** backstage. **2** in secret. **scenery** *n* **1** natural features of a landscape. **2** painted backcloths or screens used on stage to represent the scene of action. **scenic** *adj* picturesque.

scent ❶ *n* **1** pleasant smell. **2** smell left in passing, by which an animal can be traced. **3** series of clues. **4** perfume. ▷ *v* **5** detect by smell. **6** suspect. **7** fill with fragrance.

sceptic ❶ **[skep**-tik] *n* person who habitually doubts generally accepted beliefs. **sceptical** *adj* **sceptically** *adv* **scepticism** *n*.

THESAURUS

---

b = **shame**, defamation, discredit, disgrace, dishonour, ignominy, infamy, opprobrium, stigma **2** = **gossip**, aspersion, dirt, rumours, slander, talk, tattle

scant *adj* = **meagre**, barely sufficient, little, minimal, sparse

scapegoat *n* = **whipping boy**, fall guy (*inf*)

scar *n* **1** = **mark**, blemish, injury, wound ▷ *v* **3** = **mark**, damage, disfigure

scarce *adj* **1** = **in short supply**, few, few and far between, infrequent, insufficient **2** = **rare**, uncommon

scare *v* **1** = **frighten**, alarm, dismay, intimidate, panic, shock, startle, terrify ▷ *n* **2** = **fright**, panic, shock, start, terror

scathing *adj* = **critical**, biting, caustic, cutting, harsh, sarcastic, scornful, trenchant, withering

scatter *v* **1** = **throw about**, diffuse,

disseminate, fling, shower, spread, sprinkle, strew **2** = **disperse**, disband, dispel, dissipate

scenario *n* **1** = **story line**, outline, résumé, summary, synopsis

scene *n* **1** = **site**, area, locality, location, place, position, setting, spot **2** = **act**, division, episode, part **3** = **view**, landscape, panorama, prospect, vista **4** = **fuss**, carry-on (*inf, chiefly Brit*), commotion, exhibition, performance, row, tantrum, to-do **5** *Inf* = **world**, arena, business, environment

scent *n* **1** = **aroma**, bouquet, odour, smell **2** = **trail**, spoor, track **4** = **fragrance**, perfume ▷ *v* **5** = **detect**, discern, nose out, sense, smell, sniff

sceptic *n* = **doubter**, cynic, disbeliever, doubting Thomas

S

sceptre *n* ornamental rod symbolizing royal power.

schedule ● *n* 1 plan of procedure for a project. 2 list. 3 timetable. ▷ *v* 4 plan to occur at a certain time.

schematic *adj* presented as a plan or diagram.

scheme ● *n* 1 systematic plan. 2 secret plot. ▷ *v* 3 plan in an underhand manner. **scheming** *adj*, *n*.

schism ● [**skizz**-um] *n* (group resulting from) division in an organization. **schismatic** *adj*, *n*.

schizophrenia *n* 1 mental disorder involving deterioration of or confusion about the personality. 2 *informal* contradictory behaviour or attitudes. **schizophrenic** *adj*, *n*.

school¹ ● *n* 1 place where children are taught or instruction is given in a subject. 2 group of artists, thinkers, etc. with shared principles or methods. ▷ *v* 3 educate or train. **scholar** *n* 1 learned person. 2 student receiving a scholarship. 3 pupil.

school² *n* shoal of fish, whales, etc.

schooner *n* 1 sailing ship rigged fore-and-aft. 2 large glass.

science *n* systematic study and knowledge of natural or physical phenomena. **scientific** *adj* 1 of science. 2 systematic. **scientifically** *adv* **scientist** *n* person who studies or practises a science. **science fiction** stories making imaginative use of scientific knowledge.

scimitar *n* curved oriental sword.

scintillating ● *adj* very lively and amusing.

scissors *pl n* cutting instrument with two crossed pivoted blades.

scoff¹ ● *v* express derision.

scoff² ● *v* *informal* eat rapidly.

scold ● *v* 1 find fault with, reprimand. ▷ *n* 2 person who scolds.

scone *n* small plain cake baked in an oven or on a griddle.

scope ● *n* 1 opportunity for using abilities. 2 range of activity.

scorch ● *v* 1 burn on the surface. 2 parch or shrivel from heat. ▷ *n* 3 slight burn. **scorcher** *n* *informal* very hot day.

score ● *n* 1 points gained in a game or competition. 2 twenty. 3 written version

——————————— THESAURUS ———————————

schedule *n* 1 = **plan**, agenda 2 = **list**, calendar, catalogue, inventory 3 = **timetable**, programme ▷ *v* 4 = **plan**, appoint, arrange, book, organize, programme

scheme *n* 1 = **plan**, programme, project, proposal, strategy, system, tactics 2 = **plot**, conspiracy, intrigue, manoeuvre, ploy, ruse, stratagem, subterfuge ▷ *v* 3 = **plot**, collude, conspire, intrigue, machinate, manoeuvre

schism *n* = **division**, breach, break, rift, rupture, separation, split

school¹ *n* 1 = **academy**, college, faculty, institute, institution, seminary 2 = **group**, adherents, circle, denomination, devotees, disciples, faction, followers, set ▷ *v* 3 = **train**, coach, discipline, drill, educate, instruct, tutor

scintillating *adj* = **brilliant**, animated,

bright, dazzling, exciting, glittering, lively, sparkling, stimulating

scoff¹ *v* = **scorn**, belittle, deride, despise, jeer, knock (*inf*), laugh at, mock, pooh-pooh, ridicule, sneer

scoff² *v* *Inf* = **gobble (up)**, bolt, devour, gorge oneself on, gulp down, guzzle, wolf

scold *v* 1 = **reprimand**, berate, castigate, censure, find fault with, give (someone) a dressing-down, lecture, rebuke, reproach, reprove, rouse on (*Aust*), tell off (*inf*), tick off (*inf*), upbraid *n* 2 = **nag**, shrew, termagant (*rare*)

scope *n* 1 = **opportunity**, freedom, latitude, liberty, room, space 2 = **range**, area, capacity, orbit, outlook, reach, span, sphere

scorch *v* 1 = **burn**, roast, sear, singe 2 = **shrivel**, parch, wither

score *n* 1 = **points**, grade, mark, outcome, record, result, total 5 = **grievance**, grudge,

of a piece of music showing parts for each musician. **4** mark or cut. **5** grievance, e.g. *settle old scores*. ▷ *pl* **6** lots. ▷ *v* **7** gain (points) in a game. **8** keep a record of points. **9** mark or cut. **10** (foll. by *out*) cross out. **11** arrange music (for). **12** achieve a success.

scorn ❶ *n* **1** open contempt. ▷ *v* **2** despise. **3** reject with contempt. **scornful** *adj*.

scorpion *n* small lobster-shaped animal with a sting at the end of a jointed tail.

Scotch *n* whisky distilled in Scotland.

scotch *v* put an end to.

scot-free *adj* without harm or punishment.

scoundrel ❶ *n* old-fashioned cheat or deceiver.

scour¹ ❶ *v* **1** clean or polish by rubbing with something rough. **2** clear or flush out. **scourer** *n* small rough nylon pad used for cleaning pots and pans.

scour² ❶ *v* search thoroughly and energetically.

scourge ❶ *n* **1** person or thing causing severe suffering. **2** whip. ▷ *v* **3** cause severe suffering to. **4** whip.

scout ❶ *n* **1** person sent out to reconnoitre. **2** (**S-**) member of the Scout Association, an organization for boys which aims to develop character and promotes outdoor activities. ▷ *v* **3** act as a scout. **4** reconnoitre.

scowl ❶ *v, n* (have) an angry or sullen expression.

scrabble ❶ *v* scrape at with the hands, feet, or claws.

scrag *n* thin end of a neck of mutton. **scraggy** *adj* thin, bony.

scram ❶ *v* scramming, scrammed *informal* go away quickly.

scramble ❶ *v* **1** climb or crawl hastily or awkwardly. **2** struggle with others (for). **3** mix up. **4** cook (eggs beaten up with milk). **5** (of an aircraft or aircrew) take off hurriedly in an emergency. **6** make (transmitted speech) unintelligible

--- THESAURUS ---

injury, injustice, wrong ▷ *pl* **6** = **lots**, hundreds, masses, millions, multitudes, myriads, swarms ▷ *v* **7** = **gain**, achieve, chalk up (*inf*), make, notch up (*inf*), win **8** = **keep count**, count, record, register, tally **9** = **cut**, deface, gouge, graze, mark, scrape, scratch, slash **10** (foll. by *out*) = **cross out**, cancel out, delete, obliterate, strike out **11** = **arrange**, adapt, orchestrate, set

scorn *n* **1** = **contempt**, derision, disdain, disparagement, mockery, sarcasm *v* **2** = **despise**, be above, deride, disdain, scoff at **3** = **reject**, flout, slight, spurn

scoundrel *n Old-fashioned* = **rogue**, bastard (*offens*), blackguard, good-for-nothing, heel (*sl*), miscreant, ne'er-do-well, rascal, reprobate, rotter (*sl, chiefly Brit*), scally (*NW Eng dial*), scamp, swine, villain

scour¹ *v* **1** = **rub**, abrade, buff, clean, polish, scrub **2** = **wash**, cleanse

scour² *v* = **search**, beat, comb, hunt, ransack

scourge *n* **1** = **affliction**, bane, curse, infliction, misfortune, pest, plague, terror, torment **2** = **whip**, cat, lash, strap, switch, thong ▷ *v* **3** = **afflict**, curse, plague, terrorize, torment **4** = **whip**, beat, cane, flog, horsewhip, lash, thrash

scout *n* **1** = **vanguard**, advance guard, lookout, outrider, precursor, reconnoitrer ▷ *v* **3, 4** = **reconnoitre**, investigate, observe, probe, recce (*sl*), spy, survey, watch

scowl *v* = **glower**, frown, lour *or* lower ▷ *n* = **glower**, black look, dirty look, frown

scrabble *v* = **scrape**, claw, scramble, scratch

scram *v Inf* = **go away**, abscond, beat it (*sl*), clear off (*inf*), get lost (*inf*), leave, make oneself scarce (*inf*), make tracks, scarper (*Brit sl*), vamoose (*sl, chiefly US*)

scramble *v* **1** = **struggle**, climb, crawl, scrabble, swarm **2** = **strive**, contend, jostle, push, run, rush, vie ▷ *n* **8** = **climb**, trek **9** = **struggle**, commotion,

by the use of an electronic device. ▷ *n*
7 scrambling. **8** rough climb. **9** disorderly
struggle. **10** motorcycle race over rough
ground.

scrap¹ ❶ *n* **1** small piece. **2** waste metal
collected for reprocessing. ▷ *pl* **3** leftover
food. ▷ *v* **scrapping**, **scrapped 4** discard
as useless. **scrappy** *adj* fragmentary,
disjointed. **scrapbook** *n* book with blank
pages in which newspaper cuttings or
pictures are stuck.

scrap² ❶ *n, v* **scrapping**, **scrapped** *informal*
fight or quarrel.

scrape ❶ *v* **1** rub with something rough
or sharp. **2** clean or smooth thus. **3** rub
with a harsh noise. **4** economize. ▷ *n* **5** act
or sound of scraping. **6** mark or wound
caused by scraping. **7** *informal* awkward
situation. **scraper** *n* **scrape through** *v*
succeed in or obtain with difficulty.

scratch ❶ *v* **1** mark or cut with claws,
nails, or anything rough or sharp. **2** scrape
(skin) with nails or claws to relieve itching.
3 withdraw from a race or competition.

▷ *n* **4** wound, mark, or sound made by
scratching. ▷ *adj* **5** put together at short
notice. **from scratch** from the very
beginning. **up to scratch** up to standard.
scratchy *adj*.

scrawl ❶ *v* **1** write carelessly or hastily. ▷ *n*
2 scribbled writing.

scrawny ❶ *adj* **scrawnier**, **scrawniest**
thin and bony.

scream ❶ *v* **1** utter a piercing cry, esp. of
fear or pain. **2** utter with a scream. ▷ *n*
3 shrill piercing cry. **4** *informal* very funny
person or thing.

screech ❶ *v, n* (utter) a shrill cry.

screed *n* long tedious piece of writing.

screen ❶ *n* **1** surface of a television set,
VDU, etc., on which an image is formed.
2 white surface on which films or slides
are projected. **3** movable structure used
to shelter, divide, or conceal something.
▷ *v* **4** shelter or conceal with or as if with a
screen. **5** examine (a person or group) to
determine suitability for a task or to detect
the presence of disease or weapons.

———————————————————————— THESAURUS ————————

competition, confusion, mêlée, race, rush,
tussle
scrap¹ *n* **1** = **piece**, bit, crumb, fragment,
grain, morsel, part, particle, portion,
sliver, snippet **2** = **waste**, junk, offcuts ▷ *pl*
3 = **leftovers**, bits, leavings, remains ▷ *v*
4 = **get rid of**, abandon, discard, ditch (*sl*),
drop, jettison, throw away *or* out, write off
scrap² *n Inf* = **fight**, argument, battle,
disagreement, dispute, quarrel, row,
squabble, wrangle ▷ *v Inf* = **fight**, argue,
row, squabble, wrangle
scrape *v* **1** = **rub**, bark, graze, scratch, scuff
2 = **scour**, clean, erase, remove, rub, skin
3 = **grate**, grind, rasp, scratch, squeak
4 = **scrimp**, pinch, save, skimp, stint ▷ *n*
7 *Inf* = **predicament**, awkward situation,
difficulty, dilemma, fix (*inf*), mess, plight,
tight spot **scrape through** *v* = **get by** (*inf*),
just make it, struggle
scratch *v* **1** = **mark**, claw, cut, damage,
etch, grate, graze, lacerate, score, scrape

3 = **withdraw**, pull out ▷ *n* **4** = **mark**,
blemish, claw mark, gash, graze,
laceration, scrape ▷ *adj* **5** = **improvised**,
impromptu, rough-and-ready **up to
scratch** = **adequate**, acceptable,
satisfactory, sufficient, up to standard
scrawl *v, n* = **scribble**, doodle, squiggle
scrawny *adj* = **thin**, bony, gaunt, lean,
scraggy, skin-and-bones (*inf*), skinny,
undernourished
scream *v* **1, 2** = **cry**, bawl, screech, shriek,
yell ▷ *n* **3** = **cry**, howl, screech, shriek,
yell, yelp
screech *v, n* = **cry**, scream, shriek
screen *n* **3** a = **cover**, awning, canopy,
guard, mesh, net, shade, shelter, shield
b = **partition**, room divider **c** = **cloak** ▷ *v*
4 a = **protect**, defend, guard, shelter,
shield **b** = **cover**, cloak, conceal, hide,
mask, shade, veil **5** = **vet**, evaluate,
examine, filter, gauge, scan, sift, sort
6 = **broadcast**, present, put on, show

S

6 show (a film). **the screen** cinema generally. **screen saver** *Computers* a changing image on a monitor when the computer is operative but idle.

screw ⊕ *n* **1** metal pin with a spiral ridge along its length, twisted into materials to fasten them together. **2** *slang* prison guard. ▷ *v* **3** turn (a screw). **4** twist. **5** fasten with screw(s). **6** *informal* extort. **screwdriver** *n* tool for turning screws. **screw up** *v* **1** *informal* bungle. **2** distort.

scribble ⊕ *v* **1** write hastily or illegibly. **2** make meaningless or illegible marks. ▷ *n* **3** something scribbled.

scribe ⊕ *n* **1** person who copied manuscripts before the invention of printing. **2** *Bible* scholar of the Jewish Law.

scrimp ⊕ *v* be very economical.

script ⊕ *n* **1** text of a film, play, or TV programme. **2** particular system of writing, e.g. *Arabic script*. **3** handwriting.

scripture *n* sacred writings of a religion. **scriptural** *adj*.

scroll *n* **1** roll of parchment or paper. **2** ornamental carving shaped like a scroll. ▷ *v* **3** move (text) up or down on a VDU screen.

scrotum *n*, *pl* **-ta**, **-tums** pouch of skin containing the testicles.

scrounge ⊕ *v informal* get by cadging or begging. **scrounger** *n*.

scrub¹ ⊕ *v* **scrubbing**, **scrubbed 1** clean by rubbing, often with a hard brush and water. **2** *informal* delete or cancel. ▷ *n* **3** scrubbing.

scrub² *n* **1** stunted trees. **2** area of land covered with scrub. **scrubby** *adj* **1** covered with scrub. **2** stunted. **3** *informal* shabby. **scrub turkey** same as MEGAPODE.

scruff¹ *n* nape (of the neck).

scruff² *n informal* untidy person. **scruffy** *adj* unkempt or shabby.

scrum, scrummage *n* **1** *Rugby* restarting of play in which opposing packs of forwards push against each other to gain possession of the ball. **2** disorderly struggle.

scruple ⊕ *n* **1** doubt produced by one's conscience or morals. ▷ *v* **2** have doubts on moral grounds. **scrupulous** *adj* **1** very conscientious. **2** very careful or precise.

scrutiny ⊕ *n*, *pl* **-nies** close examination. **scrutinize** *v* examine closely.

scuba diving *n* sport of swimming under water using cylinders containing compressed air attached to breathing apparatus.

scud *v* **scudding**, **scudded** move along swiftly.

scuff *v* **1** drag (the feet) while walking. **2** scrape (one's shoes) by doing so. ▷ *n* **3** mark caused by scuffing.

scuffle ⊕ *v* **1** fight in a disorderly manner. ▷ *n* **2** disorderly struggle. **3** scuffling sound.

screw *v* **3** = **turn**, tighten **4** = **twist** **6** *Inf* = **extort**, extract, wrest, wring

scribble *v* **1** = **scrawl**, dash off, jot, write

scribe *n* **1** = **copyist**, amanuensis, writer

scrimp *v* = **economize**, be frugal, save, scrape, skimp, stint, tighten one's belt

script *n* **1** = **text**, book, copy, dialogue, libretto, lines, words **3** = **handwriting**, calligraphy, penmanship, writing

scrounge *v Inf* = **cadge**, beg, blag (*sl*), bludge (*Aust & NZ*), bum (*inf*), freeload (*sl*), sponge (*inf*)

scrub¹ *v* **1** = **scour**, clean, cleanse, rub **2** *Inf* = **cancel**, abolish, call off, delete, drop, forget about, give up

scruple *n* **1** = **misgiving**, compunction, doubt, hesitation, qualm, reluctance, second thoughts, uneasiness ▷ *v* **2** = **have misgivings about**, demur, doubt, have qualms about, hesitate, think twice about

scrutiny *n* = **examination**, analysis, exploration, inspection, investigation, perusal, search, study

scuffle *v* **1** = **fight**, clash, grapple, jostle, struggle, tussle ▷ *n* **2** = **fight**, brawl,

S

scull n 1 small oar. ▷ v 2 row (a boat) using sculls.

scullery n, pl **-leries** small room where washing-up and other kitchen work is done.

sculpture ⓘ n 1 art of making figures or designs in wood, stone, etc. 2 product of this art. ▷ v 3 (also **sculpt**) represent in sculpture. **sculptor**, **sculptress** n **sculptural** adj.

scum ⓘ n 1 impure or waste matter on the surface of a liquid. 2 worthless people. **scummy** adj.

scungy adj **-ier**, **-iest** Aust & NZ informal sordid or dirty.

scurrilous ⓘ adj untrue and defamatory.

scurry ⓘ v **-rying**, **-ried** 1 move hastily. ▷ n 2 act or sound of scurrying.

scurvy n disease caused by lack of vitamin C.

scuttle¹ n fireside container for coal.

scuttle² ⓘ v 1 run with short quick steps. ▷ n 2 hurried run.

scuttle³ v make a hole in (a ship) to sink it.

scythe n 1 long-handled tool with a curved blade for cutting grass. ▷ v 2 cut with a scythe.

SD South Dakota.

sea ⓘ n 1 mass of salt water covering three quarters of the earth's surface. 2 particular area of this. 3 vast expanse. **at sea 1** in a ship on the ocean. 2 confused or bewildered. **sea anemone** sea animal with suckers like petals. **seaboard** n coast. **seafaring** adj working or travelling by sea. **seafood** n edible saltwater fish or shellfish. **seagull** n gull. **sea horse** small sea fish with a plated body and horselike head. **sea lion** kind of large seal. **seaman** n sailor. **seasick** adj suffering from nausea caused by the motion of a ship. **seasickness** n **sea urchin** sea animal with a round spiky shell. **seaweed** n plant growing in the sea. **seaworthy** adj (of a ship) in fit condition for a sea voyage.

seal¹ ⓘ n 1 piece of wax, lead, etc. with a special design impressed upon it, attached to a letter or document as a mark of authentication. 2 device or material used to close an opening tightly. ▷ v 3 close with or as if with a seal. 4 make airtight or watertight. 5 affix a seal to or stamp with a seal. 6 decide (one's fate) irrevocably. **sealant** n any substance used for sealing. **seal off** v enclose or isolate (a place) completely.

seal² n amphibious mammal with flippers as limbs.

seam ⓘ n 1 line where two edges are joined, as by stitching. 2 thin layer of coal or ore. ▷ v 3 mark with furrows or wrinkles. **seamless** adj **seamy** adj sordid.

commotion, disturbance, fray, scrimmage, skirmish, tussle

sculpture v 3 (also **sculpt**) = **sculpt**, carve, chisel, fashion, form, hew, model, mould, shape

scum n 1 = **impurities**, dross, film, froth 2 = **rabble**, dregs of society, riffraff, trash (chiefly US & Canad)

scurrilous adj = **slanderous**, abusive, defamatory, insulting, scandalous, vituperative

scurry v 1 = **hurry**, dart, dash, race, scamper, scoot, scuttle, sprint ▷ n 2 = **flurry**, scampering, whirl

scuttle² v 1 = **run**, bustle, hasten, hurry, rush, scamper, scoot, scurry

sea n 1 = **ocean**, main, the deep, the waves 3 = **expanse**, abundance, mass, multitude, plethora, profusion **at sea** 2 = **bewildered**, baffled, confused, lost, mystified, puzzled

seal¹ n 1 = **authentication**, confirmation, imprimatur, insignia, ratification, stamp ▷ v 3 = **close**, bung, enclose, fasten, plug, shut, stop, stopper, stop up 5 = **authenticate**, confirm, ratify, stamp, validate 6 = **settle**, clinch, conclude, consummate, finalize **seal off** v = **isolate**, put out of bounds, quarantine, segregate

seam n 1 = **joint**, closure 2 = **layer**, lode, stratum, vein

seance [**say**-anss] n meeting at which spiritualists attempt to communicate with the dead.

sear ❶ v scorch, burn the surface of. **searing** adj **1** (of pain) very sharp. **2** highly critical.

search ❶ v **1** examine closely in order to find something. ▷ n **2** searching. **searching** adj keen or thorough. **search engine** Computers Internet service enabling users to search for items of interest. **searchlight** n powerful light with a beam that can be shone in any direction.

season ❶ n **1** one of four divisions of the year, each of which has characteristic weather conditions. **2** period during which a thing happens or is plentiful. **3** fitting or proper time. ▷ v **4** flavour with salt, herbs, etc. **5** dry (timber) till ready for use. **seasonable** adj **1** appropriate for the season. **2** timely or opportune. **seasonal** adj depending on or varying with the seasons. **seasoned** adj experienced. **seasoning** n salt, herbs, etc. added to food to enhance flavour. **season ticket** ticket for a series of journeys or events within a specified period.

seat ❶ n **1** thing designed or used for sitting on. **2** place to sit in a theatre, esp. one that requires a ticket. **3** buttocks. **4** country house. **5** membership of a legislative or administrative body. ▷ v **6** cause to sit. **7** provide seating for. **seat belt** belt worn in a car or aircraft to prevent a person being thrown forward in a crash.

secateurs pl n small pruning shears.

secede ❶ v withdraw formally from a political alliance or federation. **secession** n.

seclude v keep (a person) from contact with others. **secluded** adj private, sheltered. **seclusion** n.

second¹ ❶ adj **1** coming directly after the first. **2** alternate, additional. **3** inferior. ▷ n **4** person or thing coming second. **5** attendant in a duel or boxing match. ▷ pl **6** inferior goods. ▷ v **7** express formal support for (a motion proposed in a meeting). **secondly** adv **second-best** adj next to the best. **second-class** adj **1** inferior. **2** cheaper, slower, or less comfortable than first-class. **second-hand** adj **1** bought after use by another. **2** not from an original source. **second nature** something so habitual that it seems part of one's character. **second-rate** adj not of the highest quality. **second sight** supposed ability to predict events. **second thoughts** revised opinion on a matter already considered. **second wind** renewed ability to continue effort.

second² ❶ n **1** sixtieth part of a minute of an angle or time. **2** moment.

second³ [si-**kawnd**] v transfer (a person) temporarily to another job. **secondment** n.

S

sear v = **scorch**, burn, sizzle
search v **1, 2** = **look**, comb, examine, explore, fossick (Aust & NZ), hunt, inspect, investigate, ransack, scour, scrutinize ▷ n **2** = **look**, examination, exploration, hunt, inspection, investigation, pursuit, quest
season n **2** = **period**, spell, term, time ▷ v **4** = **flavour**, enliven, pep up, salt, spice
seat n **1** = **chair**, bench, pew, settle, stall, stool **4** = **mansion**, abode, ancestral hall, house, residence **5** = **membership**, chair, constituency, incumbency, place ▷ v **6** = **sit**, fix, install, locate, place, set,

settle **7** = **hold**, accommodate, cater for, contain, sit, take
secede v = **withdraw**, break with, leave, pull out, quit, resign, split from
second¹ adj **1** = **next**, following, subsequent, succeeding **2** = **additional**, alternative, extra, further, other **3** = **inferior**, lesser, lower, secondary, subordinate ▷ n **5** = **supporter**, assistant, backer, helper ▷ v **7** = **support**, approve, assist, back, endorse, go along with
second² n **2** = **moment**, flash, instant, jiffy (inf), minute, sec (inf), trice

secondary ❶ *adj* 1 of less importance. 2 coming after or derived from what is primary or first. 3 relating to the education of people between the ages of 11 and 18.

secret ❶ *adj* 1 kept from the knowledge of others. ▷ *n* 2 something kept secret. 3 mystery. 4 underlying explanation, e.g. *the secret of my success*. **in secret** without other people knowing. **secretly** *adv* **secrecy** *n* **secretive** *adj* inclined to keep things secret. **secretiveness** *n*.

secretary *n, pl* **-ries** 1 person who deals with correspondence and general clerical work. 2 **(S-)** head of a state department, e.g. *Home Secretary*. **secretarial** *adj*.

secrete¹ ❶ *v* (of an organ, gland, etc.) produce and release (a substance). **secretion** *n* **secretory** [sek-**reet**-or-ee] *adj*.

secrete² ❶ *v* hide or conceal.

sect ❶ *n* subdivision of a religious or political group, esp. one with extreme beliefs. **sectarian** *adj* 1 of a sect. 2 narrow-minded.

section ❶ *n* 1 part cut off. 2 part or subdivision of something. 3 distinct part of a country or community. 4 cutting. 5 drawing of something as if cut through. ▷ *v* 6 cut or divide into sections. **sectional** *adj*.

sector ❶ *n* 1 part or subdivision. 2 part of a circle enclosed by two radii and the arc which they cut off.

secular ❶ *adj* 1 worldly, as opposed to sacred. 2 not connected with religion or the church.

secure ❶ *adj* 1 free from danger. 2 free from anxiety. 3 firmly fixed. 4 reliable. ▷ *v* 5 obtain. 6 make safe. 7 make firm. 8 guarantee payment of (a loan) by giving something as security. **securely** *adv* **security** *n, pl* **-ties** 1 precautions against theft, espionage, or other danger. 2 state of being secure. 3 certificate of ownership of a share, stock, or bond. 4 something given or pledged to guarantee payment of a loan.

sedate¹ ❶ *adj* 1 calm and dignified. 2 slow or unhurried. **sedately** *adv*.

sedate² *v* give a sedative drug to. **sedation** *n* **sedative** *adj* 1 having a soothing or calming effect. ▷ *n* 2 sedative drug.

sediment ❶ *n* 1 matter which settles to the bottom of a liquid. 2 material deposited by water, ice, or wind. **sedimentary** *adj*.

——————————— THESAURUS ———————————

secondary *adj* 1 = **subordinate**, inferior, lesser, lower, minor, unimportant 2 = **resultant**, contingent, derived, indirect

secret *adj* 1 = **concealed**, close, confidential, disguised, furtive, hidden, undercover, underground, undisclosed, unknown, unrevealed ▷ *n* 3 = **enigma**, code, key 4 = **mystery in secret** = **secretly**, slyly, surreptitiously

secrete¹ *v* = **give off**, emanate, emit, exude

secrete² *v* = **hide**, cache, conceal, harbour, stash (*inf*), stow

sect *n* = **group**, camp, denomination, division, faction, party, schism

section *n* 1 = **slice** 2 = **part**, division, fraction, instalment, passage, piece, portion, segment 3 = **district**, area, region, sector, zone

sector *n* 1 = **part**, division

secular *adj* 1 = **worldly**, earthly, nonspiritual, temporal 2 = **lay**, civil

secure *adj* 1 = **safe**, immune, protected, unassailable 2 = **sure**, assured, certain, confident, easy, reassured 3 = **fixed**, fast, fastened, firm, immovable, stable, steady ▷ *v* 5 = **obtain**, acquire, gain, get, procure, score (*sl*) 7 = **fasten**, attach, bolt, chain, fix, lock, make fast, tie up

sedate¹ *adj* 1 = **calm**, collected, composed, cool, dignified, serene, tranquil 2 = **unhurried**, deliberate, slow-moving

sediment *n* 1 = **dregs**, deposit, grounds, lees, residue

sedition ❶ n speech or action encouraging rebellion against the government. **seditious** adj.

seduce ❶ v 1 persuade into sexual intercourse. 2 tempt into wrongdoing. **seducer, seductress** n **seduction** n **seductive** adj.

see¹ ❶ v **seeing, saw, seen** 1 perceive with the eyes or mind. 2 understand. 3 watch. 4 find out. 5 make sure (of something). 6 consider or decide. 7 have experience of. 8 meet or visit. 9 interview. 10 frequent the company of. 11 accompany. **seeing** conj in view of the fact that.

see² ❶ n diocese of a bishop.

seed ❶ n 1 mature fertilized grain of a plant. 2 such grains used for sowing. 3 origin. 4 obs offspring. 5 Sport player ranked according to his or her ability. ▷ v 6 sow with seed. 7 remove seeds from. 8 arrange (the draw of a sports tournament) so that the outstanding competitors will not

meet in the early rounds. **go, run to seed** 1 (of plants) produce or shed seeds after flowering. 2 lose vigour or usefulness. **seedling** n young plant raised from a seed. **seedy** adj 1 shabby. 2 informal unwell.

seek ❶ v **seeking, sought** 1 try to find or obtain. 2 try (to do something).

seem ❶ v appear to be. **seeming** adj apparent but not real. **seemingly** adv.

seep ❶ v trickle through slowly, ooze. **seepage** n.

seesaw ❶ n 1 plank balanced in the middle so that two people seated on either end ride up and down alternately. ▷ v 2 move up and down.

seethe ❶ v **seething, seethed** 1 be very agitated. 2 (of a liquid) boil or foam.

segment ❶ n 1 one of several sections into which something may be divided. ▷ v 2 divide into segments. **segmentation** n.

segregate ❶ v set apart. **segregation** n.

seize ❶ v 1 take hold of forcibly or quickly.

THESAURUS

---

sedition n = **rabble-rousing**, agitation, incitement to riot, subversion

seduce v 1 = **corrupt**, debauch, deflower, deprave, dishonour 2 = **tempt**, beguile, deceive, entice, inveigle, lead astray, lure, mislead

see¹ v 1 = **perceive**, behold, catch sight of, discern, distinguish, espy, eyeball (sl), glimpse, look, make out, notice, sight, spot, witness 2 = **understand**, appreciate, comprehend, fathom, feel, follow, get, grasp, realize 3 = **observe** 4 = **find out**, ascertain, determine, discover, learn 5 = **make sure**, ensure, guarantee, make certain, see to it 6 = **consider**, decide, deliberate, reflect, think over 9 = **visit**, receive 9 = **speak to**, confer with, consult, interview 10 = **go out with**, court, date (inf, chiefly US), go steady with (inf) 11 = **accompany**, escort, lead, show, usher, walk

see² n = **diocese**, bishopric

seed n 1, 2 = **grain**, germ, kernel, pip, spore 3 = **origin**, beginning, germ, nucleus,

source, start 4 Obs = **offspring**, children, descendants, issue, progeny **go, run to seed** 2 = **decline**, decay, degenerate, deteriorate, go downhill (inf), go to pot, let oneself go

seek v 1 = **look for**, be after, follow, hunt, pursue, search for 2 = **try**, aim, aspire to, attempt, endeavour, essay, strive

seem v = **appear**, assume, give the impression, look

seep v = **ooze**, exude, leak, permeate, soak, trickle, well

seesaw v 2 = **alternate**, fluctuate, oscillate, swing

seethe v 1 = **be furious**, be livid, be pissed (off) (taboo sl), fume, go ballistic (sl, chiefly US), rage, see red (inf), simmer 2 = **boil**, bubble, fizz, foam, froth

segment n 1 = **section**, bit, division, part, piece, portion, slice, wedge

segregate v = **set apart**, dissociate, isolate, separate

seize v = **grab**, catch up, clutch, grasp, grip, lay hands on, snatch, take

S

2 take immediate advantage of. **3** (usu. foll. by *up*) (of mechanical parts) stick tightly through overheating. **seizure** *n* **1** sudden violent attack of an illness. **2** seizing or being seized.

seldom ⊕ *adv* not often, rarely.

select ⊕ *v* **1** pick out or choose. ▷ *adj* **2** chosen in preference to others. **3** restricted to a particular group, exclusive. **selection** *n* **1** selecting. **2** things that have been selected. **3** range from which something may be selected. **selective** *adj* chosen or choosing carefully. **selectively** *adv* **selectivity** *n* **selector** *n*.

self *n*, *pl* **selves 1** distinct individuality or identity of a person or thing. **2** one's basic nature. **3** one's own welfare or interests. **selfish** *adj* caring too much about oneself and not enough about others. **selfishly** *adv* **selfishness** *n* **selfless** *adj* unselfish.

self- *prefix* used with many main words to mean: **1** of oneself or itself. **2** by, to, in, due to, for, or from the self. **3** automatic(ally). **self-coloured** *adj* having only a single colour. **self-conscious** *adj* embarrassed at being the object of others' attention. **self-contained** *adj* **1** containing everything needed, complete. **2** (of a flat) having its own facilities. **self-evident** *adj* obvious without proof. **self-made** *adj* having achieved wealth or status by one's own efforts. **self-possessed** *adj* having control of one's emotions, calm. **self-righteous** *adj* thinking oneself more virtuous than others. **selfsame** *adj* the very same. **self-seeking** *adj*, *n* seeking to promote only one's own interests. **self-styled** *adj* using a title or name that one has taken without

right. **self-sufficient** *adj* able to provide for oneself without help.

sell ⊕ *v* **selling, sold 1** exchange (something) for money. **2** stock, deal in. **3** (of goods) be sold. **4** (foll. by *for*) have a specified price. **5** *informal* persuade (someone) to accept (something). ▷ *n* **6** manner of selling. **seller** *n* **sell out** *v* **1** dispose of (something) completely by selling. **2** *informal* betray. **sellout** *n* **1** performance of a show etc. for which all the tickets are sold. **2** *informal* betrayal.

Sellotape *n* **1** ® type of adhesive tape. ▷ *v* **2** stick with Sellotape.

semaphore *n* system of signalling by holding two flags in different positions to represent letters of the alphabet.

semblance ⊕ *n* outward or superficial appearance.

semen *n* sperm-carrying fluid produced by male animals.

semi- *prefix* used with many main words to mean: **1** half, e.g. *semicircle*. **2** partly or almost, e.g. *semiprofessional*.

semibreve *n* musical note four beats long.

semicolon *n* the punctuation mark (;).

semiconductor *n* substance with an electrical conductivity that increases with temperature.

semidetached *adj* (of a house) joined to another on one side.

semifinal *n* match or round before the final.

seminal ⊕ *adj* **1** original and influential. **2** capable of developing. **3** of semen or seed.

seminar *n* meeting of a group of students for discussion.

━━━━━━━━━ THESAURUS ━━━━━━━

seldom *adv* = **rarely**, hardly ever, infrequently, not often

select *v* **1** = **choose**, opt for, pick, single out ▷ *adj* **2** = **choice**, excellent, first-class, hand-picked, special, superior, top-notch (*inf*) **3** = **exclusive**, cliquish, elite, privileged

sell *v* **1** = **trade**, barter, exchange **2** = **deal**

in, handle, market, peddle, retail, stock, trade in, traffic in

semblance *n* = **appearance**, aspect, facade, mask, pretence, resemblance, show, veneer

seminal *adj* **1** = **influential**, formative, ground-breaking, important, innovative, original

S

semiprecious adj (of gemstones) having less value than precious stones.

semolina n hard grains of wheat left after the milling of flour, used to make puddings and pasta.

send ❶ v sending, sent 1 cause (a person or thing) to go to or be taken or transmitted to a place. 2 bring into a specified state or condition. **sendoff** n demonstration of good wishes at a person's departure. **send up** v informal make fun of by imitating. **send-up** n informal imitation.

senile ❶ adj mentally or physically weak because of old age. **senility** n.

senior ❶ adj 1 superior in rank or standing. 2 older. 3 of or for older pupils. ▷ n 4 senior person. **seniority** n.

sensation ❶ n 1 ability to feel things physically. 2 physical feeling. 3 general feeling or awareness. 4 state of excitement. 5 exciting person or thing. **sensational** adj 1 causing intense shock, anger, or excitement. 2 informal very good. **sensationalism** n deliberate use of sensational language or subject matter. **sensationalist** adj, n.

sense ❶ n 1 any of the faculties of perception or feeling (sight, hearing, touch, taste, or smell). 2 ability to perceive. 3 feeling perceived through one of the senses. 4 awareness. 5 (sometimes pl) sound practical judgment or intelligence. 6 specific meaning. ▷ v 7 perceive. **senseless** adj.

sensible ❶ adj 1 having or showing good sense. 2 practical, e.g. sensible shoes. 3 (foll. by of) aware. **sensibly** adv **sensibility** n ability to experience deep feelings.

sensitive ❶ adj 1 easily hurt or offended. 2 responsive to external stimuli. 3 (of a subject) liable to arouse controversy or strong feelings. 4 (of an instrument) responsive to slight changes. **sensitively** adv **sensitivity** n **sensitize** v make sensitive.

sensor n device that detects or measures the presence of something, such as radiation.

sensory adj of the senses or sensation.

sensual ❶ adj 1 giving pleasure to the body and senses rather than the mind. 2 having a strong liking for physical pleasures. **sensually** adv **sensuality** n.

sensuous ❶ adj pleasing to the senses.

THESAURUS

---

send v 1 = **dispatch**, convey, direct, forward, remit, transmit

senile adj = **doddering**, decrepit, doting, in one's dotage

senior adj 1 = **higher ranking**, superior 2 = **older**, elder, major (Brit)

sensation n 3 = **feeling**, awareness, consciousness, impression, perception, sense 4 = **excitement**, commotion, furore, stir, thrill

sense n 1 = **faculty** 3 = **feeling**, sensation 4 = **feeling**, atmosphere, aura, awareness, consciousness, impression, perception 5 (sometimes pl) = **intelligence**, brains (inf), cleverness, common sense, judgment, reason, sagacity, sanity, sharpness, understanding, wisdom, wit(s) 6 = **meaning**, drift, gist, implication, import, significance ▷ v 7 = **perceive**, be aware of, discern, feel, get the impression, pick up, realize, understand

sensible adj 1 = **wise**, canny, down-to-earth, intelligent, judicious, prudent, rational, realistic, sage, sane, shrewd, sound 2 = **practical** 3 (foll. by of) = **aware of**, conscious of, mindful of, sensitive to

sensitive adj 1 = **easily hurt**, delicate, easily offended, easily upset, tender, thin-skinned, touchy 2 = **susceptible**, easily affected, impressionable, responsive 4 = **precise**, acute, fine, keen, responsive

sensual adj 1 = **physical**, animal, bodily, carnal, fleshly, luxurious, voluptuous 2 = **erotic**, lascivious, lecherous, lewd, lustful, raunchy (sl), sexual

sensuous adj = **pleasurable**, gratifying, hedonistic, sybaritic

sentence ❶ *n* **1** sequence of words capable of standing alone as a statement, question, or command. **2** punishment passed on a criminal. ▷ *v* **3** pass sentence on (a convicted person).

sentient ❶ [**sen**-tee-ent] *adj* capable of feeling.

sentiment ❶ *n* **1** thought, opinion, or attitude. **2** feeling expressed in words. **3** exaggerated or mawkish emotion. **sentimental** *adj* excessively romantic or nostalgic. **sentimentality** *n*.

sentinel ❶ *n* sentry.

sentry *n, pl* **-tries** soldier on watch.

separate ❶ *v* **1** act as a barrier between. **2** distinguish between. **3** divide up into parts. **4** (of a couple) stop living together. ▷ *adj* **5** not the same, different. **6** set apart. **7** not shared, individual. **separately** *adv* **separation** *n* **1** separating or being separated. **2** *Law* living apart of a married couple without divorce. **separable** *adj* **separatist** *n* person who advocates the separation of a group from an organization or country.

● **SPELLING TIP**
● There are 101 examples of *seperate* in the
● Bank of English, whic h makes it the
● most popular misspelling of **separate**.

sepia *adj, n* reddish-brown (pigment).

Sept. September.

September *n* ninth month of the year.

septet *n* **1** group of seven performers. **2** music for such a group.

septic ❶ *adj* **1** (of a wound) infected. **2** of or caused by harmful bacteria. **septic tank** tank in which sewage is decomposed by the action of bacteria.

septicaemia [sep-tis-**see**-mee-a] *n* infection of the blood.

sepulchre ❶ [**sep**-pull-ker] *n* tomb or burial vault. **sepulchral** [sip-**pulk**-ral] *adj* gloomy.

sequel ❶ *n* **1** novel, play, or film that continues the story of an earlier one. **2** consequence.

sequence ❶ *n* **1** arrangement of two or more things in successive order. **2** the successive order of two or more things. **3** section of a film showing a single uninterrupted episode. **sequential** *adj*.

sequin *n* small ornamental metal disc on a garment.

seraph *n, pl* **-aphs**, **-aphim** member of the highest order of angels. **seraphic** *adj*.

serenade *n* **1** music played or sung to a woman by a lover. ▷ *v* **2** sing or play a serenade to (someone).

serendipity *n* gift of making fortunate discoveries by accident.

————————————————————— THESAURUS ——————

sentence *n* **2** = **punishment**, condemnation, decision, decree, judgment, order, ruling, verdict ▷ *v* **3** = **condemn**, doom, penalize

sentient *adj* = **feeling**, conscious, living, sensitive

sentiment *n* **1** = **opinion**, attitude, belief, feeling, idea, judgment, view **3** = **sentimentality**, emotionalism, mawkishness, romanticism

sentinel *n* = **guard**, lookout, sentry, watch, watchman

separate *v* **2** = **single out**, isolate, segregate **3** = **divide** **4** = **part**, break up, disunite, diverge, divorce, estrange, part company, split up

▷ *adj* **6** = **unconnected**, detached, disconnected, divided, divorced, isolated, unattached **7** = **individual**, alone, apart, distinct, particular, single, solitary

septic *adj* **1** = **infected**, festering, poisoned, putrefying, putrid, suppurating

sepulchre *n* = **tomb**, burial place, grave, mausoleum, vault

sequel *n* **1** = **follow-up**, continuation, development **2** = **consequence**, conclusion, end, outcome, result, upshot

sequence *n* **1, 2** = **succession**, arrangement, chain, course, cycle, order, progression, series

serene ① *adj* calm, peaceful. **serenely** *adv* **serenity** *n*.

serf *n* medieval farm labourer who could not leave the land he worked on. **serfdom** *n*.

sergeant *n* **1** noncommissioned officer in the army. **2** police officer ranking between constable and inspector. **sergeant major** highest rank of noncommissioned officer in the army.

series ① *n*, *pl* **-ries 1** group or succession of related things, usu. arranged in order. **2** set of radio or TV programmes about the same subject or characters.

serious ① *adj* **1** giving cause for concern. **2** concerned with important matters. **3** not cheerful, grave. **4** sincere, not joking. **seriously** *adv* **seriousness** *n*.

sermon ① *n* **1** speech on a religious or moral subject by a clergyman in a church service. **2** long moralizing speech. **sermonize** *v* make a long moralizing speech.

serpent *n* snake. **serpentine** *adj* twisting like a snake.

serrated *adj* having a notched or sawlike edge.

serum [**seer**-um] *n* **1** watery fluid left after blood has clotted. **2** this fluid from the blood of immunized animals used for inoculation or vaccination.

serve ① *v* **1** work for (a person, community, or cause). **2** perform official duties. **3** attend to (customers). **4** provide with food or drink. **5** present (food or drink). **6** provide with a service. **7** be a member of the armed forces. **8** spend (time) in prison. **9** be useful or suitable. **10** *Tennis etc.* put (the ball) into play. **11** deliver (a legal document) to (a person). ▷ *n* **12** *Tennis etc.* act of serving the ball. **servant** *n* person employed to do household work for another.

service ① *n* **1** serving. **2** system that provides something needed by the public. **3** department of public employment and its employees. **4** maintenance of goods provided by a dealer after sale. **5** availability for use. **6** overhaul of a machine or vehicle. **7** set of dishes etc. for serving a meal. **8** formal religious ceremony. **9** *Tennis etc.* act, manner, or right of serving the ball. ▷ *pl* **10** armed forces. ▷ *adj* **11** serving the public rather than producing goods, e.g. *service industry*. ▷ *v* **12** provide a service or services to. **13** overhaul (a machine or vehicle).

serviette *n* table napkin.

servile ① *adj* **1** too eager to obey people, fawning. **2** suitable for a slave. **servility** *n*.

servitude *n* bondage or slavery.

sesame [**sess**-am-ee] *n* plant cultivated for its seeds and oil, which are used in cooking.

---

serene *adj* = **calm**, composed, peaceful, tranquil, unruffled, untroubled

series *n* **1** = **sequence**, chain, course, order, progression, run, set, string, succession, train

serious *adj* **1** = **grave**, acute, critical, dangerous, severe **2** = **important**, crucial, fateful, grim, momentous, no laughing matter, pressing, significant, urgent, worrying **3** = **solemn**, grave, humourless, sober, unsmiling **4** = **sincere**, earnest, genuine, honest, in earnest

sermon *n* = **homily**, address

serve *v* **1** = **work for**, aid, assist, help

2 = **perform**, act, complete, discharge, do, fulfil **3** = **attend to**, minister to, wait on **4**, **6** = **provide**, supply **5** = **present**, deliver, dish up, set out **9** = **be adequate**, answer the purpose, be acceptable, do, function as, satisfy, suffice, suit

service *n* **1** = **help**, assistance, avail, benefit, use, usefulness **6** = **overhaul**, check, maintenance **8** = **ceremony**, observance, rite, worship ▷ *v* **13** = **overhaul**, check, fine tune, go over, maintain, tune (up)

servile *adj* **1** = **subservient**, abject, fawning, grovelling, obsequious, sycophantic, toadying

S

session ❶ n 1 period spent in an activity.
2 meeting of a court, parliament, or
council. 3 series or period of such
meetings. 4 academic term or year.

set¹ ❶ v setting, **set 1** put in a specified
position or state. 2 make ready. 3 make
or become firm or rigid. 4 put (a broken
bone) or (of a broken bone) be put into a
normal position for healing. 5 adjust (a
clock) to a particular position. 6 establish,
arrange. 7 prescribe, assign. 8 arrange
(hair) while wet, so that it dries in position.
9 place (a jewel) in a setting. 10 put to
music. 11 arrange (type) for printing.
12 (of the sun) go down. 13 (of plants)
produce (fruit or seeds). 14 (of a gun
dog) face game. ▷ n 15 setting or being
set. 16 bearing or posture. 17 scenery
used in a play or film. ▷ adj 18 fixed or
established beforehand. 19 rigid or
inflexible. 20 conventional or stereotyped.
21 determined (to do something).
22 ready. **set back** v 1 hinder. 2 cost.
setback n anything that delays progress.
set off v 1 embark on a journey. 2 cause
to begin. 3 cause to explode. 4 act as a
contrast to. **set square** flat right-angled
triangular instrument used for drawing
angles. **set to** v begin working. **set-to** n

brief fight. **set up** v arrange or establish.
setup n way in which anything is
organized or arranged.

set² ❶ n 1 number of things or people
grouped or belonging together.
2 Maths group of numbers or objects
that satisfy a given condition or
share a property. 3 television or radio
receiver. 4 Sport group of games in a
match. 5 series of songs performed by
a musician or group. **set theory** branch
of mathematics concerned with the
properties of sets.

sett, set n badger's burrow.

settee n couch.

setting ❶ n 1 background or surroundings.
2 time and place where a film, book,
etc. is supposed to have taken place.
3 music written for the words of a text.
4 decorative metalwork in which a gem is
set. 5 plates and cutlery for a single place
at table. 6 position or level to which the
controls of a machine can be adjusted.

settle ❶ v 1 arrange or put in order. 2 come
to rest. 3 establish or become established
as a resident. 4 colonize. 5 make quiet,
calm, or stable. 6 pay (a bill). 7 dispose
of, conclude. 8 bestow (property) legally.
9 end (a dispute). **settlement** n 1 act

THESAURUS

session n 1 = **period** 2 = **meeting**,
discussion, hearing, sitting 3 = **congress**,
assembly, conference

set¹ v 1 = **put**, deposit, lay, locate, place,
plant, position, rest, seat, situate, station,
stick 2 = **prepare**, arrange, lay, make
ready, spread 3 = **harden**, cake, congeal,
crystallize, solidify, stiffen, thicken
6 = **arrange**, appoint, decide (upon),
determine, establish, fix, fix up, resolve,
schedule, settle, specify 7 = **assign**, allot,
decree, impose, ordain, prescribe, specify
12 = **go down**, decline, dip, disappear, sink,
subside, vanish ▷ n 16 = **position**, attitude,
bearing, carriage, posture 17 = **scenery**,
scene, setting, stage set ▷ adj 18 = **fixed**,
agreed, appointed, arranged, decided,

definite, established, prearranged,
predetermined, scheduled, settled
19 = **inflexible**, hard and fast, immovable,
rigid, stubborn 20 = **conventional**,
stereotyped, traditional, unspontaneous

set² n 1 a = **series**, assortment, batch,
collection, compendium b = **group**, band,
circle, clique, company, coterie, crowd,
faction, gang

setting n 1 = **surroundings**, backdrop,
background, location, scene, scenery, set,
site 2 = **context**

settle v 1 = **put in order**, adjust, order,
regulate, straighten out, work out 2 = **land**,
alight, come to rest, descend, light
3 = **move to**, dwell, inhabit, live, make
one's home, put down roots, reside, set

S

of settling. **2** place newly colonized. **3** subsidence (of a building). **4** property bestowed legally. **settler** *n* colonist. **settle down** *v* **1** make or become calm. **2** (foll. by *to*) concentrate on. **3** adopt a routine way of life. **settle for** *v* accept in spite of dissatisfaction.

seven *adj, n* one more than six. **seventh** *adj, n* (of) number seven in a series. **seventeen** *adj, n* ten and seven. **seventeenth** *adj, n* **seventy** *adj, n* ten times seven. **seventieth** *adj, n*.

sever ❶ *v* **1** cut through or off. **2** break off (a relationship). **severance** *n*.

several ❶ *adj* **1** some, a few. **2** various, separate. **severally** *adv* separately.

severe ❶ *adj* **1** strict or harsh. **2** very intense or unpleasant. **3** strictly restrained in appearance. **severely** *adv* **severity** *n*.

sew *v* **sewing, sewed, sewn** or **sewed 1** join with thread repeatedly passed through with a needle. **2** make or fasten by sewing.

sewage *n* waste matter or excrement carried away in sewers. **sewer** *n* drain to remove waste water and sewage. **sewerage** *n* system of sewers.

sex ❶ *n* **1** state of being male or female. **2** male or female category. **3** sexual intercourse. **4** sexual feelings or behaviour. ▷ *v* **5** find out the sex of. **sexy** *adj* **1** sexually exciting or attractive. **2** *informal* exciting or trendy. **sexism** *n* discrimination on the basis of a person's sex. **sexist** *adj, n* **sexual** *adj* **sexually** *adv* **sexuality** *n* **sexual intercourse** sexual act in which the male's penis is inserted into the female's vagina. **sex up** *v informal* make (something) more exciting.

sextet *n* **1** group of six performers. **2** music for such a group.

shabby ❶ *adj* **-bier, -biest 1** worn or dilapidated in appearance. **2** mean or unworthy, e.g. *shabby treatment*. **shabbily** *adv* **shabbiness** *n*.

shack ❶ *n* rough hut.

shackle ❶ *n* **1** one of a pair of metal rings joined by a chain, for securing a person's wrists or ankles. ▷ *v* **2** fasten with shackles.

shade ❶ *n* **1** relative darkness. **2** place sheltered from sun. **3** screen or cover used to protect from a direct source of light. **4** depth of colour. **5** slight amount. **6** *lit*

— THESAURUS —

up home, take up residence **4** = **colonize**, people, pioneer, populate **5** = **calm**, lull, outspan (*S Afr*), pacify, quell, quiet, quieten, reassure, relax, relieve, soothe **6** = **pay**, clear, discharge, square (up) **7** = **decide**, agree, confirm, determine, establish, fix **9** = **resolve**, clear up, decide, put an end to, reconcile

sever *v* **1** = **cut**, cut in two, detach, disconnect, disjoin, divide, part, separate, split **2** = **discontinue**, break off, dissociate, put an end to, terminate

several *adj* **1** = **some**, many **2** = **various**, sundry

severe *adj* **1** = **strict**, austere, cruel, drastic, hard, harsh, oppressive, rigid, unbending **2** = **intense**, acute, extreme, fierce **3 a** = **grim**, forbidding, grave, serious, stern, tight-lipped, unsmiling **b** = **plain**, austere,

classic, restrained, simple, Spartan, unadorned, unembellished, unfussy

sex *n* **1, 2** = **gender 3** = **(sexual) intercourse**, coition, coitus, copulation, fornication, lovemaking, sexual relations

shabby *adj* **1** = **tatty**, dilapidated, mean, ragged, run-down, scruffy, seedy, tattered, threadbare, worn **2** = **mean**, cheap, contemptible, despicable, dirty, dishonourable, low, rotten (*inf*), scurvy

shack *n* = **hut**, cabin, shanty

shackle *n* **1** = **fetter**, bond, chain, iron, leg-iron, manacle ▷ *v* **2** = **fetter**, bind, chain, manacle, put in irons

shade *n* **1** = **dimness**, dusk, gloom, gloominess, semidarkness, shadow **3** = **screen**, blind, canopy, cover, covering, curtain, shield, veil **4** = **hue**, colour, tinge, tint, tone **5** = **dash**, hint, suggestion,

S

ghost. ▷ *pl* **7** *slang* sunglasses. ▷ *v* **8** screen from light. **9** darken. **10** represent (darker areas) in drawing. **11** change slightly or by degrees. **shady** *adj* **1** situated in or giving shade. **2** of doubtful honesty or legality.

shadow ⓞ *n* **1** dark shape cast on a surface when something stands between a light and the surface. **2** patch of shade. **3** slight trace. **4** threatening influence. **5** inseparable companion. ▷ *v* **6** cast a shadow over. **7** follow secretly. **shadowy** *adj*.

shaft ⓞ *n* **1** long narrow straight handle of a tool or weapon. **2** ray of light. **3** revolving rod that transmits power in a machine. **4** vertical passageway, as for a lift or a mine. **5** one of the bars between which an animal is harnessed to a vehicle.

shag *n* **1** coarse shredded tobacco. **2** tangled hair or wool. ▷ *adj* **3** (of a carpet) having a long pile. **shaggy** *adj* **1** covered with rough hair or wool. **2** tousled, unkempt. **shaggy-dog story** long anecdote with a humorous twist at the end.

shake ⓞ *v* **shaking, shook, shaken** **1** move quickly up and down or back and forth. **2** make unsteady. **3** tremble.

4 grasp (someone's hand) in greeting or agreement. **5** shock or upset. ▷ *n* **6** shaking. **7** vibration. **8** *informal* short period of time. **shaky** *adj* **1** unsteady. **2** uncertain or questionable. **shakily** *adv*.

shale *n* flaky sedimentary rock.

shall *v, past tense* **should** used as an auxiliary to make the future tense or to indicate intention, obligation, or inevitability.

shallow ⓞ *adj* **1** not deep. **2** lacking depth of character or intellect. **shallows** *pl n* area of shallow water.

sham ⓞ *n* **1** thing or person that is not genuine. ▷ *adj* **2** not genuine. ▷ *v* **shamming, shammed 3** fake, feign.

shamble *v* walk in a shuffling awkward way.

shambles ⓞ *n* disorderly event or place.

shame ⓞ *n* **1** painful emotion caused by awareness of having done something dishonourable or foolish. **2** capacity to feel shame. **3** cause of shame. **4** cause for regret. ▷ *v* **5** cause to feel shame. **7** compel by shame. **shameful** *adj* causing or deserving shame. **shamefully** *adv* **shameless** *adj* with no sense of shame. **shamefaced** *adj* looking ashamed.

━━━━━━━━━━━━ THESAURUS ━━━━━━━━━━━━

trace **6** *Lit* = **ghost**, apparition, phantom, spectre, spirit ▷ *v* **8** = **cover**, conceal, hide, obscure, protect, screen, shield, veil **9** = **darken**, cloud, dim, shadow

shadow *n* **2** = **dimness**, cover, darkness, dusk, gloom, shade **3** = **trace**, hint, suggestion, suspicion **4** = **cloud**, blight, gloom, sadness ▷ *v* **6** = **shade**, darken, overhang, screen, shield **7** = **follow**, stalk, tail (*inf*), trail

shaft *n* **1** = **handle**, pole, rod, shank, stem **2** = **ray**, beam, gleam

shake *v* **1** = **wave**, brandish, flourish **2** = **jolt**, bump, jar, rock **3** = **tremble**, quake, quiver, shiver, totter, vibrate **5** = **upset**, distress, disturb, frighten, rattle (*inf*), shock, unnerve ▷ *n* **6** = **quaking**, agitation, convulsion, jerk, jolt, shiver,

shudder, trembling **7** = **vibration**, tremor

shallow *adj* **1** = **superficial**, empty, slight, surface, trivial **2** = **unintelligent**, foolish, frivolous, ignorant, puerile, simple

sham *n* **1** = **phoney** *or* **phony** (*inf*), counterfeit, forgery, fraud, hoax, humbug, imitation, impostor, pretence ▷ *adj* **2** = **false**, artificial, bogus, counterfeit, feigned, imitation, mock, phoney *or* phony (*inf*), pretended, simulated ▷ *v* **3** = **fake**, affect, assume, feign, pretend, put on, simulate

shambles *n* **1** = **chaos**, confusion, disarray, disorder, havoc, madhouse, mess, muddle

shame *n* **1** = **embarrassment**, abashment, humiliation, ignominy, mortification **3** = **disgrace**, blot, discredit, dishonour, disrepute, infamy, reproach, scandal,

shampoo n 1 liquid soap for washing hair, carpets, or upholstery. 2 process of shampooing. ▷ v 3 wash with shampoo.

shamrock n clover leaf, esp. as the Irish emblem.

shandy n, pl -dies drink made of beer and lemonade.

shanty¹ ❶ n, pl -ties shack or crude dwelling. **shantytown** n slum consisting of shanties.

shanty² n, pl -ties sailor's traditional song.

shape ❶ n 1 outward form of an object. 2 way in which something is organized. 3 pattern or mould. 4 condition or state. ▷ v 5 form or mould. 6 devise or develop. **shapeless** adj **shapely** adj having an attractive shape.

shard n broken piece of pottery or glass.

share ❶ n 1 part of something that belongs to or is contributed by a person. 2 one of the equal parts into which the capital stock of a public company is divided. ▷ v 3 give or take a share of (something). 4 join with others in doing or using (something). 5 divide and distribute. **shareholder** n.

shark n 1 large usu. predatory sea fish. 2 person who cheats others.

sharp ❶ adj 1 having a keen cutting edge or fine point. 2 not gradual. 3 clearly

defined. 4 mentally acute. 5 clever but underhand. 6 shrill. 7 bitter or sour in taste. 8 *Music* above the true pitch. ▷ adv 9 promptly. 10 *Music* too high in pitch. ▷ n 11 *Music* symbol raising a note one semitone above natural pitch. **sharply** adv **sharpness** n **sharpen** v make or become sharp or sharper. **sharpener** n **sharpshooter** n marksman.

shatter ❶ v 1 break into pieces. 2 destroy completely. **shattered** adj informal 1 completely exhausted. 2 badly upset.

shave ❶ v shaving, shaved, shaved or shaven 1 remove (hair) from (the face, head, or body) with a razor or shaver. 2 pare away. 3 touch lightly in passing. ▷ n 4 shaving. **close shave** informal narrow escape. **shaver** n electric razor. **shavings** pl n parings.

shawl n piece of cloth worn over a woman's head or shoulders or wrapped around a baby.

she pron refers to: 1 female person or animal previously mentioned. 2 something regarded as female, such as a car, ship, or nation.

sheaf n, pl sheaves 1 bundle of papers. 2 tied bundle of reaped corn.

shear v shearing, sheared, sheared or shorn 1 clip hair or wool from. 2 cut

——————— THESAURUS ———————

smear v 5 = **embarrass**, abash, disgrace, humble, humiliate, mortify 6 = **dishonour**, blot, debase, defile, degrade, smear, stain

shanty¹ n = **shack**, cabin, hut, shed

shape n 1 = **form**, build, contours, figure, lines, outline, profile, silhouette 2 = **configuration** 3 = **pattern**, frame, model, mould 4 = **condition**, fettle, health, state, trim ▷ v 5 = **form**, create, fashion, make, model, mould, produce 6 = **develop**, adapt, devise, frame, modify, plan

share n 1 = **part**, allotment, allowance, contribution, due, lot, portion, quota, ration, whack (inf) ▷ v 3 = **divide**, assign, distribute, split 4 = **partake**, participate,

receive 5 = **go halves**, go fifty-fifty (inf)

sharp adj 1 = **keen**, acute, jagged, pointed, serrated, spiky 2 = **sudden**, abrupt, distinct, extreme, marked 3 = **clear**, crisp, distinct, well-defined 4 = **quick-witted**, alert, astute, bright, clever, discerning, knowing, penetrating, perceptive, quick 5 = **cunning**, artful, crafty, dishonest, sly, unscrupulous, wily 7 = **sour**, acid, acrid, hot, piquant, pungent, tart ▷ adv 9 = **promptly**, exactly, on the dot, on time, precisely, punctually

shatter v 1 = **smash**, break, burst, crack, crush, pulverize 2 = **destroy**, demolish, ruin, torpedo, wreck

shave v 1, 2 = **trim**, crop, pare, shear

through. **shears** pl n large scissors or a cutting tool shaped like these. **shearer** n.

sheath n 1 close-fitting cover, esp. for a knife or sword. 2 condom. **sheathe** v put into a sheath.

shebeen n Irish, S Afr & Scot place where alcohol is sold illegally.

shed¹ ⊕ n building used for storage or shelter or as a workshop.

shed² ⊕ v **shedding, shed** 1 pour forth (tears). 2 cast off (skin, hair, or leaves).

sheen ⊕ n glistening brightness on the surface of something.

sheep n, pl **sheep** ruminant animal bred for wool and meat. **sheepdog** n dog used for herding sheep. **sheepskin** n skin of a sheep with the fleece still on, used for clothing or rugs.

sheer ⊕ adj 1 absolute, complete, e.g. sheer folly. 2 perpendicular, steep. 3 (of material) so fine as to be transparent. ▷ adv 4 steeply.

sheet ⊕ n 1 large piece of cloth used as an inner bed cover. 2 broad thin piece of any material. 3 large expanse. **sheeting** n material from which sheets are made. **sheet lightning** lightning that appears to flash across a large part of the sky at once.

sheikh, sheik [shake] n Arab chief.

shelf n, pl **shelves** 1 board fixed

horizontally for holding things. 2 ledge. **shelf life** time a packaged product will remain fresh.

shell ⊕ n 1 hard outer covering of an egg, nut, or certain animals. 2 external frame of something. 3 explosive projectile fired from a large gun. ▷ v 4 take the shell from. 5 fire at with artillery shells. **shellfish** n sea-living animal, esp. one that can be eaten, with a shell. **shell out** v informal pay out or hand over (money). **shell shock** nervous disorder caused by exposure to battle conditions.

shelter ⊕ n 1 structure providing protection from danger or the weather. 2 protection. ▷ v 3 give shelter to. 4 take shelter.

shelve ⊕ v 1 put aside or postpone. 2 provide with shelves. **shelving** n (material for) shelves.

shepherd ⊕ n 1 person who tends sheep. ▷ v 2 guide or watch over (people). **shepherdess** n fem **shepherd's pie** baked dish of mince covered with mashed potato.

sherbet n fruit-flavoured fizzy powder.

sheriff n 1 (in the US) chief law enforcement officer of a county. 2 (in England and Wales) chief executive officer of the Crown in a county. 3 (in Scotland)

———————————————— THESAURUS ————————————————

shed¹ n = **hut**, outhouse, shack

shed² v 1 = **cast**, drop, spill, emit, give, give out, radiate, scatter, shower 2 = **cast off**, discard, moult, slough

sheen n = **shine**, brightness, gleam, gloss, lustre, polish

sheer adj 1 = **total**, absolute, complete, downright, out-and-out, pure, unmitigated, utter 2 = **steep**, abrupt, precipitous 3 = **fine**, diaphanous, gauzy, gossamer, see-through, thin, transparent

sheet n 2 = **coat**, film, lamina, layer, overlay, panel, plate, slab, stratum, surface, veneer 3 = **expanse**, area, blanket, covering, stretch, sweep

shell n 1 = **case**, husk, pod 2 = **frame**, framework, hull, structure ▷ v 5 = **bomb**, attack, blitz, bombard, strafe

shelter n 1 = **cover**, screen 2 = **protection**, asylum, defence, guard, haven, refuge, retreat, safety, sanctuary, security ▷ v 3 = **protect**, cover, defend, guard, harbour, hide, safeguard, shield 4 = **take shelter**, hide, seek harbour

shelve v 1 = **postpone**, defer, freeze, put aside, put on ice, put on the back burner (inf), suspend, take a rain check on (US & Canad inf)

shepherd n 1 = **herdsman**, drover, grazier, stockman ▷ v 2 = **guide**, conduct, herd, steer, usher

chief judge of a district.

sherry *n*, *pl* **-ries** pale or dark brown fortified wine.

shield ⊕ *n* **1** piece of armour carried on the arm to protect the body from blows or missiles. **2** anything that protects. **3** sports trophy in the shape of a shield. ▷ *v* **4** protect.

shift ⊕ *v* **1** move. **2** transfer (blame or responsibility). **3** remove or be removed. ▷ *n* **4** shifting. **5** group of workers who work during a specified period. **6** period of time during which they work. **7** loose-fitting straight underskirt or dress. **shiftless** *adj* lacking in ambition or initiative. **shifty** *adj* evasive or untrustworthy. **shiftiness** *n*.

shilling *n* former British coin, replaced by the 5p piece.

shimmer ⊕ *v*, *n* (shine with) a faint unsteady light.

shin *n* **1** front of the lower leg. ▷ *v* **shinning**, **shinned** **2** climb by using the hands or arms and legs.

shine ⊕ *v* **shining**, **shone 1** give out or reflect light. **2** aim (a light). **3** polish. **4** excel. ▷ *n* **5** brightness or lustre. **take a shine to** *informal* take a liking to (someone). **shiny** *adj*.

shingle *n* **1** wooden roof tile. ▷ *v* **2** cover (a roof) with shingles.

shingles *n* disease causing a rash of small blisters along a nerve.

ship ⊕ *n* **1** large seagoing vessel. ▷ *v* **shipping**, **shipped 2** send or transport by carrier, esp. a ship. **3** bring or go aboard a ship. **shipment** *n* **1** act of shipping cargo. **2** consignment of goods shipped. **shipping** *n* **1** freight transport business. **2** ships collectively. **shipshape** *adj* orderly or neat. **shipwreck** *n* **1** destruction of a ship through storm or collision. ▷ *v* **2** cause to undergo shipwreck. **shipyard** *n* place where ships are built.

shire *n* county.

shirk ⊕ *v* avoid (duty or work). **shirker** *n*.

shirt *n* garment for the upper part of the body.

shirty *adj* **-tier**, **-tiest** *slang* bad-tempered or annoyed.

shiver[1] **⊕** *v* **1** tremble, as from cold or fear. ▷ *n* **2** shivering.

shiver[2] **⊕** *v* splinter into pieces.

shoal[1] *n* large number of fish swimming together.

shoal[2] *n* **1** stretch of shallow water. **2** sandbank.

shock[1] **⊕** *v* **1** horrify, disgust, or astonish. ▷ *n* **2** sudden violent emotional disturbance. **3** sudden violent blow or impact. **4** something causing this. **5** state of bodily collapse caused by physical or mental

——————— THESAURUS ———————

shield *n* **2** = **protection**, cover, defence, guard, safeguard, screen, shelter ▷ *v* **4** = **protect**, cover, defend, guard, safeguard, screen, shelter

shift *v* **1** = **move**, budge, displace, move around, rearrange, relocate, reposition ▷ *n* **4** = **move**, displacement, rearrangement, shifting

shimmer *v* = **gleam**, glisten, scintillate, twinkle ▷ *n* = **gleam**, iridescence

shine *v* **1** = **gleam**, beam, flash, glare, glisten, glitter, glow, radiate, sparkle, twinkle **3** = **polish**, brush, buff, burnish **4** = **be outstanding**, be conspicuous, excel, stand out ▷ *n* **5** = **brightness**, glare,

gleam, gloss, light, lustre, polish, radiance, sheen, shimmer, sparkle

ship *n* **1** = **vessel**, boat, craft

shirk *v* = **dodge**, avoid, evade, get out of, skive (*Brit sl*), slack

shiver[1] *v* **1** = **tremble**, quake, quiver, shake, shudder ▷ *n* **2** = **trembling**, flutter, quiver, shudder, tremor

shiver[2] *v* **1** = **splinter**, break, crack, fragment, shatter, smash, smash to smithereens

shock *v* **1 a** = **horrify**, appal, disgust, nauseate, revolt, scandalize, sicken **b** = **astound**, jolt, shake, stagger, stun, stupefy ▷ *n* **2** = **upset**, blow, bombshell,

S

shock. **6** pain and muscular spasm caused by an electric current passing through the body. **shocker** n **shocking** adj **1** causing horror, disgust, or astonishment. **2** informal very bad.

shock² n bushy mass (of hair).

shoddy ❶ adj **-dier, -diest** made or done badly.

shoe n **1** outer covering for the foot, ending below the ankle. **2** horseshoe. ▷ v **shoeing, shod 3** fit with a shoe or shoes. **shoehorn** n smooth implement inserted at the heel of a shoe to ease the foot into it. **shoestring** n **on a shoestring** using a very small amount of money.

shonky adj **-kier, -kiest** Aust & NZ informal unreliable or unsound.

shoo interj **1** go away! ▷ v **2** drive away as by saying 'shoo'.

shoot ❶ v **shooting, shot 1** hit, wound, or kill with a missile fired from a weapon. **2** fire (a missile from) a weapon. **3** hunt. **4** send out or move rapidly. **5** (of a plant) sprout. **6** photograph or film. **7** Sport take a shot at goal. ▷ n **8** new branch or sprout of a plant. **9** hunting expedition. **shooting star** meteor.

shop ❶ n **1** place for sale of goods and services. **2** workshop. ▷ v **shopping, shopped 3** visit a shop or shops to buy goods. **4** slang inform against (someone). **talk shop** discuss one's work, esp. on a social occasion. **shop around** v visit various shops to compare goods and

prices. **shop floor 1** production area of a factory. **2** workers in a factory. **shoplifter** n person who steals from a shop. **shopsoiled** adj soiled or faded from being displayed in a shop. **shop steward** trade-union official elected to represent his or her fellow workers.

shore¹ ❶ n edge of a sea or lake.

shore² ❶ v (foll. by up) prop or support.

short ❶ adj **1** not long. **2** not tall. **3** not lasting long, brief. **4** deficient, e.g. short of cash. **5** abrupt, rude. **6** (of a drink) consisting chiefly of a spirit. **7** (of pastry) crumbly. ▷ adv **8** abruptly. ▷ n **9** drink of spirits. **10** short film. **11** informal short circuit. ▷ pl **12** short trousers. **shortage** n deficiency. **shorten** v make or become shorter. **shortly** adv **1** soon. **2** rudely. **shortbread, shortcake** n crumbly biscuit made with butter. **short-change** v **1** give (someone) less than the correct amount of change. **2** slang swindle. **short circuit** faulty or accidental connection in a circuit, which deflects current through a path of low resistance. **shortcoming** n failing or defect. **short cut** quicker route or method. **shortfall** n deficit. **shorthand** n system of rapid writing using symbols to represent words. **short-handed** adj not having enough workers. **short list** selected list of candidates for a job or prize, from which the final choice will be made. **short-list** v put on a short list. **short shrift** brief and unsympathetic treatment. **short-sighted**

distress, disturbance, stupefaction, stupor, trauma, turn (inf) **3 = impact**, blow, clash, collision

shoddy adj **= inferior**, cheap, poor, rubbishy, second-rate, slipshod, tawdry, trashy

shoot v **1 = hit**, blast (sl), bring down, kill, open fire, plug (sl) **2 = fire**, discharge, emit, fling, hurl, launch, project, propel **4 = speed**, bolt, charge, dart, dash, fly, hurtle, race, rush, streak, tear ▷ n **8 = sprout**, branch, bud, offshoot, sprig

shop n **1 = store**, boutique, emporium, hypermarket, supermarket

shore¹ n **1 = beach**, coast, sands, seashore, strand (poet)

shore² v **1** (foll. by up) **= support**, brace, buttress, hold, prop, reinforce, strengthen, underpin

short adj **1 = concise**, brief, compressed, laconic, pithy, succinct, summary, terse **2 = small**, diminutive, dumpy, little, petite, squat **3 = brief**, fleeting, momentary **4 = lacking**, deficient, limited, low (on),

adj **1** unable to see distant things clearly. **2** lacking in foresight. **short-tailed shearwater** same as MEGAPODE. **short wave** radio wave with a wavelength of less than 60 metres.

shot ❶ *n* **1** shooting. **2** small lead pellets used in a shotgun. **3** person with specified skill in shooting. **4** *slang* attempt. **5** *Sport* act or instance of hitting, kicking, or throwing the ball. **6** photograph. **7** uninterrupted film sequence. **8** *informal* injection. **9** *informal* drink of spirits. **shotgun** *n* gun for firing a charge of shot at short range. **shotgun wedding** wedding enforced because the bride is pregnant.

should *v* past tense of **shall** used as an auxiliary to make the subjunctive mood or to indicate obligation or possibility.

shoulder ❶ *n* **1** part of the body to which an arm, foreleg, or wing is attached. **2** cut of meat including the upper foreleg. **3** side of a road. ▷ *v* **4** bear (a burden or responsibility). **5** push with one's shoulder. **6** put on one's shoulder. **shoulder blade** large flat triangular bone at the shoulder.

shout ❶ *n* **1** loud cry. ▷ *v* **2** cry out loudly. **3** *Aust & NZ informal* treat (someone) to (something, such as a drink). **shout down**

v silence (someone) by shouting.

shove ❶ *v* **1** push roughly. **2** *informal* put. ▷ *n* **3** rough push. **shove off** *v informal* go away.

shovel ❶ *n* **1** tool for lifting or moving loose material. ▷ *v* **-elling**, **-elled 2** lift or move as with a shovel.

show ❶ *v* **showing**, **showed**, **shown** or **showed 1** make, be, or become noticeable or visible. **2** exhibit or display. **3** indicate. **4** instruct by demonstration. **5** prove. **6** guide. **7** reveal or display (an emotion). ▷ *n* **8** public exhibition. **9** theatrical or other entertainment. **10** mere display or pretence. **showy** *adj* **1** gaudy. **2** ostentatious. **showily** *adv* **show business** the entertainment industry. **showcase** *n* **1** situation in which something is displayed to best advantage. **2** glass case used to display objects. **showdown** *n* confrontation that settles a dispute. **showjumping** *n* competitive sport of riding horses to demonstrate skill in jumping. **showman** *n* man skilled at presenting anything spectacularly. **showmanship** *n* **show off** *v* **1** exhibit to invite admiration. **2** *informal* behave flamboyantly in order to attract attention. **show-off** *n informal* person who shows off. **showpiece** *n* excellent specimen shown

scant, scarce, wanting **5** = **abrupt**, brusque, curt, discourteous, impolite, sharp, terse, uncivil ▷ *adv* **8** = **abruptly**, suddenly, without warning

shot *n* **1** = **throw**, discharge, lob, pot shot **2** = **pellet**, ball, bullet, lead, projectile, slug **3** = **marksman**, shooter **4** *Sl* = **attempt**, effort, endeavour, go (*inf*), stab (*inf*), try, turn

shoulder *v* **4** = **bear**, accept, assume, be responsible for, carry, take on **5** = **push**, elbow, jostle, press, shove

shout *n* **1** = **cry**, bellow, call, roar, scream, yell ▷ *v* **2** = **cry (out)**, bawl, bellow, call (out), holler (*inf*), roar, scream, yell

shove *v* **1** = **push**, drive, elbow, impel,

jostle, press, propel, thrust

shovel *v* **2** = **move**, dredge, heap, ladle, load, scoop, toss

show *v* **1** = **be visible**, appear **2** = **present**, display, exhibit **3** = **indicate**, demonstrate, display, manifest, register, reveal **4** = **instruct**, demonstrate, explain, teach **5** = **prove**, clarify, demonstrate, elucidate, point out **6** = **guide**, accompany, attend, conduct, escort, lead ▷ *n* **8** = **exhibition**, array, display, fair, parade, sight, spectacle **9** = **entertainment**, pageant, presentation, production **10** = **pretence**, affectation, air, appearance, display, illusion, parade, pose

S

for display or as an example. **showroom** n room in which goods for sale are on display. **show up** v **1** reveal or be revealed clearly. **2** expose the faults or defects of. **3** informal embarrass. **4** informal arrive.

shower ⊙ n **1** kind of bath in which a person stands while being sprayed with water. **2** wash in this. **3** short period of rain, hail, or snow. **4** sudden abundant fall of objects. ▷ v **5** wash in a shower. **6** bestow (things) or present (someone) with things liberally. **showery** adj.

shrapnel n **1** artillery shell filled with pellets which scatter on explosion. **2** fragments from this.

shred ⊙ n **1** long narrow strip torn from something. **2** small amount. ▷ v **shredding, shredded** or **shred 3** tear to shreds.

shrew n **1** small mouselike animal. **2** bad-tempered nagging woman.

shrewd ⊙ adj clever and perceptive.

shriek ⊙ n **1** shrill cry. ▷ v **2** utter (with) a shriek.

shrill ⊙ adj (of a sound) sharp and high-pitched. **shrillness** n **shrilly** adv.

shrimp n **1** small edible shellfish. **2** informal small person.

shrine n place of worship associated with a sacred person or object.

shrink ⊙ v **shrinking, shrank** or **shrunk, shrunk** or **shrunken 1** become or make smaller. **2** recoil or withdraw. ▷ n **3** slang psychiatrist. **shrinkage** n decrease in size, value, or weight.

shrivel ⊙ v **-elling, -elled** shrink and wither.

shroud ⊙ n **1** piece of cloth used to wrap a dead body. **2** anything which conceals. ▷ v **3** conceal.

shrub n woody plant smaller than a tree. **shrubbery** n, pl **-beries** area planted with shrubs.

shrug v **shrugging, shrugged 1** raise and then drop (the shoulders) as a sign of indifference, ignorance, or doubt. ▷ n **2** shrugging. **shrug off** v dismiss as unimportant.

shudder ⊙ v **1** shake or tremble violently, esp. with horror. ▷ n **2** shaking or trembling.

shuffle ⊙ v **1** walk without lifting the feet. **2** jumble together. **3** rearrange. ▷ n **4** shuffling. **5** rearrangement.

shun ⊙ v **shunning, shunned** avoid.

shunt v **1** move (objects or people) to a different position. **2** move (a train) from one track to another.

shut ⊙ v **shutting, shut 1** bring together or fold, close. **2** prevent access to. **3** (of a shop etc.) stop operating for the day.

━━━━━━━━━━━━━ THESAURUS ━━━━━

shower n **3, 4** = **deluge**, barrage, stream, torrent, volley ▷ v **6** = **inundate**, deluge, heap, lavish, pour, rain

shred n **1** = **strip**, bit, fragment, piece, scrap, sliver, tatter **2** = **particle**, atom, grain, iota, jot, scrap, trace

shrew n **2** = **nag**, harpy, harridan, scold, spitfire, vixen

shrewd adj = **clever**, astute, calculating, canny, crafty, cunning, intelligent, keen, perceptive, perspicacious, sharp, smart

shriek v, n = **cry**, scream, screech, squeal, yell

shrill adj = **piercing**, high, penetrating, sharp

shrink v **1** = **decrease**, contract, diminish, dwindle, grow smaller, lessen, narrow, shorten **2** = **recoil**, cower, cringe, draw

back, flinch, quail

shrivel v = **wither**, dehydrate, desiccate, shrink, wilt, wizen

shroud n **1** = **winding sheet**, grave clothes **2** = **covering**, mantle, pall, screen, veil ▷ v **3** = **conceal**, blanket, cloak, cover, envelop, hide, screen, veil

shudder v **1** = **shiver**, convulse, quake, quiver, shake, tremble ▷ n **2** = **shiver**, quiver, spasm, tremor

shuffle v **1** = **scuffle**, drag, scrape, shamble **2** = **jumble**, disarrange, disorder, mix **3** = **rearrange**

shun v = **avoid**, keep away from, steer clear of

shut v **1** = **close**, fasten, seal, secure, slam

shutter n **1** hinged doorlike cover for closing off a window. **2** device in a camera letting in the light required to expose a film. **shut down** v close or stop (a factory, machine, or business). **shutdown** n.

shuttle ❶ n **1** vehicle going to and fro over a short distance. **2** instrument which passes the weft thread between the warp threads in weaving. ▷ v **3** travel by or as if by shuttle.

shuttlecock n small light cone with feathers stuck in one end, struck to and fro in badminton.

shy¹ ❶ adj **1** not at ease in company. **2** timid. **3** (foll. by of) cautious or wary. ▷ v **shying, shied 4** start back in fear. **5** (foll. by away from) avoid (doing something) through fear or lack of confidence. **shyly** adv **shyness** n.

shy² ❶ v **shying, shied 1** throw. ▷ n, pl **shies 2** throw.

sibilant adj hissing.

sibling n brother or sister.

sick ❶ adj **1** vomiting or likely to vomit. **2** physically or mentally unwell. **3** informal amused by something sadistic or morbid. **4** (foll. by of) informal disgusted (by) or weary (of). **sickness** n **sicken** v **1** make nauseated or disgusted. **2** become ill. **sickly** adj **1** unhealthy, weak. **2** causing revulsion or nausea. **sickbay** n place for sick people, such as that on a ship.

sickle n tool with a curved blade for cutting grass, corn, or grain.

side ❶ n **1** line or surface that borders anything. **2** either of two halves into which something can be divided. **3** either surface of a flat object. **4** area immediately next to a person or thing. **5** region. **6** aspect or part. **7** one of two opposing groups or teams. **8** line of descent through one parent. **9** slang conceit. ▷ adj **10** at or on the side. **11** subordinate. **on the side 1** as an extra. **2** unofficially. **siding** n short stretch of railway track on which trains or wagons are shunted from the main line. **sideboard** n piece of furniture for holding plates, cutlery, etc. in a dining room. **sideburns, sideboards** pl n man's side whiskers. **side effect** additional undesirable effect. **sidekick** n informal close friend or associate. **sidelight** n either of two small lights on the front of a vehicle. **sideline** n **1** subsidiary interest or source of income. **2** Sport line marking the boundary of a playing area. **sidelong** adj **1** sideways. ▷ adv **2** obliquely. **side-saddle** n saddle designed to allow a woman rider to sit with both legs on the same side of the horse. **sidestep** v **1** dodge (an issue). **2** avoid by stepping sideways. **sidetrack** v divert from the main topic. **sideways** adv **1** to or from the side. **2** obliquely. **side with** v support (one side in a dispute).

sidewalk n US & Canad paved path for pedestrians.

— THESAURUS —

shuttle v **3** = **go back and forth**, alternate, commute, go to and fro

shy¹ adj **1, 2** = **timid**, bashful, coy, diffident, retiring, self-conscious, self-effacing, shrinking **3** (foll. by of) = **cautious of**, chary of, distrustful of, hesitant about, suspicious of, wary of ▷ v **5** (foll. by away from) = **recoil**, balk, draw back, flinch, start

shy² v **1** = **throw**, cast, fling, hurl, pitch, sling, toss

sick adj **1** = **nauseous**, ill, nauseated, queasy **2** = **unwell**, ailing, crook (Aust & NZ sl), diseased, indisposed, poorly (inf),

under the weather **3** Inf = **morbid**, black, ghoulish, macabre, sadistic **4** (foll. by of) Inf = **tired**, bored, fed up, jaded, weary

side n **1** = **border**, boundary, division, edge, limit, margin, perimeter, rim, sector, verge **3** = **surface**, facet **6** = **part**, aspect, face, flank, hand, view **7** = **party**, camp, cause, faction, sect, team **9** Sl = **conceit**, airs, arrogance ▷ adj **11** = **subordinate**, ancillary, incidental, lesser, marginal, minor, secondary, subsidiary **side with** v = **support**, ally with, favour, go along with, take the part of

sidle ❶ v move in a furtive manner.

siege n surrounding and blockading of a place.

siesta ❶ n afternoon nap, taken in hot countries.

sieve ❶ [siv] n 1 utensil with mesh through which a substance is sifted or strained. ▷ v 2 sift or strain through a sieve.

sift ❶ v 1 remove the coarser particles from a substance with a sieve. 2 examine (information or evidence) to select what is important.

sigh n 1 long audible breath expressing sadness, tiredness, relief, or longing. ▷ v 2 utter a sigh.

sight ❶ n 1 ability to see. 2 instance of seeing. 3 range of vision. 4 thing seen. 5 informal unsightly thing. 6 device for guiding the eye while using a gun or optical instrument. 7 thing worth seeing. 8 informal a lot. ▷ v 9 catch sight of. **sightless** adj blind. **sight-read** v play or sing printed music without previous preparation. **sightseeing** n visiting places of interest. **sightseer** n.

sign ❶ n 1 indication of something not immediately or outwardly observable. 2 gesture, mark, or symbol conveying a meaning. 3 notice displayed to advertise, inform, or warn. 4 omen. ▷ v 5 write (one's name) on (a document or letter) to show its authenticity or one's agreement. 6 communicate using sign language. 7 make a sign or gesture. **sign language** system of communication by gestures, as used by deaf people (also **signing**). **sign on** v 1 register as unemployed. 2 sign a document committing oneself to a job, course, etc. **signpost** n post bearing a sign that shows the way.

signal ❶ n 1 sign or gesture to convey information. 2 sequence of electrical impulses or radio waves transmitted or received. ▷ adj 3 formal very important. ▷ v **-nalling, -nalled** 4 convey (information) by signal. **signally** adv **signal box** building from which railway signals are operated. **signalman** n railwayman in charge of signals and points.

signatory n, pl **-ries** one of the parties who sign a document.

signature n 1 person's name written by himself or herself in signing something. 2 sign at the start of a piece of music to show the key or tempo. **signature tune** tune used to introduce a particular television or radio programme.

signet n small seal used to authenticate documents. **signet ring** finger ring bearing a signet.

significant ❶ adj 1 important. 2 having or expressing a meaning. **significantly** adv

———————————————————————————————————— THESAURUS ———

sidle v = **edge**, creep, inch, slink, sneak, steal

siesta n = **nap**, catnap, doze, forty winks (inf), sleep, snooze (inf)

sieve n 1 = **strainer**, colander ▷ v 2 = **sift**, separate, strain

sift v 1 = **sieve**, filter, separate 2 = **examine**, analyse, go through, investigate, research, scrutinize, work over

sight n 1 = **vision**, eye, eyes, eyesight, seeing 3 = **view**, range of vision, visibility 4 = **spectacle**, display, exhibition, pageant, scene, show, vista 5 Inf = **eyesore**, mess, monstrosity ▷ v 9 = **spot**, behold, catch sight of, discern, distinguish, espy, glimpse, make out, observe, perceive, see

sign n 1 = **indication**, clue, evidence, gesture, hint, mark, proof, signal, symptom, token 2 = **symbol**, badge, device, emblem, logo, mark 3 = **notice**, board, placard, warning 4 = **omen**, augury, auspice, foreboding, portent, warning ▷ v 5 = **autograph**, endorse, initial, inscribe 7 = **gesture**, beckon, gesticulate, indicate, signal

signal n 1 = **sign**, beacon, cue, gesture, indication, mark, token ▷ v 4 = **gesture**, beckon, gesticulate, indicate, motion, sign, wave

significant adj 1 = **important**, critical, material, momentous, noteworthy,

significance n.

signify ❶ v **-fying, -fied 1** indicate or suggest. **2** be a symbol or sign for. **3** be important. **signification** n.

silage [**sile**-ij] n fodder crop harvested while green and partially fermented in a silo.

silence ❶ n **1** absence of noise or speech. ▷ v **2** make silent. **3** put a stop to. **silent** adj **silently** adv **silencer** n device to reduce the noise of an engine exhaust or gun.

silhouette ❶ n **1** outline of a dark shape seen against a light background. ▷ v **2** show in silhouette.

silica n hard glossy mineral found as quartz and in sandstone. **silicosis** n lung disease caused by inhaling silica dust.

silicon n Chem brittle nonmetallic element widely used in chemistry and industry. **silicone** n tough synthetic substance made from silicon and used in lubricants, paints, and resins. **silicon chip** tiny wafer of silicon processed to form an integrated circuit.

silk n **1** fibre made by the larva (**silkworm**) of a certain moth. **2** thread or fabric made from this. **silky, silken** adj.

sill n ledge at the bottom of a window or door.

silly ❶ adj **-lier, -liest** foolish. **silliness** n.

silo n, pl **-los 1** pit or airtight tower for storing silage. **2** underground structure in which nuclear missiles are kept ready for launching.

silt ❶ n **1** mud deposited by moving water. ▷ v **2** (foll. by up) fill or be choked with silt.

silver n **1** white precious metal. **2** coins or articles made of silver. ▷ adj **3** made of or of the colour of silver. **silverbeet** n Aust & NZ leafy green vegetable with white stalks. **silverfish** n small wingless silver-coloured insect. **silverside** n cut of beef from below the rump and above the leg. **silver wedding** twenty-fifth wedding anniversary.

sim n computer game that simulates an activity such as flying or playing a sport.

similar ❶ adj alike but not identical. **similarity** n **similarly** adv.

simile [**sim**-ill-ee] n figure of speech comparing one thing to another, using 'as' or 'like', e.g. as blind as a bat.

simmer ❶ v **1** cook gently at just below boiling point. **2** be in a state of suppressed rage. **simmer down** v informal calm down.

simper ❶ v **1** smile in a silly or affected way. **2** utter (something) with a simper. ▷ n **3** simpering smile.

simple ❶ adj **1** easy to understand or do. **2** plain or unpretentious. **3** not combined

serious, vital, weighty **2** = **meaningful**, eloquent, expressive, indicative, suggestive

signify v **1, 2** = **indicate**, be a sign of, betoken, connote, denote, imply, intimate, mean, portend, suggest **3** = **matter**, be important, carry weight, count

silence n **1** **a** = **quiet**, calm, hush, lull, peace, stillness **b** = **muteness**, dumbness, reticence, taciturnity ▷ v **2** = **quieten**, deaden, gag, muffle, quiet, stifle, still, suppress **3** = **cut off**, cut short

silhouette n **1** = **outline**, form, profile, shape ▷ v **2** = **outline**, etch, stand out

silly adj = **foolish**, absurd, asinine, daft, fatuous, idiotic, inane, ridiculous, senseless, stupid, unwise

silt n **1** = **sediment**, alluvium, deposit, ooze, sludge ▷ v **2** (foll. by up) = **clog up**, choke up, congest

similar adj = **alike**, analogous, close, comparable, like, resembling

simmer v **2** = **fume**, be angry, be pissed (off) (taboo sl), rage, seethe, smoulder

simper v **1** = **smile coyly**, smile affectedly, smirk

simple adj **1** = **uncomplicated**, clear, easy, intelligible, lucid, plain, straightforward, understandable, uninvolved **2** = **plain**, classic, homely, humble, modest, naked, natural, stark, unembellished, unfussy, unpretentious, unsophisticated **3** = **pure**,

S

or complex. **4** sincere or frank. **5** feeble-minded. **simply** adv **simplicity** n **simplify** v make less complicated. **simplification** n **simplistic** adj too simple or naive. **simpleton** n foolish or half-witted person.

simulate ① v **1** make a pretence of. **2** imitate the conditions of (a particular situation). **3** have the appearance of. **simulation** n **simulator** n.

simultaneous ① adj occurring at the same time.

sin ① n **1** breaking of a religious or moral law. **2** offence against a principle or standard. ▷ v **sinning, sinned 3** commit a sin. **sinful** adj **1** guilty of sin. **2** being a sin. **sinfully** adv **sinner** n.

since prep **1** during the period of time after. ▷ conj **2** from the time when. **3** for the reason that. ▷ adv **4** from that time.

sincere ① adj without pretence or deceit. **sincerely** adv **sincerity** n.

sine n (in trigonometry) ratio of the length of the opposite side to that of the hypotenuse in a right-angled triangle.

sinew n **1** tough fibrous tissue joining muscle to bone. **2** muscles or strength. **sinewy** adj.

sing ① v **singing, sang, sung 1** make musical sounds with the voice. **2** perform (a song). **3** make a humming or whistling sound. **singer** n **singsong** n **1** informal singing session. ▷ adj **2** (of the voice) repeatedly rising and falling in pitch.

singe ① v **singeing, singed 1** burn the surface of. ▷ n **2** superficial burn.

single ① adj **1** one only. **2** distinct from others of the same kind. **3** unmarried. **4** designed for one user. **5** formed of only one part. **6** (of a ticket) valid for an outward journey only. ▷ n **7** single thing. **8** thing intended for one person. **9** record with one short song or tune on each side. **10** single ticket. ▷ pl **11** game between two players. ▷ v **12** (foll. by out) pick out from others. **singly** adv **single file** (of people or things) arranged in one line. **single-handed** adj without assistance. **single-minded** adj having one aim only.

singlet n sleeveless vest.

singular ① adj **1** (of a word or form) denoting one person or thing. **2** remarkable, unusual. ▷ n **3** singular form of a word. **singularity** n **singularly** adv.

sinister ① adj threatening or suggesting evil or harm.

---

elementary, unalloyed, uncombined, unmixed **4** = **sincere**, artless, bald, childlike, direct, frank, guileless, honest, ingenuous, innocent, naive, natural, plain, unaffected **5** = **feeble-minded**, dumb (inf), foolish, half-witted, moronic, slow, stupid

simulate v **1, 2** = **pretend**, act, affect, feign, put on, sham

simultaneous adj = **coinciding**, at the same time, coincident, concurrent, contemporaneous, synchronous

sin n **1, 2** = **wrongdoing**, crime, error, evil, guilt, iniquity, misdeed, offence, transgression ▷ v **3** = **transgress**, err, fall, go astray, lapse, offend

sincere adj = **honest**, candid, earnest, frank, genuine, guileless, heartfelt, real, serious, true, unaffected

sing v **1, 2** = **warble**, carol, chant, chirp, croon, pipe, trill, yodel **3** = **hum**, buzz, purr, whine

singe v **1** = **burn**, char, scorch, sear

single adj **1** = **one**, individual, lone, only, separate, sole, solitary **2** = **individual**, distinct, exclusive, separate, undivided, unshared **3** = **unmarried**, free, unattached, unwed **5** = **simple**, unblended, unmixed ▷ v **12** (foll. by out) = **pick**, choose, distinguish, fix on, pick on or out, select, separate, set apart

singular adj **1** = **single**, individual, separate, sole **2 a** = **remarkable**, eminent, exceptional, notable, noteworthy, outstanding **b** = **unusual**, curious, eccentric, extraordinary, munted (NZ sl), odd, peculiar, queer, strange

sinister adj = **threatening**, dire,

sink ❶ v **sinking**, **sank**, **sunk** or **sunken**
1 submerge (in liquid). 2 descend or cause
to descend. 3 decline in value or amount.
4 become weaker in health. 5 dig or drill
(a hole or shaft). 6 invest (money). 7 Golf,
snooker hit (a ball) into a hole or pocket.
▷ n 8 fixed basin with a water supply and
drainage pipe. **sinker** n weight for a fishing
line. **sink in** v penetrate the mind.

sinuous adj 1 curving. 2 lithe.

sinus [**sine**-uss] n hollow space in a bone,
esp. an air passage opening into the nose.

sip ❶ v **sipping**, **sipped** 1 drink in small
mouthfuls. ▷ n 2 amount sipped.

siphon n 1 bent tube which uses air
pressure to draw liquid from a container.
▷ v 2 draw off thus. 3 redirect (resources).

sir n 1 polite term of address for a man. 2 (**S-**
) title of a knight or baronet.

sire n 1 male parent of a horse or other
domestic animal. 2 respectful term of
address to a king. ▷ v 3 father.

siren n 1 device making a loud wailing
noise as a warning. 2 dangerously alluring
woman.

sirloin n prime cut of loin of beef.

sis interj S Afr informal exclamation of
disgust.

sissy ❶ adj, n, pl **-sies** weak or cowardly
(person).

sister n 1 girl or woman with the same
parents as another person. 2 female
fellow-member of a group. 3 senior nurse.

4 nun. ▷ adj 5 closely related, similar.
sisterhood n 1 state of being a sister.
2 group of women united by common
aims or beliefs. **sisterly** adj **sister-in-
law** n, pl **sisters-in-law** 1 sister of one's
husband or wife. 2 one's brother's wife.

sit ❶ v **sitting**, **sat** 1 rest one's body upright
on the buttocks. 2 cause to sit. 3 perch.
4 be situated. 5 pose for a portrait.
6 occupy an official position. 7 (of an
official body) hold a session. 8 take (an
examination). **sitting room** room in a
house where people sit and relax. **sit-in** n
protest in which demonstrators occupy a
place and refuse to move.

sitar n Indian stringed musical instrument.

site ❶ n 1 place where something is, was,
or is intended to be located. 2 same as
WEBSITE. ▷ v 3 provide with a site.

situate v place. **situation** n 1 state of
affairs. 2 location and surroundings.
3 position of employment. **situation
comedy** radio or television series involving
the same characters in various situations.

six adj, n one more than five. **sixth** adj, n (of)
number six in a series. **sixteen** adj, n six
and ten. **sixteenth** adj, n **sixty** adj, n six
times ten. **sixtieth** adj, n.

size¹ ❶ n 1 dimensions, bigness. 2 one of
a series of standard measurements of
goods. ▷ v 3 arrange according to size.
sizeable, **sizable** adj quite large. **size up** v
informal assess.

---

disquieting, evil, malign, menacing,
ominous

sink v 1 = **submerge**, founder, go under
2 = **descend**, dip, drop, fall, go down, lower,
plunge, subside 3 = **fall**, abate, collapse,
drop, lapse, slip, subside 4 = **decline**, decay,
decrease, deteriorate, diminish, dwindle,
fade, fail, flag, lessen, weaken, worsen
5 = **dig**, bore, drill, drive, excavate

sip v 1 = **drink**, sample, sup, taste ▷ n
2 = **swallow**, drop, taste, thimbleful

sissy adj = **wimpish** or **wimpy**, cowardly,
effeminate, feeble, namby-pamby, soft

(inf), unmanly, weak, wet (Brit inf) (inf)
▷ n = **wimp**, coward, milksop, mummy's
boy, namby-pamby, softie (inf), weakling,
wet (Brit inf) (inf)

sit v 1-3, 5 = **rest**, perch, settle
6 = **officiate**, preside 7 = **convene**,
assemble, deliberate, meet

site n 1 = **location**, place, plot, position,
setting, spot ▷ v 3 = **locate**, install, place,
position, set, situate

size¹ n 1 = **dimensions**, amount, bulk,
extent, immensity, magnitude, mass,
proportions, range, volume

S

size² n gluey substance used as a protective coating.

sizzle ❶ v make a hissing sound like frying fat.

skanky adj slang dirty or unattractive.

skate¹ n 1 boot with a steel blade or sets of wheels attached to the sole for gliding over ice or a hard surface. ▷ v 2 glide on or as if on skates. **skateboard** n board mounted on small wheels for riding on while standing up. **skate over**, **round** v avoid discussing or dealing with (a matter) fully.

skate² n large marine flatfish.

skein n 1 yarn wound in a loose coil. 2 flock of geese in flight.

skeleton ❶ n 1 framework of bones inside a person's or animal's body. 2 essential framework of a structure. ▷ adj 3 reduced to a minimum. **skeletal** adj **skeleton key** key which can open many different locks.

sketch ❶ n 1 rough drawing. 2 brief description. 3 short humorous play. ▷ v 4 make a sketch (of). **sketchy** adj incomplete or inadequate.

skew v 1 make slanting or crooked. ▷ adj 2 slanting or crooked.

skewer n 1 pin to hold meat together during cooking. ▷ v 2 fasten with a skewer.

ski n 1 one of a pair of long runners fastened to boots for gliding over snow or water. ▷ v **skiing**, **skied** or **ski'd** 2 travel on skis. **skier** n.

skid v **skidding**, **skidded** 1 (of a moving vehicle) slide sideways uncontrollably. ▷ n

2 instance of skidding.

skill ❶ n 1 special ability or expertise. 2 something requiring special training or expertise. **skilful** adj having or showing skill. **skilfully** adv **skilled** adj.

● **SPELLING TIP**
● When you make an adjective from **skill**,
● you should drop an l to make **skilful**.
● This is not the case in American English,
● and this is probably why there are over
● 100 examples of skillful in the Bank of
● English.

skim ❶ v **skimming**, **skimmed** 1 remove floating matter from the surface of (a liquid). 2 glide smoothly over. 3 read quickly. **skimmed, skim milk** milk from which the cream has been removed.

skimp ❶ v not invest enough time, money, material, etc. **skimpy** adj scanty or insufficient.

skin ❶ n 1 outer covering of the body. 2 complexion. 3 outer layer or covering. 4 film on a liquid. 5 animal skin used as a material or container. ▷ v **skinning**, **skinned** 6 remove the skin of. **skinless** adj **skinny** adj thin. **skin-deep** adj superficial. **skin diving** underwater swimming using flippers and light breathing apparatus. **skinflint** n miser. **skinhead** n youth with very short hair.

skint adj slang having no money.

skip¹ ❶ v **skipping**, **skipped** 1 leap lightly from one foot to the other. 2 jump over a rope as it is swung under one. 3 informal pass over, omit. ▷ n 4 skipping.

————————————————— THESAURUS —————————————————

sizzle v 1 = **hiss**, crackle, frizzle, fry, spit
skeleton n 2 = **framework**, frame, outline, structure
sketch n 1 = **drawing**, delineation, design, draft, outline, plan ▷ v 4 = **draw**, delineate, depict, draft, outline, represent, rough out
skill n 1 = **expertise**, ability, art, cleverness, competence, craft, dexterity, facility, knack, proficiency, skilfulness, talent, technique

skim v 1 = **separate**, cream 2 = **glide**, coast, float, fly, sail, soar 3 = **scan**, glance, run one's eye over
skimp v = **stint**, be mean with, be sparing with, cut corners, scamp, scrimp
skin n 3 = **coating**, casing, crust, film, husk, outside, peel, rind 5 = **hide**, fell, pelt ▷ v 6 = **peel**, flay, scrape
skip¹ v 1 = **hop**, bob, bounce, caper, dance, flit, frisk, gambol, prance, trip 3 Inf = **pass over**, eschew, give (something) a miss,

skip² n large open container for builders' rubbish.

skipper n, v captain.

skirmish ⓘ n 1 brief or minor fight or argument. ▷ v 2 take part in a skirmish.

skirt ⓘ n 1 woman's garment hanging from the waist. 2 part of a dress or coat below the waist. 3 cut of beef from the flank. ▷ v 4 border. 5 go round. 6 avoid dealing with (an issue). **skirting board** narrow board round the bottom of an interior wall.

skit ⓘ n brief satirical sketch.

skite v, n Aust & NZ boast.

skittish ⓘ adj playful or lively.

skive ⓘ v informal evade work or responsibility.

skivvy n, pl **-vies** female servant who does menial work.

skookum ⓘ adj Canad powerful or big.

skulduggery ⓘ n informal trickery.

skulk ⓘ v 1 move stealthily. 2 lurk.

skull n bony framework of the head. **skullcap** n close-fitting brimless cap.

skunk n 1 small black-and-white N American mammal which emits a foul-smelling fluid when attacked. 2 slang despicable person.

sky ⓘ n, pl **skies** upper atmosphere as seen from the earth. **skydiving** n sport of jumping from an aircraft and performing manoeuvres before opening one's parachute. **skylark** n lark that sings while soaring at a great height. **skylight** n window in a roof or ceiling. **skyscraper** n very tall building.

slab ⓘ n broad flat piece.

slack ⓘ adj 1 not tight. 2 negligent. 3 not busy. ▷ n 4 slack part. ▷ pl 5 informal trousers. ▷ v 6 neglect one's work or duty. **slackness** n **slacken** v make or become slack. **slacker** n.

slag ⓘ n 1 waste left after metal is smelted. ▷ v **slagging, slagged** 2 (foll. by off) slang criticize.

slake ⓘ v 1 satisfy (thirst or desire). 2 combine (quicklime) with water.

slalom n skiing or canoeing race over a winding course.

slam ⓘ v **slamming, slammed** 1 shut, put down, or hit violently and noisily. 2 informal criticize harshly. ▷ n 3 act or sound of slamming.

slang n very informal language. **slangy** adj **slanging match** abusive argument.

slant ⓘ v 1 lean at an angle, slope. 2 present (information) in a biased way.

THESAURUS

leave out, miss out, omit

skirmish n 1 = **fight**, battle, brush, clash, conflict, encounter, fracas, scrap (inf) ▷ v 2 = **fight**, clash, collide

skirt v 4 = **border**, edge, flank 5, 6 = **avoid**, circumvent, evade, steer clear of

skit n = **parody**, burlesque, sketch, spoof (inf), takeoff (inf)

skittish adj = **lively**, wired (sl)

skive v Inf = **slack**, idle, malinger, shirk, swing the lead

skookum adjective Canad = **powerful**, influential, big, dominant, controlling, commanding, supreme, prevailing, authoritative

skulduggery n Inf = **trickery**, double-dealing, duplicity, machinations, underhandedness

skulk v 1 = **sneak**, creep, prowl, slink 2 = **lurk**, lie in wait, loiter

sky n 1 = **heavens**, firmament

slab n = **piece**, chunk, lump, portion, slice, wedge

slack adj 1 = **loose**, baggy, lax, limp, relaxed 2 = **negligent**, lax, neglectful, remiss, slapdash, slipshod 3 = **slow**, quiet, slow-moving, sluggish, lazy ▷ n 4 = **room**, excess, give (inf), leeway ▷ v 6 = **shirk**, dodge, idle, skive (Brit sl)

slag v 2 (foll. by off) Sl = **criticize**, abuse, deride, insult, malign, mock, slander, slate

slake v 1 = **satisfy**, assuage, quench, sate

slam v 1 a = **bang**, crash, smash b = **throw**, dash, fling, hurl

slant v 1 = **slope**, bend, bevel, cant, heel, incline, lean, list, tilt 2 = **bias**, angle,

▷ *n* **3** slope. **4** point of view, esp. a biased one. **slanting** *adj*.

slap ❶ *n* **1** blow with the open hand or a flat object. ▷ *v* **slapping, slapped 2** strike with the open hand or a flat object. **3** *informal* place forcefully or carelessly. **slapdash** *adj* careless and hasty. **slap-happy** *adj informal* cheerfully careless. **slapstick** *n* boisterous knockabout comedy. **slap-up** *adj* (of a meal) large and luxurious.

slash ❶ *v* **1** cut with a sweeping stroke. **2** gash. **3** reduce drastically. ▷ *n* **4** sweeping stroke. **5** gash.

slat *n* narrow strip of wood or metal.

slate¹ *n* **1** rock which splits easily into thin layers. **2** piece of this for covering a roof or, formerly, for writing on. ▷ *v* **3** cover with slates. **4** *US* plan or arrange. ▷ *adj* **5** dark grey.

slate² ❶ *v informal* criticize harshly. **slating** *n*.

slaughter ❶ *v* **1** kill (animals) for food. **2** kill (people) savagely or indiscriminately. ▷ *n* **3** slaughtering. **slaughterhouse** *n* place where animals are killed for food.

slave ❶ *n* **1** person owned by another for whom he or she has to work. **2** person dominated by another or by a habit. **3** drudge. ▷ *v* **4** work like a slave. **slavery** *n* **1** state or condition of being a slave.

2 practice of owning slaves. **slavish** *adj* **1** of or like a slave. **2** imitative. **slave-driver** *n* person who makes others work very hard.

slaver [**slav**-ver] *v* dribble saliva from the mouth.

slay ❶ *v* **slaying, slew, slain** kill.

sleazy ❶ *adj* **-zier, -ziest** run-down or sordid. **sleaze** *n*.

sledge¹, sled *n* **1** carriage on runners for sliding on snow. **2** light wooden frame for sliding over snow. ▷ *v* **3** travel by sledge.

sledge², sledgehammer *n* heavy hammer with a long handle.

sleek ❶ *adj* glossy, smooth, and shiny.

sleep ❶ *n* **1** state of rest characterized by unconsciousness. **2** period of this. ▷ *v* **sleeping, slept 3** be in or as if in a state of sleep. **4** have sleeping accommodation for (a specified number). **sleeper** *n* **1** railway car fitted for sleeping in. **2** beam supporting the rails of a railway. **3** ring worn in a pierced ear to stop the hole from closing up. **4** person who sleeps. **sleepy** *adj* **sleepily** *adv* **sleepiness** *n* **sleepless** *adj* **sleeping bag** padded bag for sleeping in. **sleepout** *n* *NZ* small building for sleeping in. **sleepover** *n* *chiefly US* occasion when a person stays overnight at a friend's house. **sleep with, together** *v* have sexual intercourse (with).

---

colour, distort, twist ▷ *n* **3 = slope**, camber, gradient, incline, tilt **4 = bias**, angle, emphasis, one-sidedness, point of view, prejudice

slap *n* **1 = smack**, blow, cuff, spank, swipe ▷ *v* **2 = smack**, clap, cuff, spank, swipe

slash *v* **1, 2 = cut**, gash, hack, lacerate, rend, rip, score, slit **3 = reduce**, cut, drop, lower ▷ *n* **5 = cut**, gash, incision, laceration, rent, rip, slit

slate² *v Inf* = **criticize**, censure, rebuke, rouse on (*Aust*), scold, tear into (*inf*)

slaughter *v* **2 = slay**, butcher, kill, massacre, murder ▷ *n* **3 = slaying**, bloodshed, butchery, carnage, killing,

massacre, murder

slave *n* **1 = servant**, serf, vassal **3 = drudge**, skivvy (*chiefly Brit*) ▷ *v* **4 = toil**, drudge, slog

slay *v* = **kill**, butcher, massacre, mow down, murder, slaughter

sleazy *adj* = **sordid**, disreputable, low, run-down, scungy (*Aust & NZ sl*), seedy, squalid

sleek *adj* = **glossy**, lustrous, shiny, smooth

sleep *n* **1, 2 = slumber(s)**, doze, forty winks (*inf*), hibernation, nap, siesta, snooze (*inf*), zizz (*Brit inf*) ▷ *v* **3 = slumber**, catnap, doze, drowse, hibernate, snooze (*inf*), take a nap

sleet n rain and snow or hail falling together.

sleeve n 1 part of a garment which covers the arm. 2 tubelike cover. 3 gramophone record cover. **up one's sleeve** secretly ready.

sleigh n, v sledge.

slender ⊕ adj 1 slim. 2 small in amount.

sleuth ⊕ [**slooth**] n detective.

slice ⊕ n 1 thin flat piece cut from something. 2 share. 3 kitchen tool with a broad flat blade. 4 Sport hitting of a ball so that it travels obliquely. ▷ v 5 cut into slices. 6 Sport hit (a ball) with a slice.

slick ⊕ adj 1 persuasive and glib. 2 skilfully devised or carried out. 3 well-made and attractive, but superficial. ▷ n 4 patch of oil on water. ▷ v 5 make smooth or sleek.

slide ⊕ v sliding, slid 1 slip smoothly along (a surface). 2 pass unobtrusively. ▷ n 3 sliding. 4 piece of glass holding an object to be viewed under a microscope. 5 photographic transparency. 6 surface or structure for sliding on or down. 7 ornamental hair clip. **slide rule** mathematical instrument formerly used for rapid calculations. **sliding scale** variable scale according to which things such as wages alter in response to changes in other factors or conditions.

slight ⊕ adj 1 small in quantity or extent. 2 not important. 3 slim and delicate. ▷ v, n 4 snub. **slightly** adv.

slim ⊕ adj slimmer, slimmest 1 not heavy or stout, thin. 2 slight. ▷ v slimming, slimmed 3 make or become slim by diet and exercise. **slimmer** n.

slime n unpleasant thick slippery substance. **slimy** adj 1 of, like, or covered with slime. 2 ingratiating.

sling ⊕ n 1 bandage hung from the neck to support an injured hand or arm. 2 rope or strap for lifting something. 3 strap with a string at each end for throwing a stone. ▷ v slinging, slung 4 throw. 5 carry, hang, or throw with or as if with a sling. **slingback** n shoe with a strap that goes around the back of the heel.

slink ⊕ v slinking, slunk move furtively or guiltily. **slinky** adj (of clothes) figure-hugging.

slip¹ ⊕ v slipping, slipped 1 lose balance by sliding. 2 move smoothly, easily, or quietly. 3 place quickly or stealthily. 4 (foll. by on) (off) put on or take off easily or quickly. 5 pass out of (the mind). 6 become worse. 7 dislocate (a bone).

slender adj 1 = **slim**, lean, narrow, slight, willowy 2 = **meagre**, little, scant, scanty, small

sleuth n = **detective**, private eye (inf), (private) investigator

slice n 1, 2 = **piece**, cut, helping, portion, segment, share, sliver, wedge ▷ v 5 = **cut**, carve, divide, sever

slick adj 1 = **glib**, plausible, polished, smooth, specious 2 = **skilful**, adroit, deft, dexterous, polished, professional ▷ v 5 = **smooth**, plaster down, sleek

slide v 1 = **slip**, coast, glide, skim, slither

slight adj 2 = **small**, feeble, insignificant, meagre, measly, minor, paltry, scanty, trifling, trivial, unimportant 3 = **slim**, delicate, feeble, fragile, lightly-built, small, spare ▷ v, n 4 = **snub**, affront, disdain,

ignore, insult, rebuff, scorn, slap in the face (inf)

slim adj 1 = **slender**, lean, narrow, slight, svelte, thin, trim 2 = **slight**, faint, poor, remote, slender ▷ v 3 = **lose weight**, diet, reduce

sling v 4 = **throw**, cast, chuck (inf), fling, heave, hurl, lob (inf), shy, toss 5 = **hang**, dangle, suspend

slink v = **creep**, prowl, skulk, slip, sneak, steal

slip¹ v 1 = **fall**, skid 2 = **slide**, glide, skate, slither 3 = **sneak**, conceal, creep, hide, steal ▷ n 9 = **mistake**, blunder, error, failure, fault, lapse, omission, oversight **give someone the slip** = **escape from**, dodge, elude, evade, get away from, lose (someone) **slip up** v = **make a mistake**, blunder, err, miscalculate

S

▷ *n* **8** slipping. **9** mistake. **10** petticoat. **11** *Cricket* fielding position behind and to the offside of the wicketkeeper. **give someone the slip** escape from someone. **slippy** *adj informal* slippery. **slipknot** *n* knot tied so that it will slip along the rope round which it is made. **slip-on** *adj* (of a garment or shoe) made to be put on easily. **slipped disc** painful condition in which one of the discs connecting the bones of the spine becomes displaced. **slip road** narrow road giving access to a motorway. **slipshod** *adj* (of an action) careless. **slipstream** *n* stream of air forced backwards by a fast-moving object. **slip up** *v* make a mistake. **slipway** *n* launching slope on which ships are built or repaired.

slip² ❶ *n* **1** small piece (of paper). **2** cutting from a plant. **3** slender person.

slipper *n* light shoe for indoor wear.

slippery ❶ *adj* **1** so smooth or wet as to cause slipping or be difficult to hold. **2** (of a person) untrustworthy.

slit ❶ *n* **1** long narrow cut or opening. ▷ *v* **slitting, slit 2** make a long straight cut in.

slither ❶ *v* slide unsteadily.

sliver ❶ [**sliv**-ver] *n* small thin piece.

slob ❶ *n informal* lazy and untidy person.

slobber ❶ *v* dribble or drool. **slobbery** *adj*.

slog ❶ *v* **slogging, slogged 1** work hard and steadily. **2** make one's way with difficulty. **3** hit hard. ▷ *n* **4** long and exhausting work or walk.

slogan ❶ *n* catchword or phrase used in politics or advertising.

slop ❶ *v* **slopping, slopped 1** splash or spill. ▷ *n* **2** spilt liquid. **3** liquid food. ▷ *pl* **4** liquid refuse and waste food used to feed animals. **sloppy** *adj* **1** careless or untidy. **2** gushingly sentimental.

slope ❶ *v* **1** slant. ▷ *n* **2** sloping surface. **3** degree of inclination. ▷ *pl* **4** hills. **slope off** *v informal* go furtively.

slot ❶ *n* **1** narrow opening for inserting something. **2** *informal* place in a series or scheme. ▷ *v* **slotting, slotted 3** make a slot or slots in. **4** fit into a slot. **slot machine** automatic machine worked by placing a coin in a slot.

sloth ❶ [rhymes with **both**] *n* **1** slow-moving animal of tropical America. **2** laziness. **slothful** *adj* lazy or idle.

slouch ❶ *v* **1** sit, stand, or move with a drooping posture. ▷ *n* **2** drooping posture.

━━━━━━━━━━━━━━━━━━━━━━━━━━━━━━━━━━━━━━ THESAURUS ━━━━━

slip² *n* **1** = **strip**, piece, sliver **2** = **cutting**, offshoot, runner, scion, shoot, sprig, sprout

slippery *adj* **1** = **smooth**, glassy, greasy, icy, slippy (*inf*), unsafe **2** = **untrustworthy**, crafty, cunning, devious, dishonest, evasive, shifty, tricky

slit *n* **1** = **cut**, gash, incision, opening, rent, split, tear ▷ *v* **2** = **cut (open)**, gash, knife, lance, pierce, rip, slash

slither *v* = **slide**, glide, slink, slip

sliver *n* = **shred**, fragment, paring, shaving, splinter

slob *n Inf* = **layabout**, couch potato (*sl*), good-for-nothing, idler, loafer, lounger

slobber *v* = **drool**, dribble, drivel, salivate, slaver

slog *v* **1** = **work**, labour, plod, plough through, slave, toil **2** = **trudge**, tramp,

trek **3** = **hit**, punch, slug, sock (*sl*), strike, thump, wallop (*inf*) ▷ *n* **4 a** = **labour**, effort, exertion, struggle **b** = **trudge**, hike, tramp, trek

slogan *n* = **catch phrase**, catchword, motto, tag-line

slop *v* **1** = **spill**, overflow, slosh (*inf*), splash

slope *v* **1** = **slant**, drop away, fall, incline, lean, rise, tilt ▷ *n* **2** = **incline**, ramp, rise, slant, tilt **3** = **inclination**, gradient **slope off** *v Inf* = **slink away**, creep away, slip away

slot *n* **1** = **opening**, aperture, groove, hole, slit, vent **2** *Inf* = **place**, opening, position, space, time, vacancy ▷ *v* **4** = **fit in**, fit, insert

sloth *n* **2** = **laziness**, idleness, inactivity, inertia, slackness, sluggishness, torpor

slouch *v* **1** = **slump**, droop, loll, stoop

be no slouch *informal* be very good or talented.

slovenly ⓘ *adj* 1 dirty or untidy. 2 careless.

slow ⓘ *adj* 1 taking a longer time than is usual or expected. 2 not fast. 3 (of a clock or watch) showing a time earlier than the correct one. 4 stupid. ▷ *v* 5 reduce the speed (of). **slowly** *adv* **slowness** *n* **slowcoach** *n informal* person who moves or works slowly.

sludge ⓘ *n* 1 thick mud. 2 sewage.

slug¹ *n* land snail with no shell. **sluggish** *adj* slow-moving, lacking energy. **sluggishly** *adv* **sluggishness** *n* **sluggard** *n* lazy person.

slug² *n* 1 bullet. 2 *informal* mouthful of an alcoholic drink.

slug³ *v* **slugging, slugged** 1 hit hard. ▷ *n* 2 heavy blow.

sluice *n* 1 channel carrying off water. 2 sliding gate used to control the flow of water in this. 3 water controlled by a sluice. ▷ *v* 4 pour a stream of water over or through.

slum ⓘ *n* 1 squalid overcrowded house or area. ▷ *v* **slumming, slummed** 2 temporarily and deliberately experience poorer places or conditions than usual.

slumber ⓘ *v, n lit* sleep.

slump ⓘ *v* 1 (of prices or demand) decline suddenly. 2 sink or fall heavily. ▷ *n* 3 sudden decline in prices or demand. 4 time of substantial unemployment.

slur ⓘ *v* **slurring, slurred** 1 pronounce or utter (words) indistinctly. 2 *Music* sing or play (notes) smoothly without a break. ▷ *n* 3 slurring of words. 4 remark intended to discredit someone. 5 *Music* slurring of notes. 6 curved line indicating notes to be slurred.

slurp *informal* ▷ *v* 1 eat or drink noisily. ▷ *n* 2 slurping sound.

slurry *n, pl* **-ries** muddy liquid mixture.

slush *n* 1 watery muddy substance. 2 sloppy sentimental talk or writing. **slushy** *adj* **slush fund** fund for financing bribery or corruption.

slut ⓘ *n offens* dirty or immoral woman. **sluttish** *adj*.

sly ⓘ *adj* **slyer, slyest** or **slier, sliest** 1 crafty. 2 secretive and cunning. 3 roguish. **on the sly** secretly. **slyly** *adv* **slyness** *n*.

smack¹ ⓘ *v* 1 slap sharply. 2 open and close (the lips) loudly in enjoyment or anticipation. ▷ *n* 3 sharp slap. 4 loud

---

THESAURUS

slovenly *adj* 1 = **untidy**, disorderly 2 = **careless**, negligent, slack, slapdash, slipshod, sloppy (*inf*)

slow *adj* 1 = **late**, backward, behind, delayed, lingering, long-drawn-out, prolonged, protracted, tardy 2 = **unhurried**, dawdling, gradual, lackadaisical, laggard, lazy, leisurely, ponderous, sluggish 4 = **stupid**, braindead (*inf*), dense, dim, dozy (*Brit inf*), dull-witted, obtuse, retarded, thick ▷ *v* 5 = **reduce speed**, brake, decelerate, handicap, hold up, retard, slacken (off)

sludge *n* 1 = **sediment**, mire, muck, mud, ooze, residue, silt, slime

slum *n* 1 = **hovel**, ghetto

slumber *v, n Lit* = **sleep**, doze, drowse, nap, snooze (*inf*), zizz (*Brit inf*)

slump *v* 1 = **fall**, collapse, crash, plunge, sink, slip 2 = **sag**, droop, hunch, loll, slouch ▷ *n* 3 = **fall**, collapse, crash, decline, downturn, drop, reverse, trough 4 = **recession**, depression

slur *n* 4 = **insult**, affront, aspersion, calumny, innuendo, insinuation, smear, stain

slut *n Offens* = **tart**, scrubber (*Brit & Aust sl*), slag (*Brit sl*), slapper (*Brit sl*), trollop

sly *adj* 1, 2 = **cunning**, artful, clever, crafty, devious, scheming, secret, shifty, stealthy, subtle, underhand, wily 3 = **roguish**, arch, impish, knowing, mischievous **on the sly** = **secretly**, covertly, on the quiet, privately, surreptitiously

smack¹ *v* 1 = **slap**, clap, cuff, hit, spank, strike, swipe ▷ *n* 3 = **slap**, blow, swipe

S

kiss. **5** slapping sound. ▷ *adv* **6** *informal* squarely or directly, e.g. *smack in the middle*. **smacker** *n slang* **1** loud kiss. **2** pound note or dollar bill.

smack² *n* **1** slight flavour or trace. **2** *slang* heroin. ▷ *v* **3** have a slight flavour or trace (of).

small ⊙ *adj* **1** not large in size, number, or amount. **2** unimportant. **3** mean or petty. ▷ *n* **4** narrow part of the lower back. ▷ *pl* **5** *informal* underwear. **smallness** *n* **smallholding** *n* small area of farming land. **small hours** hours just after midnight. **small-minded** *adj* intolerant, petty. **smallpox** *n* contagious disease with blisters that leave scars. **small talk** light social conversation. **small-time** *adj* insignificant or minor.

smart ⊙ *adj* **1** well-kept and neat. **2** astute. **3** witty. **4** fashionable. **5** brisk. ▷ *v* **6** feel or cause stinging pain. ▷ *n* **7** stinging pain. **smart aleck** *informal* irritatingly clever person. **smart card** plastic card used for storing and processing computer data. **smarten** *v* make or become smart. **smartphone** *n* mobile phone with features that enable it to send emails and access the Web.

smash ⊙ *v* **1** break violently and noisily. **2** throw (against) violently. **3** collide forcefully. **4** destroy. ▷ *n* **5** act or sound

of smashing. **6** violent collision of vehicles. **7** *informal* popular success. **8** *Sport* powerful overhead shot. **smasher** *n informal* attractive person or thing. **smashing** *adj informal* excellent.

smattering ⊙ *n* slight knowledge.

smear ⊙ *v* **1** spread with a greasy or sticky substance. **2** rub so as to produce a dirty mark or smudge. **3** slander. ▷ *n* **4** dirty mark or smudge. **5** slander. **6** *Med* sample of a secretion smeared on to a slide for examination under a microscope.

smell ⊙ *v* **smelling**, **smelt** *or* **smelled** **1** perceive (a scent or odour) by means of the nose. **2** have or give off a smell. **3** have an unpleasant smell. **4** detect by instinct. ▷ *n* **5** ability to perceive odours by the nose. **6** odour or scent. **7** smelling. **smelly** *adj* having a nasty smell. **smelling salts** preparation of ammonia used to revive a person who feels faint.

smelt *v* extract (a metal) from (an ore) by heating. **smelter** *n*.

smile *n* **1** turning up of the corners of the mouth to show pleasure, amusement, or friendliness. ▷ *v* **2** give a smile. **smile on, upon** *v* regard favourably.

smirk ⊙ *n* **1** smug smile. ▷ *v* **2** give a smirk.

smith *n* worker in metal. **smithy** *n* blacksmith's workshop.

▷ *adv* **6** Inf = **directly**, exactly, precisely, right, slap (*inf*), squarely, straight

small *adj* **1** = **little**, diminutive, mini, miniature, minute, petite, pygmy *or* pigmy, teeny, teeny-weeny, tiny, undersized, wee **2** = **unimportant**, insignificant, minor, negligible, paltry, petty, trifling, trivial **3** = **petty**, base, mean, narrow

smart *adj* **1** = **neat**, spruce, trim **2** = **astute**, acute, bright, canny, clever, ingenious, intelligent, keen, shrewd **3** = **sharp**, quick **4** = **chic**, elegant, natty (*inf*), snappy, stylish **5** = **brisk**, lively, quick, vigorous ▷ *v* **6** = **sting**, burn, hurt ▷ *n* **7** = **sting**, pain, soreness

smash *v* **1** = **break**, crush, demolish,

pulverize, shatter **3** = **collide**, crash **4** = **destroy**, lay waste, ruin, trash (*sl*), wreck ▷ *n* **5** = **destruction**, collapse, downfall, failure, ruin **6** = **collision**, accident, crash

smattering *n* = **modicum**, bit, rudiments

smear *v* **1** = **spread over**, bedaub, coat, cover, daub, rub on **2** = **dirty**, smudge, soil, stain, sully **3** = **slander**, besmirch, blacken, malign ▷ *n* **4** = **smudge**, blot, blotch, daub, splotch, streak **5** = **slander**, calumny, defamation, libel

smell *v* **1** = **sniff**, scent **3** = **stink**, pong (*Brit inf*), reek ▷ *n* **6** = **odour**, aroma, bouquet, fragrance, perfume, scent

smirk *n* **1** = **smug look**, simper

S

smithereens pl n shattered fragments.

smock n 1 loose overall. 2 woman's loose blouselike garment. ▷ v 3 gather (material) by sewing in a honeycomb pattern. **smocking** n.

smog n mixture of smoke and fog.

smoke n 1 cloudy mass that rises from something burning. 2 act of smoking tobacco. ▷ v 3 give off smoke. 4 inhale and expel smoke of (a cigar, cigarette, or pipe). 5 do this habitually. 6 cure (meat, fish, or cheese) by treating with smoke. **smokeless** adj **smoker** n **smoky** adj **smoke screen** something said or done to hide the truth.

smooth ① adj 1 even in surface, texture, or consistency. 2 without obstructions or difficulties. 3 charming and polite but possibly insincere. 4 free from jolts. 5 not harsh in taste. ▷ v 6 make smooth. 7 calm. **smoothly** adv.

smother ① v 1 suffocate or stifle. 2 suppress. 3 cover thickly.

smoulder ① v 1 burn slowly with smoke but no flame. 2 (of feelings) exist in a suppressed state.

SMS short message system: used for sending data to mobile phones.

smudge ① v 1 make or become smeared or soiled. ▷ n 2 dirty mark. 3 blurred form. **smudgy** adj.

smug ① adj smugger, smuggest self-satisfied.

smuggle v 1 import or export (goods) secretly and illegally. 2 take somewhere secretly. **smuggler** n.

smut n 1 obscene jokes, pictures, etc. 2 speck of soot or dark mark left by soot. **smutty** adj.

snack ① n light quick meal. **snack bar** place where snacks are sold.

snag ① n 1 difficulty or disadvantage. 2 sharp projecting point. 3 hole in fabric caused by a sharp object. ▷ v **snagging, snagged** 4 catch or tear on a point.

snail n slow-moving mollusc with a spiral shell. **snail mail** informal conventional post, as opposed to email. **snail's pace** very slow speed.

snake n 1 long thin scaly limbless reptile. ▷ v 2 move in a winding course like a snake. **snaky** adj twisted or winding.

snap ① v snapping, snapped 1 break suddenly. 2 (cause to) make a sharp cracking sound. 3 move suddenly. 4 bite (at) suddenly. 5 speak sharply and angrily. 6 take a snapshot of. ▷ n 7 act or sound of snapping. 8 informal snapshot. 9 sudden brief spell of cold weather. 10 card game in which the word 'snap' is called when two similar cards are put down. ▷ adj 11 made on the spur of the moment. **snappy** adj

---

— THESAURUS —

smooth adj 1 = **even**, flat, flush, horizontal, level, plane 2 = **easy**, effortless, well-ordered 3 = **suave**, facile, glib, persuasive, slick, smarmy (Brit inf), unctuous, urbane 4 = **flowing**, regular, rhythmic, steady, uniform 5 = **mellow**, agreeable, mild, pleasant ▷ v 6 = **flatten**, iron, level, plane, press 7 = **ease**, appease, assuage, calm, mitigate, mollify, soften, soothe

smother v 1 a = **suffocate**, choke, strangle b = **extinguish**, snuff, stifle 2 = **suppress**, conceal, hide, muffle, repress, stifle

smoulder v 2 = **seethe**, boil, fume, rage, simmer

smudge v 1 = **smear**, daub, dirty, mark, smirch ▷ n 2 = **smear**, blemish, blot

smug adj = **self-satisfied**, complacent, conceited, superior

snack n = **light meal**, bite, refreshment(s)

snag n 1 = **difficulty**, catch, complication, disadvantage, downside, drawback, hitch, obstacle, problem ▷ v 4 = **catch**, rip, tear

snap v 1 = **break**, crack, separate 2 = **crackle**, click, pop 4 = **bite at**, nip, snatch 5 = **speak sharply**, bark, jump down (someone's) throat (inf), lash out at ▷ n 7 = **crackle**, pop ▷ adj 11 = **instant**, immediate, spur-of-the-moment, sudden

S

1 (also **snappish**) irritable. **2** *slang* quick. **3** *slang* smart and fashionable. **snapper** n food fish of Australia and New Zealand with a pinkish body covered with blue spots. **snapshot** n informal photograph. **snap up** v take eagerly and quickly.

snare ❶ n **1** trap with a noose. ▷ v **2** catch in or as if in a snare.

snarl¹ v **1** (of an animal) growl with bared teeth. **2** speak or utter fiercely. ▷ n **3** act or sound of snarling.

snarl² ❶ n **1** tangled mess. ▷ v **2** make tangled. **snarl-up** n informal confused situation such as a traffic jam.

snatch ❶ v **1** seize or try to seize suddenly. **2** take (food, rest, etc.) hurriedly. ▷ n **3** snatching. **4** fragment.

sneak ❶ v **1** move furtively. **2** bring, take, or put furtively. **3** *informal* tell tales. ▷ n **4** cowardly or underhand person. **sneaking** adj **1** slight but persistent. **2** secret. **sneaky** adj.

sneer ❶ n **1** contemptuous expression or remark. ▷ v **2** show contempt by a sneer.

sneeze v **1** expel air from the nose suddenly, involuntarily, and noisily. ▷ n **2** act or sound of sneezing.

snide ❶ adj critical in an unfair and nasty way.

sniff ❶ v **1** inhale through the nose in short audible breaths. **2** smell by sniffing. ▷ n

3 act or sound of sniffing. **sniffle** v **1** sniff repeatedly, as when suffering from a cold. ▷ n **2** slight cold. **sniff at** v express contempt for.

snigger ❶ n **1** sly disrespectful laugh, esp. one partly stifled. ▷ v **2** utter a snigger.

snip ❶ v **snipping**, **snipped 1** cut in small quick strokes with scissors or shears. ▷ n **2** informal bargain. **3** act or sound of snipping. **snippet** n small piece.

snipe ❶ n **1** wading bird with a long straight bill. ▷ v **2** (foll. by *at*) shoot at (a person) from cover. **3** make critical remarks about. **sniper** n.

snivel ❶ v**-elling**, **-elled** cry in a whining way.

snob ❶ n **1** person who judges others by social rank. **2** person who feels smugly superior in his or her tastes or interests. **snobbery** n **snobbish** adj.

snooker ❶ n **1** game played on a billiard table. ▷ v **2** leave (a snooker opponent) in a position such that another ball blocks the target ball. **3** informal put (someone) in a position where he or she can do nothing.

snoop ❶ informal ▷ v **1** pry. ▷ n **2** snooping.

snooty adj **snootier**, **snootiest** informal haughty.

snooze ❶ informal ▷ v **1** take a brief light sleep. ▷ n **2** brief light sleep.

snore v **1** make snorting sounds while

---

snare n **1** = **trap**, gin, net, noose, wire ▷ v **2** = **trap**, catch, entrap, net, seize, wire

snarl² v **2** = **tangle**, entangle, entwine, muddle, ravel

snatch v **1** = **seize**, clutch, grab, grasp, grip **2** = **grab** ▷ n **4** = **bit**, fragment, part, piece, snippet

sneak v **1** = **slink**, lurk, pad, skulk, slip, steal **2** = **slip**, smuggle, spirit **3** Inf = **inform on**, grass on (Brit sl), shop (sl, chiefly Brit), tell on (inf), tell tales ▷ n **4** = **informer**, telltale

sneer n **1** = **scorn**, derision, gibe, jeer, mockery, ridicule ▷ v **2** = **scorn**, deride, disdain, jeer, laugh, mock, ridicule

snide adj = **nasty**, cynical, disparaging,

hurtful, ill-natured, malicious, sarcastic, scornful, sneering, spiteful

sniff v **1, 2** = **inhale**, breathe, smell

snigger n, v = **laugh**, giggle, snicker, titter

snip v **1** = **cut**, clip, crop, dock, shave, trim ▷ n **2** Inf = **bargain**, giveaway, good buy, steal (inf)

snipe v **3** = **criticize**, carp, denigrate, disparage, jeer, knock (inf), put down

snivel v = **whine**, cry, grizzle (inf, chiefly Brit), moan, whimper, whinge (inf)

snob n = **elitist**, highbrow, prig

snoop Inf v **1** = **pry**, interfere, poke one's nose in (inf), spy

snooze Inf v **1** = **doze**, catnap, nap, take

sleeping. ▷ *n* **2** sound of snoring.

snorkel *n* **1** tube allowing a swimmer to breathe while face down on the surface of the water. ▷ *v* **-kelling, -kelled 2** swim using a snorkel.

snort *v* **1** exhale noisily through the nostrils. **2** express contempt or anger by snorting. ▷ *n* **3** act or sound of snorting.

snout *n* animal's projecting nose and jaws.

snow *n* **1** frozen vapour falling from the sky in flakes. **2** *slang* cocaine. ▷ *v* **3** fall as or like snow. **be snowed under** be overwhelmed, esp. with paperwork. **snowy** *adj* **snowball** *n* **1** snow pressed into a ball for throwing. ▷ *v* **2** increase rapidly. **snowboard** *n* board on which a person stands to slide across the snow. **snowboarding** *n* **snowdrift** *n* bank of deep snow. **snowdrop** *n* small white bell-shaped spring flower. **snowflake** *n* single crystal of snow. **snow gum** same as SALLEE. **snowman** *n* figure shaped out of snow. **snowplough** *n* vehicle for clearing away snow. **snowshoes** *pl n* racket-shaped shoes for travelling on snow.

snub ❶ *v* **snubbing, snubbed 1** insult deliberately. ▷ *n* **2** deliberate insult. ▷ *adj* **3** (of a nose) short and blunt. **snub-nosed** *adj*.

snuff¹ *n* powdered tobacco for sniffing up the nostrils.

snuff² *v* extinguish (a candle). **snuff it** *informal* die.

snuffle *v* breathe noisily or with difficulty.

snug ❶ *adj* **snugger, snuggest 1** warm and comfortable. **2** comfortably close-fitting. ▷ *n* **3** small room in a pub. **snugly** *adv.*

snuggle ❶ *v* nestle into a person or thing for warmth or from affection.

so *adv* **1** to such an extent. **2** in such a manner. **3** very. **4** also. **5** thereupon. ▷ *conj* **6** in order that. **7** with the result that. **8** therefore. ▷ *interj* **9** exclamation of surprise, triumph, or realization. **so-and-so** *n* **1** *informal* person whose name is not specified. **2** unpleasant person or thing. **so-called** *adj* called (in the speaker's opinion, wrongly) by that name. **so long** goodbye. **so that** in order that.

soak ❶ *v* **1** make wet. **2** put or lie in liquid so as to become thoroughly wet. **3** (of liquid) penetrate. ▷ *n* **4** soaking. **5** *slang* drunkard. **soaking** *n, adj* **soak up** *v* absorb.

soap *n* **1** compound of alkali and fat, used with water as a cleaning agent. **2** *informal* soap opera. ▷ *v* **3** apply soap to. **soapy** *adj* **soap opera** radio or television serial dealing with domestic themes.

soar ❶ *v* **1** rise or fly upwards. **2** increase suddenly.

sob ❶ *v* **sobbing, sobbed 1** weep with convulsive gasps. **2** utter with sobs. ▷ *n* **3** act or sound of sobbing. **sob story** tale of personal distress told to arouse sympathy.

sober ❶ *adj* **1** not drunk. **2** serious. **3** (of colours) plain and dull. ▷ *v* **4** make or become sober. **sobriety** *n* state of being sober.

s

THESAURUS

forty winks (*inf*) ▷ *n* **2** = **doze**, catnap, forty winks (*inf*), nap, siesta
snub *v* **1** = **insult**, cold-shoulder, cut (*inf*), humiliate, put down, rebuff, slight ▷ *n* **2** = **insult**, affront, put-down, slap in the face
snug *adj* **1** = **cosy**, comfortable, comfy (*inf*), warm
snuggle *v* = **nestle**, cuddle, nuzzle
soak *v* **1, 2** = **wet**, bathe, damp, drench, immerse, moisten, saturate, steep

3 = **penetrate**, permeate, seep **soak up** *v* = **absorb**, assimilate
soar *v* **1** = **ascend**, fly, mount, rise, wing **2** = **rise**, climb, escalate, rocket, shoot up
sob *v* **1** = **cry**, howl, shed tears, weep
sober *adj* **1** = **abstinent**, abstemious, moderate, temperate **2** = **serious**, composed, cool, grave, level-headed, rational, reasonable, sedate, solemn, staid, steady **3** = **plain**, dark, drab, quiet, sombre, subdued

soccer n football played by two teams of eleven kicking a spherical ball.

sociable ❶ adj 1 friendly or companionable. 2 (of an occasion) providing companionship. **sociability** n **sociably** adv.

social ❶ adj 1 living in a community. 2 of society or its organization. 3 sociable. ▷ n 4 informal gathering. **socially** adv **socialize** v meet others socially. **socialite** n member of fashionable society. **social security** state provision for the unemployed, aged, or sick. **social work** work which involves helping people with serious financial or family problems.

socialism n political system which advocates public ownership of industries, resources, and transport. **socialist** n, adj.

society ❶ n, pl **-ties** 1 human beings considered as a group. 2 organized community. 3 structure and institutions of such a community. 4 organized group with common aims and interests. 5 upper-class or fashionable people collectively. 6 companionship.

sociology n study of human societies. **sociological** adj **sociologist** n.

sock¹ n cloth covering for the foot.

sock² slang ▷ v 1 hit hard. ▷ n 2 hard blow.

socket n hole or recess into which something fits.

sod n (piece of) turf.

soda n 1 compound of sodium. 2 soda water. **soda water** fizzy drink made from water charged with carbon dioxide.

sodden ❶ adj soaked.

sodium n Chem silvery-white metallic element. **sodium bicarbonate** white soluble compound used in baking powder.

sodomy n anal intercourse.

sofa ❶ n couch.

soft ❶ adj 1 not hard, rough, or harsh. 2 (of a breeze or climate) mild. 3 (too) lenient. 4 easily influenced or imposed upon. 5 feeble or silly. 6 not robust. 7 (of drugs) not liable to cause addiction. 8 informal easy. 9 (of water) containing few mineral salts. **softly** adv **soften** v make or become soft or softer. **soft drink** nonalcoholic drink. **soft furnishings** curtains, rugs, lampshades, and furniture covers. **soft option** easiest alternative. **soft-pedal** v deliberately avoid emphasizing something. **soft-soap** v informal flatter. **software** n computer programs. **softwood** n wood of a coniferous tree.

soggy ❶ adj **-gier, -giest** 1 soaked. 2 moist and heavy. **sogginess** n.

soil¹ ❶ n 1 top layer of earth. 2 country or territory.

——————————————— THESAURUS ———————

sociable adj 1 = **friendly**, affable, companionable, convivial, cordial, genial, gregarious, outgoing, social, warm

social adj 2 = **communal**, collective, common, community, general, group, public ▷ n 4 = **get-together** (inf), gathering, party

society n 1 = **civilization**, humanity, mankind, people, the community, the public 4 = **organization**, association, circle, club, fellowship, group, guild, institute, league, order, union 5 = **upper classes**, beau monde, elite, gentry, high society 6 = **companionship**, company, fellowship, friendship

sodden adj = **soaked**, drenched, saturated, soggy, sopping, waterlogged

sofa n = **couch**, chaise longue, divan, settee

soft adj 1 = **pliable**, bendable, elastic, flexible, gelatinous, malleable, mouldable, plastic, pulpy, spongy, squashy, supple, yielding 2 = **mild**, balmy, temperate 3 = **lenient**, easy-going, indulgent, lax, overindulgent, permissive, spineless 6 = **out of condition**, effeminate, flabby, flaccid, limp, weak 8 Inf = **easy**, comfortable, cushy (inf), undemanding

soggy adj = **sodden**, dripping, moist, saturated, soaked, sopping, waterlogged

soil¹ n 1 = **earth**, clay, dirt, dust, ground 2 = **land**, country

soil² ❶ v 1 make or become dirty.
2 disgrace.

solace ❶ [**sol**-iss] n, v comfort in distress.

solar adj 1 of the sun. 2 using the energy of
the sun. **solar plexus** 1 network of nerves
at the pit of the stomach. 2 this part of the
stomach. **solar system** the sun and the
heavenly bodies that go round it.

solarium n, pl **-lariums, -laria** place
with beds and ultraviolet lights used for
acquiring an artificial suntan.

solder n 1 soft alloy used to join two metal
surfaces. ▷ v 2 join with solder.

soldier ❶ n 1 member of an army. ▷ v
2 serve in an army. **soldierly** adj **soldier on**
v persist doggedly.

sole¹ ❶ adj 1 one and only. 2 not shared,
exclusive. **solely** adv only, completely.
2 alone.

sole² n 1 underside of the foot. 2 underside
of a shoe. ▷ v 3 provide (a shoe) with a
sole.

sole³ n small edible flatfish.

solemn ❶ adj 1 serious, deeply sincere.
2 formal. **solemnity** n **solemnize** v
1 celebrate or perform (a ceremony).
2 make solemn.

solicit v **-iting, -ited** 1 request. 2 (of a
prostitute) offer (a person) sex for money.
solicitation n.

solid ❶ adj 1 (of a substance) keeping its
shape. 2 not liquid or gas. 3 not hollow.

4 of the same substance throughout.
5 strong or substantial. 6 sound or
reliable. 7 having three dimensions.
▷ n 8 three-dimensional shape. 9 solid
substance. **solidify** v make or become
solid or firm. **solidity** n.

soliloquy n, pl **-quies** speech made by a
person while alone, esp. in a play.

solitary ❶ adj 1 alone, single. 2 (of a place)
lonely. **solitude** n state of being alone.

solo n, pl **-los** 1 music for one performer.
2 any act done without assistance. ▷ adj
3 done alone. ▷ adv 4 by oneself, alone.
soloist n.

solstice n either the shortest (in winter) or
longest (in summer) day of the year.

solve ❶ v find the answer to (a problem).
solvable adj.

sombre ❶ adj dark, gloomy.

sombrero n, pl **-ros** wide-brimmed
Mexican hat.

some adj 1 unknown or unspecified.
2 unknown or unspecified quantity or
number of. 3 considerable number or
amount of. 4 informal remarkable. ▷ pron
5 certain unknown or unspecified people
or things. 6 unknown or unspecified
number or quantity. **somebody** pron
1 some person. ▷ n 2 important person.
somehow adv in some unspecified way.
someone pron somebody. **something**
pron 1 unknown or unspecified thing or

— THESAURUS —

soil² v 1, 2 = **dirty**, befoul, besmirch, defile,
foul, pollute, spot, stain, sully, tarnish

solace n = **comfort**, consolation, relief ▷ v
= **comfort**, console

soldier n 1 = **fighter**, man-at-arms,
serviceman, squaddie or squaddy (Brit sl),
trooper, warrior

sole adj 1 = **only**, individual, one, single,
solitary 2 = **alone**, exclusive

solemn adj 1 = **serious**, earnest,
grave, sedate, sober, staid 2 = **formal**,
ceremonial, dignified, grand, grave,
momentous, stately

solid adj 1 = **firm**, compact, concrete,

dense, hard 5 = **strong**, stable, sturdy,
substantial, unshakable 6 = **reliable**,
dependable, genuine, good, pure, real,
sound, trusty, upright, upstanding,
worthy

solitary adj 1 = **single**, alone, lone, sole
2 = **isolated**, hidden, lonely, out-of-the-
way, remote, unfrequented

solve v = **answer**, clear up, crack, decipher,
disentangle, get to the bottom of, resolve,
suss (out) (sl), unravel, work out

sombre adj = **gloomy**, dark, dim, dismal,
doleful, drab, dull, grave, joyless,
lugubrious, mournful, sad, sober

S

amount. **2** impressive or important thing.
sometime adv **1** at some unspecified time.
▷ adj **2** former. **sometimes** adv from time
to time, now and then. **somewhat** adv to
some extent, rather. **somewhere** adv in, to,
or at some unspecified or unknown place.

somersault n **1** leap or roll in which the
trunk and legs are turned over the head.
▷ v **2** perform a somersault.

son n male offspring. **son-in-law** n, pl **sons-
in-law** daughter's husband.

sonar n device for detecting underwater
objects by the reflection of sound waves.

sonata n piece of music in several
movements for one instrument with or
without piano.

song ❶ n **1** music for the voice. **2** tuneful
sound made by certain birds. **3** singing.
for a song very cheaply. **songster,
songstress** n singer. **songbird** n any bird
with a musical call.

sonic adj of or producing sound.

sonnet n fourteen-line poem with a fixed
rhyme scheme.

sonorous adj (of sound) deep or resonant.

soon ❶ adv in a short time. **sooner** adv
rather, e.g. *I'd sooner go alone.* **sooner or
later** eventually.

soot n black powder formed by the
incomplete burning of an organic
substance. **sooty** adj.

soothe ❶ v **1** make calm. **2** relieve (pain etc.).

sop n **1** concession to pacify someone. ▷ v
sopping, sopped 2 mop up or absorb
(liquid). **sopping** adj completely soaked.
soppy adj informal oversentimental.

sophistry n clever but invalid argument.

soporific ❶ adj **1** causing sleep. ▷ n **2** drug
that causes sleep.

soprano n, pl **-pranos 1** (singer with) the
highest female or boy's voice. **2** highest
pitched of a family of instruments.

sorbet n flavoured water ice.

sorcerer ❶ n magician. **sorceress** n fem
sorcery n witchcraft or magic.

sordid ❶ adj **1** dirty, squalid. **2** base, vile.
3 selfish and grasping.

sore ❶ adj **1** painful. **2** causing annoyance.
3 resentful. **4** (of need) urgent. ▷ n
5 painful area on the body. ▷ adv **6** obs
greatly. **sorely** adv greatly. **soreness** n.

sorrow ❶ n **1** grief or sadness. **2** cause
of sorrow. ▷ v **3** grieve. **sorrowful** adj
sorrowfully adv.

sorry ❶ adj **-rier, -riest 1** feeling pity or
regret. **2** pitiful or wretched.

————————————————————————— THESAURUS ————

song n **1** = **ballad**, air, anthem, carol, chant,
chorus, ditty, hymn, number, psalm, tune

soon adv = **before long**, in the near future,
shortly

soothe v **1** = **calm**, allay, appease, hush,
lull, mollify, pacify, quiet, still **2** = **relieve**,
alleviate, assuage, ease

soporific adj **1** = **sleep-inducing**, sedative,
somnolent, tranquillizing ▷ n **2** = **sedative**,
narcotic, opiate, tranquillizer

sorcerer, sorceress n = **magician**,
enchanter, necromancer, warlock, witch,
wizard

sordid adj **1** = **dirty**, filthy, foul, mean,
scungy (*Aust & NZ sl*), seedy, sleazy, squalid,
unclean **2** = **base**, debauched, degenerate,
low, shabby, shameful, vicious, vile
3 = **mercenary**, avaricious, covetous,

grasping, selfish

sore adj **1** = **painful**, angry, burning,
inflamed, irritated, raw, sensitive,
smarting, tender **2** = **annoying**, severe,
sharp, troublesome **3** = **annoyed**,
aggrieved, angry, cross, hurt, irked,
irritated, pained, pissed (*taboo sl*), pissed
(off) (*taboo sl*), resentful, stung, upset
4 = **urgent**, acute, critical, desperate, dire,
extreme, pressing

sorrow n **1** = **grief**, anguish, distress,
heartache, heartbreak, misery, mourning,
regret, sadness, unhappiness, woe
2 = **affliction**, hardship, misfortune, trial,
tribulation, trouble, woe ▷ v **3** = **grieve**,
agonize, bemoan, be sad, bewail, lament,
mourn

sorry adj **1** = **regretful**, apologetic,

S

sort ❶ n 1 group all sharing certain qualities or characteristics. 2 *informal* type of character. ▷ v 3 arrange according to kind. 4 mend or fix. **out of sorts** slightly unwell or bad-tempered.

sortie n 1 relatively short return trip. 2 operational flight made by military aircraft.

SOS n 1 international code signal of distress. 2 call for help.

so-so *adj informal* mediocre.

soufflé [soo-flay] n light fluffy dish made with beaten egg whites and other ingredients.

soul ❶ n 1 spiritual and immortal part of a human being. 2 essential part or fundamental nature. 3 deep and sincere feelings. 4 person regarded as typifying some quality. 5 person. 6 type of Black music combining blues, pop, and gospel. **soulful** *adj* full of emotion. **soulless** *adj* 1 lacking human qualities, mechanical. 2 (of a person) lacking sensitivity.

sound¹ ❶ n 1 something heard, noise. ▷ v 2 make or cause to make a sound. 3 seem to be as specified. 4 pronounce. **soundproof** *adj* 1 not penetrable by sound. ▷ v 2 make soundproof. **soundtrack** n recorded sound

accompaniment to a film.

sound² ❶ *adj* 1 in good condition. 2 firm, substantial. 3 financially reliable. 4 showing good judgment. 5 ethically correct. 6 (of sleep) deep. 7 thorough. **soundly** *adv*.

sound³ ❶ v 1 find the depth of (water etc.). 2 examine (the body) by tapping or with a stethoscope. 3 ascertain the views of. **sounding board** person or group used to test a new idea.

sound⁴ ❶ n channel or strait.

soup n liquid food made from meat, vegetables, etc. **soupy** *adj* **soup kitchen** place where food and drink is served to needy people. **souped-up** *adj* (of an engine) adjusted so as to be more powerful than normal.

sour ❶ *adj* 1 sharp-tasting. 2 (of milk) gone bad. 3 (of a person's temperament) sullen. ▷ v 4 make or become sour. **sourness** n.

source ❶ n 1 origin or starting point. 2 person, book, etc. providing information. 3 spring where a river or stream begins.

south n 1 direction towards the South Pole, opposite north. 2 area lying in or towards the south. ▷ *adj* 3 to or in the south. 4 (of a wind) from the south. ▷ *adv* 5 in,

---

— THESAURUS —

conscience-stricken, contrite, penitent, remorseful, repentant, shamefaced 2 = **wretched**, mean, miserable, pathetic, pitiful, poor, sad

sort n 1 = **kind**, brand, category, class, ilk, make, nature, order, quality, style, type, variety ▷ v 3 = **arrange**, categorize, classify, divide, grade, group, order, put in order, rank

soul n 1 = **spirit**, essence, life, vital force 2 = **essence**, embodiment, epitome, personification, quintessence, type 5 = **person**, being, body, creature, individual, man or woman

sound¹ n 1 = **noise**, din, report, reverberation, tone ▷ v 2 = **resound**, echo, reverberate 3 = **seem**, appear, look

sound² *adj* 1 = **perfect**, fit, healthy, intact,

solid, unhurt, unimpaired, uninjured, whole 4 = **sensible**, correct, logical, proper, prudent, rational, reasonable, right, trustworthy, valid, well-founded, wise 6 = **deep**, unbroken, undisturbed, untroubled

sound³ v 1 = **fathom**, plumb, probe

sound⁴ n = **channel**, arm of the sea, fjord, inlet, passage, strait, voe

sour *adj* 1 = **sharp**, acetic, acid, bitter, pungent, tart 2 = **gone off**, curdled, gone bad, turned 3 = **ill-natured**, acrimonious, disagreeable, embittered, ill-tempered, peevish, tart, ungenerous, waspish

source n 1 = **origin**, author, beginning, cause, derivation, fount, originator 2 = **informant**, authority

S

to, or towards the south. **southerly** *adj*
southern *adj* **southerner** *n* person from
the south of a country or area. **southward**
adj, *adv* **southwards** *adv* **southpaw** *n*
informal left-handed person, esp. a boxer.
South Pole southernmost point on the
earth's axis.
souvenir ❶ *n* keepsake, memento.
sou'wester *n* seaman's waterproof hat
covering the head and back of the neck.
sovereign ❶ *n* 1 king or queen. 2 former
British gold coin worth one pound.
▷ *adj* 3 (of a state) independent.
4 supreme in rank or authority.
5 excellent. **sovereignty** *n*.
sow¹ ❶ [rhymes with **know**] *v* **sowing**,
sowed, **sown** *or* **sowed** 1 scatter or plant
(seed) in or on (the ground). 2 implant or
introduce.
sow² [rhymes with **cow**] *n* female adult pig.
soya *n* plant whose edible bean (**soya
bean**) is used for food and as a source of
oil. **soy sauce** sauce made from fermented
soya beans, used in Chinese and Japanese
cookery.
spa *n* resort with a mineral-water spring.
space ❶ *n* 1 unlimited expanse in which
all objects exist and move. 2 interval.
3 blank portion. 4 unoccupied area. 5 the
universe beyond the earth's atmosphere.
▷ *v* 6 place at intervals. **spacecraft**,
spaceship *n* vehicle for travel beyond
the earth's atmosphere. **space shuttle**

manned reusable vehicle for repeated
space flights.
spacious ❶ *adj* having a large capacity
or area.
spade¹ *n* tool for digging. **spadework** *n*
hard preparatory work.
spade² *n* playing card of the suit marked
with black leaf-shaped symbols.
spaghetti *n* pasta in the form of long strings.
spam *Computers sl.* ▷ *v* **spamming**,
spammed 1 send unsolicited email or
text messages to multiple recipients. ▷ *n*
2 unsolicited email or text messages.
span ❶ *n* 1 space between two points.
2 complete extent. 3 distance from thumb
to little finger of the expanded hand. ▷ *v*
spanning, **spanned** 4 stretch or extend
across.
spangle *n* 1 small shiny metallic
ornament. ▷ *v* 2 decorate with spangles.
spaniel *n* dog with long ears and silky hair.
spank ❶ *v* 1 slap with the open hand, on
the buttocks or legs. ▷ *n* 2 such a slap.
spanking *n*.
spanner *n* tool for gripping and turning a
nut or bolt.
spar¹ *n* pole used as a ship's mast, boom,
or yard.
spar² ❶ *v* **sparring**, **sparred** 1 box or fight
using light blows for practice. 2 argue
(with someone).
spare ❶ *adj* 1 extra. 2 in reserve. 3 (of
a person) thin. ▷ *n* 4 duplicate kept in

━━━━━━━━━━━━━━━━━━━━━━━━━━━━ THESAURUS ━━━

S

souvenir *n* = **keepsake**, memento,
reminder
sovereign *n* 1 = **monarch**, chief, emperor
or empress, king *or* queen, potentate,
prince *or* princess, ruler ▷ *adj* 4 = **supreme**,
absolute, imperial, kingly *or* queenly,
principal, royal, ruling 5 = **excellent**,
effectual, efficacious, efficient
sow¹ *v* 1 = **scatter**, plant, seed 2 = **implant**
space *n* 1 = **expanse**, extent 2 = **interval**,
capacity, duration, elbowroom, leeway,
margin, period, play, room, scope, span,
time, while 3 = **gap**, blank, distance,

interval, omission
spacious *adj* = **roomy**, ample, broad,
capacious, commodious, expansive,
extensive, huge, large, sizable *or* sizeable
span *n* 1 = **period**, duration, spell, term
2 = **extent**, amount, distance, length,
reach, spread, stretch ▷ *v* 4 = **extend
across**, bridge, cover, cross, link, traverse
spank *v* 1 = **smack**, cuff, slap
spar² *v* 2 = **argue**, bicker, row, scrap (*inf*),
squabble, wrangle
spare *adj* 1 = **extra**, additional, free,
leftover, odd, over, superfluous, surplus,

case of damage or loss. ▷ *v* **5** refrain from punishing or harming. **6** protect (someone) from (something unpleasant). **7** afford to give. **to spare** in addition to what is needed. **sparing** *adj* economical.

spark ❶ *n* **1** fiery particle thrown out from a fire or caused by friction. **2** flash of light produced by an electrical discharge. **3** trace or hint (of a particular quality). ▷ *v* **4** give off sparks. **5** initiate. **sparkie** *n* NZ informal electrician.

sparkle ❶ *v* **1** glitter with many points of light. **2** be vivacious or witty. ▷ *n* **3** sparkling points of light. **4** vivacity or wit. **sparkler** *n* hand-held firework that emits sparks. **sparkling** *adj* (of wine or mineral water) slightly fizzy.

sparrow *n* small brownish bird. **sparrowhawk** *n* small hawk.

sparse ❶ *adj* thinly scattered. **sparsely** *adv* **sparseness** *n*.

spartan *adj* strict and austere.

spasm ❶ *n* **1** involuntary muscular contraction. **2** sudden burst of activity or feeling. **spasmodic** *adj* occurring in spasms. **spasmodically** *adv*.

spastic *n* **1** person with cerebral palsy. ▷ *adj* **2** suffering from cerebral palsy. **3** affected by spasms.

spate ❶ *n* **1** large number of things

happening within a period of time. **2** sudden outpouring or flood.

spatial *adj* of or in space.

spatter *v* **1** scatter or be scattered in drops over (something). ▷ *n* **2** spattering sound. **3** something spattered.

spatula *n* utensil with a broad flat blade for spreading or stirring.

spawn *n* **1** jelly-like mass of eggs of fish, frogs, or molluscs. ▷ *v* **2** (of fish, frogs, or molluscs) lay eggs. **3** generate.

spay *v* remove the ovaries from (a female animal).

speak ❶ *v* **speaking**, **spoke**, **spoken 1** say words, talk. **2** communicate or express in words. **3** give a speech or lecture. **4** know how to talk in (a specified language). **speaker** *n* **1** person who speaks, esp. at a formal occasion. **2** loudspeaker. **3** (**S-**) official chairman of a body.

spear *n* **1** weapon consisting of a long shaft with a sharp point. ▷ *v* **2** pierce with or as if with a spear. **spearhead** *v* **1** lead (an attack or campaign). ▷ *n* **2** leading force in an attack or campaign.

spearmint *n* type of mint.

special ❶ *adj* **1** distinguished from others of its kind. **2** for a specific purpose. **3** exceptional. **4** particular. **specially** *adv* **specialist** *n* expert in a particular

———— THESAURUS ————

unoccupied, unused, unwanted **3 = thin**, gaunt, lean, meagre, wiry ▷ *v* **5 = have mercy on**, be merciful to, go easy on (*inf*), leave, let off (*inf*), pardon, save from **7 = afford**, do without, give, grant, let (someone) have, manage without, part with

spark *n* **1 = flicker**, flare, flash, gleam, glint **3 = trace**, atom, hint, jot, scrap, vestige ▷ *v* **5 = start**, inspire, precipitate, provoke, set off, stimulate, trigger (off)

sparkle *v* **1 = glitter**, dance, flash, gleam, glint, glisten, scintillate, shimmer, shine, twinkle ▷ *n* **3 = glitter**, brilliance, flash, flicker, gleam, glint, twinkle **4 = vivacity**, dash, élan, life, liveliness, spirit, vitality

sparse *adj* **= scattered**, few and far between, meagre, scanty, scarce

spasm *n* **1 = convulsion**, contraction, paroxysm, twitch **2 = burst**, eruption, fit, frenzy, outburst, seizure

spate *n* **2 = flood**, deluge, flow, outpouring, rush, torrent

speak *v* **1, 2 = talk**, articulate, converse, express, pronounce, say, state, tell, utter **3 = lecture**, address, declaim, discourse, hold forth

special *adj* **1, 2, 4 = specific**, appropriate, distinctive, individual, particular, precise **3 = exceptional**, extraordinary, important, memorable, significant, uncommon, unique, unusual

S

activity or subject. **speciality** n 1 special
interest or skill. 2 product specialized
in. **specialize** v be a specialist.
specialization n.

species ⊕ n, pl **-cies** group of plants or
animals that are related closely enough to
interbreed naturally.

specific ⊕ adj 1 particular, definite. ▷ n
2 drug used to treat a particular disease.
▷ pl 3 particular details. **specifically** adv
specification n detailed description of
something to be made or done. **specify** v
refer to or state specifically.

specimen ⊕ n 1 individual or part
typifying a whole. 2 sample of blood etc.
taken for analysis.

specious [**spee**-shuss] adj apparently true,
but actually false.

speck ⊕ n small spot or particle. **speckle** n
1 small spot. ▷ v 2 mark with speckles.

spectacle ⊕ n 1 strange, interesting, or
ridiculous sight. 2 impressive public show.
▷ pl 3 pair of glasses for correcting faulty
vision. **spectacular** adj 1 impressive. ▷ n
2 spectacular public show. **spectacularly**
adv.

spectre ⊕ n 1 ghost. 2 menacing mental
image. **spectral** adj.

spectrum n, pl **-tra** 1 range of different
colours, radio waves, etc. in order of their

wavelengths. 2 entire range of anything.
spectroscope n instrument for producing
or examining spectra.

speculate ⊕ v 1 guess, conjecture. 2 buy
property, shares, etc. in the hope of
selling them at a profit. **speculation** n
speculative adj **speculator** n.

speech ⊕ n 1 act, power, or manner of
speaking. 2 talk given to an audience.
3 language or dialect. **speechify** v make
speeches, esp. boringly. **speechless** adj
unable to speak because of great
emotion.

speed ⊕ n 1 swiftness. 2 rate at which
something moves or acts. 3 slang
amphetamine. ▷ v **speeding**, **sped** or
speeded 4 go quickly. 5 drive faster than
the legal limit. **speedy** adj 1 prompt.
2 rapid. **speedily** adv **speedboat** n
light fast motorboat. **speedometer** n
instrument to show the speed of a vehicle.
speed up v accelerate. **speedway** n track
for motorcycle racing. **speedwell** n plant
with small blue flowers.

spell¹ ⊕ v **spelling**, **spelt** or **spelled** 1 give
in correct order the letters that form (a
word). 2 (of letters) make up (a word).
3 indicate. **spelling** n 1 way a word is
spelt. 2 person's ability to spell. **spell out**
v make explicit.

━━━━━━━━━━━━━━━━━━━━━━━━━━━━━━━━━━ THESAURUS ━━━━━

species n = **kind**, breed, category, class,
group, sort, type, variety
specific adj 1 = **particular**, characteristic,
distinguishing, special
specimen n 1 = **example**, exemplification,
instance, model, pattern, representative,
sample, type 2 = **sample**
speck n = **particle**, atom, bit, blemish, dot,
fleck, grain, iota, jot, mark, mite, mote,
shred, speckle, spot, stain
spectacle n 1 = **sight**, curiosity, marvel,
phenomenon, scene, wonder 2 = **show**,
display, event, exhibition, extravaganza,
pageant, performance
spectre n 1 = **ghost**, apparition, phantom,
spirit, vision, wraith

speculate v 1 = **conjecture**, consider,
guess, hypothesize, suppose, surmise,
theorize, wonder 2 = **gamble**, hazard, risk,
venture
speech n 1 = **communication**,
conversation, dialogue, discussion,
talk 2 = **talk**, address, discourse, homily,
lecture, oration, spiel (inf) 3 = **language**,
articulation, dialect, diction, enunciation,
idiom, jargon, parlance, tongue
speed n 1 = **swiftness**, haste, hurry, pace,
quickness, rapidity, rush, velocity ▷ v
4 = **race**, career, gallop, hasten, hurry,
make haste, rush, tear, zoom
spell¹ v 3 = **indicate**, augur, imply, mean,
point to, portend, signify

S

spell² ❶ n 1 formula of words supposed to have magic power. **2** effect of a spell. **3** fascination. **spellbound** adj entranced.

spell³ ❶ n period of time of weather or activity.

spend ❶ v **spending, spent 1** pay out (money). **2** use or pass (time). **3** use up completely. **spendthrift** n person who spends money wastefully.

sperm n **sperms** or **sperm 1** male reproductive cell. **2** semen. **spermicide** n substance that kills sperm.

spew ❶ v 1 vomit. **2** send out in a stream.

sphere ❶ n 1 perfectly round solid object. **2** field of activity. **spherical** adj.

spice ❶ n 1 aromatic substance used as flavouring. **2** something that adds zest or interest. ▷ v **3** flavour with spices. **spicy** adj 1 flavoured with spices. **2** informal slightly scandalous.

spick-and-span adj neat and clean.

spider n small eight-legged creature which spins a web to catch insects for food. **spidery** adj.

spike ❶ n 1 sharp point. **2** sharp pointed metal object. ▷ pl **3** sports shoes with spikes for greater grip. ▷ v **4** put spikes on. **5** pierce or fasten with a spike. **6** add alcohol to (a drink). **spike someone's guns** thwart someone. **spiky** adj.

spill ❶ v **spilling, spilt** or **spilled 1** pour from or as if from a container. **2** come out of a place. **3** shed (blood). ▷ n **4** fall. **5** amount spilt. **spill the beans** informal give away a secret. **spillage** n.

spin ❶ v **spinning, spun 1** revolve or cause to revolve rapidly. **2** draw out and twist (fibres) into thread. ▷ n **3** revolving motion. **4** continuous spiral descent of an aircraft. **5** informal short drive for pleasure. **6** informal presenting of information in a way that creates a favourable impression. **spin a yarn** tell an improbable story. **spinner** n **spin doctor** informal person who provides a favourable slant to a news item or policy on behalf of a politician or a political party. **spin-dry** v dry (clothes) in a spin-dryer. **spin-dryer** n machine in which washed clothes are spun in a perforated drum to remove excess water. **spin-off** n incidental benefit. **spin out** v prolong.

spinach n dark green leafy vegetable.

spindle n 1 rotating rod that acts as an axle. **2** weighted rod rotated for spinning thread by hand. **spindly** adj long, slender, and frail.

spine ❶ n 1 backbone. **2** edge of a book on which the title is printed. **3** sharp point on an animal or plant. **spinal** adj of the spine. **spineless** adj lacking courage. **spiny** adj covered with spines.

spinster n unmarried woman.

——— THESAURUS ———

spell² n 1 = **incantation**, charm **2, 3** = **enchantment**, allure, bewitchment, fascination, glamour, magic

spell³ n = **period**, bout, course, interval, season, stretch, term, time

spend v 1 = **pay out**, disburse, expend, fork out (sl) **2** = **pass**, fill, occupy, while away **3** = **use up**, consume, dissipate, drain, empty, exhaust, run through, squander, waste

spew v 1 = **vomit**, disgorge, puke (sl), regurgitate, throw up (inf)

sphere n 1 = **ball**, circle, globe, globule, orb **2** = **field**, capacity, department, domain, function, patch, province, realm, scope, territory, turf (US sl)

spice n 1 = **seasoning**, relish, savour **2** = **excitement**, colour, pep, piquancy, zest, zing (inf)

spike n 1 = **point**, barb, prong, spine ▷ v **5** = **impale**, spear, spit, stick

spill v 1 = **pour**, discharge, disgorge, overflow, slop over ▷ n **4** = **fall**, tumble

spin v 1 = **revolve**, gyrate, pirouette, reel, rotate, turn, twirl, whirl ▷ n **3** = **revolution**, gyration, roll, whirl **5** Inf = **drive**, joy ride (inf), ride

spine n 1 = **backbone**, spinal column, vertebrae, vertebral column **3** = **barb**, needle, quill, ray, spike, spur

S

spiral ❶ *n* **1** continuous curve formed by a point winding about a central axis at an ever-increasing distance from it. **2** steadily accelerating increase or decrease. ▷ *v* **-ralling, -ralled 3** move in a spiral. **4** increase or decrease with steady acceleration. ▷ *adj* **5** having the form of a spiral.

spire *n* pointed part of a steeple.

spirit¹ ❶ *n* **1** nonphysical aspect of a person concerned with profound thoughts. **2** nonphysical part of a person believed to live on after death. **3** prevailing feeling. **4** mood or attitude. **5** temperament or disposition. **6** liveliness. **7** courage. **8** essential meaning as opposed to literal interpretation. **9** ghost. ▷ *pl* **10** emotional state. ▷ *v* **-iting, -ited 11** carry away mysteriously. **spirited** *adj* **1** lively. **2** characterized by the mood specified, e.g. *low-spirited*.

spirit² *n* liquid obtained by distillation. **spirit level** glass tube containing a bubble in liquid, used to check whether a surface is level.

spit¹ ❶ *v* **spitting, spat 1** eject (saliva or food) from the mouth. **2** throw out particles explosively. **3** rain slightly. **4** utter (words) in a violent manner. ▷ *n*

5 saliva. **spitting image** *informal* person who looks very like another. **spittle** *n* fluid produced in the mouth, saliva. **spittoon** *n* bowl to spit into.

spit² *n* **1** sharp rod on which meat is skewered for roasting. **2** long strip of land projecting into the sea.

spite ❶ *n* **1** deliberate nastiness. ▷ *v* **2** annoy or hurt from spite. **in spite of** in defiance of. **spiteful** *adj* **spitefully** *adv*.

splash ❶ *v* **1** scatter liquid on (something). **2** scatter (liquid) or (of liquid) be scattered in drops. **3** print (a story or photograph) prominently in a newspaper. ▷ *n* **4** splashing sound. **5** patch (of colour or light). **6** extravagant display. **7** small amount of liquid added to a drink. **splash out** *v informal* spend extravagantly.

splatter *v, n* splash.

splay *v* spread out, with ends spreading in different directions.

spleen *n* **1** abdominal organ which filters bacteria from the blood. **2** bad temper. **splenetic** *adj* spiteful or irritable.

splendid ❶ *adj* **1** excellent. **2** brilliant in appearance. **splendour** *n*.

splice *v* join by interweaving or overlapping ends. **get spliced** *slang* get married.

━━━━━━━━━━━━━━━━━━━━━━━━━━━━━ THESAURUS ━━━━━━━━━━━━━━━━━━━━━━━

spiral *n* **1** = **coil**, corkscrew, helix, whorl ▷ *adj* **5** = **coiled**, helical, whorled, winding

spirit¹ *n* **2** = **life force**, life, soul, vital spark **3** = **feeling**, atmosphere, gist, tenor, tone **4, 5** = **temperament**, attitude, character, disposition, outlook, temper **6** = **liveliness**, animation, brio, energy, enthusiasm, fire, force, life, mettle, vigour, zest **7** = **courage**, backbone, gameness, grit, guts (*inf*), spunk (*inf*) **8** = **intention**, essence, meaning, purport, purpose, sense, substance **9** = **ghost**, apparition, phantom, spectre ▷ *pl* **10** = **mood**, feelings, frame of mind, morale ▷ *v* **11** = **remove**, abduct, abstract, carry away, purloin, seize, steal, whisk away

spit¹ *v* **1** = **eject**, expectorate, splutter **2** = **throw out** ▷ *n* **5** = **saliva**, dribble,

drool, slaver, spittle

spite *n* **1** = **malice**, animosity, hatred, ill will, malevolence, spitefulness, spleen, venom ▷ *v* **2** = **annoy**, harm, hurt, injure, vex **in spite of** = **despite**, (even) though, notwithstanding, regardless of

splash *v* **1, 2** = **scatter**, shower, slop, spatter, spray, sprinkle, wet **3** = **publicize**, broadcast, tout, trumpet ▷ *n* **6** = **display**, effect, impact, sensation, stir **7** = **dash**, burst, patch, spattering, touch

splendid *adj* **1** = **excellent**, cracking (*Brit inf*), fantastic (*inf*), first-class, glorious, great (*inf*), marvellous, wonderful **2** = **magnificent**, costly, gorgeous, grand, impressive, lavish, luxurious, ornate, resplendent, rich, sumptuous, superb

splint n rigid support for a broken bone.

splinter ❶ n 1 thin sharp piece broken off, esp. from wood. ▷ v 2 break into fragments. **splinter group** group that has broken away from an organization.

split ❶ v **splitting, split** 1 break into separate pieces. 2 separate. 3 share. ▷ n 4 crack or division caused by splitting. ▷ pl 5 act of sitting with the legs outstretched in opposite directions. **split second** very short period of time.

splutter v 1 utter with spitting or choking sounds. 2 make hissing spitting sounds. ▷ n 3 spluttering.

spoil ❶ v **spoiling, spoilt** or **spoiled** 1 damage. 2 harm the character of (a child) by giving it all it wants. 3 rot, go bad. **spoils** pl n booty. **spoiling for** eager for. **spoilsport** n person who spoils the enjoyment of others.

spoke n bar joining the hub of a wheel to the rim.

spokesman, spokeswoman spokesperson n person chosen to speak on behalf of a group.

sponge n 1 sea animal with a porous absorbent skeleton. 2 skeleton of a sponge, or a substance like it, used for cleaning. 3 type of light cake. ▷ v 4 wipe with a sponge. 5 live at the expense of others. **sponger** n slang person who sponges on others. **spongy** adj.

sponsor ❶ n 1 person who promotes something. 2 person who agrees to give money to a charity on completion of a specified activity by another. 3 godparent. ▷ v 4 act as a sponsor for. **sponsorship** n.

spontaneous ❶ adj 1 not planned or arranged. 2 occurring through natural processes without outside influence. **spontaneity** n.

spoof ❶ n mildly satirical parody.

spook n informal ghost. **spooky** adj.

spool n cylinder round which something can be wound.

spoon n 1 shallow bowl attached to a handle for eating, stirring, or serving food. ▷ v 2 lift with a spoon. **spoonful** n **spoon-feed** v 1 feed with a spoon. 2 give (someone) too much help. **spoonbill** n wading bird of warm regions with a long flat bill.

sporadic ❶ adj intermittent, scattered. **sporadically** adv.

spore n minute reproductive body of some plants.

sporran n pouch worn in front of a kilt.

sport ❶ n 1 activity for pleasure, competition, or exercise. 2 such activities

---

splinter n 1 = **sliver**, chip, flake, fragment ▷ v 2 = **shatter**, disintegrate, fracture, split

split v 1 = **break**, burst, come apart, come undone, crack, give way, open, rend, rip 2 a = **separate**, branch, cleave, disband, disunite, diverge, fork, part b = **separate**, break up, divorce, part 3 = **share out**, allocate, allot, apportion, distribute, divide, halve, partition ▷ n 4 a = **division**, breach, break-up, discord, dissension, estrangement, rift, rupture, schism b = **crack**, breach, division, fissure, gap, rent, rip, separation, slit, tear

spoil v 1 = **ruin**, damage, destroy, disfigure, harm, impair, injure, mar, mess up, trash (sl), wreck 2 = **overindulge**, coddle, cosset, indulge, mollycoddle,

pamper 3 = **go bad**, addle, curdle, decay, decompose, go off (Brit inf), rot, turn

sponsor n 1 = **backer**, patron, promoter ▷ v 4 = **back**, finance, fund, patronize, promote, subsidize

spontaneous adj 1 = **unplanned**, impromptu, impulsive, instinctive, natural, unprompted, voluntary, willing

spoof n Inf = **parody**, burlesque, caricature, mockery, satire, send-up (Brit inf), take-off (inf)

sporadic adj = **intermittent**, irregular, occasional, scattered, spasmodic

sport n 1, 2 = **game**, amusement, diversion, exercise, pastime, play, recreation 4 = **fun**, badinage, banter, jest, joking, teasing ▷ v 6 = **wear**, display, exhibit, show off

S

collectively. **3** enjoyment. **4** playful joking. **5** person who reacts cheerfully. ▷ *v* **6** wear proudly. **sporting** *adj* **1** of sport. **2** behaving in a fair and decent way. **sporting chance** reasonable chance of success. **sporty** *adj* **sportive** *adj* playful. **sports car** fast low-built car, usu. open-topped. **sports jacket** man's casual jacket. **sportsman**, **sportswoman** *n* **1** person who plays sports. **2** person who plays fair and is good-humoured when losing. **sportsmanship** *n* **sport utility vehicle** *n chiefly US* powerful four-wheel drive vehicle for rough terrain.

spot ❶ *n* **1** small mark on a surface. **2** pimple. **3** location. **4** *informal* small quantity. **5** *informal* awkward situation. ▷ *v* **spotting**, **spotted 6** notice. **7** mark with spots. **8** watch for and take note of. **on the spot 1** at the place in question. **2** immediately. **3** in an awkward predicament. **spotless** *adj* absolutely clean. **spotty** *adj* with spots. **spot check** random examination. **spotlight** *n* **1** powerful light illuminating a small area. **2** centre of attention. **spot-on** *adj informal* absolutely accurate.

spouse ❶ *n* husband or wife.

spout ❶ *v* **1** pour out in a stream or jet.

2 *slang* utter (a stream of words) lengthily. ▷ *n* **3** projecting tube or lip for pouring liquids. **4** stream or jet of liquid.

sprain *v* **1** injure (a joint) by a sudden twist. ▷ *n* **2** such an injury.

sprat *n* small sea fish.

sprawl ❶ *v* **1** lie or sit with the limbs spread out. **2** spread out in a straggling manner. ▷ *n* **3** part of a city that has spread untidily over a large area.

spray¹ ❶ *n* **1** (device for producing) fine drops of liquid. ▷ *v* **2** scatter in fine drops. **3** cover with a spray.

spray² ❶ *n* **1** branch with buds, leaves, flowers, or berries. **2** ornament like this.

spread ❶ *v* **spreading**, **spread 1** open out or be displayed to the fullest extent. **2** extend over a larger expanse. **3** apply as a coating. **4** send or be sent in all directions. ▷ *n* **5** spreading. **6** extent. **7** *informal* large meal. **8** soft food which can be spread. **spread-eagled** *adj* with arms and legs outstretched. **spreadsheet** *n* computer program for manipulating figures.

spree ❶ *n* session of overindulgence, usu. in drinking or spending money.

sprig *n* **1** twig or shoot.

sprightly ❶ *adj* **-lier**, **-liest** lively and brisk. **sprightliness** *n*.

——————————————————————————— THESAURUS ———————

spot *n* **1** = **mark**, blemish, blot, blotch, scar, smudge, speck, speckle, stain **2** = **pimple**, pustule, zit (*sl*) **3** = **place**, location, point, position, scene, site **5** *Inf* = **predicament**, difficulty, hot water (*inf*), mess, plight, quandary, tight spot, trouble ▷ *v* **6** = **see**, catch sight of, detect, discern, espy, make out, observe, recognize, sight **7** = **mark**, dirty, fleck, mottle, smirch, soil, spatter, speckle, splodge, splotch, stain

spouse *n* = **partner**, consort, husband *or* wife, mate, significant other (*US inf*)

spout *v* **1** = **stream**, discharge, gush, shoot, spray, spurt, surge

sprawl *v* **1** = **loll**, flop, lounge, slouch, slump **2** = **spread**, ramble, straggle, trail

spray¹ *n* **1 a** = **aerosol**, atomizer, sprinkler

b = **droplets**, drizzle, fine mist ▷ *v* **2** = **scatter**, diffuse, shower, sprinkle

spray² *n* **1** = **sprig**, branch **2** = **corsage**, floral arrangement

spread *v* **1** = **open (out)**, broaden, dilate, expand, extend, sprawl, stretch, unfold, unroll, widen **4** = **circulate**, broadcast, disseminate, make known, propagate ▷ *n* **5** = **increase**, advance, development, dispersal, dissemination, expansion, proliferation **6** = **extent**, span, stretch, sweep

spree *n* = **binge** (*inf*), bacchanalia, bender (*inf*), carousal, fling, orgy, revel

sprightly *adj* = **lively**, active, agile, brisk, energetic, nimble, spirited, spry, vivacious

spring ❶ v **springing**, **sprang** or **sprung**, **sprung 1** move suddenly upwards or forwards in a single motion, jump. **2** develop unexpectedly. **3** originate (from). **4** *informal* arrange the escape of (someone) from prison. ▷ n **5** season between winter and summer. **6** jump. **7** coil which can be compressed, stretched, or bent and returns to its original shape when released. **8** natural pool forming the source of a stream. **9** elasticity. **springy** *adj* elastic. **springboard** n flexible board used to gain height or momentum in diving or gymnastics. **spring-clean** v clean (a house) thoroughly.
springbok n S African antelope.
sprinkle ❶ v scatter (liquid or powder) in tiny drops or particles over (something). **sprinkler** n **sprinkling** n small quantity or number.
sprint ❶ n **1** short race run at top speed. **2** fast run. ▷ v **3** run a short distance at top speed. **sprinter** n.
sprite ❶ n elf.
sprocket n wheel with teeth on the rim, that drives or is driven by a chain.
sprout ❶ v **1** put forth shoots. **2** begin to

grow or develop. ▷ n **3** shoot. **4** short for BRUSSELS SPROUT.
spruce¹ n kind of fir.
spruce² ❶ *adj* neat and smart. **spruce up** v make neat and smart.
spry ❶ *adj* **spryer**, **spryest** or **sprier**, **spriest** active or nimble.
spur ❶ n **1** stimulus or incentive. **2** spiked wheel on the heel of a rider's boot used to urge on a horse. **3** projection. ▷ v **spurring**, **spurred 1** urge on, incite (someone). **on the spur of the moment** on impulse.
spurious ❶ *adj* not genuine.
spurn ❶ v reject with scorn.
spurt ❶ v **1** gush or cause to gush out in a jet. ▷ n **2** short sudden burst of activity or speed. **3** sudden gush.
spy ❶ n, pl **spies 1** person employed to obtain secret information. **2** person who secretly watches others. ▷ v **spying**, **spied 3** act as a spy. **4** catch sight of.
squabble ❶ v, n (engage in) a petty or noisy quarrel.
squad ❶ n small group of people working or training together.

—— THESAURUS ——

spring v **1** = **jump**, bounce, bound, leap, vault **2** = **appear**, develop, mushroom, shoot up **3** = **originate**, arise, come, derive, descend, issue, proceed, start, stem ▷ n **6** = **jump**, bound, leap, vault **9** = **elasticity**, bounce, buoyancy, flexibility, resilience
sprinkle v = **scatter**, dredge, dust, pepper, powder, shower, spray, strew
sprint v **3** = **race**, dart, dash, hare (*Brit inf*), shoot, tear
sprout v **1, 2** = **grow**, bud, develop, shoot, spring
spruce² *adj* = **smart**, dapper, natty (*inf*), neat, trim, well-groomed, well turned out
spry *adj* = **active**, agile, nimble, sprightly, supple
spur n **1** = **stimulus**, impetus, impulse, incentive, incitement, inducement, motive **2** = **goad**, prick ▷ v **4** = **incite**,

animate, drive, goad, impel, prick, prod, prompt, stimulate, urge **on the spur of the moment** = **on impulse**, impromptu, impulsively, on the spot, without planning
spurious *adj* = **false**, artificial, bogus, fake, phoney or phony (*inf*), pretended, sham, specious, unauthentic
spurn v = **reject**, despise, disdain, rebuff, repulse, scorn, slight, snub
spurt v **1** = **gush**, burst, erupt, shoot, squirt, surge ▷ n **2** = **burst**, fit, rush, spate, surge
spy n **1** = **undercover agent**, mole, nark (*Brit, Aust & NZ sl*), ▷ v **4** = **catch sight of**, espy, glimpse, notice, observe, spot
squabble v = **quarrel**, argue, bicker, dispute, fight, row, wrangle ▷ n = **quarrel**, argument, disagreement, dispute, fight, row, tiff
squad n = **team**, band, company, crew, force, gang, group, troop

S

squalid ❶ *adj* **1** dirty and unpleasant.
2 morally sordid. **squalor** *n* disgusting dirt and filth.

squall¹ *n* sudden strong wind.

squall² *v* **1** cry noisily, yell. ▷ *n* **2** harsh cry.

squander ❶ *v* waste (money or resources).

square ❶ *n* **1** geometric figure with four equal sides and four right angles. **2** open area in a town in this shape. **3** product of a number multiplied by itself. ▷ *adj* **4** square in shape. **5** denoting a measure of area. **6** straight or level. **7** fair and honest. **8** with all accounts or debts settled. ▷ *v* **9** multiply (a number) by itself. **10** make square. **11** be or cause to be consistent. ▷ *adv* **12** squarely, directly. **squarely** *adv* **1** in a direct way. **2** in an honest and frank manner. **square meal** substantial meal. **square root** number of which a given number is the square. **square up to** *v* prepare to confront (a person or problem).

squash¹ ❶ *v* **1** crush flat. **2** suppress. **3** push into a confined space. **4** humiliate with a crushing retort. ▷ *n* **5** sweet fruit drink diluted with water. **6** crowd of people in a confined space.

squash² *n* marrow-like vegetable.

squat *v* **squatting, squatted** **1** crouch with the knees bent and the weight on the feet. **2** occupy unused premises to which

one has no legal right. ▷ *n* **3** place where squatters live. ▷ *adj* **4** short and broad. **squatter** *n* illegal occupier of unused premises.

squawk ❶ *n* **1** loud harsh cry. ▷ *v* **2** utter a squawk.

squeak ❶ *n* **1** short shrill cry or sound. ▷ *v* **2** make or utter a squeak. **squeaky** *adj*.

squeal ❶ *n* **1** long shrill cry or sound. ▷ *v* **2** make or utter a squeal. **3** *slang* inform on someone to the police.

squeamish ❶ *adj* easily sickened or shocked.

squeeze ❶ *v* **1** grip or press firmly. **2** crush or press to extract liquid. **3** push into a confined space. **4** hug. **5** obtain (something) by force or great effort. ▷ *n* **6** squeezing. **7** amount extracted by squeezing. **8** hug. **9** crush of people in a confined space. **10** restriction on borrowing.

squelch *v* **1** make a wet sucking sound, as by walking through mud. ▷ *n* **2** squelching sound.

squid *n* sea creature with a long soft body and ten tentacles.

squiggle *n* wavy line.

squint ❶ *v* **1** have eyes which face in different directions. **2** glance sideways. ▷ *n* **3** squinting condition of the eye. **4** *informal* glance. ▷ *adj* **5** crooked.

━━━━━━━━━━━━━━━━━━━━━━━━━━━━━━ THESAURUS ━━━━━

S

squalid *adj* = **dirty**, filthy, scungy (*Aust & NZ sl*), seedy, sleazy, slummy, sordid, unclean

squander *v* = **waste**, blow (*sl*), expend, fritter away, misspend, misuse, spend

square *adj* **7** = **honest**, above board, ethical, fair, genuine, kosher (*inf*), on the level (*inf*), straight ▷ *v* **11** = **even up**, level **14** = **match**, agree, correspond, fit, reconcile, tally

squash¹ *v* **1** = **crush**, compress, distort, flatten, mash, press, pulp, smash **4** = **suppress**, annihilate, crush, humiliate, quell, silence

squawk *n, v* = **cry**, hoot, screech

squeak *v* **2** = **peep**, pipe, squeal

squeal *n* **1** = **scream**, screech, shriek, wail, yell ▷ *v* **2** = **scream**, screech, shriek, wail, yell

squeamish *adj* = **fastidious**, delicate, nauseous, prudish, queasy, sick, strait-laced

squeeze *v* **1** = **press**, clutch, compress, crush, grip, pinch, squash, wring **3** = **cram**, crowd, force, jam, pack, press, ram, stuff **4** = **hug**, clasp, cuddle, embrace, enfold **5** = **extort**, milk, pressurize, wrest ▷ *n* **8** = **hug**, clasp, embrace **9** = **crush**, congestion, crowd, jam, press, squash

squint *adj* **5** = **crooked**, askew, aslant, awry, cockeyed, skew-whiff (*inf*)

squire n 1 country gentleman, usu. the main landowner in a community. 2 *Hist* knight's apprentice.

squirm ● v 1 wriggle, writhe. 2 feel embarrassed. ▷ n 3 wriggling movement.

squirrel n small bushy-tailed tree-living animal.

squirt v 1 force (a liquid) or (of a liquid) be forced out of a narrow opening. 2 squirt liquid at. ▷ n 3 jet of liquid. 4 *informal* small or insignificant person.

st. stone (weight).

stab ● v **stabbing**, **stabbed** 1 pierce with something pointed. 2 jab (at). ▷ n 3 stabbing. 4 sudden unpleasant sensation. 5 *informal* attempt.

stabilize v make or become stable. **stabilization** n **stabilizer** n device for stabilizing a child's bicycle, an aircraft, or a ship.

stable¹ ● n 1 building in which horses are kept. 2 establishment that breeds and trains racehorses. 3 establishment that manages or trains several entertainers or athletes. ▷ v 4 put or keep (a horse) in a stable.

stable² ● adj 1 firmly fixed or established. 2 firm in character. 3 *Science* not subject to decay or decomposition. **stability** n.

staccato [stak-**ah**-toe] adj, adv 1 *Music* with the notes sharply separated. ▷ adj 2 consisting of short abrupt sounds.

stack ● n 1 ordered pile. 2 large amount. 3 chimney. ▷ v 4 pile in a stack. 5 control (aircraft waiting to land) so that they fly at different altitudes.

stadium n, pl **-diums**, **-dia** sports arena with tiered seats for spectators.

staff ● n 1 people employed in an organization. 2 stick used as a weapon, support, etc. ▷ v 3 supply with personnel. **staff nurse** qualified nurse of the rank below a sister.

stag n adult male deer. **stag night, party** party for men only.

stage ● n 1 step or period of development. 2 platform in a theatre where actors perform. 3 portion of a journey. ▷ v 4 put (a play) on stage. 5 organize and carry out (an event). **the stage** theatre as a profession. **stagecoach** n large horse-drawn vehicle formerly used to carry passengers and mail. **stage fright** nervousness felt by a person about to face an audience. **stage whisper** loud whisper intended to be heard by an audience.

stagger ● v 1 walk unsteadily. 2 astound. 3 set apart to avoid congestion. ▷ n 4 staggering.

staid ● adj sedate, serious, and rather dull.

stain ● v 1 discolour, mark. 2 colour with a penetrating pigment. ▷ n 3 discoloration or mark. 4 moral blemish or slur. 5 penetrating liquid used to colour things.

THESAURUS

squirm v 1 = **wriggle**, twist, writhe

stab v 1 = **pierce**, impale, jab, knife, spear, stick, thrust, transfix, wound ▷ n 3 = **wound**, gash, incision, jab, puncture, thrust 4 = **twinge**, ache, pang, prick 5 *Inf* = **attempt**, endeavour, go, try

stable² adj 1 = **firm**, constant, established, fast, fixed, immovable, lasting, permanent, secure, sound, strong 2 = **steady**, reliable, staunch, steadfast, sure

stack n 1, 2 = **pile**, berg (*SAfr*), heap, load, mass, mound, mountain ▷ v 4 = **pile**, accumulate, amass, assemble, heap up, load

staff n 1 = **workers**, employees, personnel, team, workforce 2 = **stick**, cane, crook, pole, rod, sceptre, stave, wand

stage n 1 = **step**, division, juncture, lap, leg, level, period, phase, point

stagger v 1 = **totter**, lurch, reel, sway, wobble 2 = **astound**, amaze, astonish, confound, overwhelm, shake, shock, stun, stupefy 3 = **alternate**, overlap, step

staid adj = **sedate**, calm, composed, grave, serious, sober, solemn, steady

stain v 1 = **mark**, blemish, blot, dirty, discolour, smirch, soil, spot, tinge 2 = **dye**, colour, tint ▷ n 3 = **mark**, blemish, blot,

S

stainless adj **stainless steel** steel alloy that does not rust.

stairs pl n flight of steps between floors, usu. indoors. **staircase**, **stairway** n flight of stairs with a handrail or banisters.

stake¹ ❶ n 1 pointed stick or post driven into the ground as a support or marker. ▷ v 2 support or mark out with stakes. **stake a claim to** claim a right to. **stake out** v slang (of police) keep (a place) under surveillance.

stake² ❶ n 1 money wagered. 2 interest, usu. financial, held in something. ▷ pl 3 prize in a race or contest. ▷ v 4 wager, risk. 5 support financially. **at stake** being risked. **stakeholder** n person who has a concern or interest in something, esp. a business.

stalactite n lime deposit hanging from the roof of a cave.

stalagmite n lime deposit sticking up from the floor of a cave.

stale ❶ adj 1 not fresh. 2 lacking energy or ideas through overwork or monotony. 3 uninteresting from overuse.

stalk¹ n plant's stem.

stalk² ❶ v 1 follow or approach stealthily. 2 pursue persistently and, sometimes, attack (a person with whom one is obsessed). 3 walk in a stiff or haughty manner. **stalking-horse** n pretext.

stall¹ ❶ n 1 small stand for the display and sale of goods. 2 compartment in a stable. 3 small room or compartment. ▷ pl 4 ground-floor seats in a theatre or cinema. 5 row of seats in a church for the choir or clergy. ▷ v 6 stop (a motor vehicle or engine) or (of a motor vehicle or engine) stop accidentally.

stall² ❶ v employ delaying tactics.

stallion n uncastrated male horse.

stalwart [**stawl**-wart] adj 1 strong and sturdy. 2 dependable. ▷ n 3 stalwart person.

stamina ❶ n enduring energy and strength.

stammer ❶ v 1 speak or say with involuntary pauses or repetition of syllables. ▷ n 2 tendency to stammer.

stamp ❶ n 1 (also **postage stamp**) piece of gummed paper stuck to an envelope or parcel to show that the postage has been paid. 2 act of stamping. 3 instrument for stamping a pattern or mark. 4 pattern or mark stamped. 5 characteristic feature. ▷ v 6 bring (one's foot) down forcefully. 7 walk with heavy footsteps. 8 characterize. 9 impress (a pattern or mark) on. 10 stick a postage stamp on. **stamping ground** favourite meeting place. **stamp out** v suppress by force.

stampede ❶ n 1 sudden rush of frightened animals or of a crowd. ▷ v 2 (cause to) take part in a stampede.

discoloration, smirch, spot 4 = **stigma**, disgrace, dishonour, shame, slur 5 = **dye**, colour, tint

stake¹ n 1 = **pole**, pale, paling, palisade, picket, post, stick

stake² n 1 = **bet**, ante, pledge, wager 2 = **interest**, concern, investment, involvement, share ▷ v 4 = **bet**, chance, gamble, hazard, risk, venture, wager

stale adj 1 = **old**, decayed, dry, flat, fusty, hard, musty, sour 2, 3 = **unoriginal**, banal, hackneyed, overused, stereotyped, threadbare, trite, worn-out

stalk² v 1, 2 = **pursue**, follow, haunt, hunt, shadow, track

stall² v = **play for time**, hedge, temporize

stalwart adj 1 = **strong**, stout, strapping, sturdy 2 = **loyal**, dependable, reliable, staunch

stamina n = **staying power**, endurance, energy, force, power, resilience, strength

stammer v 1 = **stutter**, falter, hesitate, pause, stumble

stamp n 5 = **imprint**, brand, earmark, hallmark, mark, signature ▷ v 6 = **trample**, crush 8 = **identify**, brand, categorize, label, mark, reveal, show to be 9 = **imprint**, impress, mark, print

stampede n 1 = **rush**, charge, flight, rout

stance ❶ n 1 attitude. 2 manner of standing.

stanch ❶ [stahnch] v same as STAUNCH².

stanchion n upright bar used as a support.

stand ❶ v standing, stood 1 be in, rise to, or place in an upright position. 2 be situated. 3 be in a specified state or position. 4 remain unchanged or valid. 5 tolerate. 6 offer oneself as a candidate. 7 informal treat to. ▷ n 8 stall for the sale of goods. 9 structure for spectators at a sports ground. 10 firmly held opinion. 11 US & Aust witness box. 12 rack or piece of furniture on which things may be placed. **standing** adj 1 permanent, lasting. ▷ n 2 reputation or status. 3 duration. **stand for** v 1 represent or mean. 2 informal tolerate. **stand in** v act as a substitute. **stand-in** n substitute. **standoffish** adj reserved or haughty. **stand up for** v support or defend.

standard ❶ n 1 level of quality. 2 example against which others are judged or measured. 3 moral principle. 4 distinctive flag. 5 upright pole. ▷ adj 6 usual, regular, or average. 7 of recognized authority. 8 accepted as correct. **standardize** v cause to conform to a standard. **standardization** n.

standpipe n tap attached to a water main to provide a public water supply.

standpoint ❶ n point of view.

standstill n complete halt.

stanza n verse of a poem.

staple n 1 U-shaped piece of metal used to fasten papers or secure things. ▷ v 2 fasten with staples. **stapler** n small device for fastening papers together.

star ❶ n 1 hot gaseous mass in space, visible in the night sky as a point of light. 2 star-shaped mark used to indicate excellence. 3 asterisk. 4 celebrity in the entertainment or sports world. ▷ pl 5 astrological forecast, horoscope. ▷ v **starring, starred** 6 feature or be featured as a star. 7 mark with a star or stars. ▷ adj 8 leading, famous. **stardom** n status of a star in the entertainment or sports world. **starry** adj full of or like stars. **starry-eyed** adj full of naive optimism. **starfish** n star-shaped sea creature.

starboard n 1 right-hand side of a ship, when facing forward. ▷ adj 2 of or on this side.

starch n 1 carbohydrate forming the main food element in bread, potatoes, etc., and used mixed with water for stiffening fabric. ▷ v 2 stiffen (fabric) with starch. **starchy** adj 1 containing starch. 2 stiff and formal.

——————————— THESAURUS ———————————

stance n 1 = **attitude**, position, stand, standpoint, viewpoint 2 = **posture**, bearing, carriage, deportment

stanch see STAUNCH².

stand v 1 a = **be upright**, be erect, be vertical, rise b = **put**, mount, place, position, set 4 = **exist**, be valid, continue, hold, obtain, prevail, remain 5 = **tolerate**, abide, allow, bear, brook, countenance, endure, handle, put up with (inf), stomach, take ▷ n 8 = **stall**, booth, table 10 = **position**, attitude, determination, opinion, stance 12 = **support**, base, bracket, dais, platform, rack, stage, tripod

standard n 1 = **level**, gauge, grade, measure 2 = **criterion**, average, benchmark, example, guideline, model, norm, yardstick 3 = **principles**, ethics, ideals, morals 4 = **flag**, banner, ensign ▷ adj 6 = **usual**, average, basic, customary, normal, orthodox, regular, typical 7, 8 = **accepted**, approved, authoritative, definitive, established, official, recognized

standpoint n = **point of view**, angle, position, stance, viewpoint

star n 1 = **heavenly body** 4 = **celebrity**, big name, luminary, main attraction, megastar (inf), name ▷ adj 8 = **leading**, brilliant, celebrated, major, prominent, well-known

S

stare ❶ v 1 look or gaze fixedly (at). ▷ n
2 fixed gaze.
stark ❶ adj 1 harsh, unpleasant, and
plain. 2 desolate, bare. 3 absolute. ▷ adv
4 completely.
starling n songbird with glossy black
speckled feathers.
start ❶ v 1 take the first step, begin. 2 set
or be set in motion. 3 make a sudden
involuntary movement from fright.
4 establish or set up. ▷ n 5 first part of
something. 6 place or time of starting.
7 advantage or lead in a competitive
activity. 8 sudden movement made
from fright. **starter** n 1 first course of a
meal. 2 device for starting a car's engine.
3 person who signals the start of a race.
start-up n recently launched project or
business enterprise.
startle ❶ v slightly surprise or frighten.
starve v 1 die or suffer or cause to die
or suffer from hunger. 2 deprive of
something needed. **starvation** n.
stash informal ▷ v 1 store in a secret place.
▷ n 2 secret store.
state ❶ n 1 condition of a person or thing.
2 sovereign political power or its territory.

3 (**S-**) the government. 4 informal excited or
agitated condition. 5 pomp. ▷ adj 6 of or
concerning the State. 7 involving ceremony.
▷ v 8 express in words. **stately** adj dignified
or grand. **statehouse** n NZ publicly-owned
house rented to a low-income tenant.
statement n 1 something stated. 2 printed
financial account. **stateroom** n 1 private
cabin on a ship. 2 large room in a palace,
used for ceremonial occasions. **statesman**,
stateswoman n experienced and respected
political leader. **statesmanship** n.
static ❶ adj 1 stationary or inactive. 2 (of a
force) acting but producing no movement.
▷ n 3 crackling sound or speckled
picture caused by interference in radio
or television reception. 4 (also **static
electricity**) electric sparks produced by
friction.
station ❶ n 1 place where trains stop
for passengers. 2 headquarters or local
offices of the police or a fire brigade.
3 building with special equipment for
a particular purpose, e.g. power station.
4 television or radio channel. 5 position
in society. ▷ v 6 assign (someone) to a
particular place.

──────────────────────────── THESAURUS ──────

stare v 1 = **gaze**, eyeball (sl), gape, gawk,
gawp (Brit sl), goggle, look, watch
stark adj 1, 2 = **harsh**, austere, bare,
barren, bleak, grim, hard, plain, severe
3 = **absolute**, blunt, downright, out-and-
out, pure, sheer, unmitigated, utter ▷ adv
4 = **absolutely**, altogether, completely,
entirely, quite, utterly, wholly
start v 1 = **begin**, appear, arise, commence,
embark upon, issue, make a beginning,
originate, set about, take the first step
2 = **set in motion**, activate, get going,
initiate, instigate, kick-start, open,
originate, trigger 3 = **jump**, flinch,
jerk, recoil, shy 4 = **establish**, begin,
create, found, inaugurate, initiate,
institute, launch, pioneer, set up ▷ n 5,
6 = **beginning**, birth, dawn, foundation,
inception, initiation, onset, opening,

outset 7 = **advantage**, edge, head start,
lead 8 = **jump**, convulsion, spasm
startle v = **surprise**, frighten, make
(someone) jump, scare, shock
state n 1 = **condition**, attitude,
circumstances, equation, frame of mind,
humour, mood, position, predicament,
shape, situation, spirits 2 = **country**,
commonwealth, federation, kingdom, land,
nation, republic, territory 5 = **ceremony**,
display, glory, grandeur, majesty, pomp,
splendour, style ▷ v 8 = **express**, affirm,
articulate, assert, declare, expound,
present, say, specify, utter, voice
static adj 1 = **stationary**, fixed, immobile,
motionless, still, unmoving
station n 2 = **headquarters**, base, depot
5 = **position**, post, rank, situation,
standing, status ▷ v 6 = **assign**, establish,

● SPELLING TIP
● The words **stationary** and **stationery**
● are completely different in meaning and
● should not be confused.

station wagon n US & Canad automobile with a rear door and luggage space behind the rear seats.

statue n large sculpture of a human or animal figure. **statuary** n statues collectively. **statuesque** adj (of a woman) tall and well-proportioned. **statuette** n small statue.

stature ❶ n 1 person's height. 2 reputation of a person or their achievements.

status ❶ n 1 social position. 2 prestige. 3 person's legal standing. **status quo** existing state of affairs.

statute n written law. **statutory** adj required or authorized by law.

staunch¹ ❶ adj loyal, firm.

staunch², stanch ❶ v stop (a flow of blood).

stave n 1 one of the strips of wood forming a barrel. 2 Music same as STAFF². **stave in** v **staving, stove** burst a hole in. **stave off** v **staving, staved** ward off.

stay¹ ❶ v 1 remain in a place or condition. 2 reside temporarily. 3 endure. ▷ n 4 period of staying in a place.

5 postponement. **staying power** stamina.

stay² ❶ n 1 prop or buttress. ▷ pl 2 corset.

stead n **in someone's stead** in someone's place. **stand someone in good stead** be useful to someone.

steady ❶ adj **steadier, steadiest** 1 not shaky or wavering. 2 regular or continuous. 3 sensible and dependable. ▷ v **steadying, steadied** 4 make steady. ▷ adv 5 in a steady manner. **steadily** adv **steadiness** n.

steak n 1 thick slice of meat, esp. beef. 2 slice of fish.

steal ❶ v **stealing, stole, stolen** 1 take unlawfully or without permission. 2 move stealthily.

stealth ❶ n secret or underhand behaviour. ▷ adj 1 (of technology) able to render an aircraft almost invisible to radar. 2 disguised or hidden, stealth taxes. **stealthy** adj **stealthily** adv.

steam n 1 vapour into which water changes when boiled. 2 power, energy, or speed. ▷ v 3 give off steam. 4 (of a vehicle) move by steam power. 5 cook or treat with steam. **steamer** n 1 steam-propelled ship. 2 container used to cook food in steam. **steam engine** engine worked by steam. **steamroller** n 1 steam-powered

---

THESAURUS

install, locate, post, set

stature n 2 = **importance**, eminence, prestige, prominence, rank, standing

status n 1, 2 = **position**, condition, consequence, eminence, grade, prestige, rank, standing

staunch¹ adj 1 = **loyal**, faithful, firm, sound, stalwart, steadfast, true, trusty

staunch², stanch v = **stop**, check, dam, halt, stay, stem

stay¹ v 1 = **remain**, abide, continue, halt, linger, loiter, pause, stop, tarry, wait ▷ n 4 = **visit**, holiday, sojourn, stop, stopover 5 = **postponement**, deferment, delay, halt, stopping, suspension

stay² n 1 = **support**, brace, buttress, prop,

reinforcement, shoring, stanchion

steady adj 1 = **firm**, fixed, safe, secure, stable 2 = **continuous**, ceaseless, consistent, constant, incessant, nonstop, persistent, regular, unbroken, uninterrupted 3 = **dependable**, balanced, calm, equable, level-headed, reliable, sensible, sober ▷ v 4 = **stabilize**, brace, secure, support

steal v 1 = **take**, appropriate, embezzle, filch, lift (inf), misappropriate, nick (sl, chiefly Brit), pilfer, pinch (inf), purloin, thieve 2 = **sneak**, creep, slink, slip, tiptoe

stealth n = **secrecy**, furtiveness, slyness, sneakiness, stealthiness, surreptitiousness, unobtrusiveness

S

vehicle with heavy rollers, used to level road surfaces. ▷ v **2** use overpowering force to make (someone) do what one wants.

steed n lit horse.

steel n **1** hard malleable alloy of iron and carbon. **2** steel rod used for sharpening knives. **3** hardness of character or attitude. ▷ v **4** prepare (oneself) for something unpleasant. **steely** adj.

steep¹ ⓘ adj **1** sloping sharply. **2** informal (of a price) unreasonably high.

steep² ⓘ v soak or be soaked in liquid. **steeped in** filled with.

steeple n church tower with a spire. **steeplejack** n person who repairs steeples and chimneys.

steer¹ ⓘ v **1** direct the course of (a vehicle or ship). **2** direct (one's course). **steerage** n cheapest accommodation on a passenger ship.

steer² n castrated male ox.

stellar adj of stars.

stem¹ ⓘ n **1** long thin central part of a plant. **2** long slender part, as of a wineglass. **3** part of a word to which inflections are added. ▷ v **stemming, stemmed 4 stem from** originate from.

stem² ⓘ v **stemming, stemmed** stop (the flow of something).

stench ⓘ n foul smell.

stencil n **1** thin sheet with cut-out pattern through which ink or paint passes to form the pattern on the surface below. **2** pattern made thus. ▷ v **-cilling, -cilled 3** make (a pattern) with a stencil.

step ⓘ v **stepping, stepped 1** move and set down the foot, as when walking. **2** walk a short distance. ▷ n **3** stepping. **4** distance covered by a step. **5** sound made by stepping. **6** foot movement in a dance. **7** one of a sequence of actions taken in order to achieve a goal. **8** degree in a series or scale. **9** flat surface for placing the foot on when going up or down. ▷ pl **10** stepladder. **step in** v intervene. **stepladder** n folding portable ladder with supporting frame. **stepping stone 1** one of a series of stones for stepping on in crossing a stream. **2** means of progress towards a goal. **step up** v increase (something) by stages.

stereophonic adj using two separate loudspeakers to give the effect of naturally distributed sound.

stereotype ⓘ n **1** standardized idea of a type of person or thing. ▷ v **2** form a stereotype of.

sterile ⓘ adj **1** free from germs. **2** unable to produce offspring or seeds. **3** lacking inspiration or vitality. **sterility** n **sterilize** v make sterile. **sterilization** n.

— THESAURUS —

s

steep¹ adj **1** = **sheer**, abrupt, precipitous **2** Inf = **high**, exorbitant, extortionate, extreme, overpriced, unreasonable

steep² v = **soak**, drench, immerse, marinate (Cookery), moisten, souse, submerge **steeped in** = **saturated**, filled with, imbued, infused, permeated, pervaded, suffused

steer¹ v **1** = **drive**, control, direct, guide, handle, pilot

stem¹ n **1** = **stalk**, axis, branch, shoot, trunk ▷ v **4 stem from** = **originate from**, arise from, be caused by, derive from

stem² v = **stop**, check, curb, dam, hold back, staunch

stench n = **stink**, foul smell, pong (Brit inf), reek, whiff (Brit sl)

step v **1** = **walk**, move, pace, tread ▷ n **3** = **footstep**, footfall, footprint, pace, print, stride, track **7** = **action**, act, deed, expedient, means, measure, move **8** = **degree**, level, rank

stereotype n **1** = **formula**, pattern ▷ v **2** = **categorize**, pigeonhole, standardize, typecast

sterile adj **1** = **germ-free**, aseptic, disinfected, sterilized **2** = **barren**, bare, dry, empty, fruitless, unfruitful, unproductive

sterling ❶ n 1 British money system. ▷ adj 2 genuine and reliable.

stern¹ ❶ adj severe, strict.

stern² n rear part of a ship.

sternum n, pl **-na**, **-nums** same as BREASTBONE.

steroid n organic compound containing a carbon ring system, such as many hormones.

stethoscope n medical instrument for listening to sounds made inside the body.

stew n 1 food cooked slowly in a closed pot. 2 informal troubled or worried state. ▷ v 3 cook slowly in a closed pot.

steward n 1 person who looks after passengers on a ship or aircraft. 2 official who helps at a public event such as a race. 3 person who administers another's property. **stewardess** n fem.

stick¹ ❶ n 1 long thin piece of wood. 2 such a piece of wood shaped for a special purpose, e.g. hockey stick. 3 something like a stick, e.g. stick of celery. 4 slang verbal abuse, criticism. **the sticks** informal remote country area. **stick insect** tropical insect resembling a twig.

stick² ❶ v **sticking**, **stuck** 1 push (a pointed object) into (something). 2 fasten or be fastened by or as if by pins or glue. 3 (foll. by out) extend beyond something else, protrude. 4 informal put. 5 jam. 6 come to a standstill. 7 remain for a long time. 8 slang tolerate, abide. **sticker** n adhesive label or sign. **sticky** adj 1 covered with an adhesive substance. 2 informal difficult, unpleasant. 3 (of weather) warm and humid. **stick around** v informal remain in a place. **stick-in-the-mud** n person who does not like anything new. **stick-up** n slang robbery at gunpoint. **stick up for** v informal support or defend.

stickleback n small fish with sharp spines on its back.

stickler ❶ n person who insists on something, e.g. stickler for detail.

stiff ❶ adj 1 not easily bent or moved. 2 severe, e.g. stiff punishment. 3 unrelaxed or awkward. 4 firm in consistency. 5 strong, e.g. a stiff drink. ▷ n 6 slang corpse. **stiffly** adv **stiffness** n **stiffen** v make or become stiff. **stiff-necked** adj haughtily stubborn.

stifle ❶ v 1 suppress. 2 suffocate.

stigma ❶ n, pl **-mas**, **-mata** 1 mark of social disgrace. 2 part of a plant that receives pollen. **stigmata** pl n marks resembling the wounds of the crucified Christ. **stigmatize** v mark as being shameful.

---

sterling adj 2 = **excellent**, fine, genuine, sound, superlative, true

stern¹ adj = **severe**, austere, forbidding, grim, hard, harsh, inflexible, rigid, serious, strict

stick¹ n 1, 2 = **cane**, baton, crook, pole, rod, staff, twig 4 Sl = **abuse**, criticism, flak (inf)

stick² v 1 = **poke**, dig, jab, penetrate, pierce, prod, puncture, spear, stab, thrust, transfix 2 = **fasten**, adhere, affix, attach, bind, bond, cling, fix, glue, hold, join, paste, weld 3 (foll. by out) = **protrude**, bulge, extend, jut, obtrude, poke, project, show 4 Inf = **put**, deposit, lay, place, set 7 = **stay**, linger, persist, remain 8 Sl = **tolerate**, abide, stand, stomach, take

stickler n = **fanatic**, fusspot (Brit inf), perfectionist, purist

stiff adj 1 = **inflexible**, firm, hard, inelastic, rigid, solid, taut, tense, tight, unbending, unyielding 2 = **severe**, drastic, extreme, hard, harsh, heavy, strict 3 = **awkward**, clumsy, constrained, forced, formal, graceless, inelegant, jerky (inf), stilted, ungainly, ungraceful, unnatural, unrelaxed

stifle v 1 = **suppress**, check, hush, repress, restrain, silence, smother, stop 2 = **suffocate**, asphyxiate, choke, smother, strangle

stigma n 1 = **disgrace**, dishonour, shame, slur, smirch, stain

S

stile n set of steps allowing people to climb a fence.

still¹ ⊙ adv **1** now or in the future as before. **2** up to this or that time. **3** even or yet, e.g. *still more insults*. **4** quietly or without movement. ▷ adj **5** motionless. **6** silent and calm, undisturbed. **7** (of a drink) not fizzy. ▷ n **8** photograph from a film scene. ▷ v **9** make still. **stillness** n **stillborn** adj born dead. **still life** painting of inanimate objects.

still² n apparatus for distilling alcoholic drinks.

stimulus ⊙ n, pl **-li** something that rouses a person or thing to activity. **stimulant** n something, such as a drug, that acts as a stimulus. **stimulate** v act as a stimulus (on). **stimulation** n.

sting ⊙ v **stinging, stung 1** (of certain animals or plants) wound by injecting with poison. **2** feel or cause to feel sharp physical or mental pain. **3** slang cheat (someone) by overcharging. ▷ n **4** wound or pain caused by or as if by stinging. **5** mental pain. **6** sharp pointed organ of certain animals or plants by which poison can be injected.

stingy ⊙ adj **-gier, -giest** mean or miserly. **stinginess** n.

stink ⊙ n **1** strong unpleasant smell.

2 slang unpleasant fuss. ▷ v **stinking, stank** or **stunk, stunk 3** give off a strong unpleasant smell. **4** slang be very unpleasant.

stint ⊙ v **1** (foll. by on) be miserly with (something). ▷ n **2** allotted amount of work.

stipulate ⊙ v specify as a condition of an agreement. **stipulation** n.

stir ⊙ v **stirring, stirred 1** mix up (a liquid) by moving a spoon etc. around in it. **2** move. **3** excite or stimulate (a person) emotionally. ▷ n **4** a stirring. **5** strong reaction, usu. of excitement.

stirrup n metal loop attached to a saddle for supporting a rider's foot.

stitch n **1** link made by drawing thread through material with a needle. **2** loop of yarn formed round a needle or hook in knitting or crochet. **3** sharp pain in the side. ▷ v **4** sew. **in stitches** informal laughing uncontrollably. **not a stitch** informal no clothes at all.

stoat n small mammal of the weasel family, with brown fur that turns white in winter.

stock ⊙ n **1** total amount of goods available for sale in a shop. **2** supply stored for future use. **3** financial shares in, or capital of, a company.

───────────────────────────── THESAURUS ─────────────────────────────

still¹ adj **5 = motionless**, calm, peaceful, restful, serene, stationary, tranquil, undisturbed **6 = silent**, hushed, quiet ▷ v **9 = quieten**, allay, calm, hush, lull, pacify, quiet, settle, silence, soothe

stimulus n **= incentive**, encouragement, fillip, geeing-up, goad, impetus, incitement, inducement, spur

sting v **2 = hurt**, burn, pain, smart, tingle, wound **3** Sl **= cheat**, defraud, do (sl), fleece, overcharge, rip off (sl), swindle

stingy adj **= mean**, miserly, niggardly, parsimonious, penny-pinching (inf), tightfisted, ungenerous

stink n **1 = stench**, fetor, foul smell, pong (Brit inf) ▷ v **3 = reek**, pong (Brit inf)

stint v **1** (foll. by on) **= be mean**, be frugal, be sparing, hold back, skimp on ▷ n **2 = share**, period, quota, shift, spell, stretch, term, time, turn

stipulate v **= specify**, agree, contract, covenant, insist upon, require, settle

stir v **1 = mix**, agitate, beat, shake **3 = stimulate**, arouse, awaken, excite, incite, move, provoke, rouse, spur n **5 = commotion**, activity, bustle, disorder, disturbance, excitement, flurry, fuss

stock n **1 = goods**, array, choice, commodities, merchandise, range, selection, variety, wares **2 = supply**, fund, hoard, reserve, stockpile, store **3 = property**, assets, capital, funds,

4 livestock. **5** lineage. **6** handle of a rifle. **7** liquid produced by boiling meat, fish, bones, or vegetables. **8** fragrant flowering plant. **9** standing or status. ▷ pl **10** *Hist* instrument of punishment consisting of a wooden frame with holes into which the hands and feet of the victim were locked. ▷ adj **11** kept in stock, standard. **12** hackneyed. ▷ v **13** keep for sale or future use. **14** supply (a farm) with livestock or (a lake etc.) with fish. **stockist** n dealer who stocks a particular product. **stocky** adj (of a person) broad and sturdy. **stockbroker** n person who buys and sells stocks and shares for customers. **stock car** car modified for a form of racing in which the cars often collide. **stock exchange, market** institution for the buying and selling of shares. **stockpile** v **1** store a large quantity of (something) for future use. ▷ n **2** accumulated store. **stock-still** adj motionless. **stocktaking** n counting and valuing of the goods in a shop.

stockade n enclosure or barrier made of stakes.

stocking n close-fitting covering for the foot and leg.

stodgy 🟦 adj **stodgier, stodgiest 1** (of food) heavy and starchy. **2** (of a person) serious and boring. **stodge** n heavy starchy food.

stoep [stoop] n S Afr verandah.

stoic 🟦 [stow-ik] n **1** person who suffers hardship without showing his or her feelings. ▷ adj **2** (also **stoical**) suffering hardship without showing one's feelings. **stoically** adv **stoicism** [stow-iss-izz-um] n.

stoke v feed and tend (a fire or furnace). **stoker** n.

stole n long scarf or shawl.

stolid 🟦 adj showing little emotion or interest.

stomach 🟦 n **1** organ in the body which digests food. **2** front of the body around the waist. **3** desire or inclination. ▷ v **4** put up with.

stomp v informal tread heavily.

stone n **1** material of which rocks are made. **2** piece of this. **3** gem. **4** hard central part of a fruit. **5** unit of weight equal to 14 pounds or 6.350 kilograms. **6** hard deposit formed in the kidney or bladder. ▷ v **7** throw stones at. **8** remove stones from (a fruit). **stoned** adj slang under the influence of alcohol or drugs. **stony** adj **1** of or like stone. **2** unfeeling or hard. **stony-broke** adj slang completely penniless. **stonily** adv **stone-deaf** adj completely deaf. **stonewall** v obstruct or hinder discussion. **stoneware** n hard kind of pottery fired at a very high temperature.

stooge n **1** actor who feeds lines to a comedian or acts as the butt of his jokes. **2** slang person taken advantage of by a superior.

stool n **1** chair without arms or back. **2** piece of excrement.

S

investment **4** = **livestock**, beasts, cattle, domestic animals ▷ adj
11 = **standard**, conventional, customary, ordinary, regular, routine, usual
12 = **hackneyed**, banal, overused, trite ▷ v **13** = **sell**, deal in, handle, keep, supply, trade in **14** = **provide with**, equip, fit out, furnish, supply

stodgy adj **1** = **heavy**, filling, leaden, starchy **2** = **dull**, boring, fuddy-duddy (inf), heavy going, staid, stuffy, tedious,

unexciting

stoic adj **2** (also **stoical**) = **resigned**, dispassionate, impassive, long-suffering, philosophic, phlegmatic, stolid

stolid adj = **apathetic**, dull, lumpish, unemotional, wooden

stomach n **2** = **belly**, abdomen, gut (inf), pot, tummy (inf) **3** = **inclination**, appetite, desire, relish, taste ▷ v
4 = **bear**, abide, endure, swallow, take, tolerate

stoop ❶ v 1 bend (the body) forward and downward. 2 carry oneself habitually in this way. 3 degrade oneself. ▷ n 4 stooping posture.

stop ❶ v **stopping, stopped** 1 cease or cause to cease from doing (something). 2 bring to or come to a halt. 3 prevent or restrain. 4 withhold. 5 block or plug. 6 stay or rest. ▷ n 7 stopping or being stopped. 8 place where something stops. 9 full stop. 10 knob on an organ that is pulled out to allow a set of pipes to sound. **stoppage** n plug for closing a bottle etc. **stopcock** n valve to control or stop the flow of fluid in a pipe. **stopgap** n temporary substitute. **stopover** n short break in a journey. **stop press** news item put into a newspaper after printing has been started. **stopwatch** n watch which can be stopped instantly for exact timing of a sporting event.

store ❶ v 1 collect and keep (things) for future use. 2 put (furniture etc.) in a warehouse for safekeeping. 3 stock (goods). 4 Computers enter or retain (data). ▷ n 5 shop. 6 supply kept for future use. 7 storage place, such as a warehouse. ▷ pl 8 stock of provisions. **in store** about to happen. **set great store by** value greatly. **storage** n 1 storing. 2 space for storing.

storey n floor or level of a building.

stork n large wading bird.

storm ❶ n 1 violent weather with wind, rain, or snow. 2 strongly expressed reaction. ▷ v 3 attack or capture (a place) suddenly. 4 shout angrily. 5 rush violently or angrily. **stormy** adj 1 characterized by storms. 2 involving violent emotions.

story ❶ n, pl **-ries** 1 description of a series of events told or written for entertainment. 2 plot of a book or film. 3 news report. 4 informal lie.

stout ❶ adj 1 fat. 2 thick and strong. 3 brave and resolute. ▷ n 4 strong dark beer. **stoutly** adv.

stove n apparatus for cooking or heating.

stow ❶ v pack or store. **stowaway** n person who hides on a ship or aircraft in

stoop v 1 = **bend**, bow, crouch, duck, hunch, lean 3 = **lower oneself by**, descend to, resort to, sink to ▷ n 4 = **slouch**, bad posture

stop v 1, 2 = **halt**, cease, conclude, cut short, desist, discontinue, end, finish, pause, put an end to, quit, refrain, shut down, terminate 3 = **prevent**, arrest, forestall, hinder, hold back, impede, repress, restrain 5 = **plug**, block, obstruct, seal, staunch, stem 6 = **stay**, lodge, rest ▷ n 7 = **end**, cessation, finish, halt, standstill 8 = **station**, depot, terminus

store v 1, 2 = **put by**, deposit, garner, hoard, keep, put aside, reserve, save, stockpile ▷ n 5 = **shop**, market, mart, outlet 6 = **supply**, accumulation, cache, fund, hoard, quantity, reserve, stock, stockpile 7 = **repository**, depository, storeroom, warehouse

storm n 1 = **tempest**, blizzard, gale, hurricane, squall 2 = **outburst**, agitation, commotion, disturbance, furore, outbreak, outcry, row, rumpus, strife, tumult, turmoil ▷ v 3 = **attack**, assail, assault, charge, rush 4 = **rage**, bluster, rant, rave, thunder 5 = **rush**, flounce, fly, stamp

story n 1 = **tale**, account, anecdote, history, legend, narrative, romance, yarn 3 = **report**, article, feature, news, news item, scoop

stout adj 1 = **fat**, big, bulky, burly, corpulent, fleshy, heavy, overweight, plump, portly, rotund, tubby 2 = **strong**, able-bodied, brawny, muscular, robust, stalwart, strapping, sturdy 3 = **brave**, bold, courageous, fearless, gallant, intrepid, plucky, resolute, valiant

stow v = **pack**, bundle, load, put away, stash (inf), store

order to travel free. **stow away** v hide as a stowaway.

straddle v have one leg or part on each side of (something).

straggle v go or spread in a rambling or irregular way. **straggler** n **straggly** adj.

straight ❶ adj 1 not curved or crooked. 2 level or upright. 3 orderly. 4 honest or frank. 5 in continuous succession. 6 (of spirits) undiluted. 7 Theatre serious. 8 slang heterosexual. 9 slang conventional. ▷ adv 10 in a straight line. 11 immediately. 12 in a level or upright position. ▷ n 13 straight part, esp. of a racetrack. **go straight** informal reform after being a criminal. **straighten** v **straightaway** adv immediately. **straight face** serious facial expression concealing a desire to laugh. **straightforward** adj 1 honest, frank. 2 (of a task) easy.

strain¹ ❶ v 1 cause (something) to be used or tested beyond its limits. 2 make an intense effort. 3 injure by overexertion. 4 sieve. ▷ n 5 tension or tiredness. 6 force exerted by straining. 7 injury from overexertion. 8 great demand on

strength or resources. 9 melody or theme. **strained** adj 1 not natural, forced. 2 not relaxed, tense. **strainer** n sieve.

strain² ❶ n 1 breed or race. 2 trace or streak.

strait ❶ n 1 narrow channel connecting two areas of sea. ▷ pl 2 position of acute difficulty. **straitjacket** n strong jacket with long sleeves used to bind the arms of a violent person. **strait-laced, straight-laced** adj prudish or puritanical.

strand¹ v 1 run aground. 2 leave in difficulties. ▷ n 3 poetic shore.

strand² ❶ n single thread of string, wire, etc.

strange ❶ adj 1 odd or unusual. 2 not familiar. 3 inexperienced (in) or unaccustomed (to). **strangely** adv **strangeness** n **stranger** n person who is not known or is new to a place or experience.

strangle ❶ v 1 kill by squeezing the throat. 2 prevent the development of. **strangler** n **strangulation** n strangling. **stranglehold** n 1 strangling grip in wrestling. 2 powerful control.

———— THESAURUS ————

straight adj 1 = **direct**, near, short 2 a = **level**, aligned, even, horizontal, right, smooth, square, true b adj = **upright**, erect, plumb, vertical 3 = **orderly**, arranged, in order, neat, organized, shipshape, tidy 4 a = **honest**, above board, fair, honourable, just, law-abiding, reliable, respectable, trustworthy, upright b = **frank**, blunt, bold, candid, forthright, honest, outright, plain, straightforward 5 = **successive**, consecutive, continuous, nonstop, running, solid 6 = **undiluted**, neat, pure, unadulterated, unmixed 9 Sl = **conventional**, bourgeois, conservative ▷ adv 11 = **directly**, at once, immediately, instantly

strain¹ v 2 = **strive**, bend over backwards (inf), endeavour, give it one's best shot (inf), go for it (inf), knock oneself out (inf), labour, struggle 3 = **overexert**, injure,

overtax, overwork, pull, sprain, tax, tear, twist, wrench 4 = **sieve**, filter, purify, sift ▷ n 5 = **stress**, anxiety, burden, pressure, tension 6 = **exertion**, effort, force, struggle 7 = **injury**, pull, sprain, wrench

strain² n 1 = **breed**, ancestry, blood, descent, extraction, family, lineage, race 2 = **trace**, streak, suggestion, tendency

strait n 1 = **channel**, narrows, sound ▷ pl 2 = **difficulty**, dilemma, extremity, hardship, plight, predicament

strand² n 1 = **filament**, fibre, string, thread

strange adj 1 = **odd**, abnormal, bizarre, curious, extraordinary, munted (NZ sl), peculiar, queer, uncommon, weird, wonderful 2 = **unfamiliar**, alien, exotic, foreign, new, novel, unknown, untried

strangle v 1 = **throttle**, asphyxiate, choke, strangulate 2 = **suppress**, inhibit, repress, stifle

S

strap ⓘ *n* **1** strip of flexible material for lifting, fastening, or holding in place. ▷ *v* **strapping, strapped 2** fasten with a strap or straps. **strapping** *adj* tall and sturdy.

strategy ⓘ *n, pl* **-gies 1** overall plan. **2** art of planning in war. **strategic** [strat-**ee**-jik] *adj* **1** advantageous. **2** (of weapons) aimed at an enemy's homeland. **strategically** *adv* **strategist** *n*.

stratosphere *n* atmospheric layer between about 15 and 50 kilometres above the earth.

stratum [**strah**-tum] *n, pl* **strata 1** layer, esp. of rock. **2** social class. **stratification** *n*.

straw *n* **1** dried stalks of grain. **2** single stalk of straw. **3** long thin tube used to suck up liquid into the mouth. **straw poll** unofficial poll taken to determine general opinion.

stray ⓘ *v* **1** wander. **2** digress. **3** deviate from certain moral standards. ▷ *adj* **4** having strayed. **5** scattered, random. ▷ *n* **6** stray animal.

streak ⓘ *n* **1** long band of contrasting colour or substance. **2** quality or characteristic. **3** short stretch (of good or bad luck). ▷ *v* **4** mark with streaks. **5** move rapidly. **6** *informal* run naked in public. **streaker** *n* **streaky** *adj*.

stream ⓘ *n* **1** small river. **2** steady flow, as of liquid, speech, or people. **3** schoolchildren grouped together because of similar ability. ▷ *v* **4** flow steadily. **5** move in unbroken succession. **6** float in the air. **7** group (pupils) in streams. **streamer** *n* **1** strip of coloured paper that unrolls when tossed. **2** long narrow flag.

street ⓘ *n* public road, usu. lined with buildings. **streetwise** *adj* knowing how to survive in big cities.

streetcar *n US & Canad* public transport vehicle powered by an overhead wire and running on rails laid in the road.

strength ⓘ *n* **1** quality of being strong. **2** quality or ability considered an advantage. **3** degree of intensity. **4** total number of people in a group. **on the strength of** on the basis of. **strengthen** *v*.

strenuous ⓘ *adj* requiring great energy or effort.

stress ⓘ *n* **1** tension or strain. **2** emphasis. **3** stronger sound in saying a word or syllable. **4** *Physics* force producing strain. ▷ *v* **5** emphasize. **6** put stress on (a word or syllable). **stressed-out** *adj informal* suffering from tension.

━━━━━━━━━━━━━━━━━━━ THESAURUS ━━━━━━━

strap *n* **1** = **belt**, thong, tie ▷ *v* **2** = **fasten**, bind, buckle, lash, secure, tie

strategy *n* **1** = **plan**, approach, policy, procedure, scheme

stray *v* **1** = **wander**, drift, err, go astray **2** = **digress**, deviate, diverge, get off the point ▷ *adj* **4** = **lost**, abandoned, homeless, roaming, vagrant **5** = **random**, accidental, chance

streak *n* **1** = **band**, layer, line, slash, strip, stripe, stroke, vein **3** = **trace**, dash, element, strain, touch, vein ▷ *v* **5** = **speed**, dart, flash, fly, hurtle, sprint, tear, whizz (*inf*), zoom

stream *n* **1** = **river**, bayou, beck, brook, burn (*Scot*), rivulet, tributary **2** = **flow**,

course, current, drift, run, rush, surge, tide, torrent ▷ *v* **4, 5** = **flow**, cascade, flood, gush, issue, pour, run, spill, spout

street *n* = **road**, avenue, lane, roadway, row, terrace

strength *n* **1** = **might**, brawn, courage, fortitude, muscle, robustness, stamina, sturdiness, toughness **2** = **strong point**, advantage, asset **3** = **power**, effectiveness, efficacy, force, intensity, potency, vigour

strenuous *adj* = **demanding**, arduous, hard, laborious, taxing, tough, uphill

stress *n* **1** = **strain**, anxiety, burden, pressure, tension, trauma, worry **2** = **emphasis**, force, significance, weight **3** = **accent**, accentuation, beat, emphasis

stretch ❶ v 1 extend or be extended.
2 be able to be stretched. 3 extend the
limbs or body. 4 strain (resources or
abilities) to the utmost. ▷ n 5 stretching.
6 continuous expanse. 7 period. 8 *informal*
term of imprisonment. **stretchy** *adj*
stretcher n frame covered with canvas, on
which an injured person is carried.
strew v **strewing**, **strewed**, **strewed** or
strewn scatter (things) over a surface.
stricken *adj* seriously affected by disease,
grief, pain, etc.
stricture n severe criticism.
stride v **striding**, **strode**, **stridden** 1 walk
with long steps. ▷ n 2 long step. 3 regular
pace. ▷ *pl* 4 progress.
strident ❶ *adj* loud and harsh. **stridently**
adv **stridency** n.
strife ❶ n conflict, quarrelling.
strike ❶ v **striking**, **struck** 1 cease work
as a protest. 2 hit. 3 attack suddenly.
4 ignite (a match) by friction. 5 (of a
clock) indicate (a time) by sounding a bell.
6 enter the mind of. 7 afflict. 8 discover
(gold, oil, etc.). 9 agree (a bargain).
10 take up (a posture). 11 make (a coin)
by stamping it. ▷ n 12 stoppage of work
as a protest. 13 striking. **strike camp**
dismantle and pack up tents. **strike home**
have the desired effect. **striker** n 1 striking
worker. 2 attacking footballer. **striking**
adj 1 impressive. 2 noteworthy. **strike
off, out** v cross out. **strike up** v 1 begin

(a conversation or friendship). 2 begin to
play music.
string ❶ n 1 thin cord used for tying. 2 set
of objects threaded on a string. 3 series of
things or events. 4 stretched wire or cord
on a musical instrument that produces
sound when vibrated. ▷ *pl* 5 restrictions
or conditions. 6 section of an orchestra
consisting of stringed instruments. ▷ v
stringing, **strung** 7 provide with a string
or strings. 8 thread on a string. **pull
strings** use one's influence. **stringed** *adj*
(of a musical instrument) having strings
that are plucked or played with a bow.
stringy *adj* 1 like string. 2 (of meat)
fibrous. **stringy-bark** n *Aust* eucalyptus
with a fibrous bark. **string along** v
1 deceive over a period of time. **string up** v
informal kill by hanging.
stringent ❶ [**strin**-jent] *adj* strictly
controlled or enforced. **stringency** n.
strip¹ ❶ v **stripping**, **stripped** 1 take (the
covering or clothes) off. 2 take a title
or possession away from (someone).
3 remove (paint) from (a surface).
4 dismantle (an engine). ▷ n 5 act of
stripping. **stripper** n person who performs
a striptease. **striptease** n entertainment
in which a performer undresses to music.
strip² ❶ n 1 long narrow piece. 2 clothes
a football team plays in. **strip cartoon**
sequence of drawings telling a story.
stripe n 1 long narrow band of contrasting

▷ v 5 = **emphasize**, accentuate, dwell on,
underline
stretch v 1 = **extend**, cover, put forth,
reach, spread, unroll 4 = **strain** ▷ n
6 = **expanse**, area, distance, extent,
spread, tract 7 = **period**, space, spell, stint,
term, time
strident *adj* = **harsh**, discordant, grating,
jarring, raucous, screeching, shrill
strife n = **conflict**, battle, clash, discord,
dissension, friction, quarrel
strike v 1 = **walk out**, down tools,
mutiny, revolt 2 = **hit**, beat, clobber (*sl*),

clout (*inf*), cuff, hammer, knock, punch,
slap, smack, swipe, thump, wallop (*inf*)
3 = **attack**, assail, assault, hit 6 = **occur
to**, come to, dawn on or upon, hit,
register (*inf*)
string n 1 = **cord**, fibre, twine 3 = **series**,
chain, file, line, procession, row, sequence,
succession
stringent *adj* = **strict**, inflexible, rigid,
rigorous, severe, tight, tough
strip¹ v 1 = **undress**, disrobe, unclothe
2 = **divest**, rob
strip² n 1 = **piece**, band, belt, shred

S

colour or substance. **2** chevron on a uniform to indicate rank. **striped**, **stripy**, **stripey** *adj*.

strive ❶ *v* **striving**, **strove**, **striven** make a great effort.

stroke ❶ *v* **1** touch or caress lightly with the hand. ▷ *n* **2** light touch or caress with the hand. **3** rupture of a blood vessel in the brain. **4** blow. **5** action or occurrence of the kind specified, e.g. *a stroke of luck*. **6** chime of a clock. **7** mark made by a pen or paintbrush. **8** style or method of swimming.

stroll ❶ *v* **1** walk in a leisurely manner. ▷ *n* **2** leisurely walk.

stroller *n US & Canad* chair-shaped carriage for a baby.

strong ❶ *adj* **1** having physical power. **2** not easily broken. **3** great in degree or intensity. **4** having moral force. **5** having a specified number, e.g. *twenty strong*. **strongly** *adv* **stronghold** *n* **1** area of predominance of a particular belief. **2** fortress. **strongroom** *n* room designed for the safekeeping of valuables.

stroppy *adj* **-pier**, **-piest** *slang* angry or awkward.

structure ❶ *n* **1** complex construction. **2** manner or basis of construction or organization. ▷ *v* **3** give a structure to. **structural** *adj* **structuralism** *n* approach to literature, social sciences, etc., which sees changes in the subject as caused and organized by a hidden set of universal rules. **structuralist** *n*, *adj*.

struggle ❶ *v* **1** work, strive, or make one's way with difficulty. **2** move about violently in an attempt to get free. **3** fight (with someone). ▷ *n* **4** striving. **5** fight.

strum *v* **strumming**, **strummed** play (a guitar or banjo) by sweeping the thumb or a plectrum across the strings.

strut ❶ *v* **strutting**, **strutted** **1** walk pompously, swagger. ▷ *n* **2** bar supporting a structure.

strychnine [**strik**-neen] *n* very poisonous drug used in small quantities as a stimulant.

stub ❶ *n* **1** short piece left after use. **2** counterfoil of a cheque or ticket. ▷ *v*

─────────────────── THESAURUS ───────────────────

strive *v* = **try**, attempt, bend over backwards (*inf*), break one's neck (*inf*), do one's best, give it one's best shot (*inf*), go all out (*inf*), knock oneself out (*inf*), labour, make an all-out effort (*inf*), struggle, toil

stroke *v* **1** = **caress**, fondle, pet, rub ▷ *n* **3** = **apoplexy**, attack, collapse, fit, seizure **4** = **blow**, hit, knock, pat, rap, swipe, thump

stroll *v* **1** = **walk**, amble, promenade, ramble, saunter ▷ *n* **2** = **walk**, breath of air, constitutional, promenade, ramble

strong *adj* **1** = **powerful**, athletic, brawny, burly, hardy, lusty, muscular, robust, strapping, sturdy, tough **2** = **durable**, hard-wearing, heavy-duty, sturdy, substantial, well-built **3** = **intense**, acute, deep, fervent, fervid, fierce, firm, keen, vehement, violent, zealous **4** = **persuasive**, compelling, convincing, effective, potent, sound, telling, weighty,

well-founded

structure *n* **1** = **building**, construction, edifice, erection **2** = **arrangement**, configuration, construction, design, form, formation, make-up, organization ▷ *v* **3** = **arrange**, assemble, build up, design, organize, shape

struggle *v* **1** = **strive**, exert oneself, give it one's best shot (*inf*), go all out (*inf*), knock oneself out (*inf*), labour, make an all-out effort (*inf*), strain, toil, work **3** = **fight**, battle, compete, contend, grapple, wrestle ▷ *n* **4** = **effort**, exertion, labour, pains, scramble, toil, work, yakka (*Aust & NZ inf*) **5** = **fight**, battle, brush, clash, combat, conflict, contest, tussle

strut *v* **1** = **swagger**, parade, peacock, prance

stub *n* **1** = **butt**, dog-end (*inf*), end, remnant, stump, tail, tail end **2** = **counterfoil**

stubbing, **stubbed** 3 strike (the toe) painfully against an object. 4 put out (a cigarette) by pressing the end against a surface. **stubby** adj short and broad.

stubble n 1 short stalks of grain left in a field after reaping. 2 short growth of hair on the chin of a man who has not shaved recently. **stubbly** adj.

stubborn ⓘ adj 1 refusing to agree or give in. 2 difficult to deal with. **stubbornly** adv **stubbornness** n.

stucco n plaster used for coating or decorating walls.

stud¹ ⓘ n 1 small piece of metal attached to a surface for decoration. 2 disc-like removable fastener for clothes. 3 one of several small round objects fixed to the sole of a football boot to give better grip. ▷ v **studding**, **studded** 4 set with studs.

stud² n 1 male animal, esp. a stallion, kept for breeding. 2 (also **stud farm**) place where horses are bred. 3 slang virile or sexually active man.

studio ⓘ n, pl **-dios** 1 workroom of an artist or photographer. 2 room or building in which television or radio programmes, records, or films are made.

study ⓘ v **studying**, **studied** 1 be engaged in learning (a subject). 2 investigate by observation and research. 3 scrutinize.

▷ n, pl **studies** 4 act or process of studying. 5 room for studying in. 6 book or paper produced as a result of study. 7 sketch done as practice or preparation. 8 musical composition designed to improve playing technique. **student** n person who studies a subject, esp. at university. **studied** adj carefully practised or planned. **studious** adj 1 fond of study. 2 careful and deliberate. **studiously** adv.

stuff ⓘ n 1 substance or material. 2 collection of unnamed things. ▷ v 3 pack, cram, or fill completely. 4 fill (food) with a seasoned mixture. 5 fill (an animal's skin) with material to restore the shape of the live animal. **stuffing** n 1 seasoned mixture with which food is stuffed. 2 padding.

stumble ⓘ v 1 trip and nearly fall. 2 walk in an unsure way. 3 make frequent mistakes in speech. ▷ n 4 stumbling. **stumble across** v discover accidentally. **stumbling block** obstacle or difficulty.

stump ⓘ n 1 base of a tree left when the main trunk has been cut away. 2 part of a thing left after a larger part has been removed. 3 Cricket one of the three upright sticks forming the wicket. ▷ v 4 baffle. 5 Cricket dismiss (a batsman) by breaking his wicket with the ball. 6 walk with heavy steps. **stumpy** adj short and

---

— THESAURUS —

stubborn adj = **obstinate**, dogged, headstrong, inflexible, intractable, obdurate, pig-headed, recalcitrant, tenacious, unyielding

stud¹ v 4 = **ornament**, dot, spangle, spot

studio n 1 = **workshop**, atelier

study v 1 = **learn**, cram (inf), mug up (Brit sl), read up, swot (up) (Brit inf) 2 = **contemplate**, consider, examine, go into, ponder, pore over, read 3 = **examine**, analyse, investigate, look into, research, scrutinize, survey ▷ n 4 **a** = **learning**, application, lessons, reading, research, school work, swotting (Brit inf) **b** = **examination**, analysis, consideration,

contemplation, inquiry, inspection, investigation, review, scrutiny, survey

stuff n 1 = **substance**, essence, matter 2 = **things**, belongings, effects, equipment, gear, kit, objects, paraphernalia, possessions, tackle ▷ v 3 = **cram**, crowd, fill, force, jam, pack, push, ram, shove, squeeze

stumble v 1 = **trip**, fall, falter, lurch, reel, slip, stagger ▷ v **stumble across** = **discover**, chance upon, come across, find

stump v 4 = **baffle**, bewilder, confuse, flummox, mystify, nonplus, perplex, puzzle

S

thick. **stump up** v informal give (the money required).

stun ❶ v **stunning, stunned 1** shock or overwhelm. **2** knock senseless. **stunning** adj very attractive or impressive.

stunt¹ v prevent or impede the growth of.

stunt² ❶ n **1** acrobatic or dangerous action. **2** anything spectacular done to gain publicity.

stupefy ❶ v **-fying, -fied 1** make insensitive or lethargic. **2** astound. **stupefaction** n.

stupendous ❶ adj very large or impressive.

stupid ❶ adj **1** lacking intelligence. **2** silly. **3** in a stupor. **stupidity** n **stupidly** adv.

stupor ❶ n dazed or unconscious state.

sturdy ❶ adj **-dier, -diest 1** healthy and robust. **2** strongly built. **sturdily** adv.

sturgeon n fish from which caviar is obtained.

stutter ❶ v **1** speak with repetition of initial consonants. ▷ n **2** tendency to stutter.

sty n, pl **sties** pen for pigs.

stye, sty n, pl **styes, sties** inflammation at the base of an eyelash.

style ❶ n **1** shape or design. **2** manner of writing, speaking, or doing something. **3** elegance, refinement. **4** prevailing fashion. ▷ v **5** shape or design. **6** name or call. **stylish** adj smart, elegant, and fashionable. **stylist** n **1** hairdresser. **2** person who writes or performs with great attention to style. **stylistic** adj of literary or artistic style. **stylize** v cause to conform to an established stylistic form.

stylus n needle-like device on a record player that rests in the groove of the record and picks up the sound signals.

suave ❶ [swahv] adj smooth and sophisticated in manner.

sub n **1** subeditor. **2** submarine. **3** subscription. **4** substitute. **5** informal advance payment of wages or salary. ▷ v **subbing, subbed 6** act as a substitute. **7** grant advance payment to.

subconscious ❶ adj **1** happening or existing without one's awareness. ▷ n

────────────────────────────── THESAURUS ──────────────────────────────

stun v **1** = **overcome**, astonish, astound, bewilder, confound, confuse, overpower, shock, stagger, stupefy **2** = **knock out**, daze

stunt² n = **feat**, act, deed, exploit, trick

stupefy v **2** = **astound**, amaze, daze, dumbfound, shock, stagger, stun

stupendous adj **a** = **wonderful**, amazing, astounding, breathtaking, jaw-dropping, marvellous, overwhelming, sensational (inf), staggering, superb **b** = **huge**, colossal, enormous, gigantic, mega (sl), vast

stupid adj **1** = **unintelligent**, brainless, dense, dim, half-witted, moronic, obtuse, simple, simple-minded, slow, slow-witted, thick **2** = **silly**, asinine, daft (inf), foolish, idiotic, imbecilic, inane, nonsensical, pointless, rash, senseless, unintelligent **3** = **dazed**, groggy, insensate, semiconscious, stunned, stupefied

stupor n = **daze**, coma, insensibility, stupefaction, unconsciousness

sturdy adj **1** = **robust**, athletic, brawny, hardy, lusty, muscular, powerful **2** = **substantial**, durable, solid, well-built, well-made

stutter v **1** = **stammer**, falter, hesitate, stumble

style n **1** = **design**, cut, form, manner **2** = **manner**, approach, method, mode, technique, way **3** = **elegance**, affluence, chic, comfort, ease, élan, flair, grandeur, luxury, panache, polish, smartness, sophistication, taste **4** = **fashion**, mode, rage, trend, vogue ▷ v **5** = **design**, adapt, arrange, cut, fashion, shape, tailor **6** = **call**, designate, dub, entitle, label, name, term

suave adj = **smooth**, charming, courteous, debonair, polite, sophisticated, urbane

subconscious adj **1** = **hidden**, inner, intuitive, latent, repressed, subliminal

S

2 *Psychoanalysis* that part of the mind of which one is not aware but which can influence one's behaviour.

subdivide v divide (a part of something) into smaller parts. **subdivision** n.

subdue ❶ v **-duing, -dued 1** overcome. **2** make less intense.

subject ❶ n **1** person or thing being dealt with or studied. **2** *Grammar* word or phrase that represents the person or thing performing the action of the verb in a sentence. **3** person under the rule of a monarch or government. ▷ *adj* **4** being under the rule of a monarch or government. ▷ v (foll. by to) **5** cause to undergo. **subject to 1** liable to. **2** conditional upon. **subjection** n

subjective adj based on personal feelings or prejudices. **subjectively** adv.

subjugate ❶ v bring (a group of people) under one's control. **subjugation** n.

sublet v **-letting, -let** rent out (property rented from someone else).

sublime ❶ adj **1** of high moral, intellectual, or spiritual value. **2** unparalleled, supreme. ▷ v **3** *Chem* change from a solid to a vapour without first melting. **sublimely** adv.

subliminal adj relating to mental processes of which the individual is not aware.

submarine n **1** vessel which can operate below the surface of the sea. ▷ *adj* **2** below the surface of the sea.

submerge ❶ v put or go below the surface of water or other liquid. **submersion** n.

subordinate ❶ adj **1** of lesser rank or importance. ▷ n **2** subordinate person or thing. ▷ v **3** make or treat as subordinate. **subordination** n.

subscribe ❶ v **1** pay (a subscription). **2** give support or approval (to). **subscriber** n **subscription** n **1** payment for issues of a publication over a period. **2** money contributed to a charity etc. **3** membership fees paid to a society.

subsequent ❶ adj occurring after, succeeding.

subservient ❶ adj submissive, servile. **subservience** n.

subside ❶ v **1** become less intense. **2** sink to a lower level. **subsidence** n act or process of subsiding.

THESAURUS

subdue v **1** = **overcome**, break, conquer, control, crush, defeat, master, overpower, quell, tame, vanquish **2** = **moderate**, mellow, quieten down, soften, suppress, tone down

subject n **1** = **topic**, affair, business, issue, matter, object, point, question, substance, theme **3** = **citizen**, national, subordinate ▷ *adj* **4** = **subordinate**, dependent, inferior, obedient, satellite ▷ v (foll. by to) **5** = **put through**, expose, lay open, submit, treat **subject to 1** = **liable to**, prone to **2** = **conditional on**, contingent on, dependent on

subjugate v = **conquer**, enslave, master, overcome, overpower, quell, subdue, suppress, vanquish

sublime adj **1** = **noble**, elevated, exalted, glorious, grand, great, high, lofty

submerge v = **immerse**, deluge, dip, duck, engulf, flood, inundate, overflow, overwhelm, plunge, sink, swamp

subordinate adj **1** = **lesser**, dependent, inferior, junior, lower, minor, secondary, subject ▷ n **2** = **inferior**, aide, assistant, attendant, junior, second

subscribe v **1** = **contribute**, donate, give **2** = **support**, advocate, endorse

subsequent adj = **following**, after, ensuing, later, succeeding, successive

subservient adj = **servile**, abject, deferential, obsequious, slavish, submissive, sycophantic

subside v **1** = **decrease**, abate, diminish, ease, ebb, lessen, quieten, slacken, wane **2** = **collapse**, cave in, drop, lower, settle, sink

S

subsidiary ❶ *adj* **1** of lesser importance. ▷ *n, pl* **-aries 2** subsidiary person or thing.
subsidize ❷ *v* help financially. **subsidy** *n, pl* **-dies** any financial aid, grant, or contribution.
subsist *v* manage to live. **subsistence** *n*.
substance ❶ *n* **1** physical composition of something. **2** solid, powder, liquid, or paste. **3** essential meaning of something. **4** solid or meaningful quality. **5** wealth.
substantial *adj* **1** of considerable size or value. **2** (of food or a meal) sufficient and nourishing. **3** solid or strong. **4** real. **substantially** *adv* **substantiate** *v* support (a story) with evidence. **substantiation** *n* **substantive** *n* **1** noun. ▷ *adj* **2** of or being the essential element of a thing.
substitute ❶ *v* **1** take the place of or put in place of another. ▷ *n* **2** person or thing taking the place of (another). **substitution** *n*.
subsume *v* include (an idea, case, etc.) under a larger classification or group.
subterfuge ❶ *n* trick used to achieve an objective.
subterranean *adj* underground.
subtitle *n* **1** secondary title of a book. ▷ *pl* **2** printed translation at the bottom of the picture in a film with foreign dialogue.

▷ *v* **3** provide with a subtitle or subtitles.
subtle ❶ *adj* **1** not immediately obvious. **2** having or requiring ingenuity. **subtly** *adv* **subtlety** *n*.
subtract ❶ *v* take (one number or quantity) from another. **subtraction** *n*.
suburb *n* residential area on the outskirts of a city. **suburban** *adj* **1** of or inhabiting a suburb. **2** narrow or unadventurous in outlook. **suburbia** *n* suburbs and their inhabitants.
subvert ❶ *v* overthrow the authority of. **subversion** *n* **subversive** *adj, n*.
subway *n* **1** passage under a road or railway. **2** *US & Canad* underground railway.
succeed ❶ *v* **1** accomplish an aim. **2** turn out satisfactorily. **3** come next in order after (something). **4** take over a position from (someone). **success** *n* **1** achievement of something attempted. **2** attainment of wealth, fame, or position. **3** successful person or thing. **successful** *adj* having success. **successfully** *adv* **succession** *n* **1** series of people or things following one another in order. **2** act or right by which one person succeeds another in a position. **successive** *adj* consecutive. **successively** *adv* **successor** *n* person who succeeds someone in a position.

— THESAURUS —

subsidiary *adj* **1** = **lesser**, ancillary, auxiliary, minor, secondary, subordinate, supplementary
subsidize *v* = **fund**, finance, promote, sponsor, support
substance *n* **1** = **material**, body, fabric, stuff **3** = **meaning**, essence, gist, import, main point, significance **4** = **reality**, actuality, concreteness **5** = **wealth**, assets, estate, means, property, resources
substitute *v* **1** = **replace**, change, exchange, interchange, swap, switch ▷ *n* **2** = **replacement**, agent, deputy, locum, proxy, reserve, sub, surrogate
subterfuge *n* = **trick**, deception, dodge,

manoeuvre, ploy, ruse, stratagem
subtle *adj* **1** = **faint**, delicate, implied, slight, understated **2** = **crafty**, artful, cunning, devious, ingenious, shrewd, sly, wily
subtract *v* = **take away**, deduct, diminish, remove, take from, take off
subvert *v* = **overturn**, sabotage, undermine
succeed *v* **1, 2** = **make it** (*inf*), be successful, crack it (*inf*), do well, flourish, make good, make the grade (*inf*), prosper, thrive, triumph, work **3** = **follow**, come next, ensue, result **4** = **take over**, accede, assume the office of, come into, come into possession of, inherit

● **SPELLING TIP**
● The Bank of English evidence shows
● that people are able to remember the
● double s at the end of **success** more
● easily than the double c in the middle.

succinct ❶ adj brief and clear.

succour ❶ v, n help in distress.

succulent ❶ adj 1 juicy and delicious. 2 (of a plant) having thick fleshy leaves. ▷ n 3 succulent plant. **succulence** n.

succumb ❶ v 1 (foll. by to) give way (to something overpowering). 2 die of (an illness).

such adj 1 of the kind specified. 2 so great, so much. ▷ pron 3 such things. **such-and-such** adj specific, but not known or named. **suchlike** pron such or similar things.

suck v 1 draw (liquid or air) into the mouth. 2 take (something) into the mouth and moisten, dissolve, or roll it around with the tongue. 3 (foll. by in) draw in by irresistible force. ▷ n 4 sucking. **sucker** n 1 slang person who is easily deceived or swindled. 2 organ or device which adheres by suction. 3 shoot coming from a plant's root or the base of its main stem. **suck up to** v informal flatter (someone) for one's own profit.

suckle v feed at the breast. **suckling** n unweaned baby or young animal.

suction n 1 sucking. 2 force produced by drawing air out of a space to make a vacuum that will suck in a substance from another space.

sudden ❶ adj done or occurring quickly and unexpectedly. **all of a sudden** quickly and unexpectedly. **suddenly** adv **suddenness** n.

sudoku [soo-**doh**-koo] n logic puzzle involving the insertion of numbers into each row, column, and individual grid of a larger square so that none is repeated.

suds pl n froth of soap and water.

sue ❶ v suing, sued start legal proceedings against.

suede n leather with a velvety finish on one side.

suet n hard fat obtained from sheep and cattle, used in cooking.

suffer ❶ v 1 undergo or be subjected to. 2 tolerate. **sufferer** n **suffering** n **sufferance** n **on sufferance** tolerated with reluctance.

suffice ❶ [suf-**fice**] v be enough for a purpose. **sufficiency** n adequate amount. **sufficient** adj enough, adequate. **sufficiently** adv.

suffix n letter or letters added to the end of a word to form another word.

suffocate ❶ v 1 kill or be killed by deprivation of oxygen. 2 feel uncomfortable from heat and lack of air. **suffocation** n.

suffrage n right to vote in public elections. **suffragette** n (in Britain in the early 20th century) a woman who campaigned militantly for the right to vote.

suffuse v spread through or over (something). **suffusion** n.

sugar n 1 sweet crystalline carbohydrate found in many plants and used to sweeten

S

succinct adj = **brief**, compact, concise, laconic, pithy, terse

succour v = **help**, aid, assist ▷ n = **help**, aid, assistance

succulent adj 1 = **juicy**, luscious, lush, moist

succumb v 1 (foll. by to) = **surrender**, capitulate, cave in (inf), give in, submit, yield 2 = **die**, cark (Aust & NZ sl), fall

sudden adj = **quick**, abrupt, hasty, hurried, rapid, rash, swift, unexpected

sue v = **take (someone) to court**, charge, indict, prosecute, summon

suffer v 1 = **undergo**, bear, endure, experience, go through, sustain 2 = **tolerate**, put up with (inf)

suffice v = **be enough**, be adequate, be sufficient, do, meet requirements, serve

suffocate v 1 = **choke**, asphyxiate, smother, stifle 2 = **stifle**, choke

food and drinks. ▷ v **2** sweeten or cover with sugar. **sugary** adj **sugar beet** beet grown for the sugar obtained from its roots. **sugar cane** tropical grass grown for the sugar obtained from its canes. **sugar glider** common Australian phalanger that glides from tree to tree feeding on insects and nectar.

suggest ❶ v **1** put forward (an idea) for consideration. **2** bring to mind by the association of ideas. **3** give a hint of. **suggestible** adj easily influenced. **suggestion** n **1** thing suggested. **2** hint or indication. **suggestive** adj **1** suggesting something indecent. **2** conveying a hint (of). **suggestively** adv.

suicide n **1** killing oneself intentionally. **2** person who kills himself intentionally. **3** self-inflicted ruin of one's own prospects or interests. **suicidal** adj liable to commit suicide. **suicidally** adv.

suit ❶ n **1** set of clothes designed to be worn together. **2** outfit worn for a specific purpose. **3** one of the four sets into which a pack of cards is divided. **4** lawsuit. ▷ v **5** be appropriate for. **6** be acceptable to. **suitable** adj appropriate or proper. **suitably** adv **suitability** n **suitcase** n portable travelling case for clothing.

suite ❶ n **1** set of connected rooms in a hotel. **2** matching set of furniture. **3** set of musical pieces in the same key.

suitor ❶ n old-fashioned man who is courting a woman.

sulk v **1** be silent and sullen because of resentment or bad temper. ▷ n **2** resentful or sullen mood. **sulky** adj **sulkily** adv.

sullen ❶ adj unwilling to talk or be sociable. **sullenness** n.

sully ❶ v **-lying, -lied 1** ruin (someone's reputation). **2** make dirty.

sulphur n Chem pale yellow nonmetallic element. **sulphuric**, **sulphurous** adj of or containing sulphur.

sultan n sovereign of a Muslim country. **sultana** n **1** kind of raisin. **2** sultan's wife, mother, or daughter. **sultanate** n territory of a sultan.

sultry ❶ adj **-trier, -triest 1** (of weather or climate) hot and humid. **2** passionate, sensual.

sum ❶ n **1** result of addition, total. **2** problem in arithmetic. **3** quantity of money. **sum total** complete or final total. **sum up** v summarize. **summed 1** summarize. **2** form a quick opinion of.

summary ❶ n, pl **-ries 1** brief account giving the main points of something. ▷ adj **2** done quickly, without formalities. **summarily** adv **summarize** v make or be a summary of (something). **summation** n **1** summary. **2** adding up.

summer n warmest season of the year, between spring and autumn. **summery**

suggest v **1** = **recommend**, advise, advocate, prescribe, propose **2** = **bring to mind**, evoke **3** = **hint**, imply, indicate, intimate

suit n **2** = **outfit**, clothing, costume, dress, ensemble, habit **4** = **lawsuit**, action, case, cause, proceeding, prosecution, trial ▷ v **5** = **befit**, agree, become, go with, harmonize, match, tally **6** = **be acceptable to**, do, gratify, please, satisfy

suite n **1** = **rooms**, apartment

suitor n Old-fashioned = **admirer**, beau, young man

sullen adj = **morose**, cross, dour, glowering, moody, sour, sulky, surly, unsociable

sully v **1** = **dishonour**, besmirch, disgrace, ruin, smirch **2** = **defile**, stain, tarnish

sultry adj **1** = **humid**, close, hot, muggy, oppressive, sticky, stifling **2** = **seductive**, provocative, sensual, sexy (inf)

sum n **1** = **total**, aggregate, amount, tally, whole

summary n **1** = **synopsis**, abridgment, outline, précis, résumé, review, rundown

adj **summerhouse** *n* small building in a garden. **summertime** *n* period or season of summer.

summit ⊕ *n* **1** top of a mountain or hill. **2** highest point. **3** conference between heads of state.

summon ⊕ *v* **1** order (someone) to come. **2** call upon (someone) to do something. **3** gather (one's courage, strength, etc.). **summons** *n* **1** command summoning someone. **2** order requiring someone to appear in court. ▷ *v* **3** order (someone) to appear in court.

sumo *n* Japanese style of wrestling.

sumptuous ⊕ *adj* lavish, magnificent.

sun *n* **1** star around which the earth and other planets revolve. **2** any star around which planets revolve. **3** heat and light from the sun. ▷ *v* **sunning, sunned 4** expose (oneself) to the sun's rays. **sunless** *adj* **sunny** *adj* **1** full of or exposed to sunlight. **2** cheerful. **sunbathe** *v* lie in the sunshine in order to get a suntan. **sunbeam** *n* ray of sun. **sunburn** *n* painful reddening of the skin caused by overexposure to the sun. **sunburnt, sunburned** *adj* **sundial** *n* device showing the time by means of a pointer that casts a shadow on a marked dial. **sundown** *n* sunset. **sunflower** *n* tall plant with large golden flowers. **sunrise** *n* **1** daily appearance of the sun above the horizon. **2** time of this. **sunset** *n* **1** daily disappearance of the sun below the horizon. **2** time of this. **sunshine** *n*

light and warmth from the sun. **sunspot** *n* **1** dark patch appearing temporarily on the sun's surface. **2** *Aust* small area of skin damage caused by exposure to the sun. **sunstroke** *n* illness caused by prolonged exposure to intensely hot sunlight. **suntan** *n* browning of the skin caused by exposure to the sun.

sundae *n* ice cream topped with fruit etc.

Sunday *n* first day of the week and the Christian day of worship. **Sunday school** school for teaching children about Christianity.

sundry ⊕ *adj* several, various. **sundries** *pl n* several things of various sorts. **all and sundry** everybody.

sup *v* **supping, supped 1** take (liquid) by sips. ▷ *n* **2** sip.

super ⊕ *adj informal* excellent.

super- *prefix* used with many main words to mean: **1** above or over, e.g. *superimpose*. **2** outstanding, e.g. *superstar*. **3** of greater size or extent, e.g. *supermarket*.

superannuation *n* **1** regular payment by an employee into a pension fund. **2** pension paid from this.

superb ⊕ *adj* excellent, impressive, or splendid. **superbly** *adv*.

supercilious ⊕ *adj* showing arrogant pride or scorn.

superficial ⊕ *adj* **1** not careful or thorough. **2** (of a person) without depth of character, shallow. **3** of or on the surface. **superficially** *adv* **superficiality** *n*.

S

———————————— THESAURUS ————————————

summit *n* **2** = **peak**, acme, apex, head, height, pinnacle, top, zenith

summon *v* **1** = **send for**, bid, call, invite **3** = **gather**, draw on, muster

sumptuous *adj* = **luxurious**, gorgeous, grand, lavish, opulent, splendid, superb

sundry *adj* = **various**, assorted, different, miscellaneous, several, some

super *adj Inf* = **excellent**, cracking (*Brit inf*), glorious, magnificent, marvellous, outstanding, sensational

(*inf*), smashing (*inf*), superb, terrific (*inf*), wonderful

superb *adj* = **splendid**, excellent, exquisite, fine, first-rate, grand, magnificent, marvellous, superior, superlative, world-class

supercilious *adj* = **scornful**, arrogant, contemptuous, disdainful, haughty, lofty, snooty (*inf*), stuck-up (*inf*)

superficial *adj* **1** = **hasty**, casual, cursory, desultory, hurried, perfunctory, sketchy,

superfluous ❶ [soo-**per**-flew-uss] *adj*
more than is needed. **superfluity** *n*.

superhuman ❶ *adj* beyond normal
human ability or experience.

superimpose *v* place (something) on or
over something else.

superintend *v* supervise (a person or
activity). **superintendent** *n* **1** senior
police officer. **2** supervisor.

superior ❶ *adj* **1** greater in quality,
quantity, or merit. **2** higher in position or
rank. **3** believing oneself to be better than
others. ▷ *n* **4** person of greater rank or
status. **superiority** *n*.

superlative ❶ [soo-**per**-lat-iv] *adj* **1** of
outstanding quality. **2** *Grammar* denoting
the form of an adjective or adverb
indicating *most*. ▷ *n* **3** *Grammar* superlative
form of a word.

supermarket *n* large self-service store
selling food and household goods.

supernatural ❶ *adj* of or relating to
things beyond the laws of nature. **the
supernatural** supernatural forces,
occurrences, and beings collectively.

supernumerary *adj* **1** exceeding the
required or regular number. ▷ *n, pl* **-ries**
2 supernumerary person or thing.

superpower *n* extremely powerful
nation.

supersede ❶ *v* replace, supplant.

- SPELLING TIP
- Although there is a word 'cede', spelt
- with a *c*, the word **supersede** must have
- an *s* in the middle.

supersonic *adj* of or travelling at a speed
greater than the speed of sound.

superstition *n* **1** belief in omens, ghosts,
etc. **2** idea or practice based on this.
superstitious *adj*.

superstructure *n* **1** structure erected on
something else. **2** part of a ship above the
main deck.

supervise ❶ *v* watch over to direct or
check. **supervision** *n* **supervisor** *n*
supervisory *adj*.

supine *adj* lying flat on one's back.

supper *n* light evening meal.

supplant ❶ *v* take the place of, oust.

supple ❶ *adj* **1** (of a person) moving
and bending easily and gracefully.
2 bending easily without damage.
suppleness *n*.

supplement ❶ *n* **1** thing added to
complete something or make up for a lack.
2 magazine inserted into a newspaper.

THESAURUS

slapdash **2** = **shallow**, empty-headed,
frivolous, silly, trivial **3** = **surface**, exterior,
external, on the surface, slight

superfluous *adj* = **excess**, extra, left
over, redundant, remaining, spare,
supernumerary, surplus

superhuman *adj* = **heroic**, paranormal,
phenomenal, prodigious, supernatural

superior *adj* **1 a** = **better**, grander,
greater, higher, surpassing, unrivalled
b = **first-class**, choice, de luxe, excellent,
exceptional, exclusive, first-rate
3 = **supercilious**, condescending,
disdainful, haughty, lofty, lordly,
patronizing, pretentious, snobbish ▷ *n*
4 = **boss** (*inf*), chief, director, manager,
principal, senior, supervisor

superlative *adj* **1** = **supreme**, excellent,

outstanding, unparalleled, unrivalled,
unsurpassed

supernatural *adj* = **paranormal**, ghostly,
miraculous, mystic, occult, psychic,
spectral, uncanny, unearthly

supersede *v* = **replace**, displace, oust,
supplant, take the place of, usurp

supervise *v* = **oversee**, control, direct,
handle, look after, manage, run,
superintend

supplant *v* = **replace**, displace, oust,
supersede, take the place of

supple *adj* **1** = **flexible**, limber, lissom(e),
lithe **2** = **pliant**, pliable

supplement *n* **1** = **addition**, add-on,
extra **2** = **pull-out**, insert **3** = **appendix**,
postscript ▷ *v* **4** = **add**, augment, extend,
reinforce

S

3 section added to a publication to supply further information. ▷ v **4** provide or be a supplement to (something). **supplementary** adj.

supply ❶ v **-plying, -plied 1** provide with something required. ▷ n, pl **-plies 2** supplying. **3** amount available. **4** Economics willingness and ability to provide goods and services. ▷ pl **5** food or equipment. **supplier** n.

support ❶ v **1** bear the weight of. **2** provide the necessities of life for. **3** give practical or emotional help to. **4** take an active interest in (a sports team, political principle, etc.). **5** help to prove (a theory etc.). **6** speak in favour of. ▷ n **7** supporting. **8** means of support. **supporter** n person who supports a team, principle, etc. **supportive** adj.

suppose ❶ v **1** presume to be true. **2** consider as a proposal for the sake of discussion. **supposed** adj presumed to be true without proof, doubtful. **supposed to 1** expected or required to, e.g. you were supposed to phone me. **2** permitted to, e.g. we're not supposed to swim here. **supposedly**

adv **supposition** n **1** supposing. **2** something supposed.

suppress ❶ v **1** put an end to. **2** prevent publication of (information). **3** restrain (an emotion or response). **suppression** n.

suppurate v (of a wound etc.) produce pus.

supreme ❶ adj highest in authority, rank, or degree. **supremely** adv extremely. **supremacy** n **1** supreme power. **2** state of being supreme. **supremo** n informal person in overall authority.

surcharge n additional charge.

sure ❶ adj **1** free from uncertainty or doubt. **2** reliable. **3** inevitable. ▷ adv, interj **4** informal certainly. **surely** adv it must be true that. **sure-footed** adj unlikely to slip or stumble.

surf n **1** foam caused by waves breaking on the shore. ▷ v **2** take part in surfing. **surfing** n sport of riding towards the shore on a surfboard on the crest of a wave. **surfer** n **surfboard** n long smooth board used in surfing.

surface ❶ n **1** outside or top of an object. **2** material covering the surface of an

—————————————— THESAURUS ——————————————

supply v **1** = **provide**, contribute, endow, equip, furnish, give, grant, produce, stock, yield ▷ n **3** = **store**, cache, fund, hoard, quantity, reserve, source, stock ▷ pl **5** = **provisions**, equipment, food, materials, necessities, rations, stores, tucker (Aust & NZ inf)

support v **1** = **bear**, brace, buttress, carry, hold, prop, reinforce, sustain **2** = **provide for**, finance, fund, keep, look after, maintain, sustain **3** = **help**, aid, assist, back, champion, defend, second, side with **5** = **bear out**, confirm, corroborate, substantiate, verify ▷ n **7** = **help**, aid, assistance, backing, encouragement, loyalty **8** = **prop**, brace, foundation, pillar, post

suppose v **1** = **presume**, assume, conjecture, expect, guess (inf, chiefly US & Canad), imagine, think **2** = **imagine**,

conjecture, consider, hypothesize, postulate, pretend

suppress v **1** = **stop**, check, conquer, crush, overpower, put an end to, quash, quell, subdue **3** = **restrain**, conceal, contain, curb, hold in or back, repress, silence, smother, stifle

supreme adj = **highest**, chief, foremost, greatest, head, leading, paramount, pre-eminent, prime, principal, top, ultimate

sure adj **1** = **certain**, assured, confident, convinced, decided, definite, positive **2** = **reliable**, accurate, dependable, foolproof, infallible, undeniable, undoubted, unerring, unfailing **3** = **inevitable**, assured, bound, guaranteed, inescapable

surface n **1** = **outside**, exterior, face, side, top **2** = **covering**, veneer **3** = **veneer** ▷ v **4** = **appear**, arise, come to light, come

object. **3** superficial appearance. ▷ v **4** rise to the surface. **5** put a surface on.
surfeit ❶ n excessive amount.
surge ❶ n **1** sudden powerful increase. **2** strong rolling movement, esp. of the sea. ▷ v **3** increase suddenly. **4** move forward strongly.
surgeon n doctor who specializes in surgery. **surgery** n **1** treatment in which the patient's body is cut open in order to treat the affected part. **2** pl **-geries** place where, or time when, a doctor, dentist, MP, etc. can be consulted. **surgical** adj **surgically** adv.
surly ❶ adj **-lier, -liest** ill-tempered and rude. **surliness** n.
surmise v, n guess, conjecture.
surmount v **1** overcome (a problem). **2** be on top of (something). **surmountable** adj.
surname n family name.
surpass ❶ v be greater than or superior to.
surplus ❶ n, adj (amount) left over in excess of what is required.
surprise ❶ n **1** unexpected event.

2 amazement and wonder. ▷ v **3** cause to feel amazement or wonder. **4** come upon, attack, or catch suddenly and unexpectedly.
surrealism n movement in art and literature involving the combination of incongruous images, as in a dream. **surreal** adj bizarre. **surrealist** n, adj **surrealistic** adj.
surrender ❶ v **1** give oneself up. **2** give (something) up to another. **3** yield (to a temptation or influence). ▷ n **4** surrendering.
surreptitious ❶ adj done secretly or stealthily.
surrogate ❶ n substitute. **surrogate mother** woman who gives birth to a child on behalf of a couple who cannot have children.
surround ❶ v **1** be, come, or place all around (a person or thing). ▷ n **2** border or edging. **surroundings** pl n area or environment around a person, place, or thing.
surveillance ❶ n close observation.

─────────────────────────────── THESAURUS ───────

up, crop up (inf), emerge, materialize, transpire
surfeit n = **excess**, glut, plethora, superfluity
surge n **1** = **rush**, flood, flow, gush, outpouring **2** = **wave**, billow, roller, swell ▷ v **3** = **rush**, gush, rise **4** = **roll**, heave
surly adj = **ill-tempered**, churlish, cross, grouchy (inf), morose, sulky, sullen, uncivil, ungracious
surmise v = **guess**, conjecture, imagine, presume, speculate, suppose ▷ n = **guess**, assumption, conjecture, presumption, speculation, supposition
surpass v = **outdo**, beat, eclipse, exceed, excel, outshine, outstrip, transcend
surplus n = **excess**, balance, remainder, residue, surfeit ▷ adj = **extra**, excess, odd, remaining, spare, superfluous
surprise n **1** = **shock**, bombshell,

eye-opener (inf), jolt, revelation **2** = **amazement**, astonishment, incredulity, wonder ▷ v **3** = **amaze**, astonish, stagger, stun, take aback **4** = **catch unawares** or **off-guard**, discover, spring upon, startle
surrender v **1** = **give in**, capitulate, cave in (inf), give way, submit, succumb, yield **2** = **give up**, abandon, cede, concede, part with, relinquish, renounce, waive, yield **3** = **yield**, give in ▷ n **4** = **submission**, capitulation, cave-in (inf), relinquishment, renunciation, resignation
surreptitious adj = **secret**, covert, furtive, sly, stealthy, underhand
surrogate n = **substitute**, proxy, representative, stand-in
surround v **1** = **enclose**, encircle, encompass, envelop, hem in, ring
surveillance n = **observation**, inspection, scrutiny, supervision, watch

S

survey ❶ v **1** view or consider in a general way. **2** make a map of (an area). **3** inspect (a building) to assess its condition and value. **4** find out the incomes, opinions, etc. of (a group of people). ▷ n **5** surveying. **6** report produced by a survey. **surveyor** n.

survive ❶ v **1** continue to live or exist after (a difficult experience). **2** live after the death of (another). **survival** n **1** condition of having survived. **survivor** n.

susceptible ❶ adj liable to be influenced or affected by. **susceptibility** n.

suspect ❶ v **1** believe (someone) to be guilty without having any proof. **2** think (something) to be false or questionable. **3** believe (something) to be the case. ▷ adj **4** not to be trusted. ▷ n **5** person who is suspected.

suspend ❶ v **1** hang from a high place. **2** cause to remain floating or hanging. **3** cause to cease temporarily. **4** remove (someone) temporarily from a job or team. **suspenders** pl n **1** straps for holding up stockings. **2** US braces.

suspense ❶ n state of uncertainty while awaiting news, an event, etc.

suspicion ❶ n **1** feeling of not trusting a person or thing. **2** belief that something is true without definite proof. **3** slight trace. **suspicious** adj feeling or causing suspicion.

sustain ❶ v **1** maintain or prolong. **2** keep up the vitality or strength of. **3** suffer (an injury or loss). **4** support. **sustenance** n food.

SUV sport utility vehicle.

svelte adj attractively or gracefully slim.

swab n **1** small piece of cotton wool used to apply medication, clean a wound, etc. ▷ v **swabbing, swabbed** **2** clean (a wound) with a swab. **3** clean (the deck of a ship) with a mop.

swag n slang stolen property. **swagman** n Aust tramp who carries his belongings in a bundle on his back.

swagger ❶ v **1** walk or behave arrogantly. ▷ n **2** arrogant walk or manner.

swallow¹ ❶ v **1** cause to pass down one's throat. **2** make a gulping movement in the throat, as when nervous. **3** informal believe (something) gullibly. **4** refrain from showing (a feeling). **5** engulf or absorb. ▷ n **6** swallowing. **7** amount swallowed.

——————— THESAURUS ———————

survey v **1** = **look over**, contemplate, examine, inspect, observe, scrutinize, view **2** = **plot**, measure, plan, size up **3** = **estimate**, appraise, assess ▷ n **5** = **examination**, inspection, scrutiny **6** = **study**, report, review

survive v **1, 2** = **remain alive**, endure, last, live on, outlast, outlive

susceptible adj = **liable**, disposed, given, impressionable, inclined, prone, receptive, responsive, sensitive, subject, suggestible, vulnerable

suspect v **1** = **believe**, consider, feel, guess, speculate, suppose **2** = **distrust**, doubt, mistrust ▷ adj **4** = **dubious**, doubtful, iffy (inf), questionable

suspend v **1** = **hang**, attach, dangle **3** = **postpone**, cease, cut short, defer, discontinue, interrupt, put off, shelve

suspense n = **uncertainty**, anxiety, apprehension, doubt, expectation, insecurity, irresolution, tension

suspicion n **1** = **distrust**, doubt, dubiety, misgiving, mistrust, qualm, scepticism, wariness **2** = **idea**, guess, hunch, impression, notion **3** = **trace**, hint, shade, soupçon, streak, suggestion, tinge, touch

sustain v **1** = **maintain**, continue, keep up, prolong, protract **2** = **keep alive**, aid, assist, help, nourish **3** = **suffer**, bear, endure, experience, feel, undergo, withstand **4** = **support**, bear, uphold

swagger v **1** = **show off** (inf), boast, brag, parade, skite (Aust & NZ)

swallow¹ v **1** = **gulp**, consume, devour, drink, eat, swig (inf)

swallow² *n* small migratory bird with long pointed wings and a forked tail.

swamp ❶ *n* 1 watery area of land, bog. ▷ *v* 2 cause (a boat) to fill with water and sink. 3 overwhelm. **swampy** *adj*.

swan *n* 1 large usu. white water bird with a long graceful neck. ▷ *v* **swanning**, **swanned** 2 *informal* wander about idly. **swan song** person's last performance before retirement or death.

swap ❶ *v* **swapping**, **swapped** 1 exchange (something) for something else. ▷ *n* 2 exchange.

swarm¹ ❶ *n* 1 large group of bees or other insects. 2 large crowd. ▷ *v* 3 move in a swarm. 4 (of a place) be crowded or overrun.

swarm² *v* (foll. by *up*) climb (a ladder or rope) by gripping with the hands and feet.

swarthy ❶ *adj* **-thier**, **-thiest** dark-complexioned.

swastika *n* symbol in the shape of a cross with the arms bent at right angles, used as the emblem of Nazi Germany.

swat *v* **swatting**, **swatted** 1 hit sharply. ▷ *n* 2 sharp blow.

swathe ❶ *v* 1 wrap in bandages or layers of cloth. ▷ *n* 2 long strip of cloth wrapped around something. 3 (also **swath**) the width of one sweep of a scythe or mower.

sway ❶ *v* 1 swing to and fro or from side to side. 2 waver or cause to waver in opinion. ▷ *n* 3 power or influence. 4 swaying motion.

swear ❶ *v* **swearing**, **swore**, **sworn** 1 use obscene or blasphemous language. 2 state or promise on oath. 3 state earnestly. **swear by** *v* have complete confidence in. **swear in** *v* cause to take an oath. **swearword** *n* word considered obscene or blasphemous.

sweat ❶ *n* 1 salty liquid given off through the pores of the skin. 2 *slang* drudgery or hard labour. ▷ *v* 3 have sweat coming through the pores. 4 be anxious. **sweaty** *adj* **sweatshirt** *n* long-sleeved cotton jersey. **sweatshop** *n* place where employees work long hours in poor conditions for low pay.

sweater *n* (woollen) garment for the upper part of the body.

swede *n* 1 kind of turnip.

sweep ❶ *v* **sweeping**, **swept** 1 remove dirt from (a floor) with a broom. 2 move smoothly and quickly. 3 spread rapidly. 4 move majestically. 5 carry away suddenly or forcefully. 6 stretch in a long wide curve. ▷ *n* 7 sweeping. 8 sweeping motion. 9 wide expanse. 10 sweepstake. 11 chimney sweep. **sweeping** *adj* 1 wide-ranging. 2 indiscriminate. **sweepstake**

━━━━━━━━━━━━━━━━━━━━━━━━━━━━━━━━━━━━━ THESAURUS

S

swamp *n* 1 = **bog**, fen, marsh, mire, morass, quagmire, slough, muskeg (*Canad*) ▷ *v* 2 = **flood**, capsize, engulf, inundate, sink, submerge 3 = **overwhelm**, engulf, flood, inundate, overload, submerge

swap *v* 1 = **exchange**, barter, interchange, switch, trade

swarm¹ *n* 2 = **multitude**, army, crowd, flock, herd, horde, host, mass, throng ▷ *v* 3 = **crowd**, flock, mass, stream, throng 4 = **teem**, abound, bristle, crawl

swarthy *adj* = **dark-skinned**, black, brown, dark, dark-complexioned, dusky

swathe *v* 1 = **wrap**, bundle up, cloak, drape, envelop, shroud

sway *v* 1 = **bend**, lean, rock, roll, swing 2 = **influence**, affect, guide, induce, persuade ▷ *n* 3 = **power**, authority, clout (*inf*), control, influence, mana (*NZ*)

swear *v* 1 = **curse**, be foul-mouthed, blaspheme 2 = **vow**, attest, promise, testify 3 = **declare**, affirm, assert

sweat *n* 1 = **perspiration** 2 *Sl* = **labour**, chore, drudgery, toil ▷ *v* 3 = **perspire**, glow 4 = **worry**, agonize, fret, suffer, torture oneself

sweep *v* 1 = **clear**, brush, clean, remove 2 = **sail**, fly, glide, pass, skim, tear, zoom ▷ *n* 8 = **stroke**, move, swing 9 = **extent**, range, scope, stretch

n lottery in which the stakes of the participants make up the prize.

sweet ❶ *adj* **1** tasting of or like sugar. **2** kind and charming. **3** agreeable to the senses or mind. **4** (of wine) with a high sugar content. ▷ *n* **5** shaped piece of food consisting mainly of sugar. **6** dessert. **sweetly** *adv* **sweetness** *n* **sweeten** *v* **sweetener** *n* **1** sweetening agent that does not contain sugar. **2** *slang* bribe. **sweetbread** *n* animal's pancreas used as food. **sweet corn** type of maize with sweet yellow kernels, eaten as a vegetable. **sweetheart** *n* lover. **sweetmeat** *n* old-fashioned sweet delicacy such as a small cake. **sweet pea** climbing plant with bright fragrant flowers. **sweet-talk** *v informal* coax or flatter. **sweet tooth** strong liking for sweet foods.

swell ❶ *v* **swelling**, **swelled**, **swollen** *or* **swelled 1** expand or increase. **2** (of a sound) become gradually louder. ▷ *n* **3** swelling or being swollen. **4** movement of waves in the sea. **5** *old-fashioned slang* fashionable person. ▷ *adj* **6** *US slang* excellent or fine. **swelling** *n* enlargement of part of the body, caused by injury or infection.

swerve ❶ *v* **1** turn aside from a course sharply or suddenly. ▷ *n* **2** swerving.

swift ❶ *adj* **1** moving or able to move quickly. ▷ *n* **2** fast-flying bird with pointed wings. **swiftly** *adv* **swiftness** *n*.

swig *n* **1** large mouthful of drink. ▷ *v* **swigging**, **swigged 2** drink in large mouthfuls.

swill *v* **1** drink greedily. **2** rinse (something) in large amounts of water. ▷ *n* **3** sloppy mixture containing waste food, fed to pigs. **4** deep drink.

swim *v* **swimming**, **swam**, **swum 1** move along in water by movements of the limbs. **2** be covered or flooded with liquid. **3** reel, e.g. *her head was swimming*. ▷ *n* **4** act or period of swimming. **swimmer** *n* **swimmingly** *adv* successfully and effortlessly. **swimming pool** (building containing) an artificial pond for swimming in.

swindle ❶ *v* **1** cheat (someone) out of money. ▷ *n* **2** instance of swindling. **swindler** *n*.

swine *n* **1** contemptible person. **2** pig.

swing ❶ *v* **swinging**, **swung 1** move to and fro, sway. **2** move in a curve. **3** (of an opinion or mood) change sharply. **4** hit out with a sweeping motion. **5** *slang* be hanged. ▷ *n* **6** swinging. **7** suspended seat on which a child can swing to and fro. **8** sudden or extreme change.

swingeing ❶ [**swin**-jing] *adj* punishing, severe.

swipe ❶ *v* **1** strike (at) with a sweeping blow. **2** *slang* steal. **3** pass (a credit card)

sweet *adj* **1** = **sugary**, cloying, icky (*inf*), saccharine ▷ *adj* **2** = **charming**, appealing, engaging, kind, likable *or* likeable, lovable, winning **3** = **fragrant**, agreeable, aromatic, clean, fresh, pure ▷ *n* **5** = **confectionery**, bonbon, candy (*US*), lolly (*Aust & NZ inf*) **6** = **dessert**, pudding

swell *v* **1** = **expand**, balloon, bloat, bulge, dilate, distend, enlarge, grow, increase, rise **2** = **increase**, heighten, intensify, mount, surge ▷ *n* **4** = **wave**, billow, surge

swerve *v* **1** = **veer**, bend, deflect, deviate, diverge, stray, swing, turn, turn aside

swift *adj* **1** = **quick**, fast, hurried, prompt, rapid, speedy

swindle *v* **1** = **cheat**, con, defraud, do (*sl*), fleece, rip (someone) off (*sl*), skin (*sl*), sting (*inf*), trick ▷ *n* **2** = **fraud**, con trick (*inf*), deception, fiddle (*Brit inf*), racket, rip-off (*sl*), scam (*sl*)

swing *v* **1** = **sway**, oscillate, rock, veer, wave **2** = **turn**, pivot, rotate, swivel **5** *Sl* = **hang** ▷ *n* **6** = **swaying**, oscillation

swingeing *adj* = **severe**, drastic, excessive, harsh, heavy, punishing, stringent

swipe *v* **1** = **hit**, lash out at, slap, strike, wallop (*inf*) **2** *Sl* = **steal**, appropriate, filch, lift (*inf*), nick (*sl, chiefly Brit*), pinch (*inf*),

S

through a machine which electronically reads information stored in the card. ▷ *n* **4** hard blow.

swirl ❶ *v* **1** turn with a whirling motion. ▷ *n* **2** whirling motion. **3** twisting shape.

swish *v* **1** move with a whistling or hissing sound. ▷ *n* **2** whistling or hissing sound. ▷ *adj* **3** *informal* fashionable, smart.

switch ❶ *n* **1** device for opening and closing an electric circuit. **2** abrupt change. **3** exchange or swap. **4** flexible rod or twig. ▷ *v* **5** change abruptly. **6** exchange or swap. **switchback** *n* road or railway with many sharp hills or bends. **switchboard** *n* installation in a telephone exchange or office where telephone calls are connected. **switch on, off** *v* turn (a device) on or off by means of a switch.

swivel ❶ *v* **-elling, -elled 1** turn on a central point. ▷ *n* **2** coupling device that allows an attached object to turn freely.

swoop ❶ *v* **1** sweep down or pounce on suddenly. ▷ *n* **2** swooping.

sword *n* weapon with a long sharp blade. **swordfish** *n* large fish with a very long upper jaw. **swordsman** *n* person skilled in the use of a sword.

swot ❶ *informal* ▷ *v* **swotting, swotted 1** study hard. ▷ *n* **2** person who studies hard.

sycamore *n* tree with five-pointed leaves and two-winged fruits.

sycophant ❶ *n* person who uses flattery

to win favour from people with power or influence. **sycophantic** *adj* **sycophancy** *n*.

syllable *n* part of a word pronounced as a unit. **syllabic** *adj*.

syllabus ❶ *n, pl* **-buses, -bi** list of subjects for a course of study.

syllogism *n* form of logical reasoning consisting of two premises and a conclusion.

symbol ❶ *n* sign or thing that stands for something else. **symbolic** *adj* **symbolically** *adv* **symbolism** *n* **1** representation of something by symbols. **2** movement in art and literature using symbols to express abstract and mystical ideas. **symbolist** *n, adj* **symbolize** *v* **1** be a symbol of. **2** represent with a symbol.

symmetry ❶ *n* state of having two halves that are mirror images of each other. **symmetrical** *adj* **symmetrically** *adv*.

sympathy ❶ *n, pl* **-thies 1** compassion for someone's pain or distress. **2** agreement with someone's feelings or interests. **sympathetic** *adj* **1** feeling or showing sympathy. **2** likeable or appealing. **sympathetically** *adv* **sympathize** *v* feel or express sympathy. **sympathizer** *n*.

symphony *n, pl* **-nies** composition for orchestra, with several movements. **symphonic** *adj*.

symposium *n, pl* **-siums, -sia** conference for discussion of a particular topic.

S

— THESAURUS —

purloin ▷ *n* **4** = **blow**, clout (*inf*), cuff, slap, smack, thump, wallop (*inf*)

swirl *v* **1** = **whirl**, churn, eddy, spin, twist

switch *n* **2** = **change**, reversal, shift **3** = **exchange**, substitution, swap ▷ *v* **5** = **change**, deflect, deviate, divert, shift **6** = **exchange**, substitute, swap

swivel *v* **1** = **turn**, pivot, revolve, rotate, spin

swoop *v* **1** = **pounce**, descend, dive, rush, stoop, sweep ▷ *n* **2** = **pounce**, descent, drop, lunge, plunge, rush, stoop, sweep

swot *v Inf* **1** = **study**, cram (*inf*), mug up

(*Brit sl*), revise

sycophant *n* = **crawler**, bootlicker (*inf*), fawner, flatterer, toady, yes man

syllabus *n* = **course of study**, curriculum

symbol *n* = **sign**, badge, emblem, figure, image, logo, mark, representation, token

symmetry *n* = **balance**, evenness, order, proportion, regularity

sympathy *n* **1** = **compassion**, commiseration, pity, understanding **2** = **affinity**, agreement, fellow feeling, rapport

symptom ❶ n 1 sign indicating the presence of an illness. 2 sign that something is wrong. **symptomatic** adj.

synagogue n Jewish place of worship and religious instruction.

sync, synch informal ▷ n 1 synchronization. ▷ v 2 synchronize.

synchromesh adj (of a gearbox) having a device that synchronizes the speeds of gears before they engage.

synchronize v 1 (of two or more people) perform (an action) at the same time. 2 set (watches) to show the same time. 3 match (the soundtrack and action of a film) precisely. **synchronization** n **synchronous** adj happening or existing at the same time.

syncopate v Music stress the weak beats in (a rhythm) instead of the strong ones. **syncopation** n.

syndicate n 1 group of people or firms undertaking a joint business project. 2 agency that sells material to several newspapers. ▷ v 3 publish (material) in several newspapers. 4 form a syndicate. **syndication** n.

syndrome n 1 combination of symptoms indicating a particular disease. 2 set of characteristics indicating a particular problem.

synod n church council.

synonym n word with the same meaning as another. **synonymous** adj.

synopsis n, pl -ses summary or outline.

syntax n Grammar way in which words are arranged to form phrases and sentences. **syntactic** adj.

synthesis n, pl -ses 1 combination of objects or ideas into a whole. 2 artificial production of a substance. **synthesize** v produce by synthesis. **synthesizer** n electronic musical instrument producing a range of sounds. **synthetic** adj 1 (of a substance) made artificially. 2 not genuine, insincere. **synthetically** adv.

syphilis n serious sexually transmitted disease.

syringe n 1 device for withdrawing or injecting fluids, consisting of a hollow cylinder, a piston, and a hollow needle. ▷ v 2 wash out or inject with a syringe.

syrup n 1 solution of sugar in water. 2 thick sweet liquid. **syrupy** adj.

system ❶ n 1 method or set of methods. 2 scheme of classification or arrangement. 3 network or assembly of parts that form a whole. **systematic** adj **systematically** adv **systemic** adj affecting the entire animal or body.

———————— THESAURUS ————————

symptom n 2 = **sign**, expression, indication, mark, token, warning

system n 1 = **method**, practice, procedure, routine, technique 2 = **arrangement**, classification, organization, scheme, structure

S

Tt

ta *interj informal* thank you.

tab *n* small flap or projecting label. **keep tabs on** *informal* watch closely.

Tabasco *n* ® very hot red pepper sauce.

tabby *n, pl* **-bies** *adj* (cat) with dark stripes on a lighter background.

table ❶ *n* **1** piece of furniture with a flat top supported by legs. **2** arrangement of information in columns. ▷ *v* **3** submit (a motion) for discussion by a meeting. **4** *US* suspend discussion of (a proposal). **tablespoon** *n* large spoon for serving food. **table tennis** game like tennis played on a table with small bats and a light ball.

tableau ❶ [tab-loh] *n, pl* **-leaux** silent motionless group arranged to represent some scene.

tablet *n* **1** pill of compressed medicinal substance. **2** inscribed slab of stone etc.

tabloid *n* small-sized newspaper with many photographs and a concise, usu. sensational style.

taboo ❶ *n, pl* **-boos 1** prohibition resulting from religious or social conventions. ▷ *adj* **2** forbidden by a taboo.

tacit ❶ [tass-it] *adj* implied but not spoken.

taciturn ❶ [tass-it-turn] *adj* habitually uncommunicative. **taciturnity** *n*.

tack¹ ❶ *n* **1** short nail with a large head. **2** long loose stitch. ▷ *v* **3** fasten with tacks. **4** stitch with tacks. **tack on** *v* append.

tack² ❶ *n* **1** course of a ship sailing obliquely into the wind. **2** course of action. ▷ *v* **3** sail into the wind on a zigzag course.

tack³ *n* riding harness for horses.

tackies, takkies *pl n, sing* **tacky** *S Afr informal* tennis shoes or plimsolls.

tackle ❶ *v* **1** deal with (a task). **2** confront (an opponent). **3** *Sport* attempt to get the ball from (an opposing player). ▷ *n* **4** *Sport* act of tackling an opposing player. **5** equipment for a particular activity. **6** set of ropes and pulleys for lifting heavy weights.

tacky¹ ❶ *adj* **tackier, tackiest** slightly sticky.

————————————— THESAURUS —————————————

table *n* **1** = **counter**, bench, board, stand **2** = **list**, catalogue, chart, diagram, record, register, roll, schedule, tabulation ▷ *v* **3** = **submit**, enter, move, propose, put forward, suggest

tableau *n* = **picture**, representation, scene, spectacle

taboo *n* **1** = **prohibition**, anathema, ban, interdict, proscription, restriction ▷ *adj* **2** = **forbidden**, anathema, banned, outlawed, prohibited, proscribed, unacceptable, unmentionable

tacit *adj* = **implied**, implicit, inferred, undeclared, understood, unexpressed, unspoken, unstated

taciturn *adj* = **uncommunicative**, quiet, reserved, reticent, silent, tight-lipped, unforthcoming, withdrawn

tack¹ *n* **1** = **nail**, drawing pin, pin ▷ *v* **3** = **fasten**, affix, attach, fix, nail, pin **4** = **stitch**, baste, sew **tack on** *v* = **append**, add, attach, tag

tack² *n* **2** = **course**, approach, direction, heading, line, method, path, plan, procedure, way

tackle *v* **1** = **deal with**, attempt, come or get to grips with, embark upon, get stuck into (*inf*), have a go or stab at (*inf*), set about, undertake **2** = **confront**, challenge, grab, grasp, halt, intercept, seize, stop ▷ *n* **4** *Sport* = **challenge**, block **5** = **equipment**, accoutrements, apparatus, gear, paraphernalia, tools, trappings

tacky¹ *adj* = **sticky**, adhesive, gluey, gummy, wet

t

tacky² ❶ *adj* **tackier**, **tackiest 1** *informal* vulgar and tasteless. **2** shabby.

taco [**tah-koh**] *n*, *pl* **tacos** *Mexican cookery* tortilla fried until crisp, served with a filling.

tact ❶ *n* skill in avoiding giving offence. **tactful** *adj* **tactless** *adj*.

tactics *n* art of directing military forces in battle. **tactic** *n* method or plan to achieve an end. **tactical** *adj* **tactician** *n*.

tactile *adj* of or having the sense of touch.

tadpole *n* limbless tailed larva of a frog or toad.

taffeta *n* shiny silk or rayon fabric.

tag¹ ❶ *n* **1** label bearing information. **2** pointed end of a cord or lace. **3** trite quotation. ▷ *v* **tagging**, **tagged 4** attach a tag to. **tag along** *v* accompany someone, esp. if uninvited.

tag² *n* **1** children's game where the person being chased becomes the chaser upon being touched. ▷ *v* **tagging**, **tagged 2** touch and catch in this game.

tail ❶ *n* **1** rear part of an animal's body, usu. forming a flexible appendage. **2** rear or last part or parts of something. **3** *informal* person employed to follow and spy on another. ▷ *pl* **4** *informal* tail coat. ▷ *adj* **5** at the rear. ▷ *v* **6** *informal* follow (someone) secretly. **turn tail** run away. **tailless** *adj* **tails** *adv* with the side of a coin uppermost that does not have a portrait of a head on it. **tailback** *n* queue of traffic stretching back from an obstruction. **tailboard** *n* removable or hinged rear board on a lorry etc. **tail coat** man's coat with a long back split into two below the waist. **tail off**, **away** *v* diminish gradually. **tailspin** *n* uncontrolled spinning dive of an aircraft. **tailwind** *n* wind coming from the rear.

tailor ❶ *n* **1** person who makes men's clothes. ▷ *v* **2** adapt to suit a purpose. **tailor-made** *adj* **1** made by a tailor. **2** perfect for a purpose.

taint ❶ *v* **1** spoil with a small amount of decay, contamination, or other bad quality. ▷ *n* **2** something that taints.

take ❶ *v* **taking**, **took**, **taken 1** remove from a place. **2** carry or accompany. **3** use. **4** get possession of, esp. dishonestly. **5** capture. **6** require (time, resources, or ability). **7** assume. **8** accept. **9** write down. **10** subtract or deduct. ▷ *n* **11** one of a series of recordings from which the best will be used. **take place** happen. **taking** *adj* charming. **takings** *pl n* money

tacky² *adj* **1** Inf = **vulgar**, cheap, naff (*Brit sl*), sleazy, tasteless **2** = **shabby**, seedy, shoddy, tatty

tact *n* = **diplomacy**, consideration, delicacy, discretion, sensitivity, thoughtfulness, understanding

tag¹ *n* **1** = **label**, flap, identification, mark, marker, note, slip, tab, ticket ▷ *v* **4** = **label**, mark **tag along** *v* = **accompany**, attend, follow, shadow, tail (*inf*), trail

tail *n* **1**, **2** = **extremity**, appendage, end, rear end, tailpiece ▷ *v* **6** Inf = **follow**, shadow, stalk, track, trail **turn tail** = **run away**, cut and run, flee, retreat, run off, take to one's heels

tailor *n* **1** = **outfitter**, clothier, costumier, couturier, dressmaker, seamstress ▷ *v* **2** = **adapt**, adjust, customize, fashion, modify, mould, shape

taint *v* **1** = **spoil**, blemish, contaminate, corrupt, damage, defile, pollute, ruin, stain, sully, tarnish ▷ *n* **2** = **stain**, black mark, blemish, blot, defect, demerit, fault, flaw, spot

take *v* **2** = **carry**, accompany, bear, bring, conduct, convey, convoy, escort, ferry, fetch, guide, haul, lead, transport, usher **4** = **obtain**, acquire, appropriate, catch, get, grasp, grip, misappropriate, pinch (*inf*), pocket, purloin, secure, seize, steal **5** = **capture**, seize **6** = **require**, call for, demand, necessitate, need **7** = **assume**, believe, consider, perceive, presume, regard, understand **8** = **accept**, accommodate, contain, have room for, hold **10** = **subtract**, deduct,

t

received by a shop. **take after** v look or behave like (a parent etc.). **take away** v remove or subtract. **takeaway** n **1** shop or restaurant selling meals for eating elsewhere. **2** meal bought at a takeaway. **take in** v **1** understand. **2** deceive or swindle. **3** make (clothing) smaller. **take off** v **1** (of an aircraft) leave the ground. **2** informal depart. **3** informal parody. **takeoff** n **takeover** n act of taking control of a company by buying a large number of its shares. **take up** v **1** occupy or fill (space or time). **2** adopt the study or activity of. **3** shorten (a garment). **4** accept (an offer).

talc n **1** talcum powder. **2** soft mineral of magnesium silicate. **talcum powder** powder, usu. scented, used to dry or perfume the body.

tale ⊕ n **1** story. **2** malicious piece of gossip.

talent ⊕ n **1** natural ability. **2** ancient unit of weight or money. **talented** adj.

talisman ⊕ n, pl **-mans** object believed to have magic power. **talismanic** adj.

talk ⊕ v **1** express ideas or feelings by means of speech. **2** utter. **3** discuss, e.g. let's talk business. **4** reveal information. **5** (be able to) speak in a specified language. ▷ n

6 speech or lecture. **talker** n **talkative** adj fond of talking. **talk back** v answer impudently. **talkback** n NZ broadcast in which telephone comments or questions from the public are transmitted live. **talking-to** n informal telling-off.

tall ⊕ adj **1** higher than average. **2** of a specified height. **tall order** difficult task. **tall story** unlikely and probably untrue tale.

tally ⊕ v **-lying, -lied 1** (of two things) correspond. ▷ n, pl **-lies 2** record of a debt or score.

talon n bird's hooked claw.

tambourine n percussion instrument like a small drum with jingling metal discs attached.

tame ⊕ adj **1** (of animals) brought under human control. **2** (of animals) not afraid of people. **3** meek or submissive. **4** uninteresting. ▷ v **5** make tame. **tamely** adv **tamer** n.

tamper ⊕ v (foll. by with) interfere.

tampon n absorbent plug of cotton wool inserted into the vagina during menstruation.

tan n **1** brown coloration of the skin from

———————————————————— THESAURUS ————————————————————

eliminate, remove

tale n **1** = **story**, account, anecdote, fable, legend, narrative, saga, yarn (inf)

talent n = **ability**, aptitude, capacity, flair, genius, gift, knack

talisman n = **charm**, amulet, fetish, lucky charm, mascot

talk v **1, 2** = **speak**, chat, chatter, communicate, converse, gossip, natter, utter **3** = **discuss**, confabulate, confer, negotiate, parley **4** = **inform**, blab, give the game away, grass (Brit sl), let the cat out of the bag, tell all ▷ n **6** = **speech**, address, discourse, disquisition, lecture, oration, sermon

tall adj **1** = **high**, big, elevated, giant, lanky, lofty, soaring, towering **tall order** = **difficult**, demanding, hard, unreasonable, well-nigh impossible **tall**

story = **implausible**, absurd, cock-and-bull (inf), exaggerated, far-fetched, incredible, preposterous, unbelievable

tally v **1** = **agree**, accord, coincide, concur, conform, correspond, fit, harmonize, match, square ▷ n **2** = **record**, count, mark, reckoning, running total, score, total

tame adj **1** = **broken**, amenable, disciplined, docile, gentle, obedient, tractable **2** = **domesticated 3** = **submissive**, compliant, docile, manageable, meek, obedient, subdued, unresisting **4** = **unexciting**, bland, boring, dull, humdrum, insipid, uninspiring, uninteresting, vapid ▷ v **5 a** = **domesticate**, house-train, train **b** = **subdue**, break in, master

tamper v (foll. by with) = **interfere with**,

exposure to sunlight. ▷ v **tanning, tanned**
2 (of skin) go brown from exposure to
sunlight. **3** convert (a hide) into leather.
▷ adj **4** yellowish-brown. **tannery** n place
where hides are tanned.

tandem n bicycle for two riders, one behind
the other. **in tandem** together.

tandoori adj (of food) cooked in an Indian
clay oven.

tang n **1** strong taste or smell. **2** trace or
hint. **tangy** adj.

tangent n **1** line that touches a
curve without intersecting it. **2** (in
trigonometry) ratio of the length of the
opposite side to that of the adjacent
side of a right-angled triangle. **go off at
a tangent** suddenly take a completely
different line of thought or action.
tangential adj **1** of superficial relevance
only. **2** of a tangent.

tangerine n small orange-like fruit of an
Asian citrus tree.

tangible ❶ adj **1** able to be touched. **2** clear
and definite. **tangibly** adv.

tangle ❶ n **1** confused mass or situation.
▷ v **2** twist together in a tangle. **3** (often
foll. by with) come into conflict.

tango n, pl **-gos 1** S American dance. ▷ v
2 dance a tango.

tank n **1** container for liquids or gases.
2 armoured fighting vehicle moving on

tracks. **tanker** n ship or lorry for carrying
liquid in bulk.

tankard n large beer-mug, often with a
hinged lid.

Tannoy n ® type of public-address system.

tantalize ❶ v torment by showing
but withholding something desired.
tantalizing adj.

tantamount ❶ adj **tantamount
to** equivalent in effect to.

tantrum ❶ n childish outburst of temper.

tap¹ ❶ v **tapping, tapped 1** knock lightly
and usu. repeatedly. ▷ n **2** light knock. **tap
dancing** style of dancing in which the feet
beat out an elaborate rhythm.

tap² ❶ n **1** valve to control the flow of liquid
from a pipe or cask. ▷ v **tapping, tapped
2** listen in on (a telephone call) secretly by
making an illegal connection. **3** draw off
with or as if with a tap. **on tap 1** informal
readily available. **2** (of beer etc.) drawn
from a cask.

tape ❶ n **1** narrow long strip of material.
2 (recording made on) a cassette
containing magnetic tape. **3** string
stretched across a race track to mark the
finish. ▷ v **4** record on magnetic tape.
5 bind or fasten with tape. **tape measure**
tape marked off in centimetres or inches
for measuring. **tape recorder** device
for recording and reproducing sound on

alter, fiddle with (inf), fool about with (inf),
meddle with, mess about with, tinker with

tangible adj **1 = palpable**, actual, concrete,
material, real **2 = definite**, perceptible,
positive

tangle n **1 a = knot**, coil, entanglement,
jungle, twist, web **b = confusion**,
complication, entanglement, fix (inf),
imbroglio, jam, mess, mix-up ▷ v **2 = twist**,
coil, entangle, interweave, knot, mat,
mesh, ravel **3** (often foll. by with) **= come
into conflict with**, come up against,
contend with, contest, cross swords with,
dispute with, lock horns with

tantalize v **= torment**, frustrate, lead on,

taunt, tease, torture

tantamount adj **tantamount to
= equivalent to**, commensurate with,
equal to, synonymous with

tantrum n **= outburst**, fit, flare-up,
hysterics, temper

tap¹ v **1 = knock**, beat, drum, pat, rap, strike,
touch ▷ n **2 = knock**, pat, rap, touch

tap² n **1 = valve**, stopcock, faucet (US &
Canad) ▷ v **2 = listen in on**, bug (inf),
eavesdrop on **3 = draw off**, bleed, drain,
siphon off **on tap 1** Inf **= available**, at
hand, in reserve, on hand, ready **2 = on
draught**

tape n **1 = strip**, band, ribbon ▷ v

t

magnetic tape. **tapeworm** n long flat
parasitic worm living in the intestines of
vertebrates.

taper ❶ v 1 become narrower towards one
end. ▷ n 2 long thin candle. **taper off** v
become gradually less.

tapestry n, pl **-tries** fabric decorated with
coloured woven designs.

tapioca n beadlike starch made from
cassava root, used in puddings.

tar n 1 thick black liquid distilled from coal
etc. ▷ v **tarring, tarred** 2 coat with tar.

tarantula n large hairy spider with a
poisonous bite.

tardy adj **tardier, tardiest** slow or late.
tardily adv **tardiness** n.

target ❶ n 1 object or person a missile is
aimed at. 2 goal or objective. 3 object of
criticism. ▷ v **-geting, -geted** 4 aim or
direct.

● SPELLING TIP
● Lots of people put an extra t into *targetting*
● and *targetted*, but they are wrong: the
● words are **targeting** and **targeted**.

tariff ❶ n 1 tax levied on imports. 2 list of
fixed prices.

Tarmac n 1 ® mixture of tar, bitumen, and
crushed stones used for roads etc. 2 (t-)
airport runway.

tarn n small mountain lake.

tarnish ❶ v 1 make or become stained
or less bright. 2 damage or taint. ▷ n
3 discoloration or blemish.

tarot [**tarr**-oh] n special pack of cards used
mainly in fortune-telling. **tarot card** card
in a tarot pack.

tarpaulin n (sheet of) heavy waterproof
fabric.

tarragon n aromatic herb.

tarry v **-rying, -ried** old-fashioned 1 linger or
delay. 2 stay briefly.

tart¹ ❶ n pie or flan with a sweet filling.

tart² ❶ adj sharp or bitter. **tartly** adv
tartness n.

tartan n 1 design of straight lines crossing
at right angles, esp. one associated with a
Scottish clan. 2 cloth with such a pattern.

tartar n 1 hard deposit on the teeth.
2 deposit formed during the fermentation
of wine.

task ❶ n (difficult or unpleasant) piece of
work to be done. **take to task** criticize or
scold. **task force** (military) group formed
to carry out a specific task. **taskmaster** n
person who enforces hard work.

Tasmanian tiger same as THYLACINE.

tassel n decorative fringed knot of threads.

taste ❶ n 1 sense by which the flavour of a

─────────────────────────────── THESAURUS ───────────────────────────────

4 = **record**, tape-record, video 5 = **bind**,
seal, secure, stick, wrap
taper v 1 = **narrow**, come to a point, thin
taper off v = **decrease**, die away, dwindle,
fade, lessen, reduce, subside, wane, wind
down
target n 2 = **goal**, aim, ambition, end,
intention, mark, object, objective
3 = **victim**, butt, scapegoat
tariff n 1 = **tax**, duty, excise, levy, toll
2 = **price list**, menu, schedule
tarnish v 1 = **stain**, blemish, blot, darken,
discolour 2 = **damage**, blacken, smirch,
sully, taint ▷ n 3 = **stain**, blemish, blot,
discoloration, spot, taint
tart¹ n = **pie**, pastry, tartlet
tart² adj = **sharp**, acid, bitter, piquant,

pungent, sour, tangy, vinegary
task n = **job**, assignment, chore, duty,
enterprise, exercise, mission, undertaking
take to task = **criticize**, blame, censure,
rebuke, reprimand, reproach, reprove,
rouse on (Aust), scold, tell off (inf), upbraid
taste n 2 = **flavour**, relish, savour,
smack, tang 3 = **bit**, bite, dash, morsel,
mouthful, sample, soupçon, spoonful,
titbit 5 = **liking**, appetite, fancy, fondness,
inclination, partiality, penchant,
predilection, preference 6 = **refinement**,
appreciation, discernment, discrimination,
elegance, judgment, sophistication, style
▷ v 7 = **distinguish**, differentiate, discern,
perceive 8 = **sample**, savour, sip, test, try
9 = **have a flavour of**, savour of, smack of

t

substance is distinguished in the mouth. **2** distinctive flavour. **3** small amount tasted. **4** brief experience of something. **5** liking. **6** ability to appreciate what is beautiful or excellent. ▷ v **7** distinguish the taste of (a substance). **8** take a small amount of (something) into the mouth. **9** have a specific taste. **10** experience briefly. **tasteful** adj having or showing good taste. **tasteless** adj **1** bland or insipid. **2** showing bad taste. **tastelessly** adv **tasty** adj pleasantly flavoured. **taste bud** small organ on the tongue which perceives flavours.

tattered adj ragged or torn. **in tatters** in ragged pieces.

tattle v, n gossip or chatter.

tattletale ❶ Chiefly US & Canad ▷ n a scandalmonger or gossip.

tattoo¹ n **1** pattern made on the body by pricking the skin and staining it with indelible inks. ▷ v **-tooing**, **-tooed** **2** make such a pattern on the skin. **tattooist** n.

tattoo² n **1** military display or pageant. **2** drumming or tapping.

tatty ❶ adj **-tier**, **-tiest** shabby or worn out.

taunt ❶ v **1** tease with jeers. ▷ n **2** jeering remark.

taupe adj brownish-grey.

taut ❶ adj **1** drawn tight. **2** showing nervous strain. **tauten** v make or become taut.

tavern ❶ n old-fashioned pub.

tawdry ❶ adj **-drier**, **-driest** cheap, showy, and of poor quality.

tawny adj **-nier**, **-niest** yellowish-brown.

tax ❶ n **1** compulsory payment levied by a government on income, property, etc. to raise revenue. ▷ v **2** levy a tax on. **3** make heavy demands on. **taxable** adj **taxation** n levying of taxes. **taxpayer** n **tax return** statement of personal income for tax purposes.

taxi n **1** (also **taxicab**) car with a driver that may be hired to take people to any specified destination. ▷ v **taxiing**, **taxied** **2** (of an aircraft) run along the ground before taking off or after landing. **taxi rank** place where taxis wait to be hired.

taxidermy n art of stuffing and mounting animal skins to give them a lifelike appearance. **taxidermist** n.

TB tuberculosis.

tea n **1** drink made from infusing the dried leaves of an Asian bush in boiling water. **2** leaves used to make this drink. **3** main evening meal. **4** light afternoon meal of tea, cakes, etc. **5** drink like tea, made from other plants. **tea bag** small porous bag of tea leaves. **tea cosy** covering for a teapot to keep the tea warm. **teapot** n container with a lid, spout, and handle for making and serving tea. **teaspoon** n small spoon for stirring tea. **tea towel**, **tea cloth** towel for drying dishes. **tea tree** tree of Australia and New Zealand that

---

THESAURUS

---

10 = **experience**, encounter, know, meet with, partake of, undergo

tattletale chiefly US & Canad n = **gossip**, busybody, babbler, bigmouth (slang), scandalmonger, gossipmonger

tatty adj = **shabby**, bedraggled, dilapidated, down at heel, neglected, ragged, run-down, scruffy, threadbare, worn

taunt v **1** = **jeer**, deride, insult, mock, provoke, ridicule, tease, torment ▷ n **2** = **jeer**, derision, dig, gibe, insult, provocation, ridicule, sarcasm, teasing

taut adj **1** = **tight**, flexed, rigid, strained, stressed, stretched, tense

tavern n Old-fashioned = **inn**, alehouse (arch), bar, hostelry, pub (inf, chiefly Brit), public house, beer parlour (Canad), beverage room (Canad)

tawdry adj = **vulgar**, cheap, gaudy, gimcrack, naff (Brit sl), tacky (inf), tasteless, tatty

tax n **1** = **charge**, duty, excise, levy, tariff, tithe, toll ▷ v **2** = **charge**, assess, rate **3** = **strain**, burden, exhaust, load, stretch, test, try, weaken, weary

t

yields an oil used as an antiseptic.
teach *v* **teaching**, **taught** **1** tell or show (someone) how to do something. **2** give lessons in (a subject). **3** cause to learn or understand. **teacher** *n* **teaching** *n*.
teak *n* very hard wood of an E Indian tree.
team *n* **1** group of people forming one side in a game. **2** group of people or animals working together. **teamster** *n* US lorry driver. **team up** *v* make or join a team. **teamwork** *n* cooperative work by a team.
tear¹ *n* **teardrop** *n* drop of fluid appearing in and falling from the eye. **in tears** weeping. **tearful** *adj* weeping or about to weep. **tear gas** gas that stings the eyes and causes temporary blindness. **tear-jerker** *n informal* excessively sentimental film or book.
tear² *v* **tearing**, **tore**, **torn** **1** rip a hole in. **2** rip apart. **3** rush. ▷ *n* **4** hole or split. **tearaway** *n* wild or unruly person.
tease *v* **1** make fun of (someone) in a provoking or playful way. ▷ *n* **2** person who teases. **teasing** *adj*, *n* **tease out** *v* remove tangles from (hair etc.) by combing.
teat *n* **1** nipple of a breast or udder. **2** rubber nipple of a feeding bottle.
techie *informal* ▷ *n* **1** person who is skilled in the use of technology. ▷ *adj* **2** relating to or skilled in the use of technology.
technical *adj* **1** of or specializing in

industrial, practical, or mechanical arts and applied sciences. **2** skilled in technical subjects. **3** relating to a particular field. **4** according to the letter of the law. **5** showing technique, e.g. *technical brilliance*. **technicality** *n* petty point based on a strict application of rules. **technician** *n* person skilled in a particular technical field. **technical college** higher educational institution with courses in art and technical subjects. **technique** *n* **1** method or skill used for a particular task. **2** technical proficiency.
Technicolor *n* ® system of colour photography used for the cinema.
technology *n* **1** application of practical or mechanical sciences to industry or commerce. **2** scientific methods used in a particular field. **technological** *adj* **technologist** *n*.
tedious *adj* causing fatigue or boredom. **tedium** *n* monotony.
tee *n* **1** small peg from which a golf ball can be played at the start of each hole. **2** area of a golf course from which the first stroke of a hole is made. **tee off** *v* make the first stroke of a hole in golf.
teem¹ *v* be full of.
teem² *v* rain heavily.
teens *pl n* period of being a teenager.
teeter *v* wobble or move unsteadily.
teeth *n* plural of TOOTH.

————————————— THESAURUS —————————————

teach *v* 1-3 = **instruct**, coach, drill, educate, enlighten, guide, inform, show, train, tutor
team *n* 1 = **side**, line-up, squad **2** = **group**, band, body, bunch, company, gang, set
team up = **join**, band together, cooperate, couple, get together, link, unite, work together
tear¹ *n* **in tears** = **weeping**, blubbering, crying, distressed, sobbing
tear² *v* 1 = **rip**, rend, rupture, scratch, shred, split **2** = **pull apart**, claw, lacerate, mangle, mutilate **3** = **rush**, bolt, charge, dash, fly, hurry, race, run, speed, sprint,

zoom ▷ *n* 4 = **hole**, laceration, rent, rip, rupture, scratch, split
tease *v* 1 = **mock**, goad, provoke, pull someone's leg (*inf*), taunt, torment
technical *adj* 1, 2 = **scientific**, hi-tech *or* high-tech, skilled, specialist, specialized, technological
tedious *adj* = **boring**, drab, dreary, dull, humdrum, irksome, laborious, mind-numbing, monotonous, tiresome, wearisome
teeter *v* = **wobble**, rock, seesaw, stagger, sway, totter, waver

t

teethe v (of a baby) grow his or her first teeth. **teething troubles** problems during the early stages of something.

teetotal adj drinking no alcohol. **teetotaller** n.

Teflon n ® substance used for nonstick coatings on saucepans etc.

telecommunications n communications using telephone, radio, television, etc.

telegram n formerly, a message sent by telegraph.

telegraph n **1** formerly, a system for sending messages over a distance along a cable. ▷ v **2** communicate by telegraph. **telegraphist** n **telegraphy** n.

telepathy ⊙ n direct communication between minds. **telepathic** adj **telepathically** adv.

telephone ⊙ n **1** device for transmitting sound over a distance along wires. ▷ v **2** call or talk to (a person) by telephone. **telephony** n **telephonic** adj **telephonist** n person operating a telephone switchboard.

teleprinter n apparatus like a typewriter for sending and receiving typed messages by wire.

telescope ⊙ n **1** optical instrument for magnifying distant objects. ▷ v **2** shorten. **telescopic** adj.

television ⊙ n **1** system of producing a moving image and accompanying sound on a distant screen. **2** device for receiving broadcast signals and converting them into sound and pictures. **3** content of television programmes. **televise** v broadcast on television.

teleworking n use of home computers, telephones, etc., to enable a person to work from home while maintaining contact with colleagues or customers. **teleworker** n.

telex n **1** international communication service using teleprinters. **2** message sent by telex. ▷ v **3** transmit by telex.

tell ⊙ v telling, told **1** make known in words. **2** order or instruct. **3** give an account of. **4** discern or distinguish. **5** have an effect. **6** informal reveal secrets. **teller** n **1** narrator. **2** bank cashier. **3** person who counts votes. **telling** adj having a marked effect. **tell off** v reprimand. **telling-off** n **telltale** n **1** person who reveals secrets. ▷ adj **2** revealing.

telly n, pl -lies informal television.

temerity ⊙ [tim-**merr**-it-tee] n boldness or audacity.

temp informal ▷ n **1** temporary employee, esp. a secretary. ▷ v **2** work as a temp.

temper ⊙ n **1** outburst of anger. **2** tendency to become angry. **3** calm mental condition, e.g. I lost my temper.

THESAURUS

---

telepathy n = **mind-reading**, sixth sense

telephone n **1** = **phone**, dog and bone (sl), handset, iPhone®, line, mobile (phone), smartphone ▷ v **2** = **call**, dial, phone, ring (chiefly Brit)

telescope n **1** = **glass**, spyglass ▷ v **2** = **shorten**, abbreviate, abridge, compress, condense, contract, shrink

television n **2** = **TV**, small screen (inf), telly (Brit inf), the box (Brit inf), the tube (sl)

tell v **1** = **inform**, announce, communicate, disclose, divulge, express, make known, notify, proclaim, reveal, state **2** = **instruct**, bid, call upon, command, direct, order, require, summon **3** = **describe**, chronicle, depict, narrate, portray, recount, relate, report **4** = **distinguish**, differentiate, discern, discriminate, identify **5** = **have** or **take effect**, carry weight, count, make its presence felt, register, take its toll, weigh

temerity n = **audacity**, boldness, cheek, chutzpah (US & Canad inf), effrontery, front, impudence, nerve (inf), rashness

temper n **1** = **rage**, bad mood, fury, passion, tantrum **2** = **irritability**, hot-headedness, irascibility, passion, petulance, resentment, surliness **3** = **self-control**, calmness, composure, cool (sl), equanimity

4 frame of mind. ▷ v 5 make less extreme.
6 strengthen or toughen (metal).

temperament ⓘ n person's character or disposition. **temperamental** adj 1 having changeable moods. 2 informal erratic and unreliable. **temperamentally** adv.

temperate ⓘ adj 1 (of climate) not extreme. 2 self-restrained or moderate. **temperance** n 1 moderation. 2 abstinence from alcohol.

temperature n 1 degree of heat or cold. 2 informal abnormally high body temperature.

tempest ⓘ n violent storm. **tempestuous** adj violent or stormy.

template n pattern used to cut out shapes accurately.

temple¹ ⓘ n building for worship.

temple² n region on either side of the forehead.

tempo n, pl -pi, -pos 1 rate or pace. 2 speed of a piece of music.

temporal adj 1 of time. 2 worldly rather than spiritual.

temporary ⓘ adj lasting only for a short time. **temporarily** adv.

tempt ⓘ v entice (a person) to do something wrong. **tempt fate** take foolish or unnecessary risks. **tempter, temptress** n **temptation** n 1 tempting. 2 tempting thing. **tempting** adj attractive or inviting.

ten adj, n one more than nine. **tenth** adj, n (of) number ten in a series.

tenable ⓘ adj able to be upheld or maintained.

tenacious ⓘ adj 1 holding fast. 2 stubborn. **tenacity** n.

tenant ⓘ n person who rents land or a building. **tenancy** n.

tench n, pl **tench** freshwater game fish of the carp family.

tend¹ ⓘ v 1 be inclined. 2 go in the direction of. **tendency** n inclination to act in a certain way. **tendentious** adj biased, not impartial.

tend² ⓘ v take care of.

tender¹ ⓘ adj 1 not tough. 2 gentle and affectionate. 3 vulnerable or sensitive.

——————————————————— THESAURUS ———————

4 = **frame of mind**, constitution, disposition, humour, mind, mood, nature, temperament ▷ v 5 = **moderate**, assuage, lessen, mitigate, mollify, restrain, soften, soothe, tone down 6 = **strengthen**, anneal, harden, toughen

temperament n a = **nature**, bent, character, constitution, disposition, humour, make-up, outlook, personality, temper b = **excitability**, anger, hot-headedness, moodiness, petulance, volatility

temperate adj 1 = **mild**, calm, cool, fair, gentle, moderate, pleasant 2 = **moderate**, calm, composed, dispassionate, even-tempered, mild, reasonable, self-controlled, self-restrained, sensible

tempest n = **storm**, cyclone, gale, hurricane, squall, tornado, typhoon

temple¹ n = **shrine**, church, sanctuary

temporary adj = **impermanent**, brief, ephemeral, fleeting, interim, momentary, provisional, short-lived, transitory

tempt v = **entice**, coax, invite, lead on, lure, seduce, tantalize

tenable adj = **sound**, arguable, believable, defensible, justifiable, plausible, rational, reasonable, viable

tenacious adj 1 = **firm**, clinging, forceful, immovable, iron, strong, tight, unshakable 2 = **stubborn**, adamant, determined, dogged, obdurate, obstinate, persistent, resolute, steadfast, unswerving, unyielding

tenant n = **leaseholder**, inhabitant, lessee, occupant, occupier, renter, resident

tend¹ v 1 = **be inclined**, be apt, be liable, gravitate, have a tendency, incline, lean 2 = **go**, aim, bear, head, lead, make for, move, point

tend² v = **take care of**, attend, cultivate, keep, look after, maintain, manage, nurture, watch over

tender¹ adj 2 = **gentle**, affectionate, caring, compassionate, considerate, kind, loving,

tenderly adv **tenderness** n **tenderize** v soften (meat) by pounding or treatment with a special substance. **tenderizer** n **tenderloin** n tender cut of pork from between the sirloin and the ribs.

tender² ⓿ v 1 offer. 2 make a formal offer to supply goods or services at a stated cost. ▷ n 3 such an offer. **legal tender** currency that must, by law, be accepted as payment.

tendon n strong tissue attaching a muscle to a bone.

tendril n slender stem by which a climbing plant clings.

tenement n building divided into several flats.

tenet [ten-nit] n doctrine or belief.

tennis n game in which players use rackets to hit a ball back and forth over a net.

tenor n 1 (singer with) the second highest male voice. 2 general meaning. ▷ adj 3 (of a voice or instrument) between alto and baritone.

tenpin bowling n game in which players try to knock over ten skittles by rolling a ball at them.

tense¹ ⓿ adj 1 emotionally strained. 2 stretched tight. ▷ v 3 make or become tense. **tension** n 1 hostility or suspense.

2 emotional strain. 3 degree of stretching.

tense² n Grammar form of a verb showing the time of action.

tent n portable canvas shelter.

tentacle n flexible organ of many invertebrates, used for grasping, feeding, etc.

tentative ⓿ adj 1 provisional or experimental. 2 cautious or hesitant. **tentatively** adv.

tenterhooks pl n **on tenterhooks** in anxious suspense.

tenuous ⓿ adj slight or flimsy.

tenure n (period of) the holding of an office or position.

tepee [tee-pee] n cone-shaped tent, formerly used by Native Americans.

tepid ⓿ adj 1 slightly warm. 2 half-hearted.

tequila n Mexican alcoholic drink.

term ⓿ n 1 word or expression. 2 fixed period. 3 period of the year when a school etc. is open or a lawcourt holds sessions. ▷ pl 4 conditions. 5 mutual relationship. ▷ v 6 name or designate.

terminal ⓿ adj 1 (of an illness) ending in death. 2 at or being an end. ▷ n 3 place where people or vehicles begin or end a journey. 4 point where current enters or leaves an electrical device. 5 keyboard and

——————————— THESAURUS ———————————

sympathetic, tenderhearted, warm-hearted 3 = **sensitive**, bruised, inflamed, painful, raw, sore, vulnerable

tender² v 1 = **offer**, give, hand in, present, proffer, propose, put forward, submit, volunteer ▷ n 3 = **offer**, bid, estimate, proposal, submission

tense¹ adj 1 = **nervous**, anxious, apprehensive, edgy, jumpy, keyed up, on edge, on tenterhooks, strained, uptight (inf), wired (sl) 2 = **tight**, rigid, strained, stretched, taut ▷ v 3 = **tighten**, brace, flex, strain, stretch

tentative adj 1 = **unconfirmed**, conjectural, experimental, indefinite, provisional, speculative, unsettled 2 = **hesitant**, cautious, diffident, doubtful, faltering,

timid, uncertain, undecided, unsure

tenuous adj = **slight**, doubtful, dubious, flimsy, insubstantial, nebulous, shaky, sketchy, weak

tepid adj 1 = **lukewarm**, warmish 2 = **half-hearted**, apathetic, cool, indifferent, lukewarm, unenthusiastic

term n 1 = **word**, expression, name, phrase, title 2 = **period**, duration, interval, season, span, spell, time, while ▷ v 6 = **call**, designate, dub, entitle, label, name, style

terminal adj 1 = **fatal**, deadly, incurable, killing, lethal, mortal 2 = **final**, concluding, extreme, last, ultimate, utmost ▷ n 3 = **terminus**, depot, end of the line, station

VDU having input and output links with a
computer. **terminally** adv.

terminate ❶ v bring or come to an end.
termination n.

terminology ❷ n technical terms relating
to a subject.

terminus ❸ n, pl **-ni**, **-nuses** railway or bus
station at the end of a line.

termite n white antlike insect that destroys
timber.

tern n gull-like sea bird with a forked tail and
pointed wings.

terrace n **1** row of houses built as one
block. **2** paved area next to a building.
3 level tier cut out of a hill. ▷ pl **4** (also
terracing) tiered area in a stadium where
spectators stand. ▷ v **5** form into or
provide with a terrace.

terracotta adj, n **1** (made of) brownish-red
unglazed pottery. ▷ adj **2** brownish-red.

terrain ❹ n area of ground, esp. with
reference to its physical character.

terrapin n small turtle-like reptile.

terrestrial ❺ adj **1** of the earth. **2** of or
living on land.

terrible ❻ adj **1** very serious. **2** informal very
bad. **3** causing fear. **terribly** adv.

terrier n any of various breeds of small
active dog.

terrific ❼ adj **1** great or intense. **2** informal
excellent.

terrify ❽ v **-fying**, **-fied** fill with fear.
terrified adj **terrifying** adj.

territory ❾ n, pl **-ries 1** district. **2** area
under the control of a particular
government. **3** area inhabited and
defended by an animal. **4** area of
knowledge. **territorial** adj **Territorial
Army** reserve army.

terror ❿ n **1** great fear. **2** terrifying person
or thing. **3** informal troublesome person
or thing. **terrorism** n use of violence and
intimidation to achieve political ends.
terrorist n, adj **terrorize** v force or oppress
by fear or violence.

terse ⓫ adj **1** neat and concise. **2** curt.
tersely adv.

tertiary [**tur**-shar-ee] adj third in degree,
order, etc.

Terylene n ® synthetic polyester yarn or
fabric.

test ⓬ v **1** try out to ascertain the worth,
capability, or endurance of. **2** carry
out an examination on. ▷ n **3** critical

─────────────────────────────── THESAURUS ───────────────────

terminate v = **end**, abort, cease, close,
complete, conclude, discontinue, finish,
stop

terminology n = **language**, jargon,
nomenclature, phraseology, terms,
vocabulary

terminus n = **end of the line**, depot,
garage, last stop, station

terrain n = **ground**, country, going, land,
landscape, topography

terrestrial adj **1** = **earthly**, global, worldly

terrible adj **1** = **serious**, dangerous,
desperate, extreme, severe **2** Inf = **bad**,
abysmal, awful, dire, dreadful, poor,
rotten (inf) **3** = **fearful**, dreadful,
frightful, horrendous, horrible, horrifying,
monstrous, shocking, terrifying

terrific adj **1** = **great**, enormous, fearful,
gigantic, huge, intense, tremendous

2 Inf = **excellent**, amazing, brilliant,
fantastic (inf), magnificent, marvellous,
outstanding, sensational (inf),
stupendous, superb, wonderful

terrify v = **frighten**, alarm, appal, horrify,
make one's hair stand on end, scare, shock,
terrorize

territory n **1** = **district**, area, country,
domain, land, patch, province, region, zone

terror n **1** = **fear**, alarm, anxiety, dread,
fright, horror, panic, shock **2** = **scourge**,
bogeyman, bugbear, devil, fiend,
monster

terse adj **1** = **concise**, brief, condensed,
laconic, monosyllabic, pithy, short,
succinct **2** = **curt**, abrupt, brusque, short,
snappy

test v **1** = **try out**, experiment, put to
the test **2** = **check**, analyse, assess,

examination. **4** Test match. **testing**
adj **test case** lawsuit that establishes a
precedent. **Test match** one of a series of
international cricket or rugby matches.
test tube narrow round-bottomed glass
tube used in scientific experiments.
test-tube baby baby conceived outside
the mother's body.
testament ❶ *n* **1** proof or tribute.
2 *Law* will. **3** (**T-**) one of the two main
divisions of the Bible.
testate *adj* having left a valid will.
testacy *n* **testator** [test-**tay**-tor], (*fem*)
testatrix [test-**tay**-triks] *n* maker of a will.
testicle *n* either of the two male
reproductive glands.
testify ❶ *v* **-fying, -fied** give evidence
under oath. **testify to** be evidence of.
testimony ❶ *n, pl* **-nies 1** declaration of
truth or fact. **2** evidence given under oath.
testimonial *n* **1** recommendation of the
worth of a person or thing. **2** tribute for
services or achievement.
testy *adj* **-tier, -tiest** irritable or touchy.
testily *adv* **testiness** *n*.
tetanus *n* acute infectious disease producing
muscular spasms and convulsions.
tête-à-tête *n, pl* **-têtes, -tête** private
conversation.
tether ❶ *n* **1** rope or chain for tying an
animal to a spot. ▷ *v* **2** tie up with rope.
at the end of one's tether at the limit of
one's endurance.

tetrahedron [tet-ra-**heed**-ron] *n, pl*
-drons, -dra solid figure with four faces.
text ❶ *n* **1** main body of a book as distinct
from illustrations etc. **2** passage of the
Bible as the subject of a sermon. **3** novel or
play studied for a course. **4** text message.
▷ *v* **5** send a text message to (someone).
textual *adj* **textbook** *n* **1** standard book
on a particular subject. ▷ *adj* **2** perfect, e.g.
a textbook landing. **text message** message
sent in text form, esp. by means of a cell
phone.
textile *n* fabric or cloth, esp. woven.
texture ❶ *n* structure, feel, or consistency.
textured *adj* **textural** *adj*.
than *conj, prep* used to introduce the second
element of a comparison.
thank ❶ *v* **1** express gratitude to. **2** hold
responsible. **thanks** *pl n* **1** words
of gratitude. ▷ *interj* **2** (also **thank
you**) polite expression of gratitude.
thanks to because of. **thankful** *adj*
grateful. **thankless** *adj* unrewarding or
unappreciated.
that *adj, pron* **1** used to refer to something
already mentioned or familiar, or further
away. ▷ *conj* **2** used to introduce a clause.
▷ *pron* **3** used to introduce a relative
clause.
thatch *n* **1** roofing material of reeds or straw.
▷ *v* **2** roof (a house) with reeds or straw.
thaw ❶ *v* **1** make or become unfrozen.
2 become more relaxed or friendly. ▷ *n*

—— THESAURUS ——

examine, investigate, research ▷ *n*
3 = **examination**, acid test, analysis,
assessment, check, evaluation,
investigation, research, trial
testament *n* **1** = **proof**, demonstration,
evidence, testimony, tribute, witness
2 *Law* = **will**, last wishes
testify *v* = **bear witness**, affirm, assert,
attest, certify, corroborate, state, swear,
vouch
testimony *n* **1** = **proof**, corroboration,
demonstration, evidence, indication,
manifestation, support, verification

2 = **evidence**, affidavit, deposition,
statement, submission
tether *n* **1** = **rope**, chain, fetter, halter,
lead, leash ▷ *v* **2** = **tie**, bind, chain, fasten,
fetter, secure **at the end of one's tether**
= **exasperated**, at one's wits' end, exhausted
text *n* **1** = **contents**, body
texture *n* = **feel**, consistency, grain,
structure, surface, tissue
thank *v* **1** = **say thank you**, show one's
appreciation
thaw *v* **1** = **melt**, defrost, dissolve, liquefy,
soften, unfreeze, warm

t

3 thawing. **4** weather causing snow or ice to melt.

the *adj* the definite article, used before a noun.

theatre *n* **1** place where plays etc. are performed. **2** hospital operating room. **3** drama and acting in general. **theatrical** *adj* **1** of the theatre. **2** exaggerated or affected. **theatricals** *pl n* (amateur) dramatic performances. **theatrically** *adv* **theatricality** *n*.

thee *pron obs* objective form of THOU.

theft *n* act or an instance of stealing.

their *adj* of or associated with them. **theirs** *pron* (thing or person) belonging to them.

- ● **SPELLING TIP**
- ● Do not confuse **their** and **theirs**, which
- ● do not have apostrophes, with **they're**
- ● and **there's**, which do because letters
- ● have been missed out where two words
- ● have been joined together.

them *pron* refers to people or things other than the speaker or those addressed. **themselves** *pron* emphatic and reflexive form of THEY or THEM.

theme ❶ *n* **1** main idea or subject being discussed. **2** recurring melodic figure in music. **thematic** *adj* **theme park** leisure area in which all the activities and displays are based on a single theme.

then *adv* **1** at that time. **2** after that. **3** that being so.

thence *adv* **1** from that place or time. **2** therefore.

theology *n, pl* **-gies** study of religions and religious beliefs. **theologian** *n* **theological** *adj* **theologically** *adv*.

theorem *n* proposition that can be proved by reasoning.

theory ❶ *n, pl* **-ries 1** set of ideas to explain something. **2** abstract knowledge or reasoning. **3** idea or opinion. **in theory** in an ideal or hypothetical situation. **theoretical** *adj* based on theory rather than practice or fact. **theoretically** *adv* **theorist** *n* **theorize** *v* form theories, speculate.

therapy ❶ *n, pl* **-pies** curing treatment. **therapist** *n* **therapeutic** [ther-rap-**pew**-tik] *adj* curing. **therapeutics** *n* art of curing.

there *adv* **1** in or to that place. **2** in that respect. **thereby** *adv* by that means. **therefore** *adv* consequently, that being so. **thereupon** *adv* immediately after that.

- ● **SPELLING TIP**
- ● Do not confuse **there**, which is closely
- ● connected in meaning and in spelling
- ● with 'here', and **their**, which means
- ● 'belonging to them'.

therm *n* unit of measurement of heat. **thermal** *adj* **1** of heat. **2** hot or warm. **3** (of clothing) retaining heat. ▷ *n* **4** rising current of warm air.

thermodynamics *n* scientific study of the relationship between heat and other forms of energy.

thermometer *n* instrument for measuring temperature.

Thermos *n* ® vacuum flask.

thermostat *n* device for automatically regulating temperature. **thermostatic** *adj* **thermostatically** *adv*.

thesaurus [thiss-**sore**-uss] *n, pl* **-ruses** book containing lists of synonyms and related words.

these *adj, pron* plural of THIS.

thesis ❶ *n, pl* **theses 1** written work submitted for a degree. **2** opinion supported by reasoned argument.

——————————————————————————————————— THESAURUS ———————————————

theft *n* = **stealing**, embezzlement, fraud, larceny, pilfering, purloining, robbery, thieving

theme *n* **1** = **subject**, idea, keynote, subject matter, topic **2** = **motif**, leitmotif

theory *n* **3** = **hypothesis**, assumption, conjecture, presumption, speculation,

supposition, surmise, thesis

therapy *n* = **remedy**, cure, healing, treatment

thesis *n* **1** = **dissertation**, essay, monograph, paper, treatise
2 = **proposition**, contention, hypothesis, idea, opinion, proposal, theory, view

t

thespian n **1** actor or actress. ▷ adj **2** of the theatre.

they pron refers to: **1** people or things other than the speaker or people addressed. **2** people in general. **3** informal he or she.

thick ❶ adj **1** of great or specified extent from one side to the other. **2** having a dense consistency. **3** informal stupid or insensitive. **4** informal friendly. **a bit thick** informal unfair or unreasonable. **the thick** busiest or most intense part. **thick with** full of. **thicken** v make or become thick or thicker. **thickness** n **1** state of being thick. **2** dimension through an object. **3** layer. **thickset** adj **1** stocky in build.

thicket ❶ n dense growth of small trees.

thief ❶ n, pl **thieves** person who steals. **thieve** v steal. **thieving** adj.

thigh n upper part of the human leg.

thimble n cap protecting the end of the finger when sewing.

thin ❶ adj **thinner, thinnest 1** not thick. **2** slim or lean. **3** sparse or meagre. **4** of low density. **5** poor or unconvincing. ▷ v **thinning, thinned 6** make or become thin. **thinness** n.

thing ❶ n **1** material object. **2** object, fact, or idea considered as a separate entity. **3** informal obsession. ▷ pl **4** possessions, clothes, etc.

think ❶ v **thinking, thought 1** consider, judge, or believe. **2** make use of the mind. **3** be considerate enough or remember to do something. **thinker** n **thinking** adj, n **think-tank** n group of experts studying specific problems. **think up** v invent or devise.

third adj **1** of number three in a series. **2** rated or graded below the second level. ▷ n **3** one of three equal parts. **third degree** violent interrogation. **third party** (applying to) a person involved by chance or only incidentally in legal proceedings, an accident, etc.

thirst ❶ n **1** desire to drink. **2** craving or yearning. ▷ v **3** feel thirst. **thirsty** adj **thirstily** adv.

thirteen adj, n three plus ten. **thirteenth** adj, n.

thirty adj, n three times ten. **thirtieth** adj, n.

this adj, pron **1** used to refer to a thing or person nearby, just mentioned, or about to be mentioned. ▷ adj **2** used to refer to the

— THESAURUS —

thick adj **1** = **wide**, broad, bulky, fat, solid, substantial **2** = **dense**, close, compact, concentrated, condensed, heavy, impenetrable, opaque **3** Inf = **stupid**, brainless, dense, dopey (inf), moronic, obtuse, slow, thickheaded **4** Inf = **friendly**, close, devoted, familiar, inseparable, intimate, pally (inf) **a bit thick** Inf = **unreasonable**, unfair, unjust

thicket n = **wood**, brake, coppice, copse, covert, grove

thief n = **robber**, burglar, embezzler, housebreaker, pickpocket, pilferer, plunderer, shoplifter, stealer

thin adj **1** = **narrow**, attenuated, fine **2** = **slim**, bony, emaciated, lean, scrawny, skeletal, skinny, slender, slight, spare, spindly **3** = **meagre**, deficient, scanty, scarce, scattered, skimpy, sparse, wispy

4 = **fine**, delicate, diaphanous, filmy, flimsy, gossamer, sheer, unsubstantial **5** = **unconvincing**, feeble, flimsy, inadequate, lame, poor, superficial, weak

thing n **1, 2** = **object**, article, being, body, entity, something, substance **3** Inf = **obsession**, bee in one's bonnet, fetish, fixation, hang-up (inf), mania, phobia, preoccupation ▷ pl n **4** = **possessions**, belongings, clobber (Brit sl), effects, equipment, gear, luggage, stuff

think v **1** = **believe**, consider, deem, estimate, imagine, judge, reckon, regard, suppose **2** = **ponder**, cerebrate, cogitate, contemplate, deliberate, meditate, muse, obsess, reason, reflect, ruminate

thirst n **1** = **thirstiness**, drought, dryness **2** = **craving**, appetite, desire, hankering, keenness, longing, passion, yearning

present time, e.g. *this morning*.

thistle *n* prickly plant with dense flower heads.

thither *adv obs* to or towards that place.

thong *n* **1** thin strip of leather etc. **2** skimpy article of underwear or beachwear that leaves the buttocks bare.

thorax *n, pl* **thoraxes**, **thoraces** part of the body between the neck and the abdomen. **thoracic** *adj*.

thorn ❶ *n* **1** prickle on a plant. **2** bush with thorns. **thorn in one's side**, **flesh** source of irritation. **thorny** *adj*.

thorough ❶ *adj* **1** complete. **2** careful or methodical. **thoroughly** *adv* **thoroughness** *n* **thoroughbred** *n, adj* (animal) of pure breed. **thoroughfare** *n* way through from one place to another.

those *adj, pron* plural of THAT.

thou *pron obs* singular form of YOU.

though ❶ *conj* **1** despite the fact that. ▷ *adv* **2** nevertheless.

thought ❶ *v* **1** past of THINK. ▷ *n* **2** thinking. **3** concept or idea. **4** ideas typical of a time or place. **5** consideration. **6** intention or expectation. **thoughtful** *adj* **1** considerate. **2** showing careful thought.

3 pensive or reflective. **thoughtless** *adj* inconsiderate.

thousand *adj, n* **1** ten hundred. **2** large but unspecified number. **thousandth** *adj, n* (of) number one thousand in a series.

thrash ❶ *v* **1** beat, esp. with a stick or whip. **2** defeat soundly. **3** move about wildly. **4** thresh. **thrashing** *n* severe beating. **thrash out** *v* solve by thorough argument.

thread ❶ *n* **1** fine strand or yarn. **2** unifying theme. **3** spiral ridge on a screw, nut, or bolt. ▷ *v* **4** pass thread through. **5** pick (one's way etc.). **threadbare** *adj* **1** (of fabric) with the nap worn off. **2** hackneyed. **3** shabby.

threat ❶ *n* **1** declaration of intent to harm. **2** dangerous person or thing. **threaten** *v* **1** make or be a threat to. **2** be a menacing indication of.

three *adj, n* one more than two. **threesome** *n* group of three. **three-dimensional**, **3-D** *adj* having three dimensions.

thresh *v* beat (wheat etc.) to separate the grain from the husks and straw. **thresh about** move about wildly.

threshold ❶ *n* **1** bar forming the bottom of a doorway. **2** entrance. **3** starting point. **4** point at which something begins to take effect.

THESAURUS
---

thorn *n* **1** = **prickle**, barb, spike, spine

thorough *adj* **1** = **complete**, absolute, out-and-out, outright, perfect, total, unmitigated, unqualified, utter **2** = **careful**, assiduous, conscientious, efficient, exhaustive, full, in-depth, intensive, meticulous, painstaking

though *conj* **1** = **although**, even if, even though, notwithstanding, while ▷ *adv* **2** = **nevertheless**, for all that, however, nonetheless, notwithstanding, still, yet

thought *n* **2** = **thinking**, cogitation, consideration, deliberation, meditation, musing, reflection, rumination **3** = **idea**, concept, judgment, notion, opinion, view **5** = **consideration**, attention, heed, regard, scrutiny, study **6 a** = **intention**, aim, design, idea, notion, object, plan, purpose **b** = **expectation**, anticipation,

aspiration, hope, prospect

thrash *v* **1** = **beat**, belt (*inf*), cane, flog, give (someone) a (good) hiding (*inf*), scourge, spank, whip **2** = **defeat**, beat, crush, drub, rout, run rings around (*inf*), slaughter (*inf*), trounce, wipe the floor with (*inf*) **3, 4** = **thresh**, flail, jerk, toss and turn, writhe

thread *n* **1** = **strand**, fibre, filament, line, string, yarn **2** = **theme**, direction, drift, plot, story line, train of thought ▷ *v* **4** = **string 5** = **pass**, ease, pick (one's way), squeeze through

threat *n* **1** = **menace**, threatening remark **2** = **danger**, hazard, menace, peril, risk

threshold *n* **2** = **entrance**, door, doorstep, doorway **3** = **start**, beginning, brink, dawn, inception, opening, outset, verge **4** = **minimum**, lower limit

thrice *adv lit* three times.

thrift ❶ *n* **1** wisdom and caution with money. **2** low-growing plant with pink flowers. **thrifty** *adj*.

thrill ❶ *n* **1** sudden feeling of excitement. ▷ *v* **2** (cause to) feel a thrill. **thrilling** *adj*.

thrive ❶ *v* **thriving**, **thrived** *or* **throve**, **thrived** *or* **thriven 1** flourish or prosper. **2** grow well.

throat *n* **1** passage from the mouth and nose to the stomach and lungs. **2** front of the neck. **throaty** *adj* (of the voice) hoarse.

throb ❶ *v* **throbbing**, **throbbed 1** pulsate repeatedly. **2** vibrate rhythmically. ▷ *n* **3** throbbing.

throes *pl n* violent pangs or pains. **in the throes of** struggling to cope with.

thrombosis *n, pl* **-ses** forming of a clot in a blood vessel or the heart.

throne *n* **1** ceremonial seat of a monarch or bishop. **2** sovereign power.

throng ❶ *n, v* crowd.

throttle ❶ *n* **1** device controlling the amount of fuel entering an engine. ▷ *v* **2** strangle.

through ❶ *prep* **1** from end to end or side to side of. **2** because of. **3** during.

▷ *adj* **4** finished. **5** (of transport) going directly to a place. **through and through** completely. **throughout** *prep, adv* in every part (of). **throughput** *n* amount of material processed.

throw ❶ *v* **throwing**, **threw**, **thrown 1** hurl through the air. **2** move or put suddenly or carelessly. **3** bring into a specified state, esp. suddenly. **4** move (a switch, lever, etc.). **5** shape (pottery) on a wheel. **6** give (a party). **7** *informal* baffle or disconcert. **8** direct (a look, light, etc.). **9** project (the voice) so that it seems to come from elsewhere. ▷ *n* **10** throwing. **11** distance thrown. **throwaway** *adj* **1** done or said casually. **2** designed to be discarded after use. **throwback** *n* person or thing that reverts to an earlier type. **throw up** *v* vomit.

thrush *n* brown songbird.

thrust ❶ *v* **thrusting**, **thrust 1** push forcefully. ▷ *n* **2** forceful stab. **3** force or power. **4** intellectual or emotional drive.

thud ❶ *n* **1** dull heavy sound. ▷ *v* **thudding**, **thudded 2** make such a sound.

thug ❶ *n* violent man, esp. a criminal. **thuggery** *n* **thuggish** *adj*.

thrift *n* **1** = **economy**, carefulness, frugality, parsimony, prudence, saving, thriftiness

thrill *n* **1** = **pleasure**, buzz (*sl*), kick (*inf*), stimulation, tingle, titillation ▷ *v* **2** = **excite**, arouse, electrify, move, stimulate, stir, titillate

thrive *v* **1** = **prosper**, boom, develop, do well, flourish, get on, increase, succeed **2** = **grow**

throb *v* **1** = **pulsate**, beat, palpitate, pound, pulse, thump **2** = **vibrate** ▷ *n* **3** = **pulse**, beat, palpitation, pounding, pulsating, thump, thumping, vibration

throng *n* = **crowd**, crush, horde, host, mass, mob, multitude, pack, swarm ▷ *v* = **crowd**, congregate, converge, flock, mill around, swarm around

throttle *v* **2** = **strangle**, choke, garrotte, strangulate

through *prep* **1** = **from one side to the other of**, between, by, past **2** = **because of**, by means of, by way of, using, via **3** = **during**, in, throughout ▷ *adj* **4** = **completed**, done, ended, finished

through and through = **completely**, altogether, entirely, fully, thoroughly, totally, utterly, wholly

throw *v* **1, 2** = **hurl**, cast, chuck (*inf*), fling, launch, lob (*inf*), pitch, send, sling, toss **7** *Inf* = **confuse**, astonish, baffle, confound, disconcert, dumbfound, faze ▷ *n* **10** = **toss**, fling, heave, lob (*inf*), pitch, sling

thrust *v* **1** = **push**, drive, force, jam, plunge, propel, ram, shove ▷ *n* **2** = **push**, drive, lunge, poke, prod, shove, stab **3** = **momentum**, impetus

thud *n, v* **1, 2** = **thump**, crash, knock, smack

thug *n* = **ruffian**, bruiser (*inf*), bully boy, gangster, heavy (*sl*), hooligan, tough

thumb n **1** short thick finger set apart from the others. ▷ v **2** touch or handle with the thumb. **3** signal with the thumb for a lift in a vehicle. **thumb through** flick through (a book or magazine).

thumbtack n the US and Canadian name for DRAWING PIN.

thump ❶ n **1** (sound of) a dull heavy blow. ▷ v **2** strike heavily.

thunder ❶ n **1** loud noise accompanying lightning. ▷ v **2** rumble with thunder. **3** shout. **4** move fast, heavily, and noisily. **thunderous** adj **thundery** adj **thunderbolt** n **1** lightning flash. **2** something sudden and unexpected. **thunderclap** n peal of thunder. **thunderstruck** adj amazed.

Thursday n fifth day of the week.

thus ❶ adv **1** therefore. **2** in this way.

thwart ❶ v **1** foil or frustrate. ▷ n **2** seat across a boat.

thy adj obs of or associated with you (thou). **thyself** pron obs emphatic form of THOU.

thylacine n extinct doglike Tasmanian marsupial.

thyme [**time**] n aromatic herb.

tiara n semicircular jewelled headdress.

tibia n, pl **tibiae**, **tibias** inner bone of the lower leg. **tibial** adj.

tic n spasmodic muscular twitch.

tick¹ ❶ n **1** mark (✓) used to check off or indicate the correctness of something. **2** recurrent tapping sound, as of a clock. **3** informal moment. ▷ v **4** mark with a tick. **5** make a ticking sound. **tick off** v **1** mark with a tick. **2** reprimand. **tick over** v **1** (of an engine) idle. **2** function smoothly. **ticktack** n bookmakers' sign language.

tick² n tiny bloodsucking parasitic animal.

ticket ❶ n **1** card or paper entitling the holder to admission, travel, etc. **2** label, esp. showing price. **3** official notification of a parking or traffic offence. **4** declared policy of a political party. ▷ v **-eting**, **-eted** **5** attach or issue a ticket to.

tickle v **1** touch or stroke (a person) to produce laughter. **2** itch or tingle. **3** please or amuse. ▷ n **4** tickling. **ticklish** adj **1** sensitive to tickling. **2** requiring care or tact.

tiddlywinks n game in which players try to flip small plastic discs into a cup.

tide ❶ n **1** rise and fall of the sea caused by the gravitational pull of the sun and moon. **2** current caused by this. **3** widespread feeling or tendency. **tidal** adj **tidal wave** large destructive wave. **tide over** v help (someone) temporarily.

tidings pl n news.

tidy ❶ adj **-dier**, **-diest 1** neat and orderly. **2** informal considerable. ▷ v **-dying**, **-died 3** put in order. **tidily** adv **tidiness** n.

— THESAURUS —

thump n **1 a** = **thud**, bang, clunk, crash, thwack **b** = **blow**, clout (inf), knock, punch, rap, smack, swipe, wallop (inf), whack ▷ v **2** = **strike**, beat, clobber (sl), clout (inf), hit, knock, pound, punch, smack, swipe, wallop (inf), whack

thunder n **2** = **rumble**, boom, crash, explosion ▷ v **2** = **rumble**, boom, crash, peal, resound, reverberate, roar **3** = **shout**, bark, bellow, roar, yell

thus adv **1** = **therefore**, accordingly, consequently, ergo, for this reason, hence, on that account, so, then **2** = **in this way**, as follows, like this, so

thwart v **1** = **frustrate**, foil, hinder, obstruct, outwit, prevent, snooker, stymie

tick¹ n **1** = **mark**, dash, stroke **2** = **tapping**, clicking, ticktock **3** Inf = **moment**, flash, instant, minute, second, split second, trice, twinkling ▷ v **4** = **mark**, check off, indicate **5** = **tap**, click, ticktock

ticket n **1** = **voucher**, card, certificate, coupon, pass, slip, token **2** = **label**, card, docket, marker, slip, sticker, tab, tag

tide n **2** = **current**, ebb, flow, stream, tideway, undertow **3** = **tendency**, direction, drift, movement, trend

tidy adj **1** = **neat**, clean, methodical, orderly, shipshape, spruce, well-kept, well-ordered **2** Inf = **considerable**, ample, generous,

tie ❶ *v* **tying, tied 1** fasten or be fastened with string, rope, etc. **2** make (a knot or bow) in (something). **3** restrict or limit. **4** score the same as another competitor. ▷ *n* **5** long narrow piece of material worn knotted around the neck. **6** bond or fastening. **7** drawn game or contest. **tied** *adj* **1** (of a cottage etc.) rented to the tenant only as long as he or she is employed by the owner.

tier ❶ *n* one of a set of rows placed one above and behind the other.

tiff *n* petty quarrel.

tiger *n* large yellow-and-black striped Asian cat. **tigress** *n* **1** female tiger. **2** *informal* fierce woman. **tiger snake** *n* highly venomous brown-and-yellow Australian snake.

tight ❶ *adj* **1** stretched or drawn taut. **2** closely fitting. **3** secure or firm. **4** cramped. **5** *informal* not generous. **6** (of a match or game) very close. **7** *informal* drunk. **tights** *pl n* one-piece clinging garment covering the body from the waist to the feet. **tighten** *v* make or become tight or tighter. **tightrope** *n* rope stretched taut on which acrobats perform.

tile *n* **1** flat piece of ceramic, plastic, etc. used to cover a roof, floor, or wall. ▷ *v* **2** cover with tiles. **tiling** *n* tiles collectively.

till¹ *conj, prep* until.

till² ❶ *v* cultivate (land).

till³ ❶ *n* drawer for money, usu. in a cash register.

tiller *n* lever to move a rudder of a boat.

tilt ❶ *v* **1** slant at an angle. **2** *Hist* compete against in a jousting contest. ▷ *n* **3** slope. **4** *Hist* jousting contest. **5** attempt. **at full tilt** at full speed or force.

timber ❶ *n* **1** wood as a building material. **2** trees collectively. **3** wooden beam in the frame of a house, boat, etc.

timbre ❶ [**tam**-bra] *n* distinctive quality of sound of a voice or instrument.

time ❶ *n* **1** past, present, and future as a continuous whole. **2** specific point in time. **3** unspecified interval. **4** instance or occasion. **5** period with specific features. **6** musical tempo. **7** *slang* imprisonment. ▷ *v* **8** note the time taken by. **9** choose a time for. **timeless** *adj* **1** unaffected by time. **2** eternal. **timely** *adj* at the appropriate time. **time-honoured** *adj* sanctioned by custom. **time-lag** *n* period

---

THESAURUS

goodly, handsome, healthy, large, sizable *or* sizeable, substantial ▷ *v* **3** = **neaten**, clean, groom, order, spruce up, straighten

tie *v* **1** = **fasten**, attach, bind, connect, join, knot, link, secure, tether **3** = **restrict**, bind, confine, hamper, hinder, limit, restrain **4** = **draw**, equal, match ▷ *n* **6 a** = **bond**, affiliation, allegiance, commitment, connection, liaison, relationship **b** = **fastening**, bond, cord, fetter, knot, ligature, link **7** = **draw**, dead heat, deadlock, stalemate

tier *n* = **row**, bank, layer, level, line, rank, storey, stratum

tight *adj* **1** = **taut**, rigid, stretched **2** = **close-fitting**, close **3** = **secure**, fast, firm, fixed **4** = **cramped**, constricted, narrow, snug **5** *Inf* = **miserly**, grasping, mean, niggardly, parsimonious, stingy,

tightfisted **6** = **close**, even, evenly-balanced, well-matched **7** *Inf* = **drunk**, inebriated, intoxicated, paralytic (*inf*), plastered (*sl*), tipsy, under the influence (*inf*)

till² *v* = **cultivate**, dig, plough, work

till³ *n* = **cash register**, cash box

tilt *v* **1** = **slant**, heel, incline, lean, list, slope, tip ▷ *n* **3** = **slope**, angle, inclination, incline, list, pitch, slant **4** *Hist* = **joust**, combat, duel, fight, lists, tournament **(at) full tilt** = **full speed**, for dear life, headlong

timber *n* **1** = **wood**, boards, logs, planks **2** = **trees**, forest **3** = **beams**

timbre *n* = **tone**, colour, resonance, ring

time *n* **3** = **period**, duration, interval, season, space, span, spell, stretch, term **4** = **occasion**, instance, juncture, point,

t

between cause and effect. **timepiece** n watch or clock. **timeserver** n person who changes his or her views to gain support or favour. **time sharing 1** system of part ownership of a holiday property for a specified period each year. **timetable** n plan showing the times when something takes place, the departure and arrival times of trains or buses, etc.

timid ❶ adj **1** easily frightened. **2** shy, not bold. **timidity** n **timorous** adj timid.

timpani [tim-pan-ee] pl n set of kettledrums. **timpanist** n.

tin n **1** soft metallic element. **2** (airtight) metal container. **tinned** adj (of food) preserved by being sealed in a tin. **tinny** adj (of sound) thin and metallic. **tinpot** adj informal worthless or unimportant.

tinder n dry easily-burning material used to start a fire. **tinderbox** n.

tinge ❶ n **1** slight tint. **2** trace. ▷ v **tingeing, tinged 3** give a slight tint or trace to.

tingle ❶ v, n (feel) a prickling or stinging sensation.

tinker ❶ n **1** travelling mender of pots and pans. **2** Scot & Irish Gypsy. ▷ v **3** fiddle with (an engine etc.) in an attempt to repair it.

tinkle v **1** ring with a high tinny sound like a small bell. ▷ n **2** this sound or action.

tinsel n **1** decorative metallic strips or threads.

tint ❶ n **1** (pale) shade of a colour. **2** dye for the hair. ▷ v **3** give a tint to.

tiny ❶ adj **tinier, tiniest** very small.

tip¹ ❶ n **1** narrow or pointed end of anything. **2** small piece forming an end. ▷ v **tipping, tipped 3** put a tip on.

tip² ❶ n **1** money given in return for service. **2** helpful hint or warning. **3** piece of inside information. ▷ v **tipping, tipped 4** give a tip to. **tipster** n person who sells tips about races.

tip³ ❶ v **tipping, tipped 1** tilt or overturn. **2** dump (rubbish). ▷ n **3** rubbish dump.

tipple ❶ v **1** drink alcohol habitually, esp. in small quantities. ▷ n **2** alcoholic drink. **tippler** n.

tipsy adj **-sier, -siest** slightly drunk.

tiptoe v **-toeing, -toed** walk quietly with the heels off the ground.

tiptop adj of the highest quality or condition.

tirade ❶ n long angry speech.

tire ❶ v **1** reduce the energy of, as by exertion. **2** weary or bore. **tired** adj

━━━━━━━━━━━━━━━━━━━━━━━━━━━━━━━━━ THESAURUS ━━━━━━━

stage **6** = **tempo**, beat, measure, rhythm ▷ v **9** = **schedule**, set

timid adj **1** = **fearful**, apprehensive, faint-hearted, shrinking, timorous **2** = **shy**, bashful, coy, diffident

tinge n **1** = **tint**, colour, shade **2** = **bit**, dash, drop, smattering, sprinkling, suggestion, touch, trace ▷ v **3** = **tint**, colour, imbue, suffuse

tingle v = **prickle**, have goose pimples, itch, sting, tickle ▷ n = **quiver**, goose pimples, itch, pins and needles (inf), prickling, shiver, thrill

tinker v **3** = **meddle**, dabble, fiddle (inf), mess about, play, potter

tint n **1** = **shade**, colour, hue, tone **2** = **dye**, rinse, tincture, tinge, wash ▷ v **3** = **dye**, colour

tiny adj = **small**, diminutive, infinitesimal, little, microscopic, miniature, minute, negligible, petite, slight

tip¹ n **1** = **end**, extremity, head, peak, pinnacle, point, summit, top ▷ v **3** = **cap**, crown, finish, surmount, top

tip² n **1** = **gratuity**, gift **2** = **hint**, pointer, suggestion ▷ v **4 a** = **reward**, remunerate **b** = **advise**, suggest

tip³ v **1** = **tilt**, incline, lean, list, slant **2** = **dump**, empty, pour out, unload ▷ n **3** = **dump**, refuse heap, rubbish heap

tipple v **1** = **drink**, imbibe, indulge (inf), quaff, swig, tope ▷ n **2** = **alcohol**, booze (inf), drink, liquor

tirade n = **outburst**, diatribe, fulmination, harangue, invective, lecture

tire v **1** = **exhaust**, drain, fatigue, wear out,

1 exhausted. 2 hackneyed or stale.
tiring adj **tireless** adj energetic and
determined. **tiresome** adj boring and
irritating.

tissue n 1 substance of an animal body
or plant. 2 piece of thin soft paper used as
a handkerchief etc. 3 interwoven series.

tit n any of various small songbirds.

titanic adj huge or very important.

titanium n Chem strong light metallic
element used to make alloys.

titbit ❶ n 1 tasty piece of food. 2 pleasing
scrap of scandal.

tithe n 1 esp. formerly, one tenth of one's
income or produce paid to the church as
a tax.

titillate ❶ v excite or stimulate pleasurably.
titillating adj **titillation** n.

title ❶ n 1 name of a book, film, etc.
2 name signifying rank or position.
3 formal designation, such as Mrs.
4 Sport championship. 5 Law legal right of
possession. **titled** adj aristocratic.

titter ❶ v 1 laugh in a suppressed way. ▷ n
2 suppressed laugh.

titular adj 1 in name only. 2 of a title.

TNT n trinitrotoluene, a powerful explosive.

to prep 1 indicating movement towards,
equality or comparison, etc. e.g. walking
to school; forty miles to the gallon. 2 used to
mark the indirect object or infinitive of a
verb. ▷ adv 3 to a closed position, e.g. pull
the door to. **to and fro** back and forth.

toad n animal like a large frog.

toast¹ ❶ n 1 sliced bread browned by heat.
▷ v 2 brown (bread) by heat. 3 warm or
be warmed. **toaster** n electrical device for
toasting bread.

toast² ❶ n 1 tribute or proposal of health or
success marked by people raising glasses
and drinking together. 2 person or thing so
honoured. ▷ v 3 drink a toast to.

tobacco n, pl **-cos**, **-coes** plant with large
leaves dried for smoking. **tobacconist** n
person or shop selling tobacco, cigarettes,
etc.

toboggan n 1 narrow sledge for sliding
over snow. ▷ v **-ganing**, **-ganed** 2 ride a
toboggan.

today n 1 this day. 2 the present age. ▷ adv
3 on this day. 4 nowadays.

toddle v walk with short unsteady steps.
toddler n child beginning to walk.

to-do n, pl **-dos** fuss or commotion.

toe n 1 digit of the foot. 2 part of a shoe or
sock covering the toes. ▷ v **toeing**, **toed**
3 touch or kick with the toe. **toe the line**
conform.

toffee n chewy sweet made of boiled sugar.

toga [**toe**-ga] n garment worn by citizens of
ancient Rome.

together ❶ adv 1 in company.
2 simultaneously. ▷ adj 3 informal
organized.

toggle n 1 small bar-shaped button
inserted through a loop for fastening.
2 switch used to turn a machine or
computer function on or off.

THESAURUS

weary 2 = **bore**, exasperate, irk, irritate,
weary

titbit n 1 = **delicacy**, dainty, morsel, snack,
treat

titillate v = **excite**, arouse, interest,
stimulate, tantalize, tease, thrill

title n 1 = **name**, designation, handle (sl),
term 4 Sport = **championship**, crown
5 Law = **ownership**, claim, entitlement,
prerogative, privilege, right

titter v 1 = **snigger**, chortle (inf), chuckle,
giggle, laugh

toast¹ v 2 = **brown**, grill, roast 3 = **warm**, heat

toast² n 1 = **tribute**, compliment, health,
pledge, salutation, salute 2 = **favourite**,
darling, hero or heroine ▷ v 3 = **drink to**,
drink (to) the health of, salute

together adv 1 = **collectively**, as one,
hand in glove, in concert, in unison, jointly,
mutually, shoulder to shoulder, side by
side 2 = **at the same time**, at one fell
swoop, concurrently, contemporaneously,
simultaneously ▷ adj 3 Inf = **self-possessed**,
composed, well-adjusted, well-balanced

t

toil ❶ n 1 hard work. ▷ v 2 work hard. 3 progress with difficulty.

toilet ❶ n 1 (room with) a bowl connected to a drain for receiving and disposing of urine and faeces. 2 washing and dressing. **toiletry** n, pl **-ries** object or cosmetic used to clean or groom oneself. **toilet water** light perfume.

token ❶ n 1 sign or symbol. 2 voucher exchangeable for goods of a specified value. 3 disc used as money in a slot machine. ▷ adj 4 nominal or slight. **tokenism** n policy of making only a token effort, esp. to comply with a law.

tolerate ❶ v 1 allow to exist or happen. 2 endure patiently. **tolerable** adj 1 bearable. 2 informal quite good. **tolerably** adv **tolerance** n 1 acceptance of other people's rights to their own opinions or actions. 2 ability to endure something. **tolerant** adj **toleration** n.

toll¹ ❶ v 1 ring (a bell) slowly and regularly, esp. to announce a death. ▷ n 2 tolling.

toll² ❶ n 1 charge for the use of a bridge or road. 2 total loss or damage from a disaster.

tom n male cat.

tomahawk n fighting axe of the Native Americans.

tomato n, pl **-toes** red fruit used in salads and as a vegetable.

tomb ❶ n 1 grave. 2 monument over a grave. **tombstone** n gravestone.

tombola n lottery with tickets drawn from a revolving drum.

tomboy n girl who acts or dresses like a boy.

tome n large heavy book.

tomfoolery ❶ n foolish behaviour.

tomorrow adv, n 1 (on) the day after today. 2 (in) the future.

tom-tom n drum beaten with the hands.

ton n unit of weight equal to 2240 pounds or 1016 kilograms (**long ton**) or, in the US, 2000 pounds or 907 kilograms (**short ton**). **tonnage** n weight capacity of a ship.

tone ❶ n 1 sound with reference to its pitch, volume, etc. 2 US musical note. 3 Music (also **whole tone**) interval of two semitones. 4 quality of a sound or colour. 5 general character. 6 healthy bodily condition. ▷ v 7 harmonize (with). 8 give tone to. **tonal** adj Music written in a key. **tonality** n **toneless** adj **tone-deaf** adj unable to perceive subtle differences in pitch. **tone down** v make or become more moderate.

——————————————— THESAURUS ———————————————

toil n 1 = **hard work**, application, drudgery, effort, elbow grease (inf), exertion, graft (inf), slog, sweat ▷ v 2 = **labour**, drudge, graft (inf), slave, slog, strive, struggle, sweat (inf), work, work one's fingers to the bone

toilet n 1 = **lavatory**, bathroom, convenience, gents or ladies (Brit inf), ladies' room, latrine, loo (Brit inf), privy, urinal, water closet, W.C.

token n 1 = **symbol**, badge, expression, indication, mark, note, representation, sign ▷ adj 4 = **nominal**, hollow, minimal, perfunctory, superficial, symbolic

tolerate v 1 = **allow**, accept, brook, condone, permit, put up with (inf), take 2 = **endure**, put up with (inf), stand, stomach, take

toll¹ v 1 = **ring**, chime, clang, knell, peal, sound, strike ▷ n 2 = **ringing**, chime, clang, knell, peal

toll² n 1 = **charge**, duty, fee, levy, payment, tariff, tax 2 = **damage**, cost, loss, penalty

tomb n 1, 2 = **grave**, catacomb, crypt, mausoleum, sarcophagus, sepulchre, vault

tomfoolery n = **foolishness**, buffoonery, clowning, fooling around (inf), horseplay, shenanigans (inf), silliness, skylarking (inf)

tone n 1 = **pitch**, inflection, intonation, modulation, timbre 4 = **colour**, hue, shade, tinge, tint 5 = **character**, air, attitude, feel, manner, mood, spirit, style, temper ▷ v 7 = **harmonize**, blend, go well with, match, suit

tongs pl n large pincers for grasping and lifting.

tongue ❶ n 1 muscular organ in the mouth, used in speaking and tasting. 2 language. 3 animal tongue as food. 4 thin projecting strip. 5 flap of leather on a shoe.

tonic n 1 medicine to improve body tone. ▷ adj 2 invigorating.

tonight adv, n (in or during) the night or evening of this day.

tonne [tunn] n unit of weight equal to 1000 kilograms.

tonsil n small gland in the throat. **tonsillectomy** n surgical removal of the tonsils. **tonsillitis** n inflammation of the tonsils.

tonsure n 1 shaving of all or the top of the head as a religious or monastic practice. 2 shaved part of the head. **tonsured** adj.

too ❶ adv 1 also, as well. 2 to excess. 3 extremely.

tool ❶ n 1 implement used by hand. 2 person used by another to perform unpleasant or dishonourable tasks. **toolbar** n Computers row of buttons displayed on a computer screen, allowing the user to select various functions.

toonie, twonie n inf Canadian two-dollar coin.

toot n 1 short hooting sound. ▷ v 2 (cause to) make such a sound.

tooth n, pl **teeth** 1 bonelike projection in the jaws of most vertebrates for biting

and chewing. 2 toothlike prong or point. **sweet tooth** strong liking for sweet food. **toothless** adj **toothpaste** n paste used to clean the teeth. **toothpick** n small stick for removing scraps of food from between the teeth.

top¹ ❶ n 1 highest point or part. 2 lid or cap. 3 highest rank. 4 garment for the upper part of the body. ▷ adj 5 at or of the top. ▷ v **topping, topped** 6 form a top on. 7 be at the top of. 8 exceed or surpass. **topping** n sauce or garnish for food. **topless** adj (of a costume or woman) with no covering for the breasts. **topmost** adj highest or best. **top brass** most important officers or leaders. **top hat** man's tall cylindrical hat. **top-heavy** adj unstable through being overloaded at the top. **top-notch** adj excellent, first-class. **topsoil** n surface layer of soil.

top² n toy which spins on a pointed base.

topaz [toe-pazz] n semiprecious stone in various colours.

topiary [tope-yar-ee] n art of trimming trees and bushes into decorative shapes.

topic ❶ n subject of a conversation, book, etc. **topical** adj relating to current events. **topicality** n -ties.

topography n, pl -phies (science of describing) the surface features of a place. **topographical** adj.

topple ❶ v 1 (cause to) fall over. 2 overthrow (a government etc.).

THESAURUS

---

tongue n 2 = **language**, dialect, parlance, speech

too adv 1 = **also**, as well, besides, further, in addition, likewise, moreover, to boot 2, 3 = **excessively**, extremely, immoderately, inordinately, overly, unduly, unreasonably, very

tool n 1 = **implement**, appliance, contraption, contrivance, device, gadget, instrument, machine, utensil 2 = **puppet**, cat's-paw, hireling, lackey, minion, pawn, stooge (sl)

top¹ n 1 = **peak**, apex, crest, crown,

culmination, head, height, pinnacle, summit, zenith 2 = **lid**, cap, cover, stopper 3 = **first place**, head, lead ▷ adj 5 = **leading**, best, chief, elite, finest, first, foremost, head, highest, pre-eminent, principal, uppermost ▷ v 6 = **cover**, cap, crown, finish, garnish 7 = **lead**, be first, head 8 = **surpass**, beat, better, eclipse, exceed, excel, outstrip, transcend

topic n = **subject**, issue, matter, point, question, subject matter, theme

topple v 1 = **fall over**, collapse, fall, keel over, overbalance, overturn, totter, tumble

t

topsy-turvy ❶ *adj* 1 upside down. 2 in confusion.

tor *n* high rocky hill.

torch *n* 1 small portable battery-powered lamp. 2 wooden shaft dipped in wax and set alight. ▷ *v* 3 *informal* deliberately set (a building) on fire.

toreador [torr-ee-a-dor] *n* bullfighter.

torment ❶ *v* 1 cause (someone) great suffering. 2 tease cruelly. ▷ *n* 3 great suffering. 4 source of suffering. **tormentor** *n*.

tornado ❶ *n, pl* **-dos**, **-does** violent whirlwind.

torpedo *n, pl* **-does** 1 self-propelled underwater missile. ▷ *v* **-doing**, **-doed** 2 attack or destroy with or as if with torpedoes.

torpid *adj* sluggish and inactive. **torpor** *n* torpid state.

torrent *n* 1 rushing stream. 2 rapid flow of questions, abuse, etc. **torrential** *adj* (of rain) very heavy.

torrid ❶ *adj* 1 very hot and dry. 2 highly emotional.

torsion *n* twisting of a part by equal forces being applied at both ends but in opposite directions.

torso *n, pl* **-sos** 1 trunk of the human body. 2 statue of a nude human trunk.

tortilla *n* thin Mexican pancake.

tortoise *n* slow-moving land reptile with a dome-shaped shell. **tortoiseshell** *n* 1 mottled brown shell of a turtle, used for making ornaments. ▷ *adj* 2 having brown, orange, and black markings.

tortuous ❶ *adj* 1 winding or twisting. 2 not straightforward.

torture ❶ *v* 1 cause (someone) severe pain or mental anguish. ▷ *n* 2 severe physical or mental pain. 3 torturing. **torturer** *n*.

Tory *n, pl* **Tories** 1 member of the Conservative Party in Great Britain or Canada. ▷ *adj* 2 of Tories.

toss ❶ *v* 1 throw lightly. 2 fling or be flung about. 3 coat (food) by gentle stirring or mixing. 4 (of a horse) throw (its rider). 5 throw up (a coin) to decide between alternatives by guessing which side will land uppermost. ▷ *n* 6 tossing. **toss up** *v* toss a coin. **toss-up** *n* even chance or risk.

tot¹ ❶ *n* 1 small child. 2 small drink of spirits.

tot² ❶ *v* **totting**, **totted**. **tot up** add (numbers) together.

—————————————————————————————— THESAURUS —————

2 = **overthrow**, bring down, bring low, oust, overturn, unseat

topsy-turvy *adj* 1 = **upside-down** 2 = **disorganized**, chaotic, confused, disorderly, inside-out, jumbled, messy, mixed-up

torment *v* 1 = **torture**, crucify, distress, rack 2 = **tease**, annoy, bother, harass, hassle (*inf*), irritate, nag, pester, vex ▷ *n* 3 = **suffering**, agony, anguish, distress, hell, misery, pain, torture

tornado *n* = **whirlwind**, cyclone, gale, hurricane, squall, storm, tempest, typhoon

torrent *n* 1 = **stream**, cascade, deluge, downpour, flood, flow, rush, spate, tide

torrid *adj* 1 = **arid**, dried, parched, scorched 2 = **passionate**, ardent, fervent, intense, steamy (*inf*)

tortuous *adj* 1 = **winding**, circuitous, convoluted, indirect, mazy, meandering, serpentine, sinuous, twisting 2 = **complicated**, ambiguous, convoluted, devious, indirect, involved, roundabout, tricky

torture *v* 1 = **torment**, afflict, crucify, distress, persecute, put on the rack, rack ▷ *n* 2 = **agony**, anguish, distress, pain, persecution, suffering, torment

toss *v* 1 = **throw**, cast, fling, flip, hurl, launch, lob (*inf*), pitch, sling 2 = **thrash**, rock, roll, shake, wriggle, writhe ▷ *n* 6 = **throw**, lob (*inf*), pitch

tot¹ *n* 1 = **infant**, baby, child, mite, toddler 2 = **measure**, dram, finger, nip, shot (*inf*), slug, snifter (*inf*)

tot² *v* **tot up** = **add up**, calculate, count up, reckon, tally, total

total ❶ n 1 whole, esp. a sum of parts. ▷ adj 2 complete. 3 of or being a total. ▷ v **-talling, -talled** 4 amount to. 5 add up. **totally** adv **totality** n.

totalitarian ❶ adj of a dictatorial one-party government. **totalitarianism** n.

totem n tribal badge or emblem. **totem pole** post carved or painted with totems by Native Americans.

totter ❶ v 1 move unsteadily. 2 be about to fall.

toucan n tropical American bird with a large bill.

touch ❶ v 1 come into contact with. 2 tap, feel, or stroke. 3 affect. 4 move emotionally. 5 eat or drink. 6 equal or match. 7 slang ask for money. ▷ n 8 sense by which an object's qualities are perceived when they come into contact with part of the body. 9 gentle tap, push, or caress. 10 small amount. 11 characteristic style. 12 detail. **touch and go** risky or critical. **touched** adj 1 emotionally moved. 2 slightly mad. **touching** adj emotionally moving. **touchy** adj easily offended. **touch base** make contact, renew communication. **touch down** v (of an aircraft) land. **touchline** n side line of the pitch in some games. **touch on** v refer to in passing. **touch-type** v type without looking at the keyboard.

touché [**too**-shay] interj acknowledgment of the striking home of a remark or witty reply.

tough ❶ adj 1 strong or resilient. 2 difficult to chew or cut. 3 firm and determined. 4 rough and violent. 5 difficult. 6 informal unlucky or unfair. ▷ n 7 informal rough violent person. **toughness** n **toughen** v make or become tough or tougher.

toupee [**too**-pay] n small wig.

tour ❶ n 1 journey visiting places of interest along the way. 2 trip to perform or play in different places. ▷ v 3 make a tour (of). **tourism** n tourist travel as an industry. **tourist** n person travelling for pleasure. **touristy** adj informal, often derogatory full of tourists or tourist attractions.

— THESAURUS —

total n 1 = **whole**, aggregate, entirety, full amount, sum, totality ▷ adj 2, 3 = **complete**, absolute, comprehensive, entire, full, gross, overarching, thoroughgoing, undivided, utter, whole ▷ v 4 = **amount to**, come to, mount up to, reach 5 = **add up**, reckon, tot up

totalitarian adj = **dictatorial**, authoritarian, despotic, oppressive, tyrannous, undemocratic

totter v 1 = **falter** 2 = **stagger**, lurch, reel, stumble, sway, wobble

touch v 1 = **come into contact**, abut, adjoin, be in contact, border, contact, graze, impinge upon, meet 2 = **handle**, brush, caress, contact, feel, finger, fondle, stroke, tap 3 = **affect**, impress, influence, inspire 4 = **move**, disturb, stir 5 = **consume**, drink, eat, partake of 6 = **match**, compare with, equal, hold a candle to (inf), parallel, rival ▷ n 8 = **feeling**, handling, physical contact 9 = **contact**, brush, caress, stroke, tap 10 = **bit**, dash, drop, jot, small amount, smattering, soupçon, spot, trace 11 = **style**, manner, method, technique, trademark, way **touch on** v = **refer to**, allude to, bring in, cover, deal with, mention, speak of

tough adj 1 = **resilient**, durable, hard, inflexible, leathery, resistant, rugged, solid, strong, sturdy 3 = **firm**, hard, hardy, resolute, seasoned, stern, stout, strapping, strong, sturdy, unbending, vigorous 4 = **rough**, hard-bitten, merciless, pugnacious, ruthless, violent 5 = **difficult**, arduous, exacting, hard, laborious, strenuous, troublesome, uphill 6 Inf = **unlucky**, lamentable, regrettable, unfortunate ▷ n 7 Inf = **ruffian**, bruiser (inf), bully, hooligan, roughneck (sl), thug

tour n 1 = **journey**, excursion, expedition, jaunt, outing, trip ▷ v 3 = **visit**, explore, go round, journey, sightsee, travel through

t

tournament ❶ *n* **1** sporting competition with several stages to decide the overall winner. **2** *Hist* contest between knights on horseback.

tourniquet [**tour**-nick-kay] *n* something twisted round a limb to stop bleeding.

tousled *adj* ruffled and untidy.

tout [rhymes with **shout**] *v* **1** seek business in a persistent manner. **2** recommend (a person or thing). ▷ *n* **3** person who sells tickets for a popular event at inflated prices.

tow ❶ *v* **1** drag, esp. by means of a rope. ▷ *n* **2** towing. **in tow** following closely behind. **on tow** being towed. **towbar** *n* metal bar on a car for towing vehicles. **towpath** *n* path beside a canal or river, originally for horses towing boats. **towrope** *n* rope or cable used for towing a vehicle or vessel.

towards, toward ❶ *prep* **1** in the direction of. **2** with regard to. **3** as a contribution to.

towel *n* cloth for drying things. **towelling** *n* material used for making towels.

tower ❶ *n* tall structure, often forming part of a larger building. **tower of strength** person who supports or comforts. **tower over** *v* be much taller than.

town *n* **1** group of buildings larger than a village. **2** central part of this. **3** people of a town. **township** *n* **1** small town. **2** (in

S Africa) urban settlement of Black or Coloured people.

toxic ❶ *adj* **1** poisonous. **2** caused by poison. **toxicity** *n* **toxicology** *n* study of poisons. **toxin** *n* poison of bacterial origin.

toy ❶ *n* **1** something designed to be played with. ▷ *adj* **2** (of a dog) of a variety much smaller than is normal for that breed. **toy with** *v* play or fiddle with.

toy-toy *S Afr* ▷ *n* **1** dance of political protest. ▷ *v* **2** perform this dance.

trace ❶ *v* **1** track down and find. **2** follow the course of. **3** copy exactly by drawing on a thin sheet of transparent paper set on top of the original. ▷ *n* **4** track left by something. **5** minute quantity. **6** indication. **traceable** *adj* **tracery** *n* pattern of interlacing lines. **tracing** *n* traced copy. **trace element** chemical element occurring in very small amounts in soil etc.

trachea [track-**kee**-a] *n*, *pl* **tracheae** windpipe. **tracheotomy** [track-ee-**ot**-a-mee] *n* surgical incision into the trachea.

track ❶ *n* **1** rough road or path. **2** mark or trail left by the passage of anything. **3** railway line. **4** course for racing. **5** separate section on a record, tape, or CD. **6** course of action or thought. **7** endless band round the wheels of a tank, bulldozer, etc. ▷ *v* **8** follow the trail or path

———————————————————— THESAURUS ————————

tournament *n* **1** = **competition**, contest, event, meeting, series

tow *v* **1** = **drag**, draw, haul, lug, pull, tug, yank

towards *prep* **1** = **in the direction of**, en route for, for, on the way to, to **2** = **regarding**, about, concerning, for, with regard to, with respect to

tower *n* = **column**, belfry, obelisk, pillar, skyscraper, steeple, turret

toxic *adj* **1** = **poisonous**, deadly, harmful, lethal, noxious, pernicious, pestilential, septic

toy *n* **1** = **plaything**, doll, game **toy with** *v* = **play**, amuse oneself with, dally with, fool (about *or* around) with, trifle

trace *v* **1** = **find**, detect, discover, ferret out, hunt down, track, unearth **2** = **outline**, draw, sketch **3** = **copy** ▷ *n* **4** = **track**, footmark, footprint, footstep, path, spoor, trail **5** = **bit**, drop, hint, shadow, suggestion, suspicion, tinge, touch, whiff **6** = **remnant**, evidence, indication, mark, record, sign, survival, vestige

track *n* **1** = **path**, course, line, orbit, pathway, road, trajectory, way **2** = **trail**, footmark, footprint, footstep, mark, path, spoor, trace, wake **3** = **line**, permanent way, rails ▷ *v* **8** = **follow**, chase, hunt down, pursue, shadow, stalk, tail (*inf*), trace, trail

of. **track down** v hunt for and find. **track event** athletic sport held on a running track. **track record** past accomplishments of a person or organization. **tracksuit** n warm loose-fitting suit worn by athletes etc., esp. during training.

tract¹ ❶ n 1 wide area. 2 Anat system of organs with a particular function.

tract² ❶ n pamphlet, esp. a religious one.

traction ❶ n 1 pulling, esp. by engine power. 2 Med application of a steady pull on an injured limb by weights and pulleys. 3 grip of the wheels of a vehicle on the ground. **traction engine** old-fashioned steam-powered vehicle for pulling heavy loads.

tractor n motor vehicle with large rear wheels for pulling farm machinery.

trade ❶ n 1 buying, selling, or exchange of goods. 2 person's job or craft. 3 (people engaged in) a particular industry or business. ▷ v 4 buy and sell. 5 exchange. 6 engage in trade. **trader** n **trading** n **trade-in** n used article given in part payment for a new one. **trademark** n (legally registered) name or symbol used by a firm to distinguish its goods. **trade-off** n exchange made as a compromise. **tradesman** n 1 skilled worker. 2 shopkeeper. **trade union** society of workers formed to protect their interests.

trade wind wind blowing steadily towards the equator.

tradition ❶ n 1 body of beliefs, customs, etc. handed down from generation to generation. 2 custom or practice of long standing. **traditional** adj.

traffic ❶ n 1 vehicles coming and going on a road. 2 (illicit) trade. ▷ v **-ficking, -ficked** 3 trade, usu. illicitly. **trafficker** n **traffic lights** set of coloured lights at a junction to control the traffic flow. **traffic warden** person employed to control the movement and parking of traffic.

tragedy ❶ n, pl **-dies** 1 shocking or sad event. 2 serious play, film, etc. in which the hero is destroyed by a personal failing in adverse circumstances. **tragedian** [traj-**jee**-dee-an], **tragedienne**[traj-jee-dee-**enn**] n person who acts in or writes tragedies. **tragic** adj of or like a tragedy. **tragically** adv **tragicomedy** n play with both tragic and comic elements.

trail ❶ n 1 path, track, or road. 2 tracks left by a person, animal, or object. ▷ v 3 drag along the ground. 4 lag behind. 5 follow the tracks of. **trailer** n 1 vehicle designed to be towed by another vehicle. 2 extract from a film or programme used to advertise it. **trailer park** n US site for parking mobile homes.

tract¹ n 1 = **area**, district, expanse, extent, plot, region, stretch, territory

tract² n = **treatise**, booklet, dissertation, essay, homily, monograph, pamphlet

traction n 1 = **pulling**, pull 3 = **grip**, friction, purchase, resistance

trade n 1 = **commerce**, barter, business, dealing, exchange, traffic, transactions, truck 2 = **job**, business, craft, employment, line of work, métier, occupation, profession ▷ v 4 = **deal**, bargain, cut a deal, do business, have dealings, peddle, traffic, transact, truck 5 = **exchange**, barter, swap, switch

tradition n 1 = **lore**, folklore 2 = **custom**, convention, habit, institution, ritual

traffic n 1 = **transport**, freight, transportation, vehicles 2 = **trade**, business, commerce, dealings, exchange, peddling, truck ▷ v 3 = **trade**, bargain, cut a deal, deal, do business, exchange, have dealings, peddle

tragedy n 1 = **disaster**, adversity, calamity, catastrophe, misfortune

trail n 1 = **path**, footpath, road, route, track, way 2 = **tracks**, footprints, marks, path, scent, spoor, trace, wake ▷ v 3 = **drag**, dangle, draw, haul, pull, tow 4 = **lag**, dawdle, follow, hang back, linger, loiter, straggle, traipse (inf) 5 = **follow**, chase, hunt, pursue, shadow, stalk, tail (inf), trace, track

t

train ❶ *v* **1** instruct in a skill. **2** learn the skills needed to do a particular job or activity. **3** prepare for a sports event etc. **4** aim (a gun etc.). **5** cause (an animal) to perform or (a plant) to grow in a particular way. ▷ *n* **6** line of railway coaches or wagons drawn by an engine. **7** sequence or series. **8** long trailing back section of a dress. **trainer** *n* **1** person who trains an athlete or sportsman. **2** sports shoe. **trainee** *n* person being trained.

traipse ❶ *v informal* walk wearily.

trait ❶ *n* characteristic feature.

traitor ❶ *n* person guilty of treason or treachery. **traitorous** *adj*.

trajectory ❶ *n, pl* **-ries** line of flight, esp. of a projectile.

tram *n* public transport vehicle powered by an overhead wire and running on rails laid in the road. **tramlines** *pl n* track for trams.

tramp ❶ *v* **1** travel on foot, hike. **2** walk heavily. ▷ *n* **3** homeless person who travels on foot. **4** hike. **5** sound of tramping. **6** cargo ship available for hire. **7** *US & Aust slang* promiscuous woman.

trample ❶ *v* tread on and crush.

trampoline *n* **1** tough canvas sheet attached to a frame by springs, used

by acrobats etc. ▷ *v* **2** bounce on a trampoline.

trance ❶ *n* unconscious or dazed state.

tranche *n* portion of something large, esp. a sum of money.

tranquil ❶ *adj* calm and quiet. **tranquilly** *adv* **tranquillity** *n* **tranquillize** *v* make calm. **tranquillizer** *n* drug which reduces anxiety or tension.

trans- *prefix* across, through, or beyond.

transact *v* conduct or negotiate (a business deal). **transaction** *n* business deal transacted.

transcend ❶ *v* **1** rise above. **2** be superior to. **transcendence** *n* **transcendent** *adj* **transcendental** *adj* **1** based on intuition rather than experience. **2** supernatural or mystical. **transcendentalism** *n*.

transcribe ❶ *v* **1** write down (something said). **2** record for a later broadcast. **3** arrange (music) for a different instrument. **transcript** *n* copy.

transfer ❶ *v* **-ferring, -ferred 1** move or send from one person or place to another. ▷ *n* **2** transferring. **3** design which can be transferred from one surface to another. **transferable** *adj* **transference** *n* transferring.

——————————————————————— THESAURUS ———

train *v* **1** = **instruct**, coach, drill, educate, guide, prepare, school, teach, tutor **3** = **exercise**, prepare, work out **4** = **aim**, direct, focus, level, point ▷ *n* **7** = **sequence**, chain, progression, series, set, string, succession

traipse *v Inf* = **trudge**, drag oneself, slouch, trail, tramp

trait *n* = **characteristic**, attribute, feature, idiosyncrasy, mannerism, peculiarity, quality, quirk

traitor *n* = **betrayer**, apostate, back-stabber, defector, deserter, Judas, quisling, rebel, renegade, turncoat

trajectory *n* = **path**, course, flight path, line, route, track

tramp *v* **1** = **hike**, march, ramble, roam, rove, slog, trek, walk **2** = **trudge**, plod,

stump, toil, traipse (*inf*) ▷ *n* **3** = **vagrant**, derelict, down-and-out, drifter **4** = **hike**, march, ramble, slog, trek **5** = **tread**, footfall, footstep

trample *v* = **crush**, flatten, run over, squash, stamp, tread, walk over

trance *n* = **daze**, abstraction, dream, rapture, reverie, stupor, unconsciousness

tranquil *adj* = **calm**, peaceful, placid, quiet, restful, sedate, serene, still, undisturbed

transcend *v* **1** = **rise above 2** = **surpass**, eclipse, exceed, excel, go beyond, outdo, outstrip

transcribe *v* **1** = **write out**, copy out, reproduce, take down, transfer

transfer *v* **1** = **move**, change, convey, hand over, pass on, relocate, shift, transplant, transport, transpose ▷ *n* **2** = **move**,

transfigure v change in appearance. **transfiguration** n.

transfix ❶ v 1 astound or stun. 2 pierce through.

transform ❶ v change the shape or character of. **transformation** n **transformer** n device for changing the voltage of an alternating current.

transgress ❶ v break (a moral law). **transgression** n **transgressor** n.

transient ❶ adj lasting only for a short time. **transience** n.

transistor n 1 semiconducting device used to amplify electric currents. 2 portable radio using transistors.

transit ❶ n movement from one place to another. **transition** n change from one state to another. **transitional** adj **transitive** adj Grammar (of a verb) requiring a direct object. **transitory** adj not lasting long.

translate ❶ v turn from one language into another. **translation** n **translator** n.

translucent adj letting light pass through, but not transparent. **translucency**, **translucence** n.

transmit ❶ v -mitting, -mitted 1 pass

(something) from one person or place to another. 2 send out (signals) by radio waves. 3 broadcast (a radio or television programme). **transmission** n 1 transmitting. 2 shafts and gears through which power passes from a vehicle's engine to its wheels. **transmittable** adj **transmitter** n.

transmute v change the form or nature of. **transmutation** n.

transparent ❶ adj 1 able to be seen through, clear. 2 easily understood or recognized. **transparency** n 1 transparent quality. 2 colour photograph on transparent film that can be viewed by means of a projector.

transpire ❶ v 1 become known. 2 informal happen. 3 give off water vapour through pores. **transpiration** n.

transplant ❶ v 1 transfer (an organ or tissue) surgically from one part or body to another. 2 remove and transfer (a plant) to another place. ▷ n 3 surgical transplanting. 4 thing transplanted. **transplantation** n.

transport ❶ v 1 convey from one place to another. 2 Hist exile (a criminal) to a

change, handover, relocation, shift, transference, translation, transmission, transposition

transfix v 1 = **stun**, engross, fascinate, hold, hypnotize, mesmerize, paralyse 2 = **pierce**, impale, puncture, run through, skewer, spear

transform v = **change**, alter, convert, remodel, revolutionize, transmute

transgress v = **break**, break the law, contravene, disobey, exceed, go beyond, infringe, offend, overstep, sin, trespass, violate

transient adj = **brief**, ephemeral, fleeting, impermanent, momentary, passing, short-lived, temporary, transitory

transit n = **movement**, carriage, conveyance, crossing, passage, transfer, transport, transportation

translate v = **interpret**, construe, convert, decipher, decode, paraphrase, render

transmit v 1 = **pass on**, bear, carry, convey, disseminate, hand on, impart, send, spread, transfer 3 = **broadcast**, disseminate, radio, relay, send out

transparent adj 1 = **clear**, crystalline, diaphanous, limpid, lucid, see-through, sheer, translucent 2 = **obvious**, evident, explicit, manifest, patent, plain, recognizable, unambiguous, undisguised

transpire v 1 = **become known**, come out, come to light, emerge 2 Inf = **happen**, arise, befall, chance, come about, occur, take place

transplant v 2 = **transfer**, displace, relocate, remove, resettle, shift, uproot

transport v 1 = **convey**, bear, bring, carry, haul, move, take, transfer 2 Hist = **exile**,

t

penal colony. **3** enrapture. ▷ *n* **4** business or system of transporting. **5** vehicle used in transport. **6** ecstasy or rapture. **transportation** *n* **transporter** *n* large goods vehicle.

transpose ❶ *v* **1** interchange two things. **2** put (music) into a different key. **transposition** *n*.

transverse *adj* crossing from side to side.

transvestite *n* person who seeks sexual pleasure by wearing the clothes of the opposite sex. **transvestism** *n*.

trap ❶ *n* **1** device for catching animals. **2** plan for tricking or catching a person. **3** bend in a pipe containing liquid to prevent the escape of gas. **4** stall in which greyhounds are enclosed before a race. **5** two-wheeled carriage. **6** *slang* mouth. ▷ *v* **trapping, trapped 7** catch. **8** trick. **trapper** *n* person who traps animals for their fur. **trapdoor** *n* door in floor or roof. **trap-door spider** spider that builds a silk-lined hole in the ground closed by a hinged door of earth and silk.

trapeze *n* horizontal bar suspended from two ropes, used by circus acrobats.

trapezium *n, pl* **-ziums, -zia** quadrilateral with two parallel sides of unequal length. **trapezoid** [trap-piz-zoid] *n* **1** quadrilateral with no sides parallel. **2** *Chiefly US* trapezium.

trappings ❶ *pl n* accessories that symbolize an office or position.

trash ❶ *n* **1** anything worthless. **2** *US & Canad* rubbish. **trashy** *adj*.

trauma ❶ [**traw**-ma] *n* **1** emotional shock. **2** injury or wound. **traumatic** *adj* **traumatize** *v*.

travail *n* *lit* labour or toil.

travel ❶ *v* **-elling, -elled 1** go from one place to another, through an area, or for a specified distance. ▷ *n* **2** travelling, esp. as a tourist. ▷ *pl* **3** (account of) travelling. **traveller** *n* **travelogue** *n* film or talk about someone's travels.

traverse ❶ *v* move over or back and forth over.

travesty ❶ *n, pl* **-ties** grotesque imitation or mockery.

trawl *n* **1** net dragged at deep levels behind a fishing boat. ▷ *v* **2** fish with such a net. **trawler** *n* trawling boat.

tray *n* **1** flat board, usu. with a rim, for

———————————————————— THESAURUS ————————————————————

banish, deport **3 = enrapture,** captivate, delight, enchant, entrance, move, ravish ▷ *n* **4, 5 = vehicle,** conveyance, transportation **6 = ecstasy,** bliss, delight, enchantment, euphoria, heaven, rapture, ravishment

transpose *v* **1 = interchange,** alter, change, exchange, move, reorder, shift, substitute, swap, switch, transfer

trap *n* **1 = snare,** ambush, gin, net, noose, pitfall **2 = trick,** ambush, deception, ruse, stratagem, subterfuge, wile ▷ *v* **7 = catch,** corner, enmesh, ensnare, entrap, snare, take **8 = trick,** ambush, beguile, deceive, dupe, ensnare, inveigle

trappings *pl n* **= accessories,** accoutrements, equipment, finery, furnishings, gear, panoply, paraphernalia,

things, trimmings

trash *n* **1 = nonsense,** drivel, hogwash, kak (*S Afr sl*), moonshine, poppycock (*inf*), rot, rubbish, tripe (*inf*), twaddle **2** *US & Canad* **= litter,** dross, garbage, junk (*inf*), refuse, rubbish, waste

trauma *n* **1 = shock,** anguish, ordeal, pain, suffering, torture **2 = injury,** agony, damage, hurt, wound

travel *v* **1 = go,** journey, move, progress, roam, tour, trek, voyage, wander ▷ *pl n* **3 = journey,** excursion, expedition, globetrotting, tour, trip, voyage, wandering

traverse *v* **= cross,** go over, span, travel over

travesty *n* **1 = mockery,** burlesque, caricature, distortion, lampoon, parody, perversion

carrying things. **2** open receptacle for office correspondence.

treachery ❶ *n, pl* **-eries** wilful betrayal. **treacherous** *adj* **1** disloyal. **2** unreliable or dangerous.

treacle *n* thick dark syrup produced when sugar is refined. **treacly** *adj*.

tread ❶ *v* **treading**, **trod**, **trodden** *or* **trod** **1** set one's foot on. **2** crush by walking on. ▷ *n* **3** way of walking or dancing. **4** upper surface of a step. **5** part of a tyre or shoe that touches the ground. **treadmill** *n* **1** *Hist* cylinder turned by treading on steps projecting from it. **2** dreary routine.

treadle [**tred**-dl] *n* lever worked by the foot to turn a wheel.

treason ❶ *n* **1** betrayal of one's sovereign or country. **2** treachery or disloyalty. **treasonable** *adj*.

treasure ❶ *n* **1** collection of wealth, esp. gold or jewels. **2** valued person or thing. ▷ *v* **3** prize or cherish. **treasurer** *n* official in charge of funds. **treasury** *n* **1** storage place for treasure. **2** (T-) government department in charge of finance. **treasure-trove** *n* treasure found with no

evidence of ownership.

treat ❶ *v* **1** deal with or regard in a certain manner. **2** give medical treatment to. **3** subject to a chemical or industrial process. **4** provide (someone) with (something) as a treat. ▷ *n* **5** pleasure, entertainment, etc. given or paid for by someone else. **treatment** *n* **1** medical care. **2** way of treating a person or thing.

treatise ❶ [**treat**-izz] *n* formal piece of writing on a particular subject.

treaty ❶ *n, pl* **-ties** signed contract between states.

treble *adj* **1** triple. **2** *Music* high-pitched. ▷ *n* **3** (singer with or part for) a soprano voice. ▷ *v* **4** increase three times. **trebly** *adv*.

tree *n* large perennial plant with a woody trunk. **treeless** *adj* **tree kangaroo** tree-living kangaroo of New Guinea and N Australia. **tree surgery** repair of damaged trees.

trek ❶ *n* **1** long difficult journey, esp. on foot. **2** *S Afr* migration by ox wagon. ▷ *v* **trekking**, **trekked** **3** make such a journey.

trellis *n* framework of horizontal and vertical strips of wood.

THESAURUS

---

treachery *n* = **betrayal**, disloyalty, double-dealing, duplicity, faithlessness, infidelity, perfidy, treason

tread *v* **1** = **step**, hike, march, pace, stamp, stride, walk **2** = **crush underfoot**, squash, trample ▷ *n* **3** = **step**, footfall, footstep, gait, pace, stride, walk

treason *n* = **disloyalty**, duplicity, lese-majesty, mutiny, perfidy, sedition, traitorousness, treachery

treasure *n* **1** = **riches**, cash, fortune, gold, jewels, money, valuables, wealth **2** = **darling**, apple of one's eye, gem, jewel, nonpareil, paragon, pride and joy ▷ *v* **3** = **prize**, adore, cherish, esteem, hold dear, idolize, love, revere, value

treat *v* **1** = **behave towards**, act

towards, consider, deal with, handle, look upon, manage, regard, use **2** = **take care of**, attend to, care for, nurse **4** = **provide**, entertain, lay on, regale, stand (*inf*) ▷ *n* **5 a** = **pleasure**, delight, enjoyment, fun, joy, satisfaction, surprise, thrill **b** = **entertainment**, banquet, celebration, feast, gift, party, refreshment

treatise *n* = **paper**, dissertation, essay, monograph, pamphlet, study, thesis, tract, work

treaty *n* = **agreement**, alliance, compact, concordat, contract, entente, pact

trek *n* **1** = **journey**, expedition, hike, march, odyssey, safari, slog, tramp ▷ *v* **3** = **journey**, hike, march, slog, traipse (*inf*), tramp, trudge

t

tremble ⓥ v 1 shake or quiver. 2 feel fear or anxiety. ▷ n 3 trembling. **trembling** adj.

tremendous ⓐ adj 1 huge. 2 informal great in quality or amount.

tremor ⓝ n 1 involuntary shaking. 2 minor earthquake.

tremulous adj trembling, as from fear or excitement.

trench ⓝ n long narrow ditch, esp. one used as a shelter in war. **trench coat** double-breasted waterproof coat.

trenchant adj 1 incisive. 2 effective.

trend ⓝ n 1 general tendency or direction. 2 fashion. **trendy** adj, n informal consciously fashionable (person). **trendiness** n.

trepidation ⓝ n fear or anxiety.

trespass ⓥ v 1 go onto another's property without permission. ▷ n 2 trespassing. 3 old-fashioned sin or wrongdoing. **trespasser** n **trespass on** v take unfair advantage of (someone's friendship, patience, etc.).

trestle n board fixed on pairs of spreading legs, used as a support.

trevally n, pl **-lies** Aust & NZ any of various food and game fishes.

trews pl n close-fitting tartan trousers.

tri- combining form three.

trial ⓝ n 1 Law investigation of a case before a judge. 2 trying or testing. 3 thing or person straining endurance or patience. ▷ pl 4 sporting competition for individuals.

triangle n 1 geometric figure with three sides. 2 triangular percussion instrument. 3 situation involving three people. **triangular** adj.

tribe ⓝ n group of clans or families believed to have a common ancestor. **tribal** adj **tribalism** n loyalty to a tribe.

tribulation n great distress.

tribunal ⓝ n 1 board appointed to inquire into a specific matter. 2 lawcourt.

tributary n, pl **-taries** 1 stream or river flowing into a larger one. ▷ adj 2 (of a stream or river) flowing into a larger one.

tribute ⓝ n 1 sign of respect or admiration. 2 tax paid by one state to another.

trice n **in a trice** instantly.

———————————————————————————— THESAURUS ————

tremble v 1 = **shake**, quake, quiver, shiver, shudder, totter, vibrate, wobble ▷ n 3 = **shake**, quake, quiver, shiver, shudder, tremor, vibration, wobble

tremendous adj 1 = **huge**, colossal, enormous, formidable, gigantic, great, immense, stupendous, terrific 2 Inf = **excellent**, amazing, brilliant, exceptional, extraordinary, fantastic (inf), great, marvellous, sensational (inf), wonderful

tremor n 1 = **shake**, quaking, quaver, quiver, shiver, trembling, wobble 2 = **earthquake**, quake (inf), shock

trench n = **ditch**, channel, drain, excavation, furrow, gutter, trough

trend n 1 = **tendency**, bias, current, direction, drift, flow, inclination, leaning 2 = **fashion**, craze, fad (inf), mode, rage, style, thing, vogue

trepidation n = **anxiety**, alarm, apprehension, consternation, disquiet, dread, fear, nervousness, uneasiness, worry

trespass v 1 = **intrude**, encroach, infringe, invade, obtrude ▷ n 2 = **intrusion**, encroachment, infringement, invasion, unlawful entry

trial n 1 Law = **hearing**, litigation, tribunal 2 = **test**, audition, dry run (inf), experiment, probation, test-run 3 = **hardship**, adversity, affliction, distress, ordeal, suffering, tribulation, trouble

tribe n = **race**, clan, family, people

tribunal n 2 = **hearing**, court, trial

tribute n 1 = **accolade**, commendation, compliment, eulogy, panegyric, recognition, testimonial 2 = **tax**, charge, homage, payment, ransom

trick ❶ *n* **1** deceitful or cunning action or plan. **2** joke or prank. **3** feat of skill or cunning. **4** mannerism. **5** cards played in one round. ▷ *v* **6** cheat or deceive. **trickery** *n* **trickster** *n* **tricky** *adj* **1** difficult, needing careful handling. **2** crafty.

trickle ❶ *v* **1** (cause to) flow in a thin stream or drops. **2** move gradually. ▷ *n* **3** gradual flow.

tricolour [**trick**-kol-lor] *n* three-coloured striped flag.

tricycle *n* three-wheeled cycle.

trident *n* three-pronged spear.

trifle ❶ *n* **1** insignificant thing or amount. **2** dessert of sponge cake, fruit, custard, and cream. **trifling** *adj* insignificant. **trifle with** *v* toy with.

trigger ❶ *n* **1** small lever releasing a catch on a gun or machine. **2** action that sets off a course of events. ▷ *v* **3** (usu. foll. by *off*) set (an action or process) in motion. **trigger-happy** *adj* too quick to use guns.

trigonometry *n* branch of mathematics dealing with relations of the sides and angles of triangles.

trilby *n, pl* **-bies** man's soft felt hat.

trill *n* **1** *Music* rapid alternation between two notes. **2** shrill warbling sound made by some birds. ▷ *v* **3** play or sing a trill.

trillion *n* **1** one million million, 10¹². **2** *Brit* (formerly) one million million million, 10¹⁸.

trilogy *n, pl* **-gies** series of three related books, plays, etc.

trim ❶ *adj* **trimmer**, **trimmest 1** neat and smart. **2** slender. ▷ *v* **trimming**, **trimmed 3** cut or prune into good shape. **4** decorate with lace, ribbons, etc. **5** adjust the balance of (a ship or aircraft) by shifting the cargo etc. ▷ *n* **6** decoration. **7** upholstery and decorative facings in a car. **8** trim state. **9** haircut that neatens the existing style. **trimming** *n* **1** decoration. ▷ *pl* **2** usual accompaniments.

trinitrotoluene *n* full name for TNT.

trinity *n, pl* **-ties 1** group of three. **2** (**T**-) *Christianity* union of three persons, Father, Son, and Holy Spirit, in one God.

trinket ❶ *n* small or worthless ornament or piece of jewellery.

trio ❶ *n, pl* **trios 1** group of three. **2** piece of music for three performers.

trick *n* **1** = **deception**, fraud, hoax, manoeuvre, ploy, ruse, stratagem, subterfuge, swindle, trap, wile **2** = **joke**, antic, jape, leg-pull (*Brit inf*), practical joke, prank, stunt **3** = **secret**, hang (*inf*), knack, know-how (*inf*), skill, technique **4** = **mannerism**, characteristic, foible, habit, idiosyncrasy, peculiarity, practice, quirk, trait ▷ *v* **6** = **deceive**, cheat, con (*inf*), dupe, fool, hoodwink, kid (*inf*), mislead, swindle, take in (*inf*), trap

trickle *v* **1** = **dribble**, drip, drop, exude, ooze, run, seep, stream ▷ *n* **3** = **dribble**, drip, seepage

trifle *n* **1** = **knick-knack**, bagatelle, bauble, plaything, toy **trifle with** *v* = **toy with**, dally with, mess about, play with

trigger *v* **3** = **set off**, activate, cause, generate, produce, prompt, provoke,

spark off, start

trim *adj* **1** = **neat**, dapper, natty (*inf*), shipshape, smart, spruce, tidy, well-groomed **2** = **slender**, fit, shapely, sleek, slim, streamlined, svelte, willowy ▷ *v* **3** = **cut**, clip, crop, even up, pare, prune, shave, tidy **4** = **decorate**, adorn, array, beautify, deck out, dress, embellish, ornament ▷ *n* **6** = **decoration**, adornment, border, edging, embellishment, frill, ornamentation, piping, trimming **8** = **condition**, fettle, fitness, health, shape (*inf*), state, wellness **9** = **cut**, clipping, crop, shave, tidying up

trinket *n* = **ornament**, bagatelle, bauble, knick-knack, toy, trifle

trio *n* **1** = **threesome**, triad, trilogy, trinity, triumvirate

t

trip ❶ *n* **1** journey to a place and back, esp. for pleasure. **2** stumble. **3** *informal* hallucinogenic drug experience. **4** switch on a mechanism. ▷ *v* **tripping, tripped** **5** (cause to) stumble. **6** (often foll. by *up*) catch (someone) in a mistake. **7** move or tread lightly. **8** *informal* experience the hallucinogenic effects of a drug. **tripper** *n* tourist.

tripe *n* **1** stomach of a cow used as food. **2** *informal* nonsense.

triple ❶ *adj* **1** having three parts. **2** three times as great or as many. ▷ *v* **3** increase three times. **triplet** *n* one of three babies born at one birth. **triple jump** athletic event in which competitors make a hop, a step, and a jump as a continuous movement.

triplicate *adj* triple. **in triplicate** in three copies.

tripod [**tripe**-pod] *n* three-legged stand, stool, etc.

trite ❶ *adj* (of a remark or idea) commonplace and unoriginal.

triumph ❶ *n* **1** (happiness caused by) victory or success. ▷ *v* **2** be victorious or successful. **3** rejoice over a victory. **triumphal** *adj* celebrating a triumph. **triumphant** *adj* feeling or showing triumph.

troll *n* giant or dwarf in Scandinavian folklore.

trolley *n* **1** small wheeled table for food and drink. **2** wheeled cart for moving goods.

trollop *n* promiscuous or slovenly woman.

trombone *n* brass musical instrument with a sliding tube. **trombonist** *n*.

troop ❶ *n* **1** large group. **2** artillery or cavalry unit. **3** Scout company. ▷ *pl* **4** soldiers. ▷ *v* **5** move in a crowd. **trooper** *n* cavalry soldier.

trophy ❶ *n, pl* **-phies 1** cup, shield, etc. given as a prize. **2** memento of success.

tropic *n* **1** either of two lines of latitude at 23–°N (**tropic of Cancer**) or 23–°S (**tropic of Capricorn**). *pl* **2** part of the earth's surface between these lines. **tropical** *adj* **1** of or in the tropics. **2** (of climate) very hot.

trot ❶ *v* **trotting, trotted 1** (of a horse) move at a medium pace, lifting the feet in diagonal pairs. **2** (of a person) move at a steady brisk pace. ▷ *n* **3** trotting. **trotter** *n* pig's foot. **trot out** *v* repeat (old ideas etc.) without fresh thought.

troubadour [**troo**-bad-oor] *n* medieval travelling poet and singer.

trouble ❶ *n* **1** (cause of) distress or anxiety. **2** disease or malfunctioning.

———————————————————————————— THESAURUS ————————————————

trip *n* **1** = **journey**, errand, excursion, expedition, foray, jaunt, outing, run, tour, voyage **2** = **stumble**, fall, misstep, slip ▷ *v* **5** = **stumble**, fall, lose one's footing, misstep, slip, tumble **6** = **catch out**, trap **7** = **skip**, dance, gambol, hop

triple *adj* **1** = **threefold**, three-way, tripartite ▷ *v* **3** = **treble**, increase threefold

trite *adj* = **unoriginal**, banal, clichéd, commonplace, hackneyed, stale, stereotyped, threadbare, tired

triumph *n* **1 a** = **joy**, elation, exultation, happiness, jubilation, pride, rejoicing **b** = **success**, accomplishment, achievement, attainment, conquest,

coup, feat, victory ▷ *v* **2** = **succeed**, overcome, prevail, prosper, vanquish, win **3** = **rejoice**, celebrate, crow, exult, gloat, glory, revel

troop *n* **1** = **group**, band, body, crowd, horde, multitude, team, unit **2** = **company**, squad ▷ *pl* **4** = **soldiers**, armed forces, army, men, servicemen, soldiery ▷ *v* **5** = **flock**, march, stream, swarm, throng, traipse (*inf*)

trophy *n* **1** = **prize**, award, booty, cup **2** = **memento**, laurels, souvenir, spoils

trot *v* **1, 2** = **run**, canter, jog, lope, scamper ▷ *n* **3** = **run**, canter, jog, lope

trouble *n* **1** = **distress**, anxiety, disquiet, grief, misfortune, pain, sorrow, torment,

3 state of disorder or unrest. **4** care or effort. ▷ v **5** (cause to) worry. **6** exert oneself. **7** cause inconvenience to. **troubled** adj **troublesome** adj **troubleshooter** n person employed to locate and deal with faults or problems.

trough ❶ [troff] n **1** long open container, esp. for animals' food or water. **2** narrow channel between two waves or ridges. **3** Meteorol area of low pressure.

trounce ❶ v defeat utterly.

troupe ❶ [troop] n company of performers. **trouper** n.

trousers pl n two-legged outer garment with legs reaching usu. to the ankles. **trouser** adj of trousers.

trousseau [troo-so] n, pl -seaux, -seaus bride's collection of clothing etc. for her marriage.

trout n game fish related to the salmon.

trowel n hand tool with a wide blade for spreading mortar, lifting plants, etc.

truant ❶ n pupil who stays away from school without permission. **play truant** stay away from school without permission. **truancy** n.

truce ❶ n temporary agreement to stop fighting.

truck¹ n **1** railway goods wagon. **2** lorry.

truck² n **have no truck with** refuse to be involved with.

trucker n US & Canad truck driver.

truculent [truck-yew-lent] adj aggressively defiant. **truculence** n.

trudge ❶ v **1** walk heavily or wearily. ▷ n **2** long tiring walk.

true ❶ adj **truer, truest 1** in accordance with facts. **2** genuine. **3** faithful. **4** exact. **truly** adv **truism** n self-evident truth. **truth** n **1** state of being true. **2** something true. **truthful** adj **1** honest. **2** exact.

truffle n **1** edible underground fungus. **2** sweet flavoured with chocolate.

trump n, adj **1** (card) of the suit outranking the others. ▷ v **2** play a trump card on (another card). ▷ pl n **3** suit outranking the others. **turn up trumps** achieve an unexpected success. **trumped up** invented or concocted.

trumpet n **1** valved brass instrument with a flared tube. ▷ v -peting, -peted **2** proclaim loudly. **3** (of an elephant) cry loudly. **trumpeter** n.

THESAURUS

woe, worry **2** = **ailment**, complaint, defect, disease, disorder, failure, illness, malfunction **3** = **disorder**, agitation, bother (inf), commotion, discord, disturbance, strife, tumult, unrest **4** = **effort**, care, exertion, inconvenience, labour, pains, thought, work ▷ v **5** = **bother**, disconcert, distress, disturb, pain, perturb, plague, sadden, upset, worry **6** = **take pains**, exert oneself, make an effort, take the time **7** = **inconvenience**, bother, burden, disturb, impose upon, incommode, put out

trough n **1** = **manger**, water trough **2** = **channel**, canal, depression, ditch, duct, furrow, gully, gutter, trench

trounce v = **defeat utterly**, beat, crush, drub, give a hiding (inf), hammer (inf),

rout, slaughter (inf), thrash, wipe the floor with (inf)

troupe n = **company**, band, cast

truant n = **absentee**, malingerer, piker (Aust & NZ sl), runaway, shirker, skiver (Brit sl)

truce n = **ceasefire**, armistice, cessation, let-up (inf), lull, moratorium, peace, respite

trudge v **1** = **plod**, lumber, slog, stump, traipse (inf), tramp, trek ▷ n **2** = **tramp**, hike, march, slog, traipse (inf), trek

true adj **1** = **correct**, accurate, factual, precise, right, truthful, veracious **2** = **genuine**, authentic, real **3** = **faithful**, dedicated, devoted, dutiful, loyal, reliable, staunch, steady, trustworthy **4** = **exact**, accurate, on target, perfect, precise, spot-on (Brit inf), unerring

t

truncate ❶ v cut short.
truncheon n small club carried by a policeman.
trundle v move heavily on wheels.
trunk ❶ n 1 main stem of a tree. 2 large case or box for clothes etc. 3 person's body excluding the head and limbs. 4 elephant's long nose. 5 *US* car boot. ▷ *pl* 6 man's swimming shorts. **trunk call** long-distance telephone call. **trunk road** main road.
truss ❶ v 1 tie or bind up. ▷ n 2 device for holding a hernia in place. 3 framework supporting a roof, bridge, etc.
trust ❶ v 1 believe in and rely on. 2 consign to someone's care. 3 expect or hope. ▷ n 4 confidence in the truth, reliability, etc. of a person or thing. 5 obligation arising from responsibility. 6 arrangement in which one person administers property, money, etc. on another's behalf. 7 property held for another. 8 *Brit* self-governing hospital or group of hospitals within the National Health Service. 9 group of companies joined to control a market. **trustee** n person holding property on another's behalf. **trustful**, **trusting** adj inclined to trust others. **trustworthy** adj reliable or honest. **trusty** adj faithful or reliable.
try ❶ v **trying, tried** 1 make an effort or attempt. 2 test or sample. 3 put strain

on, e.g. *he tries my patience.* 4 investigate (a case). 5 examine (a person) in a lawcourt. ▷ n, *pl* **tries** 6 attempt or effort. 7 *Rugby* score gained by touching the ball down over the opponent's goal line. **try it on** *informal* try to deceive or fool someone. **trying** adj *informal* difficult or annoying.
tryst n arrangement to meet.
T-shirt n short-sleeved casual shirt or top.
tub n 1 open, usu. round container. 2 bath. **tubby** adj (of a person) short and fat.
tuba [**tube**-a] n valved low-pitched brass instrument.
tube n 1 hollow cylinder. 2 flexible cylinder with a cap to hold pastes. **the tube** underground railway, esp. the one in London. **tubing** n 1 length of tube. 2 system of tubes. **tubular** [**tube**-yew-lar] adj of or shaped like a tube.
tuber [**tube**-er] n fleshy underground root of a plant such as a potato. **tuberous** adj.
tuberculosis [tube-berk-yew-**lohss**-iss] n infectious disease causing tubercles, esp. in the lungs. **tubercular** adj **tuberculin** n extract from a bacillus used to test for tuberculosis.
tuck ❶ v 1 push or fold into a small space. 2 stitch in folds. ▷ n 3 stitched fold. 4 *informal* food. **tuck away** v eat (a large amount of food).
tucker n *Aust & NZ informal* food.

————————————————————————— THESAURUS —————

truncate v = **shorten**, abbreviate, curtail, cut short, dock, lop, pare, prune, trim
trunk n 1 = **stem**, bole, stalk 2 = **chest**, box, case, casket, coffer, crate 3 = **body**, torso
truss v 1 = **tie**, bind, fasten, make fast, secure, strap, tether ▷ n 2 = **support**, bandage 3 = **joist**, beam, brace, buttress, prop, stanchion, stay, strut, support
trust v 1 = **believe in**, bank on, count on, depend on, have faith in, rely upon 2 = **entrust**, assign, commit, confide, consign, delegate, give 3 = **expect**,

assume, hope, presume, suppose, surmise ▷ n 4 = **confidence**, assurance, belief, certainty, conviction, credence, credit, expectation, faith, reliance
try v 1 = **attempt**, aim, endeavour, have a go, make an effort, seek, strive, struggle 2 = **test**, appraise, check out, evaluate, examine, investigate, put to the test, sample, taste ▷ n 6 = **attempt**, crack (*inf*), effort, go (*inf*), shot (*inf*), stab (*inf*), whack (*inf*)
tuck v 1 = **push**, fold, gather, insert ▷ n 3 = **fold**, gather, pinch, pleat 4 *Inf* = **food**, grub (*sl*), nosh (*sl*)

Tuesday n third day of the week.

tuft ❶ n bunch of feathers, grass, hair, etc. held or growing together at the base.

tug ❶ v **tugging, tugged** 1 pull hard. ▷ n 2 hard pull. 3 (also **tugboat**) small ship used to tow other vessels. **tug of war** contest in which two teams pull against one another on a rope.

tuition ❶ n instruction, esp. received individually or in a small group.

tulip n plant with bright cup-shaped flowers.

tumble v 1 (cause to) fall, esp. awkwardly or violently. 2 roll or twist, esp. in play. 3 rumple. ▷ n 4 fall. 5 somersault. **tumbler** n 1 stemless drinking glass. 2 acrobat. 3 spring catch in a lock. **tumbledown** adj dilapidated. **tumble dryer, drier** machine that dries laundry by rotating it in warm air. **tumble to** v informal realize, understand.

tummy n, pl -**mies** informal stomach.

tumour ❶ [**tew**-mer] n abnormal growth in or on the body.

tumult ❶ n uproar or commotion. **tumultuous** [tew-**mull**-tew-uss] adj.

tuna n large marine food fish.

tundra n vast treeless Arctic region with permanently frozen subsoil.

tune ❶ n 1 (pleasing) sequence of musical notes. 2 correct musical pitch, e.g. she sang out of tune. ▷ v 3 adjust (a musical instrument) so that it is in tune. 4 adjust (a machine) to obtain the desired performance. **tuneful** adj **tunefully** adv **tuneless** adj **tuner** n tune in v adjust (a radio or television) to receive (a station or programme).

tungsten n Chem greyish-white metal.

tunic n 1 close-fitting jacket forming part of some uniforms. 2 loose knee-length garment.

tunnel ❶ n 1 underground passage. ▷ v -**nelling, -nelled** 2 make a tunnel (through).

tupik, tupek n Canad (esp. in the Arctic) a tent of animal skins, a traditional type of Inuit dwelling.

turban n Muslim, Hindu, or Sikh man's head covering, made by winding cloth round the head.

turbine n machine or generator driven by gas, water, etc. turning blades.

turbot n large European edible flatfish.

tureen n serving dish for soup.

turf ❶ n, pl **turfs, turves** 1 short thick even grass. 2 square of this with roots and soil attached. ▷ v 3 cover with turf. **the turf** 1 racecourse. 2 horse racing. **turf accountant** bookmaker. **turf out** v informal throw out.

turgid [**tur**-jid] adj 1 (of language) pompous. 2 swollen and thick.

turkey n large bird bred for food.

Turkish adj 1 of Turkey, its people, or their language. ▷ n 2 Turkish language. **Turkish**

tuft n = **clump**, bunch, cluster, collection, knot, tussock

tug v 1 = **pull**, jerk, wrench, yank ▷ n 2 = **pull**, jerk, yank

tuition n = **training**, education, instruction, lessons, schooling, teaching, tutelage, tutoring

tumble v 1 = **fall**, drop, flop, plummet, stumble, topple ▷ n 4 = **fall**, drop, plunge, spill, stumble, trip

tumour n = **growth**, cancer, carcinoma (Path), lump, sarcoma (Med), swelling

tumult n = **commotion**, clamour, din, hubbub, pandemonium, riot, row, turmoil, upheaval, uproar

tune n 1 = **melody**, air, song, strain, theme 2 = **concord**, consonance, euphony, harmony, pitch ▷ v 3 = **adjust**, adapt, attune, harmonize, pitch, regulate

tunnel n 1 = **passage**, burrow, channel, hole, passageway, shaft, subway, underpass ▷ v 2 = **dig**, burrow, excavate, mine, scoop out

turf n 1, 2 = **grass**, sod, sward **the turf** 2 = **horse-racing**, racing, the flat

t

bath steam bath. **Turkish delight** jelly-like sweet coated with icing sugar.

turmoil *n* agitation or confusion.

turn ❶ *v* 1 change the position or direction (of). 2 move around an axis, rotate. 3 (usu. foll. by *into*) change in nature or character. 4 reach or pass in age, time, etc. e.g. *she has just turned twenty*. 5 shape on a lathe. 6 become sour. ▷ *n* 7 turning. 8 opportunity to do something as part of an agreed succession. 9 direction or drift. 10 period or spell. 11 short theatrical performance. **good, bad turn** helpful or unhelpful act. **turning** *n* road or path leading off a main route. **turncoat** *n* person who deserts one party or cause to join another. **turn down** *v* 1 reduce the volume or brightness (of). 2 refuse or reject. **turn in** *v* 1 go to bed. 2 hand in. **turning point** moment when a decisive change occurs. **turn off** *v* stop (something) working by using a knob etc. **turn on** *v* 1 start (something) working by using a knob etc. 2 become aggressive towards. 3 *informal* excite, esp. sexually. **turnout** *n* number of people appearing at a gathering. **turnover** *n* 1 total sales made by a business over a certain period. 2 small pastry. 3 rate at which staff leave and are replaced. **turnpike** *n* road where a toll is collected at barriers. **turnstile** *n* revolving gate for admitting one person at a time. **turntable** *n* revolving platform. **turn up**

v 1 arrive or appear. 2 find or be found. 3 increase the volume or brightness (of). **turn-up** *n* 1 turned-up fold at the bottom of a trouser leg. 2 *informal* unexpected event.

turnip *n* root vegetable with orange or white flesh.

turpentine *n* (oil made from) the resin of certain trees. **turps** *n* turpentine oil.

turquoise *adj* 1 blue-green. ▷ *n* 2 blue-green precious stone.

turret *n* 1 small tower. 2 revolving gun tower on a warship or tank.

turtle *n* sea tortoise. **turn turtle** capsize. **turtledove** *n* small wild dove. **turtleneck** *n* (sweater with) a round high close-fitting neck.

tusk *n* long pointed tooth of an elephant, walrus, etc.

tussle ❶ *n*, *v* fight or scuffle.

tutor ❶ *n* 1 person teaching individuals or small groups. ▷ *v* 2 act as a tutor to. **tutorial** *n* period of instruction with a tutor.

tutu *n* short stiff skirt worn by ballerinas.

tuxedo *n*, *pl* **-dos** *US & Canad* dinner jacket.

TV television.

twang *n* 1 sharp ringing sound. 2 nasal speech. ▷ *v* 3 (cause to) make a twang.

tweak ❶ *v* 1 pinch or twist sharply. ▷ *n* 2 tweaking.

twee *adj informal* too sentimental, sweet, or pretty.

——————————————— THESAURUS ———————

turmoil *n* = **confusion**, agitation, chaos, commotion, disarray, disorder, tumult, upheaval

turn *v* 1 = **change course**, move, shift, swerve, switch, veer, wheel 2 = **rotate**, circle, go round, gyrate, pivot, revolve, roll, spin, twist, whirl (usu. foll. by *into*) = **change into**, alter, convert, mould, mutate into, remodel, shape, transform into 5 = **shape**, fashion, frame, make, mould 6 = **go bad**, curdle, go off (*Brit inf*), sour, spoil, taint ▷ *n* 7 = **rotation**, circle, cycle, gyration, revolution, spin, twist,

whirl 8 = **opportunity**, chance, crack (*inf*), go, stint, time, try 9 = **direction**, drift, heading, tendency, trend

tussle *n* = **fight**, battle, brawl, conflict, contest, scrap (*inf*), scuffle, struggle ▷ *v* = **fight**, battle, grapple, scrap (*inf*), scuffle, struggle, vie, wrestle

tutor *n* 1 = **teacher**, coach, educator, guardian, guide, guru, instructor, lecturer, mentor ▷ *v* 2 = **teach**, coach, drill, educate, guide, instruct, school, train

tweak *v*, *n* 1, 2 = **twist**, jerk, pinch, pull, squeeze

tweed *n* **1** thick woollen cloth. ▷ *pl* **2** suit of tweed. **tweedy** *adj*.

tweet *n* **1** chirp. **2** a short message posted on the Twitter website. ▷ *v* **3** chirp. **4** post a short message on the Twitter website.

tweezers *pl n* small pincer-like tool.

twelve *adj*, *n* two more than ten. **twelfth** *adj*, *n* (of) number twelve in a series.

twenty *adj*, *n* two times ten. **twentieth** *adj*, *n*.

twice *adv* two times.

twiddle *v* fiddle or twirl in an idle way. **twiddle one's thumbs** be bored, have nothing to do.

twig *n* small branch or shoot.

twilight ❶ *n* soft dim light just after sunset.

twill *n* fabric woven to produce parallel ridges.

twin ❶ *n* **1** one of a pair, esp. of two children born at one birth. ▷ *v* **twinning**, **twinned** **2** pair or be paired.

twine ❶ *n* **1** string or cord. ▷ *v* **2** twist or coil round.

twinge ❶ *n* sudden sharp pain or emotional pang.

twinkle ❶ *v* **1** shine brightly but intermittently. ▷ *n* **2** flickering brightness; sparkle.

twirl ❶ *v* **1** turn or spin around quickly. **2** twist or wind, esp. idly.

twist ❶ *v* **1** turn out of the natural position. **2** distort or pervert. **3** wind or twine. ▷ *n* **4** twisting. **5** twisted thing. **6** unexpected development in the plot of a film, book, etc. **7** bend or curve. **8** distortion. **twisted** *adj* (of a person) cruel or perverted.

twit¹ *v* **twitting**, **twitted** poke fun at (someone).

twit² ❶ *n* informal foolish person.

twitch ❶ *v* **1** move spasmodically. **2** pull sharply. ▷ *n* **3** nervous muscular spasm. **4** sharp pull.

twitter *v* **1** (of birds) utter chirping sounds. ▷ *n* **2** act or sound of twittering.

Twitter *n* ® website where people can post short messages about their current thoughts and activities.

two *adj*, *n* one more than one. **two-edged** *adj* (of a remark) having both a favourable and an unfavourable interpretation. **two-faced** *adj* deceitful, hypocritical.

TX Texas.

tycoon ❶ *n* powerful wealthy businessman.

THESAURUS

twig *n* = **branch**, shoot, spray, sprig, stick

twilight *n* **1** = **dusk**, dimness, evening, gloaming (*Scot or poet*), gloom, half-light, sundown, sunset

twin *n* **1** = **double**, clone, counterpart, duplicate, fellow, likeness, lookalike, match, mate ▷ *v* **2** = **pair**, couple, join, link, match, yoke

twine *n* **1** = **string**, cord, yarn ▷ *v* **2** = **coil**, bend, curl, encircle, loop, spiral, twist, wind

twinge *n* = **pain**, pang, prick, spasm, stab, stitch

twinkle *v* **1** = **sparkle**, blink, flash, flicker, gleam, glint, glisten, glitter, shimmer, shine ▷ *n* **2** = **sparkle**, flash, flicker, gleam, glimmer, shimmer, spark

twirl *v* **1** = **turn**, pirouette, pivot, revolve, rotate, spin, wheel, whirl **2** = **twist**, wind

twist *v* **1** = **screw**, curl, spin, swivel, wrap, wring **2** = **distort**, contort, screw up **3** = **wind**, coil ▷ *n* **4** = **wind**, coil, curl, spin, swivel **6** = **development**, change, revelation, slant, surprise, turn, variation **7** = **curve**, arc, bend, meander, turn, undulation, zigzag **8** = **distortion**, defect, deformation, flaw, imperfection, kink, warp

twit² *n Inf* = **fool**, ass, chump (*inf*), halfwit, idiot, nincompoop, numbskull *or* numskull, prat (*sl*), twerp *or* twirp (*inf*)

twitch *v* **1** = **jerk**, flutter, jump, squirm **2** = **pull**, pluck, tug, yank ▷ *n* **3** = **jerk**, flutter, jump, spasm, tic

tycoon *n* = **magnate**, baron, capitalist, fat cat (*sl*, *chiefly US*), financier, industrialist, mogul, plutocrat

t

type ❶ *n* **1** class or category. **2** *informal* person, esp. of a specified kind. **3** block with a raised character used for printing. **4** printed text. ▷ *v* **5** print with a typewriter or word processor. **6** typify. **7** classify. **typist** *n* person who types with a typewriter or word processor. **typecast** *v* continually cast (an actor or actress) in similar roles. **typewriter** *n* machine which prints a character when the appropriate key is pressed.

typhoid fever *n* acute infectious feverish disease.

typhoon ❶ *n* violent tropical storm.

typhus *n* infectious feverish disease.

typical ❶ *adj* true to type, characteristic. **typically** *adv* **typify** *v* **-fying**, **-fied** be typical of.

typography *n* art or style of printing. **typographical** *adj* **typographer** *n*.

tyrant ❶ *n* **1** oppressive or cruel ruler. **2** person who exercises authority oppressively. **tyrannical** *adj* like a tyrant, oppressive. **tyrannize** *v* exert power (over) oppressively or cruelly. **tyrannous** *adj* **tyranny** *n* tyrannical rule.

tyre *n* rubber ring, usu. inflated, over the rim of a vehicle's wheel to grip the road.

— THESAURUS —

type *n* **1** = **kind**, category, class, genre, group, order, sort, species, style, variety

typhoon *n* = **storm**, cyclone, squall, tempest, tornado

typical *adj* = **characteristic**, archetypal, average, model, normal, orthodox, representative, standard, stock, usual

tyrant *n* = **dictator**, absolutist, authoritarian, autocrat, bully, despot, martinet, oppressor, slave-driver

Uu

ubiquitous ❶ [yew-**bik**-wit-uss] *adj* being or seeming to be everywhere at once. **ubiquity** *n*.

udder *n* large baglike milk-producing gland of cows, sheep, or goats.

UFO unidentified flying object.

ugly ❶ *adj* **uglier**, **ugliest** 1 of unpleasant appearance. 2 ominous or menacing. **ugliness** *n*.

ukulele, ukelele [yew-kal-**lay**-lee] *n* small guitar with four strings.

ulcer ❶ *n* open sore on the surface of the skin or mucous membrane. **ulceration** *n* **ulcerous** *adj* of, like, or characterized by ulcers.

ulterior ❶ *adj* (of an aim, reason, etc.) concealed or hidden.

ultimate ❶ *adj* 1 final in a series or process. 2 highest or supreme. **ultimately** *adv*.

ultra- *prefix* 1 beyond a specified extent, range, or limit, e.g. *ultrasonic*. 2 extremely, e.g. *ultramodern*.

ultraviolet *adj, n* (of) light beyond the limit of visibility at the violet end of the spectrum.

umbrage *n* **take umbrage** feel offended or upset.

umbrella *n* 1 portable device used for protection against rain, consisting of a folding frame covered in material attached to a central rod. 2 single organization, idea, etc. that contains or covers many different organizations, ideas, etc.

umpire ❶ *n* 1 official who rules on the playing of a game. ▷ *v* 2 act as umpire in (a game).

umpteen *adj informal* very many. **umpteenth** *n, adj*.

un- *prefix* 1 not, e.g. *unidentified*. 2 denoting reversal of an action, e.g. *untie*. 3 denoting removal from, e.g. *unthrone*.

unaccountable ❶ *adj* 1 unable to be explained. 2 (foll. by *to*) not answerable to. **unaccountably** *adv*.

unanimous ❶ [yew-**nan**-im-uss] *adj* 1 in complete agreement. 2 agreed by all. **unanimity** *n*.

unassuming ❶ *adj* modest or unpretentious.

unaware ❶ *adj* not aware or conscious. **unawares** *adv* 1 by surprise, e.g. *caught unawares*. 2 without knowing.

———— THESAURUS ————

ubiquitous *adj* = **everywhere**, ever-present, omnipresent, pervasive, universal

ugly *adj* 1 = **unattractive**, distasteful, homely (*chiefly US*), horrid, ill-favoured, plain, unlovely, unpleasant, unprepossessing, unsightly 2 = **ominous**, baleful, dangerous, menacing, sinister

ulcer *n* = **sore**, abscess, boil, gumboil, peptic ulcer, pustule

ulterior *adj* = **hidden**, concealed, covert, secret, undisclosed

ultimate *adj* 1 = **final**, end, last 2 = **supreme**, extreme, greatest, highest, paramount, superlative, utmost

umpire *n* 1 = **referee**, arbiter, arbitrator, judge ▷ *v* 2 = **referee**, adjudicate, arbitrate, judge

unaccountable *adj* 1 = **inexplicable**, baffling, mysterious, odd, puzzling, unexplainable, unfathomable 2 (foll. by *to*) = **not answerable to**, exempt, not responsible to

unanimous *adj* 1 = **agreed**, common, concerted, harmonious, in agreement, like-minded, united

unassuming *adj* = **modest**, humble, quiet, reserved, retiring, self-effacing, unassertive, unobtrusive, unpretentious

unaware *adj* = **ignorant**, not in the loop (*inf*), oblivious, unconscious, uninformed, unknowing

u

unbending *adj* rigid or inflexible.

uncanny *adj* weird or mysterious.
uncannily *adv*.

unceremonious *adj* **1** relaxed and informal. **2** abrupt or rude.

uncertain *adj* **1** not able to be accurately known or predicted. **2** not able to be depended upon. **3** changeable. **uncertainty** *n*.

uncle *n* **1** brother of one's father or mother. **2** husband of one's aunt.

unconscious *adj* **1** lacking normal awareness through the senses. **2** not aware of one's actions or behaviour. ▷ *n* **3** part of the mind containing instincts and ideas that exist without one's awareness. **unconsciously** *adv* **unconsciousness** *n*.

uncouth *adj* lacking in good manners, refinement, or grace.

unction *n* act of anointing with oil in sacramental ceremonies.

under *prep, adv* **1** indicating movement to or position beneath the underside or base. ▷ *prep* **2** less than. **3** subject to.

under- *prefix* **1** below, e.g. *underground*. **2** insufficient or insufficiently, e.g. *underrate*.

underarm *adj* **1** *Sport* denoting a style of throwing, bowling, or serving in which the hand is swung below shoulder level. ▷ *adv* **2** *Sport* in an underarm style.

undercarriage *n* **1** landing gear of an aircraft. **2** framework supporting the body of a vehicle.

undercurrent *n* **1** current that is not apparent at the surface. **2** underlying opinion or emotion.

undercut *v* charge less than (a competitor) to obtain trade.

underdog *n* person or team in a weak or underprivileged position.

undergo *v* experience, endure, or sustain.

undergraduate *n* person studying in a university for a first degree.

underground *adj* **1** occurring, situated, used, or going below ground level. **2** secret. ▷ *n* **3** electric passenger railway operated in underground tunnels. **4** movement dedicated to overthrowing a government or occupation forces.

undergrowth *n* small trees and bushes growing beneath taller trees in a wood or forest.

THESAURUS

unbending *adj* = **inflexible**, firm, intractable, resolute, rigid, severe, strict, stubborn, tough, uncompromising

uncanny *adj* = **weird**, mysterious, strange, supernatural, unearthly, unnatural

uncertain *adj* **1** = **unpredictable**, doubtful, indefinite, questionable, risky, speculative **2** = **unsure**, dubious, hazy, irresolute, unclear, unconfirmed, undecided, vague

unconscious *adj* **1** = **senseless**, insensible, knocked out, out, out cold, stunned **2 a** = **unintentional**, accidental, inadvertent, unwitting **b** = **unaware**, ignorant, oblivious, unknowing

uncouth *adj* = **coarse**, barbaric, boorish, crude, graceless, ill-mannered, loutish, oafish, rough, rude, vulgar

under *prep* **1** = **below**, beneath, underneath **3** = **subject to**, governed by, secondary to, subordinate to ▷ *adv* **1** = **below**, beneath, down, lower

undercurrent *n* **1** = **undertow**, riptide **2** = **undertone**, atmosphere, feeling, hint, overtone, sense, suggestion, tendency, tinge, vibes (*sl*)

underdog *n* = **weaker party**, little fellow (*inf*), outsider

undergo *v* = **experience**, bear, endure, go through, stand, suffer, sustain

underground *adj* **1** = **subterranean**, buried, covered **2** = **secret**, clandestine, covert, hidden ▷ *n* **3** = **the tube**, the metro, the subway (*Brit*) **4** = **the Resistance**, partisans

undergrowth *n* = **scrub**, bracken, briars, brush, underbrush

u

underhand ⊙ *adj* sly, deceitful, and secretive.

underlie *v* **1** lie or be placed under. **2** be the foundation, cause, or basis of. **underlying** *adj* fundamental or basic.

underline ⊙ *v* **1** draw a line under. **2** state forcibly, emphasize.

underling *n* subordinate.

undermine ⊙ *v* weaken gradually.

underneath *prep, adv* **1** under or beneath. ▷ *adj, n* **2** lower (part or surface).

underpants *pl n* man's undergarment for the lower part of the body.

underpass *n* section of a road that passes under another road or a railway line.

underpin *v* give strength or support to.

understand ⊙ *v* **1** know and comprehend the nature or meaning of. **2** realize or grasp (something). **3** assume, infer, or believe. **understandable** *adj* **understandably** *adv* **understanding** *n* **1** ability to learn, judge, or make decisions. **2** personal interpretation of a subject. **3** mutual agreement, usu. an informal or private one. ▷ *adj* **4** kind and sympathetic.

understudy ⊙ *n* **1** actor who studies a part in order to be able to replace the usual actor if necessary. ▷ *v* **2** act as an understudy for.

undertake ⊙ *v* **1** agree or commit oneself to (something) or to do (something). **2** promise. **undertaking** *n* **1** task or enterprise. **2** agreement to do something.

undertone ⊙ *n* **1** quiet tone of voice. **2** underlying quality or feeling.

underwear ⊙ *n* clothing worn under the outer garments and next to the skin.

underworld ⊙ *n* **1** criminals and their associates. **2** *Greek & Roman myth* regions below the earth's surface regarded as the abode of the dead.

underwrite ⊙ *v* **1** accept financial responsibility for (a commercial project). **2** sign and issue (an insurance policy), thus accepting liability. **underwriter** *n*.

undo ⊙ *v* **1** open, unwrap. **2** reverse the effects of. **3** cause the downfall of. **undone** *adj* **undoing** *n* cause of someone's downfall.

undulate *v* move in waves. **undulation** *n*.

unearth ⊙ *v* **1** reveal or discover by searching. **2** dig up out of the earth.

uneasy ⊙ *adj* **1** (of a person) anxious or apprehensive. **2** (of a condition)

———————————— THESAURUS ————————————

underhand *adj* = **sly**, crafty, deceitful, devious, dishonest, furtive, secret, sneaky, stealthy

underline *v* **1** = **underscore**, mark **2** = **emphasize**, accentuate, highlight, stress

undermine *v* = **weaken**, disable, sabotage, sap, subvert

understand *v* **2** = **comprehend**, conceive, fathom, follow, get, grasp, perceive, realize, see, take in **3** = **believe**, assume, gather, presume, suppose, think

understudy *n* **1** = **stand-in**, replacement, reserve, substitute

undertake *v* **1** = **agree**, bargain, contract, engage **2** = **promise**, guarantee, pledge

undertone *n* **1** = **murmur**, whisper **2** = **undercurrent**, hint, suggestion, tinge, touch, trace

underwear *n* = **underclothes**, lingerie, undergarments, underthings, undies (*inf*)

underworld *n* **1** = **criminals**, gangland (*inf*), gangsters, organized crime **2** *Greek & Roman myth* = **nether world**, Hades, nether regions

underwrite *v* **1** = **finance**, back, fund, guarantee, insure, sponsor, subsidize **2** = **sign**, endorse, initial

undo *v* **1** = **open**, disentangle, loose, unbutton, unfasten, untie **2** = **reverse**, annul, cancel, invalidate, neutralize, offset **3** = **ruin**, defeat, destroy, overturn, quash, shatter, subvert, undermine, upset, wreck

unearth *v* **1** = **discover**, expose, find, reveal, uncover **2** = **dig up**, dredge up, excavate, exhume

uneasy *adj* **1** = **anxious**, disturbed, edgy, nervous, on edge, perturbed, troubled,

u

precarious or uncomfortable. **uneasily**
adv **uneasiness** *n* **unease** *n* 1 feeling of
anxiety. 2 state of dissatisfaction.
unemployed 🔊 *adj* out of work.
unemployment *n*.
unexceptionable *adj* beyond criticism
or objection.
unfold 🔊 *v* 1 open or spread out from a
folded state. 2 reveal or be revealed.
ungainly 🔊 *adj* **-lier, -liest** lacking grace
when moving.
uni- *combining form* of, consisting of, or
having only one, e.g. *unicellular*.
unicorn *n* imaginary horselike creature
with one horn growing from its forehead.
uniform 🔊 *n* 1 special identifying
set of clothes for the members of an
organization, such as soldiers. ▷ *adj*
2 regular and even throughout, unvarying.
3 alike or like. **uniformly** *adv* **uniformity** *n*.
unify 🔊 *v* **-fying, -fied** make or become one.
unification *n*.
unilateral *adj* made or done by only one
person or group. **unilaterally** *adv*.
union 🔊 *n* 1 uniting or being united.
2 short for TRADE UNION. 3 association or

confederation of individuals or groups for
a common purpose. **unionist** *n* member
or supporter of a trade union. **unionize**
v organize (workers) into a trade union.
unionization *n*.
unique 🔊 [yoo-**neek**] *adj* 1 being the only
one of a particular type. 2 without equal or
like. **uniquely** *adv*.
unison 🔊 *n* 1 complete agreement.
2 *Music* singing or playing of the same
notes together at the same time.
unit 🔊 *n* 1 single undivided entity or whole.
2 group or individual regarded as a basic
element of a larger whole. 3 fixed quantity
etc., used as a standard of measurement.
4 piece of furniture designed to be fitted
with other similar pieces. **unit trust**
investment trust that issues units for
public sale and invests the money in many
different businesses.
unite 🔊 *v* 1 make or become an integrated
whole. 2 (cause to) enter into an
association or alliance.
universe 🔊 *n* 1 whole of all existing matter,
energy, and space. 2 the world. **universal**
adj 1 of or typical of the whole of mankind

——————————————— THESAURUS ———————————————

uncomfortable, worried 2 = **precarious**,
awkward, insecure, shaky, strained, tense,
uncomfortable
unemployed *adj* = **out of work**, idle,
jobless, laid off, redundant
unfold *v* 1 = **open**, expand, spread out,
undo, unfurl, unravel, unroll, unwrap
2 = **reveal**, disclose, divulge, make known,
present, show, uncover
ungainly *adj* = **awkward**, clumsy,
inelegant, lumbering, ungraceful
uniform *n* 1 = **outfit**, costume, dress,
garb, habit, livery, regalia, suit ▷ *adj*
2 = **unvarying**, consistent, constant, even,
regular, smooth, unchanging 3 = **alike**,
equal, like, same, similar
unify *v* = **unite**, amalgamate, combine,
confederate, consolidate, join, merge
union *n* 1 = **uniting**, accord, agreement,
amalgamation, blend, combination,

concord, conjunction, fusion, harmony,
joining, mixture, unanimity, unison,
unity 3 = **alliance**, association,
coalition, confederacy, federation,
league
unique *adj* 1 = **single**, lone, only, solitary
2 = **unparalleled**, matchless, unequalled,
unmatched, without equal
unison *n* 1 = **agreement**, accord, concert,
concord, harmony, unity
unit *n* 1 = **item**, entity, whole 2 = **part**,
component, constituent, element,
member, section, segment 3 = **measure**,
measurement, quantity
unite *v* 1 = **join**, amalgamate, blend,
combine, couple, fuse, link, merge, unify
2 = **cooperate**, ally, band, collaborate, join
forces, pool
universe *n* 1 = **cosmos**, creation,
macrocosm, nature

u

or of nature. **2** existing everywhere. **universally** adv **universality** n.

university n, pl **-ties** institution of higher education with the authority to award degrees.

unkempt ❶ adj **1** (of the hair) not combed. **2** slovenly or untidy.

unless conj except under the circumstances that.

unlike ❶ adj **1** dissimilar or different. ▷ prep **2** not like or typical of.

unravel ❶ v **-elling, -elled 1** reduce (something knitted or woven) to separate strands. **2** become unravelled. **3** explain or solve.

unrest ❶ n rebellious state of discontent.

unruly ❶ adj **-lier, -liest** difficult to control or organize.

unsavoury ❶ adj distasteful or objectionable.

unscathed ❶ adj not harmed or injured.

unsightly ❶ adj unpleasant to look at.

unthinkable ❶ adj out of the question, inconceivable.

until conj **1** up to the time that. ▷ prep **2** in

or throughout the period before. **not until** not before (a time or event).

unto prep old-fashioned to.

untoward ❶ adj causing misfortune or annoyance.

unwieldy ❶ adj too heavy, large, or awkward to be easily handled.

unwind ❶ v **1** relax after a busy or tense time. **2** slacken, undo, or unravel.

unwitting ❶ adj **1** not intentional. **2** not knowing or conscious. **unwittingly** adv

up prep, adv **1** indicating movement to or position at a higher place. ▷ adv **2** indicating readiness, intensity or completeness, etc. e.g. *warm up; drink up.* ▷ adj **3** of a high or higher position. **4** out of bed. ▷ v **upping, upped 5** increase or raise. **up against** having to cope with. **up and** informal do something suddenly, e.g. *he upped and left.* **ups and downs** alternating periods of good and bad luck. **what's up?** informal what is wrong? **upward** adj **1** directed or moving towards a higher place or level. ▷ adv **2** (also **upwards**) from a lower to a

unkempt adj **1** = **uncombed**, shaggy, tousled **2** = **untidy**, dishevelled, disordered, messy, scruffy, slovenly, ungroomed

unlike adj **1** = **different**, dissimilar, distinct, diverse, not alike, opposite, unequal

unravel v **1** = **undo**, disentangle, free, separate, untangle, unwind **3** = **solve**, explain, figure out (inf), resolve, work out

unrest n = **discontent**, agitation, discord, dissension, protest, rebellion, sedition, strife

unruly adj = **uncontrollable**, disobedient, mutinous, rebellious, wayward, wild, wilful

unsavoury adj = **distasteful**, nasty, nauseating, obnoxious, offensive, repellent, repulsive, revolting, sickening, unpleasant

unscathed adj = **unharmed**, safe, unhurt, uninjured, unmarked, whole

unsightly adj = **ugly**, disagreeable,

hideous, horrid, repulsive, unattractive

unthinkable adj **a** = **impossible**, absurd, out of the question, unreasonable **b** = **inconceivable**, implausible, incredible, unimaginable

untoward adj **a** = **unfavourable**, adverse, inauspicious, inopportune, unlucky **b** = **troublesome**, annoying, awkward, inconvenient, irritating, unfortunate

unwieldy adj **a** = **bulky**, clumsy, hefty, massive, ponderous **b** = **awkward**, cumbersome, inconvenient, unmanageable

unwind v **1** = **relax**, loosen up, take it easy, wind down **2** = **unravel**, slacken, uncoil, undo, unroll, untwine, untwist

unwitting adj **1** = **unintentional**, accidental, chance, inadvertent, involuntary, unplanned **2** = **unknowing**, ignorant, innocent, unaware, unconscious, unsuspecting

u

higher place, level, or condition.
upbringing *n* education of a person during the formative years.
update *v* bring up to date.
upfront *adj* **1** open and frank. ▷ *adv, adj* **2** (of money) paid out at the beginning of a business arrangement.
upgrade *v* promote (a person or job) to a higher rank.
upheaval *n* strong, sudden, or violent disturbance.
uphold *v* **1** maintain or defend against opposition. **2** give moral support to.
upholster *v* fit (a chair or sofa) with padding, springs, and covering. **upholsterer** *n* **upholstery** *n* soft covering on a chair or sofa.
upkeep *n* act, process, or cost of keeping something in good repair.
upload *v* transfer (data) from one computer system to a larger one.
upon *prep* **1** on. **2** up and on.
upper *adj* **1** higher or highest in physical position, wealth, rank, or status. ▷ *n* **2** part of a shoe above the sole. **uppermost**

adj **1** highest in position, power, or importance. ▷ *adv* **2** in or into the highest place or position. **upper class** highest social class. **upper-class** *adj* **upper crust** *informal* upper class. **upper hand** position of control.
upright *adj* **1** vertical or erect. **2** honest or just. ▷ *adv* **3** vertically or in an erect position. ▷ *n* **4** vertical support, such as a post.
uprising *n* rebellion or revolt.
uproar *n* disturbance characterized by loud noise and confusion. **uproarious** *adj* **1** very funny. **2** (of laughter) loud and boisterous.
uproot *v* **1** pull up by or as if by the roots. **2** displace (a person or people) from their native or usual surroundings.
upset *adj* **1** emotionally or physically disturbed or distressed. ▷ *v* **2** tip over. **3** disturb the normal state or stability of. **4** disturb mentally or emotionally. **5** make physically ill. ▷ *n* **6** unexpected defeat or reversal. **7** disturbance or disorder of the emotions, mind, or body. **upsetting** *adj*.

————————————— THESAURUS ————————————

upbringing *n* = **education**, breeding, raising, rearing, training
update *v* = **bring up to date**, amend, modernize, renew, revise
upgrade *v* = **promote**, advance, better, elevate, enhance, improve, raise
upheaval *n* = **disturbance**, disorder, disruption, revolution, turmoil
uphold *v* **1** = **defend**, maintain, sustain **2** = **support**, advocate, aid, back, champion, endorse, promote
upkeep *n* **a** = **maintenance**, keep, repair, running, subsistence **b** = **running costs**, expenditure, expenses, overheads
upper *adj* **1 a** = **higher**, high, loftier, top, topmost **b** = **superior**, eminent, greater, important
upright *adj* **1** = **vertical**, erect, perpendicular, straight **2** = **honest**, conscientious, ethical, good, honourable, just, principled, righteous, virtuous

uprising *n* = **rebellion**, disturbance, insurgence, insurrection, mutiny, revolt, revolution, rising
uproar *n* = **commotion**, din, furore, mayhem, noise, outcry, pandemonium, racket, riot, turmoil
uproot *v* **1** = **pull up**, dig up, rip up, root out, weed out **2** = **displace**, exile
upset *adj* **1 a** = **distressed**, agitated, bothered, dismayed, disturbed, grieved, hurt, put out, troubled, worried ▷ *v* **2** = **sick**, ill, queasy ▷ *v* **2** = **tip over**, capsize, knock over, overturn, spill **3** = **mess up**, change, disorder, disorganize, disturb, spoil **4** = **distress**, agitate, bother, disconcert, disturb, faze, fluster, grieve, perturb, ruffle, trouble ▷ *n* **6** = **reversal**, defeat, shake-up (*inf*) **7 a** = **distress**, agitation, bother, disturbance, shock, trouble, worry **b** = **illness**, bug (*inf*), complaint, disorder, malady, sickness

u

upshot ⊕ n final result or conclusion.
upside down ⊕ adj **1** turned over completely. **2** informal confused or jumbled. ▷ adv **3** in an inverted fashion. **4** in a chaotic manner.
upstage adj **1** at the back half of the stage. ▷ v **2** informal draw attention to oneself from (someone else).
upstart ⊕ n person who has risen suddenly to a position of power and behaves arrogantly.
uptight ⊕ adj informal nervously tense, irritable, or angry.
uptown adj, adv US & Canad towards, in, or relating to some part of a town that is away from the centre. ▷ n such a part of a town, esp. a residential part.
uranium n Chem radioactive silvery-white metallic element, used chiefly as a source of nuclear energy.
urban ⊕ adj **1** of or living in a city or town. **2** denoting modern pop music of African-American origin, such as hip-hop. **urbanize** v make (a rural area) more industrialized and urban. **urbanization** n.
urbane ⊕ adj characterized by courtesy, elegance, and sophistication. **urbanity** n.
urchin ⊕ n mischievous child.
urge ⊕ n **1** strong impulse, inner drive, or yearning. ▷ v **2** plead with or press (a person to do something). **3** advocate earnestly. **4** force or drive onwards.

urgent adj needing attention at once.
urine n pale yellow fluid excreted by the kidneys to the bladder and passed as waste from the body. **urinary** adj **urinate** v discharge urine. **urination** n **urinal** n sanitary fitting used by men for urination.
URL uniform resource locator: the address of a location on the Internet.
urn n **1** vase used as a container for the ashes of the dead. **2** large metal container with a tap, used for making and holding tea or coffee.
us pron objective case of WE.
USB Universal Serial Bus: standard for connecting sockets on computers.
use ⊕ v **1** put into service or action. **2** take advantage of, exploit. **3** consume or expend. ▷ n **4** using or being used. **5** ability or permission to use. **6** usefulness or advantage. **7** purpose for which something is used. **usable** adj able to be used. **usage** n **1** regular or constant use. **2** way in which a word is used in a language. **use-by date** Aust, NZ, S Afr & US date on packaged food after which it should not be sold. **used** adj second-hand. **used to** adj **1** accustomed to. ▷ v **2** used as an auxiliary to express past habitual or accustomed actions, e.g. I used to live there. **useful** adj **usefully** adv **usefulness** n **useless** adj **user** n **user-friendly** adj easy to familiarize oneself with, understand, and use. **username** n Computers name entered

upshot n = **result**, culmination, end, end result, finale, outcome, sequel
upside down adj **1** = **inverted**, overturned, upturned **2** Inf = **confused**, chaotic, disordered, higgledy-piggledy (inf), muddled, topsy-turvy
upstart n = **social climber**, arriviste, nouveau riche, parvenu
uptight adj Inf = **tense**, anxious, edgy, on edge, uneasy, wired (sl)
urban adj = **civic**, city, dorp (S Afr), metropolitan, municipal, town
urbane adj = **sophisticated**, cultivated, cultured, debonair, polished, refined,

smooth, suave, well-bred
urchin n = **ragamuffin**, brat, gamin, waif
urge n **1** = **impulse**, compulsion, desire, drive, itch, longing, thirst, wish, yearning ▷ v **2** = **beg**, beseech, entreat, exhort, implore, plead **3** = **advocate**, advise, counsel, recommend, support **4** = **drive**, compel, encourage, force, gee up, goad, impel, incite, induce, press, push, spur
use v **1** = **employ**, apply, exercise, exert, operate, practise, utilize, work **2** = **take advantage of**, exploit, manipulate **3** = **consume**, exhaust, expend, run through, spend ▷ n **4** = **usage**, application,

u

into a computer for identification purposes.

● **SPELLING TIP**
● The Bank of English shows that it's very
● common to write *usualy*, forgetting the
● double *l* of **usually**.

usher ❶ *n* **1** official who shows people to their seats, as in a church. ▷ *v* **2** conduct or escort. **usherette** *n* female assistant in a cinema who shows people to their seats.

usual ❶ *adj* of the most normal, frequent, or regular type. **usually** *adv* most often, in most cases.

usurp ❶ [yewz-**zurp**] *v* seize (a position or power) without authority. **usurper** *n*.

utensil *n* tool or container for practical use.

uterus [**yew**-ter-russ] *n* womb. **uterine** *adj*

utility ❶ *n* **1** usefulness. **2** *pl* **-ties** public service, such as electricity. ▷ *adj* **3** designed for use rather than beauty. **utility truck** *Aust & NZ* small truck with an open body and low sides.

utmost ❶ *adj, n* (of) the greatest possible degree or amount.

Utopia ❶ [yew-**tope**-ee-a] *n* any real or imaginary society, place, or state considered to be perfect or ideal. **Utopian** *adj*.

utter¹ ❶ *v* express (something) in sounds or words. **utterance** *n* **1** something uttered. **2** act or power of uttering.

utter² ❶ *adj* total or absolute. **utterly** *adv*.

————————————————————————— THESAURUS —————————————

employment, exercise, handling, operation, practice, service **6** = **good**, advantage, avail, benefit, help, point, profit, service, usefulness, value **7** = **purpose**, end, object, reason

usher *n* **1** = **attendant**, doorkeeper, doorman, escort, guide ▷ *v* **2** = **escort**, conduct, direct, guide, lead

usual *adj* = **normal**, common, customary, everyday, general, habitual, ordinary, regular, routine, standard, typical

usurp *v* = **seize**, appropriate, assume, commandeer, take, take over, wrest

utility *n* **1** = **usefulness**, benefit,

convenience, efficacy, practicality, serviceableness

utmost *adj* **a** = **greatest**, chief, highest, maximum, paramount, pre-eminent, supreme **b** = **farthest**, extreme, final, last ▷ *n* = **greatest**, best, hardest, highest

Utopia *n* = **paradise**, bliss, Eden, Garden of Eden, heaven, Shangri-la

utter¹ *v* = **express**, articulate, pronounce, say, speak, voice

utter² *adj* = **absolute**, complete, downright, outright, sheer, thorough, total, unmitigated

u

VA Virginia.

vacant ❶ adj **1** (of a toilet, room, etc.) unoccupied. **2** without interest or understanding. **vacancy** n, pl **-cies 1** unfilled job. **2** unoccupied room in a guesthouse. **3** state of being unoccupied.

vacate ❶ v **1** cause (something) to be empty by leaving. **2** give up (a job or position). **vacation** n **1** time when universities and law courts are closed. **2** US & Canad holiday.

vaccinate v inject with a vaccine. **vaccination** n **vaccine** n substance designed to cause a mild form of a disease to make a person immune to the disease itself.

vacillate [vass-ill-late] v keep changing one's mind or opinions. **vacillation** n.

vacuous ❶ adj not expressing intelligent thought. **vacuity** n.

vacuum ❶ n, pl **vacuums**, **vacua 1** empty space from which all or most air or gas has been removed. ▷ v **2** clean with a vacuum cleaner. **vacuum cleaner** electrical appliance which sucks up dust and dirt from carpets and upholstery. **vacuum flask** double-walled flask with a vacuum between the walls that keeps drinks hot or cold. **vacuum-packed** adj contained in packaging from which the air has been removed.

vagabond ❶ n person with no fixed home, esp. a beggar.

vagina [vaj-**jine**-a] n (in female mammals) passage from the womb to the external genitals. **vaginal** adj.

vagrant ❶ [**vaig**-rant] n **1** person with no settled home. ▷ adj **2** wandering. **vagrancy** n.

vague ❶ adj **1** not clearly explained. **2** unable to be seen or heard clearly. **3** absent-minded. **vaguely** adv.

vain ❶ adj **1** excessively proud, esp. of one's appearance. **2** bound to fail, futile. **in vain** unsuccessfully.

vale n lit valley.

valentine n (person to whom one sends) a romantic card on Saint Valentine's Day, February 14.

valet n man's personal male servant.

valiant ❶ adj brave or courageous.

valid ❶ adj **1** soundly reasoned. **2** having

———————————————— THESAURUS ————————————————

vacant adj **1** = **unoccupied**, available, empty, free, idle, unfilled, untenanted, void **2** = **blank**, absent-minded, abstracted, dreamy, idle, inane, vacuous, vague

vacate v **1** = **leave**, evacuate, quit

vacuous adj = **unintelligent**, blank, inane, stupid, uncomprehending, vacant

vacuum n **1** = **emptiness**, gap, nothingness, space, vacuity, void

vagabond n = **vagrant**, beggar, down-and-out, itinerant, rover, tramp

vagrant n **1** = **tramp**, drifter, hobo (US), itinerant, rolling stone, wanderer ▷ adj **2** = **itinerant**, nomadic, roaming, rootless, roving, unsettled, vagabond

vague adj **1** = **unclear**, hazy, imprecise, indefinite, loose, uncertain, unspecified, woolly **2** = **indistinct**, hazy, ill-defined, indeterminate, nebulous, unclear

vain adj **1** = **proud**, arrogant, conceited, egotistical, narcissistic, self-important, swaggering **2** = **futile**, abortive, fruitless, idle, pointless, senseless, unavailing, unprofitable, useless, worthless **in vain** = **to no avail**, fruitless(ly), ineffectual(ly), unsuccessful(ly), useless(ly), vain(ly)

valiant adj = **brave**, bold, courageous, fearless, gallant, heroic, intrepid, lion-hearted

valid adj **1** = **sound**, cogent, convincing, good, logical, telling, well-founded,

V

legal force. **validate** v make valid.
validation n **validity** n.

Valium ⊕ n ® drug used as a tranquillizer.

valley ⊕ n low area between hills, often
with a river running through it.

valour ⊕ n lit bravery.

value ⊕ n 1 importance, usefulness.
2 monetary worth. ▷ pl 3 moral principles.
▷ v **valuing**, **valued** 4 assess the worth
or desirability of. 5 have a high regard
for. **valuable** adj having great worth.
valuables pl n valuable personal property.
valuation n assessment of worth.
valueless adj **valuer** n **value-added
tax** Brit see VAT. **value judgment** opinion
based on personal belief.

valve n 1 device to control the movement
of fluid through a pipe. 2 Anat flap in a
part of the body allowing blood to flow
in one direction only. 3 Physics tube
containing a vacuum, allowing current to
flow from a cathode to an anode.

vampire n (in folklore) corpse that rises
at night to drink the blood of the living.
vampire bat tropical bat that feeds on
blood.

van¹ n 1 motor vehicle for transporting
goods. 2 Brit & Aust railway carriage for
goods, luggage, or mail.

van² n short for VANGUARD.

vandal ⊕ n person who deliberately
damages property. **vandalism** n
vandalize v.

vane n flat blade on a rotary device such as
a weathercock or propeller.

vanguard ⊕ n 1 unit of soldiers leading an
army. 2 most advanced group or position
in a movement or activity.

vanilla n seed pod of a tropical climbing
orchid, used for flavouring.

vanish ⊕ v 1 disappear suddenly or
mysteriously. 2 cease to exist.

vanity ⊕ n, pl **-ties** (display of) excessive
pride.

vanquish ⊕ v lit defeat (someone) utterly.

vantage n **vantage point** position that
gives one an overall view.

vapid ⊕ adj lacking character, dull.

vapour ⊕ n 1 moisture suspended in
air as steam or mist. 2 gaseous form of
something that is liquid or solid at room
temperature. **vaporize** v **vaporizer** n
vaporous adj.

variable ⊕ adj 1 not always the same,
changeable. ▷ n 2 Maths expression with a
range of values. **variability** n.

─────────────── THESAURUS ───────────────

well-grounded 2 = **legal**, authentic, bona
fide, genuine, lawful, legitimate, official

valley n = **hollow**, dale, dell, depression,
glen, vale

valour n Lit = **bravery**, boldness, courage,
fearlessness, gallantry, heroism,
intrepidity, spirit

value n 1 = **importance**, advantage,
benefit, desirability, merit, profit,
usefulness, utility, worth 2 = **cost**, market
price, rate ▷ pl 3 = **principles**, ethics,
(moral) standards ▷ v 4 = **evaluate**,
appraise, assess, estimate, price, rate, set
at 5 = **regard highly**, appreciate, cherish,
esteem, hold dear, prize, respect, treasure

vandal n = **hooligan**, delinquent, rowdy,
yob or yobbo (Brit sl)

vanguard n 2 = **forefront**, cutting edge,

forerunners, front line, leaders, spearhead,
trailblazers, trendsetters, van

vanish v = **disappear**, dissolve, evanesce,
evaporate, fade (away), melt (away)

vanity n = **pride**, arrogance, conceit,
conceitedness, egotism, narcissism

vanquish v Lit = **defeat**, beat, conquer,
crush, master, overcome, overpower,
overwhelm, triumph over

vapid adj = **dull**, bland, boring, flat, insipid,
tame, uninspiring, uninteresting, weak,
wishy-washy (inf)

vapour n 1 = **mist**, exhalation, fog, haze,
steam

variable adj 1 = **changeable**, flexible,
fluctuating, inconstant, mutable, shifting,
temperamental, uneven, unstable,
unsteady

V

variegated adj having patches or streaks of different colours. **variegation** n.

variety ❶ n, pl -**ties** **1** state of being diverse or various. **2** different things of the same kind. **3** particular sort or kind. **4** light entertainment composed of unrelated acts.

various ❶ adj of several kinds. **variously** adv.

varnish ❶ n **1** solution of oil and resin, put on a surface to make it hard and glossy. ▷ v **2** apply varnish to.

vary ❶ v **varying, varied** **1** change. **2** cause variations in. **varied** adj.

vase n ornamental jar, esp. for flowers.

Vaseline n ® thick oily cream made from petroleum, used in skin care.

vast ❶ adj extremely large. **vastly** adv **vastness** n.

vat n large container for liquids.

VAT Brit value-added tax: tax on the difference between the cost of materials and the selling price.

vault¹ ❶ n **1** secure room for storing valuables. **2** underground burial chamber.

vault² ❶ v **1** jump over (something) by resting one's hand(s) on it. ▷ n **2** such a jump.

veal n calf meat, used as food.

vector n **1** Maths quantity that has size and direction, such as force. **2** animal, usu. an insect, that carries disease.

veer ❶ v change direction suddenly.

vegan [**vee**-gan] n **1** person who eats no meat, fish, eggs, or dairy products. ▷ adj **2** suitable for a vegan. **veganism** n.

vegetable n **1** edible plant. **2** informal severely brain-damaged person. ▷ adj **3** of or like plants or vegetables.

vegetarian n **1** person who eats no meat or fish. ▷ adj **2** suitable for a vegetarian. **vegetarianism** n.

vegetate ❶ v live a dull boring life with no mental stimulation.

vehement ❶ adj expressing strong feelings. **vehemence** n **vehemently** adv.

vehicle ❶ n **1** machine, esp. with an engine and wheels, for carrying people or objects. **2** something used to achieve a particular purpose or as a means of expression. **vehicular** adj.

veil ❶ n **1** piece of thin cloth covering the head or face. **2** something that masks the truth, e.g. a veil of secrecy. ▷ v **3** cover with or as if with a veil. **take the veil** become a nun. **veiled** adj disguised.

variety n **1** = **diversity**, change, difference, discrepancy, diversification, multifariousness, variation **2** = **range**, array, assortment, collection, cross section, medley, miscellany, mixture **3** = **type**, brand, breed, category, class, kind, sort, species, strain

various adj = **different**, assorted, disparate, distinct, diverse, miscellaneous, several, sundry, varied

varnish n, v **1, 2** = **lacquer**, glaze, gloss, polish

vary v **1** = **change**, alter, fluctuate **2** = **alternate**

vast adj = **huge**, boundless, colossal, enormous, gigantic, great, immense, massive, monumental, wide

vault¹ n **1** = **strongroom**, depository, repository **2** = **crypt**, catacomb, cellar, charnel house, mausoleum, tomb, undercroft

vault² v **1** = **jump**, bound, clear, hurdle, leap, spring

veer v = **change direction**, change course, sheer, shift, swerve, turn

vegetate v = **stagnate**, deteriorate, go to seed, idle, languish, loaf

vehement adj = **strong**, ardent, emphatic, fervent, fierce, forceful, impassioned, intense, passionate, powerful

vehicle n **1** = **transport**, conveyance, transportation **2** = **medium**, apparatus, channel, means, mechanism, organ

veil n **1** = **cover**, blind, cloak, curtain, disguise, film, mask, screen, shroud ▷ v

v

vein ❶ n 1 tube that takes blood to the heart. 2 line in a leaf or an insect's wing. 3 layer of ore or mineral in rock. 4 streak in marble, wood, or cheese. 5 feature of someone's writing or speech, e.g. *a vein of humour*. 6 mood or style, e.g. *in a lighter vein*.

Velcro n ® fastening consisting of one piece of fabric with tiny hooked threads and another with a coarse surface that sticks to it.

velocity ❶ n, pl **-ties** speed of movement in a given direction.

velvet n fabric with a thick soft pile. **velvety** adj soft and smooth. **velveteen** n cotton velvet.

vend v sell. **vendor** n **vending machine** machine that dispenses goods when coins are inserted.

vendetta ❶ n prolonged quarrel between families, esp. one involving revenge killings.

veneer ❶ n 1 thin layer of wood etc. covering a cheaper material. 2 superficial appearance, e.g. *a veneer of sophistication*.

venerable ❶ adj worthy of deep respect. **venerate** v hold (a person) in deep respect. **veneration** n.

vengeance ❶ n revenge. **vengeful** adj wanting revenge.

venison n deer meat, used as food.

venom ❶ n 1 malice or spite. 2 poison produced by snakes etc. **venomous** adj.

vent ❶ n 1 outlet releasing fumes or fluid. ▷ v 2 express (an emotion) freely. **give vent to** release (an emotion) in an outburst.

ventilate v 1 let fresh air into. 2 discuss (ideas or feelings) openly. **ventilation** n **ventilator** n.

ventricle n Anat one of the four cavities of the heart or brain.

ventriloquist n entertainer who can speak without moving his or her lips, so that a voice seems to come from elsewhere. **ventriloquism** n.

venture ❶ n 1 risky undertaking, esp. in business. ▷ v 2 do something risky. 3 dare to express (an opinion). 4 go to an unknown place **venturesome** adj daring.

venue n place where an organized gathering is held.

veracious adj habitually truthful. **veracity** n.

verandah, veranda n open porch attached to a house.

verb n word that expresses the idea of action, happening, or being. **verbal** adj 1 spoken. 2 of a verb. **verbally** adv **verbalize** v express (something) in words.

———————————— THESAURUS ————————————

3 = **cover**, cloak, conceal, disguise, hide, mask, obscure, screen, shield
vein n 1 = **blood vessel** 3 = **seam**, lode, stratum 4 = **streak**, stripe 6 = **mood**, mode, note, style, temper, tenor, tone
velocity n = **speed**, pace, quickness, rapidity, swiftness
vendetta n = **feud**, bad blood, quarrel
veneer n 1 = **layer**, finish, gloss 2 = **mask**, appearance, facade, front, guise, pretence, semblance, show
venerable adj = **respected**, august, esteemed, honoured, revered, sage, wise, worshipped
vengeance n = **revenge**, reprisal,

requital, retaliation, retribution
venom n 1 = **malice**, acrimony, bitterness, hate, rancour, spite, spleen, virulence 2 = **poison**, bane, toxin
vent n 1 = **outlet**, aperture, duct, opening, orifice ▷ v 2 = **express**, air, discharge, emit, give vent to, pour out, release, utter, voice
venture n 1 = **undertaking**, adventure, endeavour, enterprise, gamble, hazard, project, risk ▷ v 2 = **risk**, chance, hazard, speculate, stake, wager 3 = **dare**, hazard, make bold, presume, take the liberty, volunteer 4 = **go**, embark on, plunge into, set out

V

verbose ⊙ [verb-**bohss**] *adj* speaking at tedious length. **verbosity** *n*.

verdant ⊙ *adj lit* covered in green vegetation.

verdict ⊙ *n* **1** decision of a jury. **2** opinion formed after examining the facts.

verge ⊙ *n* grass border along a road. **on the verge of** having almost reached (a point or condition). **verge on** *v* be near to (a condition).

verger *n* C of E church caretaker.

verify ⊙ *v* **-ifying, -ified** check the truth or accuracy of. **verifiable** *adj* **verification** *n*.

veritable *adj* rightly called, without exaggeration, e.g. *a veritable feast*. **veritably** *adv*.

vermilion *adj* orange-red.

vermin *pl n* animals, esp. insects and rodents, that spread disease or cause damage. **verminous** *adj*.

vernacular ⊙ [ver-**nak**-yew-lar] *n* most widely spoken language of a particular people or place.

verruca [ver-**roo**-ka] *n* wart, usu. on the foot.

versatile ⊙ *adj* having many skills or uses. **versatility** *n*.

verse *n* **1** group of lines forming part of a song or poem. **2** poetry as distinct from prose. **3** subdivision of a chapter of the Bible. **versed in** knowledgeable about. **versify** *v* write in verse. **versification** *n*.

version ⊙ *n* **1** form of something, such as a piece of writing, with some differences from other forms. **2** account of an incident from a particular point of view.

versus *prep* **1** in opposition to or in contrast with. **2** *Sport, Law* against.

vertebra *n, pl* **vertebrae** one of the bones that form the spine. **vertebral** *adj* **vertebrate** *n, adj* (animal) having a spine.

vertical ⊙ *adj* **1** straight up and down. ▷ *n* **2** vertical direction.

vertigo ⊙ *n* dizziness, usu. when looking down from a high place. **vertiginous** *adj*.

verve ⊙ *n* enthusiasm or liveliness.

very ⊙ *adv* **1** more than usually, extremely. ▷ *adj* **2** absolute, exact, e.g. *the very top*; *the very man*.

vespers *pl n* RC Church (service of) evening prayer.

vessel ⊙ *n* **1** ship. **2** *lit* container, esp. for liquids. **3** *Biol* tubular structure in animals and plants that carries body fluids, such as blood or sap.

THESAURUS

verbose *adj* = **long-winded**, circumlocutory, diffuse, periphrastic, prolix, tautological, windy, wordy

verdant *adj Lit* = **green**, flourishing, fresh, grassy, leafy, lush

verdict *n* = **decision**, adjudication, conclusion, finding, judgment, opinion, sentence

verge *n* = **border**, boundary, brim, brink, edge, limit, margin, threshold **verge on** *v* = **come near to**, approach, border

verify *v* = **check**, authenticate, bear out, confirm, corroborate, prove, substantiate, support, validate

vernacular *n* = **dialect**, idiom, parlance, patois, speech

versatile *adj* = **adaptable**, adjustable, all-purpose, all-round, flexible, multifaceted, resourceful, variable

version *n* **1 a** = **form**, design, model, style, variant **b** = **adaptation**, portrayal, rendering **2** = **account**, interpretation

vertical *adj* **1** = **upright**, erect, on end, perpendicular

vertigo *n* = **dizziness**, giddiness, light-headedness

verve *n* = **enthusiasm**, animation, energy, gusto, liveliness, sparkle, spirit, vitality

very *adv* **1** = **extremely**, acutely, decidedly, deeply, exceedingly, greatly, highly, profoundly, really, uncommonly, unusually ▷ *adj* **2** = **exact**, precise, selfsame

vessel *n* **1** = **ship**, boat, craft **2** *Lit* = **container**, pot, receptacle, utensil

V

vest ❶ *n* **1** undergarment worn on the top half of the body. **2** *US & Aust* waistcoat. ▷ *v* **3** (foll. by *in* or *with*) give (authority) to (someone). **vested interest** interest someone has in a matter because he or she might benefit from it.

vestibule ❶ *n* small entrance hall.

vestige ❶ [**vest**-ij] *n* small amount or trace. **vestigial** *adj*.

vestry *n*, *pl* **-tries** room in a church used as an office by the priest or minister.

vet ❶ *n* **1** short for VETERINARY SURGEON. ▷ *v* **vetting, vetted 2** check the suitability of.

veteran ❶ *n* **1** person with long experience in a particular activity, esp. military service. ▷ *adj* **2** long-serving.

veterinary *adj* concerning animal health. **veterinary surgeon** medical specialist who treats sick animals.

veto ❶ *n*, *pl* **-toes 1** official power to cancel a proposal. ▷ *v* **-toing, -toed 2** enforce a veto against.

vex ❶ *v* frustrate, annoy. **vexation** *n* **1** something annoying. **2** being annoyed. **vexatious** *adj* **vexed question** much debated subject.

VHF very high frequency: radio frequency band between 30 and 300 MHz.

VI Vancouver Island.

via *prep* by way of.

viable ❶ *adj* **1** able to be put into practice. **2** *Biol* able to live and grow independently. **viability** *n*.

viaduct *n* bridge over a valley.

vibrate ❶ *v* **1** move back and forth rapidly. **2** (cause to) resonate. **vibration** *n* **vibrator** *n* device that produces vibratory motion, used for massage or as a sex aid.

VIC Victoria (Australian state).

vicar *n* C of E clergyman in charge of a parish. **vicarage** *n* vicar's house.

vicarious ❶ [vick-**air**-ee-uss] *adj* **1** felt indirectly by imagining what another person experiences. **2** delegated. **vicariously** *adv*.

vice[1] ❶ *n* **1** immoral or evil habit or action. **2** habit regarded as a weakness in someone's character. **3** criminal immorality, esp. involving sex.

vice[2] *n* tool with a pair of jaws for holding an object while working on it.

vice[3] *adj* serving in place of.

viceroy *n* governor of a colony who represents the monarch.

vice versa ❶ [vie-see ver-sa] *adv Latin* conversely, the other way round.

THESAURUS

---

vest *v* **3** (foll. by *in* or *with*) = **place in**, bestow upon, confer on, consign to, endow with, entrust with, invest with, settle on

vestibule *n* = **hall**, anteroom, foyer, lobby, porch, portico

vestige *n* = **trace**, glimmer, indication, remnant, scrap, suspicion

vet *v* **2** = **check**, appraise, examine, investigate, review, scrutinize

veteran *n* **1** = **old hand**, old stager, past master, warhorse (*inf*) ▷ *adj* **2** = **long-serving**, battle-scarred, old, seasoned

veto *n* **1** = **ban**, boycott, embargo, interdict, prohibition ▷ *v* **2** = **ban**, boycott, disallow, forbid, prohibit, reject, rule out, turn down

vex *v* = **annoy**, bother, distress, exasperate, irritate, plague, trouble, upset, worry

viable *adj* **1** = **workable**, applicable, feasible, operable, practicable, usable

vibrate *v* **1** = **shake**, fluctuate, judder (*inf*) oscillate, pulsate, quiver, sway, throb, tremble **2** = **reverberate**

vicarious *adj* **1** = **indirect**, at one remove, substituted, surrogate **2** = **delegated**, deputed

vice[1] *n* **1** = **wickedness**, corruption, depravity, evil, immorality, iniquity, sin, turpitude **2** = **fault**, blemish, defect, failing, imperfection, shortcoming, weakness

vice versa *adv Latin* = **conversely**, contrariwise, in reverse, the other way round

v

vicinity ❶ [viss-**in**-it-ee] n surrounding area.

vicious ❶ adj cruel and violent. **vicious circle, cycle** situation in which an attempt to resolve one problem creates new problems that recreate the original one.

victim ❶ n person or thing harmed or killed. **victimize** v **1** punish unfairly. **2** discriminate against. **victimization** n.

victor ❶ n person who has defeated an opponent, esp. in war or in sport. **victorious** adj **victory** n winning of a battle or contest.

video n, pl **-os 1** short for VIDEO CASSETTE (RECORDER). ▷ v **videoing, videoed 2** record (a TV programme or event) on video. ▷ adj **3** relating to or used in producing television images.

vie ❶ v **vying, vied** compete (with someone).

view ❶ n **1** opinion or belief. **2** everything that can be seen from a given place. **3** picture of this. ▷ v **4** think of (something) in a particular way. **in view of** taking into consideration. **on view** exhibited to the public. **viewer** n **1** person who watches television. **2** hand-held device for looking at photographic slides. **viewfinder** n window on a camera showing what will appear in a photograph.

vigil [**vij**-ill] n night-time period of staying awake to look after a sick person, pray, etc. **vigilant** adj watchful in case of danger. **vigilance** n.

vigilante [vij-ill-**ant**-ee] n person, esp. as one of a group, who takes it upon himself or herself to enforce the law.

vignette [vin-**yet**] n **1** concise description of the typical features of something. **2** small decorative illustration in a book.

vigour ❶ n physical or mental energy. **vigorous** adj **vigorously** adv.

vile ❶ adj **1** very wicked. **2** disgusting. **vilely** adv **vileness** n.

vilify ❶ v **-ifying, -ified** attack the character of. **vilification** n.

villa n **1** large house with gardens. **2** holiday home, usu. in the Mediterranean.

village n **1** small group of houses in a country area. **2** rural community. **villager** n.

villain ❶ n **1** wicked person. **2** main wicked character in a play. **villainous** adj **villainy** n.

vindicate ❶ v **1** clear (someone) of guilt. **2** provide justification for. **vindication** n.

vindictive ❶ adj maliciously seeking revenge. **vindictiveness** n **vindictively** adv.

———————— THESAURUS ————————

vicinity n = **neighbourhood**, area, district, environs, locality, neck of the woods (inf), proximity

vicious adj **a** = **malicious**, cruel, mean, spiteful, venomous, vindictive **b** = **savage**, barbarous, cruel, ferocious, violent

victim n = **casualty**, fatality, sufferer

victor n = **winner**, champion, conqueror, prizewinner, vanquisher

vie v = **compete**, contend, strive, struggle

view n **1** = **opinion**, attitude, belief, conviction, feeling, point of view, sentiment **2** = **scene**, landscape, outlook, panorama, perspective, picture, prospect, spectacle, vista ▷ v **4** = **regard**, consider, deem, look on

vigour n = **energy**, animation, dynamism,

forcefulness, gusto, liveliness, power, spirit, strength, verve, vitality

vile adj **1** = **wicked**, corrupt, degenerate, depraved, evil, nefarious, perverted **2** = **disgusting**, foul, horrid, nasty, nauseating, offensive, repugnant, repulsive, revolting, sickening

vilify v = **malign**, abuse, berate, denigrate, disparage, revile, slander, smear

villain n **1** = **evildoer**, blackguard, criminal, miscreant, reprobate, rogue, scoundrel, wretch **2** = **antihero**, baddy (inf)

vindicate v **1** = **clear**, absolve, acquit, exculpate, exonerate, rehabilitate **2** = **justify**, defend, excuse

vindictive adj = **vengeful**, implacable, malicious, resentful, revengeful, spiteful,

v

vine n climbing plant, esp. one producing grapes. **vineyard** [**vinn**-yard] n plantation of grape vines, esp. for making wine.

vinegar n acid liquid made from wine, beer, or cider. **vinegary** adj.

vintage ❶ n 1 wine from a particular harvest of grapes. ▷ adj 2 best and most typical.

vinyl [**vine**-ill] n type of plastic, used in mock leather and records.

viola [vee-**oh**-la] n stringed instrument lower in pitch than a violin.

violate ❶ v 1 break (a law or agreement). 2 disturb (someone's privacy). 3 treat (a sacred place) disrespectfully. 4 rape. **violation** n **violator** n.

violence ❶ n 1 use of physical force, usu. intended to cause injury or destruction. 2 great force or strength in action, feeling, or expression. **violent** adj **violently** adv.

violet n 1 plant with bluish-purple flowers. ▷ adj 2 bluish-purple.

violin n small four-stringed musical instrument played with a bow. **violinist** n.

VIP ❶ very important person.

viper n poisonous snake.

viral adj of or caused by a virus.

virgin ❶ n 1 person, esp. a woman, who has not had sexual intercourse. ▷ adj 2 not having had sexual intercourse. 3 not yet exploited or explored. **virginal**

adj 1 like a virgin. ▷ n 2 early keyboard instrument like a small harpsichord. **virginity** n.

virile ❶ adj having the traditional male characteristics of physical strength and a high sex drive. **virility** n.

virtue ❶ n 1 moral goodness. 2 positive moral quality. 3 merit. **by virtue of** by reason of. **virtuous** adj morally good.

virtuoso ❶ n, pl -sos, -si person with impressive esp. musical skill. **virtuosity** n.

virulent ❶ [**vir**-yew-lent] adj 1 very infectious. 2 violently harmful.

virus n 1 microorganism that causes disease in humans, animals, and plants. 2 Computers program that propagates itself, via disks and electronic networks, to cause disruption.

visa n permission to enter a country, granted by its government and shown by a stamp on one's passport.

visage [**viz**-zij] n lit face.

vis-à-vis [veez-ah-**vee**] prep in relation to, regarding.

viscount [**vie**-count] n British nobleman ranking between an earl and a baron.

viscous ❶ adj thick and sticky. **viscosity** n.

visible ❶ adj 1 able to be seen. 2 able to be perceived by the mind. **visibly** adv **visibility** n range or clarity of vision.

———————————————————————— THESAURUS ————————

unforgiving, unrelenting

vintage adj 2 = **best**, choice, classic, prime, select, superior

violate v 1 = **break**, contravene, disobey, disregard, infringe, transgress 2 = **encroach upon** 3 = **desecrate**, abuse, befoul, defile, dishonour, pollute, profane 4 = **rape**, abuse, assault, debauch, ravish

violence n 1 = **force**, bloodshed, brutality, cruelty, ferocity, fighting, savagery, terrorism 2 = **intensity**, abandon, fervour, force, severity, vehemence

VIP n = **celebrity**, big hitter (inf), big name, heavy hitter (inf), luminary, somebody, star

virgin n 1 = **maiden**, girl (arch) ▷ adj

2 = **pure**, chaste, immaculate, uncorrupted, undefiled, vestal, virginal

virile adj = **manly**, lusty, macho, manlike, masculine, red-blooded, strong, vigorous

virtue n 1, 2 = **goodness**, incorruptibility, integrity, morality, probity, rectitude, righteousness, uprightness, worth 3 = **merit**, advantage, asset, attribute, credit, good point, plus (inf), strength

virtuoso n = **master**, artist, genius, maestro, magician

virulent adj 2 = **deadly**, lethal, pernicious, poisonous, toxic, venomous

viscous adj = **thick**, gelatinous, sticky, syrupy

visible adj 1 = **apparent**, clear, discernible,

vision ❶ *n* **1** ability to see. **2** mental image of something. **3** foresight. **4** hallucination. **visionary** *adj* **1** showing foresight. **2** idealistic but impractical. ▷ *n* **3** visionary person.

visit ❶ *v* **-iting, -ited** **1** go or come to see. **2** stay temporarily with. **3** (foll. by *upon*) *lit* afflict. ▷ *n* **4** instance of visiting. **5** official call. **visitor** *n* **visitation** *n* **1** formal visit or inspection. **2** catastrophe seen as divine punishment.

visor [**vize**-or] *n* **1** transparent part of a helmet that pulls down over the face. **2** eyeshade, esp. in a car. **3** peak on a cap.

vista ❶ *n* (beautiful) extensive view.

visual ❶ *adj* **1** done by or used in seeing. **2** designed to be looked at. **visualize** *v* form a mental image of. **visualization** *n* **visual display unit** device with a screen for displaying data held in a computer.

vital ❶ *adj* **1** essential or highly important. **2** lively. **3** necessary to maintain life. **vitals** *pl n* bodily organs necessary to maintain life. **vitally** *adv* **vitality** *n* physical or mental energy. **vital statistics 1** statistics of births, deaths, and marriages in a population. **2** *informal* woman's bust,

waist, and hip measurements.

vitamin *n* one of a group of substances that are essential in the diet for specific body processes.

viva *interj* long live (a person or thing).

vivacious ❶ *adj* full of energy and enthusiasm. **vivacity** *n*.

vivid ❶ *adj* **1** very bright. **2** conveying images that are true to life. **vividly** *adv* **vividness** *n*.

vivisection *n* performing surgical experiments on living animals. **vivisectionist** *n*.

vixen *n* **1** female fox. **2** *informal* spiteful woman.

vizor *n* same as VISOR.

vocabulary ❶ *n, pl* **-aries 1** all the words that a person knows. **2** all the words in a language. **3** specialist terms used in a given subject. **4** list of words in another language with their translation.

vocal ❶ *adj* **1** relating to the voice. **2** outspoken. **vocals** *pl n* singing part of a piece of pop music. **vocally** *adv* **vocalist** *n* singer. **vocalize** *v* express with or use the voice. **vocalization** *n* **vocal cords** membranes in the larynx that vibrate to produce sound.

— THESAURUS —

evident, in view, manifest, observable, perceptible, unconcealed

vision *n* **1** = **sight**, eyesight, perception, seeing, view **2** = **image**, concept, conception, daydream, dream, fantasy, idea, ideal **3** = **foresight**, discernment, farsightedness, imagination, insight, intuition, penetration, prescience **4** = **hallucination**, apparition, chimera, delusion, illusion, mirage, revelation

visit *v* **1** = **call on**, drop in on (*inf*), look (someone) up, stop by **2** = **stay with** ▷ *n* **4** = **call**, sojourn, stay, stop

vista *n* = **view**, panorama, perspective, prospect

visual *adj* **1** = **optical**, ocular, optic **2** = **observable**, discernible, perceptible, visible

vital *adj* **1** = **essential**, basic, fundamental, imperative, indispensable, necessary, requisite **2** = **lively**, animated, dynamic, energetic, spirited, vibrant, vigorous, vivacious, zestful **3** = **important**, critical, crucial, decisive, key, life-or-death, significant, urgent

vivacious *adj* = **lively**, bubbling, ebullient, high-spirited, sparkling, spirited, sprightly, upbeat (*inf*), vital

vivid *adj* **1** = **bright**, brilliant, clear, colourful, glowing, intense, rich **2** = **clear**, dramatic, graphic, lifelike, memorable, powerful, realistic, stirring, telling, true to life

vocabulary *n* **2** = **words**, dictionary, glossary, language, lexicon

vocal *adj* **1** = **spoken**, oral, said, uttered, voiced **2** = **outspoken**, articulate,

V

vocation ⓘ n 1 profession or trade.
2 occupation that someone feels called
to. **vocational** adj directed towards a
particular profession or trade.
vociferous ⓘ adj shouting, noisy.
vodka n (Russian) spirit distilled from
potatoes or grain.
vogue ⓘ n 1 popular style. 2 period of
popularity.
voice ⓘ n 1 (quality of) sound made when
speaking or singing. 2 expression of
opinion by a person or group. 3 property
of verbs that makes them active or
passive. ▷ v 4 express verbally. **voiceless**
adj **voice mail** electronic system for
the storage of telephone messages.
voice-over n film commentary spoken by
someone off-camera.
void ⓘ adj 1 not legally binding. 2 empty. ▷ n
3 empty space. ▷ v 4 make invalid. 5 empty.
vol. volume.
volatile ⓘ adj 1 liable to sudden change,
esp. in behaviour. 2 evaporating quickly.
volatility n.
volcano n, pl **-noes, -nos** mountain with a
vent through which molten lava is ejected.

volcanic adj.
vole n small rodent.
volition ⓘ n ability to decide things for
oneself. **of one's own volition** through
one's own choice.
volley ⓘ n 1 simultaneous discharge of
ammunition. 2 burst of questions or
critical comments. 3 Sport stroke or kick
at a moving ball before it hits the ground.
▷ v 4 discharge (ammunition) in a volley.
5 hit or kick (a ball) in a volley. **volleyball**
n team game where a ball is hit with the
hands over a high net.
volt n unit of electric potential. **voltage**
n electric potential difference expressed
in volts. **voltmeter** n instrument for
measuring voltage.
voluble ⓘ adj talking easily and at length.
volubility n **volubly** adv.
volume ⓘ n 1 size of the space occupied
by something. 2 amount. 3 loudness
of sound. 4 book, esp. one of a series.
voluminous adj 1 (of clothes) large and
roomy. 2 (of writings) extensive.
voluntary ⓘ adj 1 done by choice.
2 done or maintained without payment.

— THESAURUS —

eloquent, expressive, forthright, frank,
plain-spoken, strident, vociferous
vocation n 1 = **profession**, career, job,
pursuit, trade 2 = **calling**, mission
vociferous adj = **noisy**, clamorous,
loud, outspoken, strident, uproarious,
vehement, vocal
vogue n 1 = **fashion**, craze, custom, mode,
style, trend, way **in vogue** = **popular**,
accepted, current, in favour, in use,
prevalent
voice n 1 = **sound**, articulation, tone,
utterance 2 = **say**, view, vote, will, wish
▷ v 4 = **express**, air, articulate, declare,
enunciate, utter
void adj 1 = **invalid**, ineffective, inoperative,
null and void, useless, vain, worthless
2 = **empty**, bare, free, tenantless, unfilled,
unoccupied, vacant ▷ n 3 = **emptiness**,
blankness, gap, lack, space, vacuity,

vacuum ▷ v 4 = **invalidate**, cancel, nullify,
rescind 5 = **empty**, drain, evacuate
volatile adj 1 **a** = **changeable**, erratic,
explosive, inconstant, unsettled, unstable,
unsteady, up and down (inf), variable
b = **temperamental**, fickle, mercurial
volition n = **free will**, choice, choosing,
discretion, preference, will
volley n 1 = **barrage**, blast, bombardment,
burst, cannonade, fusillade, hail, salvo,
shower
voluble adj = **talkative**, articulate, fluent,
forthcoming, glib, loquacious
volume n 1 = **capacity**, compass,
dimensions 2 = **amount**, aggregate,
body, bulk, mass, quantity, total 4 = **book**,
publication, title, tome, treatise
voluntary adj 1 = **unforced**, optional,
spontaneous, willing 2 = **discretionary**,
free

3 (of muscles) controlled by the will. ▷ *n*, *pl* **-taries 4** organ solo in a church service. **voluntarily** *adv*.

voluptuous ❶ *adj* **1** (of a woman) sexually alluring through fullness of figure. **2** sensually pleasurable. **voluptuary** *n* person devoted to sensual pleasures.

vomit ❶ *v* **-iting, -ited 1** eject (the contents of the stomach) through the mouth. ▷ *n* **2** matter vomited.

voodoo *n* religion involving ancestor worship and witchcraft, practised by Black people in the West Indies, esp. in Haiti.

voracious ❶ *adj* **1** craving great quantities of food. **2** insatiably eager. **voracity** *n*.

vortex ❶ *n*, *pl* **-texes, -tices** whirlpool.

vote ❶ *n* **1** choice made by a participant in a shared decision, esp. in electing a candidate. **2** right to this choice. **3** total number of votes cast. **4** collective voting power of a given group, e.g. *the Black vote*. ▷ *v* **5** make a choice by a vote. **6** authorize (something) by vote. **voter** *n*.

vouch *v* **vouch for 1** give one's personal assurance about. **2** provide evidence for.

vow ❶ *n* **1** solemn and binding promise. ▷ *pl* **2** formal promises made when marrying or entering a religious order. ▷ *v* **3** promise solemnly.

vowel *n* **1** speech sound made without obstructing the flow of breath. **2** letter representing this.

voyage ❶ *n* **1** long journey by sea or in space. ▷ *v* **2** make a voyage. **voyager** *n*.

VT Vermont.

vulcanize *v* strengthen (rubber) by treating it with sulphur. **vulcanization** *n*.

vulgar ❶ *adj* showing lack of good taste, decency, or refinement. **vulgarity** *n* **vulgarian** *n* vulgar (rich) person. **vulgarism** *n* coarse word or phrase. **vulgar fraction** simple fraction.

vulnerable ❶ *adj* **1** liable to be physically or emotionally hurt. **2** exposed to attack. **vulnerability** *n*.

vulture *n* large bird that feeds on the flesh of dead animals.

——————————————— THESAURUS ———————————————

voluptuous *adj* **1** = **buxom**, ample, curvaceous (*inf*), enticing, seductive, shapely **2** = **sensual**, epicurean, hedonistic, licentious, luxurious, self-indulgent, sybaritic

vomit *v* **1** = **be sick**, disgorge, emit, heave, regurgitate, retch, spew out *or* up, throw up (*inf*)

voracious *adj* **1** = **gluttonous**, greedy, hungry, insatiable, omnivorous, ravenous **2** = **avid**, hungry, insatiable, rapacious, uncontrolled, unquenchable

vortex *n* = **whirlpool**, eddy, maelstrom

vote *n* **1** = **poll**, ballot, franchise, plebiscite,

referendum, show of hands ▷ *v* **5** = **cast one's vote**, elect, opt

vow *n* **1** = **promise**, oath, pledge ▷ *v* **3** = **promise**, affirm, pledge, swear

voyage *n* **1** = **journey**, crossing, cruise, passage, trip

vulgar *adj* = **crude**, coarse, common, impolite, indecent, ribald, risqué, rude, tasteless, uncouth, unrefined

vulnerable *adj* **1** = **susceptible**, sensitive, tender, thin-skinned, weak **2** = **exposed**, accessible, assailable, defenceless, unprotected, wide open

v

WA 1 Washington. **2** Western Australia.

wacky *adj* **wackier, wackiest** *informal* eccentric or funny.

wad ❶ *n* **1** small mass of soft material. **2** roll or bundle, esp. of banknotes. **wadding** *n* soft material used for padding or stuffing.

waddle ❶ *v* **1** walk with short swaying steps. ▷ *n* **2** swaying walk.

wade ❶ *v* **1** walk with difficulty through water or mud. **2** proceed with difficulty. **wader** *n* **1** long-legged water bird. ▷ *pl* **2** angler's long waterproof boots.

wafer *n* **1** thin crisp biscuit. **2** thin disc of unleavened bread used at Communion. **3** thin slice.

waffle¹ ❶ *informal* ▷ *v* **1** speak or write in a vague wordy way. ▷ *n* **2** vague wordy talk or writing.

waffle² *n* square crisp pancake with a gridlike pattern.

waft ❶ *v* **1** drift or carry gently through the air. ▷ *n* **2** something wafted.

wag ❶ *v* **wagging, wagged 1** move rapidly from side to side. ▷ *n* **2** wagging movement. **3** *old-fashioned* humorous witty person.

wage ❶ *n* **1** (often *pl*) payment for work done, esp. when paid weekly. ▷ *v* **2** engage in (an activity).

wager ❶ *n, v* bet on the outcome of something.

waggle ❶ *v* move with a rapid shaking or wobbling motion.

wagon, waggon *n* **1** four-wheeled vehicle for heavy loads. **2** railway freight truck.

wahoo *n* food and game fish of tropical seas.

waif ❶ *n* young person who is, or seems, homeless or neglected.

wail ❶ *v* **1** cry out in pain or misery. ▷ *n* **2** mournful cry.

waist *n* **1** part of the body between the ribs and hips. **2** narrow middle part. **waistband** *n* band of material sewn on to the waist of a garment to strengthen it. **waistcoat** *n* sleeveless garment which buttons up the front, usu. worn over a shirt and under a jacket. **waistline** *n* (size of) the waist of a person or garment.

— THESAURUS —

wad *n* **1** = **mass**, hunk **2** = **roll**, bundle

waddle *v* **1** = **shuffle**, sway, toddle, totter, wobble

wade *v* **1** = **walk through**, ford, paddle, splash **2** = **plough through**, drudge at, labour at, peg away at, toil at, work one's way through

waffle¹ *v* **1** *Inf* = **prattle**, blather, jabber, prate, rabbit (on) (*Brit inf*), witter on (*inf*) ▷ *n* **2** *Inf* = **verbosity**, padding, prolixity, verbiage, wordiness

waft *v* **1** = **carry**, bear, convey, drift, float, transport

wag *v* **1** = **wave**, bob, nod, quiver, shake, stir, vibrate, waggle, wiggle ▷ *n* **2** = **wave**, bob, nod, quiver, shake, vibration, waggle, wiggle

3 *Old-fashioned* = **joker**, card (*inf*), clown, comedian, comic, humorist, jester, wit

wage *n* **1** (often *pl*) = **payment**, allowance, emolument, fee, pay, recompense, remuneration, reward, stipend ▷ *v* **2** = **engage in**, carry on, conduct, practise, proceed with, prosecute, pursue, undertake

wager *n* = **bet**, flutter (*Brit inf*), gamble, punt (*chiefly Brit*) ▷ *v* = **bet**, chance, gamble, lay, risk, speculate, stake, venture

waggle *v* = **wag**, flutter, oscillate, shake, wave, wiggle, wobble

waif *n* = **stray**, foundling, orphan

wail *v* **1** = **cry**, bawl, grieve, howl, lament, weep, yowl ▷ *n* **2** = **cry**, complaint, howl, lament, moan, weeping, yowl

w

wait ● v **1** remain inactive in expectation (of something). **2** be ready (for something). **3** delay or be delayed. **4** serve in a restaurant etc. ▷ n **5** act or period of waiting. **waiter** n man who serves in a restaurant etc. **waitress** n fem.

waive ● v refrain from enforcing (a law, right, etc.). **waiver** n (written statement of) this act.

wake¹ ● v **waking, woke, woken 1** rouse from sleep or inactivity. ▷ n **2** vigil beside a corpse the night before the funeral. **waken** v wake. **wakeful** adj.

wake² ● n track left by a moving ship. **in the wake of** following, often as a result.

walk ● v **1** move on foot with at least one foot always on the ground. **2** pass through or over on foot. **3** escort or accompany on foot. ▷ n **4** act or instance of walking. **5** distance walked. **6** manner of walking. **7** place or route for walking. **walk of life** social position or profession. **walker** n **walkabout** n informal walk among the public by royalty etc. **walkie-talkie** n portable radio transmitter and receiver. **walking stick** stick used as a support when walking. **walk into** v meet with unwittingly. **Walkman** n ® small portable

cassette player with headphones. **walkout** n **1** strike. **2** act of leaving as a protest. **walkover** n easy victory.

wall ● n **1** structure of brick, stone, etc. used to enclose, divide, or support. **2** something having the function or effect of a wall. ▷ v **3** enclose or seal with a wall or walls. **wallflower** n **1** fragrant garden plant. **2** (at a dance) woman who remains seated because she has no partner. **wallpaper** n decorative paper to cover interior walls.

wallaby n, pl **-bies** marsupial like a small kangaroo.

wallaroo n large stocky Australian kangaroo of rocky regions.

wallet ● n small folding case for paper money, documents, etc.

walleye n fish with large staring eyes (also **dory**).

wallop ● informal ▷ v **-loping, -loped 1** hit hard. ▷ n **2** hard blow. **walloping** informal ▷ n **1** thrashing. ▷ adj **2** large or great.

wallow ● v **1** revel in an emotion. **2** roll in liquid or mud. ▷ n **3** act or instance of wallowing.

walnut n **1** edible nut with a wrinkled shell. **2** tree it grows on. **3** its wood, used for making furniture.

THESAURUS

wait v **1** = **remain**, hang fire, hold back, linger, pause, rest, stay, tarry ▷ n **5** = **delay**, halt, hold-up, interval, pause, rest, stay

waive v = **set aside**, abandon, dispense with, forgo, give up, relinquish, remit, renounce

wake¹ v **1 a** = **awaken**, arise, awake, bestir, come to, get up, rouse, stir **b** = **activate**, animate, arouse, excite, fire, galvanize, kindle, provoke, stimulate, stir up ▷ n **2** = **vigil**, deathwatch, funeral, watch

wake² n = **slipstream**, aftermath, backwash, path, track, trail, train, wash, waves

walk v **1, 2** = **go**, amble, hike, march, move, pace, step, stride, stroll **3** = **escort**, accompany, convoy, take ▷ n **4** = **stroll**,

hike, march, promenade, ramble, saunter, trek, trudge **6** = **gait**, carriage, step **7** = **path**, alley, avenue, esplanade, footpath, lane, promenade, trail **walk of life** = **profession**, calling, career, field, line, trade, vocation

wall n **1** = **partition**, enclosure, screen **2** = **barrier**, fence, hedge, impediment, obstacle, obstruction

wallet n = **holder**, case, pouch, purse

wallop Inf v **1** = **hit**, batter, beat, clobber (sl), pound, pummel, strike, swipe, thrash, thump, whack ▷ n **2** = **blow**, bash, punch, slug, smack, swipe, thump, thwack, whack

wallow v **1** = **revel**, bask, delight, glory, luxuriate, relish, take pleasure **2** = **roll about**, splash around

W

walrus *n, pl* **-ruses**, **-rus** large sea mammal with long tusks.

waltz *n* **1** ballroom dance. **2** music for this. ▷ *v* **3** dance a waltz. **4** *informal* move in a relaxed confident way.

wampum *n US & Canad* shells woven together, formerly used by N American Indians for money and ornament.

wan ❶ [rhymes with **swan**] *adj* **wanner**, **wannest** pale and sickly looking.

wand ❶ *n* thin rod, esp. one used in performing magic tricks.

wander ❶ *v* **1** move about without a definite destination or aim. **2** go astray, deviate. ▷ *n* **3** act or instance of wandering. **wanderer** *n* **wanderlust** *n* great desire to travel.

wane ❶ *v* **1** decrease gradually in size or strength. **2** (of the moon) decrease in size. **on the wane** decreasing in size, strength, or power.

wangle ❶ *v informal* get by devious methods.

want ❶ *v* **1** need or long for. **2** desire or wish. ▷ *n* **3** act or instance of wanting. **4** thing wanted. **5** lack or absence.

6 state of being in need, poverty. **wanted** *adj* sought by the police. **wanting** *adj* **1** lacking. **2** not good enough.

wanton ❶ *adj* **1** without motive, provocation, or justification. **2** *old-fashioned* (of a woman) sexually unrestrained or immodest.

war ❶ *n* **1** fighting between nations. **2** conflict or contest. ▷ *adj* **3** of, like, or caused by war. ▷ *v* **warring**, **warred** **4** conduct a war. **warring** *adj* **warlike** *adj* **1** of or relating to war. **2** hostile and eager to have a war. **warfare** *n* fighting or hostilities. **warhead** *n* explosive front part of a missile. **warmonger** *n* person who encourages war. **warship** *n* ship designed and equipped for naval combat.

warble ❶ *v* sing in a trilling voice. **warbler** *n* any of various small songbirds.

ward ❶ *n* **1** room in a hospital for patients needing a similar kind of care. **2** electoral division of a town. **3** child under the care of a guardian or court. **warder** *n* prison officer. **wardress** *n fem* **ward off** *v* avert or repel. **wardroom** *n* officers' quarters on a warship.

━━━━━━━━━━━━━━━━━━━━━━━━━ THESAURUS ━━━━━━━━━━

wan *adj* = **pale**, anaemic, ashen, pallid, pasty, sickly, washed out, white

wand *n* = **stick**, baton, rod

wander *v* **1** = **roam**, drift, meander, ramble, range, rove, stray, stroll **2** = **deviate**, depart, digress, diverge, err, go astray, swerve, veer ▷ *n* **3** = **excursion**, cruise, meander, ramble

wane *v* **1** = **decline**, decrease, diminish, dwindle, ebb, fade, fail, lessen, subside, taper off, weaken **on the wane** = **declining**, dwindling, ebbing, fading, obsolescent, on the decline, tapering off, weakening

wangle *v Inf* = **contrive**, arrange, engineer, fiddle (*inf*), fix (*inf*), manipulate, manoeuvre, pull off

want *v* **1** = **need**, call for, demand, lack, miss, require **2** = **desire**, covet, crave, hanker after, hope for, hunger for, long for, thirst for, wish, yearn for ▷ *n* **3** = **wish**, appetite, craving, desire, longing, need,

requirement, yearning **5** = **lack**, absence, dearth, deficiency, famine, insufficiency, paucity, scarcity, shortage **6** = **poverty**, destitution, neediness, penury, privation

wanton *adj* **1** = **unprovoked**, arbitrary, gratuitous, groundless, motiveless, needless, senseless, uncalled-for, unjustifiable, wilful **2** *Old-fashioned* = **promiscuous**, dissipated, dissolute, immoral, lecherous, libidinous, loose, lustful, shameless, unchaste

war *n* **1, 2** = **fighting**, battle, combat, conflict, enmity, hostilities, struggle, warfare ▷ *v* **4** = **fight**, battle, campaign against, clash, combat, take up arms, wage war

warble *v* = **sing**, chirp, trill, twitter

ward *n* **1** = **room**, apartment, cubicle **2** = **district**, area, division, precinct, quarter, zone **3** = **dependant**, charge, minor

warden ❶ *n* **1** person in charge of a building and its occupants. **2** official responsible for the enforcement of regulations.

wardrobe ❶ *n* **1** cupboard for hanging clothes in. **2** person's collection of clothes. **3** costumes of a theatrical company.

ware *n* **1** articles of a specified type or material, e.g. *silverware*. ▷ *pl* **2** goods for sale. **warehouse** *n* building for storing goods prior to sale or distribution.

warm ❶ *adj* **1** moderately hot. **2** providing warmth. **3** (of a colour) predominantly yellow or red. **4** affectionate. **5** enthusiastic. ▷ *v* **6** make or become warm. **warmth** *n* **1** mild heat. **2** cordiality. **3** intensity of emotion. **warm up** *v* **1** make or become warmer. **2** do preliminary exercises before a race or more strenuous exercise. **3** make or become more lively. **warm-up** *n*.

warn ❶ *v* **1** make aware of possible danger or harm. **2** caution or scold. **3** inform (someone) in advance. **warning** *n* **1** something that warns. **2** scolding or caution. **warn off** *v* advise (someone) not to become involved with.

warp ❶ *v* **1** twist out of shape. **2** pervert. ▷ *n* **3** state of being warped. **4** lengthwise threads on a loom.

warrant ❶ *n* **1** (document giving) official authorization. ▷ *v* **2** make necessary.

3 guarantee. **warranty** *n, pl* **-ties** (document giving) a guarantee. **warrant officer** officer in certain armed services with a rank between a commissioned and noncommissioned officer.

warren *n* **1** series of burrows in which rabbits live. **2** overcrowded building or part of a town.

warrigal *Aust* ▷ *n* **1** dingo. ▷ *adj* **2** wild.

warrior ❶ *n* person who fights in a war.

wart *n* small hard growth on the skin. **wart hog** kind of African wild pig.

wary ❶ [**ware**-ree] *adj* **warier**, **wariest** watchful or cautious. **warily** *adv* **wariness** *n*.

was *v* first and third person singular past tense of BE.

wash ❶ *v* **1** clean (oneself, clothes, etc.) with water and usu. soap. **2** be washable. **3** flow or sweep over or against. **4** *informal* be believable or acceptable, e.g. *that excuse won't wash*. ▷ *n* **5** act or process of washing. **6** clothes washed at one time. **7** thin coat of paint. **8** disturbance in the water after a ship has passed by. **washable** *adj* **washer** *n* ring put under a nut or bolt or in a tap as a seal. **washing** *n* clothes to be washed. **washing-up** *n* (washing of) dishes and cutlery needing to be cleaned after a meal. **washout** *n informal* complete failure. **wash up** *v* wash dishes and cutlery after a meal.

——————————— THESAURUS ———————————

warden *n* **1** = **keeper**, administrator, caretaker, curator, custodian, guardian, ranger, superintendent

wardrobe *n* **1** = **clothes cupboard**, closet **2** = **clothes**, apparel, attire

warm *adj* **1** = **heated**, balmy, lukewarm, pleasant, sunny, tepid, thermal **4** = **affectionate**, amorous, cordial, friendly, hospitable, kindly, loving, tender ▷ *v* **6** = **heat**, heat up, melt, thaw, warm up

warn *v* **1** = **alert**, tip off **2** = **caution** **3** = **forewarn**, advise, apprise, give notice, inform, make (someone) aware, notify

warp *v* **1** = **twist**, bend, contort, deform, distort ▷ *n* **3** = **twist**, bend, contortion, distortion, kink

warrant *n* **1** = **authorization**, authority, licence, mana (*NZ*), permission, permit, sanction ▷ *v* **2** = **call for**, demand, deserve, excuse, justify, license, necessitate, permit, require, sanction **3** = **guarantee**, affirm, attest, certify, declare, pledge, vouch for

warrior *n* = **soldier**, combatant, fighter, gladiator, man-at-arms

wary *adj* = **cautious**, alert, careful, chary, circumspect, distrustful, guarded, suspicious, vigilant, watchful

wash *v* **1** = **clean**, bathe, cleanse, launder, rinse, scrub **3** = **sweep away**, bear away, carry off, move **4** *Inf* = **be plausible**, bear scrutiny, be convincing, carry weight, hold up, hold water, stand up, stick ▷ *n*

w

wasp n stinging insect with a slender black-and-yellow striped body. **waspish** adj bad-tempered.

waste ❶ v 1 use pointlessly or thoughtlessly. 2 fail to take advantage of. ▷ n 3 act of wasting or state of being wasted. 4 anything wasted. 5 rubbish. ▷ pl 6 desert. ▷ adj 7 rejected as worthless or surplus to requirements. 8 not cultivated or inhabited. **waste away** (cause to) decline in health or strength. **wastage** n 1 loss by wear or waste. 2 reduction in size of a workforce by not filling vacancies. **wasteful** adj extravagant. **waster**, **wastrel** n layabout.

watch ❶ v 1 look at closely. 2 guard or supervise. ▷ n 3 portable timepiece for the wrist or pocket. 4 (period of) watching. 5 sailor's spell of duty. **watchable** adj **watcher** n **watchful** adj vigilant or alert. **watchdog** n 1 dog kept to guard property. 2 person or group guarding against inefficiency or illegality. **watchman** n man employed to guard a building or property. **watchword** n word or phrase that sums up the attitude of a particular group.

water ❶ n 1 clear colourless tasteless liquid that falls as rain and forms rivers etc. 2 body of water, such as a sea or lake. 3 level of the tide. 4 urine. ▷ v 5 put water on or into. 6 (of the eyes) fill with tears.

7 (of the mouth) salivate. **watery** adj **water closet** old-fashioned (room containing) a toilet flushed by water. **watercolour** n 1 paint thinned with water. 2 painting done in this. **watercress** n edible plant growing in clear ponds and streams. **water down** v dilute, make less strong. **waterfall** n place where the waters of a river drop vertically. **waterfront** n part of a town alongside a body of water. **water lily** water plant with large floating leaves. **watermark** n faint translucent design in a sheet of paper. **watermelon** n melon with green skin and red flesh. **water polo** team game played by swimmers with a ball. **waterproof** adj 1 not letting water through. ▷ n 2 waterproof garment. ▷ v 3 make waterproof. **watershed** n 1 important period or factor serving as a dividing line. 2 line separating two river systems. **water-skiing** n sport of riding over water on skis towed by a speedboat. **watertight** adj 1 not letting water through. 2 with no loopholes or weak points.

watt [**wott**] n unit of power. **wattage** n electrical power expressed in watts.

wave ❶ v 1 move the hand to and fro as a greeting or signal. 2 move or flap to and fro. ▷ n 3 moving ridge on water. 4 curve(s) in the hair. 5 prolonged spell of something.

━━━━━━━━━━━━━━━━━━━━━━━━━━━━━━━━ THESAURUS ━━━━

5 = **cleaning**, cleansing, laundering, rinse, scrub 7 = **coat**, coating, film, layer, overlay 8 = **swell**, surge, wave

waste v 1 = **squander**, blow (sl), dissipate, fritter away, lavish, misuse, throw away ▷ n 3 = **squandering**, dissipation, extravagance, frittering away, misuse, prodigality, wastefulness 5 = **rubbish**, debris, dross, garbage, leftovers, litter, refuse, scrap, trash ▷ pl 6 = **desert**, wasteland, wilderness ▷ adj 7 = **unwanted**, leftover, superfluous, supernumerary, unused, useless, worthless 8 = **uncultivated**, bare, barren, desolate, empty, uninhabited, unproductive, wild **waste away** = **decline**,

atrophy, crumble, decay, dwindle, fade, wane, wear out, wither

watch v 1 = **look at**, contemplate, eye, eyeball (sl), observe, regard, see, view 2 = **guard**, keep, look after, mind, protect, superintend, take care of, tend ▷ n 3 = **wristwatch**, chronometer, timepiece 4 = **lookout**, observation, surveillance, vigil

water n 1 = **liquid**, H2O ▷ v 5 = **moisten**, dampen, douse, drench, hose, irrigate, soak, spray

wave v 1 = **signal**, gesticulate, gesture, sign 2 = **flap**, brandish, flourish, flutter, oscillate, shake, stir, swing, wag ▷ n 3 = **ripple**, billow, breaker, ridge, roller, swell, undulation 5 = **outbreak**, flood,

w

6 gesture of waving. **7** vibration carrying energy through a medium. **wavy** *adj*
wavelength *n* distance between the same points of two successive waves.
waver ❶ *v* **1** hesitate or be irresolute. **2** be or become unsteady. **waverer** *n*.
wax¹ *n* **1** solid shiny fatty or oily substance used for sealing, making candles, etc. **2** similar substance made by bees. **3** waxy secretion of the ear. ▷ *v* **4** coat or polish with wax. **waxen** *adj* made of or like wax. **waxy** *adj* **waxwork** *n* **1** lifelike wax model of a (famous) person. ▷ *pl* **2** place exhibiting these.
wax² ❶ *v* **1** increase in size or strength. **2** (of the moon) get gradually larger.
way ❶ *n* **1** manner or method. **2** characteristic manner. **3** route or direction. **4** track or path. **5** distance. **6** room for movement or activity, e.g. *you're in the way*. **7** passage or journey. **8** *informal* state or condition. **wayfarer** *n* traveller. **waylay** *v* lie in wait for and accost or attack. **wayside** *adj, n* (situated by) the side of a road.
WC water closet.
we *pron* (used as the subject of a verb) **1** the speaker or writer and one or more others. **2** people in general. **3** formal word for 'I'

used by editors and monarchs.
weak ❶ *adj* **1** lacking strength. **2** liable to give way. **3** unconvincing. **4** lacking flavour. **weaken** *v* make or become weak. **weakling** *n* feeble person or animal. **weakly** *adv* **1** feebly. **weakness** *n* **1** being weak. **2** failing. **3** self-indulgent liking.
weal *n* raised mark left on the skin by a blow.
wealth ❶ *n* **1** state of being rich. **2** large amount of money and valuables. **3** great amount or number. **wealthy** *adj*.
wean *v* **1** accustom (a baby or young mammal) to food other than mother's milk. **2** coax (someone) away from former habits.
weapon *n* **1** object used in fighting. **2** anything used to get the better of an opponent. **weaponry** *n* weapons collectively.
wear ❶ *v* **wearing, wore, worn 1** have on the body as clothing or ornament. **2** show as one's expression. **3** (cause to) deteriorate by constant use or action. **4** endure constant use. ▷ *n* **5** clothes suitable for a particular time or purpose, e.g. *beach wear*. **6** damage caused by use. **7** ability to endure constant use. **wearer** *n*
wear off *v* gradually decrease in intensity.
wear on *v* (of time) pass slowly.

THESAURUS

rash, rush, stream, surge, upsurge
waver *v* **1** = **hesitate**, dither, falter, fluctuate, hum and haw, seesaw, vacillate **2** = **tremble**, flicker, quiver, shake, totter, wobble
wax² *v* **1** = **increase**, develop, enlarge, expand, grow, magnify, swell
way *n* **1** = **method**, fashion, manner, means, mode, procedure, process, system, technique **2** = **style**, custom, habit, manner, nature, personality, practice, wont **3** = **route**, channel, course, direction **4** = **track**, path, pathway, road, trail **5** = **distance**, length, stretch **7** = **journey**, approach, march, passage
weak *adj* **1** = **feeble**, debilitated, effete, fragile, frail, infirm, puny, sickly, unsteady **2** = **unsafe**, defenceless, exposed, helpless,

unguarded, unprotected, vulnerable **3** = **unconvincing**, feeble, flimsy, hollow, lame, pathetic, unsatisfactory **4** = **tasteless**, diluted, insipid, runny, thin, watery
wealth *n* **2** = **riches**, affluence, capital, fortune, lolly (*Aust & NZ sl*), money, opulence, prosperity **3** = **plenty**, abundance, copiousness, cornucopia, fullness, profusion, richness
wear *v* **1** = **be dressed in**, don, have on, put on, sport (*inf*) **2** = **show**, display, exhibit **4** = **deteriorate**, abrade, corrode, erode, fray, grind, rub ▷ *n* **5** = **clothes**, apparel, attire, costume, dress, garb, garments, gear (*inf*), things **6** = **damage**, abrasion, attrition, corrosion, deterioration, erosion, wear and tear

W

weary ❶ *adj* **-rier, -riest 1** tired or exhausted. **2** tiring. ▷ *v* **-rying, -ried 3** make or become weary. **wearily** *adv* **weariness** *n* **wearisome** *adj* tedious.

weasel *n* small carnivorous mammal with a long body and short legs.

weather ❶ *n* **1** day-to-day atmospheric conditions of a place. ▷ *v* **2** (cause to) be affected by the weather. **3** come safely through. **under the weather** *informal* slightly ill. **weather-beaten** *adj* worn, damaged, or (of skin) tanned by exposure to the weather. **weathercock**, **weathervane** *n* device that revolves to show the direction of the wind.

weave ❶ *v* **weaving, wove** *or* **weaved**, **woven** *or* **weaved 1** make (fabric) by interlacing (yarn) on a loom. **2** compose (a story). **3** move from side to side while going forwards. **weaver** *n*.

web ❶ *n* **1** net spun by a spider. **2** anything intricate or complex, e.g. *web of deceit*. **3** skin between the toes of a duck, frog, etc. **the Web** short for WORLD WIDE WEB. **webbed** *adj* **webbing** *n* strong fabric woven in strips. **webcam** *n* camera that transmits images over the Internet. **webcast** *n* broadcast of an event over the Internet. **weblog** *n* person's online journal (also **blog**). **website** *n* group of connected pages on the World Wide Web.

wed ❶ *v* **wedding, wedded** *or* **wed 1** marry. **2** unite closely. **wedding** *n* act or ceremony of marriage. **wedlock** *n* marriage.

wedge ❶ *n* **1** piece of material thick at one end and thin at the other. ▷ *v* **2** fasten or split with a wedge. **3** squeeze into a narrow space. **wedge-tailed eagle** large brown Australian eagle with a wedge-shaped tail.

Wednesday *n* fourth day of the week.

wee *adj* small.

weed *n* **1** plant growing where undesired. **2** *informal* thin ineffectual person. ▷ *v* **3** clear of weeds. **weedy** *adj informal* (of a person) thin and weak. **weed out** *v* remove or eliminate (what is unwanted).

week *n* **1** period of seven days, esp. one beginning on a Sunday. **2** hours or days of work in a week. **weekly** *adj, adv* **1** happening, done, etc. once a week. ▷ *n, pl* **-lies 2** newspaper or magazine published once a week. **weekday** *n* any day of the week except Saturday or Sunday. **weekend** *n* Saturday and Sunday.

weep ❶ *v* **weeping, wept 1** shed tears. **2** ooze liquid. **weepy** *adj* liable to cry.

weigh ❶ *v* **1** have a specified weight. **2** measure the weight of. **3** consider carefully. **4** be influential. **5** be

---

THESAURUS

weary *adj* **1** = **tired**, done in (*inf*), drained, drowsy, exhausted, fatigued, flagging, jaded, sleepy, worn out **2** = **tiring**, arduous, laborious, tiresome, wearisome ▷ *v* **3** = **tire**, drain, enervate, fatigue, sap, take it out of (*inf*), tax, tire out, wear out

weather *n* **1** = **climate**, conditions ▷ *v* **3** = **withstand**, brave, come through, endure, overcome, resist, ride out, stand, survive

weave *v* **1** = **knit**, braid, entwine, interlace, intertwine, plait **2** = **create**, build, construct, contrive, fabricate, make up, put together, spin **3** = **zigzag**, crisscross, wind

web *n* **1** = **spider's web**, cobweb

2 = **network**, lattice, tangle

wed *v* **1** = **marry**, get married, take the plunge (*inf*), tie the knot (*inf*) **2** = **unite**, ally, blend, combine, interweave, join, link, merge

wedge *n* **1** = **block**, chunk, lump ▷ *v* **3** = **squeeze**, cram, crowd, force, jam, lodge, pack, ram, stuff, thrust

weep *v* **1** = **cry**, blubber, lament, mourn, shed tears, snivel, sob, whimper

weigh *v* **1** = **have a weight of**, tip the scales at (*inf*) **3** = **consider**, contemplate, deliberate upon, evaluate, examine, meditate upon, ponder, reflect upon, think over **4** = **matter**, carry weight, count

burdensome. **weigh anchor** raise a ship's anchor or (of a ship) have its anchor raised.

weighbridge n machine for weighing vehicles by means of a metal plate set into the road.

weir n river dam.

weird ❶ adj 1 strange or bizarre. 2 unearthly or eerie.

- SPELLING TIP
- The pronunciation of **weird** possibly
- leads people to spell it with the vowels
- the wrong way round. The Bank of
- English shows that *wierd* is a common
- misspelling.

welcome ❶ v **-coming, -comed** 1 greet with pleasure. 2 receive gladly. ▷ n 3 kindly greeting. ▷ adj 4 received gladly. 5 freely permitted.

weld ❶ v 1 join (pieces of metal or plastic) by softening with heat. 2 unite closely. ▷ n 3 welded joint. **welder** n.

welfare ❶ n 1 wellbeing. 2 help given to people in need. **welfare state** system in which the government takes responsibility for the wellbeing of its citizens.

well¹ ❶ adv **better, best** 1 satisfactorily. 2 skilfully. 3 completely. 4 prosperously. 5 suitably. 6 intimately. 7 favourably. 8 considerably. 9 very likely. ▷ adj 10 in

good health. 11 satisfactory. ▷ interj 12 exclamation of surprise, interrogation, etc.

well² ❶ n 1 hole sunk into the earth to reach water, oil, or gas. 2 deep open shaft. ▷ v 3 flow upwards or outwards.

wellies pl n informal wellingtons.

wellingtons pl n high waterproof rubber boots.

welter n jumbled mass.

wench n facetious young woman.

wend v go or travel.

went v past tense of GO.

were v 1 form of the past tense of **be** used after *we, you, they,* or a plural noun. 2 subjunctive of BE.

werewolf n (in folklore) person who can turn into a wolf.

west n 1 (direction towards) the part of the horizon where the sun sets. 2 region lying in this direction. 3 (**W-**) western Europe and the US. ▷ adj 4 to or in the west. 5 (of a wind) from the west. ▷ adv 6 in, to, or towards the west. **westerly** adj **western** adj 1 of or in the west. ▷ n 2 film or story about cowboys in the western US. **westernize** v adapt to the customs and culture of the West. **westward** adj, adv **westwards** adv.

THESAURUS

---

weird adj 1 = **strange**, bizarre, freakish, odd, queer, unnatural 2 = **eerie**, creepy (inf), mysterious, spooky (inf)

welcome v 1 = **greet**, embrace, hail, meet 2 = **receive** ▷ n 3 = **greeting**, acceptance, hospitality, reception, salutation ▷ adj 4 = **acceptable**, agreeable, appreciated, delightful, desirable, gratifying, pleasant, refreshing 5 = **free**, under no obligation

weld v 1 = **solder**, fuse 2 = **unite**, bind, bond, connect, join, link

welfare n 1 = **wellbeing**, advantage, benefit, good, happiness, health, interest, prosperity

well¹ adv 1 = **satisfactorily**, agreeably, nicely, pleasantly, smoothly, splendidly,

successfully 2 = **skilfully**, ably, adeptly, adequately, admirably, correctly, efficiently, expertly, proficiently, properly 3 = **fully**, thoroughly 4 = **prosperously**, comfortably 5 = **suitably**, fairly, fittingly, justly, properly, rightly 6 = **intimately**, deeply, profoundly 7 = **favourably**, approvingly, glowingly, highly, kindly, warmly 8 = **considerably**, abundantly, amply, fully, greatly, heartily, highly, substantially, thoroughly, very much ▷ adj 10 = **healthy**, fit, in fine fettle, sound 11 = **satisfactory**, agreeable, fine, pleasing, proper, right

well² n 1, 2 = **hole**, bore, pit, shaft ▷ v 3 = **flow**, gush, jet, pour, spout, spring, spurt, surge

W

wet ❶ *adj* **wetter**, **wettest** **1** covered or soaked with water or another liquid. **2** not yet dry. **3** rainy. **4** *informal* (of a person) feeble or foolish. ▷ *n* **5** moisture or rain. **6** *informal* feeble or foolish person. ▷ *v* **wetting**, **wet** *or* **wetted** **7** make wet. **wet blanket** *informal* person who has a depressing effect on others. **wetland** *n* area of marshy land. **wet nurse** woman employed to breast-feed another's child. **wet suit** close-fitting rubber suit worn by divers etc.

whack ❶ *v* **1** strike with a resounding blow. ▷ *n* **2** such a blow. **3** *informal* share. **4** *informal* attempt. **whacked** *adj* exhausted. **whacking** *adj informal* huge.

wharf ❶ *n*, *pl* **wharves**, **wharfs** platform at a harbour for loading and unloading ships. **wharfie** *n Aust* person employed to load and unload ships.

what *pron* **1** which thing. **2** that which. **3** request for a statement to be repeated. ▷ *interj* **4** exclamation of anger, surprise, etc. ▷ *adv* **5** in which way, how much, e.g. *what do you care?* **what for?** why? **whatever** *pron* **1** everything or anything that. **2** no matter what. **whatnot** *n informal* similar unspecified things. **whatsoever** *adj* at all.

wheat *n* **1** grain used in making flour,

bread, and pasta. **2** plant producing this. **wheaten** *adj* **wheatmeal** *adj*, *n* (made with) brown, but not wholemeal, flour.

wheedle ❶ *v* coax or cajole.

wheel ❶ *n* **1** disc that revolves on an axle. **2** pivoting movement. ▷ *v* **3** push or pull (something with wheels). **4** turn as if on an axis. **5** turn round suddenly. **wheeling and dealing** use of shrewd and sometimes unscrupulous methods to achieve success. **wheeler-dealer** *n* **wheelbarrow** *n* shallow box for carrying loads, with a wheel at the front and two handles. **wheelbase** *n* distance between a vehicle's front and back axles. **wheelchair** *n* chair mounted on wheels for use by people who cannot walk.

wheeze ❶ *v* **1** breathe with a hoarse whistling noise. ▷ *n* **2** wheezing sound. **3** *informal* trick or plan. **wheezy** *adj*.

whelk *n* edible snail-like shellfish.

when *adv* **1** at what time? ▷ *conj* **2** at the time that. **3** although. **4** considering the fact that. ▷ *pron* **5** at which time. **whenever** *adv*, *conj* at whatever time.

where *adv* **1** in, at, or to what place? ▷ *pron* **2** in, at, or to which place. ▷ *conj* **3** in the place at which. **whereabouts** *n* **1** present position. ▷ *adv* **2** at what place. **whereas** *conj* but on the other hand. **whereby** *pron*

—————————————————— THESAURUS ——————————————————

wet *adj* **1** = **damp**, dank, moist, saturated, soaking, sodden, soggy, sopping, waterlogged, watery **3** = **rainy**, drizzling, pouring, raining, showery, teeming **4** *Inf* = **feeble**, effete, ineffectual, namby-pamby, soft, spineless, timorous, weak, weedy (*inf*) ▷ *n* **5** = **moisture**, condensation, damp, dampness, drizzle, humidity, liquid, rain, water, wetness **6** *Inf* = **weakling**, drip (*inf*), weed (*inf*), wimp (*inf*) ▷ *v* **7** = **moisten**, dampen, douse, irrigate, saturate, soak, spray, water

whack *v* **1** = **strike**, bang, belt (*inf*), clobber (*sl*), hit, smack, swipe, thrash, thump, thwack, wallop (*inf*) ▷ *n* **2** = **blow**, bang, belt (*inf*), hit, smack, stroke, swipe, thump,

thwack, wallop (*inf*) **3** *Inf* = **share**, bit, cut (*inf*), part, portion, quota **4** *Inf* = **attempt**, bash (*inf*), crack (*inf*), go (*inf*), shot (*inf*), stab (*inf*), try, turn

wharf *n* = **dock**, jetty, landing stage, pier, quay

wheedle *v* = **coax**, cajole, entice, inveigle, persuade

wheel *n* **3** = **circle**, gyration, pivot, revolution, rotation, spin, turn ▷ *v* **4**, **5** = **turn**, gyrate, pirouette, revolve, rotate, spin, swing, swivel, twirl, whirl

wheeze *v* **1** = **gasp**, cough, hiss, rasp, whistle ▷ *n* **2** = **gasp**, cough, hiss, rasp, whistle **3** *Inf* = **trick**, idea, plan, ploy, ruse, scheme, stunt

W

by which. **wherefore** *obs* ▷ *adv* **1** why.
▷ *conj* **2** consequently. **whereupon** *conj*
at which point. **wherever** *conj*, *adv* at
whatever place. **wherewithal** *n* necessary
funds, resources, etc.

whet 🔊 *v* **whetting, whetted** sharpen (a
tool). **whet someone's appetite** increase
someone's desire. **whetstone** *n* stone for
sharpening tools.

whether *conj* used to introduce an indirect
question or a clause expressing doubt or
choice.

whey [**way**] *n* watery liquid that separates
from the curd when milk is clotted.

which *adj*, *pron* **1** used to request or refer
to a choice from different possibilities.
▷ *pron* **2** used to refer to a thing already
mentioned. **whichever** *adj*, *pron* **1** any out
of several. **2** no matter which.

whiff 🔊 *n* **1** puff of air or odour. **2** trace or
hint.

while *conj* **1** at the same time that.
2 whereas. ▷ *n* **3** period of time. **whilst**
conj while. **while away** *v* pass (time) idly
but pleasantly.

whim 🔊 *n* sudden fancy. **whimsy** *n*
1 capricious idea. **2** light or fanciful humour.
whimsical *adj* unusual, playful, and fanciful.

whimper 🔊 *v* **1** cry in a soft whining way.
▷ *n* **2** soft plaintive whine.

whine 🔊 *n* **1** high-pitched plaintive cry.

2 peevish complaint. ▷ *v* **3** make such a
sound. **whining** *n*, *adj*.

whinge 🔊 *informal* ▷ *v* **1** complain. ▷ *n*
2 complaint.

whinny *v* **-nying, -nied 1** neigh softly. ▷ *n*,
pl **-nies 2** soft neigh.

whip 🔊 *n* **1** cord attached to a handle,
used for beating animals or people.
2 politician responsible for organizing
and disciplining fellow party members.
3 call made on members of Parliament
to attend for important votes. **4** dessert
made from beaten cream or egg whites.
▷ *v* **whipping, whipped 5** strike with
a whip, strap, or cane. **6** *informal* pull,
remove, or move quickly. **7** beat (esp.
eggs or cream) to a froth. **8** rouse into
a particular condition. **9** *informal* steal.
whip bird *Aust* bird with a whistle ending
in a whipcrack note. **whiplash injury** neck
injury caused by a sudden jerk to the head,
as in a car crash. **whip-round** *n informal*
collection of money.

whippet *n* racing dog like a small greyhound.

whirl 🔊 *v* **1** spin or revolve. **2** be dizzy or
confused. ▷ *n* **3** whirling movement.
4 bustling activity. **5** confusion or
giddiness. **whirlpool** *n* strong circular
current of water. **whirlwind** *n* **1** column of
air whirling violently upwards in a spiral.
▷ *adj* **2** much quicker than normal.

———— THESAURUS ————

whet *v* **1** = **sharpen**, hone **whet someone's
appetite** = **stimulate**, arouse, awaken,
enhance, excite, kindle, quicken, rouse, stir

whiff *n* **1** = **smell**, aroma, hint, odour, scent,
sniff

whim *n* = **impulse**, caprice, fancy, notion,
urge

whimper *v* **1** = **cry**, moan, snivel, sob,
weep, whine, whinge (*inf*) ▷ *n* **2** = **sob**,
moan, snivel, whine

whine *n* **1** = **cry**, moan, sob, wail, whimper
2 = **complaint**, gripe (*inf*), grouch (*inf*),
grouse, grumble, moan, whinge (*inf*) ▷ *v*
3 = **cry**, moan, sniffle, snivel, sob, wail,
whimper

whinge *Inf v* **1** = **complain**, bleat, carp,
gripe (*inf*), grouse, grumble, moan ▷ *n*
2 = **complaint**, gripe (*inf*), grouch, grouse,
grumble, moan, whine

whip *n* **1** = **lash**, birch, cane, cat-o'-nine-
tails, crop, scourge ▷ *v* **5** = **lash**, beat,
birch, cane, flagellate, flog, scourge,
spank, strap, thrash **6** *Inf* = **dash**, dart,
dive, fly, rush, shoot, tear, whisk **7** = **whisk**,
beat **8** = **incite**, agitate, drive, foment,
goad, spur, stir, work up

whirl *v* **1** = **spin**, pirouette, revolve, roll,
rotate, swirl, turn, twirl, twist **2** = **feel
dizzy**, reel, spin ▷ *n* **3** = **revolution**,
pirouette, roll, rotation, spin, swirl, turn,

w

whirr, whir *n* **1** prolonged soft buzz. ▷ *v* **whirring, whirred 2** (cause to) make a whirr.

whisk ❶ *v* **1** move or remove quickly. **2** beat (esp. eggs or cream) to a froth. ▷ *n* **3** egg-beating utensil.

whisker *n* **1** any of the long stiff hairs on the face of a cat or other mammal. ▷ *pl* **2** hair growing on a man's face. **by a whisker** *informal* only just.

whisky *n, pl* **-kies** spirit distilled from fermented cereals. **whiskey** *n, pl* **-keys** Irish or American whisky.

whisper ❶ *v* **1** speak softly, without vibration of the vocal cords. **2** rustle. ▷ *n* **3** soft voice. **4** *informal* rumour. **5** rustling sound.

whist *n* card game in which one pair of players tries to win more tricks than another pair.

whistle *v* **1** produce a shrill sound, esp. by forcing the breath through pursed lips. **2** signal by a whistle. ▷ *n* **3** whistling sound. **4** instrument blown to make a whistling sound. **blow the whistle on** *informal* inform on or put a stop to.

white ❶ *adj* **1** of the colour of snow. **2** pale. **3** light in colour. **4** (of coffee) served with milk. ▷ *n* **5** colour of snow. **6** clear fluid round the yolk of an egg. **7** white part, esp. of the eyeball. **8** (W-) member of the race of people with light-coloured skin. **whiten** *v* make or become white or whiter. **whitish** *adj* **white ant** same as TERMITE. **white-collar** *adj* denoting professional and clerical

workers. **white elephant** useless or unwanted possession.

white flag signal of surrender or truce.

white goods large household appliances such as cookers and fridges.

white-hot *adj* very hot. **white lie** minor unimportant lie.

whither *adv obs* to what place.

whittle ❶ *v* cut or carve (wood) with a knife. **whittle down, away** *v* reduce or wear away gradually.

whizz, whiz *v* **whizzing, whizzed 1** make a loud buzzing sound. **2** *informal* move quickly. ▷ *n, pl* **whizzes 3** loud buzzing sound. **4** *informal* person skilful at something. **whizz kid, whiz kid** *informal* person who is outstandingly able for his or her age.

who *pron* **1** which person. **2** used to refer to a person or people already mentioned. **whoever** *pron* **1** any person who. **2** no matter who.

whodunnit, whodunit [hoo-**dun**-nit] *n* *informal* detective story, play, or film.

whole ❶ *adj* **1** containing all the elements or parts. **2** uninjured or undamaged. ▷ *n* **3** complete thing or system. **on the whole** taking everything into consideration. **wholly** *adv* **wholefood** *n* food that has been processed as little as possible. **wholehearted** *adj* sincere or enthusiastic. **wholemeal** *adj* **1** (of flour) made from the whole wheat grain. **2** made from wholemeal flour. **whole number** number that does not contain a fraction.

whom *pron* objective form of WHO.

──────────────────────────────── THESAURUS ──────────────

twirl, twist **4** = **bustle**, flurry, merry-go-round, round, series, succession **5** = **confusion**, daze, dither, giddiness, spin

whisk *v* **1** = **flick**, brush, sweep, whip **2** = **beat**, fluff up, whip ▷ *n* **3** = **beater**

whisper *v* **1** = **murmur**, breathe **2** = **rustle**, hiss, sigh, swish ▷ *n* **3** = **murmur**, undertone **4** *Inf* = **rumour**, gossip, innuendo, insinuation, report **5** = **rustle**, hiss, sigh, swish

white *adj* **2** = **pale**, ashen, pallid, pasty, wan

whittle *v* = **carve**, cut, hew, pare, shape, shave, trim

whole *adj* **1** = **complete**, entire, full, total, unabridged, uncut, undivided **2** = **undamaged**, in one piece, intact, unbroken, unharmed, unscathed, untouched ▷ *n* **3** = **totality**, ensemble, entirety **on the whole** = **all in all**, all things considered, by and large

w

whoop v, n shout or cry to express excitement.

whooping cough n infectious disease marked by convulsive coughing and noisy breathing.

whopper ⓘ n informal **1** anything unusually large. **2** huge lie. **whopping** adj.

whore ⓘ [hore] n prostitute.

whose pron of whom or of which.

why adv **1** for what reason. ▷ pron **2** because of which.

wick n cord through a lamp or candle which carries fuel to the flame.

wicked ⓘ adj **1** morally bad. **2** mischievous. **wickedness** n.

wicker adj made of woven cane. **wickerwork** n.

wicket n **1** set of three cricket stumps and two bails. **2** ground between the two wickets on a cricket pitch.

wide ⓘ adj **1** large from side to side. **2** having a specified width. **3** spacious or extensive. **4** far from the target. **5** opened fully. ▷ adv **6** to the full extent. **7** over an extensive area. **8** far from the target.

widely adv **widen** v make or become wider.

widespread adj affecting a wide area or a large number of people.

widow n woman whose husband is dead and who has not remarried. **widowed** adj **widowhood** n **widower** n man whose wife is dead and who has not remarried.

wield ⓘ v **1** hold and use (a weapon). **2** have and use (power).

wife ⓘ n, pl **wives** woman to whom a man is married.

Wi-Fi n system of wireless access to the internet.

wig n artificial head of hair.

wiggle ⓘ v **1** move jerkily from side to side. ▷ n **2** wiggling movement.

wild ⓘ adj **1** (of animals) not tamed or domesticated. **2** (of plants) not cultivated. **3** not civilized. **4** lacking restraint or control. **5** violent or stormy. **6** informal excited. **7** informal furious. **8** random. **wilds** pl n desolate or uninhabited place. **wild-goose chase** search that has little chance of success.

wildebeest n gnu.

——————— THESAURUS ———————

whopper n Inf **1** = **giant**, colossus, crackerjack (inf), jumbo (inf), leviathan, mammoth, monster **2** = **big lie**, fabrication, falsehood, tall story (inf), untruth

whore n = **prostitute**, call girl, streetwalker, tart (inf)

wicked adj **1** = **bad**, corrupt, depraved, devilish, evil, fiendish, immoral, sinful, vicious, villainous **2** = **mischievous**, impish, incorrigible, naughty, rascally, roguish

wide adj **1** = **broad**, expansive, extensive, far-reaching, immense, large, overarching, sweeping, vast **3** = **spacious**, baggy, capacious, commodious, full, loose, roomy **4** = **distant**, off course, off target, remote **5** = **expanded**, dilated, distended, outspread, outstretched ▷ adv **6** = **fully**, completely **8** = **off target**, astray, off course, off the mark, out

wield v **1** = **brandish**, employ, flourish, handle, manage, manipulate, ply, swing, use **2** = **exert**, exercise, have, maintain, possess

wife n = **spouse**, better half (hum), bride, mate, partner

wiggle v, n **1**, **2** = **jerk**, jiggle, shake, shimmy, squirm, twitch, wag, waggle, writhe

wild adj **1** = **untamed**, feral, ferocious, fierce, savage, unbroken, undomesticated **2** = **uncultivated**, natural **3** = **uncivilized**, barbaric, barbarous, brutish, ferocious, fierce, primitive, savage **4** = **uncontrolled**, disorderly, riotous, rowdy, turbulent, undisciplined, unmanageable, unrestrained, unruly, wayward **5** = **stormy**, blustery, choppy, raging, rough, tempestuous, violent **6** Inf = **excited**, crazy (inf), enthusiastic, hysterical, raving ▷ pl n **wilds**

w

wilderness ❶ *n* uninhabited uncultivated region.

wildfire *n* **spread like wildfire** spread quickly and uncontrollably.

wilful ❶ *adj* **1** headstrong or obstinate. **2** intentional. **wilfully** *adv*.

will¹ *v, past* **would** used as an auxiliary to form the future tense or to indicate intention, ability, or expectation.

will² ❶ *n* **1** strong determination. **2** desire or wish. **3** directions written for disposal of one's property after death. ▷ *v* **4** use one's will in an attempt to do (something). **5** wish or desire. **6** leave (property) by a will. **willing** *adj* **1** ready or inclined (to do something). **2** keen and obliging. **willingly** *adv* **willingness** *n* **willpower** *n* ability to control oneself and one's actions.

will-o'-the-wisp *n* **1** elusive person or thing. **2** pale light sometimes seen over marshes at night.

willow *n* **1** tree with thin flexible branches. **2** its wood, used for making cricket bats. **willowy** *adj* slender and graceful.

willy-nilly *adv* whether desired or not.

wilt ❶ *v* (cause to) become limp or lose strength.

wimp ❶ *n informal* feeble ineffectual person.

wimple *n* garment framing the face, worn by medieval women and now by nuns.

win ❶ *v* **winning, won** **1** come first in (a competition, fight, etc.). **2** gain (a prize) in a competition. **3** get by effort. ▷ *n* **4** victory, esp. in a game. **winner** *n* **winning** *adj* **1** gaining victory. **2** charming. **winnings** *pl n* sum won, esp. in gambling. **win over** *v* gain the support or consent of (someone).

wince ❶ *v* **1** draw back, as if in pain. ▷ *n* **2** wincing.

winch *n* **1** machine for lifting or hauling using a cable wound round a drum. ▷ *v* **2** lift or haul using a winch.

wind¹ ❶ *n* **1** current of air. **2** hint or suggestion. **3** breath. **4** flatulence. **5** idle talk. ▷ *v* **6** render short of breath. **windy** *adj* **windward** *adj, n* (of or in) the direction from which the wind is blowing. **windfall** *n* **1** unexpected good luck. **2** fallen fruit. **wind farm** collection of wind-driven turbines for generating electricity. **wind instrument** musical instrument played by blowing. **windmill** *n* machine for grinding or pumping driven by sails turned by the wind. **windpipe** *n* tube linking the throat and the lungs. **windscreen** *n* front

──────────────── THESAURUS ────────────────

= **wilderness**, back of beyond (*inf*), desert, middle of nowhere (*inf*), wasteland

wilderness *n* = **desert**, jungle, wasteland, wilds

wilful *adj* **1** = **obstinate**, determined, headstrong, inflexible, intransigent, obdurate, perverse, pig-headed, stubborn, uncompromising **2** = **intentional**, conscious, deliberate, intended, purposeful, voluntary

will² *n* **1** = **determination**, purpose, resolution, resolve, willpower **2** = **wish**, desire, fancy, inclination, mind, preference, volition **3** = **testament**, last wishes ▷ *v* **5** = **wish**, desire, prefer, see fit, want **6** = **bequeath**, confer, give, leave, pass on, transfer

wilt *v* **a** = **droop**, sag, shrivel, wither

b = **weaken**, fade, flag, languish, wane

wimp *n Inf* = **weakling**, coward, drip (*inf*), mouse, sissy, softy *or* softie

win *v* **1** = **triumph**, come first, conquer, overcome, prevail, succeed, sweep the board **3** = **gain**, achieve, acquire, attain, earn, get, land, obtain, procure, secure ▷ *n* **4** = **victory**, conquest, success, triumph

wince *v* **1** = **flinch**, blench, cower, cringe, draw back, quail, recoil, shrink, start ▷ *n* **2** = **flinch**, cringe, start

wind¹ *n* **1** = **air**, blast, breeze, draught, gust, zephyr **2** = **hint**, inkling, notice, report, rumour, suggestion, warning, whisper **3** = **breath**, puff, respiration **4** = **flatulence**, gas **5** = **talk**, babble, bluster, boasting, hot air

w

window of a motor vehicle. **windscreen wiper** device that wipes rain etc. from a windscreen. **windsock** n cloth cone on a mast at an airfield to indicate wind direction. **windsurfing** n sport of riding on water using a surfboard propelled and steered by a sail.

wind² ❶ v **winding, wound 1** coil or wrap around. **2** tighten the spring of (a clock or watch). **3** move in a twisting course. **wind up** v **1** bring to or reach an end. **2** tighten the spring of (a clock or watch). **3** informal make tense or agitated. **4** slang tease.

window n **1** opening in a wall to let in light or air. **2** glass pane or panes fitted in such an opening. **3** display area behind the window of a shop. **4** area on a computer screen that can be manipulated separately from the rest of the display area. **5** period of unbooked time in a diary or schedule. **window-dressing** n **1** arrangement of goods in a shop window. **2** attempt to make something more attractive than it really is. **window-shopping** n looking at goods in shop windows without intending to buy.

windshield n the US and Canadian name for WINDSCREEN.

wine n **1** alcoholic drink made from fermented grapes. **2** similar drink made from other fruits. **wine and dine** entertain or be entertained with fine food and drink.

wing ❶ n **1** one of the limbs or organs of a bird, insect, or bat that are used for flying. **2** one of the winglike supporting parts of an aircraft. **3** projecting side part of a building. **4** faction of a political party. **5** part of a car body surrounding the wheels. **6** Sport (player on) either side of the pitch. ▷ pl **7** sides of a stage. ▷ v **8** fly. **9** wound slightly in the wing or arm. **winged** adj **winger** n Sport player positioned on a wing.

wink ❶ v **1** close and open (an eye) quickly as a signal. **2** twinkle. ▷ n **3** winking. **4** smallest amount of sleep.

winkle n shellfish with a spiral shell. **winkle out** v informal extract or prise out.

winsome adj charming or winning.

winter n **1** coldest season. ▷ v **2** spend the winter. **wintry** adj **1** of or like winter. **2** cold or unfriendly. **winter sports** open-air sports held on snow or ice.

wipe ❶ v **1** clean or dry by rubbing. **2** erase (a tape). ▷ n **3** wiping. **wipe out** v destroy completely.

wire n **1** thin flexible strand of metal. **2** length of this used to carry electric current. **3** obs telegram. ▷ v **4** equip with wires. **wiring** n system of wires. **wiry** adj **1** lean and tough. **2** like wire. **wire-haired** adj (of a dog) having a stiff wiry coat.

wise ❶ adj having intelligence and knowledge. **wisely** adv **wiseacre** n person who wishes to seem wise.

wish ❶ v **1** want or desire. **2** feel or express a hope about someone's wellbeing, success, etc. ▷ n **3** expression of a desire. **4** thing desired. **wishful** adj too optimistic. **wishbone** n V-shaped bone above the breastbone of a fowl.

wishy-washy adj informal insipid or bland.

wisp n **1** light delicate streak. **2** twisted bundle or tuft. **wispy** adj.

———————————— THESAURUS ————————————

wind² v **1** = **coil**, curl, encircle, loop, reel, roll, spiral, twist **3** = **meander**, bend, curve, ramble, snake, turn, twist, zigzag

wing n **4** = **faction**, arm, branch, group, section ▷ v **8** = **fly**, glide, soar **9** = **wound**, clip, hit

wink v **1** = **blink**, bat, flutter **2** = **twinkle**, flash, gleam, glimmer, sparkle ▷ n **3** = **blink**, flutter

wipe v **1** = **clean**, brush, mop, rub, sponge, swab **2** = **erase**, remove ▷ n **3** = **rub**, brush

wise adj = **sensible**, clever, discerning, enlightened, erudite, intelligent, judicious, perceptive, prudent, sage

wish v **1** = **want**, aspire, crave, desire, hanker, hope, long, yearn ▷ n **3** = **desire**, aspiration, hope, intention, urge, want, whim, will

W

wistful ⊕ *adj* sadly longing. **wistfully** *adv*.

wit ⊕ *n* 1 ability to use words or ideas in a clever and amusing way. 2 person with this ability. 3 (sometimes pl) practical intelligence. **witless** *adj* foolish.

witch ⊕ *n* 1 person, usu. female, who practises (black) magic. 2 ugly or wicked woman. **witchcraft** *n* use of magic. **witch doctor** (in certain societies) a man appearing to cure or cause injury or disease by magic. **witch-hunt** *n* campaign against people with unpopular views.

with *prep* indicating presence alongside, possession, means of performance, characteristic manner, etc. e.g. *walking with his dog; a man with two cars; hit with a hammer; playing with skill*. **within** *prep, adv* in or inside. **without** *prep* not accompanied by, using, or having.

withdraw ⊕ *v* **-drawing, -drew, -drawn** take or move out or away. **withdrawal** *n* **withdrawn** *adj* unsociable.

wither ⊕ *v* wilt or dry up. **withering** *adj* (of a look or remark) scornful.

withhold ⊕ *v* **-holding, -held** refrain from giving.

withstand ⊕ *v* **-standing, -stood** oppose or resist successfully.

witness ⊕ *n* 1 person who has seen something happen. 2 person giving evidence in court. 3 evidence or testimony. ▷ *v* 4 see at first hand. 5 sign (a document) to certify that it is genuine.

wizard ⊕ *n* 1 magician. 2 person with outstanding skill in a particular field. **wizardry** *n*.

wizened ⊕ [wiz-zend] *adj* shrivelled or wrinkled.

WMD weapon(s) of mass destruction.

wobble ⊕ *v* 1 move unsteadily. 2 shake. ▷ *n* 3 wobbling movement or sound. **wobbly** *adj*.

woe ⊕ *n* grief. **woeful** *adj* 1 extremely sad. 2 pitiful. **woefully** *adv* **woebegone** *adj* looking miserable.

wok *n* bowl-shaped Chinese cooking pan, used for stir-frying.

wolf *n, pl* **wolves** 1 wild predatory canine mammal. ▷ *v* 2 eat ravenously. **cry wolf** raise a false alarm. **wolf whistle** whistle by a man indicating that he thinks a woman is attractive.

wolverine *n* carnivorous mammal of Arctic regions.

——————————————————————————— THESAURUS ———————————————————————————

wistful *adj* = **melancholy**, contemplative, dreamy, longing, meditative, pensive, reflective, thoughtful

wit¹ *n* 1 = **humour**, badinage, banter, drollery, jocularity, raillery, repartee, wordplay 2 = **humorist**, card (*inf*), comedian, joker, wag 3 (sometimes *pl*) = **cleverness**, acumen, brains, common sense, ingenuity, intellect, sense, wisdom

witch *n* 1 = **enchantress**, magician, sorceress 2 = **crone**, hag

withdraw *v* = **remove**, draw back, extract, pull out, take away, take off

wither *v* = **wilt**, decline, perish, shrivel

withhold *v* = **keep back**, conceal, hide, hold back, refuse, reserve, retain, suppress

withstand *v* = **resist**, bear, cope with, endure, hold off, oppose, stand up to, suffer, tolerate

witness *n* 1 = **observer**, beholder, bystander, eyewitness, looker-on, onlooker, spectator, viewer, watcher 2 = **testifier**, corroborator ▷ *v* 4 = **see**, note, notice, observe, perceive, view, watch 5 = **sign**, countersign, endorse

wizard *n* 1 = **magician**, conjuror, magus, necromancer, occultist, shaman, sorcerer, warlock, witch

wizened *adj* = **wrinkled**, dried up, gnarled, lined, shrivelled, shrunken, withered

wobble *v* 1 = **sway**, rock, teeter, totter 2 = **shake**, tremble ▷ *n* 3 = **unsteadiness**, shake, tremble, tremor

woe *n* = **grief**, agony, anguish, distress, gloom, misery, sadness, sorrow, unhappiness, wretchedness

woman ① *n, pl* **women** 1 adult human female. 2 women collectively. **womanhood** *n* **womanish** *adj* effeminate. **womanly** *adj* having qualities traditionally associated with a woman. **womanizing** *n* practice of indulging in casual affairs with women. **womanizer** *n*.

womb *n* hollow organ in female mammals where babies are conceived and develop.

wombat *n* small heavily-built burrowing Australian marsupial.

won *v* past of WIN.

wonder ① *v* 1 be curious about. 2 be amazed. ▷ *n* 3 wonderful thing. 4 emotion caused by an amazing or unusual thing. ▷ *adj* 5 spectacularly successful, e.g. *a wonder drug.* **wonderful** *adj* 1 very fine. 2 remarkable. **wonderfully** *adv* **wonderment** *n* **wondrous** *adj* old-fashioned wonderful.

wont [rhymes with **don't**] *adj* 1 accustomed. ▷ *n* 2 custom.

woo ① *v* 1 try to persuade. 2 old-fashioned try to gain the love of.

wood ① *n* 1 substance trees are made of, used in carpentry and as fuel. 2 area where trees grow. 3 long-shafted golf club, usu. with wooden head. **wooded** *adj* covered with trees. **wooden** *adj* 1 made of wood. 2 without expression. **woody** *adj* **woodbine** *n* honeysuckle. **woodcock** *n*

game bird. **woodcut** *n* (print made from) an engraved block of wood. **woodland** *n* forest. **woodlouse** *n* small insect-like creature with many legs. **woodpecker** *n* bird which searches tree trunks for insects. **woodwind** *adj, n* (of) a type of wind instrument made of wood. **woodworm** *n* insect larva that bores into wood.

woof *n* barking noise made by a dog. **woofer** *n* loudspeaker reproducing low-frequency sounds.

wool ① *n* 1 soft hair of sheep, goats, etc. 2 yarn spun from this. **woollen** *adj* **woolly** *adj* 1 of or like wool. 2 vague or muddled. ▷ *n* 3 knitted woollen garment. **woolgathering** *n* daydreaming.

wop-wops *pl n* NZ informal remote rural areas.

word ① *n* 1 smallest single meaningful unit of speech or writing. 2 chat or discussion. 3 brief remark. 4 message. 5 promise. 6 command. ▷ *v* 7 express in words. **wordy** *adj* using too many words. **wording** *n* choice and arrangement of words. **word processor** keyboard, microprocessor, and VDU for electronic organization and storage of text. **word processing**.

wore *v* past tense of WEAR.

work ① *n* 1 physical or mental effort directed to making or doing something. 2 paid employment. 3 duty or task.

woman *n* 1 = **lady**, female, girl
wonder *v* 1 = **think**, conjecture, meditate, ponder, puzzle, query, question, speculate 2 = **be amazed**, be astonished, gape, marvel, stare ▷ *n* 3 = **phenomenon**, curiosity, marvel, miracle, prodigy, rarity, sight, spectacle 4 = **amazement**, admiration, astonishment, awe, bewilderment, fascination, surprise, wonderment
woo *v* 1 = **court**, cultivate, pursue
wood *n* 1 = **timber**, planks 2 = **woodland**, coppice, copse, forest, grove, thicket
wool *n* 1 = **fleece**, hair 2 = **yarn**
word *n* 1 = **term**, expression, name

2 = **chat**, confab (*inf*), consultation, discussion, talk, tête-à-tête 3 = **remark**, comment, utterance 4 = **message**, communiqué, dispatch, information, intelligence, news, notice, report 5 = **promise**, assurance, guarantee, oath, pledge, vow 6 = **command**, bidding, decree, mandate, order ▷ *v* 7 = **express**, couch, phrase, put, say, state, utter
work *n* 1 = **effort**, drudgery, elbow grease (*facetious*), exertion, industry, labour, sweat, toil 2 = **employment**, business, duty, job, livelihood, occupation, profession, trade 3 = **task**, assignment, chore, commission, duty, job, stint, undertaking 4 = **creation**,

W

4 something made or done. ▷ *pl*
5 factory. **6** total of a writer's or artist's
achievements. **7** *informal* full treatment.
8 mechanism of a machine. ▷ *adj* **9** of or
for work. ▷ *v* **10** (cause to) do work. **11** be
employed. **12** (cause to) operate. **13** (of
a plan etc.) be successful. **14** cultivate
(land). **15** manipulate, shape, or process.
16 (cause to) reach a specified condition.
work-to-rule *n* protest in which workers
keep strictly to all regulations to reduce
the rate of work. **workable** *adj* **worker**
n **workaholic** *n* person obsessed with
work. **workhorse** *n* person or thing
that does a lot of dull or routine work.
workhouse *n Hist* institution where the
poor were given food and lodgings in
return for work. **working class** social class
consisting of wage earners, esp. manual
workers. **working-class** *adj* **working
party** committee investigating a specific
problem. **workman** *n* manual worker.
workmanship *n* skill with which an object
is made. **workshop** *n* **1** room or building
for a manufacturing process. **worktop**
n surface in a kitchen, used for food
preparation.
world **①** *n* **1** the planet earth. **2** mankind.
3 society of a particular area or period.
4 sphere of existence. ▷ *adj* **5** of the
whole world. **worldly** *adj* **1** not spiritual.
2 concerned with material things. **3** wise in
the ways of the world. **world-weary** *adj* no

longer finding pleasure in life. **World Wide
Web** global network of linked computer
files.
worm *n* **1** small limbless invertebrate
animal. **2** *informal* wretched or spineless
person. **3** shaft with a spiral thread
forming part of a gear system. ▷ *n*
4 *Computers* type of virus. ▷ *pl* **5** illness
caused by parasitic worms in the
intestines. ▷ *v* **6** rid of worms. **worm
one's way** **1** crawl. **2** insinuate (oneself).
wormy *adj* **wormcast** *n* coil of earth
excreted by a burrowing worm. **worm-
eaten** *adj* eaten into by worms. **worm out**
v extract (information) craftily.
worn **①** *v* past participle of WEAR.
worry **①** *v* **-rying, -ried** **1** (cause to) be
anxious or uneasy. **2** annoy or bother.
3 (of a dog) chase and try to bite (sheep
etc.). ▷ *n, pl* **-ries** **4** (cause of) anxiety or
concern. **worried** *adj* **worrying** *adj, n*.
worse *adj, adv* comparative of BAD or BADLY.
worst *adj, adv* **1** superlative of BAD or
BADLY. ▷ *n* **2** worst thing. **worsen** *v* make
or grow worse.
worship **①** *v* **-shipping, -shipped**
1 show religious devotion to. **2** love
and admire. ▷ *n* **3** act or instance of
worshipping. **4** (W-) title for a mayor or
magistrate. **worshipper** *n* **worshipful** *adj*
worshipping.
worsted [**wooss**-tid] *n* type of woollen
yarn or fabric.

━━━━━━━━━━━━━━━━━━━━━━━━━━ THESAURUS ━━━

achievement, composition, handiwork,
opus, piece, production ▷ *v* **10** = **labour**,
drudge, exert oneself, peg away, slave,
slog (away), sweat, toil **11** = **be employed**,
be in work **12** = **operate**, control, drive,
handle, manage, manipulate, move,
run, use **14** = **cultivate**, dig, farm, till
15 = **manipulate**, fashion, form, knead,
mould, shape
world *n* **1** = **earth**, globe **2** = **mankind**,
everybody, everyone, humanity,
humankind, man, the public **4** = **sphere**,
area, domain, environment, field, realm

worry *v* **1** = **be anxious**, agonize, brood,
fret, obsess **2** = **trouble**, annoy, bother,
disturb, perturb, pester, unsettle,
upset, vex ▷ *n* **4 a** = **problem**, bother,
care, hassle (*inf*), trouble **b** = **anxiety**,
apprehension, concern, fear, misgiving,
trepidation, trouble, unease
worship *v* **1** = **praise**, adore, exalt,
glorify, honour, pray to, revere, venerate
2 = **love**, adore, idolize, put on a pedestal
▷ *n* **3** = **praise**, adoration, adulation,
devotion, glory, honour, regard, respect,
reverence

worth ⊙ *prep* 1 having a value of.
2 meriting or justifying. ▷ *n* 3 value or
price. 4 excellence. 5 amount to be had
for a given sum. **worthless** *adj* **worthy**
adj 1 deserving admiration or respect. ▷ *n*
2 *informal* notable person. **worthily** *adv*
worthiness *n* **worthwhile** *adj* worth the
time or effort involved.

would *v* used as an auxiliary to express a
request, describe a habitual past action,
or form the past tense or subjunctive
mood of WILL¹. **would-be** *adj* wishing or
pretending to be.

wound¹ ⊙ *n* 1 injury caused by violence.
2 injury to the feelings. ▷ *v* 3 inflict a
wound on.

wound² *v* past of WIND².

wove *v* a past tense of WEAVE. **woven** *v* a
past participle of WEAVE.

wow *interj* 1 exclamation of astonishment.
▷ *n* 2 *informal* astonishing person or thing.

wowser *n Aust & NZ slang* 1 puritanical
person. 2 teetotaller.

wraith *n* ghost.

wrangle ⊙ *v* 1 argue noisily. ▷ *n* 2 noisy
argument.

wrap ⊙ *v* **wrapping, wrapped** 1 fold
(something) round (a person or thing)
so as to cover. ▷ *n* 2 garment wrapped
round the shoulders. 3 sandwich made by
wrapping a filling in a tortilla. **wrapper** *n*
cover for a product. **wrapping** *n* material
used to wrap. **wrap up** *v* 1 fold paper
round. 2 put warm clothes on. 3 *informal*
finish or settle (a matter).

wrath ⊙ [roth] *n* intense anger. **wrathful**
adj.

wreak *v* **wreak havoc** cause chaos. **wreak
vengeance on** take revenge on.

wreath ⊙ *n* twisted ring or band of flowers
or leaves used as a memorial or tribute.
wreathed *adj* surrounded or encircled.

wreck ⊙ *v* 1 destroy. ▷ *n* 2 remains of
something that has been destroyed or
badly damaged, esp. a ship. 3 person in
very poor condition. **wrecker** *n* **wreckage**
n wrecked remains.

wren *n* 1 small brown songbird.
2 Australian warbler.

wrench ⊙ *v* 1 twist or pull violently.
2 sprain (a joint). ▷ *n* 3 violent twist or
pull. 4 sprain. 5 difficult or painful parting.
6 adjustable spanner.

wrest ⊙ *v* 1 twist violently. 2 take by force.

wrestle ⊙ *v* 1 fight, esp. as a sport, by
grappling with and trying to throw down

---

worth *n* 3 = **value**, cost, price, rate,
valuation 4 = **importance**, excellence,
goodness, merit, quality, usefulness, value,
worthiness

wound¹ *n* 1 = **injury**, cut, gash, hurt,
laceration, lesion, trauma (*Path*)
2 = **insult**, offence, slight ▷ *v* 3 a = **injure**,
cut, gash, hurt, lacerate, pierce, wing
b = **offend**, annoy, cut (someone) to the
quick, hurt, mortify, sting

wrangle *v* 1 = **argue**, bicker, contend,
disagree, dispute, fight, quarrel, row,
squabble ▷ *n* 2 = **argument**, altercation,
bickering, dispute, quarrel, row,
squabble, tiff

wrap *v* 1 = **cover**, bind, bundle up, encase,
enclose, enfold, pack, package, shroud,
swathe ▷ *n* 2 = **cloak**, cape, mantle,
shawl, stole

wrath *n* = **anger**, displeasure, fury,
indignation, ire, rage, resentment, temper

wreath *n* = **garland**, band, chaplet, crown,
festoon, ring

wreck *v* 1 = **destroy**, break, demolish,
devastate, ruin, shatter, smash, spoil ▷ *n*
2 = **shipwreck**, hulk

wrench *v* 1 = **twist**, force, jerk, pull, rip,
tear, tug, yank 2 = **sprain**, rick, strain
▷ *n* 3 = **twist**, jerk, pull, rip, tug, yank
4 = **sprain**, strain, twist 5 = **blow**, pang,
shock, upheaval 6 = **spanner**, adjustable
spanner

wrest *v* 2 = **seize**, extract, force, take, win,
wrench

wrestle *v* 1, 2 = **fight**, battle, combat,
grapple, scuffle, struggle, tussle

W

an opponent. **2** struggle hard with. **wrestler** *n* **wrestling** *n*.

wretch ❶ *n* **1** despicable person. **2** pitiful person. **wretched** [**retch**-id] *adj* **1** miserable or unhappy. **2** worthless.

wriggle ❶ *v* **1** move with a twisting action. **2** manoeuvre oneself by devious means. ▷ *n* **3** wriggling movement.

wring ❶ *v* **wringing, wrung 1** twist, esp. to squeeze liquid out of. **2** clasp and twist (the hands). **3** obtain by forceful means.

wrinkle ❶ *n* **1** slight crease, esp. one in the skin due to age. ▷ *v* **2** make or become slightly creased. **wrinkly** *adj*.

wrist *n* joint between the hand and the arm. **wristwatch** *n* watch worn on the wrist.

writ ❶ *n* written legal command.

write ❶ *v* **writing, wrote, written 1** mark paper etc. with symbols or words. **2** set down in words. **3** communicate by letter. **4** be the author or composer of. **writing** *n* **writer** *n* **1** author. **2** person who has written something specified. **write-off** *n informal* something damaged beyond

repair. **write-up** *n* published account of something.

writhe ❶ *v* twist or squirm in or as if in pain.

wrong ❶ *adj* **1** incorrect or mistaken. **2** immoral or bad. **3** not intended or suitable. **4** not working properly. ▷ *adv* **5** in a wrong manner. ▷ *n* **6** something immoral or unjust. ▷ *v* **7** treat unjustly. **8** malign. **wrongly** *adv* **wrongful** *adj* **wrongdoing** *n* immoral or illegal behaviour. **wrongdoer** *n*.

wrote *v* past tense of WRITE.

wrought [**rawt**] *v* **1** *lit* past of WORK. ▷ *adj* **2** (of metals) shaped by hammering or beating. **wrought iron** pure form of iron used for decorative work.

wrung *v* past of WRING.

wry ❶ *adj* **wrier, wriest** *or* **wryer, wryest 1** drily humorous. **2** (of a facial expression) contorted. **wryly** *adv*.

wuss *n slang chiefly US* feeble person.

WV West Virginia.

WWW World Wide Web.

WY Wyoming.

──────────────────────────── THESAURUS ────────────

wretch *n* **1** = **scoundrel**, good-for-nothing, miscreant, rascal, rogue, swine, worm

wriggle *v* **1** = **crawl**, jerk, jiggle, slink, snake, squirm, turn, twist, waggle, wiggle, worm, writhe, zigzag **2** = **manoeuvre**, dodge, extricate oneself ▷ *n* **3** = **twist**, jerk, jiggle, squirm, turn, waggle, wiggle

wring *v* **1** = **twist**, squeeze **3** = **force**, extract, screw

wrinkle *n* **1** = **crease**, corrugation, crinkle, crow's-foot, crumple, fold, furrow, line ▷ *v* **2** = **crease**, corrugate, crumple, fold, furrow, gather, pucker, rumple

writ *n* = **summons**, court order, decree, document

write *v* **1, 2** = **record**, draft, draw up, inscribe, jot down, pen, scribble, set down

writhe *v* = **squirm**, jerk, struggle, thrash, thresh, toss, twist, wiggle, wriggle

wrong *adj* **1** = **incorrect**, erroneous, fallacious, false, inaccurate, mistaken, untrue, wide of the mark **2** = **bad**, criminal, dishonest, evil, illegal, immoral, sinful, unjust, unlawful, wicked, wrongful **3** = **inappropriate**, incongruous, incorrect, unacceptable, unbecoming, undesirable, unseemly, unsuitable **4** = **defective**, amiss, askew, awry, faulty ▷ *adv* **5** = **incorrectly**, badly, erroneously, inaccurately, mistakenly, wrongly ▷ *n* **6** = **offence**, crime, error, injury, injustice, misdeed, sin, transgression ▷ *v* **7** = **mistreat**, cheat, oppress, take advantage of **8** = **malign**, abuse, dishonour, harm, hurt

wry *adj* **1** = **ironic**, droll, dry, mocking, sarcastic, sardonic **2** = **contorted**, crooked, twisted, uneven

w

X 1 indicating an error, a choice, or a kiss.
2 indicating an unknown, unspecified, or variable factor, number, person, or thing.
3 the Roman numeral for ten.
xenophobia [zen-oh-**fobe**-ee-a] *n* fear or hatred of people from other countries.

Xerox [**zeer**-ox] *n* **1** ® machine for copying printed material. **2** ® copy made by a Xerox machine. ▷ *v* **3** copy (a document) using such a machine.
Xmas ❶ [**eks**-mass] *n informal* Christmas.
X-ray, x-ray *n* **1** stream of radiation that can pass through some solid materials. **2** picture made by sending X-rays through someone's body to examine internal organs. ▷ *v*
3 photograph, treat, or examine using X-rays.
xylophone [**zile**-oh-fone] *n* musical instrument made of a row of wooden bars played with hammers.

————— THESAURUS —————

Xmas *n Inf* = **Christmas**, Noel, Yule (*arch*)

ya *interj S Afr* yes.

yacht [yott] *n* large boat with sails or an engine, used for racing or pleasure cruising. **yachting** *n* **yachtsman**, **yachtswoman** *n*.

yak *n* Tibetan ox with long shaggy hair.

yakka *n Aust & NZ informal* work.

yam *n* tropical root vegetable.

yank ❶ *v* **1** pull or jerk suddenly. ▷ *n* **2** sudden pull or jerk.

yap *v* **yapping, yapped 1** bark with a high-pitched sound. **2** *informal* talk continuously. ▷ *n* **3** high-pitched bark.

yard¹ *n* unit of length equal to 36 inches or about 91.4 centimetres. **yardstick** *n* standard against which to judge other people or things.

yard² *n* enclosed area, usu. next to a building and often used for a particular purpose, e.g. *builder's yard*.

yarn ❶ *n* **1** thread used for knitting or making cloth. **2** *informal* long involved story.

yawn *v* **1** open the mouth wide and take in air deeply, often when sleepy or bored. **2** (of an opening) be large and wide. ▷ *n* **3** act of yawning. **yawning** *adj*.

ye [yee] *pron obs* you.

year *n* **1** time taken for the earth to make one revolution around the sun, about 365 days. **2** twelve months from January 1 to December 31. **yearly** *adj, adv* (happening) every year or once a year. **yearling** *n* animal between one and two years old.

yearn ❶ *v* want (something) very much. **yearning** *n, adj*.

yeast *n* fungus used to make bread rise and to ferment alcoholic drinks.

yebo *interj S Afr informal* yes.

yell ❶ *v* **1** shout or scream in a loud or piercing way. ▷ *n* **2** loud cry of pain, anger, or fear.

yellow *n* **1** the colour of gold, a lemon, etc. ▷ *adj* **2** of this colour. **3** *informal* cowardly. ▷ *v* **4** make or become yellow. **yellow belly** *Aust* freshwater food fish with yellow underparts. **yellow fever** serious infectious tropical disease.

yelp ❶ *v, n* (give) a short sudden cry.

yen ❶ *n informal* longing or desire.

yeoman [yo-man] *n, pl* **-men** *Hist* farmer owning and farming his own land.

yes *interj* **1** expresses consent, agreement, or approval. **2** used to answer when one is addressed. **yes man** person who always agrees with their superior.

yesterday *adv, n* **1** (on) the day before today. **2** (in) the recent past.

yet ❶ *conj* **1** nevertheless, still. ▷ *adv* **2** up until then or now. **3** still. **4** now.

yeti *n* same as ABOMINABLE SNOWMAN.

yew *n* evergreen tree with needle-like leaves and red berries.

————————————————— THESAURUS —————————

yank *v, n* = **pull**, hitch, jerk, snatch, tug, wrench

yarn *n* **1** = **thread**, fibre **2** *Inf* = **story**, anecdote, cock-and-bull story (*inf*), fable, tale, tall story, urban legend, urban myth

yearn *v* = **long**, ache, covet, crave, desire, hanker, hunger, itch

yell *v* **1** = **scream**, bawl, holler (*inf*), howl, screech, shout, shriek, squeal ▷ *n*

2 = **scream**, cry, howl, screech, shriek, whoop

yelp *v* = **cry**, yap, yowl

yen *n Inf* = **longing**, ache, craving, desire, hankering, hunger, itch, passion, thirst, yearning

yet *conj* **1** = **nevertheless**, however, notwithstanding, still ▷ *adv* **2** = **so far**, as yet, thus far, until now, up to now **3** = **still**, besides, in addition, into the

y

yield ❶ v 1 produce or bear. 2 give up control of, surrender. 3 give in. ▷ n 4 amount produced. **yielding** adj 1 submissive. 2 soft or flexible.

yob, yobbo ❶ n slang bad-mannered aggressive youth.

yodel v -delling, -delled sing with abrupt changes between a normal and a falsetto voice.

yoga n Hindu method of exercise and discipline aiming at spiritual, mental, and physical wellbeing. **yogi** n person who practises yoga.

yogurt, yoghurt n slightly sour custard-like food made from milk that has had bacteria added to it, often sweetened and flavoured with fruit.

yoke n 1 wooden bar put across the necks of two animals to hold them together. 2 frame fitting over a person's shoulders for carrying buckets. 3 lit oppressive force, e.g. the yoke of the tyrant. 4 fitted part of a garment to which a fuller part is attached. ▷ v 5 put a yoke on. 6 unite or link.

yokel ❶ n offens person who lives in the country and is usu. simple and old-fashioned.

yolk n yellow part of an egg that provides food for the developing embryo.

Yorkshire pudding n baked batter made from flour, milk, and eggs.

you pron refers to: 1 the person or people addressed. 2 an unspecified person or people in general.

young ❶ adj 1 in an early stage of life or growth. ▷ pl n 2 young people in general. 3 offspring, esp. young animals. **youngster** n young person.

your adj 1 of, belonging to, or associated with you. 2 of, belonging to, or associated with an unspecified person or people in general. **yours** pron something belonging to you. **yourself** pron.

youth ❶ n 1 time of being young. 2 boy or young man. 3 young people as a group. **youthful** adj **youth club** club that provides leisure activities for young people. **youth hostel** inexpensive lodging place for young people travelling cheaply.

YT Yukon Territory.

Yule n lit Christmas (season).

yuppie n 1 young highly-paid professional person, esp. one who has a fashionable way of life. ▷ adj 2 typical of or reflecting the values of yuppies.

THESAURUS

bargain, to boot 4 = **now**, just now, right now, so soon

yield v 1 = **produce**, bear, bring forth, earn, generate, give, net, provide, return, supply 2, 3 = **surrender**, bow, capitulate, cave in (inf), give in, relinquish, resign, submit, succumb ▷ n 4 = **profit**, crop, earnings, harvest, income, output, produce, return, revenue, takings

yob, yobbo n Inf = **thug**, hooligan, lout, roughneck (sl), ruffian

yokel n Offens = **peasant**, (country)

bumpkin, countryman, hick (inf, chiefly US & Canad), hillbilly, rustic

young adj 1 = **immature**, adolescent, callow, early, fledgling, green, infant, junior, juvenile, little, new, recent, undeveloped, youthful ▷ pl n 3 = **offspring**, babies, brood, family, issue, litter, progeny

youth n 1 = **immaturity**, adolescence, boyhood or girlhood, girlhood, salad days 2 = **boy**, adolescent, kid (inf), lad, stripling, teenager, young man, youngster

Y

Zz

zany ❶ [**zane**-ee] *adj* **zanier, zaniest** comical in an endearing way.

zap *v* **zapping, zapped 1** *slang* kill (by shooting). **2** change TV channels rapidly by remote control.

zeal ❶ *n* great enthusiasm or eagerness. **zealot** [**zel**-lot] *n* fanatic or extreme enthusiast. **zealous** [**zel**-luss] *adj* extremely eager or enthusiastic.

zebra *n* black-and-white striped African animal of the horse family. **zebra crossing** pedestrian crossing marked by black and white stripes on the road.

zenith ❶ *n* **1** highest point of success or power. **2** point in the sky directly above an observer.

zephyr [**zef**-fer] *n* soft gentle breeze.

zero ❶ *n, pl* **-ros, -roes 1** (symbol representing) the number 0. **2** point on a scale of measurement from which the graduations commence. **3** lowest point. **4** nothing, nil. ▷ *adj* **5** having no measurable quantity or size. **zero in on** *v* **1** aim at. **2** *informal* concentrate on.

zest ❶ *n* **1** enjoyment or excitement.

2 interest, flavour, or charm. **3** peel of an orange or lemon.

zigzag *n* **1** line or course having sharp turns in alternating directions. ▷ *v* **-zagging, -zagged 2** move in a zigzag. ▷ *adj* **3** formed in or proceeding in a zigzag.

zinc *n Chem* bluish-white metallic element used in alloys and to coat metal.

zip ❶ *n* **1** fastener with two rows of teeth that are closed or opened by a small clip pulled between them. **2** *informal* energy, vigour. ▷ *v* **zipping, zipped 3** fasten with a zip. **4** move with a sharp whizzing sound.

zither *n* musical instrument consisting of strings stretched over a flat box and plucked to produce musical notes.

zodiac *n* imaginary belt in the sky within which the sun, moon, and planets appear to move, divided into twelve equal areas, called signs of the zodiac, each named after a constellation.

zombie, zombi *n* **1** person who appears to be lifeless, apathetic, or totally lacking in independent judgment. **2** corpse brought back to life by witchcraft.

zone ❶ *n* **1** area with particular features or properties. **2** one of the divisions of the earth's surface according to temperature. ▷ *v* **3** divide into zones. **zonal** *adj*.

zoo *n, pl* **zoos** place where live animals are kept for show.

zoology *n* study of animals. **zoologist** *n* **zoological** *adj* **zoological garden** zoo.

———————————————————————— THESAURUS ————————————

zany *adj* = **comical**, clownish, crazy, eccentric, goofy (*inf*), madcap, wacky (*sl*)

zeal *n* = **enthusiasm**, ardour, eagerness, fanaticism, fervour, gusto, keenness, passion, spirit, verve, zest

zenith *n* **1** = **height**, acme, apex, apogee, climax, crest, high point, peak, pinnacle, summit, top

zero *n* **1** = **nothing**, nil, nought **2** = **nought**

3 = **bottom**, nadir, rock bottom **4** = **nil**, nothing

zest *n* **1** = **enjoyment**, appetite, gusto, keenness, relish, zeal **2** = **flavour**, charm, interest, piquancy, pungency, relish, spice, tang, taste

zip *n* **2** *Inf* = **energy**, drive, gusto, liveliness, verve, vigour, zest

zone *n* **1** = **area**, belt, district, region, section, sector, sphere

zoom ❶ *v* **1** move or rise very rapidly. **2** make or move with a buzzing or humming sound. **zoom lens** lens that can make the details of a picture larger or smaller while keeping the picture in focus.

zygote *n* fertilized egg cell.

zoom *v* **1** = **speed**, dash, flash, fly, hurtle, pelt, rush, shoot, whizz (*inf*)

LANGUAGE FOR LIFE

CONTENTS

INTRODUCTION

A dictionary can tell you what a word means and when it can be used accurately. It cannot, though, give you guidance on how to write clearly and appropriately in a variety of situations. The *Language for Life* supplement has been written to help you express yourself effectively at work and at home. It includes advice on how to structure your writing, and how to adapt tone, style and content to different forms of communication – from letters and emails to social media.

BEFORE YOU START WRITING

It is amazing how much more effective your writing will be with a bit of thinking time beforehand. There are three questions which you should be able to answer about any piece of writing, whether it's an email, text, letter or post:

- **Who am I writing to?** This will determine the style and tone that you use. If you are writing an email to a friend, for instance, then you are likely to use less formal language than if you are writing to apply for a job.

- **What do I want to say?** Make sure that all the information you want to communicate is included, and that it is set out as clearly as possible.

- **Why do I want to say it?** In other words, what do you want to happen as a result of your communication? Whether it's for a job application, to ask someone out on a date, or to offer your condolences for a bereavement, what you want to achieve should be clearly stated.

Once you've answered these questions, writing becomes much easier.

Tone

The tone of your writing expresses your attitude towards the reader.
To achieve the tone you want, consider the following questions:

- If you were talking to your reader, what tone would your voice have?

- Is the language you are using too simple (patronising) or too difficult (pompous)?

- What is your relationship to the reader, are they your employer (formal, professional tone) or friend (informal, chatty tone)?

   Then read through your writing to make sure it conveys the tone you intended.

Here are some tips for making your writing successful and some common traps to avoid.

👍 Tips:

- **Use plain English.** Aim for concise, simple expression which will make your writing easy to read.

- **Plan.** Think about what you want to say, and how you want to say it. Planning will save you time and make your writing more effective. It needn't take a lot of time but, even if you're writing a text message, it will pay dividends.

- **Vary the length of your sentences.** Short sentences are powerful. Longer sentences can express more complicated thoughts, but try to keep them to a manageable length or else they become tiring to read! Try to stick to the principle of including one main idea in a sentence, and maybe one related point.

- **Use active rather than passive verbs.** It is usually better to use active verbs because it makes your writing simpler and less stuffy to read:
   The programme was watched by an audience of 13 million people (passive)
   13 million people watched the programme (active).
   The verb 'watched' is 'active' in the second example because it is linked to the subject - '13 million people'. The sentence is shorter and clearer as a result.

- **Read your work aloud.** If the sentences work well, it will be easy to read. Check that you have commas where there are natural pauses.

- **Think about register and tone.** Are you using the right level of formality ('register')? Does your writing accurately express your attitude to the subject and the reader ('tone')? How you address a best friend will be different from how you write to a potential employer.

- **Always check your writing before sending it – and then check it again!** You'll be surprised how easy it is to overlook mistakes. Computers have introduced new errors – for instance, did you delete the original passage that you copied and pasted later in the document? If you correct one word in a sentence, make sure the rest of it still makes sense.

> *I wish people would read through what they have written before pressing 'send'. It would save me a lot of time and make their applications more successful.*
>
> (HR manager)

Traps:

- **Jargon.** Specialist words which are understood by a particular group of people, or overly technical language. Don't talk about 'interfacing' with someone, if you simply mean 'talking' to them.

- **Clichés.** Words or phrases that are used too often, and have little meaning. They will annoy your reader and distract from what you are trying to say. Examples include sayings like, '*A different kettle of fish*,' and '*At the end of the day*'.

- **Long sentences.** Avoid sentences longer than 15-20 words – they can be difficult to read, and can usually be divided into clearer statements. If your sentences work well, they will be easy to read.

- **Repeating words.** Using the same word more than once in a sentence can be clumsy, and there is usually an alternative. For instance,
'*The date of the English exam is the same date as the French exam*,' sounds better as '*The English and the French exams are on the same date*.'

- **Long words.** Avoid using long or complex words for the sake of it, if they can be replaced by shorter, clearer ones. For example using 'proffer' when you mean 'give' or 'articulate' when you mean 'say'.

- **Redundancy.** Avoid using ten words where two will do: '*I am meeting Sophie later,*' is clearer than, '*Sophie and I are due to hook up together at some point in the day.*' Also avoid **tautology** – saying the same thing twice: '*10 a.m. in the morning*' is either '*10 a.m.*' or '*10 in the morning.*'

- **Ambiguity.** Many words can be understood in more than one way. So, '*Clarice was really cold*' could mean that Clarice was unfriendly or that she was shivering. Put yourself in the reader's place to make sure that the meaning of your statement is clear.

- **Causing offence.** A simple rule to follow is: *treat everyone equally in your writing, regardless of sex, age, race, sexual orientation, or physical difference*. Be aware of current customs and values, and also consider different cultures. This is especially relevant if you are communicating with people around the world.

These are only a few points to consider before you start writing, but if you refer to them regularly, they will help you express yourself clearly and consistently in all your communications.

EMAIL

Emails are the primary form of written communication in many people's lives. Whether at home or at work, we spend a lot of our time sending and receiving them. Email correspondence can feel more like a conversation than an exchange of letters. The tone is generally less formal, and the time between sending your message and getting a reply can be minutes or even seconds. The fact that it is instant can be good and bad. Good because it can be a very efficient way of corresponding; bad if you write quickly and carelessly.

Addressing emails

When addressing emails, the general rule of thumb is that the fewer people you email, the better. There are three address fields to consider, and each serves a different purpose:

- **'To'**: this is for the address of the main recipient, or recipients, of the information or request to do something.

- **'CC'**: if you are simply informing someone of your actions or requests, put those people in the 'CC' ('Carbon or Courtesy Copy') field.

- **'BCC'**: if you are copying someone in but you don't want the other addressees to know you should use the 'BCC' ('Blind Carbon or Courtesy Copy'). This is frequently used for mailing large groups, where you don't want individuals to know who else is receiving the email.

> *Bear in mind that if you send an email to one person you are 95 per cent likely to get a reply; if you send it to 10 people the response rate drops to 5 per cent.*
>
> (Linguistics professor)

Greeting and ending

Emails on work-related issues or personal business require a formal style. You can never go wrong with 'Dear Mr Blake' or 'Dear Peter'. If the contact is long-standing and you are on a familiar footing then 'Hi Peter' is acceptable. In initial exchanges of email it is usual to sign off in the same way that you would in a formal letter with 'Yours sincerely' or 'Yours faithfully'. As your correspondence gets onto a slightly less formal footing then 'Kind regards' or 'Best wishes' is fine.

Subject line

You can really help your correspondents by being precise in the subject line. For example if you send out a regular set of minutes by email, don't just write 'Launch Meeting Minutes', add the date so people can quickly find what they are looking for. If your email contains a specific question it is good practice to add 'Q:' followed by the question in the subject line.

Layout

Use a paragraph per point you wish to make, and put headings above each paragraph if there are more than three. If your email is long and will require the reader to scroll down the screen, consider writing it as a Word document and attaching it to an email – long emails are not easy to read and respond to.

Content

Always remember that with email, your writing can be forwarded to anyone with a single mouse click. Be careful that what you write is not defamatory, offensive, or detrimental to you or your business.

> *Never forward without reading the whole email: you never know what indiscretions or traps are in there. Never put anything in an email you don't want the world to know.*
>
> (Local authority manager)

- Restrict the email to a single subject. If you want to email the same person or people about other issues, use separate emails. It makes filing and action points much easier to follow.

- Don't reply straight away to an email that irks you. You will not be able to hide your anger and will not make the situation better. Wait until you have calmed down enough to think through your response and compose a measured reply dealing with the points raised.

- Don't assume that the person you are writing to has the same cultural reference points, sense of humour, or values.

> *I know of people who communicate regularly with colleagues in Italy, where capitalization is used to show something is urgent whereas we read it as shouting.*
>
> (Marketing executive)

Attachments

Email is great for sharing documents, photographs and audio-files in the form of attachments. But sending large files can cause headaches. Most email providers (and certainly most companies) allocate a storage limit to each email address; if an Inbox becomes too full, you cannot receive or send emails. So be considerate when you send anything as an attachment.

Replying

Sometimes you get an email which contains a series of questions. It is perfectly acceptable to reply to each of these questions by adding your comments (sometimes in a different colour or with your initials in square brackets before your answer) in the body of the original email. This saves you typing out the questions or writing replies that incorporate the original question. For example:

From: Asif Iqbal
To: Fiona McManus
SUBJECT: My paintings

Dear Fiona
Thank you very much for your email about the posters I sell. I've put my answers below your questions with [AI] after.

With thanks and all best wishes

Asif
Mobile: 011111 789456
www.asifiqbal.art.gallery.net

Do you have a website?
[AI] Yes. You can see all my work at www.asifiqbal.art.gallery.net
What sizes do the posters come in?
[AI] Anything from A5 to A1. I can also frame them to order – there's a selection of frames on the website.
What range of prices are there?
[AI] Prices start at $AUS 11.95 and can go up to $AUS 75.00
If you don't have a poster I want in stock, can you source it for me?
[AI] Of course, I'd be happy to help in any way. Have a look through the website and if you can't find what you want, just drop me a line and I'll do my best!

Formal email

The rules for writing formal emails are similar to those for formal letters.

- If you are communicating with someone for the first time you should adopt the structure of a formal letter.

- It is usual and proper to use a greeting of some sort when you begin your email. 'Dear' can never be misunderstood and rarely strikes the wrong note. If you are more familiar with the person you are writing to 'Hi' or 'Hello' is fine. If you're writing to close friends then use whichever greeting you are accustomed to in your social circle.

- If you are emailing someone for the first time without being invited to it is always proper to explain at the very start of the email who you are and why you are writing to them.

- Never leave the subject line blank. In most formal or professional correspondence you should aim to keep the email to one subject. Think clearly what the email is about and be as precise as you can. Keep the subject as short as possible as most people's inbox can only display a limited amount of the line.

- If the email is going to be long it is polite to indicate this in the opening few sentences of the email.

- Structure your email so that each point is addressed in a separate paragraph. If you wish, it is entirely acceptable to add a heading to each paragraph. Your reader can then see at a glance the points you are covering.

- In formal emails, texting abbreviations and emoticons should be avoided.

- When you end your email use the same rules as with formal letters, using 'Yours faithfully' or 'Yours sincerely' as appropriate.

 I avoid using multiple sub-clauses and long sentences and use lists or bullet points rather than block text.

(Marketing manager)

Informal emails

For emails to friends and family you can be more relaxed in your style and tone.

- 'Hi' or 'Hey' or other informal greetings are appropriate and you can sign off the email with 'See you' or 'lots of love' or other phrases.

- Even when you're writing to a friend remember that email can seem terse and abrupt if there is no greeting or sign-off.

- It is fine to use texting abbreviations and emoticons in informal emails – just make sure the person you're writing to understands them all!

> *I read the email back to myself as though I were reading someone else's email prior to sending.*
>
> (Course co-ordinator)

WRITING AT WORK

Email

Emails are the default means of communication for most businesses. Whenever you write an important email at work it needs to be concise, clear and well thought-out. The tone should in almost all cases be formal.

Some research conducted recently across a wide range of professions suggested that on average people get 100 emails per day and have to respond to about 40 per cent of them. Email adds a lot of extra reading and writing to an already busy work day. So the first question you should ask is 'Is email the best way to say what I have to say?' A frequent complaint of people in business is that they are sent or copied in on emails that they really don't need to see.

> *My tip for effective communication in an organization? Don't write. Phone or speak to someone in person.*
>
> (CEO, International Management Consultancy)

Compare these two emails which show the difference between good and bad practice in business email writing.

BAD EMAIL

Ollie

There are problems re the arrangements for the conference dinner. I met with David yesterday to finalize details and here's what we decided: The venue (Carmichael Hall) is booked for Dec 18th 7:00 - 12:00. Send out the invitations to all conference delegates the week starting November 3rd. Find out from the printers when the invitations are being returned to us and get them send out in a timely fashion to the delegates. You'll need to check against th otiginal delegate list. Hallidays need to know final numbers by Dec. 10th., latest. Call them to let them know Liaise with Sujata over the timing of the speeches and let the relevant people know when their slot is.

Can't think of anything else at the moment but it's down to you now.

- The tone is abrupt, ill-tempered and dictatorial without being helpful.

- The email is very sloppily written: there are spelling and grammatical mistakes throughout.

- Information required to carry out the actions is not provided.

- People the recipient needs to liaise with and get information from are not included in the email.

- The email generates more work for both the sender and the addressee.

- The email is one block of text which makes identifying what needs to be done laborious and time-consuming.

GOOD EMAIL

Subject: Conference dinner action points 25/10
From: "Hill, Lucy" <Lucy.Hill@bigbooks.co.uk>
To: "Ollie Walsh", "Maine, Sujata" <Sujata.Maine@bigbooks.co.uk

Hi Ollie

Thanks again for offering to help with the arrangements for the conference dinner. I do appreciate it.
David and I had a meeting yesterday to finalize the details. I've included Sujata on the email so you can liaise directly with her on a couple of the points.

Venue
The venue (Carmichael Hall) is booked for December 18th 7:00 - 12:00.
The contact there is Julia Waters.
Her number is 01354 638976.

Invitations
The invitations are currently with the printers. When they are returned to us (this Friday, 1st November) they will need checking against the original delegate list.
Sujata: could you send the list to Ollie please?
Invitations should go to all conference delegates the week starting November 3rd.

The caterers
Hallidays, the caterers, will need to know final numbers by Dec. 10th. Please call them to confirm these numbers (01354 222227).

Speeches
Finally, please could you liaise with Sujata over the timing of the speeches and let the relevant people know when their slot is? The list of speakers is on the shared drive. (K:/conference2011/speakerlist.doc)

Any questions, give me a call. I'm here all this week apart from Thursday afternoon.

Many thanks,

Lucy

- The writer includes all the people required to do something in the 'TO' box.

- There is a precise 'Subject' line.

- The paragraphs are set out so that addressing each point is easy.

- All the relevant information is included (dates, contact names and numbers, and file locations).

- The tone is collaborative, helpful and professional.

 I keep all emails as brief as possible and use short sentences to get across all important points.

(Food journalist)

When not to use email

Avoid the temptation to think that email can be used in all situations.
For example, email isn't very good at conveying tone or emotion accurately.
If you want to discuss something sensitive or personal with someone, it might be better to talk with them in person, or write them a note.

Letters at work

Formal business letters are, like memos, becoming rarer. Some professions – particularly the law – still rely on written correspondence, but for most businesses email is the default mode. When you come to write a formal letter to someone outside your organization you should observe the rules of letter writing (see section X).

I use email for almost all written communication, but I send letters to staff over HR issues: for example, around persistent absence, capability and contract issues.

(Local government manager)

A lot of letter correspondence within an organization is about HR issues – resignation letters or changes to terms and conditions, for example. These require a signature, are often 'private and confidential' and, like the work contract, may be required for future reference. For these two reasons, formal letters are the appropriate form of writing. Here is an example of a resignation letter.

Anna Wozniaki
Account Manager
Upside Down Records
Flintrock
Sussex
B45 8EP
17 June 2011

Dear Anna

Please accept this as formal notice of my resignation from the position of Account Executive, with effect from today 17th June, 2011.

In accordance with my contract of employment I am happy to continue to work until the end of my notice period which by my calculations is the 15th July.

While I believe that I am moving for good reasons, I am sorry to leave, and I thank you for your support during my time with the company, which I have found enjoyable and fulfilling.

Please let me know the arrangements for returning equipment - my company phone and laptop - and handing over outstanding work and responsibilities.

Yours sincerely

Martin Fry

Martin Fry

- The letter is polite, formal and shows that the writer wants to help to ease the process of his leaving.

- It offers no suggestions about improvements or criticisms of the company – you might be given an opportunity to do that in person at an Exit Interview.

PRESENTATIONS

The key to making a successful presentation is to be well-prepared. Make sure that you fill your available time, pitch the information at an appropriate level for your audience, and keep in mind the main points you want to get across.

Preparation

- Ask yourself why you are writing the presentation: is it to inform, to persuade your audience to accept your view, or to entertain? Structure your talk to fit in with your aim.

- Write the key points of your argument in a logical sequence on prompt cards. Keep the points to the minimum just enough to remind you what you need to say.

- Rehearse until you are confident that you know exactly what you are going to say. Make sure that you can deliver the important points clearly and confidently; practice looking at an imaginary member of the audience as you speak.

> *You should always aim to entertain – there's nothing worse than having to sit through a dull PowerPoint presentation where the speaker reads exactly what is on the slides.*
>
> (IT Manager)

Presentation slides

There are two major mistakes that inexperienced speakers make when they use PowerPoint or other presentation slide packages:

- The speaker reads out (often word for word) what is written on the slide.

- There are too many words on the slide for the audience to read and absorb.

Remember these key points about writing presentation slides:

- Presentation slides should summarize the point you want to make so that the audience can remember what you're saying.

- You should give each slide a heading to reflect the aspect of the subject you are talking about at that time in your presentation.

- Restrict each line on the slide to very short phrases or even single words. Do not use more than five or six lines per slide.

Here are some examples of good and bad presentation slides:

GOOD PRACTICE

- Use a large, simple font.
- Write only key points on slide.
- Don't use complicated backgrounds.

BAD PRACTICE

- Use a complicated font.
- Add far too many words to the slide so that people find it really hard to take in the point of the slide and spend more time reading the slide than they do listening to you.
- Repeat exactly what you have written on the slide – it's very dull for the audience and does not reinforce your point or make it more memorable.

JOB APPLICATIONS

A covering letter and CV are usually the first things any prospective employer will see of you. If you want to get an interview for a job, it is important that these documents present you in the best possible light. The following sections deal with how to construct and write your covering letter and CV, and provide tips on how to apply for a job online.

Covering letter

The covering letter should convey confidence, enthusiasm, technical knowledge and demonstrate an understanding of what the job entails. It need not be long and it should not be a rehash of the accompanying CV. A short, clear, well-written covering letter can make all the difference between two candidates.

> *Some people think the covering letter is another CV. It's not. A covering letter is a way of introducing yourself to the employer and of providing a persuasive case for reading the CV and then getting an interview.*
> (HR Director)

The covering letter should alert the employer to the key points of a CV and show the match between the candidate and the job being advertised. In general it will consist of three paragraphs or so:

- **First paragraph.** Introduce yourself, say which job you are applying for and where you saw it. You can also include a general statement of why you want to apply for the job and how you feel about the company.

- **Second paragraph.** Provide information about your skills, strengths, qualifications and experience. Give specific examples of why you are the ideal candidate and don't simply restate your CV.

- **Final paragraph.** Conclude the letter expressing your desire to get the job and requesting an interview. You should also say what the best way to contact you is, and if there are any inconvenient dates. Always thank the employer for considering your application.

FAQ

Q. *Should my letter be typed or handwritten?*

A. It should be typed on A4 paper. Only the signature should be handwritten.

Q. *Is it OK to send out the same letter to all those companies I'm interested in?*

A. No. Try to avoid general letters. Find out as much as you can about the company, and tailor your letter accordingly.

Q. *Should I mention salary in my accompanying letter?*

A. It is usually best not to touch on the subject of salary at this stage, unless requested in the advertisement.

Useful phrases

First of all, identify the job you are applying for:

- I would like to inquire as to whether there are any openings for junior telesales operators in your company.

- I am writing to apply for the post of senior marketing manager.

- I would like to apply for the position of online learning coordinator, as advertised on your website.

- I am writing to apply for the above post, as advertised in the Guardian of 8 August 2009.

Next, give some examples of personal achievements:

- I have gained experience in several major aspects of publishing.

- I co-ordinated the change-over from one accounting system to another.

- I developed designs for a new range of knitwear.

- I have supervised a team of telesales operators on several projects.

- I contributed to the development of our new database software.

Then outline your personal qualities:

- I see myself as systematic and meticulous in my approach to work.

- I am a fair and broad-minded person, with an ability to get on well with people from all walks of life.

- I am hardworking and business minded, and I tend to thrive under pressure.

Explain why you want this job:

- I am now keen to find a post with more responsibility.

- I now wish to find a more permanent full-time position.

- I would like to further my career in the field of production.

- I feel that your company's activities most closely match my own values and interests.

Express your willingness to attend an interview.

Here is an example covering letter:

Mr J Manners
15 Sandybank Drive
Derby
DX27 9LC
Joelmanners@email.com
01245 645201

27 July 2011

Mr H Carson
Personnel Manager
Allied Derby Building Society
HR House
Illingworth Way
DERBY
DX3 9DF

Dear Mr Carson

Customer Services Manager

I am responding to the job advertised in the *Derby Express* and on your website on the 22nd July. I feel the job is just what I have been looking for, and reading the job description, I am sure that I have the right level of experience, aptitude and training. Your company's support and promotion of ethical investment has always impressed and inspired me and I would very much like to contribute to your success. My CV is attached.

For the past three years I have been Senior Customer Services Adviser at Cathedral County Bank, leading a team of seven people. Since I took on the role our positive response rate has risen by 10 per cent and customer satisfaction in the area I look after by 15 per cent. I was voted Employee of the Month three times by my colleagues in the period. While I am very happy in my job, the opportunities for promotion are limited and I do want to take on a more responsible role in my area of expertise.

I would welcome the opportunity to discuss my application further. Email is the best way to contact me and I am available for interview at your convenience. Thank you for taking the time to read my application.

Yours sincerely

Mr Joel Manners

Mr Joel Manners

- Avoid just sending a letter or email with 'Please find my CV attached'. Remember that this application is a two-stage process to try to get an interview. Each step in the process (covering letter and CV) has to make the employer want to take the next step.

- Remember the basics:
  - Check all spelling and grammar two or three times.
  - Make sure you have spelled all names correctly.
  - Include all contact details.
  - Include any information that the job advertisement has specifically asked you to provide.

A speculative job application

- When applying for a job on a speculative basis, try to speak to the person responsible for recruitment in the appropriate department beforehand. This way, you will have a specific person to write to, as well as having established a relationship with them.

34 St Dunstan's Way
Vancouver
V6G 7D7

19 July 2011

Ms D Wallis
Youngs Accountancy and Finance
19 Lockwood Road
Vancouver
V9P 8K1

Dear Ms Wallis

post of software development co-ordinator

Thank you very much for taking the time to speak to me yesterday about the possibility of a position as software development co-ordinator with your company.

Please find attached a CV which highlights my prior professional experience, and the qualities which I feel make me suited to this position. You will see that I have a strong interest in, and knowledge of, staff management, and have gained extensive experience in handling large development projects and meeting deadlines.

I see myself as being well-organized and self-motivated, and have excellent communication skills. I am keen to develop my career with Youngs Accountancy and Finance, and so would very much appreciate the opportunity to discuss further my suitability for the post.

Please feel free to contact me, either by email: dgormanl@netserve.com, or by leaving a message on (604) 473 5522. I look forward to speaking to you soon.

Yours sincerely

D Gorman

Deborah Gorman

CV

Your CV exists to give a brief description of who you are, what you have done and what you can do.

> *What a lot of candidates forget is that the purpose of the CV is to get the interview – not the job. So they give way too much detail and don't tailor it to the role they are trying to get.*
>
> (HR Director)

- The language should always be 'active'. Avoid passive statements like 'Turnover growth of 25 per cent was achieved in the period,' say instead, 'I increased turnover for the period by 25 per cent.' Active language simplifies your statements and makes them easier to read.

- Use positive adverbs ('efficiently', 'successfully' 'effectively') so that your CV will convey a positive impression to your prospective employer.

CV structure

The most common CV format is called 'reverse chronological', meaning you start with your current job and work backwards. If your earliest jobs have little relevance to your current application, you can simply list the job title, company and the dates you worked there. Summarize your education after the employment section, and then add any additional skills and interests that may be of use to support your application.

You can see a sample CV on the next page:

Helena Shapur

12 Green Lane, Brighton, Sussex BT1 3EY
Email: h.sharpur@email.com
Mobile: 07123 456789

Personal profile

An enthusiastic, self-motivated professional, highly qualified in the field of online team management. My motivation is to use the web to help make the most of all businesses I work for. I have an in-depth understanding of a wide range of web technologies from Java to Flash.

Career summary

2008 - present Development Team Leader, GoGetting.com

I joined the online travel company GoGetting.com as a development officer before being promoted in August 2010 to my current position. Since becoming team leader the site has had a threefold increase in unique visitors thanks to an extensive linking program I developed. As a result of the increased traffic, the company has given me extra responsibility to drive the marketing of the site with selected web partners. I manage a team of seven development officers and am in charge of a budget of £250,000.

2004 - 2008 Web Developer, Toprank Recruitment

Having learned a lot at my first company and really enjoyed the experience of working in web development, I joined this small recruitment start-up specializing in the catering trade. During the time I helped program the site's search engine and learned ASP, Java and SQL.
I was very proud to have seen one key module of the search engine's development through from design to implementation. The module generated five per cent extra revenue for the company while I was there. I learned a lot about effective teamwork in the process.

2002-2004 Junior programmer, Oakhampton Systems

This was a perfect job after graduation. I was part of a small graduate intake whose job was to develop and code account and customer databases. I went on site visits to understand what a client needed and understand the way the business works. I taught myself HTML in this period and designed the company's first website.

Education and qualifications

1998-2001 University of Windsor, BSC Computer Science (2:1)
1991 – 1998 Greenglades School, Windsor
3 A-levels: Mathematics (A*), Physics (A), Chemistry (B)
10 O-levels

Hobbies and interests

Between leaving school and starting university I worked for six months so that I could spend three months doing charity runs for Famine Relief, whom I continue to work for as a volunteer. I run long-distance competitively, enjoy cinema, computer games and chess.

References available on request

One of the worst mistakes a candidate can make is to send employers a 6-page 'novel' about their work experience, school qualification and hobbies and pastimes - especially if it is written in size-9 font. Many managers skim read CVs so using short paragraphs and an almost report-like style will mean they are less likely to miss a candidate with relevant skills or experience. This is where editing down and making the CV relate to the job description/advert works to the candidate's advantage.

(HR Director)

BASIC GRADUATE CV

CV

Name	Kate Maxwell
Date of birth	29.02.85
Address	19, The Poplars, Bristol B10 2JU
Telephone	0117 123 4567
Email	katemaxwell@atlantic.net
Nationality	British

Education

2004–2008	**BA Hons in Modern Languages, University of Exeter** (final grade 2.1)
2002–2004	**Clifton Road Secondary School:** 3 'A' levels – French (A) German (A) History (B)
1997–2002	**Clifton Road Secondary School:** 8 GCSEs including Maths and English

Employment history

2004–2005	**Sales Assistant, Langs Bookshop, Bristol** I was responsible for training and supervising weekend and holiday staff.
2005–2006	**English Assistant, Lycée Benoit, Lyons** I taught conversational English to pupils aged 12-18, preparing the older students for both technical and more academic qualifications. I organized an educational trip to the UK for fourth year pupils.

Positions of responsibility held

2005–2006	**Entertainments Officer for University Student Social Society** I organized and budgeted for entertainment for a student society with over 1000 members.
2004–2007	**Captain of the university women's netball team** I was in charge of training, organizing and motivating the women's team.

Other skills

Fluent French and German
Extensive knowledge of Microsoft Word, Excel and Access
I hold a clean driving licence

References

on request

Top ten CV tips

1. Adapt your CV to the job or prospective employer.

2. You have 30-60 seconds to attract your reader's attention so lay out your CV clearly - use a plain typeface like Ariel, Trebuchet or Times New Roman – and keep it to the point. It should not be longer than 3 sides.

3. Remember the CV is a means of getting an interview not getting the job.

4. Avoid gimmicks like thumbnail images or pictures – they distract from the words you are writing about yourself.

5. Focus your description of your current and previous experience on achievements and the contribution you made to the organizations. If possible quantify your achievements – 'my actions led to a saving of £xx' or, 'as a result profits were up by x per cent'.

6. Give examples of your skills and qualities – don't just say 'I am a natural leader', write a brief description of when you showed this attribute.

7. Avoid bullet points when describing your current and previous jobs. It's much better to write short paragraphs because you can give examples.

8. Format the document to make sure that the printed version reflects what you see on screen. Try not to waste paper by leaving just two or three sentences at the top of the last page.

9. Use 'active' verbs such as 'achieve', 'lead', 'manage'.

10. Finally carefully proofread your CV and, if you can, ask someone else to look at it as well.

How to send your CV

You can still post your CV if you wish but most HR professionals prefer to receive the document as an attachment to an email. This means that they can share the CV with the relevant staff or store it on their computer for future reference.

Online applications

Sometimes you will be asked to complete an application form online. Here are some tips to do this effectively:

- As for written job applications, you should write in a formal style.

- The online system will probably dictate the particular text format (the font and size of type) – you should take this into account when you draft your answers.

- It is useful to prepare a draft of the application and then transfer the information to the online form.

- Copy and save your answers regularly into a normal document in case the system crashes or you have to break off your application and start again.

- Just because the application is automatically filed online, does not mean you should be any less rigorous in the editing and proofreading you do. If you can print the document out before you submit it, get someone you trust to read it over to look for errors and omissions.

WRITING FORMAL LETTERS

Emails and other digital media are the prevalent forms of communication for most of us today, at work and at home, but there are still occasions when a handwritten or typed letter is more appropriate.

This section lays out the basic structure and the rules which underpin most formal letter writing. The Domestic Correspondence, Social Communication and Job Applications sections within this supplement will look more closely at situations where formal letter writing is used, and give examples of good practice.

As with any written communication, your letter should be in three discernible parts:

- **An introduction.** This is where you introduce yourself, acknowledge any previous correspondence, and briefly state the reason why you are writing. Ideally it should be no longer than a paragraph of three or four sentences.

- **The middle.** This is the section where you expand your argument, provide further details, and raise any questions you have. The middle of the letter should be a series of paragraphs set out in a logical order. Each paragraph should make a clear, separate point. If the letter is long and covers a range of subjects, it may be appropriate to divide the contents by subheadings.

- **The ending, or conclusion.** The final paragraph should set out what you would like to happen as a result of the communication, whether that be a written response, a meeting to discuss the contents of the letter, or a demand for a refund.

Here is an example of a formal letter:

55 Torrance Close
Gorton
NSW 2234

25 August 2011

Mr L Dylan
Terrigan Building Ltd
340 Shorter Street
Terrigan
NSW 2234
Dear Mr Dylan

Estimate for extension to living room, 55 Torrance Close

I am writing to thank you for the written estimate which I received this morning. I have queries about a couple of details in your letter which I would like to be resolved before we proceed any further.

First, can you say exactly when you would propose to begin work on the extension? I realize this depends, to some extent, on how quickly you can finish your current project. I need to know which week work would commence in, however, so that I can make arrangements to store the living room furniture.

Second, can you tell me when you propose to fit the additional plumbing, so that I can arrange to stay with friends while there is no running water? Also, are there any other times when you anticipate that I shall be without water or electricity?

Finally, there is no mention of additional costs for materials? Can I assume, therefore, that these are included in the estimate you have provided for the overall cost of the extension?

Assuming I receive satisfactory answers in writing to these queries, I shall be happy to accept your proposal and go ahead with the project as discussed.

Yours sincerely

Tom Peterson

Tom Peterson

Points to remember:

- **Your address.** This should be written in the top right corner of the letter. Do not write your name here, and don't put commas after each line.

- **The date.** The date should come under your address, also on the right. It is common practice to write the date as 25 August 2011, instead of 25th August 2011.

- **The recipient's address.** Write this under the date, but on the left side of the page. Again, no punctuation is required.

- **The greeting.** If you are writing to a friend then you will use, 'Dear Luke,' for instance. Otherwise it should be 'Dear Mr Dylan'. Note that if you are writing to a woman and do not know whether she prefers to be addressed as 'Dear Mrs Dylan', or 'Dear Miss Dylan', then you should use 'Dear Ms Dylan'. If you do not know the person's name then use, 'Dear Sir or Madam'.

- **Headings.** If you are using a heading, then it should summarize the subject matter of the letter, and appear between the greeting and the first paragraph. Headings should be written in bold but not capital letters.

- **The ending.** If you have used the name of the person in the greeting, then you should end with 'Yours sincerely'. Otherwise end the letter with 'Yours faithfully'. 'Yours...' should always begin with a capital letter.

- **Punctuation.** It is not necessary to include a comma after the greeting or after the ending. Don't put full stops in initials – write 'Mr L H Dylan' instead of 'Mr L.H. Dylan'.

- **Signature.** Write your signature but include your typewritten name underneath.

- **Further contact details.** If you are including your email address or telephone number as contact details, then these should be included underneath your postal address:

55 Torrance Close
Gorton
NSW 2234
tpeterson@email.com
(02) 4254 6398

Once you have written your letter check that:

- You have explained why you are writing in the first paragraph.

- You have made all the points that you wanted to.

- Each sentence is clear, concise and unambiguous.

- You have not included too much information, or any irrelevant details.

- Your language has been courteous and polite, even if you are writing a letter of complaint.

- Check once more for spelling mistakes – it is surprisingly easy to miss them!

DOMESTIC CORRESPONDENCE

This section tackles the range of letters and correspondence that relates to you, your home, your finances and your family. The following points about content, style and tone apply equally whether you're writing a letter, an email, filling in an online form, or if you are speaking to someone on the phone:

- Use formal language.

- Include every detail that will make the letter easier to deal with.

- Lay the letter out clearly – breaking it down so that each paragraph contains a single point.

- Be explicit about what you want to happen next and introduce a timescale where appropriate.

- What you are writing may have legal implications, so take care with the details you include and the language you use.

- Provide as many contact details as you can.

- Write 'Yours sincerely' to end the letter if you know the surname of the person you are writing to. Write 'Yours faithfully' if you do not.

> *When I'm writing to a company, I always try and find out a specific person to address the letter to – or else it can just end up getting lost in the system.*
> (Teacher)

In the following section there is a selection of letters that many of us will have to write at some point:

- Insurance claims.

- Planning application objection.

- Writing to your MP.

- Deferring jury service.

- School correspondence.

- Letters of complaint.

Insurance claims

Most of us find ourselves having to make a claim to an insurance company at some stage in our lives – whether it be as the result of a car accident, burglary, incident on holiday or some other regrettable occurrence.

The claim can be made verbally, online or in a written statement but whichever form it takes, it is important to consider the kind of language you use and the information that you include.

Ms C Hall
32, Lime Road
Saddleworth
Devon
SD2 8LN
christinehall@email.com
17 June 2011

Ms Ying
Claims Assessor
Admirable Insurance Company
Claims Avenue
Spottington
Hants
SP31 4AQ

My policy number: AIC008997/CH56.

Dear Ms Ying,

I am writing to make an insurance claim, resulting from an accident I was involved in on 16 June 2011. My car is covered by a comprehensive insurance policy which I took out with you some time ago. The policy number is included above.

The incident occurred at approximately 3pm at the junction of New Street and London Road in Saddleworth. The other driver, a Mr Steve Wall, turned right out of New Street and drove into the front passenger side of my vehicle, causing extensive damage to the bodywork and the headlights. I have enclosed a picture of the damage, together with a diagram showing the relative positions of the vehicles, and the direction they were travelling in at the time of the accident.

Mr Wall has admitted liability for the accident. His insurance company's details, together with his policy number, are also enclosed.

As a result of the incident, my car is not roadworthy. I need therefore, to arrange to collect a replacement car from one of your suppliers, which I am entitled to according to the terms of my policy. Can you advise me on the nearest garage and confirm my entitlement? Please let me know if there are any other details you require to process my claim, and also give me an indication of how long it will take to arrange the repair of my vehicle.

Yours sincerely

Ms C Hall

Ms C Hall

- The letter contains all the relevant information – such as dates, policy number, details of the incident – that the company is likely to require.

- In spite of the nature of the incident, the language is restrained – emotional language will not make your claim any more likely to succeed.

- The letter politely requests information from the insurance company which will move the claim on.

Opposing a planning application

Correspondence with a local authority is often in the form of a complaint or an objection. Whether you are contesting a parking fine or opposing a planning application, the information you include should be precise and accurate to back your claims.

Mr C Hopkins
75 Birchtree Row
Lessington
County Durham
D2 8LN
chopkins@email.com

1 December 2011

Mr Anderson
Director of Planning
Lime Borough Council
Acacia Road
Lessington
County Durham
D5 1AA

Dear Mr Anderson,

Planning application number LBC123456/7A
Address of proposed extension: 77 Birchtree Row, Lessington, County Durham, D2 8LN

I am writing to object to the proposal to build an extension on the above property. There are several reasons for this.

Design
The very modern design of the proposed extension is in unsympathetic contrast to the Victorian style of all the houses in the area.

Privacy
The two-storey extension will affect the privacy of my property. The plans show a window that will look directly into my garden.

Natural light
The extension will block out the natural light I get in my conservatory all-year round.

Appropriateness of use
It is clear from the plans that the owner intends to make and sell drum kits from the property. This will have a significant impact on the local noise levels - the neighbourhood at the moment is very quiet.

I am sure that other local residents will be objecting as well, and I trust you will refuse this application on the basis that it most definitely contravenes your planning regulations.

I would be grateful if you could acknowledge this letter, confirm that it has been logged as an objection to the application within the deadline set by the council, and keep me informed as to the outcome. I can be contacted at the above address or via the email address at the top of this letter.

Yours Sincerely,

Mr C Hopkins

Mr C Hopkins

- The writer has found out the deadline for his objection and complied with it.

- He has found out and addressed the criteria on which the application will be judged.

- The headings highlight the grounds on which he is basing his objection.

Writing to your MP

When writing to your MP keep the letter to a single subject and make it as concise as possible. Remember to say what you want the MP to do as a result of your letter. At all times be courteous – just because you may disagree with his views, does not mean that you should be anything other than respectful in your writing.

You can see a letter written to an MP on the next page:

Mr R Boscombe
27 Juniper Road
Flickcroft
West Midlands
reg.boscombe@email.com

15 April 2011

Derek Firbanks MP
House of Commons
Westminster
LONDON
SW1A 1AA

Dear Derek Firbanks

I am writing to draw your attention to the imminent closure of the Priory Centre on Sandhurst Road in Flickcroft. I am a parent whose child uses the premises for a theatre group on Saturday mornings. She finds the opportunity to learn about acting and to perform stimulating and great fun. The group also provides invaluable contact with other children from the area and with the community in general.

There are 120 children aged from six to 16 who attend the theatre classes every week – divided into three age bands. Last term my daughter's group staged a production dramatizing the history of the Priory Centre and its place in the local community.

The theatre group is by no means the only one affected. There are some 30 other activities put on for a huge range of people, including for elderly and disabled groups, at weekends and during the week.

The council plans to pass the plans at a meeting in three weeks' time. I, and many others, would be grateful if you could take this matter up with the leader of the council as a matter of urgency. The loss of the centre will create a huge gap in the cultural life of our community.

Please acknowledge this letter as soon as you can and let me know of your progress.

Yours sincerely,

Mr R Boscombe

Mr R Boscombe

- The letter starts with a very specific description of the problem.

- The writer includes his full address so that the MP knows the letter is from a constituent.

- The letter is about one issue which makes it easier to deal with.

- Including anecdotes or some personal detail will help the MP to remember the letter.

- The writer refers to others who are opposed to the closure. Including supporting evidence – be it a petition, or the MP's involvement with or voting record on similar issues – will help the cause.

> *When contacting your MP, a short, handwritten or printed letter is most effective. Take the time to edit your letter for brevity and clarity. Try to make a single coherent point.*
>
> (Campaigning website)

Deferring jury service

A letter requesting you to serve on a jury is a serious matter – in the UK if you ignore it you could be prosecuted. If the dates you have been called for are very disruptive to your plans, or circumstances are such that you can't attend, then you should write asking for a deferment. The grounds for deferment will be laid out in the letter you receive.

Mr J Brown
The Moorings
Chettleworth
LINCOLNSHIRE
AG7 0BC
james.brown@email.com
01285 78945613

3 February 2011

Mr R Ball
Jury Central Summoning Bureau
Derby
DA1 9IO

Dear Mr Ball

Thank you for the letter dated January 30th inviting me to serve on a jury from March 27th. I would like to ask if it would be possible to defer this until sometime next year? My wife has recently had a car accident and suffered a serious injury. I have now had to become a full-time carer for her and as a consequence cannot leave the house for an extended period.

I would be very grateful if you could agree to this request, and if you require me to provide you with any further information, please do not hesitate to contact me.

I look forward to receiving your response.

Yours sincerely,

Mr James Brown

Mr James Brown

- It is more effective to provide specific details for your request: it decreases the likelihood of having to give more information and speeds up the process.

- Do not demand that your attendance is deferred.

School correspondence

There are a few occasions when it will be necessary to write, or email, your child's school, to keep a record of important incidents during their career. Below are an example email and letter dealing with two such incidents: when your child has more than a couple of days off school, and to put on record concerns about bullying.

To: J Chalfont <jchalfont@derwentwaterschool.ed.uk
From: kevin.bond@email.net

Subject: Charlie Bond's absence 1st - 5th March

Dear Mr Chalfont

I am writing to explain why Charlie was absent from school last week (1st to 5th March). He woke up with a very sore throat on Sunday morning. We went to the doctor on Monday and Charlie was diagnosed with laryngitis. He started to feel better on Friday morning and is able to return to school today.

Charlie is worried, as the exams approach, about keeping on top of his work, so I would be very grateful if you could let him know what he has missed and help him catch up.

If you have any concerns, please do email or phone me on the number below.

Yours sincerely

Mr K Bond
kevin.bond@email.net
Tel: 01234 456789

- The letter quickly and clearly summarizes the course of events and includes evidence of the illness by referring to the doctor's diagnosis.

- The parent, having been very clear about the reason for absence, then presents their own concerns and is explicit about what they want the teacher to do. The letter is useful and effective for the parent, teacher and pupil.

Mrs J Trewin
'The Glade'
Farm Road
Kettering
XA7 2WR
janetrewin@email.com
01234 5678913

29 January 2011

Ms L Edge
Long Oak Primary School
West End Lane
Kettering
XA5 9LD

Dear Ms Edge

I am writing to follow up on our conversation on the phone two days ago. I'm afraid that Julia is still very upset when she gets home from school. The name-calling and exclusion from playground games seems to have carried on, in spite of the warning you said you gave the other children concerned. In fact, I fear that it may have made the problem worse.

As you can imagine this is causing Julia great distress and it is certainly affecting her desire to come to school and learn. I am very anxious to get this matter resolved with all possible speed, and request a meeting with you and the head of year at your earliest convenience.

Please telephone or email me as soon as you can to arrange this.

Yours sincerely

Mrs J Trewin

Mrs J Trewin

- The letter quickly summarizes the current situation to remind the teacher of the problem.

- The parent suggests a specific course of action and a timetable.

Letters of complaint

Complaining about faulty goods or services is an unpleasant but common experience. Whatever your complaint, there are several points which you should bear in mind when composing a letter or email to increase your chances of receiving a satisfactory response:

- Make sure you are complaining to the right person. It may seem obvious, but if you have paid for something in cash or by credit card, then it is the seller of the goods or services who you should address your complaint to – not the manufacturer.

- Be aware of your rights under the Sales and Supply of Goods Act, the Trades Descriptions Act and related legislation – these decree that goods or services must be found to be 'as described' when sold.

- There are consumer watchdogs and other bodies who can help you if you are given unsatisfactory responses to your complaints. You can also write to your MP or consult a solicitor, but these should be last measures which hopefully won't be necessary.

Useful phrases

- I am writing to express my dissatisfaction with the service I received from your ...

- At the time of booking it was agreed that ...

- However, on our arrival, we discovered that ...

- I recently bought ...(include colour, model and price) in your shop in ...

- When I tried to use this item, I discovered that ...

- I have contacted you by telephone three times and each time you have promised to visit and put the faults right.

- To date these problems have not been resolved.

- Under the terms of your guarantee, I would like to request a full reimbursement of the amount paid.

- I am withholding payment of the above invoice until I have heard your response to the points outlined above.

- Under the Supply of Goods and Services Act 1982, I am entitled to expect work to be carried out using due care and skill.

- If I do not hear from you within 14 days, I will have no choice but to take the matter further.

- Because of these faults I now consider you to be in breach of contract.

Letter or email of complaint concerning faulty goods

Mr F Headley
15 High Street
Corton
LANCS
LA12 3SH
fheadley@email.com

17 August 2011

Mr D Bryant
High Fi
3 The Parade
Soulton
LANCS
LA23 8GG

Dear Mr Bryant,

I am writing to complain about the Soundalive 411 headphones which I bought from your company, High Fi in Soulton, on 14 August.

When I plugged the headphones into my compact disc player and listened to music through them, the sound in the left headphone was distorted at even low levels of volume – it was clear to me that they were faulty.

I returned them to your shop, a thirty mile round trip, but the salesperson who I originally dealt with disputed my claim - stating that the item had been sold in a satisfactory state. He suggested that I take up the complaint with you, as the owner of the shop.

The Sale of Goods Act 1979 makes it clear that goods be as described, fit for purpose and of satisfactory quality. I am therefore rejecting the headphones and request that you refund the £89 I paid, as the condition of the goods I received constitutes a breach of contract. I have enclosed a copy of my receipt.

I also require you to confirm whether you will arrange for the headphones to be collected from me at the above address, or will reimburse me for the cost of returning them by post?

I expect to receive a response detailing your proposals to satisfactorily settle my claim with seven days of this date.

Yours sincerely,

Mr F Headley

Mr F Headley

- Although the writer has being treated badly by a member of staff, the tone of the letter is formal. Emotive language is likely to produce a defensive response, whereas a detailed and factual description of the problem is more likely to succeed.

- It is quite reasonable to seek compensation for the cost of returning a faulty item.

- Don't send originals of receipts and other documentary evidence with your complaint – especially if you have paid in cash. They may be the only way you have to prove purchase should you need to take the complaint further.

Letter to a travel agency complaining about a holiday

Mrs B Pritchard
21 Churchward Close
Hintenbury
GLOS
FL34 3HQ
bpritchard@email.com

21 July 2011

Customer Services department
Sunkissed Holidays
14 The Waterglades
Hintenbury
GLOS
FL34 7HH

Dear sir or madam

I am writing to complain about the holiday I booked through your company on 5 May this year (REF: BA12303/Maga003).

The booking stated that I would have a room with a balcony with ocean views, and that I would enjoy '5 star luxury' at the Mirabelle Resort, with 'top class international cuisine', and 'a choice of four swimming pools – two of which are reserved for adult use only.' Furthermore, the booking was on an 'all-inclusive basis, guaranteeing bar snacks, soft drinks and local brands of beers, wines and spirits', as and when I requested them.

The reality of my experience was very different. On arrival at the resort, I was allocated a room at the back of the hotel, with a view over a busy street. The noise from the traffic kept me awake at night.

The 'international cuisine' turned out to be a buffet featuring the same options practically every night – mostly fried food, chips and salad.

One of the swimming pools was closed for maintenance for the duration of my stay, and there was no attempt to keep any of the three remaining pools segregated for adult use.

Finally, the availability of drinks and bar snacks was very limited – peanuts were the only snack at the poolside bar, which also only had wine stocked on two days of the fourteen I was at the hotel.

I complained about each of these issues to your firm's representative at the resort – a Mr Stephens – during my first week's holiday. He said he would 'see what he could do'. I didn't hear back from him, and he failed to turn up for the 'rep meeting' in the second week. The hotel staff were unhelpful and told me they could do nothing to rectify any of the problems.

As a result of these issues, my holiday was ruined. I am therefore writing to you seeking compensation from your firm, which has clearly failed to deliver what was contractually agreed. I request that you reply within seven days, stating your proposal to compensate me.

Yours faithfully

Mrs B Pritchard

Mrs B Pritchard

- Use the company's own description of services to compare your experience with.

- Describe each aspect of your complaint concisely; state what you have done about it, and the response that you received from the relevant authority – in this case the holiday rep and the hotel staff.

Letter of complaint to a noisy neighbour

Mr G Barton
7 Chestnut Mansions
Pibble
Cumbria
PW12 3RR
gbarton@email.com

14 October 2011

Ms R Devlin
8 Chestnut Mansions
Pibble
Cumbria
PW12 3RR

Dear Ms Devlin

I am writing to you to formally register my complaint about the excessive noise that has been generated from your flat since you moved in two months ago.

As you know, I have complained in person to you five times in the past month about extremely loud music being played after 11 pm. You have assured me that you will 'not let it happen again,' only for me and my partner to have our sleep ruined the next weekend.

We have no objection to the occasional party or celebration, but your behaviour is inconsiderate and unreasonable. The interruption to our sleep patterns is affecting our concentration at work, and therefore I am giving you notice that if this happens again, without prior notice and agreement from us, I shall instruct my solicitor to begin legal proceedings to restrain you from excessive noise pollution.

Yours sincerely

Mr G Barton

Mr G Barton

- Legal action should only be threatened after attempts to complain less formally have failed. This letter is written after five such attempts.

- Be clear about what you expect to happen as a result of your complaint – how you expect the other party to modify their behaviour in this instance.

- Also spell out what course of action you intend to take should your demands not be met. You must follow through on this course of action, if you don't get a satisfactory response, or you will not be taken seriously in the future.

SOCIAL COMMUNICATION

> *And none will hear the postman's knock*
> *Without a quickening of the heart.*
> *For who can bear to feel himself forgotten?*

(W.H. Auden)

Although seemingly belonging to a different world – predating mobile phones, texts and tablet devices, all of which convey informal messages instantly and very well – there is still a time and a place for a carefully handwritten note or card, or printed invitation.

Types of correspondence in this category include:

- Thank you notes.

- Letters of condolence.

- Invitations.

Here are some general points to consider when writing social communications:

Tone

Apart from invitations, the tone of most social communications is informal and friendly:

- Salutations can range from 'Dear' to 'Hi'.

- Language is usually quite conversational, with shortened sentences and contractions ('I'm', 'won't'); more emotive and less factual than in business correspondence.

- Endings are similarly warm – 'Lots of love'; 'Love'; 'Speak/write soon'; or slightly more formal such as 'Best wishes', 'Kind regards' or 'All the best' if you don't know your correspondent quite so well.

Format

Just because it is handwritten doesn't mean that a note shouldn't have a structure. It is still usual to have:

- An introductory line or paragraph, stating the purpose of the letter ('I was sorry to hear about your loss'; 'thank you for the birthday card...').

- A middle section expounding on the subject ('She was a wonderful woman...'; 'The party went really well, all things considered').

- An ending ('I shall hope to speak to you at the memorial service'; 'Let's meet up before another year goes by...").

> *One thing I can't stand? The computer-generated Christmas card – it's so impersonal – "Look, I can do a mail merge on my pc!" If you can't be bothered to handwrite a greetings card, don't bother!*
>
> (Publishing assistant)

Here are some examples of different kinds of social correspondence:

Thank you note for a dinner party

A thank you letter can be as varied as a formal letter: the writer's relationship with the recipient will determine the tone and language used.

Tuesday

Hi Moz,

I'm just popping this note through your letterbox to thank you so much for dinner on Saturday. Nigel and I had a wonderful evening. It was lovely to meet Sharon and Graham at last – you've talked about them so much over the years - and they were delightful company. I hope Ben has found the champagne cork (sorry about that!)

By the way, please, please send me your recipe for the chocolate mousse – it was exquisite, and Nigel talked of nothing else on Sunday.

You must come to ours for dinner soon.

Love to you both and thanks again,

Lizzie.

- Dating and address can be very informal – this is a note between friends, and knowledge of addresses and contact details can be assumed. Note that the writer uses her friend's nickname 'Moz', rather than full name. You wouldn't use this form of address if writing to a colleague, for example.

- The language is casual – contractions like 'you've' and 'I'm' are absolutely fine. "Please, please send me your recipe…" would be out of place in a formal letter, but it works here.

- In social communication you can refer to events without having to be explicit – here there was clearly an 'incident' with a champagne cork which was a shared source of humour.

Letter of condolence

46 Cork Lane
Lamington
Herts

12 May

Dear Stephen

I am writing to say how sorry I was to hear of your loss, and that I am thinking of you at this difficult time. Although I was aware that Helen was ill, I was nevertheless shocked to hear of her passing.

I know she was never happier than when she had met you, and the two of you made a lovely couple. She seemed to light up the life of everyone who met her.

I shall certainly attend the memorial service next Thursday, but if there is anything I can do in the meantime Stephen, please don't hesitate to call me. I'm sure Jo and Max are a great comfort to you at the moment.

Thinking of you all with love and affection.

Fiona

- The main point of difference with a thank you letter, is that the writer should be acutely sensitive to the addressee's feelings, rather than trying to express their own emotions. The references made to the deceased in this letter are mainly in the context of her relationship with the bereaved partner, rather than the writer.

- A handwritten note can be more appropriate than a phone call in situations of grief and loss like this. Writing a letter also gives you more time to think about what you want to say, and how you want to say it.

- Note that the letter, although it is informal in address and tone, still has a discernible structure: the introductory sentence explains the purpose of the letter; the middle paragraph expands on the theme with the writer's memories of the deceased; and the final paragraph acknowledges the future by accepting an invitation and offering support.

> *It really helped to receive letters of support from friends. Even though I didn't feel like talking to anyone at the time, it was good to know that others appreciated Jim, and that people were thinking of me and the kids.*
>
> (Widow)

Invitations

Invitations are frequently made by email or by text these days, but there are occasions when a written or printed invitation is still the prevalent form of communication.

Occasions that might require an invitation include:

- Birthday parties.
- Weddings.
- Anniversary parties.
- Christenings.
- Funerals.
- Housewarming parties.
- Dinner parties.

A wedding invitation

Boris and Isabel Andrews
request the pleasure of the company of
Phillip and Sally Bairstow
at the wedding of their daughter Florence
to James Chater
on Saturday June 18 2011
at St Bart's Church, Eggleton at 2pm.

R.S.V.P.
Isabel Andrews, The Gildings, Foxton Lane, Biblington, BB13 5TR
Tel: 01286 5543077.

- The most important feature of an invitation is that it must possess all the necessary information to allow the recipient to respond with an acceptance or a refusal. There is no point sending out wedding invitations to 400 guests without the date on them!

- Social invitations can be informal or formal. Formal invitations – to a wedding or a christening, for example – will usually be printed.

A Birthday invitation

> YIKES!
> I'm (nearly) thirty!
> Help me get over it on Saturday 21 May
> at the Stag, Riddlesway, Broxton.
> There'll be drinking, dancing and a very special
> quiz – how can you refuse?
> Please RSVP as soon as possible,
> so I can sort out some eats for the night.
> See you there,
> Charlie Bright
> cbright@email.com
> 06785 4459881

- This invitation could be sent in the form of an email, handwritten note or printed card.

- The tone is humorous and the language (and punctuation) informal, which suits the occasion.

- The font is also deliberately informal.

- Note the promise of a 'very special quiz', to intrigue the reader and hopefully persuade them to attend.

- Even with this casual approach, the host has taken care to include all the information which the recipient will need to decide whether they can attend or not.

Replying to invitations
- When replying to invitations, match the style and formality of the invite.

- If you have to decline an invitation, it is good practice to sound apologetic, regretful and explain the reason why you cannot attend.

SOCIAL MEDIA

I use email all the time; Twitter, Facebook and blogging – weekly.
(Deputy director, charity)

The development of social media has significantly changed the way we communicate with each other. It differs greatly from conventional forms of communication. You are not speaking to a few specific people but with tens, hundreds or even of thousands at once. As well as words, you use pictures, clips and internet links to share information. The best way to describe what you are doing when you use social media, like Facebook, Twitter or a blog, is that you are projecting a representation of yourself to a wide audience. This makes them very powerful and positive communication tools – for everyone from teenage friends to large corporations. The downside is that you have to be careful about what information you share, and how you share it: how you represent yourself. As social media like Facebook and Twitter are constantly developing – in terms of their reach and the purposes for which they are being used – the ground rules for successfully using them are changeable. There are, however, definitely some fundamental 'do's' and 'don'ts', which will be considered here along with the basic mechanics. This guide focuses on Facebook and Twitter, because they are currently the most popular forms of social media. There are many others – like Google+ and Linkedin – which have different formats and purposes, but most of the observations made here will still be applicable.

Social media 'do's'

- **Do decide why you're using it.** Is it to keep in touch with friends, be entertained, promote a business or service, or a mixture of all three? Blogging, Twitter and Facebook are used for all the above reasons, and they have different strengths and weaknesses.

- **Try to be consistent.** If you want to attract more followers on Twitter and other media, this is more likely to happen if people grow to trust and like your opinions or tweets.

- **Be positive.** It's a good principle to keep in mind, even if you don't always follow it. Anger and negativity do not generally translate well into social media, but a positive response to a negative issue can be effective and motivating. Consider whether you might say the same thing, or share the same information, if your audience were in the room with you. If the answer is 'no', then think twice about posting. This is true whether your audience is made up of personal or business contacts, particularly true if it contains both.

- **Be clear.** Nouns and facts work better on Facebook and Twitter than adjectives and adverbs – there is less room for misinterpretation of intention or mood if the message is clear and unambiguous. Of course, if you're casually chatting with friends on instant messenger or Twitter, then it's a different matter.

- **Check your privacy settings.** This will help you avoid inadvertently sharing private information on Facebook and other media, or being embarrassed by something posted on your wall to a wider audience than you would like.

- **Reread your message, status update or tweet before you post it.** It's very easy to make mistakes in spelling or tone, especially if you're posting from a mobile phone with a very small keyboard. Consider using emoticons if you suspect your message is ambiguous.

Social media 'don'ts'

- **'Retweet' (RT) too often.** It can be off-putting to followers. Sharing a link to a video or article you've enjoyed is often welcomed, but be sparing to make a greater impact.

- **Post, or tag, pictures of friends or acquaintances on Facebook.** Unless you're sure they won't mind, keep intimate details of shared events for private Facebook messaging.

- **Be rude.** It's very tempting to react angrily to tweets or posts that we strongly disagree with – don't. Arguments can escalate very quickly in the online environment and you will almost certainly say things, from behind your computer screen, you would not in real life. A well-reasoned objection, or counter argument, will have more infl uence than posting an abusive message but serious issues are unlikely to be resolved online. If someone you're following, or you've 'friended' on Facebook, is a continual source of annoyance, then unfollow or block them.

- **Get upset if you are 'unfollowed'.** Twitter is a more impersonal medium than Facebook, and people chop and change whom they follow with great frequency.

- **Mix up your work life and personal life.** This applies particularly on Facebook. Your work colleagues may be amused by a picture of you at last night's party but your boss, who may be a Facebook friend of one of them, might find it less amusing – especially if you call in sick the next day.

- **Post sensitive news which might be better relayed by telephone.** It's very easy to say things online which it might be difficult to express over the phone, but this doesn't necessarily make it the better option.

- **Be repetitive in your posts and tweets.** Many people repeat variations on a theme they consider important, hoping to elicit a response, while their audience gets fed up with reading the same information over and over again.

- **Ramble.** On Twitter you're usually restricted to 140 characters, which is good practice for learning how to express yourself succinctly. Try to keep Facebook updates to one or two lines, if possible. If you have a lot to say, you might be better off sending an email, or video calling.

- **Forget to punctuate.** Just because messages are short doesn't mean that they will make sense without commas, full stops and other punctuation marks.

Glossary of social media terms

> **@.** The @ sign is used in 'tweets' directly before a username to turn it into a link to that person's profile:@janesmith for example.

> **# (hashtag).** Hashtags are symbols which allow tweets on a subject to be grouped together and located by a 'hashtag search'. For instance, by including the expression, '*#spaceshuttle*' in a tweet, the user makes it possible for other tweeters to search and locate all tweets with this expression in them.

> **Blocking.** Blocking is preventing someone from reading your tweets, or Facebook posts, by denying them access to your account.

> **Links.** Webpage references included in Facebook posts and tweets, which can be clicked on to take the reader to the relevant web article or image.

> **Retweet (RT).** Resending or forwarding someone's else tweet with or without a comment of your own.

> **Status update.** The space on your Facebook account where you let your 'friends' know how you are feeling, or what you are thinking about. Entries should be kept short.

> **Tweeter.** A user of Twitter.

- » **Tweet(ing).** The act of posting a 'tweet' to Twitter.

- » **Tweets.** Posts on Twitter made up of 140 characters or less.

- » **Tweetup.** A physical meeting of tweeters – a 'twitter meet up'.

- » **Wall.** The personal page of your Facebook account where 'friends' can post messages, links and other material.

 I use Twitter all the time and have found it very useful for work. I'm on Facebook but I never use it.

(Journalist)

Blogging

A blog – or 'weblog' – is a website where someone writes their thoughts and opinions in the form of a post. Blogs range in content from online diaries to a promotional tool for business. Mostly they are expressions of personal opinions and beliefs, and so tend to be informal and chatty in tone.

Regardless of why you are blogging, some basic rules apply:

- **Think about your reader.** Are you planning to inform them? Entertain them? Persuade them? Whether it is one of the above or all three, you will have to write accordingly, and be consistent in your approach, or the reader's interest will wane.

- **Be sincere and engaging.** A blog is usually quite conversational in style, so it may help to imagine you are chatting with the reader as you write. Share your experiences and tips, particularly if you're writing about a hobby or interest.

- **Keep posts short and interesting.** People tend to 'scan' blogs for words and images of interest – they may not be paying full attention. For this reason, try to keep sentences short and punchy. Include images and links to other web pages that reinforce your opinions or make the page look attractive. Add headings to break up the text, and keep paragraphs short.

I use Facebook to keep in touch with friends around the world, and Twitter to keep tabs on the news and celebrities. Skype is great for conference calls.

(Writer)

Emoticons and Smileys

Emoticons (from 'emotion' and 'icon') and 'smileys' are typed symbols representing expressions of the human face, from happy to sad. They are used as shorthand in text messaging, email, Tweets and other real-time communications to indicate the tone of the message, when the words alone do not make this clear. For instance, 'I am going out with my parents tonight ☺', or 'I am going out with my parents tonight ☹)

Here is a selection of the most commonly used emoticons:

:-) or **:)**	happy
(-:	smiling back, also smiling
:-()	smiling with mouth open
8-)	smiling with glasses
D:-)	smiling with baseball cap
|-)	grin
:>	devilish grin
:^D	sounds good (agree)
:-))	cheerful
:-)))	really happy
:-D	laughing
|-D	belly laugh

:'-D	crying with laughter
xD	laughing really hard
:-&	tongue tied
;-)	winking, just kidding
;->	conspiratorial wink
>:)	evil grin
:p	tongue sticking out, playful, just kidding
<3	heart
:-°	kissing
:-X	big kiss
:-x	small kiss, peck
^5	high five
:-(	sad
:'-(	crying

:-C	very sad
:-@	screaming
:-O	shocked or surprised
:-o	wow
[:-(	frowning
:/	frustrated
:-	sceptical
:-||	angry
>:-|	cross
:-<>	surprised
:-(°)	you make me sick
((_x_))	kiss my ass
<:-]	stupid, idiot
:-S	confused
%-)	confused and happy
%-(	confused and unhappy

:-(o)	shouting
:-V	yelling
:-@	screaming
|-@!	swearing
]-()	yawning
|-i	sleeping
|-O	snoring